Encyclopedia of
The Persian Gulf War

Encyclopedia of
The Persian Gulf War

Mark Grossman

ABC-CLIO

Santa Barbara, California
Denver, Colorado
Oxford, England

Copyright © 1995 by Mark Grossman

Maps were adapted from the following: pages 15 and 213, *Desert Shield to Desert Storm*, "Principal Targets in Iraq" and "Troop Strength January 1991" © 1992 by Dilip Hiro; page 256, *The Longest War*, "The Northern War Sector" © 1991 by Routledge, Chapman & Hall; page 269 (two maps), *The Cambridge Atlas of the Middle East and North Africa*, "The Region on the Eve of World War I" and "The Region between the Two World Wars."

Library of Congress Cataloging-in-Publication Data

Grossman, Mark.
    Encyclopedia of the Persian Gulf War / Mark Grossman.
        p. cm.
    Includes bibliographical references and index.
    1. Weapons systems.   2. Persian Gulf War, 1991—Equipment and supplies.   I.Title.
    UF500.G8   1995   95-38945   956.7044'2—dc20

ISBN 0-87436-684-4

02 01 00 99 98 97   10 9 8 7 6 5 4 3 2

ABC-CLIO, Inc.
130 Cremona Drive, P.O. Box 1911
Santa Barbara, California 93116-1911

This book is printed on acid-free paper ∞.
Manufactured in the United States of America

Babylon's Fallen! Babylon's Fallen!
—And So Is This

Graffiti written on the side of a bomb
dropped on Iraq, based on Isaiah 21:9.

This book is dedicated to the memory of my cousin,
Sergeant Clifton Louis Davidson (1925–1944),
killed when the B-24 Liberator he was on was
shot down over Cesena, Italy, 25 April 1944;
and to my brother, David Grossman, and his wife, Pam,
who have been pestering me for years to get their
names in print and now finally
get their wish.

Table of Contents

List of Maps

Preface

"The Persian Gulf War was the first major conflict following the end of the Cold War," narrate the authors of *Conduct of the Persian Gulf War: Final Report to Congress (Pursuant to Title V of the Persian Gulf Conflict Supplemental Authorization and Personnel Benefits Act of 1991)*, a report by the Department of Defense to Congress in April 1992. Yet, why was the war fought? Was it for oil, jobs, greed, or power? Historian Kenneth Timmerman, in his work on the buildup of the Iraqi war machine, *The Death Lobby: How the West Armed Iraq* writes, "The fight against Saddam Hussein had little to do with the liberation of Kuwait, no matter how much President Bush and his advisors tried to focus publicly on that goal. It wasn't about jobs, as Secretary of State James Baker once argued, or even about oil. Simply put, the United States went to war to smash the death machine that this country and its Western allies had helped Saddam assemble in the first place. The United States and its allies had no choice but to combat Saddam Hussein on the battlefield because of the greed of western businesses, misguided analyses by the foreign policy establishment, and the incompetence of regulatory officials." Still, the war machine of Iraq, however built up by the West, had to be stopped at Kuwait, or the entire Arabian peninsula and its massive oil supply would have been at the mercy of one single dictator. As this is being written, Iraq is threatening Jordan after King Hussein took in two of Saddam's sons-in-law who had defected to the Hashemite Kingdom. Speculation still swirls as to whether Saddam will survive this latest internal struggle for power in his tortured land.

The history of U.S. foreign policy in the Persian Gulf region, including that of the 1970s and 1980s, gives some insight into the reasons behind Iraq's invasion of Kuwait and U.S. response to it. Captain Richard D. Hooker, Jr., and Captain Ricky L. Waddell wrote in the *Naval War College Review* in 1992, "Though some disagree, we can view the Iraqi invasion of Kuwait as a deterrence failure. Despite expressions of concern for the stability of the Gulf region and for the free flow of oil (such as the Carter Doctrine, the AWACs sale, the formation of [the] Central Command, and the Persian Gulf deployment of 1987–1988), the U.S. government sent mixed signals when it tilted toward Iraq in the Gulf War and when it failed to react vigorously to Iraqi rhetoric and troop deployments against Kuwait in July 1990." Still, for the first time since the end of World War II, the United States led a multinational invasion of a significant land power to recapture territory and end a major threat to world peace.

The Persian Gulf war was a turning point in military history. For the first time, air power was used almost exclusively by one side in a conflict to inflict great damage upon the other side. The casualties suffered also were extreme: while the allies suffered fewer than 500 total dead in the entire war, the Iraqis sustained perhaps 20,000 military dead and possibly upwards of 100,000 total casualties. William J. Perry, undersecretary of defense in the Carter Administration and secretary of defense in the Clinton Administration, wrote in *Foreign Affairs* magazine in fall 1991, "In Operation Desert Storm the United States employed for the first time a new class of military systems that gave American forces a revolutionary advance in military capability. Key to this capability is a new generation of military support systems—intelligence sensors, defense suppression systems and precision guidance subsystems—that serve as 'force multipliers' by increasing the effectiveness of U.S. weapons systems. An army with such technology has an overwhelming advantage over an army without it, much as an army equipped with tanks would overwhelm an army with horse cavalry." This book aims to highlight and explain the uses of the weapons used during the conflict on both sides.

When my editor, Jeff Serena, approached me with the idea for this book in Denver in April 1994, I looked at it as I do other works on American history: coverage of important people, places, events, and so on. This book, however, was different in one respect: the Persian Gulf war was still fresh enough as history so that few, if any, sources have been published on it, inside and outside the military. When I completed the text, in May 1995, only a handful of books had been published for the general public on the war. In the intervening months leading up to the editing by the project's editor, Todd Hallman, there have been several new works, but nothing in the way of a comprehensive encyclopedia such as this. This is the first book that I know of that gives an accounting not only of what weapons the United States used, but those utilized by the coalition and even Iraq. The work also explains, through the use of entries on Iraq, Kuwait, and other involved nations, as well as an extensive timeline (which extends the crisis past the resolution of war in 1991), the basis of the Persian Gulf conflict's underpinnings and beginnings.

The main problem I had in finding information for this book was this: there is not one source of information on what American and coalition ships served during the war, and these varied sources give varying listings for the ships. Calling the listings "varied" is an understatement. A ship that one source says served is reported by another not to have served. Other sources did not count ships that moved troops and equipment into the Gulf and then left the area. It was difficult to get an accurate accounting of the naval armada that served from the military. Again, because of the freshness of the war and its relation to military maneuvers still being conducted, confidentiality in many cases ruled the day.

There are several sources of information on the ships and planes that were in the Gulf that I turned to: they included Frank Chadwick's *Desert Shield Fact Book, Desert Score: U.S. Gulf War Weapons*, edited by Denise L. Almond, Norman Polmar's *Ships and Aircraft of the U.S. Fleet* (1987) and *The Naval Institute Guide to the Ships and Aircraft of the U.S. Fleet* (1993), and *Gallery of Middle East Airpower*, by John W. R. Taylor and Kenneth Munson, which appeared in Air Force magazine in October 1994. All of these sources gave varying numbers and, in some cases, conflicting names, for the coalition ships and planes that they claimed served in the war. I relied on as many conforming numbers and names as possi-

ble; however, I know that somewhere a ship that served may not be mentioned, or one that did not serve is included. I accept these as my error. Hopefully, a future writer will get a complete roster of what ships did serve, both for the United States and the coalition nations.

I would like to thank the following people without whose help and assistance this work would not have come to fruition: the reference room and interlibrary loan staffs of the Maricopa County Library, Phoenix, Arizona, and the staffs of the Scottsdale Civic Center Library and Mustang Library, Scottsdale, Arizona; the staff of the Phoenix Public Library; the Orange Coast College Library, Costa Mesa, California; the Broward County Main Library, Fort Lauderdale, Florida; the West Regional Library, Plantation, Florida; the staffs of the Newspaper Reading Room and the Main Reading Room of the Library of Congress; the staff of the New York Public Library; Rosemary Hite, Secretary in the Middle East Office of the National Council of Churches of Christ in the United States of America, for all her wonderful assistance in obtaining the NCCC statement on the Gulf War; the United States General Accounting Office, for a copy of their report on research into Gulf War Syndrome; Senator Jay Rockefeller (D-West Virginia) and the staff of the U.S. Senate Committee on Veterans' Affairs, for reams of information on hearings and other investigations into the health concerns and problems of Gulf War veterans; Senator Donald W. Riegle, Jr., and the staff of the Senate Committee on Banking, Housing, and Urban Affairs, for a copy of their report on Persian Gulf Syndrome; Senator Jesse Helms (R-North Carolina) and the staff of the Senate Foreign Relations Committee for their accession of the statement of U.S. Ambassador to the United Nations Madeleine Albright before the committee; Lionel Haas of the French Embassy in Washington, D.C., for his help in getting information on the French role in the war; the staff of the British Embassy in Washington, D.C., for their kind assistance in trying to access information on the British role in the war; the office of Dr. David P. Rall at the Institute of Medicine of the National Academy of Sciences, for a copy of the Institute's report on Gulf War Syndrome; the office of John M. Hogan, Director of the B.N.L. Task Force and

Counselor to the U.S. Attorney General, for their kindness in sharing a copy of the recently declassified summary on "The Banca Nazionale del Lavoro (BNL) Task Force—Final Report"; the Harold B. Lee Library, Brigham Young University, Provo, Utah; Martha McCaslin, Public Affairs Representative, of the Department of the Army's Communications–Electronics Command, Research, Development & Engineering Center, Night Vision & Electronic Sensors Directorate, Fort Belvoir, Virginia, for her masterful aid in obtaining information on night vision goggles; Roger Jorstad and all the wonderful people at the Headquarters, Department of the Army, Army Reserve, Program Analysis and Evaluation Division (DAAR-PAE), for their reports on the Reserve's role in the war; Professor John O. Field of the Tufts University School of Nutrition, for his wonderful sense of humor, insight into the nutrition problems in Iraq following the war, and intuitive reports and documents on the war's aftermath; and, finally, to the Public Affairs Office of the United States Central Command at MacDill Air Force Base in Tampa, Florida, for their report on the timeline leading up to the war and the history of Central Command, a little known component of the war.

Mark Grossman
18 August 1995

A-4 Skyhawk

Only 25 A-4s served during Operation Desert Shield, all for the Kuwaiti Air Force (the planes were designated as A-4KUs). They were the only Kuwaiti Air Force planes to escape the Iraqi onslaught, and went on to fly 651 sorties against various Iraqi targets.

A two-seat attack fighter, the A-4 is powered by a single Pratt & Whitney J52-P-408 turbojet engine that provides 11,200 pounds (5,080 kg) of thrust. The plane weighs 10,456 pounds (4,743 kg), and has a maximum external load of 9,195 pounds (4,171 kg). Wingspan is 27 feet 6 inches (8.38 m), and its maximum speed is between 560 and 582 knots (645–667 mph; 1,037–1,074 km/h), with allowances for the carrying of armaments. Those armaments include four AGM-45 Shrike, three AGM-62 Walleye, or four AGM-65 Maverick missiles.

References: Almond, Denise L., ed., *Desert Score: U.S. Gulf War Weapons* (Washington, DC: Carroll Publishing, 1991), 8–9; Keany, Thomas A., and Eliot A. Cohen, *Gulf War Air Power Survey, Summary Report* (Washington, DC: GPO, 1993), 185.

A-6E/TRAM Intruder

The A-6E TRAM (target recognition and attack multisensor) Intruder was one of the mainstays of the Marine Corps fleet during the Persian Gulf War, flying a total of 5,619 sorties in the Kuwaiti Theatre of Operations (KTO), which includes Kuwait, Iraq, and Saudi Arabia, according to the U.S. military.

The A-6E TRAM can deliver both conventional and nuclear weapons, and can transport about 18,000 pounds (8,165 kg) of armaments. It is an improved version of the Grumman A-6, which Walter J. Boyne, in his *Weapons of Desert Storm,* calls "a versatile two-seat, medium attack aircraft with all-weather, day-night attack capabilities." Recently updated with the TRAM system, which fits into a small pod under the nose, the aircraft is suited for deep penetration into enemy territory and close air support. With its cousins the EA-6B and the KA-6D (a refueling variant), the plane played a key role in the bombing of military installations in Libya on 15 April 1986.

The TRAM system includes what military authors Thomas A. Keaney and Eliot A. Cohen call "infrared- and laser-targeting sensors and multimode radar," which is combined with laser-guided weapon deliverance. Among these weapons is the versatile Harpoon antiship missile and so-called iron bombs. Powered by two Pratt & Whitney J52-P-8B engines giving it 18,000 pounds (8,165 kg) of total thrust, the A-6E has a wingspan of 53 feet (16.15 m), a maximum speed of 684 mph (1,100 km/h), a maximum unrefueled range of 2,740 miles (4,409 km), and a maximum weight of 60,400 pounds (27,397 kg). The variant KA-6D is a refueling carrier, and the EA-6A is an electronics warfare version.

See also EA-6B Prowler.
References: Boyne, Walter J., *The Weapons of Desert Storm* (Lincolnwood, IL: Publications International, 1991), 17; Keany, Thomas A., and Eliot A. Cohen, *Gulf War Air Power Survey, Summary Report* (Washington, DC: GPO, 1993), 184; *Sea Power: The Official Publication of the Navy League of the United States* 37:1 (January 1994), 210.

A-7 Corsair II

Nicknamed the Short Little Ugly Fellow, with a variation on the "fellow," this plane first flew in 1965 during the Vietnam War. At the time of Operations Desert Shield/Desert Storm, the craft was being phased out and therefore saw only limited action, flying from the aircraft carrier *John F. Kennedy* in close air support (CAS) missions. A-7s flew 737 sorties during Desert Storm, according to the U.S. military. They were also the first planes to operationally utilize the AGM-84E SLAM (standoff land attack missile) in combat.

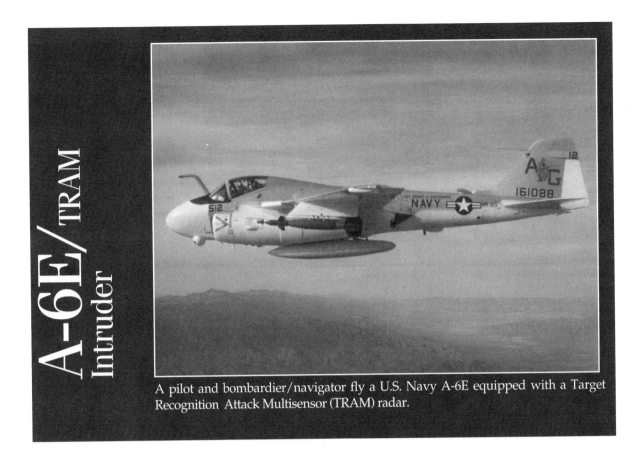

A-6E/TRAM Intruder

A pilot and bombardier/navigator fly a U.S. Navy A-6E equipped with a Target Recognition Attack Multisensor (TRAM) radar.

The A-7 Corsair II comes in several variants: A-7D, A-7E, A-7H, and A-7K (the A-7D is a slightly heavier model, and the A-7K is used as a trainer). These versions are powered by a single Allison T-F41-1 turbofan engine delivering 14,250 pounds (6,464 kg) of thrust, except the A-7E, which has a single T-F41-2 engine delivering 15,000 pounds (6,804 kg) of thrust. The A-7 has a maximum speed of 690 mph (1,110 km/h), a wingspan of 38 feet 9 inches (11.8 m), a length of 46 feet 1 inch (14 m), and a maximum weight of 42,000 pounds (19,051 kg) with armaments. The plane is armed with one 20 mm M61A-1 gun, as well as eight outboard and two inboard pylons for various armaments, including air-to-air missiles and bombs. Today, it is used mostly by units of the Air National Guard.

References: Almond, Denise L., ed., *Desert Score: U.S. Gulf War Weapons* (Washington, DC: Carroll Publishing, 1991), 16–17; *Gulf War Air Power Survey, Volume IV: Weapons, Tactics, and Training Report and Space Report* (Washington, DC: GPO, 1993), 60–61; Gunston, Bill, *An Illustrated Guide to Modern Fighters and Attack Aircraft* (New York: Prentice Hall, 1987), 148–149.

A-10 Thunderbolt II

Considered one of the most underappreciated aircraft in the service of the U.S. military before the war, the A-10 Thunderbolt—dubbed by its pilots the "Warthog" (the pilots were therefore called hogdrivers) because of its squat, flat shape—became the darling of the conflict because of its ability to destroy whole columns of Iraqi tanks and aid in speedily winning the war. The plane's engines are so quiet that the Iraqis called the plane "the silent gun."

Manufactured by the Fairchild Republic Company of Farmingdale, New York, the A-10 originally flew in 1972 as part of the military's shift to the close air support (CAS) strategy with smaller, more sturdy fighters such as the A-10, which is able to take more bullet and shrapnel hits than other craft. Dubbed A-X, the A-10A was the first model produced. A single-seat craft, the Grumman Corporation states that its mission is "to provide effective anti-armor support for ground forces; to be able to carry large ordnance payloads and have excellent range and long loiter capabilities near the battle area; to survive intense anti-aircraft fire, surface-to-air missiles,

A-7 Corsair

Two U.S. Navy A-7E Corsairs fly above the Saudi Arabian desert during Operation Desert Shield.

A-10 Thunderbolt II Warthog

An A-10A Thunderbolt, nicknamed "Warthog," stands on the flight line at the U.S. Naval Air Station in Sigonella, Italy, en route to the United States at the close of Operation Desert Storm. Two AIM-9 Sidewinder missiles hang from pylons below the plane's right wing. Warthogs were especially successful against Iraqi tanks and significantly damaged convoys of Iraqis fleeing Kuwait at the end of the war.

and attacks by other aircraft; and to maintain high sortie rates and operate from short fields, while permitting rapid servicing and easy repair of battle damage." It accomplishes much of this because the cockpit is essentially a bathtub of titanium armor that can withstand a heavy barrage of antiaircraft bombardment. In fact, of the 20 A-10s that were "significantly damaged" during the war, only one could not be returned to service because of the hits it took. Only five A-10s were lost; four were destroyed during missions and the fifth crashed on landing. Military historian Bill Gunston writes, "The basic [A-10] aircraft has a HUD [heads-up display], good communications fit and both Tacan and an inertial system, as well as ECM [electronic countermeasures] and radar homing and warning." The A-10 comes in the variants of 10A and 10/NAW (night–adverse weather); the latter is a newer, more sophisticated model with an ability to fly in poor weather and at night.

With a length of 53 feet (16.16 m) and a wingspan of 57 feet 6 inches (17.5 m), the A-10A is powered by two General Electric TF34-GE-100 turbofan engines providing 9,065 pounds (4,112

kg) of thrust. The plane has a maximum speed of 439 mph (706 km/h) and a maximum range of 2,454 miles (3,948 km). It is armed with one 30 mm General Electric GAU-8/A seven-barrel Gatling gun, known as the Avenger, which allows the gunner to deliver 1,174 rounds of high-speed bullets with depleted uranium tips that can pierce a tank's heavy skin. The craft can also be equipped with an external load of up to 16,000 pounds (7,258 kg) of air-to-ground munitions, such as smart and cluster bombs, as well as AGM-65 Maverick air-to-ground missiles and AIM-9L/M Sidewinder air-to-air missiles. According to the Air Force, the A-10s in the Kuwaiti Theatre of Operations (KTO) flew a total of 8,084 sorties.

The A-10's success at the end of the ground war phase of the conflict was formidable. Along with F-15, F-111, and F-16 fighters, the A-10s attacked the waves of retreating Iraqi tank battalions exiting in haste from Kuwait City and destroyed an unknown number of them, killing perhaps a thousand Iraqi soldiers. The *San Francisco Chronicle* quoted two pilots, Captain Eric Salomonson and First Lieutenant John Marks, who between them destroyed 13 Iraqi tanks on one day of the air war. "We've been looking for tanks since the war started," Salomonson said, and "yesterday we found a bunch." Later inspecting the devastation wrought by the planes on the Iraqi tank battalions, one Marine said, "This was just a duck shoot. It looks like they [the Iraqis] were attacked in their sleep. See, there are bedrolls near the tanks."

References: "A-10 'Warthogs' Damaged Heavily In Gulf War But Survived To Fly Again" *Aviation Week & Space Technology,* 5 August 1991, 42; Gunston, Bill, *An Illustrated Guide to USAF: The Modern US Air Force* (New York: Prentice Hall, 1986), 52–57; Keany, Thomas A., and Eliot A. Cohen, *Gulf War Air Power Survey, Summary Report* (Washington, DC: GPO, 1993), 184; Smallwood, William L., *Warthog: Flying the A-10 in the Gulf War* (McLean, VA: Brassey's, 1993).

AA-10A Alamo

This Iraqi version of a Soviet missile was part of the armament fitted aboard the Iraqi air force's MiG-29 Fulcrum. There are two versions of the AA-10A: an infrared design and a semiactive radar-guided model. An air-to-air missile, the Alamo weighs between 342 pounds (infrared version) and 441 pounds (guided radar variant) (155–200 kg). Because most of the Iraqi air force escaped to Iran, the Alamo never saw combat during the war.

Reference: Blake, Bernard, ed., *Jane's Weapon Systems, 1988–89* (Coulsdon, Surrey, UK: Jane's Information Group, 1988), 701.

AAV7A1 Tracked Personnel Vehicle (TPV)

A full-tracked amphibious assault vehicle, AAV7A1s, according to the military report *Desert Score,* were among the first armored vehicles in Saudi Arabia after Iraq's invasion. By the beginning of the ground war in February 1991, the First Marine Expeditionary Force (MEF) had 225 AAV7s ashore. Another 115 were embarked in 31 landing ships in the northern Gulf. Although the vehicle has a high silhouette and was not originally intended to venture far inland from an assault beach, it nevertheless served as two principal Marine Corps APCs (the LAV-25 being the other) during the drive to Kuwait City.

Powered by a Detroit Diesel model 8V-53T water-cooled diesel engine, the AAV7A1, which in 1986 underwent a revitalization that applied to the vehicles the RAFAEL Armament Development Authority Enhanced Appliqué Armor Kit (EAAK), is crewed by three men (commander, gunner, and driver) and can carry upwards of 25 troops. Combat weight is 52,770 pounds (23,936 kg), maximum speed is 45 mph (72.5 km/h), and maximum range on land is 300 miles (482 km) at 25 mph, while in the water the craft can move for 7 hours at 2,600 rpm. Armor is thickest at the hull sides (31–45 mm). Future improvements could include the addition of TOW or Dragon antitank guided weapon launchers, or a 40 mm grenade launcher.

References: Almond, Denise L., ed., *Desert Score: U.S. Gulf War Weapons* (Washington, DC: Carroll Publishing, 1991), 312–313; Foss, Christopher F., ed., *Jane's Armour and Artillery, 1992–93* (Coulsdon, Surrey, UK: Jane's Information Group, 1992), 501–504.

Abdulaziz, Prince Bandar Bin Sultan Bin (1949–)

In his capacity as the Saudi Arabian ambassador to the United States, Prince Bandar Bin Sultan Bin Abdulaziz played an integral role in shaping American response to the invasion of Kuwait. He was born near Taif, Saudi Arabia, on 2 March 1949, the son of Prince Sultan bin Abdulaziz al-Saud, the second deputy premier and minister of defense and aviation in the Saudi government. He graduated from the British Royal Air Force College in Cranwell, England, in 1968, and was subsequently commissioned in the royal Saudi air force (RSAF) as a second lieutenant. Over the next 17 years he was involved in the command of the Saudi air force and became experienced in piloting several aircraft, including the T-38 and F-5.

In the early 1980s Prince Bandar became involved in diplomacy. He represented King Fahd in negotiating an end to the Lebanese civil war in 1983, and he served as a member of the Saudi delegation to the United Nations. In 1982 he was

Abdulaziz, Prince Bandar Bin Sultan Bin

Ambassador Bandar Bin Sultan Bin Abdulaziz of Saudi Arabia, left, meets with U.S. president George Bush in the White House on 1 March 1991.

assigned to the Saudi embassy in Washington as the Saudi defense attaché. The following year, he was named as the Saudi ambassador to the United States.

During Operation Desert Shield, the push for congressional approval for war in the Persian Gulf, and Operation Desert Storm, Prince Bandar was a noted figure in Washington, and was present at President George Bush's address to the American people announcing the end of the ground war.

Reference: His Royal Holiness, Prince Bandar Bin Sultan Bin Abdulaziz (Washington, DC: Royal Embassy of Saudi Arabia, 1989).

AC-130A/H Spectre Gunship

A modified C-130 Hercules, these Special Operations Forces (SOF) planes first saw action during the Vietnam War. The AC-130A/Hs flew 104 sorties during Operation Desert Storm in their capacity as close air support (CAS), armed observation, and air prohibition and interdiction aircraft for the SOF. While serving the latter function, one AC-130 was shot down by an Iraqi surface-to-air missile during the crucial battle of Khafji, killing all 14 crew members aboard. The main mission of the craft during the war was to insert small teams of Special Operations troops on clandestine sorties inside Kuwait and Iraq to carry out reconnaissance and gather intelligence.

The AC-130A/H is distinguished by a sideways-firing 105 mm recoilless howitzer gun, a 40 mm Bofors cannon, and two 20 mm Vulcan Gatling guns. A new variant, the AC-130U Spectre, is being built by Rockwell International for the American military.

See also C-130 Hercules Transport; EC-130E Volant Solo; HC-130H Extended Range Aerospace Rescue and Recovery; MC-130H Combat Talon II; Special Operations Forces (SOF).
References: Gulf War Air Power Survey, Volume IV: Weapons, Tactics, and Training Report and Space Report (Washington, DC: GPO, 1993), 118–119; Lambert, Mark, ed., *Jane's All the World's Aircraft, 1991–92* (Coulsdon, Surrey, UK: Jane's Information Group, 1991), 427.

Aflaq, Michel (1910–1989)

The death of Michel Aflaq in 1989 was little noticed outside the Arab world, yet he, more than anyone, was responsible for the establishment of the Ba'ath party and for articulating the ideas that form the backbone of the movement called

Aflaq, Michel

Michel Aflaq was a leader of the post–World War II pan-Arabist movement. In 1947 he organized the Ba'ath party, which advocated a single Arab state.

pan-Arabism. Aflaq was born in 1910 in Damascus (now in Syria) to a middle-class family of Greek Orthodox background. Ba'ath party authority Kamel Abu Jaber wrote in 1966, "His father, an ardent nationalist, was arrested by both the Ottomans and the French. His mother, although advanced in years, is still very much interested in politics and a firm believer in Arab nationalism. Thus Aflaq grew up in a home where politics was a favorite topic." (She has since died.) In 1918 Aflaq traveled to Paris, where he studied at the Sorbonne for the next ten years. There he became friends with another Syrian student, Salah al-Din Bitar; together they would later found the movement known as Ba'ath.

At this time Syria was in a state of upheaval. Following the end of World War I, the French carved up the area to the north of present-day Jordan and Israel into the separate mandates of Lebanon and Syria, with the Syrian capital located at Damascus, Aflaq's birthplace. During the critical years of the 1930s and particularly 1934, when Aflaq returned from Paris to become a Syrian schoolmaster in 1934, Arab nationalism was enunciated by such scholars as Sati al-Husri

and Abd al-Rahman Bazzaz. With the outbreak of World War II, Aflaq, Salah al-Din Bitar, Bitar's cousin Midhat Bitar, and Jalal al-Sayyid wanted to form a political organization that would encompass the aspirations of pan-Arabist nationalism as well as embrace progressive social policies. In 1947 these men founded the Arab Resurrection party (al-Hizb al-Ba'ath al-Arabi), later called the Ba'ath, or the Ba'th. According to the *New York Times*, "[Aflaq's] party soon established a strong following among officers in the Syrian Army and was involved in many of the military coups that destabilized the country in the 1950s." Aflaq was arrested and held prisoner on several occasions, including detention by the French in 1939, in 1948 and 1949 by different Syrian governments, and in 1952 and 1954 by Syrian strongman Adib al-Shishakli.

Michel Aflaq served as political editor of the official party newspaper, *al-Baath*, and as the *amid*, or master, of the Ba'ath party (a title later changed to secretary-general). He resigned this latter position at the Eighth Ba'ath Congress in April 1965. Later that year, dissatisfied with the Syrian government, he attempted a takeover, but his rule lasted only briefly. In February 1966 militant elements of the party took control, sending Aflaq into exile. He spent the last 20-odd years of his life in Baghdad, Iraq, where he served as secretary-general of the Iraqi Ba'ath party from 1968 until his death.

On 10 June 1989 Aflaq underwent open heart surgery in Paris, but died on 23 June, at the age of 79. The Iraqi Ba'ath party in Baghdad issued a statement calling Aflaq "a pioneer of the human progressive Arab nationalist thought" whose work "had led Arab masses for decades in their struggle against imperialism and for Arab unity." There was no comment from Damascus.

See also Ba'ath Party; Pan-Arabism or Pan-Arabist Thought.
References: Abu Jaber, Kamel, *The Arab Ba'th Socialist Party: History, Ideology, and Organization* (Syracuse, NY: Syracuse University Press, 1966), 10–11; Devlin, John F., *The Ba'th Party: A History from Its Origins to 1966* (Stanford, CA: Hoover Institution Press, 1976), 8–9; "Michel Aflaq Dies in Paris at 79: Founder of Iraq's Baathist Party," *New York Times*, 25 June 1989, A26; Reich, Bernard, ed., *Political Leaders of the Contemporary Middle East and North Africa: A Biographical Dictionary* (Westport, CT: Greenwood, 1990), 32–33.

AGM-45 Shrike Air-to-Surface Missile (ASM)

Only 78 AGM-45 Shrike air-to-surface missiles were used during the Persian Gulf War: 53 by the U.S. Air Force, 18 by the Navy, and 7 by the Marine Corps.

According to the U.S. military report *Gulf War Air Power Survey*, the Shrike is "a completely passive missile that uses radiation emitted by a target radar for detection, homing, and detonation. Shrike was designed to detect and destroy enemy radar emitters, and was first used in 1965. Its 149-pound [68 kg] warhead is specifically designed to physically impair the operation of the radar antenna." *Jane's Weapon Systems, 1988–89* reports that the HARM (high-speed antiradiation missile) was intended to replace the older Shrike and standard antiradiation missiles used by U.S. armed forces; therefore, only limited numbers of the Shrike were used during Operation Desert Storm.

References: Blake, Bernard, ed., *Jane's Weapon Systems, 1988–89* (Coulsdon, Surrey, UK: Jane's Information Group, 1989), 722; *Gulf War Air Power Survey, Volume IV: Weapons, Tactics, and Training Report and Space Report* (Washington, DC: GPO, 1993), 104.

AGM-62 Walleye II Bomb

The Walleye II glide bomb, which weighs approximately 2,450 pounds (1,111 kg) (the Walleye I weighs 1,100 pounds [499 kg]), was used in limited numbers during the Persian Gulf War.

Built by Martin Marietta and Hughes, the AGM-62 Walleye II is 13 feet (4.0 m) in length and has a wingspan of 4 feet 3 inches (1.3 m). Because it is a glide bomb, the Walleye II is powered only by a ram air turbine, which provides energy for guidance and controls. It contains a television optical camera, enabling the pilot to see it glide into its target. Among the aircraft that can carry it are the F-4 Phantom II, the A-4 Skyhawk, and the A-7 Corsair II.

According to the U.S. military's *Gulf War Air Power Survey*, the AGM-62 is "a guided bomb for daytime, clear-weather use only. [The] Walleye is used against large targets. It is an electro-optical (2,000-pound [908 kg] class) weapon that uses proportional navigation to glide to the target. A two-way radio frequency datalink allows the pilot (in the release aircraft or another aircraft) to control the weapon by use of a small joystick. Wider fins can be attached to increase range for greater standoff distance. The weapon has a 2,015-pound [914 kg] warhead with a linearly shaped charge. Only 133 Walleyes were expended in Desert Storm, virtually all of them by the U.S. Navy."

References: *Gulf War Air Power Survey, Volume IV: Weapons, Tactics, and Training Report and Space Report* (Washington, DC: GPO, 1993), 78–79; Polmar, Norman, *Ships and Aircraft of the U.S. Fleet* (Annapolis, MD: Naval Institute Press, 1987), 488–489.

AGM-65 Maverick

During Operation Desert Storm, 5,255 AGM-65 B, D, and G missiles were fired; over 4,000, according to the U.S. military, were fired by A-10 Thunderbolts. The Marine Corps also fired 36 E-variant Mavericks (a modified D model).

Jane's Weapon Systems reports, "The AGM-65 Maverick is a precision guided tactical missile developed by the Hughes Aircraft Company . . . for use against hard targets such as tanks, armoured vehicles, field fortifications, gun positions, concrete communication centres and aircraft shelters." At a length of 16 feet 2 inches (2.49 m), the Maverick has small wings with a span of 28 inches (71.9 cm) and weighs between 463 and 677 pounds (210–307 kg). Guidance for the various models includes television cameras, lasers, and infrared. The A and B models have television cameras; D, F, and G are guided by infrared; and E is piloted by a laser.

References: Blake, Bernard, ed., *Jane's Weapon Systems, 1988–89* (Coulsdon, Surrey, UK: Jane's Information Group, 1988), 722–723; *Gulf War Air Power Survey, Volume IV: Weapons, Tactics, and Training Report and Space Report* (Washington, DC: GPO, 1993), 79–80.

AGM-69 Short Range Attack Missile (SRAM)

A supersonic air-to-surface weapon, the AGM-69 SRAM is carried primarily by B-52 G/H variants and F-111A fighter bombers of the U.S. Air

Force. The internal carriage length of the missile is 166 inches (426.7 cm) and the external carriage length is 188 inches (482.6 cm). It is 17 inches (44.5 cm) in diameter and weighs 2,240 pounds (1,016 kg) at launch. Because the SRAM is supersonic, it travels between Mach 2.8 and Mach 3.2, depending on the flight profile. Powered by an LPC-415 solid-propellant rocket, it also includes a two-pulse rocket motor. Its warhead is a single 200-kiloton W-69 explosive, the same weapon used on the Minuteman 3 rocket.

Author Max Walmer says of the AGM-69, "SRAM can be launched from high or low altitude, and can be retargeted from the aircraft prior to launch. It is likely to be used against heavily defended targets such as air defense missile sites, radar installations, airfields, or other military targets."

References: Blake, Bernard, ed., *Jane's Weapon Systems, 1988–89* (Coulsdon, Surrey, UK: Jane's Information Group, 1988), 721; Walmer, Max, *An Illustrated Guide to Strategic Weapons* (New York: Prentice Hall, 1988), 43.

AGM-84 Harpoon/SLAM Antiship Missile

The antiship missile Harpoon can be launched from surface ships, submarines, or aircraft. Many AGM-84s, as well as seven of an updated infrared version called SLAM (standoff land attack), were used in the Persian Gulf War. All of them hit their Iraqi targets.

The Harpoon varies in length depending on the craft from which it is to be released. The length of the air-launched variety is 151.5 inches (388 cm), the surface ship/submarine variant is 182.2 inches (467 cm), and the SLAM model is 177 inches (454 cm). The weight of the missile is 1,150 pounds (522 kg). *Sea Power* notes that the "ship and submarine-launched versions have an additional booster motor, with four fins, attached to the rear of the missile."

References: Blake, Bernard, ed., *Jane's Weapon Systems, 1988–89* (Coulsdon, Surrey, UK: Jane's Information Group, 1988), 724; *Sea Power: The Official Publication of the Navy League of the United States* 37:1 (January 1994), 178.

AGM-84E Stand-off Land Attack Missile (SLAM)

See AGM-84 Harpoon/SLAM Antiship Missile.

AGM-88 HARM Air-to-Surface Missile

The HARM (high-speed antiradiation missile) is one of only two antiradiation air-to-surface missiles used by the United States during the Gulf War. It is deployed on F/A-18, EA-6B, and A-6E aircraft. During Operation Desert Storm, U.S. aircraft fired 1,961 HARMs at various targets.

Jane's Weapon Systems, 1988–89 reports that the HARM was intended to replace the older AGM-45 Shrike air-to-surface missile and the standard antiradiation missiles used by U.S. armed forces, and the Shrike was used only in limited numbers during the Persian Gulf War. At 13 feet 8 inches (4.17 m) in length, the HARM's two stubby middle-to-center wings have a span of 44 inches (113 cm). Its warhead is a 145.5-pound (66 kg) prefragmented high explosive with a laser proximity fuse. It has a range of 15.5 miles (25 km), guided by a broadband, passive, radar homing seeker. The U.S. military reports that the HARM is "designed to detect, guide to, and destroy radar emitters operating throughout a wide range of frequency bands."

See also AGM-45 Shrike Air-to-Surface Missile (ASM).
References: Blake, Bernard, ed., *Jane's Weapon Systems, 1988–89* (Coulsdon, Surrey, UK: Jane's Information Group, 1988), 724–725; *Gulf War Air Power Survey, Volume IV: Weapons, Tactics, and Training Report and Space Report* (Washington, DC: GPO, 1993), 105.

AGM-114A Hellfire

An antitank missile utilized specifically by the AH-1S HueyCobra and the AH-64 Apache, the Hellfire (short for heliborne-launched, fire and forget), is the U.S. Army's antiarmor missile. Of the more than 3,000 Hellfires used by the three branches of the military during Operation Desert Storm, the U.S. Army employed all but 189 of them.

The U.S. military's *Gulf War Air Power Survey* reports on the AGM-114A, "The Hellfire's

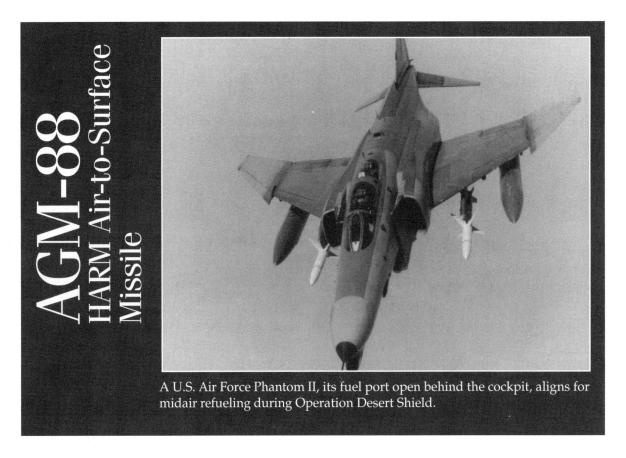

AGM-88
HARM Air-to-Surface Missile

A U.S. Air Force Phantom II, its fuel port open behind the cockpit, aligns for midair refueling during Operation Desert Shield.

semiactive seeker receives and homes in on reflected coded laser energy illuminated by a laser designator remote from the missile. Hellfire is not limited to direct line-of-sight attack, allowing launch without seeker lock-on, and thereby reducing exposure time and increasing survivability of the launch platform. The shaped-charge warhead contained 20 pounds [9 kg] of high explosives."

The AGM-114A is 5 feet 4 inches (1.63 m) in length, weighs 95 pounds (43 kg), and has a wingspan of 13 inches (330 mm). It was used mainly against armored vehicles.

References: Blake, Bernard, ed., *Jane's Weapon Systems, 1988–89* (Coulsdon, Surrey, UK: Jane's Information Group, 1988), 726; *Gulf War Air Power Survey, Volume IV: Weapons, Tactics, and Training Report and Space Report* (Washington, DC: GPO, 1993), 81.

Skipper bomb was used only 12 times during the Persian Gulf War.

According to the U.S. military's Gulf War Air Power Survey, "the AGM-123A was built around an AGM-45 Shrike solid-propellant rocket motor, a Paveway II seeker and airfoil group, and a Mk-83 bomb body. The rocket motor doubles the range of current Paveway II series munitions." The editors of *Jane's Weapon Systems, 1988–89* report that the Skipper II, an updated variant, is 14 feet 2 inches (4.33 m) in length, has a wingspan of 5 feet 3 inches (1.6 m), and weighs 1,283 pounds (582 kg).

References: Blake, Bernard, ed., *Jane's Weapon Systems, 1988–89* (Coulsdon, Surrey, UK: Jane's Information Group, 1988), 724; *Gulf War Air Power Survey, Volume IV: Weapons, Tactics, and Training Report and Space Report* (Washington, DC: GPO, 1993), 80.

AGM-123A Skipper

Designated as "a day and night, medium-range, standoff glide weapon that is directed to the target by reflected laser energy," the AGM-123A

AH-1S HueyCobra

Both this helicopter and its cousin, the AH-1T (a Marine version), are variants of the Hueys that flew during the Vietnam War. The basic AH-1 design is that of "an attack helicopter designed for close-in fire support and antitank missions." The Marine version flew 1,273 missions. Advanced versions include the AH-1W Super Cobra, another close-in fire-support craft that was used during Operation Restore Hope in Somalia, and the UH-1N Huey, an updated version of the craft that flew amphibious assault missions during the Vietnam War.

Powered by two General Electric T700-GE-401 turboshafts, the AH-1S seats a crew of two. It is capable of carrying up to eight TOW missiles, up to eight AGM-114 Hellfire missiles, or up to eight AIM-9L/M Sidewinder missiles. The craft has a wingspan of 10 feet 7 inches (3.23 m) and weighs 12,286 pounds (5,573 kg) fully fueled. The ship is designated the TH-1S Night Stalker when equipped with a FLIR (forward looking infrared radar) night-vision helmet system.

_____

See also AH-1T Sea Cobra and AH-1W Super Cobra.
References: Boyne, Walter J., *The Weapons of Desert Storm* (Lincolnwood, IL: Publications International, 1991), 28; *Gulf War Air Power Survey, Volume IV: Weapons, Tactics, and Training Report and Space Report* (Washington, DC: GPO, 1993), 62; Taylor, John W. R., ed., *Jane's All the World's Aircraft, 1989–90* (Coulsdon, Surrey, UK: Jane's Information Group, 1989), 364–365.

AH-1T Sea Cobra and AH-1W Super Cobra or Whiskey Cobra

The Marine Corps version of the AH-1S, 78 Marine Corps AH-1T Sea Cobras—39 onshore and 39 on ships in the Persian Gulf—flew 1,273 sorties, accumulating 2,014 hours of flight time during Operation Desert Storm. Forty-five models of the AH-1W variant also served, flying an undetermined number of missions.

The AH-1T is powered by two Pratt & Whitney T400-WV-402 twin turboshafts, delivering 1,970 shaft horsepower (shp). The craft has a maximum speed of 149 knots (172 mph; 276 km/h), a service ceiling of 10,550 feet (3,215 m), and a maximum unrefueled range of 310 nautical miles (356 mi; 575 km). The copter is equipped with a single 20 mm XM-197 three-barrel machine gun, and has four stores under its wings, allowing it the capability of carrying missiles or rockets. The AW-1W is powered by two

General Electric T700-GE-401 turboshafts delivering 3,200 shp. It has a maximum takeoff weight of 14,750 pounds (6,690 kg), a maximum speed of 189 knots (218 mph; 350 km/h), and an unrefueled range of 343 nautical miles (395 mi; 635 km). The AH-1W variant is suited to fly night-attack missions; this capability is provided by a pilot-worn ANVIS-AN/AVS-6 night-vision imaging system.

_____

See also AH-1S HueyCobra; ANVIS-AN/AVS-6 Night Vision Imaging System.
References: Almond, Denise L., ed., *Desert Score: U.S. Gulf War Weapons* (Washington, DC: Carroll Publishing, 1991), 62–63; Jordan, John, *An Illustrated Guide to Modern Naval Aviation and Aircraft Carriers* (London: Salamander, 1983), 94.

AH-64A Apache

Walter J. Boyne, in his *Weapons of Desert Storm*, says of this craft, "The AH-64A Apache is specifically designed for the attack role. . . . It was designed to be crashworthy. Armor made of boron carbide bonded to Kevlar protects the Apache crew and the helicopter's vital systems."

Powered by two General Electric T700-GE-701 turboshafts, the Apache is, according to the U.S. military, "the U.S. Army's principal attack helicopter." Able to conduct operations during the day or night, this two-seat attack helicopter is designed primarily to attack and destroy tanks on the field of battle. It has the capability of being armed with a Hellfire antitank missile, its primary weapon, although it is also equipped with an M230 30 mm cannon that can fire ammunition with HE (high explosive) or HEDP (high explosive, dual purpose) warheads. The Apaches that served during the war fired an estimated 5,000 Hellfires. The Apache's main rotor, "composed of stainless steel spars and glass fiber tubes," is 48 feet (14.63 m) in diameter; the tail rotor is 9 feet 2 inches (2.79 m) in diameter. It has a maximum speed of 184 mph (296 km/h), a maximum range of 300 miles (483 km), and a ceiling of 21,000 feet (6,400 m).

According to author Tom Clancy, during the Persian Gulf War the AH-64 was responsible for destroying 837 tanks and other tracked vehicles, 501 wheeled vehicles, 66 bunkers, 12 helicopters (on the ground), 10 fighter aircraft (on the ground), 120 artillery sites, and 42 SAM (surface-to-air missile) and AA (antiaircraft) gun sites.

An AH-64 Apache, the U.S. Army's principal attack helicopter, is equipped with a mast-mounted, fire-control radar system.

References: Boyne, Walter J., *The Weapons of Desert Storm* (Lincolnwood, IL: Publications International, 1991), 28; Clancy, Tom, *Armored Cav: A Guided Tour of an Armored Cavalry Regiment* (New York: Berkley, 1994), 136–137; *Gulf War Air Power Survey, Volume IV: Weapons, Tactics, and Training Report and Space Report* (Washington, DC: GPO, 1993), 62.

AIM-7 Sparrow Air-to-Air Missile

Military experts James F. Dunnigan and Austin Bay write of this projectile: "Sparrow continues to evolve due to its continued upgrades in the shipboard surface-to-air variants (RIM series) that result in upgrades to air-launched versions as well. RIM/AIM-7P now is in production and provides reprogrammable memory and better envelope expansion. A later version now in development will add dual-spectrum seeker capability for advanced electronic countermeasures threats." According to Dunnigan and Bay, the Sparrow and its mate, the AIM-9L/M Sidewinder, accounted for almost all the air-to-air kills of Iraqi aircraft during Operation Desert Storm (the Sparrow was involved in 24 of 39 kills).

The Sparrow is 12 feet (3.66 m) long, has a wingspan of 3 feet 4 inches (1 m), weighs 510 pounds (231 kg), has a maximum speed of more than 2,660 mph (4,280 km/h), has a range of more than 30 nautical miles (35 mi; 56 km), and carries a WAU-17 fragmentation warhead. The missile is powered by a Hercules Mk 58 solid-propellant rocket.

References: Dunnigan, James F., and Austin Bay, *From Shield to Storm: High-Tech Weapons, Military Strategy, and Coalition Warfare in the Persian Gulf* (New York: Morrow, 1992), 216; *Sea Power: The Official Publication of the Navy League of the United States* 37:1 (January 1994), 180.

AIM-9L/M Sidewinder Missile

One of the oldest missiles in the arsenal of the U.S. military (it evolved from the AIM-9B missiles developed in the 1940s and 1950s), the Sidewinder accounted for 11 of the 39 kills of Iraqi aircraft registered by the coalition during the war. Widely honored for its mission capability,

AIM-7 Sparrow Air-to-Air Missile

Missiles mounted on pylons under the wings of a U.S. Navy F-14A Tomcat include two AIM-7 Sparrow missiles inboard of two AIM-9 Sidewinder missiles.

the Soviets and Chinese have built their own versions of it.

Military historian Bill Gunston writes of the Sidewinder family: "Though large numbers of earlier versions remain in use, most front line United States Air Force aircraft today carry the greatly improved AIM-9J family, with part solid-state electronics and detachable double-delta control fins, or the much better still AIM-9L with control fins of greater span and pointed tips, a totally new guidance system and an annular blast/fragmentation warhead triggered by an annular proximity fuze with a ring of eight miniature lasers."

The Sidewinder version employed during the Persian Gulf War was the AIM-9M. A supersonic projectile with homing and heat-seeking capabilities, the AIM-9M was used on F-15Cs, F-15Es, and F-4Gs. One source, a military survey conducted by the U.S. government, notes, "Unlike the semiactive radar AIM-7, the Sidewinder is a 'fire and forget' missile. It does, however, require visual target acquisition. The AIM-9 seeker converts infrared (heat) energy emitted by the target into electrical signals used to guide the missile. The guidance and control units incorpo-

rate inputs from gyroscopic sensors, allowing the missile to 'lead' the target and fly what is termed a proportional navigation course. . . . Desert Storm AIM-9 variants used active optical target detectors to command detonation. The fuze functioned on either a direct hit or proximity miss."

The Sidewinder is 9 feet 4.2 inches (2.85 m) long, has a wingspan of 2 feet 1 inch (64 cm), and weighs 188 pounds (85 kg). It has a maximum speed of Mach 2.5 (1,875 mph) and a range of 10,000 to 20,000 yards (9,146–18,292 m), and is powered by a single propellant rocket. Its warhead is an annular blast fragmentation package that weighs 20.8 pounds (9.4 kg).

References: Dunnigan, James F., and Austin Bay, *From Shield to Storm: High-Tech Weapons, Military Strategy, and Coalition Warfare in the Persian Gulf* (New York: Morrow, 1992), 215–216; *Gulf War Air Power Survey, Volume IV: Weapons, Tactics, and Training Report and Space Report* (Washington, DC: GPO, 1993), 115–116; Gunston, Bill, *An Illustrated Guide to USAF: The Modern US Air Force* (New York: Prentice Hall, 1991), 158; *Sea Power: The Official Publication of the Navy League of the United States* 37:1 (January 1994), 180.

AIM-54 Phoenix Air-to-Air Missile

See Phoenix Air-to-Air Missile (AIM-54).

AIM-120A Advanced Medium-Range Air-to-Air Missile (AMRAAM)

Built by Raytheon and Hughes Missiles System, the AMRAAM is designed to fly on the F-14 Tomcat, F-15 Eagle, F-16 Fighting Falcon, and F/A-18 Hornet aircraft.

According to the military's *Gulf War Air Power Survey*, the AMRAAM is "a new generation radar-homing air-to-air missile with a blast fragmentation warhead. It has an all-weather, beyond-visual-range capability and serves as a follow-on to the AIM-7 Sparrow missile series. The AIM-120A missile is faster, smaller, and lighter than its predecessors and has improved capabilities against low altitude targets. It incorporates active radar homing in conjunction with an inertial reference unit. This unit and its microcomputer system make the missile less dependent on the fire control system than were previous radar missiles, enabling the pilot to aim and fire several missiles simultaneously at multiple targets. Like the infrared AIM-9, the AIM-120A is a 'fire and forget' missile; the pilot can fire and then perform evasive maneuvers while the missiles guide themselves to targets."

The AIM-120A is 11 feet 9 inches (3.57 m) long, has a wingspan of 1 foot 9 inches (526 mm), and weighs 300 pounds (136 kg). The missile can travel more than 760 mph (1,223 km/h) and has a range of 39 nautical miles (45 mi; 72 km). It is powered by a directed rocket motor and guided by inertial and active radar systems.

References: Blake, Bernard, ed., *Jane's Weapon Systems, 1988–89* (Coulsdon, Surrey, UK: Jane's Information Group, 1988), 702; *Gulf War Air Power Survey, Volume IV: Weapons, Tactics, and Training Report and Space Report* (Washington, DC: GPO, 1993), 117; *Sea Power: The Official Publication of the Navy League of the United States* 37:1 (January 1994), 178.

AIM-9L/M
Sidewinder Missile

An AIM Sidewinder missile, mounted next to the fuselage of an A-7E Corsair, complements the aircraft's weapons payload of eight Mark 82 500-pound bombs.

Air Tasking Order (ATO)

This process was used for the first time in the Persian Gulf War, with resounding success. Simply explained, the Air Tasking Order is a program in which potential targets are matched (in this case by computer) with the available planes and weapons that could destroy the target effectively. These decisions were made under the command of General Charles Horner, the Joint Air Forces Component commander (JFGACC), who acted under the authority of General H. Norman Schwarzkopf, commander in chief of the U.S. Central Command.

See also Schwarzkopf, General H. Norman.

Airborne Warning and Control System (AWACS)

The E-3 Sentry AWACS system, flown in Boeing 707 aircraft, provides the U.S. Air Force with airborne radar facilities.

Built by Boeing Aerospace, the E-3 can carry up to 17 crew members and is powered by four Pratt & Whitney TF33-PW-100/100A turbofan engines providing 21,000 pounds (9,525 kg) of thrust. The plane has a length of 152 feet 11 inches (46.61 m), weighs about 325,000 pounds (147,419 kg) fully loaded, and has a maximum speed of 530 mph (853 km/h) with an unrefueled range of 1,000 miles (1,609 km).

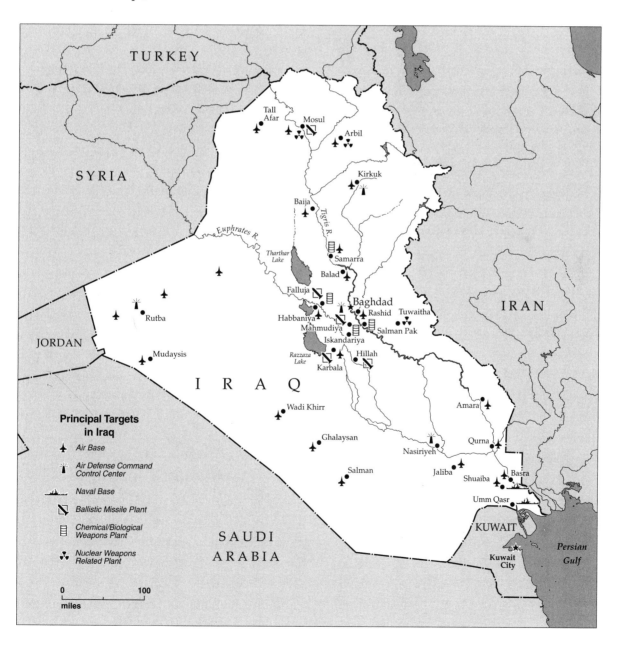

References: Gunston, Bill, *An Illustrated Guide to USAF: The Modern US Air Force* (New York: Prentice Hall, 1991), 34–39; Polmar, Norman, ed., *World Combat Aircraft Directory* (Garden City, NY: Doubleday, 1976), 256.

Aircraft Carriers, Coalition

Only one non-American aircraft carrier served during the Persian Gulf conflict: the British light aircraft carrier *Ark Royal* (CVSA-R O7), which served as a part of Task Group 323.2 to keep tabs on the machinations of Libya and perform reconnaissance over the eastern Mediterranean. The ship, which among its class boasts the *Invincible* and the *Illustrious*, displaces 20,000 tons standard (500 tons more than its two counterparts), has a flight deck that is 550 by 44.3 feet (167.8 by 13.5 m), and has a maximum speed of 28 knots (32 mph; 52 km/h) and a maximum unrefueled range of 5,000 miles (8,045 m). Among its armaments are the British Aerospace Sea Dart GWS 30 twin surface-to-air missile launcher and two General Electric/General Dynamics 20 mm Mk 15 Vulcan Phalanx guns with three separate mountings. The French sent the aircraft carrier *Clemenceau* to the Gulf, but its only mission was to deliver French troops to the Kuwaiti Theatre of Operations.

See also Task Group 323.2.
Reference: Sharpe, Richard, ed., *Jane's Fighting Ships, 1990–91* (Coulsdon, Surrey, UK: Jane's Information Group, 1990), 681.

Aircraft Carriers, United States

Aircraft carriers have been an important asset in the American military's equation in fighting wars since World War II, and were of significant benefit during the Persian Gulf War. Of the 177 American ships that served during the war, 6 were aircraft carriers.

Serving as the lead ship for Carrier Group Saratoga was the carrier *Saratoga* (CV 60). A member of the Forrestal class, the carrier displaces 59,060 tons empty (80,383 tons fully loaded) and is 1,071 feet (326.4 m) long. Powered by eight Babcock & Wilcox boilers and four Westinghouse geared turbines, the carrier has a maximum speed of 33 knots (38 mph; 61 km/h) and a range of 8,000 miles (12,872 km) at 20 knots (23 mph; 37 km/h). The *Saratoga* is complemented by a crew of 2,896 (including 136 officers) and an aircrew of 2,480 (which includes 290 officers). The ship is armed with three Raytheon Sea Sparrow Mk 29 octuple launchers and three General Electric/General Dynamics 20 mm Vulcan Phalanx guns. It is equipped to carry differing kinds of aircraft, including 20 F-14s, 20 F/A-18s, 20 A-6Es, 5 EA-6Bs, 10 S-3As, and 5 E-2Cs, as well as 6 SH-3G/H (also designated as the Canadian CH-124) Sea King helicopters.

The Carrier Group Kennedy was led by the aircraft carrier *John F. Kennedy* (CV 67), built in Newport News, Virginia, and commissioned in 1968. Powered by eight Foster-Wheeler boilers and four Westinghouse geared turbines, the *John F. Kennedy*, a member of the Kitty Hawk and John F. Kennedy class, displaces 61,000 tons standard (80,941 tons fully loaded), is 1,052 feet (320.7 m) long, and has a maximum speed of 32 knots (37 mph; 59 km/h). It carries a complement of 3,200 crew members (including 155 officers), as well as an aircrew of 2,480 (which includes 320 officers). The ship is equipped with three Raytheon Sea Sparrow Mk 20 octuple surface-to-air missile launchers and three General Electric/General Dynamics 20 mm Vulcan Phalanx guns. The *John F. Kennedy* is equipped to carry 20 F-14s, 20 F/A-18s, 5 EA-6Bs, 20 A-6s, 5 E-2Cs, and 10 S-3As, as well as 6 SH-3G/H Sea King helicopters.

The Carrier Group Midway was led by the carrier *Midway* (CV 41), a member of the Midway class (the *Coral Sea* is the only other ship). The ship displaces 51,000 tons standard (64,002 fully loaded) and is 979 feet (298.4 m) long. Powered by 12 Babcock & Wilcox boilers and 4 Westinghouse geared turbines, the *Midway* has a maximum speed of 30 knots (35 mph; 56 km/h) and a maximum range of 15,000 miles (24,135 km) at 20 knots (23 mph; 37 km/h). It is complemented by a crew of 2,826 (including 142 officers) and an aircrew of 1,854. The ship is also equipped with two Raytheon Sea Sparrow Mk 20 octuple surface-to-air missile launchers and either two or three General Electric/General Dynamics 20 mm Vulcan Phalanx guns. It is capa-

An E-3A Sentry flies patrol above Saudi Arabia during Operation Desert Shield.

AWACS Airborne Warning and Control System

ble of carrying 36 F/A-18s, 12 A-6Es, 4 EA-6Bs, and 4 E-2Cs, as well as 6 SH-3G/H Sea King helicopters.

Leading the way for the Carrier Group Roosevelt was the nuclear aircraft carrier *Theodore Roosevelt* (CVN 71), a member of the Nimitz class, a category of nuclear-powered carriers. The ship displaces 93,973 tons empty (96,386 fully loaded), and is 1,040 feet (317 m) long. Powered by two pressurized and water-cooled A4W/A1G nuclear reactors and four geared steam turbines, the *Theodore Roosevelt* has a maximum speed of 30+ knots (35 mph; 55 km/h), a complement of 3,136 (including 155 officers), and an aircrew of 2,800 (including 266 officers). The ship is equipped with two Raytheon Sea Sparrow Mk 20 octuple surface-to-air missile launchers and four General Electric/General Dynamics 20 mm Vulcan Phalanx guns. The carrier is capable of carrying 20 F-14s, 20 F/A-18s, 6 EA-6Bs, 20 A-6s, 5 E-2Cs, and 10 S-3As, as well as 6 SH-3G/H Sea King helicopters.

The lead ship of the Carrier Group America was the aircraft carrier *America* (CV 66), part of the Kitty Hawk and John F. Kennedy class. The *America* is similar to the carrier *John F. Kennedy* except for small differences, such as displacing fewer tons empty (60,300) and full (79,724), having shorter dimensions (1,046 feet [318.8 m] in length), and a smaller crew (2,963 men, including 152 officers).

The Carrier Group Ranger was led by the *Ranger* (CV 61). Like the *Saratoga*, the *Ranger* is a member of the Forrestal class, differing only in that it displaces more tons empty (60,000) and full (81,163), and carries more crew (2,889, including 161 officers).

The Carrier Group Independence was led by the carrier *Independence* (CV 62). A member of the Forrestal class, its dimensions match those of its sister ship, the *Saratoga*. The Carrier Group Eisenhower was led by the *Eisenhower* (CVN 69), a member of the Nimitz class like the *Theodore Roosevelt*.

Reference: Sharpe, Richard, ed., *Jane's Fighting Ships, 1990–91* (Coulsdon, Surrey, UK: Jane's Information Group, 1990), 707, 710, 712–714.

The nuclear-powered aircraft carrier USS *Dwight D. Eisenhower* passes through the Suez Canal in 1992.

Aircraft Carriers, U.S.

Alarm

This "short-range British antiradiation missile" was used 113 times by British Tornadoes during Operation Desert Storm.

According to *Jane's All the World's Aircraft, 1988–89*, the Alarm, an air-to-surface missile that competes with the American AGM-88 HARM missile, has a combined weight (with its launcher) of 617 pounds (280 kg), a length of 13 feet 1 inch (4 m), and a wingspan of 29 inches (0.73m). The primary British plane that carries the Alarm is the GR1 Tornado.

References: Blake, Bernard, ed., *Jane's Weapon Systems, 1988–89* (Coulsdon, Surrey, UK: Jane's Information Group, 1988), 719; *Gulf War Air Power Survey, Volume IV: Weapons, Tactics, and Training Report and Space Report* (Washington, DC: GPO, 1993), 105.

Algiers Agreement of 6 March 1975

This secret understanding between Saddam Hussein, at the time vice-chairman of Iraq's Rev-olutionary Command Council (RCC) and head of his nation's Ba'ath party, and the shah of Iran, Reza Pahlavi, settled (at least for a time) the crisis over the Shatt al-Arab waterway that threatened to plunge the two nations into war. The arrangement allowed both countries to gain some control over the disputed waterway at the *thalweg*, while dropping their claims to other sections; at the same time, Iraq got the shah to drop his support of the Kurds fighting the Iraqi government. The deal fell apart in the late 1970s, and was abrogated by Iraq on 7 September 1980 in a prelude to its invasion of Iran and the beginning of the Iran-Iraq War.

According to the agreement, "During the convocation of the OPEC summit conference in the Algerian capital of Algiers, and upon the initiative of Algerian President Houari Boumedienne, the Shah of Iran and Saddam Hussein met twice and conducted lengthy talks on the relations between Iraq and Iran. These talks, attended by President Houari Boumedienne, were characterized by complete frankness and a sincere will from both parties to reach a final and permanent solution to all problems existing between the two countries in accordance with the principles of territorial integrity, border inviolability and non-interference in internal affairs."

See also Shatt al-Arab Waterway; Thalweg Principle.
Reference: Krosney, Herbert, *Deadly Business: Legal Deals and Outlaw Weapons—The Arming of Iran and Iraq, 1975 to the Present* (New York: Four Walls Eight Windows, 1993).

Alouette III

This French helicopter was stationed aboard two Argentine warships, the Meko-class destroyer *Almirante Brown* and the 42 Meko-class frigate *Spiro*. Originally built by France's Aerospatiale (which produced 1,450 models), the craft is now built by India's Hindustan Aeronautics Limited (HAL) for the Indian air force.

The French form of the Alouette is a turbine-driven helicopter powered by one 870-shaft-horsepower (649 kW) Turbomeca Artouste IIIB turboshaft, and can seat a pilot and six other persons. In its military application, the Alouette can be outfitted with a variety of weapons systems. In addition to the positioning of a 7.62 mm machine gun on a tripod, as well as a 20 mm cannon, the craft can be implemented with wire-guided missiles or 68 mm rocket-launcher pods.

Reference: Lambert, Mark, ed., *Jane's All the World's Aircraft, 1991–92* (Coulsdon, Surrey, UK: Jane's Information Group, 1991), 103.

Amphibious Assault Ships, United States

Of the 177 American ships that served during the Persian Gulf conflict, nine were amphibious assault ships. According to *Sea Power: The Official Publication of the Navy League of the United States,* these ships can carry "a Marine battalion landing team, its weapons and equipment, a reinforced squadron of transport helicopters and support personnel." The assault ships came in two waves: those that arrived in the Kuwaiti Theater of Operations (KTO) on 6 September 1990 with the Fourth Marine Expeditionary Brigade, and those that arrived in the KTO on 12 January 1991 with the Fifth Marine Expeditionary Brigade. The ships that did serve in the Gulf War came from two of the three assault ship classes: Tarawa and Iwo Jima.

The Tarawa class is represented by the *Tarawa* (LHA 1, Fifth Marine Expeditionary Brigade), and the *Nassau* (LHA 4, Fourth Marine Expeditionary Brigade). These ships displace 25,120 tons light (39,300 tons fully loaded), and are 833.75 feet (254.2 m) in length. Powered by two Combustion Engineering boilers and two Westinghouse turbines, the Tarawa class has a maximum speed of 24 knots (28 mph; 44 km/h), and an unrefueled range of 10,000 nautical miles (18,520 km) at 20 knots (23 mph; 37 km/h). Complement for the ships differ; the *Tarawa* can carry 926 men (including 60 officers), while the *Nassau* carries 923 men (including 62 officers). The ships have the capability of carrying up to 1,900 troops, in addition to a combination of 30 CH-46 "Sea Knight" and CH-53 "Sea Stallion" helicopters, as well as 6 AV-8B Harrier VSTOL aircraft.

The Iwo Jima class is represented by the *Iwo Jima* (LPH 2, Fourth Marine Expeditionary Brigade), the *Guam* (LPH 9, Fourth Marine Expeditionary Brigade), the *Tripoli* (LPH 10, Fifth Marine Expeditionary Brigade), and the *New Orleans* (LPH 11, Fifth Marine Expeditionary Brigade). These ships displace 11,000 tons light (18,300 tons fully loaded), and are 602.25 feet (183.6 m) in length. Powered by a single Westinghouse steam turbine, which delivers 23,000 shaft horsepower, and two Combustion Engineering boilers (except for the *Guam*, which has two Babcock & Wilcox boilers), the ships have a maximum speed of 23 knots (26 mph; 43 km/h) and an unrefueled range of 16,600 nautical miles (30,743 km) at 11.5 knots (13 mph; 21 km/h). Complement for the ships range from the *Iwo Jima's* 673 (including 51 officers), to the *Guam's* 667 (including 49 officers), to the *Tripoli's* 690 (including 49 officers), to the *New Orleans's* 656 (including 46 officers). Each ship has the capability of transporting up to 1,900 troops, as well as carrying a combination of 25 CH-46 "Sea Knight" and CH-53 "Sea Stallion" helicopters.

Military author Norman Polmar writes, "In December 1990, upon arrival in the Middle East, the *Tripoli* became [the] flagship of the U.S. mine countermeasures group for operations in the Persian Gulf and took aboard Mine Counter- measures Squadron (MH) 14. On 18 February 1991 the *Tripoli* struck a moored contact mine in the Gulf that blasted a 20 x 30-foot (6.1 x 9.1-m) hole in the ship's starboard side, below the wa- terline. None of the crew were killed and injuries [were] slight. The *Tripoli* was repaired in dry dock in Bahrain; after repairs, which took one month, she returned to MCM duties in the Gulf, with her last helicopter mine mission being flown on 18 June 1991, after which she departed the Gulf on 23 June and returned to the United States."

References: Sea Power: The Official Publication of the Navy League of the United States 37:1 (January 1994), 148; Polmar, Norman, *The Naval Institute Guide to the Ships and Aircraft of the U.S. Fleet* (Annapolis, MD: Naval Institute Press, 1993), 164–167.

Amphibious Cargo Ships, United States

Of the 177 American ships that served during Operations Desert Shield/Desert Storm, 2 were amphibious cargo ships. The naval journal *Sea Power* says on these craft, "These ships, which carry heavy equipment and supplies for am- phibious assaults, are the first class of ship de- signed specifically for this role." All ships of this type come from the Charleston class. They were the *Durham*, which served as a part of the Thir- teenth Marine Expeditionary Unit from 7 Sep- tember 1990, and the *Mobile*, which as a part of the Fifth Marine Expeditionary Brigade saw ac- tion in the Kuwaiti Theater of Operations (KTO) from 12 January 1991 on. These ships displace 20,700 tons fully loaded, are 575 feet (175.26 m) in length, and have a maximum speed of 20 knots (23 mph; 37 km/h). Powered by two boil- ers and one steam turbine, which provide 22,000 shaft horsepower (shp), the ships have a comple- ment of 364, with the ability to transport up to 226 troops.

Reference: Sea Power: The Official Publication of the Navy League of the United States 37:1 (January 1994), 148.

Amphibious Command Ships, United States

Only one amphibious command ship, the USS *Blue Ridge*, served during the Gulf conflict. The *Blue Ridge* (LCC-19) served as the command ship for the naval element of CENTCOM from 28 Au- gust 1990 until the end of the war. As part of the Blue Ridge class, the *Blue Ridge* displaces 19,290 tons, is 620 feet (189 m) in length, has a maxi- mum speed of 23 knots (26 mph; 43 km/h), and carries a complement of 241 crew members. Powered by a single steam turbine and two boil- ers, the ship has a landing pad for helicopters and is armed with Sea Sparrow missile batteries, four 3-inch, 50-caliber antiaircraft weapons, and two Phalanx close-in weapons systems (CIWSs, pronounced "sea-whiz").

Reference: Sea Power: The Official Publication of the Navy League of the United States 37:1 (January 1994), 150.

Amphibious Transport Docks, United States

Of the 177 American ships that served in the Per- sian Gulf War, 8 were amphibious transport docks, of which naval authority Norman Polmar reports, "They carry Marines into forward areas and unload them by landing craft and vehicles carried into their docking well, and by using hel- icopters provided mainly from amphibious as- sault ships." The transport docks that served were of two classes: Austin and Raleigh.

The six ships that complement the Austin class were the *Shreveport* (LPD 12) and the *Tren- ton* (LPD 14), both from the Fourth Marine Ex- peditionary Brigade, which arrived in the Ku- waiti Theater of Operations on 6 September 1990; the *Denver* (LPD 9) and the *Juneau* (LPD 10), which as part of the Fifth Marine Expedi- tionary Brigade arrived in the KTO on 12 Janu- ary 1991; the *Ogden* (LPD 5), which as part of the Thirteenth Marine Expeditionary Unit arrived in the KTO on 7 September 1990; and the *Dubuque* (LPD 8), which as part of the Amphibious Ready Group Bravo arrived in the KTO on 9 September 1990 and departed on 13 October 1990. These ships displace approximately 17,000 tons fully loaded, are 570 feet (174 m) in length, and travel

A French crewman waves from atop an AMX-30 Main Battle Tank near Al-Salman, Iraq.

at a maximum speed of 21 knots (24 mph; 39 km/h). Powered by two boilers and two steam turbines, which generate 24,000 shaft horsepower (shp), the ships are complemented by 388 crew members, and can carry up to 900 troops. The ships are equipped to carry up to six CH-46 "Sea Knight" helicopters, and are armed with four 50-caliber guns and two Phalanx close-in weapons systems (CIWSs). According to Polmar, "During U.S. minesweeping operations in the Persian Gulf in 1988 the *Trenton* served as tender to six ocean minesweepers."

The two ships of the Raleigh class of transport docks (both of which were decommissioned after the war) were the *Raleigh* (LPD 1, of the Fourth Marine Expeditionary Brigade, which arrived in the KTO on 6 September 1990); and the *Vancouver* (LPD 2, of the Fifth Marine Expeditionary Brigade, which arrived in the KTO on 12 January 1991). These ships displace 8,491 tons light (14,865 tons fully loaded), and are 521.5 feet (159 m) in length. Powered by two De Laval geared steam turbines and two Babcock & Wilcox boilers, the ships have a maximum speed of 21.6 knots (25 mph; 40 km/h), and a maximum unrefueled range of 9,600 nautical miles (17,780

km) at 16 knots (18 mph; 30 km/h). The *Raleigh* had a complement of 397 (including 24 officers), while the *Vancouver*'s complement was 401 (including 27 officers). The ships were capable of carrying up to 1,140 troops. The *Raleigh* was decommissioned on 13 December 1991, and the *Vancouver* on 27 March 1992.

Reference: Almond, Denise L., ed., *Desert Score: U.S. Gulf War Weapons* (Washington, DC: Carroll Publishing, 1991), 469–474; *Sea Power: The Official Publication of the Navy League of the United States* 37:1 (January 1994), 148; Polmar, Norman, *The Naval Institute Guide to the Ships and Aircraft of the U.S. Fleet* (Annapolis, Maryland: Naval Institute Press, 1993), 172.

AMX-30 Main Battle Tank

Tanks from various countries were instrumental in the Allied victory over Iraq. Among these was the AMX-30, which was used by Qatar, France, and Saudi Arabia. France used a variant called the AMX-30B2.

Built by Giat Industries of France, the AMX-30 seats a crew of four. It is powered by a Hispano-

Suiza HS 110 12-cylinder engine and weighs 79,366 pounds (36,000 kg) (the AMX-30B2 weighs 81,570 pounds [37,000 kg]). *Jane's Main Battle Tanks* says of this vehicle, "[The] main armament of the AMX-30 is a 105 mm rifled gun designated the CN-105-F1 with a length of 56 calibres . . . the 105 mm gun can fire HEAT [High Explosive AntiTank missiles], HE, phosphorous smoke or illuminating rounds of a French design and can also fire standard 105 mm ammunition as used with the L7 series of weapons mounted in the Leopard 1 and M60 series of Main Battle Tanks." Of the AMX-30B2, one source writes, "[It] is essentially an AMX-30 with an integrated fire control system based on a laser rangefinder and a thermal system, new gearbox and other improvements."

References: Foss, Christopher F., ed., *Jane's Armour and Artillery, 1992–93* (Coulsdon, Surrey, UK: Jane's Information Group, 1992), 49; Foss, Christopher F., ed., *Jane's Main Battle Tanks* (London: Jane's Publishing Group, 1986), 22.

Analysts, American Television

The Persian Gulf War television coverage was noted for its use of analysts—experts in Middle East culture, history, and military matters—who spent countless hours offering their opinions on special reports aired by the American television networks.

Major General Perry M. Smith (USAF, ret.) comments on this use of analysts, "The networks decided before the war started that, if they were going to provide knowledgeable commentary on it, they would not rely solely on journalists and part-time military analysts. They needed to have, at the elbows of the producers, at the anchor desks, and in their research bureaus, individuals who had a thorough knowledge of military strategy, operational doctrine, tactics, and modern weapons systems."

Analysts for CBS included Fouad Ajami, director of Middle East Studies at Johns Hopkins University; General Michael Dugan, former Air Force chief of staff; and General George Crist (USMC, ret.), former commander of the U.S. Central Command. ABC offered Anthony H. Cordesman, adjunct professor of national security studies at Georgetown University; H. J. de Blij, professor of geography at Georgetown University's School of Foreign Service; Judith Kipper, guest scholar in foreign policy studies at the Brookings Institution, a Washington, D.C., think tank; Lieutenant General Bernard Trainor (USMC, ret.), a veteran of Korea and Vietnam who had worked for the *New York Times* and covered the Iran-Iraq War; and Admiral William Crowe, former chairman of the Joint Chiefs of Staff. NBC presented Colonel Harry G. Summers, Jr. (USA, ret.), a veteran of Korea and Vietnam and prolific author on military affairs; Gary Sick, former staff member of the National Security Council; Lieutenant General William Odom (USA, ret.), former director of the National Security Agency and former staff member on the National Security Council; and Edward L. Peck, former chief of the U.S. mission in Baghdad. CNN featured James Blackwell, a senior fellow at the Center for Strategic and International Studies in Washington, D.C.; Major General Perry M. Smith (USAF, ret.); Richard Perle, former assistant secretary of defense; and John Keegan, a British military and war historian.

References: "The Shooting Has Stopped, but There's No Armistice Yet in the Ratings War among TV's Pundits," *People* 36:9 (11 March 1991), 40–41; Smith, Perry M., *How CNN Fought the War: A View from the Inside* (New York: Carroll Publishing, 1991), 99.

Anglo-Iraqi Treaty (1922)

This pact, signed by the British government and King Faisal I of Iraq (the former king of Syria), increased British dominance over Iraqi affairs; however, it was a matter of irritation between the two nations, and led to increased anti-British emotions in Iraq.

The Federal Research Division of the Library of Congress, in their *Iraq: A Country Study,* explains, "The final major decision taken at the Cairo Conference [of 1921] related to the new Anglo-Iraqi Treaty. [King] Faisal was under pressure from the nationalists and the anti-British *mujtahids* [described by Middle East writer William L. Cleveland as "one who is recognized as competent to exercise ijitihad, the exercise of informed human reason in deciding matters of Islamic law"] of An Najaf and Karbala to limit both British influence in Iraq and the duration of the treaty. Recognizing that the monarchy de-

Air Force chief of staff General Michael J. Dugan joins Air Force personnel in
Saudi Arabia for breakfast in September 1990.

pended on British support—and wishing to avoid a repetition of his experience in Syria—Faisal maintained a moderate approach in dealing with Britain. The 20-year treaty, ratified in October 1922, stated that the king would heed British advice on all matters affecting British interests and on fiscal policy as long as Iraq was in debt to Britain, and that British officials would be appointed to specified posts in 18 departments to act as advisers and inspectors. Professor Malcolm B. Russell wrote: "His [Faisal's] own opposition to British demands in the treaty became so strong in 1922 that the British seemed poised to remove him . . . thus he used public opposition to the 1922 treaty as grounds in 1923 for terms that reduced its length from 20 years to four. Another treaty in 1930 provided for Iraqi independence while maintaining British bases and influence. Despite denunciations by militant nationalists in Iraq, it became the basis for the country's independence in 1932."

See also Faisal I, King of Iraq.
References: Cleveland, William L., A History of the Modern Middle East (Boulder, CO: Westview, 1994), 458–459; Metz, Helen Chapman, ed., Iraq: A Country Study (Washington, DC: GPO, 1990), 36–37; Russell, Malcolm B., "Faisal I (1883?–1933), Faisal II (1935–1958), and the Rise and Fall of the Hashemite Dynasty in Iraq," in Historic World Leaders, Vol. 1, edited by Anne Commire (Detroit: Gale, 1991), 159.

Antiaircraft Artillery, Iraqi

The Iraqis were outfitted with two types of antiaircraft artillery (AAA): self-propelled and towed. Almost all of these weapons were supplied by Eastern European nations and China. Self-propelled AAA include the ZSU-57-2 (USSR), M53/59 and M53/70 (Czechoslovakia), and ZSU-23/4 Shilka (USSR). Towed artillery units include the 130 mm KS-30 (provided by the USSR), 100 mm KS-19 (USSR), 85 mm KS-12/12A/18 (USSR), 57 mm Type 19 and S-60 (China and the USSR, respectively), 40 mm Bofors L-70 (Switzerland), 37 mm Type 55 and M1939 (China and the USSR, respectively), 35 mm Oerlikon (Switzerland), 23 mm ZU-23/2 (USSR), 20 mm M55 single (Yugoslavia), 14.5 mm ZPU-4 (USSR), 14.5 mm MR-4 (Romania), 14.5 mm Type 56 (China), and 14.5 mm ZPU-2 (USSR/Bulgaria).

Reference: Gulf War Air Power Survey, Volume IV: Weapons, Tactics, and Training Report and Space Report (Washington, DC: GPO, 1993), 16.

Antiradiation Missiles, Use of by Coalition in War

See AGM-45 Shrike Air-to-Surface Missile; AGM-88 HARM Air-to-Surface Missile; Alarm.

Antiwar Movement

Most of the public opposition to allied military action in the Persian Gulf came from the United States, although there were a small number of marches worldwide, particularly in Arab countries such as Jordan and the Occupied Territories.

As Todd Gitlin wrote in the Village Voice, "Amid the anti-imperialist rhetoric from the speaker's stand at anti-war rallies, one hears a refusal to recognize that something is at stake in the Gulf besides the lone superpower's desire to show off its smart bombs. One hears casual dismissal of Saddam Hussein's erasure of, and atrocities in, Kuwait. One hears an isolationist lack of interest in the prospect of his controlling a big bloc of world oil production, as if Iraq's military machine were a matter of indifference to global security." Some of these views were expressed on 20 October 1990, when thousands of people marched in 16 cities across the United States in opposition to the U.S. buildup and the threat of war.

Some of the leading antiwar activists in the United States included Jesse Jackson and Ramsay Clark, former attorney general under Lyndon Johnson. Another, less-known activist was Anthony Lawrence, an economist with the U.S. Treasury Department who went to Iraq after the start of the air war and condemned the U.S. government and the war as "an imperialistic attempt to wrest the oil resources of this region." Although he supported the decision of his two sons to enter the U.S. military, he disagreed with the idea of sending them to the Gulf. "My sons did not volunteer to go halfway around the world and kill Arab people in a war of aggression," he said in an interview with CNN's Peter Arnett. After spending time in a "camp near the

Antiaircraft Artillery, Iraqi

U.S. Marines relax on an abandoned Iraqi antiaircraft artillery piece near Kuwait International Airport.

Antiwar Movement

Activists opposed to U.S. policy in the Persian Gulf participate in a demonstration on 20 October 1990 in New York City.

Kuwaiti border with a 'Gulf Peace Team,'" he returned to the United States, where he wanted to form "the core of a very, very strong movement for peace on this planet."

The *New York Times* surveyed attitudes among antiwar activists following the end of the war. For them, the newspaper found, "the nation's victory is bitter." "This is one victory I'm not celebrating," said Margaret Hummel, a peace activist from Vermont. "This was a severe defeat for the international community. I was appalled at the death [*sic*] of so many Iraqis. Sanctions and diplomacy could have eventually forced them to leave Kuwait. Now I fear that war will be more and more accepted as a way to solve our problems and that we'll spend more and more money on the military instead of on problems at home that are more pressing."

References: Ayres, B. Drummond, Jr., "For Foes of Gulf War, Nation's Victory Is Bitter," *New York Times,* 17 March 1991, A20; Gitlin, Todd, "Toward a Difficult Peace Movement," *Village Voice,* 19 February 1991, quoted in *The Gulf War Reader: History, Documents, Opinions,* edited by Micah L. Sifry and Christopher Serf (New York: Times Books, 1991), 321; Harris, Scott, "U.S. Peace Movement Energized by Deadline, Plans a Wave of Protests," *Los Angeles Times,* 11 January 1991, A8; Hinds, Michael deCourcy, "Drawing on Vietnam Legacy, Antiwar Effort Buds Quickly," *New York Times,* 11 January 1991, A1; Nieves, Evelyn, "Thousands March in 16 Cities To Protest U.S. Intervention in Gulf," *New York Times,* 21 October 1990, A14; Walsh, Elsa, "Local Activist Finds Fame in Baghdad," *Washington Post,* 31 January 1991, A24.

ANVIS-AN/AVS-6 Night Vision Imaging System

Also known as night vision goggles, the Aviator's Night Vision Imaging System, according to the U.S. military, "is a lightweight, helmet-mounted, self-contained night vision system. The AN/AVS-6 provides imagery sufficient for an aviator to complete the nighttime missions down to starlight conditions." It has a field of view of 40°, a magnification of 1X, and weighs 550 grams. Its power pack, used when not powered by the aircraft, contains two lithium and four AA batteries.

Reference: "Aviator's Night Vision Imaging System," a brochure of the Night Vision and Electronic Sensors Directorate, U.S. Army Communications—Electronics Command Research, Development and Engineering Center.

Arab League. *See* League of Arab States.

Arafat, Yasir (1928? or 1929?–)

The name of Yasir (or Yasser) Arafat has become synonymous with the terrorism and brutality of the Palestine Liberation Organization (PLO). His signing of the Israeli-Palestinian peace accord in September 1993 made him an administrator of the Gaza Strip and the West Bank village of Jericho in what is called Palestinian self-rule. Yet during the Persian Gulf War he sided with Saddam Hussein, loyalty that pushed the PLO and Arafat's credibility to the brink of disaster.

Little is known about Arafat's origins. Authors Neil C. Livingstone and David Halevy report that he was born in Cairo in 1928 with the name Abed a-Rachman Abed a-Rauf Arafat al-Qudwah al-Husseini. Arafat's official biographer, Alan Hart, says Arafat was born in Cairo on 24 August 1929. His father, Abed a-Rauf Arafat al-Qudwah al-Husseini, was a somewhat prosperous landowner, but the Israeli takeover in 1948 left the family landless. Reports Middle East scholar Yaacov Shimoni, "Arafat was educated in Egypt and graduated from Cairo University as an engineer." After the state of Israel was created, which left the Palestinians stateless, Arafat began to agitate against Israeli rule. Helena Cobban writes: "In 1952, [Arafat] was one of the prime organizers of a new, highly political Palestinian Students' Union in Cairo; two key colleagues from that group, Salah Khalaf [later known as Abou Iyad] and Khalil Wazir, would later join him in founding the Palestinian group Fatah. The twin themes that marked their work in the Students' Union, as in the decades that followed, were that the Palestinians could rely on no one but themselves to regain their rights, and that Palestinian national unity was more important than any of the ideologies sweeping the Arab world at that time." In 1956 Arafat was awarded a degree in engineering. Ironically, he then went to Kuwait, where he was given a job in the Kuwaiti department of public works. At this time, he and several acquaintances who shared a passion to restore a Palestinian state founded the group called Fatah (Arabic: *Harkat al-Tachrir al-Watanni al-Falestinia*—"Palestinian National Liberation Movement"; the name is the acronym in Arabic spelled backward).

The Palestine Liberation Organization (PLO) was founded in 1967. In its nearly 30 years of existence, it has seen two bloody wars—with Jordan in 1970, which established Black September, a radical offshoot of the main Fatah organization, and with Israeli troops in Beirut in 1982. But Arafat's most important mistake came in 1990, when Saddam Hussein invaded Kuwait. Arafat sided not with his Kuwaiti supporters (who had funded much of the PLO's activities since 1967), but with Saddam Hussein, who symbolized to Arafat something even greater: the destruction of Israel and the birth of a pan-Arab state. On 4 August, two days after the invasion, Arafat helped destroy a proposed Arab summit that was to be held in Jiddah, Saudi Arabia, when he announced that he was supporting an "Arab solution" to the crisis and was pushing a peace plan formulated by Muammar el-Qaddafi of Libya. The solution never panned out, and Egypt and Syria eventually supported the introduction of American and other coalition troops into Saudi Arabia. Arafat's chief reason for siding with Saddam Hussein was that the Iraqi leader was pushing the idea of linkage—the concept that Iraqi troops would withdraw from Kuwait in exchange for the Israeli pullout from the Gaza Strip and the West Bank. At that pivotal moment, Arafat was blinded by Saddam Hussein's tempting plan (which the United States and its allies opposed completely) at the expense of his former benefactors, the Kuwaitis. Even the Temple Mount killings of 17 Palestinians on 7 October 1990 and the United States' stern condemnation of the action failed to push the linkage issue. It was dead, as was Arafat's position among the Arab leadership opposed to Saddam Hussein.

Facing certain abandonment by his staunch Persian Gulf allies, in 1993 Arafat signed a peace deal with Israel, and ended his war against the Jewish state in exchange for increased Palestinian authority in the Gaza Strip and several villages in the disputed West Bank.

Palestinian activist Edward Said writes in his "Second Thoughts on Arafat's Deal," "For at least twenty years prior to the spectacle on the White House lawn, Yasir Arafat was taken to be

Arafat, Yasir

Palestine Liberation Organization leader and president of the Occupied Territories Yasir Arafat, left, salutes with Iraqi president Saddam Hussein in 1991.

the most unattractive and morally repellent man on earth. Whenever he appeared in the media or was discussed by them, he was presented as if he had only one thought in his head: killing Jews, especially innocent women and children. But within a matter of days of the peace agreement, the 'independent' media had totally rehabilitated Arafat. He was now an accepted, even lovable figure whose courage and realism had bestowed on Israel its rightful due. He had repented, he had become a 'friend,' and he and his people were now on 'our' side." Michael Kelly wrote in the New York Times Sunday Magazine, "How can Arafat hope to create a state when there is no law, no order, not even a postage stamp? All that proliferates here [in Gaza] are romanticized violence and 720 tons of solid waste each day."

References: Allman, T. D., "Arafat in the Storm," Vanity Fair 57:5 (May 1994), 116–123, 179–187; Cobban, Helen, "Yasser Arafat," in Political Leaders of the Contemporary Middle East and North Africa: A Biographical Dictionary, ed. Bernard Reich (Westport, CT: Greenwood, 1990), 45; "Gaza: Arafat's Gamble," The Economist 333:7891 (26 November 1994), 44; Hart, Alan, Arafat: Terrorist or Peacemaker? (London: Sidgwick & Jackson, 1984), 87; Kelly, Michael, "In Gaza, Peace Meets Pathology," New York Times Sunday Magazine, 2 November 1994, 56; Livingstone, Neil C., and David Halevy, Inside the PLO: Covert Units, Secret Funds, and the War against Israel and the United States (New York: Morrow, 1990), 62; Said, Edward, "Second Thoughts on Arafat's Deal," London Review of Books, 21 October 1993, quoted in Harper's 288:1724 (January 1994), 16; Shimoni, Yaacov, Political Dictionary of the Arab World (New York: Macmillan, 1987), 88; Wallach, Janet, and John Wallach, Arafat: In the Eyes of the Beholder (New York: Lyle Stuart, 1990), xvii.

Armor-Piercing Fin Stabilized Discarding Sabot (APFSDS)

A type of antitank armor-piercing weapon used by the coalition to destroy Iraqi tanks, a sabot (pronounced SAY-bow) is, according to Webster's Third New International Dictionary of the English Language, "a thrust-transmitting lightweight carrier that positions a missile or subcaliber projectile in a tube and is normally discarded when free of the tube." Frank Chadwick remarks, in his Desert Shield Fact Book, "APFSDS is fired from both rifled and smoothbore guns. A

finned dart-shaped penetrator is encased in a two- or three-piece sabot of a lightweight material, such as aluminum. The light weight of the round means that the powder charge accelerates it to extremely high velocities. Upon leaving the gun tube the sabot falls away, while the penetrator hurtles downrange and pierces the target's armor."

See also M-1 and M-1A1 Abrams Main Battle Tanks.
Reference: Chadwick, Frank, The Desert Shield Fact Book (Bloomington, IL: Game Designers' Workshop, 1991), 16.

Armscor 155 mm G5 Howitzer

According to British writer Christopher Foss, "The G5 155 mm gun howitzer has seen combat service with the South African army in southern Angola and South West Africa (now Namibia) and by the Iraqi Army during its war with Iran. Quantities of these weapons were captured by the Allied coalition forces during Operation Desert Storm."

The G5 155 mm howitzer has a barrel length of 6.975 meters (23 feet), a weight of 13,750 kg (30,313 pounds), and is operated by a crew of five. Its towing vehicle is the Samil 100-gun tractor.

Reference: Foss, Christopher F., ed., Jane's Armour and Artillery, 1992–93 (Coulsdon, Surrey, UK: Jane's Information Group, 1992), 662–663.

Article 22 of the League of Nations Covenant

This provision of the the Versailles Treaty, the agreement that established the League of Nations in 1919, was exercised at the San Remo Conference the following year to allow Syria and Mesopotamia (now Iraq) to be "provisionally recognized as independent States, subject to the rendering of administrative advice and assistance by the mandatory until such time as they are able to stand alone. The boundaries of said States will be determined and the selection of mandatories made by the principal Allied Powers."

The exact text of the article reads:

Art. 22. To those colonies and territories which as a consequence of the late war [World War I] have ceased to be under the sovereignty of the states which formerly governed them and which are inhabited by peoples not yet able to stand by themselves under strenuous conditions of the modern world, there should be applied the principle that the well-being and development of such peoples form a sacred trust of civilisation and that securities for the performance of this trust should be embodied in this Covenant.

The best method of giving practical effect to this principle is that the tutelage of such peoples should be entrusted to advanced nations who by reason of their resources, their experience or their geographical position can best undertake this responsibility, and who are willing to accept it, and that this tutelage should be exercised by them as Mandatories on behalf of the League.

The character of the mandate must differ according to the stage of development of the people, the geographical situation of the territory, its economic conditions, and other similar circumstances.

Certain communities formerly belonging to the Turkish Empire have reached a stage of development where their existence as independent nations can be provisionally recognized subject to the rendering of administrative advice and assistance by a Mandatory until such time as they are able to stand alone. The wishes of these communities must be a principal consideration in the selection of the Mandatory.

Other peoples, especially those of Central Africa, are at such a stage that the Mandatory must be responsible for the administration of the territory under conditions which will guarantee freedom of conscience and religion, subject only to the maintenance of public order and morals, the prohibition of abuses such as the slave trade, the arms traffic, and the liquor traffic, and the prevention of the establishment of fortifications or military and naval bases and of military training of the natives for other than police purposes and the defence

of territory, and will also secure equal opportunities for the trade and commerce of other Members of the League.

————

See also San Remo Conference.
Reference: Osmañczyk, Edmund Jan, *The Encyclopedia of the United Nations and International Agreements* (Philadelphia: Taylor & Francis, 1985), 466.

Article 51 of the United Nations Charter

On 12 August 1990, just ten days after the Iraqi invasion of Kuwait, President George Bush ordered the U.S. Navy to halt the import and export of all goods to and from Iraq, asserting that he was taking action according to Security Council Resolution 661 of 6 August 1990, which imposed an embargo on Iraq. The power to enforce Resolution 661 came from Article 51 of the United Nations Charter, which reads:

Art. 51. Nothing in the present Charter shall impair the inherent right of individual or collective self-defense if an armed attack occurs against a Member of the United Nations, until the Security Council has taken measures necessary to maintain international peace and security. Measures taken by Members in the exercise of this right of self-defense shall be immediately reported to the Security Council and shall not in any way affect the authority and responsibility of the Security Council under the present Charter to take at any time such action as it deems necessary in order to maintain or restore international peace and security.

In response to the adoption of Resolution 661, the United States covertly initiated Operation Stigma, a total and complete arms embargo against Iraq.

————

Reference: Osmañczyk, Edmund Jan, *The Encyclopedia of the United Nations and International Agreements* (Philadelphia: Taylor & Francis, 1985), 838.

Articles 41 and 42 of the United Nations Charter

These provisions of the United Nations Charter were employed by the coalition forces first to implement a boycott and then to authorize the use of force against Iraq for seizing Kuwait. The text of the relevant articles reads:

> Art. 41. The Security Council may decide what measures not involving the use of armed force are to be employed to give effect to its decisions, and it may call upon the Members of the United Nations to apply such measures. These may include complete or partial interruption of economic relations and of rail, sea, air, postal, telegraphic, radio, and other means of communication, and the severance of diplomatic relations.
>
> Art. 42. Should the Security Council consider that measures provided for in Article 41 would be inadequate or have proved to be inadequate, it may take such action by air, sea, or land forces as may be necessary to maintain or restore international peace and security. Such action may include demonstrations, blockade, and other operations by air, sea, or land forces of Members of the United Nations.

Reference: Osmańczyk, Edmund Jan, *The Encyclopedia of the United Nations and International Agreements* (Philadelphia: Taylor & Francis, 1985), 838.

House Armed Services Committee chairman Les Aspin meets with members of the press at the U.S. Capitol on 9 January 1991.

Aspin, Leslie, Jr. (1938–1995)

The *Washington Post* called him "hesitant by design." His tenure as secretary of defense, January–December 1993, was marked by the U.S. military debacle in Somalia and the dispatch of American troops to Haiti, and he ultimately resigned in December 1993 in a cloud of failure. Yet, as chairman of the House Armed Services Committee, he took the lead in supporting American intervention in the Middle East during the Persian Gulf crisis.

Leslie Aspin, Jr., was born in Milwaukee, Wisconsin, on 21 July 1938, the son of Leslie Aspin, Sr., a British citizen from Yorkshire who emigrated to the United States, and Marie (née Orth) Aspin. According to the *Current Biography Yearbook 1986*, "Les Aspin graduated *summa cum laude* in history from Yale University in 1960. As a Rhodes scholar, he took an M.A. degree in economics at Oxford University in 1962, and he received a Ph.D. degree in economics at the Mas-

sachusetts Institute of Technology [M.I.T.] in 1965." At the same time, Aspin gained an education in the politics of politics as an aide to Wisconsin's firebrand senator William Proxmire in 1960, and as a staff assistant to Walter W. Heller, chief of President John F. Kennedy's Council of Economic Advisors in 1963. After earning his doctorate at M.I.T., Aspin worked from 1966 to 1968 as a member of Defense Secretary Robert McNamara's Office of Systems Analysis as a Pentagon economics analyst.

In 1968, Aspin returned to Wisconsin to help reelect President Lyndon Johnson. After Johnson's unexpected withdrawal from the race, Aspin ran an unsuccessful campaign for the Democratic nomination for Wisconsin state treasurer. Two years later, running from Wisconsin's First Congressional District, he won the Democratic nomination for Congress on a strictly anti–Vietnam War platform, and defeated a vulnerable Republican. Aspin's major committee assignment was the House Armed Services Committee. Wrote Michael R. Gordon in 1993, "[As a member of House Armed Services] he quickly became a Pentagon gadfly, issuing one weekend news release after another on wasteful Pentagon spending. The releases were astutely embargoed for the Monday newspapers for maximum exposure on what is normally a slow news day." As a member of Armed Services, Aspin was not shy to take on any aspect of the military, including the use of beagles for poison gas experiments and cost overruns for weapons systems. As Richard Madden wrote in the *New York Times* of Aspin in 1976, "Perhaps his most successful triumph came in 1973 when he won adoption by the full House of an amendment imposing a spending ceiling on a defense authorization bill over the strenuous objections of the then chairman of the [House Armed Services] committee, F. Edward Hébert, Democrat of Louisiana. Mr. Hébert became so incensed at Mr. Aspin's publicity tactics that he threatened to mount a counteroffensive to publicize what he considered Mr. Aspin's errors or misrepresentations. The counteroffensive failed to materialize and Mr. Hébert was ousted as chairman in January 1975 in part because of Mr. Aspin's lobbying among his younger fellow Democrats." Aspin helped install Rep. Melvin Price of Illinois as chairman; in 1985, Aspin worked to have Price removed, and took the chairman's spot himself, where he sat until being chosen as defense secretary in 1992. Morton Kondracke, formerly the editor of the *New Republic*, wrote in 1985 upon Aspin's promotion to the chairmanship of the House Armed Services Committee, "Aspin's elevation represents the beginning of generational transition in the House. The New Deal–era grandees are gradually and none-too-enthusiastically giving way to the Democratic 'middle managers.' . . . For nearly ten years, Rep. Aspin has been developing into one of the most thoughtful, prescient, and non-ideological defense experts in Congress. Nobody could be better prepared for the Armed Services job, which requires knowledge of economics almost as much as military affairs."

With the outbreak of the crisis in the Gulf, Aspin was in a key position, as head of Armed Services, to support or deter American policy in the region. His early and enthusiastic endorsement of sanctions was important; yet as the crisis wore on and war seemed inevitable, Aspin became a leading critic of American policy. As the editors of *Triumph without Victory: The History of the Persian Gulf War* write, "On October 2 [1990], both the House and Senate adopted resolutions supporting the President. Both stopped emphatically short of endorsing the use of force, however. Both Sam Nunn, the influential chairman of the Senate Armed Services Committee, and Les Aspin, the chair of the House Armed Services Committee, believed that the administration should allow the sanctions plenty of time to work." During this period, as chairman Aspin took a lead in trying to prevent the United States from going to war. At the same time, he released several white papers on how a possible war would fare; among these is *The Military Option: The Conduct and Consequences of War in the Persian Gulf*, released just before the outbreak of war on 8 January 1991. During the debate whether or not to give the president the power to go to war, Aspin said, "On a vote to authorize the President to use force to liberate Kuwait, the right vote is 'yes.' [But] I believe there is little possibility of achieving a 'bloodless victory.' In truth, I believe that the political risks of a war in the Persian Gulf probably exceed military risks. The long-term implications in the region and for U.S. interests are uncertain. . . ." Although he later played a relatively small role in the shaping of policy during the war, Aspin's vote and support for the war set him apart from many in his party.

With the election of Bill Clinton in 1992, many, including Defense Secretary Dick Cheney, saw Aspin as the leading contender to be the first defense secretary in a Democratic administration since Harold Brown under Jimmy Carter. Aspin was indeed chosen on 22 December 1993, yet he spent only a single year in the post. During that year, the United States got caught up in the military debacle in Somalia and a protracted occupation of Haiti, and Aspin became bogged down in the question of whether the U.S. military should allow declared homosexuals to serve. Gradually, Clinton administration officials admitted, Aspin's conservative slant caused the president to lose confidence in him, and Aspin's departure was assured. When he decided to resign as defense secretary, (rumored by many to be in response to Clinton's demand for the resignation), he said, "It's time for me to take a break and undertake a new kind of work."

Following his resignation, Aspin was involved with writing policy papers for a think tank in Washington, D.C. According to Douglas

Syrian president Hafez al-Assad, left, and Egyptian president Hosni Mubarak exchange documents upon agreeing to cooperate with one another in a meeting held in Alexandria, Egypt, on 16 July 1990.

Stanglin of *U.S. News & World Report,* "A presidential commission headed by . . . Aspin has been set up to offer guidelines [to the President] for improving the work of U.S. spy agencies." On 20 May 1995, Aspin, who had suffered with a weak heart for many years, and had had a pacemaker implanted in February 1994, suffered a massive stroke. He died the following day, on 21 May 1995, at the George Washington University Medical Center in Washington, D.C. He was 56 years old.

References: Aspin, Leslie, Jr., chairman, "The Military Option: The Conduct and Consequences of War in the Persian Gulf," a white paper of the Committee on Armed Services, U.S. House of Representatives, 8 January 1991; "Excerpts from Congress Debate on Using Force," *Los Angeles Times,* 11 January 1991, A7; Gellman, Barton, and R. Jeffrey Smith, "Hesitant by Design: Aspin's Style at Pentagon Often Leaves Important Decisions in Hands of Others," *Washington Post,* 14 November 1993, A1, A16; Gordon, Michael R., "Pathfinders of the Middle Ground: Leslie Aspin, Jr.," *New York Times,* 23 December 1992, A1, A13; Kondracke, Morton, "Les Aspin: Reagan's Friendly Foe," *Wall Street Journal,* 17 January 1985, 26; Madden, Richard L., "Aspin Gets Leverage with Press Releases," *New York Times,* 3 February 1976, A14; Moritz, Charles, ed., *Current Biography Yearbook 1986* (New York: H. W. Wilson, 1986), 24–25; Schmitt, Eric, "Aspin Resigns from Cabinet; President Lost Confidence in Defense Chief, Aides Say," *New York Times,* 16 December 1993, A1; Stanglin, Douglas, "Surprise Ending?" *U.S. News & World Report,* 9 January 1995, 12; U.S. News & World Report, *Triumph without Victory: The History of the Persian Gulf War* (New York: Times Books, 1993), 153, 200.

al-Assad, Hafez (1928? or 1930?–)

President of Syria since 1971, Hafez al-Assad is considered a strongman in the Middle East. His hard line against peace with Israel, his powerful hand in dealing with unrest in Lebanon, and his willing cooperation with the coalition to defeat Saddam Hussein show his cunning and political shrewdness in dealing with his neighbors.

Hafez al-Assad was born Hafez Suleiman in the village of Qardaha in the Alawi mountains in northwestern Syria on 6 October 1930 (the date is sometimes given as 1928), the fourth child and one of five sons of Ali Suleiman and his second wife Na'isa, both farmers belonging to the minority Alawite Shiite Islamic sect. He later changed his name to al-Assad, which translates roughly into "protector of lions." Al-Assad received his early education at the village school;

later, when he was a student at the Latakia Secondary School in the city of Latakia on the Mediterranean, he became a member of the Ba'ath (Renaissance or Resurrection) party, a radical socialist faction. Al-Assad was apparently jailed by the French during their occupation of Syria in the 1940s for supporting the Ba'athists. In 1952, after the French departed and al-Assad completed his secondary education, he joined the Military College at Homs and, later, the Air Force Training Academy at Aleppo. In 1955 al-Assad graduated from the academy as a combat pilot with the rank of lieutenant. Because Syria was at war with Israel and the West and was a client state of the Soviet Union, al-Assad was immediately sent to Moscow to further his military training.

In 1958 Syria and Egypt became partners in the short-lived United Arab Republic (UAR). Al-Assad returned to Syria three years later, where he became part of an underground Ba'athist group called the Military Committee. Although he was removed from his army post by the anti-UAR forces that took over Syria in 1961, he was a leader when the Military Committee staged a coup on 8 March 1963 that installed the Ba'athists in power for the first time. Selected as the head of the Syrian air force, al-Assad was again a leading figure when a conservative wing of the Ba'ath party toppled from power the moderate Ba'athists under the command of Lieutenant General Amin al-Hafiz. Named as minister of defense in the new government, al-Assad was in power when the Syrian air force suffered serious losses during the 1967 Arab-Israeli War.

During the 1960s al-Assad was a member of the military wing of the Ba'ath party that feuded with the more moderate civilian wing. A dispute with Major General Salah al-Jadid and President Nureddin el-Atassi led to the bloodless coup on 13 November 1970 that installed al-Assad as the president of Syria. In 1971 he was elected president in his own right. Al-Assad is accused of fostering terrorism abroad and using harsh anti–human rights measures at home to quell disorder in his country, which became a major client state of the Soviet Union before its collapse. His accomplishments, according to the *Current Biography Yearbook 1992*, include "committing a significant portion of state funds to the construction of roads, educational and medical facilities, and low-cost housing—a policy that has substan-

tially raised the standard of living of the poor." Author Judith Miller writes, "The 1980s were tough years for Assad. The Gulf Arabs cut off aid because of his support for Teheran. In 1986, Britain severed ties and trade with Damascus after Syria was implicated in the botched attempt to blow up an Israeli airliner at Heathrow Airport."

With the outbreak of the crisis in the Persian Gulf, al-Assad took the dramatic position of offering troops and supplies to the coalition, quite contrary to his former posture of intransigence toward the West and any allies of Israel. Although Syrian troops did not enter Iraqi territory, they participated in the liberation of Kuwait.

Al-Assad continues to be a major player in Middle Eastern politics. After seeing fellow Arab nations Egypt and Jordan, as well as the Palestine Liberation Organization (PLO), sign peace treaties with Israel, al-Assad may see the handwriting on the wall: He must bargain with Israel over the fate of the disputed Golan Heights, and he could conclude that peace with the Jewish state is in the best interest of his regime and his nation, or risk being cast as the pariah (with, ironically, Saddam Hussein) of the Middle East, even by his Arab brothers. Still, wrote William Safire in October 1994, "He [Assad] is dropping hints of flexibility. His controlled television shows King Hussein in Israel; his foreign minister gives an interview to Israeli journalists. . . . At the same time, he positions himself for a classic double cross. Damascus remains the capital of terrorism. Assad has conquered Lebanon and does not trouble its Hezbollah. He is adding to his force of 4,200 modern tanks, and is buying missiles from North Korea and other weaponry from Russia. If fundamentalists take over in Egypt and Assad's allies in Iran buy or develop a nuclear bomb, Syria could lead the Arabs into a Mideast Armageddon."

See also Syria.
References: Miller, Judith, "Syria's Game: Put On a Western Face," *New York Times Magazine,* 26 January 1992, 20; Moritz, Charles, ed., *Current Biography Yearbook 1992* (New York: H. W. Wilson, 1992), 24; Safire, William, "Assad: He Speaks of Concessions While Buying More Tanks," *International Herald Tribune,* 14 October 1994, 6; Seale, Patrick, *Asad: The Struggle for the Middle East* (Berkeley: University of California Press, 1988).

AT-3 Sagger Antitank Missile

A wire-guided antitank projectile, the Sagger (so nicknamed by NATO) is a Soviet design that was in the weapons cache of Iraq and Syria. Because of the lack of information from Iraq on its weapons usage during the conflict, the AT-3's use (or disuse) is only speculation.

The AT-3 comes in two types: the mounted version, which is placed on a vehicle, and the so-called suitcase Sagger, which is a smaller variant and is placed on the ground to be fired. A solid-propellant projectile with a two-stage rocket, the missile is 33.5 inches (86 cm) long and has a hollow charge. The sight allows the operator to optically track a target and then launch the rocket at it from a range of up to 9,840 feet (3,000 m). At launch, the missile weighs 25 pounds (11.3 kg), can travel at a speed of 120 mps, and can penetrate a tank's skin up to 15 inches (400 mm). The AT-3 is an older weapon, and in many Soviet client states was replaced with the AT-4 Spigot and AT-5 Spandrel.

See also AT-4 Spigot Antitank Missile.
Reference: Hogg, Ian V., ed., *Jane's Infantry Weapons, 1993–94* (Coulsdon, Surrey, UK: Jane's Information Group, 1993), 149.

AT-4 Spigot Antitank Missile

Although apparently employed by Iraq and Syria, the use of this vehicle-mounted (or man-portable), surface-to-surface, wire-guided, antitank missile in the Persian Gulf War is unknown.

Like its larger cousin, the Soviet-made AT-5 Spandrel (which has a larger propulsion system designed for longer-range target destruction), the Spigot has dual optical lenses—one to track the target, the other to follow the flight of the missile. With a solid-propellant rocket propulsion system, the AT-4's warhead is a high explosive antitank (HEAT) weapon, a charge that upon explosion directs a stream of molten metal at the target. Little is known of the missile, although one source estimates that at launch it weighs 22 to 26 pounds (10–12 kg), has a range of about 6,560 feet (2,000 m), travels at a speed of 150 to 250 mps, and can penetrate a tank's skin up to 19.5 inches (500 mm) before delivering its lethal payload.

Reference: Hogg, Ian V., ed., *Jane's Infantry Weapons, 1993–94* (Coulsdon, Surrey, UK: Jane's Information Group, 1993), 149–150.

Atrocities, Iraqi

The story of actions taken by the Iraqi army during its invasion of Kuwait, and the atrocities that spewed forth from the occupation, remains incompletely told. According to *Conduct of the Persian Gulf War*, the U.S. military's report to Congress on the conflict, "After Kuwait was firmly under Iraqi military control, Iraqi Popular Army 'volunteers' began arriving in Kuwait. They were accompanied by members of the Iraqi Intelligence Service and the Directorate of Military Intelligence." The report continues, "Iraq intelligence and security officials combed [Kuwait] city, armed with lists of names of Kuwaitis who might prove troublesome to their rule. These lists were compiled by the extensive Iraqi intelligence network. As these persons were removed from the city, bus loads of Iraqi citizens began arriving to move into their homes, part of a campaign to resettle the '19th Province' with loyal Iraqi citizens." It concluded, "Iraqi intelligence and security officials converted Kuwaiti schools and other public buildings [in]to detention and interrogation centers. Summary executions were common. The Kuwaiti government estimates [that] more than 1,000 civilians were murdered during Iraqi occupation. Hundreds of people remain unaccounted for, and Kuwait claims [that] more than 2,000 of its nationals still are being detained in Iraq [as of April 1992]."

Nora Boustany wrote in the *Washington Post* on 26 February 1991 that as the ground war began, refugees coming out of Kuwait related tales of horror occurring over the preceding six months. "The refugees' reports lend credence to allegations made in Riyadh, Saudi Arabia, today by allied commanders that Iraqi soldiers were killing, raping and mutilating hundreds of civilians in Kuwait City. The commanders described the emirate's besieged capital as a terrorized city shrouded in thick smoke from more than 500 oil wells set afire by the Iraqis."

References: Boustany, Nora, "Refugees Describe Iraqi Atrocities Seen in Kuwait," *Washington Post,* 26 February 1991, A12; *Conduct of the Persian Gulf War,* Report by the Department of Defense, April 1992, 27.

Australia

See Coalition Nations, Contributions of.

AV-8B Harrier II

Walter J. Boyne, in his *Weapons of Desert Storm*, says of this plane, "The Harrier is an outgrowth of a design pioneered by the Hawker aircraft company in Britain.... It is unique among fixed wing aircraft in its ability to take off and land vertically." The journal *Sea Power* reports that "The AV-8B is a VSTOL [Vertical Short Takeoff and Landing] jet aircraft.... During Desert Storm, Harriers were the most forward deployed tactical aircraft in the theater; they logged 4,317 flight hours with a full-mission-capable rate of 83 percent." The 86 Harriers deployed to the Kuwaiti Theater of Operations—60 flying from airstrips inside Saudi Arabia and 26 from ships in the Persian Gulf—flew a total of 3,359 sorties during Desert Storm, striking approximately 2,585 targets.

Built by McDonnell Douglas, the Harrier II is currently the only aircraft in the U.S. military with the ability to land and take off in a vertical manner. The Harrier has a wingspan of 30 feet 3 inches (9.22 m), a length of 45 feet 4 inches (13.82 m), a maximum weight of 31,000 pounds (14,062 kg) with armaments, a maximum speed of 630 mph (1,014 km/h), and a maximum range of 2,100 nautical miles (2,419 mi; 3,893 km) unrefueled. It is powered by a single Rolls-Royce F402-RR-402 turbojet engine delivering 21,500 pounds (9,752 kg) of thrust. The plane is capable of carrying cluster bombs, as well as general-purpose and laser-guided bombs and rockets, and AGM-65 Maverick and AIM-9L/M Sidewinder missiles.

References: Almond, Denise L., ed., *Desert Score: U.S. Gulf War Weapons* (Washington, DC: Carroll Publishing, 1991), 29; Boyne, Walter J., *The Weapons of Desert Storm* (Lincolnwood, IL: Publications International, 1991), 18; *Gulf War Air Power Survey, Volume IV: Weapons, Tactics, and Training Report and Space Report* (Washington, DC: GPO, 1993), 60; *Sea Power: The Official Publication of the Navy League of the United States* 37:1 (January 1994), 210.

Aviation Logistic Ships, United States

The main duty of these ships is "to provide maintenance and logistic support for Marine aircraft in forward areas," reports naval authority Norman Polmar. Both ships of the Seabridge class, the *Wright* (T-AVB 3) and the *Curtiss* (T-AVB 4), served during the Persian Gulf conflict. Built by Ingalls Shipbuilding of Pascagoula, Mississippi, the ships were originally named the *Young America* and the *Great Republic*, respectively. They displace 12,409 tons light (27,580 tons fully loaded), and are 600 feet 11 inches (183.2 m) in length. Powered by two General Electric steam turbines and two Combustion Engineering boilers, the ships have a maximum speed of 23.6 knots (27 mph; 44 km/h) and a range of 9,000 nautical miles (16,668 km). In addition to its role as logistics craft, these ships can also carry vehicles, up to 300+ troops, or 52 containers in its seven cargo holds.

Reference: Polmar, Norman, *The Naval Institute Guide to the Ships and Aircraft of the U.S. Fleet* (Annapolis, MD: Naval Institute Press, 1993), 283.

AWACS

See Airborne Warning and Control System.

Aziz, Tariq Mikhail (1936?–)

In the months between the Iraqi invasion of Kuwait and the start of Operation Desert Storm, the world saw little of President Saddam Hussein of Iraq, except for brief glimpses of him on television. Representing the nation before the world was his foreign minister, Tariq Aziz, a hardbitten veteran of Iraqi politics.

Aziz was apparently born with the name Mikhail Yuhanna to a Chaldean Arab family of the Alawite sect of Islam, presumably in the northern Iraqi city of Tell Kaif, near Mosul, in 1936. At some unknown point he changed his name to Tariq Aziz, which means "glorious past" in Arabic. After earning an English literature degree from the College of Fine Arts in Baghdad, Aziz was a teacher before becoming a radical and

Aziz, Tariq Mikhail

Iraqi foreign minister Tariq Aziz, right, meets Iranian president Akbar Hashemi Rafsanjani in Tehran on 19 February 1991.

joining the outlawed Ba'ath party. While the country's government was undergoing upheaval (including coups in 1958 and 1963), Aziz was quietly working behind the scenes, first as a staff member of the newspaper *Al-Jumhuriyah* (The Republic), then as the journal's editor just after the Ba'athists came to power in 1963.

As Elaine Sciolino wrote in the *New York Times* in 1990, "Aziz and [Saddam] Hussein became close in the 1950s when they worked together in the Ba'ath Arab Socialist Party's underground struggle to overthrow the British-imposed monarchy. While Hussein was earning his stripes in the Ba'ath hierarchy as a guerilla gunman, Aziz, armed with a degree in English from Baghdad University, became a party organizer and propagandist. In the 1950s and 1960s, he edited three party newspapers, including the main organ, *Al Thawra* [The Revolution]."

After the coup in late 1963 that drove the Ba'athists from power, Aziz sided with the Tikriti wing of the party, which included a young and revolutionary Saddam Hussein. This loyalty

to Hussein proved to be the right career move for Aziz. Just four years after the Ba'athists retook power in 1968, Aziz was named a member of the General Affairs bureau of the Revolutionary Command Council, the governing body. In 1974 he was elevated to the position of minister of information, and in essence he became the Iraqi government's chief propagandist. It was in this role that he went to Egypt in 1978 to try to dissuade President Anwar el-Sadat of Egypt from signing a peace treaty with Israel.

During the late 1970s Aziz was a key figure in his post as deputy prime minister. On 1 April 1980, however, Aziz was attacked with a grenade by members of the al-Dawa (The Call) opposition party, which the reference work *Revolutionary and Dissident Movements: An International Guide* claims is "a militant organization of the Shia community in Iraq" that "has been aligned with the Iranian Islamic revolution led by Ayatollah Khomeini." In 1983 Aziz was named foreign minister, and during the war with Iran, Aziz became Saddam Hussein's right-hand man—when the war began to go badly it was Aziz to whom the Iraqi leader turned in order to get the United Nations to broker a peace agreement, which happened in 1988.

From the time of the invasion of Kuwait to the end of the Gulf War, to many world leaders Aziz's voice was that of the Iraqi government because of the inaccessibility of Saddam Hussein. In September 1990, Aziz flew on a daring mission to Iraq's mortal enemy, Iran, where he met with Iranian foreign minister Ali Akbar Velayati to try to subvert the UN embargo. The next day, Aziz and Velayati renewed Iranian-Iraqi relations. It was Aziz who sat across from U.S. Secretary of State James A. Baker in Geneva on 9 January 1991, just seven days before the Gulf War began, in a defiant mood and demanding the linkage of an Israeli pullout from the West Bank and Gaza Strip to any withdrawal from Kuwait. During the war, Aziz shuttled between Baghdad and Moscow to try to work out a Soviet-inspired peace proposal that seemed to offer a chance to end the war early. Yet the Soviets realized that Aziz could not deal effectively. "I don't believe the Foreign Minister had the authority," related Soviet spokesman Vitaly Ignatenko. Aziz's failure to get a face-saving offer from the Soviets led to his demotion to deputy premier on 24 March 1991.

In an interview with the *Washington Post* in May 1991, Aziz "conceded" that "mistakes" had been made in the 23-year regime of Saddam Hussein. "We know we have made mistakes, which is bound to happen when you are in power that long," he acknowledged. "But we think Saddam Hussein is popular enough to be elected and the people will give us the chance to carry on the leadership in these difficult times. Besides, there is no concrete alternative." Aziz spoke of four reforms that he felt needed to be implemented, including solving the Kurdish problem once and for all, limiting a presidential term to seven years, abolishing the Revolutionary Command Council, and adopting a constitution acceptable to a majority of Iraqis.

Aziz has been in the forefront of enhancing Iraq's standing in the world since the war's conclusion. On 21 May 1994 he wrote a letter to the *New York Times* titled "U.S. Fights To Stymie Iraqi Compliance," in which he argued that many nations in the world desired to end the sanctions against Iraq, and that the United States was hindering that move. Aziz also appeared on the CNN program "Diplomatic License" on 15 January 1995. In response to a question on why Russia and France were pressuring the rest of the Security Council to lift sanctions on Iraq, Aziz commented, "I am happy that they [Russia and France] have changed their minds, and they have done it . . . they have done that after long intensive follow-up of the situation. They were not smooth with us in the last four years . . . they, like the others [on the Security Council] wanted Iraq to comply with the relevant resolutions . . . they spoke with us, and then they came to the conclusion that a great deal has already been done, and then this achievement has to be acknowledged by the Council in terms of statements, and it has to be reciprocated in terms of reduction and lifting of sanctions . . . and I hope that the other members in the Council will follow the same legal, fair, responsible attitude that Russia and France . . . and China and others have taken 'til now."

References: Aziz, Tariq, "U.S. Fights To Stymie Iraqi Compliance," *New York Times*, 21 May 1994, A20; Degenhardt, Henry W., ed., *Revolutionary and Dissident Movements: An International Guide* (New York: Longman, 1988), 171; Drozdiak, William, "Iraqi Says Regime Made 'Mistakes,' Aziz Pledges End to Baathist Monopoly," *Washington Post*, 8 May 1991, A1, A23; Sciolino, Elaine, "Tariq Aziz: Iraq's Best Face," *New York Times*, 31 August 1990, A12; "Transcript of Aziz's Comments in Moscow," *New York Times*, 24 February 1991, 19.

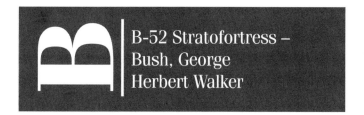

B-52 Stratofortress –
Bush, George
Herbert Walker

B-52 Stratofortress

Nicknamed the Big Ugly Fat Fellow (BUFF), the B-52 played a pivotal role in the saturation bombing phase of the air war over Kuwait and Iraq. Built by Boeing, the B-52 has survived through three generations of warriors and wars. It made its first flight in 1952 and joined the Strategic Air Command (SAC) two years later. During the Vietnam War the craft was a main component in the military's Operation Arc Light carpet-bombing of North Vietnamese targets.

Due to its long-range capabilities, the B-52D and B-52F models were used during the Vietnam War, flown out of Anderson Air Force Base in Guam. Because the B-52F could carry only 27 500-pound (227 kg) bombs, the B-52D was expanded to accommodate a heavier load. The variants of B-52 used during the Persian Gulf conflict were the B-52G and the B-52H, with only minor differences between the two. During the saturation bombing stage of the Persian Gulf War, the Air Force fully utilized the B-52's ability to drop some 60,000 pounds (27,216 kg) of bombs on the enemy at one time. Altogether, these two B-52 variants flew a total of 1,741 sorties in the Kuwaiti Theatre of Operations (KTO). With a wingspan of 185 feet (56.4 m) and a length of 160 feet 11 inches (49 m), the B-52 variants currently in use are powered by eight Pratt & Whitney TF33-P-3 turbofan engines, have an unrefueled combat radius of 10,145 miles (8,000 km), and can fly at a ceiling of 55,000 feet (16,768 m). Its armament power is mindboggling: The B-52 can carry 84 500-pound (227 kg) bombs in its internal bomb bay, and an additional 24 can be affixed to the wings with pylons.

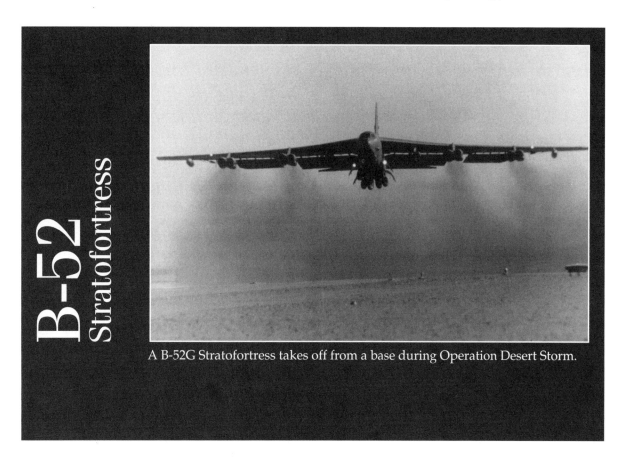

A B-52G Stratofortress takes off from a base during Operation Desert Storm.

References: Boyne, Walter J., *The Weapons of Desert Storm* (Lincolnwood, IL: Publications International, 1991), 20; Gunston, Bill, *An Illustrated Guide to Modern Bombers* (New York: Prentice Hall, 1988), 40–47.

Ba'ath Party

Arabic for "renaissance" or "resurrection," the Ba'ath party began under the leadership of Michel Aflaq in Syria in the 1930s. Its motto is "One Arab Nation, One Immortal Message." Middle East scholar Yaacov Shimoni writes, "The Ba'ath's doctrine is radically Pan-Arab; it regards the various Arab states as temporary entities to be replaced by a united all-Arab state ... by revolutionary violence or subversion if need be."

The Arab concept of *Ishtirakiyyah* (socialism) began in the first years of the twentieth century when Egyptian writer Salamah Musa wrote of his plan to copy British socialist policies in the Arab world in his *Al-Ishtirakiyyah* (Socialism; 1913), the first Arabic discourse on the subject. It was essentially a nationalization of the Arab economic order—this, in the years before the Arab lands were split amongst the victorious allies of World War I. Yet the foremost voice and scholar of the socialist, and later Ba'athist, movement was Syrian scholar Michel Aflaq. Aflaq's founding of the party in 1947 stemmed from nationalistic feelings, not from any anti-West passion. Among the fundamental principles of the Ba'ath party's constitution, adopted in 1947, are that "the Arabs form one nation. This nation has the natural right to live in a single state and to be free to direct its own destiny." Further, "the Arab fatherland constitutes an indivisible political and economic unity. *No Arab country can live apart from the others* [author's emphasis]." Helen Metz writes in her *Iraq: A Country Study*, "From its early years, the Iraqi Ba'ath recruited converts from a small number of college and high school students, intellectuals, and professionals—virtually all of whom were urban Sunni Arabs. A number of Ba'ath high school members entered the Military College, where they influenced several classmates to join the party. Important military officers who became Ba'ath members in the early 1950s included Ahmad Hassan al-Bakr, Salih Mahdi Ammash, and Abd Allah Sultan, all of whom figured prominently in Iraqi political affairs in later years."

According to Israeli writer Uriel Dann, "The Ba'ath Party was organized in Iraq in about 1954. It was an offspring of the Syrian parent party, which ignored the 'artificial frontiers' [borders] created by 'imperialism,' so far as conditions permitted. The Ba'ath leadership in Baghdad was a 'regional command' subordinate to the 'national command' in Damascus." The Iraqi Ba'ath party has been involved in three bloody coups that consolidated and solidified their power in Iraq: 1963, 1964, and 1968. Of the 1963 coup, Middle East writer U. Zaher writes, "The coup was not merely reactionary. It was carried out to bring a fascist-style party, the Ba'th, to power, a party influenced by the national socialist ideology of its principal founder and spiritual leader, Michel Aflaq. It set up a para-military body, the National Guard, whose brutal and barbarous activities were reported in the international press with undisguised revulsion. 'This sounds like an open incitement to a massacre which would make St. Bartholemew's Day look like a Sunday school picnic' ([London] *Sunday Times,* 10 February 1963), 'I have left behind many hundreds of people for whom the future holds only firing squads' ([London] *Daily Express,* 12 February 1963), 'According to the best informed sources, there are at least 1,000 dead in Baghdad alone' (*Le Monde,* 14 February 1963)." On 1 November 1963, after only nine months in power, the Ba'athists themselves were overthrown. An attempted coup in October 1964 was unsuccessful. The 1968 coup, however, was bloodless; it was led by Ahmad Hassan al-Bakr, and Saddam Hussein was named assistant general secretary of the Ba'ath party.

A fight for supremacy between Syria and Iraq led to their cold war, which was seen most notably during the Persian Gulf War. Over the years the fight has grown deeper between the two strongmen of the Middle East—Syria's Hafez al-Assad and Iraq's Saddam Hussein.

See also Aflaq, Michel; al-Assad, Hafez; Hussein al-Tikriti, Saddam; Pan-Arabism or Pan-Arabist Thought.

References: Dann, Uriel, *Iraq under Qassem: A Political History, 1958–1963* (New York: Praeger, 1969), 15; Devlin, John F., *The Ba'ath Party: A History from Its Origins to 1966* (Stanford, CA: Hoover Institution Press, 1976), 345; Metz, Helen Chapman, ed.,

Iraq: A Country Study (Washington, DC: GPO, 1990), 188; Shimoni, Yaacov, *Political Dictionary of the Arab World* (New York: Macmillan, 1987), 114; Zaher, U., "Political Developments in Iraq, 1963–1980," in CARDRI, *Saddam's Iraq: Revolution or Reaction?* (London: Zed Books, 1989), 31.

Baghdad

The commercial and political capital of modern Iraq, with a historical influence matched only by Jerusalem and Damascus, Baghdad was a key target of the Allied coalition during the Persian Gulf War. Positioned strategically 330 miles (530 km) northwest from the Persian Gulf, the city is "situated on the Tigris River at the river's closest point to the Euphrates, 25 miles (40 km) to the west. The Diyala River joins the Tigris just southeast of the city and borders its eastern suburbs. The terrain surrounding Baghdad is a flat alluvial plain 112 feet [34 m] above sea level," according to *The New Encyclopædia Britannica*.

Iraq historical experts Peter Sluglett and Marion Farouk-Sluglett write, "By the time that British Indian troops landed at Fao in the last weeks of 1914, the area that now forms modern Iraq had been at least nominally part of the Ottoman Empire for almost four centuries. The authority of the Abbasid caliphate, under which Baghdad had been the commercial, political, intellectual and spiritual capital of the Islamic world, had begun to decline as early as the tenth century; after many vicissitudes, the caliphate itself disappeared as an institution after Baghdad was sacked by the Mongols in 1258. In the next two centuries, the area was ruled first by the Mongol Ilkhans and then by the formidable Timur [Tamerlane], who died in 1405."

In the sixteenth and early seventeenth centuries, Baghdad was heavily contested and was ruled at various times by the Safavid Persians and the Ottoman Turks. Following the end of World War I, Baghdad became a major center of trade and the arts in the Middle East. In 1932, when Iraq became an independent nation, Iraqi King Faisal I proclaimed Baghdad his capital.

Over the years, Baghdad was built into a world-class capital. The al-Awqaf Library stands among the world's finest, as does the University of Baghdad as a center of education. During the Iran-Iraq War (1980–1988), the city came under heavy attack from Iranian missiles. The city's web of electrical, water, and communications were key targets of allied airstrikes during Operation Desert Storm.

References: Encyclopedia Americana: International Edition, Vol. 3 (Danbury, CT: Grolier, 1987), 50–51; Farouk-Sluglett, Marion, and Peter Sluglett, *Iraq since 1958* (London: I. B. Tauris, 1990), 1; Goetz, Philip W., ed., *The New Encyclopædia Britannica,* Vol. 14 (Chicago: Encyclopædia Britannica, 1990), 560.

Baghdad Pact (1955)

Officially called the Pact of Mutual Cooperation, the so-called Baghdad Pact was signed by representatives of Iraq and Turkey on 24 February 1955. The pact was based on a series of military and security agreements signed by the United States, Pakistan, Turkey, and Iraq in 1954. Britain, Iran, and Pakistan joined the pact in 1955 (the 1954 agreement Pakistan signed was with Turkey alone). In effect, the pact created the Central Treaty Organization.

Middle East scholar Yaacov Shimoni calls the pact "the cornerstone of Western, particularly American, plans for a Middle East defense system." Thomas Arms writes instead that "At the core of the initial agreement was a strong political and military link between Britain and Iraq. This was emphasized in the mutual defense pact when it was signed on 5 April 1955.... The agreement gave the Royal Air Force bases in Iraq and the right to help train Iraq's Air Force, and it called for close Anglo-Iraqi defense collaboration in peace and war. British foreign secretary Anthony Eden told the House of Commons that the accords could serve as the basis of a general Middle East defense plan." However, Iraq's feeling that it was still a subordinate, a colony of Great Britain, led to internal unrest. The 1958 coup that brought down King Faisal II and installed Abdul-Karim Qassem laid the foundation for the pact's ultimate destruction. On 24 March, Qassem announced that Iraq was pulling out of the pact, effective 24 February 1960, a mere five years after its signing. Israeli writer Uriel Dann said, "The withdrawal from the pact was less remarkable than the fact that it had been delayed so long. Iraq's membership had become a considerable embarrassment to the regime. It was an irritant to the Left and a providential way in

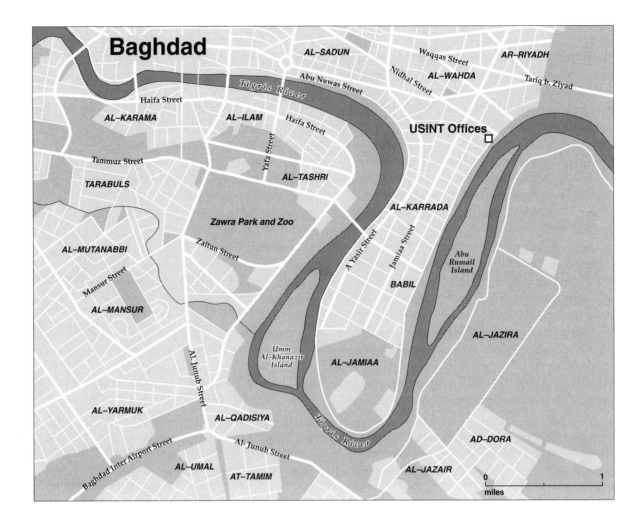

which nationalists could combine the accusation that Qassem was at once a communist and a Western agent." He adds, "Iraq's secession from the Baghdad Pact annulled the Special Agreement with Great Britain contracted on 4 April 1955. The Royal Air Force staging post at Habbaniya thereby lost its legal basis, as it had lost its strategic value with the revolution. On 26 March the British Embassy in Baghdad announced the impending withdrawal of the RAF contingent of some four hundred personnel, including eighty dependents. The withdrawal commenced on 6 April and was completed on 31 May. For the first time since November 1914, there were no British troops on Iraq[i] soil."

References: Arms, Thomas S., *Encyclopedia of the Cold War* (New York: Facts on File, 1994), 39; Dann, Uriel, *Iraq under Qassem: A Political History, 1958–1963* (New York: Praeger, 1969), 185–186; Shimoni, Yaacov, *Political Dictionary of the Arab World* (New York: Macmillan, 1987), 107.

Bahrain

Lying in the middle of the Persian Gulf, tiny Bahrain consists of 35 islands; most of the population resides on the larger island of Bahrain and the smaller al-Muharraq, Nabi Salih, and Umm Na San islands. The nation is perched between Saudi Arabia (to which it is connected by an oil pipeline running to al-Khubar) and Qatar. Although astride the world's greatest concentration of oil, its reserves are small and it is known more as an important banking center with a diversified economy. During the Gulf War it played a major role as a base for American troops.

Officially called *Dawlat al-Bahrayn,* Bahrain was once the intermediary trading stop between the vital early civilizations in Sumeria and the Indus Valley. This island, then called Dilmun, was known by the Babylonians and Sumerians as a country "where the sun rises." However, evidence from burial mounds found on the main is-

Sheik Isa Bin Salman al-Khalifa, emir of Bahrain, left, meets with U.S. president George Bush at the White House in October 1991.

Bahrain

land indicates that civilization may have thrived there about 3000 B.C. Its Arabic roots are to be found about the fourth century A.D., when it was incorporated into the Persian Sâsânian empire by Shâpûr II (c. 310–c. 380). In the eighth century, the Abbasids took control of the island, and held it until the Portuguese conquered it in 1521. Eighty-one years later, in 1602, the Persians recaptured it; however, in 1783, Ahmad ibn al-Khalifa seized authority, and his family has ruled ever since. During the period between 1783 and 1968, Britain intervened several times in Bahraini affairs; after 1820, various treaties allowed the British to trade extensively and exclusively with the island in exchange for defense obligations. In 1968 the British ended all responsibilities arising from such treaties and withdrew from the island; just three years later, in August 1971, Bahrain formally declared its independence. Iran has made several threats to annex Bahrain. In 1980 Iran renounced all claims to the nation, but was implicated in a 1988 plan to sabotage Bahrain's oil terminal. Bahrain is a close ally of the United States; in fact, it is the only Gulf nation to allow American ships to use port facil-

ities. During the Kuwaiti oil tanker reflagging crisis in 1986 and 1987, Bahrain was a strategic site for American forces in the area.

Bahrain is presently ruled by Sheik Isa Bin Salman al-Khalifa, who assumed the throne on 2 November 1961 and became the emir upon the death of his father, Sheik Salman Bin Hamad al-Khalifa, on 16 December 1961. The sheik's son, Sheik Hamad bin Isa al-Khalifa, is the heir apparent to the emirate. The Bahraini prime minister is the emir's eldest brother, Sheik Khalifa Bin Salman al-Khalifa, who has ruled since 19 January 1970. The government structure is that of an emirate, with all power resting in the hands of the head of state, the emir. A national assembly, a parliamentary form of government, was elected in 1973, but dissolved in 1975 and was not held again. The parties involved in this election included the Popular Bloc of the Left, and the Bahrain section of the Popular Front for the Liberation of Oman and the Arabian Gulf (PFLOAG), a group of leftist students. The present government is run by a 16-man council, or cabinet, dominated by the al-Khalifa family. Bahrain's area is 240 square miles (622 sq km), with an estimated population of 546,000 (1993 est.). This number includes about 164,000 non-citizens who are internal workers from other countries. The 1981 census showed about 60 percent of the nation was made up of Shiite Muslims, while the other 40 percent is from the Sunni Muslim branch. Bahrain belongs to many of the Arabic councils, including the Arab League, OPEC, and the Gulf Cooperation Council (GCC). The nation's official language is Arabic. Gross domestic product (GDP) in 1987 was $3.5 billion, or $7,550 per capita.

During the Persian Gulf War, Bahrain turned, as did all of its Gulf allies, to the United States and the coalition forces to stop Iraq's army in Kuwait and reverse the invasion of 2 August 1990. According to the military report *Desert Score*, "Bahrain has a 3,500 man military establishment. Its inventory includes 54 tanks (M603A), 140 armored combat vehicles, 55 artillery pieces, 20 fighter aircraft, and 10 naval patrol craft. [The nation's forces] flew support missions in the second week in the air war, using its four F-16 Fighting Falcon aircraft." These four aircraft flew 293 sorties.

References: Almond, Denise L., ed., *Desert Score: U.S. Gulf War Weapons* (Washington, DC: Carroll Publishing, 1991), 476; "The JDW Interview: Major General Khalifa Ibn Ahmed al-Khalifa, Bahraini Minister of Defence," *Jane's Defence Weekly* 14:14 (4 April 1992), 592; Tarr, David R., and Bryan R. Daves, eds., *The Middle East* (Washington, DC: Congressional Quarterly, 1986), 217–218.

Baker, James Addison III (1930–)

In 1989 author Marjorie Williams called him "the most powerful unelected man in America." Following the 1988 presidential election, James Baker was George Bush's first choice for a major administration post—secretary of state. Along with Secretary of Defense Dick Cheney and Joint Chiefs Chairman Colin Powell, Baker was in the president's immediate circle of advisors during the Persian Gulf crisis.

James Addison Baker III was born 28 April 1930 into a prominent Texas family in Houston, the son of James Addison Baker II and his wife Bonner (née Means) Baker. James Baker II's grandfather founded the prestigious Houston law firm of Gray & Botts (now Baker & Botts). Baker attended the prestigious Hill School near Philadelphia, Princeton University (where as a classics scholar his senior thesis was on the postwar years of the British Labour party), served two years in the Marine Corps, and earned his law degree from the University of Texas Law School in 1957. Because of Baker & Botts's policy not to hire family members, Baker took a position with another significant Houston firm, Andrews, Kurth, Campbell, and Jones, where he served from 1957 until 1981.

Baker married the former Mary Stuart McHenry, settled down, and became a famous Houston attorney. One of his neighbors became a good friend—George Bush, another millionaire's son—and Baker soon tied his political fortunes to him. As Maureen Dowd and Thomas L. Friedman wrote in 1990, "The fates of George Herbert Walker Bush and James Addison Baker III have been intertwined for three decades, ever since they teamed up to win the doubles tennis championship two years in a row at the tony Houston Country Club. 'I had a good baseline game and he had a good net game,' Baker recalls. One was the Yale-educated scion of an affluent Eastern family who had come to Texas to make his fortune in the oil business. The other was the Princeton-educated scion of a wealthy Texas family with Eastern connections. These two men were the founding members of a new breed known as Tex-prep, a patrician twist on the old bourbon-and-brass style of famous Texas pols like Lyndon B. Johnson and Sam Rayburn."

In 1970 Baker considered running for the congressional seat vacated by Bush, but his wife was dying of leukemia; his friend George Bush was at his side. Baker eventually remarried, and the friendship between the two men grew deeper. While Bush was serving as director of the Central Intelligence Agency and as the U.S. ambassador to China, Baker was undersecretary of commerce (1975–1976) and deputy chairman of President Ford's reelection committee in 1976. In 1980, when Bush made his ill-fated run for president, Jim Baker ran the campaign. When Bush lost the nomination to Ronald Reagan, he was chosen as the vice-presidential running mate, and he brought Baker on-board the campaign.

Baker, James A.

U.S. secretary of state James Addison Baker III speaks to members of the press following a meeting with Iraqi foreign minister Tariq Aziz in Geneva on 9 January 1991.

Victory allowed Baker to serve as White House chief of staff from 1981 to 1985, when he was named secretary of the treasury, a post in which he served until 1989. During the 1988 presidential campaign, Baker served as Bush's campaign chairman. The day after Bush was elected president, he named James Baker as his secretary of state, the first appointment of his administration. Bernard Weintraub wrote in the *New York Times*, "No one questions Baker's special skills as a negotiator."

While he was secretary of state, Baker was deeply involved in the formation of U.S. policy toward Iraq, both before the war and in its aftermath. In 1989 Baker met with Iraqi foreign minister Tariq Aziz, who asked that $500 million in additional food credits be issued to Iraq. At the same time, Baker's attention was drawn to an internal state department memo that alleged that Iraq was using farm credits to purchase equipment for its nuclear weapons program. The memo's authors stated that "If smoke indicates fire, we may be facing a four-alarm blaze in the near future." Nonetheless, Baker urged Secretary of Agriculture Clayton Yeutter to issue fur-

ther loan credits to Iraq, and this was done. When Iraq invaded Kuwait, Baker turned into the diplomat-in-a-suitcase and traveled the world in support of American action in the Gulf. Just before the war broke out, Baker was sent to Geneva to broker an agreement with Aziz, an attempt that failed to avert war.

After the war, Baker tried to implement a Middle East peace agreement that included Israel and her Arab enemies, but he left office before he could accomplish such an accord. In 1992 he left the state department to run George Bush's reelection campaign; the defeat left Baker out of government. He was considered a possible contender for the 1996 Republican presidential nomination, but chose not to run.

References: Dowd, Maureen, and Thomas L. Friedman, "The Fabulous Bush & Baker Boys," *New York Times Magazine*, 6 May 1990, 36; Weintraub, Bernard, "James Addison Baker 3d: First Choice for Top Cabinet Post," *New York Times*, 10 November 1988, B4; Williams, Marjorie, "Jim Baker Is Smooth, Shrewd, Tough and Coolly Ambitious. That's Why Washington Loves Him," *Washington Post Magazine*, 29 January 1989, 17.

al-Bakr, Ahmad Hassan

(1912? or 1914?–1982)

An Iraqi military officer and politician, Ahmad Hassan al-Bakr resigned as the head of the Iraqi government in 1979 and was replaced by Saddam Hussein, setting the stage for a full decade of warfare for the Iraqi people.

Ahmad Hassan al-Bakr was born in either 1912 or 1914; little else is known about him. He was a distant cousin of Khairallah Talfah, Saddam Hussein's uncle. The *New York Times* wrote of him upon his death, "A career army officer and long-standing member of the ruling Ba'ath Party, he took part in the 1958 coup d'état that overthrew the monarchy. But he opposed General Abdel Karim Qassem, who took power, and became one of the chief architects of the 1963 coup that made the more moderate Colonel Abdel Salam Aref the President. Al-Bakr soon fell out with Aref as well and, in 1968, led a bloodless coup that established the Ba'ath Party in firm control. Al-Bakr survived several assassination attempts and dealt ruthlessly with opponents."

Middle East authority Yaacov Shimoni writes, "In the Ba'ath regime that ensued he assumed, in addition to the Presidency, the premiership and the supreme command of the armed forces, and also became chairman of the Revolutionary Command Council. Al-Bakr and his associates consolidated the Ba'th's rule by cruel purges, first of non-Ba'th opposition nuclei, then of intra-Ba'th factional rivals, and an all-pervasive secret service." In July 1979, according to official Iraqi histories, al-Bakr retired to make way for his protégé, Saddam Hussein. Actually, reports Iraqi dissident Samir al-Khalil (a pseudonym), al-Bakr was purged by Saddam Hussein himself and survived the brutal executions of many high-ranking Ba'athists, dying of natural causes in 1982. Writes al-Khalil, "Through the first half of the 1970s, al-Bakr was more than a figurehead in Iraqi politics in the sense that his party seniority coupled with his high standing among officers was probably more important in facilitating the repeated purges and growing hegemony of the civilian wing of the party over the army. His decade-long partnership in power with Saddam Hussein was, to say the least, convenient for Saddam."

Iraq experts Marion Farouk-Sluglett and Peter Sluglett write of al-Bakr's resignation, "On 16 July 1979, on the eleventh anniversary of the

Iraqi president Ahmad Hassan al-Bakr, right, with his vice president, Saddam Hussein, salutes as Iraqi troops parade in Baghdad to mark the end of hostilities with Kurdish rebels in May 1975.

Ba'th takeover, al-Bakr appeared on television to announce his resignation, and Saddam Hussein was 'sworn-in' immediately as President, a transfer of power that had been as meticulously prepared as it had been long expected. In his speech, al-Bakr commended Hussein as the best man for the post and warmly endorsed his 'caricature.' Izzat al-Duri, a long-standing and loyal lieutenant of Saddam Hussein, was appointed Vice-President."

See also Hussein al-Tikriti, Saddam; Iraq.
References: "Ahmed al-Bakr Dies; Former Iraqi President," *New York Times,* 5 October 1982, IV:25; Farouk-Sluglett, Marion, and Peter Sluglett, *Iraq since 1958: From Revolution to Dictatorship* (London: I. B. Tauris, 1990), 209; al-Khalil, Samir, *Republic of Fear: The Inside Story of Saddam's Iraq* (New York: Pantheon, 1990), 71; Shimoni, Yaacov, *Political Dictionary of the Arab World* (New York: Macmillan, 1987), 109.

Basra

The capital of Basra province in Iraq, Basra (also in Arabic: Busra, Bussora, or Bassorah) is located about 75 miles (120 km) from the Persian Gulf, and sits astride the all-important Shatt al-Arab waterway. Basra's main harbor is al-Maaquil, located on the western side of the waterway. Across the waterway to the southeast is the Iranian port of Abadan. Both harbors played key roles during the eight-year Iran-Iraq War (1980–1988).

Founded about A.D. 636–638 by the Abbasid caliph Umar I, Basra was originally settled about 8 miles (13 km) southwest of its current location to take advantage of the Persian Gulf, at that time one of the most important waterways for trade and commerce in the world. Over the next several centuries, it became known for its rich culture, and was famed for its luxurious mosques and a notable public library. Under the Abbasids, it became an important center for science and commerce. With the Mongol invasions of the thirteenth century, Basra declined, but it was revitalized after Suleiman the Magnificent captured the city in 1546, making it once again an important commercial village. With the formation of the Ottoman Empire, Basra and the rest of what is now Iraq came under that authority. In the Ottoman Capitulations of 1661, the

British became the dominating influence in the area, and they held onto this possession even after the formation of Iraq in 1920. During World War II, British soldiers occupied the port, making sure its vital harbor was not used by the Nazis. The discovery of oil made the port even more important for commerce. British withdrawal and Iraqi statehood made the port a significant link in the commercial redevelopment of the area.

In 1980 Basra was caught between the two feuding powers of Iran and Iraq in their attempts to economically cripple each other. As Iraq had no other port on either waterway, for them Basra was an important connection to the Shatt al-Arab and the Persian Gulf. During the conflict, Basra and Abadan were closed by rockets fired by both sides, scuttled and shattered ships, and piled-up silt, which needed to be removed frequently. With the outbreak of the Persian Gulf War in 1991, Basra suffered rocket and missile attacks from coalition forces. After the end of the war, the city was the site of the Shiite uprising against the regime of Saddam Hussein, but the effort collapsed after only a short time.

Reference: Encyclopedia Americana: International Edition, Vol. 3 (Danbury, CT: Grolier, 1987), 333.

Battleships, United States

Only two American battleships served in the Persian Gulf War: the USS *Missouri* and the USS *Wisconsin,* both in the Iowa class of ships and the last of their kind. The *Missouri* (BB 63) was built in 1943, and the *Wisconsin* (BB 64) came out the following year. Both displace 46,177 tons light and 57,353 tons fully loaded, and are 887.2 feet (270.4 m) in length. They are powered by eight Babcock & Wilcox boilers and four geared turbines (General Electric in the *Missouri,* Westinghouse in the *Wisconsin*). The ships have a maximum speed of 35 knots (40 mph; 65 km/h), a range of 5,000 miles (8,045 km) at 30 knots (35 mph; 56 km/h) and a range of 15,000 miles (24,135 km) at 15 knots (17 mph; 28 km/h), and carry a complement of 1,518 (including 65 officers), as well as 40 marines (including 2 officers). They are armed with 32 Tomahawk missiles, a combination of Tomahawk land attack missiles (TLAMs) and Tomahawk antiship missiles

Battleships, United States

Two World War II–era battleships, the USS *Missouri* and USS *Wisconsin*, refuel from the fast combat support ship USS *Sacramento*, center, in the Persian Gulf during Operation Desert Shield.

(TASMs), as well as 16 AGM-84 Harpoon/SLAM antiship missiles.

Reference: Sharpe, Richard, ed., *Jane's Fighting Ships, 1990–91* (Coulsdon, Surrey, UK: Jane's Information Group, 1990), 736.

Bazoft, Farzad (1959–1990)

An Iranian-born journalist in Iraq representing the *London Observer*, Bazoft traveled to the Qaqa State Establishment (an hour south of Baghdad), which was rocked by a large explosion on 17 August 1989, allegedly killing hundreds of guest Egyptian workers, although such numbers cannot be confirmed. Bazoft appeared on the scene in early September, went to the Qaqa site and, working for British intelligence, took soil samples of the explosion crater and sent these back to Britain via diplomatic pouch. When he tried to leave Iraq he was arrested, charged with spying, and sentenced to death. Although world leaders spoke out for his release, Iraq executed him on 15 March 1990, effectively setting the stage for

the repression that preceded the invasion of Kuwait.

Reference: Henderson, Simon, *Instant Empire: Saddam Hussein's Ambition for Iraq* (San Francisco: Mercury House, 1991), 204–216.

Bessmertnykh, Aleksandr Aleksandrovich (1933–)

When Aleksandr Bessmertnykh stepped into the shoes of Soviet foreign minister Eduard Shevardnadze, the Georgian who had resigned from the Soviet government in protest over what he felt was the incursion of totalitarianism into the Soviet reform system, few realized just what Bessmertnykh, a career diplomat, would offer to a world locked in the deep struggle in the Persian Gulf.

Aleksandr Aleksandrovich Bessmertnykh was born in Biysk, in south-central Siberia, on 10 November 1933, the son of a civil servant. Little is known about his education. Daniel C. Diller reports in his *Russia and the Independent States*

Iranian-born Farzad Bazoft worked as a journalist for the *London Observer* before Iraqis arrested and charged him with spying. Bazoft was hanged in 1990.

that from an early age Bessmertnykh "decided to pursue a career in government." He attended the Moscow State Institute of International Relations, where he studied law and politics. After graduating in 1957, he joined the Soviet foreign ministry, where he held a number of posts: member of the United Nations Secretariat, first secretary to Soviet foreign minister Andrei Gromyko, first secretary to Soviet ambassador to the United States Anatoly Dobrinin, and chief of the United States Department in the Ministry of Foreign Affairs in Moscow.

Less than a year after Mikhail Gorbachev became the Soviet leader, Bessmertnykh was promoted to deputy foreign minister. During the next several years, he was one of Gorbachev's closest advisors, and in May 1990 was appointed Soviet ambassador to the United States. Bessmertnykh had barely settled into this post when, in December 1990, Soviet foreign minister Eduard Shevardnadze resigned, dramatically warning his country about the rise of totalitarian thought among communists. Called home just

after the new year, Bessmertnykh was installed as foreign minister just 24 hours before Operation Desert Storm began.

Because of their alliances with Iraq, the Soviets played a very small role in the coalition prior to the outbreak of Operation Desert Storm. Bessmertnykh played an even smaller role, acting after the war began as an intermediary between Middle East expert Yevgeni Primakov, who was in Baghdad trying to work out a solution to the crisis, and Soviet president Mikhail Gorbachev, who met with President George Bush in Helsinki, Finland, in September 1990 to discuss the situation in the Gulf, criticizing American moves in the area. Bessmertnykh was essentially caught in the middle, and because he was a recent addition to the Soviet foreign policy team, was not seen as a power broker. However, he did have the power to keep a dialogue running with the United States; when Secretary of State James Baker met Bessmertnykh in Moscow in late January 1991, Soviet commentators hailed the meeting, saying it had "broadened the basis of mutual understanding between Moscow and Washington."

In an interview with two reporters from *Soviet Life* magazine, Bessmertnykh said, "I have believed and still believe that we must regard relations between the Soviet Union and the United States as critically important." Responding to a question about the possibility of joint USSR-U.S. cooperation to end the Persian Gulf crisis, he remarked, "In my view, it would be wrong to set all hopes on the USSR and the USA. Conflicts should be settled by the conflicting states, but our two countries are willing to help whenever they can play a positive role. However, it is more important to strengthen the United Nations, to give preference to that organization in settling regional conflicts rather than to get involved in them."

Bessmertnykh was widely denounced by the Western press when on 21 February he presented a peace plan, one that would allow Iraq to withdraw from Kuwait without consultation with the United States and the other coalition powers. "With this move," writes Daniel C. Diller, "the Soviets distanced themselves from full cooperation with the anti-Iraq coalition and tried to preserve their traditional role as protector of the Arab world." Bessmertnykh himself became caught up in Soviet politics and served

Soviet foreign minister Aleksandr Bessmertnykh, right, is introduced by Israeli foreign minister David Levy at Tel Aviv's Ben Gurion Airport on 11 May 1991.

as foreign minister of the Soviet Union only from January to August 1991, when the coup by a number of high-ranking Soviet officials took place. Although the coup failed after a few days because of public reaction, Bessmertnykh was sacked because he had failed to criticize the coup plotters. He then joined a liberal think tank, the Soviet Foreign Policy Association, headed, ironically, by Eduard Shevardnadze.

See also Gorbachev, Mikhail Sergeivich; Shevardnadze, Eduard Amvrosiyevich.
References: Diller, Daniel C., ed., *Russia and the Independent States* (Washington, DC: Congressional Quarterly, 1993), 125; Moritz, Charles, ed., *Current Biography Yearbook 1991* (New York: H. W. Wilson, 1991), 60–65; "Portfolio: Expanding the Scope of Good Relations," *Soviet Life* 414:3 (March 1991), 14–15; *Washington Post*, 31 January 1991, A15.

BGM-71 TOW Missile
See TOW Missile.

BGM-109 Tomahawk Missile
See Tomahawk Land Attack Missile.

Blood Chit

This widely used tool is a multilanguage leaflet carried by an American pilot or aircraft crew member shot down behind enemy lines to help gain safe passage, assistance, or decent treatment from people he or she might find along the way. One such chit used by American pilots during the Persian Gulf War reads: "I am an American and do not speak your language. I will not harm you! I bear no malice towards your people. My friend, please provide me food, water, shelter, clothing, and necessary medical attention. Also, please provide safe passage to the nearest forces of any country supporting the Americans and their Allies. You will be rewarded for assisting me when you present this number and my name to American authorities."

BMP-2 Infantry Fighting Vehicle (IFV)

An Iraqi infantry fighting vehicle, the BMP-2 IFV is a Soviet model used mostly by the Republican Guards. Its use during the Persian Gulf War is unknown, as are the possible numbers employed.

The BMP-2 (*Bronevaya Maschina Pekhota*, or Armored Vehicle, Infantry) was a staple of Soviet client states throughout the 1970s and 1980s. The vehicle can carry up to seven troops and three crew members, weighs 14 tons, and can travel at a speed of 113 mph (70 km/h). Among its armaments are the AT-4 Spigot antitank missile and 30 mm guns. Its armor is 25 to 30 mm thick. The BMP-2 was said by *Newsweek* magazine to be "used mostly by [the] Republican Guards. The Soviet BMPs do double duty: They carry the infantry into battle—and help them to fight it." An updated variant of the widely used BMP-1, the BMP-2 was used by the Kuwaiti military prior to the invasion of Kuwait on 2 August 1990. *Jane's Armour and Artillery, 1992–93* reports that an Iraqi BMP-1 variant with appliqué armor fitted to its sides to provide additional protection from antitank missiles was observed in 1989, although whether it was used in the Gulf War is unknown. The *New York Times* reported in its 5 March 1995 edition that "hundreds" of BMP-2s were captured by the Iraqi army in Kuwait, taken back to Iraq, and put to use in the Republican Guard units that were rebuilt after the war.

References: "Arms and the Men," *Newsweek* magazine pullout special section on the Persian Gulf War, 18 February 1991; Chadwick, Frank, *The Desert Shield Fact Book* (Bloomington, IL: Game Designers' Workshop, 1991), 40; Foss, Christopher F., ed., *Jane's Armour and Artillery, 1992–93* (Coulsdon, Surrey, UK: Jane's Information Group, 1992), 319; Sciolino, Elaine, "With Fresh Data, U.S. Wages Fight To Keep Iraq Sanctions," *New York Times*, 6 March 1995, A5.

Buccaneer

This British dual-engined bomber flew 226 sorties in Operation Desert Storm, most, according to the U.S. miltary's Gulf War Air Power Survey,

as "buddy" laser designators, without weapons, for other British aircraft. After the arrival of the Tornado's GEC-Ferranti thermal imaging airborne laser designating (TIALD) pod, the Buccaneers flew 16 further missions on their own with weapons. The Buccaneer was supported by the Westinghouse AVQ-23E Pave Spike laser designator pod.

The Buccaneer is a two-seat, low-level strike-and-reconnaissance aircraft powered by two Rolls-Royce Spey 101 turbofan engines. Wingspan is 44 feet (13.41 m), maximum speed at 200 feet (61 m) is 645 mph (1,038 km/h), and the plane can remain in flight for up to nine hours with two in-flight refuelings. The Buccaneer can carry four 1,000-pound (454 kg) bombs, and missiles on four separate underwing pylons.

General Sir Peter de la Billière, head of British forces in the Gulf, writes of the Buccaneer in his *Storm Command: A Personal Account of the Gulf War:* "The Buccaneer was 21 years old and known as 'the flying banana' on account of the slightly undulating shape of its fuselage, but in spite of its antiquity, its crews loved it and swore that as a weapons platform it was second to none. Now it proved itself in short order; on its first live sortie—two Buccaneers escorting four Tornado GR1s, with a third Buccaneer as a backup—it achieved complete success, punching clean through an important bridge over the Euphrates with laser-guided bombs."

References: De la Billière, Sir Peter, *Storm Command: A Personal Account of the Gulf War* (New York: HarperCollins, 1992), 234; *Gulf War Air Power Survey, Volume IV: Weapons, Tactics, and Training Report and Space Report* (Washington, DC: GPO, 1993), 65; Gunston, Bill, cons. ed., *The Encyclopedia of World Air Power* (New York: Crescent, 1980), 109.

Bull, Gerald Vincent (1928–1990)

The life and death of Dr. Gerald Bull remain at the center of the story of the arming of Iraq before the Gulf War. How much was Bull responsible for modifying the deadly Scud missiles that later rained down on the cities of Saudi Arabia and Israel? Did he have a chance to arm the Iraqis with his so-called supergun, which reportedly could heave a warhead 1,000 miles (1,609

Bull, Gerald Vincent

Canadian ballistics expert Gerald Bull, left, shows Quebec premier Jean Lesage a supergun in 1965.

km) from a cannon-type rocketry unit? And, perhaps the most baffling mystery in this case, who assassinated Bull in March 1990, just months before Saddam Hussein's army invaded Kuwait?

Born in North Bay, Ontario, on 9 March 1928, Gerald Bull was the son of George Bull, an attorney, and Gertrude (née LaBrosse) Bull. He attended Regiopolis College, a Jesuit boarding school, and in 1951 became the youngest person ever to graduate from the University of Toronto with a doctorate. By then, the Canadian government saw promise in him to construct rockets.

The cold war was at its height, and skills such as his were much needed. He worked on a joint U.S.-Canadian project to build a supergun to send satellites into orbit. Frustrated by the cancellation of this undertaking because of a lack of funds, Bull turned to designing artillery shells that could be fired by guns. In the 1960s he was even involved in mapping out new shells for use by American forces in Vietnam. The project was dubbed HARP (High Altitude Research Project).

In the 1970s Bull was involved in building a supergun for the South Africans, in violation of the world arms embargo of that nation. Aided by the CIA and other interested parties, Bull was arrested when evidence of the shipments was found in Antigua. After serving a jail sentence, he worked with Iraq to build what was then called the supergun. Known as Project Babylon, the operation involved securing for the Iraqi regime parts of innocent-looking metal pipe that could be welded together to create a weapon capable of firing a projectile from the western reaches of Iraq toward Israeli population centers. In 1988 he detailed the work of this potential weapon in *Paris Kanonen—the Paris Guns (Wilhelmgeschütze) and Project HARP,* cowritten with Charles Murphy.

Bull's work to create a supergun may have led to his assassination in Brussels on 22 March 1990. Michael Wines and Jeff Gerth wrote in the *New York Times,* "On March 22, 1990, Bull was shot twice in the neck with a silencer-equipped 7.65 mm pistol outside his apartment in Brussels. The killer left behind $20,000 in American cash in the victim's pocket. Who killed him, and why, is a mystery that has consumed the European press. But a growing body of evidence suggests that Mr. Bull was a pivotal figure in a violent subculture, promoting the black-market proliferation of advanced weapons to volatile third-world

nations like Iran and Iraq." They added, "Israel has denied any role in his death. Others say Iran also had a reason to wish Mr. Bull dead. As a supplier of advanced arms, sometimes to foes on both sides of third-world conflicts, Bull collected enough potential enemies to fill several police blotters with murder suspects, American intelligence officials and others said." On 18 April 1990, shortly after Bull was murdered, in a maneuver called Operation Bertha, British customs agents seized parts of the Supergun ready for shipment to Iraq. Writing on the boxes plainly read: 'Republic of Iraq, Ministry of Industries and Minerals, Petrochemical Project, BAGHDAD, IRAQ, P.O. No. 3-839j-908, Gross wt. 11080 kgs'." The following day, Bull's company, Space Research Corporation, announced that it was going out of business "for security reasons." On 20 April, the government of Greece proclaimed that it had stopped a truck that was traveling overland to Iraq carrying parts for a large weapon.

More than five years after his murder, the killer or killers of Gerald Bull have not been identified.

References: Adams, James, *Bull's Eye: The Assassination and Life of Supergun Inventor Gerald Bull* (New York: Times Books, 1992); "Britain Is Convinced Its Customs Halted Giant Gun for Iraq," *New York Times,* 19 April 1990, A9; "Greece Seizes a Truck Carrying Arms to Iraq," *New York Times,* 21 April 1990, A3; Montgomery, Paul, "Mysterious Death of Owner, Then Arms Company Closes," *New York Times,* 20 April 1990, A3; Wines, Michael, and Jeff Gerth, "How Physicist's Weapons Genius Led Him to Greed and Then Death," *New York Times,* 22 April 1990, A14.

Bush, George Herbert Walker

(1924–)

The fortieth president of the United States, George Bush will be best remembered as the diplomat who coalesced the diversified allied Coalition front against Iraq's invasion of Kuwait during his single term in the White House.

George Herbert Walker Bush was born on 12 June 1924 in Milton, Masasachusetts, the second of five sons of Prescott Bush, a prosperous Ohio businessman, and Dorothy (née Walker) Bush.

Bush, George Herbert Walker

U.S. president George Bush, in the Oval Office of the White House, announces on 16 January 1991 that U.S. military forces had begun Operation Desert Storm against Iraq.

Bush's grandfather, Samuel Prescott Bush, was president of the Buckeye Steel Casting Company in Columbus, Ohio. Prescott Bush (1895–1972), a wealthy investment banker who was a partner in the Wall Street investment concern of Brown Brothers, Harriman and Company, served as U.S. senator from Connecticut (1952–1963). Growing up in the affluent village of Greenwich, Connecticut, George Bush attended the prestigious Greenwich Country Day School before attending Phillips Academy in Andover, Massachusetts. Bush graduated from Phillips in 1942, and put off entering Yale University so that he could volunteer to join the U.S. Navy to fight in World War II. After receiving flight training at the Corpus Christi Naval Air Station in Texas, Bush was commissioned an ensign and assigned to the aircraft carrier USS *San Jacinto* as part of Torpedo Bomber Squadron VT51. At the time, Bush, at just 18 years of age, was the youngest pilot in the Navy. Bush flew 58 missions for VT51; in one notable sortie, he was shot down in his Grumman TBF Avenger; with his two crewmates killed in the crash, Bush himself was

picked up by a submarine, with one of the men aboard capturing the rescue on camera.

Rotated back to the United States in 1944, Bush subsequently married Barbara Pierce, daughter of the publisher of *Redbook* and *McCall's* magazines. The two eventually had six children, one of whom, George Bush, Jr., was elected governor of Texas in 1994. George Bush entered Yale University in 1945 and three years later graduated as a Phi Beta Kappa with a bachelor's degree in economics. At Yale, Bush was a member of the school baseball team (he played first base), and the secretive Skull and Bones society. With his graduation, Bush was invited to join his father's firm, but instead packed up his family and traveled to Texas, where he took a job with Dresser Industries, an oilfield drilling supply company. In 1950, he founded, with partner John Overby, the Bush-Overby Company, which did business in oil and gas holdings. Three years later, Bush joined with investors Hugh and William Liedtke to form the Zapata Offshore Company, a concern that incorporated Bush-Overby and became a major offshore drilling equipment firm. In 1958, Bush transferred Zapata's headquarters from Midland, Texas, to his new home in Houston.

During the early 1960s, Bush became party chairman of the Republican Party in Harris County, Texas. In 1964, he took a leave of absence as the head of Zapata to run for the Republican nomination for the U.S. Senate. Supporting the Republican presidential candidate, Barry Goldwater, Bush ran against liberal Senator Ralph Yarborough, an ally of President Lyndon B. Johnson. Although swept to defeat by the Johnson landslide that year, Bush did manage to capture 43.5 percent of the vote—the highest share by a Republican candidate in Texas history. Two years later, in 1966, Bush ran for and was elected to the U.S. House of Representatives from the Seventh Congressional District of Texas, defeating conservative Democrat Frank Briscoe. The editors of *Current Biography Yearbook 1983* wrote about his two terms in the House (1967–1971): "Bush, the first freshman legislator in sixty years to be named to the Ways and Means Committee, pursued a basically conservative course. During his two terms the liberal Americans for Democratic Action rated him between 0 and 12 on a scale of 100, while the Americans for Constitutional Action scored him between 58 and 83. He did, however, support a number of liberal initiatives, including the enfranchisement of eighteen-year-olds, the abolition of the military draft, the adoption of a Congressional ethics code, and the passing of controversial open housing legislation that was unpopular in his own district."

In 1970, Bush gave up his safe seat for a chance to once again contest Yarborough for the U.S. Senate. Instead, a newcomer, conservative Democrat Lloyd M. Bentsen, Jr., defeated Yarborough in the Democratic primary, and the campaign was waged on the issues of law and order and support of the Vietnam War. In the end, however, Bentsen was elected by a margin of 150,000 votes out of 2.2 million cast. In recognition of his "sacrifice" for the party, Bush was given a series of appointive posts by an appreciative President Richard Nixon, beginning with U.S. ambassador to the United Nations (1971–1973), and leading up to chairman of the Republican National Committee (1973–1974), U.S. envoy to China (1974–1975), and director of the Central Intelligence Agency (1976–77). As ambassador to the United

Nations, Bush was instrumental in putting up the last defense of the West in trying to keep China from being represented. As Republican National Committee chairman, he defended Nixon against the charges of Watergate until the last moment, until even he demanded the president's resignation. Gerald Ford's choice of Bush as the first envoy to China started both countries down the road to more normalized relations and cooperation. As director of Central Intelligence, he led the agency through the turbulent period following Watergate, and steadied the organization's morale and sense of importance.

From 1977 until 1979, while the Democrats were in power and Bush was in Houston, the former ambassador planned a presidential campaign. After announcing his candidacy in May 1979, Bush seemed to be a little-known but important hopeful for the Republican nomination. Although Bush won a decisive triumph in the Iowa caucuses, he lost the important New Hampshire primary to Ronald Reagan, who began a series of victories that led him to the nomination. Although it was announced that former President Ford would be Reagan's running mate, the former California governor turned toward his rival, George Bush, as his partner. The former ambassador's foreign policy experience was seen as a major advantage for the ticket. Dissatisfaction with the regime of Jimmy Carter and a lingering hostage crisis in Iran led to Reagan and Bush's election, making George Bush the forty-third vice president of the United States. Continuing the changes made by his predecessor, Walter Mondale, in making the vice presidency more than a figurehead position, Bush oversaw the Senate, as the potential tie-breaking voter, with vigor. He was ready to assume the presidency when Reagan was shot in March 1981; he broke a tie vote in the Senate in July 1983 to have the military build more nerve gas weaponry. At the same time, Bush allegedly became involved in what was later known as the Iran–Contra Affair—the trading of arms for American hostages in the Middle East, with the profits being sent to the anti–Communist guerillas known as contras in Nicaragua. Although no evidence has ever been produced that shows that Bush knew of the intrigue, he was widely criticized.

In 1987, as the end of Reagan's second term neared, Bush announced his campaign for the

Republican presidential nomination, a prize denied him in 1980. A hard–fought primary campaign, as well as a general campaign marked by his selection of Indiana Senator Dan Quayle as his running mate, was marked by Bush's victory over Governor Michael Dukakis of Massachusetts. On 20 January 1989, George Bush took the oath of office as the forty-first president of the United States. In 1989, Hugh Sidey wrote in Fitzhugh Green's *George Bush: An Intimate Portrait*, "George Bush is the most blessed of the presidents this century. He was born with wealth (but not too much), given health, intelligence, talent, good looks, family love, discipline and the confidence that follows all of the above. He observed the Great Depression but was never scarred by it. He was called to war and his courage was summoned in combat, but he was not maimed in battle, either in mind or body. His political defeats were never of such magnitude [as] to discourage him. His victories were not so great that they bred arrogance."

George Bush served one term in the White House, his administration ending in 1993, mostly over voter fear of an extended economic recession. His successes in four years were many: the arrest of Manuel Noriega when American troops invaded Panama in 1989; the speeding up of an end to the apartheid regime in South Africa by removing American–imposed sanctions in exchange for improved racial relations; and the signing of a strategic arms limitations treaty with Soviet President Mikhail Gorbachev. Yet, Bush's greatest feat was ending the possible appeasement of Saddam Hussein and the UN coalition invasion of Iraq. He was the leader who convinced the disparate nations of the United Nations that it was in their best interest to face down and defeat the Iraqi dictator's aggression. With the end of the war in 1991, Bush set on a course of accomplishing a full-range Middle East peace, which included treaties between Israel and Syria, but negotiations were not completed before he left office in 1993. Defeated by Democrat Bill Clinton, Bush retired with his wife to his home in Houston, speaking out occasionally on public policy issues.

See also Baker, James Addison, III; Helsinki Summit; Quayle, James Danforth.
References: Bush, George, with Victor Gold, *Looking Forward* (New York: Doubleday, 1987); *Encyclopedia Americana: International Edition,* Vol. V (Danbury, CT: Grolier, 1993), 38–42; Green, Fitzhugh, *George Bush: An Intimate Portrait* (New York: Hippocrene, 1989), xii; Johnston, Bernard, exec. ed., *Colliers Encyclopedia,* Vol. V (New York: Collier, 1993), 17–19; Moritz, Charles, ed., *Current Biography Yearbook 1983* (New York: H.W. Wilson, 1983), 391.

C-5A/B Galaxy Transport

On 29 August 1990, as the U.S. military was pushing its limits to ferry cargo to Saudi Arabia, a C-5A Galaxy with the 60th Military Airlift Wing crashed on takeoff from Ramstein Air Force Base in West Germany after the pilot inadvertently sent the number one engine into full thrust reversal, killing 13 of the 17 Americans aboard—the first air fatalities of Operation Desert Shield—and seriously wounding the others. According to the military report *Desert Score,* "From 7 August 1990 [when Operation Desert Shield began] to 2 April 1991, C-5s flew more than 3,800 missions carrying 87,850 passengers and 230,600 tons of cargo to the theater of operations."

The C-5A configuration is powered by four General Electric TF39-GE-1C turbofan engines, each delivering 43,000 pounds (19,505 kg) of static thrust. Dimensions for the C-5B are staggering: weight (empty), 374,000 pounds (169,645 kg); maximum payload, 291,000 pounds (131,997 kg); wingspan, 222 feet 8½ inches (67.88 m); length, 247 feet 10 inches (75.54 m); and maximum speed, 496 knots (571 mph; 919 km/h). The plane carries five crew (pilot, copilot, flight engineer, and two loadmasters), and can carry 75 troops on its upper deck and 275 additional troops in the main cargo bay. The C-5 is the second largest military transport in the world (the largest is the Soviet AN-124 Condor, which can carry between 18 and 50 metric tons additional cargo).

See also C-130 Hercules Transport.
Reference: Almond, Denise L., ed., *Desert Score:*

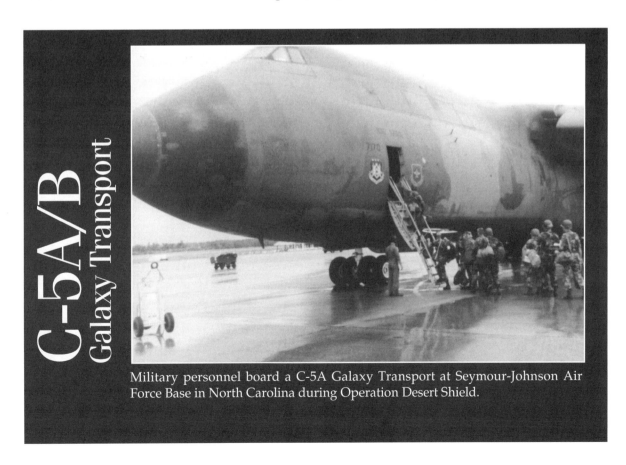

Military personnel board a C-5A Galaxy Transport at Seymour-Johnson Air Force Base in North Carolina during Operation Desert Shield.

U.S. Gulf War Weapons (Washington, DC: Carroll Publishing, 1991), 170–171.

C-21A Learjet

The C-21A Learjet, with civilian designations as the 35A and the 36A, was sold to the U.S. military for "operational support missions," according to *Jane's All the World's Aircraft, 1991–92*.

A light turbofan jet with a seating capacity of two crew members and eight passengers (the 36A carries only six passengers), the C-21A's mission is basically that of a support craft to shuttle small priority or emergency payloads, or transport medevac or other emergency medical personnel. Powered by two Garret TFE731-2-2B turbofan engines (mounted as pods on both sides at the back of the plane), the C-21A's wingspan is 39 feet 6 inches (12 m, including the single wingtip tanks at the ends), and can fly at a maximum speed of Mach 0.81. Carrying four passengers with a full tank of fuel, the C-21A can fly 1,389 miles (2,236 km), and the 36A model can fly 1,655 miles (2,664 km).

Reference: Lambert, Mark, ed., *Jane's All the World's Aircraft, 1991–92* (Coulsdon, Surrey, UK: Jane's Information Group, 1991), 417–418.

C-130 Hercules Transport

Aside from the C-5A Galaxy, the C-130 Hercules Transport is the largest carrier of U.S. military supplies in the world. Several, including variants, served in the Persian Gulf War.

Powered by four Allison T56 turboprops, the C-130 has a wingspan of 132 feet 7 inches (40.41 m), and weighs about 155,000 pounds (70,308 kg) fully loaded. These planes, as well as C-21A military-designated Learjets, were used at the beginning of the Desert Shield buildup, flying STAR (scheduled tactical airlift) flights to support Operation Desert Shield with emergency supplies. Three C-130s served as part of the New Zealand contingent in the crisis.

See also AC-130A/H Spectre Gunship; EC-130E Volant Solo; EC-130H Compass Call; MC-130H Combat Talon II.
Reference: Gunston, Bill, *USAF: An Illustrated Guide to the Modern US Air Force* (Prentice Hall, 1986), 78.

A C-130 Hercules transport easily accommodates one of the 82nd Airborne Division's M-551 Sheridan light tanks.

C-141B Starlifter

This large cargo plane was utilized to maximum benefit during Operation Desert Shield and the build-up to Operation Desert Storm in the period from August 1990 to January 1991. According to the military report *Desert Score,*

Of the 266 C-141s in service in August 1990, 90% were eventually committed to supporting the international response to the Iraqi invasion and annexation of Kuwait. In the first 100 days (up to 18 November 1990), C-141s had made 8,823 departures and averaged 91% on-time departures. Overall, from 7 August to 2 April 1991, C-141 aircraft flew more than 8,470 intertheater airlift missions carrying more than 91,000 passengers and 159,600 tons of cargo to the Persian Gulf conflict area. In the first month of redeployment (1 March to 2 April), C-141s totalled 720 missions and carried 19,400 passengers and 12,000 tons of cargo.

The C-141B is an altered version of the C-141A; simply put, the plane was "stretched" by adding a 13 foot 4 inch (4.06 m) "plug" to the fuselage in front of the wings, as well as a similar 10 foot (3.05 m) plug behind the wings, giving the plane an additional 23 feet 4 inches (7.11 m) in length. Manufactured by Lockheed Aeronautical Systems of Marietta, Georgia, the C-141B is powered, like the C-141A, by four Pratt & Whitney TF33-P-7 turbofan engines. Wingspan of the craft is 159 feet 11 inches (48.74 m). Capable of carrying a crew of 5 plus either 155 paratroops or 200 ground troops, the C-141B has a ferry range of 6,390 miles (5,550 nautical miles; 10,280 km) and a maximum payload capacity of 94,508 pounds (42,869 kg).

References: Almond, Denise L., ed., *Desert Score: U.S. Gulf War Weapons* (Washington, DC: Carroll Publishing, 1991), 182–183; Taylor, John W.R., ed., *Jane's All the World's Aircraft 1982–83* (London: Jane's Publication Company, 1982), 409.

Cairo Summit

Just eight days after Iraq's invasion of Kuwait, on 10 August 1990, a meeting of the Arab League sponsored by President Hosni Mubarak of Egypt was convened for a single day to find ways to end the crisis. The editors of *U.S. News & World Report,* in their *Triumph without Victory: The History of the Persian Gulf War,* wrote: "With Mubarak's blessing, the Arab League had issued a bland statement [in their 3 August meeting] denouncing the action by Iraqi troops in Kuwait. That had angered Saddam even further, but Mubarak nevertheless requested, through the Iraqi Ambassador in Cairo, that he send a delegation to a summit of the Arab League [to be held 10 August]. With the Iraqis present, the Egyptian president believed, and the pressure that could be brought only in a summit-type forum, perhaps a solution could still be reached."

The summit soon bogged down on the issue of whether Kuwait was still a country. As *U.S. News & World Report's* work related, "Saddam [had] dispatched Taha Yasin Ramadan to Cairo. An erstwhile bank cashier, the Iraqi envoy evidently had been authorized to adopt a hard line with Mubarak. . . . It was evident as soon as he got off the plane in Cairo on the morning of August 10 that Ramadan intended to bully the summiteers. A very nervous [Kuwaiti] Sheik Jaber al-Sabah had come to Cairo, at last, to talk. But when the Iraqi plane disgorged one hundred uniformed soldiers, each carrying a fully loaded Kalishnikov machine gun, Mubarak thought he had made a grievous mistake in asking Ramadan or any other Iraqis to the summit. . . . Once settled in his special residence, Ramadan requested a meeting with President Mubarak, and they agreed on a time. Ramadan showed up a half hour late, offering no apologies. Then, Mubarak recalled, incredulous[ly], as if there had been nothing specific on their agenda, 'he asked me what I wanted to discuss.' Mubarak indicated he was interested in talking about the independence of Kuwait. The Egyptian president said he remembered Ramadan's answer very clearly: 'He told me, "There is nothing called Kuwait, . . ." he said. "No, it is Iraqi soil. There is nothing called Kuwait!" ' "

From the first day of the crisis in the Gulf, Mubarak had endeavored to assemble a consensus on a solution to the crisis by alerting the assembled representatives that unless the Arabs solved the problem of Kuwait themselves, foreign intervention, particularly by the United States, was inevitable. In his opening statement to the summit, Mubarak said, "The options before us are clear: an Arab action to protect the higher interest of the Arab nation, preserving Iraq and Kuwait, or foreign intervention that we will have no say or control over." With the backing of Saudi Arabia, Mubarak sought to have Arab nations send "peacekeeping" troops to Saudi Arabia, and subsequently circulated a resolution railing against the potential for "foreign attack."

In the midst of the session, Saddam Hussein delivered an address from Baghdad calling for a jihad (holy war) against King Fahd of Saudi Arabia and warning of the possibility that "infidels"—American troops—would be positioned near some of Islam's holiest shrines in Saudi Arabia. "O Arabs, O Muslims and faithful everywhere, this is your day to rise and defend Mecca, which is captured by the spears of the Americans and the Zionists. Keep the foreigner away from your holy shrines, so we will all stand as one to expel darkness and expose those rulers who know no sense of honor," the Iraqi president raged.

Speaking on behalf of the Iraqi government at the conference, Foreign Minister Tariq Aziz said, "We're not coming here to discuss any Arab business under the threat of American forces and intimidation. If the Americans leave the region to its people, we are ready to discuss any questions." He continued, "If you want to find an Arab solution to the problem, there should be an Arab atmosphere around you. No solution can be found with the Americans around you."

At this point, realizing that Iraq had hijacked the summit, Mubarak asked for a vote on a resolution requesting that Arab nations send troops to defend Saudi Arabia. The resolution read: "We have decided to respond to the request by Saudi Arabia and other gulf states to deploy Arab forces to support the armed forces there to defend its lands and its regional security against any foreign attack." Quickly, 12 of the league's members (Bahrain, Djibouti, Egypt, Kuwait, Lebanon, Morocco, Oman, Qatar, Saudi Arabia, Somalia, Syria, and the United Arab Emirates) voted in favor of the resolution; Jordan, the Sudan, and Mauritania voted in favor "with reservations." Iraq, the Palestine Liberation Organization, and Libya voted no; Algeria and Yemen abstained; and Tunisia did not send a representative to the meeting. The line of Arab indifference to the Iraqi aggression had been crossed.

As John Kifner wrote in the *New York Times,* "The emergency meeting's outcome was a kind of watershed in modern Arab history, ripping aside the slogans of Arab brotherhood that had served to veil differences. It took place in a closed session so emotionally charged that the Iraqis threw plates of food at the Kuwaitis at the official luncheon, and the Kuwaiti Foreign Minister fainted during the debate, according to reports that seeped out."

References: John Kifner, "Arabs Vote To Send Troops To Help Saudis; Boycott of Arab Oil Is Reported Near 100%," *New York Times,* 11 August 1990, A1, A6; U.S. News & World Report, *Triumph without Victory: The History of the Persian Gulf War* (New York: Times Books, 1993), 99–100.

Canada

See Coalition Nations, Contributions of.

Carl-Gustaf Recoilless Gun

Used by the militaries of Great Britain, Kuwait, Qatar, Saudi Arabia, and the United Arab Republics, the Carl-Gustaf, according to *Jane's Infantry Weapons,* is "a one-manportable, recoilless gun, originally conceived for the anti-tank role but in later years upgraded to a true multi-purpose capability." An 84 mm system, the Carl-Gustaf is 3 feet 8 inches (1.13 m) in length, weighs 31.3 pounds (14.2 kg), and carries a 3.75-pound (1.7 kg) shell that can travel from 1,476 feet (450 m) with a HEAT (high-explosive anti-tank) warhead to 3,280 feet (1,000 m).

Reference: Hogg, Ian V., ed., *Jane's Infantry Weapons, 1993–94* (Coulsdon, Surrey, UK: Jane's Information Group, 1993), 423.

Carter Doctrine

This policy of American intentions in the Persian Gulf was enunciated by President Jimmy Carter in his State of the Union speech on 23 January 1980. Because of the Soviet invasion of Afghanistan the month before, and expressing deeply held military fears that in a quest to control the world's oil such an invasion would take place in

U.S. president Jimmy Carter presents his State of the Union Address to a joint session of Congress on 23 January 1980.

the Persian Gulf, Carter warned the Soviets that any such move would result in American force being used. "The region which is now threatened by Soviet troops in Afghanistan is of great strategic importance. It contains more than two-thirds of the world's exportable oil," Carter said in his remarks. "The Soviet effort to dominate Afghanistan has brought Soviet military forces to within 300 miles (483 km) of the Indian Ocean and close to the Straits of Hormuz—a waterway through which most of the world's oil must flow. The Soviet Union is now attempting to consolidate a strategic position therefore that poses a grave threat to the free movement of Middle East oil." He continued:

This situation demands careful thought, steady nerves and resolute action—not only for this year, but for many years to come. It demands collective efforts to meet this new threat to security in the Persian Gulf and in Southwest Asia. It demands the participation of those who rely on oil from the Middle East and who are concerned with global peace and stability. And it demands consultation and close cooperation with countries in the area which might be threatened.

Meeting this challenge will take national will, diplomatic and political wisdom, economic sacrifice and, of course, military capability. We must call on the best that is in us to preserve the security of this crucial region.

Let our position be absolutely clear: An attempt by any outside force to gain control of the Persian Gulf region will be regarded as an assault on the vital interests of the United States of America. And such an assault will be repelled by any means necessary, including military force.

The Carter Doctrine is important for three reasons: For the first time, the American government articulated a policy that involved the potential use of American forces in the Persian Gulf. Further, it set the stage for a new working relationship in trade and the military with the Persian Gulf states, including Oman, Bahrain, the United Arab Emirates, Saudi Arabia, and, for a period during the 1980s, Iraq. It also led to the establishment of the Rapid Deployment Force

(RDF), which the United States utilized during the early 1980s for quick responses to worldwide crises. The RDF evolved into the U.S. Central Command, the military "supervisor" of sorts, that played such a pivotal role in the prosecution of the Persian Gulf War. Hedrick Smith called the Carter discourse "an echo of President Truman facing Soviet threats to Greece and Turkey in 1947 and President Eisenhower dealing with the instability of the Middle East a decade later."

Reference: Smith, Hedrick, "The Carter Doctrine: Stern Warning on Gulf Area Is in Sharp Contrast to Nixon's Avoidance of Regional Confrontation," *New York Times,* 26 January 1980, A1, A12.

Casualties, Coalition

As a whole, the coalition suffered few casualties, counted as killed in action and wounded in action. According to authors Lawrence Freedman and Efraim Karsh, the totals are: the United States, 148 killed in action and 458 wounded in action; and other coalition countries, 92 killed in action and 318 wounded in action, for a total of 240 killed in action and 776 wounded in action.

Reference: Freedman, Lawrence, and Efraim Karsh, *The Gulf Conflict: Diplomacy and War in the New World Order, 1990–1991* (Princeton, NJ: Princeton University Press, 1993), 409.

Casualties, Iraqi

It may be an impossible task to determine the number of military and civilian casualties on the Iraqi side during the Persian Gulf War. Guy Gugliotta wrote in the *Washington Post,* "[Schwarzkopf] said the coalition did not have any estimate of Iraqi casualties for the six weeks [from the start of the war until its conclusion]. Assessments from other sources, including the Saudi Arabian ambassador to the United States, Prince Bandar bin Sultan, suggest that Iraqi dead and wounded number 60,000 to 100,000, the majority killed in the massive allied bombing campaign that preceded the ground offensive." However, according to a study commissioned by the House Armed Services Committee, "the committee estimated that 9,000 Iraqi soldiers had been killed in the air war and 120,000 had died

or escaped the battlefield in the ground war. Rep. Les Aspin (D–Wisconsin) said the 'bulk' of the 120,000 had probably fled north into Iraq."

References: Gugliotta, Guy, "Iraqi Battle Casualties May Exceed 60,000," *Washington Post,* 28 February 1991, A32; Schmitt, Eric, "Study Lists Lower Tally of Iraqi Troops in Gulf War," *New York Times,* 24 April 1992, 6.

Casualties, United States

From the beginning of Operation Desert Shield on 7 August 1990 to the conclusion of Operation Desert Storm on 28 February 1991, 191 American servicemen and servicewomen were counted as killed in action; 72 of these deaths were considered nonhostile. Three hundred servicemen and servicewomen were wounded and 7 remain missing in action.

See also Appendix 1, Selected Statistics Comparing American Casualties in Past Wars Appendix 1, U.S. Casualty List
Reference: Fort Lauderdale Sun-Sentinel, 10 March 1991, 8G, 9G.

CBU Bomb Series

In the Persian Gulf War these cluster bombs were dropped on various targets that needed to be destroyed by small, high-explosive bomblets. The classification includes the CBU-52, CBU-58, CBU-59 APAM, CBU-71, and CBU-72. In total, 17,831 of these weapons were used during Operation Desert Storm.

CBU-52 This weapon is loaded with 220 small bomblets, and weighs 785 pounds (356 kg).

CBU-58 Amassed with 650 bomblets, these embody "5-gram titanium pellets, making them incendiary and useful against flammable targets."

CBU-59 APAM Short for antipersonnel antimaterial weapon, the CBU-59 was created to succeed the MK-20 Rockeye. Although it looks the same as the MK-20 (it is contained in the same casing), the CBU-59 carries 717 small BLU-77 bomblets instead of 247 larger bomblets; 186 APAMs were used during the war.

CBU-71 Packed with 650 bomblets, the CBU-71 "has two separate kill mechanisms, one

Casualties, Iraqi

Burned-out vehicles outside Kuwait City provide evidence of Coalition air power against the Iraqis.

fragmentation, one incendiary. Both incorporate a time delay fuze, which detonates at random times after impact."

CBU-72 This 550-pound (249 kg) weapon contains a fuel air explosive (FAE), which acts like a small nuclear weapon upon impact but without the radiation.

Reference: Gulf War Air Power Survey, Volume IV: Weapons, Tactics, and Training Report and Space Report (Washington, DC: GPO, 1993), 72–74.

Censorship of the War, Coalition

The alarm went up almost immediately: "Covering the [Persian Gulf] War is CENSORED," wrote NBC president Michael Gartner in the *Wall Street Journal* on 30 August 1990, when the crisis in the Gulf was barely a month old and it would be four and a half months before hostilities broke out. Yet postwar analyses, particularly by reporters and news editors (newspapers, magazines, and television), consistently show that as a whole they felt the sting of censorship, whether real or unintended, from the Pentagon in their coverage of Operations Desert Shield and Desert Storm.

"Reporters are told where they can go and can't go in Saudi Arabia," Gartner explained. "Put simply, they can't go [to] very many places—and the television reporters are forbidden from telling their viewers just where the reporters [themselves] are other than 'someplace in Saudi Arabia.'" But was this just the beef of American reporters and journalists? Gara La-Marche, executive director of the Fund for Free Expression, wrote in 1991, "Regrettably, the U.S. had plenty of company in the censorship business during Operation Desert Storm . . . Turkish television used much of CNN's material on the war, but when the coverage turned to such matters as U.S. strikes at Iraq from Turkish bases or the shortage of gas masks in the country, programming was interrupted for a 'commercial break' or scenic waterfall footage." He continued, "The Egyptian Organization for Human Rights reported that as many as 200 political activists and students were detained. Israel closed nine press offices in the occupied territories and arrested the Palestinian writer and peace activist Sari Nusseibeh on 'spying' charges widely be-

lieved to be spurious. Syria detained 80 writers and intellectuals for expressing support for Iraq. In Great Britain, the BBC blocked a documentary on the export to Iraq of British-built superguns, on the grounds that the 'tone is wrong,' and the government detained dozens of Iraqi nationals as prisoners of war and deported others. France banned the distribution, publication or sale of three publications deemed pro-Iraqi on the grounds that they 'defend interests that are contrary to France's interests' concerning the war, and expelled one of the editors. The Australian Broadcasting Corporation faced a government inquiry following complaints from Prime Minister Hawke about its war coverage."

The Pentagon's official policy on the reporting process was established on 14 August 1990 when a ten-page memorandum named Annex Foxtrot was sent out from USCENTCOM (U.S. Central Command) headquarters in Tampa, Florida. Written by Captain Ron Wildermuth, chief aide for public affairs, to General H. Norman Schwarzkopf, Annex Foxtrot made one point noticeably clear: "News media representatives will be escorted at all times. Repeat, at all times." This attitude developed from the disastrous Vietnam War experience, in which reporters were allowed to wander across the entire theater of operations, sending back horrible pictures that brought the dramatic reality of war into the living rooms of the American people. It is argued that had pictures from D-Day been sent home, American resolve to move on to Berlin and defeat Hitler would have eroded. The Annex Foxtrot policy sought to avoid this outcome from the Gulf War.

On 7 January 1991 Pete Williams, assistant secretary of defense, sent a Memorandum for Washington Bureau Chiefs of the Pentagon Press Corps that outlined Pentagon rules for what could and could not be printed in newspapers and magazines or displayed on television. These restrictions remained in force for much of the war, although journalists bent or simply ignored them, such as the incident where CBS reporter Bob Simon and a television crew went to the Saudi-Iraqi border and were captured, and when CBS reporter Bob McKeown charged past U.S. troops to become the first reporter to "liberate" Kuwait City. "I never saw any organized efforts at censorship," reported Lieutenant Charles E. Hoskinson, Jr., a reservist and pool escort. "All I saw was the natural tendency in the military to keep things under control."

Tom Wicker wrote in the *New York Times,* "Nor did the press and television, to their discredit, protest as effectively as they should have, or always make it as clear as they could have, that much of what they conveyed was not only controlled by the military but prettified for home consumption. Thus was the First Amendment badly wounded in Desert Storm—though war-giddy Americans seemed not to know or mourn this national casualty."

See also Joint Information Bureau; Journalists; Media; National Media Pool.
References: DeParle, Jason, "Long Series of Military Decisions Led to Gulf War News Censorship," *New York Times,* 5 May 1991, A1, A20; Fialka, John J., *Hotel Warriors: Covering the Gulf War* (Washington, DC: Woodrow Wilson Center Press, 1992), 57; Gartner, Michael, "Covering the War Is CENSORED," *Wall Street Journal,* 30 August 1990, A9; LaMarche, Gara, "In Bad Company: Censorship in the Gulf War," *New York Times,* 18 May 1991, A22; Wicker, Tom, "An Unknown Casualty," *New York Times,* 20 March 1991, A29.

CENTCOM. *See* U.S. Central Command.

CH-46E Sea Knight

A three-man shipborne assault and troop-carrying helicopter, the CH-46E was a vital supply line for the U.S. Marines during Operation Desert Storm.

The CH-46E is powered by two 1,870 shaft horsepower General Electric T58-16 turboshafts, has a maximum speed of 143 knots (165 mph; 265 km/h), an unfueled range of 206 nautical miles (237 mi; 381.5 km), and can carry either 17 troops or 10,000 pounds (4,536 kg) of cargo. According to the military report *Desert Score,* "120 Marine Corps Sea Knights—60 operating from shore bases and 60 from ships—flew 1,601 sorties during Operation Desert Storm. They supported the drive into Kuwait that began the ground war on 24 February 1991. Two CH-46s were lost during the seven-week war, both to non-combat causes."

References: Almond, Denise L., ed., *Desert Score: U.S. Gulf War Weapons* (Washington, DC: Carroll Publishing, 1991), 71; Jordan, John, *An Illustrated Guide to Modern Naval Aviation and Aircraft Carriers* (New York: Prentice Hall, 1983), 46.

CH-47D Chinook

This transport and shuttle helicopter was used by the United States (specifically by U.S. Special Operations Command Central [USSOCCENT]) and Britain during the Persian Gulf War. The 160 American Chinooks flew several hundred sorties, while the 21 British versions, known as HC Mk 1Bs, flew an undetermined number.

Powered by two Avco Lycoming T55-L-712 turboshaft engines each delivering 3,750 shaft horsepower (shp), the Chinook has a crew of three (pilot, copilot, and crew chief/combat commander), and is capable of transporting a minimum of 44 soldiers. The craft weighs 22,452 pounds (10,184 kg) empty, and can support a maximum internal and external load of 26,679 pounds (12,102 kg). Maximum speed is 159 knots (183 mph; 295 km/h), while the unrefueled range varies because of mission radius and internal and external payload capacity. The rotor of the craft is 60 feet (18.29 m) in length.

According to the military report *Desert Score,* "10 Chinooks supported the eight AH-64 Apaches that staged an attack on Iraqi radars to open Desert Storm on 17 January. One of them was a 'fat cow' CH-47 loaded with fuel that served as a forward-based refueling depot." No CH-47s were lost during the seven-week-long war.

See also Task Force Normandy.
Reference: Almond, Denise L., ed., *Desert Score: U.S. Gulf War Weapons* (Washington, DC: Carroll Publishing, 1991), 74–75.

CH-53E Super Stallion

This helicopter, a Marine Corps and Navy variant of the MH-53 Sea Dragon, a minesweeping helicopter, was used by the Marine Corps during Operation Desert Storm. In all, 75 CH-53Es—53 on shore and 22 on ships in the Persian Gulf—flew 2,045 sorties. The ship is identical to the

A CH-53E Super Stallion helicopter, one of 22 based on ships during Operation Desert Storm, lifts off from the flight deck of the USS *New Orleans*.

more sophisticated MH-53 except that the MH-53 has an increased internal fuel capacity of 2,183 gallons.

See also MH-53E Sea Dragon.
Reference: Almond, Denise L., ed., *Desert Score: U.S. Gulf War Weapons* (Washington, DC: Carroll Publishing, 1991), 78–79.

CH-124 Sea King
See SH-3G/H Sea King.

Challenger Main Battle Tank

Considered state-of-the-art in armor protection and fighting capability, this main battle tank (MBT) served with the British in the Persian Gulf. Powered by a Rolls-Royce Condor 12V 1200 12-cylinder diesel engine, the tank has a crew capacity of four, a combat weight of 136,685 pounds (62,000 kg), and a maximum road speed of 60 km/h. It has a a single 120 mm gun and two 7.62 mm guns. In the rear of the vehicle is an NBC (nuclear, biological, and chemical) weapons environmental control system.

References: Foss, Christopher F., ed., *Jane's Armour and Artillery, 1992–93* (Coulsdon, Surrey, UK: Jane's Information Group, 1992), 126; Foss, Christopher F., ed., *Jane's Main Battle Tanks* (London: Jane's Publishing Group, 1986), 99.

Chemical and Biological Warfare

The potential usage of chemical and/or biological weapons by the Iraqis during the Allied invasion of Kuwait hung over preparations for the assault like a cloud.

The Iraqis were notorious for having used chemical weapons on both their Iranian opponents and their own Kurdish population during the Iran-Iraq war. Authors Marion Farouk-Sluglett and Peter Sluglett write that the United Nations sent two missions, one between 13 and 19 March 1984 and the second between 26 February and 3 March 1986, to investigate these rumors. Their report in March 1986 confirmed that "in the areas around Abadan inspected by the United Nations mission, chemical weapons have been extensively used against Iranian positions

Muslims at morning prayer in Saudi Arabia wear gas masks during the early days of Operation Desert Storm.

Chemical and Biological Warfare

by Iraqi forces." In 1988 Secretary of State George Shultz condemned the use of such weapons in a San Francisco speech. Although Shultz did not mention any specific nations in his speech, he commented to the *Washington Post* that "he strongly criticized Iraq two months" earlier "for its alleged use of chemical weapons against its Kurdish minority. The [Reagan] Administration earlier had criticized Iran and Iraq for using chemical weapons. It had said that Iraq used them more extensively."

The U.S. position on the usage of chemical and biological weapons in the Persian Gulf was clear. On 16 November 1990, President George Bush signed Executive Order 12735, which found that the proliferation of chemical and biological weapons "constitutes an unusual and extraordinary threat to the national security and foreign policy of the United States"; along with the order, Bush declared a national emergency to deal with the problem. A month before the Persian Gulf air war started, CIA Director William Webster stated in congressional testimony that he calculated that Iraq had "1,000 tons of poisonous agents, much of it capable of being loaded into two types of missiles: the FROG (free rocket over ground) and the SCUD B (SS-1)," according to a

report released in May 1994 by the Senate Banking Committee, which was investigating western deliveries to Iraq that resulted in a stockpile of nerve gas and other agents.

The U.S. military, in its final report to Congress on the war, wrote that "the most effective contamination detection system fielded during Operations Desert Shield and Desert Storm was the German-donated Fuchs [Fox] NBC reconnaissance vehicle. Fielding of the vehicle and training of the crews began in August. Units had just three weeks of training at the German NBC School at Sonthofen or the Army Chemical School at Fort McClellan."

Following the war, CWO Joseph P. Sorrel discussed his training in the recognition of poison gases that might come during possible chemical attacks:

My experiences in Southwest Asia [the geographic determinant of the Persian Gulf] . . . comes from serving as the Nuclear, Biological, Chemical (NBC) defense officer for the Seventh Marine Regiment/Task Force Ripper (TFR). The first occurrence happened at both breach sites . . . the FOX vehicle attached to TFR detected blister agent[s] at levels below [an] IMMEDIATE threat to personnel. Levels that are below levels required to cause effects on humans. It was determined at that time that the rapid movement through the breach sites would not pose a threat to continued combat operations or require decontamination. Exposure time for individuals was not tracked or limited.

The next occurrence happened the evening of the first day of the ground attack. As TFR held positions around the Ahmed Al Jaber Airbase, . . . the Fox vehicle detected Lewisite blister vapors. The levels detected were also low. . . . The only other case known to me happened around the 'bunker complex.' . . . The FOX crew was directed to check the area for chemical munitions. A report that some chemical vapors were found and reported. TFR was ordered back to the division support area and further detection operations were not carried out by TFR. This report cannot be confirmed.

After examining Iraq's potential biological weapons resources, on 30 July 1991 Rolf Ekeus, director of UNSCOM, the United Nations Special Commission on Iraq, told the UN Security Council that his group had found Scud missiles, ready for launch and armed with chemical warheads. On 13 February, a secret radio network in Iraq, the "Voice of the Iraqi People," reported that Saddam Hussein still had chemical weapons stockpiles, which it claimed he had hidden in closed oil pipelines, away from the UN inspectors.

See also Fuchs (Fox) M93 NBC Vehicle; Nuclear Weapons, Iraq's Potential for Constructing.
References: Carus, Seth, *The Genie Unleashed: Iraq's Chemical and Biological Weapons Programs* (Washington, DC: Washington Institute for Near East Policy, 1989); *Conduct of the Persian Gulf War: Final Report to Congress,* Report by the Department of Defense, April 1992, 643; Executive Order 12735 of 16 November 1990, 55 Federal Register 48587; Farouk-Sluglett, Marion, and Peter Sluglett, *Iraq since 1958: From Revolution to Dictatorship* (London: I. B. Tauris, 1990), 261, 324; "2 Weapons Troubling to Shultz," *Washington Post,* 30 October 1988, A35; "U.S. Chemical and Biological Warfare–Related Dual Use Exports to Iraq and Their Possible Impact on the Health Consequences of the Persian Gulf War," Report of Chairman Donald W. Riegle, Jr., and Ranking Member Alfonse M. D'Amato of the Committee on Banking, Housing and Urban Affairs with Respect to Export Administration, U.S. Senate Report, 103rd Congress, 2nd Session, 25 May 1994, 17, 23; "Use of Chemical Weapons in Desert Storm," Hearing before the Oversight and Investigations Subcommittee of the House Commitee on Armed Services, 103rd Congress, 1st Session, 1994, 9.

Cheney, Richard Bruce (1941–)

In a large measure, it was the strong leadership of U.S. Secretary of Defense Dick Cheney during the Persian Gulf crisis that shaped American foreign policy more than anyone other than President George Bush and Secretary of State James Baker.

Richard Bruce Cheney was born in Lincoln, Nebraska, on 30 January 1941, the son of Richard Herbert Cheney, a soil conservation agent with the U.S. Department of Agriculture, and Marjorie Lauraine (née Dickey) Cheney. After attending local schools, Cheney went to Yale University for three semesters before earning a B.S. and an M.S. in political science at the University of Wyoming in 1965 and 1966. He married the former Lynne Anne Vincent in 1964.

In 1968 the Cheneys moved to Washington, D.C., where Dick Cheney served in a number of official positions, first with Republican congressman William Steiger of Wisconsin, and then former congressman Donald Rumsfield, then director of the Office of Economic Opportunity under President Richard Nixon. Because of his work with Rumsfield, Cheney was named as President Gerald R. Ford's chief of staff in 1975 at the age of 34, the youngest man to hold that post. As chief of staff, he became good friends with two men who would play important positions during the Gulf War: Brent Scowcroft, national security advisor under Ford (as well as later under Bush), and James A. Baker III, a hard-nosed politico from Texas who was hired to head Ford's reelection campaign in 1976.

After Ford's defeat in 1976, Cheney returned to Wyoming, where two years later he was elected to the state's only congressional seat. He continued to be reelected until 1988, when he resigned his seat to become secretary of defense. He quickly moved up the ladder of seniority, and in his second term, 1981–1983, he was

Cheney, Richard Bruce

Secretary of Defense Richard Cheney, center, meets with Joint Chiefs of Staff chairman General Colin Powell, left, and Central Command commander General Norman H. Schwarzkopf, right, in Riyadh, Saudi Arabia, on 10 February 1991.

named as head of the Republican Policy Committee, considered by some to be one of the top jobs in the Republican House hierarchy. In December 1988, shortly before he was appointed secretary of defense, he was named as House minority whip—the number two position behind the minority leader.

President George Bush's first choice for secretary of defense, former senator John Tower of Texas, was rejected by the Senate, and Bush turned to the loyal Cheney for the post. In March 1989 Cheney won almost unanimous approval from the Senate. Gloria Borger wrote in *U.S. News & World Report*, "In a city in which continual turmoil breeds nervousness, Cheney seems tranquil, even secure. Perhaps that is because he has played the game from almost every vantage point—from that of a congressional aide, White House chief of staff at age 34, a member of Congress, and now second in the military chain of command." Cheney oversaw the end of the cold war, and he used his position to work closely with the Soviets in the post–cold war world, particularly in the area of reducing nuclear weapons and cutting waste from the defense budget.

The crisis that struck the Middle East with the Iraqi invasion of Kuwait on 2 August 1990 gave Cheney the opportunity, as part of the adminis-

tration's inner circle, to shape and formulate American foreign policy. The day before the invasion, Cheney had met with U.S. Central Command chief General H. Norman Schwarzkopf to draw up possible plans in the event of an Iraqi attack on Kuwait. Three days after the attack, Cheney was sent to Saudi Arabia to confer with the Saudi leadership on how to confront the Iraqi aggression. On 23 August Cheney announced that more troops would be sent to the Kuwaiti Theatre of Operations. Cheney was also forced to fire Air Force chief of staff Michael Dugan on 17 September after Dugan told the *Washington Post* that the Pentagon was formulating a battle plan involving a massive air war followed by a ground attack, and that Saddam Hussein would be targeted. After the start of the war, Cheney was also in the forefront. On 24 February 1991 he appeared on CBS's "Face the Nation," in which he reiterated that friendly Arab governments— such as Saudi Arabia, Egypt, and Kuwait— should take up the mantle of postwar security. "The leading responsibility for putting together a new [security] system will rest with the countries of the region." He added that "We [the United States] don't have an interest in a long-term, major ground presence for U.S. forces in the gulf."

With the defeat of George Bush in 1992, Cheney left government but continued speaking out on issues of public policy. In late 1994 he decided not to seek the 1996 Republican presidential nomination. He is the author, with his wife Lynne, of *Kings of the Hill: Power and Personality in the House of Representatives* (New York: Continuum, 1983).

———

References: Borger, Gloria, "The Politician at the Pentagon," *U.S. News & World Report,* 2 October 1989, 24–25; CBS, "Face the Nation" interview quoted in "Cheney Says Security Should Rest with Arabs," by Don Oberdorfer, *Washington Post,* 25 February 1991, A11, A17.

Civil Reserve Air Fleet (CRAF)

The Civil Reserve Air Fleet, known by the acronym CRAF, is a standby group of civilian aircraft to be used by the military to transport material and/or troops in the event of a military emergency. The Pentagon's report, *Gulf War Air Power Survey,* discusses the CRAF's elements: "When Desert Shield began, CRAF comprised five segments: long-range international, short-range international, aeromedical evacuation, domestic, and Alaskan." Under the command of the commander in chief of the Military Airlift Command (CINCMAC), Stage I (emergency) carriers had 24 hours to respond to tasking (assignment) from MAC heaquarters. Stage II carriers were activated by the secretary of defense; these planes, numbering about 177, also had 24 hours to respond after being notified. At Stage III, involving 506 commercial aircraft, planes had to be used within 48 hours. According to the military, Stage III "would only be activated short of a defense oriented national emergency as determined by the President or the Congress." The commercial carriers included in the CRAF prior to 2 August 1990 included Delta Airlines, Continental Airlines, Eastern Airlines, Pan American World Airways, Federal Express, Southern Air Transport, United Airlines, Tower Air, and Air Transport International. CRAF aircraft flew a total of 800 flights in and out of Saudi Arabia to deliver men and materiel. The following table illustrates the participation and numbers of flights for the various airlines that served in the Civil Reserve Air Fleet:

U.S. CARRIERS	MISSIONS:	
	WITH PASSENGERS	WITH CARGO
Air Transport International	—	156
American Airlines	98	—
American International Airways	—	370
American TransAir	494	—
America West Airlines	39	—
Arrow Air	—	119
Buffalo Airways	—	22
Continental Airlines	91	—
Delta Airlines	26	—
Eastern Airlines	33	—
Emery Worldwide	—	152
Evergreen International Airlines	—	347
Federal Express	29	576
Flagship Express	—	249
Florida West	—	54
Hawaiian Airlines	263	—
Northwest Airlines	268	117
Pan Am	335	69
Rich International Airways	14	—
Southern Air Transport	—	252
Sun Country Air Lines	30	—
Tower Air	242	1
Trans Continental Airlines	5	—
Trans World Airlines	236	—
United Airlines	177	—
United Parcel Service	—	123
World Airways	188	149
TOTAL MISSIONS U.S. CARRIERS	2,568	2,756
Foreign Carriers		
Alitalia	—	27
Cargolux Airlines International (Luxembourg)	17	—
Korean Air (South Korea)	—	70
Kuwait Airways	—	1
Martinair Holland (Netherlands)	—	16
TOTAL MISSIONS FOREIGN CARRIERS	17	114
TOTAL MISSIONS ALL CARRIERS	2,585	2,870

Source: "Commercial Airlines Participation in Desert Shield/Storm, Aug. 7, 1990–June 30, 1991," *Aviation Week & Space Technology,* 9 September 1991, 58.

———

Reference: Gulf War Air Power Survey, Volume II: Operations Report and Effectiveness Report (Washington, DC: GPO, 1993).

Cluster Bombs. *See* CBU Bomb Series.

Coalition Nations, Contributions of

Without the international assemblage of troops, planes, and ships from more than 30 nations (including the six countries of the Gulf Cooperation Council), the United States would not have been able to face down Saddam Hussein alone. The contributions of the coalition partners follow.

Afghanistan

According to the military work *Desert Score,* "300 Mujahideen fighters, out of a total pledge of 2,000, were confirmed in-theater at the start of the ground war." There is no information on their role during the conflict.

Argentina

This South American nation contributed 100 troops, 2 warships (the 4 Meko-class destroyer *Almirante Brown* and the 4+2 Meko-class frigate *Spiro*), and 1 Boeing 707-320 and 2 C-130H Hercules transports, as well as 2 Alouette III helicopters on-board the *Almirante Brown,* 1 of which was lost during Gulf operations.

Australia

Australia's assistance to the coalition forces consisted of several ships, which housed some 600 crew members, and included the Royal Australian Navy's DDG-2-class destroyer *Brisbane;* the Perry-class frigates *Adelaide, Darwin,* and *Sydney;* and the underway replenishment tankers *Success* and *Westralia.* No troops or planes played a part, although both the *Adelaide* and the *Darwin* were fitted with AS 550 B Ecureuil helicopters and several S-70B Seahawk helicopters, used in the embargo against Iraq. The *Adelaide* left the Gulf area in December 1990, as did the *Darwin,* and the *Success* left in late January 1991. The others stayed throughout the entirety of the conflict. According to *Desert Score,* "Australian ships in the Gulf were under U.S. tactical command, although the Australian command and control center in Sidney was reactivated for administrative control."

Bangladesh

Bangladesh contributed 2,000 troops to the effort. There is no information on their area of deployment or role during the conflict.

Coalition Nations, Contributions of

Egyptian troops patrol the border between Saudi Arabia and Iraqi-held Kuwait during Operation Desert Storm.

Belgium

No troops or planes represented Belgium, but six ships (the Weilingen-class frigate *Wielingen*; the Tripartite minesweepers *Iris*, *Myosotis*, and *Dianthus*; the support ship *Zinnia*; and the command and logistic support ship *Wandelaar*, which served an an escort for two logistic landing ships) did sail the Belgian flag. The minesweepers were armed with Stinger antiaircraft missiles. There was heated discussion in Belgium about sending a squadron of F-16s to the conflict, but this idea was rejected because the planes were not fitted with electronic countermeasures equipment. The Belgian government refused to allow the minesweepers to be used during the war, but consented to their use to clean up after the war.

Canada

Although no Canadian troops saw combat, 1,700 troops from the Canadian Naval and Air Task Group were stationed in Qatar for patrol duties from northern Bahrain to the Strait of Hormuz. As part of its air contribution to the coalition cause, 24 CF-18 "Hornet" fighter planes (which flew a total of 1,302 sorties), as well as 12 CC-130 "Hercules" transports, 5 CH-124A "Sea King" helicopters, 1 CC-130 converted tanker aircraft, 1 KC-130 tanker, 2 CE-144A electronic warfare planes, 1 CP-140 Aurora maritime reconnaissance aircraft, and 1 T-33 trainer plane, saw action in the Gulf theater of operations. Further, as part of what was known in Canada as Operation Friction, 4 ships (the Tribal-class destroyer *Athabaskan*, the Improved Restigouche-class frigate *Terra Nova*, the St. Laurent-class frigate *Margaree*, and the Protecteur-class underway replenishment tanker *Protecteur*) did serve.

Czechoslovakia

This East European nation dispatched 169 soldiers, all anti–chemical warfare troops, at the behest of the Saudi government. The contingent consisted of one field hospital and three chemical warfare units. Later installments upped the number of troops, both chemical warfare and support personnel, to approximately 190.

Denmark

This country's only contribution was the frigate *Olfert Fischer*.

Egypt

Hosni Mubarak's anger at being lied to by Saddam Hussein led the Egyptian president to send more troops to the Kuwait Theatre of Operations than any other Arab nation (approximately 40,000 soldiers from the Fourth Egyptian Armored Division and the Fourth Egyptian Mechanized Infantry Division, as well as 5,000 paratroopers, commandos, and chemical warfare specialists stationed in the United Arab Emirates during the duration of the war). Although Mubarak offered Saudi Arabia the use of Egyptian Air Force F-16s and Mirage 2000s (an offer that was rejected), no Egyptian air or naval forces participated in the war. The troops that did see action utilized American-built M60A3 tanks.

France

The French contribution was the third highest among the NATO allies (NATO itself also sent a contingent of ships). Some 15,200 French soldiers were sent to the Kuwait Theatre of Operations (plus an additional 4,000 rapid deployment troops and 1,200 chemical warfare troops). Forty-two French planes participated in the war, including the Gabriel and the Jaguar, flying 2,258 sorties. Twenty-one French ships served in the Gulf: the aircraft carrier *Clemenceau*, which served only to deliver French troops to the Gulf before going back to France; the destroyers *Du Chayla*, *Dupleix*, *Jeanne de Vienne*, *La Motte-Picquet*, and *Montcalm*; the frigates *Commandant Bory*, *Commandant Ducuing*, *Doudart de Lagree*, *Premier Maitre L'Her*, and *Protet*; the underway replenishment tankers *Durance*, *Marne*, and *Var*; the maintenance ship *Jules Verne*; the coastal tug *Buffle*; the support ship *Rhin*; the hospital ships *Foudre* and *Rance*; and three tripartite minehunters/sweepers from the Éridan class, the *Pegase*, the *Aigle*, and the *Sagittaire*, as well as six unnamed commercial transports leased by the French government.

Germany

Due to the provision of its constitution that forbids the deployment of German troops outside of its border (as does Japan's), Germany contributed no air or land forces to the Gulf conflict, although it did send seven ships to participate in support activities to act as surrogates for NATO ships that usually serve in the Standing Naval

Force Atlantic (STANAVFORLANT), and were used during the Gulf conflict. These ships included the Rhein-class depot ship *Werra*, the Westerwald-class ammunition transport *Westerwald*, the Lindau-class minehunters *Koblenz*, *Marburg*, and *Wetzlar*, and the Hamelin-class minesweepers *Laboe* and *Überherrn*. Five minehunters/minesweepers and six Troika-class minesweeper drones contributed to the postwar cleanup, and arrived in the Persian Gulf on 4 April 1991. The Germans later contributed at least $6.6 billion (U.S.) to pay for the cost of the war, excluding refugee assistance.

Great Britain

The United States' closest ally in NATO contributed 25,000 troops (including the First Armoured Division under the command of Brigadier General Patrick Cordingley, the Seventh Armoured Brigade under the command of Major General Rupert Smith, and 9,000 support troops), dispatched 54 planes (including the Buccaneer, Tornado, and Nimrod, which flew a total of 5,417 sorties), and, aside from the United States, supplied the largest naval force to the region. Among the ships sent were the Type 42 Batch I destroyer *Cardiff;* the Type 42 Batch II destroyer *Exeter;* the Type 42 Batch III destroyers *York* and *Gloucester;* the Type 22 Batch I frigates *Brazen* and *Battleaxe;* the Type 22 Batch II frigate *London;* the Batch IIIA frigate *Jupiter;* the Hunt-class minesweepers *Atherstone, Cattistock, Dulverton, Hurworth,* and *Ledbury;* the survey ships *Herald* and *Hecla;* the underway replenishment ship *Fort Grange;* the Appleleaf-class support tanker *Orangeleaf;* the OL-class large fleet tanker *Olna;* the repair ship *Diligence;* the logistic land ships (LSL) *Sir Bedivere, Sir Galahad, Sir Percival,* and *Sir Tristam;* the aviation training ship–turned–hospital ship *Argus;* and the Oberon-class diesel-electric submarines *Opossum* and *Otus.* In addition, the Royal Navy dispatched a group of ships to the Mediterranean Sea to monitor that area and check for any potential activity from Libya. This squad, nicknamed Task Group 323.2, consisted of the aircraft carrier *Ark Royal*, the destroyer *Manchester* (which was replaced in the group by the Batch IIIA conversion-class frigate *Charybdis* after 23 January 1991), and the Batch II frigate *Sheffield*. For information on this grouping, see Task Group 323.2.

Greece

Greece supplied two frigates from the Netherlands Kortenaer class: the *Limnos* and its eventual replacement, the *Elli.*

Gulf Cooperation Council (GCC)

The nations of Bahrain, Kuwait, Oman, Qatar, Saudi Arabia, and the United Arab Emirates (UAE) fall into this grouping. Collectively, the GCC contributed 145,000 total troops (including a rapid deployment force of up to 10,000 troops, plus an additional 7,000 Kuwaitis who escaped during the invasion and later participated in liberating their homeland), 330 aircraft flying 8,077 sorties (6,852 by Saudi Arabia, 780 by Kuwait, 293 by Bahrain, 109 by the UAE, and 43 by Qatar), and a small number of ships, including the Kuwaiti craft *Istiqlal* and *Al Sanbouk* and the oil platform ship *Sawahil*. The Kuwaitis used these ships to harass the Iraqis; they were later employed to successfully liberate the first Kuwaiti territory.

Honduras

This Central American nation sent 150 troops as part of the coalition.

Italy

Although no Italian troops saw land combat (700 did serve in some capacity or another in the Persian Gulf Theater of Operations), 10 Italian planes did participate in the air campaign (all Tornado fighter-bombers), as well as 9 ships, including the Maestrale-class frigates *Libeccio* and *Zeffiro*, the Lupo-class frigates *Lupo, Orsa,* and *Sagittario*, the Audace-class missile destroyer *Audace*, the Stromboli-class replenishment tankers *Vesuvio* and *Stromboli*, and the San Georgio-class helicopter assault ship *San Marco* (supplied with 4 CH-124 "Sea King" helicopters), which also doubled as a hospital ship.

Japan

Because its constitution prohibits this Asian nation from dispatching troops overseas (even in a peacekeeping role), Japan was able only to contribute $13 billion (U.S.) to pay for the war effort, excluding refugee assistance and U.N. operations payments. At the end of the conflict, the Japanese government was able to send four unnamed Japanese minesweepers, a flagship, and two supply ships, which arrived in the Gulf on 3 June 1991.

Morocco

This northern African nation sent 1,200 troops to the Gulf, plus an additional 3,500 that were stationed in the United Arab Emirates.

The Netherlands

This northern European nation dispatched eight ships to the Gulf: the Jacob Van Heemskerck–class frigates *Jacob Van Heemskerck* and *Witte de With*, the Kortenaer-class frigates *Pieter Florisz* and *Philips can Almonde*, and the Poolster-class fast combat support ship (FCSS) *Zuiderkruis*. Three Tripartite minehunters/sweepers from the Alkmaar class assisted in postwar cleanup.

New Zealand

This nation's assistance to the coalition was in the form of three C-130 transports.

Niger

This African nation contributed 481 troops to the Gulf.

Norway

This nation's single contribution was the Nordkapp-class tug *Andenes*, sent primarily to assist the Danish frigate *Olfert Fischer*.

Pakistan

This neighbor of Iran provided an initial 7,000 men to the Persian Gulf buildup, plus an additional 2,000 stationed in the United Arab Emirates. By the start of the air war (16 January 1991), 6,000 more arrived in the Kuwaiti Theatre of Operations (KTO), although none took part in combat operations.

Poland

Poland dispatched two ships to the Gulf: the Piast-class salvage ship *Piast* and the Wodnik-class training ship *Wodnik*, modified into a hospital ship.

Portugal

This European nation's only contribution to the coalition forces was the logistic support ship and underway replenishment tanker *Sâo Miguel*, which aided the British in moving supplies from Britain to the Gulf. The Portuguese government did not allow any of its troops to serve in either combat or noncombat roles.

Romania

This country donated a mobile field hospital team as well as 180 chemical warfare experts.

Senegal and Sierra Leone

These two African nations assisted the coalition with 500 troops each. Ninety-two of the Senegalese troops were killed in a crash of a Saudi C-130 near Khafji on 22 March 1991.

Singapore

Singapore sent a 30-member medical team that served in a British hospital.

South Korea

This country sent five C-130s and 150 Korean air force pilots.

Soviet Union

Although the Soviets supplied no troops, planes, or ships to the conflict in the Gulf, they dispatched four ships to the area to oversee coalition operations; these included the Udaloy-class destroyer *Admiral Tributs,* a missile destroyer, a frigate, and an Amur-class repair ship.

Spain

Eight Spanish ships were deployed to the Gulf: the Santa Maria–class frigates *Santa Maria* and *Numancia*, the Descubierta class-frigates *Cazadora, Descubierta, Diana, Infanta Elena,* and *Infanta Christina* and an unnamed amphibious troop transport (which did not ferry any troops but acted in a support role only).

Syria

Iraq's greatest Arab political enemy was persuaded to supply 18,000 total troops to the KTO, which included some stationed in the United Arab Emirates. Although many were involved in the liberation of Kuwait, none of the troops were allowed to enter Iraqi territory. The troops that did participate in ground combat against Iraqi soldiers in Kuwait include the 12,000 troops of the Second Syrian Armored Division, the 4,000 soldiers of the Ninth Syrian Armored Division elements, and 2,000 special forces troops.

He is the standard

Turkey

This country dispatched 120,000 troops to the Turkey-Iraq border to deter a potential Iraqi invasion. Turkish fighter aircraft operating from Incirlik Air Force Base also participated in the air war.

See also Aircraft Carriers, Coalition; Destroyers, Coalition; Frigates, Coalition; Minesweepers/ Minehunters, Coalition; Submarines, Coalition; Underway Replenishment Ships, Coalition.
References: Friedman, Norman, *Desert Victory: The War for Kuwait* (Annapolis, MD: Naval Institute Press, 1991), 310–319; Sharpe, Richard, ed., *Jane's Fighting Ships 1990–91* (Coulsdon, Surrey, UK: Jane's Information Group, 1990).

Congressional Debate

The U.S. Congress began its heated consideration on giving President George Bush the authorization to go to war on 10 January 1990, just six days before the war actually started. In its 11 January 1990 edition, the *Los Angeles Times* headlined that Congress was split evenly in deciding whether or not to authorize the war. The Republicans in the House and Senate backed the president by a healthy majority, but the Democrats in both Houses were divided. In the Senate debate, the leading Democrats rose to speak against the war resolution. "[Stability in the Middle East] has never in 5,000 years been accomplished for very long.... Who do we think we are?" said Senator Joseph Biden (D–Delaware). He added, "Let me say this, Mr. President: President Bush, if you're listening, I implore you to understand that even if you win today [with the Senate voting for war] you still lose. The Senate and the nation are divided on this issue. You have no mandate for war." Senator Claiborne Pell (D–Rhode Island) warned, "An effort to oust Iraqi forces from Kuwait would, according to estimates, cost the lives of 20,000 American soldiers." Senator Paul Wellstone (D–Minnesota) opined, "We stand on the brink of catastrophe." He added, "I believe if we rush to war, it will be a nightmare in the Persian Gulf, our country will be torn apart, and very little good will happen in the United States for a long, long, long time." Rep. Lee Hamilton (D–Indiana), chairman of the House Foreign Affairs Committee, predicted, "War will split the coalition, estrange us from

Democrats, including Senator Joseph Biden, had reservations about the long-term success of military action in the historically unstable Middle East.

our closest allies, make us the object of Arab hostility, endanger friendly governments in the region, and not be easy to end, once started." Senator Edward M. Kennedy (D–Massachusetts) added, "Now is not the time for war. A war will be brutal and costly. It will take weeks, even months, and will quickly turn from an air war to a ground war with thousands, perhaps tens of thousands, of American casualties."

The vote on 12 January in the House was 250 to 183 for war (164 Republicans and 86 Democrats voted yes; 179 Democrats, 3 Republicans, and 1 Independent voted no), while in the Senate the vote was 52 for, 47 against (42 Republicans and 10 Democrats voted yes, 46 Democrats and 1 Republican voted no).

After the war came to its victorious conclusion, Rep. Hamilton wrote an angry article in the *Washington Post,* in which he asked, "Who Voted 'Wrong?'" "It is flawed logic to assert that if one strategy proved successful, the other strategy was wrong," he argued. "I believe the original strategy against Iraq [that of using sanctions to drive Iraq out of Kuwait] stood a reasonable chance of success."

References: "Excerpts from Congress Debate on Using Force," *Los Angeles Times*, 11 January 1991, A7; Hamilton, Lee H., "Who Voted 'Wrong?'" *Washington Post*, 10 March 1991, D7; Houston, Paul, and Dwight Morris, "Times Survey: Congress Split on Giving Bush Its Vote for War," *Los Angeles Times, 11 January 1991, A1*; Robbins, James, "Echoes of 1939 on Capitol Hill," *Wall Street Journal*, 14 January 1991, A12.

Cruisers, United States

Of the 177 American ships that served in the Gulf, 17 were cruisers. A majority were from the Ticonderoga class, by far the largest class of cruisers. By carrier group and class, they are:

Belknap Class

Ships from this class that served in the Persian Gulf include the *Jouett* (CG 29, Carrier Group Independence), the *Horne* (CG 30), and the *Biddle* (CG 34, Carrier Group Saratoga). The ships of this class displace 7,930 tons fully loaded, are 547 feet (174 m) in length, and have a maximum speed of 32.5 knots (37 mph; 60 km/h). Complemented by a crew of approximately 489 (which includes 29 officers), they are powered by 2 General Electric geared steam turbines, which provide 85,000 shaft horsepower (shp). Equipped with a single LAMPS Mk1 helicopter, the ships are armed with Harpoon and Standard missiles and two Phalanx close-in weapon systems (CIWSs). The *Jouett* has a helicopter hangar that is approximately 55 feet (16.8 m) in length.

California Class

The only ship that served in the Gulf from this class was the *South Carolina* (CGN-37). This class of ships displace 10,450 tons full, are 596 feet in length (182 m), and have a maximum speed of 60+ knots (69 mph; 111 km/h). Powered by 2 nuclear reactors, providing 60,000 shaft horsepower (shp), these ships have a complement of 648 and are armed with Harpoon and Standard missiles.

Leahy Class

This class includes the cruisers *Richmond K. Turner* (CG 20, Carrier Group Roosevelt) and *England* (CG 22, Persian Gulf Squadron). The Leahy-class cruisers displace 8,200 tons fully

The USS *Valley Forge*, above, was one of 17 U.S. cruisers to serve during the Persian Gulf War.

loaded, are 533 feet (162.5 m) in length, and have a maximum speed of 32.7 knots (38 mph; 61 km/h). They are powered by four boilers (Babcock & Wilcox in the *Richmond K. Turner* and Foster-Wheeler in the *England*) and two General Electric/De Laval/Allis Chalmers geared turbines delivering 85,000 shaft horsepower (shp). Armaments include Harpoon and Standard missile systems, as well as two Phalanx close-in weapons systems (CIWS, pronounced "sea-whiz").

Ticonderoga Class

This class includes the *Valley Forge* (CG 50, Carrier Group Ranger), *Thomas S. Gates* (CG 51, Carrier Group Kennedy), *Bunker Hill* (CG 52, Carrier Group Midway), *Mobile Bay* (CG 53, Carrier Group Midway), *Leyte Gulf* (CG 55, Carrier Group Roosevelt), *San Jacinto* (CG 56, Carrier Group Kennedy), *Philippine Sea* (CG 58, Carrier Group Saratoga), the *Princeton* (CG 59, Carrier Group Ranger), and *Normandy* (CG 60, Carrier Group America). The ships of the Ticonderoga class displace 7,015 tons light, 9,466 loaded (except the *Valley Forge* and *Thomas S. Gates*, which displace 9,407 tons fully loaded). They are 567 feet (172.8 m) in length, are pow-

ered by four General Electric LM 2500 gas turbines delivering 80,000 hp, have a maximum speed of 30+ knots (35 mph; 56 km/h), have a range of 6,000 miles (9,654 km) at 20 knots (23 mph; 37 km/h), and are complemented by a crew of 358 (including 24 officers). All ships are equipped with sea-launched cruise missiles (SLCMs), but those numbered CG 52 and upward are armed with a combination of Tomahawk missiles.

Virginia Class

These include the *Virginia* (CGN 38, Carrier Group Kennedy) and the *Mississippi* (CGN 40, Carrier Group Kennedy). These ships displace 11,000 tons fully loaded, are 585 feet (178.35 m) in length, and have a maximum speed of 30+ knots (35 mph; 56 km/h). They are powered by two nuclear reactors and two geared turbines that deliver 100,000 shaft horsepower (shp). Armaments include Tomahawk, Harpoon, and Standard missile batteries.

References: *Sea Power: The Official Publication of the Navy League of the United States* 37:1 (January 1994), 128–133; Sharpe, Richard, ed., *Jane's Fighting Ships, 1990–91* (Coulsdon, Surrey, UK: Jane's Information Group, 1990), 738–742.

Damascus Agreement. *See* Bahrain.

De Cuéllar, Javier Pérez

See Pérez de Cuéllar, Javier.

Defense Intelligence Agency (DIA)

A supersecret agency within the Department of Defense, the Defense Intelligence Agency played a small part in shaping American prewar policy.

John R. Brinkerhoff, in a monograph on the U.S. Army Reserve's role during the Persian Gulf War, writes, "The Defense Intelligence Agency is the primary producer of strategic intelligence within the Department of Defense. DIA is a defense agency manned by civilian employees and military personnel from all of the armed forces. DIA recognizes that it needs to be able to expand rapidly in time of crisis, and it relies extensively on reservists to provide that rapid expansion capability. About 1,300 reservists are assigned to or designated for DIA. DIA regards these reservists as an important part of its staff."

DIA was a small but important component in the Bush administration's shaping of policy before the war. On 23 July, less than two weeks before Iraq invaded Kuwait, the DIA reported to the White House that, after assessing Iraq's military strengths and weaknesses, the possibility of an Iraqi invasion of Kuwait had abated. Only eight days later, on 31 July, the DIA analysts reversed their assessment, agreeing with a USCENTCOM (U.S. Central Command) appraisal that an Iraqi invasion was imminent.

On the role of DIA during Operations Desert Shield and Desert Storm, Brinkerhoff further reports, "When Iraq threatened Kuwait in late July 1990, DIA responded by establishing on 1 August 1990 a Task Force to focus on the Persian Gulf area. The Middle East–Africa Division of DIA's Research Directorate, headed by Mr. John Moore, provided the core of the task force, which grew from 115 to over 800 intelligence analysts. The mission of the task force was to provide strategic intelligence to the Office of the Secretary of Defense, the Joint Chiefs of Staff, the U.S. Central Command, and other members of the coalition. In addition, the task force provided intelligence to Congress and the White House."

Reference: Brinkerhoff, John R., "United States Army Reserve in Operation Desert Storm—Strategic Intelligence Support: Military Intelligence Detachments for the Defense Intelligence Agency," Monograph of the Department of the Army, Army Reserve—Program Analysis and Evaluation Division (DAAR-PAE), 1991, 1–2.

Defense Meteorological Satellite Program (DMSP)

This little-known and highly classified satellite system was used during the Persian Gulf War. The military magazine *Air Force* wrote in 1994 of the program, "[It provides] global and infrared coverage. DMSP satellites work in pairs, each scanning an area 1,800 miles (2,896 km) wide and surveying the entire Earth four times a day. Because of DMSP, during the Gulf War aircrews knew which targets were clear and which were obscured by clouds or other weather phenomena." Vice Admiral William Dougherty wrote in the *U.S. Naval Institute Proceedings* in 1992, "Weather satellites also played a key role during the war. U.S. and coalition forces used data from Defense Meteorological Satellite Program spacecraft and civil weather satellites to predict rapidly changing weather patterns and monitor burning oil wells."

References: Dougherty, William A., "Storm from Space," *U.S. Naval Institute Proceedings* 118:8 (August 1992), 51; "Space Almanac," *Air Force* 77:8 (August 1994), 51.

Dellums et al. v. Bush

Representatives Ronald Dellums, left, and Thomas Foglietta, right, meet with reporters outside U.S. District Court in Washington, D.C.

Defense Satellite Communications System (DSCS)

Unknown to most people before the Gulf War except for those in the military, this satellite system was used to provide various communications transmissions for coalition forces in the Gulf theater of operations.

The first DSCS, named DSCS-1, was launched into geostationary orbit on 3 November 1971, and several more have followed, creating a web in the sky. Discussing the work of the satellite in 1994, the military journal *Air Force* reported, "[It delivers] continuous, long-distance transmissions (voice, data, digital, TV) between major military terminals and national command authorities. [It supplies] secure voice and high-data-rate communications. Replacements continue to be produced as on-orbit assets end their useful mission life. During the Gulf War, a DSCS II satellite was repositioned in geosynchronous orbit above the Indian Ocean and used to excellent effect."

References: Caprara, Giovanni, *Space Satellites: Every Civil and Military Satellite of the World since 1957* (New York: Portland House, 1986), 100; "Space Almanac," *Air Force* 77:8 (August 1994), 51.

Dellums et al. v. Bush (752 F.Supp. 1141 [D.C. Circ., 1990])

This case, heard before the district court for the District of Columbia, was an attempt to force the president of the United States to go to Congress for a declaration of war against Iraq before sending troops into battle in the Persian Gulf. Rep. Ronald Dellums (D–California) was among 53 representatives and 1 senator who sued President George Bush. The Congress, through various resolutions, had expressed its support of the president's actions *only* in his buildup of troops in the Gulf. The plaintiffs argued that under Article I, Section 8, Clause 11 of the U.S. Constitution, which grants the Congress the power "to declare war," the president was obligated to go to Congress to get a declaration of war.

Dellums and the other signatories to this lawsuit felt that the president would go to war without congressional authorization. District Judge Harold H. Greene denied the plaintiffs' motion in ruling that although it was preferable for the president to ask the Congress for a declaration of war, he was not required to do so by the Constitution. Greene wrote, "No one knows the position of the Legislative Branch on the issue of war or peace with Iraq; certainly no one, including this Court, is able to ascertain the congressional position on that issue on the basis of this lawsuit brought by fifty-three members of the House of Representatives and one member of the U.S. Senate. It would be both premature and presumptuous for the Court to render a decision on the issue of whether a declaration of war is required at this time or in the near future when the Congress itself has provided no indication whether it deems such a declaration either necessary, on the one hand, or imprudent, on the other."

Desert Express

This operation (as well as its counterpart, European Desert Express) was established to shuttle highly needed materiel to the coalition armed forces in the Gulf from points in the United States and Europe. In October the U.S. Military Air Command (MAC) instituted Desert Express, which, according to the U.S. Department of Defense, "provided overnight delivery of spare parts considered absolutely crucial to accomplish the mission and ensure maximum wartime readiness." Each day a single C-141 Starlifter would leave Charleston Air Force Base in South Carolina for the Gulf. Charleston AFB was designated as the spare parts collection point for all four branches of the military. Cargo from Rhein Main AFB in Germany was sent via "European Desert Express."

Reference: *Conduct of the Persian Gulf War: Final Report to Congress,* Report by the Department of Defense, April 1992, 415–416.

Desert Shield

See Operation Desert Shield.

Desert Storm

See Operation Desert Storm.

Destroyer Tenders, United States

The publication *Sea Power: The Official Journal of the Navy League of the United States* reports on these ships, "These classes, which have a helicopter platform and hangar and are equipped with two 30-ton and two 6.5-ton cranes, can provide services to as many as six destroyers moored alongside. Their importance to the fleet was emphasized by the deployment of four destroyer tenders to the Middle East during Desert Shield/Storm, where they provided repair services for U.S. and coalition ships." The four tenders that served were the *Puget Sound* (AD 38), the *Yellowstone* (AD 41), the *Acadia* (AD 42), and the *Cape Cod* (AD 43), all elements of the Samuel Gompers and Yellowstone classes.

These ships differ from each other slightly in almost all of their dimensions. The *Puget Sound* displaces 13,600 tons light (20,500 tons full), while the rest displace 13,318 tons light (20,224 tons full). They are all of equal length: 643.83 feet (196.3 m) overall, and share the same propulsion system: one De Laval steam turbine and two Combustion Engineering boilers. Maximum speed is 20 knots (23 mph; 37 km/h). Comple-

ment for the ships range from 680 for the *Puget Sound* to 631 for the *Acadia*. The *Puget Sound* has a landing platform and hangar for helicopters.

References: *Sea Power: The Official Publication of the Navy League of the United States* 37:1 (January 1994), 159; Polmar, Norman, *The Naval Institute Guide to the Ships and Aircraft of the U.S. Fleet* (Annapolis, MD: Naval Institute Press, 1993), 220.

Destroyers, Coalition

Just after the start of the Gulf crisis, British, French, Dutch, and Italian commanders met on the French destroyer *Dupleix* to map out coalition responsibility for patrol zones. This was the beginning of a massive coalition response to the crisis through the use of destroyers. In addition to the United States, 17 countries supplied destroyers.

The countries and their contributions include:

Argentina

This South American nation's contribution to the allied effort in this area of study was limited to the destroyer *Almirante Brown*, deployed as part of the coalition blockade flotilla. The *Almirante Brown* (D10) displaces 2,900 tons (3,360 fully loaded), and is 413 feet (125.9 m) in length. It carries 200 men, and is usually armed with eight Aerospatiale MM 40 Exocet launchers, a Selenia/Elsag Albatros octuple launcher, and one OTO Melara 127 mm gun as well as eight Breda/Bofors 40 mm 4–twin gun launchers. All four ships of the Almirante Brown class, including the above-named ship and three sister ships, were at one time to have been equipped with Lynx helicopters from Britain, but after the Falklands War the order was canceled.

Australia

The sole effort in the area of destroyers from the land down under was the destroyer *Brisbane*. Part of the Adams class, the *Brisbane* (No. 41) is normally fitted with Harpoon antiship missiles, 40 GDC Pomona Standard SM-1MR surface-to-air missiles, and 2 FMC 5-inch (127 mm) guns, but during the Gulf crisis it was also fitted with Phalanx close-in guns for use in a defensive posture. Author Norman Friedman reports that prior to the end of the war, the Royal Australian Navy was planning to supply a second destroyer. He does not identify which ship this may have been, but the *Hobart* and *Perth* remained among the Adams class.

Canada

Among the three ships Canada deployed as part of its Gulf contribution were the destroyers *Atabaskan* and *Terra Nova*. The *Atabaskan*, a member of the Tribal class, displaces 4,700 tons loaded (5,100 modified), and normally carries two Raytheon Sea Sparrow SAM quad launchers, one Martin Marietta Mk 41 VLS launcher to handle 29 GDC Standard SM-2MR missiles, and one OTO Melara 5-inch (127 mm) gun. The *Terra Nova*, from the Improved Restigouche class, was formerly a frigate. It displaces 2,390 tons (2,900 fully loaded) and carries 285 men. Among its armaments are an A/S (antisubmarine) Honeywell ASROC Mk 112 octuple mortar launcher and two Vickers 3-inch (76 mm) twin guns. For duty in the Persian Gulf, both ships were refitted with Phalanx missile units, as well as two single Bofors guns and 50-caliber machine guns; the *Terra Nova* was also adapted with two quadruple Harpoon launchers. The third ship in the Canadian unit was the operational support ship *Protecteur*. All three ships were supplemented with Javelin surface-to-air missiles and escorted by five CH-124 Sea King helicopters.

France

Besides providing the fifth largest army in the desert, the French sent the third largest contingent of ships to the Gulf, after the United States and Great Britain. Five of these were destroyers: the *Du Chayla*, *Dupleix*, *Jeanne de Vienne*, *La Motte-Picquet*, and *Montcalm*. The *Du Chayla* (D 630), based in the Du Chayla class with the *Dupetit-Thouars*, was initially constructed as a fleet escort for ships of the French Surcouf class, but was converted in the late 1960s so that it could be equipped with the American Tartar missile system. During the Gulf War it was implemented with 40 GDC Pomona Standard SM-1MR surface-to-air missiles, an Mk 12 launcher, and 3 twin DCN 57 mm guns. Displacing 2,750 tons standard (3,740 fully loaded), the *Du Chayla* is 421.9 feet (128.5 m) long, and has a complement of 275. The *Dupleix* (D 641), the *Montcalm* (D 643), and the *La Motte-Picquet* (D 645) are part of the Georges Leygues class of French destroyers. All of the ships displace 3,830 tons standard, while all of the ships save the *La Motte-Picquet* displace 4,300 tons full (the *La Motte-Picquet* displaces 4,380 full). The Georges Leygues–class ships are 455.9 feet (139 m) in length and are powered by two Rolls-Royce Olympus TM38 gas turbines and two SEMT-Pielstick 16PA6 CV280 diesel engines. The complement for this class is 218 crew members, which includes 16 officers. The *Montcalm* is equipped with four MM-38 Exocet missiles, while the other ships have the newer MM-40 model. All of the ships have the ability to carry two Lynx MK 2/4 helicopters.

Great Britain

The nation that once ruled the seas dispatched 31 ships to the Gulf, among them four destroyers: the *Cardiff*, the *Exeter*, the *York*, and the *Gloucester*. The *Cardiff* (D108), a part of the Sheffield class, was built in 1974. It displaces 3,500 tons standard (4,100 fully loaded), is 410 feet (125 m) long, and can carry 299 crew members. The *Cardiff* and her Sheffield sister ship *Exeter* (D89), which shares the same characteristics, are equipped with a twin British Aerospace Sea Dart GWS surface-to-air missile launcher and a single Vickers 4.5-inch (114 mm) 55 Mk 8 gun. The *York* (D104) and the *Gloucester* (D95), both from the Manchester class, displace 3,500 tons standard (4,775 fully loaded), and are 463 feet (141.1 m) long. Both ships are implemented with twin British Aerospace Sea Dart GWS surface-to-air missile launchers, and single Vickers 4.5-inch (114 mm) 55 Mk 8 guns.

Italy

Of the eight Italian ships that saw action in the Persian Gulf War, only one, the *Audace*, was a destroyer. The *Audace* (D 551), of the Audace class, displaces 3,600 tons standard (4,400 fully loaded), and is 448 feet (136.6 m) long. Complemented with a crew of 380, it is equipped with 40 GDC Pomona Standard SM-1MR surface-to-air missiles in an Mk 13 Mod 1 launcher, a single OTO Melara 5-inch (127 mm) gun, and is armed with six 324 mm US Mk 32 torpedoes.

Soviet Union

Although not considered a coalition partner, the Soviets monitored activities in the Gulf through four ships, including the Udaloy-class destroyer *Admiral Tributs*. Built at the Zhdanov Yard in

Leningrad in 1983, the *Admiral Tributs* displaces 6,700 tons standard (8,400 fully loaded), and has a complement of 310, including 35 officers. Armed with eight SA-N-9 vertical-launched surface-to-air missile launchers and two SS-N-14 Silex quad antisubmarine missile launchers, the ship is also fitted with two 3.9-inch (100-mm) guns and eight 21-inch torpedoes.

See also Coalition Nations, Contributions of.
References: Friedman, Norman, *Desert Victory: The War for Kuwait* (Annapolis, MD: Naval Institute Press, 1991), 310–319; Jordan, John, *An Illustrated Guide to Modern Destroyers* (London: Salamander, 1986); Sharpe, Richard, ed., *Jane's Fighting Ships, 1990–91* (Coulsdon, Surrey, UK: Jane's Information Group, 1990), 12, 24.

Destroyers, United States

The most versatile fighting ships in the arsenal of the U.S. Navy, destroyers played a significant part in the execution of the war against Iraq. Fourteen of the United States' 177 ships were destroyers. They are grouped into distinct classes: the Spruance, the Farragut, the Charles F. Adams, and the Kidd.

In the Spruance class are the destroyers *Spruance* (DD 963), *Paul F. Foster* (DD 964), *Hewitt* (DD 966), *Caron* (DD 970), *David R. Ray* (DD 971), *Oldendorf* (DD 972), *Moosbrugger* (DD 980), and *Harry W. Hill* (DD 986). At 529 feet (161.28 m) in length, the Spruance-class destroyers displace 8,040 tons and travel at a top speed of 32.5 knots (37 mph; 60 km/h). Powered by four gas turbine engines that generate 80,000 horsepower, these ships employ four types of radar, including air search and surface radar. The crew consists of 300 sailors (including 25 officers). Operations aboard the destroyers are conducted from the Combat Information Center (CIC), where input from radar and other observations are fed into computers. These modern destroyers are fitted with various weaponry systems, among them Mark 26 and Sea Sparrow missiles for airborne threats, tube-launched Harpoon surface-to-air missiles and 12.75-inch (32.4 cm) torpedoes for sea hazards, and, for danger from land sources, two rapid-fire 5-inch (12.7 cm) guns. Gatling guns mounted on a turret on the deck serve as a last line of defense. Sea threats are discerned through the use of the hull-mounted SQS-53

sonar; a backup is supplied by two helicopters that can use sonar buoys. Air dangers are monitored by the Aegis fixed-array radar system.

In the Farragut class are the destroyers *Mac-Donough* (DDG 39), *William V. Pratt* (DDG 44), and *Preble* (DDG 46). Able to displace 4,700 tons standard (up to 6,150 tons full), the ships are powered by 2 De Laval/Allis-Chambers geared turbines and 4 Foster Wheeler/Babcock & Wilcox boilers. Their maximum speed is 33 knots (38 mph; 61 km/h), with a maximum range of 5,000 miles at 20 knots (23 mph; 37 km/h). With a complement of 402 (including 25 officers), the crew is also supplemented with a flag staff of 26 (7 of them officers). The class is equipped with 4 quad McDonnell Douglas Harpoon surface-to-surface missile launchers and 40 GDC Pomona Standard ER-SM2 surface-to-air missiles. Although prepared with a landing platform, it is for limited helicopter use. The *MacDonough* arrived in the Kuwaiti Theater of Operations from 17 to 28 October 1990 as part of the Mid-East Force, and departed from the area on 24 February 1991.

In the Charles F. Adams class is the destroyer *Sampson* (DDG 10). Weighing 3,370 tons standard (4,825 fully loaded), the ships of the Charles F. Adams class are 437 feet (133.2 m) long, are powered by 4 Babcock & Wilcox boilers and 2 General Electric geared turbines, have a maximum speed of 30 knots (35 mph; 56 km/h), and have a range of 6,000 miles (9,654 km) at 15 knots (17 mph; 28 km/h). Complemented by a crew of 360, which includes 20 officers, the *Sampson* is armed with either 4 or 6 Harpoon surface-to-surface missiles and either 40 or 42 GDC Standard MR-SM1 surface-to-air missiles. Sonar elements include the Sperry SQQ 23 or the Sangamo SQS 23D. The *Goldsborough*, patrolling the Gulf of Oman, became the first American ship to stop, search, and seize an Iraqi freighter; on 4 September it stopped and boarded the Iraqi cargo ship *Zanoobia*. After being diverted to the Port of Muscat in Oman, the *Zanoobia* was found to be carrying tea to the Iraqi port of Basra, and the cargo was confiscated. The ships of this class are being removed from service; the *Sampson* was decommissioned on 24 June 1991, the *Tattnall* on 18 January 1991, and the *Goldsborough* was due to be removed from service in 1992.

The Kidd class was represented by the *Kidd* (DDG 993) and the *Scott* (DDG 995). All of these ships, of which there are four, were originally built for the Shah of Iran, but not delivered before the Iranian revolution. Of all American destroyers, they are endowed with the most sophisticated antisubmarine warfare (ASW) weaponry. The ships of this class displace 8,300 tons fully loaded, are 563 feet (172 m) in length, and have a maximum speed of 33 knots (38 mph; 61 km/h). Powered by four General Electric LM 2500 gas turbines, which provide 80,000 shaft horsepower (shp), they have a complement of approximately 357 (including 23 officers), are equipped with one LAMPS I helicopter (future plans may allow for three LAMPS III helicopters), and are armed with Harpoon and Standard missiles as well as two Phalanx close-in weapon systems.

References: Jordan, John, *An Illustrated Guide to Modern Destroyers* (New York: Prentice Hall, 1986), 139–145; Sharpe, Richard, ed., *Jane's Fighting Ships 1990–91* (Coulsdon, Surrey, UK: Jane's Information Group, 1990), 728–730.

Dhahran

The major air base at Dhahran was used by the coalition for supplying their troops. It was also the site of a Scud missile attack, in which more American soldiers were killed than in any other incident.

Authors Thomas A. Keany and Eliot A. Cohen recount in their "Summary Report" of the U.S. military's report, *Gulf War Air Power Survey* "The Saudi air bases owed so much to long-standing security assistance relations with the United States. Dhahran served during World War II as a resupply point for U.S. forces in Asia, and the U.S. Army Corps of Engineers rebuilt Dhahran Airfield in 1956. In the 1960s and 1970s, U.S. Army and Air Force engineers designed and constructed several more bases, including the major bases [at] Taif, King Khalid Military City, and Khamis Mushait. These bases and support facilities, which accounted for three quarters of U.S. military sales to Saudi Arabia over the past forty years [1953–1993], provided the needed infrastructure to help absorb deployment of the size and speed of Desert Shield."

John R. Brinkerhoff wrote in a monograph on the U.S. Army Reserve role during Operations Desert Shield and Desert Storm, "When the 1030th Engineer Battalion arrived in Saudi Arabia on 14 December 1990, the housing situation at Dhahran was in serious trouble. Several hundred thousand troops had already arrived, but the Directorate of Engineering and Housing (DEH) operations were being handled by just three personnel from the ARCENT [U.S. Army Forces, Central Command] Engineering Staff—a captain, a warrant officer, and a sergeant.– Upon arrival in Dhahran, the 1030th Engineer Battalion Headquarters immediately established and staffed a DEH for the Dhahran area as part of its overall responsibility as the Facilities Engineering Activity for ARCENT."

On Monday, 25 February 1991, at 8:40 P.M. (12:40 P.M. EST), a Scud missile hit the barracks housing the 476th Quartermaster Group in Dhahran, killing 27 American personnel and wounding another 98. It was the highest number of Americans killed in a single attack in the war.

Reference: Brinkerhoff, John R., "United States Army Reserve in Operation Desert Storm—Engineer Support at Echelons above Corps: The 416th Engineer Command," Monograph of the Department of the Army, Army Reserve—Program Analysis and Evaluation Division (DAAR-PAE), 1992, A1; Claiborne, William, "Scud Kills 27 GIs at Dhahran Billet," *New York Times,* 26 February 1991, A1; Keany, Thomas A., and Eliot A. Cohen, *Gulf War Air Power Survey, Summary Report* (Washington, DC: GPO, 1993), 175.

Dinarte Incident

This accident, in which 26 Allied soldiers were killed when two Blackhawk helicopters were shot down by American F-15 aircraft, occurred on 14 April 1994 and was a tremendous embarrassment for the United States.

The two F-15s, operating out of Incirlik Air Force Base in Turkey, visually sighted two UH-60 Blackhawk helicopters transferring 15 American and 11 British, French, and Turkish troops near Irbil over northern Iraq, but misidentified them as Soviet Mi-24 Hind helicopters violating the northern no-fly zone. The helicopters, carrying a radar system called IFF (Identification Friend or Foe), were not on the F-15s' wavelengths and did not respond to their queries. After requesting identification from nearby AWACs jets, the two F-15 pilots assumed that the helicopters were Iraqi and proceeded to fire a single AIM-120 advanced medium-range air-to-air missile (AMRAAM) and a single AIM-9L/M Sidewinder missile, destroying the two helicopters instantly and killing all 26 troops aboard. In September 1994 the Pentagon announced that the two pilots would go on trial for murder and would be dishonorably discharged. Only one pilot was subsequently tried, and he was found not guilty on 20 June 1995.

Reference: "U.S. F-15s Down U.S. Helicopters," *Aviation Week & Space Technology,* 18 April 1994, 17.

Dock Landing Ships, Coalition

Only one of the ships sent by the international coalition to the Persian Gulf was a dock landing ship: the Ouragan-class dock landing ship *Ouragan.* The *Ouragan* (L 9021) displaces 5,800 tons light (8,500 tons fully loaded; 15,000 tons when "fully docked down"), and is 488.9 feet (149 m) in length. Powered by two SEMT-Pielstick diesel engines, the ship has a maximum speed of 17 knots (20 mph; 31 km/h), with a range of 9,000 miles (14,484 km) at 15 knots (17 mph; 28 km/h), and a complement of 213 (including 10 officers). Its maximum lift can include 343 troops, 2 landing craft with 11 light tanks, and 2 cranes (35 tons each). It has the capability of allowing to land four SA 321G Super Frelon or Super Puma helicopters, or ten SA 319B Alouette III helicopters. The *Ouragan* is fitted with an EDO SQS-17 sonar mechanism. The dock landing ship *Foudre* was converted to a hospital ship and served in the Gulf as well.

Reference: Sharpe, Richard, ed., *Jane's Fighting Ships, 1990–91* (Coulsdon, Surrey, UK: Jane's Information Group, 1991), 194.

Dock Landing Ships, United States

Eight of these versatile ships served during the conflict in the Persian Gulf, four each from the Anchorage class and four from the Whidbey Island class. Distinguished by class, they are:

Anchorage Class

This class includes the *Anchorage* (LSD 36, part of the Fifth Marine Expeditionary Brigade which arrived in the Kuwaiti Theater of Operations [KTO] on 12 January 1991), the *Portland* (LSD 37, part of the Fourth Marine Expeditionary Brigade, which arrived in the KTO on 6 September 1990), the *Pensacola* (LSD 38, part of the Fourth Marine Expeditionary Brigade), and the *Mount Vernon* (LSD 39, part of the Fifth Marine Expeditionary Brigade). The ships displace 8,600 tons light (14,000 tons full), and are 553.25 feet (168.66 m) in length. Powered by 2 De Laval steam turbines and 2 Foster Wheeler (except in the *Anchorage,* which contains Combustion Engineering) boilers, the ships have a maximum speed of 22 knots (25 mph; 41 km/h). Manned by a crew of approximately 358 (which includes 20 officers), these LSDs can carry approximately 330 troops, and their docking well can accommodate 3 LCACs (cushioned landing craft), or 52 AAV7A1 Tracked Personnel Vehicles.

Whidbey Island Class

This class includes the *Whidbey Island* (LSD 41), the *Germantown* (LSD 42, part of the Fifth Marine Expeditionary Brigade), the *Gunston Hall* (LSD 44, a part of the Fourth Marine Expeditionary Brigade), and the *Ashland* (LSD 48). These ships displace 15,726 tons full, and are 609 feet (186 m) in length. Powered by 4 medium-speed diesel engines, they have a maximum speed of 20+ knots (23mph; 37 km/h). Complemented by 340 men, the ships are capable of carrying 338 troops, as well as having a pad for helicopter and VSTOL aircraft.

Reference: Polmar, Norman, *The Naval Institute Guide to the Ships and Aircraft of the U.S. Fleet* (Annapolis, MD: Naval Institute Press, 1993), 177; *Sea Power: The Official Publication of the Navy League of the United States* 37:1 (January 1994), 149.

Dragon Antitank/Assault Missile

Seen in the weapons assemblages of Morocco, Saudi Arabia, and the United States, this wire-guided antitank weapon was used by the United States against Iraqi tanks in the Persian Gulf War.

Dragon
Antitank/Assault
Missile

The Dragon Antitank/Assault Missile was used against Iraqi tanks during the Persian Gulf War.

Developed by McDonnell Douglas for the Army and Marine Corps, the Dragon is a man-portable, recoilless, launched projectile with a solid-propellant rocket engine. According to *Jane's Infantry Weapons*, "The missile is ejected from the tube by a gas generator using a recoilless technique. When it emerges folding fins flip open and the missile starts to roll. Thereafter propulsion and control forces are provided by the 60 small sustainers which fire in pairs on demand from the tracker." With a shaped charge, the missile weighs 30 pounds (13.8 kg) at launch, and has a range of 0.6 mile (1 km). The updated Dragon III launcher has improved night vision and infrared capabilities with a larger missile and 50 percent more range.

Reference: Hogg, Ian V., ed., *Jane's Infantry Weapons, 1993–94* (Coulsdon, Surrey, UK: Jane's Information Group, 1993), 154–155.

Drones, Unmanned
See Remotely Piloted Vehicles.

Dupleix Meetings
See Destroyers, Coalition.

E-2C Hawkeye

The Grumman E-2C Hawkeye is an airborne early warning and air control plane; these five-crew aircraft flew 1,183 sorties during Operation Desert Storm.

The company that built the E-2C says of the plane, "With its distinctive 24-foot diameter rotating radome and 12,000 pounds [5,443 kg] of sophisticated electronic equipment, the E-2C can monitor three million cubic miles of airspace . . . from its operating altitude, about 30,000 feet [9,146 m], the Hawkeye overcomes limitations the earth's curvature imposes on ground-based radar systems. With its General Electric APS-125 advanced radar processing system, the Hawkeye automatically detects, identifies, and tracks enemy aircraft, over both land and water, at ranges approaching 300 miles [483 km]." Powered by two Allison T56-425 turboprop engines that produce 4,910 shaft horsepower, the E-2C has a maximum speed of 326 knots (375 mph; 604 km/h), and a ferry range of 1,394 nautical miles (2,583 km).

Reference: Jordan, John, *An Illustrated Guide to Modern Naval Aviation and Aircraft Carriers* (New York: Prentice Hall, 1983), 102.

E-3 Sentry

See Airborne Warning and Control System.

E-8A/C Joint Surveillance Target Attack Radar System (JSTARS or JOINT STARS)

See Joint Surveillance and Target Attack Radar System.

EA-6B Prowler

A four-seat electronic countermeasures (ECM) craft, the EA-6B flew 504 missions for the Marines and 1,126 for the Navy during the Gulf War.

Built by Grumman, the EA-6B is perhaps the most sophisticated electronic warfare craft in operation. The plane mimics its older cousin, the EA-6A Intruder, in all ways except for the addition of ECM gear. Aircraft writer John Jordan states that "the EA-6B . . . is a completely redesigned aircraft incorporating a very advanced and comprehensive suite of ECM equipment, both internal and podded. Five ALQ-99 high-power tactical jamming pods, each with windmill generators to supply their power requirements, can be carried, and enemy radar transmissions are monitored and countered by two electronics warfare (EW) operators seated side by side in the rear. The pilot sits on the left, and on his right is an ECM officer who manages navigation, communications, defensive ECM and the dispensing of chaff."

Powered by two Pratt & Whitney J52-406 two-shaft turbojet engines providing 11,200 pounds (5,080 kg) of thrust, the EA-6B weighs a maximum of 65,100 pounds (29,530 kg), has a maximum speed of 566 knots (1,048 km/h), and has an unrefueled range of 2,085 nautical miles (3,861 km).

See also A-6E/TRAM Intruder.
Reference: Jordan, John, *Modern Naval Aviation and Aircraft Carriers* (New York: Prentice Hall, 1983), 100.

EC-130E Volant Solo

The EC-130E Volant Solo, an updated version of the C-130 Hercules, is used mainly to conduct

E-2C Hawkeye

The Grumman E-2C Hawkeye, with a crew of five, is an airborne early warning and air control craft capable of monitoring three million cubic miles of airspace.

psychological operations (PSYOP) against enemy forces.

The U.S. military summary *Gulf War Air Power Survey* reports on the use of the Volant Solo: "In the Persian Gulf Theater of Operations, six broadcast platforms were established and used: aerial platforms—EC-130s—and ground radio stations. The Volant Solo aircraft were available in August; however, their use was put on hold until late November. Volant Solo was first used on Thanksgiving Day, 22 November, when the aircraft broadcasted the Voice of America (VOA) service in Arabic in areas VOA could not reach. Volant Solo operations had the positive effect of establishing an airborne platform as a credible broadcaster."

Volant Solo aircraft flew 450 sorties for the U.S. Air Force and 155 for the U.S. Central Command in PSYOP raids. The EC-130E has the same structure as the C-130 Hercules.

See also C-130 Hercules Transport.
Reference: Gulf War Air Power Survey, Volume IV: Weapons, Tactics, and Training Report and Space Report (Washington, DC: GPO, 1993), 329–337.

EC-130H Compass Call

A variant of the C-130 Hercules, this craft served with ground-based radar stations to monitor Iraqi command, control, and communications (known as C^3CM) capabilities.

Because the EC-130H varies from the original C-130 only in internal improvements, its engine power, maximum speed, and traveling distance are the same. The EC-130 is modified with an electronic countermeasures system, an improved air refueling ability, and an updated navigation and maintenance support system. According to the Air Force, the plane carries a complement of up to 13 crew members; 9 are responsible for operating the electronic warfare and countermeasures system and 4 are in charge of flying the aircraft.

Three Compass Calls arrived in Riyadh, Saudi Arabia, on 21 August 1990, at the beginning of Operation Desert Shield; eventually, EC-130s flew 450 sorties during Desert Storm.

See also C-130 Hercules Transport; EC-130E Volant Solo; HC-130H Extended Range Aerospace Rescue and Recovery; MC-130H Combat Talon II.

The EA-6B was designed as carry equipment to jam or monitor enemy radar and radio transmissions.

References: Gulf War Air Power Survey, Volume IV: Weapons, Tactics, and Training Report and Space Report (Washington, DC: GPO, 1993), 96–97; Lambert, Mark, ed., *Jane's All the World's Aircraft, 1991–92* (Coulsdon, Surrey, UK: Jane's Information Group, 1991), 427.

Economic Effects of the Persian Gulf War (on Iraq)

Because of the embargo imposed against it by the United Nations, Iraq has suffered economically in the areas of food and medicine. Child mortality has risen, as have malnutrition and morbidity.

In 1991 Dr. John O. Field and Dr. Robert M. Russell, both of Tufts University in Massachusetts, were selected by UNICEF to travel to Iraq to examine the situation. In an article published in the scientific journal *GeoJournal*, Field writes, "Iraq in 1990–91 experienced an unusually dramatic shift in its food security/food insecurity profile. The reasons for the shift are clear: the in-

vasion of Kuwait in August 1990 and what followed, notably the UN-mandated embargo on trade between Iraq and other countries, the Gulf War, the civilian uprisings in the Kurdish north and Shiite south of Iraq following the war and their suppression, UN Security Council sanctions against Iraq accompanying the cease-fire, and persisting irresolution of differences between Iraq and the Security Council that has impeded the flow of humanitarian assistance to the Iraqi people, food and medicines in particular."

The Field and Russell mission traveled through southern Iraq and Baghdad from 18 June to 28 June 1991. According to their report, "While there, and with support from local UNICEF staff, the team examined 680 children, measuring weight, height, and mid-upper arm circumference and observing clinical signs of anemia, vitamin A deficiency, and dehydration." The conclusions of the team were: "Child malnutrition in southern Iraq is a serious problem. The team believes it is a chronic problem that has existed for some time, albeit undetected,

Economic Effects of the Persian Gulf War

UNICEF executive director James P. Grant, left, UN secretary general Javier Pérez de Cuéllar, center, and World Health Organization director-general Hiroshi Nakajima, right, report findings of a UN mission to Iraq in 1991.

on which an acute deterioration has been super-imposed within the past year. Whatever its origins, the problem is real, severe, and wide-spread; and it reflects a simultaneous failure of health and food consumption in the present and—we believe—a similar, if lesser failure in the past." In an article on the mission, the two men reported, "The rapid nutritional assessment conducted in June 1991 revealed a high preva-lence and severity of protein-calorie malnutri-tion among children 0–5 years old in southern Iraq, accompanied in some cases by anemia."

Because Iraq has refused to follow the UN res-olutions passed in the wake of the invasion of Kuwait, the embargo is still in force as of this writing. The effects of the embargo were felt par-ticularly by mid-1994, when Iraq began a series of steps culminating in an advance toward the Kuwaiti border that was checked by a massive buildup of American troops.

References: Ascherio, Albert, et al., "Effect of the Gulf War on Infant and Child Mortality in Iraq," *The New England Journal of Medicine* 327:13 (24 September 1992), 931–936; Field, Dr. John Osgood, "From Food Security to Food Insecurity: The Case of Iraq, 1990–91," *GeoJournal* 30:2 (June 1993), 185; Field, Dr. John Osgood, and Dr. Robert M. Russell,

"Nutrition Mission to Iraq: Final Report to UNICEF by Tufts University, August 14, 1991," 1, 3; Field, Dr. John Osgood, and Dr. Robert M. Russell, "Nutrition Mission to Iraq for UNICEF," *Nutrition Reviews* 50:2 (February 1992), 46.

Ecureuil Helicopter

This French craft served on-board the Australian frigates *Adelaide* and *Darwin*.

Built by the French manufacturer Aérospa-tiale, the Ecureuil, numbered AS 350B, serves as a reconnaisance and/or attack helicopter for European forces, although its main duties con-sist of materiel transport for troops from sea to land. Powered by a Turboméca Arriel engine that provides 641 shaft horsepower (shp), the craft's maximum speed is 169 mph (272 km/h). The copter has a capacity of six persons (a pilot and five passengers), a maximum unrefueled range of 466 miles (750 km), and a service ceiling of 19,028 feet (5,800 m). It is also capable of car-rying a HeliTOW (the helicopter version of the TOW) antitank missile.

References: Rees, Elfan Ap, *World Military Helicop-ters* (London: Jane's Publication Company, 1986),

19; Taylor, John W. R., ed., *Jane's All the World's Aircraft, 1989–90* (Coulsdon, Surrey, UK: Jane's Information Group, 1989), 64.

EF-111A Raven. *See* F-111 Aardvark.

Egypt
See Coalition Nations, Contributions of; Mubarak, Muhammad Hosni.

Enemy Prisoners of War (EPWs)

For the first time, the prisoners taken by the United States and other Allied nations were designated as enemy prisoners of war, to distinguish them from the prisoners of war (POWs) of the Allies.

A total of 86,743 EPWs were taken by the Allies during Operations Desert Shield and Desert Storm. This includes 63,948 by the United States (including 1,492 considered as displaced civilians), 16,921 taken by the combined Arab forces, 5,005 seized by the British forces, and 869 taken by the French. Eleven camps were built to accommodate these prisoners. They include four named camps of the United States, two of which were given the collective name Bronx and the other two collectively named Brooklyn. These camps enclosed prisoners held by the Army's VII Corps and the XVII Airborne Corps as well as British and French captives. A fifth camp was set up by MARCENT, the U.S. Marines Central Command. The British camp, Maryhill, was located near al-Qaysumah near the Iraq-Saudi border, while the French enclosure, Clemence, was situated farther west near Raffa. The Saudis ran four camps, dubbed no. 1 through no. 4. According to the Department of Defense report, *Conduct of the Persian Gulf War: Final Report to Congress,* "on 2 May 1991 the last EPW in U.S. custody was transferred to the Saudi Arabian government. . . . A total of 13,418 EPWs refused repatriation, including 191 officers."

John R. Brinkerhoff, in a monograph on the U.S. Army Reserve's role during the war, reports, "Of the EPW in U.S. custody, 2,940 were officers, 2,688 were warrant officers, 61,620 were

Enemy Prisoners of War

An Iraqi surrenders to a Saudi Arabian soldier in southeastern Kuwait on the second day of Operation Desert Storm.

enlisted personnel, and 1,492 were civilian internees. Another 1,082 were of indeterminate status. Thirteen general officers were captured, including three full generals."

References: Brinkerhoff, John, "United States Army Reserve in Operation Desert Storm—Enemy Prisoner of War Operations: The 800th Military Police Brigade," Monograph of the Department of the Army, Army Reserve—Program Analysis and Evaluation Division (DAAR-PAE), 1992, 21; *Conduct of the Persian Gulf War: Final Report to Congress,* Report by the Department of Defense, April 1992, 578–587.

Environmental Effects of the Persian Gulf War

For the first time in the history of warfare, a retreating army destroyed the environment, and set fire to oil wells, to deny the victors the spoils of war. Although many of the more immediate environmental threats to that part of the world—including climate impact and massive contamination of the Persian Gulf—have not yet materialized, the total result of this shocking action has yet to be realized.

In an article for the British magazine *Nature,* Richard D. Small writes, "The Iraqi invasion of Kuwait on 2 August 1990 set in motion actions threatening the environment on a grand scale. Iraq demonstrated its intent to use environmental destruction as an instrument of national policy. Several million barrels of oil have been released into the Persian Gulf; several hundred oil-well fires have been started. Smoke clouds have covered Kuwait and spread over Iran reaching toward Pakistan. Black rain has fallen over Kuwait, the Gulf and Iran from Qasr-E-Shirin in the north to Bushehr in the south, adversely affecting population, water supply and agriculture." However, Small adds, "Estimates of the smoke mass produced by [the] destruction of Kuwait's oil wells and refineries and the smoke stabilization altitude do not support any of the purported climate impacts. The smoke is not injected high enough to spread over large areas of the North Hemisphere, nor is enough produced to cause a measurable temperature change or failure of the monsoons. Similarly, only a small increase in the global CO_2 budget results." In another article, a team of German scientists measured the climate response to the

Environmental Effects of the Persian Gulf War

Black smoke from burning oil wells in Kuwait darken the sky as a U.S. Navy F-14 Tomcat makes an overflight in September 1991.

oil-well fires, and concluded, "The results [of their tests] show a decrease in surface air temperature of −4 degrees Celsius in the Gulf region. Outside this region the changes are small and statistically insignificant. No weakening of the Indian summer monsoon is observed."

Author T. M. Hawley reports that in March 1991, "A task force of scientists from the United States, representing the Centers for Disease Control, the Environmental Protection Agency, and other federal organizations, began work in Kuwait. Under orders that appeared to have come down from President George Bush, the team, known as the 'Interagency Task Force,' could issue only innocuous statements about the war's environmental consequences—reporting, for example, that the 'catastrophic predictions of the fires' effects are exaggerated.' It was almost a month before they released their first findings, which emphasized surprisingly low values for the toxic gases hydrogen sulfide and sulfur dioxide."

On 13 April 1991 the Kuwaiti oil minister, Dr. Rashid al-Amiri, announced that he intended to hire more fire-fighting contractors to end the fires in seven months instead of the estimated two years some experts predicted the job would require. The last of the Kuwaiti oil fires was extinguished on 6 November 1991.

References: Bakan, S., et al., "Climate Response to Smoke from Burning Oil Wells in Kuwait," *Nature* 361:6325 (30 May 1991), 367; Hawley, T. M., *Against the Fires of Hell: The Environmental Disaster of the Gulf War* (New York: Harcourt Brace Jovanovich, 1992), 26–27; Small, Richard D., "Environmental Impact of Fires in Kuwait," *Nature* 350:6313 (7 March 1991), 11; Wald, Matthew L., "Kuwait Will Hire More Firefighters," *New York Times*, 14 April 1991, A12.

ERA (Explosive Reactive Armor). *See* M60A1/3 MBT.

European Economic Community (EEC)

The European Economic Community (since 1993 the European Union) is the commercial equiva-

lent of a "United States of Europe": a viable, sustainable, common "economic, political and social" consortium of primarily Western European nations (although some of the former East Bloc countries may join in the future) that unites some 330 million consumers and gives the EEC a gross domestic product of $4,287, second only to the United States' $4,473. The nations involved are Belgium, Denmark, France, Germany, Greece, Ireland, Italy, Luxembourg, the Netherlands, Portugal, Spain, and the United Kingdom. As writer Robert Burns reported in 1987, "At the center of Europe's effort to integrate is the European Economic Community, or Common Market . . . the 12 EEC countries are working together to fashion not only a common market for their products and a common approach to the environment, unemployment and other related problems, but also a common view of the world outside their frontiers." This common view was an important factor in the backing that the EEC gave to the coalition during the crisis leading up to the outbreak of war in the Gulf.

The concept of a united Europe is not a new one. The British newspaper *Financial Times* covered the EC92 celebration in early 1993 with this feature: "Charlemagne, Barbarossa [Frederick the Great], Charles V, Napoleon and Hitler all belong on the list of continental Europeans who have tried to build and maintain a trans-European empire, although using more coercive methods than today's rulers." Caesar Augustus, also known as Octavius, founded Europe's first "common market" in 31 B.C., but it lasted only as long as the Roman Empire. Its collapse in the fifth century led to further attempts at union, but all failed, leaving it up to French foreign minister Robert Schuman to suggest in 1950 that France and what was then West Germany collaborate to boost their respective steel productions. On 18 April 1951 the European Coal and Steel Community (ECSC) was instituted, the first brick in the wall of full European economic integration. This cooperation led to the signing on 25 March 1957 of the Treaty of Rome, which established the European Economic Community and the European Atomic Energy Community (EAEC), a cousin to the United States' Atomic Energy Commission. The treaty was later expanded to create the Court of Justice and the European Investment Bank. In 1976 the EEC, EAEC, and

ECSC were condensed into what is now called the EEC.

The European Community itself reports that "what makes the Community unique among the world's international organizations is that it can pass laws which are directly binding on the countries" in the Union; in addition, "In some cases it can pass laws which are directly binding on the citizens of some of these countries." Maria Antonietta Macchiocchi, professor of philosophy at the Sorbonne in Paris, said in an interview in 1989, "We are entering a new era of true free trading in culture that goes beyond our nationalistic structure." On 31 December 1992 the project called EC92 became reality as the borders between these 12 nations seemingly evaporated. To further the goal of integration, the 12 nations were asked to vote on the Maastricht Treaty; it was signed by the 12 members at the Dutch city of Maastricht in December 1991. This charter commits the 12 EEC members to fashion closer ties through the formation of a central bank, establish "common foreign and security policies," and expand the legislative reach of the 518-member European Parliament to include matters of "internal trade, the environment, education, health, and consumer protection."

After the foreign ministers of the 12-nation European Community met in session in Luxembourg in what is called the Council of Ministers on 4 January 1991, they released the following statement:

In accordance with the positions adopted by the community and its member states since the beginning of the crisis, ministers reiterate their firm commitment in favor of the full and unconditional implementation of the relevant resolutions of the U.N. Security Council. Should this happen, the Twelve consider that Iraq should receive the assurance not to be subject to a military intervention. They consequently recall that the entire responsibility for war or peace rests with the Iraqi Government alone, as is spelled out in Resolution 678 of the U.N. Security Council.

Any initiative tending to promote partial solutions, or to establish a link between the full implementation of the resolutions of the U.N. Security Council and other problems is unacceptable.

Reaffirming their attachment to a peaceful solution in the full respect of the relevant resolutions of the U.N. Security Council, the community and its member states welcome the agreement reached on the meeting between the American Secretary of State, Mr. James Baker, and the Iraqi Minister of Foreign Affairs, Mr. Tariq Aziz.

In accordance with the declaration adopted by the European Council in Rome on December 15, 1990, Ministers have asked the Presidency [Jacques Poos, Foreign Minister of Luxembourg] to invite the Iraqi Foreign Minister to a meeting with the troika in Luxembourg on January 10. The presidency will remain in close consultation with the United States, the Arab countries concerned, and the presidency of the movement of the nonaligned, to prepare the two meetings.

In the spirit of the foregoing, and as soon as the present crisis will have been settled peacefully and in full respect of the resolutions of the U.N. Security Council, the community and its member states reaffirm their commitment to contribute actively to a settlement of the other problems of the region and establish a situation of security, stability and development there.

Further European union action failed to stop the world's slide toward war. Although many of the major European powers did not send troops to the war, they participated in other ways.

See also Coalition Nations, Contributions of. **References:** Balls, Edward, "Europe 1993," *Financial Times,* 4 January 1993, 3; Burns, Robert, "Toward a 'United States of Europe,' " Council of Ministers, Text of Statement, *New York Times,* 5 January 1991, A5. *Fort Lauderdale News/Sun-Sentinel,* 15 March 1987, 1G, 8G; *The European Parliament* (Luxembourg: Secretariat of the European Parliament, Directorate-General for Information and Public Relations, 1980), 6; Fabricio, Roberto, "Europe Soon To Wield Global Power," *Fort Lauderdale Sun-Sentinel,* 15 May 1989, 1G, 3G; Stitt, Iain P. A., cons. ed., *The Arthur Andersen European Community Sourcebook* (Chicago: Triumph Books, 1991), 50–54; Waxman, Sharon, "Gut Feeling Likely To Guide French Vote on Unity: Maastricht Treaty Hangs in Balance," *Miami Herald,* 20 September 1992, 27A.

Executive Orders

See Appendix 3; International Emergency Economic Powers Act.

Exocet Missile

This missile system, built by the French, was a staple of the Iraqi air force, but because most of the Iraqi planes either fled to Iran or were destroyed on the ground by the coalition attack, its use during the Persian Gulf War was limited or unknown.

There are several versions of the Exocet; AM 39, the air-to-surface (ATS) variant, is an extension of the antiship Exocet, while the MM-40 is a coastal defense version. The ATS Exocet is powered by a two-stage solid-rocket motor that provides the missile with subsonic speeds. The projectile is 15 feet 5 inches (4.70 m) in length, has a diameter of 13.5 inches (35 cm), has a wingspan of 43 inches (1.10 m), weighs 1,437 pounds (652 kg), and has a range of 31 miles (50 km).

On 17 May 1987 the Exocet was used with brutal accuracy when an Iraqi pilot flying a French-made Iraqi Mirage F-1 fighter fired two Exocets at the guided-missile frigate USS *Stark*, which was patrolling the Persian Gulf during the Iran-Iraq War, killing 37 American sailors.

Reference: Blake, Bernard, ed., *Jane's Weapon Systems, 1988–89* (Coulsdon, Surrey, UK: Jane's Information Group, 1988), 709.

F-4E Phantom II

See F-4G Phantom II Wild Weasel.

F-4G Phantom II Wild Weasel

The F-4G, nicknamed the Wild Weasel, is a two-seat, all-weather interceptor and attack craft with electronic warfare capabilities. These aircraft flew 2,683 sorties during Operation Desert Storm (a variant, the F-4E, flew only four missions).

Built by McDonnell Douglas, the F-4 (which first flew as the F4-H1 in 1958) is powered by two General Electric J79-15 afterburning turbojet engines delivering 17,900 pounds (8,120 kg) of thrust. The plane holds up to 16,000 pounds (7,258 kg) of armaments, including up to four AIM-7 Sparrow missiles or three AGM-65 Maverick missiles. The F-4Gs are specifically designed for electronic warfare; one source says that the plane "covers all dedicated EW and anti-SAM missions in which specially equipped electronic aircraft hunt down hostile SAM installations (using radar for lock-on, tracking or missile guidance) and destroy them before an attack by other friendly aircraft on nearby targets."

See also RF-4C Phantom II.
References: Gunston, Bill, *An Illustrated Guide to USAF: The Modern US Air Force* (New York: Prentice Hall, 1991), 109; ''Wild Weasels: Electronic Wizards of Desert Storm,'' *Popular Science* 238:5 (May 1991), 73.

F-14 Tomcat

The most formidable fighter of its kind, the two-seat F-14 is matched in the air only by its coun-

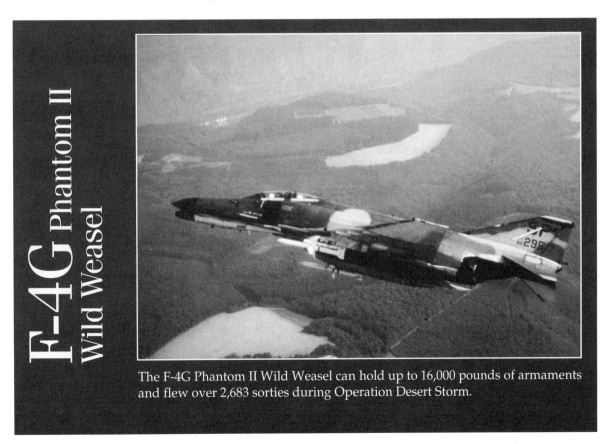

The F-4G Phantom II Wild Weasel can hold up to 16,000 pounds of armaments and flew over 2,683 sorties during Operation Desert Storm.

terparts, the F-15 and F-16. The F-14 squadrons deployed to the Gulf were used for three distinct missions: target combat air patrol (TARCAP), barrier combat air patrol (BARCAP), and MiG patrols.

The F-14 has a swept-wing capability. Swept, the wings are 28 feet (8.53 m); unswept, 64 feet (19.5 m). The F-14's maximum weight is 74,348 pounds (33,724 kg) with weaponry included. It is powered by two Pratt & Whitney TF30-P414 turbofan engines with afterburners, delivering over 40,000 pounds (18,144 kg) of thrust each. Maximum speed is 1,544 mph (2,484 km/h), and maximum weight is 74,348 pounds (33,724 kg). Besides the pilot, the two-seat craft accommodates a "radar intercept officer who monitors and operates the AWG-9 weapons control system," according to Grumman (now Northrop-Grumman), the builder. The plane is armed with AIM-54 Phoenix missiles, AIM-7 Sparrow missiles, AIM-9 Sidewinder missiles, and a single M61-A1 Vulcan 20 mm cannon.

Sea Power reports on the plane, "The F-14 has been one of the nation's premier fighter aircraft for more than two decades. Its sophisticated radar-missile combination enables it to simultaneously track 24 targets and attack six while continuing to scan the airspace. It can attack and destroy targets up to 100 miles [161 km] away." During Operation Desert Storm, the F-14s flew 4,005 sorties, solely for the Navy. For the campaign, the planes were fitted with new equipment, including an important data link pod. As Bruce Nordwall writes in *Aviation Week & Space Technology,* "F-14 flight crews had a big edge in coordinated tactics during Desert Storm because of a new data link installed shortly before they deployed to the gulf . . . the new equipment, Harris Corp.'s AN/ASW-27C digital data link, allowed the F-14 to link tactical data directly to other F-14s, without the presence of a command and control platform." Commander Thomas F. Enright, who commanded one of the F-14 squadrons, reported: "The result was fantastic situational awareness."

References: Nordwall, Bruce, "New Data Link Gave F-14 Pilots Major Advantage in Desert

F-14 Tomcat

U.S. Navy fighter pilots flew 4,000 sorties in the F-14 Tomcat during Operation Desert Storm.

Storm," *Aviation Week & Space Technology*, 5 August 1991, 46; *Sea Power: The Official Publication of the Navy League of the United States* 37:1 (January 1994), 185–186.

References: *Gulf War Air Power Survey, Volume IV: Weapons, Tactics, and Training Report and Space Report* (Washington, DC: GPO, 1993), 45; Gunston, Bill, cons. ed., *The Encyclopedia of World Air Power* (New York: Crescent, 1980), 253.

F-15E Eagle

A two-seat, high-performance, supersonic, all-weather, dual-role, air-to-air, and air-to-surface fighter developed from the F-15C air-superiority fighter, the F-15E Eagle is considered the premier fighter aircraft of the U.S. military. The plane flew a total of 2,172 sorties during Operation Desert Storm, hitting approximately 2,124 targets in both Kuwait and Iraq.

The F-15 is powered by two Pratt & Whitney F100-PW-100 turbofan engines, each delivering 23,800 pounds (10,976 kg) of thrust with afterburning. Maximum speed is 921 mph (1,482 km/h) at low altitude, while its unrefueled range (carrying three 600-gallon fuel tanks) is 2,878 miles (4,631 km). Armaments include a single General Electric 20 mm M61A1 rotating-barrel cannon, and up to eight air-to-air missiles (usually four AIM-7F Sparrows and four AIM-9L Sidewinders) on outer wing pylons.

F-16 Fighting Falcon

Built by General Dynamics, the F-16 is a high performance Air Force attack fighter. The U.S. military reports of the F-16, "A multirole, single-seat fighter . . . highly maneuverable, it has both air-to-air and air-to-surface capability . . . since more F-16s [248] were deployed to Operation Desert Storm than any other U.S. fighter aircraft, they flew the most sorties." This number was 13,087, striking some 11,698 targets in Kuwait and Iraq. A total of four F-16s were lost during the Persian Gulf War: two to surface-to-air missiles (SAMs), and two to antiaircraft fire.

Powered by a single Pratt & Whitney F100-PW-110(3) afterburning turbofan engine, the F-16 has a maximum speed of 1,289 mph (Mach 1.95; 2,074 km/h) at 36,000 feet (10,970 m) with two Sidewinder missiles. Weight figures include the plane, which unfueled weighs 14,567

A Royal Saudi F-15 Eagle closes with a KC-135 Stratotanker in order to refuel during Operation Desert Shield.

pounds (6,607 kg), fuel at 6,972 pounds (3,162 kg), and maximum external armaments at 15,200 pounds (6,894 kg). Armaments include a single General Electric 20 mm M61A1 multibarrel cannon that delivers 500 rounds; two wingtip AIM-9J/L Sidewinder missiles, and seven additional underwing and underfuselage pylons for auxiliary missile systems.

References: Gulf War Air Power Survey, Volume IV: Weapons, Tactics, and Training Report and Space Report (Washington, DC: GPO, 1993), 47–48; Gunston, Bill, cons. ed., *The Encyclopedia of World Air Power* (New York: Crescent, 1980), 180.

F-111 Aardvark

Built by General Dynamics, this swing-wing, twin-engine, two-seat aircraft is a long-range, deep-penetration plane that saw major action during the Persian Gulf War. Used exclusively by the Air Force, the two variants used in the conflict—the F-111E and F-111F—flew a total of 2,881 sorties (2,443 by the F-111F; 458 by the F-111E) without a single loss, striking 3,335 tar-

gets. Forty-six percent of the laser-guided bomb strikes involved in the war were accomplished with the F-111.

The total number of distinct F-111 models currently in use include the A, D, E, and F versions (with all-weather attack capabilities), as well as the variants FB-111 (strategic attack ability) and EF-111 (utilizing a tactical electronic countermeasures jammer). Powered by two Pratt & Whitney TF30 afterburner turbofan engines, the F-111's spread-wing system allows it to achieve a full wingspan from 63 feet (19.2 m) out in the A, D, E, F, and EF versions to 70 feet (21.3 m) out for the FB version only. Length is 73 feet 6 inches (22.4 m) except for the EF, which is 77 feet 1.6 inches (23.5 m). The military notes that the F-111F includes improved turbofan engines, and was equipped during the war with the Pave Tack infrared target acquisition and laser designation pod, allowing the plane to attack targets during day and night missions using laser-guided missiles. The plane contains an internal bomb bay that can hold 31,500 pounds (14,288 kg) of bombs, as well as three pylons under each wing for further ordnance. The EF variant has no

F-111 Aardvark

The U.S. Air Force used the F-111 Aardvark to deliver GBU-15 infrared guided bombs as well as 4,700-pound GBU-28 laser-guided bombs to Iraqi targets during Operation Desert Storm.

armament capabilities. The F-111 was the only fighter in the Gulf War that carried and delivered the GBU-15 infrared-guided bomb. It also used the massive 4,700-pound (2,132 kg) GBU-28 laser-guided bomb against the North Taji command bunker on the last day of the war. No F-111s were lost during the conflict, although one EF-111 Raven was shot down. EF-111s flew 1,105 sorties during the war for the U.S. Air Force.

See also GBU-10 GP Bomb Series.
References: Gulf War Air Power Survey, Volume IV: Weapons, Tactics, and Training Report and Space Report (Washington, DC: GPO, 1993), 42–45; Gunston, Bill, *An Illustrated Guide to USAF: The Modern US Air Force* (New York: Prentice Hall, 1991), 68–73.

F-117A Stealth Fighter

The F-117A Stealth fighter was employed extensively in the attack role in the Persian Gulf conflict, specializing in precision bombing of ground targets. The U.S. Air Force 37th Fighter Wing, led by wing commander Colonel Alton C. Whitley, Jr., and squadron commanders Lieutenant Colonel Ralph D. Getchell, Lieutenant Colonel Gregory Gonyea, and Lieutenant Colonel Robert Maher, was the first unit to use this virtually untried craft in the first air missions of the war against heavily fortified targets in downtown Baghdad, and flew a total of 1,299 sorties without the loss of a single fighter. The U.S. military reported that "they scored 1,664 direct hits with laser-guided bombs without suffering battle damage."

Powered by two General Electric F404-GE-F1D2 turbofan engines that produce 11,000 pounds of thrust, the F-117A is a single-seat, two-engine fighter/bomber aircraft. Developed under a super-secret program at Lockheed Aircraft's "skunk works" plant in Burbank, California, the plane has been in service since 1983, but its existence was not disclosed until Operation Just Cause in Panama in 1989 when two F-117As, flying experimental combat flights, each dropped a 2,000-pound (907 kg) laser-guided bomb on the Panamanian defense barracks at Rio Hato. With a wing span of 43 feet 4 inches (13.20 m), the craft is 65 feet 11 inches (20.08 m) in length overall. The F-117A variant is the sole plane of this type.

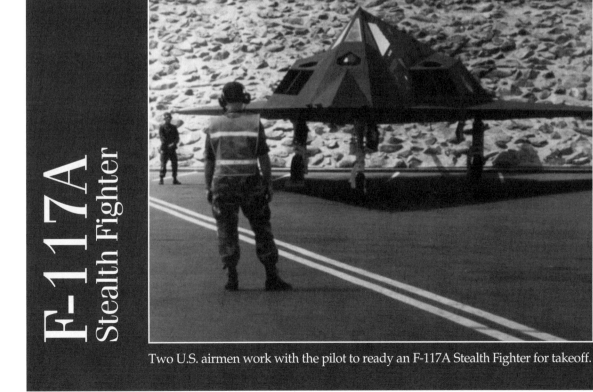

Two U.S. airmen work with the pilot to ready an F-117A Stealth Fighter for takeoff.

The F-117A, perhaps the most space-age fighter ever introduced, features two distinct types of radar systems: forward-looking infrared radar (FLIR), and downward-looking infrared radar (DLIR). The plane uses an inertial navigation system (INS) to direct the forward-looking radar to its target. The FLIR then utilizes wide-field-of-view (WFOV) and narrow-field-of-view (NFOV) optical systems to lock onto the target with precise measurements. Because the F-117A moves so fast, it can fly over a target before bombs hit the intended objective. This is where DLIR comes in. The system works with laser-guided bombs, such as the GBU-10 Paveway II (a normal MK-84 bomb mated to a Paveway II laser system) and GBU-24 Paveway III (also called the low-level laser-guided bomb [LLLGB]) to give the pilot a downward-looking view instead of the normal front view so that he can aim, release, and allow the weapon to hit the target effectively.

References: Gulf War Air Power Survey, Volume IV: Weapons, Tactics, and Training Report and Space Report (Washington, DC: GPO, 1993), 40; "Strategic Campaign Focused on Targets and Cut Casualties, Pentagon Maintains," Aviation Week & Space Technology, 27 January 1992, 11; Sweetman, Bill, and James Goodall, Lockheed F-117A: Operation and Development of the Stealth Fighter (Osceola, WI: Motorbooks International, 1990), 55–61.

F/A-18C Hornet

Military authors Thomas A. Kearny and Eliot Cohen report on the F/A-18C, "The multimission Hornet was designed and developed as both a fighter and an attack aircraft. It has replaced Navy and Marine Corps F-4s and A-7s. It can carry up to 17,000 pounds (7,711 kg) of ordnance, including Sparrow, Sidewinder, Harpoon, and Harm missiles, on nine stations." The U.S. military reports that "during the initial hours of Desert Storm, 89 Navy and 72 Marine Corps F/A-18Cs conducted both defense suppression and strike missions against Iraqi targets. The Navy Hornets flew 4,449 sorties and the Marine Corps' F/A-18Cs flew 4,936 sorties resulting in a combined total of 4,551 strikes against targets during Operation Desert Storm." A total of 174 American Hornets (90 Navy; 84 Marines) participated in the war; 26 Canadian

models, known as the CF-18, also participated in Desert Storm. Only three Hornets were lost during the war, one of them in a noncombat accident.

During the air war, F/A-18Cs served as forward air controllers (FACs) for other fighter aircraft. Captain R. A. Padilla, a pilot of the F/A-18C, writes, "After the first period [of the war], the FACs cycled back to the tanker and then returned to their assigned area for another 30 minutes before returning home. Typical target areas were more than 200 miles [322 km] from Bahrain. We used high-altitude tactics during the early part of the war, identifying targets through 7- and 10-power binoculars. Secondary explosions after initial strike aircraft runs often confirmed active Iraqi positions."

A single-seat fighter, the F/A-18C is the most up-to-date variant of the plane (the F/A-18D is a trainer craft). It is powered by two General Electric F404-GE-402 turbofan engines that with afterburning produce 17,600 pounds (7,983 kg) of thrust each. The plane itself has a maximum weight of 49,224 pounds (22,327 kg); it has a maximum speed of Mach 1.6 (about 1,190 mph), and a service ceiling of 50,000 feet (15,244 m). The F/A-18C is armed with a single 20 mm six-barrel M61A1 machine gun in its nose and has nine "external stations" (usually underwing pylons) to carry a variance of missile systems, including the AIM-9 Sidewinder, the AIM-7 Sparrow, the AIM-20 AMRAAM, the AGM-84 Harpoon, and the AGM-65 Maverick air-to-ground missiles.

References: Gulf War Air Power Survey, Volume IV: Weapons, Tactics, and Training Report and Space Report (Washington, DC: GPO, 1993), 58; Padilla, R. A. (USMC), "F/A-18s Go to War," U.S. Naval Institute Proceedings 118:8 (August 1991), 40; Sea Power: The Official Publication of the Navy League of the United States 37:1 (January 1994), 185.

Faisal I, King of Iraq (1883?–1933)

The only man to serve as king of both Syria and Iraq, Faisal I was responsible for helping to achieve Iraqi independence in 1932 and shaping the early years of the Iraqi nation-state.

Born about 1883 as the son of Sharif Hussein of the Hejaz, Faisal's early years remain a mystery. According to Professor Malcolm B. Russell,

King Faisal II of Iraq, at the microphones, addresses the newly elected Iraqi parliament in Baghdad on 10 May 1958.

"In 1911, Faisal accompanied his father in battle against a neighboring ruler and later led a Bedouin fighting force himself. The next year, though hardly old enough, he was elected to the Ottoman Parliament as the deputy from the port of Jiddah [now in Saudi Arabia]." In 1918 Faisal once again led a revolt against Ottoman rule and, with his army, entered Damascus (now the capital of Syria) to take control over the Syrian mandate. He then proclaimed himself Faisal I, king of Syria. However, he was the sovereign for only a short time. Because he summarily rejected French rule over Syria as mandated by the San Remo Agreement of 1920, the French army defeated Faisal's forces at the battle of Maisalun, stormed Damascus, and removed him from power. Faisal fled to Italy. The following year, 1921, the British asked him to take the throne of their mandate in Iraq; Faisal consented, and was crowned Faisal I, king of Iraq, ruling until 1933. In those 12 years, he was considered a difficult leader by the British. Winston Churchill wrote of him in 1922, "King Feisal [*sic*] had been making great difficulties and confusing the situation in

Iraq. He had made objections to the [British] Mandate but had stated his willingness to agree to a Treaty. He was not, however, prepared to recognize the mandatory basis as he thought that the mandatory system was a slur on Iraq. No argument had been of any effect with him. He had recently taken up [with] the Extremists who now regarded him as their patron." Faisal ultimately signed the Anglo-Iraqi treaties of 1922 and 1930, which gave the British expanded powers over Iraqi affairs.

Helen Metz, in her *Iraq: A Country Study*, writes, "Ultimately, the British-created monarchy suffered from a chronic legitimacy crisis: the concept of a monarchy was alien to Iraq. Despite his Islamic and pan-Arab credentials, Faisal was not an Iraqi, and, no matter how effectively he ruled, Iraqis saw the monarchy as a British creation." Samir al-Khalil adds, "Faisal never abandoned his pan-Arabism. His early experiences, however, made him more cautious and explicitly gradualist. In the end Faisal's achievements during his twelve years in Iraq stemmed not from this 'foreign' policy orientation but from his personal role in consolidating the institutions of a modern state out of a patchwork of conflicting tribes, sects, and ethnic and religious groups. His major accomplishment, and the central preoccupation of his reign, was the abrogation of the British mandate and the recognition by the League of Nations of the independent state of Iraq in 1932." Faisal's death came after a trip to England and Switzerland in 1933, during which there was a small rebellion in northern Iraq. He died in September in Switzerland, leaving his son, the playboy Ghazi, to rule. Ghazi's death in 1939 in an automobile accident gave the throne to Faisal's grandson, Faisal II.

See also Anglo-Iraqi Treaty (1922); Faisal II, King of Iraq.
References: al-Khalil, Samir, *Republic of Fear: The Inside Story of Saddam's Iraq* (New York: Pantheon Books, 1990), 150; Metz, Helen Chapman, ed., *Iraq: A Country Study* (Washington, DC: GPO, 1990), 36; Report of Churchill to Cabinet Ministers' Conference, quoted in Fromkin, David, *A Peace To End All Peace: The Fall of the Ottoman Empire and the Creation of the Modern Middle East* (New York: Avon, 1989), 509; Russell, Malcolm B., "Faisal I (1883?–1933), Faisal II (1935–1958), and the Rise and Fall of the Hashemite Dynasty in Iraq," in *Historic World Leaders*, Vol. 1, edited by Anne Commire (Detroit: Gale, 1991), 157; Russell, Malcolm B., *The First Modern Arab State: Syria under Faysal, 1918–1920* (Minneapolis: Bibliotheca Islamica, 1985).

Faisal II, King of Iraq (1935–1958)

In his short life, King Faisal II of Iraq attempted to link his country closely with the West, but failed. Faisal II was born in 1935, the son of King Ghazi of Iraq, killed in an automobile accident in 1939, and Princess Aliya, whose brother, Abdul Illah, was named regent in Faisal's name and served until Faisal took the throne on his eighteenth birthday. Faisal II was the great-grandson of Sharif Hussein of the Hejaz, the founder of the TransJordan mandate, the foundation for the modern state of Jordan. He was the grandson of Faisal I, king of Syria and Iraq, and a first cousin to King Hussein ibn Talal, king of Jordan.

The *New York Times* wrote in 1958 that "Faisal's early education was begun in the family palace in Baghdad by British governesses and tutors. During a brief pro-Nazi revolt in 1941 he was kidnapped, but soon released unharmed."

According to Malcolm B. Russell, professor of history and economics at Andrews University in Michigan, Faisal finished his education in Britain at Harrow in 1952. He returned to Iraq and took the throne in 1953.

Faisal ruled as king for five years, a period in which Iraqi politician Nuri as Said served as prime minister. Helen Metz writes in her work, *Iraq: A Country Study*, "The monarchy's major foreign policy mistake occurred in 1955, when Nuri as Said announced that Iraq was joining a British-supported mutual defense pact with Iran, Pakistan, and Turkey. The Baghdad Pact constituted a direct challenge to Egyptian president Gamal Abdul Nasser. In response, Nasser launched a vituperative media campaign that challenged the legitimacy of the Iraqi monarchy and called on the officer corps to overthrow it. The 1956 British-French-Israeli attack on Sinai further alienated Nuri as Said's regime from the growing ranks of the opposition. In 1958 King Hussein of Jordan and Abd al Ilah [Abdul Illah] proposed a union of Hashemite monarchies to counter the recently formed Egyptian-Syrian union [the United Arab Republic]. At this point, the monarchy found itself completely isolated. Nuri as Said was able to contain the rising discontent only by resorting to even greater repression and to tighten control over the political process."

Middle East experts Peter Sluglett and Marion Farouk-Sluglett write, "The Revolution of 14 July 1958 was almost universally welcomed by the people of Iraq. For the poor, particularly the *sarifa* dwellers and the masses of unemployed, as well as for most other social groups, it was a time of great hope and optimism for the future. At last, many believed, a government had come to power that would not only free the country from the tutelage of Britain and her clients, but would pursue policies directed towards the fulfillment of their own interests." During the revolt, led by Iraqi Free Officer leader Abdul-Karim Qassem, Faisal, Abdul Illah, and Nuri as Said were all executed.

See also Faisal I, King of Iraq; Qassem, Abdul-Karim.
References: Belair, Felix, Jr., "President Bids U.N. Act Today on Mideast after Pro-Nasser Coup Ousts Iraq's King; U.S. May Intervene; Britain Alerts Troops," *New York Times,* 15 July 1958, A1; "British-Educated Faisal Finds Main Interest in Realm of Sports," *New York Times,* 15 July 1958, A3;

Caruthers, Osgood, "Faisal Vanishes; Rebels Offer Reward for Premier as-Said after He Escapes," *New York Times,* 15 July 1958, A1; Farouk-Sluglett, Marion, and Peter Sluglett, *Iraq since 1958: From Revolution to Dictatorship* (London: I. B. Tauris, 1990), 47; Metz, Helen Chapman, ed., *Iraq: A Country Study* (Washington, DC: GPO, 1990), 49; Russell, Malcolm B., "Faisal I (1883?–1933), Faisal II (1935–1958), and the Rise and Fall of the Hashemite Dynasty in Iraq," in *Historic World Leaders,* Vol. 1, edited by Anne Commire (Detroit: Gale, 1991), 159–160.

Fast Combat Support Ships, Coalition

Of the ships that participated in the international naval armada that served during the Persian Gulf conflict, two, the Poolster-class fast combat support ships *Zuiderkruis* (A 832) and *Poolster* (A 835) helped supply those nations that fought alongside the United States. Although both belong to the same class, they have some minor differences between them. The *Poolster* displaces 16,800 tons fully loaded (16,900 for the *Zuiderkruis*), and is 552.2 feet (168.3 m) in length (556 feet [169.6 m] for the *Zuiderkruis*). The *Poolster* is powered by two turbines, which provide 22,000 shaft horsepower (the *Zuiderkruis* is powered by two Werkspoor TM 410 diesel engines, which provide 21,000 horsepower). Both ships have a maximum speed of 21 knots. Complement for the *Poolster* is 200 (with 17 officers), while it is 266 (including 17 officers) for the *Zuiderkruis.* Cargo capacity for both ships is 10,300 tons, which includes 8,000-9,000 tons of oil fuel; both ships have the capability to carry Westland UH-14A Lynx helicopter.

Reference: Sharpe, Richard, ed., *Jane's Fighting Ships, 1990–91* (Coulsdon, Surrey, UK: Jane's Information Group, 1991), 404.

February 26th

Originally published secretly under Iraqi occupation, *February 26th* was a newspaper printed by the Kuwaiti underground. From early March until 20 March 1991, it was the first free, nongovernmentally controlled newspaper in liberated Kuwait.

Field Army Ballistic-Missile Defense System (FABMDS)

See Patriot Tactical Air Defense Missile System.

France

The role of France, led by President François Mitterrand, in the coalition against Iraq is little known. The French deployment of forces to the Gulf was called Operation Daguet.

France was entangled in the Middle East long before Saddam Hussein came to power or the forces that propelled the world to war in the sands of the Iraqi desert came together. As early as the turn of the twentieth century, France was using its muscle to capture strategic portions of the Middle East, which was then borderless and led by tribal leaders rather than men like Saddam Hussein. It was in this vein that one of the leaders to become involved in the partitioning of the Middle East into states was Charles François Georges-Picot, who served for several terms as consul–general for France in Syria, and negotiated on behalf of the French Foreign Office in Paris to increase French control over as much of the region as possible in talks with his counterparts, Sir Mark Sykes of Great Britain and Russian Foreign Minister Sergei Sazanov. Their communications culminated in the so–called Sykes–Picot–Sazanov Agreement of 9 May 1916, which divided the Middle Eastern territories into zones of influence. In a letter from British Foreign Secretary Sir Edward Grey to Paul Cambon, French ambassador to Great Britain, Grey wrote that "I have the honour to acknowledge the receipt of your Excellency's note of the 9th instant, stating that the French Government accept the limits of a future Arab State, or Confederation of States, and of those parts of Syria where French interests predominate, together with certain conditions attached thereto, such as they result from recent discussions in London and Petrograd on the subject." France later participated in strengthening their possessions in the area (confined to modern-day Syria and Lebanon), in their entirety labeled the Levant States, under the San Remo Agreement of 1920 and the Treaty of Lausanne of 1923. In 1920, dissatisfied with the governance of King Faisal of Syria, whom the

French had installed as a puppet, French troops invaded Syria and overthrew Faisal. They held power over that region despite anti–French revolts in 1924 and 1925. The onset of the Second World War forced France to dedicate its military elsewhere, and Syria was established as an independent state, obtaining its status of nationhood five years later. French influence in the area was limited to Lebanon, a poor cousin of Syria. Britain, and eventually the United States, grew in power in the region after the end of the Second World War. France's lone reintroduction into the area came in October and November 1956, when French forces joined British troops in trying to reopen the Suez Canal, which had been closed in fighting between Israel and Egypt.

From 1956 until 1990, France's activities in the Middle East were purely economic. As Lester Brune wrote in his essay on the origins of the 1991 Persian Gulf War, "During the 1970s, France not only sent Iraq some of its best warplanes and missiles, but also supplied it with nuclear materials to inaugurate Iraq's nuclear weapons project. According to Steve Weissman and Herbert Krosney, France agreed in 1976 to build an Iraqi nuclear reactor for peaceful purposes, even though Saddam Hussein told a Beirut newspaper in 1975 that he wanted nuclear power to begin 'the first Arab attempt at nuclear arming.' Nevertheless, the Western powers accepted Iraq's acquisition of nuclear materials because France had already helped Israel and Pakistan develop 'peaceful' nuclear reactors. In addition, because Iraq had signed the nuclear non-proliferation treaty (NPT), other nations assumed Iraq would be inspected by the Internation Atomic Energy Agency." From 1976 until its destruction by Israeli planes in 1981, the Tammuz I nuclear reactor constructed at Osirak in Iraq was manufactured chiefly by France.

Between the Iraqi invasion and the start of Operation Desert Storm, French policy was to mollify the restive Arabs over whom they had once ruled. Time and time again, the French attempted to persuade Iraq to withdraw from Kuwait before a war started. As Alan Riding wrote in the New York Times in January 1991, "By taking the lead in promoting a European formula to end the Persian Gulf crisis, France appears to be responding to mounting fears in this country and elsewhere in Europe that the United States is intent on using force to push Iraq out of Kuwait.

But by demonstrating that it does not automatically follow Washington's leadership, France's initiative also seems aimed at its credibility in the Arab world five months after its Mideast policy was shattered by the Iraqi invasion."

The French forces in the Kuwaiti Theater of Operations (KTO), in which were incorporated several units of the French Foreign Legion, were commanded by General Michel Roquejoffre. On G–day, the first day of the ground offensive against Iraqi army holdouts in Kuwait, French troops pushed deep into Iraqi territory. As the editors of *Triumph without Victory* explain, "Three hundred miles west of the Persian Gulf, the fast mechanized division composed of French forces and one brigade of the 82nd Airborne Division had raced 60 miles north into Iraq across a rocky desert floor. This was the Sixth Light Armored Division, called the Daguet Division, combining American paratroopers with a variety of French armor. Its two light tank regiments were equipped with AMX–10RCs, small, fast, six–wheeled vehicles with 105–mm guns. 'They just flew,' said Colonel Bob Kee, the American liaison officer to the French forces. 'They can go fifty miles an hour, and at times they were going that fast.'"

France proved to be more of an ally to the coalition before the war started than after its conclusion. Almost from the start, the French (joined by the Russians) were involved in attempting to lift sanctions against Iraq so as to start up a lucrative business relationship with Baghdad. The leadership of the United States in the United Nations Security Council vetoed this plan. As Alan Riding commented in January 1991, "Unlike Washington, France is convinced that Iraq should be offered some incentive to withdraw from Kuwait, and it has repeatedly argued the need for an international peace conference to tackle all outstanding conflicts in the Middle East [even] if the current crisis is settled peacefully." Led first by Mitterrand and then by former Paris mayor Jacques Chirac, the move to end sanctions may culminate in their lifting by the end of 1995 or some time in 1996.

See also Coalition Nations, Contributions of; Operation Artimon; Operation Meteil.
References: Brune, Lester H., *America and the Iraqi Crisis, 1990–1992: Origins and Aftermath* (Clairmont, CA: Regina Books, 1993), 25; Fromkin,

David, *A Peace to End All Peace: The Fall of the Ottoman Empire and the Creation of the Modern Middle East* (New York: Avon, 1989), 190–191; Letter from Grey to Cambon, 16 May 1916, in Helmreich, Paul C., *From Paris to Sèvres: The Partition of the Ottoman Empire at the Peace Conference of 1919–1920* (Columbus: Ohio State University Press, 1974), 343; Riding, Alan, ''French Maneuvering: Taking the Lead for Europe,'' *The New York Times*, 6 January 1991, A4; U.S. News & World Report, *Triumph without Victory: The History of the Persian Gulf War* (New York: Times Books, 1993), 313.

Free Rocket over Ground
See FROG.

Friendly Fire

Of the 613 casualties (deaths and wounded) suffered by the United States from military action during Operation Desert Storm, 146 were killed in action. A total of 28 friendly fire incidents accounted for 35 of these (23.9 percent), with 72 (11.7 percent) wounded.

The U.S. Department of Defense, in a report issued on the Persian Gulf War in 1992, stated: ''During Operation Desert Storm, approximately 39 percent of the incidents (11 out of 29) appeared to be as a result of target misidentification. Misidentification was a result of several factors—weather and battlefield conditions being the most predominant reasons. Coordination problems also accounted for approximately 29 percent (8 out of 28) of friendly fire incidents. Of the remaining six incidents that occurred, six were due to technical and/or ordnance malfunctions; three incidents had insufficient or inconclusive findings to determine cause.''

The military is hard at work trying to solve the dilemma of how to prevent American forces from firing on one another. Writes Eric Schmitt in the *New York Times*, ''Senior Army officers say that training has been increased for Apache helicopter crews to help them distinguish American tanks and armored vehicles at night and in bad weather from those of the enemy. In addition, tank gunners must watch under fire in drills for 'friendly' robotic tanks that pop out on training courses in California's Mojave Desert.''

Charles R. Schrader (Lieutenant Colonel, USA, ret.) writes, ''Many Americans were shocked to learn that 23 percent of all our casualties in the Gulf War were from our own weapons. The knowledge that about 77 percent of all combat vehicles lost (seven of ten Abrams tanks and 20 of 25 Bradley infantry fighting vehicles) were destroyed by friendly fire was perhaps more shocking. The featureless desert terrain; poor weather and reduced visibility; large, complex, fast-moving operations; and very lethal sophisticated weapons firing at long ranges all contributed to these incidents.''

References: *Conduct of the Persian Gulf War: Final Report to Congress,* Report by the Department of Defense, April 1992, 589; Johnson, Robert, and Caleb Solomon, ''Chilling Tapes Show How Soldiers Died in 'Friendly Fire,''' *Wall Street Journal*, 7 November 1991, A1; Johnson, Robert, and Caleb Solomon, '' 'Friendly Fire' Downs the Soaring Career of a Gung-Ho Colonel,'' *Wall Street Journal*, 10 September 1991, A1; Schmitt, Eric, ''U.S. Striving To Prevent 'Friendly Fire,''' *New York Times*, 9 December 1991, A12; Schmitt, Eric, ''War's Accidental Deaths Spur Push for Solutions,'' *New York Times*, 5 June 1992, A14; Shrader, Charles R., ''Friendly Fire: The Inevitable Price,'' *Parameters: U.S. Army War College Quarterly* 22:3 (Autumn 1992), 29–30.

Frigates, Coalition

Of the nearly 180 coalition ships that saw action in the Gulf conflict, 29 were frigates. The nations and their contributions in this area include:

Argentina

This South American country's sole contribution in this category was the 4+2 Meko-class frigate *Spiro* (No. 42). Commissioned in 1987, the *Spiro* has a complement of 93 (including 11 officers), displaces 1,790 tons fully loaded, and is powered by two Type 16PC2-5V400 SEMT-Peilstick 16-cylinder diesel engines. It is equipped with four Aerospatiale Exocet missiles, as well as a single OTO Melara 3-inch (76mm) gun and six 324mm ILAS tubes for launching torpedoes. It has several countermeasures aboard, including chaff and decoys.

Australia

Three of Australia's six ships that saw action in the Kuwaiti Theatre of Operations (KTO) were frigates; they are the Perry-class frigates *Adelaide*, *Sydney*, and *Darwin*. Since all three come from the same class, they are nearly identical; all three were built by the Todd Pacific Shipyard in Seattle, Washington. *Adelaide* (No. 01) was commissioned in 1980, *Sydney* (No. 03) in 1983, and *Darwin* (No. 04) in 1984. Complemented by a crew of 181 (including 15 officers), the Perry-class crafts displace 3,962 tons fully loaded, and are powered by two General Electric LM 25090 gas turbine engines. Each ship is equipped with Harpoon antiaircraft missiles, as well as a GDC Pomona SM-1MR SAM system; further, they have the capability to support Sikorsky S-70B Seahawk and AS 550 B Ecureuil helicopters.

Belgium

Of Belgium's four ships in the Gulf, only one was a frigate—the Wielingen-class *Wielingen*. The *Wielingen* (F 910) was commissioned in 1978; it displaces 2,430 tons fully loaded and has a complement of 160, including 15 officers. Powered by a single Rolls-Royce Olympus TM3B gas turbine and two Cockerill CO-240 V122400 diesel engines, the ship is equipped with four Aerospatiale Exocet missile launchers, as well as a Raytheon Sea Sparrow SAM launcher and a single Creusot Loire 3.9-inch (100mm) gun. Its countermeasures include chaff and a towed antitorpedo decoy.

Denmark

This northern European nation sent the Niels Juel–class frigate *Olfert Fischer* to serve in the Gulf. The *Olfert Fischer* (F 355) was commissioned in 1981 as the second ship in its class. Displacing 1,320 tons fully loaded, the ship is complemented by a crew of 98, which includes 18 officers. It is powered by one General Electric LM 2500 gas turbine and a single MTU 20 V 956 TB82 diesel engine, and is equipped with eight McDonnell Douglas Harpoon surface-to-surface missile launchers, as well as an octuple Sea Sparrow Mk 29 launcher and an OTO Melara 76mm gun. Countermeasures include a Breda SCLAR chaff launcher.

France

In addition to sending several thousand troops to the Persian Gulf, the French dispatched 21 ships, which included five frigates: the *Commandant Bory*, the *Doudart de Lagree*, and the *Protet* of the Commandant Rivière class, and the *Commandant Ducuing* and the *Premier Maitre L'Her* of the D'Estienne D'Orves class. Of the former three ships, they were among three of the first six, commissioned between 1963 and 1964. They displace 2,250 tons fully loaded (1,750 standard), and carry complements of 159 crew (including 9 officers). Powered by four SEMT-Pielstick 12PC diesel engines, two SEMT-Pielstick 16-cylinder diesel engines, and two SEMT-Pielstick 12PC2-V200 diesel engines, the ships are equipped with four Aerospatiale Exocet missile launchers and two DCN 3.9-inch (100mm) 55 Mod automatic guns. Their countermeasures include two CSEE Dagaie trained launchers. The latter two ships belong to a class that included 17 ships as of 1991. Both the *Premier Maitre L'Her* (F 792), commissioned in 1981, and the *Commandant Ducuing* (F 795), commissioned in 1983, displace between 1,170 and 1,250 tons fully loaded, and have a complement of 90 (including 7 officers). They are powered by two SEMT-Pielstick 12PC2-V200 diesel engines, and are equipped with four Aerospatiale Exocet missiles, a single DCN 3.9-inch (100mm) CADAM automatic gun, and four torpedo tubes. Countermeasures include chaff, flares, and two CSEE Dagaie ten-barreled trainable launchers.

Great Britain

Under the leadership of Margaret Thatcher and John Major, Great Britain sent 33 ships to the Gulf, which included eight frigates: the Type 22 Batch I *Battleaxe* and *Brazen*, the Type 22 Batch II frigates *London* and *Sheffield*, the Batch III frigates *Chatham* and *Campeltown*, and the Batch IIIA conversion frigates *Jupiter* and *Charybdis*. The *Battleaxe* (F 89) and the *Brazen* (F 91) each displace 3,500 tons standard (4,400 tons fully loaded), and carry a complement of 222 (including 17 officers). Powered by two Rolls-Royce Olympus TM3B gas turbines and two Rolls-Royce Tyne RM1C gas turbines, the two ships have a maximum speed of 30 knots. The *London* (F 95), formerly called *The Bloodhound*, and its sister ship the *Sheffield* (F 96) are larger ships than the Batch I class, displacing 4,100 tons standard (4,800 tons loaded). Powered by the same engines as the Batch I fleet, the *London* and the *Sheffield* are complemented by a crew of 273 (including 30 officers). Both classes are equipped by four Aerospatiale Exocet missiles, two British Aerospace Seawolf surface-to-air missiles, two twin DES/Oerlikon 30mm guns, and two triple

324mm Plessey STWS Mk 2 torpedo tubes. Both classes are also fitted out to carry two Westland Lynx helicopters or, in the case of the *London* and the *Sheffield*, a Westland Sea King HAS 5 or EH 101 "Merlin" helicopter. The Batch III frigates *Campeltown* (F 86) and *Chatham* (F 87) are from the so-called Cornwall class. These ships displace 4,200 tons standard (4,900 tons fully loaded), and are 485.9 feet (148.1 m) in length. Powered by two Rolls-Royce Spey SM1A gas turbines, which provide 37,540 shaft horsepower, and two Rolls-Royce Tyne RM3C gas turbines, which provide 9,700 shaft horsepower, the ships have a maximum speed of 30 knots and an unrefueled range of 4,500 miles at 18 knots. Complement is 250 (including 31 officers), and an accommodation for 301 total. Each ship is armed with a single Vickers 4.5-inch (55mm) gun and a single Signaal/General Electric 30mm 7-barrelled Gatling "Goalkeeper" gun.

The last frigate to join the British fleet was the *Charybdis*, from the Batch IIIA conversion fleet. Joining the *Jupiter*, also from the same class, the *Charybdis* replaced the destroyer *Manchester* after 23 January 1991. Both ships displace 2,500 tons standard (2,962 fully loaded), and are powered by two White/English Electric double-reduction geared turbines, as well as two Babcock & Wilcox boilers. Complemented by a crew of 260 (including 19 officers), the ships are equipped with four Aerospatiale Exocet missiles, the Seawolf surface-to-air missile, and two Oerlikon/BMARC 20mm guns. Further, both ships are equipped with a platform to carry a single Westland Lynx HAS 3 helicopter.

Greece

The Mediterranean nation supplied two frigates to the coalition cause from the Netherlands Kortenaer class: the *Limnos* (F 451) and the *Elli* (F 450), serving consecutively. Commissioned less than a year apart, they are identical in every form. Both displace 3,050 tons standard (3,630 tons fully loaded) and have a complement of 176 (including 17 officers). Powered by two Rolls-Royce Olympus TM3B gas turbines and two Rolls-Royce Tyne RM1C gas turbines, they have a maximum speed of 30 knots (35 mph; 56 km/h). The ships are equipped with two quad Harpoon missile launchers, the Sea Sparrow surface-to-air missile, an OTO Melara 76mm gun, and two twin 324mm Mk 32 torpedo tubes. Both

are fitted with a platform to enable two AB 212ASW helicopters to land.

Italy

Of the eight Italian ships that saw duty in the Persian Gulf, five were frigates: the Maestrale-class frigates *Libeccio* and *Zeffiro*, and the Lupo-class frigates *Lupo*, *Orsa*, and *Sagittario*. The *Libeccio* (F 572) and *Zeffiro* (F 577) are relatively new ships, both commissioned in the 1980s. They displace 2,500 tons standard (3,200 fully loaded), have a complement of 232 (including 24 officers), are powered by two Fiat LM 2500 gas turbines and two GMT B 230.20 DVM diesel engines, and have a maximum speed of 32 knots (37 mph; 59 km/h) using the gas turbines or 21 knots (24 mph; 39 km/h) using the diesel engines. Both ships are equipped with four OTO Melara/Matra Teseo Otomat Mk 2 missiles, a Selenia Albatros octuple surface-to-air missile launcher, a single OTO Melara 127mm gun, and six 324mm Mk 32 torpedo tubes. Both operate with a platform that can hold two AB 212ASW helicopters.

The *Lupo* (F 564), *Sagittario* (F 565), and *Orsa* (F 567), all of the Lupo class, are smaller cousins of the Maestrale class. They displace 2,208 tons standard (2,500 fully loaded), and are powered by two Fiat LM 2500 gas turbines and two GMT A230.20M diesel engines. Their complement is 185 (including 15 officers). All three are equipped with eight OTO Melara/Matra Otomat Teseo Mk 2 missiles, an octuple Sea Sparrow surface-to-air missile launcher, a single OTO Melara 127mm gun, and six 324mm Mk 32 torpedo tubes. They are also fitted with a platform able to hold a single AB 212ASW helicopter.

The Netherlands

The Netherlands sent no troops and no planes, but among the eight ships it assigned to the Gulf were five frigates: the Jacob Van Heemskerck–class frigates *Jacob Van Heemskerck* and *Witte de With*, and the Kortenaer-class frigates *Pieter Florisz*, *Van Kinsbergen*, and *Philips can Almonde*. The *Jacob Van Heemskerck* (F 812) and the *Witte de With* (F 813) were commissioned in 1986. They displace 3,750 tons fully loaded, are powered by 2 Rolls-Royce Olympus TM3B gas turbines and 2 Rolls-Royce Tyne RM1C gas turbines, and have a maximum speed of 30 knots (35 mph; 56 km/h). They are implemented with 2 quad Harpoon missile launchers, 40 GDC Pomona

Standard SM-1MR surface-to-air missile launchers and an Mk Mod 1 SAM launcher, a single Signaal SGE-30 Goalkeeper 7-barreled 30mm gun, and 2 twin 324mm Mk 32 torpedo tubes.

The Kortenaer-class frigates *Philips can Almonde* (F 823), *Van Kinsbergen,* and *Pieter Florisz* (F 826) each displace 2,050 tons standard (2,630 tons fully loaded), and are complemented by a crew of 176 (including 18 officers). Powered by 2 Rolls-Royce Olympus TM3B gas turbines, the ships are equipped with 2 quad Harpoon missile launchers, a Sea Sparrow octuple surface-to-air missile launcher, a single OTO Melara 76mm gun, and 2 twin Mk 32 torpedo tubes. Unlike those in the Jacob Van Heemskerck class, these ships are fitted with a platform that allows the landing of two Westland SH-14B Lynx helicopters.

Spain

Spain sent no planes or troops to the Gulf. Of the eight Spanish ships that were deployed to participate in Operations Desert Shield and Desert Storm, six were frigates: the Santa Maria–class frigates *Santa Maria* and *Numancia,* and the Descubierta-class frigates *Cazadora, Descubierta, Infanta Elena,* and *Infanta Christina.* The Santa Maria–class ships are much larger than their other sister ships that served in the war. Both the *Santa Maria* (F 81) and the *Numancia* (F 83) were commissioned in the late 1980s. They displace 4,017 tons fully loaded, and have a crew complement of 223 (including 13 officers). Powered by 2 General Electric LM 2500 gas turbines, they have a maximum speed of 29 knots. Both ships are equipped with 8 Harpoon missiles, 32 GDC Pomona Standard SM-1MR surface-to-air missiles and an Mk 13 Mod 4 missile launcher, a single OTO Melara 76mm gun, and 2 triple 324mm torpedo tubes. Further, each has a platform that harbors two Sikorsky S-70L "Seahawk" helicopters (designated HS.23). The Descubierta-class frigates *Descubierta* (F 31), *Infanta Elena* (F 33), and *Cazadora* (F 35) each displace 1,233 tons standard (1,482 tons fully loaded), and have a complement of 118 (including 10 officers) and room for 30 marines. Powered by 4 MTU-Bažin 16V 956 TB 91 diesel engines, the ships have a maximum speed of 25 knots (29 mph; 46 km/h). All three are equipped with two quad Harpoon missile launchers, a Selenia Albatros octuple sur-

face-to-air missile launcher, 24 Sea Sparrow surface-to-air missiles, a single OTO Melara 76mm gun, and 2 triple 324mm Mk 32 torpedo tubes. Countermeasures include chaff and decoys.

See also Westland Lynx.
Reference: Sharpe, Richard, ed., *Jane's Fighting Ships, 1990–91* (Coulsdon, Surrey, UK: Jane's Information Group, 1990).

Frigates, United States

Of the 177 American ships that served in the Persian Gulf, 15 were frigates in two classifications—the Oliver Hazard Perry class and the Knox class. With their specific battle groups listed, the ships that served are:

Knox Class

The *Vreeland* (1068, Carrier Group Roosevelt), *Francis Hammond* (FF 1067, Carrier Group Ranger), *Elmer Montgomery* (FF 1082, Carrier Group Saratoga), *Barbey* (FF 1088, Persian Gulf Squadron), and *Thomas C. Hart* (FF 1092, Carrier Group Saratoga). The Knox-class ships are broken down into two divisions—those like the *Vreeland* and *Francis Hammond,* and the others, all built at later dates, differing only in their empty weight. The *Vreeland* and the *Francis Hammond* weigh 3,877 tons standard (4,260 fully loaded), as opposed to the later ships, which weigh 3,011 tons standard (4,260 fully loaded). All Knox-class ships are powered by two Combustion Engineering boilers and a single Westinghouse geared turbine, have a maximum speed of 27 knots (31 mph; 50 km/h) and a range of 4,000 miles (6,436 km), and have a complement of 288, including 17 officers. Armaments include eight Harpoon surface-to-surface missiles, and a General Electric/General Dynamics 20mm Mk 15 Vulcan Phalanx gun.

Oliver Hazard Perry Class

The *Curts* (FFG 38, Carrier Group Midway), *Halyburton* (FFG 40, Carrier Group America), *Rentz* (FFG 46, Persian Gulf Squadron), *Vandegrift* (FFG 48, Persian Gulf Squadron), *Robert G. Bradley* (FFG 49, Persian Gulf Squadron), *Taylor* (FFG 50, Persian Gulf Squadron), *Hawes* (FFG 53, Carrier Group Roosevelt), *Samuel B. Roberts* (FFG 58,

Carrier Group Kennedy), and *Rodney M. Davis* (FFG 60, Carrier Group Midway) displace 2,750 tons empty (4,100 tons fully loaded), and the *Reid* (FFG 30, Persian Gulf Squadron) displaces 3,638 tons. They are all powered by two General Electric LM 2500 gas turbines producing 41,000 shaft horsepower (shp), and have two auxiliary retractable propeller pods to provide emergency thrust. Maximum speed is 29 knots (33 mph; 54 km/h), with a range of 4,500 miles (7,240 km), and the complement is 206 sailors (which includes 13 officers) and 19 airmen. Armaments include four Harpoon surface-to-surface missiles and a single OTO Melara 76mm Mk 75 gun.

Among the ships in this class are the *Stark* and the *Samuel B. Roberts.* Both the *Stark,* hit by an Iraqi Exocet missile on 17 May 1987, killing 37 sailors, and the *Roberts,* which struck a mine in the Persian Gulf on 14 April 1988, were nearly lost because of activity in the troubled Persian Gulf area.

Reference: Sharpe, Richard, ed., *Jane's Fighting Ships, 1990–91* (Coulsdon, Surrey, UK: Jane's Information Group, 1990), 752, 754.

FROG (Free Rocket over Ground)

Known by its initials, this missile, a variant of the Soviet FROG-7, was in the Iraqi arsenal for the delivery of chemical, and perhaps nuclear, weapons. Because it is obsolete, its basic usage—had it been applied in the war—would have been more as a weapon of terror than for the proper delivery of weaponry.

With a single solid-propellant, single-stage rocket motor surrounded by smaller rocket nozzles, the FROG (called Luna by the Soviets) can thrust a 990-pound (449 kg) chemical warhead about 37 miles (60 km) from a mobile erected launcher. Most likely the FROG would have been used against coalition forces in Saudi Arabia rather than the civilian population of Israel. The FROG is 29 feet 6 inches (9 m) in length, weighs 5,511 pounds (2,500 kg) without a warhead, and is guided by radio.

See also Laith.
References: Blake, Bernard, ed., *Jane's Weapon Systems, 1988–89* (Coulsdon, Surrey, UK: Jane's Information Group, 1988), 128; Boyne, Walter J., *The*

U.S. Marines in Kuwait examine a captured Iraqi FROG-7 (Free Rocket over Ground) artillery rocket system transporter-erector-launcher.

Weapons of Desert Storm (Lincolnwood, IL: Publications International, 1991), 88.

Fuchs (Fox) M93 NBC Vehicle

This state-of-the-art vehicle's main assignment is to study a battlefield scene for nuclear, biological, and chemical (NBC) weapons contamination. The German government donated about 60 vehicles to the U.S. military specifically for use during military action in the Persian Gulf.

Called the Fuchs (or simply Fox in English), the M93 NBC is built conjunctively by General Dynamics Land Systems and Thyssen Henschel of Germany. Crew for this vehicle includes a driver and two technicians who conduct soil and air sample collection. The M93 is 22 feet 2 inches (6.76 m) in length, weighs 17.9 tons (16,238 kg), has a maximum speed of 65 mph (105 km/h), and has a maximum unrefueled range of 500 miles (805 km).

See also Chemical and Biological Warfare.
References: Clancy, Tom, *Armored Cav: A Guided Tour of an Armored Cavalry Regiment* (New York: Berkley Books, 1994), 81–83; Shenon, Philip, ''Vehicles Roam the Front To Detect Gas Attacks,'' *New York Times,* 24 February 1991, A18.

G5 155mm Gun Howitzer – Gulf War Syndrome

G5 155mm Gun Howitzer

This weapon was used by Iraq during the Persian Gulf War, although its exact numbers and technique of application remain unknown.

The informative journal *Jane's Armour and Artillery* relates, "The G5 155mm gun howitzer has seen combat with the South African Army in Southern Angola and South West Africa [now Namibia] and by the Iraqi Army during its war with Iran. Quantities of these weapons were captured by Allied coalition forces during Operation Desert Storm, the liberation of Kuwait." Carried on a large chassis with four massive tires, the gun as a whole weighs 30,313 pounds (13,750 kg), has a maximum firing range of 98,400 feet (30,000 m), and is operated by a crew of five.

Reference: Foss, Christopher F., ed., *Jane's Armour and Artillery, 1992–93* (Coulsdon, Surrey, UK: Jane's Information Group, 1992), 662–663.

GBU-10 GP Bomb Series

This 2,000-pound (908 kg) general-purpose bomb is a redesignated MK-84 mated with a laser guidance kit. According to the military, "the kits consist of a computer-control group (CCG), guidance canards attached to the front of the warhead to provide steering commands, and a wing assembly attached to the aft end to provide lift." The bomb is essentially fire-and-forget—it is controlled strictly by an internal guidance system that tracks laser traces and follows them, utilizing a laser reference that is flashed on the

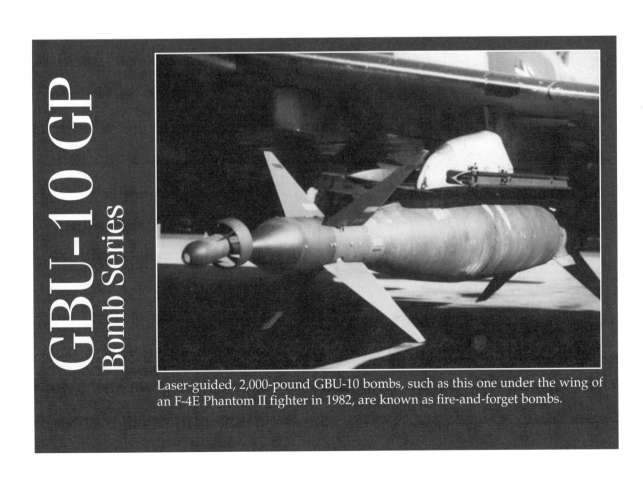

GBU-10 GP Bomb Series

Laser-guided, 2,000-pound GBU-10 bombs, such as this one under the wing of an F-4E Phantom II fighter in 1982, are known as fire-and-forget bombs.

target by any number of sources, including the firing aircraft or another craft nearby. Included in the list of GBU-related weaponry used during Desert Storm is the GBU-10I, a derivation of the GBU-10 that is actually a BLU-109B bomb hitched to a Paveway II laser guidance package. Both the GBU-10 and GBU-10I series were used by F-15Es and F-111Fs against bridges, C³I (command, control, communications, intelligence) bunkers, Scud missile launchers, and other bunkers. Numbering 2,637 weapons, one-third were dropped by F-111s. Other GBUs used were the GBU-12 (4,493), the GBU-16 (219), the GBU-24 (1,181), and the GBU-27 (739).

Reference: Gulf War Air Power Survey, Volume IV: Weapons, Tactics, and Training Report and Space Report (Washington, DC: GPO, 1993), 75–76.

GKN Desert Warrior Mechanised Combat Vehicle (MCV)

British writer Christopher Foss writes of this vehicle, "During Operation Desert Storm, all six variants [of the Desert Warrior vehicle] were deployed including the Artillery Observation and Battery Command Vehicles which entered service for the first time. A number of Warriors were converted for use in the Milan ATGW [antitank guided weapon] role. The order was placed on 22 October 1990 and the first kits were designed, produced and delivered in one week. This allowed Milan to be launched from the vehicle with provision being made for internal missile stowage. This version was subsequently adopted by the British Army . . . Warrior Command vehicles were also deployed in the forward observation role for armoured regiments, a new task for the vehicle . . . To improve battlefield survivability, the Warriors deployed to Saudi Arabia were fitted with passive armour developed by Vickers Defence Systems; this was fitted in Saudi Arabia." Of the six variants deployed, it is not known exactly how many Desert Warriors served during the Gulf conflict.

The British GKN Desert Warrior, which is exported particularly to the Middle East under the name Fahris, can be equipped with either a Milan, HOT, or TOW antitank guided weapon

(ATGW). Driven by a three-man crew, the vehicle is fitted with the capability of carrying up to seven additional troops. Powered by a Perkins Engines CV8 TCA V-8 diesel engine, the Desert Warrior MCV has a combat weight of 24,000 kg (52,911 pounds), a forward maximum road speed of 75 km/h (47 mph), and a maximum unrefueled range of 660 km at 60 km/h (410 miles at 40 mph).

See also Milan Antitank Missile.
Reference: Foss, Christopher F., ed., *Jane's Armour and Artillery, 1992–93* (Coulsdon, Surrey, UK: Jane's Information Group, 1992), 445–449; Shifrin, Carole A., "GKN Bids for Westland," *Aviation Week & Space Technology,* 14 February 1994, 58.

Glaspie, April Catherine (1942–)

"Envoy No Longer Silent," headlined the *New York Times* in its biographical profile of diplomat April Glaspie. Caught between a rock and a hard place, she remained the only one who could answer an important question: Did she, in a meet-

April Glaspie, U.S. ambassador to Iraq, testifies before the House Foreign Affairs Committee in 1991.

ing with Saddam Hussein on 25 July 1990, tell the Iraqi leader that the United States would not stand in the way of an Iraqi assault on Kuwait? Did this "appeasement" assure Iraq's invasion? Or did she, as she vehemently insists, tell Hussein "orally [that] we [the United States] would defend our vital interests, we would support our friends in the Gulf, we would defend their sovereignty and their integrity," as she testified in March 1991?

April Catherine Glaspie was born 26 April 1942 in Vancouver, Canada, the daughter of a British mother whose family had served in British Palestine and from whom she learned of the Arab world. After receiving a bachelor's degree in history and government from Mills College in Oakland, California, in 1963 and a master's degree from the Johns Hopkins School of International Studies two years later, Glaspie joined the U.S. Foreign Service. When she asked to take classes in Arabic, she had to battle with superiors who felt that the Arab world was not the place for a woman diplomat.

Glaspie eventually served as political officer at the U.S. embassies in Amman, Jordan (1966), and Kuwait City, Kuwait (1967–1969), as chief of language training at the U.S. embassy in Beirut, Lebanon (1972–1973), as political officer at the U.S. embassy in Cairo, Egypt (1973–1977), political officer at the U.S. mission to the United Nations in New York (1980–1981), director of the Language Institute at the American embassy in Tunis, Tunisia (1981–1983), and political officer/deputy chief of mission at the U.S. embassy in Damascus, Syria (1983–1985). In this latter position she played a key behind-the-scenes role in arranging for the release of American hostages abducted from TWA Flight 847 by Islamic terrorists and held for 39 days in Beirut. In 1985, after a short stint as director of the Department of State's Office of Jordan, Syria, and Lebanon, Glaspie was selected as the American ambassador to Baghdad, the first American woman to be named as the chief diplomat to an Arab country.

Nevertheless, she was merely one of the many anonymous diplomats handling American affairs across the world until the third week of July 1990. On 25 July Saddam Hussein summoned her to his office to discuss the situation along the Iraq-Kuwait border. According to transcripts later released by the Iraqi government, Glaspie denounced a piece done on Iraq for ABC television by Diane Sawyer. "I saw the Diane Sawyer program on ABC," Glaspie is reported to have said. "And what happened in that program was cheap and unjust. And this is a real picture of what happens in the American media—even to American politicians themselves. These are the methods the western media employs," the transcript says. Glaspie is then supposed to have said to Hussein, "I am pleased that you add your voice to the diplomats who stand up to the media. Because your appearance in the media, even for five minutes, would help us to make the American people understand Iraq. This would increase mutual understanding. If the American President had control of the media, his job would be much easier."

Glaspie was en route to London later that week when Iraq invaded Kuwait. Because she never returned to Baghdad, her duties were taken up by Joseph Charles Wilson IV. On 22 September 1990 Iraq released a "transcript" of what it claimed had happened during the Glaspie-Hussein meeting. For the next seven months, probably under orders from the State Department, Glaspie said nothing, and her possible role in giving a green light to Iraq went unreported.

In March 1991 Glaspie broke her silence. In front of the Senate Foreign Relations Committee on 20 March, she claimed that "she warned Saddam Hussein a week before his invasion of Kuwait that the United States would defend Kuwaiti sovereignty and its own vital interests against Iraqi aggression." Thomas L. Friedman wrote in the *New York Times*, "Glaspie . . . has been widely depicted as the designated scapegoat for what is termed the Bush Administration's policy of appeasing Iraq before its invasion of Kuwait."

Glaspie's career has been permanently damaged by the crisis in the Gulf; her reputation has been destroyed, and soon after the end of the ground war her post was given to a close friend, Peter A. Burleigh.

See also Appendix 4, Alleged Excerpts from the Saddam Hussein–April Glaspie Meeting, 25 July 1990.
References: "Ambassador Says U.S. Gave Iraq Warning about Kuwait," *Arlington Heights [IL] Daily Herald*, 21 March 1991, 3; "April Catherine Glaspie," *Presidential Appointments Staff*, U.S. Department of State information sheet, August 1987;

Friedman, Thomas L., "Envoy to Iraq, Faulted in Crisis, Says She Warned Hussein Sternly," *New York Times,* 21 March 1991, A1; Sciolino, Elaine, "Envoy No Longer Silent: April Catherine Glaspie," *New York Times,* 21 March 1991, A15.

Global Positioning System (GPS)

The Global Positioning System, a series of 24 satellites that hover in Earth orbit, allows for pinpoint accuracy in determining the position of a person on the planet. GPS was widely used during the Persian Gulf conflict.

The U.S. Department of Defense called the use of space-based navigation and positioning "an unqualified success." One of the main components in this scheme was the GPS, which with the use of a small receiver (dubbed a "slugger" by the soldiers of Desert Shield and Desert Storm), pinpointed the location of downed pilots and lost troops to within a few inches in the borderless desert. General Donald J. Kutyna, commander in chief of the U.S. Space Command, said in 1991, "During Operation Earnest Will in the Persian Gulf four years ago, U.S. and allied commanders employed Global Positioning System terminals on ships and helicopters to assist in minesweeping operations." In its final report to Congress, the Department of Defense listed eight reasons for the success of the GPS during the Gulf War:

1. Assistance with midcourse guidance for the stand-off land attack missile (SLAM), which allowed for more efficient terminal sensor target acquisition;
2. Improvement in navigation accuracy for the F-16s and B-52s;
3. Improvement in the emitter source location for RC-135s;
4. Enhancement in the deep penetration of enemy territory to rescue downed aircrews and other personnel;
5. Improvement in land navigation for ground forces;
6. Aiding in Patriot missile system radar emplacements;
7. Improvement in navigational system data for the Tomahawk land attack missile (TLAM);
8. Improved minefield mapping.

References: Conduct of the Persian Gulf War: Final Report to Congress, Report by the Department of Defense, April 1992, 569–570; Kutyna, Donald J., "SPACECOM: We Lead Today, but What about Tomorrow?" *Defense '91* (July/August 1991), 25.

Gorbachev, Mikhail Sergeivich

(1931–)

Gorbachev played a small but important role in the months leading up to the outbreak of hostilities in the Persian Gulf. On 1 January 1990 *Time* magazine named Mikhail Gorbachev as its "Man of the Decade." Writer Gail Sheehy called him "The Man Who Changed the World." Except for the leadership of Ronald Reagan, Gorbachev changed the political and geographical landscape more than any other figure in the 1980s. He was the last general secretary of the Communist party of the Soviet Union and the last leader of that nation before its breakup.

Mikhail Sergeivich Gorbachev was born on 2 March 1931. (Spellings of his middle name differ, and include Sergeevich and Sergeyevich.) Russian historian Zhores Medvedev writes, "[He] was born . . . in the village of Privol'noye in the Krasnogvardeisk district of Stavropol *krai* [Russian: "region"; Robert G. Kaiser reports that the word is used mainly to describe territories that were autonomous administrative units in the former Soviet Union]. His parents were peasants. His grandfather was a member of the Party and the chairman of the first collective farm founded in Privol'noye in 1931." *Current Biography,* looking at his life in 1985 as he became the Soviet leader, reported, "Although he was only eleven when the Germans occupied Stavropol during World War II, the experience left a deep impression on him. From 1946 to 1950 he worked summers at a machine and tractor station as an assistant combine harvester operator in the grain fields of the collective farms of his home area." The *New York Times* said of this period, "There, he joined the party and became a Communist Youth League organizer. He returned to Stavropol to start a career in party work, broken only by a correspondence course in agricultural economics for which he received a degree in 1967. He enjoyed a steady rise until 1970, when he was named the first secretary of the regional organization, a post that also brought him into the Central Committee." Thomas S. Arms adds, "Gorbachev made a name for himself boosting local agricultural production and came to the attention of Mikhail Suslov, the head of party ideology under Leonid Brezhnev, and KGB chief Yuri Andropov. Acting as Gorbachev's mentors, they arranged for him to be elected to the Supreme Soviet in 1970 and the Central Committee in 1971 and placed him on overseas delegations to Belgium, West Germany and France. In 1978 Gorbachev was taken to Moscow to join the secretariat of the Central Committee and oversee national agricultural production."

Gorbachev gradually rose in the ranks of the Soviet leadership. With the deaths of Leonid Brezhnev in 1982 and Yuri Andropov in 1984, Gorbachev found himself appointed as party ideologue (essentially the number two post) under General Secretary Konstantin Chernenko. With Chernenko's death, on 11 March 1985 Gorbachev became the general secretary of the Soviet Union. "Shortly after Mikhail Gorbachev attained supreme authority as General Secretary of the Communist Party, he made a symbolic choice," wrote Christian Schmidt-Häuer in 1986. "He set February 25 as the date for the opening of the 27th [Communist] Party Congress in 1986. February 25 has a particular significance in Soviet history. It was the date on which Nikita Khrushchev concluded his disclosure of Stalin's crimes to the 20th Party Congress 30 years earlier. . . . The social transformation Gorbachev is seeking to achieve is the second attempt at de-Stalinization. Khrushchev had fought with Stalin's shadow spontaneously, individually and personally. Gorbachev, 30 years later, is trying to mount a well-planned, large-scale assault on Stalin's legacy—the Soviet Union's hide-bound, centralized economic system." Daniel C. Diller said, "During Gorbachev's first year in power . . . he distinguished himself from past Soviet leaders more through his style of leadership than through the policies he promoted. From the day he took power he projected an image different from his three aging predecessors. He exploited his relative youth, presenting himself as a vigorous leader capable of improving the Soviet way of life. He frequently appeared in public with his wife and other family members and startled Soviet people with his penchant for wading into crowds of citizens to shake hands."

In describing his revolutionary plan for his country, Gorbachev wrote in his work *Perestroika*, "Perestroika is an urgent necessity arising from the profound processes of development in our socialist society. This society is ripe for change. It has been long yearning for it. Any delay in beginning perestroika could have led to an exacerbated internal situation in the near future, which, to put it bluntly, would have been fraught with serious social, economic and political crises."

Gorbachev's role in the formation of a clear and concise coalition policy toward Iraq was small at best, although at one point his personal emissary to Iraq, Yevgeni Primakov, was close to extracting a promise of withdrawal from Saddam Hussein. However, the Iraqi leader backed off. Gorbachev had a personal impact on the crisis during three time periods. On 8–9 September, Gorbachev met with President Bush in Helsinki, Finland, to discuss the crisis. In their joint statement released at the end of the summit the two leaders said, "Our preference is to resolve the crisis peacefully, and we will be united against Iraq's aggression as long as the crisis exists. However, we are determined to see this aggression end, and if the current steps fail to end it, we are prepared to consider additional ones consistent with the U.N. Charter." Less than two months later, in an interview on 27 October, Gorbachev suggested in couched terms that the Iraqi government might be "reconsidering" its position on whether to withdraw from Kuwait. At Gorbachev's direction, Soviet diplomats at the United Nations requested that body to postpone considering a resolution condemning Iraq's failure to withdraw from Kuwait, at least until after Russian envoy Primakov had talked with Saddam Hussein in Baghdad about an agreement to an unconditional withdrawal of Iraqi troops from Kuwait. The trip ended in failure. On 20 November Gorbachev announced his refusal to back a U.S.-sponsored resolution in the United Nations requiring force in the Gulf. The Soviets later relented, albeit reluctantly, to the adoption of a war resolution. And although the Soviets supplied no troops, planes, or ships to the coalition effort in the Gulf, they dispatched four ships to the area to observe coalition operations, including the Udaloy-class destroyer *Admiral Tributs*, a missile destroyer, a frigate, and an Amur-class repair ship. Even after the war began,

Primakov attempted to get the Iraqis to withdraw. Again he failed.

Gorbachev's reign came to a quick end in 1991. In August an assemblage of the Soviet hierarchy took over in a coup while Gorbachev was vacationing. Due to the machinations of Boris Yeltsin, president of the Russian Federated Republic, the coup failed, and Gorbachev returned to power, although for only a short time. That December the Soviet Union was disbanded, and Gorbachev was ousted from power legally. In the years since, he has remained a leading voice within Russia, and reportedly plans to run for president of Russia in 1996.

See also Helsinki Summit; Primakov, Yevgeni Maksimovich; Shevardnadze, Eduard Amvrosiyevich.
References: Arms, Thomas S., *Encyclopedia of the Cold War* (New York: Facts on File, 1994), 250; Butson, Thomas G., *Gorbachev: A Biography* (New York: Stein & Day, 1985); Diller, Daniel C., ed., *Russia and the Independent States* (Washington, DC: Congressional Quarterly, 1993), 105; Doder, Dusko, and Louise Branson, *Gorbachev: Heretic in the Kremlin* (New York: Viking, 1990); Gorbachev, Mikhail, *Perestroika: New Thinking for Our Country and the World* (New York: Harper & Row, 1988), 3; "A Kremlin Leader with Style—and Impatience," *New York Times*, 12 March 1985, A16; Medvedev, Zhores A., *Gorbachev* (New York: W. W. Norton, 1986), 22; Moritz, Charles, ed., *Current Biography Yearbook 1985* (New York: H. W. Wilson, 1985), 151; Morrow, Bruce, et al., "Mikhail Gorbachev: Man of the Decade," *Time*, 1 January 1990, 42–45; Schmidt-Häuer, Christian, *Gorbachev: The Path to Power* (Topsfield, MA: Salem House, 1986), 1; Sheehy, Gail, *The Man Who Changed the World* (New York: HarperCollins, 1990).

Great Britain

The contributions of Great Britain during the embargo of Iraq, as well as Operations Desert Shield and Desert Storm, have yet to be fully described in the United States. Few people know the full extent of British cooperation in the air, naval, and army facets of the conflict aside from the able leadership of Prime Minister Margaret Thatcher (who was replaced during the crisis by John Major), the skilled diplomacy of Foreign Secretary Douglas Hurd, and the direction of Lieutenant General Sir Peter de la Cour de la Billière, who commanded British troops in Saudi Arabia.

Besides the closeness between President George Bush and Prime Minister Margaret Thatcher, it was in Britain's interest to be active in the coalition—Britain had been a major power in the region until the early 1960s. Britain sent to the Gulf 25,000 troops, as well as 9,000 support troops, 54 planes (including the Buccaneer, Tornado, and Nimrod), and, with the exception of the United States, supplied the largest naval force to the region, a total of 31 ships. The Royal Air Force (RAF) was separated into various squadrons inside and outside the Kuwaiti Theatre of Operations (KTO); British jets flew the fourth highest number of sorties during the war, estimated at 5,417. At the start of the crisis, 36 Tornado GR.1s were stationed in three groups of 12 at Muharraq in Bahrain, Tabuk, and Dhahran, while a fourth wing composed of six GR.1A reconnaisance craft was also situated at Dhahran. In addition, 18 Tornado F.3 fighters at Dhahran, 6 Jaguar GR.Mk 1As at Muharraq, and 4 Nimrod MR.Mk 2 maritime patrol craft at Oman (consisting of parts of the Kinloss Wing) completed the KTO positioning. Outside the KTO, three Nimrod R.Mk 1P ESMs operated out of Akrotiri, Cy-

Lieutenant General Sir Peter de la Billière commanded 34,000 British troops, as well as aircraft and naval vessels, during Operation Granby.

prus, and RAF tankers were present in the Gulf vicinity. VC1 K.Mk 2s, VC K.Mk 3s, and Victor K.Mk 2s, as well as Buccaneer S.2Bs, also saw combat in some form or another.

The Persian Gulf War was not the first time Britain was involved in Arab—particularly Kuwaiti and Iraqi—affairs. On 23 January 1899 the British government signed an agreement with Sheik Mubarak ibn Sabah al-Sabah, the sheik of Kuwait, making Kuwait a protectorate of Great Britain. The exact text of the agreement reads:

Praise be to God alone [interpreted from *Bissim Illah Ta'alah Shanuho*, or "in the name of God Almighty"]—

The object of writing this lawful and honourable bond is that it is hereby covenanted and agreed between Lieutenant-General Malcolm John Meade, I.S.C., Her Britannic Majesty's Political Resident, on behalf of the British Government on the one part, and Sheikh Mubarak-bin-Sheikh Subah, Sheikh of Koweit, on the other part, that the said Sheikh Mubarak-bin-Sheikh Subah of his own free will and desire does hereby pledge and bind himself, his heirs, and successors not to receive the Agent or Representative of any Power or Government at Koweit, or at any other place within the limits of his territory, without the previous sanction of the British Government; and he further binds himself, his heirs and successors not to cede, sell, lease, mortgage, or give for occupation or for any other purpose any portion of his territory to the Government or subjects of any other Power without the previous consent of Her Majesty's Government for these purposes. This engagement also to extend to any portion of the territory of the said Sheikh Mubarak, which may now be in the possession of the subjects of any other Government.

In token of the conclusion of this lawful and honourable bond, Lieutenant-Colonel Malcolm John Meade, I.S.C., Her Britannic Majesty's Political Resident in the Persian Gulf, and Sheikh Mubarak-bin-Sheikh Subah, the former on behalf of the British Government and the latter on behalf of himself, his heirs and successors do each, in the presence of witnesses, affix their signa-

tures on this, the tenth day of Ramazam 1316, corresponding with the twenty-third day of January 1899.

After the 1899 agreement, Britain took firm control of political matters in the Middle East area. In 1913 Kuwait was declared an independent state under the protection of the British, a situation that lasted until 1961. The following year, the British took the side of Sharif Hussein, the king of the Hashemites, in his quest to eject the Ottoman Empire from the area known today as Jordan, and thus solidified British influence there. During World War I, British envoy Sir Mark Sykes worked together with French emissary Charles François Georges-Picot and Russian foreign minister Sergei Sazanov to draft what was later called the Sykes-Picot-Sazanov Agreement, an arrangement in which the British, French, and Russians essentially carved up the Middle East into spheres of influence. The sections given to Britain under the 1920 San Remo Agreement included what is now Iraq, Israel, and Kuwait. In 1919 British troops were needed in Kuwait to drive away an attempt by Saudi fundamentalists to overrun the small semiautonomous state. In Iraq, however, the people were agitated by British rule, and started an insurrection against the British that lasted from July to October 1920. The following 21 August, the British installed Faisal, the former king of Syria who had been overthrown by the French, as the first king of Iraq. With Faisal in control, the British were able to force the Iraqis to sign the Anglo-Iraqi Treaty of 1922, which allowed Britain to have unprecedented intervention in Iraqi affairs. The treaty was conducted under the stern management of Sir Percy Zachariah Cox, the British representative in the Persian Gulf. In 1923 Britain was a cosignatory of the Treaty of Lausanne, which carved up northern Iraq into a viable border with Turkey, the former Ottoman Empire. In that same year, under British sponsorship Iraq became the first Arab nation to enter the League of Nations as an independent state.

The landmark study of Iraq's years after independence is Hanna Batatu's 1978 work, *The Old Social Classes and the Revolutionary Movements of Iraq*. Wm. Roger Louis comments on the study, "The subject of British imperialism in Iraq, indirectly at least, is basic to Hanna Batatu's overall interpretation. He draws at least three conclusions that are significant. The first is that the British themselves were uneasily aware as early as the period of the Second World War that, in their own self-interest, too much depended on their principal collaborator, Nuri [as] Said. . . . From the British vantagepoint, the long-range future appeared to be unsatisfactory. What could be done about it? Could revolution be averted? The second conclusion is that the British miscalculated, like Nuri, on the pace and way in which [Iraqi] resources should be developed and the revenues invested. The third point, certainly the most fundamental, is that the British helped create the set of shifting alliances among the propertied classes, the shaikhs, and the political and military leaders of the country. One of the principal arguments, as I read it, is that during the 1920s and 1930s the British represented part of the triangular basis of power in Iraq. They rivalled the monarchy and the socially-dominant landed classes. The institutional policies initiated by the British continued to work in favor of the existing social order." Such a program, argues Louis, caused the resentment that culminated in the revolution of 1958 that installed the Ba'ath party into power in Iraq.

The British move, with France and Israel, to seize the Suez Canal in October 1956 spoiled Britain's relations with the rest of its former Arab surrogates. British writer T. O. Lloyd relates, "Co-operation with Israel and the failure of the operation combined to undermine Britain's position in the Arab world. Iraq had been her main ally there for a generation; the King [Faisal II] had been educated in Britain, the leading politician Nuri es-Said [sic], who had been Prime Minister much of the time since the 1930s, was a devoted anglophile, and the country's oil was managed by British companies." In 1961 Britain gave independence to Kuwait and pulled its troops out of the Persian Gulf emirate. After Iraqi leader Qassem declared that Kuwait was a part of Iraq, the British were forced to redeploy those troops. The issue seemed to calm.

British operations during Operations Desert Shield and Desert Storm were extensive. With their buildup designated as Operation Granby (separate from the Americans' Operations Desert Shield and Desert Storm and the French Operation Daguet), the British furnished 25,000 soldiers (plus another 9,000 support troops), 53 planes, and 30 ships. Lieutenant Commander Kenneth Napier of the Royal British Navy wrote: "[The] British Forces Middle East headquarters was located in Riyadh, close to other allied headquarters. In the United Kingdom, the recently completed Strike Command headquarters at High Wycombe, between London and Oxford, quickly became a joint headquarters. The naval team at the joint headquarters was supported by the staff at Northwood. Air Marshal Patrick Hime was in overall command, and Lieutenant Sir Peter de la Billière was in command in the Gulf." General Sir Peter de la Billière, commander of the British forces in Saudi Arabia, worked closely with his two assistants, Commander in Charge of the United Kingdom Air Force Air Marshal Sir Patrick Hime, and Deputy Commander of the Royal Air Force Vice Marshal Bill Wrattan.

See also Faisal I, King of Iraq; Sykes, Sir Mark; Task Group 323.2; Thatcher, Margaret Hilda Roberts, Baroness Thatcher of Kesteven.
References: Batatu, Hanna, *The Old Social Classes and the Revolutionary Movements of Iraq: A Study of Iraq's Old Landed and Commercial Classes and of Its Communists, Ba'thists and Free Officers* (Princeton, NJ: Princeton University Press, 1978); De la Billière, Sir Peter, *Storm Command: A Personal Account of the Gulf War* (New York: HarperCollins, 1992); Lauterpacht, E., et al., eds., *The Kuwait Crisis: Basic Documents* (Cambridge, UK: Grotius, 1991), 10; Lloyd, T. O., *The British Empire, 1558–1983* (New York: Oxford University Press, 1984), 338–339; Louis, Wm. Roger, "The British and the Origins of the Iraqi Revolution," in *The Iraqi Revolution of 1958: The Old Social Classes Revisited,* edited by Robert A. Fernea and Wm. Roger Louis (London: I. B. Tauris, 1991), 31; Napier, Kenneth, "With the British in the Gulf," *U.S. Naval Institute Proceedings* 117:6 (June 1991), 65.

Greece

See Coalition Nations, Contributions of.

Ground-Launched Cruise Missile (GLCM)

See Tomahawk Land Attack Missile.

Gulf Cooperation Council (GCC)

The Gulf Cooperation Council was initially formed in Riyadh, Saudi Arabia, on 4–5 February 1981, and established with a constitution in Abu Dhabi, United Arab Emirates, on 25–26 May 1981. The GCC (officially, the Cooperation Council of the Arab States of the Gulf) is a leading Arab congress involving the states that border the Persian Gulf. The original idea for such a council came from the Kuwaiti delegation to a meeting of Persian Gulf states meeting in Riyadh in February 1981. The delegation called for a congregation of Persian Gulf states to cooperate in economic, social, and financial affairs. The six members of the GCC are Bahrain, Kuwait, Oman, Qatar, Saudi Arabia, and the United Arab Emirates.

Historians James F. Dunnigan and Austin Bay write of the council: "The GCC began as less of a defensive 'pact' than as a political statement announcing that the member nations were already linked by common interests of trade, culture, language, and custom." These authors disclose the fact that in the 1980s the GCC nations held combined-forces mock military drills, and that the name of their operation was Desert Shield. The group's purpose, as stated in its constitution, is "(1) to achieve coordination, integration and cooperation among the member states in all fields in order to bring about their unity; (2) to deepen and strengthen the bonds of cooperation existing among the peoples in all fields; (3) to draw up similar plans in all fields; . . . and (4) to promote scientific and technical progress in the fields of industry, minerals, agriculture, sea wealth and animal wealth . . . for the good of the peoples of the member states."

Researchers Alfred Prados and Clyde Mark of the Foreign Affairs Division of the Congressional Research Service, an arm of the Library of Congress, wrote in 1990 of the GCC's armed forces: "The combined force strength of Saudi Arabia and its Gulf allies is less than 15% of the Iraqi level. Although they have acquired modern weapons from the United States and other western countries and long-range missiles from China, Saudi Arabia's armed forces have had little combat experience. Air and air defense forces (including the U.S.-supplied AWACS aircraft) took part in some actions tangential to the Iran-Iraq war, and in 1987 Saudi pilots succeeded in downing at least one Iranian F-4 fighter that violated Saudi airspace. Saudi Arabia's partners in the GCC have very small military establishments with capabilities largely limited to internal security duties. Nonetheless, these countries have had long-standing military training and supply relationships with western powers, and, unlike Iraq, have access to reliable sources of weapons resupply."

During the Gulf War, the GCC nations as a whole furnished 145,000 troops, in addition to a rapid deployment force of up to 10,000 troops. In addition, 7,000 Kuwaitis who escaped during the invasion were trained and later aided in the liberation of Kuwait. The GCC nations supplied 330 aircraft, which flew a total of 8,077 sorties (6,852 by Saudi Arabia, 780 by Kuwait, 293 by Bahrain, 109 by the UAE, and 43 by Qatar), and a small number of ships, including several small Kuwaiti craft that avoided capture during the invasion.

_____

References: Banks, Arthur S., ed., *Political Handbook of the World: 1993* (Binghamton, NY: CSA Publications, 1993), 1028–1029; Dunnigan, James F., and Austin Bay, *From Shield to Storm: High-Tech Weapons, Military Strategy, and Coalition Warfare in the Persian Gulf* (New York: Morrow, 1992); Prados, Alfred B., and Clyde R. Mark, *Iraq-Kuwait Crisis: U.S. Policy and Options,* Report of the Congressional Research Service, 30 August 1990.

Gulf War Syndrome

This disease, at the time of this writing, remains a mysterious chapter in the Persian Gulf War. Why are Gulf War veterans (as well as some of their children) experiencing ailments that seem to be related to their service in the Gulf? Are these ailments related to possible chemical and/or biological weapons contamination? And if not, what virus did these veterans pick up that mystifies the American medical community?

Mary Fischer wrote in *GQ* magazine in May 1994, "Perfectly healthy when they left for the Mideast, these veterans came home with a baffling array of debilitating symptoms that so far have defied diagnosis. Some are tormented by large blisters and rashes. Others have headaches, diarrhea, bleeding gums and chronic fatigue. Some of the afflicted hobble around on canes because of the pain in their joints and muscles. Some have been diagnosed as having cancer. Others have died." Tina Adler wrote in *Science News,* "The ailing U.S. veterans are not alone. Canadian, British, and Australian troops who served during the Gulf War have told [Senator

Gulf War Syndrome

Army sergeant Stephen Miller, holding a picture of his wife and son, testifies before the Senate Veterans Affairs Committee in 1994. His son, born in March 1992, has multiple birth defects.

Donald] Riegle's staff [on the Senate Committee on Banking, Housing and Urban Affairs, chaired since January 1995 by Alphonse M. D'Amato (R–NY)] and U.S. veterans' groups that they too suffer from Gulf War Syndrome. Nor are these veterans unique in medical history, says Stephen E. Straus of the National Institute of Allergy and Infectious Diseases. 'There is a spectrum of illness that is seen with all military adventures,' he says. In 1871, J. M. Da Costa, a physician, studied 300 Civil War veterans who had undiagnosable symptoms, including fatigue, breathlessness, chest pains, and gastrointestinal problems. Some 60,000 British troops suffered from a mysterious 'effort syndrome' after World War I."

The U.S. government has passed several pieces of legislation to deal with the problem of veterans' illnesses. The first, the Persian Gulf Conflict Supplemental Authorization and Personnel Benefits Act of 1991, was enacted on 6 April 1991. This legislation established, under section 335, the Persian Gulf Rehabilitative Services system to treat symptoms of posttraumatic stress disorder (PTSD) among Gulf War veterans. The second, passed on 5 December 1991, was the National Defense Authorization Act, which mandated that the Department of De-

fense establish a "Registry of Members of the Armed Forces Exposed to Fumes of Burning Oil in Connection with Operation Desert Storm." A third, on 4 November 1992, was the Veterans Health Care Act of 1992, which established the Persian Gulf Health Registry in the Department of Veterans Affairs.

In August 1994 the General Accounting Office released a report in which it noted that "the Pentagon did little to protect gulf war troops from exposure to toxins linked to birth defects, infertility and other reproductive problems." However, other possibilities—including that the illnesses may be caused from home-grown drugs—have been examined. According to the Institute of Medicine's report, *Health Consequences of the Service during the Persian Gulf War: Initial Findings and Recommendations for Immediate Action* (1995), "troops were given packets of pyridostigmine bromide (PB) pills to be taken as a prophylactic to the threat of nerve gas exposure, at the direction of their commanding officer. PB by itself, in recommended doses, is a safe drug. Additionally, DEET (N,N-diethyl-m-toluamide) and permethrin were used by the troops to prevent insect bites. There is some information about the possible long-term toxicity to humans of DEET absorbed through the skin; however, there appears to be little or no information about dermal absorption of permethrin from residues left on clothing, bedding or elsewhere. Although permethrin is generally not applied to [the] skin, animal studies have shown that permethrin is transferred from cloth to skin, and subsequently absorbed. There is little information about how PB, DEET and permethrin might interact; interactions among these compounds are possible and are inadequately studied." A New Orleans physician, Dr. James Moss, says that his studies link the use of DEET and PB to the ailments Gulf War veterans exhibit, and that he has a treatment to combat the syndrome, but that the Pentagon refuses to acknowledge his work.

The issue is still under intense examination. In November 1994 the Department of Veterans Affairs reported that "several panels of government physicians and private-sector experts have been unable to discern any new illness or unique symptom complex such as that popularly called 'Persian Gulf Syndrome.' 'No single disease or syndrome is apparent, but rather multiple illnesses with overlapping symptoms and causes,' wrote an outside panel led by professors from Harvard and Johns Hopkins University that convened for an April 1994 National Institutes of Health (NIH) workshop."

See also Persian Gulf Conflict Supplemental Authorization and Personnel Benefits Act of 1991; Veterans Health Care Act of 1992.

References: Adler, Tina, "Desert Storm's Medical Quandary: Do Iraqi Chemical and Biological Agents Explain Gulf War Syndrome?" *Science News* 145:25 (18 June 1994), 394–395; Committee To Review the Health Consequences of Service during the Persian Gulf War Medical Follow-up Agency, the Institute of Medicine, *Health Consequences of Service during the Persian Gulf War: Initial Findings and Recommendations for Immediate Action* (Washington, DC: National Academy Press, 1995), 15; "Denial of Poison Gas in Gulf War Irks Vets," *Arizona Republic,* 26 May 1994, A2; Fischer, Mary A. "Dying for Their Country," *GQ* 64:5 (May 1994), 148; "Gulf War Illness May Be Spreading to Veterans' Families," *Arizona Republic,* 6 March 1994, A10; Ritter, John, "Gulf Troops Lacked Protection from Toxins," *USA Today* (5 August 1994), A1; U.S. Department of Defense, "Persian Gulf Veterans' Problems," Report of the Persian Gulf Veterans Coordinating Board, 13 December 1994; U.S. General Accounting Office, "Operation Desert Storm: Questions Remain on Possible Exposure to Reproductive Toxicants," Report to the Chairman, Committee on Veterans' Affairs, U.S. Senate, August 1994, 14–19; U.S. Senate, Committee on Veterans' Affairs, "Is Military Research Hazardous to Veterans' Health? Lessons Spanning Half a Century," Senate Report 103-97, 103rd Congress, 2nd Session, 1994, 1–2; "VA Fact Sheet: VA Programs for Persian Gulf Veterans," Department of Veterans Affairs, November 1994, 1.

Hawk Air Defense System (MIM-23B)

Several Kuwaiti batteries of this missile system were captured by Iraq, but because that nation did not have Hawk missiles, the gunnery units were never used. The U.S. military report *Gulf War Air Power Survey* said of the batteries, "Hawk was a highly capable missile with excellent low altitude and ECM capabilities. Since the Iraqis proved unable to operate the Hawk, it was not a factor in Desert Storm, although there was initial concern that it might be used."

Reference: Gulf War Air Power Survey, Volume IV: Weapons, Tactics, and Training Report and Space Report (Washington, DC: GPO, 1993), 15.

HC-130H Extended Range Aerospace Rescue and Recovery

Five Coast Guard HC-130Hs, a variant of the C-130 that is exclusively part of "the Aerospace Rescue and Recovery Service of the U.S. Air Force for aerial recovery of personnel or equipment or other duties," were dispatched to the Kuwaiti Theatre of Operations on 21 August 1990, along with their sister ship, the MC-130H Combat Talon II. The ships flew 107 missions.

See also C-130 Hercules Transport; EC-130E Volant Solo; MC-130H Combat Talon II.
Reference: Blake, Bernard, ed., *Jane's Weapon Systems, 1988–89* (Coulsdon, Surrey, UK: Jane's Information Group, 1988), 440.

HEAT (High Explosive Antitank) Weapon

An ammunition used to destroy tanks, according to one source HEAT is "a shaped charge warhead that directs the explosion forward ... in HEAT, the penetrator is a stream of molten metal created by the explosion of a warhead."

Reference: Chadwick, Frank, *The Desert Shield Fact Book* (Bloomington, IL: Game Designers' Workshop, 1991), 16.

Helicopter Carriers, United States

Two ships that served in the Persian Gulf conflict were classified as helicopter carriers: the USS *Inchon,* which served with the Persian Gulf Amphibious Group, and the USS *Tripoli,* which was reclassified as an amphibious assault ship (AAS), although it carried MH-53C Sea Dragon mine countermeasure (MCM) helicopters.

The *Tripoli* (LPH 10) was commissioned in 1966 and the *Inchon* (LPH 12) in 1970. From the Iwo Jima class of amphibious assault ships, they have a displacement of 11,000 tons (18,000 loaded), are 602.3 feet (183.7 m) long, are powered by two Combustion Engineering boilers and one geared turbine (De Laval in the *Tripoli;* General Electric in the *Inchon*), and can attain a speed of 23 knots (26 mph; 43 km/h). Both have a complement of 686 (which includes 48 officers), and can carry up to 1,746 troops or 405,000 gallons of aviation fuel or petrol. Each is equipped with a Raytheon Sea Sparrow surface-to-air missile battery, as well as four U.S. Navy 3-inch (76mm) guns. Each ship has the capability of carrying four AV-8B Harriers, or 20 CH-46D/E Sea Knight, or 11 CH-53C Sea Dragon or CH-53D Sea Stallion helicopters.

Reference: Taylor, John W. R., ed., *Jane's All the World's Aircraft, 1989–90* (Coulsdon, Surrey, UK: Jane's Information Group, 1989), 743.

Helsinki Summit

Held in Helsinki, Finland, on 8–9 October 1990, this meeting between President George Bush of

Soviet president Mikhail Gorbachev and U.S. president George Bush share a laugh over a cartoon depicting the end of the cold war.

the United States and President Mikhail Gorbachev of the USSR was held to discuss the Iraqi invasion of Kuwait. Upon Bush's arrival he said, "Here in Helsinki, President Gorbachev and I meet, hopefully to strengthen our common approach to the unjustifiable act of aggression." He added, "If the nations of the world, acting together, continue as they have been to isolate Iraq and deny Saddam the fruits of aggression, we will set in place the cornerstone of an international order more stable and secure than any we have known." Arriving several hours later, Gorbachev echoed Bush's sentiments. "I hope this will be an important meeting," the Soviet president declared. "We have things to discuss, although we are constantly exchanging views, maintaining contact by telephone and letter and through our representatives. But at such times personal contact is essential."

Hosted by President Mauno Kovisto of Finland, the conference started off with the release of a strange note from Saddam Hussein to the two men. In part it read, "At the time you are in, being in a position to decide whatever relates to the future of good or evil for humanity, the angels will be hovering above you on one side and devils on the other. Each says his prayer, and

each would hope it to be in accordance with his nature and what God has chosen for him. God will be above all. I am not saying to either of you, neither appealing to any of you on what your decision should be. . . ."

After meeting for seven full hours, the two leaders emerged to issue a joint statement that called for Iraq's complete and unconditional withdrawal from Kuwait. "Our preference is to resolve the crisis peacefully, and we will be united against Iraq's aggression as long as the crisis exists," the two leaders declared in the statement. "However, we are determined to see this aggression end, and if the current steps fail to end it, we are prepared to consider additional ones consistent with the U.N. Charter."

See also Appendix 4: Letter From Saddam Hussein to George Bush, 16 August 1990; Text of Joint Statement Released by Presidents Bush and Gorbachev, 9 September 1990; Transcript of Press Conference with President George Bush and President Mikhail Gorbachev, 9 September 1990.
References: Keller, Bill, "Bush and Gorbachev, in Helsinki, Face the Gulf Crisis," *New York Times*, 9 September 1990, A1; Keller, Bill, "Bush and Gorbachev Say Iraqis Must Obey U.N. and Quit Kuwait," *New York Times*, 10 September 1990, A1, A6–A9, A14.

HN-5 Series Manportable Surface-to-Air (SAM) Missile

This Chinese SAM system was a part of Iraq's arsenal to be used against coalition forces. Because the full story of Iraq's weapons usage in the war has never been told, the application of the HN-5 has not been confirmed.

The HN-5 is a Chinese version of the Soviet SA-7 Grail SAM system. *Jane's Land-Based Air Defence* says of the weapon, "The missile itself consists of a launch tube which serves as an aiming device and launcher as well as a carrying case; a gripstock firing unit (designated SK-5A), mounted under the forward part of the launcher which provides launch information and ensures correct firing of the missile and, lastly, a thermal battery mounted on the forward part of the gripstock to provide power." A single-stage, one-rocket weapon, the HN-5 variant that Iraq possessed weighs 35.3 pounds (16 kg), including launcher, and can operate from 164 feet to 8,200 feet (50–2,500 m). The missile can hit head-on a target that is going 150 miles per second (241 km/sec).

Reference: Cullen, Tony, and Christopher F. Foss, eds., *Jane's Land-Based Air Defence, 1989–90* (Coulsdon, Surrey, UK: Jane's Information Group, 1989), 26.

Honduras

See Coalition Nations, Contributions of.

Hospital Ships, Coalition

Among the many ships that served the coalition forces during the Persian Gulf conflict are so-called hospital ships, whether they were built for that purpose or transformed for that use. Among these are the ships that served with Operation Artimon, the name for the French contingent of naval armor that served in the Gulf War. The two French ships are the Rhin-class support-hospital ship *Rance* (A 618), and the Foudre-class amphibious assault ship (changed to the transport hospital ship) *Foudre* (L 9011). The *Rance*, a depot and support ship at one time, displaces 2,075 tons standard (2,445 tons fully loaded), and is 331.5 feet (101.1 m) in length. Powered by two SEMT-Pielstick 12PA4 diesel engines, the ship has a speed of 13 knots (15 mph; 24 km/h). Complement, in its depot and support role, is 165 (including 11 officers). The *Foudre* displaces 8,190 tons standard (11,800 tons fully loaded), and is 511 feet (168 m) in length. Powered by two SEMT-Pielstick 16 PC 2.5 V400 diesel engines, the *Foudre* has a speed of 21 knots and a range of 11,000 miles at 15 knots. Complement is 210.

The Italians sent the San Georgio–class helicopter assault ship *San Marco*, which was transformed into a hospital ship. The *San Marco* weighs 6,687 tons standard (7,665 tons fully loaded), is 437.2 feet (133.3 m) long, is powered by two GMT A420.12 4-stroke diesel engines, each of which delivers 16,800 shaft horsepower (shp), and is usually complemented by a crew of 170. Speed is 20 knots (23 mph; 37 km/h), with maximum unrefueled range at 7,500 miles at 16 knots (18 mph; 30 km/h) or 4,500 miles at 20 knots.

The British sent the aviation training ship HMS *Argus* (formerly the *Contender Bezant*, A 135), as its hospital ship. The *Argus* displaces 18,280 tons standard (28,480 tons full), and is 574.5 feet in length (175 m). Powered by two Lindholm SEMT-Pielstick 18PC2.5V diesel engines, the ship is usually complemented by a crew of 254 Royal Air Force personnel.

The Polish Wodnik-class training ship *Wodnik* was transformed to serve as a hospital ship. The *Wodnik* (251) displaces 1,800 tons fully loaded, and is 236.2 feet (72 m) in length. Powered by two Cegielski-Sulzer 6TD48 diesel engines, which deliver 3,600 horsepower, the *Wodnik* has a maximum speed of 17 knots (20 mph; 31 km/h), a maximum unrefueled range of 7,500 miles at 11 knots (13 mph; 20 km/h), and a complement of 75.

Reference: Almond, Denise L., ed., *Desert Score: U.S. Gulf War Weapons* (Washington, DC: Carroll Publishing, 1991), 478–482; Sharpe, Richard, ed., *Jane's Fighting Ships, 1990–91* (Coulsdon, Surrey, UK: Jane's Information Group, 1991), 194, 199, 459, 703.

Hospital Ships, United States

Two American hospital ships served during the Persian Gulf conflict, both from the Mercy class

(AH) of craft. They are the *Mercy*, formerly the SS *Worth*, and the *Comfort*, formerly the SS *Rose City*, both previously used as San Clemente–class tankers. The *Mercy* (T-AH-19) was commissioned in 1986 and stationed in Oakland, California; the *Comfort* (T-AH-20) was commissioned in 1987 and berthed in Baltimore, Maryland. According to *Jane's Fighting Ships*, both have "1000 beds, 12 operating theatres, laboratories, pharmacies, dental, radiology and optometry departments, physical therapy and burn care units, and radiological services." Both ships saw action in the Persian Gulf awaiting battlefield casualties, although that number was so low that the ships did not play the kind of role they were expected to. In 1994 the *Mercy* was used to house Cubans escaping to the United States.

Reference: Sharpe, Richard, ed., *Jane's Fighting Ships 1993–94* (Coulsdon, Surrey, UK: Jane's Information Group, 1993), 817.

HOT Missile

Utilized in the weapons caches of France, Iraq, Kuwait, Qatar, Saudi Arabia, and the United Arab Emirates, this antitank weapon was used on both sides of the Persian Gulf conflict.

The HOT (*Haut Subsonique Optiquement téléguidé tiré d'un Tube*) was developed by French and German companies as a weapon that can be fired from a tube and is wire-guided. The HOT is mounted on a vehicle, either an armored personnel carrier (such as the AMX-10P) or a helicopter (including the Lynx, Gazelle, and Alouette III). Upon firing, the HOT spins out of its tube and extends fins to allow for cleaner flight. *Jane's Infantry Weapons 1993–94* reports, "When the missile is launched, infrared radiation from its tracer flares is detected by a precision goniometer that is associated with the optical sight and that has its reference axis accurately parallel to the optical axis. . . . Once the target has been visually acquired, all that the operator has to do is aim carefully, launch the missile, and maintain his aim steadily during the missile's flight."

The HOT missile is composed of a solid-propellant missile with folded fins, weighs 50.7 pounds (23 kg) at launch, has a maximum speed of 240 miles per second (386 km/sec), and has a range of up to 2.5 miles (4 km).

Reference: Hogg, Ian V., ed., *Jane's Infantry Weapons, 1993–94* (Coulsdon, Surrey, UK: Jane's Information Group, 1993), 140–142.

Howell, Wilson Nathaniel (1939–)

When Iraqi troops ordered the American embassy in Kuwait to close, little did they know that the tenacious W. Nathaniel Howell would face them down until he was ready to go. A career diplomat, he was one of the minor heroes of the Gulf conflict.

Barely known outside the diplomatic community, Howell was born in Portsmouth, Virginia, on 14 September 1939, according to his State Department appointments sheet. His education includes a bachelor of arts degree from the University of Virginia in 1961, a Ph.D. from that same institution in 1965, and a diploma from the National War College in 1983. He is skilled in languages such as Arabic and French. He joined the Foreign Service in 1965; served in the American embassy in Cairo; was a political officer to the U.S. Mission to the North Atlantic Treaty Organization in Brussels, Belgium, from 1967 to 1968; and served as the political officer at the American embassy in Beirut, Lebanon, from 1974 to 1976.

Howell began serving as U.S. ambassador to Kuwait on 11 August 1987. Ironically, he was supposed to leave Kuwait about the time the crisis began; his replacement, Edward W. Gnehm, Jr., had already been confirmed by the U.S. Senate. But Gnehm had not yet taken his post, which left Howell to face the storm of the Iraqi assault. From the time of the invasion until he was forced to abandon the American embassy to Iraqi troops, Howell stood firm, and during the few times he appeared on camera, he was seen to be at the forefront of the crisis. The *Miami Herald* compared Howell to "the captain of the ship." After he was allowed to leave Kuwait through Iraq, Howell returned to the United States to his official office at U.S. Central Command (USCENTCOM) at MacDill Air Force Base in Florida, where from 1986 until 1987 he served as the political advisor to the commander in chief of USCENTCOM. He has not served as a diplomat since 1990.

References: Bennett, Susan, "U.S. Envoy Stands Firm in Kuwait," *Miami Herald*, 24 August 1990,

W. Nathaniel Howell, U.S. ambassador to Kuwait at the time of the Iraqi invasion in 1990, addresses a news conference in Atlanta, Georgia.

16A; "Wilson Nathaniel Howell," *U.S. Department of State Presidential Appointments Staff,* April 1987.

Humvee

See M998 High Mobility, Multipurpose Wheeled Vehicle.

Human Shields

Saddam Hussein's use of Westerners caught in Iraq and Kuwait after the Iraqi invasion of Kuwait as human shields to prevent a possible American attack on Iraq may have done more than any other action to rally Western public opinion against the Iraqi regime. Even President Colonel Muammar el-Quaddafi of Libya condemned the use of Westerners as shields. A total of 2,395,000 people (910,000 in Kuwait, and 1,485,000 in Iraq) from numerous countries were held. Between 26 August, when President Kurt Waldheim of Austria left Iraq with 95 Austrian hostages given to him as a goodwill gesture, and 8 December, when the last of the shields—23 Americans—left Baghdad on a private jet chartered by former Texas governor John Connally, all hostages were released.

See also Appendix 1, Human Shields by Nationality and Location.

Hussein ibn Talal, Hashemite King of Jordan (1935–)

King Hussein ibn Talal of Jordan was one of the staunchest supporters of Saddam Hussein during the Gulf crisis and war, a stance that put him at odds with his allies in the West and threatened for a time to destabilize Jordan itself.

Hussein ibn Talal was born in Amman, the capital of Jordan (then Transjordan), in 1935, the son of Talal, king of Jordan (1909–1972; ruled 1951–1952), and Queen Zein, a member of another important Jordanian family. His brother Hassan was the crown prince of Jordan (1947–). His grandfather, Abdullah, was the emir of Transjordan (1921–46), king of Jordan (1946–51), and himself the son of Sharif Hussein ibn Ali, sharif of the Hejaz (1852–1931). (The Hejaz, or Hijiz, was a small strip of land from the southern tip of what is now Israel down the Arabian peninsula and ending just below the site of present-

Human Shields

Austrian president Kurt Waldheim, left, meets with Iraqi president Saddam Hussein to negotiate the release of Westerners held hostage in Iraq following the Kuwaiti invasion of 2 August 1990.

Hussein ibn Talal, Hashemite King of Jordan

Amman, Jordan

CNN LIVE

Jordan's king Hussein supported the actions of Iraq's president Saddam Hussein against Kuwait in 1990.

day Mecca.) Hussein ibn Talal was also the first cousin of Faisal II, the king of Iraq, who was assassinated in 1958. On 20 July 1951 a Palestinian assassin, angered by King Abdullah's loss of Jerusalem in the 1948 Arab-Israeli War, assassinated the Jordanian monarch at the Haram al–Sharif, Jerusalem's holiest Muslim shrine. The killing made Hussein's father, Talal, the new king of Jordan. However, Talal suffered from schizophrenia, and was removed from the monarchy after only a year. His son Hussein, a minor at the time, allowed a regency council to rule in his name. This enabled the young prince to complete his education in England; he and his cousin Faisal II of Iraq attended Harrow and the Sandhurst military academy. In May 1953 he returned to Jordan where he was crowned king.

King Hussein has never been fully accepted in the Arab world. As Yaacov Shimoni wrote in 1991, "Hussein succeeded in preserving his throne despite numerous plots sponsored by Egypt or Syria. His relations with Nasser's Egypt fluctuated. Sometimes, in the course of vitriolic propaganda attacks, Nasser called Hussein a traitor and imperialist stooge with whom Arab leaders could not cooperate; at other times, when currents of inter-Arab unity were emphasized, Hussein was the noble king of an Arab sister country." In 1967 Hussein sent his forces to disastrous defeat against Israel in the Six Day War. The loss of the West Bank in that war and the inter-Arab rivalry for control over the destiny of the Palestinian population in Jordan culminated in the September 1970 clash with Palestine Liberation Organization (PLO) forces that led to the formation of the offshoot sect called "Black September." Hussein made another mistake during the 1973 Yom Kippur War: Jordanian troops arrived too late to aid Syrian soldiers, and Israel was again victorious. Peter Gubser writes, "Not an intellectual, but serious and intelligent, [Hussein] is thought at times to be moody. However, for a leader of a small country buffeted by major Middle East forces beyond his control, he retains a consistent moderation in his policies ..."

Hussein appeared to repeat his mistake by siding with Saddam Hussein when the latter invaded Kuwait. Battered by criticism from Western nations such as the United States (which had supplied Jordan with millions of dollars in economic and military aid), Hussein declared that Saddam Hussein was a "patriot" for the major-

ity of the Arab world because of his actions in the Persian Gulf. Hussein met with President George Bush in the United States in August and with Prime Minister Margaret Thatcher in London just after the New Year in 1991, but he failed to get the coalition to see things his way, and the defeat of Saddam Hussein left King Hussein a pariah among the victorious coalition nations. However, perhaps he foresaw a revolution among his countrymen in search of peace and economic stability. In July 1994 Hussein and Prime Minister Yitzhak Rabin of Israel signed an accord in which the two countries officially recognized each other and declared an end to their nearly half-century-old war.

References: Gubser, Peter, "Hussein Ibn Talal," in *Political Leaders of the Contemporary Middle East and North Africa,* edited by Bernard Reich (Westport, CT: Greenwood, 1990), 234–235; Shimoni, Yaacov, *Biographical Dictionary of the Middle East* (New York: Facts on File, 1991), 111; Shimoni, Yaacov, *Political Dictionary of the Arab World* (New York: Macmillan, 1987), 212.

Hussein al-Tikriti, Saddam (1937–)

Ironically, his name means "one who confronts." One of the most powerful leaders in the Middle East, Saddam Hussein took his country from a small, backward, agricultural nation to a leading military state in just a single decade. He believes himself to be the reincarnation of the ruler Nebuchadnezzar, someone who will ultimately unite the "Arab nation" into a single entity. Yet his miscalculation as to how the world would react to his assault on Kuwait was key to his collapse as such a leader, and may lead to his ultimate downfall.

Saddam Hussein al-Tikriti was born in the small northern Iraqi village of al-Auja, near the town of Tikrit, on 28 April 1937. Little is known of his immediate family, and the shining biographies of him produced by the Iraqi government shed little light on this period of his life. In a semiofficial biography published in Paris in 1981, his "family tree" was disclosed. In it, he claimed to be related to Ali, the fourth caliph (a successor to the prophet Muhammad) and the father, or patron, of Shiite Islam. The known facts are that his father, Hussein al-Majid, died before he was born (authors Judith Miller and

Iraqi president Saddam Hussein with his wife Sajida and family in 1989. He became leader of the Iraqi government in 1979.

Laurie Mylroie speculate that his father in fact abandoned the family), and that his mother, Subha, sent him to live with her brother, Khair-allah Talfah, an army officer who later served as the mayor of Baghdad. Talfah's stern upbringing served as a model for the young Saddam. He fell in love with Talfah's daughter, Sajida (Saddam's first cousin), and eventually married her. Because of the influence of Talfah's son Adnan, Saddam sought an education; however, while in school he became involved in revolutionary activities with the growing Iraqi Ba'athist party, an offshoot of the Syrian wing. Adnan later served as defense minister under Saddam Hussein.

As a student, Saddam became a young revolutionary and joined the Ba'ath party. Although many details are lacking, Saddam and his biographers note that he was involved in an attempted coup against the regime of Abdul-Karim Qassem in 1959, and that Saddam himself shot at Qassem but missed; he was subsequently arrested and jailed. After escaping to Egypt, he was taken under the wing of Egyptian strongman Gamer Abdel Nasser, who encouraged the young Iraqi revolutionary to study law in Egypt. Nine years later, Hussein was back in Iraq at the side of his Ba'ath party elders in a bloodless coup that installed Hussein's cousin Ahmad Hassan

al-Bakr as president of Iraq. Considered an up-and-coming leader, Hussein was made vice-president of the Revolutionary Command Council (RCC) (although author Simon Henderson reports that Hussein was not officially acknowledged as RCC vice-president until November 1969). In 1979 Hussein edged out al-Bakr and took full control of the Iraqi regime, imprisoning his cousin until his death in 1982.

Many of Saddam's biographers point to several imprints that he uses to stand tall as a leader among the Arab people. Among these are unpredictability, brutality, an unceasing desire to be the conqueror of Israel, and his ability as a great commander, tactician, and strategist. In November 1988 a low-ranking Iraqi official was expected to visit Egypt to discuss Palestinian issues; however, when the plane's door opened, Saddam himself came down the steps, surprising his Egyptian guests. His methods of dominating his people are brutal. In 1989 Iraqi dissident Samir al-Khalil (a pseudonym) wrote of Saddam's Iraq in his *Republic of Fear*. The *London Daily Telegraph* said of the work, "[it] paints a nightmarish picture of what al-Khalil calls 'the most ruthless regime in the world.' "

His hatred of Israel is overwhelming. Much of it may be tied to Israel's 1981 attack on the Osirak nuclear power plant, outside Baghdad, that had been in the planning and building stages for many years. Did this attack cost Saddam the chance to own a nuclear weapon? And if so, did it prevent him from using it to end the bloody Iran-Iraq War? Or was his real target Israel? After all, as Nebuchadnezzar had done many centuries earlier, Saddam wanted to capture Jerusalem, and a strong Israel stood in his way. The final imprint of Hussein, as a great and tactical military commander, was destroyed by his monstrous failure in the war against the coalition during Operation Desert Storm. General H. Norman Schwarzkopf, when asked about his impression of Hussein, jokingly replied, "Ha! As far as Saddam Hussein being a great military strategist, he is neither a strategist, nor is he schooled in the operational arts, nor is he a tactician, nor is he a general, nor is he a soldier. Other than that, he is a great military man." Nora Boustany wrote in the *Washington Post*, "Whether . . . Hussein goes down in history as a war criminal or a war hero, Arab glorification of his defiance of the West has, for many, turned to [a] disillusionment that will mark the regional memory for years."

Iraqi military officials, concerned with the deterioration of their nation, have sought to assassinate Saddam on more than one occasion. All attempts have failed, resulting in several hundred, and perhaps several thousand, executions. British writer Gareth Smyth wrote, "Who could replace Saddam? Western policy-makers feel the Iraqi opposition is an unknown quantity. In any case, what goes on at the margins of the country—where the opposition is at its strongest—is less important than at first sight. For Saddam, strengthening his hold on the center of the country is more important than reasserting authority over the Kurdish north and the southern marshlands. The imposition of 'no fly zones' and recent renewed Allied military action have done nothing to break the stalemate. If anything, they strengthen Saddam." The 5 April 1994 edition of the *Guardian* in London quoted a former high Iraqi official who had defected as stating that "the Iraqi leader was mentally unstable and might strike at Kuwait again."

Representative Tom Lantos (D–CA) asked the important question in 1994: "Will Saddam strike again?" He writes, "In the last three years, Saddam—with the same deception and drive he used to amass his war machine in the first place—has rebuilt 80 percent of Iraq's military manufacturing capability. Saddam has an insatiable desire for power and territory. As a result, Iraq is likely to reemerge as the predominant Arab military power in the Mideast—unless the West acts." Lantos issued a four-step process to deny this power to Iraq:

1. The United Nations should set a deadline for Iraq to provide a complete list of its military suppliers. If the deadline is ignored, punitive action is called for.
2. Companies and individuals who knowingly violate their country's laws and supply Saddam should be prosecuted.
3. Western countries must be much more vigilant in containing Iraq's ambitions. Germany must enforce its export laws, instead of looking the other way as it so often has. France, Britain, and the United States should enact and enforce whatever regulations are necessary to prevent any future flow of arms to Iraq.
4. The United Nations should rescind permission for Iraq to sell oil to Jordan. This is a major weakness in our sanctions against Baghdad, and alternative oil supplies for Jordan can be found. At this point, the sales are no more than a way for Saddam to build up his war machine.

Commander William F. Hickman, in his article "Confrontation in the Gulf: Unintended Consequences," summed up why the Gulf War occurred: "As in the case of his decision to invade and annex the oil fields of southwestern Iran in 1980, he may have calculated that he could achieve his 1990 goals in Kuwait quickly; but just as he did not foresee the fanatical response from Iran, he did not foresee that his actions in Kuwait would forge a new coalition of nations to oppose him."

See also Ba'ath Party; Iran-Iraq War; Iraq; Kuwait; Operation Desert Shield; Operation Desert Storm. *References:* Atkinson, Rick, and Steve Coll, "Bush Announces Cease-Fire, Declares Kuwait Liberated," *Washington Post*, 28 February 1991, A28; Boustany, Nora, "Saddam: The Hero Who Crumpled," *Washington Post*, 28 February 1991, A31;

Cowell, Alan, "Iraqi Chief Pays an Impromptu Call on Egypt," *New York Times,* 29 November 1988, A6; Henderson, Simon, *Instant Empire: Saddam Hussein's Ambition for Iraq* (San Francisco: Mercury House, 1991), 72; Hickman, Comdr. William F., "Confrontation in the Gulf: Unintended Consequences," *Naval War College Review* 44:1 (Winter 1991), 49; Hirst, David, "The Father of Battles," *Manchester (U.K.) Guardian,* 5 April 1994, quoted in the *New York Times,* 15 April 1994, A12; Karsh, Efraim, and Inari Rautsi, *Saddam Hussein: A Political Biography* (New York: Free Press, 1991); al-Khalil, Samir, *Republic of Fear: The Inside Story of Saddam's Iraq* (New York: Pantheon Books, 1990); Kramer, Michael, "Deadline: Jan. 15," *Time,* 10 December 1990, 26; Lantos, Tom, "Will Saddam Strike Again?" *Reader's Digest* 144:865 (May 1994), 100, 103; Miller, Judith, and Laurie Mylroie, *Saddam Hussein and the Crisis in the Gulf* (New York: Times Books, 1990), 26; Smyth, Gareth, "Divided in Unity," *The New Statesman & New Society,* 22 January 1993, 18.

IL-76 Illyushin (Candid) –
Italy

IL-76 Ilyushin (Candid)

This huge Soviet transport plane (NATO code name: Candid) was used to a limited degree by the Iraqis for intelligence capabilities during the Persian Gulf War, but its precise application, as well as the exact numbers of the craft employed during the conflict, cannot be determined. Military aviation expert John W. R. Taylor states, "Before Desert Storm, Iraqi Airways operated a fleet of around 30 IL-76Ts and IL-76Ms, mainly for military duties, of which 15 were flown to sanctuary in Iran. This total may include two of the three AEW&C [airborne early warning and control system] conversions produced in Iraq under the name *Adnan 1*; the third was put out of commission during an attack on the Al Taqaddum Airfield." In *Military Aircraft of the World*, coauthored with Gordon Swanborough, Taylor writes, "The first export deliveries of IL-76s—a counterpart to the C-141A Starlifter—were reported in mid-1978, when a small batch went to Iraq."

The standard Soviet (and now Russian) version of the IL-76 is powered by four Soloviev D-30KP turbofan engines, each delivering 26,455 pounds (12,000 kg) of thrust. The plane has a wingspan of 165 feet 8 inches (50.50 m), a gross weight of 374,785 pounds (170,000 kg), and a payload capacity of 88,185 pounds (40,000 kg). Maximum speed is 528 mph (850 km/h), and maximum unrefueled range is 4,163 miles (6,700 km).

References: Taylor, John W. R., ed., *Jane's All the World's Aircraft, 1986–87* (London: Jane's Publications, 1986), 234–236; Taylor, John W. R., and Kenneth Munson, "Gallery of Middle East Airpower," *Air Force* 77:10 (October 1994), 70; Taylor, John W. R., and Gordon Swanborough, *Military Aircraft of the World* (New York: Scribner's, 1979), 63.

Intelligence Operations

In August 1993 the Oversight and Investigation Subcommittee of the House Armed Services Committee surveyed and reported on successes and failures during Operations Desert Shield and Desert Storm. The subcommittee concluded that: (a) Intelligence *collection* was generally very good and deserving of praise, but major problems were found; (b) Intelligence *distribution* within the Kuwaiti Theatre of Operations (KTO) was very poor from the standpoint of many Air Force units; (c) Intelligence *analysis* was mixed; the counting of Iraqi dead and destroyed tanks, for instance, had no generally accepted doctrine or methodology.

Reference: "Intelligence Successes and Failures in Operations Desert Shield/Storm," Report of the Oversight and Investigations Subcommittee of the House Committee on Armed Services, 103rd Congress, 1st Session, 1993.

International Emergency Economic Powers Act (35 U.S.C. 1701)

This legislation, enacted by Congress on 28 December 1977, was used by President George Bush to impose wide-reaching economic sanctions against Iraq at the onset of the Persian Gulf crisis. Under its authority, the president of the United States is granted sweeping powers in the event of an "unusual and extraordinary threat" to make a "declaration of [a] national emergency." The legislation reads: "(a) Any authority granted to the President by section 1702 of this title may be exercised to deal with any unusual and extraordinary threat, which has its source in whole or substantial part outside the United States, to the national security, foreign policy, or economy of the United States, if the President declares a national emergency with respect to such threat."

See also Appendix 4: Executive Order 12722 of 2 August 1990; Executive Order 12723 of 2 August

1990; Executive Order 12724 of 9 August 1990; Executive Order 12725 of 9 August 1990.
Reference: Celada, Raymond J., *Iraq, Kuwait, and IEEPA, CRS Report for Congress,* Congressional Research Service, 7 August 1990.

Intifada

Arabic for "uprising," this revolt against Israeli rule that began in the town of Jabaliya on 9 December 1987 played an important role in the Persian Gulf crisis. Saddam Hussein tried to link the "possible" pullout of Iraqi troops from Kuwait with an Israeli withdrawal from what are called the Occupied Territories—the Gaza Strip and the West Bank. Because the coalition stood steadfast against such linkage of issues, the Palestinian problem was not solved until 1993, when Israel and the Palestine Liberation Organization (PLO) signed a peace agreement giving the Palestinians limited autonomy over the Gaza Strip and the city of Jericho in the West Bank.

See also Arafat, Yasir; Linkage.

Iran

Now officially named the Islamic Republic of Iran, the nation once called Persia was at one time an ally of the United States. The spread of Islamic fundamentalism, as well as the rise of Ayatollah Ruhollah Khomeini, led to a break with the West, a hostage crisis that brought down an American president, and a crushing eight-year war with Iraq. Certainly, because of this war that killed perhaps a million people on both sides, Iran was no friend of Iraq's as the latter nation struggled to fight off crippling sanctions imposed on it and the threat of military action if its armies were not removed from Kuwait. Yet during the Persian Gulf War, the possibility that Iran would somehow enter the war *on either side* could not have been very far from the minds of military strategists. For a long period of time during the crisis, the possibility of Iranian intervention hung high.

Although Persia as an entity has existed for several millennia, modern Persia came into being during the sixth century B.C., when Cyrus the Great established the Persian Empire. Near what is today the city of Shiraz lie the ruins of Persepolis, the ceremonial capital of Persia built by Cyrus's son Darius I in 520 B.C. and destroyed by Alexander the Great in 330 B.C. after his defeat of Darius at Gaugamela near the Tigris River. The rise of the Greek, followed by the Roman, empires marked the beginning of the Persian Empire's long and slow decline from one of mastery of that portion of the world to what one source calls "internal disintegration." Invasion by Arabs from the Middle East brought a different culture and one of the three great religions of the world, Islam, which dominates modern Iran more than other Arab nations.

From the late nineteenth century onward, the land that had been Persia became a colony of European powers. After a 1905 uprising, it was partitioned two years later into two zones of influence by its neighbor, Russia, and Great Britain. During World War I, Persia sided with the Allies because it was occupied by the British and Russians. However, caught up in a revolution after the war, the Russians withdrew their troops. In return for its "cooperation" during the war, the state signed an agreement with Britain establishing it as an independent state with protectorate status, and in 1919 it was allowed entry into the League of Nations, of which it was a member for 20 years.

In 1925 the Pahlavi dynasty came to power in the person of Reza Khan, who had been the initiator of a revolt against foreign rule four years earlier. He was crowned Reza Shah Pahlavi, emperor of Persia. In 1935 he changed the name of the country to Iran. Although he attempted to modernize his country, his flirtation with the Nazis during the opening days of World War II led to his removal by invading British troops. His son Muhammad Reza Pahlavi was installed as the shah of Iran on 18 September 1941 (he was crowned emperor in 1967).

In 1965 John Fischer wrote in *Harper's* magazine, "The Moslem religious leaders hate him because the Shah is trying to modernize the country—and Islam cannot thrive in a modern atmosphere. In particular the *mullahs* resent the introduction of public schools, which threaten to break their near monopoly of literacy, and the liberation of women from the old Koranic rules." The new shah became a close friend of the West, particularly the United States. This close relationship even drew the leaders of the Allies to Teheran for the Teheran Conference in 1943.

Iran

Ali Akbar Hashemi Rafsanjani, speaker of the Iranian Majlis, the country's Parliament, votes in the July 1989 election that brought him the presidency of the country.

Historians R. R. Palmer and Joel Colton write, "The Shah identified himself with the west. When the Iranian parliament and a reform prime minister sought to nationalize the oil industry after the end of the war, the Shah, with American and British encouragement, blocked them and assumed full control. Embarking on an extensive modernization program, he introduced Western-style industry and education and, with American aid, revamped the armed forces. Using the oil wealth of his country for his economic and military plans, he also received loans and assistance from the United States. At the same time, he solidified authoritarian rule, crushing opposition from traditionalist clerical leaders (*mullahs*) and leftists." On 6 March 1975 the shah and Iraqi leaders (including a rising Ba'ath party political star named Saddam Hussein) signed the Algiers Agreement, in which Iraq pledged to give up its border aspirations between the two nations in exchange for a smaller piece of the Shatt al-Arab waterway and Iranian aid in crushing the pro-Iranian Kurds in Iraq.

By the end of the 1970s, the shah was hated by his people, and the beginnings of an Islamic revolution were starting to show. The fall of the shah in 1978–1979 came at the same time as the rise of the Islamic cleric, the Ayatollah Ruhollah Khomeini (1902?–1989). The ayatollah had been exiled to Iraq by the shah in the 1960s and was his mortal enemy. When the shah fled in 1979, Khomeini returned from a short stay in France. Shortly after the shah fell, one source notes, "a civilian form of government was established under a Revolutionary Council headed by Khomeini [and abolished in 1980]," which "became dominated increasingly by fundamentalists, driving most leftist and moderate groups into armed opposition to the regime." Among these groups are the Communist party of Iran, the *Fedayeen e-Khalq* (People's Fighters), and the *Mujaheddin e-Khalq* (People's Holy Warriors).

The Iran-Iraq War, which began with the Iraqi invasion of western Iran in September 1980, was a military disaster for both sides. It was clearly a battle between the well-trained and militarily stocked Iraqis against the fanatical waves of Iranians, who plunged into battle only to be wiped out in grotesque numbers. The balance was slightly tipped during the war because of American foodstuffs supplied to Iraq and the arms sent to Iran in exchange for the release of American hostages in Lebanon, but not much. The so-called War of the Cities in 1988—in which both sides fired weapon-ladened missiles into major city centers, killing scores of civilians, and the use of poison gases by Iraq against Iranian soldiers and pro-Iranian Kurdish *peshmerga* (Arabic: "Those who confront death") guerrillas in eastern Iraq—made the war one of the bloodiest in the annals of man. The end of the war came out of desperation, as each side (declaring victory) was too tired and its armies too decimated to carry on. A cease-fire, arranged by the United Nations, seemed to bring a peaceful end to conflict in the Persian Gulf. But it was not to be. The invasion of Kuwait was a mere two years away.

In the years since the end of its war with Iraq, Iran has in some ways attempted to get closer to the West, although this rapprochement has been deliberately vague. The key figure behind this slow reconciliation is President Hojatoislam (or Hojat al-Islam, a ceremonial title meaning one step below ayatollah) Ali Akbar Hashemi Rafsanjani (1934–), one-time speaker of the Iranian *Majlis,* or Parliament. Rafsanjani must steer a careful course between the radicals and moderates in Iran. He can look toward the West, as when he commended Western (and particularly American and British) relief agencies during the 1990 earthquake, which killed more than 40,000, or rail against it, such as when he denounced American-brokered Arab-Israeli peace talks by disclaiming "overreliance on the arrogant powers, the United States in particular, [which] contradicts the lofty interests of the Muslim world." It was this nebulous and nonspecific policy that led coalition commanders during the Gulf crisis to question whether Iran would stay neutral, side with the Allies against her enemy Iraq, or position itself with Iraq against the coalition. Fears of an Iranian-Iraqi union were fostered when, on 9 September 1990, Iraqi foreign minister Tariq Aziz flew to Teheran to meet with his counterpart, Iranian foreign minister Ali Akbar Velayati, to coordinate Iraqi efforts to circumvent the economic embargo. The following day, the two nations restored diplomatic relations. The alliance, however, was tenuous at best, and involved only the Iranians safeguarding Iraqi jets that fled from the war over Iraq—planes that to this day have not been returned.

The future for Iran looks murky at best. Middle East experts Daniel Pipes and Patrick Claw-

son write, "Under Rafsanjani's command, Iran resumed ties with the International Monetary Fund, borrowed from the World Bank, and implemented the economic reforms recommended by those organizations. He steeply cut the budget deficit and greatly reduced government control over imports. One exchange rate for the rial [the Iranian currency], set by the market, will replace several old unrealistic rates. . . . These steps led to a 20 percent increase in per capita real income during the first three years of Rafsanjani's presidency [1989–1992]; imports in that period rose from $11 billion a year to $25 billion." However, Rafsanjani is not all-powerful. The *Economist* reported in its 25 June 1994 issue that Rafsanjani's harsh economic measures have in many ways stalled the country's progress. The magazine reports that at least seven attempts (the last known was in February 1994) have been made on Rafsanjani's life. "Mr. Rafsanjani himself looks ever more isolated," Pipes and Clawson continue. "It is said he has tried three times to resign, but each time was told to soldier on. He is a useful fall guy, says a western diplomat. Will he last to the end of his second term in 1997? Iranians speculate on a successor. The frontrunner is the parliamentary Speaker, Ali Akbar

Nateq-Nouri, a conservative mullah who has distanced himself from Rafsanjani's economic reforms." The religious fundamentalism of the country continues to make it a pariah even in the Middle East. Dilip Hiro commented in the *Washington Post*, "The regime's Islamization program has left no aspect of life untouched. The legislative assembly and the courts are under [the] firm control of clergy and other committed Moslems. The banking system is now run according to religious guidelines and the clergy control the education system, from kindergarten to graduate school, as well as the publishing industry." Iran came under increasing suspicion about other intentions during 1994, when reports surfaced that during Rafsanjani's six-day trip to Southeast Asia for a state visit, several members of the Iranian security apparatus were meeting with members of clandestine Islamic fundamentalist groups to fund opposition to more moderate Islamic governments. Iranian designs on fomenting rebellion even outside of the Middle East led *U.S. News & World Report* writers Stephen Hedges and Peter Cary to call Rafsanjani's Iran "the other problem in the Persian Gulf." In 1995 came reports that Iran was using the world's focus on Iraq to concentrate on building an extensive chemical and biological weapons complex.

See also Algiers Agreement of 6 March 1975; Iran-Iraq War.

References: Degenhardt, Henry W., ed., *Revolutionary and Dissident Movements: An International Guide* (New York: Longman, 1988), 163–164; Fischer, John, "The Editor's Easy Chair: The Shah and His Exasperating Subjects—A Report from Iran, Part II," *Harper's* 230:1379 (April 1965), 24; Graves, William, "Iran: Desert Miracle," *National Geographic* 147:1 (January 1975), 35; Hedges, Stephen J., et al., "The Other Problem in the Persian Gulf," *U.S. News & World Report*, 14 November 1994, 87–88; Hiro, Dilip, "Iran Moves To Perpetuate Rule by Islamic Clergy," *Washington Post*, 13 February 1986, A25; "Iran: Explosive Circles," *The Economist*, 25 June 1994, 43–44; Morello, Carol, "[Iranian] Quake Reveals a Deeper Split: National Schizophrenia," *Miami Herald*, 2 July 1990, 7A; Palmer, R. R., and Joel Colton, *A History of the Modern World* (New York: Knopf, 1984), 875; Pipes, Daniel, and Clawson, Patrick, "Ambitious Iran; Troubled Neighbors," *Foreign Affairs: America and the World 1992/93* 72:1 (January 1993), 124–141; "Washington Whispers: A Lesson in Fundamentals," *U.S. News & World Report*, 14 November 1994, 37; Williams, Nick B., Jr., "Iran's Rafsanjani, Guarding His Political Flanks, Steers a More Militant Course," *Los Angeles Times*, 13 January 1992, 8A.

Iran-Iraq War (1980–1988)

The conflict between these two great powers of the Middle East haunted every move made during the subsequent Persian Gulf hostilities. Many factors, as well as many sensitive questions, involved in the eight-year-long struggle came into play: Would Iran enter the coalition's war to drive the Iraqi army from Kuwait, and if so, against whom—Iraq, or Iraq's mortal enemy the United States? How would Iranian fundamentalism affect the warring powers, including the delicate Persian Gulf states and Saudi Arabia? What role would the Sunni Muslims in Iraq (known to be allied with Iran) play?

Except for the slim piece of land adjoining the Shatt al-Arab waterway, Iraq has no port access

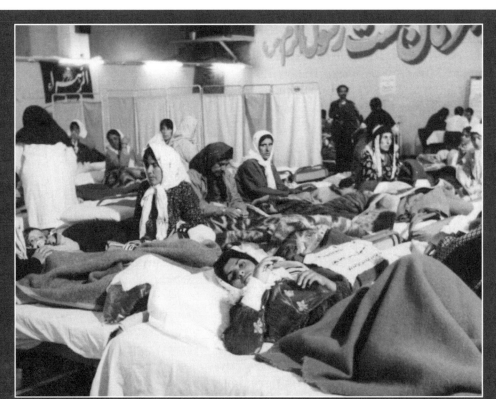

Iran-Iraq War (1980–1988)

Kurdish women and children from Halabla, Iraq, recover in a makeshift hospital in Tehran, Iran, after suffering from an alleged Iraqi chemical warfare attack in March 1988.

to the Persian Gulf and thus no real water border. In 1975 a treaty between Iran and Iraq allowed for their dual access to this vital waterway; however, in 1980 Saddam Hussein nullified the treaty, claiming that Iraq owned the waterway completely. When Iran refused to withdraw from its half of the Shatt al-Arab, Iraq attacked. This was not the sole purpose for Iraq's move. One source on the Iraqi dictator said, "His ambition to become a regional leader, along with his fear of the impact of the Islamic revolution, motivated his decision" to invade Iran. Another source, a paper written by military historians Stephen Pelletiere and Douglas Johnson II, says of the conflict, "Iraq emerged from its war with Iran as a superpower in the Persian Gulf. This had not been its original intent; it did not deliberately use the war to transform its strategic position or to impose its domination over the region. Iraq achieved regional superpower status through a series of escalatory steps that were required to repel Iran's Islamic fundamentalist crusade. Iraqi leaders mobilized a diverse population, strengthened Iraq's armed forces, and transformed its society to take the offensive and terminate the war with Iran."

The move to claim the Shatt al-Arab was not Iraq's first assertion on that Iranian territory; as early as 1958, Iran and Iraq battled over the waterway. After a peaceful period lasting from 1963 to 1968, the Ba'ath party's ascension to power in Iraq resurrected all the old hatreds. In a series of speeches that brings to mind those delivered over Kuwait, Iraq claimed that some parts of Iran belonged to Iraq. In a 1969 speech the deputy prime minister of Iraq proclaimed, "Iraq has not had [a] serious dispute with Iran over [the] Shatt al-Arab, since this is part of Iraq's territory. The dispute is in connection with Arabistan [Iran's Khuzestan], which is part of Iraq's soil and was annexed to Iran during foreign [Ottoman] rule." Thus, the atmosphere was established regarding Iraqi claims against Iranian territory. From 1972 to 1974 a series of border skirmishes occurred, in which Iraq claimed that Iran had occupied 5 square kilometers of Iraqi territory. A meeting of the UN Security Council was convened, but found no solutions to the demands of each side. The region was gradually slipping toward one of the worst wars in human history.

A series of actions starting in mid-1979 and ending in April 1980 began this long slide toward armed conflict between Iran and Iraq. In June 1979 Âyat Allah Bakir (Baqir), a Shiite cleric in the city of al-Najaf in Iraq, came out in favor of the militant Islamic revolution of Ayatollah Khomeini in Iran over the socialist regime of Saddam Hussein. On 1 April 1980 a grenade was thrown at Tariq Aziz, the foreign minister of Iraq, by members of the al-Dawa ("the Call") opposition party, believed by many to be allied with Iran. Although Aziz was only slightly injured, a number of students listening to him speak at a rally were killed. On 9 April, Iraqi Shiite dissidents Mohammed Baqir al-Sadr and his sister, Bint al-Huda, who had been arrested the previous year for supporting the Iranian revolution, were executed by the Iraqi government. Finally, on 12 April Latif Nsayyif Jâsim, the Iraqi minister of culture and information, was assassinated; his killers were assumed to be Iranian-backed. These events led the Iraqi regime to begin rounding up members of the pro-Iranian al-Dawa party and proceed with the forcible deportation of some 35,000 Shiites of Iranian descent to Iran by that summer. However, author Samir al-Khalil, in his *Republic of Fear: The Inside Story of Saddam's Iraq*, finds that Iran was to blame for the ensuing conflict: "Iran had already abrogated the Algiers Agreement through 187 border violations, all of which had allegedly taken place in the four-month period preceding the war (any violation, Iraq claimed, nullified the entire document). Numerous statements by Iranian leaders also proved their intent to 'export' the Islamic revolution. It followed, once the treaty was abrogated, that the Shatt al-Arab waterway had to revert back to Iraqi sovereignty according to all previous agreements. All naval craft along the Shatt were henceforth to fly the Iraqi flag, and navigation fees should be paid to Iraq. In addition, the region of Ahwaz, or 'Arabistan' [as the Iraqis called it] had been wrongfully ceded in the second treaty of Erzerum in 1847; its inhabitants were overwhelmingly Arab and their ancestry could be traced back to the Islamic conquest of Iran."

On 4 September 1980, border skirmishes between Iraqi troops and Kurdish guerrillas supported by Iran began to flare up. Iranian artillery batteries shelled the Iraqi cities of Khaniqîn and Mandalî, killing an untold number of civilians. The shelling was repeated on 7 September. Although Iraq delivered a diplomatic protest to the government in Tehran, no reply was given, and the stage was set for war. That same day, Iraq nullified the 1975 Algiers Agreement, effectively declaring war against Iran. Two weeks later, on 22 September 1980, Iraqi fighter-bombers strafed across the border and bombed ten Iranian air bases, while Iraqi foot soldiers raced across the border, claiming that by 25 September they had laid siege to Ahvaz, Dezful, and Khorramshahr. On 24 October, Iraqi troops overran Khorramshahr. In honor of the Arab victory over the Persians in the A.D. 636 battle of Qadissiyat, Saddam Hussein called this 1980 offensive "Qadissayat Saddam." The "war against oil" began soon after the occupation of Khorramshahr. Iraq shelled and destroyed the Iranian oil centers of Abadan and Bandar Khomeini (formerly Bandar Abbas), while Iran demolished the Iraqi oil stations at Kirkuk and Mosul. The Iranian counteroffensive began in May 1981, and eventually pushed the retreating Iraqis back across the Karûn River. In May 1982 the Iranians retook Khorramshahr. After the summer of 1982, when Iranian troops tried to take the Iraqi city of Basra with frightening losses, the war bogged down into a bloody stalemate like that of the trench warfare of World War I.

The war became unpopular at home for Iraq. Saddam Hussein continually faced the possibility of his army falling apart—because most of them were Shiites, there was a great fear that they might defect to Iran. Further, many Iraqis felt that the country's defenses were being weakened, while the real enemy of Iraq—Israel—remained strong. Further, by 1984 the Iraqis had suffered at least 65,000 killed, with 50,000 to 60,000 prisoners of war in Iranian hands (Iran had 180,000 killed and 8,000 taken prisoner). Although at one point Iran was in the midst of the embassy hostage crisis, and later the diplomat hostage dilemma in Lebanon with the United States, and was in a horrible economic situation, it appeared to have an endless well of young men to send in waves to be slaughtered by Iraqi guns.

The destruction of oil facilities of both countries led to the so-called Tanker War in 1986 and 1987; both mined the Persian Gulf to stop the other side from selling oil to finance the war effort. This led to the first direct American involvement in the Gulf when tankers reflagged with American flags sailed the Gulf with American military escort. Other factors that kept the war going include the selling of American foodstuffs to Iraq in an effort to stop an Iranian victory, the sending of American weapons (with the help of Israel) to keep Iran in the war and to achieve the release of American hostages held by Islamic terrorists in Lebanon, and the funding by Persian Gulf states (particularly Kuwait) of Iraq with billions of dollars to keep Baghdad's economy afloat.

If anything, the world looked upon the Iran-Iraq War with some relief. Iraq's close ally, the Soviet Union, was distressed with Iraqi expansionist moves but happy to see the spread of Iran's Muslim fundamentalism checked. The West, including the United States, felt that the war aided in both the containment of Iran and the exhaustion of Iraq.

On 29 February 1988, the "War of the Cities" began. Iraq began this most brutal of military strategies by sending Scuds loaded with explosives crashing into the civilian populations of Teheran, killing untold numbers of innocents. Through March and April of that year, as Iran struck back, the two nations evacuated their main cities, sending tens of thousands of civilians into the countryside. Historian Herbert Krosney writes, "With the winter rainy season coming to an end, both Iran and Iraq girded themselves for the offensives that each hoped would be decisive in turning the tide of war in its favor. Two weeks after Iraq launched the 'War of the Cities,' the Iranians retaliated with ground offensives deep in Iraqi territory. The main attacks were in northern Iraq, in Kurdistan. On March 14th, Iranian soldiers approached the Iraqi provincial capital of Suleymaniyah, also a center for the country's Kurdish population. Spokesmen announced that this was in retaliation for the firing of SCUD-B missiles at Iranian civilians in Teheran and the holy city of Qom." The Kurds, enemies of the Iraqi government, sided with the Iranians. When the Iranians occupied the Kurdish city of Halabja, Saddam Hussein unleashed his stockpile of chemical weapons on the civilians of Halabja; untold numbers were killed. Except for a few stories in the Western press, the full story of the massacre at Halabja remains a well-kept secret. One source on the Iran-Iraq War reports, "Four major battles were fought from April to August 1988, in which the Iraqis routed or defeated the Iranians. In the first offensive, named Blessed Ramadan, Iraqi Republican Guard and regular Army units recaptured the al-Faw peninsula. The 36-hour battle was conducted in a militarily sophisticated manner with two main thrusts, supported by heliborne and amphibious landings, and low-level fixed-wing attack sorties. In this battle, the Iraqis effectively used chemical weapons, using nerve and blister agents against Iranian command and control facilities, artillery positions, and logistics points." This battle and three subsequent pushes to quickly end the war resulted in 375,000 Iraqi casualties and 60,000 POWs. Still, Iraq had plunged deep into Iran, and effectively finished the Iranians' chances of winning the war outright. Later that year, both nations signed a United Nations–brokered cease-fire. One of the oversight missions set up under this cease-fire was the United Nations Iran-Iraq Military Observer Group (UNIIMOG), set up in August 1988 under the command of General Slavko Jovic of Yugoslavia, with 350 officers from 24 nations.

Saddam Hussein passed off a bloody war and eventual stalemate as victory. In a parade honoring returning war veterans, he led the procession on a white horse, symbolizing victory. In Baghdad he erected the Arch of Swords—two huge arms, modeled after his own but 48 times normal size, embracing touching swords—out of armor and helmets captured from slaughtered Iranians. At the foot of the monument is a cascade of Iranian helmets. Author Simon Henderson relates of another monolith, "The Martyrs' Memorial in Baghdad consists of two glazed blue domes, parted and offset to symbolize the course to heaven along which the spirits of all Muslim martyrs are said to travel. Constructed in an open area to imitate other famous monuments from Iraq's history, such as ziggurats and the spiral minaret at Samarra, the monument is over 180 feet wide and 130 feet high. It took more than two years to build and was completed in 1983." Along the shores of the Iraqi side of the Shatt al-Arab are statues of 99 Iraqi commanders killed during the war, their accusing fingers pointed at Iran.

One of the main arguments Saddam Hussein used for his invasion of Kuwait in 1990 was that with the Iran-Iraq War he saved the Gulf states from a horrible fate at the hands of Iran. Discussing the Iraqi argument, Middle East scholar Walid Khalidi writes, "At horrendous cost in Iraqi lives (Saddam's favorite phrase in Arabic is *anhar al-damn,* 'rivers of blood') and material assets, he, Saddam, blocked al-bawwabah al-sharqiyyah, 'the Eastern Gateway' to the Arab world in the face of Khomeini's hordes. It is this that saved the other Gulf states, notably Kuwait, from certain ruin." However, Saddam Hussein refused to acknowledge the dangerous fact that it was Kuwait, more than any other country, that kept Iraq afloat during the war through the exportation of Iraqi oil in Kuwaiti tankers.

In the end, Iran refused to play a role in the Persian Gulf War, for whatever reason, although it condemned both the Iraqi invasion of Kuwait and the subsequent buildup of American troops in Saudi Arabia. However, did Iran arm the Sunni Muslims in Iraq, who rose up at the end of the war to do battle with Saddam Hussein's troops during the massacres in the marshes of Basra? There is no evidence of this at this time. Obviously, Iran has yet to recover from the Iran-Iraq War, and may not do so until well into the twenty-first century.

The outlook for relations between Iran and Iraq as of this writing are impossible to predict. Although considered mortal enemies because of the costly war the two fought, there have been overtures in recent years, particularly at the height of Operation Desert Shield in September 1990, when Iraqi foreign minister Aziz flew to Teheran to meet with his counterpart, Ali Akbar Velayati, to discuss ways in which the Iranians could help the Iraqis circumvent the world embargo. The following day, the two countries restored full diplomatic relations. However, during the air war, although Iraqi planes flew to safety in Iran, Iran has so far refused to return them.

See also Algiers Agreement of 6 March 1975; Iran; Iraq; Persian Gulf; Shatt al-Arab Waterway.
References: *Conduct of the Persian Gulf War: Final Report to Congress,* Report by the Department of Defense, April 1992, 9; Henderson, Simon, *Instant Empire: Saddam Hussein's Ambition for Iraq* (San Francisco: Mercury House, 1991); Khalidi, Walid, "Iraq vs. Kuwait: Claims and Counterclaims," in *The Gulf War Reader: History, Documents, Opinions,* edited by Micah L. Sifry and Christopher Serf (New York: Times Books, 1991), 60; al-Khalil, Samir, *Republic of Fear: The Inside Story of Saddam's Iraq* (New York: Pantheon, 1990), 269; Krosney, Herbert, *Deadly Business: Legal Deals and Outlaw*

Weapons—The Arming of Iran and Iraq, 1975 to the Present (New York: Four Walls Eight Windows, 1993), 124; Pelletiere, Stephen C., and Douglas V. Johnson II, *Lessons Learned: The Iran-Iraq War* (Carlisle Barracks, PA: U.S. Army War College Strategic Studies Institute, 1991), vii.

Iraq

At 168,927 square miles (437,522 sq km), Iraq is the third largest nation in size (behind Saudi Arabia and Iran) in the Middle East, and at one time had one of the ten largest standing armies in the world. Because of its strategic position in the Middle East, it played an integral part in the shaping of politics in the region. The Persian Gulf War may have been inevitable because of Iraq's history, its current political situation, and the ego of its leader, Saddam Hussein.

Modern Iraq sits on the location of Mesopotamia, the "land between the rivers." Those rivers, the Tigris and the Euphrates, were and are two of the most vital and important waterways in the area. Approximately 1,200 miles (1,931 km) long, the Tigris is fed by the Diyala and the Greater and Lesser Zab rivers, while the Euphrates, whose main tributaries are the Balikh and Khabur rivers, saw the building of the great cities of Nippur and Ur along its banks. Both rivers are used for transportation, trade, energy, and sustenance. Recent discoveries at Nippur, the religious center of Mesopotamia, show that the people who lived there about 8,000 years ago believed that Enlil, the wind god and supreme deity, created man in that city. Iraq is also on the Fertile Crescent, that area of the Middle East where Egyptian and Sumerian culture thrived from the end of the Stone Age to the beginning of the Golden Age of Greece.

After the Muslim conquest of Mesopotamia in the seventh century, the Abassids established a caliphate with Damascus as their capital. The Abassids were a dynasty of caliphs (successors to Muhammad) who ruled the entire Islamic empire from 750 until the Mongol conquest of the Middle East in 1258. The dynasty takes it name from its ancestor *al-Abbas,* the uncle of the prophet Muhammad. In 750 the Abbasids defeated the Umayyad dynasty and shifted the capital of the caliphate from Damascus to Baghdad, thereby moving the empire's center and changing its main sphere of influence from what is now Syria to Iraq. The Abbasid caliphate affirmed the theocratic idea of the caliph as supreme leader and faithfulness to orthodox Islam as the foundation of harmony and supremacy in the empire. Thus, because of the Abassids, Baghdad, now the Iraqi capital, became one of the region's most important centers of trade, learning, and the arts. By 1638 the city was incorporated into the Ottoman Empire, and it remained a parcel that belonged to the "sick man of Europe" until after World War I. Military authority John Keegan writes, "Between the death of Timur the Lame (also known as Tamerlane, c. 1336–1405) in 1405 and 1831, Iraq was successively conquered by two Turcoman confederations, the Kara Koyunlu ("Black Sheep") and the Ak Koyunlu ("White Sheep"), by the Safavid dynasty of Iran, by the Ottoman Turks, by the Persians again, and finally by the Ottomans in 1638 after two unsuccessful invasions."

Because of Great Britain's influence in the region before, during, and after World War I, Iraq became part of the British mandate during the Versailles Peace Conference, and it remained so until its independence was declared in 1932. This British influence became a major factor in how the area was controlled. In 1920 some Arabs in Mosul revolted against British rule; their rebellion, *Ath Thawra al Iraqiyya al Kubra* (The Great Iraqi Revolution), was put down with British fighter planes and troops from Iran and India. This unsuccessful insurrection was later duplicated by the Kurds after the Persian Gulf War. To calm the potential for further strife, in 1921 the British installed Faisal, the former leader of Syria who had been driven out of his homeland by the French, as the first king of Iraq. According to Middle East writer Phebe Marr, "On 11 July 1921, under [Sir Percy] Cox's persuasion, the Iraqi Council of State passed a unanimous resolution declaring Faisal of Syria King. He was installed 27 August 1921."

The following year the Anglo-Iraqi Treaty was signed by Faisal and Cox, allowing for British control of Iraqi affairs. The 1923 Treaty of Uqair established the boundaries of Kuwait, Iraq, and Saudi Arabia, while the Treaty of Lausanne, enacted the same year, gave Turkey a share of Iraq's northern border. Two years later, oil was discovered in Iraq. This commodity would change the fortunes of almost every Middle Eastern nation. In 1932, under British sponsor-

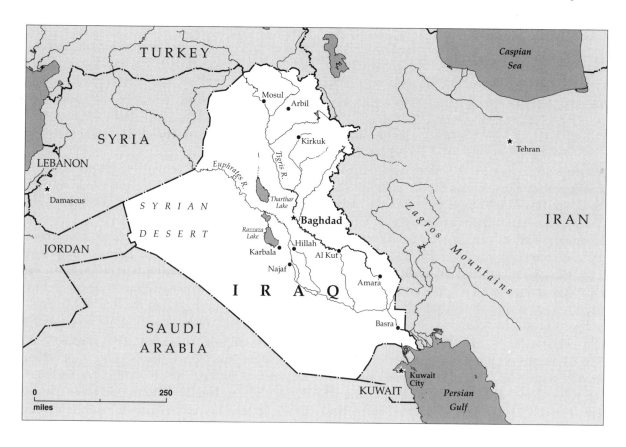

ship, Iraq became a member of the League of Nations, the first Arab nation to do so. The following year King Faisal died, to be replaced by his son King Ghazi. Although Ghazi seemed to stabilize the country, in 1936 Bakr Sidqi, a military officer, launched a military coup and deposed Prime Minister Yassin al-Hashemi. Bakr Sidqi would be assassinated by dissatisfied members of his own military that same year. It was at this time, about April 1937, that Saddam Hussein—who would play the most important role in twentieth-century Iraq—was born near the small northern Iraqi town of Tikrit.

Like other Iraqi leaders who followed him, Bakr Sidqi took total control of the government apparatus, which in turn led to his assassination in August 1937 by a group of disaffected army officers. The return of King Ghazi was followed by his death in a car accident in 1939, and he was succeeded by a series of despotic and monarchical leaders. In Iraq the periods before and immediately after World War II were noted for the increase in pan-Arabist thought, which led the way for the founding of the Iraqi wing of the Syrian Ba'athist party, originally founded by Syrian Michel Aflaq. Iraqi pan-Arabism was fostered by educator Sati al-Husri. Iraq authorities

Marion Farouk-Sluglett and Peter Sluglett write, "In broad terms al-Husri developed a new form of Arab nationalism, which held that although the Arab countries had been liberated from Ottoman rule, the post-war situation in the Arab world simply amounted to the substitution of one form of control for another, and that the Arab world was essentially a single geopolitical entity, which had been divided artificially and arbitrarily by the Western powers after the First World War." Part of this philosophy, embraced by Saddam Hussein, holds that Kuwait was a natural part of Iraq and, as such, both "nations" should be reunited. In January 1948 student riots broke out over the signing of the Portsmouth Treaty, which gave Great Britain control over Iraqi military bases in time of war. Again, the issue of self-determination came to the forefront of Iraqi domestic affairs.

In 1952 Iraq officially announced for the first time that Kuwait was a part of Iraq, but Great Britain forestalled any attempt at union when it warned the Iraqis that the British agreement with Kuwait would compel them to come to Kuwait's defense. For the next decade, the issue remained dormant. In that time, Iraq became a signatory of the Pact of Mutual Cooperation (the so-called Baghdad Pact) with Turkey, and stability appeared to envelop the country. Then, on 14 July 1958, a group of Communists and military officers called the Free Officers, who were followers of Egypt's strong pan-Arabist leader Gamel Abdel Nasser and were led by Iraqi military officer Abdul-Karim Qassem, overthrew the pro-British government in a bloodless coup. Qassem's strong pan-Arabist thinking led him to proclaim that Kuwait was a part of Iraq. This event, in June 1961, took place in the same month that Great Britain declared Kuwait an independent nation and free of British control. Qassem's announcement led to British and Arab League troops being sent to Kuwait, the first (but not the last) time that Kuwait would need to be defended from a potential outside attack or to drive out hostile invaders.

In February 1963, Iraqi Ba'athists dissatisfied with Qassem's administration staged a bloody coup in which 10,000 people were killed in the first week alone. Although the Ba'athists gained power, it was a tenuous hold, and in November, Abd al-Salaam Aref (1920–1966), a military officer, overthrew the Ba'athist regime in a bloodless coup. The following October, the Ba'athists tried to regain power but failed. A young revolutionary, Saddam Hussein, was arrested as one of the plotters, convicted, and spent two years in prison. In 1968 the Ba'athists again staged a coup, regaining the power that they hold to this day. Led by military officer Ahmad Hassan al-Bakr, who was named president, the Ba'athists chose the young Saddam Hussein as assistant general secretary of the Ba'ath party.

Under al-Bakr's regime, which lasted until 1979, Iraq signed a defense pact with Syria and a treaty of friendship with the Soviet Union, which began to pump millions of dollars' worth of arms into the country. Like his predecessors, al-Bakr saw Kuwait as part of Iraq, and in 1972 started a small crisis when Iraqi construction crews began building a road 2 miles inside Kuwait at the site of a village called Samita, or al-Samita. In March of the next year, the al-Bakr government submitted a pact in which Iraq would have the right to drill for oil inside Kuwait, particularly at the disputed Rumailia oilfield (which both countries share and at the same time claim whole ownership of), and establish oil export facilities. Kuwait refused to sign such a treaty, and the crisis began to build. Later in the

month of March 1973, Kuwait ordered its soldiers to halt Iraqi construction at Samita and expel the interlopers. The Iraqis resisted, and the shooting incident that followed left two Kuwaitis and one Iraqi dead. Syrian foreign minister Abdel Halim Khaddam and Arab League secretary Mahmoud Riad began intensive negotiations to settle the dispute, mediation that led to the early April 1973 retreat by Iraqi troops. A joint Iraqi-Kuwaiti committee was eventually set up in 1977 to resolve the border problems arising from the Samita incident.

In 1975 Iraq signed the Algiers Agreement with its longtime rival, Iran. Because Iraq does not have a major deepwater port, it must rely on the Shatt al-Arab waterway, which is owned by Iran. Consistently, Iraq claimed that the Shatt al-Arab was a part of Iraq and should be returned to its sovereignty. Iran disagreed. Further tensions were highlighted by Iranian support of Kurdish guerrillas inside Iraq. The Algiers Agreement, signed by Saddam Hussein (who at this time was the vice-chairman of the Revolutionary Command Council [RCC]) and the shah of Iran, allowed Iraq to have a small piece of the Shatt al-Arab while relinquishing the rest as Iranian territory; in exchange, Iranian support of the Kurds would end. Iraq also expelled the Ayatollah Ruhollah Khomeini, an Iranian cleric and fundamentalist Muslim who had been in exile in Iraq for several years.

In 1979 the Islamic Revolution broke out in Iran, leading to major instability in the area. Saddam Hussein, who became the RCC's leader that same year after pushing aside an ailing al-Bakr, saw such instability as a chance to grab the Shatt al-Arab for Iraq. Publicly, however, he showed a different face. In February 1980, in his "National Covenant" speech, he renounced "the use of force by any Arab country against another and the resolution of all inter-Arab disputes by peaceful means." In the meantime, he began a crackdown on Shiite Muslims sympathetic to Iran. He abrogated the Algiers Agreement on 7 September, and three weeks later Iraqi troops invaded Iran.

The Iran-Iraq War was possibly the bloodiest twentieth-century conflict, with uncounted tens of thousands, and perhaps upward of one million, dead on both sides, both military and civilian. On paper, the war changed Iraq; no longer was it the economic powerhouse it had been before the war; it had to depend on its neighbors, particularly the Gulf states, for monetary sustenance. Before the Persian Gulf War, modern-day Iraq was both a military and a police state, one of the most extreme in both cases in the world, and remains so even after the Gulf conflict. According to the U.S. Defense Department's *Final Report to Congress* on the Gulf War, "Iraq's 1990 military budget was $12.9 billion, or approximately *$700 per citizen* [author's emphasis] in a country where the average annual income was $1,950. By mid-1990, Iraq had only enough cash reserves for three months of imports and an inflation rate of 40 percent." Much of this spending on arms (which came from both the Soviet Union and the West, including Germany, France, and the United States) was financed by loans from lender nations and short-term credits from both world banks, including those of the Persian Gulf states, especially Kuwait. Iraq demanded that they be written off after the end of the Iran-Iraq War, but they weren't, and these creditors demanded payment. This boxed in Iraq, and pushed them toward the 2 August 1990 invasion of Kuwait.

Through the use of terror, primarily secret police agencies, Saddam Hussein keeps a firm grip over the majority of Iraqi society. These agencies include the General Intelligence Department (GID), a segment of the Ba'ath party; the *Amn,* or Government Security Service, which is in control of criminal administration and prosecution; the Military Intelligence Department (MID), which oversees the military's loyalty to the regime; and the *Amn al-Khas* (Special Security [SS]), which is responsible for protecting Saddam Hussein himself. The latter agency was developed in 1985 during the height of the Iran-Iraq War to replace a presidential sentry after the Republican Guard was sent to the front to strengthen the frontline units.

Is it possible for Iraq to once again be accepted by the Arab world's leadership? Yes, declares British journalist Julie Flint. "The new fear of Iraq is dramatically illustrated in Saudi Arabia, where the editor of the weekly *al-Majalla . . .* was earlier this month [January 1993] one of the first Arab journalists to consider the possibility of a reconciliation between the Gulf [states] and Saddam's Iraq. . . . After Iraq's raids into the 'buffer zone' with Kuwait, *al-Majalla* argued that the high-risk operation to recover a few medium

range missiles demonstrated the depletion of Baghdad's main arsenal and asked: 'Can we still talk about forgiveness?' Its answer was an unqualified yes. 'Iraq the invader is gone for years to come.' "

Of Iraq's ethnic groups, Arabs make up 75 percent, while ethnic Kurds, mainly in the northern part of the country, comprise 15–20 percent. The country's main cities, besides Baghdad, include Mosul, Irbil, An Najaf, and Basra.

_____

See also Ba'ath Party; Baghdad; Basra; Hussein al-Tikriti, Saddam; Iran-Iraq War; Mosul.
References: Conduct of the Persian Gulf War: Final Report to Congress, Report by the U.S. Department of Defense, April 1992, 5–6; Dunnigan, James F., and Austin Bay, *From Shield to Storm: High-Tech Weapons, Military Strategy, and Coalition Warfare in the Persian Gulf* (New York: William Morrow, 1992), 103; Farouk-Sluglett, Marion, and Peter Sluglett, *Iraq since 1958: From Revolution to Dictatorship* (London: I. B. Tauris, 1990), 19; Flint, Julie, "The Lion and the Wolf," *The New Statesman & New Society,* 22 January 1993, 16; *Iraq: Background Notes* (Washington, DC: U.S. Department of State Bureau of Public Affairs, 1982); Keegan, John, *World Armies* (Detroit: Gale, 1983), 283; Marr, Phebe, *The Modern History of Iraq* (Boulder, CO: Westview, 1985); Metz, Helen Chapman, ed., *Iraq: A Country Study* (Washington, DC: GPO, 1990).

Iraq, Claims on Kuwait by

Several times since 1937 Iraq has claimed that Kuwait is in fact its nineteenth province. This point was driven home with the 2 August 1990 invasion.

Authors Judith Miller and Laurie Mylroie write, "Tensions between Kuwait and Iraq are deeply rooted in history, geography and ideology, not to mention dramatic differences in culture and style. In the weeks [after] the invasion of Kuwait, the *Baghdad Observer,* the regime's English-language newspaper, [ran] almost daily articles on the historical underpinnings of Iraq's claim to Kuwait. One report in August [1990], for example, dated an Iraqi presence there to the second millennium B.C., thanks to the discovery of a clay statue on the Kuwaiti island of Feilaka that bears a resemblance to the Assyrian kings. A second 'proof,' the paper argued, was the fact that Kuwait is listed on eighth-century maps as one of the Arab army headquarters of the Iraqi city of Basra." The authors of an article that appeared in the *Congressional Digest* in March 1991 stated that after its declaration of independence in 1932, "nationalist sentiment in Iraq was opposed to the creation of a separate Kuwaiti state; however, as long as Iraq remained under varying degrees of British influence, it rarely pressed claims to Kuwait. In 1937, King Ghazi advocated the absorption of Kuwait into Iraq and criticized the ruler of Kuwait as an outdated feudal monarch. Again, in 1958, Iraqi prime minister Nuri as-Said invited Kuwait to join a short-lived federation which had just been concluded between the two monarchies of Iraq and Jordan. Both proposals were abandoned in the face of British opposition."

References: Miller, Judith, and Laurie Mylroie, *Saddam Hussein and the Crisis in the Gulf* (New York: Times Books, 1990), 194; "Recent Iraqi Claims on Kuwait," *Congressional Digest* 70:3 (March 1991), 72.

Iraq, Purported Atrocities in Kuwait by. *See* Atrocities, Iraqi.

Iraq, Supplying Arms to

Did the Reagan and Bush Administrations secretly funnel, or allow to be funneled, armaments to Iraq in the 1980s? That is the premise of journalist Alan Friedman in his book *Spider's Web: The Secret History of How the White House Illegally Armed Iraq.* Yet was such supplying the policy of the Western powers, or was a blind eye turned for profit and to stop Iran?

Among the important military complexes constructed with the aid of Western technology was Zaafaraniya, about 8 miles north of Baghdad. According to the *New York Times*, "The precision equipment [at Zaafaraniya] had been made by Matrix Churchill, according to Gary Milhollin, an expert on nuclear proliferation. Matrix Churchill has offices in London and Ohio that procured military technology for Iraq. British intelligence services have acknowledged they were aware of Matrix Churchill's role, saying the company was allowed to operate to help them keep tabs on Iraq's weapons program. Mr. Milhollin also said that sophisticated machinery

made by German companies was found in the complex: a large milling machine made by Schwäbische Hüttenwerke and a lathe made by Dorries." On 25 November 1991, *U.S. News & World Report* cataloged some of the firms that supplied Iraq between 1984 and 1990, all with the help of licenses issued by the U.S. Department of Commerce. Included in the group are Canberra Industries Inc. of Meriden, Connecticut, which sold Iraq $26,567 worth of computer equipment to measure neutrons; Carl Zeiss of Thornwood, New York, which sold $104,545 worth of computer equipment for the measurement and calculation of photographic data; Databit Inc. of Hauppauge, New York, which sold $4 million worth of circuit switches for data transmission; Forney International Inc. of Carrolton, Texas, which sold computer equipment to be used in the al-Musayyib thermal power station, located southeast of Baghdad; and Hewlett-Packard of Palo Alto, California, which sold Iraq $3.1 million worth of "computer equipment, frequency synthesizers, calibration equipment, optical fiber cables, and precision electronic and photo equipment."

See also Appendix 1, Tanks and Armored Vehicles Sold to Iraq in the 1980s.
References: Friedman, Alan, *Spider's Web: The Secret History of How the White House Secretly Armed Iraq* (New York: Bantam, 1991); Gordon, Michael R., "Jets Bomb Iraq Again; U.S. Admits Hitting Hotel," *New York Times*, 19 January 1993, A8; Hedges, Stephen J., et al., "Saddam's Secret Bomb," *U.S. News & World Report*, 25 November 1991, 36.

Iraq Sanctions Act of 1990 (104 Stat. 2047)

See Appendix 4, Iraq Sanctions Act of 1990, 5 November 1990.

Iraqi-Soviet Relations

The issue of how the Soviets viewed Iraq's invasion of Kuwait was always a concern to the coalition, yet through hard work the United States was able to keep the Soviets out of the crisis militarily. From the high point of its 15-year treaty of friendship in 1972 to Moscow demanding that Iraq release Soviet citizens that it was holding as human shields, the Iraqi-Soviet relationship has been a rocky one.

Previous to 1972, Iraq counted mostly on aid from Britain, or was a semi-independent state. Russia's involvement in the area came from the signing of the Sykes-Picot-Sazanov agreement of 1916, allowing Russian influence in the Middle East, but which was preempted by the Bolshevik Revolution. For the next 50 years, Russian, and then Soviet, influence was almost nonexistent. Finally, with the ascendance to power of Ba'athist rule in Iraq in the 1960s, the attitude toward the Soviets changed. The editors of the important work *Iraq: A Country Study*, report, "In 1972 the Ba'athist regime signed a Treaty of Friendship and Cooperation with the Soviet Union. Article 1 stated that the treaty's objective was to develop broad cooperation between Iraq and the Soviet Union in economic, trade, scientific, technical, and other fields on the basis of 'respect for sovereignty territorial integrity and non-interference in one another's internal affairs.'" Six years later, Iraq initiated an arrangement with the Soviet Union in which the USSR sold them 138 MiG-23 and MiG-27 fighter/bombers, Scud missile launchers, troop and equipment transports, and MI8 transport helicopters worth an estimated $3 billion. This formed the basis of the buildup of Iraq's powerful military.

The Iran-Iraq War presented Iraq with a grand opportunity: Continue its cozy relationship with the Soviets, while reaching out to the United States. At the same time, Iran, a mortal enemy of communism, embraced some aspects of the Soviet program. As did the United States, the Soviets played both sides of the Persian Gulf street. By 1987 Iraq owed Moscow in excess of $5 billion (U.S.).

On 2 August 1990, when Iraq invaded Kuwait, the Soviet Union had 8,364 workers and other personnel and their families in the Persian Gulf (7,830 in Iraq, and 534 in Kuwait). On that same day, the Soviet government announced the cessation of its arms fulfillment to Iraq. The next day, both the United States and the Soviet Union mutually procured a pledge from the international community to end all arms shipments to Iraq.

Although taking the side of the coalition in the matter of the invasion because of their close friendship with Iraq, the Soviets made sure not to station troops in the Gulf area. However, they dispatched four ships to the area to oversee coalition operations, including the Udaloy-class destroyer *Admiral Tributs,* a missile destroyer, a frigate, and an Amur-class repair ship, and the Soviet leadership took the lead in trying to negotiate a peaceful end to the crisis. President Mikhail Gorbachev, Foreign Minister Eduard Shevardnadze (later replaced by Alexandr Bessmertnykh), and Middle East envoy Yevgeni Primakov all played key roles in attempting to get Iraq to withdraw peacefully from Kuwait. Gorbachev met with President George Bush in Helsinki, Finland, in September 1990 to confer on the Gulf situation, and Secretary of State James Baker met Foreign Minister Bessmertnykh in Moscow in late January 1991. After the beginning of the air war on 16 January, the Soviets played a minor role in the crisis, attempting through the machinations of envoy Primakov to get the Iraqis to remove their troops from Kuwait—all to no avail.

In the five years since the end of the war, the Soviets have tried to get the UN Security Council to lift economic sanctions against Iraq on the pretense that the profits from the sale of Iraqi oil would be used to pay off the debt Iraq owes the Russians.

See also Bessmertnykh, Aleksandr Aleksandrovich; Gorbachev, Mikhail Sergeivich; Primakov, Yevgeni Maksimovich; Sazanov, Sergei Dmitryevich; Shevardnadze, Eduard Amvrosiyevich.
Reference: Metz, Helen Chapman, ed., *Iraq: A Country Study* (Washington, DC: GPO, 1990), 203.

Israel

When Saddam Hussein attempted to link his possible pullout from Kuwait with the Israeli withdrawal from the West Bank and Gaza Strip, and when he fired Scuds at the Jewish state to get it militarily involved in the Persian Gulf War, he used a calculated strategy that the union of nations arrayed against him would fracture. With Israeli enemies Syria, Saudi Arabia, and Turkey in the Allied front, the entrance of Israel into the fray would no doubt have caused a rupture in the alliance.

Modern-day Israel sits on some of the holiest land in the Middle East. First colonized by unknown settlers about 7000 B.C., the area was later taken over by the Jebusites. David captured

Israeli rescue workers search through rubble in Tel Aviv for survivors of an Iraqi Scud missile attack in February 1991.

what is now Jerusalem and called it Zion, which translates into the "City of God," and established the workings of old Israel's government and military administration. Forced by a great famine to depart for Egypt, the Israelites soon became slaves in their new land, and it took the machinations of Moses to lead his people back to Israel. He stood upon Mount Sinai and accepted from God the Ten Commandments, the basis of the Torah (Judaic law) and the essential foundation and tenets that make up Christianity's basic beliefs. Although the Israelites eventually took back their homeland, they soon were forced to confront the Romans, who had designs of a great empire. The Israelites twice rose up in unsuccessful revolt against their new oppressors; the final insurrection caused the Roman destruction of Jerusalem and the alteration of its name to Aeolia Capitolina. Scattered to the far corners of the world, the former Israelites, now called Jews, wanted to return to their home. This formed the basis of the Diaspora (dispersal), the goal of the Jews being to one day return and re-create Israel.

Thus the dream of a Jewish state was the ultimate design of Zionists (those wanting to establish a Jewish homeland in Israel), a group of Jew-ish intellectuals who assembled in the last years of the nineteenth century. They were led by Hungarian writer Theodore Herzl and Russian chemist Dr. Chaim Weizmann, and spurred into action by the pogroms (anti-Jewish murders and rampages) in Russia and the notorious anti-Semitic trial of French captain Alfred Dreyfus. Herzl's book, *The Jewish State* (1896), led to the beginnings of Jewish emigration from Europe to the area then called Palestine, populated mainly by Palestinian Arabs. Over time, the population of Jews, while small compared to the Palestinians, grew. In 1917 British foreign secretary Arthur Balfour declared that the British government approved of the formation in Palestine of "a National Home for the Jewish people." The Balfour Declaration led the League of Nations to establish the British mandate of Palestine in 1920. Over the next 28 years, during the worst years of the Nazi Holocaust, Jewish emigration picked up, to the detriment of the Arabs in Palestine. Before the end of World War II, East European Jewish terrorists formed units, including the Stern gang and the Irgun Zvau Leumi (National Miltary Organization), which brought violence home to the British troops in Palestine.

Some of the leaders of this group included Menachem Begin and Yitzhak Yzernitzky, who later took the name Shamir. The group's efforts to destroy British resolve to remain an active participant in the fate of Palestine led to decisions by the British government in May 1948 to withdraw from the area, end the British mandate, and partition the area into Jewish and Arab quarters.

At the same moment that David Ben-Gurion was declaring the existence of an Israeli state, the armies of five Arab nations—Egypt, Iraq, Lebanon, Syria, and Transjordan—attacked the small state with all their might. Israel clearly bettered the Arabs on the battlefield. The war's ultimate conclusion, in January 1949, established a ceasefire and diplomatic recognition of Israel from the United States, the Soviet Union, and many other countries. In May 1949 Israel was admitted into the United Nations.

From 1948 until 1973, Israel struggled in four hard-fought wars with its Arab neighbors, including Egypt, Jordan, Syria, and Iraq. In 1981 it attacked Iraq's Osirak nuclear power plant after Israeli intelligence surmised that Saddam Hussein might have a nuclear weapon within several months. Although Israel again clashed with Syria during the Lebanese invasion in 1982, by 1990

only Iraq remained as a major military enemy. (Iran is also considered a major enemy, but its tactics are more terroristic in style.) Israeli intelligence had more information on Iraqi troop movements and were able to surmise Saddam Hussein's intentions well before any Western governments. Israeli authors Dan Raviv and Yossi Melman relate: "Israel had repeatedly warned the United States about Iraq, but hardly anyone in Washington had seemed to be listening. Only a week before the invasion [Israeli] Defense Minister Moshe Arens gave Pentagon officials the latest Israeli intelligence estimate, and its prediction of an Iraqi military move into Kuwait proved prophetic. The truth is, however, that Arens did not push the point. It was not a matter of high priority, in part because it was classically good for Israel when two Arab countries battled each other."

In an interview on 27 December 1990, Saddam Hussein broadcast his intentions concerning Israel if a war broke out: "If aggression were to take place, we should assume that Israel has taken part in it. Therefore, without asking any questions we will strike at Israel. If the first strike is dealt to Baghdad or the front, the second strike will target Tel Aviv," he warned. When the war

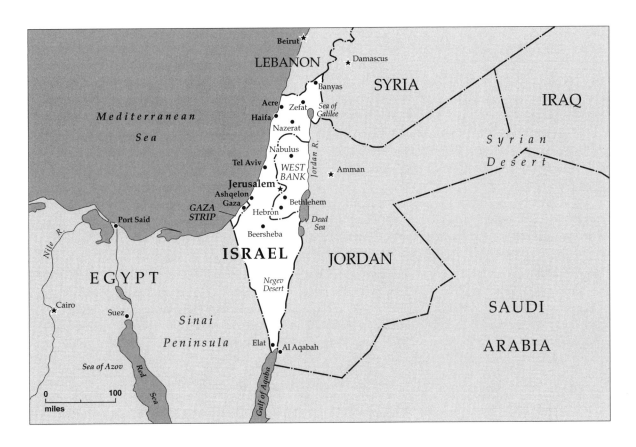

broke out, Saddam Hussein carried out his threat by shooting off Scuds at civilian population centers in Israel. Several deaths and minor damage resulted, and it took incredible restraint for Israel not to become involved in the war. Patriot missile batteries sent by the United States warded off later Scud attacks.

In the end, Israel never became involved in the war, and may have benefited highly from its passive stance. Middle East expert Dr. Shibley Telhami wrote, "The Persian Gulf War and the decline of the Soviet Union left Israel in a superbly advantageous position: Much of the military machinery of Iraq, Israel's most powerful Arab adversary, was destroyed; the Arab world was divided and confused; and the inheritors of the Soviet empire were no longer in a position to offer an alternative to the United States." With the election of Yitzhak Rabin as prime minister in 1992, Israel set out on a course of peacemak-

ing, which led to peace agreements with the Palestine Liberation Organization (PLO) and Jordan. In 1994 these efforts resulted in a Nobel Peace Prize for Rabin and Foreign Minister Shimon Peres, shared with Yasir Arafat.

————

See also Arafat, Yasir; Palestine Liberation Organization; Shamir, Yitzhak.
References: "Israel's 40-Year Quandary," *Congressional Quarterly's Editorial Research Reports* 1:14 (15 April 1988), 192–193; Raviv, Dan, and Yossi Melman, *Every Spy a Prince: The Complete History of Israel's Intelligence Community* (Boston: Houghton Mifflin, 1990), 425; Telhami, Shibley, "Israeli Foreign Policy after the Gulf War," *Middle East Policy* 1:2 (1992), 192–193.

Italy
See Coalition Nations, Contributions of.

Jaguar. *See* Sepecat Jaguar.

Japan

See Coalition Nations, Contributions of.

Jianjiji-6 (J-6)

This Chinese fighter aircraft, also known as Fighter Aircraft 6, was one of the staples of the Iraqi air force. It is assumed that those that were not destroyed fled to Iran.

A duplicate of the Mikoyan Gureyan (MiG-19) Soviet fighter, the J-6 is also classified the Farmer-C (MiG-19SF variant) and Farmer-D (MiG-19PF variant) by NATO. Originally built in the Soviet Union, the craft was copied after relations between the Soviets and Chinese broke down in the 1960s. This single-seat fighter is considered an important tool in fighter attack and tactical reconnaisance missions. Powered by two Shenyang Wopen-6 turbojets, the J-6 has a wingspan of 20 feet 2.25 inches (6.15 m), can travel at a maximum ceiling of 58,725 feet (17,900 m), and has a maximum unrefueled range of 863 miles (685 km) without external fuel tanks.

See also Jianjiji-7.
Reference: Taylor, John W. R., ed., *Jane's All the World's Aircraft, 1986–87* (London: Jane's Information Group, 1986), 39–40.

Jianjiji-7 (J-7)

A single-seat Chinese version of the MiG-21F Fishbed (NATO gives this fighter the same designation), the Jianjiji-7, or Fighter Aircraft 7, was part of the Iraqi air force's squadron of close air support and air superiority fighters. Because so few Iraqi aircraft were shot down, it is impossible to know whether Iraq's J-7s were destroyed on the ground or simply fled to Iran.

According to *Jane's All the World's Aircraft,* the variant supplied to Iraq (as well as to Egypt when it was a client of Soviet and Chinese armaments) was the J-7B, an export version of the Chinese People's Liberation Army force craft J-7 I, which had a limited run because of an inadequate escape system. Armed with two 30 mm belt-fed cannons (with pods to carry various types of Soviet-type missiles, including the PL-2, PL-5B, or a Matra R.550), the J-7 is powered by a single Chengdu WP7B(BM) turbojet. It has a wingspan of 23 feet 5.625 inches (7.154 m), a maximum speed of Mach 2.05 (1,350 mph; 2,172 km/h), a service ceiling of 59,710 feet (18,200 m), and an unrefueled range (with three external drop tanks) of 1,081 miles (1,740 km).

See also Jianjiji-6.
Reference: Lambert, Mark, ed., *Jane's All the World's Aircraft, 1991–92* (Coulsdon, Surrey, UK: Jane's Information Group, 1991), 33–34.

Jihad

When terrorist Abu Abbas, mastermind of the *Achille Lauro* affair in 1985, called for a "jihad" against the coalition for their attack against Iraq, he was using a well-known and highly successful technique little understood outside the Muslim world. Described by one authority on Islam as "striving on behalf of the faith; known also as the 'holy war,'" jihad has been used effectively against enemies of Islam. Islamic authority Fazlur Rahman, in his *Islam,* writes, "The Qur'an ă [Koran] calls upon believers to undertake *jihad* . . . , which is to surrender 'your properties and yourselves in the path of Allah . . . '; the purpose of which in turn is to 'establish prayer, give *zak-ată* [a rate of lending to avoid usury], command good and forbid evil'—i.e. to establish the Islamic socio-moral order." Simply put, they are armed attacks, using terroristic methods, undertaken in the name of the believer's faith. Such jihads were conducted against American forces in Lebanon

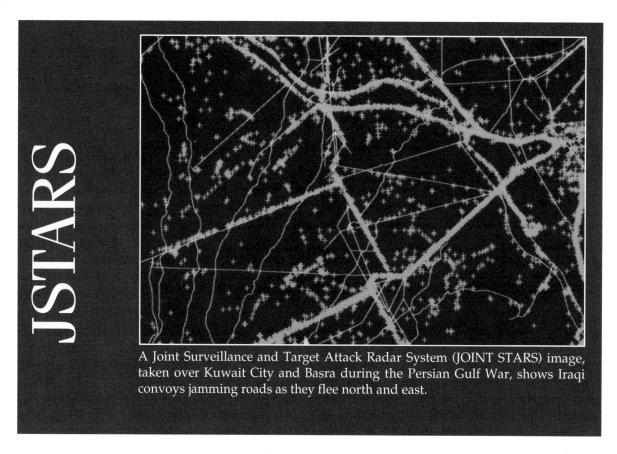

JSTARS

A Joint Surveillance and Target Attack Radar System (JOINT STARS) image, taken over Kuwait City and Basra during the Persian Gulf War, shows Iraqi convoys jamming roads as they flee north and east.

in the early 1980s, against Soviet troops in Afghanistan from 1979 to 1989, and against Israel since that nation's creation.

References: Farah, Caesar E., *Islam: Beliefs and Observances* (Hauppauge, NY: Barrons, 1987); Rahman, Fazlur, *Islam* (Chicago: University of Chicago Press, 1979).

Joint Information Bureau (JIB)

The U.S. military's *Final Report to Congress* remarks on the formation of this media outlet and authority: "To facilitate media coverage of U.S. forces in Saudi Arabia, CENTCOM [Central Command] established a Joint Information Bureau (JIB) in Dhahran and, later, another in Riyadh. Saudi Ministry of Information representatives also were located with the JIB in Dharhan, which let visiting media register with the Saudi government and the JIB at one location. The JIB coordinated with reporters and worked to arrange visits to units the reporters desired to cover. The Saudi government required that a U.S. official escort reporters visiting Saudi bases.

The CENTCOM Public Affairs Office (PAO) assumed this responsibility and provided escorts to facilitate coverage on Saudi bases and to U.S. units on the ground and sea and throughout the theater."

See also Censorship of the War, Coalition; Journalists; Media; National Media Pool.
Reference: Conduct of the Persian Gulf War: Final Report to Congress, Report by the Department of Defense, April 1992, 652.

Joint Surveillance and Target Attack Radar System (JOINT STARS or JSTARS)

The JOINT STARS system was developed in the 1980s as a means to monitor, from the sky, ground conflicts and small, slow-moving enemy aircraft with precise computerized tracking and relay mechanisms. Operating out of two Grumman E-8A/C aircraft, the system as a whole is not due to be operational until 1997. Yet during the Gulf War both planes were utilized to maximum capability and worked to perfection. The system as a whole works in two areas: the E-8A aircraft, a modified Boeing 707-300 series aircraft jam-packed with advanced radar and communications technology, is complemented with mobile ground station modules (GSMs).

The key to JOINT STARS is, as its name implies, its radar system. Housed in a 24-foot-long (7.3 m) phased array mounted under the forward fuselage in a cigar-shaped radome, the system has three operating conditions: wide-area-surveillance moving target indicator (WAS/MTI), sector-search moving target indicator (SS/MTI), and synthetic-aperture radar fixed target indicator (SAR/FTI). The first two modes detect, position, and identify slow-moving targets, while SAR/FTI generates a photographic radar image of chosen geographic sites. As part of its latter mission, the JOINT STARS aircraft were pressed into service in an attempt to locate Scud missile launchers. Working hand in hand with F-15E fighters, JOINT STARS produced images to help look for the deadly Scuds.

Because the JOINT STARS system is housed in a modified Boeing 707-320 airliner, its specifications are those of the civilian 707. Powered by four JT3D-3 turbofan engines, the plane weighs 168,000 pounds (76,204 kg) empty, with a maximum weight of 333,600 pounds (151,320 kg). Maximum speed is 600 mph (965 km/h), with a cruising speed of 550 mph (885 km/h), a service ceiling of 39,000 feet (11,885 m), and an unrefueled range of 6,000 miles (9,655 km).

References: Francillon, Rene J., *Grumman Aircraft since 1929* (Annapolis, MD: Naval Institute Press, 1989), 531; *Gulf War Air Power Survey, Volume IV: Weapons, Tactics, and Training Report and Space Report* (Washington, DC: GPO, 1993), 101.

Jordan

Once called Transjordan, this former mandate, located in the geographically strained position between Iraq and Israel, took a position against the coalition and with Iraq in the Persian Gulf crisis—a decision for which it may have paid a dear price.

Officially called *al-Mamlakah al-Urdunniyah al-Hashemiya* (the Hashemite Kingdom of Jordan), the present-day nation of Jordan is a consolida-tion of lands around Israel and Iraq that were established as the mandate of Transjordan just after World War I. Although essentially a creation of the League of Nations in the twentieth century, Jordan had the character of a nation prior to this time. Jordan originally was the land of Edom and Moab. Cities such as Petra, known as the ancient city of the rock and located in Edom; Ezion-Geber (now called Aqaba), Jordan's strategic port on the Red Sea; Mount Nebo, southwest of the Jordan Valley, where Moses glimpsed the Promised Land, are all part of modern Jordan. Peter Ryan writes, "The area which is now Jordan became largely Muslim after A.D. 636, when the Byzantine forces of the Emperor Heraclius were defeated by the Arab armies of Khalid ibn al-Walid at the battle of Yarmuk in northern Jordan. Then followed Umayyad and Abbasid rule and a short period of Seljuk rule in the late eleventh century. Parts of Jordan were then included in the Latin Kingdom established by the Crusaders in Jerusalem in 1099. After their defeat at the battle of Hittin in 1187, crusader rule was replaced by that of Saladin. After an ensuing period of Mamluk rule, the 400-year rule of the Ottomans began." The editors of *The Middle East and North Africa 1989* add, "For centuries, nothing more is heard of the country; it formed normally a part of Syria, and as such was generally governed from Egypt. From the beginning of the 16th century it was included in the Ottoman *vilayet* [administrative district] of Damascus, and remained in a condition of stagnation until the outbreak of the First World War in 1914."

While World War I raged in Europe, Sharif Hussein ibn Ali (1852? 1853? 1854?–1931), the emir of Mecca, was consolidating power in the Transjordanian area. Sharif (an Arab title meaning a descendant of the Prophet Muhammad through his daughter Fatima and her son Hassan) Hussein forged an alliance with the British and led an Arab revolt against the Ottomans with his sons Abdullah, who later served as emir of Transjordan, and Faisal, who became king of both Syria and Iraq. In 1916 Hussein was named king of the Hejaz. In return for his war against the Turks, Hussein expected the British to grant independence to his small kingdom. Instead, the British and the French carved the area into mandates, and Transjordan was created with Sharif

Hussein as titular head, but with the British in charge. After raids by the forces of King ibn Saud (who founded the neighboring nation of Saudi Arabia), Hussein abdicated in favor of his son Ali. Hussein died in Amman, now the capital of Jordan, and was buried in Jerusalem's Temple Mount. From Ali's brother, Abdullah (1882–1951), came two future leaders of Jordan: Talal (1909–1972), and Talal's son Hussein ibn Talal, the present king of Jordan. Middle East expert Fouad Ajami writes, "King Abdullah . . . was the great pragmatist of his time. He paid for it, was made the sacrificial lamb for the Arab debacle in Palestine, when he was struck down by a Palestinian assassin at the al-Aqsa mosque in Jerusalem in 1951. It was a terrible time of panic and shame. Abdullah was turned into a scapegoat for the flight of the Palestinian upper and middle classes from the land and for the incompetence of the larger Arab armies of Syria, Egypt and Iraq. When the end came for Abdullah, his grandson and political heir, Hussein, a young boy of 16, was by his grandfather's side."

Under King Hussein, Jordan has become one of the leading powers in the Middle East. Christopher Wren commented in the *New York Times*, "Hussein's success in forging a disparate population with limited resources into one of the Arab world's most literate and progressive societies prompts comparison with the failure of the wealthier, more powerful Shah of Iran to rally his people."

Jordan's position on the corner of Iraq, Syria, and Israel, however, makes it a hesitant and sometimes unwilling participant in regional affairs. When Israeli planes attacked and bombed Iraq's Osirak nuclear facility in 1981, they flew surreptitiously over Jordanian territory. Further, as the leader of a nation that has a large Palestinian population, Hussein must be careful to side with them when their interests are threatened. (His battles with Yasir Arafat in the 1970s led to the expulsion of the Palestine Liberation Organization [PLO] from Jordan.) Thus, when the crisis in the Persian Gulf exploded, it was King Hussein who tried to mediate between Iraq and the rest of the Arab world. In the end, he calculated that siding with Iraq—to which Jordan did most of its exporting, and from which it got almost all its oil—was an option preferable to sending troops against an Arab brother.

This posture, however, put him in difficulty with the West, particularly the United States, with which he had always had good relations, and which contributed a substantial amount of aid to Jordan every year. On 22 September 1990, King Hussein went on American television to plead his case and ask for understanding for his country's position. Joel Brinkley wrote in the *New York Times*, "As he has from the beginning, the King said that he did not support Iraq's seizure of Kuwait and added that 'despite its close relationship with Iraq, Jordan had no prior knowledge of or involvement in' Iraq's invasion of Kuwait. And he noted that Jordan still recognizes the Kuwaiti government; its embassy is still open there."

Because Jordan sided with Iraq, and voted with it to block UN sanctions, the American response to such "disloyalty" came quickly. On 20 March 1991 the U.S. Senate passed a bill that rescinded the annual $55 million Jordan received from the United States in military and economic aid unless the president certified that the issuance of such aid was "in the nation's national interest." As Martin Tolchin wrote in the *New York Times*, "The funds would be restored if the President certified to Congress that 'Jordan has taken steps to advance the peace process in the Middle East,' according to the bill." Although even more pressure was brought to bear, Jordan has never apologized for positioning itself against the coalition. On 26 September 1991, President Bush unfroze $21 million in military aid allocated to Jordan in fiscal year 1991, calling such aid "beneficial to the peace process in the Middle East."

See also Hussein ibn Talal, Hashemite King of Jordan.

References: Ajami, Fouad, "Stalked by the Memory of the Dead," *U.S. News & World Report*, 1 August 1994, 48; Brinkley, Joel, "Jordan's Monarch Appeals on TV to American Public," *New York Times*, 23 September 1990, A20; *The Middle East and North Africa 1989* (London: Europa, 1988), 531; "Military Aid to Jordan Is Unfrozen by Bush," *New York Times*, 27 September 1991, A9; Mostyn, Trevor, exec. ed., *The Cambridge Encyclopedia of the Middle East and North Africa* (New York: Cambridge University Press, 1988), 359; Tolchin, Martin, "Senate Backs Bill That Withholds $55 Million Aid Plan for Jordan," *New York Times*, 21 March 1991, A14; Wren, Christopher, "Man on the Spot: Sadat's Peace Becomes Hussein's Trial," *New York Times Sunday Magazine*, 8 April 1979, 19.

Journalists

The part played by the journalistic community (including television and the print media) during the Persian Gulf War set new standards and broke new ground. The growing crisis and the subsequent conflict became part of the first "television war," with moment-by-moment events captured live and immediately beamed into the living rooms of the world's viewers. When Saddam Hussein was interviewed by Dan Rather of CBS, the conversation was broadcast almost immediately for American public consumption. When Charles Jaco of CNN came on live with a report that Scud missile warning sirens were going off across the expanse of the Saudi Arabian city of Dharhan and put on a gas mask, proclaiming that he thought it was a chemical weapons attack, the world was watching the action live and could at that very moment hold its collective breath.

Journalists were not just a part of the story; at times they *were* the story. CBS's Bob Simon attempted to cross the border into Kuwait to see for himself the Iraqi troops; his arrest by the Iraqis and his subsequent imprisonment as a prisoner of war, at times threatened with death, demonstrated the potentiality of journalists making the news, instead of just reporting it. CNN's Peter Arnett became the target of international outrage when he broadcast Iraqi government responses to external events and appeared to be Saddam Hussein's spokesman. Arnett came under further fire when he backed Iraqi claims that a destroyed military target was a "baby milk factory," when intelligence had confirmed it as a military post. Elizabeth O. Colton, a reporter representing Arundel newspapers in Virginia, was approached by a battalion of Iraqi soldiers who surrendered to her, dropping their rifles and exclaiming, "No water, no eat. We want peace. George Bush good. Saddam Hussein bad." In April 1991 the *Washington Post* reported that *Newsweek* photographer Gad Gross was killed near the Iraqi city of Kirkuk by Iraqi soldiers while he was covering the Kurdish rebellion.

The reporters in Iraq before the war broke out employed the latest technology to transmit their stories. Among these was the INMARSAT, which CNN producer Robert Wiener describes as "a suitcase-sized satellite phone." The reporters came from many nations and represented many television networks, newspapers and magazines, and other media. Included in this group were Jeremy Thompson and Nigel Handcock from the British network ITN; John Simpson of the British Broadcasting Company (BBC); Mohammed Amin, cameraman for VISNEWS, an international video organization; Patrick Cockburn of the London daily *Independent*; Michael Haj, a cameraman for the British network WTN; ABC correspondent Gary Shepard, who was on the air live with Peter Jennings on ABC's "World News Tonight" when the attack began over Baghdad; and CNN reporters Christiane Amanpour, Peter Arnett, Richard Blystone, Jim Clancy, John Holliman, and Tom Mintier.

Based in Saudi Arabia were CNN's Charles Jaco, NBC's Arthur Kent (later known as the "Scud Stud" for his reporting during Scud attacks), and CBS's Bob McKeown, who was the first Western reporter to enter a liberated Kuwait City.

CNN journalist Christiane Amanpour suits up in a helmet, goggles, and gas mask for covering Operation Desert Shield in Saudi Arabia. Journalists brought an immediacy to the war with live coverage.

References: "Iraqi Troops Killed Journalist, Two Freed Companions Say," *Washington Post,* 18 April 1991, A40; Weil, Martin, "Iraqis Surrender to Reporter," *Washington Post,* 27 February 1991, A32; Wiener, Robert, *Live from Baghdad: Gathering News at Ground Zero* (New York: Doubleday, 1992), 7.

JP-233

This all-purpose weapon, whose main mission is to destroy airfield runways, was used exclusively by Great Britain during Operation Desert Storm.

Utilized solely by the Tornado GR1, the JP-233 blasts a hole in the concrete, settles into the ground, and then explodes, forming a crater that renders the runway useless. The editors of *Jane's Weapons Systems, 1988–89* state: "The weapon is designed for the high-speed, low level, simultaneous delivery of two complementary weapons—a cratering weapon to attack and render unusable runways, taxiways and grass operating strips, and an area denial weapon to pose a continuing threat to vehicles and crew engaged in airfield repair. The JP-233 weapon comprises a cratering weapon designated SG357 and an area denial weapon designated HB876."

Reference: Blake, Bernard, ed., *Jane's Weapon Systems, 1988–89* (Coulsdon, Surrey, UK: Jane's Information Group, 1988), 755.

KC-10 Extender Refueling Tanker

This military version of the civilian DC-10 aircraft flew an undetermined number of sorties during Operations Desert Shield and Desert Storm in its capacity as a refueling tanker. The craft carries six crew members (pilot, copilot, flight engineer, and three refueling crew) and is powered by three General Electric CF6-50C2 turbofan engines providing 52,500 pounds (23,814 kg) of static thrust. The plane can accommodate 36,500 gallons (138,165 liters) of fuel and, with added internal fuel bladders, an additional 18,125 gallons (68,610 liters). Maximum speed is 530 knots (610 mph; 982 km/h) and the maximum range (carrying full fuel capacity) is 3,797 nautical miles (4,370 miles; 7,032 km).

See also KC-135 Refueling Tanker.
Reference: Almond, Denise L., ed., *Desert Score: U.S. Gulf War Weapons* (Washington, DC: Carroll Publishing, 1991), 186–187.

KC-135 Refueling Tanker

This plane, in the variant KC-135Q, began service in the Gulf crisis on 21 August 1990 when nine were dispatched to Riyadh Air Force Base. According to the military report *Desert Score*, "Hundreds of American KC-135A/E/Rs supported the airlift to Saudi Arabia. During Operation Desert Storm, KC-135s and French C-135FRs refueled strike aircraft from several countries. KC-135s orbited nearer Kuwait and Iraq airspace. In one instance, a KC-135 searched for an F-117 Stealth fighter that was so low on fuel that it was in danger of flaming out. The KC-135 connected with the F-117 and dove with it from over 30,000 feet to 12,000 feet (to keep the F-117's engines from stalling) while transferring fuel."

The KC-135, related to the Boeing 707 civilian aircraft, has the capability of carrying four crew members (pilot, copilot, navigator, and fuel boom operator). The three variants—A, E, and R—are all powered by different engine designs; the A has four Pratt & Whitney J57-59W or J57-43W turbojets, the E has four Pratt & Whitney JT3D turbofan engines; and the R has four CFM International F108-CF-100 turbofan engines. The plane carries about 31,300 gallons (118,471 liters) of transferrable fuel.

See also Appendix 1, KC-10 Extender and KC-135 Missions; RC-135W Rivet Joint.
Reference: Almond, Denise L., ed., *Desert Score: U.S. Gulf War Weapons* (Washington, DC: Carroll Publishing, 1991), 190–191.

KH-11 and KH-12 Reconnaissance Satellites

Known by the nickname Keyhole, the KH-11 and KH-12 reconnaissance satellites are the most sophisticated military surveillance satellites in existence. During the Gulf War, they were used to photograph and monitor Iraqi troop movements.

Known by the Big Bird classification, the later models of the KH series differ from the earlier models in that they send back digital imaging of surveillance photographs instead of ejecting film capsules that splash down and are retrieved. One source notes that the KH-11 and KH-12 are equipped with "sensing systems and high-resolution cameras . . . to distinguish military from civilian personnel . . . [and] infrared and multispectral sensing devices [that] can locate missiles, trains and launchers by day or night, and [can] distinguish camouflage and artificial vegetation from real plants and trees. Its sideways looking radar can see through cloud cover."

Reference: Bulkeley, Rip, and Graham Spinardi, *Space Weapons: Deterrence or Delusion?* (Totowa, NJ: Barnes & Noble, 1986), 41.

KC-135 Refueling Tanker

Six carrier-based aircraft, five A-7E Corsairs and an A-6E Intruder, rendezvous with a KC-135E Stratotanker over Saudi Arabia for in-flight refueling.

al-Khalifa, Emir Sheik Isa Bin Sulman. *See* Bahrain.

Reference: Dunnigan, James F., and Austin Bay, *From Shield to Storm: High-Tech Weapons, Military Strategy, and Coalition Warfare in the Persian Gulf* (New York: Morrow, 1992), 30.

Khawr Abd-Allah

A briny channel located between Kuwait's Bubiyan Island and the Iraqi coast, the Khawr Abd-Allah was coveted by Saddam Hussein in order to permit his nation to bypass the Shatt al-Arab waterway, and thus allow Iraq to have a port on the Persian Gulf. Kuwait refused to lease Bubiyan to Iraq, and this may have been one of the reasons Saddam Hussein invaded Kuwait.

The conflict over the fate of the Khawr Abd-Allah began in August 1988, just after the end of the Iran-Iraq War. Iraqi officials met with their Kuwaiti counterparts to ask for the right to lease Bubiyan and Warba islands. Kuwait refused. Iraq demanded the lease of the islands twice more, in December 1988 and again in February 1989. At the time of the last refusal, American intelligence determined that Iraq was building fixed ballistic missile launchers for Scud missiles in western Iraq.

Kurds

Christopher Hitchens wrote in *National Geographic* in August 1992, "Who are the Kurds? They number 25 million and are scattered from the Middle East to Europe, North America, and Australia, which makes them one of the largest ethnic groups in the world without a state of its own. Once nomadic, most are now farmers or have migrated to cities. . . . Like the majority of their neighbors, most Kurds are Sunni Muslims; a few are Jews or Christians. Their language is fractured—like the Kurds themselves—by region and dialect, but it is distinct from Turkish, Persian, and Arabic. They are neither Turks, nor Persians, nor Arabs, and they regard their own survival as proof in itself of a certain integrity."

What some people consider "Greater Kurdistan" encompasses an area from the western border of Armenia, south across Turkey, through northeastern Syria and northern Iraq,

Kurds, an ethnic minority in Iraq, ferry supplies on a makeshift raft across the Habur River in northern Iraq.

Kurds

and slashing through Iran. Following the British mandate of what is now Iraq, the Kurds in northern Iraq desired independence from both Iraqi and Turkish influence. In 1920 the British declared the Treaty of Sèvres with the Ottoman Empire, which would have made Mosul, now and then a Kurdish stronghold, the capital of an independent Kurdistan. The treaty was rejected, writes historian Helen Chapman Metz, after Turkish leader Mustafa Kamal (known as Ataturk, 1881–1938) extended Turkish control over the Kurdish areas. The British eventually melded Kurdish areas into an independent Iraq, and set the stage for several decades of hostility, oppression, and warfare.

In 1937 the anti-Kurdish dictator Saddam Hussein was born in the southern Iraqi town of Tikrit; ironically, this is the same village where the Kurdish champion Saladin (Salah ad-Din Yusuf ibn Ayyub, 1138–1193) was born. Through military adventures, Saladin was able to unite the Muslim regions of northern Mesopotamia, Palestine, and Egypt into a single administrative authority; later, he was one among many who conquered Jerusalem. In 1945 the Kurds established the Republic of Mahabad,

based in what is now the Iranian city of the same name, but the experiment lasted for only a single year. During the Iran-Iraq War, Saddam Hussein used the Kurds as guinea pigs in a brutal experiment, dropping canisters of cyanide and mustard gas on the civilians of the Kurdish villages around Halabja. The operation was initiated to punish the Kurdish *peshmerga* (Arabic: "Those who confront death") guerrillas who had aided and abetted Iran during the war.

After the end of the Persian Gulf War, the Kurds in the north and the Shiites in the south turned on the Iraqi government, initiating a program of rebellion that lasted for several weeks until the Revolutionary Guards, Saddam Hussein's most trusted and loyal troops, fought back and defeated the insurgents. Fleeing into southern Turkey, northwestern Iran, and some parts of Syria, the Kurds were driven to imminent destruction. The relief of Operation Provide Comfort, launched by the United States, saved them.

Tariq Aziz wrote in the *New York Times* on 21 May 1994, "As to the Kurdish issue in Iraq, between April and August of 1991 extensive and serious talks took place in Baghdad between the Government of Iraq and the leaders of six

Kurdish parties, including those of Massoud Barzani and Jalal Talabani. A comprehensive agreement was reached on such issues as the shape and extent of autonomy in the Kurdish region of Iraq, the participation and role of the leaders of those parties in the Government, and [the] election of a new legislative council." The British magazine *Economist*, in its 25 June 1994 edition, called attention to the treatment of the Kurds in Turkey. "A military campaign against the separatist Kurds in the southeast is being conducted with increased severity, making life hell for thousands of innocent villagers caught in the middle. . . . Some ugly clauses in the constitution are being invoked in order to lock up elected deputies who are deemed sympathetic to Kurdish separatism (a dozen have been arrested or chased abroad)."

See also Iran-Iraq War; Operation Provide Comfort.
References: Hitchens, Christopher, "Struggle of the Kurds," *National Geographic* 182:2 (August 1992), 32–61; Metz, Helen Chapman, ed., *Iraq: A Country Study* (Washington, DC: GPO, 1990); "The Stateless Nation," *The Economist*, 25 June 1994, 15; "U.S. Fights to Stymie Iraq Compliance: A Letter from Tariq Aziz to the *New York Times*," *New York Times*, 21 May 1994, A20.

Kuwait

What stands now as Kuwait proper is an entity that was created by many men over many years in an effort by the Western powers to control the Middle Eastern peoples. Discussing the geography of the nation in its final report to Congress on the Gulf War, U.S. Department of Defense analysts wrote, "Kuwait, a country slightly smaller than New Jersey, consists of flat to slightly undulating desert plains. It has almost no defensible terrain. The only significant elevation in the country is the al-Mutl'a Ridge, just north of the city of al-Jahra. A pass in this ridge at al-Jahra is the traditional defensive position against an approach from the north. British troops occupied the position in the 1961 defense of Kuwait when Iraq threatened to seize the newly independent country. In the Gulf War, Iraqi troops mined and fortified this pass as a defense against potential coalition attacks north toward the Iraq-Kuwait frontier."

J. G. Lorimer, in his 1915 work *Gazetteer of the Persian Gulf, Omân and Central Arabia*, wrote, "The foundation of the *town* [author's emphasis] of Kuwait, though a modern event, is the subject of various and conflicting traditions. The first settlers, however, almost certainly belonged to the [Bani] Utub, a tribe consisting of three principal traditions, the Jalahimah, Al Khalifah and Al Subah [Sabah], and said to be derived from the Anizah of northern Central Arabia." In 1752 these tribes left their homes in central Arabia and formed an alliance with the al-Sabahs, a clannish family that had settled a tent village on the site of what is now Kuwait City. The al-Sabahs were then constituted by the British as the rulers of a separate entity from the Ottoman Empire called Kuwait. Sheik Sabah bin Jabir al-Sabah, the leader of the clan, became the ruler of this nation-state. Although in 1871 his successor, Sheik Abdullah ibn Sabah al-Sabah, was consigned to the position of provincial governor of Basra, 28 years later, in 1899, Great Britain agreed to establish Kuwait as a protectorate under British rule. The *Congressional Digest*, in its issue on the congressional debate over whether to go to war in the Gulf, stated that, as part of Iraq's stand, "Kuwait formed an integral part of the Ottoman province of Basra, one of three Ottoman provinces that were combined to constitute the modern state of Iraq. The Kuwait district was never detached from the Ottoman province of Basra by any decree of the Ottoman Government, internationally recognized document, or valid diplomatic instrument."

This relationship between the British and Kuwaitis continued until 1961, when Britain gave the small Persian Gulf nation its independence. Twice since then Britain has had to come to Kuwait's defense, both times when Iraq threatened to annex Kuwait. After the first incident, in 1961, Iraq retracted its demands for what is now Kuwait in exchange for an $84 million grant from Kuwait's rulers after the surrounding Arab nations endorsed Kuwaiti independence. Kuwait had been a primary conduit for money to Iraq for many years; in fact, Kuwait floated multibillion-dollar loans to Saddam Hussein so that he could fight Iran during the 1980s.

The border between Iraq and Kuwait is a mere 149 miles (240 km). Because of this closeness and Kuwait's size, only 6,880 square miles (17,820 sq km), Saddam Hussein had little opposition if he

Kuwait

Kuwaitis celebrate their liberation by coalition troops, including those of the United States and Great Britain, from Iraqi forces on 27 February 1991.

wanted to swallow Kuwait militarily. In July 1990 the small Kuwaiti defense force consisted of an army that was more a constabulary than a standing army, an air force with two squadrons (one of French Mirage F-1s, and the other composed of A-4 Skyhawk fighters purchased from the United States), and a navy of four small ships, two of which were eventually captured in the first waves of the invasion on 2 August. More fighters in the form of F/A-18 Hornets were on order, but would not arrive until late 1991. The standing army comprised mainly non-Kuwaiti citizens. To say the least, it was an incredibly ineffective force against the massive Iraqi army just across the border. However, Kuwait was prepared, in the case of an emergency such as an invasion, with revenues—billions of dollars' worth (some estimate the fund at $150–200 billion)—tucked away in banks across the globe. So when the invasion came, the emir and his family, as well as other Kuwaiti citizens who had an opportunity to flee, were well stocked with cash reserves for their wait in exile.

In the early morning hours of 2 August 1990, a wave of Iraqi soldiers and tanks swept south-ward from Iraqi soil toward Kuwait City and the outward reaches of the Kuwaiti nation. Youssef M. Ibrahim wrote in the *New York Times*, "One of the first tasks assigned to Iraqi troops when they invaded Kuwait in the early hours of August 2 was to capture or kill Sheik Jaber al-Ahmed al-Sabah, the Emir of Kuwait." Killing Sheik al-Sabah would be a feather in the cap of the Iraqi army. Al-Sabah, emir since 1977, was born in Kuwait City on 29 June 1926, the son of Sheik Ahmad al-Jaber al-Sabah, the emir of Kuwait from 1921 to 1950. After succeeding his cousin, Sheik Sabah al-Salem al-Sabah, upon his death, the new emir continued the pastoral and monarchical reign of his small nation. The *New York Post* described him as "the quintessential Kuwaiti," while praising him as a "shrewd and astute politician." He ruled Kuwait with an iron hand, dissolving Parliament in 1986 and refusing to call it back into session. Although many people said that he was detached from day-to-day affairs, he was widely loved by his people. In 1985 he was the subject of an assassination attempt by members of a shadowy Muslim terrorist group called Islamic Holy War. According to the U.S. Department of Defense's 1992 *Final Re-*

port to Congress on the Gulf War, "[Iraqi] commando teams made amphibious assaults against the Emir's palace and other key facilities. The Emir was able to escape into Saudi Arabia, but his brother was killed in the Iraqi assault on the Dasman Palace." The *New York Times* said of the action, "Without warrant or warning, Iraq has struck brutally at a tiny Kuwait, a brazen challenge to world law. Iraq stands condemned by a unanimous U.N. Security Council. . . . President Bush's taste for bluntness stands him in good stead: 'Naked Aggression!' is the correct term for President Saddam Hussein's grab at a vulnerable, oil-rich neighbor." Over the next six months, an underground Kuwaiti resistance fought valiantly against the massive Iraqi army. Although the resistance was little felt, it nonetheless demonstrated the Kuwaiti people's resolve to free themselves and their nation from the grasp of a dictator.

The destruction of Kuwait was so brutal, and so complete, that of this writing—four full years after liberation—the nation as a whole has yet to recover adequately to allow the citizens to enjoy the life they had before. Historian Joseph Wright

Twinam said, "The major economic blow [of the invasion] fell on Kuwait, a blow so severe that the early damage estimates were almost meaningless except as a rough order of magnitude. Initial guesses that Kuwait's infrastructure had suffered as much as $100 billion in destruction have been gradually scaled down since the liberation and beginning of reconstruction closer to the $20 billion level. Still, $20 billion is a lot of money in an economy the size of Kuwait's. In the 1980s two years of Kuwait's oil export earnings hardly equaled this amount."

In late 1991, Kuwait and the United States signed a ten-year enhanced defense cooperation covenant between the two nations. One source said of the agreement, "The pact covers U.S. access to Kuwaiti port facilities, Kuwaiti logistics support for U.S. forces, joint military training and exercises, and [the] prepositioning of defense materials for use by U.S. forces." This was amptly demonstrated in October 1994, when Saddam Hussein's armies again moved to confrontation at the Kuwaiti border and the United States dispatched troops to defend the small monarchy.

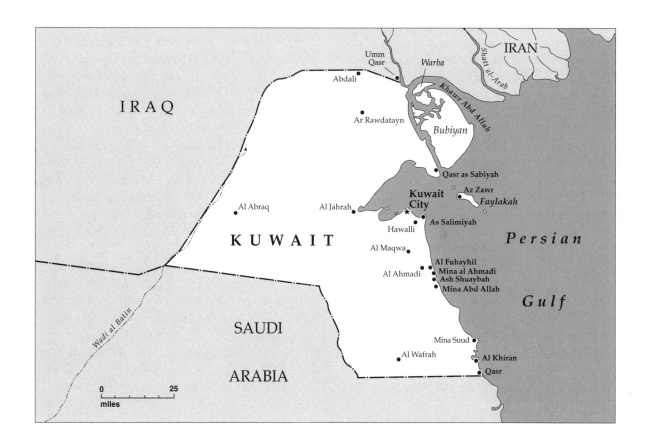

References: *Conduct of the Persian Gulf War: Final Report to Congress,* Report by the Department of Defense, April 1992, 4; Dunnigan, James F., and Austin Bay, *From Shield to Storm: High-Tech Weapons, Military Strategy, and Coalition Warfare in the Persian Gulf* (New York: Morrow, 1992), 44–45; Ibrahim, Youssef M., "Sheik Jaber al-Ahmed al-Sabah: The Exiled Emir," *New York Times,* 26 September 1990, A9; Lorimer, J. G., *Gazetteer of the Persian Gulf, Omân and Central Arabia,* quoted in *The Kuwait Crisis: Basic Documents,* edited by E. Lauterpacht et al. (Cambridge, UK: Grotius, 1991), 3; "Naked Aggression," *New York Times,* 3 August 1990, A26; Tarr, David R., and Bryan R. Daves, *The Middle East* (Washington, DC: Congressional Quarterly, 1986), 219; Twinam, Joseph Wright, "The Gulf Cooperation Council since the Gulf War: The State of the States," *Middle East Policy* 1:4 (1992), 98; "Washington Roundup: Gulf Pact," *Aviation Week & Space Technology,* 9 September 1991, 21.

Laith

This Iraqi missile is a variant of the Soviet FROG-7 (Free Rocket over Ground) rocket. The Laith is 30 feet (9 m) long, weighs approximately 2 tons, can carry a 500-pound (226.8 kg) projectile, and has a range of about 37 miles (60 km).

See also FROG.

Reference: Dunnigan, James F., and Austin Bay, *From Shield to Storm: High-Tech Weapons, Military Strategy, and Coalition Warfare in the Persian Gulf* (New York: Morrow, 1992), 84.

Landing Craft Air Cushion (LCAC)

Key to the Navy's precision plan to land troops and personnel onto shore to establish beachheads, the Landing Craft Air Cushion, according to naval authority Norman Polmar, "are the first advanced-technology surface ships to be produced in series by the U.S. Navy. They carry vehicles and cargo from amphibious ships onto the beach at higher speeds and for longer distances than can conventional landing craft." Built by Bell Aerospace/Textron Marine and Land Systems of New Orleans, Louisiana, 17 LCACs served the Navy during the Persian Gulf conflict.

The LCAC is essentially a large landing craft with lightweight material on its sides to allow for a cushioned trip on water. It displaces 102.2 tons light, 169 tons fully loaded, and can even reach 184 tons if overloaded. Length, including cushion, is 87.92 feet (24.7 m). Powered by 4 Avco-Lycoming TF-40B gas turbines, the ships are distinguished by 2 large propeller fans at the rear of the craft. While carrying cargo, a complement of 5, and a maximum of 24 troops, the LCAC has the ability to travel on its cushion at a speed of 50 knots (58 mph; 93 km/h). Range at 40 knots (46 mph; 74 km/h) is 200 nautical miles (230 miles; 370 km).

Reference: Polmar, Norman, *The Naval Institute Guide to the Ships and Aircraft of the U.S. Fleet* (Annapolis, MD: Naval Institute Press, 1993), 183–184.

LANDSAT

This satellite was employed during the Gulf War, according to the U.S. military's *Final Report to Congress* on the Persian Gulf War, to "provide multi-spectral surface imaging for geological and ecological mapping and surface-change detection." Officially named the Multi-Spectral Imagery LANDSAT (MSI), the satellite "provided direct war-fighting support during Desert Storm. Because of MSI's unique nature, military planners were able to obtain information normally not available. Furthermore, MSI showed features of the earth beyond human visual detection capability." Because maps of Kuwait, Iraq, and Saudi Arabia were not reliable, the military called upon the Defense Mapping Agency (DMA) to prepare maps that were more up-to-date. Further, because MSI technology allows for the examination of the earth 30 feet (9 m) below the surface, MSI mapping was used to highlight Iraqi mines and booby traps.

Vice Admiral William A. Dougherty, deputy commander in chief of the U.S. Space Command in Colorado, writes, "When U.S. forces deployed to the Persian Gulf region, the maps of Kuwait, Iraq, and Saudi Arabia were old and out-of-date. To correct this deficiency, multispectral imagery satellite systems were used to prepare up-to-date and precise maps of the areas of operation." The leading satellite used for this mission was the LANDSAT.

General Donald J. Kutyna, commander in chief of the U.S. Space Command, said in 1991, "The first troops deploying to Saudi Arabia . . . were equipped with maps prepared from LANDSAT multispectral satellite imagery. During Desert Shield, our ground forces received thousands of high-quality maps and charts that were based on LANDSAT imagery. While this system is currently funded by the Department of Commerce, it has clearly demonstrated its military utility."

References: Conduct of the Persian Gulf War: Final Report to Congress, Report by the Department of Defense, April 1992, 808; Dougherty, William A., "Storm from Space," *U.S. Naval Institute Proceedings* 118:8 (August 1992), 51; Kutyna, Donald J., "SPACECOM: We Lead Today, but What about Tomorrow?" *Defense '91,* July/August 1991, 27.

LASTE

See Low Altitude Safety and Target Enhancement.

Lausanne, Treaty of (1923)

Taking the place of the controversial Treaty of Sèvres, the Treaty of Lausanne, signed on 24 July 1923 by France, Greece, Japan, Yugoslavia, Romania, Great Britain, Italy, and Turkey, sought to establish borders between former satellite powers of the Ottoman Empire and newly formed Turkey, as well as spheres of influence in the Middle East, following the end of World War I. Summarized, the 60-page treaty contains the following provisions: Part I embodies the "Political Clause" (articles 1–45); article 1 reads: ". . . the state of peace will be definitely re-established between the Contracting Powers. . . . Official relations will be resumed on both sides, . . ." while article 4 says, "The frontiers [with Bulgaria, Greece, Iraq, and Syria] described by the present Treaty are traced on the one-in-a-million maps attached to the present Treaty. . . ."

See also Sèvres, Treaty of.
Reference: Osmańczyk, Edmund Jan, *The Encyclopedia of the United Nations and International Agreements* (Philadelphia: Taylor & Francis, 1985), 456.

LAV-25 Infantry Fighting Vehicle

Built in Canada by General Motors, the Land Attack Vehicle, designated the LAV-25, entered service in the Marine Corps in 1984. Copied from a Swiss design, it is a mobile semitank that can carry six Marines into combat. It has an operating crew of three: the driver, the gunner, and the commander. The LAV carries a turret-mounted

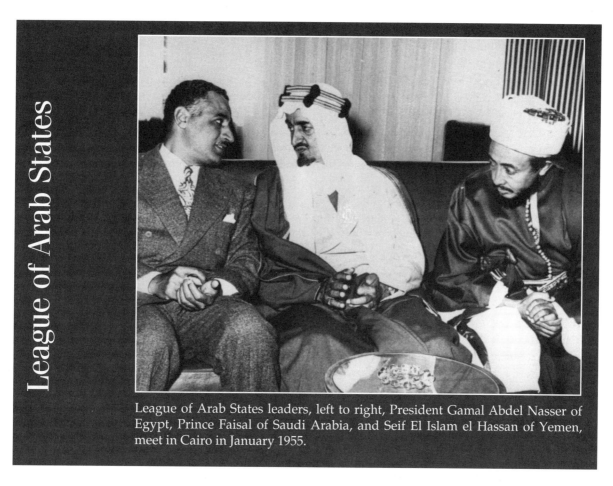

League of Arab States leaders, left to right, President Gamal Abdel Nasser of Egypt, Prince Faisal of Saudi Arabia, and Seif El Islam el Hassan of Yemen, meet in Cairo in January 1955.

25 mm Bushmaster chain gun and two 7.62 mm machine guns, both of which have a firing radius of 3,000 yards (2,744 m). It has a road speed of 63 mph (101 km/h) on land and 6 mph (9.7 km/h) in water. Its foam-filled tires, which take bullet holes without deflating, make the LAV an important vehicle for operation close to the front lines. Over 300 served in Saudi Arabia and Kuwait during Operations Desert Shield and Desert Storm. An updated version, the LAV/AD (Air Defense), has antiaircraft capability by carrying General Electric Aerospace's *Blazer* turret, which includes a 22 mm Gatling gun and two missile pods with four Stinger antiaircraft missiles in each pod.

Reference: Chadwick, Frank, *The Desert Shield Fact Book* (Bloomington, IL: Game Designers' Workshop, 1991), 41.

LAW 80

Used by Great Britain, the LAW 80 is an anti-armored tank missile. The acronym stands for Light Antitank Weapon.

Jane's Weapons Systems, 1988–89 calls the LAW "a one-shot low cost disposable short range anti-tank weapon designed to replace existing weapons which are either light and ineffective or of a size which demands crew operation to achieve lethality." The LAW 80 launcher is 4 feet 11 inches (1.5 m) long in its ready-to-fire mode, with a shoulder weight of 20 pounds (9 kg) and a missile weight of 10 pounds (4.6 kg) in the launcher. With a maximum effective range of 1,640 feet (500 m), the weapon has an effective armor penetration limit of 25 inches (650 mm).

Reference: Blake, Bernard, ed., *Jane's Weapon Systems, 1988–89* (Coulsdon, Surrey, UK: Jane's Information Group, 1988), 151–152.

League of Arab States (al-Jami'a al-'Arabiyah)

The League of Arab States, considered the United Nations of the Arab world, played an integral role in the early days of the Persian Gulf crisis. Officially formed on 22 March 1945 by a treaty signed at Cairo, its purpose is to "strengthen relations among member states by coordinating policies in political, cultural, economic, social, and related affairs; to mediate disputes between members, or between members and third parties." The charter nations of the league are Egypt, Iraq, Jordan, Lebanon, Saudi Arabia, Syria, and the Yemen Arab Republic (then North Yemen). Added to the membership over the years are Libya (1953), Sudan (1956), Tunisia (1958), Morocco (1958), Kuwait (1961), Algeria (1962), Bahrain (1971), Qatar (1971), Oman (1971), United Arab Emirates (1971), Mauritania (1973), Somalia (1974), and Djibouti (1977). The Palestine Liberation Organization (PLO) was made a member on 7 September 1976, while the Comoro Islands applied for membership in 1993, and the new nation of Eritrea announced that it intended to apply. Egypt was thrown out of the league in 1979 for signing the peace treaty with Israel, but was allowed to reapply in 1989.

From almost the time of its founding, the Arab League has been preoccupied with the "Palestine Question." Through the machinations of the league, contributions to lessen the plight of Palestinian refugees were gathered from the league's wealthiest members (including, ironically enough, Kuwait, which heavily subsidized the PLO and was repaid by having Yasir Arafat support Saddam Hussein during the Gulf crisis).

In May 1990, in a special summit held in Baghdad, the league members condemned increased Jewish emigration from the Soviet Union to Israel, with the harshest comments coming from President Saddam Hussein of Iraq. Eight days after the Iraqi invasion of Kuwait, the league met in special session. At the outset Saddam Hussein objected when the league decided to seat the exiled Kuwaiti emir, Sheik Jabir al-Ahmad al-Jabir al-Sabah, as the representative of Kuwait. Just prior to the conference it appeared that the Arab nations hesitant over Iraq's role in Kuwait had brokered a solution to the crisis, in which Iraqi troops would withdraw from Kuwait in exchange for Kuwaiti land and monetary concessions. But the deal broke down when one of Iraq's representatives, Foreign Minister Tariq Aziz, demanded that U.S. troops leave Saudi Arabia before any Iraqi withdrawal could be negotiated. "We are not going to discuss any Arab business here under the threat of American

forces, under American intimidation," Aziz stated. "If the Americans leave the region, leave it to their people, then we are ready to discuss any question." The summit's host, President Hosni Mubarak of Egypt, was so angered by Aziz's demands that in his opening statement he demanded an outright Iraqi withdrawal from Kuwait. "We can only overcome the current crisis in the Gulf and envisage a solution from the situation through the departure of Iraqi troops from Kuwait," the Egyptian president said. After a midday recess, the Iraqis responded that such a solution was impossible, as Kuwait was now part of Iraq. This statement by Iraqi delegate Taha Yassin Ramadan, combined with a speech that morning by Hussein in which he called for all the petromonarchies to be overthrown by Islamic militants to protect Iraq, threw the summit into a spin. King Fahd of Saudi Arabia and other emirate leaders then submitted a resolution condemning both the Iraqi invasion and Hussein's clamor for a jihad, as well as calling for more U.S. troops in the region and demanding the restoration of the exiled emir as "the legitimate government that was in place [in Kuwait] before the Iraqi invasion." The proclamation was approved by 12 of the League's 20 members, with Iraq, Libya, and the PLO voting against it (Algeria and Yemen abstained, Tunisia was absent, and Jordan, the Sudan, and Mauritania took no position). Thus, the Arab League's action in the early days of the crisis accelerated the world's march toward war.

The league's permanent headquarters is located in Cairo, Egypt. (During the period of Egypt's banishment from the league, 1979–1989, the league's main offices were moved to Tunis, Tunisia. In 1990, the league voted to move most, but not all, of its offices back to Cairo. The partial transfer was completed on 1 January 1991.) Under the power of a secretary general (in 1995 this was Ahmad Esmat Abdel-Maguid of Egypt), the league sits in the same fashion as the UN Security Council, with each member receiving an equal vote in all affairs. However, on many matters before the league, only unanimous decisions are binding on all members, and because of the division in the Arab world during the Gulf crisis, there was no official league policy on Iraq's occupation of Kuwait. Because the league oversees matters of trade among its member states, a full boycott of Israel, both materially and commercially, has been its main business, although at the time of this writing some Arab states, particularly those in the Persian Gulf, have moved toward ending the boycott. Aside from this, the league also handles elements of trade among its members, including all-important economic cooperation.

References: Banks, Arthur S., ed., *Political Handbook of the World: 1993* (Binghamton, NY: CSA Publications, 1993), 980–981; Osmańczyk, Edmund Jan, *The Encyclopedia of the United Nations and International Agreements* (Philadelphia: Taylor & Francis, 1985), 460–462.

Linkage

Was Saddam Hussein's attempt to link a proposed Iraqi pullout from Kuwait with an Israeli withdrawal from the occupied territories a stunt, or a missed chance to avoid war in the Middle East? Was the coalition wrong to ignore this so-called linkage of the two unrelated issues?

Yasir Arafat, head of the Palestine Liberation Organization (PLO), hung his group's future on Saddam Hussein's stunning ploy, and in so doing turned his back on his benefactors, the Kuwaitis, who had supplied the PLO and the Palestinian people with jobs and millions in aid over the years. And yet, the idea of linkage was never even considered by the coalition. Even though on 1 December 1990 Iraq welcomed President Bush's offer to resolve the Persian Gulf crisis as an opportunity to have "a serious and deep dialogue," the Iraqi Revolutionary Command Council reiterated that "Palestine and the other occupied Arab territories remain before our eyes and at the forefront of the issues that we will discuss in any dialogue." In an interview with CNN, Vice-president Dan Quayle restated American policy: "Palestine is not an issue on the table. The issue on the table is Saddam Hussein's invasion of Kuwait. . . . You're not going

to link Palestine up to Saddam's invasion of Kuwait." The issue was effectively dead.

Colonel Trevor N. Dupuy wrote in 1991, "It is neither possible nor desirable to link talks on Kuwait with discussion of the totally unrelated Palestinian issue. It was not necessary for Saddam to invade Kuwait in order to promote talks on the Palestinian question. . . . Is Israeli cooperation in [a Middle Eastern Peace Conference] likely? Consider: the Israelis have said that they are prepared to address the Palestinian issue by 'political means' provided there is an end to endemic violence in the occupied territories and in Israel proper. It may be expected that in the wake of a decisive coalition victory, Palestinian extremists will recognize that the intifada—now turning on itself with grotesque violence directed against 'collaborators'—has served its purpose and that it is time to move toward the political settlement all sides desire."

See also Arafat, Yasir.
Reference: Dupuy, Trevor N., et al., *How To Defeat Saddam Hussein: Scenarios and Strategies for the Gulf War* (New York: Warner Books, 1991), 135.

Low Altitude Safety and Target Enhancement (LASTE)

This module, situated on the A-10 Warthog, consists of a radar altimeter, a three-axis autopilot, and a computer that improves the plane's precision while using its guns and during bombing runs. The LASTE system was not yet in operation in 1990–1991 and therefore not used in the Persian Gulf War, but it makes the A-10, once considered a useless plane, one of the better fighter jets to come out of the war.

Reference: Smallwood, William L., *Warthog: Flying the A-10 in the Gulf War* (McLean, VA: Brassey's, 1993), 209.

M-1 and M-1A1 Abrams Main Battle Tanks

The M-1 and its updated cousin, the M-1A1, are the main battle tanks of the U.S. military. At 32 feet (with guns, which includes the 105 mm for the M-1 and the 120 mm for the M-1A1), the tanks are 9 feet 6 inches (2.9 m) tall and weigh 63 tons. The power source for both models is a 1,500-horsepower gas turbine engine that, while sturdy, is very fuel-inefficient and goes only about 40 mph (64 km/h). There was controversy about its possible duty in the Gulf because historically the engine quit when clogged with sand or dust. The Saudi Arabian desert seemed to present the machine with an obvious handicap compared to the Soviet-made Iraqi opposition. Sophisticated armor protection for the crew and an internal fire-extinguishing system round out

the superior qualities of both these machines, as well as their updated variants, including the M-1A2. The M-1 and M-1A1 tanks are armed with armor-piercing sabots (pronounced say-bows), metal darts that pierce the skin of an opposing tank and explode inside, and HEAT (high-explosive antitank) missiles, which deliver a stream of molten metal into an enemy tank's interior.

Charles Babcock, in the *Washington Post,* said of the tank, ''When the first two U.S. divisions were rushed to Saudi Arabia last August from Georgia and Texas, they were equipped with about 650 original model M-1 tanks, which were lighter and carried a small 105 mm main gun. In October, the Army announced it was replacing those tanks with newer M-1A1s. 'We wanted to give our men the best,' explained Major Pete Keating, an Army spokesman. 'We wanted an

M-1A1 Abrams main battle tanks, 4 of the 1,800 that were posted to the Persian Gulf region, fire test rounds on a range in Saudi Arabia during Operation Desert Shield.

overmatch.'" A total of 1,800 M-1A1s served in the Persian Gulf conflict. The U.S. government reported that the 18 M-1A1s were lost as follows: "seven to friendly fire, two to enemy fire; four to antitank mines; two to onboard fires of unknown origin; and three that broke down and were destroyed by U.S. forces to prevent their capture."

See also Armor-Piercing Fin Stabilized Discarding Sabot (APFSDS).
References: Babcock, Charles, "M-1 Tanks Quickly Demonstrate Superiority," *Washington Post,* 27 February 1991, A28; "Facing Off in the Desert: The Two Best Main Battle Tanks," *New York Times,* 27 January 1991, A13.

M2 Bradley Infantry Fighting Vehicle (IFV) and M3 Bradley Cavalry Fighting Vehicle (CFV)

These vehicles were one of the key components of troop movement during Operation Desert Storm. The only difference between the two is that the M2 is an infantry carrier and the M3 is a cavalry vehicle. The M2's armor is 30 mm thick, while the M2A1, a variant, is 60 mm thick.

In his *Armored Cav* Tom Clancy writes, "What does the Bradley do? The M2/3 is not designed to fight tanks, though it is equipped with a missile launcher for the TOW-2 anti-tank guided missile (ATGM) and a 25 mm M242 Bushmaster cannon. It is *not* designed to absorb damage from MBT [Main Battle Tank] gun rounds and heavy ATGMs, though it is highly survivable against such weapons.... What it is, though, is a well-armed, armored battle taxi designed to deliver a squad of infantry or a team of scouts to the edge of a battle field, support them with fire as necessary, and then re-embark them for movement under armor to the next objective."

In either configuration, the Bradley weighs 22.59 tons and is powered by a Cummins VTA-903T turbocharged 8-cylinder diesel engine providing 2,600 rpm. It has a top speed on the road of 41 mph (66 km/h) and 4.5 mph (7.2 km/h) in the water, and carries a crew of three, with a capability of carrying up to seven troops. As mentioned, the vehicle is fitted to carry

M-2 Bradley Infantry Fighting Vehicles are designed as armored taxis capable of carrying seven infantry personnel and providing covering fire with TOW missiles if necessary.

TOW and TOW-2 missile launchers. It is also equipped with an NBC (nuclear, biological, and chemical) M13A1 gas particulate breathing-filter system.

In March 1991 the U.S. military printed a report on the effectiveness of the M2/3 Bradley fighting vehicle during Operation Desert Storm: "Crews reported that the sights were very effective, even during sand storms. Other crews reported that the 25 mm Bushmaster cannon was more lethal than they expected. There were no reports of transmission failure during offensive operations. Of the 220 Bradleys in theater, three were disabled. To date, we have no information on the number damaged. Overall Bradley operational readiness rates remained at 90 per cent or above during combat."

References: Chadwick, Frank, *The Desert Shield Fact Book* (Bloomington, IL: Game Designers' Workshop, 1991), 40; Clancy, Tom, *Armored Cav: A Guided Tour of an Armored Cavalry Regiment* (New York: Berkley Books, 1994), 71; Foss, Christopher F., ed., *Jane's Armour and Artillery, 1992–93* (Coulsdon, Surrey, UK: Jane's Information Group, 1992), 470.

M60A1/3 MBT (Main Battle Tank)

The M60, one of the U.S. military's most significant main battle tanks, was used by the U.S. Marine Corps and Egyptian and Saudi troops during the ground war in Operation Desert Storm.

The M60 series began with the U.S. military in 1960, and has undergone significant changes. The Marines carried the M60A1 into battle with ERA (explosive reactive armor) plates attached to the tank. (The Egyptians used the regular M60A1, while the Saudis employed the updated M60A3.) All three tanks can carry four crewmen. The tanks' weights range from 109,600 pounds (49,714 kg) for the M60 to 116,000 pounds (52,617 kg) for the M60A1 and M60A3. The M60 and M60A1 are powered by a Continental AVDS-1790-2A 12-cylinder air-cooled diesel engine providing 2,400 rpm (the M60A3 is powered by a Continental AVDS-1790-2C engine that provides the same power). Speed is 30 mph (48.28 km/h). Armaments include 7.62 mm and 12.7 mm guns.

Tom Clancy writes that ERA is "an add-on armor system that uses high explosive[s] sand-

M-60A1/3
Main Battle Tank

While one U.S. Marine naps, the rest of the four-man crew of a M-60A1 tank check the vehicle's power pack.

wiched in between steel plates. The explosive detonates upon impact from a shaped-charge jet or long-rod penetrator. First-generation ERA was designed to reduce the effectiveness of a shaped-charge jet by breaking it up. Second-generation ERA provides improved performance against shaped-charge jets, but can also break long-rod penetrators. Once used, the ERA tile has to be replaced."

References: Clancy, Tom, *Armored Cav: A Guided Tour of an Armored Cavalry Regiment* (New York: Berkley Books, 1994), 297; Foss, Christopher F., ed., *Jane's Armour and Artillery, 1992–93* (Coulsdon, Surrey, UK: Jane's Information Group, 1992), 150.

M113A3 Armored Personnel Carrier (APC)

Several variants of this armored personel carrier served during the Gulf War, in the models of the M113A3 APC, the M109 Improved TOW Vehicle (ITV), and the M557A2 Command Vehicle with telescopic antenna. During the Iraqi invasion of Kuwait on 2 August 1990, 50 Kuwaiti M113s were captured, although whether they were used during Operation Desert Storm remains unknown at this time.

Powered by a Detroit Diesel model 6V-53T (the M577A2 is powered by a model 6V-53), the M113A3 can carry a commander and a driver, as well as transport 11 troops. Weight of the M113A3 is 27,000 pounds (12,247 kg, plus an additional 4,000 pounds [1,772 kg] of external armor). Maximum speed is 40 mph (65 km/h), with a maximum unrefueled range of 300 miles (483 km).

References: Almond, Denise L., ed., *Desert Score: U.S. Gulf War Weapons* (Washington, DC: Carroll Publishing, 1991), 304–305; Foss, Christopher F., ed., *Jane's Armour and Artillery, 1992–93* (Coulsdon, Surrey, UK: Jane's Information Group, 1992), 478–388.

M117 GP Bomb

This free-fall, nonguided, general-purpose bomb was used primarily by B-52 bombers during the Gulf War. A 750-pound (1,653 kg) weapon, it carries 386 pounds (175 kg) of explosives and is equipped with an M904 fuse in the nose and an M905 fuse in its tail. During Operation Desert Storm, 43,435 were dropped in the Kuwaiti Theatre of Operations.

See also MK-80 Bomb Series.
Reference: Gulf War Air Power Survey, Volume IV: Weapons, Tactics, and Training Report and Space Report (Washington, DC: GPO, 1993), 70–71.

M551 Sheridan Light Tank/Reconnaissance Vehicle

According to British writer Christopher Foss, "M551 Sheridan tanks were among the first U.S. Army vehicles to arrive in Saudi Arabia in the summer of 1990 following the Iraqi invasion of Kuwait. These vehicles of the Second Battalion, 73rd Armored Regiment, subsequently took part in Operation Desert Storm." The M551, named the "Sheridan" after the Civil War general Philip Sheridan, is an aluminum-hulled reconnaissance machine with the capabilities of a small tank, although because of its age (many were built in the 1960s) it served in a purely reconnaissance role during the war.

The M551 can carry four men (commander, gunner, loader, and driver). With a combat weight of 34,900 pounds (15,830 kg), the vehicle is powered by Detroit Diesel 6V-53T 318-cubic-inch (5.21 liter) water-cooled engine. It has the ability to fire the MGM-51 "Shillelagh" antitank missile, with other ammunition ranging from white phosphorus (WP) to High Explosive Anti-Tank with Tracer (HEAT-T-MP [Multi-Purpose]) warheads.

References: Foss, Christopher F., ed., *Jane's Armour and Artillery, 1992–93* (Coulsdon, Surrey, UK: Jane's Information Group, 1992), 188–190; Almond, Denise L., ed., *Desert Score: U.S. Gulf War Weapons* (Washington, DC: Carroll Publishing, 1991), 292–293.

M998 High Mobility, Multipurpose Wheeled Vehicle (HMMWV)

Also known as the Hummer (its civilian designation when sold by AM General) or Humvee, the HMMWV replaced the standard Army jeep

U.S. Marines establish a motor pool of M998 High Mobility, Multi-Purpose Wheeled Vehicles (HMMWV) in Saudi Arabia during Operation Desert Shield.

in the early 1980s. Tony Swan wrote in *Popular Mechanics*, "The Hummer was already solidly established with the U.S. Army, Marine Corps, Navy and Air Force by the time Desert Storm broke . . . but like so many other elements of American military technology, the crucible of combat put this vehicle's exceptional capabilities into sharp focus. While the 20,000 Hummers involved in Desert Storm didn't command the kind of media attention given to Patriot missiles and smart bombs, they performed their multiple workhorse chores in the gear-grinding grit of Saudi Arabia, Kuwait and Iraq with a level of reliability that exceeded expectations."

The Humvee replaced the U.S. Army jeep because it had the ability to do the job of several vehicles used by the U.S. military. As Tom Clancy writes in his *Armored Cav*, "The U.S. Army calls it a four-wheeled vehicle in the medium (4,000–to–10,000 lb./1,818–to–4,545 kg.) class. But the forces that use the HMMWV (all four branches of the U.S. military, along with numerous foreign countries) look upon it as an 'everything' vehicle. It performs all of the missions that used to be accomplished by the old M151 jeep, as well as the old 1½ ton truck (called a 'five quarter') and six other truck types. This simplifies the skills needed to operate and maintain it, and greatly reduces the need for separate lines of spare parts."

References: Clancy, Tom, *Armored Cav: A Guided Tour of an Armored Cavalry Regiment* (New York: Berkley Books, 1994), 87; Swan, Tony, "Earth Mover: The Civilian Hummer—For Those Who Would Go Where No 4x4 Has Gone Before," *Popular Mechanics* 169:6 (June 1992), 28.

Major, John Roy (1943–)

A player behind the scenes in the British government, John Major stunned the world when, in the midst of the Persian Gulf crisis, he replaced Margaret Thatcher as prime minister of Great Britain.

Described as "a dry, wooden speaker with limited experience in the public eye," John Roy Major was born in the borough of Merton in London, England, on 29 March 1943, the son of Thomas Major and his wife Gwendolyn (née Coates) Major. According to Glenn Frankel in the *Washington Post*, Thomas Major "was 66 and nearly blind when Major was born in 1943 . . . he had tried and failed at many strange and colorful jobs, including trapeze artist, vaudeville performer and minor-league baseball player in the United States." John Major spent many of his early years in the poor London suburb of Brixton; he then attended Rutlish Grammar School, an educational institution for gifted children. From the age of eight he worked as a laborer to

Prime Minister John Major of Great Britain responds to questions about Allied air attacks on Iraq from his London residence on 17 January 1991, two days after the initiation of Operation Desert Storm.

support his family, and dropped out of school at the age of 16. After struggling in several jobs, Major failed the entrance examination to become a bus conductor. Later, he passed an entrance exam that allowed him to become a junior clerk at the Standard Chartered Bank of London, where he worked for the next 14 years, rising to become the bank's chief spokesman before leaving in 1979.

In 1968 Major got his first taste of politics when he ran for (and won) a seat on the city council representing the south London district of Lambeth as a member of the Conservative party. After two unsuccessful runs for the House of Commons, in 1979 he joined Margaret Thatcher's coalition and won a seat as a member of Parliament from Huntingdonshire. Thatcher aides later said that they saw great potential in Major; in 1985, she selected him as junior minister for social security and the disabled. A year later, he was named minister of the same department.

In 1987 Major began the upward climb toward becoming prime minister when Thatcher named him as chief secretary of the treasury (considered equal to the American Office of Management and Budget), where he served until 1989. In July of that year he was appointed British foreign secretary, holding the office until October. He was then chosen for the office of chancellor of the exchequer (the equivalent of the American secretary of the treasury), replacing Nigel Lawson. By this time, it was evident that Thatcher was grooming Major to be her successor.

That chance came in November 1990, at the height of the crisis in the Persian Gulf. Because of a worsening economic situation in Britain, the Conservative members of Parliament gave Thatcher a vote of no-confidence, in essence removing her from the Conservative party's leadership. In a three-way race a week later between Major, former defense secretary Michael Hesseltine, and Foreign Minister Douglas Hurd, Major won a majority of votes among his party to become the leader of the Conservatives; since they controlled Parliament, he was named the new British prime minister, the youngest man to hold that post in this century.

Major acted quickly to reinforce British support for Operation Desert Shield. He told an interviewer that "there will be no difference in policy in the Persian Gulf. . . . There is absolute unity that what has happened there is unforgivable and that it has to be reversed." Because troops and materiel had already been dispatched under Thatcher's leadership, Major's role was more of a supportive one, with his staff, including Foreign Secretary Douglas Hurd, playing a key role in the creation of coalition policy. With the end of the war, Major basked in the glow of an Allied victory. Craig Whitney reported in the *New York Times* in February 1991 that "the war and his direct style have made Mr. Major . . . one of the most popular British politicians of the last 30 years." In June 1995, after an internal fight within his Conservative party, Major won a stunning vote of confidence.

See also Thatcher, Margaret Hilda Roberts, Baroness Thatcher of Kesteven.
References: Frankel, Glenn, "Major Followed Unlikely Path from Rags to Rule," *Washington Post,* 28 November 1990, A1; Frankel, Glenn, "Thatcher's Protege Major To Be British Leader," *Washington Post,* 28 November 1990, A26; Whitney, Craig R., "Gray Flannels or Not, John Major Is Riding the

Crest of Popularity in Britain," *New York Times*, 28 February 1991, A3.

MC-130H Combat Talon II

This variant of the C-130, designated for "day and night infiltration and exfiltration, resupply of Special Operations Forces, psychological warfare and aerial reconnaissance," was ordered to the Kuwaiti Theatre of Operations on 21 August 1990, along with its sister ship, the Coast Guard HC-130H. The U.S. military report *Gulf War Air Power Survey* reports that the MC-130 flew 84 missions dedicated to various special operations for USSOCCENT (U.S. Special Operations Command Central). "During Desert Storm," the report states, "the aircraft was used primarily for infiltration missions and to resupply special operations units on the ground. [Its] special navigation and aerial delivery systems were used to locate small drop zones and deliver people and equipment. The aircraft also was able to penetrate hostile airspace at low altitude, and the crews were specially trained in night and adverse weather conditions. . . . [The crews also]

conducted psychological operations by flying multiple leaflet-drop missions."

See also AC-130A/H Spectre Gunship; C-130 Hercules Transport; EC-130E Volant Solo; HC-130H Extended Range Aerospace Rescue and Recovery; Special Operations Forces.
Reference: Gulf War Air Power Survey, Volume IV: Weapons, Tactics, and Training Report and Space Report (Washington, DC: GPO, 1993), 119.

Media

Although many argue the opposite, the facts bear out that the Persian Gulf War was the *most covered* conflict by the media, American and otherwise, ever. At the height of the Vietnam War, during the 1968 Tet Offensive, there were 637 journalists from many nations "in-country" covering all aspects of the war. In Grenada, again a source of controversy, there were at most 96 reporters specifically placed in so-called media pools by the Pentagon. However, in the Gulf there were (at the time of the start of the air war) 1,200 reporters (with 130 of these in pools); at the start of the ground war, the number expanded to 1,500 reporters (which includes 192 in pools).

Assistant Secretary of Defense Pete Williams talks with reporters at the Pentagon on 18 January 1991, three days after the beginning of Operation Desert Storm.

And although Pentagon rules prohibited excursions without military escorts (a rule broken by CBS reporter Bob Simon and his crew), by the height of the ground war many reporters were running willy-nilly across the battlefield trying to capture a story that was outdistancing even their own cameras. CBS's Bob McKeown was the first reporter into a liberated Kuwait City, having hired a jeep and raced ahead of American troops.

On 7 January 1991 Pete Williams, assistant secretary of defense, sent a note to bureau chiefs in the Washington press corps defining rules for journalists covering the war in Saudi Arabia:

Memorandum for Washington Bureau Chiefs of the Pentagon Press Corps

SUBJ: Ground rules and guidelines for correspondents in the event of hostilities in the Persian Gulf

Last Monday [31 December 1990], I sent you copies of our revised ground rules for press coverage of combat operations and guidelines for correspondents that are intended to meet the specific operational environment of the Persian Gulf. I appreciate the comments I have received from some of you and understand your concerns, particularly with respect to security review and pooling in general. I also was pleased by the general consensus that the one-page version of the ground rules was an improvement.

The ground rules have been reviewed and approved with no major changes. They became effective today.

The guidelines were revised to comply with operational concerns in Saudi Arabia. We added a provision that media representatives will not be permitted to carry weapons, clarified the escort requirement, added a sentence giving medical personnel the authority to determine media guidelines at medical facilities, and deleted the sentence saying the JIB [Joint Information Bureau] in Dhahran would verify next of kin notification on casualties. We also added a section, in response to many questions, which clarifies our policy on unilateral media coverage of the forward areas during the period when the pools are operational.

Last Saturday [5 January 1991], I conducted a conference call with the majority of the CENTCOM [Central Command] public affairs officers, who were gathered in Riyadh and Dhahran, and discussed the ground rules and guidelines to ensure that the intent and purpose of the ground rules is clearly understood.

I appreciate your counsel and remain ready to discuss any problems or questions you may have.

Pete Williams
Assistant Secretary of Defense
(Public Affairs)

OPERATION DESERT SHIELD
GROUND RULES

The following information should not be reported because its publication or broadcast could jeopardize operations and endanger lives:

(1) For U.S. or coalition units, specific numerical information on troop strength, aircraft, weapons systems, on-hand equipment, or supplies (e.g., artillery tanks, radars, missiles, trucks, water), including amounts of ammunition or fuel moved by or on hand in support and combat units. Unit size may be described in general terms such as "company-size," "multibattalion," "multidivision," "naval task force," and "carrier battle group." Number or amount of equipment and supplies may be described in general terms such as "large," "small," or "many."

(2) Any information that reveals details of future plans, operations, or strikes, including postponed or canceled operations.

(3) Information, photography, and imagery that would reveal the specific location of military forces or show the level of security at military installations or encampments. Locations may be described as follows: all navy embark stories can identify ship upon which embarked as a dateline and will state that the report is coming from the "Persian Gulf," "Red Sea," or "North Arabian Sea." Stories written in Saudi Arabia may be datelined "Eastern Saudi Arabia," "Near the Kuwaiti border," etc. For specific countries outside Saudi Arabia, stories will state that the report is coming from the Persian Gulf region unless

that country has acknowledged its participation.

(4) Rules of engagement details.

(5) Information on intelligence collection activities, including targets, methods, and results.

(6) During an operation, specific information on friendly force troop movements, tactical deployments, and dispositions that would jeopardize operational security or lives. This would include unit designations, names of operations, and size of friendly forces involved, unless released by CENTCOM.

(7) Identification of mission aircraft points of origin, other than as land- or carrier-based.

(8) Information on the effectiveness or ineffectiveness of enemy camouflage, cover, deception, targeting, direct and indirect fire, intelligence collection, or security measures.

(9) Specific identifying information on missing or downed aircraft or ships while search and rescue operations are planned or underway.

(10) Special operations forces' methods, unique equipment, or tactics.

(11) Specific operating methods and tactics (e.g., air angles of attacks or speeds, or naval tactics and evasive maneuvers). General terms such as "low" or "fast" may be used.

(12) Information on operational or support vulnerabilities that could be used against U.S. forces, such as details of major battle damage or major personnel losses of specific U.S. or coalition units, until that information no longer provides tactical advantage to the enemy and is, therefore, released by CENTCOM. Damage and casualties may be described as "light," "moderate," or "heavy."

GUIDELINES FOR NEWS MEDIA

News media personnel must carry and support any personal and professional gear they take with them, including protective cases for professional equipment, batteries, cables, converters, etc.

Night Operations—Light discipline restrictions will be followed. The only approved light source is a flashlight with a red lens. No visible light source, including flash or television lights, will be used when operating with forces unless specifically approved by the on-scene commander.

Because of host-nation requirements, you must stay with your public affairs escort while on Saudi bases. At other U.S. tactical or field locations and encampments, a public affairs escort may be required because of security, safety, and mission requirements as determined by the host commander.

Casualty information, because of concern of the notification of the next of kin, is extremely sensitive. By executive directive, next of kin of all military fatalities must be notified in person by a uniformed member of the appropriate service. There have been instances in which the next of kin have first learned of the death or wounding of a loved one through the news media. The problem is particularly difficult for visual media. Casualty photographs showing a recognizable face, name tag, or other identifying feature or item should not be used before the next of kin have been notified. The anguish that sudden recognition at home can cause far outweighs the news value of the photograph, film, or videotape. News coverage of casualties in medical centers will be in strict compliance with the instructions of doctors and medical officials.

To the extent that individuals in the news media seek access to the U.S. area of operation, the following rule applies: Prior to or upon commencement of hostilities, media pools will be established to provide initial combat coverage of U.S. forces. U.S. news media personnel present in Saudi Arabia will be given the opportunity to join CENTCOM media pools, providing they agree to pool their products. News media personnel who are not members of the official CENTCOM media pools will not be permitted into forward areas. Reporters are strongly discouraged from attempting to link up on their own with combat units. U.S. commanders will maintain extremely tight security throughout the operational area and will exclude from the area of operation all unauthorized individuals.

For news media personnel participating in designated CENTCOM media pools:

(1) Upon registering with the JIB, news media should contact their respective pool coordinator for an explanation of pool operations.

(2) In the event of hostilities, pool products will be subject to review before release to determine if they contain sensitive information about military plans, capabilities, operation, or vulnerabilities (see attached ground rules) that would jeopardize the outcome of an operation or the safety of U.S. or coalition forces. Material will be examined solely for its conformance to the attached ground rules, not for its potential to express criticism or cause embarrassment. The public affairs escort officer on scene will review pool reports, discuss ground rule problems with the reporter, and in the limited circumstances when no agreement can be reached with a reporter about disputed materials, immediately send the disputed materials to JIB Dhahran for review by the JIB Director and the appropriate news media representative. If no agreement can be reached, the issue will be immediately forwarded to OASD(PA) [Office of the Secretary of Defense, Public Affairs] for review with the appropriate bureau chief. The ultimate decision on publication will be made by the originating reporter's news organization.

(3) Correspondents may not carry a personal weapon.

CENTCOM POOL MEMBERSHIP AND OPERATING PROCEDURES

General. The following procedures pertain to the CENTCOM news media pool concept for providing news to the widest possible American audience during the initial stages of U.S. military activities in the Arabian Gulf area. Their composition and operation should not be confused with that of the Department of Defense National Media Pool. The pools are a cooperative arrangement designed to balance the media's desire for unilateral coverage with the logistics realities of the military operation, which make it impossible for every media representative to cover every activity of his or her choice, and with CENTCOM's responsibility to maintain operational security, protect the safety of the troops, and prevent interference with military operations. There is no intention to discriminate among media representatives on the basis of reporting content or viewpoint. Favoritism or disparate treatment of the media in pool operations by pool coordinators will not be tolerated. The purpose and intention of the pool concept is to get media representatives to and from the scene of military action, to get their reports back to the Joint Information Bureau–Dhahran for filing, rapidly and safely, and to permit unilateral media coverage of combat and combat-related activity as soon as possible. There will be two types of pools: 18-member pools for ground combat operations and small, 7-member pools for ground combat and other coverage. Pools will be formed and governed by the media organizations that are qualified to participate and will be administered through pool-appointed coordinators working in conjunction with the JIB-Dhahran. The media will operate under the ground rules issued by CENTCOM on January 15, 1991.

Pool participation. Due to logistics and space limitations, participation in the pools will be limited to media that principally serve the American public and that have had a long-term presence covering Department of Defense military operations, except for pool positions specifically designated as "Saudi" or "international." Pool positions will be divided among the following categories of media: television, radio, wire service, news magazine, newspaper, pencil, photo, Saudi and international. Media that do not principally serve the American public are qualified to participate in the CENTCOM media pool in the international category.

Pool procedures. Because of the extensive media presence in the Arabian Gulf, the fact that some media organizations are represented by many individuals, and the likelihood that more organizations and individuals will arrive in the future, membership in the categories except pencil will be by organization rather than specific individual. An organization will be eligible to participate in pool activities only after being a member of the appropriate media pool category for three continuous weeks. Members of a single-medium pool may use their discretion to allow participation by organizations which have had a significant stay in country, but which have had breaks in their stay that would otherwise cause them to be ineligible to participate under the three-continuous-weeks rule.

The single-medium pools will be formed and governed by the members. The members of each category will appoint a pool coordinator who will serve as the spokesperson and single point of contact for that medium. The print media will select a coordinator who will serve as the point of contact for the pencil category. Any disputes about membership in or operation of the pool shall be resolved by the pool coordinator.

Each single-medium pool coordinator will maintain a current list of members and a waiting list prioritized in the order in which they should be placed on the pools. The same order will be used to replace pool members during normal rotations and those individual members who return from the field prematurely and who do not have another individual in Dhahran from their field organization to replace them.

Membership of standing pools will rotate approximately every two to three weeks as the situation permits.

Pool Categories and Composition

Television: The television category will be open to the major television networks.

Radio: The radio category will be open to those radio networks that serve a general (nonprivate) listening audience.

Wire Service: The wire service category will be open to the major wire services.

News Magazine: The news magazine category will be open to those major news magazines that serve a general news function.

Newspaper: The newspaper category will be divided into two subcategories for participation in the 18-member pools. One will be open to those major papers and newspaper groups that have made a commitment since the early stages of Operation Desert Shield to cover U.S. military activities in Saudi Arabia and which have had a continuous or near-continuous presence in Saudi Arabia since the early stages of the operations, such as the *New York Times*, Cox, Knight-Ridder, the *Wall Street Journal*, *Chicago Tribune*, the *Los Angeles Times*, the *Washington Post*, *USA Today* and *Boston Globe*. The second category will include all other newspapers.

Pencil: The general category of "pencil" (print reporter) may be used by the print media pool coordinator in assigning print reporters to the smaller pools. All eligible print reporters may participate.

Photo: The photography category will be divided into the four subcategories of wire, newspaper, magazine, and photo agency. Participants may take part in only one subcategory.

Saudi: The Saudi category will be open to Saudi reporters as determined by the Saudi Ministry of Information liaison in the JIB-Dhahran. They must speak and write English and must file their reports in English.

International: The international category will be open to reporters from organizations which do not principally serve the American public from any news medium. They must speak and write English and must file their reports in English.

Sharing of Media Products
within the CENTCOM Pools

Pool participants and media organizations eligible to participate in the pools will share all media products within their medium; e.g., television products will be shared by all other television pool members and photo products will be shared with other photo pool members. The procedures for sharing those products and the operating expenses of the pool will be determined by the participants of each medium.

Alert Procedures for Combat
Correspondent Pool Activation

When the pools are to be activated, the JIB-Dhahran director or his designated representative will call each of the pool coordinators and announce the activation of the pools. The pool coordinators will be told when and where the pool members are to report (the reporting time will be within, but not later than, two hours of alert notification).

Operational security (OPSEC) considerations are of the utmost concern. JIB personnel, pool coordinators, and pool members need to be especially cognizant of OPSEC. All involved with the activation of the pools need to remain calm and unexcited. Voice inflection, nervous behavior, etc., are all indicators that something extraordinary is underway and could signal that operations are imminent.

Neither pool coordinators nor pool members will be told if the activation is an "exercise" or actual "alert."

Pool members should report to the predesignated assembly area dressed for deployment, with the appropriate equipment and supplies.

Recommendations for changes to pool membership or other procedures will be considered on a case-by-case basis.

The press as a whole was completely unhappy with these rules. Burl Osborne, president of the American Society of Newspaper Editors (ASNE), wrote two letters detailing his criticisms of the regulations.

January 8, 1991

Dear Mr. Williams:

The newly revised (January 7) set of ground rules and guidelines for news coverage in the gulf are a major improvement over the previous proposals. Still, we have concern in two areas.

First, we must strongly protest the use of a "security review" of any type. Even though you have told us that "material will not be withheld just because it is embarrassing or contains criticism," there is no guarantee that on-site commanders will not do what was done in July, 1987, when the commodore in charge during the reflagging of Kuwaiti tankers insisted on censoring material that in no way violated news media ground rules but merely embarrassed him.

In a world where "spin control" of the news has become commonplace, this form of prior restraint is a tool to gain control over what the American public sees or hears from the battlefield. There was no such prior review in Vietnam, and there were few security breaches of any consequence.

Finally, we are concerned that the entire emphasis of your ground rules is on the pool coverage, over which you will assert direct control. Our view of the pool situation is that it should be in effect only as long as it absolutely has to be, say for the first day or so of fighting, because of the logistical difficulty of getting the press in quickly. But as soon as possible the press should be allowed coverage that would be free of many of the pool constraints. We see no evidence of any attempt to prepare for that circumstance.

There are 250 U.S. reporters on site in Saudi Arabia today. The American public would be best served by a system that allows them to do their job as quickly as possible after hostilities break out.

We ask that you devote more time to preparation for that situation.

Sincerely,

Burl Osborne   Larry Kramer
President, ASNE   ASNE Press, Bar &
                                Public Affairs Committee

January 25, 1991

Dear Mr. Williams:

Now that we are in the second week of the war, I ask on behalf of my colleagues in the American Society of Newspaper Editors that you consider changes in ground rules for coverage of the war in order to better balance the need for timely reporting with the need for security. We propose changes in two areas about which most concern has been expressed.

We recognize, as a predicate, that security ought to be a paramount in your considerations. Reporters have demonstrated in the past that they will abide by reasonable security guidelines. As has been pointed out frequently, they did so in Vietnam, and there were very, very few breaches of security. The experience of the past two weeks tends to confirm that even in this new environment of instant communications capability, journalists recognize the need to maintain military security. In these circumstances, we believe the requirement for "security review" is neither necessary nor helpful to the military, and it unnecessarily restrains the ability of journalists to do their jobs properly.

We propose that you at least try out a ground rule that provides security guidelines for journalists, but does not impose the requirement of prior review. We believe that the military and the press, and by extension the American public, all would benefit.

The second area of concern is access. We understand that the initial circumstance of the war may have dictated pool coverage as the only practical way for reporters to be present. We also appreciate your willingness to consider and implement some modifications to the original plan.

It does seem that it now is appropriate to find a way to expand access to the various areas of operation, and we ask that you permit this to happen. We believe that all interests are best served if access to and distribution of news from the gulf is expanded. If a system of rotation is required to avoid overburdening some locations, that is fine. If some areas require military escorts to get there, that is fine too. But we ask that escorts be limited to escorting, and that journalists be permitted to do their work once on the scene without the inhibiting presence of a public affairs officer looking over their shoulders. The sight of a PAO declaring chaplains to be off-limits to journalists doesn't do anyone any good.

We ask that you give these proposals serious consideration and that you call on us if we can be of any help in further discussions.

With best wishes.
Sincerely,
Burl Osborne
President, ASNE

There have been some arguments from the political left that the media of the coalition nations did their best to dehumanize and ignore the Iraqis. Alexander Cockburn wrote in the liberal commentary magazine *The Nation*, "With virtually no exception the press in both the United States and Britain omitted all reports, let alone critical discussion, of Iraq's negotiating positions, as publicly proclaimed August 12, as communicated to National Security Advisor Brent Scowcroft later that month, and as relayed to the White House through Yugoslav emissaries in the Non-Aligned Movement in late December."

―――

See also Joint Information Bureau; Journalists; National Media Pool.
References: Cockburn, Alexander, "Beat the Devil: The Press and the 'Just War,'" *The Nation*, 18 February 1991, 186–187; *Gulf War Air Power Survey, Volume III: Logistics Report and Support Report* (Washington, DC: GPO, 1993), 286–288; Smith, Hedrick, ed., *The Media and the Gulf War* (Washington, DC: Seven Locks Press, 1992), 4–15.

MH-53E Sea Dragon

The largest and most powerful helicopter in the Navy's arsenal, the MH-53E is a mine countermeasures (MCM) craft, able to utilize mechanical, acoustic, and magnetic antimine equipment. It can tow an Edo AN/ALQ-166 MCM magnetic influence sledge (a small hydrofoil sled) to detect and detonate such mines in the water. The MH-53E was first sent to the Gulf as part of a special operations squadron deployed to Riyadh on 13 August 1990, and the fleet served on the amphibious assault ship USS *Tripoli* as part of the U.S. Mine Countermeasures Group (USMCMG). The six craft in the grouping eventually flew 282 sorties.

Powered by three General Electric T64-GE-416 turboshafts, each with up to 4,380 shaft horsepower, the Sea Dragon has an operational speed of 170 knots (196 mph; 315 km/h), a service ceiling of 18,500 feet (5640 m), and a range of 1,000 nautical miles (1,850 km). Because its main mission is over water, its fuselage is a watertight container composed of a steel and aluminum alloy. In addition to the MCM sledge, it can carry a Westinghouse AN/AQS-14 towed sonar, an AN/AQS-17 mine neutralization device, and an AN/AQS-141 electronic sweeper. Built by Sikorsky Helicopter, its export version is called the Sikorsky S-80, with its own E (basic transport) and M (mine countermeasures) variants available. The MH-53E differs from the CH-53E because of a larger fuel capacity (1,017 gallons vs.

3,200 gallons [3,850 liters vs. 13,530 liters]), which allows the MH-53E to fly longer missions.

See also CH-53E Super Stallion; Helicopter Carriers, United States
References: Almond, Denise L., ed., *Desert Score: U.S. Gulf War Weapons* (Washington, DC: Carroll Publishing, 1991), 78–79; Lambert, Mark, ed., *Jane's All the World's Aircraft 1993–94* (Coulsdon, Surrey, UK: Jane's Information Group, 1993), 559–560.

MH-53J Pave Low III

In the late 1980s, Sikorsky reconfigured 31 HH-53B/C Super Jolly Green Giant helicopters to the configuration of the MH-53J Pave Low III Enhanced craft. The 13 Pave Lows that were sent to the Persian Gulf flew 282 sorties.

The MH-53J is essentially the result of two craft updates. Originally, the Pentagon took S-61 helicopters and modernized them for use in Vietnam for armed search-and-rescue missions, giving them the designation of HH-53. Self-sealing external fuel tanks and a refueling probe were added to allow the craft to participate in longer sorties. Because of its green color, the copter was nicknamed the Jolly Green Giant. After the Vietnam War the copters had no further discernible missions, but in the 1980s a need was seen for a deep-penetration helicopter that could serve as escort to other attacking aircraft into potentially dangerous situations. The installation of the FLIR (forward-looking infrared radar) system, which can map a safe flight at low altitudes, as well as use of the Global Positioning Satellite (GPS) navigation system, made the former S-61 a modern craft. The standard S-61, updated to its Jolly Green Giant configuration, is powered by two General Electric T58-GE-5 turboshaft engines, each delivering 1,500 shaft horsepower (shp). Maximum speed is 164 mph (264 km/h), with a service ceiling of 13,600 feet (4,145 m) and an unrefueled range of 497 miles (800 km). The ship holds three crew members.

The U.S. military's *Gulf War Air Power Survey* reports on the Pave Low III: "In Desert Storm, the MH-53J proved capable of penetrating deep into Iraqi airspace. The Pave Low's forward-looking infrared radar and terrain-following radar permitted safe flight at extremely low altitudes at night. The Global Positioning Satellite (GPS) permitted precise navigation. Poor vis-

ibility and lack of visual cues rendered attempts to fly and navigate with only night vision goggles (NVGs) dangerous except under optimum conditions."

The MH-53J Pave Lows participated in the first combat operations in the air war portion of Operation Desert Storm. Just after midnight on 16 January, four Pave Lows accompanied ten CH-47D Chinook helicopters (including one that was used for carrying fuel) and eight AH-64 Apache helicopters in a raid on Iraqi radar installations, an operation called Task Force Normandy. Pave Lows were also responsible for rescuing a downed American pilot inside Iraq.

See also ANVIS-AN/AVS-6 Night Vision Imaging System; CH-47D Chinook; Task Force Normandy.
References: Gulf War Air Power Survey, Volume IV: Weapons, Tactics, and Training Report and Space Report (Washington, DC: GPO, 1993), 120–121; Rees, Elfan Ap, *World Military Helicopters* (London: Jane's Publications, 1986), 139; Taylor, John W. R., ed., *Jane's All the World's Aircraft, 1989–90* (Coulsdon, Surrey, UK: Jane's Information Group, 1989), 436.

MH-60G Pave Hawk

The MH-60G Pave Hawk is a modified UH-60A Blackhawk (like its cousin, the S-70B Seahawk) that saw action during the Persian Gulf War with a search-and-rescue mission profile as well as the transportation of Special Operations Forces (SOF) "reconnaissance teams" of USSOCCENT's (U.S. Special Operations Central Command's) 55th Special Operations Squadron into Kuwait and Iraq. A total of eight MH-60s saw action, flying a total of 284 sorties.

Like the UH-60A, the MH-60G is powered by two General Electric T700-GE-701C turboshaft engines providing 1,800 shaft horsepower each. It has a a fuselage length of 50.75 feet (15.26 m) and a rotor diameter of 53 feet 8 inches (16.37 m), and weighs 11,500 pounds (5,216 kg) empty, or up to 23,500 pounds (10,660 kg) loaded with crew and/or armaments. The copter has a maximum cruising speed of 173 mph (278 km/h), and an unrefueled range of 363 miles (584 km); with four external fuel tanks, the range is 1,380 miles (2,220 km). Its range of armaments includes a 12.7 mm machine gun, as well as the use of Hellfire missiles and ECM (electronic countermeasures) pods. According to the U.S. military report *Gulf War Air Power Survey,* "The Pave Hawk has several special-mission, night, all-weather upgrades. These upgrades include an additional 117-gallon internal fuel tank, [an] in-flight refueling capability, a doppler/inertial navigation system, [an] electronic map display, Pave Low II FLIR [forward looking imaging radar], satellite communications, and a 600-pound [272 kg] capacity external rescue hoist that anchors a 'fast-rope' repelling system" for retrieving downed pilots.

See also S-70B Seahawk; UH-60 Blackhawk.
References: Gulf War Air Power Survey, Volume IV: Weapons, Tactics, and Training Report and Space Report (Washington, DC: GPO, 1993), 121; Taylor, John W. R., and Kenneth Munson, "Gallery of Middle East Airpower," *Air Force* 77:10 (October 1994), 67.

Mi-8 Hip-C/E Helicopter

Aviation authorities John W.R. Taylor and Kenneth Munson write of this helicopter, "Of at least 40 air forces worldwide that fly MI-8s and uprated MI-17s, six are in the Middle East/North Africa region. Equipped largely with standard military Mi-8 armed transports ('Hip-C' and 'E'), they are the air forces of Algeria (32), Egypt (about 50), Iraq (possibly 70 following Desert Storm), Libya (seven), Syria (at least 100), and Yemen (about 50)." Little is known about the Iraqi Mi-8s, except that one was shot down on 15 February 1991 by an A-10 Thunderbolt.

A two-seat (for two pilots) transport helicopter with a missile-carrying capacity, capable of expanding to make room for a flight engineer, the Mi-8 comes in the variants of the "Hip-D" airborne communications craft and the "Hip-K" electronic countermeasures copter. Powered by two Isotov TV2-117A turboshaft engines, the standard Mi-8 has a fuselage length (excluding tail rotor) of 59 feet 7.38 inches (18.17 m), and an empty weight of 16,007 pounds (7,260 kg), while full capacity weight is 24,470–26,455 pounds (11,100–12,000 kg). The Mi-8 can accommodate up to 24 troops internally, as well as 8,820 pounds (4,000 kg) of cargo internally and 6,614 pounds (3,000 kg) externally (usually wingtip missiles). Armaments for this craft include a 12.7 mm machine gun in the nose, as well as racks placed on the sides of the fuselage that can serve to carry four 32-round packs of 57 mm rockets or other missiles.

References: Lambert, Mark, ed., *Jane's All the World's Aircraft, 1991–92* (Coulsdon, Surrey, UK: Jane's Information Group, 1991), 263–264; Taylor, John W. R., and Kenneth Munson, "Gallery of Middle East Airpower," *Air Force* 77:10 (October 1994), 67.

Mi-24D Hind-D Helicopter

This state-of-the-art Soviet helicopter was sold to the Iraqis, although its numbers and utilization during the Gulf War remain unknown.

A two-seater helicopter gunship, the Mi-24D is powered by two Leningrad Klimov (Isotov) TV3-117 turboshaft engines, each of which provides 2,200 shaft horsepower (shp). Fuel capacity is 3,307 pounds (1,500 kg), supplemented by an auxiliary tank in the cabin which can carry an additional 2,205 pounds (1,000 kg) of fuel. Thus, range without the additional fuel tank is 270 nautical miles (500 km; 310 miles), while with it the range can reach 540 nautical miles (1,000 km; 620 miles). The craft is armed with a single remotely controlled 4-barrel Gatling 12.7 mm machine gun, and has rails and pylons for AT-2 "Swatter" antitank missiles, S-5 57 mm rockets, and PFM-1 mine dispensers.

Reference: Lambert, Mark, ed., *Jane's All the World's Aircraft, 1991–92* (Coulsdon, Surrey, UK: Jane's Information Group, 1991), 268–270.

Midhat Pasha (1822–1883)

Little known outside the Middle East, Midhat Pasha ruled as governor of Baghdad from 1869 to 1872, and instituted the all-important *tanzimat* reforms. Born in Constantinople in October 1882, he was the son of Hadji Ali Effendi, a *qădì* (judge). Midhat was trained as an administrator in the Ottoman Empire. He worked his way up the governmental ladder, occupying positions in the office of the grand vizier (chief minister) where he worked as an advisor in Damascus and Constantinople, as secretary to Sami Bekir Pasha's council, and as president of the *Medjlissi Vala* (grand council of the state). In this latter position he was elevated first to the rank of *Sanie,* which his son and biographer, Ali Haydar Midhat Bey, calls "the first rank in the Ottoman hierarchy," and, in 1851, to the rank of *Mutemaiz.*

Because of his contacts, in 1861 Midhat Pasha was named governor of the Ottoman government at Niš (now in southern Yugoslavia near the Bulgarian border), where for the next eight years he promulgated many reforms, including the organization of a gendarmerie (police force), the establishment of a system that allowed for the peaceful and safe collection of taxes from those who had refused to pay in the past, the ending of religious persecution among those over whom he ruled, and oversight over the construction of schools and hospitals for the use of all, regardless of religious persuasion. These reforms settled down this contentious area, and Midhat Pasha's work impressed many, including Ottoman Sultan Abdülaziz, who recalled Midhat to Constantinople to reorganize the Ottoman council of state and execute these reforms empirewide. After this work was completed in 1869, Midhat Pasha was named governor of Baghdad.

Midhat's administration at Baghdad, 1869–1872, was marked by the implementation of the same reform-minded measures put into practice at Niš. Historian David H. Finnie wrote, "Midhat's vigorous tenure was marked by the introduction into Iraq of a version of the sweeping *tanzimat* reforms, originally adopted by the central government in Constantinople and thereafter applied in various parts of the empire." The Tanzimat (the Reorganization) was a succession of reforms unlike any ever tried in the Middle Eastern area of the world. Historian Lord Kinross said, "The earliest constitutional document in any Islamic country, the Tanzimat was in effect a charter of legal, social, and political rights, a Magna Carta for the subjects of the Empire." Thus, Midhat Pasha's reign was the first true blueprint for democracy in what is now Iraq.

After leaving his post in 1872, and replacing Grand Vizier Mahmud Nedim, Midhat became involved in a scheme in which Sultan Abdülaziz was deposed and murdered. Although Midhat was again appointed grand vizier, and he set up the first Ottoman constitution, he was dismissed. Later, after serving as governor of Smyrna, he was arrested for the death of Abdülaziz, tried, and sentenced to death. The British called for his life to be spared, and he was banished to at-Tā'if

(now in Saudi Arabia), where he was murdered on 8 May 1883.

See also Pasha, or Pasa (Turkish).
References: Bey, Ali Hadyar Midhat, *The Life of Midhat Pasha: A Record of His Services, Political Reforms, Banishment, and Judicial Murder* (London: John Murray, 1903); Finnie, David H., *Shifting Lines in the Sand: Kuwait's Elusive Frontier with Iraq* (Cambridge: Harvard University Press, 1992), 6–8; Goetz, Philip W., ed., *The New Encyclopædia Britannica,* Vol. 8 (Chicago: Encyclopædia Britannica, 1990), 112; Kinross, Lord John Patrick Douglas Balfour, *The Ottoman Centuries: The Rise and Fall of the Turkish Empire* (New York: William Morrow, 1977), 474.

MiG-21MF Fishbed (or Mongol)

The MiG-21, designated Fishbed or Mongol by NATO, is a single-seat multirole fighter that plays a major part in the Soviet air force and was a key component of the Iraqi air force. The Iraqis purchased 150 MiG-21MFs from the Soviets and 40 from the People's Republic of China, which manufactures its own version, called the MiG J-7.

The Soviet variant of the Fishbed, the MiG-21MF, also known as the Fishbed J series, is an updated version of an earlier plane, the MiG-21PFMA, with four underwing pylons for carrying weapons, particularly Atoll air-to-air missiles. It is a small, maneuverable fighter, weighing 20,725 pounds (9,400 kg) at takeoff; it has a length of 51 feet 8.5 inches (15.76 m) and a wingspan of 23 feet 5.5 inches (3.21 m). Powered by a single Tumansky R-13-300 turbojet engine, the MiG-21MF has a maximum speed of Mach 2.1, and a maximum range of 1,118 miles (1,800 km), with a ceiling of 50,000 feet (15,244 m). According to *Jane's All the World's Aircraft 1991–92,* the MiG-21MF is distinguished from other MiG jets by the appearance of a "gun gas deflector situated beneath the suction relief door forward of each wingroot." Each plane in the MiG-21 series is armed with a single twin-barrel 23 mm GSh-23 gun, holding 200 rounds.

See also Jianjiji-7.
References: Boyne, Walter J., *The Weapons of Desert Storm* (Lincolnwood, IL: Publications International, 1991), 14; Lambert, Mark, ed., *Jane's All the World's Aircraft 1991–92* (Coulsdon, Surrey, UK:

Jane's Information Group, 1991), 255–256; U.S. Department of Defense, *Soviet Military Power 1986* (Washington, DC: GPO, March 1986), 77.

MiG-23 Flogger B/G

The Mikoyan-Gurevich MiG-23, nicknamed Flogger by NATO, was designed in the 1960s as a vanguard aviation aircraft to operate as a specialty in the domain of an attack craft, intercepter, and ground-attack plane. The Iraqis had about 90 of them in their arsenal, although they never saw combat—they were part of the armada that fled to Iran at the height of the air war.

Like its American counterpart, the F-111, the Flogger became the first Soviet jet to have the swept-wing variable, in which the wings start off pinned back to the plane's sides, but during flight swing or sweep outward to give the plane more lift and smooth its flight. Unswept, the Flogger's wings extend outward 26 feet 9.5 inches (8.17 m); swept, they are 46 feet 9 inches (14.25 m). Its speed, Mach 2.35, makes it a quick and efficient fighter. Because of these qualities, the plane was a staple of the militaries of most Warsaw Pact nations up until the end of the cold war (and continues to remain so in the free East-

ern European armed forces). The Flogger was included in Iraq's arsenal, although it played no role in the Persian Gulf War (retreating to Iran as did most of Iraq's airplane squadron). The Flogger's length is 59 feet 6.5 inches (18.15 m), and its radius is 715 miles (1,150 km). It is capable of carrying six antiaircraft missiles, as well as the AS-7 air-to-surface (ATS) missile. Powered by a single Tumansky 29B turbojet, its updated version is the MiG-27 Flogger D/J, which is slower (Mach 1.7) and has a shorter radius, 373 miles (600 km), but carries 6,614-pound (3,000 kg) bombs, allowing it to act as a ground-attack fighter and bomber.

References: Boyne, Walter J., *The Weapons of Desert Storm* (Lincolnwood, IL: Publications International, 1991), 15; U.S. Department of Defense, *Soviet Military Power 1986* (Washington, DC: GPO, 1986), 54.

MiG-25 Foxbat A/E

Code-named by NATO as the Foxbat, the MiG-25A and its close variant, the MiG-25E, are considered two of the premier fighter/attack aircraft conceived by the former Soviet Union. The

MiG-23 Flogger

Two troopers of the U.S. Army's 2nd Armored Cavalry Regiment check the cockpit of a camouflaged hulk of an Iraqi MiG-23 Flogger near Ur, Iraq.

Iraqis had an estimated 25 of these craft in their air force, but because most of the force fled to Iran, their capability was never tested. Military aviation authority John W. R. Taylor reports that "about 20 Iraqi Air Force [MiG-25] interceptors may have survived the Persian Gulf War."

A single-seat craft, the MiG-25 is powered by two Soyuz/Tumansky R-15B-300 turbojets, each producing 22,500 pounds (10,206 kg) of thrust with afterburning. The MiG-25 has a weight of 76,985 to 80,950 pounds (34,920–36,719 kg), a wingspan of 45 feet 11 inches (14 m), a maximum speed of Mach 2.83, and a service ceiling of 67,900 feet (20,701 m). Its maximum unrefueled radius is 805 miles (1,300 km) (which includes what the Pentagon calls a "subsonic area intercept with external fuel"). It has the ability, with four underwing pylons, to carry four R-40R/T Acrid, R-23 Apex, R-60T Aphid, or R-73A Archer antiaircraft missiles.

References: Taylor, John W. R., and Kenneth Munson, "Gallery of Middle East Airpower," *Air Force* 77:10 (October 1994), 63; Taylor, John W. R., and Gordon Swanborough, *Military Aircraft of the World* (New York: Scribner's, 1979), 85; U.S. Department of Defense, *Soviet Military Power 1986* (Washington, DC: GPO, 1986), 54.

MiG-29 Fulcrum

A state-of-the-art military aircraft, the Soviet MiG-29, dubbed the Fulcrum by NATO, is "a single-seat all-weather counter-air fighter with secondary attack capability," as highlighted by Mike Spick in his *Modern Fighter Combat.* The Iraqis purchased 41 MiG-29s from the Soviet Union, which included 35 single-seat MiG-29 Fulcrum A craft as well as 6 MiG-29UB Fulcrum B trainers. According to military air expert John W. R. Taylor, half of these "may still be serviceable" following the end of the Persian Gulf War; he further notes that four of the craft fled to Iran. All were confiscated by Teheran and repainted in the colors of the Iranian air force.

The MiG-29 is powered by two Klimov/Sarkisov RD-33 turbofan engines, each providing 18,300 pounds (8,300 kg) of thrust with afterburning. The plane is 56 feet 10 inches (17.33 m) in length, and weighs 24,030 pounds (10,906 kg) empty; fully loaded with fuel and weapons, weights range from 33,600 pounds to 40,785 pounds (15,240–18,500 kg). It has a maximum

speed of Mach 2.3 and a service ceiling of 55,775 feet (17,005 m). Armaments include one 30 mm GSh-301 gun, and six underwing attachments to hold R-27R1 Alamo-A, R-60MK Aphid, or R-73E Archer antiaircraft missiles. The plane is also equipped to handle a variety of bombs and other munitions. During the Gulf War, the Iraqi variants were apparently armed with AA-10A Alamo missiles.

See also AA-10A Alamo.
References: Spick, Mike, *An Illustrated Guide to Modern Fighter Aircraft* (New York: Prentice Hall, 1987); Taylor, John W. R., and Kenneth Munson, "Gallery of Middle East Airpower," *Air Force* 77:10 (October 1994), 63.

MIL Mi-24 Hind

A twin-turbine gunship craft, the Mi-24, dubbed the Hind by NATO, was part of Iraq's armada of craft that could have been used during the Gulf War. Several variants of the ship exist, including the Hind A, B, and C (all early versions, and probably not in the Iraqi fleet), the Mi-24D, Mi-24W, Mi-24P, Mi-24R (known as the Hind-G1), and the Mi-24K (known as the Hind-G2). Iraq used at least one of its Mi-24s during the Iran-Iraq War; it shot down an Iranian F-4 Phantom II with a Spiral antitank missile, a lesson that potentially haunted the coalition in the Gulf.

The Mi-24's basic character is that of a gunship helicopter with short, stubby wings used for the deployment of missile launch tubes. Powered by two Leningrad/Klimov TV3-117 turboshafts, it can travel at 208 mph (335 km/h), with a ceiling of 14,750 feet (4,500 m) and a range of 310 miles (500 km) with standard fuel tanks, or 620 miles (1,000 km) with added-on internal tanks. It is usually armed with the standard four-barrel Gatling 12.7 mm machine gun turret, but can also be equipped with rocket pods connected to four pylons under the wings.

Reference: Lambert, Mark, ed., *Jane's All the World's Aircraft 1991–92* (Coulsdon, Surrey, UK: Jane's Information Group, 1991), 268–270.

Milan Antitank Missile

A wire-guided antitank projectile, the Milan is used by Egypt, France, Great Britain, Oman, Qatar, and the United Arab Emirates, but its employment during the Persian Gulf War is unknown. Iraq used the missile during its war with Iran, but whether or not the weapon was used during the Gulf War remains in doubt.

The Milan (Missile d'Infanterie Léger Antichar) is a small missile only 30 inches (0.77 m) in length, with tiny folded wings that extend after the missile is ejected from the canister by way of a gas generator. The missile itself is powered by a small solid-propellant engine in the rear of the missile body. The firing container is a compact unit weighing 26.5 pounds (12 kg), including the missile, that can be laid on the ground for target acquisition or mounted on a tripod. To acquire the target, the operator uses an infrared guidance system (such as the one utilized with the HOT missile); however, updated versions of the Milan have night-vision capability with the addition of a MIRA thermal imaging device. Moving at a speed of up to 200 meters per second (656 ft/sec), the hollow-charge warhead has the ability of piercing between 33 and 39 inches (850–1,000 mm) of a tank's armor.

Reference: Hogg, Ian V., ed., *Jane's Infantry Weapons, 1993–94* (Coulsdon, Surrey, UK: Jane's Information Group, 1993), 142.

Minesweepers/Minehunters, Coalition

Of the numerous ships sent to the Gulf by the coalition powers, 16 were minesweepers, minehunters, or dual-use craft. Belgium deployed the minesweepers *Iris* and *Myosotis*, armed with Stinger antiaircaft missiles; however, the Belgian government declined to permit their minesweepers to be used during the war, only after its conclusion. Among the seven ships Germany sent to the Gulf were the Lindau-class minehunters *Koblenz*, *Marburg*, and *Wetzlar*, and the Hamelin-class minesweepers *Laboe* and *Überherrn*, as well as five minehunters/minesweepers and six Troika-class minesweeper drones to the postwar cleanup. Great Britain dispatched the Hunt-class minesweepers *Atherstone*, *Cattistock*, *Dulverton*, *Hurworth*, and *Ledbury*. The United Arab Emirates provided two foreign vessels, the *Vivi* and the *Celina*, that were reflagged and used as escort and support ships for the U.S.

Mine Countermeasures Group (USMCMG). Saudi Arabia's four MCM ships were the minesweepers *Addriyah* (MSC 412), *Al Quysumah* (MSC 414), *Al-Wadi'ah* (MSC 416), and *Safwa* (MSC 418). After the war ended, MCM craft from Italy, Japan, and the Netherlands joined those already in the Gulf.

See also Coalition Nations, Contributions of.
Reference: *Conduct of the Persian Gulf War: Final Report to Congress,* Report by the Department of Defense, April 1992, 205–207.

Minesweepers/Minehunters, United States

As part of the U.S. Mine Countermeasures Group (USMCMG), the United States deployed four ships involved in mine detection and minesweeping to the Persian Gulf: the minesweepers USS *Impervious* (MSO 449), USS *Adroit* (MSO 509), USS *Leader* (MSO 490), and the mine countermeasures (MCM) ship USS *Avenger* (MCM 1). The USS *Tripoli,* a part of the amphibious task force, served as both a support ship and a command center. In addition, six MH-53E Sea Dragon airborne mine countermeasure (AMCM) helicopters were assigned to the *Tripoli.*

The *Impervious* and the *Leader* belong to the Aggressive class of ocean minesweepers. They displace 720 tons unloaded (780 fully loaded), are 172.5 feet (52.6 m) long, and are powered by four Waukesha diesel engines (older models from this class are powered by four Packard diesel engines). Much of the fleet was modernized in the mid-1960s to include SQQ sonar with the ability for mine detection and classification.

The *Adroit* is part of a class of Naval Reserve Force mine warfare ships, while the *Avenger* is a member of the Avenger class of MCM vessels. Avenger-class ships displace 1,312 tons fully loaded, are 224 feet (68.3 m) long, and are powered by four Waukesha L-1616 diesel engines. They are equipped with two AN/SLQ-48 MCM sleds, as well as magnetic/acoustic–influence sweep equipment.

The operations of minesweepers from the United States and seven other nations resulted in the detection and destruction of more than 1,300 mines. According to the editors of *Sea Power,*

Minesweepers/Minehunters, U.S.

The minesweeper USS *Adroit* in the Persian Gulf following the Iraqi cease-fire.

"On the first day of mine-clearance operations *Avenger* detected with its sophisticated SQQ-32 sonar an Iraqi influence mine believed undetectable by sonar and destroyed it; later it would detect and destroy a number of other such mines. Moored mines comprised 58 percent of mines destroyed; bottom mines, including some 200 acoustic influence mines not then known to western nations, 24 percent; floating mines, 11 percent; and beached mines, 6 percent."

See also MH-53E Sea Dragon; Minesweepers/Minehunters, Coalition.
References: Conduct of the Persian Gulf War: Final Report to Congress, Report by the Department of Defense, April 1992, 205; Lambert, Mark, ed., *Jane's All the World's Aircraft 1993–94* (Coulsdon, Surrey, UK: Jane's Information Group, 1993), 559–560, 751–752; *Sea Power: The Official Publication of the Navy League of the United States* 37:1 (January 1994), 153.

Mirage F-1EQ, F-1CR, and EQ5-200 (M-2000) Models

Built by Dassault-Breguet, the leading aerospace manufacturer of French air force planes, the Mirage variants under this entry are updated, state-of-the-art jets that replace and modernize earlier versions such as the IVA and IVP models. The F-1CR and the 2000, or EQ5-200 (M-2000), variant served with the French air force during Operation Desert Storm; the F-1EQ was a staple of the Iraqi air force, which bought 64 from the French. The craft was a potentially lethal weapon in the Iraqi arsenal against the Allies, although there is little evidence that it was used, as all Iraqi planes not destroyed on the ground or in the air fled to Iran.

Equipped with the Super Matra 530 Magic or AIM-9 Sidewinder air-to-air missiles, these French air force planes flew 92 (F-1CR) and 512 (M-2000) sorties. Both are single-seat, multimission attack fighters; the F-1CR is powered by a single SNECMA Atar 9K-50 turbojet engine, which delivers 15,873 pounds (7,200 kg) of thrust and the M-2000 is powered by one SNECMA M-53-P2 turbofan engine delivering 21,385 pounds (9,700 kg) of thrust. Both have a wingspan of 29 feet 11.5 inches (9.13 m), a maximum speed of Mach 2.26, and an unrefueled range of 1,118 miles (1,800 km).

The U.S. Defense Department said of the French Mirages that were part of the Iraqi air force, "The 65 French-built F-1s and their pilots were the Iraqi Air Force elite. Iraq had acquired a wide range of weapons and electronic warfare gear for the F-1, including laser-guided air-to-surface missiles. French-trained pilots exhibited a high degree of skill and determination when attacking Iranian surface targets, and were more willing to engage in air-to-air combat than their colleagues flying Soviet-built aircraft."

References: Boyne, Walter J., *The Weapons of Desert Storm* (Lincolnwood, IL: Publications International, 1991), 12; *Conduct of the Persian Gulf War: Final Report to Congress,* Report by the Department of Defense, April 1992, 12; Gunston, Bill, *An Illustrated Guide to Modern Bombers* (New York: Prentice Hall, 1988), 48–51.

Missile Systems, Iraqi

The Iraqi missile arsenal was not limited to the inaccurate Scud. Included in this armory were the FROG-7, al-Hussein, al-Abbas, al-Hijarah, Silkworm, and SA-6 missiles.

The FROG-7, a surface-to-surface missile, was apparently employed during the Iran-Iraq War to transport deadly mustard gas payloads toward Iran. Its specific usage, as a terror weapon, was amply demonstrated during the "War of the Cities" campaign in 1988, when civilian populations in Iran were ruthlessly targeted. Previous to the outbreak of the Persian Gulf War there was a serious threat that Saddam Hussein would use the same tactics against Allied troops, or Saudi civilians, just over the border in Saudi Arabia. The FROG-7, modeled on a Soviet design, has a single solid-propellant engine that is able to deliver a nearly 1,000-pound (454 kg) chemical warhead about 37 miles (60 km). At 29 feet 6 inches (9 m) in length, the Iraqi version weighs 5,511 pounds (2,500 kg), and is controlled by radio command.

The al-Hussein and al-Abbas missiles are both modified Scuds to fit the Iraqi model. Although they were not used during the Persian Gulf War, they were employed during the Iran-Iraq conflict to apparently deliver chemical payloads to civilian populations, and the threat existed during the war for Kuwait that these weapons would be targeted against Allied troops in Saudi Arabia or civilians in Israel. With ranges of 375

Mirage F-1EQ, F-1CR, and EQ5-200 Models

A Mirage F-1, belonging to the air force of Qatar, gets a pre-flight check at a base in Saudi Arabia during Operation Desert Storm.

and 575 miles (603 and 925 km), respectively—compared to the Scud's short 175 miles (282 km)—the two missiles can deliver only small warheads, and their increased range makes them unreliable at best. The al-Hussein was the first Iraqi-produced/modified Scud, and it is estimated that at least 200 were fired during the "War of the Cities" in the Iran-Iraq War. According to the U.S. Department of Defense, the projectile was named "for the grandson of the Prophet Muhammad and the son of Ali."

The last of the Scud variants was the al-Hijarah. A play on the words "the Stones" in English, it was named in honor of the Palestinian youths who hurled stones at Israeli soldiers during the Intifada, the Palestinian uprising. The missile has a range of 466 miles (750 km) and the capability of carrying conventional or high-explosive warheads.

The number of Chinese-made Silkworm missiles in the Iraqi arsenal before and after the war remains unknown. Like the other Iraqi missile systems, the Silkworm is notable for its delivery of terror rather than for a powerful punch. On 25 February 1991 Iraqi forces fired two Silkworms at the battleship USS *Missouri*. A Navy radar warning system detected one incoming missile, which was destroyed by the British destroyer *Gloucester*, and the second fell harmlessly into the Persian Gulf. The Navy then ordered strike aircraft to attack and destroy the missile site.

_____

See also Scud Missiles.
References: Allen, Thomas B., F. Clifton Berry, and Norman Polmar, *CNN: War in the Gulf: From the Invasion of Kuwait to the Day of Victory and Beyond* (Atlanta, GA: Turner, 1991), 176; *Conduct of the Persian Gulf War: Final Report to Congress,* Report by the Department of Defense, April 1992, 13–15.

Mitterrand, François Maurice Adrien Marie (1916–)

President of France since 1981, François Mitterrand has been a leading player in French politics since the 1950s. He was born on 26 October 1916 in Jarnac, in the western department of Charente in France. He was the fifth of eight children of Joseph Mitterrand, a railroad stationmaster, and his wife Yvonne (née Lorrain) Mitterrand. François Mitterrand received an education in the law and political science at the College Saint-Paul, Angoulême, at the University of Paris, and at the École Libre Des Sciences Politiques (School of Liberal Sciences and Politics), from which he earned a law degree.

In August 1994 a scandal hit Mitterrand that connected him with Nazi collaborationists in the French government just prior to the collapse of France in 1940. As Roger Kaplan, editor of *Freedom Review,* related in 1995, "The scandal that hit Paris last August was provoked by Pierre Péan's *Une Jeunesse Française,* a meticulously researched book on Mitterrand's career in the 1930s and '40s. The shock was not so much in the broad fact of Mitterrand's participation in the Vichy regime that ran France under the German shadow from the summer of 1940 until the summer of 1944. That was already known. Rather, it was in the details; the sincerity with which he had engaged himself, the enduring loyalties that he formed while there. What was intolerable to those who for years had bought Mitterrand's own rationale—[that] Vichy was a cover for Resistance work—was the feeling of having been had. Which is exactly how Jean Daniel put it in a lead editorial in his weekly *Le Nouvel Observateur,* the conscience and weathervane of the French left and the Paris intelligentsia. What Daniel expressed was not only exasperation with the fifty-year game of 'love me, love me not' that Mitterrand has played with the French people, and the French left, but the feeling that the French had never sufficiently expiated the sins of the fascist Vichy regime." After enlisting in the French infantry at the outbreak of World War II, Mitterrand saw limited action before being wounded and taken prisoner by the Germans. The *Encyclopædia Britannica* says of this episode in Mitterrand's life, "It was not enough for Mitterrand . . . to demonstrate a keen political sense—which he undoubtedly possessed. He also learned not to give up and to keep on taking risks rather than bowing to events. Three times during World War II he tried to escape from German prisoner-of-war camps before finally succeeding." After his escape, Mitterrand joined the French resistance, later served as head of the resistance's National Movement of War Prisoners and Deportees, and made several trips to London and Algiers to aid war prisoners. With the liberation of France, he was named by Gen-

French president François Mitterrand announces on 15 September 1990 that France will contribute troops, helicopters, and tanks to the coalition buildup in the Persian Gulf.

eral Charles de Gaulle as secretary-general for war prisoners and deportees in the new French government, serving for a short time. Later in 1945 he left to become editor of the French newspaper *Libres,* and for a time acted as president of the Société d'Editions du Rond-Point, a publishing house. In 1946 Mitterrand was elected to the French assembly, where he served until 1958. (He was later elected to a second term, from 1962 to 1991.) In the interim period, 1959 to 1962, he served in the upper house of the French legislature (the Senate), but returned to the lower—and more powerful—house. During these years he also served in various posts in the French government: minister of overseas territories (1950–1951), minister of state (1952–1953), and minister of the interior (1954–1955).

From his first run for office in 1946, Mitterrand had been identified with the Left in France, even being accused during the 1950s of collaboration with the French Communist party. Yet because of his popularity among the French electorate he was never far from the peak of power. In 1965 he staged a failed but close-fought challenge against Charles de Gaulle for the French presidency. He ran again in 1974, but was unsuccessful once more. Mitterrand made a comeback in 1981, defeating Gaullist Valery Giscard d'Estaing as the

Socialist party candidate and becoming president of France at age 65; he was reelected in 1988. Because of surgery for prostate cancer and because of his age, he is expected to retire in 1995.

Mitterrand played a major role at the start of the crisis in the Persian Gulf. On 15 September 1990 he assailed the Iraqi assault of the French embassy in Kuwait, and in response to the worsening situation in the Middle East, he dispatched several thousand troops, materiel, and planes to the area. This support became vital to the coalition cause to oust Iraqi troops from Kuwait. On 24 September Mitterrand spoke at the United Nations, where he proposed to the Iraqi leader that if Iraqi troops were to leave Kuwait voluntarily, Saddam Hussein's demand that all Middle Eastern problems be addressed at once would become a major focus of his. No reply was ever received.

As Mitterrand limped toward the end of his last presidential term in May 1995, he was ill with cancer. Alan Riding wrote in the *New York Times* in October 1994, "While the ailing Socialist looks increasingly like a figure from the past, with even his Presidential powers largely neutralized by a rightist Government and a conservative-dominated Parliament, he still seems to fascinate the French more than any of the politicians in line to succeed him."

References: Kaplan, Roger, "Vichy François," *The American Spectator* 28:2 (February 1995), 42; Moritz, Charles, ed., *Current Biography Yearbook 1968* (New York: H. W. Wilson, 1968), 256–258; Moritz, Charles, ed., *Current Biography Yearbook 1982* (New York: H. W. Wilson, 1982), 270–274; *1982 Britannica Book of the Year* (Chicago: Encyclopædia Britannica, 1982), 85; Northcutt, Wayne, *Mitterrand: A Political Biography* (New York: Holmes & Meier, 1992); Riding, Alan, "At 78, Mitterrand Drawing Admiration and Criticism," *New York Times,* 30 October 1994, A4.

MK-20 Rockeye

The U.S. military calls this air-to-ground weapon "a free-fall, unguided cluster weapon designed to kill tanks and armored vehicles." Rockeyes used during the Gulf War numbered 27,987, including 15,828 by the Marines.

Reference: Gulf War Air Power Survey, Volume IV: Weapons, Tactics, and Training Report and Space Report (Washington, DC: GPO, 1993), 74.

MK-80 Bomb Series

These three variants of air-to-ground explosive devices, including the MK-82, MK-83, and MK-84, were expended in the Persian Gulf War because of their optimum blast effect. All three models are equipped with conical fins for flight stabilization, which delivers the missile on a steady and smooth slide to its target. All three bombs are cylindrical in shape, and come in variables of 500, 1,000, and 2,000 pounds (227, 454, and 908 kg).

MK-82

This 500-pound (227 kg), general-purpose, free-fall nonguided bomb was a basic component of the ordnance dropped in the Kuwaiti Theatre of Operations (KTO), with 77,653 units delivered into action, mostly by B-52s but also by Air Force F-16s and Marine Corps F/A-18s and AV-8Bs. The weapon is equipped with a mechanical M904 nose fuse and an M905 tail fuse, or a single FMU-113 air-burst fuse. It is suitable for internal loading (B-52s) or external mounting (F-16s, etc.). When equipped with a BSU-49 balloon retard system (BALLUTE), it is designated the MK-82 RE GP (general purpose) bomb. Its explosive alone weighs 192 pounds (87 kg).

MK-83

Like its smaller cousin the MK-82, the MK-83 is a free-fall, nonguided general-purpose bomb, although it weighs twice as much—1,000 pounds (454 kg). The explosive alone weighs 416 pounds (189 kg). The MK-83's use during the Gulf conflict was limited to Marine jets conducting close air support/battlefield air interdiction (CAS/BAI), with a total of 19,018 hits.

MK-84

The largest of the M-80 series, this 2,000-pound (908 kg) general-purpose weapon mimics the smallest (the MK-82), except for its larger shell and its 945 pounds (429 kg) of explosives, making for greater incendiary power. Normally equipped with an M904 fuse in the nose and an M905 fuse in the tail, it can be implemented with a BSU-50 BALLUTE balloon retard system to produce an MK-84 RE general-purpose bomb.

Reference: Gulf War Air Power Survey, Volume IV: Weapons, Tactics, and Training Report and Space Report (Washington, DC: GPO, 1993), 70–71.

Morale, Iraqi

Destroying an enemy's morale—military, civilian, or both—is a key strategy toward defeating that enemy. As Allied troops stormed forth into Kuwait and, ultimately, southern Iraq, Iraqi troop morale completely collapsed. Pictures of grateful Iraqi soldiers surrendering to an American soldier by kissing his hand best illustrate this.

Early assessments of Iraqi morale were not promising. Based on the testimony of about 800 total defectors, the military estimated that troop morale was not unusually low. Yet after Desert Storm's land attack, it became evident that *whole masses* of Iraqi troops had not given up to the Allies, but instead had fled homeward and blended into the civilian population. Why did one of the most trained, disciplined, and feared armies in the world—one that had endured eight years of massive casualties during the Iran-Iraq war—literally collapse, even before the coalition launched its ground assault?

The first reason for the breakdown in morale may lie in a debate on the use of massive carpet bombing to wear down an enemy. In congressional testimony it was revealed that after the war, captured Iraqi officers disclosed that the numerous and constant B-52 strikes were the main cause of the collapse of morale. This reinforces information obtained during and after the Vietnam War, when captured Vietcong (VC) soldiers credited the B-52 strikes for shortages of morale. Yet in Vietnam, such morale was not destroyed, but merely worn down; the VC continued to work and operate against American forces. The dynamics in the Kuwaiti Theatre of Operations (KTO) were different. Iraqi troops were stuck in bunkers for long periods; they had no intelligence warnings of incoming aircraft and no direct enemy kills (the latter two are known morale-boosters). Therefore, the B-52s delivered a more powerful wallop. A second part of the theory is that the "truth in Allied advertising" also destroyed the Iraqis' resolve to fight. Planes flew over bunkers and dropped leaflets that said, in effect, "Get out of this area. Tomorrow we will carpet bomb here, and you could get hurt. This is our last warning." The bombing came, on a massive scale, and the lower-echelon troops knew that when the Allies said something was going to happen, it did. This "truth in advertising" later helped convince other Iraqi EPWs (enemy prisoners of war) to surrender peacefully because they had been promised through other leaflets that they would not be hurt. A third and final reason may be that after having fought an Iranian enemy for eight years, many Iraqi soldiers were shell-shocked, and did not want to fight the United States and its allies for what seemed to many of them an unimportant goal—Kuwait. This lack of spirit to fight for Saddam Hussein's cause, as with any army and any leader, is a major reason for a lack of resolve among troops.

Examining the effects of morale or its lack provides students of the war with great insight into what happened. Juan Tomayo wrote in the *Miami Herald* after the end of the war, "An Iraqi military once touted as the world's fourth largest has simply vanished into the desert sands, leaving behind only pulverized debris and a host of troubling questions. Ten days after the war ended, U.S. commanders are still no better prepared to answer some of the most nagging ones." Included in his report from Dhahran was this one query: "Why did the Iraqi army collapse so quickly? Only 100 hours into ground combat, its troops were surrendering by the droves, including some who simply gathered in a knot, put coils of barbed wire around themselves, raised a white flag and waited for the allies to capture them."

References: "Intelligence Successes and Failures in Operations Desert Shield/Storm," Report of the Oversight and Investigations Subcommittee of the House Committee on Armed Services, 103rd Congress, 1st Session, 1993; Tomayo, Juan, "Weakness Surprised U.S. Force; Were Defenses Overrated?" *Miami Herald*, 10 March 1991, 18A.

Morocco
See Coalition Nations, Contributions of.

Mosul
The third largest city in Iraq, Mosul (Arabic: al-Mawsil) is the capital of the Ninawa province, which derives its name from the ancient Assyrian capital of Nineveh. Situated 220 miles (354 km) northwest of Baghdad, Iraq's capital, Mosul is located in northwestern Iraq on the Tigris River. It has an elevation of 730 feet on an upland plain, and is located near the towns of Dohuk, Suleimaniyah, Kirkuk, and Arbil, all strongholds of Kurdish resistance to Iraqi authority.

Mosul has several historically important mosques, including the Great Mosque with its leaning minaret, built in the twelfth century. During the Gulf War, Mosul was the center of several coalition attacks, but the amount of damage caused is unknown.

The Mother of All Battles
Saddam Hussein used this phrase to declare what would happen after the coalition forces attacked the Iraqi army in Kuwait. The phrase was not a new one; he had used it in another speech to the Iraqi troops in Kuwait on 6 January 1991.

In the more famous address, Saddam Hussein's voice was heard on Iraqi radio on 16 January at 4:18 A.M. local time, just two hours after the bombs began to rain down on Baghdad. "O great Iraqi people, sons of great people, valiant men of our courageous armed forces," Hussein said. "Satan's follower Bush committed his treacherous crime, he and the criminal Zionism. The great duel, *the mother of all battles,* between victorious right and the evil that will certainly be defeated has begun, God willing." The speech was a rambling, jingoistic diatribe. The phrase "mother of all battles" is now a part of the English language, used to refer mockingly to the enormity of events.

See also Appendix 4, Address by Saddam Hussein, 20 January 1991.
References: Karsh, Efraim, and Inari Rautsi, *Saddam Hussein: A Political Biography* (New York: Free Press, 1991), 245; Sifry, Micah L., and Christopher Serf, eds., *The Gulf War Reader: History, Documents, Opinions* (New York: Times Books, 1991), 315–316.

The Mother of All Briefings

So dubbed by the media, this briefing, held by General H. Norman Schwarzkopf in the fourth-floor ballroom of the Hyatt Regency Hotel in Riyadh, Saudi Arabia, on 27 February 1991, oriented the media as well as the American public on the land war operations in Kuwait and Iraq.

Schwarzkopf opened the briefing by stating, "Good evening, ladies and gentlemen. Thank you for being here. I promised you a complete rundown on what we were doing and, more important, why we were doing it—the strategy behind what we were doing. I've been asked by Secretary [of Defense Dick] Cheney to do that this evening, so if you will bear with me, we're going to go through a briefing."

See also Appendix 4, General H. Norman Schwarzkopf, CENTCOM Briefing, 27 February 1991.
Reference: Pyle, Richard, *Schwarzkopf: The Man, the Mission, the Triumph* (New York: Signet, 1991), 239.

Mubarak, Muhammad Hosni

(1928–)

The *New York Times* called him a "Mediator Turned Risk-Taker." A former Egyptian air force commander, hero of the 1973 Arab-Israeli War, and for six years (1975–1981) vice-president of his nation, Hosni Mubarak stepped quickly into the shoes of his predecessor, Anwar el-Sadat, after Sadat was assassinated by Egyptian fundamentalists in 1981. He became one of the Arab

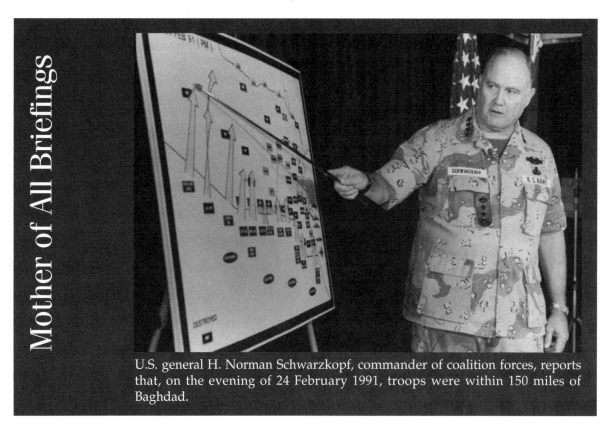

U.S. general H. Norman Schwarzkopf, commander of coalition forces, reports that, on the evening of 24 February 1991, troops were within 150 miles of Baghdad.

Mubarak, Muhammad Hosni

Egyptian president Hosni Mubarak speaks to the People's Assembly, the Egyptian parliament, in Cairo on 24 January 1991.

leaders in the Allied coalition against Iraq during the Persian Gulf crisis. Born on 4 May 1928 in the small village of Kafr-El Meselha in the Nile delta province of Minuffya (or Menoufia), the same province as his mentor Sadat, Mubarak received his military and educational training at the Egyptian military academy in Cairo and at the air academy at Bilbeis; in 1950 he joined the Egyptian air force.

In 1967 Mubarak was named the director-general of the Egyptian Air Academy, where he served until 1969. For the next three years he was the chief of staff of the Egyptian air force. John Kifner wrote in the *New York Times*, "The young officer gained a reputation as an able commander and he was promoted rapidly. In 1972, he was appointed commander of the air force, and was largely credited with its success in the early days of the October 1973 war with Israel. Anwar el-Sadat appointed him Vice President in 1975." Adds *The Encyclopædia Britannica*, "For Sadat, Mubarak was a model of what he called the 'October Generation'—the class of technocrats capable of meeting the Israelis on their own grounds and restoring Egypt's pride damaged by the 1967 defeat [at the hands of Israel]."

Mubarak continued in that position until 1981,

becoming involved in Middle Eastern and sub-Saharan issues. Upon Sadat's assassination by Muslim fundamentalists in October 1981, Mubarak became president of Egypt, a position he continues to hold. Reelected in 1987 and 1993, he is one of the foremost democratically elected leaders in the Middle East. His work against the influence of fundamentalism, as well as his close alliance with the United States, has won him wide respect. In February 1989 he took the initiative to become a leader of the "Arab nation" when he led Egypt into an alliance with Jordan, Iraq, and Yemen, called the Arab Cooperation Council (ACC). Because of the Persian Gulf War that erupted in 1991, the ACC was disbanded.

At the start of the Persian Gulf crisis, Mubarak took a hard line against Saddam Hussein, even going so far as to dispatch Egyptian troops to Saudi Arabia—troops that later fought for the coalition. Why did Mubarak take such a hard stand against his Arab brother, a man to whom he had been making important overtures in the previous half dozen years? As Edward Cody discussed in the *Washington Post*, "Mubarak thus had no reason to suspect he was being lied to when Saddam reportedly told him shortly before August 2 that he would not invade Kuwait despite threatening Iraqi troops movements. Mubarak relayed these assurances to President Bush and other world leaders. In addition, as Bashir [Tahseen Bashir, a former Egyptian government official and news commentator] pointed out, he [Mubarak] made the assurances public, making him look gullible before his own people when the news" of the invasion came out.

American secretary of defense Dick Cheney said of the Egyptian president, "We worked closely with the Egyptians and President Mubarak. President Mubarak and King Fahd were really the two very strong leaders in the Arab world that we worked with throughout this period. . . . I asked him [Mubarak] for a number of things—overflights rights, because we had a lot of aircraft coming from the United States that would have to overfly Egypt to get to Saudi Arabia—which he readily agreed to. I also asked permission to pass one of our aircraft carriers through the Suez Canal. The carrier was the *Eisenhower*, which was deployed in the Med[iterranean], and we wanted to immediately move it down to the Red Sea just off the Saudi coast and provide air cover in case Saddam Hussein did make a move south. President Mubarak said when do you want to move the carrier? I said tonight. He said okay, and immediately signed up for it." Mubarak sent soldiers and weapons (he even offered Egyptian planes to Saudi Arabia, but the offer was refused) to the Gulf; they saw limited action in the liberation of Kuwait.

On 26 June 1995, Mubarak was the subject of an unsuccessful assassination attempt while he was in Addis Ababa, Ethiopia, for an African summit. Mubarak was unharmed, Sudanese and Egyptian fundamentalists were blamed for the attack.

References: Cody, Edward, "Anger at Saddam, Financial Need Seen Motivating Mubarak," *Washington Post*, 6 November 1990, A15; *Conduct of the Persian Gulf War: Final Report to Congress*, Report by the Department of Defense, April 1992, 23; Kifner, John, "Hosni Mubarak: Mediator Turned Risk-Taker," *New York Times*, 13 August 1990, A10; *1982 Britannica Book of the Year* (Chicago: Encyclopædia Britannica, 1982), 86.

Muhammarah, Treaty of
See Uqair, Treaty of.

Multiple Launch Rocket System (227-MM MLRS)

About 90 MLRS launchers were committed to Operations Desert Shield/Desert Storm, with more than 10,000 rockets fired during battle. The military report *Desert Score* summarizes of this system, "The MLRS is also identified as the M270 Armored Vehicle Mounted Rocket Launcher (AVMRL). It consists of an M269 Launcher Loader Module (LLM) with two 6-cell rocket Launch Pods/Containers (LP/c) mounted on an M993 carrier vehicle. Its role is to bombard enemy formations from as far as 20 miles (32 km) away. A full salvo of twelve 227 mm ripple-fired rockets with the Dual-Purpose Improved Conventional Munitions (DPICM) submunition warhead will saturate a 60-acre (24 hectare) area with 8,256 anti-personnel bomblets in less than one minute." The editors of *Jane's Weapons Systems, 1989–89* write, "The multiple launch rocket system is a highly mobile automatic rocket system developed to enable a firing crew with a minimum amount of training to shoot a complete 12-rocket load, reload rapidly and fire again."

With two 6-rocket launchers, the MLRS can fire a warhead a maximum of 19 miles (30.5 km) with the M77 submunition warhead and up to 24 miles (38.6 km) with the AT-2 antitank mine warhead. Rocket size is 13 feet x 9 inches (4 m x 33 cm). Powered by a Cummins VTA-903 903 cubic inch (14.8 liter) liquid-cooled V-8 diesel engine, the vehicle, which is essentially a modified M2 Bradley APC, is crewed by three men (section chief, gunner, and driver). It is built by FMC of San Jose, California, and LTV of Dallas, Texas.

References: Almond, Denise L., ed., *Desert Score: U.S. Gulf War Weapons* (Washington, DC: Carroll Publishing, 1991), 378–379; "America's Arsenal," *Popular Mechanics*, 168:4 (April 1991), 30; Blake, Bernard, ed., *Jane's Weapon Systems, 1988–89* (Coulsdon, Surrey, UK: Jane's Information Group, 1988), 133–134.

National Defense Authorization Act for the Fiscal Years 1992 and 1993 (Public Law 102-190, 105 Stat. 1290)

This legislation, enacted on 5 December 1991, appropriated funds for "military activities of the Department of Defense" for the years 1992 and 1993. Important in the bill was section 734, which established a "Registry of Members of the Armed Forces Exposed to Fumes of Burning Oil in Connection with Operation Desert Storm" in the Department of Defense.

See also Persian Gulf Conflict Supplemental Authorization and Personnel Benefits Act of 1991; Veterans Health Care Act of 1992.

National Emergency Construction Authority

See Appendix 4, Executive Order 12734 of 14 November 1990.

National Media Pool (NMP)

Established "in response to protests over the news blackout effected in the first two days of the invasion in Grenada" in 1983, the Defense Department's National Media Pool was first used during the invasion of Panama in 1989, with some protests from the media. It was revived for Operations Desert Shield and Desert Storm to keep a firm handle on press reporting during a delicate situation.

In its *Final Report to Congress,* the U.S. military wrote of the NMP, "The pool enables reporters to cover the earliest possible military action in a remote area where there is no other presence of the American news media, while still protecting

the element of surprise, an essential part of operational security. Starting with those initial 17 press pool members, representing Associated Press, United Press International, Reuters, Cable News Network, National Public Radio, *Time,* Scripps-Howard, the *Los Angeles Times,* and the *Milwaukee Journal,* the number of reporters, editors, photographers, producers, and technicians grew to nearly 800 by December [1990]. Except during the first two weeks of the pool, those reporters filed all their stories independently, directly to their news organizations." According to journalist John J. Fialka, the NMP was deployed on 12 August 1990 and arrived in Dhahran the next day. The pool was dissolved because of protests on 26 August, giving way to a system of individual pools of reporters assigned to various units.

See also Censorship of the War, Coalition; Joint Information Bureau; Journalists; Media.
References: Conduct of the Persian Gulf War: Final Report to Congress, Report by the Department of Defense, April 1992, 652; Fialka, John J., *Hotel Warriors: Covering the Gulf War* (Washington, DC: Woodrow Wilson Center Press, 1992), 67; MacArthur, John R., *Second Front: Censorship and Propaganda in the Gulf War* (New York: Hill & Wang, 1992), 8–9.

National Security Council

Under the direction and leadership of Brent Scowcroft, the National Security Council played an important role in advising the President on national security matters during the crisis in the Persian Gulf. The council was constituted by the National Security Act of 1947 (61 Stat. 497), which established that "the function of the Council shall be to advise the President with respect to the integration of domestic, foreign, and military policies relating to the national security so as to enable the military services and the other departments and agencies of the Government to cooperate more effectively in matters involving the national security." The council is made up of the president, the vice-president, the secretary of state, and secretary of defense, with the president serving as the head of the council when it meets, but otherwise delegating authority to a National Security Adviser (NSA). During the Bush Administration, the NSA was Brent Scowcroft.

Scowcroft was a member of the three-man panel that comprised the President's Special Review Board, which examined the Iran-Contra Affair in 1987. (The other members were former Senator John Tower and former Senator Edmund Muskie; the board was better known as the Tower Commission.) The report noted: "The National Security Council has from its inception been a highly personal instrument. Every President has turned for advice to those individuals and institutions whose judgment he has valued and trusted. For some presidents, such as President Eisenhower, the National Security Council served as a primary forum for obtaining advice on national security matters. Other presidents, such as President Kennedy, relied more on more informal groupings of advisers, often including some but not all of the council members."

On 15 January 1991, President Bush met in the Oval Office with the men inside his inner circle: Vice President Quayle, Secretary of State James Baker, Secretary of Defense Dick Cheney, CIA Director Robert Gates, Joint Chiefs Chairman Colin Powell, and National Security Adviser Brent Scowcroft. The group was called to discuss a top-secret National Security Directive (NSD) drawn up by Scowcroft's National Security Council assistants as per Secretary of State Baker's order of 1 January. As *Washington Post* editor Bob Woodward writes, "It [the directive] had been modified [from an earlier draft] to include two conditions. It now authorized the execution of Operation Desert Storm, provided that: (1) there was no last–minute diplomatic breakthrough, and (2) Congress had been properly notified. The document basically laid out the administration's case for launching the offensive soon after the [15 January] deadline. It stated that it was the policy of the United States to get Iraq to leave Kuwait; all peaceful means, including diplomacy, economic sanctions and a dozen U.N. resolutions, had failed to persuade Iraq to withdraw; waiting would be potentially damaging to U.S. interests because Iraq was continuing to move additional forces into the Kuwaiti theater of operations, and was improving its fortifications in occupied Kuwait; Iraq continued to pillage Kuwait and brutalize its people; Iraq's military had to be attacked in order to defend U.S. and allied forces. It also directed that civilian casualties and damage to Iraq should be minimized consistent with protecting friendly forces, and that Islamic holy places should be protected. The President signed it. The NSD was intentionally not dated. The date and time would be added when and if the two conditions were met."

See also Scowcroft, Brent.
References: Shane, Peter, and Harold H. Bruff, *The Law of Presidential Power: Cases and Materials* (Durham, NC: Carolina Academic Press, 1988), 492; *The Tower Commission Report: The Full Text of the President's Special Review Board* (New York: Bantam Books and Times Books, 1987), 7; Woodward, Bob, *The Commanders* (New York: Simon & Schuster, 1991), 366.

Naval Blockade, Coalition

On 6 August 1990 the UN Security Council authorized an embargo against Iraq for its invasion of Kuwait four days earlier. Resolution 661 allowed for an imposition of this embargo to stop all materials short of foodstuffs and medicine being sent to Iraq.

Rear Admiral E. W. Carter III wrote, "The President of the United States announced that the U.S. Navy would be employed, either unilaterally or as part of a multinational force, to enforce these sanctions by interdicting all maritime traffic carrying goods to and from Iraq. The President refused to describe these actions as a blockade because, by some definitions, blockade is an act of war."

Commander Tom Delery, who served with the Maritime Interception Force, said, "The sudden and decisive end of Operation Desert Storm did not bring immediate compliance by Saddam Hussein with all outstanding U.N. resolutions, and thus did not bring an end to interceptions and board-and-search operations. At the time of the initial cease-fire, interceptions totaled nearly 7,000 and were continuing at the rate of 30–40 per day. Boardings totalled near 1,000 and were continuing at the rate of five to ten per day. In terms of oil revenue, Iraq was losing upwards of 30 million dollars every day that it remained in this sea-based stranglehold."

References: Carter, E. W., III, "Blockade," *U.S. Naval Institute Proceedings* 116:11 (November 1990), 42; Delery, Tom, "Away, the Boarding Party!" *U.S. Naval Institute Proceedings* 117:5 (May 1991), 71.

New Zealand
See Coalition Nations, Contributions of.

Niger
See Coalition Nations, Contributions of.

No Fly Zone
See Operation Southern Watch.

Norway
See Coalition Nations, Contributions of.

Nuclear Weapons, Iraq's Potential for Constructing

In March 1991 the *Bulletin of the Atomic Scientists* posed an important question on Iraq's capability for manufacturing a nuclear weapon before the coalition forces destroyed most, if not all, of their nuclear program: "Were They Even Close?" As far back as the early 1970s, Iraq and its leaders (even before Saddam Hussein's ascension to power) were interested in constructing a nuclear weapon, and it was the French, through their Osirak plant near Baghdad, who helped them. The Israelis' bold 1981 attack on Osirak destroying the complex put a major dent in the Iraqi nuclear program, and warned the world what the Iraqis were up to.

References: Albright, David, and Mark Hibbs, "Hyping the Iraq Bomb," *Bulletin of the Atomic Scientists* 47:2 (March 1991), 26–28; Albright, David, and Mark Hibbs, "Iraq and the Bomb: Were They Even Close?" *Bulletin of the Atomic Scientists* 47:2 (March 1991), 16–25.

al-Nuhayyan, Sheik Zayid Bin Sultan. *See* United Arab Emirates.

OH-58 Kiowa and the OH-58D Kiowa Warrior Scout

Flown from the frigate *Nicholas* to attack offshore oil platforms that Iraqi troops were using to harass Allied aircraft flying over the Gulf, the OH-58D Kiowa Warrior Scout was said by aviation writer Elfan Ap Rees in 1986 to be "the newest variant of the Bell OH-58 'Kiowa' to enter service . . . the subject of a major updating program which includes the introduction of a four-bladed main rotor, new avionics and a mast-mounted sight/sensor system." According to the military report *Desert Score*, "During the run-up to the ground war that ended Operation Desert Storm, OH-58s were used for reconnaissance, forward air control training, and personal transports for commanders. They performed similar functions during the ground war. Two were lost, one as a combat casualty and one to non-combat causes."

Of the two craft, the one used most by U.S. forces during the war was the OH-58D, of which 118 saw action in the Gulf. Only 15, all stationed on the frigate *Nicholas,* were equipped with Hellfire missiles. The Saudis also used the export variant, the 406CS, as forward air controllers (FACs) for other coalition craft. The OH-58D is powered by a single Allison 250-C30U turboshaft providing 650 shaft horsepower (shp). The craft has a fuselage length of 34 feet 4.75 inches (10.5 m) and is able to seat two crew members (pilot and co-pilot) and carry two troops. Modifications (not including those done to the models sold to the Saudis) comprise, according to author Tom Clancy, "the installation of weapons pylons capable of taking AGM-114 Hellfire missiles, air-to-air Stingers, 2.75 inch Hydra-70 rockets, and a .50-caliber machine-gun pod." He adds, "In September 1987, under a 'black' program (the very existence of the program was secret) code-named PRIME CHANCE, the Joint Chiefs of Staff directed Bell Helicopter-Textron to convert fifteen OH-58Ds to an armed configuration."

Originally called the Kiowa Scout, it was renamed the Kiowa Warrior Scout in honor of its duty during the Iran-Iraq War, when it worked to save tankers from Iranian mines, and its accomplishments during Operations Desert Shield and Desert Storm. An OH-58D craft was shot down over North Korea in December 1994, an incident in which one U.S. airman, CWO David Hilemon, was killed.

References: Allen, Thomas B., F. Clifton Berry, and Norman Polmar, *CNN: War in the Gulf: From the Invasion of Kuwait to the Day of Victory and Beyond* (Atlanta, GA: Turner, 1991), 170; Almond, Denise L., ed., *Desert Score: U.S. Gulf War Weapons* (Washington, DC: Carroll Publishing, 1991), 94–95; Clancy, Tom, *Armored Cav: A Guided Tour of an Armored Cavalry Regiment* (New York: Berkley Books, 1994), 145–146; Rees, Elfan Ap, *World Military Helicopters* (London: Jane's Publications, 1986), 40–41.

Oil

The chief argument of those who opposed American involvement in the Persian Gulf was that the war was essentially fought over oil. After all, the Persian Gulf is the world's preeminent oil shipping lane, and control by Iraq of Kuwait's and Saudi Arabia's oil reserves could make Saddam Hussein the preeminent power over world oil supplies.

Just exactly what part did oil play in the prosecution of the war against Iraq? Government analyst Carl Behrens, in a Congressional Research Service brief, "Oil and Iraq's Invasion of Kuwait," wrote in 1990: "Almost 40% of oil produced by market economies, 17.2 million barrels per day (mbd), comes from Persian Gulf countries. Of that total, Iraq and Kuwait produced 3 mbd and 1.9 mbd respectively, representing almost 30% of Gulf production." Thus, it was extremely important that Iraqi troops be stopped from taking Saudi Arabi, if that was their intent.

Oil and its power became a huge part of the argument against going to war in the Persian Gulf. Todd Gitlin wrote in the *Village Voice*, "Given the reality of the world economy, as

Oil

Retreating Iraqi forces set Kuwaiti oil-well heads afire. The Kuwaiti government contracted fire fighting companies from around the world to extinguish the fires.

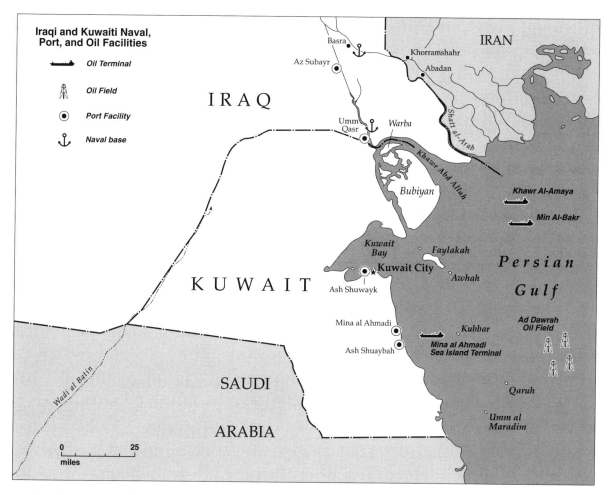

Iraqi and Kuwaiti Naval, Port, and Oil Facilities

- Oil Terminal
- Oil Field
- Port Facility
- Naval base

IRAN

Basra
Khorramshahr
Az Subayr
Abadan

IRAQ

Umm Qasr
Warba
Shatt al-Arab
Khawr Abd Allah
Bubiyan

Khawr Al-Amaya
Min Al-Bakr

Kuwait Bay
Faylakah
Persian
Kuwait City
Awhah
Gulf
Ash Shuwayk

KUWAIT

Mina al Ahmadi
Kubbar
Ad Dawrah Oil Field
Ash Shuaybah
Mina al Ahmadi Sea Island Terminal

SAUDI

Qaruh

ARABIA

Umm al Maradim

Wadi al Batin

0   25
miles

reality that cannot be washed away, oil is, as Arthur Waskow says, not only heroin but life-blood—witness the dire impact of increasing oil prices on the non-oil producing Third World." James R. Schlesinger, secretary of defense in the Nixon administration and secretary of energy in the Carter administration, said in an interview in the *New York Times* in September 1990, "Why is Saudi Arabia so important? Because it is the world's largest producer of oil, and the U.S. is becoming increasingly dependent on foreign sources of supply."

Agis Salpukas wrote in March 1995 in the *New York Times*, "The Middle East holds two-thirds of the world's oil reserves. At the rate the world is increasing its use of oil, it will need 10 million more barrels a day by the year 2000. Some analysts and economists say the Middle East is the only place where that extra 10 million barrels a day can be brought into production fast enough." He added, "Now, in the aftermath of the Persian Gulf War, with Arab unity shattered and with oil prices long depressed, a new oil embargo is no longer a threat. What appears more

likely is a creeping price rise as oil companies and Arab lands jockey for the financial resources with which to develop new oil fields."

References: Behrens, Carl, Robert Bamberger, and Marc Humphries, *Oil and Iraq's Invasion of Kuwait,* Report of the Congressional Research Service, 7 September 1990, 1; Gitlin, Todd, "Toward a Difficult Peace Movement," *Village Voice,* 19 February 1991, quoted in *The Gulf War Reader: History, Documents, Opinions,* edited by Micah L. Sifry and Christopher Serf (New York: Times Books, 1991), 321; "Resistance to Blatant Aggression, Defense of Allies and, above All, Oil," *New York Times,* 23 September 1990, A11; Salpukas, Agis, "Still Looking to the Persian Gulf," *New York Times,* 26 March 1995, E5.

Oman

Known as Saltanan 'Umăn (the Sultanate of Oman), this small country, originally called Muscat and Trucial Oman, takes up the south end of the Gulf, at the mouth of the Persian Gulf, and wraps south along the Arabian peninsula

Oman's leader, Sultan Qaboos bin Al Sa'id, arrives in London, England, for a state visit in 1982.

beside the Arabian Sea. It is bordered by Saudi Arabia to the west, South Yemen to the southwest, and the United Arab Emirates to the northwest. According to writer Alison Brown, "With an area of 271,949 sq km [105,000 sq mi] and a population of around one million [in 1988 figures], Oman is the second largest country on the Arabian peninsula. The country is divided into five main geographical regions: the Batina Plain and Hajar Mountains in the north; the Naj Desert; Dhofar in the south; and Musandam, the rocky peninsula which is divided from the rest of Oman by a 70 kilometer [43.5 mile] strip of the United Arab Emirates."

Oman's recent history is sparse. Formed through an agreement by the Albusa'id family in 1856, the area was ruled mainly by tribal factions for many years. In 1920 Sultan Sa'id bin Taimur signed the Agreement of Seeb, which established Muscat and Sohar as main trading facilities. The isolationist sultan misused the oil royalties his country earned in the 1950s and 1960s, making Oman an economic basket case. As the present sultan of Oman, Qaboos bin Al Sa'id rules over a nation of approximately 1.4 million (1988 est.), of whom about 300,000 are expatriate workers. He was born on 18 November 1940 in Salalah, in

what was then known as Muscat and Trucial Oman. A member of the ruling Albusa'id family, Qaboos bin Said received his education at Bury Saint Edmunds, Suffolk, Britain. Thereafter, he received military training at the Royal Military Academy at Sandhurst, Berkshire. In a palace coup in July 1970, Qaboos overthrew his father and declared himself the new sultan. He abrogated the rigid Islamic laws, and established a cabinet and municipal councils. Although the system of absolute ruler gave way to a council of rulers, the country did not move toward a constitutional monarchy. The royal family retains a monopoly over power and decision-making.

Oman played a small role in aiding the coalition during the Gulf War. Having trained with Egyptian and American troops in the Egyptian desert during Operation Bright Star in November 1980, Omani troops were accustomed to Americans. Just after the start of the air war portion of Operation Desert Storm, Oman allowed 6,000 American Marines to train on their soil in what was called Exercise Sea Soldier IV. Oman also stood by the coalition at a ministerial meeting of the Arab League in Tunis, Tunisia, voting with other Arab nations against a PLO-sponsored resolution to condemn the United States for the Temple Mount killings in Israel on 7 October.

References: Adams, Michael, ed., *The Middle East* (New York: Facts on File, 1988), 94–95; Brown, Alison, "Oman," in *The Cambridge Encyclopedia of the Middle East and North Africa*, edited by Trevor Mostyn (Cambridge: Cambridge University Press, 1988), 395.

Operation Artimon

This was the French name for that nation's naval contribution to the coalition forces. It consisted of 30 ships, which included 6 leased transport ships.

See also Coalition Nations, Contributions of.

Operation Busiris

Under this little-known maneuver by the French, according to the military report *Desert Score*, "a reconnaissance squadron of ERC 90 [Sagaie armored cars] as well as 2 Croatale and 1 Mistrale SAM missile sections were deployed to the United Arab Emirates."

Reference: Almond, Denise L., ed., *Desert Score: U.S. Gulf War Weapons* (Washington, DC: Carroll Publishing, 1991), 479.

Operation Camel Sand

This little-known exercise conducted during Operation Desert Shield was intended to convince Saddam Hussein that an Allied attempt to wrest control of Kuwait from his armies would come from the sea. Just after dawn on 1 October 1990, some 6,000 Marines from the Fourth Marine Expeditionary Brigade and sailors from the USS *Cuyuga,* USS *Durham,* USS *Fort McHenry,* USS *Ogden,* and USS *Okinawa* stormed ashore in southern Oman near Ras al-Madrakah to "test their plans, operational timing, combat readiness, and communications." The operation lasted for five days and, as the authors of *Triumph without Victory: The History of the Persian Gulf War* relate, "It would have been hard for Saddam, even with his limited intelligence capabilities, to have missed it." As is now known, the feint was never used.

See also Operation Imminent Thunder.
References: *Gulf War Air Power Survey, Volume V: A Statistical Compendium and Chronology* (Washington, DC: GPO, 1993), 75; U.S. News & World Report, *Triumph without Victory: The History of the Persian Gulf War* (New York: Times Books, 1993), 170.

Operation Desert Hell

So nicknamed by its participants, Desert Hell was the mission to extinguish the Kuwaiti oil-well fires set by the Iraqi army. It lasted until the last fires were doused on 6 November 1991.

Reference: "New Hellfighters Battle Mother of All Infernos," *Popular Mechanics* (July 1991), 14.

Operation Desert Shield

For the first time in the history of warfare, a major combat army, consisting of coalition forces, was allowed time to build up and train, then bomb an enemy without threat to its ground forces. This buildup became Operation Desert Shield.

Rick Atkinson, in his *Crusade: The Untold Story of the Persian Gulf War,* writes, "The Central Command that Schwarzkopf inherited in 1989 had focused on a Soviet thrust south into Iran, a hypothesis obviated by the collapse of central authority in Moscow. Almost immediately after assuming command, he began looking at other threats; in September 1989, with encouragement from Under Secretary Paul Wolfowitz, the CINC [commander in chief, U.S. Central Command; also called USCINCCENT] asked the Defense Intelligence Agency to scrutinize Iraq as a potential foe. By July 1990, he had assembled portions of a secret battle plan, Operations Plan 1002-90, *Defense of the Arabian Peninsula,* which was designed to parry an Iraqi invasion of Saudi Arabia through Kuwait."

Started on 2 August 1990, the first day of the crisis, in effect Desert Shield was the establishment of a buffer to stop a potential Iraqi invasion of Saudi Arabia. Iraq's biggest mistake in the war may have been its failure to take the war to Riyadh, which would have denied the coalition a base from which to attack and liberate Kuwait. Alfred Prados and Clyde Mark, of the Congressional Research Service's Foreign Affairs and National Defense Division, wrote in August 1990, "Significant logistical factors would complicate, though not preclude, a further Iraqi move into Saudi Arabia. Approximately 200 miles [321 km] of inhospitable desert separate Kuwait from the Saudi core of oil facilities centered on the western shore of the Persian Gulf at Ras Tunura, the first likely objective of an Iraqi invading force. The largely six-lane coastal road would facilitate rapid advance but the distances involved together with lack of water resources would create major supply burdens. Open terrain with sparse vegetation would afford little cover or concealment and leave forces vulnerable to interdiction, although Iraq's air force and Soviet-supplied air defense system would provide some protection against air strikes."

The U.S. military's *Gulf War Air Power Survey* reports that "Many of [Saddam Hussein's] commanders did not seriously believe that Saddam would lead Iraq to war and felt that he would withdraw from Kuwait at the last moment. One saw the systematic looting of Kuwait as evidence that Iraq would eventually withdraw."

References: Atkinson, Rick, *Crusade: The Secret History of the Gulf War* (Boston: Houghton Mifflin, 1993), 107; *Gulf War Air Power Survey, Volume I: Planning Report* and Command and Control Report (Washington, DC: GPO, 1993), 71; Murphy, Carlye, "Papers Left in Kuwait Offer Glimpse of Iraqi Occupiers," *Washington Post,* 6 October 1991, A30; Prados, Alfred B., and Clyde R. Mark, *Iraq-Kuwait Crisis: U.S. Policy and Options,* Report of the Congressional Research Service, 30 August 1990.

Operation Desert Shield/Desert Storm Supplemental Appropriations Act of 1991(Public Law 102-88; 105 Stat. 161)

Enacted on 10 April 1991, this congressional legislation secured supplemental appropriations for military actions during Operations Desert Shield and Desert Storm. As part of the legislation, a Persian Gulf Regional Defense Fund was established. It was created "for incremental costs of the Department of Defense and the Department of Transportation associated with operations in and around the Persian Gulf as part of operations currently known as Operation Desert Shield (including Operation Desert Storm), $15,000,000,000 is appropriated to the Persian Gulf Regional Defense Fund, which is hereby established in the Treasury of the United States, and in addition such sums as necessary are appropriated from current and future balances in the Defense Cooperation Account, to be available only for transfer in a total amount not to exceed $42,625,822,000."

Operation Desert Storm

Known for its two phases, the air war and the ground war, Operation Desert Storm was the obvious and eventual extension of the buildup in the Gulf called Operation Desert Shield. It was apparent that such a continuing phase was necessary because the economic sanctions slapped on Iraq by most of the world were hurting the Iraqi people, not Saddam Hussein, and thus put no pressure on him to withdraw from Kuwait.

Most importantly, however, the line drawn in the sand by President George Bush and the Allied coalition's aim to liberate Kuwait were a clash of egos and cultures—American military might and its wish to stand up for a small nation against a larger bully imposing Arab pride and intransigence against outside pressure. Operation Desert Storm was also a turning point in man's ever-progressing march toward new ways of fighting war, an advance marked for the first time by television and minute-by-minute accounts of developments. It was also the first "video game war."

Thomas A. Keany and Eliot A. Cohen, the editors of the U.S. military's *Gulf War Air Power Survey, Summary Report,* stated: "On 25 August 1990, General Schwarzkopf briefed General Powell on a four-phase plan, code named Desert Storm, to eject Iraqi forces from Kuwait. The first phase, called the strategic air campaign, was essentially the Instant Thunder plan, with an added aim of preventing reinforcement of Iraqi forces in Kuwait; the second phase would gain air superiority over Kuwait; the third phase consisted of air operations to reduce Iraqi ground forces capability before the ground attack; and the fourth phase, which still required much work, was a ground attack into Kuwait—a planning concept identical to the one executed the following January and February."

Theoretically the war began just after midnight EST on 16 January 1991. The previous evening, President George Bush had concluded that Iraq would not withdraw voluntarily from Kuwait, and he ordered air strikes to begin as soon as the UN-imposed deadline passed. At 7:02 P.M. on 15 January, Secretary of State James Baker called Senator Jesse Helms (R–NC), the ranking Republican on the Senate Foreign Relations Committee, with the code "the balloon is up," the signal that the war would soon be under way. Journalist Carl Mollins wrote in *Maclean's,* a Canadian news magazine, "Hour after hour, night and day, by the accounting of U.S.-led coalition forces, high-explosion destruction rained down on Iraq's army in occupied Kuwait and along its northern border. Armadas of warplanes bombed and strafed entrenched soldiers and their dug-in tanks at attack rates that averaged 25 an hour. For the first time in the Gulf War, the U.S. battleships *Missouri* and *Wisconsin,* whose big guns last bellowed in anger off Korea

Operation Desert Storm

The battleship USS *Wisconsin* fires a salvo of one-ton shells while on station in the Persian Gulf during Operation Desert Storm.

40 years ago, fired 2,700-lb. shells at Iraqi placements ashore. Artillery in Saudi Arabia opened up against Iraqi gun positions across the Kuwait frontier." In an important discussion in "Early Gulf War Lessons," Vice Admiral Robert F. Dunn (USN, Ret.), wrote, "The first and most obvious lesson of the Gulf War to date [March 1991] is that technology works. In fact, Buck Rogers or Luke Skywalker would be at home in the Gulf War. Cruise missiles launched from ships far at sea destroy enemy air defense systems and other point targets. Iraqi ballistic missiles spread terror among the civilians in Israel and Saudi Arabia, although Patriot missiles intercept and destroy most of these ballistic missiles. Aegis-controlled missiles are on standby, should Iraqi weapons reach seaward. Missiles from fighter planes destroy other aircraft, and laser-guided weapons from tactical bombers pound heavily defended targets on the ground—the targets having been located with the aid of satellite-based navigation systems, television, infrared, and night-vision devices. Several types of missiles suppress and attack enemy radars. Meanwhile, other satellites gather intelligence, give warning, relay communications, and help commanders assess target damage. The

money allocated to technology has been well spent. The new gear works . . . over and over again." Authors Keaney and Cohen report that by the end of Desert Storm, coalition aircraft had shot down 33 fixed-wing Iraqi aircraft and 5 helicopters.

What were the causes of the war; its origins, its meanings? Charles William Maynes, the editor of *Foreign Policy* magazine, wrote in 1991, "When historians examine the reasons behind the U.S. decision to go to war in the Persian Gulf . . . they are likely to identify four: oil, order, security, and Israel." Add a fifth: greed—greed for land, greed for oil, greed for the opportunity to control a major world commodity. Yet was the Gulf War a *just* war? In an important article, Captain Yuval Joseph Zacks of the U.S. Army said, "Kuwait, an independent state with internationally recognized borders, was clearly the victim of Iraqi aggression. This aggression constituted a criminal act. . . . Ill-equipped to either defend itself or regain its independence through unilateral action, Kuwait was necessarily dependent on the international community for its rescue."

The coalition air forces' impact in determining the Iraqi troops' ability to fight, their resolve to resist calls for their surrender, and their adequacy in defending their frontier were nothing short of incredible. In an interview in December 1990, Saddam Hussein boasted, "The United States depends on the air force. The air force has never decided a war in the history of wars. In the early days of the war between us and Iran, the Iranians had an edge in the air. They had approximately 600 aircraft, all U.S.-made and whose pilots received training in the United States. They flew to Baghdad like black clouds, but they did not determine the outcome of the battle. In later years, our air force gained supremacy, and yet it was not our air force that settled the war. The United States may be able to destroy cities, factories and to kill, but it will not be able to decide the war with the air force."

General Sir Peter de la Billière, commander of British forces in the Gulf, wrote of the first phase of the campaign against Saddam Hussein: "The air war was an operation of astonishing complexity. Devised by Buster Glosson and his targeting teams, under the overall guidance of Chuck Horner, it was a masterpiece of human planning and computer-controlled aggression, directed with a degree of precision which far surpassed that of any air attack in the past. Each day's ATO, or Air Tasking Order, ran to well over 100 pages of minutely detailed orders, which coordinated sorties by allied aircraft from all over the theatre in 'force packages' for every period of twenty-four hours."

According to the briefing conducted by General H. Norman Schwarzkopf, the *Washington Post* reported that "Before the air war began, Iraqi forces outnumbered coalition troops 3-to-2. U.S. and coalition forces were concentrated and aligned opposite the enemy in Kuwait, reinforcing Iraq's belief that an attack would come over the Saudi-Kuwait border. An active naval presence in the gulf presented the threat of an amphibious landing." General Schwarzkopf said of the ground war, "It is not a Nintendo game. It is a tough battlefield where people are risking their lives at all times . . . and we ought to be very, very proud of them." Colonel J. D. Morelock wrote, "Saddam Hussein apparently expected his dug-in troops to inflict an increasingly large number of casualties on the U.S.-led forces, which would surely find it difficult to force their way through the interlocking system of bunkers, trenches, antitank ditches, and supporting strong points. If the battle developed into a re-

play of the grinding, bloody attrition warfare of the eight-year long Iran-Iraq War, Saddam confidently expected the United States and its coalition partners eventually to give up in the face of ever-increasing domestic opposition." However, at the moment that the ground war began, coalition commanders' plans went according to design. In a full frontal attack from western Kuwait to the Persian Gulf, Allied units stormed over dozens of penetration points across the Kuwaiti border. According to the *Washington Post,* on the first day, "The U.S. Army VII Corps and elements of the XVIII Airborne Corps joined with British and French forces in a broad flanking maneuver aimed at cutting off and killing Iraq's Republican Guard divisions dug in along the northern and western Kuwaiti border."

The allies of the United States paid $54 billion of the $61 billion that it cost to fight the war. Two-thirds of this amount was paid by the Gulf states, and the other third by Germany and Japan.

The final chapter on the conflict in the Gulf may not be written for many years to come. In an interview with the *Washington Post* in May 1991, Iraq's deputy foreign minister, Tariq Aziz, attempted to lessen the Allied victory and explain the situation post–Desert Storm: "Ten years from now, we will see that everybody, including the West, will be worse off [for fighting and defeating Iraq] because wars always create messier situations than before." He added, "I really doubt the situation is better than before last January 15 for the United States and its Arab allies. Israel is more ambitious and expansionist than ever, and you will see in a few years how the Arab members of the so-called coalition will suffer seriously because of it." In his *Future Wars: The World's Most Dangerous Flashpoints,* Colonel Trevor N. Dupuy writes, "The aftermath of Operation Desert Storm in some ways exacerbated the situation in the region. The economic, social and political infrastructure of Iraq was thrown into disarray. Massive migrations by refugees from Iraq created new problems in Iran and Turkey. In Kuwait the economic dislocation was on a greater scale than that in Iraq. In Saudi Arabia massive wartime expenditures resulted in a situation unique in that country's modern history: a cash-flow crisis. Jordan's attempt to maintain neutrality in Middle Eastern affairs had collapsed during the crisis under pressure from the

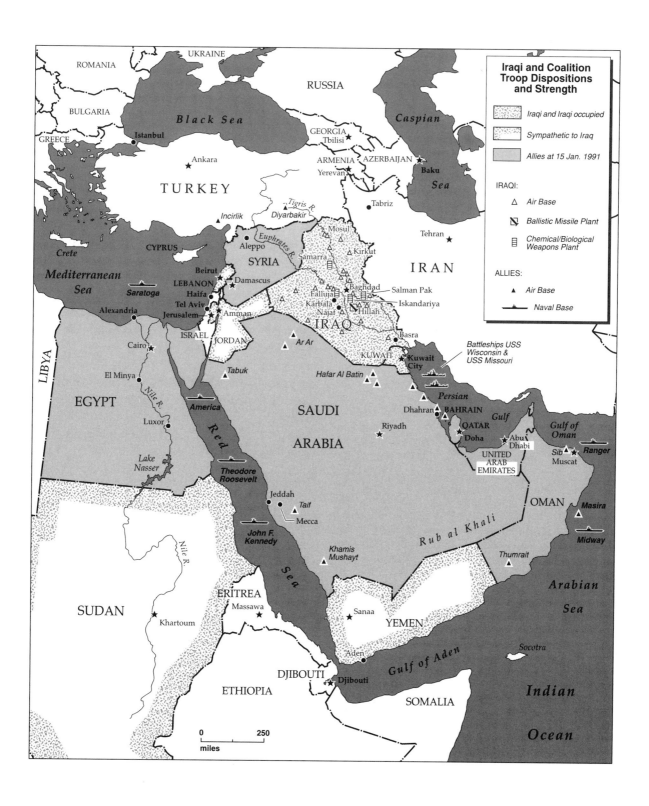

Iraqi and Coalition Troop Dispositions and Strength

Iraqi and Iraqi occupied

Sympathetic to Iraq

Allies at 15 Jan. 1991

IRAQI:

△ Air Base

◨ Ballistic Missile Plant

▤ Chemical/Biological Weapons Plant

ALLIES:

▲ Air Base

⚓ Naval Base

ROMANIA

UKRAINE

RUSSIA

BULGARIA

Black Sea

GEORGIA
Tbilisi

Caspian

GREECE

Istanbul

ARMENIA
Yerevan

AZERBAIJAN

Baku

Sea

Ankara

TURKEY

Incirlik

Diyarbakir

Tigris R.

Mosul

Tabriz

Tehran

IRAN

Crete

CYPRUS

Aleppo

Euphrates R.

Samarra

Kirkut

Mediterranean Sea

Beirut

SYRIA

Damascus

Saratoga

LEBANON
Haifa
Tel Aviv
Jerusalem

Alexandria

ISRAEL

Amman

JORDAN

Falluja

Baghdad

Salman Pak

Karbala

Iskandariya

Najaf

Hillah

IRAQ

Basra

LIBYA

Cairo

El Minya

Nile R.

Tabuk

Ar Ar

KUWAIT

Kuwait City

Battleships USS
Wisconsin &
USS Missouri

EGYPT

Luxor

Red

America

Hafar Al Batin

Persian

Dhahran

BAHRAIN

Gulf

Gulf of Oman

Lake Nasser

SAUDI

Riyadh

QATAR

Doha

Abu Dhabi

Sib

Ranger

Muscat

Theodore Roosevelt

ARABIA

UNITED ARAB EMIRATES

OMAN

Masira

SUDAN

Nile R.

Jeddah

Taif

Mecca

Sea

John F. Kennedy

Khamis Mushayt

Rub al Khali

Thumrait

Arabian

Midway

ERITREA

Massawa

Sanaa

Sea

Khartoum

ETHIOPIA

Aden

YEMEN

DJIBOUTI

Djibouti

Gulf of Aden

Socotra

Indian

SOMALIA

Ocean

0   250
miles

pro-Iraqi Palestinian majority, and King Hussein had trouble in regaining lost stature. The general (but not universal) euphoria following the 'end' to the Kuwait war was replaced by a new realization of the depth of regional problems. A major result of the Kuwait war was further polarization of the Arab nations in the region. It seemed certain that, if and when the immediate economic problems were solved, Saudi Arabia and Kuwait would amply reward the nations which supported them during the war. Debt-ridden Egypt, its economy moribund, was expected to benefit most from the largesse of the oil-rich Arab states. Other states, including Syria and Morocco, also expected to profit. However, the world oil glut, the shattered Kuwaiti economy, and the estimated $64 billion Saudi war debt, ensured that the rewards for loyalty would be years away."

References: "Anatomy of a Briefing," *Washington Post,* 28 February 1991, A29; Aziz, Tariq, interview in the *Washington Post,* 8 May 1991, A23; *Conduct of the Persian Gulf War: Final Report to Congress,* Report by the Department of Defense, April 1992, 20; De la Billière, Sir Peter, *Storm Command: A Personal Account of the Gulf War* (New York: HarperCollins, 1992), 205; Dunn, Robert F., "Early Gulf War Lessons," *U.S. Naval Institute Proceedings* 117:3 (March 1991), 25; Dupuy, Trevor N., *Future Wars: The World's Most Dangerous Flashpoints* (New York: Warner Books, 1993), 151–152; Hussein, Saddam, interview on Radio Baghdad, 20 August 1990, quoted in *Gulf War Air Power Survey, Volume I: Planning Report and Command and Control Report* (Washington, DC: GPO, 1993), 65; Keany, Thomas A., and Eliot A. Cohen, *Gulf War Air Power Survey, Summary Report* (Washington, DC: GPO, 1993), 38, 58; Maynes, Charles William, "Dateline Washington: A Necessary War?" *Foreign Policy* 82 (Spring 1991), 159–177; Mollins, Carl, "Countdown to Battle," *Maclean's* 107:7 (18 February 1991), 26; Morelock, J. D., *The Army Times Book of Great Land Battles from the Civil War to the Gulf War* (New York: Berkley Books, 1994), 295; "Schwarzkopf: Strategy behind Desert Storm," *Washington Post,* 28 February 1991, A35; Zacks, Yuval Joseph, "Operation *Desert Storm* a Just War?" *Military Review* LXXII:1 (January 1992), 30.

Operation Eastern Exit

Although unconnected to the Gulf War, this military action of 3 January 1991 was conducted during Operation Desert Shield to rescue and evacuate all American embassy personnel from the U.S. embassy in Mogadishu, Somalia, as the civil war that had been raging for two weeks engulfed that small African nation. Engrossed as the world was in the events in the Persian Gulf, few people realized the implications this situation would create: American troops would eventually be deployed there, and more than 40 would die before the military pulled out in virtual defeat.

Operation Granby

This is the little-known name for the British buildup in the Gulf. General Sir Peter de la Billière, commander of British forces in the Gulf, wrote of the designation, "The name baffled our American allies, who had never heard of the Marquess of Granby, the distinguished eighteenth-century commander who fought in the battle of Minden during the Seven Years War. The name was chosen from a list in the Ministry of Defence computer, awaiting the next major operation." The battle of Minden was a key turning point in the Seven Years' War, when foot soldiers of the British and Hanoverian armies defeated the French at Minden in Germany on 1 August 1759, stopping the last threat by the French to overtake Prussia.

Reference: De la Billière, Sir Peter, *Storm Command: A Personal Account of the Gulf War* (New York: HarperCollins, 1992), 10.

Operation Imminent Thunder

This military exercise, held from 15 to 21 November 1990, was a repeat of the October operation called Camel Sand, which dealt with amphibious landings in Saudi Arabia as a rehearsal for similar landings during the liberation of Kuwait. Its intent was to confuse Saddam Hussein as to the actual battle strategy that would be employed by the coalition if war should break out. Because General H. Norman Schwarzkopf felt that the Iraqis had shifted their battle plans to accommodate possible coalition amphibious landings, he ordered American ships to be anchored off the Kuwaiti coast on the night of the opening of Operation Desert Storm to confuse them more. Marine Corps historian Colonel Charles J. Quilter II writes of the operation, "General Schwarzkopf wanted to provide 'an environment within which joint/combined operational issues c[ould] be identified, analyzed, and resolved' by faithfully simulating theater situations and conditions in a defensive scenario. It was the first major joint and combined force exercise in-theater to have fully integrated air, ground, and naval activity.... The proximity of Iraqi forces in Kuwait added an element of unpredictability that gave Imminent Thunder actual as well as simulated combat conditions."

See also Operation Camel Sand.
Reference: Quilter, Charles J., II, "U.S. Marines in the Persian Gulf, 1990–1991: With the I Marine Expeditionary Force in Desert Shield and Desert Storm" (Washington, DC: History and Museums Division, Headquarters, U.S. Marine Corps, 1993), 24–25.

Operation Ivory Justice
See United Arab Emirates.

Operation Meteil

According to the military report *Desert Score*, "In early October [1990], France sent eight Mirage F1C fighter aircraft and two Crotale SAM batteries to Qatar for that country's defense" in what was dubbed Operation Meteil. The maneuver mirrored the United States' Operation Ivory Justice, in which two KC-135 refueling aircraft were sent to Al Dahfra Airport in the United Arab Emirates after the UAE requested the planes for security reasons.

Reference: Almond, Denise L., ed., *Desert Score: U.S. Gulf War Weapons* (Washington, DC: Carroll Publishing, 1991), 479.

Operation Provide Comfort

This major action was coordinated in response to the collapse of the Kurdish rebellion against Saddam Hussein following the end of the Persian Gulf War.

Under the authority of Combined Task Force (CTF) Provide Comfort, headquartered at Incirlik Airbase, Turkey, the operation was commanded by Lieutenant General John Shalikashvili, who was named head of the Joint Chiefs of Staff of the U.S. military in 1993. For several

months, food and shelter were airlifted into the mountains of northern Iraq and southern Turkey. The major Kurd concentrations were along the border at Isikveren, Gulyabi, Uzumlu, Kuracu, and Cukurca, totaling perhaps 600,000 to 700,000 people, and possibly as many as 850,000. From the beginning of the operation, American intentions were to simply supply the refugees with equipment and food for survival.

Captain Timothy W. LaFleur reported in congressional testimony: "About 16 April our mission changed. The National Command Authority felt that we needed to put people on the ground to help out the refugees, to help build some tents, and to get a better feel for what they needed. We also were getting reports early on that our air drops were falling on people; that in the rush and panic to get to the food, some of the people were literally running underneath the loads and were maybe getting injured, or even killed. We did not ever firm up the report that there were any fatalities. It was reported on the news, but we never could confirm that on the ground, any that actually did get killed."

Although the action to assist the Kurdish refugees in northern Iraq was called Provide Comfort, a similar program was instituted to aid the Shiite rebels in southern Iraq. Lieutenant Commander Dana C. Covey of the U.S. Naval Reserve Medical Corps writes of this assistance, "In late March [1991], members of the medical team learned of the plight of the refugees in southern Iraq.... Steadily increasing numbers of refugees, fleeing the fighting in Basra and its surrounding suburbs, were taking refuge in the U.S. security zone that was established in southern Iraq after the cessation of Desert Storm hostilities. This zone was controlled by the Third Armored Division, which took on the herculean task of providing humanitarian assistance to more than 35,000 refugees." Between the end of March and 23 April 1991, the humanitarian assistance included food, as well as medical supplies and the opening of a clinic. Through three convoys, this medical team was able to stave off hunger and disease before the operation was closed down.

References: Covey, Dana C., "Offering a Helping Hand in Iraq," *U.S. Naval Institute Proceedings* 118: 5 (May 1992), 106–109; "Operations Desert Shield/

Kurdish children wave as they leave a rough, temporary camp in the mountains of northern Iraq for a refugee camp built by coalition forces during Operation Provide Comfort near Zakho, Iraq.

Operation Provide Comfort

Desert Storm," Hearings before the Committee on Armed Services, United States Senate, 102nd Congress, 1st Session, 1991, 17.

Operation Sharp Edge

This operation, conducted by American forces during the buildup in the Persian Gulf (but wholly unconnected with the conflict itself), was in execution from July 1990 until January 1991 in Liberia as that country crumbled into chaos during a civil war. Sharp Edge was conducted, according to Norman Polmar, "to provide security for the U.S. Embassy and to evacuate over 2,400 civilians from the country during a violent insurrection."

Reference: Polmar, Norman, *The Naval Institute Guide to the Ships and Aircraft of the U.S. Fleet* (Annapolis, MD: Naval Institute Press, 1993), 5.

Operation Southern Watch

This military exercise was established on 27 August 1992, and continues as of this writing, by the coalition to conduct surveillance flights over southern Iraq to prohibit Iraqi military flights

against the Kurds and Shiite rebels south of the 32nd parallel. Southern Watch includes American Air Force F-15s and Navy F/A-18s, an E-3 AWACS, and RC-135 electronic intelligence craft. Among the planes that have flown surveillance over this so-called no-fly zone are several EF-111s, three British Tornado GR-1 strike planes and three Tornado GR-1A reconnaissance craft, and ten French Mirages. A further zone was established over the northern section of Iraq at the 36th parallel; it was here that the tragic friendly-fire accident called the Dinarte Incident occurred, in which 26 Allied troops were killed when their helicopters were mistaken for Iraqi craft and shot down.

See also Dinarte Incident.
Reference: "Allies Flying over Iraq To Enforce U.N. Sanctions," *Aviation Week & Space Technology* (31 August 1992), 26.

Operation Stigma

This secret policy, initiated by the United States on 12 August 1990, was a clandestine attempt to commence a total, worldwide arms embargo against Iraq.

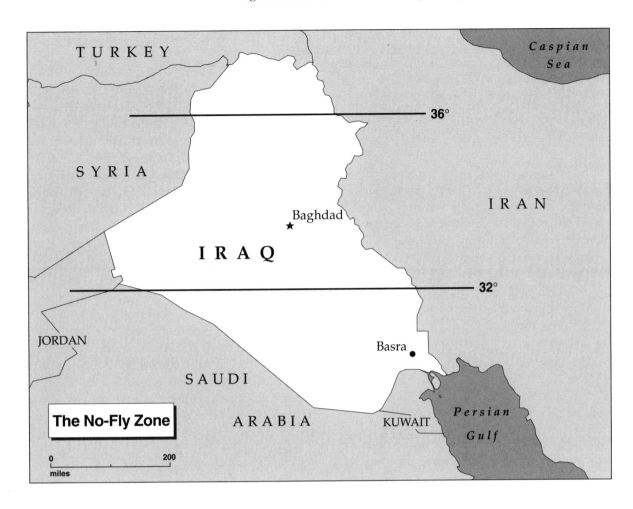

IRAQ

TURKEY

SYRIA

IRAN

36°

Baghdad ★

32°

JORDAN

SAUDI

ARABIA

Basra ●

KUWAIT

The No-Fly Zone

Caspian Sea

Persian Gulf

0   200
miles

Operation Vigilant Warrior

This military buildup was conducted in October 1994 to halt the potential aggression of the Iraqi army as they moved once again toward the Kuwaiti border. The buildup reached its peak strength on 19 October when 26,213 American troops were in Kuwait.

Organization of Petroleum Exporting Countries (OPEC)

The oil cartel of the Arab countries, OPEC was established so that uniform oil prices could be set. As Dr. Paul Stevens wrote, "OPEC was formed in 1968 by Saudi Arabia, Kuwait and Libya. Its purpose was to provide the three conservative oil-producing states with a counterbalance to the pressures growing within the Arab League to use oil as a weapon in the struggle against Israel. The 1969 Libyan revolution effectively destroyed its original purpose, which was to provide the 'traditional' states with a bul-

wark against the 'radical' states—mainly [at that time] Algeria and Egypt. However, in its place was developed an organization with an expanded membership and significant potential for policy coordination. By 1972, all the Arab oil producers had joined the organization." OPEC's influence in causing an oil shortage in the United States during the 1970s made it an important voice in Arab affairs. On 8 August 1990, OPEC attempted to intercede in the Persian Gulf crisis by issuing a statement. Louis Uchitelle, in an article in the *New York Times* in March 1991, wrote that "by virtue of its military victory, the United States is likely to have more influence in the Organization of Petroleum Exporting Countries than any industrialist nation has ever exercised." As of this writing, that influence has yet to be applied.

See also Appendix 4, Statement by the President of the Opec Conference, 8 August 1990.
References: Lauterpacht, E., et al., eds., *The Kuwait Crisis: Basic Documents* (Cambridge, UK: Grotius, 1991), 317; Mostyn, Trevor, exec. ed., *The Cam-*

bridge Encyclopedia of the Middle East and North Africa (New York: Cambridge University Press, 1988), 110; Uchitelle, Louis, "Gulf Victory May Raise U.S. Influence in OPEC," *New York Times*, 5 March 1991, D1.

Osirak

The Israeli attack on Iraq's Osirak nuclear power complex on 7 June 1981 may have saved the world from the use of nuclear weapons more than ten years later during the Persian Gulf War.

Situated on the plain of Osirak—an Iraqi slant on the name Osiris, the Egyptian god of the lower world and judge of the dead, who was slain by his brother and exiled to hell—the French-built Tammuz I nuclear reactor made up the largest part of the nuclear weapons experiment complex at al-Tuwaitha, 10.5 miles (17 km) southeast of Baghdad. In 1974 Saddam Hussein went to Paris as a high-ranking member of the Iraqi government to shop for French technology with which to build a nuclear reactor "for peaceful purposes only." French president Valery Giscard d'Estaing and Premier Jacques Chirac, both Arabists, signed a deal with Saddam Hussein in which French materials and technicians would be supplied to Baghdad. Within a year, the 70-megawatt reactor, dubbed Tammuz I and supported by an 800-kilowatt minireactor, was being assembled.

During the building of the reactor and its weapons complex, the Israeli government watched nervously through the use of satellite photographs and spies. At 3:15 A.M. on 7 April 1979, just two days before the reactor's core was due to be shipped from France, several men broke into the Compagnie des Constructions Navales et Industrielles nuclear manufacturing plant at La Seyne-sur-Mer, attached explosives to the core, and escaped. The resulting explosion crippled the core, delaying its shipment for two years. On 14 June 1980, more than a year later, unknown assassins murdered Yahia El-Meshad, the head of Iraq's nuclear power program, in his Paris hotel room. Meshad's death mirrors the 1990 assassination of Dr. Gerald Bull, the Canadian scientist who was helping Iraq obtain a supergun to fire large projectiles from Iraq as far as Israel. In both the core sabotage and the assassination of El-Meshad, French authorities suspected the Israeli Mossad (Secret Service), but had no proof.

On 30 September 1980, at the start of the Iran-Iraq War, Iranian jets flew over Osirak and fired at the Tammuz reactor, but did little damage. Unknown to many, at that exact time unmarked Israeli spy planes were over central Iraq, and were able to photograph the entire incident. Although Iran denied that the attack happened, Iraq tried to calm the fears of the Persian nation with which it was locked in a death struggle. "The Iranian people should not fear the Iraqi nuclear reactor, which is not intended to be used against Iran, but against the *Zionist enemy*, [author's emphasis]" a Baghdad newspaper article pronounced.

About the last week of May 1981, Prime Minister Menachem Begin of Israel received intelligence reports that the Iraqis were planning to start up the Tammuz reactor sometime in July. On 5 June he ordered the Israeli air force (IAF) to launch an attack on the plant within two days. The IAF had planned for such an attack, going so far as to construct a full-size model of the complex in the Sinai desert and practicing hit-and-run bombing missions on it.

Sometime before 5 P.M. on 7 June, six F-15 interceptor and support fighters took off from Israel's Etzion Air Force Base and headed east, joined by eight F-16 fighters. As they slipped south of Jordan, Jordanian radar picked them up and asked for identification; the Israeli pilots calmed the Jordanians by answering in perfect Arabic, allowing the flight to proceed. The flight advanced over northern Saudi Arabia until it entered Iraqi airspace. While the six F-15s provided protective cover, the F-16s settled into their bombing runs. According to *Time* magazine, "the lead plane fired a pair of video-precision 'smart' bombs to punch through predetermined spots in the [reactor's] domed concrete. The following aircraft launched their own explosives through the jagged holes: a dozen conventional bombs weighing 2,200 pounds [998 kg] apiece." In less than three minutes, what had taken the Iraqis five years to build was destroyed. The Israelis flew home with no casualties. The world soon condemned the raid, although it was found out later that the Reagan administration secretly applauded Israel's tenacity. Secretary of State Alexander Haig was at the forefront of the support inside the U.S. government. The *New York Times* called the attack "an act of inexcusable and short-sighted aggression."

The Osirak raid may have saved many lives during the Persian Gulf War just ten years later. Had Osirak not been destroyed, and had it been used to build nuclear bombs, such weapons might have been used against Iran during the Iran-Iraq War or, worse, against Saudi Arabian oilfields or American troops. This worry is best illustrated by a comment from Joseph S. Nye, Jr., an authority on nuclear proliferation, who said in 1981 after the Israeli attack of Iraq's potential nuclear capacity: "They [Iraq] were between five and ten years away from a serious nuclear-weapons program. But they did have a theoretical capability to produce two or three bombs by 1985 if they had chosen to go that route for symbolical political purposes."

References: "Raiders Undetected by U.S. Radar Plane," New York Times, 10 June 1981, A12; Russell, George, David Aikman, and William Stewart, "Attack and Fallout," Time, 22 June 1981, 24–38; Shipler, David K., "Israeli Jets Destroy Iraqi Atomic Reactor; Attack Condemned by U.S. and Arab Nations," New York Times, 9 June 1981, A1, A8, A9, A14; Webb, Al, Robert S. Dudney, and Dennis Mullin, "After the Israeli Shocker," U.S. News & World Report, 22 June 1981, 20–23.

OV-1D Mohawk/RV-1D Quick Look I

Built by Grumman Corporation of Bethpage, New York, this small aircraft, in the two variants of OV-1D and RV-1D, flew 161 (OV-1D) and 111 (RV-1D) unarmed tactical reconnaissance missions for the U.S. Army during the Gulf War. Little is known of this aircraft, which has a VSTOL (vertical short takeoff and landing) capability. Able to carry a pilot and an observer, the plane is powered by two Lycoming T53-L-701A turboprop engines, each delivering 1,400 shaft horsepower (shp). It has an internal fuel capacity of 297 gallons (1,125 liters) and a speed of 265 knots (305 mph; 491 km/h) with infrared radar and cameras, or 251 knots (289 mph; 465 km/h) with side-looking airborne radar (SLAR).

Reference: Almond, Denise L., ed., Desert Score: U.S. Gulf War Weapons (Washington, DC: Carroll Publishing, 1991), 146–147.

OV-10 Bronco

This small, armed but light observation aircraft flew 482 sorties (411 as part of close air support missions) as an element of the Marine contingent in Operation Desert Storm.

The Bronco weighs only 9,908 pounds (4,494 kg) loaded, is 41 feet 7 inches (12.68 m) long, and has a wingspan of 40 feet (12.2 m). Powered by two 715 engine horsepower (ehp) Garrett T76416/417 turboprop engines, its maximum speed is 281 mph (452 km/h). It is designed with forward-looking imaging radar (FLIR) and laser designation capabilities. Its cockpit, with two tandem ejection seats, affords both the pilot and copilot outstanding all-around vision. Originally built for use in the Vietnam War, the Bronco saw action mostly in the role of attacking small surface targets. After the war, the plane was redesigned and updated with forward air control ability by having sensors attached that allow it to detect targets at night. It is armed solely with four 7.62 M60 machine guns carrying 500 rounds each. During the Persian Gulf War, its main missions were reconnaissance, escort for helicopters, and, using the FLIR radar, supplying laser designation and night observation for other aircraft.

References: Gulf War Air Power Survey, Volume IV: Weapons, Tactics, and Training Report and Space Report (Washington, DC: GPO, 1993); Gunston, Bill, An Illustrated Guide to USAF: The Modern US Air Force (New York: Prentice Hall, 1991), 140–142.

Özal, Turgut (1927–1993)

Turkish politician and Middle Eastern strongman, the short, rotund Turgut Özal was one of the leaders who sided with the coalition against Iraq during the Persian Gulf War, allowing American airplanes to fly out of the vital Incirlik Air Force Base to targets inside Iraq. His death in 1993 left the Turkish nation with a tremendous vacuum in its leadership.

Turgut Özal was born in 1927 in the central Anatolian village of Malataya, Turkey (Malataya is located about 465 miles [748 km] east of the Turkish capital of Ankara), the son of Mehmet Özal, a bank clerk, and Hafize Özal, a teacher. A devout Muslim, Turgut Özal's early education was at Istanbul's Technical University, where in 1950 he was awarded a master's degree in electrical engineering. For the next two years he worked at Turkey's Electrical Power Resources Survey Administration, where, according to Louise Mooney Collins and Lorna Mpho Mabunda, "he worked on hydroelectric projects as part of the country's electrification program." His boss at the time was Suleyman Demirel, who would later serve as Turkey's prime minister.

From 1952 to 1953, Özal studied electrical power in the United States. For the next several years after his return to Turkey he worked at several state ministries, including the State Planning Organization and the Scientific Advisory Council of the Ministry of Defense. Demirel's ascension to prime minister in 1965 allowed him to elevate Özal to the post of technical advisor to the prime minister. Two years later Özal was appointed as undersecretary of the State Planning Organization. In 1971 Demirel was overthrown by a military coup, and Özal went to the United States, where he worked as an economist with the World Bank in Washington, D.C. In 1973 he returned to Turkey. According to the *Current Biography Yearbook 1985*, "On his return, he entered the private sector, working first as a managing director of the Sabanki Combine, and then for the Asil Celik Steel Works." With Demirel's election as prime minister in 1975, Özal was named governor of Turkey's Central Bank, but political opposition thwarted the nomination. In 1977 Özal ran for a seat in the Turkish Parliament; he was unsuccessful, but two years later Demirel named him as undersecretary of the State Planning Organization.

In 1980 the military once again overthrew the civilian government, and for the next three years Özal sided with the coup plotters and served as the military government's deputy prime minister. Özal's economic policies began to work, and by 1982 inflation had dropped and exports were up. Özal resigned from the government to participate in the national elections. When the military government ended the ban on political parties, Özal helped found the Anatavan Partisi (Motherland party) in May 1983; on 6 November 1983, the group won more than half the seats in Parliament, making Özal the new prime minister; he served from 1983 until 1989. Middle East expert Yaacov Shimoni wrote, "In his foreign policy, Özal was considered a moderate. He endeavored to improve relations with Greece and met with Greek Prime Minister Andreas Papandreou in 1988, the first Turkish statesman to visit Athens in a quarter of a century. He tried to strengthen Turkey's relations with Western Europe, and in 1987 formally requested to change Turkey's status in the European Community to full membership. He also strengthened Turkey's relations with the Arab and Islamic countries. Özal's economic plans suffered a setback in the late 1980s when inflation rose again to 80%, the economy showed signs of a crisis, and the gap between the rich and the poor grew. His leadership was challenged by Demirel's right-wing True Path Party and Erdal Inonu's left-wing Social Democratic Party, as well as by factions in his own Motherland Party, whose standing in public opinion declined in the late 1980s." In 1987 Özal underwent triple-bypass surgery, and a year later survived an assassination attempt. Because of his party's position, Özal was elected president of Turkey on 31 October 1989, the second civilian to hold the post since the founding of the Turkish republic in 1960. In October 1991 his party lost its majority in Parliament, coming in second to Demirel's True Path Party.

Alan Cowell wrote of Özal in the *New York Times*, "In 1990, he showed no hesitation in committing his predominantly Muslim country, a member of the NATO alliance, to the United States–led coalition against Iraq in the Persian Gulf War. That [action] was crucial to the coalition's planning because it meant the severing of Iraq's principal oil-export routes, which remain closed by United Nations sanctions, and gave allied warplanes access to tactically important air bases," including Incirlik Air Force Base.

On 17 April 1993 Özal died at his home in Ankara at the age of 66. Although in seemingly good health, he had just completed a laborious 12-day journey throughout Asia to lend support to Azerbaijan in its war with neighboring Armenia.

See also Lausanne, Treaty of.

References: Collins, Louise Mooney, and Lorna Mpho Mabunda, *The Annual Obituary 1993* (Detroit: St. James Press, 1994), 340; Cowell, Alan, "Turgut Özal, 66, Dies in Ankara; Pugnacious President of Turkey," *New York Times*, 18 April 1993, 46; Moritz, Charles, ed., *Current Biography Yearbook 1985* (New York: H. W. Wilson, 1985), 322; Shimoni, Yaacov, *Biographical Dictionary of the Middle East* (New York: Facts on File, 1991), 180.

P-3 Orion

Military aviation authorities John W. R. Taylor and Gordon Swanborough describe the P-3 Orion in their *Military Aircraft of the World* as "a shore-based anti-submarine reconnaissance aircraft." The P-3 saw some action during the Persian Gulf War, flying 4 missions for the U.S. Air Force (as the variant EP-3, which are "special reconnaisance aircraft with radomes above and below the fuselage"), and 23 for the U.S. Navy.

Built by Lockheed, the P-3 is powered by four Allison T56-A-14 turboprop engines delivering 4,910 shaft horsepower (shp). At 99 feet 8 inches (30.37 m) in length, the P-3 weighs 61,491 pounds (27,890 kg) empty; its ability to carry assorted antisubmarine equipment and weaponry allows its maximum weight to boost to 142,000 pounds (64,410 kg). The P-3 has a maximum speed of 473 mph (761 km/h) and an unrefueled range of 1,550 miles (2,494 km).

In an article on the P-3's work during the Persian Gulf War, it was said of the craft, "As a true multimission aircraft, the P-3 is constantly in high demand to perform a host of missions, including search and rescue, reconnaissance, communications relay, and intelligence gathering. . . . As in the maritime patrols of Vietnam, surveillance flights in support of Desert Shield, also known as maritime interdiction force operations, and in the North Arabian Gulf in support of Desert Storm, were the primary missions of the P-3s. The distinct advantage brought to maritime interdiction and the North Arabian Gulf by maritime patrol was the highly accurate standoff surveillance capability of the inverse synthetic aperture radar, complemented by its standoff weapons capability (Harpoon). Although the weapons were not employed by P-3s, the ability to identify surface contacts at an extended range and to provide accurate targeting to strike aircraft proved to be major contributing factors to the attrition of the Iraqi inventory of naval combatants and supporting units."

References: Brooks, Richard, Skip Hiser, and T. K. Hohl, "If It Was There, P-3s Found It," *U.S. Naval Institute Proceedings* 118:8 (August 1991), 41; Taylor, John W. R., and Gordon Swanborough, *Military Aircraft of the World* (New York: Scribner's, 1979), 72.

Pakistan

See Coalition Nations, Contributions of.

Palestine Liberation Organization (PLO)

See Arafat, Yasir; Palestinian Militia.

Palestinian Militia

The Iraqi occupation army in Kuwait assembled about a thousand Palestinians to act as a garrison to fight Kuwaiti resistance. Authors James F. Dunnigan and Austin Bay describe the small force as "somewhere between an armed mob and a rabble in effectiveness." The militia did not play a role in the eventual fight for the liberation of Kuwait.

Reference: Dunnigan, James F., and Austin Bay, *From Shield to Storm: High-Tech Weapons, Military Strategy, and Coalition Warfare in the Persian Gulf* (New York: Morrow, 1992), 78.

Pan-Arabism or Pan-Arabist Thought

One of the fundamental principles of the constitution of the Arab Ba'ath party is that "the Arabs form one nation. This nation has the natural right to live in a single state and to be free to direct its own destiny." This belief comprises what can be called the pan-Arabist movement, or pan-Arabist thought.

The idea that Arabs were of a common heritage, and had a joint interest in forming a unified "nation," started just after World War II, when several of the mandates under the control of the European powers began their march toward independence. The leaders of these mandates, however, were concerned more for the well-being of their own nation-states; unity was a faraway concept. However, due to the influence of Syrian teacher Michel Aflaq, a new movement—the Ba'ath, or renaissance, party—advanced the idea of pan-Arab union.

See also Aflaq, Michel.
Reference: Abu Jaber, Kamel, *The Arab Ba'th Socialist Party: History, Ideology, and Organization* (Syracuse, NY: Syracuse University Press, 1966), 167.

Pasha, or Pasa (Turkish)

The rank or title accorded to an official in the Ottoman Empire. Specifically bestowed on civil officials, and not religious leaders, the word followed a person's name, e.g., Midhat Pasha. In the latter stages of the Ottoman Empire it was used for civil and provincial administrators in the lands ruled by the empire, including Persian Gulf states such as Iraq; during the period of the *tanzimat* reforms, it was bestowed particularly on the four highest classes of civil and military authorities.

See also Midhat Pasha.
Reference: Goetz, Philip W., et al., eds., *The New Encyclopædia Britannica*, Vol. 9 (Chicago: Encyclopædia Britannica, 1990), 181.

Patriot Tactical Air Defense Missile System (MIM-104)

Built for the U.S. government by Raytheon, the Patriot missile became an overnight sensation during the Gulf War for shooting down incoming Iraqi Scud missiles in Saudi Arabia and Israel. Dana Gardner said in *Design News*, "The antimissile era officially began on 18 January 1991, when a Patriot rocketed from its mobile launcher in Saudi Arabia and destroyed an incoming Scud missile."

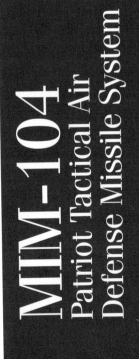

A Patriot Tactical Air Defense Missile emerges from a crate-shaped multiple launch rack during a test.

In the morning hours of 18 January 1991, just after the start of the air war, radar in Saudi Arabia picked up an incoming Iraqi Scud missile and a warning was sent to the Patriot defense teams stationed at Saudi Arabia's Dhahran Royal Saudi Air Force Base. The Patriot system's automatic control defenses traced the arc of the crude Scud while its computer estimated an interception point. At 4:28 A.M, the Patriot was fired upward at 2,000 mph (322 km/h), locked onto the Scud's homing system, and collided into the wayward missile, sending a shower of sparks across the Saudi Arabian sky and plunging the pieces of the two cigar-shaped weapons to the desert below.

The working concept of a surface-to-air missile (SAM) that could manually track, home in on, and destroy an incoming missile of a similar nature began in 1961 as the Field Army Ballistic-Missile Defense System (FABMDS). Several years of testing by the U.S. Army's Missile Command (MICOM) led to a contract award in 1966 for the building of this new-generation SAM to Raytheon, Hughes, and RCA, with Raytheon getting the bulk of the contract. By 1974 the Track-via-Missile (TVM) system was in testing, and by 1976 the renamed MIM-104 Patriot was designed and ready to undergo full company trials. The MIM-104 was first delivered to the U.S. Army in 1982 and tests began in 1983. Although several difficulties with hardware were found, by 1984 the Army declared the Patriot operational. They were not used, however, until the Persian Gulf War.

In a *Wall Street Journal* article, Bob Davis wrote: "A Patriot manager says that during the first Scud attack on Saudi Arabia, on January 17, the U.S. satellite tracking missile launches reported the launch of five Scuds. But about six minutes later, as the missiles were descending over Dhahran, they shredded so badly that Patriot radar screens showed 14 different objects. The Patriot batteries, programmed to launch two missiles at every object, showered the Scud parts with 28 of the $600,000 Patriot missiles, the manager says." Davis reports that over the course of the war, 158 Patriots were fired at 47 Scuds that came into range. Except for the attack on 28 February in which a Scud crashed into a U.S. Army barracks, killing 28 Americans, the Patriot was successful in warding off other Scud fatalities in Saudi Arabia.

The Patriot is essentially an antimissile missile, although it is officially categorized as a SAM—a surface-to-air missile. The Patriot itself is 17.4 feet (5.3 m) in length, and has a range of up to 38 miles (61 km). The warhead alone weighs only 70 pounds (32 kg); the entire missile system weighs approximately 2,000 pounds (908 kg).

References: Davis, Bob, "Patriot Missile, High-Tech Hero in Gulf, Comes under Attack as Less Than Scud's Worst Enemy," *Wall Street Journal*, 15 April 1991, A16; Gardner, Dana, "How Patriot Launched the Smart War Era," *Design News* 44:8 (22 April 1991), 66.

Pérez de Cuéllar, Javier (1920–)

The fifth secretary general of the United Nations (1982–1992), Peruvian diplomat Javier Pérez de Cuéllar played a significant role during the Persian Gulf crisis in shaping the United Nations' actions toward the Iraqi invasion of Kuwait and the subsequent coalition military response.

Javier Pérez de Cuéllar was born in Lima, the capital of Peru, on 19 January 1920, the son of a

Javier Pérez de Cuéllar, former UN secretary general, talks with reporters in New York.

well-to-do businessman who died when his son was four. Pérez de Cuéllar attended local Roman Catholic schools before earning a law degree from the Catholic University in Lima. In 1944 he entered the Peruvian diplomatic service. The *New York Times* said of him, "He stumbled into diplomacy by accident. As a law student at the Catholic University in Lima, he looked for a job to earn pocket money and found one as a $50-a-month clerk in the Foreign Ministry. By the time he graduated he decided that the foreign service was a good life—'It helps you to know countries and at someone else's expense'—and he signed on as First Secretary in the Paris Mission." Subsequent offices that Pérez de Cuéllar held include Peruvian ambassador to the Soviet Union and Poland (1969–1971), permanent Peruvian representative to the United Nations (1971–1975), and Peruvian ambassador to Venezuela (1978–1981).

After Secretary General Kurt Waldheim failed to win a third term as head of the United Nations, there was a long deadlock to choose his replacement. On 11 December 1981, Pérez de Cuéllar was chosen, beating out Prince Sadruddin Aga Khan. Under Pérez de Cuéllar's administration, which ended in 1992, the United Nations became more of a peacekeeping operation; in 1988, the Nobel Peace Prize was awarded to the UN peacekeepers.

As the secretary general oversaw the talks on a cease-fire in the Iran-Iraq War in 1988, Don Shannon of the *Los Angeles Times* said of him, "He is an international bureaucrat whose past successes owe more to persistence and patience than to brilliance and leadership. And even his legendary patience wore thin at times during the two weeks that he sought to bring Iraq and Iran to agreement, resulting in occasional testy lectures to reporters." A year later Shannon wrote, "As a result [of his negotiations to end hostilities in Angola, Namibia, the Iran-Iraq War, and Cambodia], the reserved, almost invisible chief of a financially troubled organization that had seemed to have lost relevance to the real world suddenly emerged as a valuable player in global politics."

From the start of the crisis in the Persian Gulf, Pérez de Cuéllar acted with immediate speed and thoughtful intent. On 26 August, just three weeks after the Iraqi invasion of Kuwait, he announced that he would meet with Iraqi foreign minister Tariq Aziz in Jordan in an attempt to end the crisis. The meeting failed to resolve the situation. Pérez de Cuéllar continued to try, right up to the beginning of the ground war, to get Iraq to agree to a withdrawal. After the war, he oversaw the U.N.'s attempt to get Iraq to comply with U.N.-imposed sanctions. In 1992, he was succeeded by Boutros-Boutros Ghali of Egypt.

References: "Javier Pérez de Cuéllar: Cautious, Gentle Pilot for the U.N.," *New York Times,* 12 December 1981, A6; Shannon, Don, "Pérez de Cuellar Emerges as Key Player in World Chess Board," *Los Angeles Times,* 4 November 1989, A13; Shannon, Don, "U.N.'s Pérez de Cuellar: It's Persistence over Personality," *Los Angeles Times,* 14 August 1988, A12.

Persian Gulf

The body of water that stretches for 615 miles (990 km) from the Shatt al-Arab waterway on the three-cornered border between Iran, Iraq, and Kuwait, and moves first south, then turns north, and then swings south again before emptying into the Gulf of Oman and ultimately the Indian Ocean is called the Persian Gulf, after the former name of Iran, Persia. From this waterway thousands of barrels of oil, about one-fourth of the world's oil supply in total, flow to the world via tankers.

One of the world's main waterways, the Persian Gulf has shaped the path and direction of commerce, trade, and military campaigns for thousands of years. Historian Sir Arnold T. Wilson wrote of the Gulf in his 1928 work, *The Persian Gulf: An Historical Sketch from the Earliest Times to the Beginning of the Twentieth Century,* "No arm of the sea has been, or is of greater interest, alike to the geologist and archaeologist, the historian and the geographer, the merchant, the statesman, and the student of strategy, than the inland water known as the Persian Gulf." Even before the strategic fight over oil and the "battles" of the cold war, the Gulf was pictured as both a crucial and essential waterway for the world. Originally, small seagoing vessels plied the Gulf in search of trade; later, larger ships sailed the expanse of the waterway seeking military advantage. This was how Portugal, an early sea power, expanded its sphere of dominance into the Gulf from about 1515 to 1622, when it owned the port of Hormuz, near what is now the Iranian city of Bandar Abbas. Later, this expansion of European dominance into Middle Eastern affairs led the British, Dutch, and French to divvy up the entire Middle Eastern area following the end of World War I.

American influence also started to develop in the Persian Gulf region just after the formation of the republic. Historian Michael A. Palmer wrote, "In the first quarter of the nineteenth century, American trade in the Indian Ocean continued to expand, prompting the United States government to consider the establishment of a formal commercial relationship with the Sultan of Muscat. . . . While many people in the United States considered those of the Islamic world heathen barbarians living in darkness, the Americans who rounded the Cape of Good Hope found the Arabs to be shrewd businessmen whose societies were generally well ordered and civil. In the nineteenth century American naval officers considered 'Mohammedan' ports unusually safe, if somewhat boring, venues for sailors." The United States has had a naval presence in the Gulf since 1949, overseeing its one-time friendly alliance with Iran (which changed after 1979) and Israel, the amicable alliance with some Gulf sheikdoms, and its stormy relationship with other Arab nations. Although administrations have come and gone, the goal of American policy in the Gulf has remained the same: to oversee vital strategic, political, and (because of oil) economic interests in the area.

The Iran-Iraq War, which lasted from 1980 to 1988, changed the American mission in the Gulf. For the first time, the United States found a way to play two enemies off each other by arming both sides. R. W. Apple, Jr., commented in the *New York Times,* "American policy in the gulf in the late 1980s was rooted sometimes in the notion that Iraq and Iran had equally despicable governments and other times in the notion that Iraq, however tyrannical its government under Saddam Hussein, had at least never seized American diplomats or portrayed the United States as the satanic enemy from whom all evil flowed." Although this course may have led to the Persian Gulf War in 1991, other directions might have led to similar, if not worse, outcomes.

Middle East historian Yaacov Shimoni writes of the Gulf, "Connected with the Gulf of Oman and the Arabian Sea by the shallow Straits of Hormuz, the Persian Gulf is rather shallow, its maximum depth not exceeding 328 feet [100 m]. It is about 500 miles [800 km] long and of varying width (125–200 miles [200–320 km]), and its area is about 90,000 square miles [235,000 sq km]."

References: Palmer, Michael A., *Guardians of the Gulf: A History of America's Expanding Role in the Persian Gulf, 1833–1992* (New York: Free Press, 1992), 2–3; Shimoni, Yaacov, *Political Dictionary of the Arab World* (New York: Macmillan, 1987), 400; *U.S. Policy in the Persian Gulf,* Special Report 166 of the United States Department of State, July 1987.

Persian Gulf Conflict Supplemental Authorization and Personnel Benefits Act of 1991 (Public Law 102-25; 105 Stat. 77; 10 U.S.C. 1010 note).

This legislation, enacted by Congress on 6 April 1991, approved appropriations for fiscal year 1991 for Operation Desert Storm, increased benefits for certain members of the armed forces serving in the Persian Gulf, and, with the passage of Title V of the act, requested a report on the conflict by the Department of Defense. The report was published in April 1992 as *Conduct of the Persian Gulf War: Final Report to Congress (Pursuant to Title V of the Persian Gulf Conflict Supplemental Authorization and Personnel Benefits Act of 1991).* The act also established, under section 335, the Persian Gulf Rehabilitative Services system to treat symptoms of posttraumatic stress disorder (PTSD) among Gulf War veterans. Section 335 reads:

SEC. 335: REPORTS BY SECRETARY OF DEFENSE AND SECRETARY OF VETERANS AFFAIRS CONCERNING SERVICES TO TREAT POST-TRAUMATIC STRESS DISORDER

(a) IN GENERAL.—The Secretary of Defense and the Secretary of Veterans Affairs shall each submit to Congress two reports containing, with respect to their respective Departments, the following:

(1) An assessment of the need for rehabilitative services for members of the

Armed Forces participating in the Operation Desert Storm who experience post-traumatic stress disorder.

(2) A description of the available programs and resources to meet those needs.

(3) The specific plans of that Secretary for treatment of members experiencing post-traumatic stress disorder, particularly with respect to any specific needs of members of reserve components.

(4) An assessment of needs for additional resources necessary in order to carry out such plans.

(5) A description of plans to coordinate treatment services for post-traumatic stress disorder with the other Departments.

(b) TIMES FOR SUBMISSIONS OF REPORTS.—The first report by each of the Secretaries shall be submitted not later than 90 days after the date of the enactment of this Act, and the second report by each of the Secretaries shall be submitted a year later.

Phoenix Air-to-Air Missile (AIM-54)

Used only by the Navy's F-14 Falcon fighter, the Phoenix air-to-air missile is an updated variant of the AIM-54A, which had been sold to the Iranians in the 1970s. The more modern version is the U.S. Navy fleet's long-range air defense missile.

The Phoenix is 13 feet (4 m) long, has a wingspan of 3 feet (0.9 m), weighs 969 pounds (440 kg), has a maximum speed of more than 3,040 mph (4,891 km/h), has a range of more than 100 nautical miles (115 miles; 185 km), and is powered by an Mk 47 solid-propellant rocket. The more recent versions of the Phoenix include reprogrammable memory (RPM) and modern software upgrades.

References: Blake, Bernard, ed., *Jane's Weapon Systems, 1988–89* (Coulsdon, Surrey, UK: Jane's Information Group, 1988), 755; Dunnigan, James F., and Austin Bay, *From Shield to Storm: High-Tech Weapons, Military Strategy and Coalition Warfare in the Persian Gulf* (New York: Morrow, 1992), 216; *Sea Power: The Official Publication of the Navy League of the United States* 37:1 (January 1994), 178–179.

Poland

See Coalition Nations, Contributions of.

"Poobah's Party"

See Tomahawk Land Attack Missile.

Portugal

See Coalition Nations, Contributions of.

Powell, Colin Luther (1937–)

The first black man to serve as chairman of the Joint Chiefs of Staff of the U.S. military, Colin Powell is one of the most highly regarded military authorities. His service as part of the Carter mission to resolve the potential invasion of Haiti in September 1994 only added to his resume.

Powell was born in Harlem, New York, on 5 April 1937, the son of Luther Theopolis Powell, a shipping clerk who worked in New York City's garment district, and Maud Ariel (née McKoy) Powell, a seamstress. Both parents were Jamaican immigrants who instilled a sense of duty to country and wielded a stern hand in the discipline and education of their children, Marilyn and Colin. Powell attended local schools before receiving a bachelor's degree from New York's City College and a master's in business administration from George Washington University in Washington, D.C. In 1958 Powell entered the U.S. military, accepting a commission as a second lieutenant in the Army. Over the next four years, reports one source, Powell was shifted from one military base to another. In 1962 he married Alma Vivian Johnson, but soon after was sent to Vietnam as an advisor to the government of Ngo Dinh Diem, an American ally. Powell served from 1962 to 1963 in Vietnam, where he was awarded the Purple Heart and the Bronze Star. After a period of reassignment in the United States and more education, Powell served a second tour in Vietnam (1968–1969). His bravery during a rescue of a downed helicopter in which he had been riding earned him the Soldier's Medal. He returned to the United States, where he was promoted to major and as-

General Colin Powell, chairman of the Joint Chiefs of Staff, speaks to U.S. airmen at a base in Saudi Arabia during Operation Desert Storm.

signed as a White House fellow. In this capacity he was spotted by Caspar Weinberger, head of the Office of Management and Budget, and Weinberger's second-in-command, Frank Carlucci (both men would eventually serve as secretary of defense in the Reagan administration). Because of his work with the two, Powell was eventually assigned as the commander of the Second Brigade of the 101st Airborne Division at Fort Campbell, where he served from 1976 to 1977. He later served as assistant commander of the Fourth Infantry Division at Fort Carson, Colorado.

In 1983 Powell was named by President Ronald Reagan as the military assistant to Secretary of Defense Caspar Weinberger, serving for three years. Powell showed his military shrewdness during the invasion of the island of Grenada when he advised that allowing the military a free hand in fighting was the best course of action. In 1986 Reagan named Powell as commander of the V Corps in Europe. The following year, Reagan brought him back to the United States to serve as deputy national security advisor to

Frank Carlucci. When Carlucci succeeded Weinberger as secretary of defense in 1987, Powell became the first black to become the national security advisor. Although he left this post in 1988 to become commander of the Armed Forces Command, in 1989 President George Bush named Powell as chairman of the Joint Chiefs of Staff, making him the highest ranking black military official in U.S. history.

Because of his position at the time of the Gulf War, Colin Powell may have been one of four people (President George Bush, Secretary of State Dick Cheney, General H. Norman Schwarzkopf, and Powell) who truly knew what the coalition was going to do and when they were going to do it.

Joe Klein considered the question of whether Colin Powell would run for president in his cover story "The Powell Scenario" for *Newsweek* magazine: "It is likely that Colin Powell's race has worked to his advantage along the way—no doubt, the bright, young army major's skin color didn't hurt when such Republican sponsors as Caspar Weinberger and Frank Carlucci selected him from the White House fellows list to work in the Nixon budget office in 1972. More to the point, Powell never seems to have allowed his race to be a disadvantage, either."

References: Adler, Bill, *The Generals: The New American Heroes—The Commanders behind Desert Storm—General H. Norman Schwarzkopf and General Colin Powell* (New York: Avon, 1991), 15–16, 44–45; Klein, Joe, "Can Colin Powell Save America?" *Newsweek*, 10 October 1994, 26.

Primakov, Yevgeni Maksimovich

(1928–)

Russian envoy Yevgeni (also called Evgenii in some Russian-language journals and books) Primakov was a senior policy advisor to Soviet president Mikhail Gorbachev in Arab and Asian affairs, and a key player in the effort to forestall a coalition attack against Iraq. Born in Kiev on 29 October 1928, he graduated from the Moscow Institute of Oriental Studies in 1953 and worked for the State Radio and Television Committee from 1953 to 1962. In 1959 he became a member of the Communist party of the Soviet Union (CPSU) and remained so until the party's downfall in 1991. From 1962 to 1970 he was a columnist and deputy editor of the Asian and African desk at the Russian newspaper *Pravda*. After 1970 he was the deputy director of the Institute of World Economy and International Relations of the USSR Academy in Moscow, where he became a leading Soviet authority on Arab affairs. In 1972 and 1975 he was the editor of two Russian journals, and in the latter year he was awarded the Nasser Prize from Egypt. In 1985 he was named director of the institute.

As a prominent expert in Arab matters, Primakov was called by Soviet president Mikhail Gorbachev to join his foreign policy team when Gorbachev rose to power in 1985. He was at Gorbachev's side throughout the Persian Gulf crisis, shuttling back and forth between Moscow and Baghdad in an unsuccessful attempt to resolve the issue of Kuwait before a war broke out. In a *Time* magazine article called "My Final Visit with Saddam Hussein," Primakov wrote of his visit to Baghdad on 11 February 1991: "After hearing rebukes that Soviet policy had given the 'green light' to the 'U.N. war against Iraq' and declarations about Iraq's 'unshakable' stand, I asked to be left alone with Saddam. Then I said to him, 'The Americans are determined to launch a large-scale ground operation to crush Iraqi forces in Kuwait.' Politics, I reminded him, was the art of the possible. On [Soviet General Secretary Mikhail] Gorbachev's instructions, I made a proposal: to announce the pullout of troops from Kuwait. The deadline should be the shortest possible, and the withdrawal should be total and without conditions. . . . We had reached a turning point. Saddam began to ask specific questions—evidence that he was not flatly rejecting the proposals. Would there be guarantees that Iraqi soldiers leaving Kuwait would not be 'shot in the back'? Would attacks on Iraq be halted after the pullout? Would the U.N. sanctions against Iraq then be lifted?" Primakov relates that although at first the Iraqis agreed with the Soviet demands, they later added conditions, and demanded that they be allowed up to six weeks to withdraw all Iraqi troops from Kuwait. The talks bogged down and, on 24 February, the ground war began.

References: Lewytzkyj, Borys, ed., *Who's Who in the Soviet Union* (München, Germany: K. G. Saur, 1984), 264; Primakov, Yevgeni, "My Final Visit with Saddam Hussein," *Time*, 11 March 1991, 44–45; Vronskaya, Jeanne, with Vladimir Chuguev, *A Biographical Dictionary of the Soviet Union, 1917–1988* (London: K. G. Saur, 1989), 338.

Prisoners of War, United States

Twenty Americans were taken prisoner by the Iraqi forces, including—for the first time in American history—uniformed women. Alphabetically, they are: Acree, Clifford M., Lieutenant Colonel, USMC; Andrews, William F., Captain, USAF; Berryman, Michael C., Captain, USMC; Coleman, Melissa A., Specialist, USA; Cornum, Rhonda L., Major, USA; Dunlap, Troy A., Specialist, USA; Eberly, David W., Colonel, USAF; Fox, Jeffrey D., Lieutenant Colonel, USAF; Griffith, Thomas E., Jr., Major, USAF; Hunter, Guy L., Jr., Chief Warrant Officer Four, USMC; Lockett, David, Specialist, USA; Roberts, Harry M., Captain, USAF; Sanborn, Russell A. C., Captain, USMC; Slade, Lawrence R., Lieutenant, USN; Small, Joseph J. II, Major, USMC; Stamaris, Daniel J., Jr., Staff Sergeant, USA; Storr, Richard D.,

Captain, USAF; Sweet, Robert J., First Lieutenant, USAF; Tice, Jeffrey S., Lieutenant, USN; and Zaun, Jeffrey N., Lieutenant, USN.

See also Enemy Prisoners of War.
Reference: *Conduct of the Persian Gulf War: Final Report to Congress,* Report by the Department of Defense, April 1992, 317.

Project Babylon
See Bull, Gerald Vincent.

Propaganda, Iraqi

In order to keep coalition force morale low, the Iraqi government used various types of propaganda, from the funny to the ludicrous.

Bill Licatovich, a public affairs specialist in the U.S. Army's Office of the Chief of Public Affairs in Washington, D.C., discussed the various types of propaganda used by the Iraqis prior to the outbreak of the war.

Common allegations include:

—American soldiers are all addicted to wine, women, and song, and constantly and openly violate Arab morals;

—American soldiers have very low morale and can't stand up to the tough conditions of the desert;

—American soldiers are afraid of Iraqi soldiers and will break and run once combat starts.

Reference: Licatovich, Bill, "Iraqi Propaganda Ploys," *Soldiers* 46:1 (January 1991), 6–8.

Provisional Free Government of Kuwait

On 2 August, shortly after the Iraqi assault cleaned up the last pockets of Kuwaiti resistance, the government in Baghdad announced that a new provisional government (rumored by some to involve pro-Iraqi Kuwaitis opposed to the ruling Sabah family) would take power in Kuwait.

Propaganda, Iraqi

In this cartoon an Iraqi soldier says to U.S. president George Bush, "How long are we going to sit here pointlessly? I have a baby at home. I want to go back before the cannon starts firing."

This so-called Provisional Free Government of Kuwait had apparently taken power *before* the coup, and had "requested" that Iraq deliver military relief against the al-Sabahs. The new "government," in its first official act, informed the Kuwaiti people that elections would eventually be held in their country, presumably under Iraqi authority. As well, it ordered that the assets of the al-Sabahs not taken during the emir's rush to safety in Saudi Arabia would be confiscated. Iraq declared to the rest of the Arab world that the Kuwait situation was "an internal matter," and asked for Arab unity. The United States denounced the deceptive Kuwaiti rulers as a "puppet regime."

The following day, as the Arab world attempted to deal with the burgeoning crisis, Iraq announced that it would withdraw its forces from Kuwait on 5 August, but that the provisional government would remain in power after they departed. On 4 August Baghdad television announced that the new nine-man Kuwaiti "government" would be led by Colonel Ala Hussein Ali; he would hold the posts of Kuwaiti prime minister, commander in chief of the armed forces, minister of defense, and interior minister. Eight other men were also named. Analysts of Iraqi strategy noted that all nine men were Iraqi military officers or mayors of Iraqi cities, and that Colonel Ali was a son-in-law of Saddam Hussein, which Iraq angrily and forcefully denied. On 4 August the new provisional government announced that it was forming a "popular Arab army" to be open to all Arabs who wished to defend Iraq and Kuwait. Radio Baghdad said of the armed force, "They are volunteering to aid brethren in Kuwait to defend the Kuwait revolution and to stand as strong barriers and drawn swords to confront all those who may think of encroaching upon our great Iraq or the soil of Kuwait." The following day, in response to calls from the United States for sanctions to be imposed on Iraq, the new Kuwaiti foreign minister, Walid Saud Abdullah, said on Iraqi radio, "Countries that resort to punitive measures against the provisional free Kuwait government and fraternal Iraq should remember that they have interests and nationals in Iraq. These countries should also not expect us to act honorably at a time when they are conspiring against us and other brothers in Iraq in an aggressive way. If these countries insist on aggression against Kuwait and Iraq, the Kuwaiti government will then reconsider the method of dealing with these countries."

The so-called Kuwaiti provisional government lasted until 28 August when, instead of withdrawing all Iraqi troops from Kuwait and declaring it to be an independent state (nonetheless under Iraqi authority), Saddam Hussein announced that Kuwait was to become Iraq's nineteenth province, that Kuwait City would hereafter be referred to as Kadhima, and that the province would officially be called Saddam. The need for a provisional government evaporated, and nothing more was heard from it.

References: "Arabs Put Off Talks as Iraqis Consolidate in Kuwait," *New York Times,* 5 August 1990, 14; Kifner, John, "Bush, Hinting Force, Declares Iraqi Assault 'Will Not Stand'; Proxy in Kuwait Issues Threat," *New York Times,* 6 August 1990, A1.

Qaqa State Establishment Explosion. *See* Bazoft, Farzad.

Qassem, Abdul-Karim (1914–1963)

An Iraqi army officer, Abdul-Karim Qassem was the head of the Free Officers who overthrew the government of King Faisal II of Iraq in 1958. Qassem was himself overthrown by a Ba'athist coup in 1963.

Israeli writer Uriel Dann's considerable work *Iraq under Qassem: A Political History, 1958–1963*, relates, "Qassem himself was near the lower end of the social scale of the Free Officer membership. He was born in Mahdiyya, a poor quarter of Baghdad on the left side of the river, on December 21, 1914, the youngest of the three sons of Qasim bin Muhammad bin Bakr. According to official data published while he held office, Qassem's parents were both of pure Arab descent. His father's family derived from the Qahtăniyya [southern Arab] clan and his mother's from a clan of Adnăniyya [northern Arab] origin. Hostile biographers have denied his Arab blood, alleging that his father was a Turcoman and his mother a Kurd. According to the most reliable evidence, Qassem's father was a Sunni Arab while his mother's parents were Faylîs—Shi'i Kurds who had migrated to Baghdad in large numbers from territory beyond the Iranian border."

Qassem joined the Iraqi military and was commissioned as an officer in 1938. His only known military service was as a member of the Iraqi contingent sent to fight against Israel in the 1948 Arab-Israeli War. In 1956 he became a member of the "Free Officers," members of Iraq's military hierarchy who plotted to overthrow the monarchy of King Faisal II. On 14 July 1958, with the aid of the other Free Officers, including Abdul-Salam Aref, Qassem overpowered the government of Faisal and Prime Minister Nuri as-Said. The two men and the former

regent, Abdul Illah, were executed. The British ambassador to Iraq, Sir Michael Wright, cabled London, "The Prime Minister, Brigadier Abdul Karim Qassim [*sic*] is soft-spoken and friendly to meet. He is said to be a devout Muslim and dedicated to the service of his country. He is unmarried and lives very simply. Apart from a few remarks in some of his speeches his conduct so far has been essentially moderate and restrained. . . . He has a good reputation as a competent army officer and as far as it is possible to judge enjoys confidence in the army."

Middle East author Yaacov Shimoni wrote, "Qassem was interested in social affairs, and in September 1958 [he] enacted a major land reform law. Early in 1960 he tried to revive political parties; but the attempt failed, and it remains in doubt to what extent Qassem had taken it seriously in the first place. He became increasingly erratic—to an extent that he was nicknamed 'The Mad Dictator.' Endowed with an exalted sense of his own missions, he had not created a political base to his rule, and by 1961 he had no supporters left among the political groupings and was in serious political difficulty." In 1961 Qassem declared that Kuwait was part of Iraq, setting the stage for the reintroduction of British troops into that small emirate, as well as for a 30-year battle for the right to own Kuwait that culminated in the Persian Gulf War of 1991.

One of Qassem's leading critics was Abdul Hassan al-Bakr, another of the Free Officers, along with Qassem's former partner, Aref. On 8 February 1963, known as the Fourteenth Ramadan, Free Officers belonging to the Ba'ath party used the military to attack the Qassem government. Early the next morning, according to Uriel Dann, Qassem and several of his followers surrendered. They were given a brief court martial, led into a courtyard, and summarily executed.

See also al-Bakr, Ahmad Hassan; Faisal II, King of Iraq.
References: Dann, Uriel, *Iraq under Qassem: A Political History, 1958–1963* (New York: Praeger, 1969),

Qassem, Abdul-Karim

Brigadier General Abdul-Karim Qassem of Iraq salutes as he leaves army headquarters in Baghdad on 23 July 1958.

21; Fernea, Robert A., and Wm. Roger Louis, *The Iraqi Revolution of 1958: The Old Social Classes Revisited* (London: I. B. Tauris, 1991), 57; Shimoni, Yaacov, *Political Dictionary of the Arab World* (New York: Macmillan, 1987), 409–410.

Qatar

Simply called Dawlat Qatar (the state of Qatar), this member of the Gulf Cooperation Council was an important part of the Allied coalition during Operations Desert Shield and Desert Storm.

Geographically, Qatar seems to be a small, insignificant peninsula inside the Persian Gulf. Yet a closer look reveals its strategic and military importance. Located to the southeast of Bahrain and connected by land to Saudi Arabia and the United Arab Emirates, according to writer Tony Odone, Qatar has "an area of 180 km by 85 km [112 by 53 mi]" that "is mainly desert." Middle East writer and authority Rosemarie Said Zahlan wrote of the nation, "The location and geographical features of Qatar have played a predominant role in the shaping of its political and social characteristics. A narrow limestone peninsula. . . . Qatar juts out midway onto the Arab [western]

coast of the Persian Gulf around 30 km [18.6 mi] south of the Bahrain Islands. The peninsula is largely desert with undulating rock rising out of it, making the soil generally unfit for anything but nomadic pastoralism; in fact, until the discovery of oil enabled limited agricultural activity to be financed, the only natural vegetation in Qatar, apart from a few date gardens, was coarse grass and occasional stunted brushwood."

The al-Thani family has been in control of Qatar since the 1860s. The editors of *The Middle East* write, "During the period of Ottoman occupation (1872–1915), the al-Thani [family] retained their eminence and in 1916 Abdullah bin Qasim al-Thani, as de facto ruler, signed an agreement with Britain by which he received British protection in return for surrendering the responsibility for Qatar's external relations." The present ruler, Sheik Khalifa bin Hamad al-Thani, holds the positions of head of state and prime minister. In 1981 Qatar was one of the founding members of the Gulf Cooperation Council. The Qatari army was implemented largely with French-made equipment, and, although small, saw action during the Persian Gulf War at the crucial battle of Khafji, where a tank battalion outmaneuvered the Iraqis in that city.

Qatar

Sheik Khalifa bin Hamad al-Thani, crown prince of Qatar, reviews Irish Guards at Whitehall, the British Foreign Office, in London in 1988.

References: Adams, Michael, ed., *The Middle East* (New York: Facts on File, 1988), 103; Dunnigan, James F., and Austin Bay, *From Shield to Storm: High-Tech Weapons, Military Strategy, amd Coalition Warfare in the Persian Gulf* (New York: Morrow, 1992), 13; Odone, Tony, "Qatar," in *The Cambridge Encyclopedia of the Middle East and North Africa*, Trevor Mostyn, exec. ed. (New York: Cambridge University Press, 1988), 400; Zahlan, Rosemarie Said, *The Creation of Qatar* (London: Croom Helm, 1979), 48.

Quayle, James Danforth (1947–)

This American politician was a congressman and senator from the state of Indiana before being chosen in 1988 as George Bush's running mate. Dan Quayle became an important member of Bush's inner circle during the Persian Gulf crisis and subsequent conflict.

Born James Danforth Quayle on 4 February 1947 in Indianapolis, Indiana, he is the son of James C. Quayle and Corinne (née Pulliam) Quayle. His maternal grandfather, Eugene Pulliam, was the founder of the *Huntington Herald-Press* and the *Arizona Republic*. Named after

James Danforth, a family friend who was killed in World War II, Quayle received his education in public schools in Arizona and Indiana, and earned a bachelor's degree in political science at Indiana's DePauw University in 1969. At this time Quayle joined the Indiana National Guard to serve his country, but others later claimed that he used the National Guard to avoid going to Vietnam. Whatever the case, Quayle served as a reporter for the National Guard until his discharge in 1975.

During a three-month period in 1971, Quayle served as an investigator with the Indiana attorney general's Consumer Protection Division office. From 1971 to 1973 he served as an administrative assistant to Edgar Whitcomb, the governor of Indiana, simultaneously attending law school at Indiana University–Indianapolis. From 1973 to 1974 he was the director of the Inheritance Tax Division in Indiana. In 1974 he passed the Indiana bar exam and was admitted to the bar; that same year, he joined the Indiana Bar Association. In 1975 he taught business law at Indiana's Huntington College, and also served as the associate publisher and general manager

Quayle, James Danforth

U.S. vice president Dan Quayle, left, meets with Saudi king Fahd, right, and his interpreter, center, in Riyadh, Saudi Arabia, on 31 December 1990.

of his family's newspapers from 1974 to 1976. In 1976 Quayle was elected to the U.S. House of Representatives from Indiana's Fourth Congressional District by defeating eight-term Democratic congressman J. Edward Roush, whom he accused of being a liberal.

In 1980 Quayle challenged three-term incumbent senator Birch E. Bayh, whose election was seen as a certainty. Yet Quayle was able to accuse Bayh of being out of the mainstream for supporting abortion and, as luck would have it, 1980 was the year of the Reagan revolution. Quayle won 54 percent of the vote (the largest margin in Indiana history) to become, at 33, the youngest man to serve Indiana in the U.S. Senate. In the Senate, Quayle deviated from his far-right voting record, voting for a Clean Air Act reauthorization, the Martin Luther King holiday, and to override Reagan's veto of sanctions on South Africa. He even worked with Senator Edward Kennedy, a darling of liberals, on the Job Training and Partnership Act of 1982. Quayle was reelected in 1986.

In August 1992, Republican presidential nominee George Bush chose Quayle as his running mate, making the Indiana senator an instant media sensation. Brought into focus was his military and voting record, as well as his relative inexperience on the national scene and his seeming immaturity to be one heartbeat away from the presidency. Although the campaign was rough, Quayle was elected the forty-fourth vice-president of the United States. In his four years on the job, he was a faithful companion to Bush and to the administration's policies.

With the outbreak of the crisis in the Gulf, Quayle became a member of the administration's inner circle. On 1 December he appeared on CNN to give the administration's view on the linking of the withdrawal of Iraqi troops from Kuwait to a similar Israeli withdrawal from the Occupied Territories: "Palestine is not an issue on the table. The issue on the table is Saddam Hussein's invasion of Kuwait. . . . You're not going to link Palestine up to Saddam's invasion of Kuwait." On 29 December Quayle met in Riyadh with King Fahd and the deputy prime minister, Crown Prince Abdullah, of Saudi Arabia to solicit an agreement that the Saudis and Kuwaitis should bear a greater burden of the financial cost of the American military buildup in the Gulf. After the start of the ground war, Quayle remained just a heartbeat from the president's side, and may have helped make important policy decisions.

In 1992 journalists Bob Woodward and David Broder wrote of Quayle in *The Man Who Would Be President,* and predicted that the Indiana politician, so unknown just a few years ago, might someday be president of the United States. Although Quayle was defeated when the Bush-Quayle ticket lost in the 1992 election, he was considered a prime contender for the 1996 Republican presidential nomination. He announced in January 1995, however, that he would not run.

Reference: Woodward, Bob, and David S. Broder, *The Man Who Would Be President: Dan Quayle* (New York: Simon & Schuster, 1992).

Rapid Deployment Force

See Carter Doctrine; U.S. Central Command.

RC-135W Rivet Joint

The RC-135W Rivet Joint, a derivation of the KC-135 tanker, flew 197 missions, all for the U.S. Air Force during Operation Desert Storm. The mission of the RC-135W is cloaked in secrecy; the U.S. military's *Gulf War Air Power Survey* will merely say that "throughout Desert Shield and Desert Storm, Rivet Joint crews collected valuable information about enemy forces." The same survey's *Summary Report* says, "A second category of U.S. reconnaissance assets were the strategic airborne reconnaissance platforms, a group of nine RC-135 Rivet Joint aircraft and nine U-2/TR-1 aircraft operated by [the] Strategic Air Command. These aircraft had sophisticated sensors for collecting imagery and electronic intelligence, but they were vulnerable while flying in Iraqi airspace." *Aviation Week & Space Technology* called the plane a "signals intelligence aircraft which can monitor Iraqi communications."

The Rivet Joint is one of several derivations of the KC-135 tanker. These include the RC-135A Looking Glass, used by the president and other top officials during a nuclear attack; the RC-135U Combat Scent, an ELINT/COMINT (electronic intelligence/communications intelligence) collection aircraft; and the RC-135V, a Strategic Air Command (SAC) aircraft whose mission remains a closely guarded secret.

See also KC-135 Refueling Tanker.
References: Almond, Denise L., ed., *Desert Score: U.S. Gulf War Weapons* (Washington, DC: Carroll Publishing, 1991), 135; *Gulf War Air Power Survey, Volume IV: Weapons, Tactics, and Training Report and Space Report* (Washington, DC: GPO, 1993), 100; Keany, Thomas A., and Eliot A. Cohen, *Gulf War Air Power Survey, Summary Report* (Washington, DC: GPO, 1993), 194; "Special Mission Aircraft Support Desert Storm Air Campaign," *Aviation Week & Space Technology*, 25 February 1991, 45.

Refueling Aircraft

See KC-10 Extender Refueling Tanker; KC-135 Refueling Tanker.

Remotely Piloted Vehicles (RPVs)

A shorter-range RPV used during the Persian Gulf War in a limited capacity was the Pointer RPV. With a maximum flying time of one hour, a maximum range of up to 3 miles (5 km) from the operator, susceptibility to desert winds (because of its weight of about 50 pounds [23 kg]), and an altitude limit of 500 to 1,000 feet (152.5–305 m), the Pointer RPV had a limited scope and did not see much action.

See also Unmanned Aerial Vehicle.

Repair Ships, United States

This class of ships, whose main task is to repair other ships on short notice in the area of assignment, was represented by the *Vulcan* (AR 5) and the *Jason* (AR 8), both of which arrived in the Kuwaiti Theater of Operations (KTO) in January 1991; the *Vulcan* departed from the area on 15 February 1991. These ships displace 16,245 tons loaded; the *Vulcan* is 529.33 feet (161.4 m) in length, while the *Jason* is 530 feet (161.6 m) in length. Powered by two Allis Chalmers steam turbines (the *Jason* has New York Shipbuilding steam turbines) and four Babcock & Wilcox boilers, the ships have a maximum speed of 19.2 knots (22 mph; 36 km/h) and a range of 18,000 nautical miles (33,336 km) at 12 knots (14 mph; 22 km/h). Complement for the *Vulcan* is 593 (including 23 officers); for the *Jason* it is 888 (including 35 officers). The *Vulcan* was decommissioned on 20 September 1991. With this move, the *Jason*, commissioned in 1943, became the oldest ship in the U.S. Navy.

Reference: Polmar, Norman, *The Naval Institute Guide to the Ships and Aircraft of the U.S. Fleet* (Annapolis, MD: Naval Institute Press, 1993), 267.

Republican Guard

In most wars, individual units in any army are never really highlighted (save for the "Big Red One" from World War II, the title of a somewhat successful Hollywood picture). Yet the Iraqi Republican Guard became more well known, by both friends and foes, than perhaps any military element of this century.

The U.S. Defense Department called the Republican Guards "Iraq's most capable and loyal force, and [they] had received the best training and equipment." Composed of men recruited from Saddam Hussein's hometown of Tikrit, these men expressed incredible devotion to their leader; in return, they received the best pay, food, and weapons.

Frank Chadwick writes, "The Iraqi Republican Guard was originally intended to provide President Saddam Hussein with a body of troops of unquestioning loyalty. As the principal means of presidential succession in Iraq has become coup and murder, these troops were more political than military. They originally consisted of three brigades recruited from Tikrit, Saddam's hometown in northern Iraq." The number of divisions was later expanded to eight; by the time of the outbreak of the war, they included the First Armored Division, known as the Hammurabi; the Second Armored Division (the Medina), the Third Mechanized Division (the Tawakalna), the Fourth Motorized Division (the Al Faw), the Fifth Motorized Division (the Baghdad), the Sixth Motorized Division (the Nebuchadnezzar), the Seventh Motorized Division (the Adnan), and the Eighth Division, known as the Special Forces Division.

The U.S. Defense Department reports, "At the end of the war with Iran, the Republican Guard consisted of eight divisions. Combined with its independent infantry and artillery brigades, the Guard comprised almost 20 percent of Iraqi ground forces. Most Republican Guard heavy divisions were equipped with Soviet T-72 main battle tanks, Soviet BMP armored personnel carriers, French GCT self-propelled howitzers and Austrian GHN-45 towed howitzers—all modern, state-of-the-art equipment."

Yet how well trained, and experienced, were Guard fighters? In *From the House of War*, the BBC's John Simpson wrote, "The Republican Guard, which journalists and politicians insisted on calling 'elite,' was increased by several divisions during the period of the crisis, largely by means of taking men from regular units and giving them red berets. Anyone who could march in step was considered eligible. The officers of the Republican Guard were usually better trained, but that generally meant that they too had to be taken from other units. The mass dilution meant that the Republican Guards' standards, which in the war against Iran had been above average, were little different from those of the rest of the Iraqi army. . . . When the ground offensive came, the 'elite' Republican Guard showed little more inclination to fight than the regular army divisions and reservists."

References: Chadwick, Frank, *The Desert Shield Fact Book* (Bloomington, IL: Game Designers' Workshop, 1991), 51; *Conduct of the Persian Gulf War: Final Report to Congress*, Report by the Department of Defense, April 1992, 10; Simpson, John, *From the House of War*, quoted in *Second Front: Censorship and Propaganda in the Gulf War*, by John R. MacArthur (New York: Hill & Wang, 1992), 243.

Revolutionary Command Council (RCC)

As Helen Chapman Metz writes in her work, *Iraq: A Country Study*, "The most powerful decision-making body in Iraq, the ten-member Revolutionary Command Council (RCC), which functioned as the top executive and legislative organ of the state, was for all practical purposes an arm of the Ba'ath Party. All members of the RCC were also members of the party's Regional Command, or state apparatus. President Saddam Hussein was both chairman of the RCC and the secretary general of the Ba'ath's Regional Command." Samir al-Khalil argues, in his work *Republic of Fear: The Inside Story of Saddam's Iraq,*

Revolutionary
Command Council

Iraqi president Saddam Hussein, center, listens to Foreign Minister Tariq Aziz, second from right, during a February 1991 meeting of the Revolutionary Command Council.

that with the ascension of Saddam Hussein, the RCC, an arm of the Ba'ath party, has in effect taken control of the nation, instead of the nation controlling the party.

Because it is the prevailing government in Iraq, the RCC played a major role in Iraq's prosecution of the Gulf War, although the words of the RCC were more likely the words of Saddam Hussein. On 8 August, just six days after the invasion of Kuwait, the RCC announced that Iraq and Kuwait were unified as a nation. On 1 December 1990, in replying to President Bush's offer for talks to avert war, the RCC reiterated that "Palestine and the other occupied Arab territories remain before our eyes and at the forefront of the issues that we will discuss in any dialogue." Because Saddam Hussein rules the nation with an iron hand, the other members of the RCC may be considered little more than puppets who could be replaced at any time.

References: al-Khalil, Samir, *Republic of Fear: The Inside Story of Saddam's Iraq* (New York: Pantheon, 1990), 145; Metz, Helen Chapman, ed., *Iraq: A Country Study* (Washington, DC: GPO, 1990), 175.

RF-4C Phantom II

An aircraft similar to the F-4 Phantom Wild Weasel, the RF-4 flew 822 sorties for the U.S. Air Force during Operation Desert Storm: 719 as the RC-4 and 103 as the RF-4C, all in a bomb damage assessment (BDA) capacity.

The RF-4C has almost the same specifications as the F-4, except for the inclusion of several cameras for optical reconnaissance. Built by McDonnell Douglas, the RF-4C is a two-seat craft (pilot and radar intercept officer) powered by two General Electric J79-GE-10 turbojet engines, each producing 17,659 pounds (8,010 kg) of thrust with afterburners. The plane weighs 30,776 pounds (13,960 kg) empty, has a wingspan of 38 feet 5 inches (17.76 m), a maximum speed of 1,450 mph (Mach 2.1), and a range of up to 334 nautical miles (385 mi; 619 km) in an attack role. Armaments can include AIM-7 Sparrow and AIM-9L Sidewinder air-to-air missiles.

The U.S. military's *Gulf War Air Power Survey* reports that the RF-4C is "a multisensor aircraft capable of all-weather day and night reconnaissance in a high- or low-threat environment." It adds, "RF-4Cs deployed to Saudi Arabia during Desert Shield, and collected intelligence on Iraqi positions near the Saudi Arabian–Iraqi border before Desert Storm. During Desert Storm, 18 RF-4s flew 822 sorties conducting bomb damage assessment flights, and no RF-4s were lost in combat."

See also F-4G Phantom II Wild Weasel.
References: *Gulf War Air Power Survey, Volume IV: Weapons, Tactics and Training Report and Space Report* (Washington, DC: GPO, 1993), 100–101; Polmar, Norman, *Ships and Aircraft of the U.S. Fleet* (Annapolis, MD: Naval Institute Press, 1987), 401.

Roland Surface-to-Air Missile System

The U.S. military report *Gulf War Air Power Survey* said of the system, "The French Roland was another short-range missile designed to protect tactical ground units. It has a range of approximately three and one half miles [5.6 km]. Approximately thirteen Roland I (clear weather) systems and one hundred Roland II (all weather) systems had been sold to Iraq. By the beginning of the Gulf War, it appeared that most Rolands had been incorporated into the strategic air defense system protecting high-value targets."

Reference: *Gulf War Air Power Survey, Volume IV: Weapons, Tactics, and Training Report and Space Report* (Washington, DC: GPO, 1993), 14.

Romania

See Coalition Nations, Contributions of.

RPG-7 Manportable Antitank Rocket Launcher

Found in the weapons reserves of Egypt, Iraq, and Syria, this manportable short-range rocket launcher may have been used in the Persian Gulf War by Iraq, although this cannot be confirmed. Originally built exclusively by the Soviet Union and sold to its client states, the RPG-7 is 37 inches (950 mm) in length. The launcher weighs 17.4 pounds (7.9 kg), while the added grenade is 5 pounds (2.25 kg). Range for a moving target is 984 feet (300 m), and that of a stationary target is 16,400 feet (5,000 m). It can penetrate a tank's armor up to 22 inches (330 mm).

Reference: Hogg, Ian V., ed., *Jane's Infantry Weapons, 1993–94* (Coulsdon, Surrey, UK: Jane's Information Group, 1993), 741–743.

S-3B Viking

A two-engine, four-seat Navy antisubmarine warfare (ASW) carrier aircraft, the S-3B Viking was used in an electronics warfare role during Operation Desert Storm, flying 1,674 sorties chiefly, reports one source, "in force-interdiction operations in the Persian Gulf and Red Sea," as well as "SCUDCAP (Scud Combat Air Patrol) missions in western Iraq." Other missions included the bombing of "an Iraqi AA site in Kuwait, providing emergency tanker service throughout the theater, and taking part in mine-detection operations in the Persian Gulf." The S-3B's main mission during Operation Desert Storm was as a reconnaisance craft and sometimes, equipped with a D-704 refueling package, as a refueling tanker.

With a wingspan of 68 feet 8 inches (20.93 m), the S-3 is 53 feet 4 inches (16.26 m) in length.

Powered by two General Electric TF34-GE-400B turbofan engines, the plane's maximum speed is 450 knots (518 mph; 834 km/h), its maximum unrefueled range is more than 2,300 nautical miles (2,650 mi; 4,263 km), and the plane can be equipped with various types and combinations of missiles, rockets, and depth charges for anti-submarine warfare. Under a weapons system improvement program instituted by the S-3's manufacturer (Lockheed), original S-3As were turned into S-3Bs with the inclusion of updated avionics packages and weapons systems, expanding the plane's capability to carry modernized Harpoon missiles.

References: Dunnigan, James F., and Austin Bay, *From Shield to Storm: High-Tech Weapons, Military Strategy and Coalition Warfare in the Persian Gulf* (New York: Morrow, 1992), 200; *Gulf War Air Power Survey, Volume IV: Weapons, Tactics, and*

Original S-3A Viking aircraft, such as this one on the flight deck of the USS *Independence* during Operation Desert Shield, were updated and converted to S-3Bs.

Training Report and Space Report (Washington, DC: GPO, 1993), 101; *Sea Power: The Official Publication of the Navy League of the United States* 37:1 (January 1994), 192; Taylor, John W. R., ed., *Jane's All the World's Aircraft, 1978–79* (London: Jane's Yearbooks, 1978), 362; Taylor, John W. R., ed., *Jane's All the World's Aircraft, 1989–90* (Coulsdon, Surrey, UK: Jane's Information Group, 1989), 439.

S-70B Seahawk

This Navy helicopter (also classified as the SH-60B/F Mark III Seahawk) was employed during the Persian Gulf crisis as part of Australia's contribution to the operations, mostly to enforce the embargo against Iraq. As well, 46 SH-60B Mark IIIs (34 LAMPS III SH-60Bs and 12 LAMPS I SH-2F/Gs, a slight variant) also served with American forces, "performing maritime interception operations, detection and targeting missions, mine hunting and destruction, explosive ordnance disposal, team support, special warfare operations, battle damage assessment, combat search and rescue, and coastal surveillance," according to the U.S. military's final report to Congress on the war. The Spanish navy also used a variant, the S-70L, which they have designated as the HS.23.

The S-70B Seahawk is an antiship surveillance and targeting helicopter, according to *Jane's All the World's Aircraft,* although its more modernized version, the SH-60, is better known as the LAMPS (light airborne multipurpose system) Mark III helicopter, and is really an updated UH-60 Blackhawk helicopter designed for the U.S. Navy. In *The Illustrated Encyclopedia of Helicopters,* Georgio Apostolo writes, "The SH-60 is intended principally for the U.S. Navy LAMPS Mk.III role—antisubmarine and antiship warfare and target acquisition, with the following complementary roles: SAR [search and rescue], casevac [casualty evacuation], and fleet replenishment."

Powered by two General Electric T700-GE-401 turboshaft engines delivering 1,690 shaft horsepower (shp), the Seahawk has an endurance range of 2 to 4 hours, or 2 to 3½ hours, on station, in its antisubmarine warfare (ASW) mode. The S-70Bs mainly served on the Australian frigates *Adelaide, Sydney,* and *Darwin.*

See also Frigates, Coalition; SH-2F/G Seasprite LAMPS I.

References: Apostolo, Georgio, *The Illustrated Encyclopedia of Helicopters* (New York: Bonanza, 1984), 92; *Conduct of the Persian Gulf War: Final Report to Congress,* Report by the Department of Defense, April 1992, 715–716; Lambert, Mark, ed., *Jane's All the World's Aircraft 1993–94* (Coulsdon, Surrey, UK: Jane's Information Group, 1993), 565–566; *Sea Power: The Official Publication of the Navy League of the United States* 37:1 (January 1994), 197.

SA-2, 3, 6, 8, 9, and 13 Surface-to-Air Missile Systems

The Iraqi military was equipped with many types of Soviet-designed SAM systems, including the SA-2 Guideline, the SA-3 Goa, the SA-6 Gainful, the SA-8 Gecko, the SA-9 Gaskin, and the SA-13 Gopher.

The U.S. military's *Gulf War Air Power Survey* reports: "The SA-2 and SA-3 systems formed the backbone of the Iraqi air defense system. The older systems were usually supplemented by an SA-6 battery. The SA-2, while updated somewhat, was originally designed to go against the B-52 and presented few problems to modern, fast moving, maneuverable fighter aircraft. It had a range of twenty-seven nautical miles [31 mi; 50 km] and was designed for high-altitude targets. The SA-3, developed shortly after the SA-2, had a range of fourteen miles [16 mi; 26 km] and was designed to defeat low- to medium-altitude craft.... During Desert Shield, SA-6s were placed at fixed sites defending airfields, key logistics centers, and command and control positions. SA-6 systems were also concentrated around Baghdad and the H3 areas.... The SA-8 was another tactical SAM designed to protect maneuver units. However, most SA-8s had been incorporated into the joint defense of strategically important areas, as had the SA-6s. ... As Desert Storm approached, the only mounted systems organic to Army Air Defense units apparently were the SA-9 and SA-13s."

Reference: Gulf War Air Power Survey, Volume IV: Weapons, Tactics, and Training Report and Space Report (Washington, DC: GPO, 1993), 11–14.

al-Sabah, Emir Sheik Jabir al-Ahmad al-Jabir. *See* Kuwait.

Sa'id, Qaboos Bin Al. *See* Oman.

Salvage and Rescue Ships, United States

Of the 177 American ships that served in the Persian Gulf conflict, only one, the Diver and Bolster–class ship *Opportune,* was a salvage and rescue ship. Built by the Basalt Rock Company of Napa, California, in 1945 and commissioned that same year, the *Opportune* (ARS 41) arrived in the Kuwait Theater of Operations (KTO) in November 1990. The ship displaces 1,530 tons standard (2,045 tons fully loaded), and is 213.5 feet (65.1 m) in length. Powered by four Cooper Bessemer diesel engines, the ship has a maximum speed of 16 knots (18 mph; 30 km/h) and a range of 20,000 nautical miles (23,016 mi; 37,040 km) at 7 knots (8 mph; 13 km/h). Complement for this class is approximately 103, which includes 7 officers. In December 1990, the *Opportune* became the first ship in the history of the U.S. Navy to be commanded by a woman.

See also Salvage and Rescue Tugs, United States.
Reference: Polmar, Norman, *The Naval Institute Guide to the Ships and Aircraft of the U.S. Fleet* (Annapolis, MD: Naval Institute Press, 1993), 271.

Salvage and Rescue Tugs, United States

Differing from salvage and rescue ships, the two tugs of the Powhatan class, the *Powhatan* (T-ATF 166) and the *Apache* (T-ATF 172) are also known as fleet tugs. The publication *Sea Power: The Official Journal of the Navy League of the United States,* reports, "[These ships] have a 300-brake-horsepower bow thruster, a 10-ton-capacity crane, and a 53.6-ton bollard pull. Space is provided for light armament in time of war." The Powhatan class displaces 2,000 tons standard (2,260 tons full), and are 240 feet 1 inch (73.2 m) in length. Powered by two General Electric EMD 20-645X7 diesel engines, the tugs have a maximum speed of 15 knots (17 mph; 28 km/h) and a range of 10,000 nautical miles (18,520 km) at 13 knots (15 mph; 24 km/h). Complement is 16 civilian crew and 4 Navy personnel.

See also Salvage and Rescue Ships, United States.
References: Polmar, Norman, *The Naval Institute Guide to the Ships and Aircraft of the U.S. Fleet* (Annapolis, MD: Naval Institute Press, 1993), 281; *Sea Power: The Official Publication of the Navy League of the United States* 37:1 (January 1994), 167.

Samita Incident

This crisis along the Iraqi-Kuwaiti border in March–April 1973 forecast the eventual war that broke out between the two nations less than 18 years later. In April 1969 Iraq requested the right to occupy a small slice of Kuwaiti territory to defend the Iraqi outpost of Umm Qasr against possible Iranian attacks. Although Kuwait never signed a written agreement to allow for such occupation, Kuwaiti minister of defense Shaikh Sa'id al-Sabah nonetheless orally agreed to the arrangement. There the matter stood for nearly four years.

In December 1972 Kuwait discovered that Iraqi construction crews were building a paved road inside Kuwaiti territory at al-Samita, or Samita. Four months later, Iraq submitted to Kuwait a treaty allowing Iraqi troops full access to the area, as well as oil drilling rights. Kuwait refused, and on 20 March 1973 a contingent of Kuwaiti soldiers approached the construction crews with orders to eject them from Kuwaiti territory. Instead, Iraqi troops opened fire on the group, killing two Kuwaitis and one Iraqi. After lodging a protest with the Iraqi government, Kuwait turned to the Arab world for help in resolving the matter. Syrian foreign minister Abdel Halim Khaddam and Arab League Secretary General Mahmoud Riad traveled to both Kuwait City and Baghdad before Iraq decided to withdraw its troops on 5 April 1973.

References: Finnie, David H., *Shifting Lines in the Sand: Kuwait's Elusive Frontier with Iraq* (Cambridge: Harvard University Press, 1992); "Iraq and Kuwait Clash at Border," *New York Times,* 21 March 1973, 6.

San Remo Conference

Held 19–26 April 1920, this international conference was assembled at San Remo, on the Italian Riviera, for the purposes of deciding the future of the former territories of the Ottoman Empire, one of the central powers defeated in World War I. The gathering was the direct result of Arab anger over the secret deal cut between the French, British, and Russians under the Sykes-Picot-Sazanov Agreement of 1916.

Attending the conference were Prime Minister David Lloyd George of Great Britain, Prime Minister Vittorio Orlando of Italy, and Premier Georges Clemenceau of France, as well as representatives from Belgium, Greece, and Japan. The discussions hinged on the degree of independence the victorious World War I powers would give to the small tribal states in the Arab world. Britain and France partitioned the area, giving Palestine, Transjordan (later the Hashemite Kingdom of Jordan), and Iraq to England, and Syria and Lebanon to France. When King Faisal of Damascus objected to French rule over Syria, he was sent into exile by the French army in Syria. In August 1921 Faisal was installed as king of Iraq.

Two smaller issues also dominated the meeting. The conferees approved the Treaty of Sèvres, which obliterated the Ottoman Empire, and set strict rules for Kurdish sovereignty and independence for Armenia (which Turkey later rejected), and allowed for the sale of 25 percent of Iraq's oil from Britain to France in exchange for the inclusion of the town of Mosul into the Iraqi mandate, controlled by the British.

The text of the decision of the Supreme Council of the San Remo Conference, passed on 25 April 1920, is as follows:

> The high contracting parties agree that Syria and Mesopotamia shall, in accordance with the fourth paragraph of article 22, Part I [of the Covenant of the League of Nations], be provisionally recognized as independent States, subject to the rendering of administrative advice and assistance by the mandatory until such time as they are able to stand alone. The boundaries of said States will be determined and the selection of mandatories made by the principal Allied Powers.

See also Article 22 of the League of Nations Covenant; Lausanne, Treaty of; Sèvres, Treaty of; Sykes-Picot-Sazanov Agreement.
Reference: Lauterpacht, E., et al., eds., *The Kuwait Crisis: Basic Documents* (Cambridge, UK: Grotius, 1991), 38.

Satellites, Use of by Coalition

See Global Positioning System; KH-11 and KH-12 Reconnaissance Satellites.

al-Saud, King Fahd Bin Abdul Aziz *See* Saudi Arabia.

Saudi Arabia

The largest nation in the Middle East in terms of size, Saudi Arabia lies at the crossroads of the Persian Gulf, reaching out to touch Iraq, the two Yemens, Jordan, and the Red Sea. It is also one of the leading oil producers in the world, and it was for this reason, and a possible attempt by Saddam Hussein's armies to cross from Kuwait toward the Saudi oilfields, that Operation Desert Shield was established.

P. W. Harrison wrote in the *Atlantic Monthly* in 1920, "The centre of this great brotherhood is the territory of the Hejaz on the coast of the Red Sea, and the two cities, Mecca and Medina, which that territory contains." The modern Saudi state was founded about 1747, when the central Arabian peninsula's sovereign, Muhammad Bin Saud, forged a federation with Muslim scholar Muhammad Bin Abdul Wahhab. Thus Bin Saud became al-Saud, and his family began a rule that has lasted to the present. However, credit for the consolidation of modern Saudi Arabia goes to Abdul Aziz (1876–1953), known as ibn Sa'ud (son of Saud). Chased from Riyadh in 1891 by the clan known as the Rasheed (al-Rashid), he fled to what is now Kuwait. Eric Pace related in the *New York Times* at the start of the Persian Gulf crisis in 1990, "Professor Jon E. Mandaville, a historian at Portland State College in Oregon, observed that Emir Mubarak of Kuwait, a forebear of the exiled Kuwaiti ruler, Sheik Jaber al-Ahmed al-Sabah, gave shelter to the future King Ibn Saud and his family for a short time before Ibn Saud's raid on the Riyadh fort." Captain William Shakespear, Britain's political agent in Kuwait in the early twentieth century, wrote of Abdul Aziz, "He is a fair, handsome man . . . with a particularly frank and open face and, after the first shyness, genial and courteous manners. . . . His reputation among Arabs is that of a no-

Saudi Arabia

Although initially hesitant to cooperate with the United States against Iraq, King Fahd of Saudi Arabia became a major contributor to the success of Operation Desert Storm.

ble, generous and just man." Military historians James F. Dunnigan and Austin Bay agreed that "Saudi Arabia was very much the creation of one man, Abdul al-Aziz ibn Sa'ud, born in 1876. His father, Abdul Rahmăn (185?–1928) and the rest of the Sa'ud clan were driven fron the Sa'ud hometown of Riyadh in 1891. Taking refuge in Kuwait, Abdul Aziz led a small band of followers and retook Riyadh in 1902." During the next 30 years, Abdul Aziz was able to unite the various tribes in Saudi Arabia. On 23 September 1932, the kingdom of Saudi Arabia was born. The country now celebrates that date as National Day.

The rise of Saudi Arabia from a backward desert shiekdom to one of the world's leading petromonarchies is a story in itself. Juan Tamayo, reported in the *Miami Herald* in 1987, "Massive industrial cities sprout where camels once roamed. An educational system that includes seven spanking-new universities groans under the weight of two million students. Color television reaches the most remote corners of the kingdom—as big as all of the United States east of the Mississippi—and satellites beam its communications to the world." The capital, Riyadh (Ar Riyâd, Arabic for "gardens"), is a sprawling me-

tropolis in the northeast corner of the nation. Of this former sleepy village Tamayo relates, "Riyadh, a capital city where bicycles were banned until 20 years ago as a Western evil, is now a suburban sprawl of one million people with eight-lane freeways and cloverleaf junctions, air-conditioned shopping malls stocked with the latest in Japanese electronics and French fashions, stunning glass high-rises, the world's largest airport, a few Kentucky Fried Chickens and Radio Shacks and one Safeway supermarket."

Saudi Arabia and Iraq share a common border from Kuwait to Jordan; at one time there was a neutral zone, which both countries declared as their own. On 27 December 1981, Prince Nayef, the Saudi minister of the interior, and his counterpart, Interior Minister Sa'adun Chaker of Iraq, signed an agreement that, while not made public, did "provide for certain border adjustments satisfactory to both sides."

Although at the start of the Gulf conflict Saudi Arabia was hesitant to accept American troops on its soil, King Fahd and his advisors saw that stopping the imminent threat of an invasion by Saddam Hussein's troops was more important. The Saudis ultimately played a major military role in the fighting of the Gulf War, lending troops, military materiel, and planes. One of the coalition commanders, a key aide to General H. Norman Schwarzkopf, was Lieutenant General Prince Khalid bin Sultan, head of the Saudi military forces.

The Saudi defense system is safeguarded by two basic units: the regular Saudi army and the Saudi national guard. Their mission is to protect the nation, guard the Saudi royal family, and offer security during the hajj (pilgrimage) to Mecca. Because of security concerns, as well as cooperative relations, Saudi Arabia is closer to the United States than any other Arab nation. It was for this reason that one of the first foreigners to fly on an American space shuttle was Prince Sultan bin Salman Abdelaziz al Saud; he flew on the space shuttle *Discovery* in 1985.

Occupying most of the Arabian peninsula, Saudi Arabia is bounded by Jordan to the northwest; Iraq and Kuwait to the north; the Persian Gulf, Qatar, and the United Arab Emirates to the east; and Yemen and the Red Sea to the southwest. Total land area is 864,869 square miles (2,240,000 sq km), with 1,559 miles (2,510 km) of coastline. Total population, according to the 1989 census, is 16,108,539.

References: Azzi, Robert, "Saudi Arabia: The Kingdom and Its Power," *National Geographic* 158:3 (September 1980), 286–333; Dunnigan, James F., and Austin Bay, *From Shield to Storm: High-Tech Weapons, Military Strategy, and Coalition Warfare in the Persian Gulf* (New York: Morrow, 1992), 45–46, 114; Harrison, P. W., "The Situation in Arabia," *Atlantic Monthly,* December 1920, 849; Lacey, Robert, *The Kingdom: Arabia and the House of Sa'ud* (New York: Avon, 1981), 103; Miller, Judith, "Saudi General Has Kinship for 'Norm,'" *New York Times,* 5 May 1991, A20; *Saudi Arabia* (Washington, DC: Royal Saudi Embassy, n.d.); "Saudis and Iraq Sign Pact Ending Border Dispute," *New York Times,* 28 December 1981, A9; Tamayo, Juan, "The Dilemma of Saudi Arabia," *Miami Herald,* 3 May 1987, 6C.

Sazanov, Sergei Dmitryevich
(1861?–1927)

A Russian diplomat and statesman, Sergei Sazanov served as the Russian negotiator during the talks that resulted in the Sykes-Picot-Sazanov Agreement of 1916. His date of birth is in dispute; two sources give the year as either 1860 or 1861. Sazanov joined the Russian diplomatic

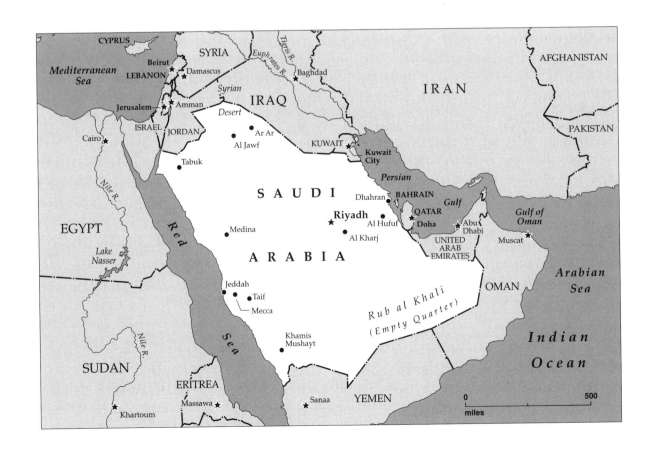

Coalition commander, U.S. Army general Norman Schwarzkopf, meets some of his troops on 13 January 1991 in Saudi Arabia.

service in 1883 and made his way up the ladder of seniority, serving as secretary of the Russian embassy to the Vatican (1889–1898) and Russian ambassador to the Vatican (1906–1908). The brother-in-law of Russian interior minister Peter Arkadevich Stolypin (1863–1911), Sazanov was named Russian foreign minister in 1910 and served until shortly before the fall of the Romanov dynasty in 1917. Although many histories of these last years before the Bolshevik Revolution mention Sazanov (he is held responsible for pressuring the czar to mobilize Russian troops in defense of Bosnia-Herzegovina following the assassination of Archduke Franz Ferdinand), he is barely credited for his work in trying to exact Russian influence in the carving up of the Middle East after World War I was over. He was the last Russian ambassador to London, and during the Russian civil war served as foreign minister for Admiral Aleksandr Vasilyevich Kolchak (1875–1920), who was fighting the Bolsheviks for the control of Russia. After the Bolshevik takeover, Sazanov settled on an estate in Poland. He died in Nice, France, on 25 December 1927.

See also Sykes-Picot-Sazanov Agreement.
References: Paxton, John, *Companion to Russian History* (New York: Facts on File, 1983); Vronskaya, Jeanne, with Vladimir Chuguev, *A Biographical Dictionary of the Soviet Union, 1917–1988* (London: K. G. Saur, 1989), 369.

Schwarzkopf, General H. Norman (1934–)

Unlike General William Westmoreland, whose hands were tied during the Vietnam War as to what he could or could not do on the battlefield, General H. Norman Schwarzkopf, commander in chief of the U.S. Central Command (USCENT-COM) during Operations Desert Shield and Desert Storm, was given a free hand to do as he saw fit during the conflict. His skill and training led to one of the greatest American military victories in the history of the nation.

Born 22 August 1934 in Trenton, New Jersey, H. Norman Schwarzkopf is the son of Herbert Norman Schwarzkopf, an American of German ancestry who attended West Point, and Ruth (née Bowman) Schwarzkopf. Herbert Schwarzkopf, who detested his first name so much that he gave his son the initial "H," was the state police chief of the New Jersey police, and was in charge of the Lindbergh baby kidnapping in 1932; he later served as chief of the Imperial Iranian Gendarmerie, the Iranian national police force, where he was instrumental in returning the shah of Iran, Mohammad Reza Pahlavi, to power after a coup in 1953. Of Herbert Schwarzkopf's time at West Point, authors Roger Cohen and Claudio Gatti write, "He became known to his West Point friends as 'Schwarzie'—the nickname that would also be given to his son thirty-nine years later. In the end, he graduated 88 in a class of 139—a passable performance. And in May 1917, one month after the United States entered the war, the young lieutenant from Newark left for France with the Second Cavalry Regiment. According to the family, he was not in the least ambivalent about donning an American uniform and fighting the country of his ancestors. The motto of West Point was clear—'Duty, Honor, Country'—and his country was the United States of America."

H. Norman Schwarzkopf was educated at Bordentown Military Institution and Valley Forge Military Academy. A soldier by profession, Schwarzkopf received his military training at the U.S. Military Academy in West Point (1952–1956). In 1956 he was commissioned as a second lieutenant in the U.S. Army, graduating forty-third in a class of 480. In 1964 he earned a master's degree in mining engineering from the University of Southern California. In that same year, and also from 1966 to 1968, Schwarzkopf returned to the military academy at West Point as an instructor. In 1965 Schwarzkopf volunteered to do a full tour of duty in Vietnam. The editors of *Current Biography* wrote, "Soon after taking up his duties in the summer of 1965 as a task-force advisor to a South Vietnamese Airborne Division, Schwarzkopf, by then a captain, withstood a ten-day siege at Dak To a month before being promoted to major. He developed a close relationship with his South Vietnamese counterparts and at least once defied American orders to ensure their safety. 'After my first tour,' he told C. B. D. Bryan, who interviewed him in 1971 for his book *Friendly Fire* (1976), 'I came home with probably the greatest feeling of satisfaction I've ever had in anything I've ever done. I slept in the mud, ate rice and Vietnamese food with chopsticks for one solid year. Everywhere the Vietnamese went, I went. I was one of them. And I felt, I really felt that I was honestly helping people.' "

From 1983 to 1985 Schwarzkopf served as the commanding general of the 24th Infantry Division Mechanized at Fort Stewart, Georgia. During the invasion of Grenada in 1983, he was the commander of American ground forces and deputy commander of the joint task force involved in the fighting. The work he did during the invasion, including correcting mistakes he felt had been made in Vietnam, earned him praise from his Pentagon superiors. During 1986 and 1987 he served as the commanding general of the First Corps at Fort Lewis, Washington. His work during the Grenada invasion earned him the post of commander in chief of the U.S. Central Command at MacDill Air Force Base near Tampa, Florida, where he served from 1988 until 1992.

As Operation Desert Shield revved up, Schwarzkopf took control of the situation and helped formulate the battle plans. Because President George Bush allowed the general a free hand to control the buildup and later to prosecute the war, Schwarzkopf was once again able to correct problems he had experienced with the military hierarchy during Vietnam. Eric Schmitt of the *New York Times* called him a "Tough but Politic Chief." He wrote, "If generals like George Patton cultivated images of harshness, General Schwarzkopf has not tried to hide his fatherly personality and he has been known to choke up with tears talking about his troops." In an interview with *People* magazine, Air Force Staff Sergeant Andrew Glaze said of the general, "He's a legend over here. All the guys in the field love him." The magazine added, "The 6'3", 240-lb. commander—nicknamed Bear for both his grizzly and teddyish sides—'is a fighter's fighter,' says retired General John 'Doc' Bahnsen, a friend. 'There are a lot of armchair generals but damn few combat generals.' " At the end of the ground war, on 27 February 1991, Schwarzkopf conducted what has been called "The Mother of All Briefings," in which he briefed reporters on the status of the war at that time. The conference was broadcast around the world, and earned Schwarzkopf further accolades for the calm and humorous manner in which he conducted it.

After retirement, Schwarzkopf shunned all possible political posts and plum assignments, opting instead for a quiet life to write his memoirs. In September 1992 he joined The Nature Conservancy's (TNC) national board of governors.

See also Appendix 4, General H. Norman Schwarzkopf, CENTCOM Briefing, 27 February 1991.

References: Cohen, Roger, and Claudio Gatti, *In the Eye of the Storm: The Life of H. Norman Schwarzkopf* (New York: Farrar, Straus & Giroux, 1991), 27; Moritz, Charles, ed., *Current Biography Yearbook 1991* (New York: H. W. Wilson, 1991), 507–508; "Profile: The Bear, Alias Norman of Arabia," *London Sunday Times,* 3 February 1991, 14; Schmitt, Eric, "Tough but Politic Chief," *New York Times,* 28 January 1991, A10; "Stormin' Norman: Born To Win," *People* 36:9 (11 March 1991), 34.

Scowcroft, Brent (1925–)

National security adviser to Presidents Gerald R. Ford and George Bush, General Brent Scowcroft served the Bush Administration and the nation with particular distinction during the Persian Gulf crisis, contributing advice that ultimately shaped the blueprint of the action that became known as Operations Desert Shield and Desert Storm. The son of James and Lucille Scowcroft, Brent Scowcroft was born in Ogden, Utah, on 19 March 1925. After completing his primary education at local schools, he entered the United States Military Academy at West Point, New York, where he received a bachelor of science degree in 1947. He subsequently earned a master's degree in 1953 and a doctorate in 1967, both from Columbia University and both in the field of international relations. Although commissioned as a second lieutenant in the U.S. Air Force in 1947, Scowcroft's flying career was ended when, just a few months after earning his wings, a plane he was piloting crashed, leaving him seriously injured and grounded.

Forced to find new areas of Air Force employment, Scowcroft "rose through the ranks in a series of diplomatic, administrative and academic jobs, including stints teaching Russian history at West Point and as a military attaché at the United States Embassy in Belgrade, Yugoslavia."

At that time, Scowcroft became fluent in Serbian and Croatian, and later learned the Russian language. Another source added in 1972 that "He has attended the Naval Intelligence School, the Armed Forces Staff College and the National War College. He has served in the Defense Department's Office of International Security Affairs, which has been called the Pentagon's State Department, and in the Air Force's headquarters dealing with matters concerning the National Security Council." In the 1960s, Scowcroft served on the staff of the assistant secretary of defense for international security affairs and as an assistant to the Joint Chiefs of Staff. In 1971, President Richard Nixon brought him on board as a military aide to the president, where he served the president on historic trips to China and the Soviet Union. Impressed by his military knowledge and capability, Henry Kissinger, who held the dual titles of secretary of state and national security adviser, brought Scowcroft in as the deputy assistant to the president for national security affairs. In 1975, when Kissinger resigned from the NSC to be secretary of state full time, Scowcroft was named to succeed him, although he was forced to resign his commission in the Air Force (he was a lieutenant general at the time). In his less than two years as NSC adviser, Scowcroft was involved in the arrangement and instrumentation of the interim SALT II arms control treaty, the closing of American involvement in the Vietnam War, and the settlement of the *Mayaguez* incident in Cambodia. In 1977, with the end of the Ford Administration, Scowcroft left office. From 1977 until 1981, he served in an advisory capacity on arms control matters to the Carter Administration.

Because of his support for arms control measures that many conservatives detested, Scowcroft was not given a major post when Ronald Reagan became president in 1981. However, in 1983, Reagan tapped the former NSC adviser to head the 11-man Commission on Strategic Forces, known as the Scowcroft Commission, to study the placement of the controversial MX missile. When the Commission's interim findings were leaked in April 1983, *The New York Times* editorialized on its weak conclusions in an editorial titled "Mr. Scowcroft's MX Mouse": "The Commission was given the opportunity to step free of past dogma and find a fresh approach. Having interviewed a mountain of witnesses, it has labored mightily—and now seems likely to produce a mouse." The Commission's final report was released in 1984 to heavy criticism from both sides of the MX missile debate. However, Scowcroft was consulted by the Reagan Administration on national security issues, and it was he to whom Reagan turned in 1987 as one of three members of the so-called President's Special Review Board to investigate what went wrong at the National Security Council and led to the Iran-Contra Affair. The board, named after its chairman, former Texas Senator John Tower (it also included former Senator and former Secretary of State Edmund S. Muskie), analyzed the NSC and concluded in its 1987 report that mistakes had been made in the way the Reagan Administration conducted foreign policy. Scowcroft, who issued the report's section on the history of the NSC, was praised for his nonpartisan reporting.

With the election of George Bush to the White House in 1988, Scowcroft was once again elevated to National Security Adviser. As historian John Prados relates, " 'I realized on day one of the 1988 campaign,' James Baker recalled, 'that George would probably like to have him [Scowcroft] as NSC adviser. This came from a close Bush associate, the man George made secretary of state, who had once almost convinced Ronald Reagan to name him the keeper of the keys [the nickname of the NSC adviser].' Jim Baker knew what he was talking about. Bush had seen Scowcroft in action in the last year of Jerry Ford's presidency, when Bush directed the CIA and Brent ran the NSC staff; then again, when the vice-president observed the Tower Board, of which Scowcroft was a member. The appointment became the second time in NSC history that an individual got the call for a return engagement as keeper of the keys." Scowcroft served as NSC adviser from 1989 until 1993. Key during that period was when he was bitterly criticized for a secret trip to meet with Chinese leaders in Beijing just days after the Tiananmen Square massacre in June 1989. With the outbreak of the Gulf crisis, Scowcroft took a leading role among the president's advisers. As Andrew Rosenthal wrote of him in *The New York Times*, "[Scowcroft,] who believes in narrowly drawn military goals, was pivotal in defining the aims of the war in the gulf, especially the decision not to make the overthrow of Saddam Hussein a publicly stated

objective." In particular, he was outspoken when in December 1990, after the Iraqi leadership rejected dates to meet with Secretary of State Baker over settling the crisis, Scowcroft called the action "another ploy that he [Saddam Hussein] is trying to use to drag things out and to avoid seriously facing up to what the world community is demanding that he do." Following the war, in March 1991, Bush sent Scowcroft on a clandestine mission to the Middle East to discuss with leaders there "recent developments in the Gulf." Scowcroft continued to be a close confidante to the president for the remainder of the Bush Administration; Bush referred to the general as "a trusted friend who understands how the White House, the Congress and the intelligence community work."

See also National Security Council.
References: Arms, Thomas S., *Encyclopedia of the Cold War* (New York: Facts on File, 1994), 504; "Brent Scowcroft: Advance Man in Moscow" *New York Times,* 21 April 1972, 8; Clines, Francis X., "Reagan Appoints a Panel To Study MX Missile System," *New York Times,* 4 January 1983, A1, A15; Editorial, "Mr. Scowcroft's MX Mouse" *New York Times,* 7 April 1983, A22; "Men Behind the [Tower Commission] Report: 3 Wise in the Capital's Ways" *New York Times,* 27 February 1987, A14; Mohr, Charles, "Longtime Security Aide Leads MX Panel," *New York Times,* 4 January 1983, A15; Prados, John, *Keepers of the Keys: A History of the National Security Council from Truman to Bush* (New York: William Morrow, 1991), 549; Rosenthal, Andrew, "Scowcroft and Gates: A Team Rivals Baker," *New York Times,* 21 February 1991, A14.

Scud Missiles

Perhaps the most frightening weapons in the Iraqi arsenal (with the exception of chemical weapons, which were not used in the Gulf War) were Scud missiles, originally built by the Soviets as short-range, no-nonsense weaponry that dealt more in terror than actual damage potential. Iraqi Scuds included the al-Hussein, al-Hijarah, FROG (a variant of the Soviet FROG-7), and Laith.

In a speech on 18 April 1990, Saddam Hussein declared, "He who launches an aggression against Iraq or the Arab nation will now find someone to repel him. If we can strike him with a stone, we will. With a missile, we will . . . and

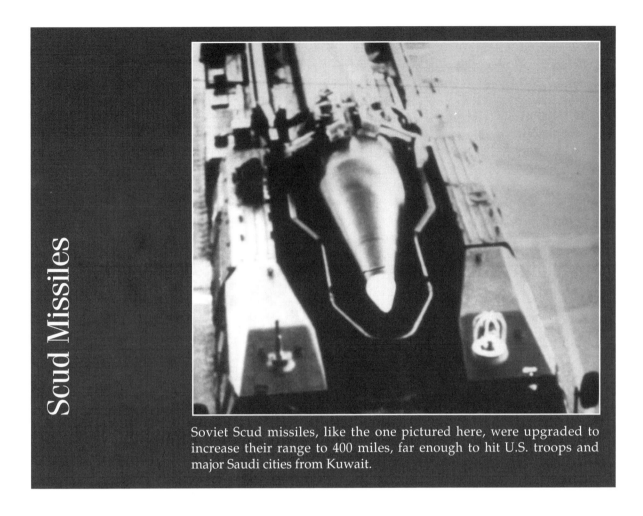

Soviet Scud missiles, like the one pictured here, were upgraded to increase their range to 400 miles, far enough to hit U.S. troops and major Saudi cities from Kuwait.

Scud Missiles

with all the missiles, bombs, and other means at our disposal."

With the onset of the air war, coalition pilots began "The Great Scud Hunt," searching across the Iraqi plain for mobile Scud launchers. Destruction of such launchers made the pilots instant heroes. Except for one incident, in which parts of a Scud crashed into the U.S. Army barracks in Dhahran on 25 February 1991, killing 28 members of the 14th Quartermaster Detachment, Scud fatalities among military personnel were zero. In Israel, two people are confirmed to have been killed during Scud attacks, and their deaths have been attributed to heart attacks or collapsed apartments. Thus, of 91 Scud launches, only 13 direct hits were made (all in Israel), with moderate damage and few casualties.

See also Appendix 1, Results of Scud Attacks; Missile Systems, Iraqi.
References: Conduct of the Persian Gulf War: Final Report to Congress, Report by the Department of Defense, April 1992, 5; Friedman, Norman, *Desert*

Victory: The War for Kuwait (Annapolis, MD: Naval Institute Press, 1991), 365–366.

SEAL Teams
See Special Operations Forces.

Senegal and Sierra Leone
See Coalition Nations, Contributions of.

Sennacherib

Historian Richard Hallion, in his *Storm over Iraq: Air Power and the Gulf War,* calls attention to the story of Sennacherib, the Assyrian dictator. Hallion speculates that the Bible predicted the ultimate defeat of Saddam Hussein through the story of Sennacherib, whose defeat in 701 B.C. at the battle of Eltekeh (Assyrian: Altaku) may have foreshadowed the events that would occur in the Persian Gulf nearly 27 centuries later.

Known as Akkadian Sin-Akhkheeriba (?–681 B.C.), Sennacherib was the king of Assyria from 705/704 B.C. to 681 B.C. He was the son of Sargon II, who had left his protégé a major empire stretching from Asia Minor to Palestine and into what is now Iraq. Sennacherib decided to extend his hold on the world, and this insatiable appetite for conquest led to his various attempts to subjugate major portions of the known world. Among his triumphs was a victory over the Babylonians at the Battle of Halule in 691 B.C., which set the stage for the destruction of Babylon two years later. His next attempt at glory was an attempt to grab the great city of Eltekeh from the Egyptians in 701 B.C. What happened there is pure conjecture; biblical studies suggest that while Sennacherib's men were camped outside town the night before heading off to battle, a plague swept down on the men and slew most of them. Sennacherib's defeat is recounted in 2 Kings 19:35: "And it came to pass that night, that the angel of the LORD went out, and smote in the camp of the Assyrians an hundred fourscore and five thousand; and when they arose early in the morning, behold, they were all dead corpses."

After his defeat, Sennacherib was exiled to Nineveh, where his demise, at the hands of his sons, is chronicled in 2 Chronicles 32:21: "And the LORD sent an angel, which cut off all the mighty men of valour, and the leaders and captains in the camp of the king of Assyria, so he returned with shame of face to his own land. And when he was come into the house of his god, they that came forth of his own bowels slew him there with the sword."

The story of Sennacherib is, of course, biblical in nature, and thus open to skepticism and conjecture. Hallion writes of the great losses Sennacherib's army sustained at Eltekeh: "Cynics credit a plague [for the defeat], but a miraculous intervention of some sort cannot be denied." The narrative's possible ties to Saddam Hussein's clash with the great coalition armies 2,600 years later must be considered, until further evidence is discovered, nothing more than mere coincidence. George Gordon, Lord Byron, wrote about the mystical figure in his poem "The Destruction of Sennacherib" (1815).

Reference: Hallion, Richard P., *Storm over Iraq: Air Power and the Persian Gulf War* (Washington, DC: Smithsonian Institution Press, 1992), 360.

Sepecat Jaguar

This coalition aircraft, in what is perhaps its final mission, saw action in the air armadas of Great Britain and France as a tactical support fighter. A twin-engine craft, Jaguars had most recently seen action against Libya in the French campaign to defend the African nation of Chad. The French took the lead in using the Jaguar to the utmost advantage. Gulf air war authority Richard P. Hallion reported, "French Jaguars went into Kuwait from the first night, striking airfields and other targets at low altitude with both smart and dumb bombs." Operating from Al Ahsa, an airport in eastern Saudi Arabia, in tandem with Mirage F1CRs and Mirage 2000s, the 24 French Jaguars flew 571 sorties and fired 60 AS30L laser-guided missiles at various Iraqi objectives. Twelve British Jaguars flew in Operation Desert Storm, flying 600 sorties, including 26 reconnaissance missions for both the French and British. In addition, these British Jaguars fired 741 British UK-1000 bombs, 387 CBU-87 cluster bombs, eight BL-755 cluster bombs, and 608 rockets.

A single-seat, all-weather attack-and-strike aircraft originally developed as a tactical support craft, the Jaguar is powered by two RB.172 Adour Mk 104 turbofan engines providing 8,040 pounds (3,647 kg) of thrust each. More recent models have been fitted with the Mk 811 engine, which supplies 8,400 pounds (3,810 kg) of thrust. The Jaguar has a ceiling of 46,000 feet (14,000 m), weighs 16,975 pounds (7,700 kg) empty, and can carry a maximum external armament load of up to 10,500 pounds (4,763 kg). These jets have seen limited service, being employed outside the Persian Gulf in the war of the African nation of Chad against Libya.

References: *Gulf War Air Power Survey, Volume IV: Weapons, Tactics, and Training Report and Space Report* (Washington, DC: GPO, 1993), 65; Hallion, Richard P., *Storm over Iraq: Air Power and the Gulf War* (Washington, DC: Smithsonian Institution Press, 1992), 215–216; Keany, Thomas A., and Eliot A. Cohen, *Gulf War Air Power Survey, Summary Report* (Washington, DC: GPO, 1993), 185; Lenorovitz,

Jeffrey M., "French AS30L Laser Missiles Scored High Hit Rate in Air-Ground Attacks," *Aviation Week & Space Technology*, 22 April 1991, 108–109; Spick, Mike, *An Illustrated Guide to Modern Attack Aircraft* (New York: Prentice Hall, 1987), 76–77.

Sèvres, Treaty of (1920)

This unratified contract signed by the Allied Powers and Turkey (formerly the Ottoman Empire) on 10 August 1920 in the Paris suburb of Sèvres set the boundaries for what would become Iraq. Article 27(3) of Part II of the treaty notes this frontier to be from the island on which is situated the town of Djezire-ibn-Omar, "thence in a general easterly direction to a point to be chosen on the northern boundary of the vilayet [town] of Mosul, a line to be fixed on the ground; thence eastwards to the point where it meets the frontier between Turkey and Persia, the northern boundary of the vilayet of Mosul, modified, however, so as to pass south of Amadia." Article 37 of Part III reads: "The navigation of the straits, including the Dardanelles, the Sea of Mamara and the Mosporus, shall in [the] future be open, both in peace and war, to every vessel of commerce or of war and to military and commercial aircraft, without distinction of flag. These waters shall not be subject to blockade, nor shall any belligerent right be exercised nor any act of hostility be committed within them, unless in pursuance of a decision of the Council of the League of Nations."

In Article 94 of Part II, Section VII of the treaty, the signatories agreed

> that Syria and Mesopotamia shall, in accordance with the fourth paragraph of Article 22, Part I [of the Covenant of the League of Nations], be provisionally recognized as independent States subject to the rendering of administrative advice and assistance by the mandatory until such time as they are able to stand alone.
>
> A Commission shall be constituted within fifteen days from the coming into force of the present Treaty to trace on the spot the frontier described in article 27, II (2) and (3). This Commission will be composed of three members nominated by France, Great Britain and Italy respectively, and one member nominated by Turkey; it will be assisted by a representative of Syria for the Syrian frontier, and by a representative of Mesopotamia for the Mesopotamia frontier.
>
> The determination of the other frontiers of the said States and the selection of the Mandatories, will be made by the Principal Allied Powers.

Articles 96, 97, and 132 were also controversial. The texts of these sections read:

> Article 96. The terms of the mandates in respect to the above territories will be formulated by the principal Allied Powers and submitted to the Council of the League of Nations for approval.
>
> Article 97. Turkey hereby undertakes, in accordance with the provisions of Article 132, to accept any decision which may be taken in relation to the questions dealt with in this Section.
>
> Article 132. Outside her frontiers as fixed in the present treaty, Turkey hereby renounces in favour of the Principal Allied Powers all rights and title which she could claim on any ground over or concerning any territories outside Europe which are not otherwise disposed of by the present Treaty.
>
> Turkey undertakes to recognise and conform to the measures which may be taken now or in the future by the Principal Allied Powers, in agreement where necessary with third Powers, in order to carry the above stipulation into effect.

Because several sections of the agreement were so controversial and seemed to strip Turkey of many of its lands and powers, the Treaty of Sèvres was never ratified by the Turks. A subsequent meeting produced the more palatable Treaty of Lausanne, which they signed.

See also Lausanne, Treaty of.
References: Lauterpacht, E., et al., eds., *The Kuwait Crisis: Basic Documents* (Cambridge, UK: Grotius, 1991), 39; Osmańczyk, Edmund Jan, *The Encyclopedia of the United Nations and International Agreements* (Philadelphia: Taylor & Francis, 1985), 751.

SH-2F/G Seasprite LAMPS I

Currently in use for several classes of American ships in an antisubmarine warfare (ASW) attack mode, the SH-2F and G variants of this helicopter carry the LAMPS (light airborne multipurpose system) mission profile (as compared to the larger SH-60 LAMPS III model). Several SH-2s were deployed during the Gulf War, on Belknap class cruisers, Kidd class destroyers, and Knox class frigates, flying an undetermined number of sorties.

The Seasprite, in either the F or G variant, has a fuselage length of 38 feet (11.6 m) and an overall length of 53 feet (16 m). With the ability to carry a crew of three (two pilots and an ASW systems operator), the craft is powered either by two General Electric T58-GE-8F turboshaft engines (F variant) or two General Electric T700-GE-401 turboshaft engines (G variant). Unrefueled range for both copters is 367 nautical miles (423 mi; 680 km), although both can be equipped with three extra external fuel tanks for extended ASW forays and search-and-rescue (SAR) missions of downed pilots.

See also S-70B Seahawk.
References: Almond, Denise L., ed., *Desert Score: U.S. Gulf War Weapons* (Washington, DC: Carroll Publishing, 1991), 98–99; *Sea Power: The Official Publication of the Navy League of the United States* 37: 1 (January 1994), 200.

SH-3G/H Sea King

About 30 American SH-3G/H helicopters served during the Gulf War, flying, according to the military report *Desert Score*, "1,800 sorties as plane guards, search and rescue [SAR], and utility aircraft." Nine others saw action in the war—five as part of the Canadian contingent, and four with the Italians. The export models are classified as CH-124s, built to resemble the SH-3G/Hs. Constructed by Sikorsky Aircraft of Stratford, Connecticut, the SH-3 model is powered by two General Electric T58-GE-10 turboshaft engines each delivering 1,400 shaft horsepower (shp). The length of the craft is 54 feet 9 inches (16.69 m), with a gross weight of 18,626 pounds (8,449 kg), a maximum speed of 166 mph (267 km/h), and an unrefueled range of 625 miles (1,005 km). Armaments include two Mk 46 homing torpedoes.

References: Almond, Denise L., ed., *Desert Score: U.S. Gulf War Weapons* (Washington, DC: Carroll Publishing, 1991), 102–103; Taylor, John W. R., and Gordon Swanborough, *Military Aircraft of the World* (New York: Scribner's, 1979), 204.

SH-60 Seahawk LAMPS III

See S-70B Seahawk.

Shamir, Yitzhak (1914? or 1915?–)

The seventh prime minister of Israel, feisty Yitzhak Shamir held the people of his nation at bay while dangerous Iraqi Scud missiles were fired at Israel to break up the Allied coalition. Born Yitzhak Yizernitsky in the small Hasidic Jewish village of Kuzinoy, in eastern Poland, Shamir is the son of Shlomo and Penina Yizernitsky (also spelled Yzernitzky and Jazernicki). The date of his birth varies widely; some sources report 3 November 1914, while others declare 15 October 1915. Shamir's education was religious in nature; he attended Hebrew elementary schools before graduating from a Hebrew gymnasium in Bialystok, Poland.

Almost from the beginning, Yitzhak Shamir was involved in speeding up the liberation of Palestine for the Jews. He was especially involved in the group called B'rit Trumpeldor, a radical Zionist student organization. One of the leaders in this Polish movement was Menachem Begin, a future prime minister of Israel and the man Shamir would succeed. Shamir entered the University of Warsaw to study law, but withdrew in 1935 to emigrate to Palestine, where he picked up the study of law at the Hebrew University in Jerusalem. After his arrival in Palestine, he changed his name to Shamir, which is the Hebrew word for "sharp thorn" or "hard substance."

As the *New York Times* reported in 1983, "Shamir joined the Jewish underground during the anti-Jewish Arab riots in 1936, and fought the British in defiance of the official Jewish policy of military self-restraint. In 1940, the *Irgun Zvai Leumi* (National Military Organization), of which Menachem Begin was a leader, split, and Shamir went with the more radical faction, the *Lohamei Herut Yisrael* (or LHY, the Israel Freedom Fight-

Israeli prime minister Yitzhak Shamir answers questions at a meeting near Tel Aviv in June 1990.

ers), otherwise known as the Stern Gang after its leader, Abraham Stern." After Stern was killed by the British in 1942, Shamir and his small group of terrorists became an ineffectual guerrilla band, compared to the better-supplied Irgun. Still, the LHY was responsible for the attempted assassination of Sir Harold Mac-Michael, the British high commissioner of Palestine, and for the murder of Lord Moyne, the British minister of state in the Middle East, in November 1944. In fact, LHY and the Irgun worked hand-in-hand with members of the Haganah until the terrorist explosion at the King David Hotel, which killed hundreds of British soldiers. Shamir was arrested and sent into exile in Eritrea, but he escaped with leaders of the Irgun and went first to Ethiopia, then to French Djibouti, where they were jailed simply for entering French territory illegally. By the time of their release, Israel had become an independent state, and the men could return as heroes instead of wanted felons.

Until his emergence as Israel's seventh prime minister in 1983, Yitzhak Shamir kept a low profile in Israel, working only to transform the LHY into a political party (which became the Lohamim, or Fighter's, party, and which was rep-

resented in Israel's Knesset, or Parliament, in the 1950s) and serving as a senior advisor to the Mossad, Israel's secret intelligence agency comparable to the CIA. Later he became a prosperous businessman and worked for the freedom of Soviet Jews.

In 1970 Shamir joined the Herut party of which Menachem Begin was a member. Elected in 1973 to the Knesset, he became Speaker in 1977 when Begin was elected prime minister. After the resignation of Foreign Minister Moshe Dayan, Begin named Shamir as his replacement. David K. Shipler wrote in the *New York Times*, "Shamir is staid, cautious in his public comments and rather difficult to draw out in conversation, perhaps as a hangover from his earlier days when, schooled in secrecy, he donned disguises and evaded British authorities as a leader of the Stern Gang." On 30 August 1983 Begin told his followers that "he could not continue" as their leader, a reference to his then-declining health. A few days later, on 1 September, the Herut party voted for Shamir as their new party leader, and he was sworn in as Israel's seventh prime minister. His regime was marked by an increase of construction in Israeli settlements in the West Bank.

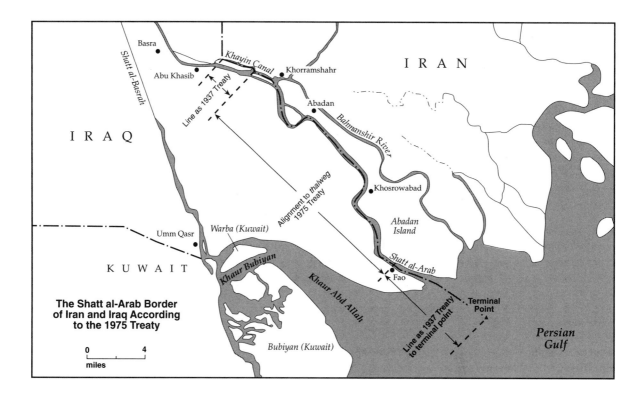

The Shatt al-Arab Border
of Iran and Iraq According
to the 1975 Treaty

0   4
miles

Yitzhak Shamir's reign as prime minister was coming to an end by the time of the crisis in the Persian Gulf. Much of the role he played during the buildup to the war and the war itself was that of a back-room player. On 26 August 1990 Israel announced that it would block the shipment of Palestinian-made goods to Jordan for transport to Iraq. Five days later, the *New York Times* reported that the Bush administration was sending an additional $1 billion to Israel to reinforce its defense against a possible Iraqi attack. Following the onset of the war, Scuds fired at Tel Aviv and other civilian population centers seemed about to drive Israel to go to war, but Patriot missile batteries helped calm the fears of the Israelis, and an expected chemical weapons attack did not happen.

Unpopular because of discord among the Israeli electorate, in 1993 Shamir saw his coalition government defeated by the more liberal Labor party of Yitzhak Rabin. Shamir left government, retiring to his home in Israel.

References: Moritz, Charles, ed., *Current Biography Yearbook 1983* (New York: H. W. Wilson, 1983), 361–365; Shipler, David K., "Yitzhak Shamir: A Taciturn Israeli Foreign Minister," *New York Times*, 11 March 1980, A3; "Yitzhak Shamir: Begin's Heir Apparent," *New York Times*, 2 September 1980, A3.

Shatt al-Arab Waterway

Formed by the confluence of the Tigris and Euphrates rivers, the Shatt al-Arab (Arabic: "stream of the Arabs") begins at Al Qurnah (or Al Qurna), 64 kilometers from Basra. *Chambers World Gazetteer* relates that from Al Qurnah "it flows 192 kilometers southeast through marshland to discharge into the Arabian Gulf [at the head of the Persian Gulf]; in its lower course it forms part of the Iran-Iraq border; the delta is wide and swampy, containing the world's largest date-palm groves; [it is] navigable for ocean-going vessels as far as the port of al Basrah [Basra]." The river's chief tributary is the Karun River, which flows into Iran.

The Shatt al-Arab's geographical significance is crucial to the foundation of trade among the small villages, and later nation-states, that sprang up along the Tigris and Euphrates. As the *Reader's Digest* reports, "Nourishing the eastern half of the Fertile Crescent, which stretched from the Persian Gulf to the Nile delta, the waters of the Tigris and Euphrates gave life to the first civilizations of ancient Mesopotamia. Among the cities that flourished along their courses were Nineveh on the banks of the Tigris and Babylon on the Euphrates. Indeed, the area where the two rivers converge is believed by some biblical scholars to have been the site of the Garden of Eden." Because it plays a major trade role in the region, control of the waterway is vital. Since 1932 Iran and Iraq have verbally fought over which nation physically controls the Shatt al-Arab. The argument was considered settled when the shah of Iran and Saddam Hussein (then vice-chairman of Iraq's Revolutionary Command Council) signed the Algiers Agreement in 1975, in which Iraq resigned itself to controlling only a small section of the waterway in exchange for an end to Iran's support of Kurdish rebels fighting inside Iraq. The agreement did not last long, however. In 1979 the shah was overthrown by Islamic fundamentalists and, as Iraqi author Samir al-Khalil said, "Iran had already abrogated the Algiers Agreement through 187 border violations, all of which had allegedly taken place in the four-month period preceding the [start of the Iran-Iraq War, September 1980]. Numerous statements by Iranian leaders also proved their intent to 'export' the Islamic revolution. It followed, once the treaty was abrogated, that the Shatt al-Arab waterway had to revert back to Iraqi sovereignty according to all previous agreements. All naval craft along the Shatt were henceforth to fly the Iraqi flag, and navigation fees should be paid to Iraq."

During the eight years of the Iran-Iraq War, the Shatt al-Arab was the scene of bitter fighting; untold numbers of troops on both sides were slaughtered in an attempt to control the waterway. At the end of the war, the Shatt al-Arab was filled with silt (it needed to be dredged constantly, and had not been for a long time because of the war) and the hulks of sunken ships. Except for the smallest of channels, it is now considered completely unusable, an ironic outcome considering its importance before the war.

See also Algiers Agreement of 6 March 1975; Basra; Thalweg Principle.
References: al-Khalil, Samir, *Republic of Fear: The Inside Story of Saddam's Iraq* (New York: Pantheon, 1990), 268–269; Metz, Helen Chapman, ed., *Iraq: A Country Study* (Washington, DC: GPO, 1990), 232–235; Munro, David, ed., *Chambers World Gazetteer: An A–Z of Geographical Information* (Edinburgh: W&R Chambers, 1988), 585; *Reader's Digest Natural Wonders of the World* (Pleasantville, NY: Reader's Digest Association, 1980), 342.

Shevardnadze, Eduard Amvrosiyevich (1928–)

One newspaper called him "the co-architect of perestroika." This Georgia-born Soviet foreign minister was instrumental in Soviet cooperation with the Allied coalition in the early days of the Persian Gulf crisis.

Born in the village of Mamati, about 40 miles (64 km) north of the Black Sea in Soviet Georgia on 25 January 1928, Shevardnadze was the son of a teacher who later served in the Soviet Union's Supreme Soviet. According to E. Kaye Fulton in the Canadian magazine *MacLeans,* "In the rough dialect of the Georgian farmland he calls home, his name, Shevardnadze, means 'the falcon.'" *Current Biography* said of him, "Shevardnadze's older brother and mentor, Ippokrat, who died about 1978, was a powerful department chief in the central committee of the Georgian Communist Party." In 1946 Shevardnadze himself became a coach at the local Komsomol, or Communist Youth League, and two years later a member of the Communist party. He graduated from the local Communist party school, and later studied history at the Kutaisi Teachers College in Georgia. After his graduation in 1959, he became a member of the Georgian Supreme Soviet, and six years later was promoted to the posts of Georgian minister of maintenance of public order and minister of internal affairs.

Sometime between his graduation and promotion, Shevardnadze became acquainted with a young up-and-coming engineer named Mikhail Gorbachev. As Soviet authority Robert G. Kaiser relates, "Gorbachev and Shevardnadze apparently first met in the 1960s, when both were working in the Komsomol. Shevardnadze's native Georgia was next door to Gorbachev's Stavropol krai [region]. Like Gorbachev, he went from the Komsomol to Party work, then was named Georgia's minister of internal affairs in the 1960s."

In 1990 *Time* magazine's Bruce Melan called Shevardnadze "Perestroika's Other Father." Carrol Bogert wrote, "As Mikhail Gorbachev tells it, he and Eduard Shevardnadze cooked up *perestroika* together during a walk on the beach. It was December 1984, when the future Soviet president was the Communist Party secretary

Shevardnadze, Eduard

Soviet foreign minister Eduard Amvrosiyevich Shevardnadze, right, meets U.S. secretary of state James Baker at the Soviet Mission in New York City on 29 November 1990.

for ideology and his future foreign minister was party chief in Soviet Georgia. While vacationing at the Black Sea resort of Pitsunda, Gorbachev invited Shevardnadze to go for a stroll. The two men found they had a lot in common. Gorbachev had been a party chief in a southern province and, like Shevardnadze, was frustrated with the Brezhnev regime. 'Everything's gone rotten,' Shevardnadze reported gloomily, and Gorbachev agreed."

The *Wall Street Journal* commented in 1985, "He will be tough to intimidate. He braved death threats, and perhaps also assassination attempts, from Georgian mobsters who opposed his anticorruption campaign while he was Georgian interior minister and party secretary. U.S. officials say they have heard reports that Shevardnadze's driver was killed in one such attempt; and a Georgian emigré who knew Shevardnadze recalls rumors of attempts to bribe his bodyguards. Regardless of the details, it's clear that Shevardnadze played in a rough league in Soviet Georgia and survived."

In a speech to the Supreme Soviet on 23 Octo-

ber 1989, Shevardnadze condemned the 1979 Soviet invasion of Afghanistan as an "illegal act," and he further admitted that the Krasnoyarsk radar complex violated the 1972 ABM treaty with the United States. Thus, he made it known that he was straightforward and candid in his ideas on Soviet policies. This outspokenness led to the shocking announcement while speaking before the Congress of People's Deputies on 20 December 1990 that he was resigning because "revolutionary forces" were threatening the country. He said in his discourse, "Comrade democrats . . . you have run away. . . . The reformers have headed for the hills. Dictatorship is coming. No one knows what kind of dictatorship it will be, who will come to power." Shevardnadze was immediately replaced by Aleksandr Bessmertnykh. For a short time, Shevardnadze became the leading speaker and writer for the Soviet Foreign Policy Association, a think tank.

The loss of Shevardnadze to the Soviet Union was shocking, but his exit triggered much soul-searching in Washington, D.C., and other world capitals caught in the ever-growing crisis in the

Persian Gulf. U.S. Secretary of State James Baker said, "I have known Eduard Shevardnadze to be a man of his word, a man of courage, conviction and principle. I am proud to call him my friend." As Margaret Warner wrote in *Newsweek*, "The secretary [Baker] may be losing much more than a friend. Baker's relationship was essential to the administration progress toward ending the superpower rivalry. It was equally important to forging a united front in the Persian Gulf. His departure threatens to weaken Bush's hand at a critical moment in his war of nerves with Saddam Hussein. . . . Shevardnadze was the first Soviet official to warn Saddam publicly that he could be forced from Kuwait if he didn't leave on his own. By his public statements and behind-the-scenes arm twisting, the Soviet foreign minister was indispensable in marshaling support for the anti-Saddam resolutions at the United Nations." As George J. Church added, "The biggest problem [with Shevardnadze's resignation] may be the Persian Gulf. Shevardnadze helped draft the U.N. resolution approving the use of force by the U.S. and its allies if Iraq does not leave Kuwait by January 15. But that policy has been very unpopular with much of the Soviet military, which looks back nostalgically on the long years when Iraq was Moscow's closest ally in the Middle East. In fact, hard-liners in the Congress of People's Deputies talked up a declaration forbidding the Kremlin to send troops to the gulf force opposing Iraq, and Shevardnadze described this as the last straw prompting his resignation. He insisted that there were no plans to send a single soldier but regarded the resolution as a blatant attempt to undermine his policy by raising doubts about it."

Shevardnadze's return to his native Georgia began in January 1992, when he was elected honorary chairman of the Georgian Democratic party after the ouster of President Zviad Gamsakhurdia. On 7 March, Shevardnadze was named chairman of the four-man ruling council that replaced Gamsakhurdia. He returned, he said, "because I thought that if my presence here would do something for [the] stabilization of the situation, I would think that my historic mission, if you like, is fulfilled, even if I have to pay for it with my death as a politician." In October 1993 Shevardnadze signed a proclamation making Georgia a member of the Confederation of In-

dependent States (CIS), a treaty ratified by the Georgian Parliament on 2 March 1994. On 3 February 1994 Shevardnadze and Boris Yeltsin, president of Russia, signed a military treaty and other documents of cooperation, all endorsed with the goal of improving the tension between Georgia and Russia. Shevardnadze visited Washington, D.C., where he received backing from President Bill Clinton to have UN peacekeepers sent to the breakaway Georgia region of Abkhazia.

See also Bessmertnykh, Aleksandr Aleksandrovich; Gorbachev, Mikhail Sergeivich.
References: Bogert, Carroll, "From the Beach to the Breach," *Newsweek,* 31 December 1990, 52; Church, George J., "Next: A Crackdown—Or a Breakdown?" *Time,* 31 December 1990, 22; Coleman, Fred, "A Soviet Bombshell," *Time,* 31 December 1990, 50; Fabricio, Roberto, "No Regrets: Eduard Shevardnadze, Who Helped Bring about the End of the Soviet Union, Is Feeling History Pass Him By," *Fort Lauderdale Sun-Sentinel,* 8 March 1992, 1E; Ignatius, David, "Soviet Foreign Minister Is a Georgian Who Knows How To Charm, or Be Ruthless," *Wall Street Journal,* 31 July 1985, 23; Kaiser, Robert G., *Why Gorbachev Happened: His Triumphs, His Failure, and His Fall* (New York: Simon & Schuster, 1992), 104; Melan, Bruce, "Shevardnadze: Perestroika's Other Father," *Time,* 31 December 1990, 22; Moritz, Charles, ed., *Current Biography 1986* (New York: H. W. Wilson, 1986), 523; Shargorodsky, Sergei, "Backers of Ousted Georgian Protest," *New Orleans Times-Picayune,* 9 January 1992, A9; "Shevardnadze Comes Home to a Nightmare," *Miami Herald,* 16 March 1992, 8A; Warner, Margaret Garrard, "The Loss of a Friend in Court," *Newsweek,* 31 December 1990, 53.

Singapore
See Coalition Nations, Contributions of.

Slang

Like other wars before it, the Persian Gulf conflict was filled with slang words used by the troops who fought in it. *Time* magazine reported, "In the war, the top brass and the G.I.s seem[ed] to be speaking two different languages—neither of them English." For instance, the "body bag" that the ground troops came to know in the Vietnam War became a "human remains pouch" in the Persian Gulf War. Any food not considered appetizing was "camel meat." Although the standard ration was officially labeled an MRE—a Meal Ready To Eat—the troops dubbed them as Meals Rejected by Ethiopians, Meals Refusing To Exit, Meals Refused by Everyone, or, simply, Rees.

See also Appendix 2, Glossary of English Language Slang.
Reference: "The Two Sides of Warspeak," *Time,* 25 February 1991, 13.

South Korea
See Coalition Nations, Contributions of.

Southwest Asia Service Medal
See Appendix 4, Executive Order 12754 of 12 March 1991.

Soviet Union

The fact that the Soviets militarily stayed out of the conflict said a great deal about the changing social structure of the world's two superpowers and the collapse of the Soviet economy. The Soviets looked on warily as the situation in the Gulf went from bad to worse. After all, it was their allies, the Iraqis, using Soviet weaponry and training to do their dirty work in Kuwait. For Mikhail Gorbachev, desperately trying to have his country join the family of nations, it was a no-win situation. How does one of the world's two greatest superpowers turn its back on a former, strategically important ally? At the start of the crisis, Gorbachev sent Yevgeny Primakov to Iraq as his special envoy to the Middle East, but Iraq was not to be persuaded to withdraw from its spoils in Kuwait. Gorbachev then made a calculated decision. He instructed his ambassador to the United Nations, Vitaly Vorontsov, to vote for UN resolutions requiring an Iraqi withdrawal, and supported his two foreign ministers, Eduard Shevardnadze (who served until January 1991) and Alexandr Bessmertnykh in siding with the coalition. Gorbachev himself went to Helsinki, Finland, where on 8–9 September 1990 he ironed out an agreement with President Bush on the potential use of force against Iraq.

Slang

U.S. soldiers eat pre-packaged meals, Meals Ready to Eat (MRE), in the Saudi Arabian desert.

In order to keep tabs on what the coalition was doing to its former ally, the Soviets dispatched four ships to the Gulf during Operation Desert Storm; among these were the Udaloy-class destroyer *Admiral Tributs,* a missile destroyer, a frigate, and an Amur-class repair ship. They did not participate in the after-war cleanup, and little has been said since the end of the war regarding their former role in Iraq.

Space Shuttle *Atlantis,* Military Mission of

This secret Department of Defense (DoD) space mission was sent aloft to deposit the classified military satellite known simply as Air Force Project 658 (AFP-658). Its purpose was to spy on Iraq and aid coalition military commanders in case war broke out. The crew for this mission, which blasted off on 15 November 1990 and returned on 20 November, were: Air Force Colonel Richard C. Covey (commander), Navy Commander Frank L. Culbertson (pilot), and mission specialists Army Captain Charles D. Gemar, Air Force Lieutenant Colonel Carl J. Meade, and Marine Corps Colonel Robert C. Springer. The main mission of AFP-658, which weighed about 22,000 pounds (9,980 kg), was to "focus on the Persian Gulf region to provide both strategic and tactical reconnaissance information for Desert Shield air and ground commanders," according to the *New York Times.*

References: Broad, William J., "Spy Satellite Aim Is To Track Iraq," *New York Times,* 20 October 1990, A4; Kolcum, Edward H., "Next Shuttle Flight To Carry Sensors for Providing Intelligence on Persian Gulf," *Aviation Week & Space Technology,* 22 October 1990, 29.

Spain

See Coalition Nations, Contributions of.

Special Operations Forces (SOF)

The military's secret corps of operational troops, such as the Navy SEALs, Special Forces Attach-ment Delta (more popularly known as the Delta Force), and others, are incorporated in the U.S. military as the Special Operations Forces. Located within all four branches of the military, these teams were used by the American military during Operations Desert Shield and Desert Storm. The full story of their participation remains shrouded in secrecy.

In a monograph prepared for the U.S. military, John R. Brinkerhoff wrote, "The mission of the United States Special Operations Command (USSOCOM) is to provide Special Operations Forces for the theater unified commands. USSOCOM was formed in April 1987 to consolidate command, control, training, and funding for all special operations forces in the Department of Defense. USSOCOM was mandated by Congress because of perceptions that the SOF were not receiving adequate funding, policy guidance, oversight, and operational emphasis from their own services. The Defense Authorization Act for FY 1987 directed DoD to do several things with respect to the SOF. To assure high level oversight and support for the consolidation of SOF forces and functions, the office of the Assistant Secretary of Defense for Special Operations and Low Intensity Conflict (SO/LIC) was established."

In an article entitled "America's Secret Commandos," Abe Dane wrote, "The tools and tactics of these special warriors are as diverse as their missions. But with the creation of the United States Special Operations Command (USSOCOM) in 1987, they have found a unified and newly prominent identity. Members of the Army, Navy and Air Force now work together within this structure, complemented by select Marine Corps units." These units are established as the U.S. Army Special Operations Command (USASOC), which includes the Army Rangers, Green Berets, Special Operations Aviation Force, Psychological Operations, and Civil Affairs (the handling of prisoners of war, etc.); Naval Special Warfare Command (NSWC), which includes the Navy SEALs; the Air Force Special Operations Command (AFSOC), which utilizes such weaponry as the MC-130H Combat Talon II gunship (a variant of the C-130 Hercules aircraft), used principally, as the U.S. military's *Gulf War Air Power Survey* reports, "for infiltration missions and to resupply special operations units on the ground. [Its]

Space Shuttle *Atlantis*, Military Mission of

Data collection on behalf of the U.S. Department of Defense and delivery of a U.S. secret satellite into Earth orbit dominated the *Atlantis* space shuttle mission.

special navigation and aerial delivery systems were used to locate small drop zones and deliver people and equipment"; Marine Reconnaissance Battalions (MRB); and Joint Special Operations Command (JSOC).

General Carl W. Stiner of the U.S. Army wrote in June 1991, "In *Desert Shield* and *Desert Storm*, the U.S. Central Command [USCENTCOM] employed SOF to support its campaign plan. Army Special Forces and Navy SEALS were among the first forces employed in the theater of operations and provided coalition forces training in individual and small-unit skills. This training program focused on nuclear, biological and chemical (NBC) skills, integrating joint and combined arms into tactical plans, land navigation, beach surveillance and reconnaissance, and close air support operations. Navy SEALS actively supported maritime embargo operations, conducted area reconnaissance operations, and supported countermine warfare missions. In addition, the SOF was the primary trainer in reconstituting the Kuwaiti armed forces. With every coalition Arab battalion that went into battle in *Desert Storm*, there were Special Forces units with them."

See also AC-130A/H Spectre Gunship.
References: Brinkerhoff, John R., "United States Army Reserve in Operation Desert Storm—Civil Affairs in the War with Iraq," Monograph of the Department of the Army, Army Reserve—Program Analysis and Evaluation Division (DAAR-PAE), 1991, 5; Dane, Abe, "America's Secret Commandos," *Popular Mechanics* 169:9 (September 1992), 26–27; *Gulf War Air Power Survey, Volume IV: Weapons, Tactics, and Training Report and Space Report* (Washington, DC: GPO, 1993), 119; Stiner, Carl W., "The Strategic Employment of Special Operations Forces," *Military Review* LXXI:6 (June 1991), 9–10.

STANAVFORLANT (Standing Naval Force Atlantic)

See Coalition Nations, Contributions of; United States, Naval Contributions of.

Stark Incident. *See* USS *Stark* Incident.

Stinger Missile (FIM-92A)

The Stinger surface-to-air missile was a little-known entity until used with great effect by Afghan guerrillas against Soviet troops in Afghanistan. In the Persian Gulf it was employed with limited effect by American forces.

A one-manportable launch tube equipped with the Identification Friend or Foe (IFF) classification, the Stinger can be carried on one's shoulder. The missile, which delivers a wallop of 6.6 pounds (3 kg) of explosive to its target, contains infrared heat-seeking technology. At 5 feet 6 inches (1.52 m), the Stinger weighs 34.76 pounds (15.8 kg). As Colonel Walter J. Boyne's *Weapons of Desert Storm* reports, the missile is "powered by a dual-thrust, solid-fuel rocket motor" that shoots the missile forward at Mach 2 (1,500 mph) toward the target, which can be a fixed-wing aircraft (high speed or propeller).

References: Blake, Bernard, *Jane's Weapon Systems, 1988–89* (Coulsdon, Surrey, UK: Jane's Information Group, 1988), 217; Boyne, Walter J., *The Weapons of Desert Storm* (Lincolnwood, IL: Publications International, 1991), 86.

SU-7B Fitter-A

The Iraqis purchased 30 models of the Sukhoi SU-7B, code-named Fitter-A and Moujik by NATO. Military aviation authority John W. R. Taylor relates that few models of the original Soviet design exist, mostly in the air forces of Algeria and Iraq. Iraq's Fitter-A craft fled to Iran during the Persian Gulf War; their fate remains unknown. The official Soviet export model of the plane is called the SU-20, code-named the Fitter-C.

John W. R. Taylor describes the SU-7B as "a single-seat ground attack fighter." Powered by a single Lyulka AL-7F-1 afterburning turbojet, the craft is 29 feet 3.5 inches (8.93 m) in length, with a gross weight of 29,750 pounds (13,495 kg). It has a maximum speed of Mach 1.6 (1,055 mph; 1,700 km/h) and a maximum unrefueled range of 900 miles (1,450 km). The Fitter-A supports two 30 mm cannons, as well as underwing pylons for a multitude of bombs or rocket pods that weigh a total of 5,512 pounds (2,500 kg).

References: Taylor, John W. R., and Kenneth Munson, "Gallery of Middle East Airpower," *Air Force* 77:10 (October 1994), 64; Taylor, John W. R., and Gordon Swanborough, *Military Aircraft of the World* (New York: Scribner's, 1979), 105.

SU-20 Fitter-C

This single-seat Soviet ground attack fighter, dubbed the "Fitter-C" by NATO, was part of Iraq's air force, but its use during the Gulf War, considering that most of Iraq's planes fled to Iran, remains little known. What is known is that on 7 February 1991, three SU-20s were shot down by coalition air force aircraft.

The "Fitter-C" is an export model of the Soviet-built Sukhoi SU-17 "Fitter," and as such it appears in the air forces of many former Soviet Union client states. Powered by one Saturn Lyulka AL-21F-3 turbojet, which provides (with afterburning) 24,700 pounds of thrust, this plane, which has a swept-wing variable (allowing its wings to remain locked forward during takeoff and landing, or "dirty," and swing back swept, or "clean," during flight), has a wingspan of 45 feet 3 inches (13.80 m) forward or 32 feet 10 inches (10 m) swept. Armaments include two 30 mm NR-30 machine guns, as well as underwing pylons that can accommodate Kh-23 "Kerry," Kh-24 "Kyle," or Kh-25 "Karen" air-to-surface missiles.

Reference: Lambert, Mark, ed., *Jane's All the World's Aircraft, 1991–92* (Coulsdon, Surrey, UK: Jane's Information Group, 1991),

SU-24 Fencer

At least 15 models of the Soviet two-seat (for the pilot and a weapons officer) bomber aircraft, the Sukhoi SU-24, designated by NATO as the "Fencer," were sold to Iraq, but their utilization during the war remains little known.

Powered by two Saturn Lyulka AL-21F-3A turbojets, which each provide (with afterburning) 24,700 pounds (11,204 kg) of thrust, the SU-24, which has a swept-wing variable, has a spread wingspan of 57 feet 10 inches (17.5 m) and a swept span of 34 feet (10.3 m). Length of the craft overall is 80 feet 5.75 inches (24.53 m). Armaments include underwing pylons for

Kh-23 "Kerry," AS-11 "Kilter," AS-12 "Kegler," AS-13 "Kingbolt," and Kh-29 "Kedge" air-to-surface missiles.

Reference: Lambert, Mark, ed., *Jane's All the World's Aircraft, 1991–92* (Coulsdon, Surrey, UK: Jane's Information Group, 1991), 277–278.

SU-25 Frogfoot-A

Military aircraft specialist John W. R. Taylor writes of this aircraft, code-named Frogfoot-A by NATO, "The Sukhoi SU-25 . . . is the CIS [Confederation of Independent States, the alliance of former Soviet republics formed in 1991) counterpart to the U.S. Air Force's A-10A Thunderbolt II." He also reports that "the Iraqi Air Force ordered 45 SU-25s. Seven of those delivered by 1991 were flown to Iran during Desert Storm, and two others were shot down en route by F-15Cs. An estimated 22 remain in service."

The SU-25 is powered by two Soyuz/Tumansky R-195 turbojet engines, each generating 9,921 pounds (4,500 kg) of thrust. With a maximum cruising speed of Mach 0.8 and a maximum attack speed of 428 mph (689 km/h), the SU-25 remains the state-of-the-art Soviet (and now Russian) single-seat attack fighter. The plane can be armed with a single twin-barrel 30 mm gun, and is arrayed with pylons to handle numerous air-to-surface (ASM) weapons, including Kh-23 Kerry, Kh-25 Karen, and Kh-29 Kedge ASM missiles, and air-to-air missiles (AAM) such as the R-3S Atoll and R-60 Aphid AAMs.

Reference: Taylor, John W. R., and Kenneth Munson, "Gallery of Middle East Airpower," *Air Force* 77:10 (October 1994), 64.

Submarines, Coalition

The only coalition submarines to serve in the Gulf War belonged to Great Britain. They were the *Opossum* and the *Otus*, two Oberon-class diesel-electric subs. The Oberon class is an improvement on the original British class of submarines, the Porpoise class, which originated soon after World War II. The Oberon class contains improved internal equipment and a superstructure composed of tough woven-glass fibers. A sister ship, the *Onyx*, played a key role during the Falklands War in the South Atlantic in 1982.

References: Miller, David, *An Illustrated Guide to Modern Sub Hunters* (London: Salamander, 1984), 104–105; Sharpe, Richard, ed., *Jane's Fighting Ships 1990–91* (Coulsdon, Surrey, UK: Jane's Information Group, 1990), 710.

Submarines, United States

The United States deployed five nuclear-powered submarines to the Persian Gulf area. Two of them fired Tomahawk cruise missiles at Iraqi targets, the first time American submarines had fired shots in battle since World War II. All the subs deployed were from the Los Angeles class: the USS *Philadelphia* (SSN 690), USS *Pittsburgh* (SSN 720), USS *Chicago* (SSN 721), USS *Louisville* (SSN 724), and USS *Newport News* (SSN 750). These submarines weigh 6,080 tons standard (6,927 in a diving mode) and are 360 feet (109.7 m) in length. Powered by a single General Electric pressurized water-cooled S6G reactor and two geared turbines providing 35,000 shaft horsepower (shp), the subs have a maximum speed (dive) of 30+ knots (35 mph; 56 km/h) and a complement of 133, which includes 13 officers. Both the *Louisville* and the *Pittsburgh*, the subs that fired the Tomahawk cruise missiles, are armed with Tomahawk land attack missiles (TLAM-Ns) and Tomahawk antiship missiles (TASMs).

Reference: Sharpe, Richard, ed., *Jane's Fighting Ships 1990–91* (Coulsdon, Surrey, UK: Jane's Information Group, 1990), 724.

Sudan

This African country, a member of the Arab League, which in November 1980 participated in the joint military exercises called Operation Bright Star with the United States, Egypt, Oman, and Somalia, sided with Iraq during the Persian Gulf crisis and war.

The pro-Iraqi positioning of Sudan began on 3 August 1990, a day after the Iraqi invasion, when, at an Arab League Council, Sudan abstained rather than vote for a resolution that condemned Iraq's aggression, joining with Yemen, Jordan, Mauritania, and the Palestine delegation.

On 15 December, while visiting Tehran, Iran, Sudanese President Omar Hassan al-Bashir declared that he felt the end of the crisis would come only through "the necessity of a complete withdrawal of Iraqi forces from Kuwait and of the foreign forces from the region." With the outbreak of the war, according to the military report *Desert Score,* "Sudan sent a 13-person medical team to Baghdad to assist with Iraqi casualties."

Reference: Almond, Denise L., ed., *Desert Score: U.S. Gulf War Weapons* (Washington, DC: Carroll Publishing, 1991), 484.

Support and Supply Ships, United States

Among the 177 American ships that participated in Operations Desert Shield/Desert Storm, 44 were support or supply ships. They include the following.

Ammunition Supply Ships

The nine ammunition supply ships (six from the Kilauea class and three from the Suribachi class); these are basically underway-replenishment ships whose sole duty is to resupply ships and troops with ammunition. Representing the Kilauea class were the *Kilauea* (AE 26), the *Santa Barbara* (AE 28), the *Mount Hood* (AE 29), the *Flint* (AE 32), the *Shasta* (AE 33), and the *Kiska* (AE 35). These ships displace 9,238 tons light (19,937 tons fully loaded), and are 563.83 feet (171.9 m) in length. Powered by a single General Electric steam turbine and three Foster Wheeler boilers, they have a maximum speed of 22 knots (25 mph; 41 km/h), and have a maximum unrefueled range of 18,000 nautical miles (33,336 km) at 11 knots (13 mph; 20 km/h) and 10,000 nautical miles (20,714 miles; 18,520 km) at 20 knots (23 mph; 37 km/h). Manned by approximately 409 men (21 officers) (excepting the *Kilauea*, which has a complement of 123 civilian and 67 Navy personnel), the ships are capable of carrying up to two CH-46D "Sea Knight" helicopters. The Suribachi class was represented by the *Suribachi* (AE 21), the *Nitro* (AE 23), and the *Haleakala* (AE 25). These ships displace 10,000 tons light (the *Suribachi* displaces 17,000 tons fully loaded; the others 17,450 tons fully loaded), and are 512 feet (156.1 m) in length. Powered by a single

Bethlehem steam turbine and two Combustion Engineering boilers, the ships have a maximum speed of 20.6 knots (24 mph; 38 km/h) and a range of 12,000 nautical miles (13,809 miles; 22,224 km) at 15 knots (10,000 nautical miles [11,508 miles; 18,520 km] at 20 knots (23 mph; 37 km/h). Complement is 346 (including 21 officers), and the ships are implemented with a pad for helicopter alighting.

Combat Support Ships

The fast combat support ships *Seattle* (AOE 3) and *Detroit* (AOE 4). The *Seattle* displaces 51,400–53,600 tons fully loaded, measures 793 feet (241.7 m) long, is powered by four Combustion Engineering boilers and two General Electric geared turbines, and has a maximum speed of 26 knots (30 mph; 48 km/h). With a complement of 601 (including 24 officers), the ships of this class have a cargo capacity of 177,000 barrels of fuel, 2,150 tons of munitions, 500 tons of dry stores, and 250 tons of refrigerated stores. Each ship also has the capability of handling the landing and storage of two CH-46E "Sea Knight" helicopters.

Oil Supply Ships

The Henry J. Kaiser–class fleet oil supply ships *Henry J. Kaiser*, *Joshua Humphreys*, *John Lenthall, Jr.*, and *Andrew J. Higgins*; the Cimmaron-class oilers *Cimmaron* and *Platte*; the Neosho-class oilers *Neosho* and *Ponchatoula*; and the Mispillion-class fleet oiler *Passumpsic*. The *Henry J. Kaiser* (T-AO 187), the *Joshua Humphreys* (T-AO 188), the *John Lenthall, Jr.* (T-AO 189), and the *Andrew J. Higgins* (T-AO 190) displace 9,500 tons light (40,700 tons fully loaded) and are 677.5 feet (206.6 m) in length. Powered by two Colt-Pielstick 10PC4.2V diesel engines, the ships have a maximum speed of 20 knots (23 mph; 37 km/h) and an unrefueled range of 6,000 miles (11,112 km) at 20 knots (23 mph; 37 km/h). Complemented by 95 civilian and 21 Navy personnel, they have a landing area, but no hangar facilities, for helicopters. From the Cimmaron class, the *Cimmaron* (AO 177) and the *Platte* (AO 186) displace 37,000 tons fully loaded, are 708.33 feet (215.95 m) in length, and have a maximum speed of 19.4 knots (22 mph; 36 km/h). The ships are powered by two Combustion Engineering boilers and a single steam turbine, which deliver 24,000 shaft horsepower (shp). Complement is approximately 226 (including 16 offi-

cers), making these ships the only fully Navy-manned oilers in the fleet. The Neosho-class oilers *Neosho* (T-AO 143), *Hassayampa* (T-AO 145), *Truckee* (T-AO 147), and *Ponchatoula* (T-AO 148) displace 11,750 tons light (36,840 tons fully loaded), and are 655.66 feet (200 m) in length. Powered by two General Electric steam turbines and two Babcock & Wilcox boilers, the ships have a maximum speed of 20 knots (23 mph; 37 km/h) and a maximum unrefueled range of 34,000 nautical miles (62,968 km) at 19 knots (22 mph; 35 km/h). Complement for these ships is approximately 125 civilian and approximately 23 Navy personnel (including 1 officer). The Mispillion-class fleet oiler *Passumpsic* (T-AO 107), the only member of its class to serve, displaces 9,486 tons light (35,090 tons fully loaded), and is 646 feet (197 m) in length. Powered by two Westinghouse steam turbines and four Babcock & Wilcox boilers, has a maximum speed of 16 knots (18 mph; 30 km/h). Complemented by a crew of approximately 110 civilian and approximately 21 Navy personnel (including 1 officer), the ship is furnished with a landing pad for a helicopter.

Replenishment Oilers

The two Wichita-class replenishment oilers *Kalamazoo* and *Kansas City*. The *Kansas City* (AO 3) and the *Kalamazoo* (AO 6) displace approximately 27,500 tons fully loaded, are 659 feet (201 m) in length, and have a maximum speed of 20 knots (23 mph; 37 km/h). They are powered by three boilers and two steam turbines, which deliver 32,000 shaft horsepower (shp). Complement is 452; armaments include two Phalanx close-in weapons systems (CIWS), either 20 mm or 40 mm, and Sea Sparrow SAM missiles. The ships are equipped to carry two CH-46E "Sea Knight" helicopters.

Store Ships

The store ship *Rigel*. The *Rigel* (T-AF 58), the only ship of its class, is the only refrigerated store ship or "reefer" in the U.S. Navy. The *Rigel*, built by Ingalls Shipbuilding of Pascagoula, Mississippi, displaces 9,696 tons light (15,540 tons fully loaded), and is 502 feet (153.1 m) in length. Powered by a single General Electric steam turbine and two Combustion Engineering boilers, the *Rigel* has a maximum speed of 21 knots (24 mph; 39 km/h) and a range of 15,000 nautical miles

(17,262 miles; 27,780 km) at 15 knots (28 mph; 37 km/h). Complemented by 113 civilians and 19 Navy personnel, the *Rigel* is also outfitted with a helicopter pad aft.

The former British combat store ships *Sirius* (T-AFS 8) and *Spica* (T-AFS 9). Built by Swan Hunter & Wighman Richardson in Wallsend-on-Tyne, England, these two Royal Navy replenishment ships were originally named the *Lyness* and the *Tarbatness,* respectively. The U.S. government purchased them in 1982 for a total of $37 million. They displace 9,010 tons light (16,792 tons full loaded), and are 523.35 feet (159.5 m) in length. Powered by a single Wallsend-Sulzer 8RD76 turbo-charged engine, the ships have a maximum speed of 19 knots (22 mph; 36 km/h), and a range of 27,500 nautical miles (31,643 miles; 50,930 km) at 12 knots (14 mph; 22 km/h) and 11,000 nautical miles (12,659 miles; 20,372 km) at 19 knots (22 mph; 35 km/h). Complemented by a civilian crew that ranges from 110 to 125 men, and approximately 47 Navy personnel (including 5 officers), the ships are fitted out with a helicopter pad that can accommodate two CH-46 "Sea Knight" helicopters.

The six combat store ships of the Mars class of support ships include the *Mars* (AFS 1), the *Sylvania* (AFS 2), the *Niagara Falls* (AFS 3), the *White Plains* (AFS 4), the *San Diego* (AFS 6), and the *San Jose* (AFS 7). These ships displace from 9,200 to 9,400 tons light (from 15,900 to 18,663 tons fully loaded), and measure 581 feet (177.1 m) in length. Powered by three Babcock & Wilcox boilers and three De Laval steam turbines, they have a maximum speed of 21 knots (24 mph; 39 km/h) and a range of 18,000 nautical miles (20,714 miles; 33,336 km) at 11 knots (13 mph; 21 km/h). With a complement of 428 (including 25 officers), the Mars-class ships can carry 2,625 tons of dry stores and upwards of 1,300 tons of refrigerated stores. Because it is fitted with a helicopter pad aft, the Mars class can handle the landing and storage of two CH-46E "Sea Knight" helicopters.

Surveyor Ships

The two surveyor ships of the Chauvenet class, the *Chauvenet* (T-AGS 29) and the *Harkness* (T-AGS 32). These ships, whose main task was to prepare and supply hydrographic charts of the Persian Gulf to the four branches of the military,

displace 4,830 tons fully loaded, and are 393.17 feet (119.9 m) in length. Powered by two Alco diesel engines and two Westinghouse electric motors, the ships have a maximum speed of 15 knots (17 mph; 28 km/h) and a range of 12,000 nautical miles (13,809 miles; 22,224 km) at 15 knots. Equipped with two helicopter pads, the Chauvenet-class ships utilize two SH-2F/G "Seasprite" helicopters for survey missions.

Transport Oiler

The Sealift-class transport oiler *Sealift Pacific* (T-AOT 168). This ship, in service since 1974, displaces 6,487 tons light (33,000 tons fully loaded), and is 587 feet (179 m) in length. Powered by two Colt-Pielstick 14PC-2V400 turbo-charged diesel engines, the ship has a maximum speed of 16 knots (18 mph; 30 km/h) and a maximum range of 12,000 nautical miles (13,809 miles; 22,224 km) at 16 knots. Complement is 24 civilian and 2 Navy personnel.

Vehicle Cargo and Fast Transport Ships

The converted SL-7 type vehicle cargo and fast transport ships the *Algol* (T-AKR 287), the *Bellatrix* (T-AKR 288), the *Denebola* (T-AKR 289), the *Pollux* (T-AKR 290), the *Altair* (T-AKR 291), the *Regulus* (T-AKR 292), the *Capella* (T-AKR 293), and the *Antares* (T-AKR 294). These ships displace 31,017 tons light (55,425 tons fully loaded), and are 946.17 feet (288.5 m) in length. Powered by two General Electric steam turbines and two Foster Wheeler boilers, the ships have a maximum speed of 33 knots (38 mph; 61 km/h) and a maximum unrefueled range of 12,200 nautical miles (14,040 miles; 22,594 km) at 27 knots (31 mph; 50 km/h). Complement for the ships is 49 civilian personnel, with an additional 56 or 57 troops that can be carried. The *Antares*, like the other ships, was dispatched to the Gulf, but she broke down in the eastern Atlantic in August 1990, and she was towed to a Spanish port, where her cargo was transferred to another ship.

The C7-S-95a type vehicle cargo ship *Mercury* (T-AKR 10). Built by the Bath Iron Works of Bath, Maine, this ship displaces 14,222 tons light (33,765 tons fully loaded), and is 684.66 feet (208.8 m) in length. Powered by two General Electric steam turbines and two Babcock & Wilcox boilers, the ship has a maximum speed of 24 knots (28 mph; 44 km/h) and a maximum range of 12,600 nautical miles (14,500 miles; 23,335 km) at 23 knots (26 mph; 43 km/h). Complement is 21 civilian personnel.

References: Polmar, Norman, *The Naval Institute Guide to the Ships and Aircraft of the U.S. Fleet* (Annapolis, MD: Naval Institute Press, 1993), 223–224, 226–228, 251, 293–295, 320; *Sea Power: The Official Publication of the Navy League of the United States* 37:1 (January 1994), 148, 154–155; Sharpe, Richard, *Jane's Fighting Ships, 1990–91* (Coulsdon, Surrey, UK: Jane's Information Group, 1991), 754–756, 776–777.

Sykes, Sir Mark (1879–1919)

Unknown outside his native Britain, Sir Mark Sykes played a key role in the early formation of the borders of the Middle East. Born into a wealthy family in London on 16 March 1879, he was the son of Sir Tatton Sykes and Jessica (née Cavendish-Bentinck) Sykes, the daughter of a member of the British Parliament. Mark Sykes did not receive a full education; because of his father's travels, he could never stay in one school for very long. What little instruction he did obtain came from private tutors and some periods in Jesuit institutions in Monaco and Brussels. He attended Jesus College at Cambridge, but left without earning a degree.

Sykes apparently suffered from wanderlust, and his intense travels led to several works, including *Through Five Turkish Provinces* (1900) and *Dar ul-Islam* (1904), an account of his journeys through Mesopotamia and Syria. In 1905 he was sent to Turkey as the honorary attaché to the British embassy. Later voyages to the Middle East led to his *Five Mansions of the House of Othman* (1909) and *The Caliphs' Last Heritage* (1915), which *The Dictionary of National Biography* called "the most ambitious of his books."

Because of his knowledge of the Middle East and his ability to speak French, Sykes was a perfect choice to deal with Charles François Georges-Picot, sometime consul-general of French-occupied Syria and negotiator for the French foreign office, during talks held in 1915 and 1916 to settle the matter of who would own what in the Middle East after the end of World War I. Included in the talks was Foreign Minister Sergei Sazanov of Russia, but because of the disastrous way in which the war was being prosecuted by the Russians on the eastern front, his role was limited. Historian David Fromkin writes, "Sykes possessed some of the qualifications necessary to carry out his assignment. He passionately wanted to succeed in reaching an agreement with the other side. He was pro-French. As a result of his early schooling abroad, he spoke French—though it is not clear how well. As a Roman Catholic himself, he was not prejudiced against France's goal of promoting Catholic interests in Lebanon. He had lived and traveled in the East, and had met with and knew the views of Britain's soldiers and civil servants there." After the signing of the so-called Sykes-Picot-Sazanov Agreement of 9 May 1916, Sykes and Picot went to Transjordan to convince King Hussein, the sharif of Mecca, that the agreement would be to his benefit. After General Sir Edmund Allenby of Britain entered Jerusalem, it was Sykes who wanted a more pro-Zionist British influence exacted in the area. As a member of the British foreign office who consulted the bureau on Arab policy, for a time he lived in Aleppo, in what is now Syria.

In order to make sure that the peace in the Middle East was equitable, Sykes had himself recalled to London in 1919 in order to discuss the situation with members of the British Government. Weakened by travel, he stopped in Paris, where he came down with influenza. Three days later, on 16 February 1919, he died, just a month short of his fortieth birthday.

References: David, H. W. C., and J. R. H. Weaver, eds., *The Dictionary of National Biography, Vol. 1912–1921* (London: Oxford University Press, 1980), 522–524; Fromkin, David, *A Peace To End All Peace: The Fall of the Ottoman Empire and the Creation of the Modern Middle East* (New York: Avon, 1989), 189.

Sykes-Picot-Sazanov Agreement

This secret deal between British diplomat Sir Mark Sykes, French negotiator Charles François Georges-Picot, and Russian foreign minister Sergei Sazanov was arranged on 9 May 1916 between Great Britain, France, and Russia in an effort to carve up the territories of the Ottoman Empire following the end of World War I. The compact created the states of Syria, Iraq, Lebanon, Palestine (governed by the Balfour Declaration as to its later disposition) and Transjordan, which later became Jordan. All would be dominated by either the British or the French. Any

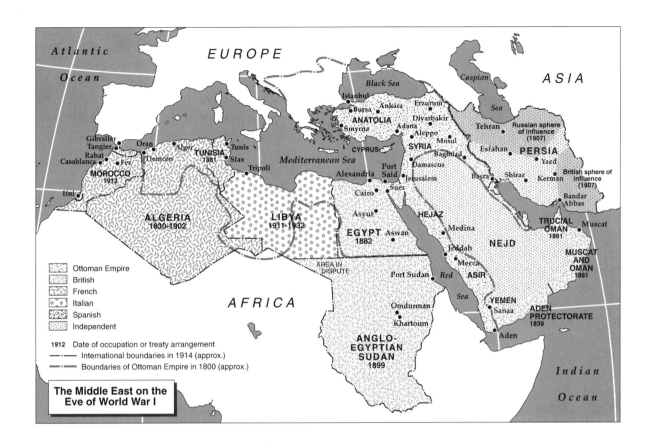

The Middle East on the Eve of World War I

Atlantic Ocean
EUROPE
ASIA
Black Sea
Caspian Sea
Istanbul
Bursa
Ankara
Erzurum
ANATOLIA
Diyarbakir
Tehran
Russian sphere of influence (1907)
Smyrna
Adana
Aleppo
Mosul
Esfahan
PERSIA
CYPRUS
SYRIA
Baghdad
Yazd
Gibralter
Tangier
Oran
Alger
TUNISIA
Tunis
Mediterranean Sea
Damascus
Basra
Shiraz
Kerman
British sphere of influence (1907)
Rabat
Tlemcen
1881
Sfax
Alexandria
Port Said
Jerusalem
Casablanca
Fez
Tripoli
Bandar Abbas
MOROCCO
1912
Cairo
Suez
Ifni
Asyut
HEJAZ
TRUCIAL OMAN 1861
Muscat
ALGERIA
1830-1902
LIBYA
1911-1932
EGYPT
1882
Aswan
Medina
NEJD
MUSCAT AND OMAN 1861
Jeddah
Mecca
ASIR
AREA IN DISPUTE
Port Sudan
Red Sea
AFRICA
Omdurman
YEMEN
Sanaa
ADEN PROTECTORATE 1839
Khartoum
Aden
ANGLO-EGYPTIAN SUDAN 1899
Indian Ocean

Ottoman Empire
British
French
Italian
Spanish
Independent

1912 Date of occupation or treaty arrangement
International boundaries in 1914 (approx.)
Boundaries of Ottoman Empire in 1800 (approx.)

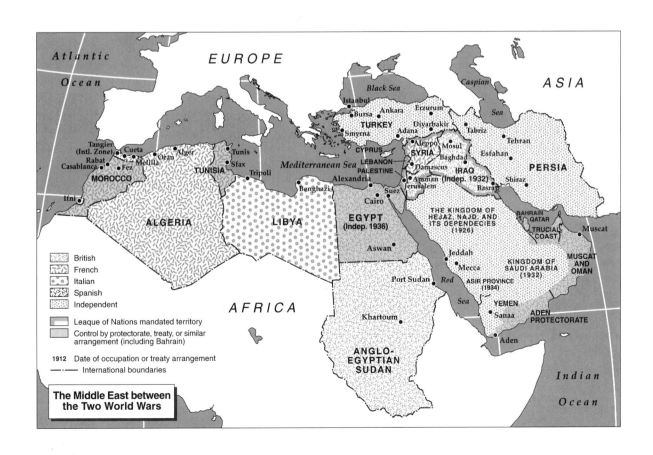

The Middle East between the Two World Wars

Atlantic Ocean
EUROPE
ASIA
Black Sea
Caspian Sea
Istanbul
Bursa
Ankara
Erzurum
TURKEY
Diyarbakir
Tabriz
Tehran
Smyrna
Adana
Aleppo
Mosul
Esfahan
PERSIA
Tangier (Intl. Zone)
Cueta
Oran
Alger
CYPRUS
LEBANON
SYRIA
Baghdad
Rabat
Melilla
Tunis
Mediterranean Sea
PALESTINE
Damascus
IRAQ
Shiraz
Casablanca
Fez
TUNISIA
Sfax
Alexandria
Jerusalem
Amman (Indep. 1932)
Basra
Tripoli
BAHRAIN
MOROCCO
Benghazi
Suez
THE KINGDOM OF HEJAZ, NAJD, AND ITS DEPENDECIES (1926)
QATAR
Ifni
Cairo
EGYPT (Indep. 1936)
TRUCIAL COAST
Muscat
ALGERIA
LIBYA
Aswan
MUSCAT AND OMAN
Jeddah
KINGDOM OF SAUDI ARABIA (1932)
Mecca
Port Sudan
Red Sea
ASIR PROVINCE (1934)
AFRICA
Khartoum
YEMEN
Sanaa
ADEN PROTECTORATE
Aden
ANGLO-EGYPTIAN SUDAN
Indian Ocean

British
French
Italian
Spanish
Independent
League of Nations mandated territory
Control by protectorate, treaty, or similar arrangement (including Bahrain)

1912 Date of occupation or treaty arrangement
International boundaries

Russian involvement ended with the ascension to power of the Bolsheviks and the succeeding civil war that captured that nation's entire attention.

The terms of the agreement were: (1) Russia would secure possession of the Armenian provinces of Erzurum, Lake Van, Trebizond (Trabzon), and Bitlis in Anatolia, as well as some Kurdish territory north of what is now Turkey; (2) France would have control over Syria, including Damascus, Homs, Hama, and Aleppo, and the eastern areas of Aintab, Urfa, Mardin, Diyarbakir, and Mosul, as well as Cilicia in Asia Minor and all of coastal Syria and Lebanon; (3) Great Britain would obtain control over southern Mesopotamia, the Palestine ports of Haifa and Acre, the Negev desert, and the area east of the Jordan River, and the provinces of Baghdad and Basra would come under direct British administration; (4) Alexandretta (Iskenderun) in Syria would be designated as a free port; and (5) Palestine would come under international control because of its great number of holy places important to the three religions, Catholicism, Judaism, and Islam.

The Sykes-Picot-Sazanov Agreement was a slap in the face to the Arabs who had pledged to fight for the Allies during World War I in exchange for their independence after the conflict was over. The secret exchange became public after Russia was conquered by the Bolsheviks and Lenin issued Minister Sazanov's copy of the letter to the Arabs who were fighting the Turks. Among these Arabs was Hussein ibn Ali, the sharif of Mecca and the master of the Hashemite kingdom (which later became the nation of Jordan). Because of Ali's anger with the accord, it was later adjusted at the San Remo Conference in April 1920.

See also Appendix 4, Letter from British Foreign Secretary Sir Edward Grey to Paul Cambon, 16 May 1916; San Remo Conference; Sazanov, Sergei Dmitryevich; Sykes, Sir Mark.
Reference: "Sykes-Picot Agreement," in *The New Encyclopædia Britannica,* Vol. II, edited by Philip W. Goetz (Chicago: Encyclopædia Britannica, 1990), 454.

Syria

It is one of the most remarkable of ironies that Syria, an avowed enemy of Israel—and by ex-

tension, of Israel's ally the United States—joined the United States in opposing Iraq during the Persian Gulf War. However, a careful study of Syria's relations with its larger and, until recently, more prosperous neighbor to the east explains why Syria put aside its hatred of the West for this one moment in history.

Bounded on the north by Turkey, on the east and southeast by Iraq, on the south and southwest by Jordan, and Israel and Lebanon on the southwest and west, respectively, the modern state known as Syria was founded as the Syrian Arab Republic in 1946 on the site of many thousands of years of history. Damascus (Arab: *Dimashq;* it is also known among locals as *Esh-Sham*) is the world's oldest continually occupied city (since about 2000 B.C.) The Bible mentions an "Assyria"—and many scholars freely use the terms "Syria" and "Assyria" to denote the area of upper Mesopotamia's western regions, although the inclusion of southern Mesopotamia in fact makes the territory as a whole "Aram," which the Bible also mentions. What is now Syria came under the control of many peoples, including the Babylonians, Macedonians, and Persians; a small portion of it was conquered by the Assyrian dictator Seleucus I, nicknamed Nicator ("Conqueror"), who established his capital at Antioch. His successors, the Seleucids, gave Syria its name. In the twelfth century, Arab journeyman Ibn Jubayr called the site of Damascus, the capital of modern Syria, "the paradise of the Orient." In this city where Saul of Tarsus renamed himself Paul the Apostle is the Umayyad Mosque, the fourth holiest site in Islam, built in the eighth century. Damascus, located to the northeast of Mount Hermon at an elevation of approximately 2,200 feet (671 m), was the capital of the Syrian Empire under the authority of Benhadd I, and it is also mentioned in the Bible in several psalms.

Syria was eventually incorporated into the Ottoman Empire in 1517, and remained a part of that authority until it became, with a semi-independent Lebanon, a French-dominated mandate known as the Levant states, which were established by the League of Nations in 1920. Under the Sykes-Picot-Sazanov Agreement of 1916, Syria's northern port of Alexandretta, or Iskenderun, was allocated as a free harbor. Revolts in Syria proper in 1924 and 1925 were followed by a division between Lebanon and Syria, and a nation called "Syria" was established five years later with the cities of Damascus and Aleppo included within its geographical borders. In 1941, with the outbreak of World War II, the British and French gave Syria its independence. Five years later, all foreign troops left Syrian soil, leading to the formation of the independent nation of Syria on 17 April 1946.

Syria soon joined its Arab League brethren in a war against the newly formed state of Israel, a conflict that brought the first taste of bitter defeat to the Arab nation. Syria also suffered from internal strife. The civilian government of President Shukri al-Kuwatly, elected in 1943, was overthrown by a military coup in 1949, the first of many. In 1943 a new political group was formed that eventually became the Arab Socialist Resurrection party, known as the Ba'athists. Although left wing in nature, the party stressed pan-Arabism and the objective of a single Arab state. The leader of the party, a Syrian named Michel Aflaq, had formed the group with Salah al-Din al-Bitar. Ironically, during the 1940s Aflaq was a leader in the so-called Syrian Committee To Aid Iraq to assist that nation in shaking off its British colonial rulers. Almost 50 years later, Syria and Iraq would find themselves on opposing sides in the largest war in the Middle East to date.

Syria was a member of the United Arab Republic (UAR), an economic and military union with Egypt, from 1958 until 1961. In 1966 a group of army officers helped overthrow a more moderate Ba'ath-led government. Four years later, one of the officers, a 40-year-old general named Hafez al-Assad, took power in a second coup; in 1971 he was elected president, and has served ever since. As the *New York Times* commented, "Assad's government has systematically suppressed political dissent. Human rights groups say hundreds, perhaps more, have died in prison. In recent months [up until August 1993], nine political prisoners rounded up immediately after the 1970 coup have been freed. Assad unexpectedly freed 3,500 political prisoners in late 1991, and 1,000 [more] were released [in 1992]." Among the prisoners not released was Salah Jadid (1930?–1993), whom the *New*

York Times called "one of the world's longest-held political prisoners." Jadid was the Syrian armed forces chief of staff when he and al-Assad overthrew the more moderate Ba'ath government headed by General Amin al-Hafiz. In September 1970 Jadid sent tanks into neighboring Jordan to aid battling Palestinian rebels in their war against King Hussein. Fearing the possibility of a war with Israel, al-Assad refused to send the Syrian air force into the fray. King Hussein won the war, sending the Syrians home in defeat. Jadid was blamed, and in a move to oust al-Assad, Jadid was himself deposed in a bloody coup. Al-Assad then imprisoned Jadid until the latter's death on 18 August 1993.

During the Persian Gulf War, al-Assad was a leading figure, taking a chance on the possibility of discontent among his people in the hope that armed intervention against a fellow Ba'athist nation, Iraq, on the side of Israel's ally, the United States, would somehow work to Syria's benefit. In many ways, al-Assad's clever strategy paid off. At the same time that he was fostering closer ties to the West and defeating a potential adversary (politically as a leader among Arabs and militarily) in Saddam Hussein, al-Assad was also consolidating his hold on Lebanon, of which he gained almost total control after his troops entered Beirut. (The Israelis still dominate the small southern section of that nation.) Because of this shrewd ability, al-Assad played, and continues to play, a leading role in the brokering of a wide-ranging and comprehensive Middle East peace agreement that would for the first time include Israel and her most voracious enemies. Foreign Minister Farouq al-Shara and Mustafa Tlas, the minister of defense, played prominent parts in arranging for Syrian troops to fight for Kuwaiti independence, although no Syrian troops invaded Iraq itself.

See also al-Assad, Hafez.
References: Moritz, Charles, ed., *Current Biography Yearbook 1992* (New York: H. W. Wilson, 1992), 24; "Salah Jadid, 63, Leader of Syria Deposed and Imprisoned by Assad," *New York Times*, 24 August 1993, D19; Tarr, David R., and Bryan R. Daves, eds., *The Middle East* (Washington, DC: Congressional Quarterly, 1986), 181–182.

T-54 Main Battle Tank

Designed just after the end of World War II, the T-54 became one of the premier main battle tanks in the world of military hardware. By 1991, it was considered obsolete, replaced by the T-55, the T-62 and, the 1980s-era T-80, regarded as a near-equivalent of the U.S. M-1A1 Abrams Main Battle Tank. Still, the Iraqis had a considerable number, but their use (as well as how many were destroyed by the coalition forces) remains a secret.

With a crew of four, the T-54 has a combat weight of 36,000 kg (79,366 pounds), and a length of 6.45 meters (21.16 feet). Powered by a V-12 water-cooled diesel engine, the tank is implemented with a single 100 mm gun, two 7.62 mm machine guns, and a 12.7 mm antiaircraft machine gun. Different ammunition types used include AP-T (armor-piercing tracer), APC-T (armor-piercing capped tracer), HE (high explosive), HE-FRAG (high explosive fragmentation), and HVAPDS-T (high-velocity armor-piercing discarding sabot). The Iraqi variants of the tank include an additional 160 mm mortar and a T-54 with observation mast. The chassis of the T-54 is used as the base for the ZSU-57/2 "SPAAG" self-propelled antiaircraft gun.

Reference: Foss, Christopher F., ed., *Jane's Armour and Artillery, 1992–93* (Coulsdon, Surrey, UK: Jane's Information Group, 1992), 77; Foss, Christopher F., *Jane's Main Battle Tanks* (London: Jane's Publishing Group, 1986), 90, 94.

T-55 Main Battle Tank

The Iraqis had 1,600 of these tanks in their arsenal, enough to make them one of the leading land armies in the world.

The T-55 has long been a mainstay of the Soviet army and its client states for many years. Powered by a V-12 water-cooled diesel engine, the tank carries a crew of four, has a combat weight of 79,366 pounds (36,000 kg), and has a single 100 mm main gun and a single 7.62 mm machine gun.

References: Foss, Christopher F., ed., *Jane's Armour and Artillery* (Coulsdon, Surrey, UK: Jane's Information Group, 1992), 34–36; Foss, Christopher F., ed., *Jane's Main Battle Tanks* (London: Jane's Publishing Group, 1986), 94.

T-62 Main Battle Tank

Called "an inferior relative of the T-72 battle tank," the Iraqis had 1,500 of these tanks in their arsenal. The tanks weigh 81,570 pounds (37,000 kg), have a speed of 31 mph (50 km/h), and are equipped with a 115 mm gun, their main armament.

References: "Arms and the Men," special pullout section from *Newsweek*, 18 February 1991; U.S. Department of Defense, *Soviet Military Power 1986* (Washington, DC: GPO, 1986), 66.

T-72 Main Battle Tank

The T-72 was Iraq's main battle tank during the Persian Gulf War, but because it was outclassed by the American Abrams M-1 and M-1A1, as well as other coalition tanks, its full potential was not realized.

Deployed in many battles, the Soviet-made T-72 is an older model but is packed with power nonetheless. Said Army Major General Donn Starry, who was one of the developers of the Abrams tanks, "I wouldn't sell it [the T-72] short." Starry was quoted in the *Washington Post* as saying that, inside of a mile, the T-72 can be "a devastating piece of equipment." Still, reports Orr Kelly, author of a 1989 work on the Abrams, in comparing the T-72 and the M-1, "They're really two different generation tanks." Armed with a 125 mm smoothbore gun, the T-72 is fitted with "reactive armor," which comes off if hit during an attack and shields the occupants from penetrating missiles; its low position, and thus a low silhouette, gives it additional protection. It weighs 45 tons (18 tons less than the M-1 and M-1A1), has a length of 30 feet 4 inches (9.25 m) including the gun, and seats a crew of three. The Iraqis had approximately 1,000 of these tanks in their arsenal; more than 500 were strategically placed in the Kuwaiti Theatre of Operations with the highly trained Republican Guard.

Reference: Babcock, Charles R., "M-1 Tanks Quickly Demonstrate Superiority," *Washington Post,* 27 February 1991, A28.

Tank Landing Ships, United States

Naval authority Norman Polmar reports on the LSTs, tank landing ships, "these ships represent the 'ultimate' design in landing ships that can be 'beached.' However, they generally unload onto pontoon causeways. They depart from the traditional LST bow-door design to obtain a hull design for a sustained speed of 20 knots." These ships were deployed to the Persian Gulf in three separate waves: as part of the Fourth Marine Expeditionary Brigade, which arrived in the Kuwaiti Theater of Operations (KTO) on 6 September 1990 as part of the Amphibious Ready Group Bravo, which arrived in the KTO on 9 September 1990, and as part of the Fifth Marine Expeditionary Brigade, which arrived in the KTO on 12 January 1991. All of the ships belong to the Newport class. They are the *Manitowoc* (LST 1180), *Peoria* (LST 1183), *Frederick* (LST 1184), *Schenectady* (LST 1185; departed the KTO 10 October 1990), *Cayuga* (LST 1186), *Saginaw* (LST 1188), *San Bernardino* (LST 1189; departed the KTO 13 October 1990), *Spartanburg County* (LST 1192), *La Moure County* (LST 1194), and *Barbour County* (LST 1195). These ships displace 4,793 tons light (8,450 tons fully loaded), and are 561.83 feet (159.2 m) in length. Powered by six Arco 15-251 diesel engines (except for the *Manitowoc,* which has six General Motors 16-645-E5 diesels), the ships have a maximum speed of 22 knots (25 mph; 41 km/h). Complement of the ships is approximately 253 (including 15 officers). The ships can accommodate 430 troops, as well as carrying 23 AAV7A1 tracked personnel vehicles (TPVs) or 41 2.5-ton cargo trucks, and

T-55 Main Battle Tank

A Soviet-built T-55, one of 1,600 in the Iraqi arsenal, lies burned out at the edge of an oilfield in Kuwait.

are furnished with a landing pad for helicopters, although they do not have hangar facilities.

Reference: Polmar, Norman, *The Naval Institute Guide to the Ships and Aircraft of the U.S. Fleet* (Annapolis, MD: Naval Institute Press, 1993), 179.

Tanzimat ("The Reorganization")

See Midhat Pasha.

Task Force Normandy

On the first night of the air war of Desert Storm, three separate missions were launched against Iraqi positions almost simultaneously. One of these sorties was an attack by three MH-53J Pave Low helicopters belonging to the Air Force's First Special Operations Wing against two Iraqi early-warning-radar sites. Just before the beginning of H-hour (the approximate moment the war began), three Pave Lows left their station at Al Jouf, Saudi Arabia, and headed across the

Iraqi border to serve as navigational guides for nine AH-64 Apache helicopters. They were accompanied by ten CH-47D Chinook helicopters, one of which served as a forward-based refueling depot for the other craft. Because the Pave Low pilots used night-vision goggles, they were able to direct the Apaches to the target, set chemical lights to illuminate the two targets, and veer off, allowing the Apaches to destroy the radar sites with 27 Hellfire missiles, 100 Hydra unguided rockets, and some 4,000 rounds of 30 mm gunfire. Task Force Normandy was supposed to silence potential Iraqi responses to the ensuing F-117A Stealth fighter attacks on Baghdad, but the attack was somehow reported to the capital, and the Stealth fighters came under heavy anti-aircraft fire.

See also ANVIS-AN/AVS-6 Night Vision Imaging System; CH-47D Chinook.

Task Group 323.2

This special assemblage of British ships was formed by the Royal Navy to watch the situation in Libya and the eastern Mediterranean during the Gulf crisis. The armada consisted of the aircraft carrier *Ark Royal*, the destroyer *Manchester* (replaced after 23 January 1991 by the frigate *Charybdis*), and the frigate *Sheffield*. In the eastern Mediterranean, the ships worked closely with the USS *Virginia* and the USS *Spruance*.

Reference: Friedman, Norman, *Desert Victory: The War for Kuwait* (Annapolis, MD: Naval Institute Press, 1991), 317–318.

Thalweg Principle

The thalweg, or talweg, is described as "the middle of the chief navigable channel of a waterway which constitutes a boundary between states." The Algiers Agreement of 1975 between Iran and Iraq established this principle to properly divide the all-important Shatt al-Arab waterway. Iraqi author Samir al-Khalil (a pseudonym) said, "In 1975 [with the signing of the Algiers Agreement] Iraq formally conceded to an Iranian demand (first made in 1932) that the border [of the Shatt al-Arab] be adjusted according to the *thalweg* principle, which translates into its running

The Iraqis had approximately 1,000 Soviet-built T-72 main battle tanks, such as this one captured near Kuwait City, at the beginning of Operation Desert Storm.

T-72 Main Battle Tank

along the midpoint of the river's navigational channel."

See also Algiers Agreement of 6 March 1975; Iran-Iraq War; Shatt al-Arab Waterway.
Reference: al-Khalil, Samir, *Republic of Fear: The Inside Story of Saddam's Iraq* (New York: Pantheon, 1990), 268.

al-Thani, Sheik Khalifa bin Hamad. *See* Qatar.

Thatcher, Margaret Hilda Roberts, Baroness Thatcher of Kesteven (1925–)

As prime minister of Great Britain and perhaps the most powerful female politician in the world during the 1980s, Margaret Thatcher stood head and shoulders above many male politicians during the crises her nation experienced. When the Iraqi army rolled into Kuwait, she worked together with President George Bush to formulate the coalition that eventually expelled Saddam Hussein's army from that nation.

Born Margaret Hilda Roberts on 13 October 1925 in her parents' flat above the grocery store where her father worked in the London suburb of Grantham, she was the younger daughter of Alfred Roberts and Beatrice (née Stephenson) Roberts. Alfred Roberts was the son of an impoverished shoemaker, but his poor eyesight precluded him from following in his father's occupational footsteps; he became a grocer. Kenneth Harris wrote, "[Margaret] thought the world of him, and for him she was not only his daughter, but pupil, protégé and potential alter ego, the offspring who could and would achieve the greater, wider life which circumstances and the accident of birth had denied him."

Margaret Roberts attended Grantham High School and Somerville College in Oxford; she studied research chemistry from 1947 to 1951, when she married Denis Thatcher. Called to the bar at Lincoln's Inn (a college of law), she was elected to the lower House of Parliament, the House of Commons, from Barnet, and served from 1959 to 1992. In 1961 she began an upward climb within the British government that led to the halls of power: secretary of the ministry of pensions and national insurance (1961–1964), chief opposition spokesman on education (1969–1970), secretary of state for education and science (1970–1974), leader of the Conservative party (1975–1990), and leader of the opposition (1975–1979). On 11 February 1979 she defeated Edward Heath to become leader of the Conservatives in the elections that May. On 4 May, after the Conservatives won a majority of the House of Commons, Thatcher became the first female British prime minister. In her nearly 12 years on the job (the fourth longest rule of one person in that position), Thatcher was known by the nickname "The Iron Lady." She sent British forces halfway across the world to fight a short but bloody war against the Argentinians for control of the Falkland Islands, came close to being assassinated by the Irish Republican Army, put down a 51-week-long strike by British miners, and used her talents to desocialize the British economy. Thatcher worked hand-in-hand with President Ronald Reagan on several foreign relations matters, including the air strike on Libya in 1986. Thatcher worked as well with President George Bush, and aided him in formulating coalition strategy to face down Saddam Hussein.

On 16 March 1990 Iraq executed Farzad Bazoft, an Iranian-born journalist who was working for the *London Observer*. Thatcher had been working behind the scenes to get amnesty for Bazoft, but failed. She called the hanging "an act of barbarism." At the same time, however, Iraq had a $400-million line of credit for commodities with the British government, and the line was not canceled. It was just another sign that Western governments were covertly supplying to Iraq the materiel with which it built up its war machine.

From 1985 to 1990, Thatcher apparently groomed John Major, a Conservative from the district of Huntingdonshire in the House of Commons, as her heir apparent. Major began his upward climb in 1985 as junior minister for social security and the disabled; a year later, he was named minister of the same department. In 1987 Thatcher was instrumental in his becoming chief secretary of the treasury (an office on a par with the American position of the Office of Management and Budget), where Major served until July 1989, when he was appointed British

British prime minister Margaret Thatcher walks with U.S. president George Bush during a meeting on 2 August 1990 in Woody Creek, Colorado.

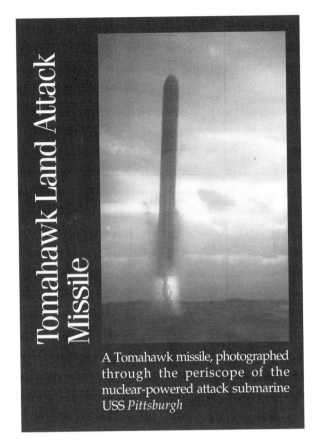

A Tomahawk missile, photographed through the periscope of the nuclear-powered attack submarine USS *Pittsburgh*

foreign secretary. Eventually he was named chancellor of the exchequer (the chief of the British monetary system and comparable to the American secretary of the treasury). In November 1990, because of the heightening economic downturn in the British economy, Thatcher's Conservative party members on the House of Commons gave her a no-confidence vote, effectively asking her to step aside as party leader and, thus, prime minister. Three weeks later Major was named as her replacement, and he saw the British through the rest of the Persian Gulf War. The stalwart Thatcher was later elected to a seat in the House of Lords, and in 1992 she was knighted Baroness Thatcher of Kesteven. Alan Riding wrote in the *New York Times* that while other Western European governments welcomed Thatcher's removal so that European union could be speeded up, by March 1991 the loss seemed to "slow unity." Her writings include *In Defence of Freedom* (1986) and *The Downing Street Years, 1979–1990* (1993).

References: Harris, Kenneth, *Thatcher* (Boston: Little, Brown, 1988), 41; Junor, Penny, *Margaret Thatcher: Wife, Mother, Politician* (London: Sidgwick & Jackson, 1983); Riding, Alan, "Europe's

Loss of Thatcher Slows Unity," *New York Times*, 17 March 1991, A8; "The Thatcher Years: Rise and Fall of an Iron-Willed Leader," *New York Times*, 23 November 1990, A14.

TLAM. *See* Tomahawk Land Attack Missile.

Tomahawk Land Attack Missile (BGM-109)

Known as TLAM, the Tomahawk is, according to *Sea Power*, "an all-weather, subsonic cruise missile that can be fired as a conventional anti-ship weapon or as a land-attack weapon using both nuclear and conventional warheads." The Tomahawk is 18 feet 3 inches long (5.56 m); an expendable rocket booster adds 2 feet 3 inches (0.69 m). The missile has a wingspan of 8 feet 9 inches (2.67 m), weighs 2,650 pounds (1,179 kg) or 3,200 pounds (1,452 kg) with the booster, and can fly 700 nautical miles (806 mi; 1,298 km) with a conventional warhead and 1,500 (1,728 mi; 2,780 km) with a nuclear warhead. The missile is powered by a Williams International F107-W-R-400 cruise turbofan engine, as well as a solid-fuel booster, and travels at a high subsonic speed. When attached to a ground mobile-launch unit, the combination of missile and rocket is called a ground-launched cruise missile (GLCM) system.

At the precise moment that Operation Desert Storm began, the Aegis cruiser USS *San Jacinto*, part of the Carrier Group Kennedy, fired the first Tomahawk from the Red Sea; an instant later, in the Persian Gulf, the Aegis cruiser *Bunker Hill* also fired one; both were aimed at Iraqi targets. In all, 298 Tomahawks would be fired; TLAM-C variants used 1,000-pound (454 kg) warheads, and TLAM-Ds fired 24 small bundles of explosives carrying 166 bomblets each. Another variant is the Tomahawk antiship missile (TASM).

Commander Steve Froggett of the U.S. Navy wrote of the Tomahawk in 1992, "Tomahawk missiles use an inertial navigator, updated by reference to terrain elevation maps and visual reference scenes near the target. The terrain contour maps (TerComs) contain a matrix of elevation data over a specific area. The missile samples the terrain profile over the maps, compares the profile with the stored data, and calculates its actual position. The corrected position is used to update the inertial navigator, and course corrections necessary to regain the preplanned route are calculated and implemented."

References: Froggett, Steve, "Tomahawk in the Desert," *U.S. Naval Institute Proceedings* 118:1 (January 1992), 72; Kandebo, Stanley W., "U.S. Fires over Twenty-five of Its Conventional Land Attack Tomahawks in First Week of War," *Aviation Week & Space Technology,* 29 January 1991, 29; *Sea Power: The Official Publication of the Navy League of the United States* 37:1 (January 1994), 177–178.

Tornado

A multipurpose two-seat fighter belonging to the militaries of Great Britain, Germany, Italy, and Saudi Arabia, 74 of these aircraft saw action in the Gulf War; the British flew 1,644 sorties, the Italians 224, and the Saudis 451.

The British version of the plane is called the GR1, the Saudi variant is the IDS, and the Italian form is called the Tornado. Powered by two Turbo-Union RB-199 Mk 103 turbofan engines delivering a maximum of 16,920 pounds (7,675 kg) of thrust each, the Tornado is built by a consortium in which the British (BAe) and Germans (MBB) split 85 percent of the building responsibility, with Italy picking up the remaining 15 percent. With a swing-wing variable, the Tornado has a wingspan of 45 feet 7 inches (13.9 m) swept and 28 feet 2 inches (8.6 m) unswept, a maximum speed of Mach 2.2, and a maximum unrefueled range of 1,525 miles (2454 km).

The U.S. military account *Gulf War Air Power Survey* reports that "the Tornado initially used its JP-233 runway denial weapon, which was designed for low-level attacks on airfields in Europe. With [the] JP-233, Tornados flew level deliveries at extremely low altitudes and attacked runways and aircraft parking areas. Fifty-three sorties were flown in the first four days, expending 106 JP-233s. . . . With the arrival of Buccaneer aircraft equipped with the Pave Spike laser designating pod on day 17 of Desert Storm, Tornados dropped laser-guided bombs that were buddy-lased by Buccaneers. Tornados flew 488 strikes against targets such as bridges, hardened aircraft shelters, and other elements of air base infrastructure." Tornados carried Alarm missiles, British antiradiation missiles like the United States' AGM-45 Shrike. Alarms were utilized by Tornados on SEAD (suppression of enemy air defense) missions.

The British GR series comes in several variants that were utilized during the war: the GR1, an all-weather bomber; the GR3, an interceptor/attack craft; the GR1A, an all-weather reconnaissance plane used specifically to hunt mobile Scud launchers. The Italians deployed 10 Tornadoes for air superiority missions. The Tornado suffered the most severe casualties of any allied aircraft in the war; making up only 4 percent of allied aircraft, they sustained 26 percent of all shoot-downs. Five allied Tornado pilots were killed in action, with an additional five taken prisoner.

See also Buccaneer.
References: Boyne, Walter J., *The Weapons of Desert Storm* (Lincolnwood, IL: Publications International, 1991), 22; *Gulf War Air Power Survey, Volume IV: Weapons, Tactics, and Training Report and Space Report* (Washington, DC: GPO, 1993), 63–64.

TOW Missile

A wire-tracked antitank missile, the TOW, designated BGM-71, was in the weapons supplies of Bahrain, Egypt, Morocco, Oman, Saudi Arabia, and the United Arab Emirates, although its use during the Persian Gulf War is unknown.

The TOW (tube-launched, optically-tracked, wire-guided) missile, mounted on a small tripod, can be installed with the tripod on the U.S. Army's Humvee vehicle or without it on the AH-1S HueyCobra helicopter. The missile, a solid-propellant weapon, has a small launch engine and boost motor, which burn for 15 seconds after launch. The missile is 46 inches (117.4 cm) in length and weighs slightly over 42 pounds (18.9 kg) at launch; the BGM-71C variant weighs 42 pounds (19.1 kg). The missile has a maximum speed of 656 feet per second (200 m/sec) and a maximum range of 12,300 feet (3,750 m). The BGM-71C variant is called I-TOW.

See also TOW II Missile.
Reference: Blake, Bernard, ed., *Jane's Weapon Systems, 1988–89* (Coulsdon, Surrey, UK: Jane's Information Group, 1988), 155–156.

Tornado

A Royal Saudi Air Force Tornado, one of 74 such fighters used during Operation Desert Storm, sits on a flight line.

TOW II Missile

Used by the United States in the Persian Gulf, the TOW II is an updated version of the TOW. It is similar to its cousin except, as one source notes, it "incorporates a heavier 6-inch-diameter [152.4 mm] warhead of still greater penetration performance and this occupies the full diameter of the missile body."

Reference: Blake, Bernard, ed., *Jane's Weapon Systems, 1988–89* (Coulsdon, Surrey, UK: Jane's Information Group, 1988), 155–156.

TR-1A

A single-seat reconnaisance craft similar to the U-2 spyplane that became so famous during the cold war, four TR-1As flew 89 sorties during Operation Desert Storm. Five U-2s flew 149 missions.

The TR-1A is "equipped with a variety of sensors to provide continuous day or night, all-weather, standoff surveillance of a battle area in direct support of U.S. and allied ground and air forces," according to the U.S. military. *Jane's All the World's Aircraft* reports that the plane "has the same basic airframe as the U-2R, with a J75-P-13B engine, but with the significant addition of an advanced synthetic aperture radar system (ASARS)." The plane is 63 feet (19.20 m) long, has a wingspan of 103 feet (31.39 m), and weighs under 10,000 pounds (4,535 kg) empty, without pods.

References: Blake, Bernard, ed., *Jane's Weapon Systems, 1988–89* (Coulsdon, Surrey, UK: Jane's Information Group, 1988), 436; *Gulf War Air Power Survey, Volume IV: Weapons, Tactics, and Training Report and Space Report* (Washington, DC: GPO, 1993), 99.

Transport Dock Vessels, Amphibious, United States

According to the reference authority *Sea Power*, "these versatile ships replace amphibious transports, amphibious cargo ships, and the older

TOW II Missile

Four frames in one picture show the launch of a U.S. Army TOW II (tube-launched, optically-tracked, wire-guided) missile.

dock landing ships. Although their capabilities are less than those of the new Whidbey Island class of dock landing ships, they effectively demonstrated their utility during Desert Shield/Storm, during which both Raleigh-class ships and eight of the Austin class were deployed to the Middle East, where they participated in a myriad of operations." As of 1995 both ships of the Raleigh class have been decommissioned, and those of the Austin class are expected to suffer the same fate in the near future. The Austin-class ships include the USS *Nashville* (LPD 13), which participated in the Persian Gulf War. They are powered by two boilers, two steam turbines, and two shafts, which deliver 24,000 shaft horsepower (shp). The ships displace approximately 17,000 tons fully loaded, are 570 feet (174 m) in length, have a maximum speed of 21 knots (24 mph; 39 km/h), and have a complement of 388. They can carry up to six CH-46E Sea Knight helicopters and up to 900 troops.

Reference: Sea Power: The Official Publication of the Navy League of the United States 37:1 (January 1994), 148.

TU-16 Badger Bomber

Although several sources confirm that the Iraqis were a purchaser of this Soviet bomber, the variant and type (from electronics countermeasures craft to tanker), number, and what role they played during the Persian Gulf War remain a mystery.

A six-man (two pilots, navigator, tail observer, and two other rear observers) bomber, reconnaissance, attack, and electronic warfare aircraft, the Tupolev TU-16 is powered by two Mikulin RD-3M-500 turbojet engines, which deliver 20,920 pounds (9,489 kg) of thrust each. The plane, with a length of 114 feet 2 inches (34.8 m), has a wingspan of 108 feet 3 inches (32.99 m) and an unfueled weight of 82,000 pounds (37,200 kg). Maximum speed, at 19,700 feet (6,000 m), is 566 knots (1,050 km/h; 652 mph). It can carry a bomb load of up to 19,800 pounds (9,000 kg) of bombs.

References: Dupuy, Trevor N., et al., *How to Defeat Saddam Hussein: Scenarios and Strategies for the Gulf War* (New York: Warner Books, 1991), 170;

Lambert, Mark, ed., *Jane's All the World's Aircraft, 1991–92* (Coulsdon, Surrey, UK: Jane's Information Group, 1991), 284–285.

TU-22 Blinder-A Bomber

Considered one of the most sophisticated Soviet supersonic attack bombers, the Tupolev TU-22 bomber, christened the "Blinder" by NATO, was apparently part of the Iraqi air force. *Jane's All the World's Aircraft, 1991–92* reports that Iraq, along with Libya, "have a few." The plane's use during the Persian Gulf War, because it is a supersonic bomber, and because few Iraqi planes got into the air, was probably minimal at best.

There are many TU-22 variants, including the "Blinder-C," a maritime version, the "Blinder-E," an electronics warfare and reconnaissance variant, and the TU-22M, called by NATO the "Backfire" bomber. The plane, in the standard "Blinder-A" model, is powered by two Koliesov VD-7 turbojets, each of which delivers 30,900 pounds (14,016 kg) of thrust. With a length of 132 feet 11.5 feet (40.53 m), a wingspan of 78 feet (23.75 m), and a crew of three (all pilots), the TU-22 is equipped specifically with a huge fuselage bay for conventional (and nuclear) weaponry, with the "Blinder-B" model being fitted with panels for AS-4 "Kitchen" air-to-surface missiles.

Reference: Dupuy, Trevor N., et al., *How To Defeat Saddam Hussein: Scenarios and Strategies for the Gulf War* (New York: Warner Books, 1991), 170; Lambert, Mark, ed., *Jane's All the World's Aircraft, 1991–92* (Coulsdon, Surrey, UK: Jane's Information Group, 1991), 287–288.

Turkey. *See* Özal, Turgut.

U-2R Spyplane. *See* TR-1A.

UAV. *See* Unmanned Aerial Vehicle.

UH-1H/N Huey Iroquois

Built by Bell Helicopter Textron of Fort Worth, Texas, the UH-1H/N saw action with U.S. Army and Marine contingents during the Gulf War. According to the military report *Desert Score,* "Two Marine UH-1Ns flying from the U.S.S. *Okinawa* were lost in the Northern Arabian Sea in October [1990]. One from the USS *Tripoli* crashed into the Pacific in December while en-route to the Persian Gulf. During the buildup and execution of Desert Storm, the UH-1Ns were the Marine Corps' principal light utility helicopter. Some were fitted with Nite Eagle Forward Looking Infrared Radar (FLIR)/laser designator pods . . . used to designate targets at night. During Desert Storm, 50 Marine Corps UH-1Ns—30 flying from shore bases and 20 from amphibious ships—flew 1,016 sorties."

The UH-1 variants have a fuselage length of 42 feet 4 inches (12.9 m) and an overall length of 56 feet 3 inches (17.15 m). Empty weight is 5,550 pounds (2,517 kg) for the UH-1H and 5,997 pounds (2,720 kg) for the UH-1N. The helicopter is powered by either a single Lycoming T53-L-13 turboshaft, which provides 1,400 shaft horsepower (shp) (the H variant) or by two Pratt & Whitney of Canada PT6T-3B-1 turboshafts, which together provide 1,800 shp. It has the capability of carrying two crew (pilot and copilot), with the option of a third crew member, and from 11 to 14 troops.

References: Almond, Denise L., ed., *Desert Score: U.S. Gulf War Weapons* (Washington, DC: Carroll Publishing, 1991), 110–111; *Sea Power: The Official Publication of the Navy League of the United States* 37: 1 (January 1994), 214.

UH-60 Blackhawk

Brigadier General Robert H. Scales, Jr., called the Blackhawk one of the "Big Five" weapons systems of the U.S. military. The U.S. Army's version of the exportable S-70B Seahawk, the UH-60 flew ten sorties for USSOCCENT (U.S. Special Operations Command Central) during the Persian Gulf War.

Powered by two General Electric T700-GE-701C turboshaft engines providing 1,800 shaft horsepower (shp) each, the UH-60 has a fuselage length of 50 feet ¾ inch (15.26 m) and a rotor diameter of 53 feet 8 inches (16.36 m). The copter weighs 11,500 pounds (5,216 kg) empty and up to 23,500 pounds (10,660 kg) loaded. It has a maximum cruising speed of 173 mph (278 km/h), with an unrefueled range of 363 miles (584 km); with the addition of four external fuel tanks, the range increases to 1,380 miles (2,220 km). It carries a crew of 3 and either 11 to 14 troops, or 6 litters and 1 to 3 attendants for medical evacuation and/or treatment. Armaments include pylons for Hellfire missiles, mine distributors, and ECM (electronic countermeasures) pods. Israel is currently forming a small squadron of ten UH-60s, which it has renamed Nammer (Tiger).

See also S-70B Seahawk.
References: Scales, Robert H., Jr., *Certain Victory: The United States Army in the Gulf War* (Washington, DC: Office of the Chief of Staff, U.S. Army, 1993); Taylor, John W. R., and Kenneth Munson, "Gallery of Middle East Airpower," *Air Force* 77:10 (October 1994), 67.

Underway Replenishment Ships, Coalition

Underway replenishment ships (URSs) were used by five coalition nations to replenish their supplies during the Gulf War. Such tankers and ships furnish a nation's overseas military forces with food, oil, munitions, and other combat supplies and materiel.

UH-1H/N
Huey Iroquois

A U.S. Navy UH-1H Huey Iroquois helicopter leaves the flight deck of the USS *Tripoli* during minesweeping operations following the close of Desert Storm.

A U.S. Army UH-60L Black Hawk lifts a howitzer.

From Australia came two URSs: the *Success* and the *Westralia*. The *Success* (OR 304), from the Durance class, displaces 17,933 tons fully loaded, measures 157.2 feet long (515.7 m), has a maximum speed of 20 knots (23 mph; 37 km/h), and has a complement of 193 men (including 17 officers). Its much larger sister ship in the Leaf class is the *Westralia* (O 195). It displaces 40,870 tons fully loaded, measures 170.7 feet long (560 m), has a maximum speed of 16 knots (18 mph; 30 km/h), and has a complement of 57 men (including 8 officers).

The underway replenishment tanker *Protecteur* served for Canada. This ship (AOR 509), displacing 24,700 tons fully loaded, is 564 feet long (171.9 m), and is powered by a General Electric steam turbine. Its maximum speed is 21 knots (24 mph, 39 km/h), although it usually travels between 11.5 and 20 knots (13–23 mph; 21–37 km/h).

French forces were served by the underway replenishment tankers *Durance, Marne,* and *Var,* all of the Durance class. The *Durance* (A 629), like its two sister ships (*Marne*: A 607; *Var*: A 608),

displaces 17,800 tons fully loaded, can travel at 19 knots (22 mph; 35 km/h), and has a complement of 164, with 18 officers. Powered by two SEMT-Pielstick diesel engines, it can also be equipped with a single Lynx Mk 2/4 helicopter.

Great Britain's single underway replenishment ship, *Fort Grange* (A 385), is of the Fort Grange class (Portugal's *Sâo Miguel* also supplied British troops; see Portugal in this entry). Commissioned in 1978, the ship displaces 23,384 tons fully loaded, measures 603 feet (183.9 m), and can travel at 22 knots (25 mph; 41 km/h). Powered by a single Sulzer RND90 8-cycle diesel engine, it has a complement of 208, which includes 36 civilian supply staff.

The Vesuvio-class replenishment tanker *Vesuvio* was Italy's sole contribution in this category. Displacing 8,706 tons fully loaded, the *Vesuvio* (A 5329) has a complement of 115 (including 9 officers), can travel at 18.5 knots (21 mph; 34 km/h) powered by two GMT diesel engines, is 423.1 feet (129 m) long, and can carry 4,700 tons of cargo. The Italians built a similar Vesuvio-class ship that it sold to Iraq, but there is no evidence that Iraq used it in the Persian Gulf War.

Portugal's only offering to the coalition forces was the logistic support ship and underway replenishment tanker *Sâo Miguel,* which aided the British. Formerly called the *Cabo Verde,* the *Sâo Miguel* (A 5208) was built in 1962. It displaces 8,209 tons fully loaded, is 354.6 feet (108 m) long, and is powered by a single MAN K62 60/105C diesel engine. It has a complement of 30, including 5 officers.

Reference: Sharpe, Richard, ed., *Jane's Fighting Ships, 1990–91* (Coulsdon, Surrey, UK: Jane's Information Group, 1990), 31, 317.

UNIKOM (UN Iraq-Kuwait Observation Commission)
See United Nations.

United Arab Emirates (UAE)

A member of the all-important Gulf Cooperation Council (GCC), the United Arab Emirates is placed strategically inside the crucial Persian Gulf.

The UAE is positioned to the east of Saudi Arabia; to the southeast of Iraq, Kuwait, and Qatar; to the north of Oman; and to the southwest of Iran. Most of its coast faces the Persian Gulf, but a small portion touches the Gulf of Oman. The United Arab Emirates (al-Imărăt al-'Arabì-yah al-Muttabidah), according to one source, "was formed in 1976 by the merging of the former Trucial States of Abu Dhabi, Ajman, Dubai, Fujairah, Ras al Khimah, Sharjah and Umm al Oaiwain." The editors of the work *The Middle East* write, "From the late 18th century onward, many of the activities—including outright piracy—of the seafaring Arab tribes of the central and southern Gulf, in particular along the Trucial Coast, became detrimental to the maritime trade of Britain and other powers." Thus until 1971 Britain was the dominant power in these Trucial States. The area has been ruled by two major tribes, the Qawasim and the Bani Yas. Adds Andrew Mango, "Britain's first formal treaty with the Gulf states was the 1820 General Treaty for Peace for the Cessation of Plunder and Piracy. In 1835 the sheiks of Sharja[h], Dubai, Ajman, and Abu Dhabi bound themselves in an inviolable truce, pledging not to retaliate against aggression but to report it to the British. This undertaking was renewed at intervals until, in 1853, a 'Perpetual Maritime Truce' was signed, calling a halt to all hostilities at sea. A major side effect of these treaties, in curbing the power of the Qawasim, was to allow the rise of Bani Yas. By the start of the twentieth century, meetings of the Trucial sheiks were presided over by the sheik of Abu Dhabi." In December 1971 the British canceled all treaties with the Trucial States, and these small entities—except Ras al-Khaimah, which joined in February 1972—formed the United Arab Emirates.

The UAE played a small role in the shaping of policy before and during the Gulf War. On 23 July 1990, just before Iraq invaded Kuwait, the Pentagon ordered that two KC-135 aircraft be dispatched to Al Dahfra Airport in the United Arab Emirates in response to an official UAE request; the maneuver was called Operation Ivory Justice. With the outbreak of the Persian Gulf crisis, the UAE played a more substantial part, sending an unknown number of troops as part of the GCC's 162,000-troop deployment (which includes 7,000 Kuwaitis who fought to liberate their homeland). Of the GCC's 330 aircraft, UAE craft flew 109 sorties during Operation Desert Storm.

References: Adams, Michael, ed., *The Middle East* (New York: Facts on File, 1988), 153–154; Foss, Christopher F., ed., *Jane's Main Battle Tanks* (London: Jane's Publishing Group, 1986), 194; Mango, Andrew, "The United Arab Emirates," in *The Cambridge Encyclopedia of the Middle East and North Africa,* Trevor Mostyn, exec. ed. (Cambridge: Cambridge University Press, 1988), 443.

United Nations (UN)

The Security Council of this international organization was the foundation for the resolutions demanding that Iraqi troops leave Kuwait, and ultimately provided the backing to go to war to force Iraq out of the tiny emirate. As a whole, the United Nations played a small role in the shaping of policy dealing with the Persian Gulf, mostly in the form of a platform for world leaders to speak out on the issues.

The United Nations is the second organization dedicated to ending conflicts among nations (it was modeled after its predecessor, the League of Nations). From 21 August to 7 October 1944, representatives at the Dumbarton Oaks Conference in Washington, D.C., laid out a plan for the world body. The UN Charter was signed in San Francisco on 26 June 1945. The actions of the Security Council (a special arm of the United Nations) to call for a withdrawal of Iraqi troops from Kuwait, authorize an embargo against Iraq, and decree that force be used to end the Iraqi occupation were based on the provisions of the UN Charter.

The two main bodies of the United Nations are the Security Council and the General Assembly. In the General Assembly, all nations are represented, and all representatives have a chance to speak on issues that concern their respective nations. However, this body has no authority to commit UN peacekeepers, or order UN members to submit to the will of the organization. These functions are handled by the Security Council, which is in effect the executive advisory board of the United Nations. According to the UN Charter, the United States, the United Kingdom, Taiwanese China (replaced by Mainland China), France, and the Soviet Union (now Russia) are the five permanent members of the Council. The Charter also specifies that six nonpermanent, or rotating, members sit on the

U.S. president George Bush speaks to the United Nations General Assembly on 1 October 1990 about the Middle East crisis caused by the Iraqi invasion of Kuwait.

Council, but in 1965 the Charter was amended to increase this number to ten.

Although most of the United Nations' concern in the Kuwaiti crisis was expressed in the Security Council, other matters were carried before the General Assembly. On 1 October 1990, President George Bush spoke to the latter body:

Two months ago, in the waning weeks of one of history's most hopeful summers, the vast, still beauty of the peaceful Kuwaiti desert was fouled by the stench of diesel and the roar of steel tanks. And once again, the sound of distant thunder echoed across a cloudless sky. And once again, the world awoke to face the guns of August.

But this time, the world was ready. The United Nations Security Council's resolute response to Iraq's unprovoked aggression has been without precedent. Since the invasion on August 2, the Council has passed eight major resolutions setting the terms for a solution to the crisis. The Iraqi regime has yet to face the facts. But as I said last month, the annexation of Kuwait will not be permitted to stand. And this is not simply the view of the United States. It is the view of every Kuwaiti, the Arab League, the United Nations. Iraq's leaders should listen. It is Iraq against the world.

Let me take this opportunity to make the policy of my Government clear. The United States supports the use of sanctions to compel Iraq's leaders to withdraw immediately and without condition from Kuwait. We also support the provision of medicine and food for humanitarian purposes, so long as distribution can be properly monitored. Our quarrel is not with the people of Iraq. We do not wish for them to suffer. The world's quarrel is with the dictator who ordered that invasion.

Along with others, we have dispatched military forces to the region to enforce sanctions, to deter and if need be defend against further aggression. And we seek no advantage for ourselves, nor do we seek to maintain our military forces in Saudi Arabia for one day longer than is necessary. U.S. forces were sent at the request of the Saudi Government. The American people and this President want every single American

soldier brought home as soon as this mission is completed.

Previous to Bush's speech, President François Mitterrand of France and Soviet foreign minister Eduard Shevardnadze also addressed the General Assembly, communicating the views of their respective nations on the situation in the Gulf. On 24 September, in what was the opening assemblage of the General Assembly for the 1990–1991 session, Mitterrand proposed that if Iraq withdrew from Kuwait, the potential issues involved in so-called linkage—that Iraqi withdrawal from Kuwait be tied to a similar Israeli withdrawal from the Gaza Strip and West Bank, as well as a Syrian evacuation of Lebanon— would be under discussion. Mitterrand was alone among the coalition nations in this view, and his idea went nowhere. The following day, Shevardnadze cautioned the same group: "We should remind those who regard aggression as an acceptable form of behavior that the United Nations has the power to suppress acts of aggression. There is ample evidence that this right can be exercised. It will be, if the illegal occupation of Kuwait continues."

After the war ended, the United Nations marshaled itself into forming a watchdog agency with powers to oversee the truce between Kuwait and Iraq. This UNIKOM (UN Iraq-Kuwait Observation Commission) was established to enforce the peace agreement and police the border. Beginning in April 1991, the United Nations sent peacekeepers to the Iraq-Kuwait area. By June 1994 a total of 1,147 troops and observers were deployed, at a cost of $73 million a year. Other agency bodies established at the end of the war include the UN Special Commission (UNSC), formed "to oversee the destruction, removal or rendering harmless of all Iraq's chemical and biological weapons and related capabilities and facilities, and its ballistic missiles with a range greater than 150 kilometers"; the Iraq-Kuwait Boundary Demarcation Commission (IKBDC), organized "to demarcate the international boundary" between Iraq and Kuwait; the UN Compensation Commission (UNCC), whose duty is "to administer the Fund to pay compensation for 'any direct loss, damage, including environmental damage and the depletion of natural resources, or injury to foreign Governments, nationals and corporations, as a result of Iraq's unlawful invasion and occupation of Kuwait"; and the Security Council Sanction Committee (SCSC), which "monitors the prohibitions against the sale or supply of arms to Iraq and related sanctions set out in resolution 687."

See also Pérez de Cuéllar, Javier; United Nations Security Council.
References: *Resolutions of the United Nations Security Council and Statements by Its President Concerning the Situation between Iraq and Kuwait* (New York: United Nations Department of Public Information, April 1994), 2–3; "Transcript of the President's Address to the U.N. General Assembly," *New York Times*, 2 October 1990, A12; "United Nations Peacekeeping: Trotting to the Rescue," *The Economist*, 25 June 1994, 19.

United Nations Security Council

The United Nations is divided into two distinct bodies: the General Assembly, in which all nations are represented, and the Security Council, which is composed of five permanent members and ten rotating members. This entry concentrates on the Security Council and its impact on the Persian Gulf conflict.

The editors of *The Worldmark Encyclopedia of the Nations* write of the Security Council, "Under the Charter, the members of the U.N. vest in the Security Council primary responsibility for maintaining international peace and security. To facilitate its work and to ensure quick and effective action when required, the Council has certain powers and attributes not accorded the other organs of the U.N. Thus, the Council is empowered by the Charter to enforce its decisions and prescribe them as a course of action legally binding upon all U.N. members. However, the prerogatives can be invoked only in times of gravest crisis and under explicit conditions laid down in the Charter. Otherwise, the Council, like the General Assembly, can only recommend and advise."

The five permanent powers, all with veto power over any potential resolutions, are China, France, Great Britain, Russia (formerly the Soviet Union), and the United States. The ten rotating members of the Council are elected in the General Assembly to sit on the Council for two-year terms. From the beginning of the crisis until 1 January 1991, these members included Canada, Colombia, the Ivory Coast, Cuba, Ethiopia, Fin-

land, Malaysia, Romania, Yemen, and Zaire. On 1 January 1991, Austria, Belgium, Ecuador, India, and Zimbabwe replaced Canada, Colombia, Ethiopia, Finland, and Malaysia.

See also Appendix 4, The Complete U.N. Resolutions, 2 August 1990–15 August 1991.
Reference: *The Worldmark Encyclopedia of the Nations: United Nations* (New York: Worldmark, 1988), 22.

United Nations Security Council Resolutions

Between 2 August 1990 and 15 October 1994, the United Nations Security Council passed 29 resolutions dealing with the crisis in the Persian Gulf. The first of these was Resolution 660, passed unanimously, in which the Security Council condemned the invasion, demanded that Iraq withdraw immediately and unconditionally, and called on Iraq and Kuwait to meet and discuss their differences. Resolution 661, adopted by a vote of 13–0 (with two abstentions, Cuba and Yemen) on 6 August, established an embargo against Iraq for failing to withdraw from Kuwait. Resolution 662 of 9 August, adopted by a unanimous vote, declared Iraq's annexation of Kuwait to be "null and void," and expressly forbade other UN members from recognizing Kuwait as part of Iraq. Resolution 664, adopted unanimously on 18 August, demanded that so-called human shields held by Iraq be released immediately. Resolution 665, passed on 25 August by a vote of 13–0 (with two abstentions, Cuba and Yemen), authorized military force to be used to uphold the economic embargo of Iraq. Resolution 666, adopted on 13 September, allowed for medicine and foodstuffs to be exempted from the UN embargo. Resolution 667, adopted on 16 September, condemned Iraq for its invasions of diplomatic offices and embassies in Kuwait to abduct diplomatic personnel. Resolution 669, adopted on 24 September, called for the Committee of the Security Council, set up under resolution 660, to examine requests for assistance made by various countries in dealing with the Persian Gulf crisis. Resolution 670, ratified on 25 September, extended the economic embargo against Iraq to include aircraft. Resolution 674, enacted on 29 October, demanded that "Iraqi authorities and occupying forces immediately cease and desist from taking third-State nationals [in Kuwait] hostage, mistreating and oppressing Kuwaiti and third-State nationals," actions that "violate the decisions of this Council, the Charter of the United Nations, the Fourth Geneva Convention, the Vienna Conventions on Diplomatic and Consular Relations and international law." Resolution 667, passed on 28 November by a unanimous vote, condemned Iraq for its attempts "to alter the demographic composition of the population of Kuwait and destroy the civil records maintained by the legitimate government of Kuwait." Resolution 686, enacted on 2 March 1991 by a vote of 11–1 (Cuba voted no; there were three abstentions, China, India, and Yemen), demanded that Iraq, after being thoroughly defeated in the Persian Gulf War, submit to all previous Security Council resolutions. Resolution 687, adopted on 3 April by a vote of 12–1 (Cuba voted no; there were two abstentions, Ecuador and Yemen), established a commission to legally demarcate a boundary between Iraq and Kuwait, and called on Iraq to destroy its chemical and biological weapons stocks. Resolution 689, ratified by unanimous vote on 9 April 1991, approved the report of the United Nations Iraq-Kuwait Observer Mission (UNIKOM) to monitor the Iraq-Kuwait border. Resolution 692, passed on 20 May 1991 by a vote of 14–0 (with one abstention, Cuba), acknowledged the secretary-general's report of 2 May and established the United Nations Compensation Commission to pay reparations to those harmed by Iraq's invasion. Resolution 699, ratified on 17 June 1991 by a unanimous vote, affirmed the authority of the International Atomic Energy Agency (IAEA) to send inspectors to Iraq to search out and destroy all chemical and biological weapons and ballistic missiles in Iraqi stocks. Resolution 700, adopted by unanimous vote on 17 June 1991, approved the guidelines to implement sections 24, 25, and 27 of resolution 687 of 3 April 1991. Resolution 705, approved 15 August 1991 by a unanimous vote, called for Iraq to pay no more than 30 percent of its oil revenues as compensation once it was allowed to sell oil. Resolution 706, enacted on 15 August by a vote of 13–1 (Cuba voted no; there was one abstention, Yemen), set out the circumstances under which Iraq would be allowed to sell oil. Resolution 707, approved 15 August 1991 by a

unanimous vote, condemned Iraq after it failed to comply with nuclear inspectors investigating Iraq's chemical weapons stocks. With the passage of resolution 712 on 19 September 1991, the Security Council mandated that funds from the compensation fund be "available to meet Iraq's humanitarian needs." Resolution 715, adopted 11 October 1991 by a unanimous vote, solicited from the secretary-general a report to the Council every six months on Iraq's implementation of the provisions of resolution 687. With the adoption of resolution 773 on 16 August 1992 by a vote of 14–0 (with 1 abstention, Ecuador), the Security Council reassured Iraq that it "is not reallocating territory between Kuwait and Iraq, but is simply carrying out the technical task necessary to demarcate for the final time the precise coordinates of the boundary set out in the Minutes between the State of Kuwait and the Republic of Iraq . . . of 4 October 1963." Resolution 778, ratified on 2 October 1992 by a vote of 14–0 (with one abstention, Cuba), requested that all nations that had frozen Iraqi funds because of the invasion of Kuwait place the money in an escrow account established under resolutions 706 and 712. Resolution 806, passed on 5 February 1993, expanded UNIKOM's authority to allow mission members to use physical action for self-defense. Resolution 833, adopted by a unanimous vote on 27 May 1993, demanded that both Iraq and Kuwait respect the decisions of the United Nations Iraq-Kuwait Observer Commission to demarcate a border between the two nations. Resolution 899, ratified 4 March 1994 by a unanimous vote, doled out payments from the fund of the UN Compensation Commission. The last resolution, 949 of 15 October 1994, was adopted in response to Iraq's movement of troops toward the Kuwaiti border, and demanded that Iraq refrain from threatening its neighbors. This resolution also barred Iraq from sending Republican Guard soldiers south of the Thirty-second parallel.

See also Appendix 4, The Complete U.N. Resolutions, 2 August 1990–15 August 1991.

United States

Under the effective civilian leadership of President George Bush and the skillful military tactical command of General H. Norman Schwarz-kopf, commander in chief of the U.S. Central Command (USCENTCOM), Joint Chiefs of Staff chairman Colin L. Powell, and Secretary of Defense Dick Cheney, the United States led a coalition of nations as diverse as Syria and England, and forces as disparate in size as the American contingent of 425,000 and Argentina's 170-man army, in reversing the Iraqi domination of Kuwait.

Historian Michael A. Palmer writes, "The origins of American involvement and interest in the [Persian] gulf are to be found in the early history of the United States. Over two hundred years ago commercial necessity, revolutionary political passions, and missionary zeal carried representatives of 'God's American Israel' to the four corners of the globe." This situation lasted until the middle of the twentieth century, when America became inextricably linked with the Middle East by siding with, and financially supporting, the state of Israel. With the augmentation of the United States into a world leader and superpower, it played a larger and larger role in the area. The Iranian hostage crisis, which lasted for 444 days, the reflagging of Kuwaiti tankers with U.S. flags to save them from attack during the Iran-Iraq War, and the rapprochement toward Iraq that led to the widespread build-up of Iraq's conventional arms forces (a policy not fully known until the start of Operation Desert Storm in 1991), pulled the United States deeper into the region's political and military dilemmas. When Iraq invaded Kuwait, and the world decided to stand up to the aggression, it was natural that the United States, with the aid of France, Great Britain, and Saudi Arabia, took the lead in teaming the military coalition to drive Saddam Hussein from Kuwait.

See also Aspin, Leslie, Jr.; Baker, James Addison III; Bush, George Herbert Walker; Cheney, Richard Bruce; Operation Desert Shield; Operation Desert Storm; Powell, Colin Luther; Quayle, James Danforth; Schwarzkopf, General H. Norman; U.S. Central Command.
References: Brune, Lester H. Palmer, *America and the Iraqi Crisis, 1990–1992: Origins and Aftermath* (Claremont, CA: Regina Books, 1993), 24–25; Michael, A., *Guardians of the Gulf: A History of America's Expanding Role in the Persian Gulf, 1833–1992* (New York: Free Press, 1992), 1.

United States, Naval Contributions of

A total of 177 American ships, in 7 different carrier groups and other groupings, served in the Persian Gulf War. Prior to 2 August, and just after the beginning of the conflict in the Gulf, the following ships were in the Middle East area as part of the Sixth and Seventh Fleet Mid-East forces, with their dates of departure, if any: USS *LaSalle* (AGF-3), LaSalle-class command ship; USS *Barbey* (FF 1088), Knox-class frigate (departed 3 November 1990); USS *Reid* (FFG 30), Perry-class guided-missile frigate (departed 9 September 1990); USS *Robert G. Bradley* (FFG 49), Perry-class guided-missile frigate (departed 12 November 1990); USS *Taylor* (FFG 50), Perry-class guided-missile frigate (departed 12 November 1990); USS *England* (CG 22), Leahy-class guided-missile cruiser (departed 3 November 1990); USS *David R. Ray* (DD 971), Spruance-class destroyer (departed 18 September 1990); USS *Vandergrift* (FFG 48), Perry-class guided-missile frigate (departed 9 September 1990); and USS *Antietam* (CG 54), Ticonderoga-class cruiser (departed 3 November 1990).

As the tenseness of the situation in the Gulf grew, the United States began to dispatch groups of ships to the area. Broken down by carrier group, with dates of arrival into the Kuwaiti Theater of Operations (KTO) and date of departure, if any, are the following.

Carrier Group Independence

This grouping, which arrived in the KTO on 5 August 1990, included the aircraft carrier *Independence*, the guided-missile destroyer *Goldsborough*, the frigates *Reasoner* and *Brewton*, the guided-missile cruiser *Jouett*, the combat stores craft *White Plains*, the oiler *Cimmaron*, and the ammunition supply ships *Flint* and *Nitro*. The *Independence* departed on 4 November 1990, as did the *Goldsborough*, the *Reasoner*, the *Brewton*, the *Jouett*, and the *Cimmaron*. The *White Plains* departed on 15 October 1990. The other ships remained in the area to service other members of the fleet.

Carrier Group Eisenhower

This grouping, which arrived in the KTO on 8 August 1990, included the aircraft carrier

Eisenhower, the Aegis cruiser *Ticonderoga,* the destroyer *John Rodgers,* the guided-missile destroyers *Tattnall* and *Scott,* the frigates *Paul* and *John L. Hall,* and the ammunition supply ship *Suribachi.* All of the ships, save the *Suribachi,* departed from the area on 24 August 1990 (the *Suribachi* left on 22 August).

Carrier Group Saratoga

This grouping, which arrived in the KTO on 22 August 1990, included the aircraft carrier *Saratoga,* the nuclear-propelled guided-missile cruiser *South Carolina,* the Aegis cruiser *Philippine Sea,* the guided-missile cruiser *Biddle,* the destroyers *Sampson* and *Spruance,* the frigate *Thomas C. Hart,* the combat support ship *Detroit,* the destroyer tender *Yellowstone,* and the combat stores ship *Sirius* (part of the Military Sealift Command). The *South Carolina* departed on 11 December 1990, the *Biddle* on 9 February 1991, and the *Yellowstone* on 27 February 1991.

Carrier Group Kennedy

This grouping, which arrived in the KTO on 14 September 1990, included the aircraft carrier *John F. Kennedy,* the Aegis cruisers *Thomas S. Gates* and *San Jacinto,* the missile cruiser *Mississippi,* the destroyer *Moosbrugger,* the frigates *Samuel B. Roberts* and *Elmer Montgomery,* and the support ships *Seattle* and *Sylvania.* The *Elmer Montgomery* departed on 9 January 1991, and the *Sylvania* on 17 February 1991.

Battle Group Missouri

This grouping, which arrived in the KTO on 1 January 1991, included the battleship *Missouri,* the guided-missile frigate *Ford,* and the fast combat support ship *Sacramento.*

Carrier Group Ranger

This grouping, which arrived in the KTO on 13 January 1991, included the aircraft carrier *Ranger,* the Aegis cruisers *Valley Forge* and *Princeton,* the destroyers *Harry W. Hill* and *Paul F. Foster,* the frigate *Francis Hammond,* the ammunition supply ship *Shasta,* and the oil supply ship *Kansas City.*

Carrier Group Roosevelt

This grouping, which arrived in the KTO on 14 January 1991, included the nuclear aircraft carrier *Theodore Roosevelt,* the Aegis cruiser *Leyte Gulf* and the missile cruiser *Richmond K. Turner,* the destroyer *Caron,* the frigates *Hawes* and *Vreeland,* the oil supply ship *Platte,* and the ammunition supply ship *Santa Barbara.*

Carrier Group America

This grouping, which arrived in the KTO on 15 January 1991, included the aircraft carrier *America,* the Aegis cruiser *Normandy,* the missile cruiser *Virginia,* the destroyers *Preble* and *William V. Pratt,* the frigate *Halyburton,* the oil supply ship *Kalamazoo,* and the ammunition supply ship *Nitro* (the latter of which also serviced the ships of the Carrier Group Independence).

Carrier Group Midway

This grouping, which arrived in the KTO on 15 January 1991, included the aircraft carrier *Midway,* the Aegis cruisers *Bunker Hill* and *Mobile Bay,* the destroyers *Oldendorf* and *Fife,* the ammunition supply ship *Kiska,* and the oil supply ship *Walter S. Diehl.*

Other Naval Vessels

Other ships which served in the Gulf, with their appropriate groupings, if any, are: USS *Wisconsin* (battleship; arrived in KTO 18 August 1990) and USS *Blue Ridge* (served as CENTCOM command ship; arrived in KTO 28 August 1990).

Mid-East Force (arrived in KTO 31 August 1990; both departed 9 December 1990): USS *Rentz* (guided-missile frigate) and USS *O'Brien* (destroyer).

Fourth Marine Expeditionary Brigade (MEB, arrived in KTO 6 September 1990): USS *Nassau* (amphibious assault ship) and USS *Guam* (amphibious assault ship); USS *Raleigh* (amphibious transport docks); USS *Shreveport* (amphibious transport docks); USS *Trenton* (amphibious transport docks); USS *Iwo Jima* (amphibious assault ship); USS *Portland* (dock landing ship); USS *Pensacola* (dock landing ship); USS *Gunston Hall* (dock landing ship); USS *Manitowoc* (tank landing ship); USS *Saginaw* (tank landing ship); USS *Spartanburg County* (tank landing ship); and USS *La Moure County* (tank landing ship).

Thirteenth Marine Expeditionary Unit (MEU, arrived in KTO 7 September 1990): USS *Durham* (amphibious cargo ship) and USS *Ogden* (amphibious transport dock ship).

Amphibious Ready Group Bravo (arrived in KTO 9 September 1990): USS *Dubuque* (transport dock ship, departed 13 October 1990); USS *Schenectady* (tank landing ship, departed 10 October 1990); and USS *San Bernardino* (tank landing ship, departed 13 October 1990).

Standing Naval Force Atlantic (STANA-VFORLANT; U.S. only; extended operations from 10 September 1990 to 25 March 1991): USS *Pharris* (frigate).

Detached ships (arrived in KTO September 1990): USS *San Jose* (combat stores ship).

Mine Countermeasures Task Force (arrived in KTO 2 October 1990): USS *Avenger* (mine-hunter); USS *Impervious* (minesweeper); USS *Leader* (minesweeper); and USS *Adroit* (minesweeper).

Mid-East Force (arrived in KTO 17-28 October 1990): USS *Marvin Shields* (frigate, departed 15 February 1991); USS *Worden* (guided-missile cruiser, departed 15 February 1991); USS *MacDonough* (guided-missile destroyer, departed 24 February 1991); and USS *Nicholas* (guided-missile frigate, departed 14 February 1991).

Detached ships (arrived in KTO October 1990): USS *Savannah* (replenishment tanker, departed 13 October 1990) and USS *Acadia* (destroyer tender).

Detached ships (arrived in KTO November 1990): USS *Opportune* (salvage ship).

Desert Shield Command Ship (arrived in KTO 4 December 1990): USS *Leftwich* (destroyer).

Detached ships (arrived in KTO December 1990): USS *Mars* (combat stores ship).

Fifth Marine Expeditionary Brigade (MEB, arrived in KTO on 12 January 1991): USS *Tarawa* (amphibious assault ship); USS *Tripoli* (amphibious assault ship); USS *Mobile* (amphibious cargo ship); USS *Denver* (amphibious transport ship); USS *Vancouver* (amphibious transport docks); USS *Juneau* (amphibious transport docks); USS *New Orleans* (amphibious assault ship); USS *Anchorage* (dock landing ship); USS *Mount Vernon* (dock landing ship); USS *Germantown* (dock landing ship); USS *Peoria* (tank landing ship); USS *Frederick* (tank landing ship); and USS *Barbour County* (tank landing ship).

Mid-East Force (Arrived in KTO 24 January 1991): USS *Horne* (guided-missile cruiser) and USS *Jarrett* (guided-missile frigate).

Detached ships (arrived in KTO January 1991): USS *Vulcan* (repair ship, departed 15 February 1991); USS *Niagara Falls* (combat stores ship); USS *San Diego* (combat stores ship); USS *Jason* (repair ship); and USS *Beaufort* (salvage tug).

Mid-East Force (arrived in KTO 1-5 February 1991): USS *Kidd* (guided-missile destroyer); and USS *McInerny* (guided-missile frigate).

Detached ships (arrived in KTO February 1991): USS *Puget Sound* (destroyer tender); USS *Cape Cod* (destroyer tender); USS *Haleakala* (ammunition supply and transport); and USS *Mount Hood* (ammunition supply and transport).

Military Sealift Command Ships (those not included in previously mentioned battle or carrier groups): USNS *Algol* (fast transport ship); USNS *Bellatrix* (fast transport ship); USNS *Denebola* (fast transport ship); USNS *Pollux* (fast transport ship); USNS *Altair* (fast transport ship); USNS *Regulus* (fast transport ship); USNS *Capella* (fast transport ship); USNS *Antares* (fast transport ship); USNS *Rigel* (stores supply ship); USNS *Spica* (combat stores supply ship); USNS *Mercury* (resupply ship); USNS *Kilauea* (ammunition transport ship); USNS *Sealift Pacific* (transport oiler); USNS *Henry J. Kaiser* (oil supply); USNS *Andrew J. Higgins* (oil supply); USNS *Joshua Humphreys* (oil supply); USNS *John Lenthall, Jr.* (oil supply); USNS *Neosho* (oil supply); USNS *Hassayampa* (oil supply); USNS *Ponchatoula* (oil supply); USNS *Truckee* (oil supply); USNS *Passumpsic* (oil supply); USNS *Mercy* (hospital ship); USNS *Comfort* (hospital ship); USNS *Wright* (aviation support ship); USNS *Curtiss* (aviation support ship); USNS *Chauvenet* (surveyor); USNS *Harkness* (surveyor); USNS *Powhatan* (salvage and rescue tug); and USNS *Apache* (salvage and rescue tug).

See also Aircraft Carriers, United States; Amphibious Assault Ships, United States; Amphibious Cargo Ships, United States; Amphibious Command Ships, United States; Amphibious Transport Docks, United States; Aviation Logistic Ships, United States; Battleships, United States; Cruisers, United States; Destroyer Tenders, United States; Destroyers, United States; Dock Landing Ships,

United States; Frigates, United States; Helicopter Carriers, United States; Hospital Ships, United States; Minesweepers/Minehunters, United States; Repair Ships, United States; Salvage and Rescue Ships, United States; Salvage and Rescue Tugs, United States; Support and Supply Ships, United States; Tank Landing Ships, United States; Transport Dock Vessels, Amphibious, United States.
Reference: Almond, Denise L., ed., *Desert Score: U.S. Gulf War Weapons* (Washington, DC: Carroll Publishing, 1991), 469–474; Chadwick, Frank, *Desert Shield Fact Book* (Bloomington, IL: Games Designers' Workshop, 1991), 29.

U.S. Central Command (USCENTCOM)

Known by the acronym USCENTCOM, the U.S. Central Command is, according to Lieutenant General William G. Pagonis, "one of ten unified and specified commands, under which members of the four armed services are placed while in the theatres of combat." USCENTCOM was led by General H. Norman Schwarzkopf during the Persian Gulf War.

Based at MacDill Air Force Base near Tampa, Florida, USCENTCOM evolved from the Rapid Deployment Force (RDF) formulated under the Carter Doctrine, enunciated as part of President Jimmy Carter's State of the Union speech on 23 January 1980. Thus, the president foresaw a need for the expeditious deployment of American troops to far-off international hot spots. However, the formulation of such a force and the requirements to assemble it became mired in governmental bureaucracy. One joke ran: "What is the RDF? You and me and our M16s and two tickets on Pan Am."

During the first term of President Ronald Reagan, the Rapid Deployment Joint Task Force (RDJTF) was used specifically during the Operation Bright Star exercises with Egypt to train American troops for potential desert warfare. In 1983, under Reagan's command, the RDJTF evolved into the U.S. Central Command, devoted to establishing a single battle preparation and logistics program under one central command, a leader to be designated USCINCCENT (U.S. Commander in Chief, Central Command). According to the command, USCENTCOM "is the administrative headquarters for U.S. military affairs in 19 countries of the Middle East, Southwest Asia and Northeast Africa including the Arabian Gulf . . . it supports U.S. and free world

interests by assuring access to Mideast oil resources, helping friendly regional states maintain their own security and collective defense, maintaining an effective and visible U.S. military presence in the region, deterring threats by hostile regional states and by projecting U.S. military force into the region if necessary."

In November 1988, General H. Norman Schwarzkopf was named as USCINCCENT, and stationed at CENTCOM's headquarters at MacDill Air Force Base in Tampa, Florida. He immediately began a rapid buildup of American experience in fighting a desert war somewhere in the Middle East. This buildup came about because of the rapidly waning influence of the Soviet Union in the area, and the rise of dictatorships (including those in Iraq, Iran, and Syria). Schwarzkopf made sure that CENTCOM was at the forefront in estimating the possibility of crises erupting in the region.

On 25 April 1990, CENTCOM estimated that the main source of tension in the Persian Gulf area was Iraq; consequently, it established the "Iraq Regional Warning Problem" to develop and extend the collection of military intelligence on issues involving Iraq. Less than a month later, on 21 May, CENTCOM evaluated the key trouble spot in the region as the border between Iraq and Kuwait, and issued an assessment that "Iraq is not expected to use military force to attack Kuwait or Saudi Arabia to seize disputed territory or resolve a dispute over oil policy." Still, there was wide concern inside CENTCOM that Iraq was a threat to its small neighbor. In July, Schwarzkopf ordered a covert computerized war game called Internal Look, which indicated that while Saudi Arabia could be defended from a mythical Iraqi invasion, the cost in American casualties would be high. The editors of *Triumph without Victory: A History of the Persian Gulf War* reported: "A senior officer who was deeply involved in the running of the exercise said, 'Schwarzkopf wanted to have an exercise to test the war plan as it was developing so that we could refine it.'"

At the beginning of July 1990, as Iraq began to threaten Kuwait over the oil question, American military planners began to get nervous, and started a full month of military moves and plans leading up to the Iraqi invasion of Kuwait. On 18 July, the day after Saddam Hussein accused several Persian Gulf states of "stabbing Iraq in the back" with a "poisoned dagger" by exceeding OPEC oil production quotas, USCENTCOM issued a Worldwide Warning Indicator Monitoring System (WWIMS) status change to establish the growing American concern with the situation. On 19 July, CENTCOM secured its first intelligence reports of Iraqi troop movements near the Kuwaiti border. On 21 July, CENTCOM intelligence sources reported that 3,000 Iraqi military vehicles were spotted moving from Baghdad on the roads to Kuwait. This final action led to another internal war program (unnamed) in which CENTCOM planned for a possible Iraqi invasion of Kuwait using some 300,000 American troops and 640 combat aircraft. Finally, on 31 July, Schwarzkopf reported to President Bush that according to all standards, an Iraqi invasion of Kuwait was "imminent." The Defense Intelligence Agency, which had differed with CENTCOM over the seriousness of the Iraqi threat, concurred with Schwarzkopf's appraisal. On 1 August, while meeting with Secretary of Defense Dick Cheney, Schwarzkopf foresaw that while Iraq would invade and quickly conquer Kuwait, an Iraqi advance would end there and not proceed into Saudi Arabia. Further, Schwarzkopf presented Cheney with a blueprint of potential Iraqi targets that would be hit if American forces got into the fray.

Once the Iraqi onslaught on Kuwait began on 2 August, Schwarzkopf became the chief foot soldier of coalition forces in the Gulf. President Bush's hands-off attitude—in effect allowing the military, with Schwarzkopf's advice, to carry out its best plan for the war—allowed the conflict to be fought in a nonpolitical manner. Thus the war culminated in Schwarzkopf's celebrated press conference on 27 February known as "The Mother of All Briefings."

See also Carter Doctrine; Schwarzkopf, General H. Norman.
Reference: Dunnigan, James F., and Austin Bay, *From Shield to Storm: High-Tech Weapons, Military Strategy, and Coalition Warfare in the Persian Gulf* (New York: Morrow, 1992), 51; U.S. News & World Report, *Triumph without Victory: The History of the Persian Gulf War* (New York: Times Books, 1993), 29.

Unmanned Aerial Vehicle (UAV)

These small, remotely piloted craft served a vital function during the Persian Gulf War: aerial re-

connaissance, battle damage assessment (BDA), and target selection.

Fifty UAVs served in the Gulf for three of the four branches (Army, Navy, and Marines) of the U.S. military. Only 14 feet (4.3 m) long, UAVs have a wingspan of 17 feet (5.2 m), weigh 448 pounds (203 kg), and are powered by a 26-horsepower aviation-gas engine. The Pioneer model UAV can fly about 120 miles (138 mi; 222 km) at an altitude between 1,000 and 12,000 feet (1,610–19,308 m). It is handled by three controllers and managed by three additional ground crew members. The Navy used the craft from the battleships USS *Missouri* and USS *Wisconsin* for 151 sorties; the Army UAVs flew 46 sorties, and the Marine UAVs flew 138 sorties.

See also Remotely Piloted Vehicles.
Reference: Conduct of the Persian Gulf War: Final Report to Congress, Report by the Department of Defense, April 1992, 211–212, 722–724.

Uqair, Treaty of (1922)

In May 1922 Sir Percy Zachariah Cox, Britain's representative in the Persian Gulf, brought together representatives of King Faisal I of Iraq and King ibn Saud of Najd (Saudi Arabia) to settle their boundary disputes. Ahmad al-Sabah, the sheik of Kuwait, was represented by Major J. C. Moore, the British political agent in Kuwait. The parties met at Muhammarah on what is now the Iranian side of the Shatt al-Arab waterway. The result was the Treaty of Muhammarah, which called for the creation of a delineation committee to iron out boundary differences. Cox did not attend this first meeting, but saw promise in the exchange and called for a further set of meetings. The resulting conference of Uqair was held from 28 November to 3 December 1922 at the Saudi port of the same name on the Persian Gulf near what is now the nation of Bahrain. In his *Kuwait and Her Neighbours,* Harold R. P. Dickson, a witness at the conference, wrote:

On the sixth day Sir Percy entered the lists. He told both sides that, at the rate they were going, nothing would be settled for a year.... At a general meeting of the conference, Sir Percy took a red pencil and very carefully drew on the map of Arabia a boundary line from the Persian Gulf to Ja-

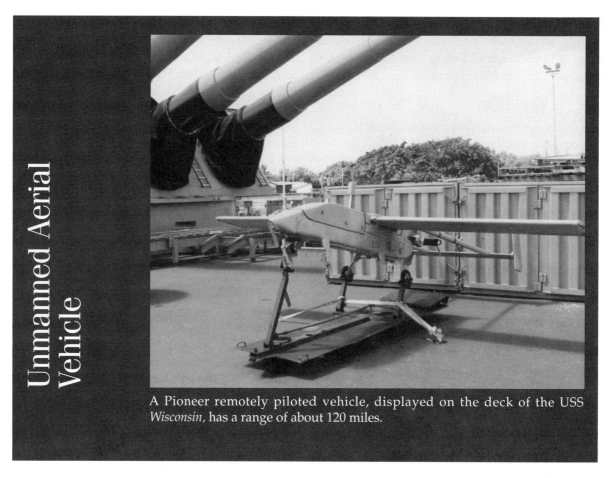

A Pioneer remotely piloted vehicle, displayed on the deck of the USS *Wisconsin*, has a range of about 120 miles.

Unmanned Aerial Vehicle

bal 'Anaizan, close to the Transjordan frontier. This gave Iraq a large area of the territory claimed by Najd. Obviously to placate Ibn Sa'ud, he ruthlessly deprived Kuwait of nearly two-thirds of her territory and gave it to Najd, his argument being that the power of the Ibn Saba [the desert title of the Kuwaiti sheik] was much less in the desert than it had been when the Anglo-Turkish Agreement had been drawn up. South and west of Kuwait proper, he drew out two zones, which he declared should be neutral and known as the Kuwait Neutral Zone and the Iraq Neutral Zone. . . . Throughout the talks, Major Moore, who was supposed to be watching the interests of the Sheikh of Kuwait, had said nothing. Sir Percy had dominated everything and everybody. . . .

Both Major More [*sic*] and myself, I only in a secretarial capacity, were present when Sir Percy broke the news to the ruler of Kuwait that he had been obliged to give away to Ibn Sa'ud nearly two-thirds of the kingdom claimed by Shaikh Ahmad. Shaikh Ahmad pathetically asked why he had

done this without even consulting him. Sir Percy replied that, on this unfortunate occasion, the sword had been mightier than the pen, and that had he not conceded the territory, Ibn Sa'ud would certainly have soon picked a quarrel and taken it, if not more, by force of arms. . . .

Thus faced with a *fait accompli* Shaikh Ahmad agreed to add his signature to the agreement. . . .

The text of the Treaty of Uqair, which delineated the border between Iraq and Saudi Arabia, reads:

IN THE NAME OF GOD THE
MERCIFUL, THE COMPASSIONATE
The frontier between Najd and Kuwait begins in the West from the junction of the Wadi al Aujah, with the Batin [el Batin]; leaving Raq'i [Rikai] to Najd, from this point it continues in a straight line until it joins latitude 29 degrees and red semi-circle referred to in Article 5 of the Anglo-Turkish Agreement of 29th July 1913. The line then follows the side of the red semi-circle until it reaches a point terminating on the coast

south of Ras al Qali'ah [Ras el Kaliyah] and this is the indisputable southern frontier of Kuwait territory. The portion of territory bounded on the North by this line and which is bounded on the West by a low mountainous ridge called Shaq [Esh Shakk] to 'Ain al 'Abd [Ain el Abd] and thence to the coast north of Ras al Mish'ab [Ras Mishaab], in this territory the Governments of Najd and Kuwait will share equal rights until through the good offices of the Government of Great Britain a further agreement is made between Najd and Kuwait concerning it. The map on which this boundary has been made is Asia 1-1,000,000, made at the Royal Geographical Society under the direction of the Geographical Section General Staff and printed at the War Office in the year 1918.

Written in the port of 'Uqair and signed by the representatives of both governments on the second day of December 1922 corresponding to the 13th of Rabi'al Thani, 1341.

References: Dickson, Harold Richard Patrick, *Kuwait and Her Neighbours* (London: Allen & Unwin, 1956), 274; Lauterpacht, E., et al., eds., *The Kuwait Crisis: Basic Documents* (Cambridge, UK: Grotius, 1991), 47–48.

USS *Stark* Incident

The Iraqi attack on the Navy frigate *Stark* during the Iran-Iraq War was classified as "inadvertent," but whether it was an accident on Iraq's part, or an accident caused by U.S. policy in the Gulf, remains a matter of speculation.

The *Stark* (FFG-21), one of the Oliver Hazard Perry class of guided missile frigates, is 445 feet (136 m) long and displaces 3,585 tons fully loaded. Powered by two General Electric LM 2500 gas turbines and one propeller shaft delivering 41,000 shaft horsepower (shp), the ship is armed with Harpoon missiles, a single 76 mm/ 62-caliber gun, six torpedo tubes, and a General Electric/General Dynamics 20 mm Vulcan Phalanx gun. It carries a crew of 206 (193 crew and 13 officers), and 19 airmen.

On 17 May 1987 the *Stark* was about 85 miles (137 km) northeast of Bahrain, in the Persian Gulf, when a French-made Iraqi Mirage F-1 fighter fired two Exocet missiles at the ship from 11 miles (17.7 km) away. One of the missiles struck the *Stark* on the port (left) side of the ship, causing an explosion. Twenty-eight sailors were immediately killed and the lives of nine more were eventually claimed. The ship was announced to be "dead in the water"; however, according to military aviation and naval authority Norman Polmar, "The *Stark* was able to return to the United States under her own power and underwent 15 months of repairs at the Litton/Ingalls yard. The repairs cost an estimated $90 million."

A Pentagon spokesman, Robert Sims, said that the attack appeared to be "inadvertent." Iraq apologized for the assault, and the day after the attack Saddam Hussein issued a message to President Ronald Reagan, iterating that "I hope this unintentional accident will not affect relations between Iraq and the United States of America." A month later, on 19 June 1987, *Stark* commanding officer Captain Glenn R. Brindel, executive officer Lieutenant Commander Raymond J. Gajan, Jr., and tactical action officer Lieutenant Basil E. Moncrief, Jr., were relieved of duty because of their performance during the attack (the ship did not issue a warning that a foreign plane involved in a war was coming close enough to fire missiles). On 28 March 1989 the U.S. Department of State announced that it approved an Iraqi offer of $27.3 million as compensation for the 37 men killed.

On 14 April 1988 the USS *Samuel B. Roberts*, another Perry-class frigate, struck an Iranian mine in the Persian Gulf, suffering a considerable amount of damage to its hull. Although the *Stark* never again saw action in the Gulf, the *Samuel B. Roberts* was one of the 177 American ships that served during Operations Desert Shield and Desert Storm.

References: Cushman, John H., Jr., "Captain of *Stark* and Two Others Relieved of Duty," *New York Times*, 20 June 1987, A1; Cushman, John H., Jr., "Iraqi Missile Hits U.S. Navy Frigate in Persian Gulf," *New York Times*, 18 May 1987, A1; Halloran, Richard, "Why Didn't *Stark* Defend Herself? U.S. Awaits the Captain's Report," *New York Times*, 19 May 1987, A1; Johnston, David, "Reagan Report to Congress Will Assess Gulf Peril," *New York Times*, 15 June 1987, A8; Polmar, Norman, *The Naval Institute Guide to the Ships and Aircraft of the U.S. Fleet* (Annapolis, MD: Naval Institute Press, 1993), 145; Roberts, Steven V., "Missile Toll on Frigate Is 28; Ship Did Not Fire in Defense; U.S. Orders a Higher Alert," *New York Times*, 19 May 1987, A1.

Veterans' Benefits Improvements Act of 1994

See Veterans Persian Gulf Health Registry.

Veterans Health Care Act of 1992 (Public Law 102-585; 106 Stat. 4943)

This congressional legislation, enacted on 4 November 1992, includes provisions that established the Persian Gulf War Veterans Health Registry in the Department of Veterans Affairs (DVA).

See also National Defense Authorization Act for the Fiscal Years 1992 and 1993; Veterans Persian Gulf Health Registry.

Veterans Persian Gulf Health Registry (VHR)

Following reports of possible poison-chemical victims from the Persian Gulf War, in 1991 the Veterans Administration (VA) established the Veterans Health Registry, a manifest of troops eligible for medical examination, treatments, and, if such evidence of chemical weapons use is found, benefits from the government. Modeled on the VA's Agent Orange and Ionizing Radiation registries, the VHR was authorized by the Veterans Health Care Act of 1992 (Public Law 102-585; 106 Stat. 4943) to "improve the delivery of health care services to eligible veterans and clarify the authority of the Secretary of Veterans Affairs."

Reference: "VA Fact Sheet: Programs for Persian Gulf Veterans," Department of Veterans Affairs, November 1994.

Vietnam Syndrome

"By God, we've licked the Vietnam syndrome once and for all!" exclaimed President George Bush on 1 March 1991, at the close of the land portion of the Gulf War. Was he right? Many analysts, both in the military and civilian sectors, argue impressively that the key factor behind the syndrome—America's fear that its days as a major military power were effectively over—was changed by the quick and decisive victory in the Persian Gulf.

In an editorial in the *Washington Post*, Jim Hoagland laid out his reasons why he felt Bush's early handling of the crisis, before the outbreak of the air and ground wars, brought about a conclusion that was different in every way from the American experience in Vietnam. "Playing against type, America's generals are refusing to fight the last war again in the Persian Gulf," Hoagland wrote. "They have learned the lessons of Vietnam, which is more than can be said for the politicians and retread anti-war activists who argue today that the threat to world peace comes not from Saddam Hussein but from President Lyndon Baines Bush. . . . The Persian Gulf crisis represents the professional military's revenge for Vietnam. By ruling out a deceptive 'incremental' buildup in the Gulf, the generals are forcing the politicians in Washington to take immediate and clear responsibility for the decisions (including those of the generals) on how this confrontation should be waged."

Comparisons with Vietnam were ruled out early. Rep. Les Aspin (D–Wisconsin), chairman of the House Armed Services Committee in 1990–1991, wrote in the white paper "The Military Option: The Conduct and Consequences of War in the Persian Gulf": "I am convinced that we do not face another Vietnam in the Persian Gulf. There are four principal reasons why there is little risk of a long, drawn-out war: 1) A war in the Gulf would not be fought in the jungle, but in the desert, where there is little cover and

Veterans Persian Gulf Health Registry

Veterans Affairs secretary Jesse Brown testifies before the House Veterans' Affairs subcommittee on 9 June 1994.

concealment for Iraqi forces; 2) There are no friendly countries around Iraq and we would not have to worry about any Cambodian sanctuaries or Ho Chi Minh trails; 3) We would not be fighting a guerilla force supported by a sympathetic population, but a uniformed military that has occupied and largely depopulated Kuwait; and 4) In Vietnam, our military forces were constrained by policies of gradualism and concern about escalating the war to bring in the Soviet Union or China; these constraints will not apply in the Persian Gulf."

References: Aspin, Rep. Les, chairman, "The Military Option: The Conduct and Consequences of War in the Persian Gulf," a white paper of the Committee on Armed Services, U.S. House of Representatives, 8 January 1991, 23–24; Hoagland, Jim, "Congress, Bush and the Generals," *Washington Post,* 22 November 1990, A31.

War Powers Act

Congress's abrogation of its oversight responsibility after the passage of the Gulf of Tonkin Resolution, which authorized to President Lyndon B. Johnson "unlimited means" to conduct the Vietnam War, led to the passage of this still controversial legislation on 7 November 1973. Although vetoed by President Richard Nixon, both houses of Congress overrode the veto.

The War Powers Act, introduced by Senator Jacob K. Javits in the Senate and cosponsored by 58 other senators, establishes a standard set of guidelines for congressional notification when and if a president decides to commit American troops to a combat zone. American leaders since George Washington have dealt with the issue of whether a chief executive can undertake American foreign policy without congressional approval; in 1793, Secretary of State Thomas Jefferson conceded that even Washington's issuing of a proclamation of American neutrality (in the ongoing war between Britain and France at that time) was "an encroachment on the congressional war power." Presidents since Richard Nixon have resisted triggering the War Powers Act itself, labeling it an infringement of the president's powers as commander in chief as set forth in Article II, section 2 of the U.S. Constitution.

Congressional debate surrounding the resolution approving the beginning of Operation Desert Storm was both heated and partisan, but in the end, both houses of Congress sanctioned the use of force by American troops.

The Supreme Court has yet to determine whether or not the War Powers Act is constitutional. However, in *Woods v. Miller Company* (U.S., 1948), Supreme Court Justice Robert H. Jackson wrote, "No one will question that [the war] power is the most dangerous one to free government in the whole catalogue of powers. It usually is invoked in haste and excitement when calm legislative consideration of constitutional limitation is difficult. It is executed in a time of patriotic fervor that makes moderation impossible. And, worst of all, it is interpreted by judges under the influence of the same passions and pressures."

See also Appendix 4, The War Powers Act, 7 November 1973; Joint Congressional Resolution, on the Use of Force in the Persian Gulf, 12 January 1991; Letter from President George Bush to Speaker of the House Thomas S. Foley, 18 January 1991; Congressional Debate.
References: Javits, Jacob K., with Don Kellerman, *Who Makes War: The President versus Congress* (New York: Morrow, 1973), 22; Shane, Peter M., and Harold H. Bruff, *The Law of Presidential Power: Cases and Materials* (Durham, NC: Carolina Academic Press, 1988), 642–645.

Westland Lynx

This Anglo-French helicopter served on several frigates with the British marine fleet during Operations Desert Shield and Desert Storm.

The Westland Lynx is powered by two Rolls-Royce Gem 2 turboshaft engines, each providing 900 shaft horsepower. The craft seats two crew (pilot and copilot or observer), and can carry up to ten troops. With an overall length of 49 feet 9 inches (15.17 m), the Lynx's maximum speed is 205 mph (330 km/h) with an unrefueled range of 475 miles (764 km). Armaments comprise an assortment of missiles, cannons, or torpedoes. Variants of the copter include the AH.1 (British army), HAS.2 (British Royal Navy and French navy), and the HT.Mk 3 Trainer used by the British Royal Air Force.

References: Polmar, Norman, ed., *World Combat Aircraft Directory* (Garden City, NY: Doubleday, 1976), 338–339; Taylor, John W. R., *Jane's All the World's Aircraft, 1980–81* (London: Jane's Publications, 1980), 255–257.

Women, Role of, in Operations Desert Shield/Desert Storm

For the first time in American history, women played an integral role in military operations. The Pentagon's official summary on the war reported to Congress: "By late February [1991], more than 37,000 military women were in the Persian Gulf, making up approximately 6.8 percent of U.S. forces. By service, there were approximately 26,000 Army, 3,700 Navy, 2,200 Marine, and 5,300 Air Force women deployed." And "while many flew helicopters and reconnaissance aircraft," it was "as a matter of law and policy [that] women were excluded from certain specific combat military occupational specialties."

Women were not just a part of the military buildup for Operations Desert Shield and Desert Storm—they became part of the fabric of the war itself. Although women were not situated in positions where they could engage or be engaged by the enemy, several women were killed, including three during the Scud attack on 25 February 1991 that leveled a military barracks, and two others in military missions. For the first time in American history, among Allied prisoners of war were two women, Specialist Melissa A. Coleman and Major Rhonda L. Cornum, both serving with the U.S. Army. Four women who served with the Marines were given the Combat Action Ribbon, awarded to those who have been attacked by and have returned fire on the enemy.

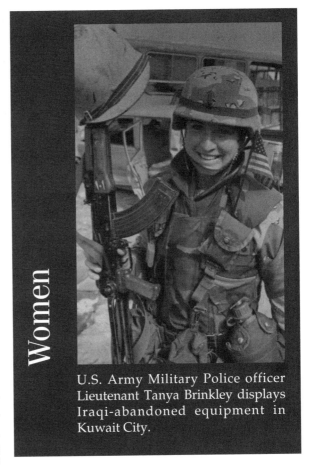

U.S. Army Military Police officer Lieutenant Tanya Brinkley displays Iraqi-abandoned equipment in Kuwait City.

References: Conduct of the Persian Gulf War: Final Report to Congress, Report by the Department of Defense, April 1992, 647; Elicott, Susan, "American Forces: Pentagon Reviews Role of Women," *London Times,* 5 March 1991, 7; Jolidon, Laurence, "Females on the Front Lines: No Easy Task," *USA Today,* 13 December 1990, 5A; Priest, Dana, "Women at the Front: Gulf War More Diverse Than in Past Wars," *Washington Post,* 1 March 1991, A1, A31; Terry, Don, "Scud's Lethal Hit Takes First 3 Female Soldiers," *New York Times,* 28 February 1991, A13.

Yemen

Yemen and the Sudan were the two most vocal Arab nations in defense of Saddam Hussein. Although their governments claimed that thousands of Yemeni citizens and Sudanese enlisted as part of Saddam Hussein's army, and some Yemeni and Sudanese troops were captured, Allied forces estimate that at most a few hundred people from both countries served with Iraqi forces. "Support from these quarters was more in the nature of a nuisance to the coalition than an actual threat," the U.S. Department of Defense reported on the situation. "However, because of the long-standing border disputes between Saudi Arabia and Yemen, that country's alignment with Iraq had to be treated as a potentially serious threat. A Yemeni invasion of southern Saudi Arabia or western Oman could not have succeeded; however, such a move would have diverted resources and attention away from the primary threat. Saudi Arabia remained concerned about potential threats to the kingdom's security from the Sudan and Yemen throughout Operations Desert Shield and Desert Storm. Saudi concerns led to the expulsion of hundreds of thousands of Yemenis—a problem that continues in Saudi-Yemeni relations."

Reference: Conduct of the Persian Gulf War: Final Report to Congress, Report by the Department of Defense, April 1992, 25.

Yuhanna, Mikhail
See Aziz, Tariq Mikhail.

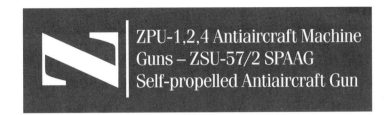

ZPU-1, ZPU-2, ZPU-4 Antiaircraft Machine Guns

Essentially a 14.5 mm Vladimirov KPV machine gun anchored to a multi-legged carriage, these antiaircraft machine guns were part of Iraq's ground defense force, but their effectiveness, considering that few allied aircraft were shot down, is considered inconclusive.

The ZPU series of AA machine guns originated with the ZPU-1, built just after World War II; the ZPU-2 and ZPU-4 models entered service together in 1949. All are two-wheeled, except for the ZPU-4, which has four wheels that lay flat on the ground to support the gun's weight. Weights for the vehicles range from 413 kg (911 pounds) for the ZPU-1 to 1,810 kg (3,990 pounds) for the ZPU-4. Outfitted with a crew of five (except the ZPU-1, which has a crew of four), this AA gun has a maximum range of 8,000 meters (26,247 feet, or 5 miles). The ZPU-4, the most modern of the guns, can fire as many as 4,800 rounds at one time.

References: Dupuy, Trevor N., et al., *How to Defeat Saddam Hussein: Scenarios and Strategies for the Gulf War* (New York: Warner Books, 1991), 168–169; Cullen, Tony, and Christopher F. Foss, eds., *Jane's Land-Based Air Defence, 1989–90,* (Coulsdon, Surrey, UK: Jane's Information Group, 1989), 213–215.

ZSU-23/4 Shilka Self-propelled Antiaircraft Gun

Built by the Soviet Union, the ZSU-23/4 was a staple of the Iraqi air defense. With a crew of four, the ZSU-23/4 gun is a four-barreled 23 mm cannon; it fires bursts of up to 50 rounds. It weighs 41,888 pounds (19,000 kg), and can travel on its chassis at a maximum of 27 mph (43 km/h).

The ZSU-23/4 (*Zenitnaia Samokhodnaia Ustanovka,* self-propelled antiaircraft mount) is so named because it has four 23 mm guns, hence 23/4. Shilka is Russian for "awl." In his *Bullseye: Iraq*, Dan McKinnon writes, "This weapon is a modified tank that is fully tracked, armor plated for protection of the crew, and self-propelled with a turret that can rotate 360 degrees in four to five seconds to easily track incoming bombers. It has a radar dish in the turret that seeks out and locks on aircraft targets at which the four 23 mm guns open fire. Each of the guns pumps out 400 rounds per minute which takes about seven seconds to reach the target. The guns are effective up to 10,000 feet (3,049 m). Accuracy of the fire greatly diminishes when the aircraft fly at speeds greater than 300 knots [350 mph; 560 km/h]."

Reference: McKinnon, Dan, *Bullseye: Iraq* (New York: Berkley, 1987), 145.

ZSU-57/2 SPAAG Self-propelled Antiaircraft Gun

This self-propelled antiaircraft gun was in the Iraqi military store, but its use during the Persian Gulf War remains unknown.

During the 1950s and 1960s, the ZSU series of guns were widely sold to the Soviet Union's client states, among them Iraq. Both the ZSU-23/4 and the ZSU-57/2, essentially antiaircraft guns mounted on a rotating turret atop a small tank chassis, found their way into Iraq's military. The ZSU-57/2 (*Zenitnaia Samokhodnaia Ustanovka,* self-propelled antiaircraft mount or gun) is so named because it has two 57 mm guns, hence 57/2.

In *Bullseye: Iraq*, Dan McKinnon's work on the Israeli attack on Iraq's Osirak nuclear complex, he writes of the ZSU-57/2: "This twin 57 mm [gun] fires about 100 rounds per minute from each barrel with a maximum effective range between 10,000 and 14,000 feet when visually directed. If radar directed, they can accurately hit aircraft in the 15,000 to 20,000 [foot] altitude [range]. When the shell explodes, lethal shrapnel blasts 30 feet in all directions, ripping apart any airplane. This weapon also fires orange and red tracers that look like flaming beer cans to the pilot. When the projectile explodes, the airburst gives a deadly white puff as the fragments seek to penetrate the skin of an airplane."

Reference: McKinnon, Dan, *Bullseye: Iraq* (New York: Berkley, 1987), 146.

Appendix Tables

Size of Nations Involved in the Persian Gulf War

Nation	Size (square miles)	Size (sq km)
Saudi Arabia	829,995	2,149,690
Iran	636,000	1,642,240
Egypt	386,900	1,002,000
Yemen (North and South)	203,645	528,106
Iraq	168,927	437,522
Oman	120,000	300,000
Syria	71,043	184,050
United Arab Emirates	30,000	77,700
Israel*	7,992	20,770
Kuwait	6,880	17,818
Qatar	4,000	10,400
Bahrain	267	691

*Marks 1949 boundaries. The West Bank and Gaza Strip add 2,759 square miles (7,145 sq km), with an additional 171 square miles (44 sq km) from the Golan Heights.

Populations and Economies of Nations Involved in the Persian Gulf War

Nation	Population (millions, 1990)	Per Capita GNP (1988 U.S.$)
Bahrain	.5	n.a.
Egypt	54.7	650
Iran	55.6	n.a.
Iraq	18.8	n.a.
Israel	5.2	8,650
Jordan	4.1	1,500
Kuwait	2.1	13,680
Oman	1.5	5,070
Qatar	.5	11,610
Saudi Arabia	15.0	6,170
Syria	12.6	1,670
Turkey	56.7	1,280
United Arab Emirates	1.6	15,720

Source: *Great Decisions 1991: The Middle East* (New York: Foreign Policy Association, 1991), 9.

Tanks and Armored Vehicles Sold to Iraq in the 1980s

Weapon	Total	Types
Main Battle Tanks	5,500	1,500 Soviet T-54s/55s/M-77s
		1,500 Chinese T-59s/69s
		1,000 Soviet T-62s
		1,000 Soviet T-72s
		470 American M-60s, M-47s
		30 British Chieftains
Light Tanks	100	Soviet PT-76s
Infantry Fighting Vehicles (IFVs)	1,500	Soviet BMPs
Armored Personnel Carriers (APCs)	6,000	Soviet BTR-50s, 60s, 152s, and MTLB
		Czech OT-62-64
		Chinese YW-531s
		French Panhard M-3s
		Brazilian EE-11s
		American M-113A1s/A2s
Self-propelled Artillery	500	Soviet 2S1 122mm
		American M-109 155mm
		French AUF-1 155mm
		Soviet 2S3 152mm

Source: "Iraq and Beyond: Post-Cold War Military Choices," *Congressional Quarterly's Editorial Research Reports* 1:42 (16 November 1990), 658.

Results of Scud Attacks

Target Result	Saudi Arabia	Israel	Bahrain
Total fired at	48	40	3
Missed target area	11	15	1
Intercepted by Patriot(s)	34	11	0
Hit target	0	13	0
Debris Hit	7	7	0
Missed Country	3	1	2
Direct Deaths	28*	2	0

*All 28 deaths were American servicemen and women in the barracks.

Accounting for the Iraqi Army

I: Rough Estimates

Assigned Strength: 547,000 (accounting for an estimate of all Iraqi divisions in the Kuwaiti Theatre of Operations [KTO] at normal strength).

Understrength: 186,000 (based on an average of 34 percent, arrived at through interviews with captured Iraqi officers, who estimated their own forces to be between 0 percent and 66 percent understrength).

Captured: 85,251 (63,000 by the United States, 22,251 by other Allied nations).

Deserted: Estimated at 153,000 (an average determined from conversations with senior Iraqi officers who were captured, who estimated that between 20 and 50 percent of their forces deserted from the KTO after the start of the air war and before the start of the ground war; this figures to about 42 percent for front line units).

Injured: 17,000 (based on EPW [enemy prisoner of war] interviews in which units suffered injuries from 2 percent to 16 percent; air war only).

Killed: (air war only): 9,000 (based on interviews with senior Iraqi officer EPWs; the numbers ranged from 1 percent to 6 percent in the Iraqi units; does not include ground war fatalities).

On Leave: Very few.

Escaped at the end of the ground war: Estimated at about 120,000 (aerial reconnaisance estimated that more than 100,000 men escaped back to Iraq, but because men cannot be counted from the air, the number is more a scientific estimate than a hard figure).

II: Estimated Breakdown of Iraqi Troop Strength

Assigned Strength:	547,000
Understrength:	185,000
Deserted:	153,000
Injured in Air War:	17,000
Killed in Air War:	9,000
Estimated Remainder at Start of Ground War:	183,000
Captured in Ground War:	85,251
Escaped/Killed in Ground War:	97,749

Source: "Defense for a New Era: Lessons of the Persian Gulf War," *Report for the House Armed Services Committee,* 1992, 29-33.

Number and Disposition of Armed Forces Deployed in the Persian Gulf

	Combat Troops	Aircraft	Warships
COALITION FORCES			
Argentina	100	0	2
Australia	0	0	2
Bangladesh	2,000	0	0
Belgium	0	0	4
Canada	0	24[1]	3
Czechoslovakia	170[2]	0	0
Denmark	0	0	1
Egypt	40,000[3]	0	0
France	15,200[4]	42[5]	21
Germany	0	0	18
Great Britain	25,000[6]	54[7]	31
Greece	0	0	2
Gulf Cooperation Council[8]	145,000	330	—
Honduras	150	0	0
Italy	0	10[9]	8
Morocco	1,200[10]	0	0
Netherlands	0	0	8
Niger	480	0	0
Norway	0	0	1
Pakistan	7,000[11]	0	0
Poland	0	0	2
Portugal	0	0	1
Senegal	500	0	0
Sierra Leone	500	0	0
Spain	0	0	6
Syria	15,000[12]	0	0
Soviet Union	0	0	4
United States	425,000	1,200	66
IRAQI FORCES[13]	540,000	665[14]	174[15]

[1] CF-18 Hornets only.
[2] Antichemical warfare troops.
[3] 5,000 Egyptians were based in the United Arab Emirates.
[4] The number includes 4,000 rapid deployment troops and 1,200 antichemical warfare troops.
[5] Broken down as 24 Jaguars and 18 Mirages.
[6] Includes the First Armoured Division as well as 9,000 support troops.
[7] Broken down as 42 Tornado and 12 Jaguar fighters.
[8] Includes Bahrain, Kuwait, Saudi Arabia, Oman, Qatar, and the United Arab Emirates.
[9] All were Tornado fighter-bombers.
[10] Another 3,500 were stationed in the United Arab Emirates.
[11] Plus an additional 2,000 stationed in the United Arab Emirates; up to 6,000 more arrived by the start of the air war.
[12] Includes an undetermined number stationed in the United Arab Emirates.
[13] Total estimated number deployed to the entire Kuwait Theatre of Operations (KTO).
[14] Some of these were shot down in dogfights with coalition aircraft, others were destroyed in their hangars, but many escaped to Iran.
[15] Includes no major battleships. Many of these were patrol boats used for harassment and armed attacks.

Sources: Allen, Thomas B., F. Clifton Berry, and Norman Polmar, *CNN: War in the Gulf: From the Invasion of Kuwait to the Day of Victory and Beyond* (Atlanta, GA: Turner Publishing, 1991), 97; Friedman, Norman, *Desert Victory: The War for Kuwait* (Annapolis, MD: Naval Institute Press, 1991), 310-319.

KC-10 Extender and KC-135 missions

Desert Shield (7 Aug–16 Jan)	Desert Storm (17 Jan–5 Mar)	After Desert Storm (5 Mar–3 April)
17,000+ sorties	16,000+ sorties	2,200+ sorties
75,000+ flying hours	64,000+	12,000+
33,500+ refuelings	49,000+	3,700+
70 million gals. of fuel used	120 million gals. of fuel used	8.4 million gals. of fuel used

Operation Desert Storm Air-to-Air Victories by Joint Coalition Forces, 17 January to 28 February 1991

From 17 January 1991 until the end of the war, allied pilots shot down 32 Iraqi airplanes and 5 Iraqi helicopters utilizing a varied inventory of missiles and guns. The units involved were the 33d Tactical Fighter Wing (TFW), the 36th Tactical Fighter Wing, the Royal Saudi Air Force, Fighter Strike Squadron (VFA) 81, the 32d Tactical Fighter Group, the 926th Tactical Fighter Group, Fighter Squadron (VF) 1, and the Tenth Tactical Fighter Wing.

Date	Unit	Shooter Aircraft	Type Downed	Weapon Used
17 Jan.	33 TFW	F-15C	MiG-2	AIM-7
17 Jan.	1 TFW	F-15C	F-1 Mirage	AIM-7
17 Jan.	33 TFW	F-15C	2 F-1 Mirages	AIM-7 (both)
17 Jan.	33 TFW	F-15C	MiG-29	AIM-7
17 Jan.	33 TFW	F-15C	MiG-29	AIM-7
17 Jan.	VFA-81	F/A-18	MiG-21	AIM-9
17 Jan.	VFA-81	F/A-18	MiG-21	AIM-7
19 Jan.	33 TFW	F-15C	MiG-25	AIM-7
19 Jan.	33 TFW	F-15C	MiG-25	AIM-7
19 Jan.	33 TFW	F-15C	MiG-29	AIM-7
19 Jan.	33 TFW	F-15C	MiG-29	AIM-7
19 Jan.	33 TFW	F-15C	F-1 Mirage	AIM-7
19 Jan.	33 TFW	F-15C	F-1 Mirage	AIM-7
24 Jan.	RSAF	F-15C	2 F-1 Mirages	AIM-9 (both)
26 Jan.	33 TFW	F-15C	MiG-23	AIM-7
26 Jan.	33 TFW	F-15C	MiG-23	AIM-7
26 Jan.	33 TFW	F-15C	MiG-23	AIM-7
27 Jan.	36 TFW	F-15C	2 MiG-23s	AIM-9 (both)
27 Jan.	36 TFW	F-15C	MiG-23	AIM-7
27 Jan.	36 TFW	F-15C	F-1 Mirage	AIM-7
28 Jan.	32 TFG	F-15C	MiG-23	AIM-7
29 Jan.	33 TFW	F-15C	MiG-23	AIM-7
2 Feb.	36 TFW	F-15C	IL-76	AIM-7
6 Feb.	36 TFW	F-15C	2 SU-25s	AIM-9 (both)
6 Feb.	36 TFW	F-15C	2 MiG-21s	AIM-9 (both)
6 Feb.	926 TFG	A-10	helicopter*	gun
6 Feb.	VF-1	F-14A	helicopter*	AIM-9
7 Feb.	33 TFW	F-15C	2 SU-20s	AIM-7 (both)
7 Feb.	33 TFW	F-15C	SU-20	AIM-7
7 Feb.	36 TFW	F-15C	helicopter*	AIM-7
11 Feb.	36 TFW	F-15C	helicopter*	AIM-7
15 Feb.	10 TFW	A-10	MI-8 helicopter	gun

*Signifies helicopter that could not be identified.

Source: *Conduct of the Persian Gulf War: Final Report to Congress (Pursuant to Title V of the Persian Gulf Conflict Supplemental Authorization and Personnel Benefits Act of 1991)*, Report by the Department of Defense, April 1992, 160; Polmar, Norman, *The Naval Institute Guide to the Ships and Aircraft of the U.S. Fleet* (Annapolis, MD: Naval Institute Press, 1993), 374.

Human Shields by Nation and Location

Country	In Kuwait	In Iraq
Argentina	51 (in both)	
Australia	90	69
Austria	70	70
Bangladesh	59,800	15,000
Belgium	21	38
Brazil	?	450
Canada	500	200
Chile	7 (in both)	
China	3,000	5,000
Cyprus	30	10
Czechoslovakia	26	366
Denmark	83	17
Egypt	120,000	1,200,000
Finland	23	23
France	290	270
Germany	290	450
Greece	180	47
Hong Kong	19	0
Hungary	5	182
India	172,000	10,000
Indonesia	709	?
Iran	40,000	0
Ireland	50	300
Italy	152	350
Japan	278	230
Luxembourg	2	4
Malaysia	10	10
Mexico	17 (in both)	
Morocco	6,000	30,000
Netherlands	83	150
New Zealand	11	24
Norway	17	35
Pakistan	30,000	15,000
Phillipines	45,000	3,000
Poland	40	2,700
Portugal	50	50
South Korea	96	612
Soviet Union	534	7,830
Spain	106	34
Sri Lanka	85,000	?
Sweden	120	40
Switzerland	71	69
Syria	30,000	N.A.
Taiwan	41	?
Thailand	5,600	6,200
Tunisia	1,565	2,000
Turkey	2,480	4,800
United Kingdom	4,000	640
United States	2,500	600
Yugoslavia	300	7,000
Palestinians	300,000	170,000
TOTAL	910,000	1,485,000

Source: Freedman, Lawrence, and Efraim Karsh, *The Gulf Conflict: Diplomacy and War in the New World Order* (Princeton, NJ: Princeton University Press, 1993), 140.

U.S. Casualty List

OPERATION DESERT SHIELD

Adams, Thomas Ray, Jr., 20, Marine lance corporal, Baton Rouge, Louisiana

Avey, Hans Christian Richard, 21, Army p.f.c., Okangan, Washington State

Bates, Tommie William, 27, Army captain, Coventry, Rhode Island

Belliveau, Michael Louis, 24, Navy, Evansville, Indiana

Betz, Dennis William, 22, Marine sergeant, Alliance, Ohio

Blue, Tommy Angelo, 33, Army sergeant, Spring Lake, North Carolina

Bnosky, Jeffrey John, 25, Army captain, Monongahela, Pennsylvania

Brooks, Tyrone Michael, 19, Navy, Detroit, Michigan

Brown, Christopher Bernard, 19, Navy, Leslie, Georgia

Brown, Darrell Kenneth, 19, Navy, Rockford, Illinois

Caldwell, Thomas Robert, 32, Air Force captain, Columbus, Ohio

Calloway, Kevin Lee, 20, Army p.f.c., Arpin, Wisconsin

Campisi, John Francis, 30, Air Force staff sergeant, West Covina, California

Carrington, Monray Corzere, 22, Navy seaman, North Braddock, Pennsylvania

Chinburg, Michael Leo, 26, Air Force captain, Durham, New Hampshire

Clark, Larry Marcellous, 21, Navy seaman, Decatur, Georgia

Clark, Steven Douglas, 22, Army specialist, Cedar Rapids, Iowa

Cronin, William David, Jr., 29, Marine captain, Elmhurst Dupage, Illinois

Cunningham, James Bernard, 22, Marine lance corporal, Glendale, Arizona

Danielson, Donald, 35, Army sergeant, Sylvania, Ohio

Dees, Tatiana, 34, Army sergeant, Congers, New York

Delgado, Delwin, 26, Navy, Jacksonville, Florida

Diffenbaugh, Thomas Michael, 34, Marine warrant officer, Bakersfield, California

Dillon, Gary Scott, 29, Marine captain, Concord, New Hampshire

Dolvin, Kevin Ray, 29, Marine captain, Canton, Ohio

Fleming, Anthony Javanne, 25, Navy, Buffalo, New York

Fontaine, Gilbert A., 22, Navy seaman, Spring Valley, New York

Gilliland, David Alan, 21, Navy, Warrenburg, Missouri

Hampton, Tracy, 26, Army sergeant, Tutwiler, Mississippi

Hancock, Joe Henry, Jr., 39, Army lieutenant colonel, Nashville, Tennessee

Henderson, Barry Keith, 40, Air Force major, Tuscumbia, Alabama

Hills, Kevin John, 19, Navy, Genoa, Illinois

Hogan, Larry Gene, 33, Marine sergeant, Montgomery, Alabama

Hook, Peter Samuel, 25, Air Force major, Bishop, California

Horwath, Raymond Louis, Jr., 26, Marine corporal, Waukegan, Illinois

Hurley, William Joseph, 27, Marine captain, Chicago, Illinois

Hutchison, Mark Edward, 27, Navy, Elkins, West Virginia

Huyghue, Wilton L., 20, Navy seaman, St. Thomas, Virgin Islands

Jackson, Arthur, 36, Army staff sergeant, Brent, Alabama

Jackson, Timothy Jerome, 20, Navy, Anniston, Alabama

James, Jimmy Wesley, 22, Army, Willingboro, New Jersey

Jock, Dale William, 28, Navy, Malone, New York

Jones, Alexander, 19, Navy, St. Louis, Missouri

Jones, Daniel Mooers, 19, Navy, Wakefield, Massachusetts

Keller, Kenneth Thomas, Jr., 26, Marine sergeant, Glenview, Illinois

Kelley, Shannon Patrick, 23, Army 2nd lieutenant, Gulf Breeze, Florida

Kemp, Nathaniel Henry, 18, Navy, Greenwood, Florida

Kilkus, John Robert, 26, Marine staff sergeant, Norwood, Massachusetts

Lamoureux, Dustin Craig, 20, Army p.f.c., Bremerton, Washington

Lupatsky, Daniel, 22, Navy, Centralia, Pennsylvania

Mahan, Gary Wayne, 23, Army specialist, Bellmead, Texas

Manns, Michael Nunnally, Jr., 23, Navy seaman, Bowling Green, Virginia

McCreight, Brent Allen, 23, Navy seaman, Brooklyn, New York

McDougle, Melvin Dennis, 35, Army sergeant, Fayetteville, North Carolina

McKinsey, Daniel Clayton, 21, Navy, Hanover, Pennsylvania

Monroe, Michael Neal, 27, Marine 1st lieutenant, Seattle, Washington

Monsen, Lance Milo, 25, Marine staff sergeant, Pembine, Wisconsin

Moran, Thomas Joseph, 29, Marine staff sergeant, Cornwells Heights, Pennsylvania

Mullin, Jeffrey Edward, 24, Army staff sergeant, Weymouth, Massachusetts

Neel, Randy Lee, 19, Navy, Albuquerque, New Mexico

Nelson, Rocky John, 21, Air Force airman 1st class, New Auburn, Wisconsin

Noonan, Robert Allan, 21, Army specialist, Cincinnati, Ohio

Parker, Fred Russell, Jr., 24, Navy, Reidsville, North Carolina

Plummer, Marvin Jerome, 27, Navy, Detroit, Michigan

Poulet, James Bernard, 34, Air Force captain, San Carlos, California

Ried, Frederick Arthur, 32, Air Force captain, Harrisburg, Pennsylvania

Rivers, Ernest, 26, Marine sergeant, Burton, South Carolina

Romei, Timothy William, 22, Marine corporal, San Francisco, California

Schiedler, Matthew James, 20, Navy, Hubbard, Oregon

Schramm, Stephen Gerald, 43, Air Force lieutenant colonel, Birmingham, Alabama

Seay, Timothy Bernard, 22, Navy, Thomaston, Georgia

Settimi, Jeffrey A., 25, Navy, Ft. Wayne, Indiana

Shukers, Jeffrey Warren, 28, Navy, Union, Iowa

Smith, James Arthur, Jr., 22, Navy, Somerville, Tennessee

Snyder, John Mather, 25, Navy lieutenant, Shelton,Connecticut

Speicher, Jeffrey William, 20, Army p.f.c., Camp Hill, Pennsylvania

Stewart, Anthony Deshawn, 19, Marine lance corporal, Yonkers, New York

Stewart, Roderick Ternail, 20, Navy seaman, Shreveport, Louisiana

Thomas, Phillip Jesse, 25, Navy, Chapel Hill, North Carolina

Vigrass, Scott Nolie, 28, Army p.f.c., Batavia, New York

Volden, Robert Lee, 38, Navy, Rego Park, New York

Weaver, Brian Paul, 22, Navy, Lockport, New York

Wilcher, James, 25, Army sergeant, Crystal Springs, Mississippi

Wilkinson, Philip L., 35, Navy, Savannah, Georgia

OPERATION DESERT STORM

Alaniz, Andy, 20, Army specialist, Corpus Christi, Texas

Allen, Frank Choai, 22, Marine lance corporal, Walanae, Hawaii

Allen, Michael Ray, 31, Marine lance corporal, West Point, Mississippi

Ames, David Robert, 29, Army staff sergeant, Schuyler, New York

Anderson, Michael Fredrick, 36, chief warrant officer 3rd class, Frankfort, Indiana

Applegate, Tony Ray, 28, Army sergeant, Portsmouth, Ohio

Arteaga, Jorge Isaac, 26, Air Force captain, Trumbull,Connecticut

Atherton, Steven Eric, 26, Army specialist, Nurmine, Pennsylvania

Auger, Alan Randy, 22, Marine lance corporal, Worcester, Massachusetts

Awalt, Russell Frank, 34, sergeant first class, Lynchburg, Tennessee

Bartusiak, Stanley Walter, 34, Army specialist, Romulus, Michigan

Bates, Donald Ray, 43, Army staff sergeant, College Park, Georgia

Beaudoin, Cindy Marie, 20, Army specialist, Plainfield, Connecticut

Belas, Lee Arthur, 22, Army sergeant, Port Orchard, Washington

Benningfield, Alan Harden, 22, Navy, Evansville, Indiana

Bentzlin, Stephen Eric, 23, Marine corporal, Wood Lake, Minnesota

Benz, Kurt Allen, 22, Marine corporal, Garden City, Michigan

Bianco, Scott Francis, 21, Marine corporal, Troy, Missouri

Bland, Thomas Clifford, Jr., 26, Air Force captain, Gaithersburg, Maryland

Blessinger, John Perry, 33, Air Force staff sergeant, Suffolk, New York

Boliver, John August, Jr., 27, Army specialist, Monongahela, Pennsylvania

Bongiorni, Joseph Phillip, III, 20, Army sergeant, Morgantown, West Virginia

Bowers, Tyrone Roneya, 33, Army specialist, Trenton, New Jersey

Bowman, Charles Leroy, Jr., 20, Army specialist, Manchester, Maryland

Boxler, John Thomas, 44, Army sergeant, Johnstown,Pennsylvania

Brace, William Carl, 24, Army specialist, Bath, Pennsylvania

Bradt, Douglas Lloyd, 29, Air Force captain, Houston, Texas

Bridges, Cindy DeAnna Jane, 20, Army p.f.c., Trinity, Alabama

Brilinski, Roger Paul, Jr., 24, Army sergeant, Ossineke, Michigan

Brogdon, Tracey Darlene, 27, Army sergeant, Bartow, Florida

Brown, James Robert, 26, Army specialist, Dade City, Florida

Budzian, Steven A., 21, Navy sergeant, Waterbury, Connecticut

Buege, Paul Garfield, 43, Air Force master sergeant, Milwaukee, Wisconsin

Bunch, Ricky Lee, 29, Army staff sergeant, Corbin Whitley, Kentucky

Burt, Paul Lawrence, 24, Army sergeant, Hingham, Massachusetts

Butch, Michael Richard, 25, Navy, Aurora, Colorado

Butler, Tommy Don, 22, Army specialist, Amarillo, Texas

Butts, William Thomas, 30, Army staff sergeant, Waterford, Connecticut

Carr, Jason Charles, 24, Army sergeant, Halifax, Virginia.

Carranza, Hector, Jr., 38, Army lieutenant colonel, Herndon, Virginia

Cash, Clarence Allen, 20, Army specialist, Ashland, Ohio

Chapman, Christopher Jones, 25, Army staff sergeant, Charlotte, North Carolina

Clark, Barry Maxwell, 26, Air Force sergeant, Fairhope, Alabama

Clark, Beverly Sue, 23, Army specialist, Armagh, Pennsylvania

Clark, Otto Frank, 35, Army master sergeant, Corinth, New York

Codispodo, Edward Michael, 25, Marine lance corporal, Philadelphia, Pennsylvania

Cohen, Gerard Anthony, 30, Army p.f.c., St. Louis, Missouri

Collins, Melford Ray, 34, Army p.f.c., Uhland, Texas

Connelly, Mark Alan, 34, Army major, Lancaster, Pennsylvania

Conner, Michael Ray, Sr., 32, Marine staff sergeant, CastroValley, California

Connor, Patrick Kelly, 25, Navy lieutenant, Columbia, Missouri

Cooke, Barry Thomas, 35, Navy lieutenant commander, Austin, Texas

Cooke, Michael Dennis, 22, Marine corporal, Montgomery County, Pennsylvania

Cooper, Ardon Bradley, 23, Army p.f.c., Seattle, Washington

Cooper, Charles William, 33, Army captain, St. Charles,Illinois

Cormier, Dale Thomas, 30, Air Force captain, Crystal Lake, Illinois

Costen, William Thompson, 27, Navy lieutenant, St. Louis, Missouri

Cotto, Ismael, 27, Marine corporal, Bronx, New York

Crask, Gary Wayne, 21, Army specialist, Cantrall, Illinois

Craver, Alan Brent, 32, Army sergeant, Penn Hills, Pennsylvania

Crockford, James Frederick, 30, Navy, Venice, California

Cronquist, Mark Richard, 20, Army specialist, Columbia Falls, Montana

Cross, Shirley Marie, 36, Navy, Fountain, Florida

Crumby, David Ray, Jr., 26, Army sergeant, Long Beach, California

Curtain, John Joseph, 52, Army chief warrant officer, Brooklyn, New York

Dailey, Michael Craig, Jr., 19, Army p.f.c., Klamath Falls, Oregon

Damian, Roy Tydingo, Jr., 21, Army specialist, Toto, Guam

Daniel, Candace Morgan, 20, Army p.f.c., West Palm Beach, Florida

Daniels, Michael David, 20, Army specialist, Ft. Leavenworth, Kansas

Daugherty, Robert Lawrence, Jr., 20, Army p.f.c., Hollywood, Florida

Davila, Manuel Michael, 22, Army specialist, Gillette, Wyoming

Davis, Marty Revohn, 19, Army p.f.c., Salina, Kansas

Delagneau, Rolando Adolfo, 30, Army corporal, Gretna, Louisiana

Delgado, Luis Roberto, 30, Army specialist, Laredo, Texas

Dierking, Ross Alan, 25, Army sergeant, Lakewood, New York

Dillon, Young Min, 27, Army sergeant, Aurora, Colorado

Donaldson, Patrick Anthony, 30, Army chief warrant officer, Houston, Texas

Dougherty, Joseph Douglas III, 20, Marine lance corporal, St. Petersburg, Florida

Douthit, David Allen, 41, Army lieutenant colonel, Herndon, Virginia

Douthit, David Quentin, 24, Army sergeant, Tacoma, Washington

Durrell, Robert Lee, 29, Army sergeant, Ashland, Alabama

Dwyer, Robert John, 32, Navy lieutenant, Worthington, Ohio

Edwards, Jonathan Ross, 34, Marine captain, Athens, Ohio

Eichenlaub, Paul Richard, II, 29, Air Force captain, Bentonville, Arkansas

Fails, Dorothy Lee, 25, Army private 2nd class, Taylor, Arizona

Fajardo, Mario, 29, Army captain, Flushing, New York

Farnen, Steven Paul, 22, Army specialist, Columbia, Missouri

Felix, Eliseo Celestino, 19, Marine lance corporal, Avondale, Arizona

Fielder, Douglas Lance, 22, Army specialist, Nashville, Tennessee

Finneral, George Scott, 21, Navy, Lowell, Massachusetts

Fitz, Michael Lloyd, 18, Army private 2nd class, Horicon, Wisconsin

Fleming, Joshua John, 20, Army p.f.c., Kent, Washington

Foreman, Ira Lynn, 30, Army sergeant, Sacramento, California

Fowler, John Clinton, 26, Army specialist, Beaumont, Texas

Galvan, Arthur, 33, Air Force captain, Newport Beach, California

Garrett, Mike Alan, 31, Army sergeant, Laurel, Mississippi

Garvey, Philip H., 39, Army chief warrant officer, Pensacola, Florida

Garza, Arthur Oscar, 20, Marine lance corporal, Houston, Texas

Gay, Pamela Yvette, 20, Army p.f.c., Spring Grove, Virginia

Gentry, Kenneth Blane, 32, Army staff sergeant, Ringgold, Virginia

Gillespie, John Howard, 34, Army major, Philadelphia, Pennsylvania

Godfrey, Robert Gary, 32. Army c.w.o., Phenix City, Alabama

Gologram, Mark Joseph, 23, Army sergeant, Homeworth, Ohio

Graybeal, Daniel Eugene, 25, Army captain, Johnson City, Tennessee

Gregory, Troy Lorenzo, 21, Marine lance corporal, Richmond, Virginia

Grimm, William David, 28, Air Force captain, Manhattan, Kansas

Guerrero, Jorge Luis, 21, Navy seaman, Chicago, Illinois

Haddad, Albert George, Jr., 22, Marine corporal, Lewisville, Texas

Haggerty, Thomas Joseph, 26, Army 1st lieutenant, West Harwich, Massachusetts

Hailey, Garland Vance, 27, Army staff sergeant, Baltimore, Maryland

Hansen, Steven Mark, 28, Army staff sergeant, Ludington, Michigan

Harris, Michael Anthony, Jr., Army sergeant, Pollocksville, North Carolina

Harrison, Timothy Roger, 31, Air Force staff sergeant, Maxwell, Iowa

Hart, Adrian Jay, 28, Army specialist, Albuquerque, New Mexico

Hatcher, Raymond Elijah, Jr., 32, Army staff sergeant, Monticello, Florida

Haws, Jimmy DeWayne, 28, Army staff sergeant, Traver, California

Hawthorne, James Dale, 24, Marine sergeant, Stinnett, Texas

Hector, Wade Elliott, 22, Army specialist, Newport, New Hampshire

Hedeen, Eric Douglas, 27, Air Force 1st lieutenant, Malaga, Washington

Hein, Kerry Peter, 28, Army chief warrant officer 2nd class, Daytona Beach, Florida

Hein, Leroy Emil, Jr., 22, Air Force sergeant, Sacramento, California

Henry<196>Garay, Luis A., 28, Army sergeant, Brooklyn, New York

Herr, David Rohrer, Jr., 28, Marine captain, Fort Worth, Texas

Heyden, James Paul, 24, Army specialist, Chicago, Illinois

Heyman, David Lawrence, 28, Army specialist, Hazelwood, Missouri

Hill, Timothy Eugene, 23, Army specialist, Detroit, Michigan

Hoage, Adam Todd, 19, Marine p.f.c., Corona, California

Hodges, Robert Kevin, 28, Ai Force sergeant, Panama City, Florida

Holland, Donnie Ray, 42, Air Force lieutenant colonel, Bastrop, Louisiana

Hollen, Duane Writner, Jr., 24, Army specialist, Bellwood, Pennsylvania

Hollenbeck, David Clarence, 19, Army specialist, Buncombe, North Carolina

Holt, William Aaron, 26, Navy, Sand Springs, Oklahoma

Holyfield, Ron Randall, 21, Navy, Junction City, Louisiana

Howard, Aaron Winship, 20, Army p.f.c., Battle Creek, Michigan

Hughes, Robert Joseph, 35, Army chief warrant officer 3rd class, Vernon, Connecticut

Hurley, Patrick Robert, 37, Army, New Douglas, Illinois

Hutto, John Wesley, 19, Army p.f.c., Andalusia, Alabama

Jackson, Kenneth Jerome, 22, Army p.f.c., Concord, North Carolina

Jackson, Mark David, 27, Navy lieutenant, Washburn, Maine

Jarrell, Thomas Randall, 20, Army specialist, Alexander City, Alabama

Jenkins, Thomas Allen, 20, Marine lance corporal, Coulterville, California

Joel, Daniel Dean, 23, Marine corporal, Fairbault, Minnesota

Jones, Glen Dean, 21, Army specialist, Grand Rapids, Michigan

Jones, Phillip John, 21, Marine corporal, Atlanta, Georgia

Kamm, Jonathan Hall, 25, Army sergeant, Mason, Ohio

Kanuha, Damon Valentine Keaw, 28, Air Force staff sergeant, San Diego, California

Keough, Frank Scott, 22, Army specialist, North Huntington, Pennsylvania

Kidd, Anthony Wayne, 21, Army specialist, Lima, Ohio

Kime, Joseph Gordon, III, 38, Army captain, Charlestown, West Virginia

King, Jerry Leon, 20, Army p.f.c., Winston-Salem, North Carolina

Kirk, Reuben Gideon, III, 19, Army p.f.c., Dunlow, West Virginia

Koritz, Thomas Flagg, 37, Air Force major, Davenport, Iowa

Kramer, David Walter, 20, Army p.f.c., Palm Desert, California

Kutz, Edwin Brian, 26, Army sergeant, Sunnymead, California

Lake, Victor Theodore, Jr., 22, Marine corporal, Marmet, West Virginia

Lane, Brian Lee, 20, Marine lance corporal, Bedford, Indiana

Lang, James Michael, 20, Marine lance corporal, Oxon Hill, Maryland

Larson, Thomas Stewart, 30, Navy lieutenant, St. James, New York

Lawton, Lorraine Kerstin, 28, Army 2nd lieutenant, West Lafayette, Indiana

Lee, Richard Ruffin, 36, Army chief warrant officer 3rd class, Independence, Missouri

Linderman, Michael Eugene, Jr., 19, Marine lance corporal, Silverdale, Washington

Lindsey, J. Scott, 27, Army specialist, Diamond Springs, California

Long, William Edward, 40, Army major, Frankford, Delaware

Lumpkins, James Henry, 22, Marine lance corporal, New Richmond, Ohio

McCarthy, Eugene Thomas, 35, Marine major, Brooklyn, New York

McCoy, James Robert, 29, Army corporal, Wilmington, Delaware

McKnight, Bobby Lewis, 52, Army specialist, Dallas, North Carolina

Madison, Anthony Erik, 27, Army specialist, Monessen, Pennsylvania

Maks, Joseph Dillon, 38, Army 1st lieutenant, Roseburg, Oregon

Malak, George Nassif, 34, Army warrant officer 1st class, Santa Monica, California

Martin, Christopher Andre, 29, Army warrant officer 1st class, Chino, California

Mason, Steven Glen, 23, Army specialist, Paragould, Arkansas

Matthews, Kelly Lynn, 28, Army sergeant, Buckley, Michigan

May, James Blaine, II, 40, Air Force, Jonesboro, Tennessee

Mayes, Christine Lynn, 23, Army specialist, Rochester Mills, Pennsylvania

Middleton, Jeffrey Thomas, 26, Army specialist, Decatur, Indiana

Miller, James Robert, Jr., 20, Army specialist, Decatur, Indiana

Miller, Mark Alan, 20, Army p.f.c., Cannelton, Indiana

Mills, Michael Ward, 23, Army specialist, Jefferson, Iowa

Mills, Randal Craig, 29, Army sergeant, Waynesboro, Mississippi

Mitchell, Adrienne Lynette, 20, Army p.f.c., Moreno Valley, California

Mitchem, Earnest Frank, Jr., 41, Army sergeant first class, Granite City, Illinois

Mobley, Phillip Dean, 26, Army specialist, Blue Springs, Missouri

Moller, Nels Andrew, 23, Army sergeant, Paul, Idaho

Mongrella, Garett Adam, 25, Marine sergeant, Belividere, New Jersey

Montalvo, Candelario, Jr.25, Marine sergeant, Eagle Pass, Texas

Morgan, Donald Wayne, 30, Army staff sergeant, Ford, Virginia

Morgan, John Kendall, 28, Army warrant officer 1st class, Bellevue, Washington

Murphy, Donald Thomas, Jr., 34, Army sergeant first class, Munhall, Pennsylvania

Murphy, Joe, 57, Army sergeant 1st class, Roosevelt, New York

Murray, James Clarence, Jr., 20, Army p.f.c., Conroe, Texas

Myers, Donald Ray, 29, Army specialist, Paducah, Kentucky

Noble, Shawnacee Loren, 18, Army p.f.c., Albany, New York

Noline, Michael A., 20, Marine p.f.c., Phoenix, Arizona

O'Brien, Cheryl Lorraine, 24, Army sergeant, Long Beach, California

Oelschlager, John Lee, 28, Air Force, Pensacola, Florida

Oliver, Arthur Dwayne, 20, Marine lance corporal, College Park, Georgia

Olson, Jeffry Jon, 37, Air Force captain, Grand Fork, North Dakota

Olson, Patrick Brian, 25, Air Force first lieutenant, Washington, North Carolina

Ortiz, Patbouvier Enrique, 27, Army staff sergeant, Brooklyn, New York

Pack, Aaron Alan, 22, Marine corporal, Phoenix, Arizona

Paddock, John Michael, 43, Navy chief warrant officer 4th class, Indianapolis, Indiana

Palmer, William Fitzgerald, 23, Army specialist, Hillsdale, Michigan

Patterson, Anthony Troy, 22, Army private, Oxnard, California

Paulson, Dale Leonard, 36, Army p.f.c., Sacramento, California

Perry, Kenneth James, 23, Army specialist, Lake Waccamaw, North Carolina

Phillips, Kelly D., 22, Army sergeant, Madison Heights, Michigan

Phillis, Stephen Richard, 30, Air Force captain, Rock Island, Illinois

Plasch, David Gordon, 23, Army warrant officer, Portsmouth, New Hampshire

Plunk, Terry Lawrence, 25, Army first lieutenant, Lexington, Virginia

Poole, Ramono Levias, 21, Air Force, Muscle Shoals, Alabama

Poremba, Kip Anders, 21, Marine lance corporal, Springfield, Virginia

Porter, Christian Jay, 20, Marine lance corporal, Wood Dale, Illinois

Powell, Dodge Randell, 28, Army sergeant, Hollywood, Florida

Rainwater, Norman Ray, Jr., 35, Army specialist, Erin, Tennessee

Randazzo, Ronald Milton, 24, Army sergeant, Glen Burnie, Maryland

Reel, Jeffrey David, 21, Army specialist, Vincennes, Indiana

Reichle, Hal Hooper, 27, Army chief warrant officer 2nd class, Marietta, Georgia

Rennison, Ronald David, 21, Army specialist, Dubuque, Iowa

Ritch, Todd Christopher, 20, Army private second class, Charlestown, New Hampshire

Rivera, Manuel, Jr., 31, Marine captain, Bronx, New York

Robinette, Stephen Ray, 35, Army staff sergeant, Saraland, Alabama

Robson, Michael Robert, 30, Army staff sergeant, Seminole, Florida

Rodriquez, Eloy Angel, Jr., 34, Army master sergeant, Key West, Florida

Rollins, Jeffrey Allan, 23, Army staff sergeant, Bountiful, Utah

Rossi, Marie Therese, 32, Army major, Oradell, New Jersey

Rush, Scott Alan, 19, Army p.f.c., Blaine, Minnesota

Russ, Leonard Allen, 26, Army staff sergeant, Pleasantville, New Jersey

San Juan, Archimedes Panabe, 21, Marine lance corporal, Newport News, Virginia

Sanders, Henry Junior, 42, Army sergeant, Cocoa, Florida

Sapien, Manuel Bernardo, Jr., 22, Army specialist, Denver, Colorado

Satchel, Baldwin Lovell, 21, Army staff sergeant, Courtland, Alabama

Schmauss, Mark John, 29, Air Force staff sergeant, Waggaman, Louisiana

Scholand, Thomas James, 20, Marine lance corporal, Spencerport, New York

Schroeder, Scott Arthur, 20, Marine p.f.c., Milwaukee, Wisconsin

Scott, Brian Patrick, 22, Army sergeant, Park Falls, Wisconsin

Shaw, David Alan, 33, Marine staff sergeant, Harrisville, Michigan

Shaw, Timothy Alan, 21, Army p.f.c., Suitland, Maryland

Sherry, Kathleen Marie, 23, Army 2nd lieutenant, Tonawanda, New York

Siko, Stephen Julius, 24, Army specialist, Latrobe, Pennsylvania

Simpson, Brian Keith, 22, Army captain, Indianapolis, Indiana

Smith, James Melvin, Jr., 51, Army staff sergeant, Ft. Mitchell, Alabama

Smith, Michael Sean, 25, Army sergeant, Erie, Pennsylvania

Smith, Russell Griffin, Jr., 44, Army sergeant, Fall River, Massachusetts

Snyder, David Timothy, 21, Marine lance corporal, Kenmore, New York

Speicher, Michael Scott, 33, Navy lieutenant commander, Jacksonville, Florida

Spellacy, David, 28, Marine captain, Washington, Ohio

Squires, Otha Bennett, Jr., 23, Army specialist, Indianapolis, Indiana

Stephens, Christopher Hoyt, 27, Army staff sergeant, Houston, Texas

Stephens, John Bradley, 26, Army staff sergeant, Morristown, Tennessee

Stephenson, Dion James, 22, Marine p.f.c., Bountiful, Utah

Stokes, Adrian Leonard, 20, Army p.f.c., Riverside, California

Stone, Thomas Gerald, 20, Army specialist, Falconer, New York

Streeter, Gary Eugene, 39, Army sergeant 1st class, Manhattan, Kansas

Strehlow, William Allen, 27, Army sergeant, Kenosha, Wisconsin

Stribling, Earl K., 35, Army major, Gilbert, Louisiana

Summerall, Roy Junior, 29, Army staff sergeant, Ocala, Florida

Swano, Peter Lawrence, Jr., 20, Army specialist, Salem, New York

Swartzendruber, George Richard, 24, Army chief warrant officer 2nd class, San Diego, California

Sylvia, James Henry, Jr., 23, Marine corporal, Putnam, Connecticut

Talley, Robert D., 18, Army p.f.c., Newark, New Jersey

Tapley, David Lloyd, 38, Army sergeant first class, Winston, California

Tatum, James David, 22, Army specialist, Athens, Tennessee

Thorp, James Kevin, 30, Marine captain, Louisville, Kentucky

Tillar, Donaldson Preston, III, 25, Army first lieutenant, Miller School, Virginia

Tormanen, Thomas Robert, 22, Marine lance corporal, Cokato, Minnesota

Trautman, Steven Robert, 21, Army sergeant first class, Houstonia, Missouri

Turner, Charles John, 29, Navy lieutenant, Richfield, Michigan

Underwood, Reginald Courtney, 33, Marine captain, Lexington, Kentucky

Valentine, Craig Eugene, 26, Navy lieutenant junior grade, Augusta, Michigan

Valentine, Roger Edward, 19, Army private, Memphis, Tennessee

Vega<196>Velazquez, Mario, 35, Army staff sergeant, Ponce, Puerto Rico

Viquez, Carlos Alberto, 47, Army lieutenant colonel, Bronx, New York

Wade, Robert Curtis, 31, Army p.f.c., Hackensack, New Jersey

Waldron, James Eric, 25, Marine lance corporal, Jeannett, Pennsylvania

Walker, Charles Scott, 19, Army p.f.c., Jonesboro, Georgia

Walker, Daniel B., 20, Marine lance corporal, Flint, Texas

Wallington, Michael Craig, 39, Army lieutenant colonel, Gibsonia, Pennsylvania

Walls, Frank James, 20, Army specialist, Hawthorne, Pennsylvania

Walrath, Thomas Eugene, 25, Army specialist, Santiara Springs, New York

Walters, Dixon Lee, Jr., 29, Air Force captain, Columbia, South Carolina

Wanke, Patrick Anthony, 20, Army p.f.c., Watertown, Wisconsin

Ware, Bobby Maurice, 21, Army specialist, New Bern, North Carolina

Weaver, Paul Jennings, 34, Air Force major, Alamosa, Colorado

Wedgwood, Troy Mitchell, 22, Army specialist, The Dalles, Oregon

Welch, Lawrence Norman, 31, Army sergeant, Chisholm, Minnesota

West, John Doege, 22, Navy seaman, West Fork, Arkansas

Whittenburg, Scotty Lynn, 22, Army sergeant, Carlisle, Arkansas

Wieczorek, David Mark, 21, Army p.f.c., Gentry, Arkansas

Wilbourn, James Newton, III, 29, Marine captain, Huntsville, Alabama

Williams, Jonathan Mathew, 23, Army corporal, Portsmouth, Virginia

Winkle, Corey Lee, 21, Army p.f.c., Lubbock, Texas

Winkley, Bernard Sean, 27, Marine chief warrant officer 2nd class, Kennebec, Maine

Witzke, Harold Paul, III, 28, Army staff sergeant, Caroga Lake, New York

Wolverton, Richard Vincent, 22, Army specialist, Lattrobe, Pennsylvania

Worthy, James Earl, 22, Army specialist, Albany, Georgia

Wright, Kevin Edward, 22, Army sergeant, Louisville, Kentucky

Zabel, Carl Wesley, 25, Army specialist, Appleton, Wisconsin

Zeugner, Thomas C.M., 36, Army major, Petersburg, Virginia

Source: U.S. Active Duty Military Deaths, Alphabetical By Name, Operations Desert Shield/Desert Storm, as of February 1995, printout prepared by the Washington Headquarters Service, Directorate for Information Operations and Reports (DIOR), April 1995; *Fort Lauderdale Sun-Sentinel,* 10 March 1991, 8G, 9G.

American Casualties, Civil War
through Desert Storm

War or Battle Theatre	Strength	KIA	WIA	Total Casualties	Casualties per Day*
Civil War (1861-1865)	400,000	69,000	318,200	387,200	0.07
Little Big Horn (1876)	600	257**	44**	301**	25.08
Spanish-American War (1898)	50,000	272	1,600	1,872	0.02
World War I (1918)	990,000	37,568	224,089	261,657	0.45
World War II (1941-1945)	1,500,000	175,407	625,328	800,735	0.05
Korean War (1950-1953)	220,000	19,453	77,788	97,241	.04
Vietnam War (1965-1973)	240,000	23,373	104,032	127,405	0.03
Desert Storm (1991)	530,000	111	256	367	0.0016

*As a percentage of theatre strength.
**Does not include Native American casualties.
Source: *National Review,* 1 April 1991, 30.

Appendix
Glossary of English-Language Slang Words

Abdul—any Arab.

Area Denial Weapons—cluster bombs that wreak havoc over a particular zone.

BACK—acronym for the drill given to American soldiers in case they are captured: don't Bow in public, stay off the Air (in other words, avoid participating in enemy propaganda), don't admit Crimes, and don't Kiss them (your captors) goodbye.

Baldrick—British camp named after a character in the British television series Blackadder.

Ballistically Induced Aperture in the Subcutaneous Environment (BIASE)—a bullet hole in a human being.

BAM—big assed Marine; any female Marine.

Bang out—to eject from an aircraft.

BFPO—British Forces Post Office, the link between British soldiers in the Gulf and their families.

BMOs—black moving objects; derogatory term for Saudi women, who are forced by the Muslim religion to wear veils over the faces.

Boloed—destroyed, as in "that plane was boloed."

Bondook—British slang for their weapons.

Bovine scatology—General H. Norman Schwarzkopf's name for press reports on the war.

Boxed out—excluded from planning or exercises.

Brew up—the act of destroying an enemy tank.

British aces—the name for the British pilots who flew the Tornado during night-time raids into Iraq.

Cleansed—term used to describe the condition of the Saudi town of Khafji after Allied troops "cleansed" it of Iraqi soldiers.

Crabs—nickname given to the air forces of the coalition by other services, such as the Navy and Marines.

Crimp—squeezed (e.g., "The Iraqi oil spill has put a crimp in our water supply.")

CSR—combat stress reaction, the new official name for battle fatigue. It was called shell shock in World War I and is diagnosed as posttraumatic stress disorder for Vietnam veterans.

De-air—destroy the enemy's air defenses.

Dhobi—British term for washing up.

Dossbag—a British sleeping bag.

Environmental terrorism—invented strictly for the Gulf War, the first instance in which the destruction of the environment became part of a nation's war strategy.

EPW—enemy prisoner of war; used to distinguish them from Allied POWs.

Fizzog—face. In the desert, one had to "dhobi his fizzog" frequently.

Gobbling rods—British name for their knives, forks, and spoons.

Going up (or down) town—used to describe air missions, as in "going uptown to Baghdad."

Gonk—British term for going to sleep.

Hellacious—American term describing the combat that went on in Khafji.

High-speed, low-drag—emphasizing state-of-the-art technology, or respect for any thing or person.

Him—Saddam Hussein.

HMFIC—head military fucker in charge, the name used for senior officers.

Hog—troop name for the A-10 Thunderbolt II tank killer, known more commonly as the Warthog. Pilots were called hogdrivers.

Homer—troop name for Iraqi soldiers, named after the father figure in the cartoon series The Simpsons.

Humvee (also Hummer)—name for the M998 high-mobility, multipurpose wheeled vehicle, which became popular after the war when it was sold for civilian use in the United States.

Hunkering down—what the Iraqi Army did during the massive coalition air strikes that marked the first phase of Operation Desert Storm.

Intercontinent ordnance—bombs and artillery shells that fall wide of their targets and hit civilians.

JIB rats—nickname for journalists who worked through the Joint Information Bureau.

Johnny Weissmuller shower—a shower so cold that you scream like Tarzan.

Minging—troop talk for the state of (or lack of) cleanliness after being in the desert for an extended period of time. The British used the term "gopping" to describe their similar problem.

MOPP 4—the condition one is in after donning all the protective gear needed to be safe from chemical attack (named after Military Oriented Protective Posture). To reach MOPP 4 is to arrive at the highest state of readiness.

Mother of Battles Radio—Iraqi radio stations hastily set up in Kuwait to spew propaganda at the coalition troops in Saudi Arabia.

Mud movers—bomber pilots, as described by fighter pilots.

9-4—a chummy version of the trucker-oriented "10-4" of the 1970s.

Nuclear coffee—Saudi Arabian water given to the troops. Coffee, sugar, and other ingredients were added to kill its bad taste.

OBOGS—on-board oxygen-generating system; the air supply in the coalition aircraft.

Penguins—British name for the air force ground crews.

POL—petrol, oil, and lubricants.

REMF—rear echelon motherfucker. Name given to the men in the rear who were seen as protecting themselves.

RGs—Republican Guards.

Rope-a-dope tactics—surprise moves by the enemy.

Rotor-head—British term for a helicopter pilot.

The Rudolph Hess—British slang for the mess.

Sammy—Saddam Hussein.

Scenario-dependent, post-crisis development—what happens *after* the war.

Scud—British slang for a potato; a "spud."

Scud-a-Vision—CNN, the Cable News Network, noted for its round-the-clock coverage of the war.

Septic tanks—British slang for American troops, whom they referred to as Yanks.

Shreddies—British serviceman's underwear.

SLUD—the effect on the human body if one is not protected from a chemical weapons attack; an acronym for salivate, lachrymate, urinate and defecate.

Smooge (or Splooge)—the extrusion of smoke and other particles from an underground target, indicating that the pilot had hit the target's outside cover and had penetrated inside (e.g., "After dropping his bombs on the bunker, the pilot saw a massive explosion but no smooge"). This word is being tracked by the American Heritage Dictionary for possible future use.

Snake eaters—Special Forces troops.

Spammed—given an unpleasant task.

Splash—pilot jargon for a hit (e.g., "First Target: Splash! Second target: Splash!")

Suicide circles—American term for the often-confusing Saudi highway signs, which led to the deaths of about 13 Allied soldiers.

Switched on cookie—British slang for a good soldier.

Tread heads—tank drivers.

Tree eaters—Special Forces, or Green Berets.

Ulu—in the middle of nowhere.

Unhappy Teddy—British term for a sad soldier.

Unwelcome visit—British for any plunge into enemy territory.

Varks—shortened name for Aardvark, the unofficial name of the F117 Stealth fighter. Pilots were also called "varks."

Zoomie—anyone in the Air Force.

Source: "A to Z of Warspeak," *Sunday Times* (London), 3 February 1991, 18; Dickson, Paul, *War Slang: American Fighting Words and Phrases from the Civil War to the Gulf War* (New York: Pocket Books, 1994), 298–333; Dunnigan, James F., and Austin Bay, *From Shield to Storm: High-Tech Weapons, Military Strategy, and Coalition Warfare in the Persian Gulf* (New York: Morrow, 1992), 360–362; "The Two Sides of Warspeak," *Time* (25 February 1991), 13.

yat Allah—model or exemplar of God. A title and high rank given in Shi'a Islam.

Ayatollah or Ayatullah—the highest Shiite religious title; literally means "verses of Allah."

Ba'ath or Baath—rennaissance or resurrection

bint—daughter

daawa or dawa—call

din—faith

fatah—victory

hajj—pilgrimage to Mecca

Hashemite or Hashimite—literally "of the Prophet's Clan." All the members of this family claim direct lineage from the Prophet Mohammad. This includes the sons of the sharif Hussein of Mecca, who settled on the thrones of Syria and Iraq, and now rule Jordan.

hojatoislam or hojataislam—proof of Islam

ibn—son

islam—state or act of submission to the will of Allah

jihad—struggle or crusade in the name of Islam

majlis—assembly

mubarak—blessed

mujahid, mujahedin—those who carry on jihad

mullah—cleric

Muslim—one who accepts Islam

nasr—victory

Qadissiyat—site of epic battle between Arabs and Persians in A.D. 637.

quran/koran—Islamic holy book; literally means "recitation or discourse"

Safavid—dynasty that ruled Persia from 1500 to 1794. Its first ruler, Shah Ismail Safavi, was responsible for establishing Shi'a Islam as the official religion of Persia.

shah—king

sharif—literally, "a descendant of the Prophet."

shatt—river

sheikh, shaikh—title of respect bestowed on old, wise men

thalweg—the middle of a river

wathbah—uprising or revolt, applied specifically to the 1948 rebellion in Iraq against the signing of the Portsmouth Treaty.

Sources: Gowers, Andrew, and Tony Walker, *Behind the Myth: Yasser Arafat and the Palestinian Revolution* (New York: Olive Branch Press, 1991), viii–ix; Marr, Phebe, *The Modern History of Iraq* (Boulder, CO: Westview Press, 1985); Tapsell, R. F., comp., *Monarchs, Rulers, Dynasties and Kingdoms of the World* (New York: Facts on File, 1983), 116–117.

Appendix
Documents

Chronological List of Documents

Documents

Agreement between the British Government and Sheik Mubarak ibn Sabah Al-Sabah, the Sheik of Kuwait, 23 January 1899

Praise be to God alone [interpreted from *"Bissim Illah Ta'alah Shanuho,"* or "in the name of God Almighty"]—The object of writing this lawful and honourable bond is that it is hereby covenanted and agreed between Lieutenant-General Malcolm John Meade, I.S.C., Her Britannic Majesty's Political Resident, on behalf of the British Government on the one part, and Sheikh Mubarak-bin-Sheikh Subah, Sheikh of Koweit, on the other part, that the said Sheikh Mubarak-bin-Sheikh Subah of his own free will and desire does hereby pledge and bind himself, his heirs, and successors not to receive the Agent or Representative of any Power or Government at Koweit, or at any other place within the limits of his territory, without the previous sanction of the British Government; and he further binds himself, his heirs and successors not to cede, sell, lease, mortgage, or give for occupation or for any other purpose any portion of his territory to the Government or subjects of any other Power without the previous consent of Her Majesty's Government for these purposes. This engagement also to extend any portion of the territory of the said Sheikh Mubarak, which may now be in the possession of the subjects of any other Government.

In token of the conclusion of this lawful and honourable bond, Lieutenant-Colonel Malcolm John Meade, I.S.C., Her Britannic Majesty's Political Resident in the Persian Gulf, and Sheikh Mubarak-bin-Sheikh Subah, the former on behalf of the British Government and the latter on behalf of himself, his heirs and successors do each, in the presence of witnesses, affix their signatures on this, the tenth day of Ramazam 1316, corresponding with the twenty-third day of January 1899.

Reference: Lauterpacht, E., et al., eds., *The Kuwait Crisis: Basic Documents* (Cambridge, Eng.: Grotius Publications, 1991), 10.

Letter from British Foreign Secretary Sir Edward Grey to Paul Cambon, French Ambassador to Great Britain, Regarding the Sykes-Picot-Sazanov Agreement, 16 May 1916

Your Excellency,

I have the honour to acknowledge the receipt of your Excellency's note of the 9th instant, stating that the French Government accept the limits of a future Arab State, or Confederation of States, and of those parts of Syria where French interests predominate, together with certain conditions attached thereto, such as they result from recent discussions in London and Petrograd on the subject.

I have the honour to inform your Excellency in reply that the acceptance of the whole project, as it now stands, will involve the abdication of considerable British interests, but, since His Majesty's Government recognise the advantage to the general cause of the Allies entailed in producing a more favourable internal political situation in Turkey, they are ready to accept the arrangement now arrived at, provided that the cooperation of the Arabs is secured, and that the Arabs fulfill the conditions and obtain the towns of Homs, Hama, Damascus, and Aleppo.

It is accordingly understood between the French and British Governments—

1. That France and Great Britain are prepared to recognise and uphold an independent Arab State or a Confederation of Arab States in the areas (A) and (B) marked on the annexed map, under the suzerainty of an Arab chief. That in area (A) France, and in area (B) Great Britain shall alone supply advisers or foreign functionaries at the request of the Arab State or Confederation of Arab States.

2. That in the blue area France, and in the red area Great Britain, shall be allowed to establish such direct or indirect administration or control as they desire and as they may think fit to arrange with the Arab State or Confederation of Arab States.

3. That in the brown area there shall be established an international administration, the form of which is to be decided upon consultation with Russia, and subsequently in consultation with the other Allies, and the representatives of the Shereef of Mecca.

4. That Great Britain be accorded (1) the ports of Haifa and Acre, (2) guarantee of a given supply of water from the Tigris and Euphrates in area (A) for area (B). His Majesty's Government, on their part, undertake that they will at no time enter into negotiations for the cessation of Cyprus to any third Power without the previous consent of the French Government.

5. That Alexandretta shall be a free port as regards the trade of the British Empire, and that there shall be no discrimination in port charges or facilities as regards British shipping and British goods; that there shall be freedom of transit for British goods through Alexandretta and by railway through the blue area, whether those goods are intended for or originate in the red area, or (B) area, or area (A); and there shall be no discrimination, direct or indirect, against British goods on any railway or against British goods at any port serving the areas mentioned.

6. That in area (A) the Bagdad Railway shall not be extended southwards beyond Mosul, and in area (B) northwards beyond Sammara until a railway connecting Bagdad with Aleppo via the Euphrates Valley has been completed, and then only with the concurrence of the two Governments.

7. That Great Britain has the right to build, administer, and be sole owner of a railway connecting Haifa with area (B), and shall have a perpetual right to transport troops along such a line at all times.

It is to be understood by both Governments that this railway is to facilitate the connexion of Bagdad with Haifa by rail, and it is further understood that, if the engineering difficulties and expense entailed by keeping this connecting line in the brown area only make the project unfeasible, that the French Government shall be prepared to consider that the line in question may also traverse the polygon Banias-Keis Marib-Salkhad Tell Otsda-Mesmie before reaching area (B).

8. For a period of twenty years the existing Turkish customs tariff shall remain in force throughout the whole of the blue and red areas, as well as in areas (A) and (B), and no increase in the rates of duty or conversion from *ad valorem* to specific rates shall be made except by agreement between the two powers.

There shall be no interior customs barriers between any of the above-mentioned areas. The customs duties leviable of goods destined for the interior shall be collected at the port of entry and handed over to the administration of the area of designation.

9. It shall be agreed that the French Government will at no time enter into any negotiations for the cessation of their rights and will not cede such rights in the blue area to any third Power, except the Arab State or Confederation of Arab States, without the previous agreement of His Majesty's Government, who, on their part, will give similar undertaking to the French Government regarding the red area.

10. The British and French Governments as the protectors of the Arab State, shall agree that they will not themselves acquire and will not consent to a third Power acquiring territorial possessions in the Arabian peninsula, nor consent to a third Power installing a naval base either on the east coast, or on the islands, of the Red Sea. This, however, shall not prevent such adjustment of the Aden frontier as may be necessary in consequence of recent Turkish aggression.

11. The negotiations with the Arabs as to the boundaries of the Arab State or Confederation of Arab States shall be continued through the same channel as heretofore on behalf of the two Powers.

12. It is agreed that measures to control the importation of arms into the Arab territories will be considered by the two powers.

I have further the honour to state that, in order to make the agreement complete, His Majesty's Government are proposing to the Russian Government to exchange notes analogous to those exchanged by the latter and your Excellency's Government on the 26th April last. Copies of these notes will be communicated to your Excellency as soon as exchanged.

I would also venture to remind your Excel-

lency that the conclusion of the present agreement raises, for practical consideration, the question of the claims of Italy to share in any partition or rearrangement of Turkey in Asia, as formulated in article 9 of the agreement of the 26th April 1915, between Italy and the Allies.

His Majesty's Government further consider that the Japanese Government should be informed of the arrangements now concluded.

I have, &c.

E. Grey

Reference: Paul C. Helmreich, *From Paris to Sèvres: The Partition of the Ottoman Empire at the Peace Conference of 1919–1920* (Columbus: Ohio State University Press, 1974), 343–345.

The War Powers Act (now 50 U.S.C. 1541-48), as Introduced as Legislation on 7 November 1973

WAR POWERS RESOLUTION

Section 1. This joint resolution may be cited as the "War Powers Resolution."

PURPOSE AND POLICY

Sec. 2. (a) Congressional declaration

It is the purpose of this chapter to fulfill the intent of the framers of the Constitution of the United States and insure that the collective judgment of both the Congress and the President will apply to the introduction of United States Armed Forces into hostilities, or into situations where imminent involvement in hostilities is clearly indicated by the circumstances, and to the continued use of such forces in hostilities or in such situations.

(b) Congressional legislative power under necessary and proper clause

Under article I, section 8, of the Constitution, it is specifically provided that the Congress shall have the power to make all laws necessary and proper for carrying into execution, not only its own powers but also all other powers vested by the Constitution in the Government of the United States, or in any department or officer thereof.

(c) President executive power as Commander-in-Chief; limitation

The constitutional powers of the President as Commander-in-Chief to introduce United States Armed Forces into hostilities, or into situations where imminent involvement in hostilities is clearly indicated by the circumstances, are exercised only pursuant to (1) a declaration of war, (2) specific statutory authorization, or (3) a national emergency created by attack upon the United States, its territories or possessions, or its armed forces.

CONSULTATION

Sec. 3. The President in every possible instance shall consult with Congress before introducing United States

Armed Forces into hostilities or into situations where imminent involvement in hostilities is clearly indicated by the circumstances, and after every such introduction shall consult regularly with the Congress until United States Armed Forces are no longer engaged in hostilities or have been removed from such situations.

REPORTING

Sec. 4. Written Report; time of submission; circumstances necessitating submission; information reported

(a) In the absence of a declaration of war, in any case in which the United States Armed Forces are introduced—

(1) into hostilities or into situations where imminent involvement in hostilities is clearly indicated by the circumstances;

(2) into the territory, airspace or waters of a foreign nation, while equipped for combat, except for deployments which relate solely to supply, replacement, repair, or training of such forces; or

(3) in numbers which substantially enlarge United States Armed Forces equipped for combat already located in a foreign nation;

the President shall submit within 48 hours to the Speaker of the House of Representatives and to the President pro tempore of the Senate a report, in writing, setting forth—

(A) the circumstances necessitating the introduction of United States Armed Forces;

(B) the constitutional and legislative authority under which the introduction took place; and

(C) the estimated scope and duration of the hostilities or involvement.

(b) the President shall provide such other information as the Congress may request in the fulfillment of its constitutional responsibilities with respect to committing the Nation to war and to the use of the Armed Forces abroad.

(c) Whenever United States Armed Forces are introduced into hostilities or into any situation described in subsection (a) of this section, the President shall, so long as such armed forces continue to be engaged in such hostilities or situation, report to the Congress periodically on the status of such hostilities or situation as well as on the scope and duration of such hostilities or situation, but in no event shall he report to the Congress less often than once every six months.

CONGRESSIONAL ACTION

Sec. 5. Transmittal of report and referral to Congressional committees; joint request for convening Congress

(a) Each report submitted pursuant to section 4(a)(1) shall be transmitted to the Speaker of the House of Representatives and to the President pro tempore of the Senate on the same calendar day.—If, when the report is transmitted, the Congress has adjourned sine die or has adjourned for any period in excess of three calendar days, the Speaker of the House of Representatives and the President pro tempore of the Senate, if they deem it advisable (or if petitioned by at least 30 percent of the membership of their respective Houses) shall jointly request the President to convene Congress in order that it may consider the report and take appropriate action pursuant to this section.

(b) Within sixty calendar days after a report is submitted or is required to be submitted pursuant to section 4(a)(1), whichever is earlier, the President shall terminate any use of United States Armed Forces with respect to which such report was submitted (or required to be submitted), unless the Congress (1) has declared war or has enacted a specific authorization for such use of United States Armed Forces, (2) has extended by law such sixty-day period, or (3) is physically unable to meet as a result of an armed attack upon the United States. Such sixty-day period shall be extended for not more than an additional thirty days if the President determines and certifies to the Congress in writing that unavoidable military necessity respecting the safety of United States Armed Forces requires the continued use of such armed forces in the course of bringing about a prompt removal of such forces.

(c) Notwithstanding subsection (b), at any time that United States Armed Forces are engaged in hostilities outside the territory of the United States, its possessions and territories without a declaration of war or specific statutory authorization, such forces shall be removed by the President if the Congress so directs by concurrent resolution.

PRIORITY OF CONGRESSIONAL REACTION WITH RESPECT TO A JOINT RESOLUTION OR BILL

Sec. 6. Time requirement; referral to Congressional committee; single report; pending business; vote; referral to other House committee; disagreement between Houses

(a) Any joint resolution or bill introduced pursuant to section 5(b) of this resolution at least thirty calendar days before the expiration of the sixty-day period specified in such section shall be referred to the Committee on Foreign Affairs of the House of Representatives or the Committee on Foreign Relations of the Senate, as the case may be, and such committee shall report one such joint resolution or bill, together with its recommendations, not later than twenty-four calendar days before the expiration of the sixty-day period specified in each section, unless such House shall otherwise determine by the yeas and nays.

(b) Any joint resolution or bill so reported shall become the pending business of the House in question (in the case of the Senate the time for debate shall be equally divided between proponents and the opponents), and shall be voted on within three calendar days thereafter, unless such House shall otherwise determine by yeas and nays.

(c) Such joint resolution or bill passed by one House shall be referred to the Committee of the other House named in subsection (a) of this section and shall be reported out not later than fourteen calendar days before the expiration of the sixty-day period specified in section 5(b) of this resolution. The joint resolution or bill so reported shall become the pending business of the House in question and shall be voted on within three calendar days after it has been reported, unless such House shall otherwise determine by yeas and nays.

(d) In the case of any disagreement between the two Houses of Congress with respect to a joint resolution or bill passed by both Houses, conferees shall be promptly appointed and the committee of the conference shall make and file a report with respect to such resolution or bill not later than four calendar days before the expiration of the sixty-day period specified in section 5(b) of this resolution. In the event the conferees are unable to agree within 48 hours, they shall report back to their respective Houses in disagreement. Notwithstanding any rule in either House concerning the printing of conference reports in the Record or concerning any delay in consideration of such reports, such report shall be acted on by both Houses not later than the expiration of such sixty-day period.

PRIORITY OF CONGRESSIONAL REACTION WITH RESPECT TO A CONCURRENT RESOLUTION

Sec. 7. Referral to Congressional committee; single report; pending business; vote; referral to other House committee; disagreement between Houses;

(a) Any concurrent resolution introduced pursuant to section 5(b) of this resolution shall be referred to the Committee on Foreign Affairs of the House of Representatives or the Committee on Foreign Relations of the Senate, as the case may be, and one such concurrent resolution shall be reported out by such committee together with its recommendations within fifteen calendar days, unless such House shall otherwise determine by the yeas and nays.

(b) Any concurrent resolution so reported shall become the pending business of the House in question (in the case of the Senate the time for debate shall be equally divided between proponents and the opponents), and shall be voted on within three calendar days thereafter, unless such House shall otherwise determine by yeas and nays.

(c) Such a concurrent resolution passed by one House shall be referred to the committee of the other House named in subsection (a) of this section and shall be reported out by such committee within fifteen calendar days and shall thereupon become the pending business of such House and shall be voted upon within three calendar days, unless such House shall otherwise determine by yeas and nays.

(d) In the case of any disagreement between the two Houses of Congress with respect to a concurrent reso-

lution passed by both Houses, conferees shall be promptly appointed and the committee of conference shall make and file a report with respect to such concurrent resolution within six calendar days after the legislation is referred to the committee of conference. Notwithstanding any rule in either House concerning the printing of conference reports in the Record or concerning any delay in the consideration of such reports, such report shall be acted on by both houses not later than six calendar days after the conference report is filed. In the event the conferees are unable to agree within 48 hours, they shall report back to their respective Houses in disagreement.

INTERPRETATION OF JOINT RESOLUTION

Sec. 8. Inferences from any law or treaty; Joint headquarters operations of high-level military commands; introduction of United States Armed Forces; constitutional authorities or existing treaties unaffected; construction against grant of Presidential authority respecting use of United States Armed Forces.

(a) Authority to introduce United States Armed Forces into hostilities or into situations wherein involvement in hostilities is clearly indicated by the circumstances shall not be inferred—

(1) from any provision of law (whether or not in effect before the date of the enactment of this joint resolution) including any provision contained in any appropriation Act, unless such provision specifically authorizes the introduction of United States Armed Forces into hostilities or into such situations and states that it is intended to constitute specific statutory authorization within the meaning of this joint resolution; or

(2) from any treaty heretofore or hereafter ratified unless such treaty is implemented by legislation specifically authorizing the introduction of United States Armed Forces into hostilities or into such situations and stating that it is intended to constitute specific statutory authorization within the meaning of this joint resolution.

(b) Nothing in this chapter shall be construed to require any further specific statutory authorization to permit members of United States Armed Forces to participate jointly with members of the armed forces of one or more foreign countries in the headquarters operations of high-level military commands which were established prior to the enactment of this resolution, and pursuant to the United Nations Charter or any treaty ratified by the United States prior to such date.

(c) For purposes of this joint resolution, the term "introduction of United States Armed Forces" includes the assignment of members of such armed forces to command, coordinate, participate in the movement of, or accompany the regular or irregular military forces of any foreign country or government when such military forces are engaged, or there exists an imminent threat that such forces will become engaged, in hostilities.

(d) Nothing in this joint resolution—

(1) is intended to alter the constitutional authority of the Congress or of the President, or the provisions of existing treaties; or

(2) shall be construed as granting any authority to the President with respect to the introduction of United States Armed Forces into hostilities or into situations wherein involvement in hostilities is clearly indicated by the circumstances which authority he would not have had in the absence of this joint resolution.

SEPARABILITY CLAUSE

Sec. 9. If any provision of this joint resolution or the application thereof to any person or circumstance is held invalid, the remainder of the joint resolution and the application of such provision to any other person or circumstance shall not be affected thereby.

The Algiers Agreement, 6 March 1975

To settle the dispute over the Shatt al-Arab waterway, Saddam Hussein, then vice-president at Iraq's Revolutionary Command Council, and the shah of Iran met and signed the Algiers Agreement, which allowed Iraq to gain more access to the waterway and a cessation of the tension over it in exchange for an ending to Iranian support for anti-Iraq guerrillas in Iran.

During the convocation of the OPEC summit conference in the Algerian capital and upon the initiative of (Algerian) President Houari Boumedienne, the Shah of Iran and Saddam Hussein met twice and conducted lengthy talks on the relations between Iraq and Iran. These talks, attended by President Houari Boumedienne, were characterized by complete frankness and a sincere will from both parties to reach a final and permanent solution to all problems existing between the two countries in accordance with the principles of territorial integrity, border inviolability and non-interference in internal affairs.

The two High Contracting Parties have decided to:

First: Carry out a final delineation of their land boundaries in accordance with the Constantinople Protocol of 1913 and the Proceedings of the Border Delineation Commission of 1914.

Second: Demarcate their river boundaries according to the thalweg line.

Alleged Excerpts from the Saddam Hussein–April Glaspie Meeting in Baghdad, 25 July 1990

The following transcript of what is purported to be the Hussein-Glaspie dialogue held on 25 July 1990 was released by the Iraqi government on 22 September 1990. On 20 March 1991, in testimony before the Senate Foreign Relations Committee, Glaspie loudly denounced the transcript as "fabricated."

Saddam Hussein: I have summoned you today to hold comprehensive political discussion with you. This is a message to President Bush.

You know that we did not have relations with the U.S. until 1984 and you know the circumstances and reasons which caused them to be severed. The decision to establish relations with the U.S. were [sic] taken in 1980 during the two months prior to the war between us and Iran.

When the war started, and to avoid misinterpretation, we postponed the establishment of relations hoping that the war would end soon.

But because the war lasted for a long time, and to emphasize the fact that we are a non-aligned country, it was important to re-establish relations with the U.S. And we chose to do this in 1984.

It is natural to say that the U.S. is not like Britain, for example, with the latter's historic relations with Middle Eastern countries, including Iraq. In addition, there were no relations between Iraq and the U.S. between 1967 and 1984. One can conclude it would be difficult for the U.S. to have a full understanding of many matters in Iraq. When relations were re-established we hoped for a better understanding and for better cooperation because we too do not understand the background of many American decisions.

We dealt with each other during the war, and we had dealings on various levels. The most important of those levels were with the foreign ministers.

We had hoped for a better common understanding and a better chance of cooperation to benefit both our peoples and the rest of the Arab nations.

But these better relations have suffered from various rifts. The worst of these was in 1986, only two years after establishing relations, with what was known as Irangate, which happened during the year that Iran occupied the Fao peninsula.

It was natural then to say that old relations and complexity of interests could absorb many mistakes. But when interests are limited and relations are not that old, then there isn't a deep understanding and mistakes could leave a negative effect. Sometimes the effect of an error can be larger than the error itself.

Despite all of that, we accepted the apology, via his envoy, of the American President regarding Irangate, and we wiped the slate clean. And we shouldn't unearth the past except when new events remind us that old mistakes were not just a matter of coincidence.

Our suspicions increased after we liberated the Fao peninsula. The media began to involve itself in our politics. And our suspicions began to surface anew, because we began to question whether the U.S. felt uneasy with the outcome of the war when we liberated our land.

It was clear to us that certain parties in the United States—and I don't say the President himself—but certain parties who had links with the intelligence community and the State Department—and I don't say the Secretary of State himself—I say that these parties did not like the fact that we liberated our land. Some parties began to prepare studies entitled, "Who Will Succeed Saddam Hussein?" They began to contact gulf states to make them fear Iraq, to persuade them not to give Iraq economic aid. And we have evidence of these activities.

Iraq came out of the war burdened with $40 billion debts [sic], excluding the aid given by Arab states, some of whom consider that too to be a debt although they knew—and you knew too—that without Iraq they would not have had these sums and the future of the region would have been entirely different.

We began to face the policy of the drop in the price of oil. Then we saw the United States, which always talks of democracy but which has no time for the other point of view. Then the media campaign against Saddam Hussein was started by the official American media. The United States thought that the situation in Iraq was like Poland, Romania or Czechoslovakia. We were disturbed by this campaign but we were not disturbed too much because we hoped that, in a few months, those who are decision makers in America would have a chance to find the facts and see whether this media campaign had any effect on the lives of Iraqis. We had hoped that soon the American authorities would make the correct decision regarding their relations with Iraq. Those with good relations can sometimes afford to disagree.

But when planned and deliberate policy forces the price of oil down without good commercial interests, then that means another war against Iraq. Because military war kills people by bleeding them, and economic war kills their humanity by depriving them of their chance to have a good standard of living. As you know, we gave rivers of blood in a war that lasted eight years, but we did not lose our humanity. Iraqis have a right to live proudly. We do not accept that anyone could injure Iraqi pride or the Iraqi right to have high standards of living.

Kuwait and the UAE were at the front of this policy aimed at lowering Iraq's position and depriving its people of higher economic standards. And you know that our relations with the Emirates and Kuwait have been good. On top of that, while we were busy at war, the state of Kuwait began to expand at the expense of our territory.

You may say this is propaganda, but I would direct you to one document, the Military Patrol Line, which is the borderline endorsed by the Arab League in 1961 for military patrols not to cross the Iraq-Kuwait border.

But go and look for yourselves. You will see the Kuwaiti border patrols, the Kuwaiti farms, the Kuwaiti oil installations—all built as closely as possible to this line to establish that land as Kuwaiti territory.

Since then, the Kuwaiti Government has been stable while the Iraqi Government has undergone many changes. Even after 1968 and for 10 years afterwards, we were too busy with our own problems. First in the north, then the 1973 war [with Israel], and other problems. Then came the war with Iran which started 10 years ago.

We believe that the United States must understand that people who live in luxury and economic security can reach an understanding with the United States on what are legitimate joint interests. But the starved and the economically deprived cannot reach the same understanding.

We do not accept threats from anyone because we do not threaten anyone. But we say clearly that we hope that the U.S. will not entertain too many illusions and will see new friends rather than increase the number of its enemies.

I have read the American statements speaking of friends in the area. Of course, it is the right of everyone to choose their friends. We can have no objections. But you know you are not the ones who protected your friends during the war with Iran. I assure you, had the Iranians overrun the region, the American troops would not have stopped them, except by the use of nuclear weapons.

I do not belittle you. But I hold this view by looking at the geography and nature of America into account. Yours is a society that cannot accept 10,000 dead in one battle.

You know that Iran agreed to the cease-fire not because the United States bombed one of the oil platforms after the liberation of the Fao. Is this Iraq's reward for its role in securing the stability of the region and for protecting it from an unknown flood?

So what can it mean when America says it will now protect its friends? It can only mean prejudice against Iraq. This stance plus maneuvers and statements which have been made has encouraged the U.A.E. and Kuwait to disregard Iraqi rights.

I say to you clearly that Iraq's rights, which are mentioned in the memorandum, we will take one by one. That might not happen now or after a month or after one year, but we will take it all. We are not the kind of people who will relinquish their rights. There is no historic right, or legitimacy, or need, for the UAE and Kuwait to deprive us of our rights. If they are needy, we too are needy.

The United States must have a better understanding of the situation and declare who it wants to have relations with and who its enemies are. But it should not make enemies simply because others have different points of view regarding the Arab-Israeli conflict.

We clearly understand America's statement that it wants an easy flow of oil. We understand America saying that it seeks friendship with the states in the region, and to encourage their joint interests. But we cannot understand the attempt to encourage some parties to harm Iraq's interests.

The United States wants to secure the flow of oil. This is understandable and known. But it must not deploy methods which the United States says it disapproves of—flexing muscles and pressure.

If you use pressure, we will deploy pressure and force. We know that you can harm us although we do not threaten you. But we too can harm you. Everyone can cause harm according to their ability and their size. We cannot come all the way to you in the United States, but individual Arabs may reach you.

You can come to Iraq with aircraft and missiles but do not push us to the point where we cease to care. And when we feel that you want to injure our pride and take away the Iraqis' chance of a high standard of living, then we will cease to care and death will be the choice for us. Then we would not care if you fired 100 missiles for each missile we fired. Because without pride life would have no value.

It is not reasonable to ask our people to bleed rivers of blood for eight years, then to tell them, "Now you have to accept aggression from Kuwait, the U.A.E., or from the U.S. for from Israel."

We do not put all these countries in the same boat. First, we are hurt and upset that such disagreement is taking place between us and Kuwait and the U.A.E. The solution must be found within an Arab framework and through direct bilateral relations. We do not place America among the enemies. We place it where we want our friends to be and we try to be friends. But repeated American statements last year made it apparent that America did not regard us as friends. Well, the Americans are free.

When we seek friendship we want pride, liberty and our right to choose.

We want to deal according to our status as we deal with others according to their statuses.

We consider the others' interests while we look after our own. And we expect the others to consider our interests while they are dealing with their own. What does it mean when the Zionist war minister is summoned to the United States now? What do they mean, these fiery statements coming out of Israel during the past few days, and the talk of war being expected now more than at any other time?

I do not believe that anyone would lose by making friends with Iraq. In my opinion, the American President has not made mistakes regarding the Arabs, although his decision to freeze dialogue with the P.L.O. was wrong. But it appears that this decision was made to appease the Zionist lobby or as a piece of strategy to cool the Zionist anger, before trying again. I hope that our latter conclusion is the correct one. But we will carry on saying it was the wrong decision.

You are appeasing the usurper in so many ways—economically, politically and militarily as well as in the media. When will the time come when, for every three appeasements to the usurper, you praise the Arabs just once?

April Glaspie: I thank you, Mr. President, and it is a great pleasure for a diplomat to meet and talk directly to the President. I clearly understand your message. We studied history at school. They taught us to say freedom or death. I think you know well that we as a people have our experience with the colonialists.

Mr. President, you mentioned many things during this meeting which I cannot comment on on behalf of my Government. But with your permission, I will comment on two points. You spoke of friendship and I believe it was clear from the letters sent by our President to you on the occasion of your National Day that he emphasizes—

Saddam Hussein: He was kind and his expressions met with our regard and respect.

April Glaspie: As you know, he directed the United States Administration to reject the suggestion of implementing trade sanctions.

Saddam Hussein: There is nothing left for us to buy from America. Only wheat. Because every time we want to buy something, they say it is forbidden. I am afraid that one day you will say, "You are going to make gunpowder out of wheat."

April Glaspie: I have a direct instruction from the President to seek better relations with Iraq.

Saddam Hussein: But how? We too have this desire. But matters are running contrary to this desire.

April Glaspie: This is less likely to happen the more we talk. For example, you mentioned the issue of the article published by the American Information Agency and that was sad. And a formal apology was presented.

Saddam Hussein: Your stance is generous. We are Arabs. It is enough for us that someone says, "I am sorry, I made a mistake." Then we carry on. But the media campaign continued. And it is full of stories. If the stories were true, no one would get upset. But we understand from its continuation that there is a determination.

April Glaspie: I saw the Diane Sawyer program on ABC. And what happened in that program was cheap and unjust. And this is a real picture of what happens in the American media—even to American politicians themselves. These are the methods the Western media employs. I am pleased that you add your voice to the diplomats who stand up to the media. Because your appearance in the media, even for five minutes, would help us make the American people understand Iraq. This would increase mutual understanding. If the American President had control of the media, his job would be much easier.

Mr. President, not only do I want to say that President Bush wanted better and deeper relations with Iraq, but he also wants an Iraqi contribution to peace and prosperity in the Middle East. President Bush is an intelligent man. He is not going to declare an economic war against Iraq.

You are right. It is true what you say that we do not want higher prices for oil. But I would ask you to examine the possibility of not charging too high a price for oil.

Saddam Hussein: We do not want too high prices for oil. And I remind you that in 1974 I gave Tariq Aziz the idea for an article he wrote which criticized the policy of keeping oil prices high. It was the first Arab article which expressed this view.

Tariq Aziz [interrupting]: Our policy in OPEC opposes sudden jumps in oil prices.

Saddam Hussein: Twenty-five dollars a barrel is not a high price.

April Glaspie: We have many Americans who would like to see the price go above $25 because they come from oil-producing states.

Saddam Hussein: The price at one stage had dropped to $12 a barrel. A reduction in the modest Iraqi budget of $6 billion to $7 billion is a disaster.

April Glaspie: I think I understand this. I have lived here for years. I admire your extraordinary efforts to rebuild your country. I know you need funds. We understand that and our opinion is that you should have the opportunity to rebuild your country. But we have no opinion of the Arab-Arab conflicts, like your border disagreement with Kuwait.

I was in the American Embassy during the late 1960s. The instruction we had during this period was that we should express no opinion on this issue and that the issue is not connected with America. James Baker has directed our official spokesman to emphasize this instruction. We hope you can solve this problem using any suitable methods via Klibi [Chadly Klibi, secretary-general of the League of Arab States] or via President Mubarak. All that we hope is that these issues are solved quickly. With regard to all of this, can I ask you to see how the issue appears to us?

My assessment after 25 years' service in this area is that your objective must have strong backing from your Arab brothers. I now speak of oil. But you, Mr. President, have fought through a horrific and painful war. Frankly, we can only see that you have deployed massive troops in the south. Normally that would not be any of our business. But when this happens in the context of what you said on your national day, then when we read the details in the two letters of the Foreign Minister, then when we see the Iraqi point of view that the measures taken by the U.A.E. and Kuwait is, in the final analysis, parallel to military aggression against Iraq, then it would be reasonable for me to be concerned. And for this reason, I received an instruc-

tion to ask you, in the spirit of friendship—not in the spirit of confrontation—regarding your intentions.

I simply describe the concern of my Government. And I do not mean that the situation is a simple situation. But our concern is a simple one.

Saddam Hussein: We do not ask people to be concerned when peace is at issue. This is a noble human feeling which we all feel. It is natural for you as a superpower to be concerned. But what we ask is not to express your concern in a way that would make an aggressor believe that he is getting support for his aggression.

We want to find a just solution which will give us our rights but not deprive others of their rights. But at the same time, we want the others to know that our patience is running out regarding their action, which is harming even the milk our children drink, and the pensions of the widow who lost her husband during the war, and the pensions of the orphans who lost their parents.

As a country, we have the right to prosper. We lost so many opportunities, and the others should value the Iraqi role in their protection. Events this Iraqi [indicates interpreter] feels bitter like all other Iraqis. We are not aggressors but we do not accept aggression either. We sent them envoys and handwritten letters. We tried everything. We asked the Servant of the Two Shrines—King Fahd—to hold a four-member summit, but he suggested a meeting between the Oil Ministers. We agreed. And as you know, the meeting took place in Jidda. They reached an agreement which did not express what we wanted, but we agreed.

Only two days after the meeting, the Kuwaiti Oil Minister made a statement that contradicted the agreement. We also discussed the issue during the Baghdad summit. I told the Arab Kings and Presidents that some brothers are fighting an economic war against us. And that not all wars use weapons and we regard this kind of war as a military action against us. Because if the capability of our army is lowered, then, if Iran renewed the war, it could achieve goals which it could not achieve before. And if we lowered the standard of our defenses, then this could encourage Israel to attack us. I said that before the Arab Kings and Presidents. Only I did not mention Kuwait and [the] U.A.E. by name, because they were my guests.

Before this, I had sent them envoys reminding them that our war had included their defense. Therefore the aid they gave us should not be regarded as a debt. We did no more than the United States would have done against someone who attacked its interests.

I talked about the same thing with a number of other Arab states. I explained the situation to brother King Fahd a few times, by sending envoys and on the telephone. I talked with brother King Hussein and with Sheik Zaid after the conclusion of the summit. I walked with the Sheik to the plane when he was leaving Mosul. He told me, "Just wait until I get home." But after he had reached his destination. the statements that came from there were very bad—not from him, but from his Minister of Oil.

Also after the Jidda agreement, we received some intelligence that they were talking of sticking to the agreement for two months only. Then they would change their policy. Now tell us, if the American President found himself in this situation, what would he do? I said it was very difficult for me to talk about these issues in public. But we must tell the Iraqi people who face economic difficulties who was responsible for that.

April Glaspie: I spent four beautiful years in Egypt.

Saddam Hussein: The Egyptian people are kind and good and ancient. The oil people are supposed to help the Egyptian people, but they are mean beyond belief. It is painful to admit it, but some of them are disliked by Arabs because of their greed.

April Glaspie: Mr. President, it would be helpful if you could give us an assessment of the effort made by your Arab brothers and whether they have achieved anything.

Saddam Hussein: On this subject, we agreed with President Mubarak that the Prime Minister of Kuwait would meet with the deputy chairman of the Revolution Command Council in Saudi Arabia, because the Saudis initiated contact with us, aided by President Mubarak's efforts. He just telephoned me a short while ago to say the Kuwaitis have agreed to that suggestion.

April Glaspie: Congratulations.

Saddam Hussein: A protocol meeting will be held in Saudi Arabia. Then the meeting will be transferred to Baghdad for deeper discussion directly between Kuwait and Iraq. We hope we will reach some result. We hope that the long-term view and the real interests will overcome Kuwaiti greed.

April Glaspie: May I ask you when you expect Sheik Saad to come to Baghdad?

Saddam Hussein: I suppose it would be on Saturday or Monday at the latest. I told brother Mubarak that the agreement should be in Baghdad Saturday or Sunday. You know that brother Mubarak's visits have always been a good omen.

April Glaspie: This is good news. Congratulations.

Saddam Hussein: President Mubarak told me they were scared. They said troops were only 20 kilometers north of the Arab League line. I said to him that regardless of what is there, whether they are police, border guards or army, and regardless of how many are there, and what they are doing, assure the Kuwaitis and give them our word that we are not going to do anything until we meet with them. When we meet and when we see that there is hope, then nothing will happen. But if we are unable to find a solution, then it will be natural

that Iraq will not accept death, even though wisdom is above everything else. There you have good news.

Tariq Aziz: This is a journalistic exclusive.

April Glaspie: I am planning to go to the United States next Monday. I hope I will meet with President Bush in Washington next week. I thought to postpone my trip because of the difficulties we are facing. But now I will fly on Monday.

Reference: "Excerpts from Iraqi Document on Meeting with U.S. Envoy," *New York Times,* 23 September 1990, A19.

The Complete U.N. Resolutions

RESOLUTION 660
August 2, 1990
The Security Council,

Alarmed by the invasion of Kuwait on 2 August 1990 by the military forces of Iraq,

Determining that there exists a breach of international peace and security as regards the Iraqi invasion of Kuwait,

Acting under Articles 39 and 40 of the Charter of the United Nations,

1. *Condemns* the Iraqi invasion of Kuwait;

2. *Demands* that Iraq withdraw immediately and unconditionally all its forces to the positions in which they were located on 1 August 1990;

3. *Calls upon* Iraq and Kuwait to begin immediately intensive negotiations for the resolution of their differences and supports all efforts in this regard, and especially those of the League of Arab States;

4. *Decides* to meet again as necessary to consider further steps to ensure compliance with the present resolution.

VOTE: 14 for, 0 against, 1 abstention (Yemen)

RESOLUTION 661
August 6, 1990
The Security Council,

Reaffirming its resolution 660 (1990) of 2 August 1990,

Deeply concerned that that resolution has not been implemented and that the invasion by Iraq of Kuwait continues with further loss of human life and material destruction,

Determined to bring the invasion and occupation of Kuwait by Iraq to an end and to restore the sovereignty, independence and territorial integrity of Kuwait,

Noting that the legitimate Government of Kuwait has expressed its readiness to comply with resolution 660 (1990),

Mindful of its responsibilities under the Charter of the United Nations for the maintenance of international peace and security,

Affirming the inherent right of individual or collective self-defense, in response to the armed attack by Iraq against Kuwait, in accordance with Article 51 of the Charter,

Acting under Chapter VII of the Charter of the United Nations,

1. *Determines* that Iraq so far has failed to comply with paragraph 2 of resolution 660 (1990) and has usurped the authority of the legitimate Government of Kuwait;

2. *Decides,* as a consequence, to take the following measures to secure compliance of Iraq with paragraph 2 of resolution 660 (1990) and to restore the authority of the legitimate Government of Kuwait;

3. *Decides* that all States shall prevent;

(a) The import into their territories of all commodities and products originating in Iraq or Kuwait exported therefrom after the date of the present resolution;

(b) Any activities by their nationals or in their territories which would promote or are calculated to promote the export or transshipment of any commodities or products from Iraq or Kuwait; and any dealings by their nationals or their flag vessels or in their territories in any commodities or products originating in Iraq or Kuwait and exported therefrom after the date of the present resolution, including in particular any transfer of funds to Iraq or Kuwait for the purposes of such activities or dealings;

(c) The sale or supply by their nationals or from their territories or using their flag vessels of any commodities or products, including weapons or any other military equipment, whether or not originating in their territories but not including supplies intended strictly for medical purposes, and, in humanitarian circumstances, foodstuffs, to any person or body in Iraq or Kuwait or to any person or body for the purposes of any business carried on in or operated from Iraq or Kuwait, and any activities by their nationals or in their territories which promote or are calculated to promote such sale or supply of such commodities or products;

4. *Decides* that all States shall not make available to the Government of Iraq or to any commercial, industrial or public utility undertaking in Iraq or Kuwait, any funds or any other financial or economic resources and shall prevent their nationals and any persons within their territories from removing from their territories or otherwise making available to that Government or to any such undertaking any such funds or resources and from remitting any other funds to persons or bodies within Iraq or Kuwait, except payments exclusively for strictly medical or humanitarian purposes and, in humanitarian circumstances, foodstuffs;

5. *Calls upon* all states, including States nonmembers of the United Nations, to act strictly in accordance with the provisions of the present resolution notwithstanding any contract entered into or license granted before the date of the present resolution;

6. *Decides* to establish, in accordance with rule 28 of the provisional rules of procedure of the Security Council, a Committee of the Security Council consisting of all the members of the Council, to undertake the following tasks and to report on its work to the Council with its observations and recommendations:

(a) To examine the reports on the progress of the implementation of the present resolution which will be submitted by the Secretary-General;

(b) To seek from all States further information regarding the action taken by them concerning the effective implementation of the provisions laid down in the present resolution;

7. *Calls upon* all States to cooperate fully with the Committee in the fulfillment of its task, including supplying such information as may be sought by the Committee in pursuance of the present resolution;

8. *Requests* the Secretary-General to provide all necessary assistance to the Committee and to make the necessary arrangements in the Secretariat for the purpose;

9. *Decides* that, notwithstanding paragraphs 4 through 8 above, nothing in the present resolution shall prohibit assistance to the legitimate Government of Kuwait, and *calls upon* all States:

(a) To take appropriate measures to protect assets of the legitimate Government of Kuwait and its agencies;

(b) Not to recognize any regime set up by the occupying Power,

10. *Requests* the Secretary-General to report to the Council on the progress of the implementation of the present resolution, the first report to be submitted within thirty days;

11. *Decides* to keep this item on its agenda and to continue its efforts to put an early end to the invasion by Iraq.

VOTE: 13 for, 0 against, 2 abstentions (Cuba and Yemen)

RESOLUTION 662
August 9, 1990
The Security Council,

Recalling its resolutions 660 (1990) and 661 (1990),

Gravely alarmed by the declaration by Iraq of "comprehensive and eternal merger" with Kuwait,

Demanding, once again, that Iraq withdraw immediately and unconditionally all its forces to the positions in which they were located on 1 August 1990,

Determined to bring the occupation of Kuwait by Iraq to an end and to restore the sovereignty, independence and territorial integrity of Kuwait,

Determined also to restore the authority of the legitimate Government of Kuwait,

1. *Decides* that annexation of Kuwait by Iraq under any form and whatever pretext has no legal validity, and is considered null and void;

2. *Calls upon* all States, international organizations and specialized agencies not to recognize that annexation, and to refrain from any action or dealing that might be interpreted as an indirect recognition of the annexation;

3. Further Demands that Iraq rescind its actions purporting to annex Kuwait;

4. Decides to keep this item on its agenda and to continue its efforts to put an early end to the occupation.

VOTE: Unanimous (15-0)

RESOLUTION 664
August 18, 1990
The Security Council,

Recalling the Iraqi invasion and purported annexation of Kuwait and resolutions 660, 661 and 662,

Deeply concerned for the safety and well-being of third state nationals in Iraq and Kuwait,

Recalling the obligations of Iraq in this regard under international law,

Welcoming the efforts of the Secretary-General to pursue urgent consultations with the Government of Iraq following the concern and anxiety expressed by the members of the Council on 17 August 1990,

Acting under Chapter VII of the United Nations Charter,

1. *Demands* that Iraq permit and facilitate the immediate departure from Kuwait and Iraq of the nationals of third countries and grant immediate and continuing access of consular officials to such nationals;

2. *Further* demands that Iraq take no action to jeopardize the safety, security or health of such nationals;

3. *Reaffirms* its decision in resolution 662 (1990) that annexation of Kuwait by Iraq is null and void, and therefore demands that the Government of Iraq rescind its orders for the closure of diplomatic and consular missions in Kuwait and the withdrawal of the immunity of their personnel, and refrain from any such actions in the future;

4. *Requests* the Secretary-General to report to the Council on compliance with this resolution at the earliest possible time.

VOTE: Unanimous (15-0)

RESOLUTION 665
August 25, 1990
The Security Council,

Recalling its resolutions 660 (1990), 661 (1990), 662 (1990) and 664 (1990) and demanding their full and immediate implementation,

Having decided in resolution 661 (1990) to impose economic sanctions under Chapter VII of the Carter of the United Nations,

Determined to bring an end to the occupation of Kuwait by Iraq which imperils the existence of a Member State and to restore the legitimate authority, the sovereignty, independence and territorial integrity of Kuwait which requires the speedy implementation of the above resolutions,

Deploring the loss of innocent life stemming from the Iraqi invasion of Kuwait and determined to prevent further such losses,

Gravely alarmed that Iraq continues to refuse to comply with resolutions 660 (1990), 661 (1990), 662 (1990) and 664 (1990) and in particular at the conduct of the Government of Iraq in using Iraqi flag vessels to export oil,

1. *Calls upon* those Member States cooperating with the Government of Kuwait which are deploying maritime forces to the area to use such measures commensurate to the specific circumstance as may be necessary under the authority of the Security Council to halt all inward and outward maritime shipping in order to inspect and verify their cargoes and destinations and to ensure strict implementation of the provisions related to such shipping laid down in resolution 661 (1990);

2. *Invites* Member States accordingly to cooperate as may be necessary to ensure compliance with the provisions of resolution 661 (1990) with maximum use of political and diplomatic measures, in accordance with paragraph 1 above;

3. *Requests* all States concerned to coordinate their actions in pursuit of the above paragraphs of this resolution using as appropriate mechanisms of the Military Staff Committee and after consultation with the Secretary-General to submit reports to the Security Council and its Committee established under resolution 661 (1990) to facilitate the monitoring of the implementation of this resolution;

4. *Further requests* the States concerned to coordinate their actions in pursuit of the above paragraphs of this resolution using as appropriate mechanisms of the Military Staff Committee and after consultation with the Secretary-General to submit reports to the Security Council and its Committee established under resolution 661 (1990) to facilitate the monitoring of the implementation of this resolution;

5. Decides to remain actively seized of the matter.

VOTE: 13 for, 0 against, 2 abstentions (Cuba and Yemen)

RESOLUTION 666
September 13, 1990
The Security Council,

Recalling its resolution 661 (1990), paragraphs 3 (c) and 4 of which apply, except in humanitarian circumstances, to foodstuffs,

Recognizing that circumstances may arise in which it will be necessary for foodstuffs to be supplied to the civilian population in Iraq or Kuwait in order to relieve human suffering,

Noting that in this respect the Committee established under paragraph 6 of that resolution has received communications from several Member States,

Emphasizing that it is for the Security Council, alone or acting through the Committee, to determine whether humanitarian circumstances have arisen,

Deeply concerned that Iraq has failed to comply with its obligations under Security Council resolution 664 (1990) in respect of the safety and well-being of third State nationals, and reaffirming that Iraq retains full responsibility in this regard under international humanitarian law including, where applicable, the Fourth Geneva Convention,

Acting under Chapter VII of the Charter of the United Nations,

1. *Decides* that in order to make the necessary determination whether or not for the purposes of paragraph 3 (c) and paragraph 4 of resolution 661 (1990) humanitarian circumstances have arisen, the Committee shall keep the situation regarding foodstuffs in Iraq and Kuwait under constant review;

2. *Expects* Iraq to comply with its obligations under Security Council resolution 664 (1990) in respect of third State nationals and reaffirms that Iraq remains fully responsible for their safety and well-being in accordance with international humanitarian law including, where applicable, the Fourth Geneva Convention;

3. *Requests,* for the purposes of paragraphs 1 and 2 of this resolution, that the Secretary-General seek urgently, and on a continuing basis, information from relevant United Nations and other appropriate humanitarian agencies and all other sources on the availability of food in Iraq and Kuwait, such information to be communicated by the Secretary-General to the Committee regularly;

4. *Requests* further that in seeking and supplying such information particular attention will be paid to such categories of persons who might suffer specially, such as children under 15 years of age, expectant mothers, maternity cases, the sick and the elderly;

5. *Decides* that if the Committee, after receiving the reports from the Secretary-General, determines that circumstances have arisen in which there is an urgent humanitarian need to supply foodstuffs to Iraq or Kuwait in order to relieve human suffering, it will report promptly to the Council its decision as to how such need should be met;

6. *Directs* the Committee that in formulating its decisions it should bear in mind that foodstuffs should be provided through the United Nations in cooperation with the international Committee of the Red Cross or their appropriate humanitarian agencies and distributed by them or under their supervision in order to ensure that they reach the intended beneficiaries;

7. *Requests* the Secretary-General to use his good offices to facilitate the delivery and distribution of foodstuffs to Kuwait and Iraq in accordance with the provisions of this and other relevant resolutions;

8. *Recalls* that resolution 661 (1990) does not apply to supplies intended strictly for medical purposes, but in this connection recommends that medical supplies should be exported under the strict supervision of the Government of the exporting State or by appropriate humanitarian agencies.

VOTE: 13 for, 0 against, 2 abstentions (Cuba and Yemen)

RESOLUTION 667
September 16, 1990
The Security Council,

Reaffirming its resolutions 660 (1990), 661 (1990), 662 (1990), 664 (1990), 665 (1990) and 666 (1990),

Recalling the Vienna Conventions of 18 April 1961 on diplomatic relations and of 24 April 1963 on consular relations, to both of which Iraq is a party,

Considering that the decision of Iraq to order the closure of diplomatic and consular missions in Kuwait and to withdraw the immunity and privileges of these missions and their personnel is contrary to the decisions of the Security Council, the international Conventions mentioned above and international law,

Deeply concerned that Iraq, notwithstanding the decisions of the Security Council and the provisions of the Conventions mentioned above, has committed acts of violence against diplomatic missions and their personnel in Kuwait,

Outraged at recent violations by Iraq of diplomatic premises in Kuwait and at the abduction of personnel enjoying diplomatic immunity and foreign nationals who were present in these premises,

Considering that the above actions by Iraq constitute aggressive acts and a flagrant violation of its international obligations which strike at the root of the conduct of international relations in accordance with the Charter of the United Nations,

Recalling that Iraq is fully responsible for any use of violence against foreign nationals or against any diplomatic or consular mission in Kuwait or its personnel,

Determined to ensure respect for its decisions and for Article 25 of the Charter of the United Nations,

Further considering that the grave nature of Iraq's actions, which constitute a new escalation of its violations of international law, obliges the Council not only to express its immediate reaction but also to consult urgently to take further concrete measures to ensure Iraq's compliance with Council's resolutions,

Acting under Chapter VII of the Charter of the United Nations,

1. *Strongly condemns* aggressive acts perpetrated by Iraq against diplomatic premises and personnel in Kuwait, including the abduction of foreign nationals who were present in those premises;

2. *Demands* the immediate release of those foreign nationals as well as all nationals mentioned in resolution 664 (1990);

3. *Further demands* that Iraq immediately and fully comply with its international obligations under resolutions 660 (1990), 662 (1990) and 664 (1990) of the Security Council, the Vienna Conventions on diplomatic and consular relations and international law;

4. *Further demands* that Iraq immediately protect the safety and well-being of diplomatic and consular personnel and premises in Kuwait and in Iraq and take no action to hinder the diplomatic and consular missions in the performance of their functions, including access to their nationals and the protection of their person and interests;

5. *Reminds* all States that they are obliged to observe strictly resolutions 661 (1990), 662 (1990), 664 (1990), 665 (1990) and 666 (1990);

6. *Decides* to consult urgently to take further concrete measures as soon as possible, under Chapter VII of the Charter, in response to Iraq's continued violation of the Charter, of resolutions of the Council and of international law.

VOTE: Unanimous (15-0)

RESOLUTION 669
September 24, 1990
The Security Council,

Recalling its resolution 661 (1990) of 6 August 1990,

Recalling also Article 50 of the Charter of the United Nations,

Conscious of the fact that an increasing number of requests for assistance have been received under the provisions of Article 50 of the Charter of the United Nations,

Entrusts the Committee established under resolution 661 (1990) concerning the situation between Iraq and Kuwait with the task of examining requests for assistance under the provisions of Article 50 of the Charter of the United Nations and making recommendations to the President of the Security Council for appropriate action.

VOTE: Unanimous (15-0)

RESOLUTION 670
September 25, 1990
The Security Council

Reaffirming its resolutions 660 (1990), 661 (1990), 662 (1990), 664 (1990), 665 (1990), 666 (1990), and 667 (1990);

Condemning Iraq's continued occupation of Kuwait, its failure to rescind its actions and end its purported annexation and its holding of third State nationals against their will, in flagrant violation of resolutions 660 (1990), 662 (1990), 664 (1990), and 667 (1990) and of international humanitarian law;

Condemning further the treatment by Iraqi forces of Kuwaiti nationals, including measures to force them to leave their own country and mistreatment of persons and property in Kuwait in violation of international law,

Noting with grave concern the persistent attempts to evade the measures laid down in resolution 661 (1990),

Further noting that a number of States have limited the number of Iraqi diplomatic and consular officials in their countries and that others are planning to do so,

Determined to ensure by all necessary means the strict and complete application of the measures laid down in resolution 661 (1990),

Determined to ensure respect for its decisions and the provisions of Articles 25 and 48 of the Charter of the United Nations,

Affirming that any acts of the Government of Iraq which are contrary to the above-mentioned resolutions or to Articles 25 or 48 of the Charter of the United Nations, such as Decree No. 377 of the Revolution Command Council of Iraq of 16 September 1990, are null and void,

Reaffirming its determination to ensure compliance with Security Council resolutions by maximum use of political and diplomatic means,

Welcoming the Secretary-General's use of his good offices to advance a peaceful solution based on the relevant Security Council resolutions and noting with appreciation his continuing efforts to this end,

Underlining to the Government of Iraq that its continued failure to comply with the terms of resolutions 660 (1990), 661 (1990), 662 (1990), 664 (1990), 666 (1990), and 667 (1990) could lead to further serious action by the Council under the Charter of the United Nations, including under Chapter VII,

Recalling the provisions of Article 103 of the Charter of the United Nations,

Acting under Chapter VII of the Charter of the United Nations,

1. *Calls upon* all States to carry out their obligations to ensure strict and complete compliance with resolution 661 (1990) and in particular paragraphs 3, 4 and 5 thereof;

2. *Confirms* that resolution 661 (1990) applies to all means of transport, including aircraft;

3. *Decides* that all States, notwithstanding the existence of any rights or obligations conferred or imposed by any international agreement or any contract entered into or any license or permit granted before the date of the present resolution, shall deny permission to any aircraft to take off from their territory if the aircraft would carry any cargo to or from Iraq or Kuwait other than food in humanitarian circumstances, subject to authorization by the Council or the Committee established by resolution 661 (1990) and in accordance with resolution 666 (1990), or supplies intended strictly for medical purposes or solely for UNIIMOG [the United Nations Iran-Iraq Military Observer Group];

4. *Decides further* that all States shall deny permission to any aircraft destined to land in Iraq or Kuwait, whatever its State of registration, to overfly its territory unless;

(a) The aircraft lands at an airfield designated by that State outside Iraq or Kuwait in order to permit its inspection to ensure that there is no cargo on board in violation of resolution 661 (1990) or the present resolution, and for this purpose the aircraft may be detained for as long as necessary; or

(b) The particular flight has been approved by the Committee established by resolution 661 (1990); or

(c) The flight is certified by the United Nations as solely for the purposes of UNIIMOG;

5. *Decides* that each State shall take all necessary measures to ensure that any aircraft registered in its territory or operated by an operator who has his principal place of business or permanent residence in its territory complies with the provisions of resolution 661 (1990) and the present resolution;

6. *Decides further* that all States shall notify in a timely fashion the Committee established by resolution 661 (1990) of any flight between its territory and Iraq or Kuwait to which the requirement to land in paragraph 4 above does not apply, and the purpose for such a flight;

7. *Calls upon* all States to cooperate in taking such measures as may be necessary, consistent with international law, including the Chicago Convention, to ensure the effective implementation of the provisions of resolution 661 (1990) or the present resolution;

8. *Calls upon* all States to detain any ships of Iraqi registry which enter their ports and which are being or have been used in violation of resolution 661 (1990), or to deny such ships entrance to their ports except in circumstances recognized under international law as necessary to safeguard human life;

9. *Reminds* all States of their obligations under resolution 661 (1990) with regard to the freezing of Iraqi assets, and the protection of the assets of the legitimate Government of Kuwait and its agencies, located within their territory and to report to the Committee established under resolution 661 (1990) regarding those assets;

10. *Calls upon* all States to provide to the Committee established by resolution 661 (1990) information regarding the action taken by them to implement the provisions laid down in the present resolution;

11. *Affirms* that the United Nations Organization, the specialized agencies and other international organizations in the United Nations system are required to take such measures as may be necessary to give effect to the terms of resolution 661 (1990) and this resolution;

12. *Decides* to consider, in the event of evasion of the provisions of resolution 661 (1990) or of the present resolution by a State or its nationals or through its territory, measures directed at the State in question to prevent such evasion;

13. *Reaffirms* that the Fourth Geneva Convention applies to Kuwait and that as a High Contracting Party to the Convention Iraq is bound to comply fully with all its terms and in particular is liable under the Convention in respect of the grave breaches committed by it, as are individuals who commit or order the commission of grave breaches.

VOTE: 14 for, 1 against (Cuba)

RESOLUTION 674
October 29, 1990
The Security Council,

Recalling its resolutions 660 (1990), 661 (1990), 662 (1990), 664 (1990), 665 (1990), 666 (1990), 667 (1990) and 670 (1990),

Stressing the urgent need for the immediate and unconditional withdrawal of all Iraqi forces from Kuwait, for the restoration of Kuwait's sovereignty, independence and territorial integrity and of the authority of its legitimate government,

Condemning the actions by the Iraqi authorities and occupying forces to take third-State nationals hostage and to mistreat and oppress Kuwaiti and third-State nationals, and the other actions reported to the Security Council, such as the destruction of Kuwaiti demographic records, the forced departure of Kuwaitis, the relocation of population in Kuwait and the unlawful destruction and seizure of public and private property in Kuwait, including hospital supplies and equipment, in violation of the decisions of the Council, the Charter of the United Nations, the Fourth Geneva Convention, the Vienna Conventions on Diplomatic and Consular Relations and international law,

Expressing grave alarm over the situation of nationals of third States in Kuwait and Iraq, including the personnel of the diplomatic and consular missions of such States,

Reaffirming that the Fourth Geneva Convention applies to Kuwait and that as a High Contracting Party to the Convention Iraq is bound to comply fully with all its terms and in particular is liable under the Convention in respect of the grave breaches committed by it, as are individuals who commit or order the commission of grave breaches,

Recalling the efforts of the Secretary-General concerning the safety and well-being of third-State nationals in Iraq and Kuwait,

Deeply concerned at the economic cost and at the loss and suffering caused to individuals in Kuwait and Iraq as a result of the invasion and occupation of Kuwait by Iraq,

Acting under Chapter VII of the Charter of the United Nations,

Reaffirming the goal of the international community of maintaining international peace and security by seeking to resolve international disputes and conflicts through peaceful means,

Recalling the important role that the United Nations and its Secretary-General have played in the peaceful solution of disputes and conflicts in conformity with the provisions of the Charter,

Alarmed by the dangers of the present crisis caused by the Iraqi invasion and occupation of Kuwait, which directly threaten international peace and security, and seeking to avoid any further worsening of the situation,

Calling upon Iraq to comply with the relevant resolutions of the Security Council, in particular its resolutions 660 (1990), 662 (1990) and 664 (1990),

Reaffirming its determination to ensure compliance by Iraq with the Security Council resolutions by maximum use of political and diplomatic means,

1. *Demands* that the Iraqi authorities and occupying forces immediately cease and desist from taking third-State nationals hostage, mistreating and oppressing Kuwaiti and third-State nationals and any other actions, such as those reported to the Security Council and described above, that violate the decisions of this Council, the Charter of the United Nations, the Fourth Geneva Convention, the Vienna Conventions on Diplomatic and Consular Relations and international law;

2. *Invites* States to collate substantiated information in their possession or submitted to them on the grave breaches by Iraq as per paragraph 1 above and to make this information available to the Security Council;

3. *Reaffirms* its demand that Iraq immediately fulfill its obligations to third-State nationals in Kuwait and Iraq, including the personnel of diplomatic and consular missions, under the Charter, the Fourth Geneva Convention, the Vienna Conventions on Diplomatic and Consular Relations, general principles of international law and the relevant resolutions of the Council;

4. *Also reaffirms* its demand that Iraq permit and facilitate the immediate departure from Kuwait and Iraq of those third-State nationals, including diplomatic and consular personnel, who wish to leave;

5. *Demands* that Iraq ensure the immediate access to food, water and basic services necessary to the protection and well-being of Kuwaiti nationals and of nationals of third States in Kuwait and Iraq, including the personnel of diplomatic and consular missions in Kuwait;

6. *Reaffirms* its demand that Iraq immediately protect the safety and well-being of diplomatic and consular personnel and premises in Kuwait and in Iraq, take no action to hinder these diplomatic and consular missions in the performance of their functions, including access to their nationals and the protection of their person and interests and rescind its orders for the closure of diplomatic and consular missions in Kuwait and the withdrawal of the immunity of their personnel;

7. *Requests* the Secretary-General, in the context of the continued exercise of his good offices concerning the safety and well-being of third-State nationals in Iraq and Kuwait, to seek to achieve the objectives of paragraphs 4, 5 and 6 above and in particular the provision of food, water and basic services to Kuwaiti nationals and to the diplomatic and consular missions in Kuwait and the evacuation of third-State nationals;

8. *Reminds* Iraq that under international law it is liable for any loss, damage or injury arising in regard to Kuwait and third States, and their nationals and corporations, as a result of the invasion and illegal occupation of Kuwait by Iraq;

9. *Invites* States to collect relevant information regarding their claims, and those of their nationals and corporations, for restitution or financial compensation by Iraq with a view to such arrangements as may be established in accordance with international law;

10. *Requires* that Iraq comply with the provisions of the present resolution and its previous resolutions, failing which the Security Council will need to take further measures under the Charter;

11. *Decides* to remain actively and permanently seized of the matter until Kuwait has regained its independence and peace has been restored in conformity with the relevant resolutions of the Security Council;

12. *Reposes* its trust in the Secretary-General to make available his good offices and, as he considers appropriate, to pursue them and to undertake diplomatic efforts in order to reach a peaceful solution to the crisis caused by the Iraqi invasion and occupation of Kuwait on the basis of Security Council resolutions 660 (1990), 662 (1990) and 664 (1990), and calls upon all States, both those in the region and others, to pursue on this basis their efforts to this end, in conformity with the Charter, in order to improve the situation and restore peace, security and stability;

13. *Requests* the Secretary-General to report to the Security Council on the results of his good offices and diplomatic efforts.

VOTE: 13 for, 2 against (Cuba and Yemen)

RESOLUTION 677
November 28, 1990
The Security Council,

Recalling its resolutions 660 (1990) of 2 August 1990, 662 (1990) of 9 August 1990 and 674 (1990) of 29 October 1990,

Reiterating its concern for the suffering caused to individuals in Kuwait as a result of the invasion and occupation of Kuwait by Iraq,

Gravely concerned at the ongoing attempt by Iraq to alter the demographic composition of the population of Kuwait and to destroy the civil records maintained by the legitimate Government of Kuwait,

Acting under Chapter VII of the Charter of the United Nations,

1. *Condemns* the attempts by Iraq to alter the demo-

graphic composition of the population of Kuwait and to destroy the civil records maintained by the legitimate Government of Kuwait,

2. *Mandates* the Secretary-General to take custody of a copy of the population register of Kuwait, the authenticity of which has been certified by the legitimate Government of Kuwait and which covers the registration of the population up to 1 August 1990;

3. *Requests* the Secretary-General to establish, in cooperation with the legitimate Government of Kuwait, an Order of Rules and Regulations governing access to and use of the said copy of the population register.

VOTE: Unanimous (15-0)

RESOLUTION 678

November 29, 1990
The Security Council,

Recalling, and reaffirming its resolutions 660 (1990) of 2 August 1990, 661 (1990) of 6 August 1990, 662 (1990) of 9 August 1990, 664 (1990) of 18 August 1990, 665 (1990) of 25 August 1990, 666 (1990) of 13 September 1990, 667 (1990) of 16 September 1990, 669 (1990) of 24 September, 670 (1990) of 25 September 1990, 674 (1990) of 29 October 1990 and 677 (1990) of November 1990,

Noting that, despite all efforts by the United Nations, Iraq refuses to comply with its obligation to implement resolution 660 (1990) and the above-mentioned subsequent relevant resolutions, in flagrant contempt of the Security Council,

Mindful of its duties and responsibilities under the Charter of the United Nations for the maintenance and preservation of international peace and security,

Determined to secure full compliance with its decisions,

Acting under Chapter VII of the Charter of the United Nations,

1. *Demands* that Iraq comply fully with resolution 660 (1990) and all subsequent relevant resolutions, and decides, while maintaining all its decisions, to allow Iraq one final opportunity, as a pause of goodwill, to do so;

2. *Authorizes* Member States cooperating with the Government of Kuwait, unless Iraq on or before 15 January 1991 fully implements, as set forth in paragraph 1 above, the foregoing resolutions, to use all necessary means to uphold and implement resolution 660 (1990) and all subsequent relevant resolutions and to restore international peace and security in the area;

3. *Requests* all States to provide appropriate support for the actions undertaken in pursuance of paragraph 2 of the present resolution;

4. *Requests* the States concerned to keep the Security Council regularly informed on the progress of actions undertaken pursuant to paragraphs 2 and 3 of the present resolution;

5. *Decides* to remain seized of the matter.

VOTE: 12 for, 2 against (Cuba and Yemen), 1 abstention (China)

RESOLUTION 686

March 2, 1991
The Security Council,

Recalling and reaffirming its resolutions 660 (1990), 661 (1990), 662 (1990), 664 (1990), 665 (1990), 666 (1990), 667 (1990), 669 (1990), 670 (1990), 674 (1990), 677 (1990) and 678 (1990),

Recalling the obligations of member states under Article 25 of the Charter,

Recalling paragraph 9 of resolution 661 (1990) regarding assistance to the Government of Kuwait and paragraph 3 (c) of that resolution regarding supplies strictly for medical purposes and, in humanitarian circumstances, foodstuffs,

Taking note of the suspension of offensive combat operations by the forces of Kuwait and the member states cooperating with Kuwait pursuant to resolution 678 (1990),

Bearing in mind the need to be assured of Iraq's peaceful intentions, and the objective in resolution 678 (1990) of restoring international peace and security in the region,

Underlining the importance of Iraq taking the necessary measures which would permit a definitive end to the hostilities,

Affirming the commitment of all member states to the independence, sovereignty and territorial integrity of Iraq and Kuwait, and noting the intention expressed by the member states cooperating under paragraph 2 of Security Council resolution 678 (1990) to bring their military presence in Iraq to an end as soon as possible consistent with achieving the objective of the resolution,

Acting under Chapter VII of the Charter of the United Nations,

1. *Affirms* that all 12 resolutions noted above continue to have full force and effect;

2. *Demands* that Iraq implement its acceptance of all 12 resolutions noted above and in particular that Iraq:

(a) Rescind immediately its actions purporting to annex Kuwait;

(b) Accept in principle its liability under international law for any loss, damage or injury arising in regard to Kuwait and third states, and their nationals and corporations, as a result of the invasion and illegal occupation of Kuwait by Iraq;

(c) Arrange for immediate access to and release of all prisoners of war under the auspices of the International Committee of the Red Cross and return the remains of any deceased personnel of the forces of Kuwait and the member states cooperating with Kuwait pursuant to resolution 678 (1990); and

(d) Immediately begin to return all Kuwaiti property seized by Iraq, to be completed in the shortest possible period;

3. *Further* demands that Iraq:

(a) Cease hostile or provocative actions by its forces against all member states, including missile attacks and flights of combat aircraft;

(b) Designate military commanders to meet with counterparts from the forces of Kuwait and the member states cooperating with Kuwait pursuant to resolution 678 (1990) to arrange for the military aspects of a cessation of hostilities at the earliest possible time;

(c) Arrange for immediate access to and release of all prisoners of war under the auspices of the International Committee of the Red Cross and return the remains of any deceased personnel of the forces of Kuwait and the member states cooperating the Kuwait pursuant to resolution 678 (1990); and

(d) Provide all information and assistance in identifying Iraqi mines, booby traps and other explosives as well as any chemical and biological weapons and material in Kuwait, in areas of Iraq where forces of member states cooperating with Kuwait pursuant to resolution 678 (1990) are present temporarily, and in adjacent waters.

4. *Recognizes* that during the period required for Iraq to comply with paragraphs 2 and 3 above, the provisions of paragraph 2 of resolution 678 (1990) remain valid;

5. *Welcomes* the decision of Kuwait and the member states cooperating with Kuwait pursuant to resolution 678 (1990) to provide access and to commence immediately the release of Iraqi prisoners of war as required by the terms of the Third Geneva Convention of 1949, under the auspices of the International Committee of the Red Cross;

6. *Requests* all member states, as well as the United Nations, the specialized agencies and other international organizations in the United Nations system, to take all appropriate action to cooperate with the Government and people of Kuwait in the reconstruction of their country;

7. *Decides* that Iraq shall notify the Secretary-General and the Security Council when it has taken the actions set out above;

8. *Decides* that in order to secure the rapid establishment of a definitive end to the hostilities, the Security Council remains actively seized of the matter.

VOTE: 11 for, 1 against (Cuba), 3 abstentions (Yemen, China, and India)

RESOLUTION 687
April 2, 1991
The Security Council,

Recalling its Resolutions 660 (1990), 661 (1990), 662 (1990), 664 (1990), 665 (1990), 666 (1990), 667 (1990), 669 (1990), 670 (1990), 674 (1990), 677 (1990), 678 (1990), 686 (1991) [and]

Welcoming the restoration to Kuwait of its sovereignty, independence, and territorial integrity and the return of its legitimate Government,

1. *Affirms* all 13 resolutions noted above, except as expressly changed below to achieve the goals of this resolution, including a formal cease-fire;

2. *Demands* that Iraq and Kuwait respect the inviolability of the international boundary and the allocation of islands set out in the "Agreed Minutes Between the State of Kuwait and the Republic of Iraq Regarding the Restoration of Friendly Relations and Related Matters," signed at Baghdad on 4 October 1963 . . . ;

3. *Calls on* the Secretary-General to lend his assistance to make arrangements with Iraq and Kuwait to demarcate the boundary between Iraq and Kuwait . . . ;

4. *Decides to* guarantee the inviolability of the above-mentioned international boundary and to take as appropriate all necessary measures to that end in accordance with the Charter;

5. *Requests the* Secretary-General, after consulting with Iraq and Kuwait, to submit within three days to the Security Council for its approval a plan for the immediate deployment of a United Nations observer unit to monitor the Khor Abdullah and a demilitarized zone, which is hereby established, extending 10 kilometers into Iraq and 5 kilometers into Kuwait from the boundary . . . ;

6. *Notes* that the deployment of the United Nations observer unit as soon as possible will establish the conditions for the forces of the member states cooperating with Kuwait in accordance with resolution 678 (1990) to bring their military presence in Iraq to an end consistent with resolution 686 (1991);

7. *Invites* Iraq to reaffirm unconditionally its obligations under the Geneva Protocol for the Prohibition of the Use in War of Asphyxiating, Poisonous or Other Gases, and of Bacteriological Methods of Warfare . . . and to ratify the Convention on the Prohibition of the Development, Production and Stockpiling of Bacteriological (Biological) and Toxin Weapons and on Their Destruction . . . ;

8. *Decides* that Iraq unconditionally accept the destruction, removal, or rendering harmless, under international supervision, of:

(a) all chemical and biological weapons and all stocks of agents; and all related subsystems and components and all research, development, support and manufacturing facilities;

(b) all ballistic missiles with a range greater than 150 kilometers and related major parts, and repair and production facilities;

9. *Decides*, for the implementation of paragraph 8 above, the following:

(a) Iraq shall submit to the Secretary-General, within 15 days of the adoption of this resolution, a declaration of the locations, amounts and types of all items specified in paragraph 8 and agree to urgent, on-site inspection as specified below;

(b) the Secretary-General, in consultation with the appropriate governments and, where appropriate, with the director general of the World Health Organization, within 45 days of the passage of this resolution, shall develop, and submit to the Council for approval, a plan calling for the completion of the following acts within 45 days of such approval:

(I) The forming of a special commission which shall carry out immediate on-site inspection of Iraq's biological, chemical and missile capabilities . . . ;

(ii) The yielding by Iraq of possession to the special commission for destruction, removal or rendering harmless . . . of all other items notified under paragraph 8 (a) above . . . and the destruction by Iraq, under supervision of the special commission, of all its missile capabilities including launchers as specified under paragraph 8 (b) above;

10. *Decides* that Iraq shall unconditionally undertake not to use, develop, construct or acquire any of the items specified in paragraphs 8 and 9 above and requests the Secretary-General, in consultation with the Special Commission, to develop a plan for the future ongoing monitoring and verification of Iraq's compliance with this paragraph, to be submitted to the Council for approval with 120 days of the passage of this resolution;

11. *Invites* Iraq to reaffirm unconditionally its obligations under the Treaty on the Non-Proliferation of Nuclear Weapons . . . ;

12. *Decides* that Iraq shall unconditionally agree not to acquire or develop nuclear weapons or nuclear-weapons-usable material or any subsystems or components or any research, development, support or manufacturing facilities related to the above; to submit to the Secretary-General and the Director-General of the International Atomic Energy Agency within 15 days of the adoption of this resolution a declaration of the locations, amounts and types of all items specified above; to place all of its nuclear-weapons-usable materials under the exclusive control, for custody and removal, of the IAEA, with the assistance and cooperation of the Special Commission as provided for in the plan of the Secretary-General discussed in paragraph 9 (b) above; to accept, in accordance with the arrangements provided for in paragraph 13 below, urgent, on-site inspection and the destruction, removal, or rendering harmless of all items specified above; and to accept the plan discussed in paragraph 13 below for the future ongoing monitoring and verification of its compliance with these undertakings;

13. *Requests* the Director-General of the International Atomic Energy Agency . . . to carry out immediate on-site inspection of Iraq's nuclear capabilities based on Iraq's declarations and the designation of any additional locations by the special commission; to develop a plan for the submission to the Security Council within 45 days calling for the destruction, removal or render-ing harmless of all items listed in paragraph 12 above, to carry out the plan within 45 days following approval by the Security Council; and to develop a plan . . . for the future ongoing monitoring and verification of Iraq's compliance with paragraph 12 above . . . ;

14. *Takes* note that the actions to be taken by Iraq in paragraphs 8, 9, 10, 11, 12 and 13 of this resolution represent steps toward the goal of establishing in the Middle East a zone free from weapons of mass destruction and all missiles for their delivery and the objective of a global ban on chemical weapons;

15. *Requests* the Secretary-General to report to the Security Council on the steps taken to facilitate the return of all Kuwaiti property seized by Iraq, including a list of any property which Kuwait claims has not been returned or which has not been returned intact;

16. *Reaffirms* that Iraq . . . is liable under international law for any direct loss, damage, including environmental damage and the depletion of natural resources, or injury to foreign governments, nationals and corporations, as a result of Iraq's unlawful invasion and occupation of Kuwait;

17. *Decides* that all Iraqi statements made since August 2, 1990, repudiating its foreign debt are null and void, and demands that Iraq scrupulously adhere to all of its obligations concerning servicing and repayment of its foreign debt;

18. *Decides* to create a fund to pay compensation for claims that fall within paragraph 16 above and to establish a commission that will administer the fund;

19. *Directs* the Secretary-General to develop and present to the Council for decision, no later than 30 days following the adoption of this resolution, recommendations for the fund to meet the requirement for the payment of claims established in accordance with paragraph 18 above and for a program to implement the decisions in paragraphs 16, 17, and 18 above, including: administration of the fund; mechanisms for determining the appropriate level of Iraq's contribution to the fund based on a percentage of the value of the exports of petroleum and petroleum products from Iraq not to exceed a figure to be suggested to the Council by the Secretary-General, taking into account the requirements of the people of Iraq and in particular humanitarian needs, Iraq's payment capacity as assessed in conjunction with the international financial institutions taking into consideration external debt service, and the needs of the Iraqi economy; arrangements for ensuring that payments are made to the fund . . . ;

20. *Decides*, effective immediately, that the prohibitions against the sale or supply to Iraq of commodities or products, and prohibitions against financial transactions related thereto, contained in resolution 661 (1990) shall not apply to foodstuffs notified to the committee established in resolution 661 (1990) or, with the approval of that Committee, under simplified and accel-

erated procedures, to materials and supplies for essential civilian needs as identified in the report of the Secretary-General dated 20 March 1991, and in any further findings of humanitarian need by the Committee;

21. *Decides* that the Council shall review the provisions of paragraph 20 above every 60 days in light of the policies and practices of the government of Iraq, including the implementation of all relevant resolutions of the Security Council, for the purpose of determining whether to modify further or lift the prohibitions referred to therein;

22. *Decides* that upon the approval of the Security Council of the program called for in paragraph 19 above and of the completion by Iraq of all actions contemplated in paragraphs 8, 9, 10, 11, 12 and 13 above, the prohibitions against financial transactions related thereto contained in resolution 661 (1990) shall have no further force or effect;

23. *Decides* that, pending action by the Security Council under paragraph 22 above, the committee established under resolution 661 shall be empowered to approve, when required to assure adequate financial resources on the part of Iraq to carry out the activities under paragraph 20 above, exceptions to the prohibition against the import of commodities and products originating in Iraq;

24. *Decides* that, in accordance with resolution 661 (1990) and subsequent related resolutions and until a further decision is taken by the Council, all states shall continue to prevent the sale or supply, or promotion or facilitation of such sale or supply, to Iraq by their nationals, or from their territories or using their flag vessels or aircraft, of:

(a) arms and related materiel of all types, specifically including the sale or transfer through other means of all forms of conventional military equipment, including for paramilitary forces, and spare parts and components and their means of production, for such equipment;

(b) items specified and defined in paragraph 8 and paragraph 12 above not otherwise covered above;

(c) technology under licensing or other transfer arrangements used in the production, utilization or stockpiling of items specified in subparagraphs (a) and (b) above;

(d) personnel or materials training or technical support services relating to the design, development, manufacture, use, maintenance or support of items specified in subparagraphs (a) and (b) above;

25. *Calls upon* all states and international organizations to act strictly in accordance with paragraph 24 . . . ;

26. *Requests* the Secretary-General . . . to develop within 60 days, for approval of the Council, guidelines to facilitate full international implementation of paragraphs 24 and 25 above and paragraph 27 below . . . ;

27. *Calls upon* all states to maintain such national controls and procedures and to take such other actions consistent with the guidelines to be established by the Security Council under paragraph 26 above as may be necessary to insure compliance with the terms of paragraph 24 above, and calls upon international organizations to take all appropriate steps to assist in insuring such full compliance;

28. *Agrees* to review its decisions in paragraphs 22, 23, 24 and 25 above, except for the items specified and defined in paragraphs 8 and 12 above, on a regular basis and in any case 120 days following passage of this resolution, taking into account Iraq's compliance with this resolution and general progress toward the control of armaments in the region;

29. *Decides* that all states, including Iraq, shall take the necessary measures to ensure that no claim shall lie at the instance of the Government of Iraq, or of any person or body in Iraq, or of any person claiming through or for the benefit of any such person or body, in connection with any contract or other transaction where its performance was affected by reason of the measures taken by the Security Council in resolution 661 (1990) and related resolutions;

30. *Decides* that, in furtherance of its commitment to facilitate the repatriation of all Kuwaiti and third-country nationals, Iraq shall extend all necessary cooperation to the International Committee of the Red Cross, providing lists of such persons, facilitating the access of the International Committee of the Red Cross to all such persons wherever located or detained and facilitating the search by the International Committee of the Red Cross for those Kuwaiti and third-country nationals still unaccounted for;

31. *Invites* the International Committee of the Red Cross to keep the Secretary General apprised as appropriate of all activities undertaken in connection with facilitating the repatriation or return of all Kuwaiti and third-country nationals or their remains present in Iraq on or after August 2, 1990;

32. *Requires* Iraq to inform the Council that it will not commit or support any act of international terrorism or allow any organization directed toward commission of such acts to operate within its territory and to condemn unequivocally and renounce all acts, methods, and practices of terrorism;

33. *Declares* that, upon official notification by Iraq to the Secretary-General and to the Security Council of its acceptance of the provisions above, a formal cease-fire is effective between Iraq and Kuwait and the member states cooperating with Kuwait in accordance with resolution 678 (1990);

34. *Decides* to remain seized of the matter and to take such further steps as may be required for the implementation of this resolution and to secure peace and security in the area.

VOTE: 12 for, 1 against (Cuba), 2 abstentions (Ecuador and Yemen)

RESOLUTION 688
April 5, 1991
The Security Council,

Mindful of its duties and its responsibilities under the Charter of the United Nations for the maintenance of international peace and security,

Also mindful of Chapter 1, Article 2, paragraph 7 of the Charter of the United Nations,

Gravely concerned by the repression of the Iraqi civilian population in many parts of Iraq, including most recently in Kurdish populated areas which led to a massive flow of refugees toward and across international frontiers and to cross border incursions, which threaten international peace and security in the region,

Deeply disturbed by the magnitude of the human suffering involved,

Taking note of the letters sent by the representatives of Turkey and France to the United Nations dated 2 April 1991 and 4 April 1991, respectively (S/22435 and S/22442),

Reaffirming the commitment of all Member States to the sovereignty, territorial integrity and political independence of Iraq and of all States in the area,

Bearing in mind the Secretary-General's report of 20 March 1991 (S/22366),

1. *Condemns* the repression of the Iraqi civilian population in many parts of Iraq, including most recently in Kurdish populated areas, the consequences of which threaten international peace and security in the region;

2. *Demands* that Iraq, as a contribution to remove the threat to international peace and security in the region, immediately end this repression and express the hope in the same context that an open dialogue will take place to ensure that the human and political rights of all Iraqi citizens are respected;

3. *Insists* that Iraq allow immediate access by international humanitarian organizations to all those in need of assistance in all parts of Iraq and to make available all necessary facilities for their operations;

4. *Requests* the Secretary-General to pursue his humanitarian efforts in Iraq and to report forthwith, if appropriate on the basis of a further missions to the region, on the plight of the Iraqi civilian population, and in particular the Kurdish population, suffering from the repression in all its forms inflicted by the Iraqi authorities;

5. *Requests* further the Secretary-General to use all the resources at his disposal, including those of the relevant United Nations agencies, to address urgently the critical needs of the refugees and displaced Iraqi population;

6. *Appeals* to all Member States and to all humanitarian organizations to contribute to these humanitarian relief efforts;

7. *Demands* that Iraq cooperate with the Secretary-General to these ends;

8. *Decides* to remain seized of the matter.
VOTE: 10 for, 3 against (Cuba, Yemen, and Zimbabwe), 2 abstentions (China and India)

RESOLUTION 689
April 9, 1991
The Security Council,

Recalling its resolution 687 (1991),

Acting under Chapter VII of the Charter of the United Nations,

1. *Approves* the report of the Secretary-General on the implementation of paragraph 5 of Security Council resolution 687 (1991) contained in document S/22454 and Add. 1-3 of 5 and 9 April 1991, respectively;

2. *Notes* that the decision to set up the observer unit was taken in paragraph 5 of resolution 687 (1991) and can only be terminated by a decision of the Council; the Council shall therefore review the question of termination or continuation every six months;

3. *Decides* that the modalities for the initial six-month period of the United Nations Iraq-Kuwait Observation Mission shall be in accordance with the above-mentioned report and shall also be reviewed every six months.
VOTE: Unanimous (15-0)

RESOLUTION 692
May 20, 1991
The Security Council,

Recalling its resolutions 674 (1990) of 29 October 1990, 686 (1991) of 2 March 1991 and 687 (1991) of 3 April 1991, concerning the liability of Iraq, without prejudice to its debts and obligations arising prior to 2 August 1990, for any direct loss, damage, including environmental damage and the depletion of natural resources, or injury to foreign Governments, nationals and corporations as a result of Iraq's unlawful invasion and occupation of Kuwait,

Taking note of the Secretary-General's report of 2 May 1991 (S/22559), submitted in accordance with paragraph 19 of resolution 687 (1991),

Acting under Chapter VII of the Charter of the United Nations,

1. *Expresses its appreciation* to the Secretary-General for his report of 2 May 1991;

2. *Welcomes the fact* that the Secretary-General will now undertake the appropriate consultations requested by paragraph 19 of resolution 687 (1991) so that he will be in a position to recommend to the Security Council for decision as soon as possible the figure which the level of Iraq's contribution to the Fund will not exceed;

3. *Decides* to establish the Fund and the Commission referred to in paragraph 18 of resolution 687 (1991) in accordance with section I of the Secretary-General's report, and that the Governing Council will be located

at the United Nations Office at Geneva and that the Governing Council may decide whether some of the activities of the Commission should be carried out elsewhere;

4. *Requests* the Secretary-General to take the actions necessary to implement paragraphs 2 and 3 above in consultation with the members of the Governing Council;

5. *Directs* the Governing Council to proceed in an expeditious manner to implement the provisions of section E of resolution 687 (1991), taking into account the recommendations in section II of the Secretary-General's report;

6. *Decides* that the requirement for Iraqi contributions will apply in the manner to be prescribed by the Governing Council with respect to all Iraqi petroleum and petroleum products exported from Iraq after 2 April 1991 as well as such petroleum and petroleum products exported earlier but not delivered or not paid for as a specific result of the prohibitions contained in Security Council resolution 661 (1990);

7. *Requests* the Governing Council to report as soon as possible on the actions it has taken with regard to the mechanisms for determining the appropriate level of Iraq's contribution to the Fund and the arrangements for ensuring that payments are made to the Fund, so that the Security Council can give its approval in accordance with paragraph 22 of resolution 687 (1991);

8. *Requests* that all States and international organizations cooperate with the decisions of the Governing Council taken pursuant to paragraph 5 of the present resolution, and also requests that the Governing Council keep the Security Council informed on this matter;

9. *Decides* that, if the Governing Council notifies the Security Council that Iraq has failed to carry out decisions of the Governing Council taken pursuant to paragraph 5 of the present resolution, the Security Council intends to retain or to take action to reimpose the prohibition against the import of petroleum and petroleum products originating in Iraq and financial transactions related thereto;

10. *Decides* also to remain seized of this matter and that the Governing Council will submit periodic reports to the Secretary-General and the Security Council.

VOTE: 14 for, 0 against, 1 abstention (Cuba)

RESOLUTION 699
June 17,1991
The Security Council,

Recalling its resolution 687 (1991),

Taking note of the report of the Secretary-General of 17 May 1991 (S/22614), submitted to it in pursuance of paragraph 9 (b) of resolution 687 (1991),

Also taking note of the Secretary-General's note of 17 May 1991 (S/22615), transmitting to the Council the

letter addressed to him under paragraph 13 of the resolution by the Director-General of the International Atomic Energy Agency (IAEA),

Acting under Chapter VII of the Charter of the United Nations,

1. *Approves* the plan contained in the report of the Secretary-General;

2. *Confirms* that the Special Commission and the IAEA have the authority to conduct activities under section C of resolution 687 (1991), for the purpose of the destruction, removal or rendering harmless of the items specified in paragraphs 8 and 12 of that resolution, after the 45-day period following the approval of this plan until such activities have been completed;

3. *Requests* the Secretary-General to submit to the Security Council progress reports on the implementation of the plan referred to in paragraph I every six months after the adoption of this resolution;

4. *Decides* to encourage the maximum assistance, in cash and in kind, from all Member States to ensure that activities under section C of resolution 687 (1991) are undertaken effectively and expeditiously; further decides, however, that the Government of Iraq shall be liable for the full costs of carrying out the tasks authorized by section C; and requests the Secretary-General to submit to the Council within 30 days for approval recommendations as to the most effective means by which Iraq's obligations in this respect may be fulfilled.

VOTE: Unanimous (15-0)

RESOLUTION 700
June 17, 1991
The Security Council,

Recalling its resolutions 661 (1990) of 6 August 1990, 665 (1990) of 25 August 1990, 670 (1990) of 25 September 1990 and 687 (1991) of 3 April 1991,

Taking note of the report of the Secretary-General of 2 June 1991 (S/ 22660), submitted pursuant to paragraph 26 of resolution 687 (1991),

Acting under Chapter VII of the Charter of the United Nations,

1. *Expresses* its appreciation to the Secretary-General for his report of 2 June 1991 (S/22660);

2. *Approves* the Guidelines to Facilitate Full International Implementation of paragraphs 24, 25, and 27 of Security Council resolution 687 (1991), annexed to the report of the Secretary-General (S/22660);

3. *Reiterates* its call upon all States and international organizations to act in a manner consistent with the Guidelines;

4. *Requests* all States, in accordance with paragraph 8 of the Guidelines, to report to the Secretary-General within 45 days on the measures they have instituted for meeting the obligations set out in paragraph 24 of resolution 687 (1991);

5. *Entrusts* the Committee established under resolu-

tion 661 (1990) concerning the situation between Iraq and Kuwait with the responsibility, under the Guidelines, for monitoring the prohibitions against the sale or supply of arms to Iraq and related sanctions established in paragraph 24 of resolution 687 (1991);

6. *Decides* to remain seized of the matter and to review the Guidelines at the same time as it reviews paragraphs 22, 23, 24, and 25 of resolution 687 (1991) as set out in paragraph 28 thereof.

VOTE: Unanimous (15-0)

RESOLUTION 705
August 15, 1991
The Security Council,

Having considered the note of 30 May 1991 of the Secretary-General pursuant to paragraph 13 of his report of 2 May 1991 (S/22559) which was annexed to the Secretary-General's letter of 30 May 1991 to the President of the Security Council (S/22661),

Acting under Chapter VII of the Charter of the United Nations,

1. *Expresses its appreciation* to the Secretary-General for his note of 30 May 1991 which was annexed to his letter to the President of the Security Council of the same date (S/22661),

2. *Decides* that in accordance with the suggestion made by the Secretary-General in paragraph 7 of his note of 30 May 1991, compensation to be paid by Iraq (as arising from section E of resolution 687) shall not exceed 30 percent of the annual value of the exports of petroleum and petroleum products from Iraq;

3. *Decides further,* in accordance with paragraph 8 of the Secretary-General's note of 30 May 1991, to review the figure established in paragraph 2 above from time to time in light of data and assumptions contained in the letter of the Secretary-General (S/22661) and other relevant developments.

VOTE: Unanimous (15-0)

RESOLUTION 706
August 15, 1991
The Security Council,

Recalling its previous relevant resolutions and in particular resolutions 661 (1990), 686 (1991) 687 (1991), 688 (1991), 692 (1991), 699 (1991) and 705 (1991),

Taking note of the report (S/22799) dated 15 July 1991 of the inter-agency mission headed by the executive delegate of the Secretary-General for the United Nations inter-agency humanitarian program for Iraq, Kuwait and the Iraq/Turkey and Iraq/Iran border areas,

Concerned by the serious nutritional and health situation of the Iraqi civilian population as described in this report, and by the risk of a further deterioration of this situation,

Concerned also that the repatriation or return of all Kuwaitis and third-country nationals or their remains

present in Iraq on or after 2 August 1990, pursuant to paragraph 2 (c) of resolution 686 (1991), and paragraphs 30 and 31 of resolution 687 (1991) has not yet been fully carried out,

Taking note of the conclusions of the above-mentioned report, and in particular of the proposal for oil sales by Iraq to finance the purchase of foodstuffs, medicines and materials and supplies for essential civilian needs for the purpose of providing humanitarian relief,

Taking note also of the letters dated 14 April 1991, 31 May 1991, 6 June 1991, 9 July 1991 and 22 July 1991 from the Minister of Foreign Affairs of Iraq and the Permanent Representative of Iraq to the Chairman of the committee established by resolution 661 (1990) concerning the export from Iraq of petroleum and petroleum products,

Convinced of the need for equitable distribution of humanitarian relief to all segments of the Iraqi civilian population through effective monitoring and transparency,

Recalling and reaffirming in this regard its resolution 688 (1991) and in particular the importance which the Council attaches to Iraq allowing unhindered access by international humanitarian organizations to all those in need of assistance in all parts of Iraq and making available all necessary facilities for their operation, and in this connection stressing the important and continuing role played by the Memorandum of Understanding between the United Nations and the Government of Iraq of 18 April 1991 (S/22663).

Recalling that, pursuant to resolutions 687 (1991(, 692 (1991) and 699 (1991), Iraq is required to pay the full costs of the Special Commission and IAEA in carrying out the tasks authorized by section C of resolution 687 (1991), and that the Secretary-General in his report to the Security Council of 15 July 1991 (S/22792), submitted pursuant to paragraph 4 of resolution 699 (1991), expressed the view that the most obvious way of obtaining financial resources from Iraq to meet the costs of the Special Commission and the IAEA would be to authorize the sale of some Iraqi petroleum and petroleum produces; recalling further that Iraq is required to pay its contributions to the Compensation Fund and half the costs of the Iraq-Kuwait Boundary Demarcation Commission, and recalling further that in its resolutions 686 (1991) and 687 (1991) the Security Council demanded that Iraq return in the shortest possible time all Kuwaiti property seized by it and requested the Secretary-General to take steps to facilitate this,

Acting under Chapter VII of the Charter of the United Nations,

1. *Authorizes* all States, subject to the decision to be taken by the Security Council pursuant to paragraph 5 below and notwithstanding the provisions of paragraphs 3 (a), 3 (b) and 4 of resolution 661 (1990), to per-

mit the import, during a period of 6 months from the date of passage of the resolution pursuant to paragraph 5 below, of petroleum and petroleum products originating in Iraq sufficient to produce a sum to be determined by the Council following receipt of the report of the Secretary-General requested in paragraph 5 of this resolution by not to exceed 1.6 billion United States dollars for the purposes set out in this resolution and subject to the following conditions:

(a) Approval of each purchase of Iraqi petroleum products by the Security Council Committee established by resolution 661 (1990) following notification to the Committee by the State concerned;

(b) Payment of the full amount of each purchase of Iraqi petroleum and petroleum products directly by the purchaser in the State concerned into an escrow account to be established by the United Nations and to be administered by the Secretary-General, exclusively to meet the purposes of this resolution;

(c) Approval by the Council, following the report of the Secretary-General requested in paragraph 5 of this resolution, of a scheme for the purchase of foodstuffs, medicines and materials and supplies for essential civilian needs as referred to in paragraph 20 of resolution 687 (1991), in particular health related materials, all of which to be labeled to the extent possible as being supplied under this scheme, and for all feasible and appropriate United Nations monitoring and supervision for the purpose of assuring their equitable distribution to meet humanitarian needs in all regions of Iraq and to all categories of the Iraqi civilian population, as well as all feasible and appropriate management relevant to this purpose, such a United Nations role to be available if desired for humanitarian assistance from other sources;

(d) The sum authorized in this paragraph to be released by successive decisions of the Committee established by resolution 661 (1990) in three equal portions after the Council has taken the decision provided for in paragraph 5 below on the implementation of this resolution, and notwithstanding any other provision of this paragraph, the sum to be subject to review concurrently by the Council on the basis of its ongoing assessment of the needs and requirements;

2. *Decides* that a part of the sum in the account to be established by the Secretary-General shall be made available by him to finance the purchase of foodstuffs, medicines and materials and supplies for essential civilian needs, as referred to in paragraph 20 of resolution 687, and the cost to the United Nations of its roles under this resolution and of other necessary humanitarian activities in Iraq;

3. *Decides further* that a part of the sum in the account to be established by the Secretary-General shall be used by him for appropriate payments to the United Nations Compensation Fund, the full costs of carrying

out the tasks authorized by Section C of resolution 687 (1991), the full costs incurred by the United Nations in facilitating the return of all Kuwaiti property seized by Iraq, and half the costs of the Boundary Commission;

4. *Decides* that the percentage of the value of exports of petroleum and petroleum products from Iraq, authorized under this resolution to be paid to the United Nations Compensation Fund, as called for in paragraph 19 of resolution 687 (1991), and as defined in paragraph 6 of resolution 692 (1991), shall be the same as the percentage decided by the Security Council in paragraph 2 of resolution 705 (1991) for payments to the Compensation Fund, until such time as the Governing Council of the Fund decides otherwise;

5. Requests the Secretary-General to submit within 20 days of the date of adoption of this resolution a report to the Security Council for decision of measures to be taken in order to implement paragraphs I (a), (b) and (c), estimates of the humanitarian requirements of Iraq set out in paragraph 2 above and of the amount of Iraq's financial obligations set out in paragraph 3 above up to the end of the period of the authorization in paragraph I above, as well as the method for taking the necessary legal measures to ensure that the purposes of this resolution are carried out and the method for taking account of the costs of transportation of such Iraqi petroleum and petroleum products;

6. *Further requests* the Secretary-General in consultation with the International Committee of the Red Cross to submit within 20 days of the date of adoption of this resolution a report to the Security Council on activities undertaken in accordance with paragraph 31 of resolution 687 (1991) in connection with facilitating the repatriation or return of all Kuwaiti and third-country nationals or their remains present in Iraq on or after 2 August 1990;

7. *Requires* the Government of Iraq to provide to the Secretary-General and appropriate international organizations on the first day of the month immediately following the adoption of the present resolution and on the first day of each month thereafter until further notice, a statement of the gold and foreign currency reserves it holds whether in Iraq or elsewhere;

8. *Calls upon* all States to cooperate fully in the implementation of this resolution;

9. *Decides* to remain seized of the matter.

VOTE: 13 for, 1 against (Cuba), 1 abstention (Yemen)

RESOLUTION 707
August 15, 1991
The Security Council,

Recalling its resolution 687 (1991), and its other resolution on this matter,

Recalling the letter of 11 April 1991 from the President of the Security Council to the Permanent Representative of Iraq to the United Nations (S/22485) noting that on the basis of Iraq's written agreement (S/22456) to implement fully resolution 687 (1991) the preconditions established in paragraph 33 of that resolution for a cease-fire had been met,

Noting with grave concern the letters dated 26 June 1991 (S/22739), 28 June 1991 (S/22743) and 4 July 1991 (S/22761) from the Secretary-General, conveying information obtained from the Executive Chairman of the Special Commission and the Director-General of the IAEA which establishes Iraq's failure to comply with its obligations under resolution 687 (1991),

Recalling further the statement issued by the President of the Security Council on 28 June 1991 (S/22761) requesting that a high-level mission consisting of the Chairman of the Special Commission, the Director-General of the IAEA, and the Under-Secretary-General for Disarmament Affairs be dispatched to meet with officials at the highest levels of the Government of Iraq at the earliest opportunity to obtain written assurance that Iraq will fully and immediately cooperate in the inspection of the locations identified by the Special Commission and present for immediate inspection any of those items that may have been transported from those locations,

Dismayed by the report of the high-level mission to the Secretary-General (S/22761) on the results of its meetings with the highest levels of the Iraqi Government,

Gravely concerned by the information provided to the Council by the Special Commission and the IAEA on 15 July 1991 (S/22788) and 25 July 1991 (S/22837) regarding the actions of the Government of Iraq in flagrant violation of resolution 687 (1991),

Gravely concerned also by the evidence in the letter of 7 July 1991 from the Minister of Foreign Affairs of Iraq to the Secretary-General and in subsequent statements and findings that Iraq's notifications of 18 and 28 April were incomplete and that it had concealed activities, which both constituted material breaches of its obligations under resolution 687 (1991),

Noting also from the letters dated 26 June 1991 (S/22739), 28 June 1991 (S/22743) and 4 July 1991 (S/22761) from the Secretary-General that Iraq has not fully complied with all of its undertakings relating to the privileges, immunities and facilities to be accorded to the Special Commission and the IAEA inspection teams mandated under resolution 687 (1991),

Affirming that in order for the Special Commission to carry out its mandate under paragraph 9 (b) (i), (ii) and (iii) of resolution 687 (1991) to inspect Iraq's chemical and biological weapons and ballistic missile capabilities and to take possession of them for destruction, removal or rendering harmless, full disclosure on the part of Iraq as required in paragraph 9 (a) of resolution 687 (1991) is essential,

Affirming that in order for the IAEA, with the assistance and cooperation of the Special Commission, to determine what nuclear-weapons-usable material or any subsystems or components or any research, development, support or manufacturing facilities related to them need, in accordance with paragraph 13 of resolution 687 (1991), to be destroyed, removed or rendered harmless, Iraq is required to make a declaration of all its nuclear programs including any which it claims are for purposes not related to nuclear-weapons-usable material,

Affirming that the aforementioned failures of Iraq to act in strict conformity with its obligations under resolution 687 (1991) constitutes a material breach of its acceptance of the relevant provisions of resolution 687 (1991) which established a cease-fire and provided the conditions essential to the restoration of peace and security in the region,

Affirming further that Iraq's failure to comply with its safeguards agreement with the International Atomic Energy Agency, concluded pursuant to the Treaty on the Non-Proliferation of Nuclear Weapons of 1 July 1968, as established by the resolution of the Board of Governors of the IAEA of 18 July 1991 (GOV/2532),1 constitutes a breach of its international obligations,

Determined to ensure full compliance with resolution 687 (1991) and in particular its section C,

Acting under Chapter VII of the Charter of the United Nations,

1. *Condemns* Iraq's serious violation of a number of its obligations under section C of resolution 687 (1991) and of its undertakings to cooperate with the Special Commission and the IAEA, which constitutes a material breach of the relevant provisions of resolution 687 (1991) which established a cease-fire and provided the conditions essential to the restoration of peace and security in the region;

2. *Further condemns* non-compliance by the Government of Iraq with its obligations under its safeguards agreement with the International Atomic Energy Agency, as established by the resolution of the Board of Governors of 18 July, which constitutes a violation of its commitments as a party to the Treaty on the Non-Proliferation of Nuclear Weapons of 1 July 1968;

3. *Demands* that Iraq

(i) provide full, final and complete disclosure, as required by resolution 687 (1991), of all aspects of its programs to develop weapons of mass destruction and ballistic missiles with a range greater than 150 kilometers, and of all holdings of such weapons, their components and production facilities and locations, as well as all other nuclear programs, including any which it claims are for purposes not related to nuclear-weapons-usable material, without further delay;

(ii) allow the Special Commission, the IAEA and their Inspection Teams immediate, unconditional and unrestricted access to any and all areas, facilities, equipment, records and means of transportation which they wish to inspect;

(iii) cease immediately any attempt to conceal, or any movement or destruction of any material or equipment relating to its nuclear, chemical or biological weapons or ballistic missile programmes, or material or equipment relating to its other nuclear activities without notification to and prior consent of the Special Commission;

(iv) make available immediately to the Special Commission, the IAEA and their Inspection Teams any items to which they were previously denied access;

(v) allow the Special Commission, the IAEA and their Inspection Teams to conduct both fixed wing and helicopter flights throughout Iraq for all relevant purposes including inspection, surveillance, aerial surveys, transportation and logistics without interference of any kind and upon such terms and conditions as may be determined by the Special Commission, and to make full use of their own aircraft and such airfields in Iraq as they may determine are most appropriate for the work of the Commission;

(vi) halt all nuclear activities of any kind, except for use of isotopes for medical, agricultural or industrial purposes until the Security Council determines that Iraq is in full compliance with this resolution and paragraphs 12 and 13 of resolution 687 (1991), and the IAEA determines that Iraq is in full compliance with its safeguards agreement with that Agency;

(vii) ensure the complete implementation of the privileges, immunities and facilities of the representatives of the Special Commission and the IAEA in accordance with its previous undertakings and their complete safety and freedom of movement;

(viii) immediately provide or facilitate the provision of any transportation, medical or logistical support requested by the Special Commission, the IAEA and their Inspection Teams;

(ix) respond fully, completely and promptly to any questions or requests from the Special Commission, the IAEA and their Inspection Teams;

4. *Determines* that Iraq retains no ownership interest in items to be destroyed, removed or rendered harmless pursuant to paragraph 12 of resolution 687 (1991);

5. *Requires* that the Government of Iraq forthwith comply fully and without delay with all its international obligations, including those set out in the present resolution, in resolution 687 (1991), in the Treaty on the Non-Proliferation of Nuclear Weapons of 1 July 1968 and its safeguards agreement with the IAEA;

6. *Decides* to remain seized of this matter.
VOTE: Unanimous (15-0)

Executive Order 12722 of 2 August 1990

This order, signed by President George Bush, blocked Iraqi access to any bank accounts and property in the United States and barred any transactions with Iraq.

I, George Bush, President of the United States of America, find the policies and actions of the Government of Iraq constitute an unusual and extraordinary threat to the national security and foreign policy of the United States and hereby declare a national emergency to deal with that threat.

I hereby order:

Section 1. All property and interests in property of the Government of Iraq, its agencies, instrumentalities and controlled entities and the Central Bank of Iraq that are in the United States, that hereafter come within the United States or that are or hereafter come within the possession of control of United States persons, including their overseas branches, are hereby blocked.

Section 2. The following are prohibited, except to the extent provided in regulations which may hereafter be issued pursuant to this Order:

(a) The import into the United States of any goods or services of Iraqi origin, other than publications and other informational materials;

(b) The export to Iraq of any goods, technology (including technical data or other information controlled for export pursuant to section 5 of the Export Administration Act (50 U.S.C. Appendix 2404)) or services from the United States, except publications and other informational materials, and donations of articles intended to relieve human suffering, such as food, clothing, medicine and medical supplies intended strictly for medical purposes;

(c) Any transaction by a United States person relating to transportation to or from Iraq; the provision of transportation to or from the United States by any Iraqi person or any vessel or aircraft of Iraqi registration; or the sale in the United States by any person holding authority under the Federal Agency Act of 1958, as amended (49 U.S.C. 1514) of any transportation by air which includes any stop in Iraq;

(d) The purchase by any United States person of goods for export from Iraq to any country;

(e) The performance by any United States person of any contract in support of an industrial or other commercial or governmental project in Iraq;

(f) The grant of or extension of credits or loans by any United States person to the Government of Iraq, its instrumentalities and controlled entities;

(g) Any transaction by a United States person relating to travel by any United States citizen or permanent resident alien to Iraq, or to activities by any such person within Iraq, after the date of this Order, other than transactions necessary to effect such person's departure from Iraq, or travel for journalistic activities by persons regularly employed in such capacity by a newsgathering organization; and

(h) Any transaction by any United States person which evades or avoids, or has the purpose of evading or avoiding, any of the prohibitions set forth in this Order.

For purposes of this Order, the term "United States person" means any United States citizen, permanent resident alien, juridical person organized under the laws of the United States, or any person in the United States.

Section 3. This Order is effective immediately.

Section 4. The Secretary of the Treasury, in consultation with the Secretary of State, is hereby authorized to take such actions, including the promulgation of rules and regulations, as may be necessary to carry out the purposes of this Order. Such actions may include prohibiting or regulating payments or transfers of property or any transactions involving the transfer of anything of economic value by any United States person to the Government of Iraq, its instrumentalities and controlled entities, or to any Iraqi national or entity controlled, directly or indirectly, by Iraq or Iraqi nations. The Secretary may redelegate any of these functions to other officers and agencies of the Federal government. All agencies of the United States government are directed to take all appropriate measures within their authority to carry out the provisions of this Order, including the suspension or termination of licenses or other authorizations in effect as of the date of this Order.

Executive Order 12723 of 2 August 1990

With this presidential decree, President George Bush impeded Iraqi procurement of Kuwaiti property and funds in the United States.

By the authority vested in me as President by the Constitution and laws of the United States of America, including the International Emergency Economic Powers Act (50 U.S.C. 1701 et seq.), the National Emergencies Act (50 U.S.C. 1601 et seq.), and 3 U.S.C. 301,

I, George Bush, President of the United States, find that the situation caused by the invasion of Kuwait by Iraq constitutes an unusual and extraordinary threat to the national security, foreign policy and economy of the United States and have declared a national emergency to deal with that threat.

I hereby order blocked all property and interests in property of the Government of Kuwait or any entity purporting to be the Government of Kuwait, its agencies, instrumentalities and controlled entities of the Central Bank of Kuwait that are in the United States, that hereafter come within the United States or that are or hereafter come within the possession or control of United States persons, including their overseas branches.

For purposes of this Order, the term "United States person" means any United States citizen, permanent resident alien, juridical person organized under the laws of the United States, or any person in the United States.

The Secretary of the Treasury is authorized to employ all powers granted to me by the International Emergency Economic Powers Act to carry out the provisions of this Order.

Initial U.S. Reaction to the Iraqi Invasion of Kuwait: Statement by President Bush, 2 August 1990

At 8:05 A.M. on 2 August 1990, President George Bush appeared in the Cabinet Room in the White House and delivered a statement on the United States government's initial reaction to the Iraqi invasion of Kuwait. The following is an extract of that statement.

Let me make a brief statement here about recent events. The United States strongly condemns the Iraqi military invasion of Kuwait. We call for the immediate and unconditional withdrawal of all Iraqi forces. There is no place for this sort of naked aggression in today's world, and I've taken a number of steps to indicate the deep concern that I feel over the events that have taken place.

Last night, I instructed our Ambassador at the United Nations, Tom Pickering, to work with Kuwait in convening an emergency meeting of the Security Council. It was convened, and I am grateful for that quick, overwhelming vote condemning the Iraqi action and calling for immediate and unconditional withdrawal. Tom Pickering will be here in a bit, and we are contemplating with him further United Nations action.

Second, consistent with my authority under the International Economic Powers Act, I've signed an Executive order early this morning freezing Iraqi assets in this country and prohibiting transactions with Iraq. I've also signed an Executive order freezing Kuwaiti assets. That's to insure that those assets are not interfered with by the illegitimate authority that is now occupying Kuwait. We call upon other governments to take similar actions.

Third, the Department of State has been in touch with governments around the world urging that they, too, condemn the Iraqi aggression and consult to determine what measures should be taken to bring an end to this totally unjustified act. It is important that the international community act together to ensure that Iraqi forces depart Kuwait immediately.

Needless to say, we view the situation with the utmost gravity. We remain committed to take whatever steps are necessary to defend our longstanding, vital interests in the Gulf, and I'm meeting this morning with my senior advisers here to consider all possible opinions available to us. I've talked to Secretary Baker just now; General Scowcroft and I were on the phone with him. And after this meeting, I will proceed to deliver a longstanding speech. I will have consultations— short ones—there in Aspen with Prime Minister

Thatcher, and I will be returning home this evening, and I'll be here in Washington tomorrow.

Reference: *Weekly Compilation of Presidential Documents*, 6 August 1990, quoted in Wells, Sherrill Brown, ed., *American Foreign Policy Current Documents 1990* (Washington, DC: U.S. Department of State, 1991), 456.

Press Conference by President Bush and British Prime Minister Thatcher, 2 August 1990

On 2 August 1990, President George Bush flew to Aspen, Colorado, where he met with British Prime Minister Margaret Thatcher. Later that day, at about 2:10 P.M., the two held a press conference, of which excerpts appear below, in front of the residence of Henry Catto, U.S. ambassador to the United Kingdom.

President Bush: Let me first welcome Prime Minister Thatcher back to the United States. It's a very timely visit, and as you can well imagine, we have been exchanging views of the Iraq-Kuwait situation. Not surprisingly, I find myself very much in accord with the views of the Prime Minister. I reported to her on contacts that I've had since I left Washington: personal contacts with King Hussein; Mr. Mubarak of Egypt, President Mubarak; President Salih of Yemen—a long conversation just now. I can tell you that Jim Baker has been in close touch with the Soviet leadership, and indeed, the last plan was for him to stop in Moscow on his way back here.

We are concerned about the situation, but I find that Prime Minister Thatcher and I are looking at it on exactly the same wavelength: concerned about this naked aggression, condemning it and hoping that a peaceful solution will be found that will result in the restoration of the Kuwaiti leaders to their rightful places and, prior to that, a withdrawal of Iraqi forces.

Prime Minister, welcome to Colorado and to the United States. And if you care to say a word on that, then we can take the questions.

Prime Minister Thatcher: Thank you, Mr. President, and thank you for the welcome.

We have, of course, been discussing the main question as the President indicated. Iraq has violated and taken over the territory of a country which is a full member of the United Nations. That is totally unacceptable, and if it were allowed to endure, then there would be many other small countries that could never feel safe.

The Security Council acted swiftly last night under the United States' leadership, well-supported by the votes of 14 members of the Security Council, and rightly demanded the withdrawal of Iraqi troops. If that withdrawal is not swiftly forthcoming, we have to consider the next step. The next step would be further consideration by the Security Council of possible mea-

sures under Chapter VII [of the United Nations Charter, which addresses "Action with Respect to Threats to the Peace, Breaches of the Peace, and Acts of Aggression."]

The fundamental question is this: whether the nations of the world have the collective will effectively to see [that] the Security Council resolution is upheld; whether they have the collective will effectively to do anything, which the Security Council further agrees, to see that Iraq withdraws and that the Government of Kuwait is restored to Kuwait. None of us can do it separately. We need a collective and effective will of the nations belonging to the United Nations—first the Security Council and then the support of all the others to make it effective.

Questions and Answers

Q. Mr. President, when Kuwaiti shipping was in danger in the Gulf War, you put those ships under American flags. Now Kuwait itself has been invaded. The Kuwaiti Ambassador says that they're desperate for help and that American intervention is of paramount importance. Will you answer that call, and how will you?

President Bush: I answer that we're considering what the next steps by the United States should be, just as we strongly support what Prime Minister Thatcher said about collective action in the United Nations.

Q. Are you contemplating military intervention?

President Bush: No. I mentioned at the time we were going to discuss different options, which I did after that first press conference this morning, And we're not ruling any options in, but we're not ruling any options out. And so, that is about right where we are right now. We had thorough briefings—you know who was at the meeting today—by General Powell, General Schwarzkopf and others. But I think it would be inappropriate to discuss options.

Q. Mr. President, isn't Saddam Hussein at the root of this problem? Hasn't he replaced [Libyan leader Muammar] Qadhafi as sort of the bad boy of the region? Would you like to see him removed? And what can you do about him?

President Bush: I would like to see him withdraw his troops and the restoration of the legal government of Kuwait to the rightful place, and that's the step that should be taken. I might say that I am somewhat heartened by the conversations I had with Mubarak and with King Hussein, Mr. Salih—all of whom I consider friends of the United States—and all of them who are trying to engage in what they call an Arab answer to the question, working diligently behind the scenes to come to an agreement that would satisfy the United Nations and the rest of the world. So, there are collective efforts beginning to be undertaken by these worthy countries, and let's hope that they result in a satisfactory resolution of this international crisis.

Q. But, Mr. President, Saddam Hussein has been the source of the most recent mischief in the region—nuclear triggers, missiles, the big gun—as Prime Minister Thatcher knows about. Is he going to be a constant source of problems there in that region?

President Bush: If he behaves this way, he's going to be a constant source. We find his behavior intolerable in this instance, and so do the rest of the United Nations countries that met last night. And reaction from around the world is unanimous in being condemnatory. So, that speaks for itself.

Q. Prime Minister, is there any action short of military intervention that Britain or the other United Nations countries could take—

Prime Minister Thatcher: Yes, of course.

Q.—that would be effective against Iraq?

Prime Minister Thatcher: Yes, of course. Yes, of course there is—you know, the whole Chapter VII measures. And that, of course—obviously we're in consultation now as to which measures we could all agree on so the Security Council would vote on them. And then they'd become mandatory. The question then is whether you can make them effective over the rest of the nations. And obviously, the 14 [members of the Security Council] couldn't do it on their own. And so, there will be a good deal of negotiation as to what to put in the next Security Council resolution if Iraq does not withdraw.

Q. But are you confident that you'd be able to mobilize that kind of international support?

Prime Minister Thatcher: I believe that further Chapter VII measures would have a good chance of going through. We certainly would support them.

President Bush: May I add to that, that the United States has demonstrated its interest in that by the action that I took this morning by Executive order cutting off imports from Iraq to this country.

Q. At the risk of being hypothetical, if Iraq does not move out quickly and has gained a foothold among the small Gulf nations, what can the United States and other nations do militarily?

President Bush: We have many options, and it is too hypothetical, indeed, for me to comment on them. And I'd refer that also to the Prime Minister.

Prime Minister Thatcher: That's precisely what you're looking at the next stage in the Security Council; second, what other measures can be put into action mandatorily, and why the very nations to whom you refer—we should also need their cooperation in putting other actions into effect.

Q. Mr. President, have you dispatched the USS *Independence* to the region, and have you heard from Saudi Arabia?

President Bush: Well, I would not discuss [the] movement of any U.S. forces. And what was the second part of your question?

Q. Have you heard from Saudi Arabia?

President Bush: No, but I have a call to King Fahd and I was supposed to have taken that call before now, but its been delayed by a few minutes. And so, I hope before I leave here I will talk to him. I think its very important I do talk to him. And I'd leave it there.

Q. What do you expect him to say?

President Bush: Well, that's too hypothetical, too. I know he'll be expressing the same kind of concern that we feel.

Reference: "A Shared Anglo-American Approach to the [Gulf] Crisis," in Wells, Sherrill Brown, ed., *American Foreign Policy Current Documents 1990* (Washington, DC: U.S. Department of State, 1991), 456–458.

Senate Resolution 318, Commending the President for "His Initial Actions" in the Gulf Crisis, 2 August 1990

On 2 August 1990, the U.S. Senate voted to commend President Bush for his initial response to the Gulf crisis. The document mentions two pieces of legislation: an amendment passed by the Senate on 27 July 1990 to the farm bill that year which would have cut off credits to Iraq, and the amendment's final wording, which was in the Iraqi Sanctions Act of 1990 (104 Stat. 2047).

Whereas Iraq during the 1980s, under the leadership of Saddam Hussein, has demonstrated a blatant disregard for international law and all standards of human decency, building a heinous record of atrocity and carnage;

Whereas in 1980 Iraq's invasion of Iran began the Iran-Iraq war, which became one of history's bloodiest;

Whereas, beginning in 1983, Iraq initiated and made extensive use of chemical weapons in the Iran-Iraq war;

Whereas this chemical slaughter constituted the most significant violation of the Geneva Protocol in the 65 year history of that international treaty, to which Iraq is a party;

Whereas Iraq's use of chemical weapons culminated in 1988 in a massive attack on its own Kurdish minority, causing tens of thousands of deaths and more than 65,000 refugees;

Whereas Iraq may be proceeding to develop biological weapons in violation of the 1972 international convention prohibiting the manufacture or possession of such weapons;

Whereas Iraq has continued illegal efforts to acquire nuclear weapons technology in violation of United States export laws and Iraq's obligations under the Nuclear Non-Proliferation Treaty;

Whereas the Iraqi effort to develop an indigenous

ballistic missile capability represents an additional dimension of Iraq's threat to the Persian Gulf region;

Whereas, domestically, Iraq's human rights record is one of continuing barbarism, characterized by arbitrary imprisonment, government-sanctioned murder, and even the torture, mutilation, and killing of children as a means of terror against their parents;

Whereas Iraq's efforts to eradicate Kurds and depopulate the Kurdish regions of Iraq are tantamount to a policy of genocide;

Whereas Iraq stands in flagrant violation of its obligations under the United Nations Charter and the International Covenant on Civil and Political Rights;

Whereas, in 1988, in response to Iraq's use of chemical weapons against the Kurds, the United States Senate on three occasions passed legislation imposing comprehensive sanctions against Iraq;

Whereas, on July 27 this year, the Senate passed the Iraq International Law Compliance Act in a continuing effort to secure Iraqi compliance with the rule of law;

Whereas in recent days Iraq mobilized forces on its border with Kuwait, issuing a series of bellicose threats, aimed not only at Kuwait but also at Israel and the United Arab Emirates;

Whereas Iraq, on August 1, without provocation, and under contrived pretense, invaded the sovereign nation of Kuwait, seizing control of its capital and all national territory;

Whereas the President, on August 2, issued an Executive order freezing Iraqi and Kuwaiti assets in the United States, and embargoing all trade with Iraq;

Whereas Iraq's military power in the Persian Gulf area is virtually unchallenged, and its record of callous brutality, opportunism, and belligerency demonstrates that no policy of appeasement or cooperation will constrain the threat Iraq now poses to the security of nations throughout the entire Persian Gulf region and to the international order; Now, therefore be it

Resolved, That Congress commends the President for his initial actions and urges the President to act immediately, using unilateral and multilateral measures, to seek the full and unconditional withdrawal of all Iraqi forces from Kuwait territory; and, specifically to:

(1) Proceed to enforce against Iraq, unilaterally, all provisions of United States law, including the International Emergency Economic Powers Act, to impose—

(a) sanctions against a country engaged in a consistent pattern of gross violations of internationally recognized human rights,

(b) a sustained freeze of all Iraqi assets, and

(c) a sustained ban on any export of United States goods and services to Iraq; and

(2) Undertake, multilaterally, a concerted diplomatic effort, through the United Nations Security Council and all other available channels, to achieve collective international sanctions against Iraq, to include—

(a) a cessation of all arms shipments and all transfer of military technology to Iraq, with emphasis on—

(i) all Soviet-supplied arms and spare parts, as promised by the Soviet Union immediately after Iraq's invasion;

(ii) all arms and spare parts supplied by other major suppliers; and

(iii) all material and technical assistance from any source that could contribute to the development or employment of ballistic missiles and nuclear, biological, and chemical weapons;

(b) a cessation of trade with Iraq and a worldwide freeze on Iraqi and Kuwaiti assets;

(c) a suspension of all economic activities within Iraq, with emphasis on—

(i) oil development activities; and

(ii) construction and other projects supported by American, European, and Japanese industry;

(d) the imposition, under Article 41 of the United Nations Charter, a full economic blockade against Iraq; and

(e) if such measures prove inadequate to secure Iraq's withdrawal from Kuwait, additional multilateral actions, under Article 42 of the United Nations Charter, involving air, sea, and land forces as may be needed to maintain or restore international peace and security in the region.

Reference: "Congress Commends the President for His Initial Actions," in Wells, Sherrill Brown, ed., *American Foreign Policy Current Documents 1990* (Washington, DC: U.S. Department of State, 1991), 459-460.

Iraq's Statement of Withdrawal from Kuwait, 3 August 1990

On 3 August 1990, just a day after it invaded and swallowed up the nation of Kuwait, the Iraqi government issued a statement to the world announcing that its forces would be withdrawing back to Iraq, leaving a puppet government in charge in Kuwait City. Herewith is the text of that statement, delivered by a spokesman for Iraq's ruling Revolutionary Command Council and reported by the official Iraqi news agency, INA.

The statement issued by the Revolution [*sic*] Command Council [on Thursday, 2 August] was clear in defining the reasons and circumstances which made Iraq extend help to the free provisional government of Kuwait. Our forces have performed their pan-Arab and national duty in supporting our people in Kuwait and maintaining security and stability with a high degree of faithfulness and discipline, as everyone saw, even our enemies.

In accordance with the statement yesterday on the mission of our brave forces, and according to the understanding with the free provisional government of

Kuwait, a plan has been laid down to start withdrawing these forces under a timetable as of Sunday[,] August 5, unless factors appear that would threaten the security of Kuwait or Iraq. We announce and emphasize to our people and our glorious Arab nation that by doing this we are not responding to the hollow fuss launched from various places by ill-meaning people to whom we give no consideration whatsoever. We are committed to our principles, and in harmony with ourselves and the duty rendered by our brave forces in accordance with the statement yesterday.

Any party whatever, great or small, of whatever sort, that might try and interfere with Kuwait and Iraq would be confronted with a decisive stand that would chop its arms off from its shoulders. There can be no return for the extinct regime now that the sun of dignity and honour has shone over Kuwait. Present and future relations between Kuwait and Iraq will be determined only by the people of Iraq and Kuwait.
Reference: "Iraq's Statement of Withdrawal," *Times* (London), 4 August 1990, 7.

Message from President Bush to Congress on Declaration of National Emergency, 3 August 1990

On 3 August 1990, President George Bush wrote to the Congress about his declaration of a National Emergency regarding the Persian Gulf crisis. In his message, the president mentions two executive orders; they are order 12722 of 2 August 1990 and order 12723 of 2 August 1990.

To the Congress of the United States:
Pursuant to section 204(b) of the International Emergency Economic Powers Act, 50 U.S.C. section 1703(b), and section 201 of the National Emergencies Act, 50 U.S.C. section 1621, I hereby report that I have exercised my statutory authority to declare a national emergency and to issue two Executive orders that:
—prohibit exports and imports of goods and services between the United States and Iraq and the purchase of Iraqi goods by U.S. persons for sale in third countries;
—prohibit transactions related to travel to or from Iraq, except for transactions necessary for journalistic travel or prompt departure from Iraq;
—prohibit transactions related to transportation to or from Iraq, or the use of vessels or aircraft registered in Iraq by U.S. persons;
—prohibit the performance of any contract in support of the Government of Iraq projects;
—ban all extensions of credit and loans by U.S. persons to the Government of Iraq;
—block all property of the Government of Iraq now or hereafter located in the United States or in the possession or control of U.S. persons, including their foreign branched; and
—prohibit all transfers or other transactions involving assets belonging to the Government of Kuwait now or hereafter located in the United States or in the possession or control of U.S. persons, including their foreign branches.

The Secretary of the Treasury is authorized to issue regulations implementing these prohibitions. These two orders were effective 5 A.M. e.d.t. August 2, 1990.

I am enclosing a copy of each Executive order that I have issued making these declarations and exercising these authorities.

I have authorized these measures in response to the Iraqi invasion of Kuwait, which clearly constitutes an act of aggression and a flagrant violation of international law. This action is in clear violation of the national sovereignty and independence of Kuwait and the Charter of the United Nations. It threatens the entire structure of peaceful relations among nations in this critical region. It constitutes an unusual and extraordinary threat to the national security, foreign policy, and economy of the United States.

The measures we are taking to block Iraqi assets will have the effect of expressing our outrage at Iraq's actions, and will prevent that government from drawing on monies and properties within U.S. control to support its campaign of military aggression against a neighboring state. Our ban on exports to Iraq will prevent the Iraqi Government from profiting from the receipt of U.S. goods and technology. Our ban on imports, while not preventing sales of Iraqi oil to third countries, denies Iraq access to the lucrative U.S. market for its most important product.

At the same time, in order to protect the property of the legitimate Government of Kuwait from possible seizure, diversion, or misuse by Iraq, and with the approval of the Kuwaiti Government, we are blocking Kuwaiti assets within the jurisdiction of the United States or in the possession or control of U.S. persons.

We are calling upon our friends and allies, and all members of the world community who share our interest in the peaceful resolution of international disputes, to join us in similar actions against Iraq and for the protection of Kuwait.
Reference: "Declaration of National Emergency Regarding Iraq," in Wells, Sherrill Brown, ed., *American Foreign Policy Current Documents 1990* (Washington, DC: U.S. Department of State, 1991), 462–463.

Joint U.S.-Soviet Statement Calling for the Withdrawal of Iraqi Forces from Kuwait, 3 August 1990

On 3 August 1990, Secretary of State James Baker met with his counterpart, Soviet Foreign Minister Eduard Shevardnadze, in Moscow, to discuss, among other matters, the crisis in the Persian Gulf. Baker and Shevardnadze emerged from the meeting to issue a joint statement calling for the immediate and unconditional withdrawal of Iraqi troops from Kuwait. Herewith is the complete transcript of that statement, which refers to United Nations Security Council Resolution 660 (1990).

The Soviet Union and the United States, as members of the United Nations Security Council, consider it important that the Council promptly and decisively condemn the brutal and illegal invasion of Kuwait by Iraqi military forces. The United States and the Soviet Union believe that now it is essential that the Security Council Resolution be fully and immediately implemented. By its action, Iraq has shown its contempt for the most fundamental principles of the United Nations Charter and international law.

In response to this blatant transgression of the basic norms of civilized conduct, the United States and the Soviet Union have each taken a number of actions, including the Soviet suspension of arms deliveries and the American freezing of assets. The Soviet Union and the United States reiterate our call for the unconditional Iraqi withdrawal from Kuwait. The sovereignty, national independence, legitimate authorities, and territorial integrity of the State of Kuwait must be completely restored and safeguarded. The United States and the Soviet Union believe the international community must not only condemn this action, but also take practical steps in response to it.

Today we take the unusual step of jointly calling upon the rest of the international community to join with us in an international cut-off of all arms supplies to Iraq. In addition, the Soviet Union and the United States call on regional organizations, especially the League of Arab States, all Arab governments, as well as the Non-Aligned Movement and the Islamic Conference to take all possible steps to ensure that the United Nations Security Council Resolution is carried out. Governments that engage in blatant aggression must know that the international community cannot and will not acquiesce in nor facilitate aggression.

Reference: "U.S.-Soviet Call for Unconditional Iraqi Withdrawal," in Wells, Sherrill Brown, ed., *American Foreign Policy Current Documents 1990* (Washington, DC: U.S. Department of State, 1991), 460–461.

Statement by U.S. Representative to the United Nations Thomas Pickering on Sanctions on Iraq, 6 August 1990

On 6 August 1990, U.S. Permanent Representative to the United Nation Thomas Pickering, spoke before the United Nations Security Council to justify the emerging anti-Iraq coalition's necessity to impose economic sanctions against Iraq, as contained in U.N. Security Council Resolution 661 (1990), passed later that day by a vote of 13-0 with two abstentions (Cuba and Yemen). Herewith is Pickering's complete statement.

Mr. President, my government has joined nine other countries in sponsoring the resolution before us today. It is in response to Iraq's blatant aggression against Kuwait, a sovereign member state of the United Nations, and Iraq's unacceptable failure to comply with Resolution 660, a mandatory resolution which is binding on all member states. By his actions, Saddam Hussein has plunged into crisis the strategically critical area of the Persian Gulf. Thirty percent of the region's oil production is now under Iraqi control, thus threatening international economic health and stability.

These actions follow Iraq's declarations 11 days ago that it would not invade Kuwait. Events have proven this untrue. Friday, Radio Baghdad announced Iraq would withdraw from Kuwait on Sunday. This too was false. Today, Iraqi troops deployments in Kuwait are enhanced, consolidated, and dangerously provocative to other states in the region. The family of nations has come to the point where it cannot believe anything the Baghdad regime has to say on this matter.

The international community, by this resolution, demands immediate implementation of U.N. Security Council Resolution 660. The many statements from individual states around the world, the European Community, the Gulf Cooperation Council, the Arab League, and the Non-Aligned States condemn the Iraqi invasion and demand withdrawal. We will, by our resolution today, give effect to their condemnations of this invasion, and to all of our calls for immediate and unconditional withdrawal. This is only the second occasion on which we have taken such a sweeping and weighty step in this Council. It will reflect a new order of international cooperation.

There are some who hope that Baghdad's purported promises to withdraw immediately and unconditionally will be implemented without international insistence. Unfortunately, reality indicates the contrary. 'Promises' not to invade, and subsequent 'promises' to withdraw already have proven to be mendacious. In a matter of 6 hours, Iraq took over Kuwait; in a matter of 24 hours, Iraq established a marionette 'provisional government'; in a matter of 48 hours, Iraqi troops—upwards of 100,000 strong—were 'volunteered' to serve quickly as cobbled puppets and moved south to the Saudi border. Moreover, Iraq had effectively held hostage and threatened over one million foreigners, and Iraq's puppets have declared that they will not behave honorably should the international community seek to respond to Iraq aggression. We will, of course, want to respect the rights of all states to continue to maintain necessary contacts with Baghdad effectively to protect their citizens.

Iraq, through its actions, has rejected U.N. Security Council Resolution 660, the calls from its own region and from the Non-Aligned States. Its response to the world community has been scorn. The U.N. Security

Council states unequivocally today that the family of all nations will not tolerate this behavior. By this resolution, we declare to Iraq that we will use the means available to us provided in Chapter VII of the U.N. Charter to give effect to U.N. Security Council Resolution 660. Iraq must learn that its disregard for international law will have crippling political and economic costs, including, but not limited to, arms cutoffs. Our concerted resolve will demonstrate that the international community does not—and will not—accept Baghdad's preference for the use of force, coercion and intimidation.

Mr. President, today's resolution is binding upon all member states of the United Nations. Indeed, as paragraph 5 makes clear, the resolution speaks to all states, members and nonmembers alike. As you know, my government acted swiftly to freeze all Iraqi and Kuwaiti assets, and barred all trade with Iraq, and we welcomed the issuance of many governments' decisions to cease all arms transfers to Iraq. Today, the Council acts to consolidate and enforce all of actions. Iraq's aggression must be—and will be—stopped, lest Iraq, or others, conclude that its will can prevail. Our obligation to Kuwait, a sovereign member state of this body, is to implement U.N. Security Council Resolution 660, and restore Kuwait's legitimate authority, sovereignty, and territorial integrity. By our action today, we pledge to the legitimate Government of Kuwait that there will be an international redress for the Iraqi invasion. And, by our action today, we declare for all that we will not countenance the continuation or repetition of this aggression.

Thank you, Mr. President.

Reference: "Need To Impose Economic Sanctions," in Wells, Sherrill Brown, ed., *American Foreign Policy Current Documents 1990* (Washington, DC: U.S. Department of State, 1991), 468-469.

Address by President Bush on the Deployment of U.S. Forces to the Persian Gulf, 8 August 1990

At 9 A.M. on 8 August 1990, President George Bush went before the American people in a national address to discuss his plan to send American troops to Saudi Arabia to start up what was to be called Operation Desert Shield. His remarks, which appear in full below, were carried live by all of the national television and radio networks.

In the life of a nation we're called upon to define who we are and what we believe. Sometimes these choices are not easy. But today as President, I ask for your support in a decision I've made to stand up for what's right and condemn what's wrong, all in the cause of peace.

At my direction, elements of the 82nd Airborne Division as well as key units of the United States Air Force are arriving today to take up key defensive positions in Saudi Arabia. I took this action to assist the Saudi Arabian Government in the defense of its homeland. No one commits America's armed forces to a dangerous mission lightly, but after perhaps unparalleled international consultation and exhausting every alternative, it became necessary to take this action. Let me tell you why.

Less than a week ago, in the early morning hours of August 2nd, Iraqi armed forces, without provocation or warning, invaded a peaceful Kuwait. Facing negligible resistance from its much smaller neighbor, Iraq's tanks stormed in blitzkrieg fashion through Kuwait in a few short hours. With more than 100,000 troops, along with tanks, artillery, and surface-to-surface missiles, Iraq now occupies Kuwait. This aggression came just hours after Saddam Hussein specifically assured numerous countries in the area that there would be no invasion. There is no justification whatsoever for this outrageous and brutal act of aggression.

A puppet regime imposed from the outside is unacceptable. The acquisition of territory by force is unacceptable. No one, friend or foe, should doubt our desire for peace; and no one should underestimate our determination to confront aggression.

Four simple principles guide our policy. First, we seek the immediate, unconditional, and complete withdrawal of all Iraqi forces from Kuwait. Second, Kuwait's legitimate government must be restored to replace the puppet regime. And third, my administration, as has been the case with every President from President Roosevelt to President Reagan, is committed to the security and stability of the Persian Gulf. And fourth, I am determined to protect the lives of American citizens abroad.

Immediately after the Iraqi invasion, I ordered an embargo of all trade with Iraq and, together with many other nations, announced sanctions that both freeze all Iraqi assets in this country and protected Kuwait's assets. The stakes are high. Iraq is already a rich and powerful country that possesses the world's second largest reserves of oil and over a million under arms. Its the fourth largest military in the world. Our country now imports nearly half the oil it consumes and could face a major threat to its economic independence. Much of the world is even more dependent upon imported oil and is even more vulnerable to Iraqi threats.

We succeeded in the struggle for freedom in Europe because we and our allies remain stalwart. Keeping the peace in the Middle East will require no less. We're beginning a new era. This era can be full of promise, an age of freedom, a time of peace for all peoples. But if history teaches us anything, it is that we must resist aggression or it will destroy our freedoms. Appeasement does not work. As was the case in the 1930s, we see in Saddam Hussein an aggressive dictator threatening his neighbors. Only 14 days ago, Saddam Hussein promised his friends he would not invade Kuwait. And 4 days ago, he promised the world he would withdraw. And twice we have seen what his promises mean: His promises mean nothing.

In the last few days, I've spoken with political leaders from the Middle East, Europe, Asia, and the Americas; and I've met with Prime Minister Thatcher, [Canadian] Prime Minister [Brian] Mulroney, and NATO Secretary General [Manfred] Woerner. And all agree that Iraq cannot be allowed to benefit from its invasion of Kuwait.

We agree that this is not an American problem or a European problem or a Middle East problem; it is the world's problem. And that's why, soon after the Iraqi invasion, the United Nations Security Council, without dissent, condemned Iraq, calling for the immediate and unconditional withdrawal of its troops from Kuwait. The Arab world, through both the Arab League and the Gulf Cooperation Council, courageously announced its opposition to Iraqi aggression. Japan, the United Kingdom, and France, and other governments around the world have imposed severe sanctions. The Soviet Union and China ended all arms sales to Iraq.

And this past Monday, the United Nations Security Council approved for the first time in 23 years mandatory sanction under Chapter VII of the United Nations Charter. These sanctions, now enshrined in international law, have the potential for denying Iraq the fruits of aggression while sharply limiting its ability to either import or export anything of value, especially oil.

I pledge here today that the United States will do it part to see that these sanctions are effective and to induce Iraq to withdraw without delay from Kuwait.

But we must recognize that Iraq may not stop using force to advance its ambitions. Iraq has massed an enormous war machine on the Saudi border capable of initiating hostilities with little or no additional preparation. Given the Iraqi Government's history of aggression against its own citizens as well as its neighbors, to assume Iraq will not attack again would be unwise and unrealistic.

And therefore, after consulting with King Fahd, I sent Secretary of Defense Dick Cheney to discuss cooperative measures we could take. Following those meetings, the Saudi Government requested our help, and I responded to that request by ordering U.S. air and ground forces to deploy to the Kingdom of Saudi Arabia.

Let me be clear: The sovereign independence of Saudi Arabia is of vital interest to the United States. This decision, which I shared with the Congressional leadership, grows out of the longstanding friendship and security relationship between the United States and Saudi Arabia. U.S. forces will work together with those of Saudi Arabia and other nations to preserve the integrity of Saudi Arabia and to deter further Iraqi aggression. Through their presence, as well as through training and exercises, these multinational forces will enhance the overall capability of Saudi armed forces to defend the Kingdom.

I want to be clear about what we are doing and why. America does not seek conflict, nor do we seek to chart the destiny of other nations. But America will stand by her friends. The mission of our troops is wholly defensive. Hopefully, they will not be needed long. They will not initiate hostilities, but they will defend themselves, the Kingdom of Saudi Arabia, and other friends in the Persian Gulf.

We are working around the clock to deter Iraqi aggression and to enforce U.N. sanctions. I'm continuing my conversations with world leaders. Secretary of Defense Cheney has just returned from valuable consultations with President Mubarak of Egypt and King Hassan of Morocco. Secretary of State Baker has consulted with his counterparts in many nations, including the Soviet Union, and today he heads for Europe to consult with President Ozal of Turkey, a staunch friend of the United States. And he'll then consult with the NATO foreign ministers.

I will ask oil-producing nations to do what they can to increase production in order to minimize any impact that oil flow reductions will have on the world economy. And I will explore whether we and our allies should draw down our strategic petroleum reserves. Conservative measures can also help; Americans everywhere must do their part. And one more thing: I'm asking the oil companies to do their share. They should show restraint and not abuse today's uncertainties to raise prices.

Standing up for our principles will not come easy. It may take time and possibly cost a great deal. But we are asking no more of anyone than of the brave young men and women of our Armed Forces and their families. And I ask that in the churches around the country prayers be said for those who are committed to protect and defend America's interests.

Standing up for our principles is an American tradition. As it has so many times before, its may take time and tremendous effort, but most of all, it will take unity of purpose. As I've witnesses throughout my life in both war and peace, America has never wavered when her purpose is driven by principle. And on this August day, at home and abroad, I know she will do no less.

Thank you and God bless the United States of America.

Reference: "Deployment of U.S. Armed Forces to Saudi Arabia," in Wells, Sherrill Brown, ed., *American Foreign Policy Current Documents 1990* (Washington, DC: U.S. Department of State, 1991), 469-471.

Statement by the President of the OPEC Conference, 8 August 1990

We have been following with deep concern the reactions on the oil scene to the events taking place in the Gulf since August 2nd 1990.

Having registered the various opinions expressed so far by most of the oil executives and leading analysts in the industry, where it appears that according to all reliable informations the level of world oil stocks on land as well as on water and the fact that the level of the production ceiling set by OPEC at its last Geneva Conference exceeds the real call on OPEC oil for the 3rd Quarter, fears expressed regarding possible disruptions in oil supply in the short term are rather the result of psychological and speculative factors, than of real market fundamentals.

Nonetheless we are fully aware that the developments induced by the events in the Gulf are fraught with uncertainties as regards the equilibrium and stability of the international oil market as well as the integrity of the Organization.

Therefore and following a series of consultations, a conclusion has been reached to carefully monitor the evolution of the situation and to assess all its possible implications on world oil supply, on Member Countries' revenues and lasting interests of both producers and consumers and take whatever measures are deemed necessary.

All Their Excellencies, the Heads of Delegation consulted are of the view that individual initiatives which will necessarily have limited impacts, should be avoided so as to preserve OPEC unity and not hamper its capacity to collectively play its role as a factor of market stability.

While reaffirming OPEC responsibility in performing this task to the extent of its ability, I take this opportunity to strongly stress that ensuring stability of supply to the international oil market is the shared responsibility of all oil producers, the international oil industry as well as the consuming countries' governments and international energy agencies.

Reference: Lauterpacht, E. , et al., eds., *The Kuwait Crisis: Basic Documents* (Cambridge, UK: Grotius Publications, 1991), 317.

Executive Order 12724 of 9 August 1990

Seven days after blocking Iraq's access to its money and property in the United States, President George Bush issued this directive, which effectively and completely froze all Iraqi government property and assets in the United States and prohibited all transactions with Iraq.

By the authority vested in me as President by the Constitution and the laws of the United States of America, including the International Emergency Economic Powers Act (50 U.S.C. 1701 et seq.), the National Emergencies Act (50 U.S.C. 1601 et seq.), section 301 of Title 3 of the United States Code, and the United Nations Participation Act (22 U.S.C. 287c), in view of United Nations Security Council Resolution No. 661 of August 6, 1990, and in order to take additional steps with respect to Iraq's invasion of Kuwait and the national emergency declared in Executive Order No. 12722,

I, George Bush, President of the United States, hereby order:

Section 1. Except to the extent provided in regulations that may hereafter be issued pursuant to this order, all property and interests in property of the Government of Iraq that are in the United States, that hereafter come within the United States, or that are or hereafter come within the possession or control of United States persons, including their overseas branches, are hereby blocked.

Section 2. The following are prohibited, except to the extent provided in regulations that may hereafter be issued pursuant to this order:

(a) The importation into the United States of any goods or services of Iraqi origin, or any activity that promotes or is intended to promote such importation;

(b) The exportation to Iraq, or to any entity operated from Iraq, or owned or controlled by the Government of Iraq, directly or indirectly, of any goods, technology (including technical data or other information), or services either (i) from the United States, or (ii) requiring the issuance of a license by a Federal agency, or any activity that promotes or is intended to promote such exportation, except donations of articles intended to relieve human suffering, such as food and supplies intended strictly for medical purposes;

(c) Any dealing by a United States person relating to property of Iraqi origin exported from Iraq after August 6, 1990, or property intended for exportation from Iraq to any country, or exportation to Iraq from any country, or any activity of any kind that promotes or is intended to promote such dealing;

(d) Any transaction by a United States person relating to travel by any United States citizen or permanent resident alien to Iraq, or to activities by any such person within Iraq, after the date of this order, other than transactions necessary to effect (i) such person's departure from Iraq, (ii) travel and activities for the conduct of the official business of the Federal Government of the United Nations, or (iii) travel for journalistic activity by persons regularly employed in such capacity by a news-gathering organization;

(e) Any transaction by a United States person relating to transportation to or from Iraq; the provision of transportation to or from the United States by any Iraqi person or any vessel or aircraft of Iraqi registration; or the sale in the United States by any person holding authority under the Federal Aviation Act of 1958, as amended (49 U.S.C. 1301 et seq.), of any transportation by air that includes any stop in Iraq;

(f) The performance by any United States person of any contract, including a financing contract, in support of an industrial, commercial, public utility, or governmental project in Iraq;

(g) Except as otherwise authorized herein, any commitment to transfer, direct or indirect of funds, or other financial or economic resources by any United States person to the Government of Iraq or any person in Iraq;

(h) Any transaction by any United States person that evades or avoids, or has the purpose of evading or avoiding, any of the prohibitions set forth in this order.

Section 3. For purposes of this order:

(a) the term "United States person" means any United States citizen, permanent resident alien, juridical person organized under the laws of the United States (including foreign branches), or any person in the United States, and vessels of U.S. registration.

(b) the term "Government of Iraq" includes the Government of Iraq, its agencies, instrumentalities and controlled entities, and the Central Bank of Iraq.

Section 4. This order is effective immediately.

Section 5. The Secretary of the Treasury, in consultation with the Secretary of State, is hereby authorized to take such actions, including the promulgation of rules and regulations, as may be necessary to carry out the purposes of this order. Such actions may include prohibiting or regulating payments or transfers of property or any transactions involving the transfer of anything of economic value by any United States person to the Government of Iraq, or to any Iraqi national or entity owned or controlled, directly or indirectly, by the Government of Iraq or Iraqi nationals. The Secretary of the Treasury may redelegate any of these functions to other officers and agencies of the Federal Government. All agencies of the Federal Government are directed to take all appropriate measures within their authority to carry out the provisions of this order, including the suspension or termination of licenses or other authorizations in effect as of the date of this order.

Section 6. Executive Order 12722 of August 2, 1990, is hereby revoked to the extent inconsistent with this order. All delegations, rules, regulations, orders, licenses, and other forms of administrative action made, issued, or otherwise taken under Executive Order 12722 and not revoked administratively shall remain in full force and effect under this order until amended, modified, or terminated by proper authority. The revocation of any provision of Executive Order 12722 pursuant to this section shall not effect any violation of any rules, regulations, orders, licenses, or other forms of administrative action under that order during the period that such provision of that order was in effect.

Executive Order 12725 of 9 August 1990

On 9 August 1990, President George Bush completed the barrier against the accession of Kuwaiti property and assets in the United States by Iraq or its agents.

By the authority vested in me as President by the Constitution and laws of the United States, including the International Emergency Economic Powers Act (50 U.S.C. 1701 et seq.), the National Emergencies Act (50 U.S.C. 1601 et seq.), section 301 of Title 3 of the United States Code, and the United Nations Participation Act (22 U.S.C. 287c), in view of United Nations Security Council Resolution No. 661 of August 6, 1990, and in order to take additional steps with respect to Iraq's invasion of Kuwait and the national emergency declared in Executive Order 12722,

I, George Bush, President of the United States, hereby order:

Section 1. Except to the extent provided in regulations that may hereafter be issued pursuant to this order, all property and interests of the Government of Kuwait that are in the United States, that hereafter come within the United States, or that are or hereafter come within the possession or control of United States persons, including their overseas branches, are blocked.

Section 2. The following are prohibited, except to the extent provided in regulations that may hereafter be issued to this order:

(a) The importation into the United States of any goods or services of Kuwaiti origin, or any activity that promotes or is intended to promote such importation;

(b) The exportation to Kuwait, or to any entity operated from Kuwait or owned and controlled by the Government of Kuwait, directly or indirectly, of any goods, technology (including technical data or other information), or services either (i) from the United States, or (ii) requiring the issuance of a license by a Federal agency, or any activity that promotes or is intended to promote such exportation, except donations of articles intended to relieve human suffering, such as food and supplies intended strictly for medical purposes.

(c) Any dealing by a United States person related to property of Kuwaiti origin exported from Kuwait after August 6, 1990, or property intended for exportation from Kuwait to any country or exportation to Kuwait from any country, or any activity of any kind that promotes or is intended to promote such dealing;

(d) Any transaction by a United States person relating to travel by any United States citizen or permanent resident alien to Kuwait, or to activities by any such person within Kuwait, after the date of this order, other than transactions necessary to effect (i) such person's departure from Kuwait, (ii) travel and activities for the conduct of the official business of the Federal Government of the United Nations, or (iii) travel for journalistic activity by persons regularly employed in such capacity by a news-gathering organization;

(e) Any transaction by a United States person relating to transportation to or from Kuwait; the provision of transportation to or from the United States by any Kuwaiti person or any vessel or aircraft of Kuwaiti registration; or the sale in the United States by any person holding authority under the Federal Aviation Act of 1958, as amended (49 U.S.C. 1301 et seq.), of any transportation by air that includes any stop in Kuwait;

(f) The performance by any United States person of any contract, including a financing contract, in support of an industrial, commercial, public utility, or governmental project in Kuwait;

(g) Except as otherwise authorized herein, any commitment to transfer, direct or indirect of funds, or other financial or economic resources by any United States person to the Government of Kuwait or any person in Kuwait;

(h) Any transaction by any United States person that evades or avoids, or has the purpose of evading or avoiding, any of the prohibitions set forth in this order.

Section 3. For purposes of this order:

(a) the term "United States person" means any United States citizen, permanent resident alien, juridical person organized under the laws of the United States (including foreign branches), or any person in the United States, and vessels of U.S. registration.

(b) the term "Government of Kuwait" includes the Government of Kuwait, its agencies, instrumentalities and controlled entities, and the Central Bank of Kuwait.

Section 4. This order is effective immediately.

Section 5. The Secretary of the Treasury, in consultation with the Secretary of State, is hereby authorized to take such actions, including the promulgation of rules and regulations, as may be necessary to carry out the purposes of this order. Such actions may include prohibiting or regulating payments or transfers of property or any transactions involving the transfer of anything of economic value by any United States person to the Government of Kuwait, or to any Kuwaiti national or entity owned or controlled, directly or indirectly, by the Government of Kuwait or Kuwaiti nationals. The Secretary of the Treasury may redelegate any of these functions to other officers and agencies of the Federal Government. All agencies of the Federal Government are directed to take all appropriate measures within their authority to carry out the provisions of this order, including the suspension or termination of licenses or other authorizations in effect as of the date of this order.

Section 6. Executive Order 12723 of August 2, 1990, is hereby revoked to the extent inconsistent with this

order. All delegations, rules, regulations, orders, licenses, and other forms of administrative action made, issued, or otherwise taken under Executive Order 12723 and not revoked administratively shall remain in full force and effect under this order until amended, modified, or terminated by proper authority. The revocation of any provision of Executive Order 12723 pursuant to this section shall not effect any violation of any rules, regulations, orders, licenses, or other forms of administrative action under that order during the period that such provision of that order was in effect.

Statement by President Bush about U.S. Moves against Iraq, 12 August 1990

The following statement by President George Bush was delivered by his press secretary, Marlin Fitzwater.

This morning, the President received a letter from His Highness, Sheik Jaber al-Ahmed al-Sabah, the Emir of Kuwait, requesting on behalf of the Government of Kuwait, and in accordance with Article 51 of the U.N. Charter and the right of individual and collective self-defense, that the United States Government take appropriate steps as necessary to ensure that U.N.-mandated economic sanctions against Iraq and Kuwait are immediately and effectively implemented.

In view of the Emir's request, the President has decided that the United States will do whatever is necessary to see that relevant U.N. sanctions are enforced. The President stressed that these efforts will complement, not substitute, for individual and collective compliance that has been highly successful thus far. The United States will coordinate its efforts with the governments of other nations to whom the Kuwaiti Government has made similar requests.

Regarding Saddam Hussein's proposals announced today, the United States categorically rejects them. We join the rest of the U.N. Security Council in unanimously calling for the immediate, complete and unconditional withdrawal of Iraqi forces from Kuwait, and the restoration of Kuwait's legitimate government. These latest conditions and threats are another attempt at distracting from Iraq's isolation and at imposing a new status quo. Iraq continues to act in defiance of U.N. resolutions 660, 661 and 662, the basis for resolving Iraq's occupation. The United States will continue to pursue the application of those resolutions in all their parts.

Reference: New York Times, 13 August 1990, A11.

Letter from Saddam Hussein to President Bush, 16 August 1990

On 16 August 1990, Saddam Hussein issued an open letter to President George Bush, in what may considered an attempt to explain the roots of the situation in the Persian Gulf which led to the Iraqi invasion of Kuwait, and denounce American actions in the first weeks of the crisis. Herewith is the full text of that letter, translated from the Arabic.

In the name of God, the merciful, the compassionate: An open letter to the President of the United States.

I have heard your feverish utterances and remarks before the U.S. Defense Department staff in which expressed your determination to continue the policy of harming Iraq and occupying and insulting the holy places and land of the Arabs and Muslims in Hejaz and Najd [Saudi Arabia]. Frankly speaking, Mr. President, as I was reading your remarks, which clearly show an underestimation of and disregard for the Arab mentality and popular and official sentiments, your shallow thinking came into sharp focus, when I had thought you were more farsighted. Also, my faith has been strengthened in the right path chosen by the people of Iraq, and down which I am leading them and through which I am serving them. My conviction of the soundness of every jealous Arab and Muslim choosing the route of jihad against invading forces has been reinforced.

President of the superpower: Along with your little agents, you have sought to stigmatize Saddam Hussein with the epithet of liar, having failed to tarnish him otherwise—you, who have access to fat files about others, from them—foremost of whom are your supporters in the region. You and your agents and your business partners in the region have been saying that Saddam Hussein promised [Egyptian President Hosni] Husni Mubarak that he would not do such-and-such a thing and yet went ahead and did it. This is despite the fact that you know that your greatest dream is for Saddam Hussein to lie, since the one who lies will lose the power to influence things and will relent in his determination, having lost the staples of faith, since what you hate most in terms of plotters in the United States and in terms of your little isolated agents in the region is the truthfulness of men. And the man you hate most is Saddam Hussein, inasmuch as his faithfulness towards principle, his honesty with himself and his people and nation make him the servant and leader of the people and nation and not the servant of the foreigner, while you look at liars in the region as true friends, and you know who the ultimate liars in the region are.

President of the United States: You have chosen to be a liar so that you may be in harmony with the band you have chosen and regard as representatives of the Arab nation. In your statements, you have lied to the people and public opinion, because you accused Saddam Hussein of being a liar, on the strength of the tale of Husni Mubarak in which he alleges that Saddam Hussein had promised not to use military force and yet he did. This tale has been disproved by evidence witnessed by at least eight Iraqi and Egyptian officials who are still alive and can bear witness.

I did not promise Husni Mubarak anything, except that I would not use force until after the Jeddah meeting had convened. This was explained in detail by an official Iraqi spokesman on 10 August 1990. I suppose that you must have taken cognizance of this statement. As you must be well aware, I used force only after the failure and end of the Jeddah meeting.

Besides, you lied to your people when you said that the majority of Arabs support your measures to occupy the Gulf, Arab lands, and the Islamic holy lands of Hejaz and Najd. The Arabs, O President of the United States, are not the rulers who serve you, obey your orders, and share with you the plundering of the nation's wealth. The Arabs are the people. They are the sons of the nations—the poor, the honorable, and the sincerest patriots. They are the patriotic leaders and rulers who clearly expressed their opinion of your policy and the policy of your agents in their statements, in their rejection of your conspiracy that you termed the Cairo Summit, and in the mass demonstrations and protests that will turn into a flood and sweep away the thrones of those who fail to resist your schemes, which humiliate the Arab nation and the Muslims' holy sites—the schemes in which you made clear how much you hate the Arabs and how much you despise their will as well as the will of Muslims.

The West, and even the U.S. public, will be on the side of right. When the fight escalates and the tensions worsen, your distorted image, as well as the distorted images of your allies, will be exposed to all well-meaning parties in the world. The Americans will then tell you: We united America with blood. Why are you working against the unity of the Iraqi people, who were divided by colonial powers? And why are you making yourself a hostage to the whims of the backward and the exploiters? They will ask you: Where are our legitimate interests that are threatened by Iraq? When the American people realize that legitimate interests are more than welcomed by Iraq, their wrath against you will increase, and then you will fall off your seat after the defeat of your brute force, which you deluded yourself into believing would terrorize the Arab nation. This is the great nation chosen by God to be the nation of prophets and messengers and the nation of heavenly books.

You, U.S. President, lied to your people when you told them that you were massing troops to protect American interests in Saudi Arabia. Now, you are telling them that they are there to force Iraq to withdraw from Kuwait. You have not asked yourself: Is it permissible for Iraq to ask you to withdraw your troops from the southern United States? And would you respond favorably if we were to request you to do this? We are on our land. The Kuwaitis and Iraqis have been Iraqis since the beginning of time. Since time immemorial, Iraqi borders extended from Zakho in the north to the city of al-Nida' [also known as al-Ahmadi] and the city of Kuwait [the capital, Kuwait City] on the sea coast in the south.

With their irreversible manifestation of willpower, the Iraqis have become one people, just as they have always been throughout history. The people were divided by colonial powers at a certain phase. They were destined to live, during a short period of time, within the confines of the fences created by colonial powers. However, this has become a thing of the past. Besides, there is no chance for the backward oil amirs who distorted the Arab image to Westerners, including Americans, to return to the throne which disgraced the Arabs by its characteristics and by its rulers and those of their ilk among you allies.

You must be truthful to your people, O elected President of the United States, and tell them that you have miscalculated and that you have been hasty in your decision, thanks to those who involved you in this decision. You must say this to us, to, and ask us to help you so as to save face through measures and arrangements that do not change the essence of things as they have become, as regards the unity of Iraq—the land and the people. Moreover, you must also be truthful to your people and say that Arab public opinion—in fact, Islamic as well—are against your presence on the land of messages from heaven and the land of prophets, and against your aggression in the holy places and on Iraq, and that the Arab and Islamic public opinion will fight your schemes and will sacrifice blessed life in defense of faith, the values of the Islamic teachings, the holy places, and the honor of nationalism. You will be defeated, because falsehood cannot triumph after right has found its claimants, and the people have found their genuine reflection in right, justice, and fairness.

Moreover, are you not sad—being the President of the state which brags about being democratic—that your allies are those Arabs who are backward, thieves, and liars, while the enlightened, struggling, and mujahidin Arabs and the vanguard of the nation stand on the opposite side. However, we will continue to pray to God that the two sides will not collide, for then thousands of Americans wrapped up in sad coffins will reach you after you have sent them into a dark tunnel.

O Arabs, the doors of Heaven have been laid open to you, and you can smell its pure aroma; the opportunity for an honorable living has been made available to you.

O Muslims, your faithful role has come, and the door of jihad has been laid open—the door which angered the shameless fraud Bush—so, proceed toward it.

God is great. Accursed be the lowly. God is great, Accursed be the infidels and aggressors. Might for the Arabs and the Muslims and all honorable people who stand for right in the world.

Reference: "Open Letter to U.S. President George Bush from Saddam Hussein, dated 16 August 1990," in Moore, Fred, comp., *Iraq Speaks: Documents on the Gulf Crisis* (Palo Alto, CA: privately printed, 1991), 11–12.

Executive Order 12727 of 22 August 1990

This presidential dictate was signed by President George Bush to order the Selected Reserve of the armed forces to active duty.

By the authority vested in me as President by the Constitution and the laws of the United States of America, including sections 121 and 673b of title 10 of the United States Code, I hereby determine that it is necessary to augment the active armed forces of the United States for the effective conduct of operational missions in and around the Arabian Peninsula. Further, under the stated authority, I hereby authorize the Secretary of Defense, and the Secretary of Transportation with respect to the Coast Guard when the latter is not operating as a service in the Department of the Navy, to order to active duty units and individual members not assigned to units, of the Selective Reserve.

This order is intended only to improve the internal management of the executive branch, and is not intended to create any right or benefit, substantive or procedural, enforceable at law by a party against the United States, its agencies, its officers, or any person.

Executive Order 12728 of 22 August 1990

This executive order, signed by President George Bush, delegated the president's authority to suspend any provision of law relating to the promotion, retirement, or separation of members of the armed forces.

By the authority vested in me as President by the Constitution and the laws of the United States of America, including section 673c of title 10 of the United States Code and section 301 of title 3 of the United States Code, I hereby order:
Section 1. The Secretary of Defense, and the Secretary of Transportation with respect to the Coast Guard when it is not operating as a service in the Department of the Navy, are hereby designated and empowered to exercise, without the approval, ratification, or other action of the President, the authority vested in the President by section 673c of title 10 of the United States Code:
(1) to suspend any provision of law relating to promotion, retirement, or separation applicable to any member of the armed forces determined to be essential to the national security of the United States, and (2) to

determine, for the purposes of said section, that members of the armed forces are essential to the national security of the United States.

Sec. 2. The authority delegated to the Secretary of Defense and the Secretary of Transportation by this order may be redelegated and further subdelegated to subordinates who are appointed to their offices by the President, by and with the advice and consent of the Senate.

Sec. 3. This order is intended only to improve the internal management of the executive branch and is not intended to create any right or benefit, substantive or procedural, enforceable at law by a party against the United States, its agencies, its officers, or any person.

Dan Rather Interview with Saddam Hussein in Baghdad, 29 August 1990

On 29 August 1990, CBS News anchor Dan Rather went to Baghdad to conduct a lengthy interview with Saddam Hussein, which appeared on the CBS Evening News *that night. The following is the complete transcript of that interview.*

Rather: Mr. President, your Deputy Prime Minister [Sa'-dun Hammadi] and Foreign Minister [Tariq Aziz] said a few days ago that the door was not closed to any idea. Does that include the idea of possibly Iraq withdrawing from Kuwait under any circumstances?

Saddam Hussein: At any rate, the Foreign Minister spoke within the framework of the general situation; Kuwait is part of the general situation. You know that the U.S. troops are currently occupying the lands considered to be holy to Arabs and Muslims. Moreover, a blockade is being imposed on Iraq. There is a military buildup. There is a massive buildup of troops by the United States and its allies. One of the issues relating to this is possible aggression against Iraq. Then comes Kuwait as one of these numerous factors.

Rather: But is it negotiable? Is it negotiable or non-negotiable?

Saddam Hussein: If you are talking about withdrawal, then there would be nothing left to negotiate about. When a man, including government officials in any world state, faces any problem, he cannot say that there is no solution or that there is no room for proposing any new idea. When you say that there is no room for any new ideas, then life, as we said a short while ago, would cease to function. Only a rigid mentality would say there is no room for new ideas.

Rather: So, is it negotiable?

Saddam Hussein: Negotiable with whom?

Rather: With the United States.

Saddam Hussein: Is Kuwait the 52nd state of the United States?

Rather: No, you said it is the 19th province of Iraq.

Saddam Hussein: So, we are talking about dialogue, not negotiations. Negotiations are held with the concerned parties. The United States has thus far been saying that it has been asked to send troops by Saudi Arabia, by the Saudi government, and that it came in response to this request. The United States did not tell us that it was the legitimate heir of the previous government of Kuwait so we would hold negotiations with it. Consequently, we would negotiate the withdrawal of the United States from the holy places if the Muslims and Arabs asked us to negotiate on their behalf. But since the Arabs and Muslims have not asked us to perform this duty, we should say that we are ready to enter into a dialogue, rather than negotiations, with the United States.

Rather: But that would include the possibility of your withdrawing from Kuwait?

Saddam Hussein: Kuwait is part of Iraq.

Rather: Forever?

Saddam Hussein: We have made our words clear on this. The Iraqi legislative authorities issued a clear decision saying Kuwait is an Iraqi governorate. Do you think that U.S. citizens or the U.S. officials have a sufficient background about Kuwait being a part of Iraq? Or have they viewed the issue only from the perspective that Kuwait was a state, that the Iraqi Army is now in Kuwait, and that the Kuwaiti Government is now out of Kuwait? And that therefore, in accordance with human and international criteria, the only duty for everyone is to denounce this action? For instance, do Americans know that the Kuwaiti Legislative Council decided in 1938 to rejoin Iraq on the basis that Kuwait was part of Iraq? Do they know, moreover, that this Council was dissolved because it decided twice to rejoin Iraq? This was done on instructions from the British authorities carried out by the Kuwaiti sheikhs. Do Americans know, for instance, that the Iraqi Government has not recognized the presence of any other legislative body that can make such a decision within or outside the state of Kuwait? So, Kuwait is different from Saudi Arabia. We could understand when someone says that he is worried about Saudi Arabia if there were a real danger threatening Saudi Arabia. Saudi Arabia is an independent state that has never been a part of Iraq. Neither has Iraq been at any time a part of it. As for Kuwait, the matter is different.

Rather: May I change this subject for just a moment, Mr. President? There was a report today in the United States—from several back channels, from several sources—that you have offered to negotiate an Iraqi withdrawal from Kuwait provided that you will get some of the islands that belong to Kuwait [in the Persian Gulf] and you will get one of Kuwait's major oil fields, and that the debt to Kuwait for the war would be forgiven. Is that report true?

Saddam Hussein: So far we have not met with the U.N. Secretary General. We have not said this to anyone. Nevertheless, when any proposal is presented to us, we will give our opinion on it. But who would suggest the proposal to us?

Rather: Well, Mr. [Javier] Pérez de Cuéllar has been submitting proposals.

Saddam Hussein: So far we have not met with Mr. Pérez de Cuéllar. If he suggests any idea to the Foreign Minister when they meet, the Foreign Minister will discuss the idea with him. We respect Mr. Pérez de Cuéllar in his capacity as a U.N. representative.

Rather: Do you expect a United States military strike against you?

Saddam Hussein: We have taken this into consideration and are preparing ourselves for such a possibility. Yet, despite the fact that we are preparing to face such a possibility, we are not working toward this end.

Rather: I think many Americans are concerned that there may be a war. The question they want to know is: who is that man Saddam Hussein? How would you describe yourself?

Saddam Hussein [at first, addressing the interpreter]: Before thinking that they are greatly interested to know who Saddam Hussein is, does he not think they would first like to know the way to prevent war? [to Rather] I believe the Americans' concern is correct and legitimate. The Iraqis, like the Americans, do not want war. Therefore, in the name of the Iraqis, I say that I do not want war. What Mr. Bush needs to do is tell the Americans that he does not want war. Then, war will not take place. As for whom Saddam Hussein is, Saddam Hussein is the man sitting in front of you. You and all politicians and media men in the United States know who Saddam Hussein is because Saddam Hussein is not locked up in a vault. A human being is known from his history, so you can tell the public exactly who Saddam Hussein is.

Rather: President Bush has said that you are to be equated with Hitler, that you are a bully and a very dangerous man.

Saddam Hussein: From which angle did Mr. Bush choose to compare me with Hitler?

Rather: You invaded a weak neighbor who is no threat to you.

Saddam Hussein: Do you realize how wicked those in authority in that country, which you call weak, were? As a U.S. citizen who should honor his U.S. citizenship by telling the truth, you must know who wicked the al-Sabah family were. Only in 1963, the border station between what was formerly called the state of Kuwait and Iraq was in an are called al-Mitla. That was in 1963. From 1963 until 2 August 1990, this point continued to move until it reached an area called al-Abdali. Do you know how far al-Abdali is from al-Mitla? Over 70 kilometers. All this took place because we in Iraq did not have stable governments from 1963 to 1968. From 1968 to 1970 the new government was not stable enough. I am talking about something based on documents we

can provide you with. Before the war with Iran in 1980, the value of the Iraqi dinar was higher than that of the Kuwait dinar. Do you know what the value of the Iraqi dinar was on 2 August? The value was only 54 Kuwaiti fils [a unit of the Kuwaiti dinar], which means 1/19th of the former value of the Iraqi dinar. The party responsible for this state of affairs was Kuwait. Is this a weak government? It is a wicked government. It was the claw of the wolf. The rulers of this part wanted Iraq, which is larger than their part, to be brought down to earth.

Rather: If I may, I know that you did not like Kuwait. I would like to know the circumstances.

Saddam Hussein: I hope that you will see the documents in which we warned against this behavior, and I also hope that you will see the statements that I made at the Baghdad summit held prior to the events.

Rather: Americans simply can't accept a man who takes hostages. How can you defend that?

Saddam Hussein: Taking hostages means to hold a person and demand something in return. What have we asked from the United States in return? We have asked for nothing.

Rather: But you asked not to be attacked.

Saddam Hussein: We said we want peace. And we said that perhaps the U.S. Administration would be influenced by U.S. public opinion if they knew that it would attack Iraq despite the fact that there were U.S. citizens in Iraq. Therefore, we kept a number of foreigners in Iraq and did not allow them to travel outside Iraq—for a while, not for good. And when I visited and met with the foreign families yesterday, I felt that they wanted their children and women to be allowed to leave. I consulted with the speaker of the National Assembly [Saadi Mahdi Saleh], exercised my powers, and allowed them to depart. Therefore, we have not taken anyone hostage in exchange for anything. We do not want anything. We do not want war to break out, because if it does, it will harm the United States, Iraq, and humanity in general.

Rather: Mr. President, respectfully, a hostage is a hostage is a hostage. I have to believe that you, an intelligent person, know that these people are hostages.

Saddam Hussein: If this is understood as such, why did the Americans detain tens of thousands of Japanese during World War II. Some of them, most of them, were U.S. nationals. Therefore, the Americans committed two acts of detention. First they detained a human being, and second, they detained a U.S. national with citizenship rights.

Rather: I do not want to defend that, but it was a long time ago, a different situation. Would you consider letting all the hostages go?

Saddam Hussein: Why different? Was not the justification for detaining those Japanese and Americans that you did want the war to drag on?

Rather: No, it was done for internal security.

Saddam Hussein: We are doing it for the sake of peace, which is a more sublime objective than internal security.

Rather: Let me ask: One of your Iraqi officials said to me in private: What we have now is a kind of balance of terror. Do you agree that what we have now is a kind of balance of terror between the United States and Iraq; you have the hostages and we have a huge military force?

Saddam Hussein: No, we do not believe this. The man who told you this does not know our policy; that is, if someone really told you this. You must have heard my remarks to our foreign guests. I recommend that if a raid were launched against this place where they are and there is a shelter, those in charge should allow the foreigners to enter the shelter first and then the Iraqis. If we wanted to strike a balance of so-called terror, we would not have given preference to foreigners over Iraqis in entering the shelters. But we are still considering them our guests. In Arab tradition, the guest is dealt with on this basis. He comes before the people in the house. Let me ask you as an American: I will also ask you questions if you will allow me—don't you in America wonder how this situation is different from that in Grenada and Panama? We say that Kuwait is a part of Iraq and we have documents to prove it. As for Panama and Grenada, they have never been parts of the United States of America. Yet, you invaded Panama and Grenada. You brought the leader of Panama to the United States to try him there. Don't the American people ask their government about this double standard treatment? On the one hand, armies are dispatched to Iraq because it extended into its other part, namely Kuwait; and on the other hand, the U.S. action in Grenada and Panama is considered to be a correct action, a legitimate and constitutional action.

Rather: First of all, my job is to ask questions and not to answer questions. These questions are better directed to President Bush.

Saddam Hussein: Then I put it to President Bush, and were he to answer that he went to Grenada and Panama, but he kept neither, I would tell him that had they been part of the United States, he would have retained them.

Rather: When I saw you on television with the families, with what you call "guests" and I call "hostages," with the British boy [identified as Stuart Lockwood of Great Britain] and his family, I was very uncomfortable with that, and I think many Americans and others were uncomfortable and outraged by it. Why did you do it?

Saddam Hussein: We have said that foreigners, those you call "hostages," are our guests. It is a habit with me to see the field before I decide anything, and when the issue has to do with human beings, then I take great care to see the situation for myself before I decide on

anything. It is my duty to see for myself how these foreigners are doing rather than depend on secondhand accounts. Which is why I have been to see them twice. And I asked them about their private and general affairs, and I learned some very valuable human lessons. For example, regardless of assurances given to the foreigners as to the women's safety and comfort, I discovered that the women were not really comfortable. And my conversation with them led me to believe that Arab mentality and morality might be misunderstood—old values and our glorious past that we want to maintain. I, therefore, talked to a number of my comrades and the speaker of the National Assembly, and we decided to let the children and women leave the country, stay, or return whenever they want. The aim of the meeting was prompted by humanitarian grounds.

Rather: Would you consider letting all of the hostages leave, Mr. President?

Saddam Hussein: We wish this thing had not happened in the first place. It is only natural for us to feel the heavy burden of the situation on us just as the guests we were compelled to host feel the heavy burden of the situation.

Rather: I want to make sure I understand: so the answer is no, you will not consider letting the other hostages go?

Saddam Hussein: As we consider it, a decision will be made.

Rather: Mr. President, you have proposed a debate with President Bush and with Prime Minister Thatcher; are you serious about it?

Saddam Hussein: I am very serious.

Rather: But why; what will that accomplish?

Saddam Hussein: Do not the Western nations like dialogues through which they can learn facts? We are often told the Western nations like dialogues, discussions, and innovation. However, we see some of them avoiding dialogue and innovation. They also refuse to view matters flexibly. For instance, based on declared Western values, we thought that as we used to be abused by others because of the practices of Jabir al-Ahmad al-Sabah [the Kuwaiti Emir], his removal would be greeted with relief in some quarters regardless of disagreements on other viewpoints. However, we found that the biggest power in the world—the United States—came to invade the region under the slogan of returning this backward person—a person who knows nothing but possessing women and money and who can hardly manage to construct a full sentence. This power came to invade the land of the Ka'aba [the Islamic holy site at Mecca] and the tomb of the prophet in order to return Jabir al-Ahmad to power. These is a contradiction in this.

Rather: Excuse me, Mr. President. Respectfully, it is you who invaded another country, not the United States who invaded any country.

Saddam Hussein: Yes, but did you not use to abuse the

Arabs because of the behavior of Jabir al-Ahmad and the like, whom you see in Europe and America?

Rather: My answer to that is no. But let me move on. I want to get back to this idea of the debate. Where would this take place and when?

Saddam Hussein: Any time, starting this moment. I meant a televised debate. But if dialogue is wanted, I am ready as of this moment for a direct dialogue with Mr. Bush and Mrs. Thatcher, together or separately. If they wish a televised debate, my essential condition is that it be live, with no chance for editing the tape, so that citizens could see exactly what takes place.

Rather: Would you see this happening, for example, at the United Nations?

Saddam Hussein: Through whatever means and form. What is important is for the dialogue to take place. It does not matter how.

Rather: Why is this so important to you?

Saddam Hussein: Is dialogue not important for human beings so they can learn the viewpoints of each other and so that the mistaken can correct his mistake and he who is correct can stick to his position?

Arab Interpreter to Rather: We are talking about the televised debate?

Rather: Yes.

Saddam Hussein: Yes.

Interpreter [to Hussein]: Why is it important?

Saddam Hussein: The televised debate is important for me so that public opinion will know the facts as they truly are, not as the rulers say; whether this opinion is Arab—in which I am interested—or foreign, in which Mr. Bush and Mrs. Thatcher are interested. This is important as well for the common denominator among the three of us, which is the human dimension, so that all world peoples will know the facts as they truly are through their own assessment of the debate between the three concerned parties.

Rather: The Bush Administration today calls this idea, and I quote, "sick."

Saddam Hussein: Why is it sick? You, as a U.S. national, have to ask the U.S. Administration why an open and direct dialogue that would make citizens in the countries concerned and the world public in general aware of facts as they are, or as they can be deduced through a dialogue, should be described as sick.

Rather: Mr. President, are you willing to take your claim to Kuwait to the World Court and abide by its decision, to the World Court, the International Court of Justice?

Saddam Hussein: Such a measure could have been taken before 2 August. However, if a comprehensive and durable peace is to be attained in the region, we know that all concerned parties must make some sacrifices. On the basis of this feeling, we proposed our initiative on 12 August. We said that if all the region's problems were to be resolved to ensure that regional problems are settled in accordance with the same bases and standards, the international community must heed all resolutions issued on similar issues by the U.N. Security Council and which have so far been left implemented. The reference here is to the Palestine question, the Arab-Zionist conflict, the occupation of Lebanon, and—before we launched our initiative toward Iran—the issue of the Iraq-Iran war. We included in our initiative the Western Sahara issue, as well as the Kuwait issue. This initiative was declared before the launching of the initiative that resolved matters with Iran. We proposed that all these issues be resolved in accordance with clear standards and principles. As for the Kuwait issue, historical facts and the status quo should provide the background for any solution to it. However, Mr. Bush rejected the initiative within hours, even before asking for the official text of the initiative.

Rather: Well, I believe he considered it to be unrealistic.

Saddam Hussein: Why unrealistic? When the occupation is Zionist, it is considered to be legitimate. When the Zionists occupied Arab lands, it was considered legitimate by Bush. But when the mother restores her child who was snatched away from her, this is considered illegal for Iraq, this is a reason for him to bring in his troops, and to occupy the Ka'aba, and the prophet's tomb. This is the double standard in Mr. Bush's way of thinking.

Rather: Mr. President, again: You are an intelligent person, and you recognize the difference. Israel, which has been surrounded by neighbors who want to destroy her, and a weak neighbor of yours who didn't want to destroy you.

Saddam Hussein: First, regarding the talk that Israel's neighbors seek her destruction, I do not believe any Arab is calling for destroying the Israel of the Jewish identity. But, it is only natural for the Arabs to say that the occupier must leave our lands and that if he does not leave our lands through politics, he must realize that the Arabs will be forced one day to make him leave their lands in other ways. With regard to the rulers of Kuwait: yes, they did want to destroy Iraq. The rulers of Kuwait wanted to destroy Iraq. We clearly said this to them in front of all the Arab kings and presidents who were meeting in Baghdad. We have a document which we can give to you showing that we said this to them. What is taking place against Iraq is war. If you do not mean to wage war, you should review your policy that aims to destroy the Iraqi economy. But what happened later is that things became worse and worse.

Rather: I want to ask you Mr. President: This last weekend I interviewed your friend Hosni Mubarak, [the] President of Egypt.

Saddam Hussein: He was my friend.

Rather: He says he is still a friend.

Saddam Hussein: To me, he no longer is.

Rather: Here's what he told me. This is a paraphrase, but it is accurate, He said: "Either way, Saddam Hussein is through, finished. If he stays in Kuwait, he will be destroyed by military power. If he withdraws from Kuwait, he will lose credibility, he will lose face, and so he will be finished.

Saddam Hussein: If this is what he said, he should be one of the decision-makers in the Pentagon, not the president of the Arab state of Egypt. If he is really the president of the Arab state of Egypt, he would not have said this, even if he wished it. If he is one of the decision makers of the Pentagon, he will commit the same mistake the relevant people in the Pentagon will commit if they believe they can destroy Iraq. History will show us. That is, within a few months, weeks, and years, the one who knows the right course of history and who knows what the real feelings among Arabs is, will emerge. I am saying this, of course, supposing that what you told me about Mr. Mubarak is correct.

Rather: That's it exactly, Mr. President. Your deputy Prime Minister and Foreign Minister told me in an interview that Iraq would not use poison gas to biological weapons unless attacked with nuclear weapons itself. Are you prepared to give this commitment?

Saddam Hussein: We have made enough statements on this issue. If what is meant is the situation with Israel, we spoke about this a great deal.

Rather: No, we properly speak about the situation with the United States.

Saddam Hussein: In all cases, we will not give Iraq to anybody. Iraq exists to live in dignity.

Rather: So, you might use poison gas in defense of Iraq, to save Iraq?

Saddam Hussein: I have not said that. I say: Iraq is an independent and sovereign state. And whoever attacks Iraq to change the ruling system and destroy this country should know that Iraq will not be an easy target.

Rather: Do you think, Mr. President, that this will be Vietnam in the sand for the United States?

Saddam Hussein: We do not hope that the United States will face the tragedies it faced in Vietnam, and neither do we hope that the Iraqis and the Arabs will face the same tragedies the Vietnamese faced in the war between the United States and the Vietnamese. But, if the war breaks out between the United States and Iraq, representing the Arabs, I think the United States will no longer be superpower number one. And the harm that will be inflicted on the invaders will be even more severe than what they experienced in Vietnam, and Iraq will come out on top.

Rather: I think that you underestimate the power of the United States. What are the chances that a quick, powerful strike could knock you out immediately?

Saddam Hussein: There is no powerful and quick strike that any nation could deliver, whatever their overall power. The United States depends on the Air Force. The

Air Force has never decided a war in the history of wars. In the early days of the war between us and Iran, the Iranians had an edge in the air. They had approximately 600 aircraft, all U.S.-made and whose pilots received training in the United States. They flew to Baghdad like black clouds, but they did not determine the outcome of the battle. In later years, our air force gained supremacy, and yet it was not our air force that settled the war. The United States may be able to destroy cities, factories and to kill, but it will not be able to decided the war with its Air Force. This is in terms of the relationship between technology and our fighters, within the framework of war. But otherwise, God is with us, and Satan is with the U.S. Administration. Can Satan defeat God?

Rather: Every soldier I ever met believes God is on his side.

Saddam Hussein: Yet there remains a difference between one coming all the way from the United States to occupy Hejaz and Najd and one sitting in his home among his kinfolk without committing aggression against the United States.

Rather: If you attacked by the United States from Saudi territory or any place else, will your promise not to attack Saudi Arabia still hold?

Saddam Hussein: In the event we are attacked from Saudi territory, the situation will be different. And if we are attacked from other territories, the situation will also be different.

Rather: Sir, we are nearing the end of our time. I appreciate your generosity. But what is happening now is going to drastically change the balance of forces in the Middle East. Do you agree with that?

Saddam Hussein: Yes, I agree, if the situation should develop into war. But if the crisis finds a political solution, things will take a different course.

Rather: Is there anything that you want to say to President Bush, if you could speak to him directly?

Saddam Hussein: I have nothing to say, except that before he involves the United States in a difficult situation, he should think a great deal and consult with people who might be able to give him accurate and correct information on the region and the background of the issue of Kuwait in regard to Iraq.

Rather: Do you have any new proposals to make?

Saddam Hussein: If a dialogue begins, we are sure to have a good many things to say, just as they would have many things to tell us. But if war breaks out, we will not bear the sin of starting it.

Rather: Mr. President, I thank you for your time.

Saddam Hussein: My pleasure.

Reference: "Interview with Saddam Hussein by Dan Rather of CBS Television Network in Baghdad on 29 August 1990," in Moore, Fred, comp., *Iraq Speaks: Documents on the Gulf Crisis* (Palo Alto, CA: privately printed, 1991), 24–28.

Letter from Saddam Hussein to Presidents Bush and Gorbachev in Conference in Helsinki, Finland, 9 September 1990

In the name of God, from Saddam Hussein to Presidents Mikhail Gorbachev and George Bush.

You are meeting tomorrow, 9 September 1990, 19 Safar 1411 A.H. When you meet, the world will follow with unusual interest, including the people of the region in which God has privileged us with the honor of being part of a nation, the Arab nation, a nation which God had honored to be the cradle of divine messages and prophecy throughout the ages.

At the time you are in, being in a position to decide whatever relates to the future of good or evil for humanity, the angels will be hovering above you on one side and devils on the other. Each says his prayer, and each would hope it to be in accordance with his nature and what God has chosen for him. God will be above all. I am not saying to either of you, neither appealing to any of you on what your decision should be. . . . However, after relying on God, the great determiner, I say that before taking any decision, you should bear in mind the following.

First, Iraq did not invade with its armies either of your countries, nor has it premeditated intention to harm peoples, countries or legitimate interests. It is a country that loves peace based on justice, fairness and respect, of human choices, each in accordance with his judgment and in accordance with what pleases God and peoples.

Despite the fact that Nuri As Said, Iraq's Prime Minister and a friend of the West in 1958, and Abdul Karim Quasim, head of the Iraq Government and a friend of the Soviet Union in 1961, had decided to annex or to claim Kuwait on the basis that it is part of Iraq, those who stand against us today did not do so against them at that time. Although the current situation has given today's decision an added weight, this is because the backward and corrupt ex-rulers of Kuwait conspired against Iraq and its great people to the point that placed it on the verge of the abyss.

If your talks lead you to the approach of the defender of the international organization's resolution, then you should remember that this international organization had taken before the resolutions relating to Iraq many other resolutions since its establishment. Among them were decisions relating to Arab issues, their parties being Arabs and foreigners. Principal among these issues was the question of the patient people of Palestine and the people of Golan.

Despite the fact that such resolutions were adopted under circumstances in which there was a balance of power between the superpowers, unlike presently, the Security Council has never taken such hasty and agitated resolutions. Its resolutions never reached this level of cruelty and injustice, which exposes a premeditated intention. Those who remember the unjust campaign which preceded the events of August 2, led by the U.S.A. and Zionism against Iraq, will find out for sure the real purpose of the feverish campaign led in the Security Council by the U.S.A., which, apart from the Security Council, made unilateral and even more unjust decisions against Iraq by applying its own blockade measure. . . .

Probably what may come under discussion when you both meet is only Iraq. . . . If this is true, then it will prompt you to make decisions that would restore your part of the responsibility that may save our region the evil of war and the ensuing sorrows. Goodness lies in what God may choose.

Reference: *New York Times,* 9 September 1990, 14.

Joint Statement by Presidents Bush and Gorbachev at the Helsinki Summit, 9 September 1990

With regard to Iraq's invasion and continued military occupation of Kuwait, President [George] Bush and President [Mikhail] Gorbachev issue the following joint statement:

We are united in the belief that Iraq's aggression must not be tolerated. No peaceful international order is possible if larger states can devour their smaller neighbors.

We reaffirm the joint statement of our foreign ministers of August 3, 1990, and our support for United Nations Security Council Resolutions 660, 661, 662, 664 and 665.

Today, we once again call upon the Government of Iraq to withdraw unconditionally from Kuwait, the restoration of Kuwait's legitimate Government, and to free all hostages now held in Iraq and Kuwait.

Nothing short of the complete implementation of the United Nations Security Council resolutions is acceptable.

Nothing short of a return to the preAugust 2 status of Kuwait can end Iraq's isolation.

We call upon the entire world community to adhere to the sanctions mandated by the United Nations, and we pledge to work, individually and in concert, to insure full compliance with the sanctions. At the same time, the United States and the Soviet Union recognize that U.N. Security Council Resolution 661 permits, in humanitarian circumstances, the importation into Iraq and Kuwait of food. The Sanctions Committee will make recommendations to the Security Council on what would constitute humanitarian circumstances. The United States and the Soviet Union further agree that any such imports must be strictly monitored by the appropriate international agencies to insure that food reaches only those for whom it is intended, with special priority being given to meeting the needs of children.

Our preference is to resolve the crisis peacefully, and

we will be united against Iraq's aggression as long as the crisis exists. However, we are determined to see this aggression end. and if the current steps fail to end it, we are prepared to consider additional ones consistent with the U.N. Charter. We must demonstrate beyond any doubt that aggression cannot and will not pay.

As soon as the objectives mandated by the U.N. Security Council resolutions mentioned above have been achieved and we have demonstrated that aggression does not pay, the Presidents direct their foreign ministers to work with countries in the region and outside it to develop regional security structures and measures to promote peace and stability. It is essential to work actively to resolve all remaining conflicts in the Middle East and Persian Gulf. Both sides will continue to consult each other and initiate measures to pursue these broader objectives at the proper time.

*Reference: New York Times,*10 September 1990, A7.

Press Conference with Presidents Bush and Gorbachev, 9 September 1990

On 9 September 1990, after a two-day summit in Helsinki, Finland, President George Bush of the United States and President Mikhail Gorbachev of the Soviet Union held a news conference. A transcript of that conference follows.

Q [Helen Thomas]. I'd like to ask both Presidents whether we are going to have a war in the Persian Gulf? And I'd like to follow up.
Bush: Well, with your permission, Mr. President, I hope that we can achieve a peaceful solution, and the way to do that is to have Iraq comply with the United Nations resolutions.

And I think that part of our joint statement, two short lines, said it most clearly—nothing short of the complete implementation of United Nations Security Council resolutions is acceptable. As soon as Saddam Hussein realizes that, then there certainly will be a peaceful resolution to that question.
Q. President Gorbachev? What do you think?
President Gorbachev: In replying to your question, I should say that the whole of our seven hours of meeting today were devoted to the quest for a political resolution of that conflict. And I believe that we're on the right road.
Q. Mr. President, if I may follow up with you, President Bush. You are indicating that hostilities could break out if this is not resolved peacefully?
Bush: The question is what?
Q. I said, are you indicating that there could be hostilities?
Bush: The United—The United States is determined to see these resolutions enforced, and I like to feel that they will be enforced and that will result in a peaceful resolution.

Q. My question to Mr. President [Bush]—my name is Panyi. Do you think, Mr. President, that the conflict of the—do you think, Mr. President, that the conflict of the Gulf gives the opportunity to solve the Palestinian problem through an international peace conference for the Middle East? And my second question is if this problem was discussed today with Mr. Gorbachev?
Bush: Well, let me say that I see the implementation of the United Nations resolutions separate and apart from the need to solve the other question. That question has been on the agenda of many countries for many years, and it is very important that that question be resolved.

The Secretary of State said the other day, and I strongly support that, that under certain circumstances the consideration of a conference of that nature would be acceptable—indeed, it's been a part of our policy from time to time. But the thing that I feel strongly about is that these issues are not linked. And any effort to link them is an effort to dilute the resolutions of the United Nations.
Q. A question to President Bush from Soviet radio and television. How long will United States be—troops be present in the Persian Gulf area?
Bush: They will be present in the—in the area until we are satisfied that the security needs of the area have been met, and that these resolutions have been complied with. And they sooner that they are out of there, as far as I am concerned, the better. I made very clear to President Gorbachev, as I think he will confirm, that we have no intention keeping them a day longer than is required. And so, I'd leave it right there.
Q. Tom Raum with the Associated Press—
Gorbachev (interrupting): I'd like to add something, and to confirm what President—the President of the United States has just said to me in our conversation, that the United States of America do not intend [*sic*] to leave their forces in the zone.

And in connection with the change or the normalization of the situation, the United States Administration, and personally the President, will do everything possible to insure that the forces are withdrawn from the region—from the zone. And that's a very important statement.
Marlin Fitzwater: Tom, please go ahead.
Q. I have a question for both Presidents. The unity that you're expressing today doesn't ignore the fact that there are still some irritants between the two countries. President Bush, are you more sympathetic now to suggestions of Western economic aid to the Soviet Union? And President Gorbachev, would you be willing to withdraw Soviet military advisers from Iraq?
Bush: For my part, I am very much interested in assisting to be sure that *perestroika* is successful. We indeed have a mission of high-level businessmen on their way to the Soviet Union right now. They happen to be in Helsinki.

This is but a manifestation of the fact that we are trying to encourage economic cooperation in as many ways as possible. And we had a good, long discussion in our expanded meeting this afternoon about that. And I—I am given the—the common stand that the Soviet Union and the United States have taken at the United Nations. It seems to me that we should be as forthcoming as we possibly can in terms of economics, and I plan to do that.

There are certain constraints, as you say, there are certain nuances of difference. There are certain differences, real differences. But on the other hand, I have said before and I'll repeat it here in front of all this—journalists from all around the world—we, of course, want *perestroika* to succeed.

It is an internal matter of the—of the Soviet union, but I think this remarkable cooperation that has been demonstrated by the Soviet Union at the United Nations gets me inclined to recommend as close cooperation in the economic field as possible, and I will be saying this to the Congress when I get back.

We still have problems. Look, we've got some problems ourselves in our economy, and we are not in the position, operating at the enormous deficits, to write out large checks. Having said that, there are many ways, that we can endeavor to be of assistance to the—to the emerging economy in the Soviet Union.

Gorbachev: And there was a question also addressed to me. I would like, nevertheless, on the question which did appear also to be addressed to me—the Western assistance to the Soviet [Union]—I would like to continue.

The conversation with President Bush is continuing on the Western assistance to the Soviet Union. I see that there is an attempt being made to link—to establish a link between this and disagreements or the lack of disagreements. And in response to that, I would say the following.

We began our conversation today together by reviewing the situation and realizing that the whole of world society and our two great states are undergoing a trial. This is a test of the durability of the new approach to resolving world problems. And as we enter upon a new peaceful period and as we emerge from the cold war, we see that no less [inaudible] are necessary in order to find ways and means in this period of peace to meet the new situation and to tackle all problems that may arise.

I think if it hadn't been for Malta, it would have been very difficult for us to act in the very difficult situation connected with the unification of Germany. I think that if, following that, there hadn't been Washington and Camp David and the other meetings on this level with other partners in international relations, we would now be in a difficult situation facing the crisis in the Persian Gulf.

And the fact that today we have taken a common approach to such difficult problems, problems which may well have tragic consequences for the whole world, not just for the peoples of that region, demonstrates that we still are moving forward in the right direction and that we are capable of resolving the most difficult and the most acute problems and to find appropriate responses to the challenges of our time. And the greater part of our conversation together was devoted to this.

And I believe that this is the most important point to bear in mind. Differences, nuances in the differences of view, arguments—these can be—these are natural. It's natural that those should arise. But what we have seen today is that we have confirmed the most important progress of recent time. Now I should like to say something about the Iraqi question, but in fact, I haven't quite finished on the first subject.

I wouldn't want President Bush's reply to give rise to the opinion that the Soviet Union is going to align a certain sum with a certain behavior. We are acting in a different situation. We are finding a solution—we shall find a solution which will be satisfactory and, above all, which will remove the danger of an explosion. And this is becoming a normal element of the new kind of cooperation in trade, in technology and human exchange. All of these elements characterize the new peaceful period upon which we are just now embarked and which we have to get used to.

It would be very oversimplified and very superficial to judge that the Soviet Union could be bought for dollars, because although we do look forward to cooperation in this very serious time of far-reaching changes in our economy, and that's normal, let's remember the reforms of recent years.

In a number of states, they always, in addition to the principal efforts made by the peoples concerned themselves, they always involved also the participation of the world community in one form or another. So if anybody wants to try and impose a different view, that's unacceptable to us. It's unacceptable to the United States. It's unacceptable to the Soviet Union, and it would be unacceptable to any other state.

Now, to move on to the second part of your question concerning our experts in Iraq. They are not so much advisers as specialists or experts who are working under contract, and their number is being reduced.

Whereas at the beginning of the conflict, I think there were still 196 of them, there now some 150 of them. And the Iraqi leadership looks upon the matter thus: that if they haven't completed their work—their normal work under contract, even though it might be a matter of weapons, then they are, nevertheless, leaving Iraq and the process is going forward. So I really don't think there's a problem.

Q. Isvestia. Question to both Presidents. Did you discuss any possible military options for curbing Iraqi aggression? And what would be the conditions, and would be the point where you would consider that the political options were exhausted and it was time to go to the Security Council and talk about—through the Security Council demanding an Iraqi withdrawal from Kuwait?

Bush: The answer to your question is no. We did not discuss military options. And your question is too hypothetical. And I would like to see this matter peacefully resolved.

Gorbachev: I would like to support what was said by President Bush, and I stress once more that the whole of our time together was spent on talking about this conflict in a mutual search for a political solution. And I think we can look with optimism in the final analysis on the efforts being taken by the international community working together within the Security Council at the U.N.

Q. Mikhail Sergeyevich, you were just saying that if Iraq doesn't withdraw its force peacefully, then it will be necessary to take military steps. What kind of Soviet contribution will there be to those military steps? And what will happen then to the Soviet citizens who are in Iraq now? And what will the Arab factor be?

Gorbachev: Firstly, I did not say that if Iraq does not withdraw peacefully, we're going to have recourse to military methods. I did not state that. I do not state that. And moreover, in my view, that would draw us into consequences which we can't at this stage forecast and therefore, our country and the United Nations as a whole has a whole range of possibilities of finding a political solution to this problem. Therefore, I would limit ourselves to that and therefore the second part of your question is irrelevant.

Q. If I could ask President Gorbachev, specifically, Iraq had been your ally. What directly have you done with Saddam Hussein to reverse the situation there? And President Bush, what specifically have you asked Mr. Gorbachev to do directly? Have you asked him to make direct contact with Saddam Hussein?

Gorbachev: I should say that from the start of the crisis, we've been actively exchanging views and carrying forth dialogue not only within the Security Council, not only with the administration of the USA. These types of contact have great importance to us, but we are also holding active leadership of China, of India, of all the other European states, especially those which are members of the Security Council. And in my view, it's this dialogue which has helped us toward the Security Council resolution which was passed.

On top of that, we are also actively cooperating with the Arab states, the countries of the Arab world. And here our dialogue is no less intensive than with our partners in the countries I previously mentioned, including dialogue with President Hussein.

And I can state that what we have announced publicly is also being said to President Hussein in our dialogue with him, which all means that the President and the leadership of Iraq are expected to show a reasonable approach to stop and to understand what is implied by the position taken by the Security Council on this issue.

This is the dialogue which we have undertaken with him. And we are trying to make sure that our arguments are convincing. We discussed various options for ending the situation with him and we are also attempting, as I already said, to make it quite clear to Saddam Hussein that if Iraq were to provoke military action, then the result would be tragedy first and foremost for the Iraqi people themselves, for the whole of the region and for the whole of the world.

You know, this is, of course, a dialogue in a very difficult situation. But we consider it a very useful dialogue, and we don't exclude the possibility of establishing new contacts, of having new meetings at various levels. And the type of communication which we have had up until now with the Iraqis gives us hope that those links we have with them can be used positively for the sake of all of us, for the sake of finding a peaceful solution to this problem, and especially of preventing the situation turning into aggression, in this situation.

Bush: My [inaudible] would be simply that there is no need to ask Mr. Gorbachev to contact Saddam Hussein. Clearly, from his answer, you can see that they have been in contact—

Interpreter: The President cannot be heard. The microphone seems to be off.

Bush: Not working?

Interpreter: The President could not be heard for a few seconds there. The microphone was off.

Bush [Working with microphone]: Is that better? Well—

Gorbachev: It's a little better, but hit it again.

Bush: President Gorbachev answered the question about the contact with Saddam Hussein. And clearly your question to me is, have I asked him to contact Saddam Hussein? The answer is no. But the Soviet Union is in contact.

He himself received the Foreign Minister, Aziz. But I would just simply sum it up by saying the best answer to Saddam Hussein, or the best contact is the contact that took place at the United Nations when there was worldwide condemnation of the aggression.

And I happen to feel that this statement showing the Soviet Union and the United States in essential agreement here is another good statement for Saddam Hussein. And hopefully he will see that he is not going to divide us and divide other countries, and that he will do what he should have done some time ago, and that is comply with the United Nations sanctions.

So—but I did not ask him to do that, because they're way ahead of us on that. They are having contacts and trying to be helpful in that regard.

Q. Pravda. I have a question to Mr. Bush. Mr. President, what is your position on the question of signing a treaty limiting strategic offensive weapons? And when do you think that such a treaty will in fact be signed?

Bush: We still remain committed to a strategic arms treaty. We vowed that we would encourage our negotiators to move forward more rapidly on both the strategic arms treaty and the conventional force agreement. And I'm still hopeful that by the end of the year we will have such an agreement.

Interpreter: Microphone please for Mr. Gorbachev.

Gorbachev: Should I hit it again? I think it's working. I'd like to confirm what President Bush has just said, that we really have agreed to make fresh efforts to give further instructions, because we see that there is a possibility successfully to complete the negotiating process in those two fora and to come up with positive results in the course of this year.

Q. O.K., my question is—good evening. Doris Akatarian from the Palestine news agency, WAFA. My question is for President Bush, and I would also like to hear President Gorbachev's comments on that.

Interpreter: The question is to President Bush, and [she] also wants to hear President Gorbachev's comment.

Q. President Bush mentioned that you failed to see the link between the Palestinian question and the present situation. I would like to know how come it is so important to implement the U.N. resolutions in this particular instance when other standing ones have—have been frozen and overlooked and disregarded for so long? So, I'd like to know how come this aggression is so different from other ones? And I would also like to add that I personally feel that the Palestinian dilemma and question need the attention of the superpowers more than ever. Thank you very much.

Bush: I agree that it needs it, and we are very much interested in implementing resolution 242 of the United Nations. We've been zealously trying to do that, as have many powers for many years.

But the fact that that resolution hasn't been fulfilled when it calls for withdrawal to secure and recognized boundaries, and it should be, and hopefully we can be catalytic in seeing that happen, does not mean that you stand idly by in the face of a naked aggression against Kuwait.

And the United Nations has moved, and the United Nations' resolutions should be implemented on their face without trying to tie it into some other undissolved—unresolved dispute. But I couldn't agree more that it is important, it is very important that that question eventually, and hopefully sooner than later, be resolved.

Q. I have a question for both Presidents—Oh, excuse me, sir.

Interpreter: Microphone, please, for Mr. Gorbachev.

Gorbachev: I think that everything that is taking place in the Middle East is a matter of concern to us, of equal concern. And even more than in the case of the Persian Gulf, we need to act more energetically in order to resolve the complex of problems in the Middle East, and to come up with decisions and to devise a system, to devise guarantees that would insure the interests of all peoples and of the whole world community, because it's a matter which is of vital concern to all of us.

And it seems to me that these is a link here because the failure to find a solution in the Middle East at large also has a bearing on the acuteness of the particular conflict we've been talking about here.

Q. A question for both Presidents, please. In your statement, you pledged to work individually and in concert to insure full compliance with the U.N. sanctions against Iraq. May I inquire what, if any, specific and concrete steps you have agreed to take in furtherance of that.

Bush: We didn't agree to specific and concrete steps. I think President Gorbachev in the contacts he's had with Saddam Hussein, and if—I mean the Iraqis—and if they continue, will be a step in that direction. Clearly, this message itself will be a step in that direction. But we did not sit at this meeting and try to assign each other or ask each other to undertake specific measures in keeping with that particular—particular paragraph.

Q. May I follow up, President Bush; the statement also says that you are prepared to offer additional [inaudible].

Gorbachev: I'd like to add to that that the emphasis here is on the significance of the political fact that we feel necessary to reflect in this statement, which testifies to our political will to act jointly, or in parallel—independently really—in search of these new steps toward peaceful resolution of the problem.

I think that for the meeting and the document on—that we've just adopted is more important than our enumerating various steps that might have been taken here. That forms the basis for the further active quest for solutions.

Q. Tass—Soviet Tass agency. I also have a question to the Presidents of both countries. Mr. President—Mr. Gorbachev first of all. Since the last meeting, it seems to be that you've had a good mutual understanding. Have you succeeded in deepening that mutual understanding in the course of today's meeting and how, in general, what bearing in general is that factor having on the results of your negotiations?

Bush: Well, I think clearly there has been a developed—a developing mutual understanding over the years. I like to feel, and I think President Gorbachev agrees, that our meeting in Malta had something to do with furthering that understanding.

I'm convinced that our meeting in the United States at Camp David particularly furthered that understanding. But I'm not—I think the world sees clearly that if this had occurred 20 years ago, there wouldn't have been this cooperative feeling at the United Nations. And I think that it's very important.

So I don't know how one qualified mutual understanding, but I feel we're moving on the right track. Neither of us when we talk try to hide our differences. Neither of us try to indicate that we look at exactly every problem exactly the same way. But the very fact that we can talk with that degree of frankness, without rancor, I think, enhances mutual understanding.

And then when we see us on a question of this nature, standing shoulder to shoulder with many other countries at the United Nations, I think it is [the] obvious manifestation of this developing mutual understanding. It's a very broad philosophical question, but differences still remain. But the common ground, in my view, at least, surges ahead of these differences. And we will continue to cooperate with President Gorbachev.

Gorbachev: I don't know if I would be allowed to tell you a secret here. I haven't asked President Bush if he'll let me. But I must admit that I'm dying to take the risk and tell you, but it's too important to give you an answer to this particular question.

But that last sentence does really give me the hope that we'll get by. In our talks, the President said: "You know, there was a long time when our view was that the Soviet Union had nothing to do in the Middle East. There was—had no business there." This was something that we had to talk through during this meeting here in Helsinki, and what was said here is that it's very important for us to cooperate in the Middle East, just as it is on other issues of world politics. So that is an answer to your question.

It is very important that at each meeting we move forward. We enrich our relationship, and I think I should say that we increase our trust. If trust is engendered between the leaders of two such nations during meetings of this kind, then I'm sure you'll agree with me that that is to the good of all of us.

Whether we want it or not, history dictates that a lot is going to depend on whether the two countries can work together. That's not our ambition, it's just the way that history has gone.

So far from excluding such a possibility, we intend to cooperate with all sorts of other countries as well, more and more. That's how we see our role in the world developing.

And my last comment is also very important. Its seems to me that the way the world is, the way the world is changing, in today's world, no single country, however powerful, will be able to provide the leadership which individual countries formerly tried to provide, including some countries which are represented here.

We can only succeed if we work together and solve our problems together. That is what is emerging from these negotiations, and that we consider the most important aspect.

Q. Mikhail Sergeyevich, from French television—I'm going to speak French if I may. Could I ask Mr. Gorbachev whether the Soviet Union is still Iraq's friend, as Minister Tariq Aziz declared in Moscow last week? Are you still the friend of Saddam Hussein? And another question, also directed to Mr. Gorbachev. President Saddam Hussein stated yesterday that the Soviet Union would demonstrate that it is a great power by resisting George Bush's pressure and supporting the Baghdad regime. Could you indicate to me, if you would, what your reply would be to Saddam Hussein?

Gorbachev: I will reply to you, and so I don't have to repeat it also to Saddam Hussein, the same reply that I've given to previous questions. My position is unchanged.

We see our role and our responsibility, and within the framework of that responsibility we shall act in cooperation with the other members of the Security Council. And in this instance, I can once again say, since we are sitting here, two Presidents together, I shall interact and cooperate with the President of the United States.

I'd very much like to express the hope that President Saddam Hussein will—will display—I really hope that he will—will display sobriety, will look carefully at the whole situation and will respond to the appeals and the demands of the world community and that he will take steps that are suitable to the situation, that are carefully weighed in their worldwide implications and their implications for the Arab world too.

No one has any intention of trying to exclude Iraq from the community of nations, but what the present Iraqi leadership is doing is—is driving into a dead end, and I hope that President Saddam Hussein will heed this appeal to him.

Q. I'm sorry it's always time—other kind of—as a neighboring country of the conflict—we're from Turkey—

Q. [Another reporter] I think I'm next. Thank you very much.

Q. [Turkish reporter] But I didn't have a chance—microphone—people are trying to grab it from me.

Q. Let me just press on here, if I may. I have a—ladies first, right? Oh, okay, okay. I'd like to ask Mr. Gorbachev if you have ruled out the possibility of a Soviet military participation in this effort in any sense, either as part of the naval blockade or as part of some future peacekeeping force in the region? And I would follow up with a question to Mr. Bush. To what degree that would be a disappointment to you if—if that's Mr. Gorbachev's position?

Gorbachev: I don't see the point of doing that now, and we shall continue to act in cooperation within the Security Council and in strict compliance with all of its decisions.

Bush: I'm not disappointed in that answer.

Q. You said you're determined to see this aggression

end, and you're—and current steps are being considered. What does this mean? What comes next?

Bush: It's too hypothetical. We want to see this—we want to see the message get through to Saddam Hussein. We want to see him do what the United Nations calls on him to do. And that statement can be interpreted any way you want to interpret it, but it's out there and I would simply not go into any hypothetical questions that would lead me beyond what that statement says.

Gorbachev: Could I add a couple of words?

Interpreter: Mr. Gorbachev wishes to add a couple of words.

Gorbachev: Please, if you'd—if you would—excuse me, I'll add a couple of words—just to what Mr. Bush has already said.

You know, in my view, I have the impression that both the press and public opinion in some countries is in some ways saying that there's a lack of decision on somebody's part. that we're withdrawing in the face of those who are trampling on international law. I cannot agree with that view. In fact, it's a view which causes a certain amount of embarrassment to the leadership of nations which are acting through the Security Council in this respect. What has been done up till now in answer to Iraqi aggression is very important because action has been taken not only within the framework of the Security Council, but there has been unanimous world opinion—a kind of solidarity which has never been expressed before in the history of the world. And we have prevented the aggression [from] going any further.

We have preserved the functioning of the structures which are of economic importance, which would affect so many other countries as well. And finally, the resolution has been taken on an embargo, which is a very stiff measure, in reaction to the aggression.

In my view, this is a strategic way of tackling the question, which has been tackled successfully at the first stages. And we are convinced that the next stage of a political solution, achieved politically, to put an end to this acute international crisis and make sure that a political settlement should be possible, that in this situation decisiveness, willpower and the responsibility and political faith in the possibility of a political solution to this very difficult issue shows that the political leaders of the world are being responsible to their own nations and to the world. And we do not want to get caught up in arguments about prestige and so on.

Q. From Finnish television. Concerning the humanitarian aid, does your joint statement mean in practice that you consider that food should now be allowed [in]to Iraq?

Gorbachev: The Presidents feel it necessary to reflect in our joint declaration that we see the need to uphold what was decided by the Security Council on this subject and the Security Council was prepared to admit for humanitarian purposes the supply of medicines and of foodstuffs required first and foremost for children. We've actually stated this quite plainly in our statement. And so we've taken a very clear-cut position on that. But we've also made it clear this must take place within the framework of certain international organizations and being monitored by them at stages in the operation. So I think that this has been stated in the correct terms.

Bush: [inaudible] President Gorbachev on that point, and that language is very good because it does express the concern that both countries feel in the event there actually are children and others who are suffering because of lack of food.

I hope that nobody around the world interprets this as our view now that now there should be wholesale food shipments to Iraq because I can only speak here for the—the United States when I would call attention to the fact that we need some kind of international agency to see that there is this humanitarian concern as expressed, this exception in the United Nations embargo for humanitarian purposes, and not only is it required for this humanitarian circumstance, but that the food gets where it is supposed to go.

So this should not be from the U.S. standpoint as interpreted as a wholesale big—big whole in this embargo. It is not the—it was not our intention and I think the language is very clear on that point.

Marlin Fitzwater: John Cochran, please.

Q. A few things if you could clear up for us. First of all, you seem to disagree on the military option. And when you talk about further steps being taken to implement the—the U.N. sanctions, President Bush, you seem to be saying [that] the military option is still out there. President Gorbachev seems to disagree. Do you disagree on that? Did you ask President Gorbachev to pull his experts out of Iraq and did you ask him to send his troops into the gulf region?

Bush: I did not ask him to send troops in. If the Soviets decided to that at the invitation of the Saudis, that would be fine with us. But I did not ask him to do that.

I believe there—with the 23 countries that are participating on the ground or—23 countries that are participating on the ground and at sea that the security of Saudi Arabia is close to safeguarded. What were the other two points?

Q. Did you ask him to pull the experts out of Iraq and do you disagree on the use of military force? You seem to say it's still an option. He seems to say it's not an option, ever.

Bush: We may have a difference on that. I'm just—as I think I've answered over and over again at home—I'm not going to discuss what I will or won't do. And President Gorbachev made an eloquent appeal, with which I agree, that a peaceful solution is the best. So I've left it open. He can comment on the other. But I—and again, John, I'm sorry—the second point?

Q. The experts; pulling the experts out?

Bush: Well, I think it would facilitate things, but on the other hand, he's given his answer here. And that it is not a major irritant. You've said that he's already—I think that he said that he is reducing the numbers there, but I think I tried to make clear that this was a question that was widely being raised in the United States, and it would facilitate things if they were out of there in terms of total understanding.

But I heard his answer, listened to it very, very carefully, and I must say that I would let it stand at that. If I was just saying, "Would I like to see them all out of there?" I think I'd say absolutely. But I'd let him add to that.

Gorbachev: In answer to all these questions which you gave us such a clear list of, I've already given answers. I really don't have anything to add to the answers I've already given.

Q. Al Ahram newspaper of Cairo, Egypt. Question to the two Presidents, please. You mentioned something about the security arrangement. Is the Soviet Union going to participate in any kind of security arrangement, and what is the role of the region and the countries of that region of the Middle East?

Gorbachev: On the first question, as we began, we intend to continue to cooperate closely and actively in the framework of the Security Council and on the basis of the decisions that have been adopted, we shall act accordingly. That's the first point.

Secondly, as concerns the role of the countries of the region, yes, I think that generally speaking I would stress [that] the importance of the Arab factor, not yet, really hadn't been brought to bear in efforts to help resolve this crisis situation. I don't want to offer you our analysts right now as to why that's the case, but nevertheless I am convinced that there is an obvious activization of the quest on the part of Arab states to find the response to the urgent situation which faces us—faces us all here.

We cooperate with all the Arab countries, and I might say not unusefully. The outlines of possible steps are beginning to emerge but it is too soon to be specific. We are continuing our cooperation with Arab countries and at a certain stage, when the situation has changed and has been somewhat—when the tension has been reduced, then perhaps we might carry this further.

But we shall continue in the Security Council—the permanent members of the Security Council—to guarantee security. I have no doubt that we shall succeed in resolving the problem by political means.

Marlin Fitzwater: [Inaudible] the hour. Thank you very much.

Bush: May I comment on that one, please? I am very glad that the Arab states, at the Arab League and in other ways, have stated their condemnation of Saddam Hussein. He is trying to make this a contest between the Arab world and the United States. And it is no such thing if you will look at how the United Nations has overwhelmingly condemned him.

So the Arab states have a very key role in this. Many Arab states have responded in the defense of Saudi Arabia—Syria, Morocco, Egypt, to say nothing of the G.C.C. countries. So it is not Saddam Hussein and the Arab world against the United States. It is Saddam Hussein against the United Nations and against a majority of the Arab League. And that is a very important point that I will continue—continue to make because the Arab League itself has stood up to him and urged his compliance with the sanctions and condemned his aggression.

So in this case I see the Arab states as having a very important role to play in the resolution of this question, and they have not been taken in by his attempt to make this the—the Arab world versus the United States of America, when it is nothing of the kind. . .

Reference: New York Times, 10 September 1990, A8, A9.

Joint Statement by Presidents Bush and Gorbachev at the Helsinki Summit, 9 September 1990

With regard to Iraq's invasion and continued military occupation of Kuwait, President [George] Bush and President [Mikhail] Gorbachev issue the following joint statement:

We are united in the belief that Iraq's aggression must not be tolerated. No peaceful international order is possible if larger states can devour their smaller neighbors.

We reaffirm the joint statement of our foreign ministers of August 3, 1990, and our support for United Nations Security Council Resolutions 660, 661, 662, 664 and 665.

Today, we once again call upon the Government of Iraq to withdraw unconditionally from Kuwait, the restoration of Kuwait's legitimate Government, and to free all hostages now held in Iraq and Kuwait.

Nothing short of the complete implementation of the United Nations Security Council resolutions is acceptable.

Nothing short of a return to the pre–August 2 status of Kuwait can end Iraq's isolation.

We call upon the entire world community to adhere to the sanctions mandated by the United Nations, and we pledge to work, individually and in concert, to insure full compliance with the sanctions. At the same time, the United States and the Soviet Union recognize that U.N. Security Council Resolution 661 permits, in humanitarian circumstances, the importation into Iraq and Kuwait of food. The Sanctions Committee will make recommendations to the Security Council on what would constitute humanitarian circumstances. The United States and the Soviet Union further agree that any such imports must be strictly monitored by the appropriate international agencies to insure that food reaches only those for whom it is intended, with special priority being given to meeting the needs of children.

Our preference is to resolve the crisis peacefully, and we will be united against Iraq's aggression as long as the crisis exists. However, we are determined to see this aggression end. and if the current steps fail to end it, we are prepared to consider additional ones consistent with the U.N. Charter. We must demonstrate beyond any doubt that aggression cannot and will not pay.

As soon as the objectives mandated by the U.N. Security Council resolutions mentioned above have been achieved and we have demonstrated that aggression does not pay, the Presidents direct their foreign ministers to work with countries in the region and outside it to develop regional security structures and measures to promote peace and stability. It is essential to work actively to resolve all remaining conflicts in the Middle East and Persian Gulf. Both sides will continue to consult each other and initiate measures to pursue these broader objectives at the proper time.

Reference: New York Times, 10 September 1990, A7.

Statement of General Colin Powell before the Senate Committee on Armed Services, 11 September 1990

On 11 September 1990, General Colin Powell, Chairman of the Joint Chiefs of Staff, appeared with Secretary of Defense Dick Cheney in front of the Senate Committee on Armed Services to discuss the American deployment of troops to the Persian Gulf. Powell's testimony appears verbatim. Presiding over the hearing was committee chairman Senator Sam Nunn (D-Georgia).

Mr. Chairman, members of this committee, I am pleased to have this opportunity to discuss the military aspects of U.S. actions in the Persian Gulf region.

As Secretary Cheney indicated in his statement, U.S. forces are in the Persian Gulf region to support the President's national policy objectives. Our military objectives are to deter further aggression by Iraq, and to enforce the mandatory Chapter VII sanctions of the U.N. Charter and U.N. Security Council Resolutions 661, 662, and 665. In accomplishing these objectives, we are working very closely with allied and friendly nations—today, over 25 in number—who have sent or are in the process of sending military forces to the region. Saddam Hussein is facing a multinational military force. This multinational force will be capable of a successful defense if Iraqi forces invade Saudi Arabia. It will also have the capability to respond should Iraqi forces invade any other nation in the area.

Because of the tremendous distances involved, we phased our overall operation for the defense of Saudi Arabia. In the initial phase, naval, air superiority, and light ground forces moved swiftly to provide an immediate deterrent presence. In the second phase, attack aircraft, additional fighter aircraft, and maritime forces were deployed. In the current phase, we are building up heavy ground forces and additional air, maritime, and sustainment forces to insure a successful defense of Saudi Arabia.

With respect to enforcing the U.N. sanctions, a multinational naval force, consisting of U.S. naval forces and naval forces from 12 other allied nations—with additional forces from four other nations en route—is intercepting maritime vessels in the relevant ocean areas to determine their destination and whether they are in compliance with the U.N. sanctions regarding prohibited cargo. U.S. Navy support for this operations includes 11 ships in the Persian Gulf, 23 ships in the North Arabian Sea, and 12 ships in the Red Sea. To date, we have intercepted over 750 ships and we have boarded and diverted 4 ships that were not in compliance with U.N. sanctions, including two Iraqi ships.

U.S. investment in forces and equipment capable of deploying quickly to any part of the world has paid off. The movement of U.S. forces to Saudi Arabia and surrounding Gulf Coast countries is the largest rapid deployment of U.S. forces since World War II. We moved more forces and equipment in the first three weeks of Desert Shield than we moved during the first three months of the Korean War. This massive deployment of troops and equipment is the equivalent of moving and sustaining a city the size of Chattanooga, Tennessee.

Desert Shield has also convincingly demonstrated the value of a full range of balanced forces. In Desert Shield we have needed and deployed light forces, maritime forces, heavy forces, tactical and strategic air forces, mobility and sustainment forces.

As you know, we had to move as quickly as possible. As a result, Operation Desert Shield has taxed U.S. airlift and sealift to the maximum. The Military Airlift Command's organic fleet of aircraft is fully employed, with nearly 90 percent currently dedicated to Desert Shield missions. The remaining aircraft continue to support DoD's other worldwide requirements. According to established plans, for the first time in history we activated a portion of the Civil Reserve Air Fleet (CRAF). CRAF Stage I made 38 civil aircraft available for DoD use. If required, Stages II and III can make an additional 78 and 277 aircraft available. To date, airlift has deployed over 75,000 people and over 65,000 tons of equipment. Moreover, the extent of Strategic Air Command's tanker support has been impressive—all combat aircraft deploying to the region required multiple aerial refuelings.

More than 180,000 tons of cargo has been sealifted to

the area of operations—with an additional 55 ships loading or en route. All eight of the Navy's fast sealift ships are supporting the deployment. As of today, seven of those ships have completed the 15-day journey and offloaded their cargoes in Saudi Arabia. Nine Maritime Prepositioning Ships (MPS-2 and MPS-3) from Diego Garcia and Guam have unloaded. These ships carried combat equipment and 30 days of supplies for the I Marine Expeditionary Force. Forty-one Ready Reserve Force (RRF) ships have been ordered activated and thirty-two are ready for sea. We are exploring options to increase our sealift capability, including getting ships from our allies.

Committee members will be pleased to hear that in all of these lift efforts, the U.S. Transportation Command had performed superbly. Coordinating the largest rapid lift in America's history has not been an easy task, but the new unified command has proven its worth.

You are aware than on 23 August, the President invoked, for the first time, the provisions of section 673b, Title 10, United States Code, the Selected Reserve Callup Authority. This augmentation of the Active Armed Forces provides us with the capability to perform certain critical military activities. The Reserves and National Guard are an integral part of our Armed Forces. Currently we are ordering to active duty units and individuals to perform a wide variety of tasks both in this country and in and around the Arabian Peninsula.

We are all aware of the personal sacrifices being made by the reservists being called up. I assure you that we will only call those we need, and will retain them for only the period of service that is absolutely necessary to accomplish the mission. The most immediate need is for Army logistics forces to sustain the growing combat power in the theater of operations. We also will be calling up Air Force, Navy and Coast Guard units and individuals to support strategic lift and enhance the flow of forces and supplies to the U.S. Central Command (USCENTCOM) area. Finally, individual Army and Navy reservists are being called up to backfill critical medical specialists who have deployed to meet theater medical requirements.

In addition to those called up under the Presidential Callup Authority, many more reservists and guardsmen have supported this operation on a volunteer basis, logging thousands of air miles in support of strategic airlift, aerial refueling and tactical reconnaissance requirements, and pitching in to assist where needed in the deployment process. These are patriotic men and women, totally dedicated to our national defense. In short, our Total Force policy is working well in Operation Desert Shield.

All of the U.S. forces in Operation Desert Shield are organized as a joint force under the Central Command's Commander in Chief (USCINCCENT), General H. Norman Schwarzkopf. This joint force includes Army, Navy, Air Force, and Marine Corps component commanders.

Major U.S. forces deployed to the Middle East come under the operational control of USCINCCENT when they enter the USCENTCOM area of responsibility. USCINCCENT has primary responsibility for Operation Desert Shield and is supported by the other combatant commands and numerous federal departments and agencies. General Schwarzkopf's naval component commander commands both U.S. naval forces for the defense of Saudi Arabia and U.S. naval forces for the multinational Marine Intercept Force.

General Schwarzkopf's mission is to "deploy forces to the U.S. Central Command area of responsibility and take actions in concert with host nation forces, friendly regional forces and other allies to defend against an Iraqi attack on Saudi Arabia and be prepared to conduct other operations as directed." General Schwarzkopf is coordinating closely with the military forces of Saudi Arabia and the other allied forces in the theater.

U.S. forces in Saudi Arabia and in other Arab countries are part of a command arrangement that has established an effective coalition of Arab and Western forces. These forces are organized along national lines with national forces being assigned separate areas of operations. National Force Commanders are maintaining close coordination and cooperation on all issues.

Host nation support has been outstanding. Saudi Arabia and other Gulf States have provided unprecedented use of airfields, port facilities, beddown locations, heavy equipment transport, and water for all allied forces.

A large Iraqi military force remains in Kuwait. It has the capability to attack Saudi Arabia with very little warning. As of this week, approximately 173,000 Iraqi troops with over 1,500 tanks continue to occupy positions in Kuwait. Moreover, 11 Iraqi divisions are deployed in southern Iraq position to support the Iraqi forces in Kuwait.

U.S. military forces in the Persian Gulf are well trained and well supported. Together with the military forces of participating Arab and Western countries, these forces will be capable of defending Saudi Arabia from an Iraqi attack and enforcing the U.N. sanctions.

Reference: Crisis in the Persian Gulf Region: U.S. Policy Options and Implications: Hearings Before the Committee on Armed Services, United States Senate, 101st Congress, 1990, 29-33.

Remarks of Secretary of State Baker before the UN Security Council, 25 September 1990

On 25 September 1990, Secretary of State James Baker appeared before the United Nations Security Council to speak on the crisis in the Gulf and the council's response to it, en-

dorsing the passage of another resolution to further punish Iraq. Later that day, the council passed Resolution 670 by a vote of 14-1 (Cuba). Herewith are Baker's remarks.

Our meeting here today is extraordinary. This marks only the third time in the 45-year history of this organization that all of the permanent five foreign ministers of the Security Council are meeting. Rarely has the United Nations been confronted by so blatant an act of aggression as the Iraqi invasion of Kuwait. Rarely has the international community been so united and determined that aggression should not succeed.

Acts have consequences. The stakes are clear. For international society to permit Iraq to overwhelm a small neighbor and to erase it from the map would send a disastrous message. The hopes of the world for a new, more peaceful post-Cold War era would be dimmed. The United Nations Charter would be devalued—at the very moment when its promise is closer to fulfillment than at any time in its history.

Speaking for the United States, I want to tell the council that our hopes for a better world are real. The United Nations Charter embodies the values of the American people and people everywhere who know that might alone cannot be allowed to make right.

Elementary justice and a prudent regard for our own interests have brought together an unprecedented solidarity on this issue. We are engaged in a great struggle and test of wills. We cannot allow our hopes and aspirations to be trampled by a dictator's ambitions or his threats.

Our purpose must be clear and clearly understood by all, including the government and people of Iraq. Security Council Resolutions 660 and 662 establish the way to settle the crisis: complete, immediate, and unconditional Iraqi withdrawal from Kuwait, the restoration of Kuwait's legitimate government, and the release of all hostages. Until that time, the international community through Resolution 661 and its successor resolutions has set a high and rising penalty upon Iraq for each passing day that it fails to abandon its aggression.

These penalties are beginning to take effect, and bellicose language from Baghdad cannot compensate for the perils of isolation. Threats only prolong the needless suffering of the Iraqi people. Iraq has been quarantined because its brutal actions have separated it from the community of nations. There can be no business as usual. In fact, there can be no economic exchanges with Iraq at all.

Today, the United States, together with other members of this council, supports a new resolution and additional measures:

First, the council explicitly states that United Nations Security Council Resolution 661 includes commercial air traffic. This demonstrates again that the international community is prepared to plug any loophole in the isolation of Iraq.

Second, we agree to consider measures against any government that might attempt to evade the international quarantine. No temptation of minor gain should lead any government to complicity with Iraq's assault on international legality and decency. I would even say that the more effective the enforcement of sanctions, the more likely the peaceful evolution of this conflict.

Third, we remind the government of Iraq that it is not free to disregard its international obligations, especially the humanitarian provisions of the Fourth Geneva Convention. Each day that Iraqi officials flout norms of elementary decency makes it that much more difficult for Iraq to resume its place in the international community and to repair the damage it has done. On this point, I would note the call of the Arab League for reparations.

Many thousands of innocent people have been dislocated as well. That is why the United States supports a coordinated and unitary approach to refugee assistance and relief efforts. The appointment of Saddrudin Aga Khan is a major step in this direction.

Fourth, the council puts the government of Iraq on notice that its continued failure to comply could lead to further action, including action under Chapter Seven. The international community has made clear its desire to exhaust every peaceful possibility for resolving this matter in accordance with the principles of the United Nations Charter. But we are all well aware that the Charter envisages the possibility of further individual and collective measures to defend against aggression and flagrant violations of international humanitarian law.

Eduard Shevardnadze [Foreign Minister, U.S.S.R.] spoke for all of us when he said earlier today: "This is a major affront to mankind. In the context of recent events, we should remind those who regard aggression as an acceptable form of behavior that the United Nations has the power to suppress acts of aggression. There is ample evidence that this right can be exercised. It will be, if the illegal occupation of Kuwait continues."

It is important to emphasize that the sanctions we have adopted are aimed at reversing the aggressive policies of the Iraqi government. They are not aimed at the people of Iraq, who are being forced to live with the consequences of a misguided policy.

The council has acknowledged that its sanctions, as with any disruption, can be costly to many of our member states. We have a duty to make sure that no nation is crippled because it stood for the principles of international order. The United States has worked with other nations to coordinate an international effort to provide assistance to those desperately in need.

The passing of the Cold War has meant many things—above all, a rebirth of hope. The horizons of democracy, of human rights, of national dignity, and of economic progress have all been extended. The result has been a rebirth of the United Nations as well. Suddenly, the vision of the Charter and the promise of international cooperation seem within reach. In Central America, in Namibia, and perhaps soon in Cambodia and Afghanistan, this organization makes signal contributions as a peacemaker. We are beginning to control at last the proliferation of conflicts, major and minor, that have exacted so high a price from humanity.

Now, together we all confront a supreme challenge to the United Nations and all that it represents. If the United Nations is to fulfill its mission, if peace is to prevail, then Iraq's leader must not be allowed to gain from his assault on decency and basic human values. We must do what justice, honor, and international peace demand that we do: reverse Saddam Hussein's brutal aggression.

Reference: "Secretary Baker: U.S. Support for Additional U.N. Action against Iraq," *Current Policy Paper 1302,* U.S. Department of State, Bureau of Public Affairs, September 1990, 12.

Testimony by Secretary of State Baker before the Senate Foreign Relations Committee, 17 October 1990

On 17 October 1990, Secretary of State James Baker appeared before the Senate Foreign Relations Committee to discuss the Bush administration's "isolation strategy" against Iraq. Herewith is his statement before the committee.

Six weeks ago, it was my privilege to speak to this committee and, through you, to the American people about Iraq's aggression against Kuwait. At that time, I outlined the President's goals:

First, the immediate, complete, and unconditional withdrawal of all Iraqi forces from Kuwait as mandated in U.N. Security Council Resolution 660;

Second, the restoration of Kuwait's legitimate government;

Third, the protection of the lives of American citizens held hostage by Iraq, both in Iraq and Kuwait; and

Fourth, a commitment to the security and stability of the Persian Gulf.

I also described our strategy for achieving these goals. The key element of that approach is American leadership of a global alliance that isolates Iraq—politically, economically, and militarily.

Today, I would like to discuss with you what we have done to carry out that strategy since early September, including how responsibilities are being shared and what results have been achieved.

First, we have been working successfully through the U.N. Security Council to isolate Iraq politically and to impose penalties for its refusal to comply with the U.N. resolutions. That effort is continuing today as the council considers its tenth resolution on the Gulf.

Second, we have secured notable cooperation from the Soviet Union. We have described this conflict as the first real crisis of the post–Cold War period. This positive approach of the Soviet Union has validated that label. In their Helsinki joint statement, President Bush and President Gorbachev declared, "We are united in the belief that Iraq's aggression must not be tolerated. No peaceful international order is possible if larger states can devour their smaller neighbors."

Since then I have met with Foreign Minister Shevardnadze on several occasions, both in Moscow and New York, and have talked to him on the phone frequently. The Soviets continue to support the objectives of the Security Council resolutions.

Third, from the beginning, we recognized that maintaining such an unprecedented international coalition would necessitate special efforts. The United States could lead—indeed, had to lead—but we should not carry the responsibility alone. The principle of shared responsibility had to be observed.

We must jointly face the military threat. But we must also act collectively to support the many nations observing the economic embargo or contributing forces for the defense of Saudi Arabia. Iraq's pillage of Kuwait continues to displace thousands of workers, straining the resources of neighboring states and the fragile economies of their homelands.

Immediately after testifying before this committee last month, I left at the president's request to visit our major allies and partners in the Arabian peninsula, the European Community, Italy, and Germany to put responsibility-sharing into effect. The secretary of the treasury [Nicholas Brady] led a similar missions to London, Paris, Tokyo, and Seoul. This exercise in sharing responsibilities produced commitments of $20 billion in resources, equally divided between support for the front-line states of Egypt, Turkey, and Jordan, and assistance to the multinational military effort. This includes support for a substantial portion of incremental defense costs, now running about $1 billion per month.

I would summarize the results of our ongoing efforts as follows:

—Fifty four nations have contributed or offered to contribute militarily and/or economically to the Gulf effort.

—The three Gulf states of Saudi Arabia, Kuwait, and the United Arab Emirates have agreed to contribute more than $12 billion to this effort in 1990. All of the states in the Gulf Cooperation Council (GCC) have contributed troops to the multinational force in Saudi Arabia and are providing access and services in support of U.S. forces. Host-nation support for our deployed forces includes the free use of ports, logistical facilities, bases, and fuel.

—The United Kingdom is deploying over 6,000 combat troops, over 50 aircraft, and 12 warships.

—France has deployed over 4,000 combat troops, 30 aircraft, and 12 warships.

—Japan has pledged $4 billion: $2 billion in support of the military effort plus $2 billion in economic aid. And we hope to see that commitment fulfilled promptly and in a form immediately usable.

—Germany has pledged $2 billion: $1 billion in support of the military effort plus $1 billion in economic aid.

—The European Economic Community has pledged $670 million in economic aid, along with member state commitments of an additional $1.3 billion.

—Italy has deployed four warships and eight aircraft.

—Korea has pledged $220 million: $95 million in support of the military effort plus $125 million in economic aid.

To coordinate timely and effective economic assistance to the front-line states, the president launched the Gulf Crisis Financial Coordinating Group on September 25th. This group unites the major donors of Europe, Asia, and the Gulf under U.S. chairmanship, with technical support from the I.M.F. [International Monetary Fund] and World Bank. We see it as an important vehicle for maintaining the international coalition.

The most important demonstration of America's commitment to bolstering the economic stability of our front-line allies is the president's proposal to cancel Egypt's FMS [foreign military sales] debt. No other signal would send the same powerful message to our friends in the region that we are determined to stand by them, even on the toughest issues. Last Thursday's assassination of the Speaker of Egypt's Parliament is a tragic reminder of how far Egypt's enemies are prepared to go to divert President Mubarak from his responsible and courageous course. Strong Congressional endorsement of Egyptian debt cancellation would provide Egypt critical economic relief and send a powerful and timely signal that the United States stands by its friends.

The political and economic isolation of Iraq has been achieved. The costs and responsibilities for enforcing this isolation are being fairly distributed. Economic leakage is minimal. The Iraqi economy will suffer badly, and the Iraqi war machine will be hurt, too.

A discussion of diplomacy and economic sanctions, however, should not blind us to the other essential track of our policy: the military build-up in the Gulf. I have just detailed for you the contributions made by our allies, including combat units, aircraft, and warships. In addition, Arab states such as Egypt and Syria are sending major units. There are now many thousands of Arab and Muslim soldiers deployed with the multinational forces in and around Saudi Arabia. And, of course, very large numbers of American marines,

soldiers, sailors, and airmen are there already. All told, over 25 countries are now supplying men or materiel in support of the Security Council resolutions.

Our military objectives are to deter an Iraqi attack on Saudi Arabia and to ensure the effective implementation of the U.N. sanctions. Economic sanctions against an aggressor like Saddam Hussein would never be effective unless the international community could help ensure the security of those nations, such as Saudi Arabia and Turkey, who must apply those sanctions. Our military forces are also there to protect American lives and to provide an effective and decisive response should Iraq escalate its aggression to active combat with the multinational force.

Saddam Hussein must know that he lacks not only the political and economic options of holding Kuwait but also the military option to succeed with his aggression. The political, economic, and military aspects of our strategy reinforce each other.

As the strategy takes effect, we face a difficult task. We must remain firm, not wavering from the goals we have set or our focus on the blatant aggression committed by Iraq. We must exercise patience as the grip of sanctions tightens with increasing severity.

Some may urge action for action's sake. But the only truly effective action we can take now is to continue to heighten Iraq's political, economic, and military isolation. Every day—in Washington, in New York, in the region—we continue our search for a peaceful solution.

Action that moves toward a partial solution would be self-defeating appeasement.

And should there be any doubt about the awful consequences of a partial solution, I would urge a close look at what Saddam Hussein is doing to the people of Kuwait. Because Saddam Hussein controls access to the true story of Kuwait, this is a story that is not told frequently enough. So I commend the Congress' effort to secure eyewitness testimony of the brutalities now taking place.

It is the rape of Kuwait. Hospitals have been looted without regard for the sick. Parents have been tortured and executed in front of the their children. Children have been tortured and executed in front of their parents. Even after his military conquest, Saddam has continued to make war on the people of Kuwait.

Let me be blunt: Saddam Hussein has invaded and tortured a peaceful Arab neighbor purely for self-aggrandizement. He is not raping to advance the Palestinian cause.

We cannot allow this violent way to become the wave of the future in the Middle East. Saddam Hussein must fail if peace is to succeed. The prospects for a just and lasting peace between Israel and its Arab neighbors will be shattered if he prevails.

It is time to clear the air once and for all about the relationship between Saddam's aggression in Kuwait and other conflicts and problems in the region. I will put it to you simply: Does anyone seriously think that if this aggression succeeds, that prospects will be better for peace between Israel and the Palestinians? Can anyone seriously believe that if Iraq wins this contest with the international community, it will be easier to eliminate chemical weapons or biological weapons or nuclear weapons in the region? Of course not.

Every hope for peace in this conflict-ridden region depends on stopping Iraq's aggression and ultimately reversing its capacity for future aggression.

Since we met last, a great coalition of nations has gathered to isolate Iraq and its dictator. Where before his aggression Saddam Hussein found allies of consequence, today he finds none. Where before the invasion, the Iraqi economy had important international links, today it has none. And where once there were prospects for successful Iraqi aggression against Saudi Arabia, today there are none.

Unity remains essential. I do not believe we could have come this far if most nations did not agree with President Bush that we all have a stake in a world where conflicts are settled peacefully. And that unity, expressed in political, economic, and military terms, remains the best hope for a peaceful solution to this conflict as well.

It is gratifying that the vast majority of Americans have rallied behind the president in support of both our goals and our strategy in the Persian Gulf. Indeed, most of the world has done so, as well. Saddam Hussein cannot be allowed to ruin the region. He cannot be allowed to spoil this time of hope in the world for a more secure and prosperous future. There is a morality among nations. That morality must prevail.

Reference: "Secretary Baker: Isolation Strategy toward Iraq," Current Policy Paper 1308, U.S. Department of State, Bureau of Public Affairs, October 1990, 13.

Iraq Sanctions Act of 1990 (104 Stat. 2047)

This legislation was attached by Congress to the Foreign Operations Appropriations Budget Act for the year 1990 (sections 586586]) and enacted into law on 5 November 1990.

SEC. 586A. DECLARATIONS REGARDING IRAQ'S INVASION OF KUWAIT.

The Congress—

(1) condemns Iraq's invasion of Kuwait on August 2, 1990;

(2) supports the actions that have been taken by the President in response to that invasion;

(3) calls for the immediate and unconditional withdrawal of Iraqi forces from Kuwait;

(4) supports the efforts of the United Nations Security Council to end this violation of international law and threat to international peace;

(5) supports the imposition and enforcement of multilateral sanctions against Iraq;

(6) calls on the United States allies and other countries to support fully the efforts of the United Nations Security Council, and to take other appropriate actions, to bring about an end to Iraq's occupation of Kuwait; and

(7) condemns the brutal occupation of Kuwait by Iraq and its gross violations of internationally recognized human rights in Kuwait, including widespread arrests, torture, summary executions, and mass extrajudicial killings.

SEC. 586B. CONSULTATIONS WITH CONGRESS

The President shall keep the Congress fully informed, and shall consult with the Congress, with respect to current and anticipated events regarding the international crisis caused by Iraq's invasion of Kuwait, including with respect to United States actions.

SEC. 586C. TRADE EMBARGO AGAINST IRAQ

(a) CONTINUATION OF EMBARGO—Except as otherwise provided in this section, the President shall continue to impose the trade embargo and other economic sanctions with respect to Iraq and Kuwait that the United States is imposing, in response to Iraq's invasion of Kuwait, pursuant to Executive Orders numbered 12724 and 12725 (August 9, 1990) and, to the extent that they are still in effect, Executive Orders numbered 12722 and 12723 (August 2, 1990). Notwithstanding any other provision of law, no funds, credits, guarantees, or insurance appropriated or otherwise made available by this or any other Act for fiscal year 1991 or any fiscal year thereafter shall be used to support or administer any financial or commercial operations of any United States Government department, agency, or other entity, or of any person subject to the jurisdiction of the United States, for the benefit of the Government of Iraq, its agencies or instrumentalities, or any person working on behalf of the Government of Iraq, contrary to the trade embargo and other economic sanctions imposed in accordance with this section.

(b) HUMANITARIAN ASSISTANCE—To the extent that transactions involving foodstuffs or payments for foodstuffs are exempted "in humanitarian circumstances" from the prohibitions established by the United States pursuant to United Nations Security Council Resolution 661 (1990), these exemptions shall be limited to foodstuffs that are to be provided consistent with United Nations Security Council Resolution 666 (1990) and other relevant Security Council resolutions.

(c) NOTICE TO CONGRESS OF EXCEPTIONS TO AND TERMINATION OF SANCTIONS.—

(1) NOTICE OF REGULATIONS—Any regulations issued after the date of enactment of this Act with respect to the economic sanctions imposed with respect to Iraq and Kuwait by the United States under Executive Orders numbered 12722 and 12723 (August 2, 1990) and

Executive Orders numbered 12724 and 12725 (August 9, 1990) shall be submitted to the Congress before those regulations take effect.

(2) NOTICE OF TERMINATION OF SANCTIONS.—The President shall notify the Congress at least 15 days before the termination, in whole or part, of any sanction imposed with respect to Iraq or Kuwait pursuant to those Executive Orders.

(d) RELATION TO OTHER LAWS.

(1) SANCTIONS LEGISLATION.—The sanctions that are described in subsection (a) are in addition to, and not in lieu of the sanctions provided for in section 586G of this Act or any other provision of law.

(2) NATIONAL EMERGENCIES AND UNITED NATIONS LEGISLATION.—Nothing in this section supersedes any provision of the National Emergencies Act of any authority of the President under the International Emergency Economic Powers Act or section 5(c) of the United Nations Participation Act of 1945.

SEC. 586D. COMPLIANCE WITH UNITED NATIONS SANCTIONS AGAINST IRAQ.

(a) DENIAL OF ASSISTANCE.—None of the funds appropriated or otherwise made available pursuant to this Act to carry out the Foreign Assistance Act of 1961 (including title IV of chapter 2 of part I, relating to the Overseas Private Investment Corporation) or the Arms Export Control Act may be used to provide assistance to any country that is not in compliance with the United Nations Security Council sanctions against Iraq unless the President determines and so certifies to the Congress that

(1) such assistance is in the national interest of the United States;

(2) such assistance will directly benefit the needy people in that country; or

(3) the assistance to be provided will be humanitarian assistance for foreign nationals who have fled Iraq and Kuwait.

(b) IMPORT SANCTIONS.—If the President considers that the taking of such action would promote the effectiveness of the economic sanctions of the United Nations and the United States imposed with respect to Iraq, and is consistent with the national interest, the President may prohibit, for such a period of time as he considers appropriate, the importation into the United States of any or all products of any foreign country that has not prohibited

(1) the importation of products of Iraq into its customs territory; and

(2) the exports of its products to Iraq.

SEC. 586E. PENALTIES FOR VIOLATIONS OF EMBARGO. Notwithstanding section 206 of the International Emergency Economic Powers Act (50 U.S.C. 1705) and section 5(b) of the United Nations Participation Act of 1945 (22 U.S.C. 287(b))

(1) a civil penalty of not to exceed $250,000 may be imposed on any person who, after the date of enactment of this Act, violates or evades or attempts to violate or evade Executive Orders numbered 12722, 12723, 12724, or 12725 or any license, order, or regulation issued under any such Executive order; and

(2) whoever, after the date of enactment of this Act, willfully violates or evades or attempts to violate or evade Executive Orders numbered 12722, 12723, 12724, or 12725 or any license, order, or regulation issued under any such Executive Order

(A) shall, upon conviction, be fined not more than $1,000,000, if a person other than a natural person; or

(B) if a natural person, shall, upon conviction, be fined not more than $1,000,000, be imprisoned for not more than 12 years, or both.

Any officer, director, or agent of any corporation who knowingly participates in a violation, evasion, or attempt described in paragraph (2) may be punished by imposition of the fine or imprisonment (or both) specified in subparagraph (B) of that paragraph.

SEC. 586F. DECLARATIONS REGARDING IRAQ'S LONG-STANDING VIOLATIONS OF INTERNATIONAL LAW.

(a) IRAQ'S VIOLATIONS OF INTERNATIONAL LAW.—The Congress determines that—

(1) the Government of Iraq has demonstrated repeated and blatant disregard for its obligations under international law by violating the Charter of the United Nations, the Protocol for the Prohibition of the Use in War of Asphyxiating, Poisonous or Other Gases, and of Bacteriological Methods of Warfare (done at Geneva, June 17, 1925), as well as other international treaties;

(2) the Government of Iraq is a party to the International Covenant on Civil and Political Rights and the International Covenant on Economic, Social, and Cultural Rights as is obligated under the covenants, as well as the Universal Declaration of Human Rights, to respect internationally recognized human rights;

(3) the State Department's Country Reports on Human Rights Practices for 1989 again characterized Iraq's human rights record as "abysmal";

(4) Amnesty International, Middle East Watch, and other independent human rights organizations have documented extensive, systematic, and continuing human rights abuses by the Government of Iraq, including summary executions, mass political killings, disappearances, widespread use of torture, arbitrary arrests and prolonged detention without trial of thousands of political opponents, forced relocation and deportation, denial of nearly all civil and political rights such as the freedom of association, assembly, speech, and the press, and the imprisonment, torture, and execution of children;

(5) since 1987, the Government of Iraq has intensified its severe repression of the Kurdish minority of Iraq, deliberately destroyed more than 3,000 villages

and towns in the Kurdish regions, and forcibly expelled more than 500,000 people, thus effectively depopulating the rural areas of Iraqi Kurdistan;

(6) Iraq has blatantly violated international law by initiating [the] use of chemical weapons in the Iran-Iraq war;

(7) Iraq has also violated international law by using chemical weapons against its own Kurdish citizens, resulting in tens of thousands of deaths and more than 65,000 refugees;

(8) Iraq continues to expand its chemical weapons capability, and President Saddam Hussein has threatened to use chemical weapons against other nations;

(9) persuasive evidence exists that Iraq is developing biological weapons in violation of international law;

(10) there are strong indications that Iraq has taken steps to produce nuclear weapons and has attempted to smuggle from the United States, in violation of United States law, components for triggering devices used in nuclear warheads whose manufacture would contravene the Treaty on the Non-Proliferation of Nuclear Weapons, to which Iraq is a party; and

(11) Iraqi President Saddam Hussein has threatened to use terrorism against other nations in violation of international law and has increased Iraq's support for the Palestine Liberation Organization and other Palestinian groups that have conducted terrorist acts.

(b) HUMAN RIGHTS VIOLATIONS.—The Congress determines that the Government of Iraq is engaged in a consistent pattern of gross violations of internationally recognized human rights. All provisions of law that impose sanctions against a country whose government is engaged in a consistent pattern of gross violations of internationally recognized human rights shall be fully enforced against Iraq.

(c) SUPPORT FOR INTERNATIONAL TERRORISM.—(1) The Congress determines that Iraq is a country which has repeatedly provided support for acts of international terrorism, a country which grants sanctuary from prosecution to individuals or groups which have committed an act of international terrorism, and a country which otherwise supports international terrorism. The provisions of law specified in paragraph (2) and all other provisions of law that impose sanctions against a country which has repeatedly provided support for acts of international terrorism, which grants sanctuary from prosecution to an individual or group which has committed an act of international terrorism, or which otherwise supports international terrorism shall be fully enforced against Iraq.

(2) The provisions of law referred to in paragraph (1) are—

(A) section 40 of the Arms Export Control Act;

(B) section 620A of the Foreign Assistance Act of 1961;

(C) sections 555 and 556 of this Act (and the corresponding sections of predecessor foreign operations appropriations Acts);

(D) section 555 of the International Security and Development Cooperation Act of 1985.

(d) MULTILATERAL COOPERATION.—The Congress calls on the President to seek multilateral cooperation—

(1) to deny dangerous technologies to Iraq;

(2) to induce Iraq to respect internationally recognized human rights; and

(3) to induce Iraq to allow appropriate international humanitarian and human rights organizations to have access to Iraq and Kuwait, including areas in northern Iraq traditionally inhabited by the Kurds.

SEC. 586G. SANCTIONS AGAINST IRAQ.

(a) IMPOSITION.—Except as provided in section 586H, the following sanctions shall apply with respect to Iraq:

(1) FMS SALES.—The United States Government shall not enter into any sale with Iraq under the Arms Export Control Act.

(2) COMMERCIAL ARMS SALES.—Licenses shall not be issued for the export to Iraq of any item on the United States Munitions List.

(3) EXPORTS OF CERTAIN GOODS AND TECHNOLOGY.—The authorities of section 6 of the Export Administration Act of 1979 (50 U.S.C. App. 2405) shall be used to prohibit the export to Iraq of any goods or technology listed pursuant to that section or section 5(c)(1) of that Act (50 U.S.C. App. 2404(c)(1) on the control list provided for in section 4(b) of that Act (50 U.S.C. App. 2403(b)).

(4) NUCLEAR EQUIPMENT, MATERIALS, AND TECHNOLOGY. —

(A) NRC LICENSES.—The Nuclear Regulatory Commission shall not issue any license or other authorization under the Atomic Energy Act of 1954 (42 U.S.C. 2011 and following) for the export to Iraq of any source or special nuclear material, any production or utilization facility, any sensitive nuclear technology, any component, item, or substance determined to have significance for nuclear explosive purposes pursuant to section 109b of the Atomic Energy Act of 1954 (42 U.S.C. 2139(b)), or any other material or technology requiring such a license or authorization.

(B) DISTRIBUTION OF NUCLEAR MATERIALS.—The authority of the Atomic Energy Act of 1954 shall not be used to distribute any special nuclear material, source material, or byproduct material to Iraq.

(C) DOE AUTHORIZATIONS.—The Secretary of Energy shall not provide a specific authorization under section 57b.(2) of the Atomic Energy Act of 1954 (42 U.S.C. 2077(b)(2)) for any activity that would constitute directly or indirectly engaging in Iraq in activities that require a specific authorization under that section.

(5) ASSISTANCE FROM INTERNATIONAL FINANCIAL INSTITUTIONS.—The United States shall oppose any loan or

financial or technical assistance to Iraq by international financial institutions in accordance with section 701 of the International Institutions Act (22 U.S.C. 262d).

(6) ASSISTANCE THROUGH THE EXPORT-IMPORT BANK.—Credits and credit guarantees through the Export-Import Bank of the United States shall be denied to Iraq.

(7) ASSISTANCE THROUGH THE COMMODITY CREDIT CORPORATION.—Credit, credit guarantees, and other assistance through the Commodity Credit Corporation shall be denied to Iraq.

(8) FOREIGN ASSISTANCE.—All forms of assistance under the Foreign Assistance Act of 1961 (22 U.S.C. 2151 and following) other than emergency assistance for medical supplies and other forms of emergency humanitarian assistance, and under the Arms Export Control Act (22 U.S.C. 2751 and following) shall be denied to Iraq.

(b) CONTRACT SANCTITY.—For purposes of the export controls imposed pursuant to subsection (a)(3), the date described in subsection (m)(1) of section 6 of the Export Administration Act of 1979 (50 U.S.C. App. 2405) shall be deemed to be August 1, 1990.

SEC. 586H. WAIVER AUTHORITY.

(a) IN GENERAL.—The President may waive the requirements of any paragraph of section 586G9A0 if the President makes a certification under subsection (b) or subsection (c).

(b) CERTIFICATION OF FUNDAMENTAL CHANGES IN IRAQI POLICES AND ACTIONS.—The authority of subsection (a) may be exercised 60 days after the President certifies to the Congress that

(1) the Government of Iraq

(A) has demonstrated, through a pattern of conduct, substantial improvement in its respect for internationally recognized human rights;

(B) is not acquiring, developing, or manufacturing (i) ballistic missiles, (ii) chemical, biological, or nuclear weapons, or (iii) components for such weapons; has forsworn the first use of such weapons; and is taking substantial and verifiable steps to destroy or otherwise dispose of any such missiles and weapons its possesses; and

(C) does not provide support for international terrorism;

(2) the Government of Iraq is in substantial compliance with its obligations under international law, including

(A) the Charter of the United Nations;

(B) the International Covenant on Civil and Political Rights (done at New York, December 16, 1966) and the International Covenant on Economic, Social, and Cultural Rights (done at New York, December 16, 1966);

(C) the Convention on the Prevention and Punishment of the Crime of Genocide (done at Paris, December 9, 1948);

(D) the Protocol for the Prohibition of the use in War of Asphyxiating, Poisonous or Other Gases, and of Bacteriological Methods of Warfare (done at Geneva, June 17, 1925);

(E) the Treaty on the Non-Proliferation of Nuclear Weapons (done at Washington, London, and Moscow, July 1, 1968); and

(F) the Convention on the Prohibition of the Development, Production and Stockpiling of Bacteriological (Biological) and Toxin Weapons and on Their Destruction (done at Washington, London, and Moscow, April 10, 1972); and

(3) the President has determined that it is essential to the national interests of the United States to exercise the authority of subsection (a).

(c) CERTIFICATION OF FUNDAMENTAL CHANGES IN IRAQI LEADERSHIP AND POLICIES.—The authority of subsection (a) may be exercised 30 days after the President certifies to the Congress that

(1) there has been a fundamental change in the leadership of the Government of Iraq; and

(2) the new Government of Iraq has provided reliable and credible assurance that -

(A) it respects internationally recognized human rights and it will demonstrate such respect through its conduct;

(B) it is not acquiring, developing, or manufacturing and it will not acquire, develop, or manufacture (i) ballistic missiles, (ii) chemical, biological, or nuclear weapons, or (iii) components for such weapons; and is taking substantial and verifiable steps to destroy or otherwise dispose of any such missiles and weapons it possesses;

(C) it is not and will not provide support for international terrorism; and

(D) it is and will continue to be in substantial compliance with its obligations under international law, including all the treaties specified in subparagraphs (A) through (F) of subsection (b)(2).

(d) INFORMATION TO BE INCLUDED IN CERTIFICATIONS.—Any certification under subsection (b) or (c) shall include the justification for each determination required by that subsection. The certification shall also specify which paragraphs of section 586(a) the President will waive pursuant to that certification.

SEC. 586I. DENIAL OF LICENSES FOR CERTAIN EXPORTS TO COUNTIRES ASSISTING IRAQ'S ROCKET OR CHEMICAL, BIOLOGICAL, OR NUCLEAR WEAPONS CAPABILITY.

(a) RESTRICTION OF EXPORT LICENSES.—None of the funds appropriated by this or any other Act may be used to approve the licensing for export of any supercomputer to any country whose government the President determines is assisting, or whose government officials the President determines are assisting, Iraq to improve its rocket technology or chemical, biological, or nuclear weapons capability.

(b) NEGOTIATIONS.—The President is directed to begin immediate negotiations with those governments with which the United States has bilateral supercomputer agreements, including the Government of the United Kingdom and the Government of Japan, on conditions restricting the transfer to Iraq of supercomputer or associated technology.

SEC. 586J. REPORTS TO CONGRESS

(a) STUDY AND REPORT ON THE INTERNATIONAL EXPORT TO IRAQ OF NUCLEAR, BIOLOGICAL, CHEMICAL, AND BALLISTIC MISSILE TECHNOLOGY.

—(1) the President shall conduct a study on the sale, export, and third party transfer or development of nuclear, biological, chemical, and ballistic missile technology to or with Iraq, including

(A) an identification of specific countries, as well as companies and individuals, both foreign and domestic, engaged in such sale or export of nuclear, biological, chemical, and ballistic missile technology;

(B) a detailed description and analysis of the international supply, information, support, and coproduction network, individual, corporate, and state, responsible for Iraq's current capability in the area of nuclear, biological, chemical, and ballistic missile technology; and

(C) a recommendation of standards and procedures against which to measure and verify a decision of the Government of Iraq to terminate the development, production, coproduction, and deployment of nuclear, biological, chemical, and offensive ballistic missile technology as well as the destruction of all existing facilities associated with such technologies.

(2) The President shall include in the study required by paragraph (1) specific recommendations on new mechanisms, to include, but not be limited to, legal, political, economic and regulatory, whereby the United States might contribute, in conjunction with its friends, allies, and the international community, to the management, control, or elimination of the threat of nuclear, biological, chemical, and ballistic missile proliferation.

(3) Not later than March 30, 1991, the President shall submit to the Committee on Appropriations and the Committee on Foreign Relations of the Senate and the Committee on Appropriations and the Committee on Foreign Affairs of the House of Representatives, a report, in both classified and unclassified form, setting forth the findings of the study required by paragraph (1) of this subsection.

(b) STUDY AND REPORT ON IRAQ'S OFFENSIVE MILITARY CAPABILITY.—(1) The President shall conduct a study on Iraq's offensive military capability and its effect on the Middle East balance of power including an assessment of Iraq's power projection capability, the prospects of another sustained conflict with Iran, joint Iraqi-Jordanian military cooperation, and [the] threat Iraq's arms transfers pose to United States allies in the Middle East,

and the extension of Iraq's political-military influence into Africa and Latin America.

(2) Not later than March 30, 1991, the President shall submit to the Committee on Appropriations and the Committee on Foreign Relations of the Senate and the Committee on Appropriations and the Committee on Foreign Affairs of the House of Representatives, a report, in both classified and unclassified form, setting forth the findings of the study required by paragraph (1).

(c) REPORT ON SANCTIONS TAKEN BY OTHER NATIONS AGAINST IRAQ.

(1) The President shall prepare a report on the steps taken by other nations, both before and after the August 2, 1990, invasion of Kuwait, to curtail the export of goods, services, and technologies to Iraq which might contribute to, or enhance, Iraq's nuclear, biological, chemical, and ballistic missile capability.

(2) The President shall provide a complete accounting of international compliance with each of the sanctions resolutions adopted by the United Nations Security Council against Iraq since August 2, 1990, and shall list, by name, each country which, to his knowledge, has provided any assistance to Iraq and the amount and type of that assistance in violation of each United Nations resolution.

(3) The President shall make effort to encourage other nations, in whatever forum or context, to adopt sanctions toward Iraq similar to those contained in this section.

(4) Not later than every 6 months after the date of enactment of this Act, the President shall submit to the Committee on Appropriations and the Committee on Foreign Relations of the Senate and the Committee on Appropriations and the Committee on Foreign Affairs of the House of Representatives, a report, in both classified and unclassified form, setting forth the findings of the study required by paragraph (1).

Executive Order 12734 of 14 November 1990

Signed by President George Bush, this order established the National Emergency Construction Authority, which is mandated under 10 U.S.C. 2808.

By the authority vested in me as President by the Constitution and the laws of the United States of America, including the International Emergency Economic Powers Act (50 U.S.C. 1701 et seq.), the National Emergencies Act (50 U.S.C. 1601 et seq.), and 3 U.S.C. 301, I declared a national emergency by Executive Order No. 12722, dated August 2, 1990, to deal with the threat to the national security and foreign policy of the United States caused by the invasion of Kuwait by Iraq. To provide additional authority to the Department of Defense to respond to that threat, and in accordance with section 301 of the National Emergencies Act (50 U.S.C. 1631), I hereby order that emergency construction authority at 10 U.S.C. 2808 is invoked and made available in accordance with its terms to the Secretary of Defense and, at the discretion of the Secretary of Defense, to the Secretaries of the military departments.

Message against the War by the National Council of the Churches of Christ of the United States, 15 November 1990

Theological and Moral Imperative

I, therefore, the prisoner of the Lord beg you to lead a life worthy of the calling to which you have been called, with all humility and gentleness, with patience, bearing with one another in love, making every effort to maintain the unity of the Spirit in the bond of peace. (Eph. 4:13)

Throughout the history of the church, the question of the admissibility of war as a means of resolving disputes has been a source of differences, and at times division, in the body of Christ. Among our own communions, there is a wide diversity of approaches to this question. For all Christians, however, war is a sign of the sinful human condition, of human alienation from God, of alienation between human beings who are all children of God.

We stand at a unique moment in human history, when all around us seemingly impregnable walls are being broken down and deep historical enmities are being healed. And yet, ironically, at such a moment, our own nation seems to be poised at the brink of war in the Middle East. "What then are we to say about these things?" (Romans 8:31)

The quest for peace and the quest for Christian unity, which is the very reason for our existence as a Council, are intimately related. As churches seeking to recover our unity, we are called to be the salt and leaven of our societies. Together with other faith communities, we are called to address moral and spiritual dimensions in the debate on a national policy that seems to be careening toward war. Believing that Christ is our peace, we cannot do other than to strive to be the incarnation of creation's cry for peace.

Unanswered Questions

Two months ago, on September 14, 1990, the Executive Coordinating Committee of the National Council of the Churches of Christ in the U.S.A. addressed a message to its member communions on the Gulf crisis. That message condemned Iraq's invasion and occupation of Kuwait, raised serious questions about the decision of the U.S. government to send troops to the Gulf region and about the growing magnitude of U.S. presence, noting that the extent of the commitment of U.S. forces and weaponry was the largest since the Vietnam War. Since then, the U.S. has more than doubled the number of troops sent to the region to a number approaching half a million persons.

The message also questioned the apparent open-ended nature of U.S. military involvement in the Middle East and the failure on the part of the administration clearly to state its goals. President Bush and administration officials have done little to clarify either of these points. Indeed the rationales offered for the steady expansion of U.S. presence have often been misleading and sometimes contradictory. Early statements that U.S. forces had been deployed for the defense of Saudi Arabia or the enforcement of U.N. sanctions have been supplanted by suggestions of broader goals, including expulsion of Iraqi forces from Kuwait by military means, or even offensive action against Iraq itself. The nation still has not been told in clear and certain terms what would be required for the withdrawal of U.S. troops.

The Prospect of War

The initial response of the NCCC/USA was carefully measured, recognizing the magnitude of the injustice inflicted by Iraq against Kuwait, and the unprecedented reliance by the U.S. on the mechanisms of the U.N. In contrast, the U.S. administration increasingly prepares for war, a war that could lead to the loss of tens of thousands of lives and the devastation of the region. Such talk has given rise to widespread speculation in our country, in the Middle East and elsewhere that the United States will initiate war.

In the face of such reckless rhetoric and imprudent behavior, as representatives of churches in the United States we feel that we have a moral responsibility publicly and unequivocally to oppose actions that could have such dire consequences.

The Wider Implications

Our earlier message also pointed out that the active U.S. effort to implement United Nations Security Council resolutions relating to the occupation of Kuwait by Iraq stands in marked contrast to U.S. negligence regarding the implementation of Security Council resolutions 242 and 338. These call for the withdrawal of Israeli troops from the territories occupied in the 1967 War and the convening of an international conference to resolve the Israeli-Palestinian issue. There has also been negligence regarding the implementation of Security Council resolutions 359, 360, and 361 which call for the withdrawal "without delay" of Turkish troops from Cyprus and solving the problems of the island through negotiations.

During the intervening weeks the situation in the Israeli-Occupied Territories has, in fact, worsened. The U.S. government's condemnation of the massacre on the Haram al-Sharif/Temple Mount and its endorsement of a U.N. mission to the Occupied Territories was a welcome departure from past policies. The failure of the U.S. government to take any substantive measures to oppose the Israeli occupation, however, weakens the effect of its appropriate outrage over Iraqi aggression against Kuwait. The region cries out for a U.S. policy that seeks to redress all cases of injustice, including those of Israel and Palestine, Lebanon and Cyprus.

The Dangers of Militarization

The presence of U.S. troops in the Middle East has led to an expansion of the military capacity of an already grossly overmilitarized region. The proposed billions of dollars of arms sales to Saudi Arabia, the forgiveness of military debts to Egypt and Israel, and the supplying of both with new and more sophisticated weaponry, combined with a seeming lack of initiative to resolve the region's unsettled disputes, can only be seen as morally irresponsible.

The Price of War

The price of war and the preparation for further conflict is already being paid in human terms. Hundreds of thousands of foreign workers and their families have been compelled to leave Kuwait and Iraq, creating enormous strains on the Kingdom of Jordan and the Republic of Egypt and, ultimately, on the societies to which they are returning.

The cost of the current U.S. military presence in the Gulf is estimated at $1 billion per month. This "extra-budgetary expenditure" is once again likely to reduce further the nation's capacity to address human needs in our own society. Thus, among the early victims of this tragic engagement will certainly be the growing number of the poor, homeless, sick and elderly. The corrosive effects on our own nation will be felt especially by racial/ethnic communities who make a disproportionate number both of the poor and those who are on the front lines of military confrontation.

We are appalled by the past and present behavior of the regime in Iraq, one which has previously enjoyed U.S. support. But the demonization of the Iraqi people and their leader has led us to an increased incidence of defamation of or discrimination against persons of Arab descent or appearance.

A New World Order

We stand on the threshold of a "new world order." Indeed, the near unanimous condemnation by the nations of the world of Iraq's illegal occupation of its neighbor, Kuwait, shows the promise of a new approach to the vocation of peacemaking for which the United Nations was created 45 years ago. There are present in this moment seeds either of a new era of the international cooperation under the rule of international law or of rule based upon superior power, which holds the prospect of continuing dehumanizing chaos.

Our churches have long sought to nurture and bring to fruition the seeds of hope. The power we would invoke is not the power of the gun, nor is it the power of wealth and affluence; we would invoke the power of the cross and the resurrection, symbols for us of love and hope. As Christians in the U.S. we must witness against weak resignation to the illogical pursuit of militarism and war. We must witness to our belief in the capacity of human beings and human societies to seek and achieve reconciliation.

The General Board of the NCCC/USA commends this message to the churches, all Christians, and persons of other faiths, inviting them to join with us in continuing prayer and urgent action to avert war in the Persian/Arabian Gulf region, and to join in the quest for a just and durable peace in the Middle East.

Resolution on the Gulf and Middle East Crisis

The General Board of the National Council of Churches, meeting in Portland, Oregon, November 14–16, 1990, recognizing its solidarity with the Christians of the Middle East and with the Middle East Council of Churches,

Urges the government of Iraq to release immediately all those citizens of other nations being held against their will in Kuwait or Iraq and to withdraw immediately its troops and occupation forces from Kuwait.

Calls for the continued rigorous application of the sanctions against Iraq authorized by the United Nations Security Council until such time as it withdraws its forces from Kuwait.

Reiterates its opposition to the withholding of food and medicine as a weapon against civilian populations.

Encourages the Secretary-General of the United Nations to exercise fully his own good offices in pursuit of a rapid negotiated resolution of the present conflict in the Gulf.

Calls upon the President and U.S. Congress to pursue every means for a negotiated political solution to the crisis in the Gulf, including direct negotiations with Iraq.

Reiterates support for the convening under U.N. auspices of an international conference for a comprehensive peace in the Middle East, as a means of implementing United Nations Security Council resolutions on Israel and Palestine, Lebanon and Cyprus, recognizing that the present crisis cannot be isolated from the unresolved issues of the region as a whole.

Calls for an immediate halt to the buildup and the withdrawal of U.S. troops from the Gulf region except those which might be required and explicitly recommended by the Security Council of the United Nations in accordance with the relevant provisions of the United Nations Charter.

Calls upon the U.S. government to give leadership to the institution of an immediate and complete embargo under U.N. auspices on arms transfers to the Middle East.

Calls upon member communions, congregations, local and regional ecumenical agencies and individuals to make peace in the Middle East a paramount and urgent priority for prayer, study and action.

Expresses its profound gratitude for the witness of the Middle East Council of Churches and commits itself to continued partnership with the MECC in its efforts for peace, justice and development.

Requests the President and General Secretary engage in dialogue and to coordinate where possible and appropriate with the National Council of Churches Bishops and Evangelical Organizations with regard to the development of statements or actions in an effort to provide a common Christian witness.

Requests the President and General Secretary to communicate this resolution to the President and the Secretary of State, to the members of Congress, to the President of Iraq, to the Secretary General of the United Nations, the World Council of Churches, and to the Middle East Council of Churches.

Remarks by President Bush to American and British Troops in Saudi Arabia, 22 November 1990

Visiting American and British troops at a Marine outpost somewhere in northeastern Saudi Arabia, President Bush delivered some remarks, excerpted here.

You know, Thanksgiving is the oldest, some may say the most American of holidays, dating back to our origins as a people. And it's a day, I think we would all agree, separate and apart from others. It's a day of peace, it's a day of thanks, a day to remember what we stand for, and what it means to be an American, and why our forebears sacrificed so much to cross an ocean and build a great land.

And on this day, with all that America has to be thankful for, is it fair for Americans to say, "Why are we here?" It's not all that complicated. There are three key reasons why we're here with our U.N. allies making a stand in defense of freedom; we're here to protect our future, and we're here to protect innocent life.

And number one, protecting freedom means standing up to aggression. You know, the brutality inflicted on the people of Kuwait and on innocent citizens of every country must not be rewarded, because a bully unchecked today is a bully unleashed for tomorrow. And last August second this brutal dictator set out to wipe another country from the face of the earth, and Kuwait, a little tiny country, awoke to flashing guns of cold, cold-blooded troops, the fire and ice of Saddam Hussein's invasion.

And now Kuwait is struggling for survival, an entire nation ransacked, looted, held hostage. And maybe you can strike a name from the maps, but you can't strike a country from the hearts of its people. The invasion of Kuwait was without provocation, the looting of Kuwait is without excuse, and the occupation of Kuwait will not stand.

And number two, our mission is about protecting national security, which is to say protecting our future, because energy security is national security for us and, indeed, for every country.

Last year on a snowy Thanksgiving eve up there at Camp David, I spoke to the American people about the newly fallen Berlin Wall, and the piece of the wall that sits on my desk is a reminder of our steadfast role in the worldwide explosion of freedom. But now, the march of freedom must not be threatened by the man whose invasion of Kuwait is causing great economic hardship in the countries which can afford it least.

We saw it in Czechoslovakia. Barbara and I are just back from Czechoslovakia, where the progress of their peaceful revolution has already been damaged by the shock waves of Iraq's aggression. President Havel told me that Saddam's aggression is having a severe effect on his struggling economy. And every day that goes by increases the damage.

But when he was asked if our action in the Gulf was taking too much money away from the problems of Eastern Europe, he answered plainly. He said, "All the resources that are expended on resisting aggression anywhere in the world are finally turned to the good of all humankind." This from that playwright that was jailed not so many months ago by aggression itself. Listen to the words of this man who stands for freedom.

Vaclav Havel is right. Iraq's aggression is not just a challenge to the security of Kuwait and the other Gulf neighbors but to the better world we all hope to build in the wake of the Cold War. We're not talking simply about the price of gas. We are talking about the price of liberty.

Number three, we're here because innocent lives are at stake. We've all heard of atrocities in Kuwait that would make the strongest among us weak.

Turns your stomach when you listen to the tales of those that have escaped the brutality of Saddam the invader. Mass hangings. Babies pulled from incubators and scattered like firewood across the floor. Kids shot for failing to display the photos of Saddam Hussein. And he has unleashed a horror on the people of Kuwait.

And our diplomats and our citizens held hostage must be freed. And it's time to stop toying with the American hostages . . . because if we let Iraq get away with this abuse now, Americans will pay a price in future hostage-taking for decades to come. And so will other nations.

Three simple reasons: protecting freedom, protecting our future, protecting innocent lives. And any one is reason enough why Iraq's unprincipled, unprovoked aggression must not go unchallenged. And together they make a compelling case. For you to be away from your families on this special Thanksgiving Day, they make a compelling case for your mission. No president is quick to order American troops abroad. But there are times when any nation that values its own freedom must confront aggression.

As in World War II, the threat to American lives from a seemingly distant enemy must be measured against the nature of the aggression itself. A dictator who has gassed his own people, innocent women and children, unleashing chemical weapons of mass destruction, weapons that were considered unthinkable in the civilized world for over 70 years. And let me say this: those who would measure Saddam Hussein's, those who would measure the timetable for Saddam's atomic program in years may be seriously underestimating the reality of that situation and the gravity of the threat.

Every day that passes brings Saddam one step closer to realizing his goal of a nuclear weapons arsenal. And that's why, more and more, your mission is marked by a real sense of urgency. You know, no one knows precisely when this dictator may acquire atomic weapons, or exactly who they may be aimed at down the road. But we do know this for sure: He has never possessed a weapon that he didn't use.

What we're confronting is a classic bully who thinks he can get away with kicking sand in the face of the world. So far I've tried to act with restraint and patience. I think that's the American way. But Saddam is making the mistake of his life if he confuses an abundance of restraint, confuses that with a lack of resolve.

Over the past four months you have launched what history will judge as one of the most important deployments of allied military power since 1945, and I have come here today to personally thank you. The world is watching. Our objectives in the Gulf have never varied; we want to free and restore Kuwait's government, protect American citizens abroad, [and] safeguard the security and stability of the region. A united world has spelled out these objectives in 10 United Nations Security Council resolutions,

To force Iraq to comply, we and our allies have forged a strong diplomatic, economic and military strategy. But the Iraqi dictator still hasn't gotten the message . . .

We have been patient. We've gone to the United Nations, time and time again. We still hope for a peaceful settlement. But the world is a dangerous place. And we must make all of these options credible.

Those in uniform, [it] seems to me, will always bear the heaviest burden. We understand something of what you endure: the waiting, the uncertainty, the demands of family and military life. And we want every single troop home. We want every Brit to be able to go home as soon as possible. We want every single American home. And this I promise: no single American will be kept in the Gulf a single day longer than is necessary. But we won't pull punches. We are not here on some exercise. This is a real-world situation. And we're not

walking away until our mission is done, until the invader is out of Kuwait. And that may well be where you'll come in.

As we meet, it is dawn in America. It is Thanksgiving Day. The church bells ring. An hour of prayer. A day of rest. A nation at peace. And especially today, Americans understand the contribution that you are all making to world peace and to our country.

Year after year, on this special day, no doubt each of you has given thanks for your country. This year your country gives thanks for you. Thanksgiving is a day of prayer, a day when we thank God for our many, many blessings. And I've done that today.

This has been an unforgettable visit, an unforgettable visit. And I leave, as I know our congressmen do, and I know Barbara does, with pride in our hearts, a prayer on our lips.

God bless you all. God bless our faithful allies, the United Kingdom. God bless the marines. And may God bless the greatest freest country on the face of the earth, the United States of America. Thank you and bless you all. Thank you. Good luck to all you guys.
Reference: New York Times, 23 November 1990, A16.

Iraqi Revolutionary Command Council Response to President Bush's Solicitation for Talks, 1 December 1990

On 1 December 1990, in response to President Bush's call for talks to be held between Secretary of State James Baker and Iraqi Foreign Minister Tariq Aziz in either Washington or Baghdad, the Iraqi Revolutionary Command Council (RCC) released a statement.

We learned about a statement made by Bush yesterday as it was disseminated by news agencies. In his statement, he proposes inviting the Iraqi Foreign Minister to Washington for a meeting with him, and sending his Secretary of State to Baghdad to meet leader President Saddam Hussein . . .

We believe that human interaction, for it to be sincere, must be based on justice and equality eliminating all forms of tyranny, political intransigence, threats, social oppression and exploitation. On the debris of the era of oppression and dictation practiced by the superpowers, foremost of which is the United States, we must build a new form of democratic relations among the peoples of the world . . .

We believe that, in order to accomplish cooperation, it should be the result of deep interaction among nations and peoples. And in order to achieve cooperation, dialogue should be preferred over any other method. Our announcements on this have been frequent.

The enemy of God, the arrogant President of the United States, George Bush, always rejected dialogue, voicing his contempt of the Arabs and Muslims, and all those who believe in God and human values in the world.

Despite the fact that Bush's call for the meeting came after he had mobilized all the criminal forces on the holy places of the Arabs and Muslims, after he had issued unjust resolutions through the so-called Security Council against the people of Iraq and despite the arrogant language he used in his call . . . and in harmony with our principles and the ethics and morals that Almighty God called on us to abide by, we accept the idea of the invitation and the meeting.

When we receive the invitation officially, those concerned in Iraq and those concerned in the United States will agree on the timing and practical arrangements of the exchange of visits to suit both sides.

Because the call for the meeting contains an idea whose purposes are not clear enough—namely, the U.S. President's invitation to several countries' ambassadors to attend the meeting between himself and the Iraqi Foreign Minister, we will inquire from the American side about this idea and the reasons for it.

If the American side believes that it is necessary, Iraq, for its part, will call on representatives of countries and parties that are connected with unresolved disputes and issues to attend the meetings between Iraq and the U.S. Administration, whether in Washington or Baghdad. This will take place after consultations with the concerned parties on the basis of reciprocity.

In any case, our efforts will continue, as always, to hold an in-depth, serious dialogue, not formal meetings as sought by the American President to use as a pretext for American public opinion, the U.S. Congress, world public opinion and the international community to achieve objectives that he planned in the first place.

Iraq will continue to follow up and expand any room for dialogue instead of using threats and warnings. The principles of leader President Saddam Hussein's initiative of August 12, 1990, will be our guide in any serious dialogue.

Palestine and the other occupied Arab territories will remain before our eyes and at the forefront of the issues that we will discuss in any dialogue.

Reference: New York Times, 2 December 1990, A18.

Saddam Hussein Interview with French Television and Radio, 1 December 1990

On 1 December 1990, Antenne 2, a French television network, and Radio France Inter interviewed Saddam Hussein at length in Baghdad. The interview was broadcast in Paris on 2 December. Transmitted in Arabic, the interview, of which excerpts appear here, was translated by the Associated Press.

Q. Do you accept the dialogue proposed to you by President Bush?

A. If President Bush wishes to establish a balanced dia-

logue, such a dialogue must not get under way on the basis of preconditions. . . . President Bush has proposed two meetings. . . . We have accepted.

Q. What gesture are you ready to make to convince the world of your good will as you begin this dialogue?

A. There is no proposition more important than a dialogue that reaches a solution to all the problems of the region, and at their head the Palestinian problem. . . . We have taken a series of initiatives [concerning the Western hostages], and we have even fixed a date, March 25, as the last date for all of them to go home if nothing happens to disturb the peace.

This is not a tactic to sow discord on the ranks of whomever, but it is one of the means which we think are capable of preventing war. Such a method has perhaps proven its effectiveness, because so far there has been no war.

We will free them . . . as soon as we have President Bush's assurance that he will not attack the Iraqi people between now and March 25. If after March 25 he still has the devil in his head, we will count on God to face any eventuality."

Q. Now that President Bush has proposed dialogue, and you can save face to an extent, why not open up some possibility regarding Kuwait?

A. Our face is saved. We don't need Bush for that. Our face is saved because we are believers. . . . You know that Bush has not taken the same measures vis-à-vis the Israeli occupation of Palestine and doesn't even lift his little finger when he sees on the television screens women, children and old people being killed, humiliated and tortured in Palestine by the Israelis.

The problem is that President Bush and the other Western heads of state have two United Nations charters . . . a criteria based on evaluations of their own needs and interests and a criteria for the oppressed peoples of the third world, oppressed by the policies of the Western bloc and by the United States in particular.

Q. Is it necessary for a country like Iraq to provide itself with a nuclear capability? The Americans say this will happen in a year or two.

A. I speak of the present. If we had nuclear weapons, we wouldn't have any problem saying so. . . . But we don't possess a nuclear weapon. . . . Why doesn't the West protest and worry at the destructive capabilities of Israel?

Q. And this evening, are we closer to war or to peace?

A. Fifty-fifty. If this meeting is to be a true path to dialogue, then we are closer to peace. But if this meeting is to be nothing more than a formal exhibition for the American Congress, the American people and for international public opinion, simply to salve consciences and say, "There, we've tried to talk to Iraq without Iraq renouncing its position"—in that case, we are closer to war.

Reference: "Excerpts from the Interview with President Hussein," *New York Times*, 3 December 1990, A12.

Message of Saddam Hussein to the Iraqi National Assembly, 6 December 1990

On 6 December 1990, Saddam Hussein addressed the Iraqi National Assembly, calling for the release of all Western hostages immediately. Baghdad radio carried the discourse. The National Assembly (the rubber-stamp parliament) quickly endorsed the proclamation. Hussein's message follows.

In the name of God, the merciful, the compassionate, Mr. National Assembly Speaker, members: Peace be upon you. Under difficult conditions, the strength of the believers' affiliation and loyalty is put to the test. Their action in the service of principles is also put to the test. Iraqis in general, and you among them, have proved that on very dark nights, the spark of faith glows in a much nicer way than on ordinary nights. Adherence to the supreme principles governing the relation between Man and his Creator and his duty toward Him, as well as the relation between the Iraqis with all peoples, becomes even stronger in the more difficult circumstances.

And, just as the continued endeavor is required on earth, the correct answers to the continuous test are also required, without making the test or success in it dependent on a certain phrase and time.

On the basis of these principles and what we desire—that the influence of the believers expands, and that the knowledge of mankind in general expands with the believers' principles and the truth of their missions—we believe that, this time, the National Assembly is asked to take a decisive and final decision concerning a humanitarian issue, which you, and the whole world, know about.

National Assembly members, the thing that worries the faithful struggler, the honorable struggler, and the brave fighter—who has the values of the chivalrous believer—most is when the trenches in the battle arena get mixed and when some people, who do not want to fight and who are not among the evildoers, get trapped in the space between the two trenches. This worry becomes deep grief what that kind of people are harmed because of the level and type of the conflict.

The foreigners who were prevented from traveling are among those people in the battle between right, led by Iraq's great people and valiant armed forces, and evil, whose failing mass is led by Bush, the enemy of God. As you and my brothers in the leadership know, I realize that despite what they had to put up with, denying those people the freedom to travel has rendered a great service to the cause of peace. And because God has taught us that forbidden things should never be resorted to except in very urgent cases and without any excesses, we must not keep these emergency measures, especially this measure, any longer.

These days, weeks, and months through which our people and nation have passed have been such that our options, even those concerning the nature and form of defense, were not open or without limits in every area and all conditions. For instance, our valiant forces did not have the chance to complete their concentrations in order to confront the possibilities of military aggression against them in the Kuwaiti governorate. So any measure that was taken to delay the war may not have been correct from the humanitarian and practical standpoints and under established norms, but it has provided an opportunity for us to prepare for any eventuality.

We have now reached the time when, with God's care, our blessed force has become fully prepared, if God wills that we should fight in defense of his values and ideals against the infidels, profligates and traitors, and also in defense of the great national, pan-Arab and humanitarian gains.

Gentlemen: Good people, men and women of different nationalities and political trends have come to Iraq. Dear brothers from Jordan, Yemen, Palestine, Sudan, and the Arab Maghreb have also consulted with us on this issue, as on others. We have felt, guided by our humanitarian feelings, that the time has come to make a firm decision on this subject. We had considered a timing different from the present one; namely, the occasion of Christmas and [the] New Year, which are of special significance to Christians in the world, including Christians in the West.

However, the appeal by some brothers, the decision of the Democratic majority in the U.S. Senate, and the European Parliament's invitation to our Foreign Minister for dialogue; all these have encouraged us to respond to these good, positive changes—changes that will have a major impact on world public opinion in particular, in restraining the evil ones who are seeking and pushing for war as the option they have chosen out of their evil tendencies and premeditated intentions to do harm.

In view of all this, we have found that the exigencies that permitted the impermissible, and thus prevented the travel of foreigners, have weakened and have been replaced by something stronger; namely, this positive change in public opinion, including the change in U.S. public opinion, which will constitute a restraint in the intentions and decisions of the evil ones, who are led in their evil intentions and steps by the enemy of God, Bush.

Therefore, I call on you, brothers, to make your just decision and allow all foreigners on whom restrictions of travel were placed to enjoy the freedom of travel and to lift these restrictions, with our apologies for any harm done to any one of them. God, the Almighty, grants forgiveness.

Brothers, I ask you, and through you I ask the Iraqi

people and our brave armed forces, to maintain your alertness and vigil because the armies of aggression are still on our holy lands, in the Arabian Peninsula, and the evil ones are talking of war. Bush's invitation for talks, as far as we can discern, has continued to bear the possibilities or the inclination toward aggression and war. The buildup is growing.

Therefore, the steadfast believers, both on the level of the public and on the level of our armed forces, should not fall in the trap in which some have fallen in the past.

May God protect you and protect our people and nation, steer humanity from what God hates, help the faithful to carry out what God wishes, and smite the infidels and traitors after exposing them and their shameful deeds. He is the best supporter and backer. God is great, accursed be the infidels and traitors, who gave the oppressors and infidels the opportunity to invade the holy land.

Glory and greatness to the mujahedeen of the occupied land and all the steadfast mujahedeen and fighters of our great Arab nation.

Reference: "Iraqi Leader's Message to National Assembly," *New York Times,* 7 December 1990, A20.

President Bush's News Conference, 14 December 1990

On November 30th, in offering direct meetings between the United States and Iraq, I offered to go the extra mile for a peaceful solution to the gulf question. And I wanted to make clear to Saddam Hussein the absolute determination of the coalition that he comply fully with the Security Council resolutions. Iraqi aggression cannot be rewarded.

And so I have asked the Secretary of State to be available to go to Baghdad any time up to and including January 3rd, which is over five months after the invasion of Kuwait and only 12 days before the United Nations deadline for withdrawal. That deadline is real.

To show flexibility I have offered one of 15 dates for Secretary Baker to go to Baghdad, and the Iraqis have offered only one date. In offering to go the extra mile for peace, however, I did not offer to be a party to Saddam Hussein's manipulation. Saddam Hussein is not too busy to see, on short notice, Kurt Waldheim, Willy Brandt, Muhammad Ali, Ted Heath, John Connally, Ramsay Clark and many, many others on very short notice. And it simply is not credible that he cannot, over a two-week period, make a couple of hours available for the Secretary of State on an issue of this importance, unless, of course, he is seeking to circumvent the United Nations deadline.

Look, I want a peaceful solution to this crisis. But I will not be a party to circumventing or diluting the United Nations deadline, which I think offers the very best chance for a peaceful solution. And so I wanted to get out my feeling about these . . . these proposed meetings. . . .

Q. Mr. President, what's wrong with the January 12th date that he [Saddam Hussein] set? Why would that dilute it, unless you're afraid that he will come with up some offer?

A. Well, in the first place, the United Nations resolutions that pertain say that he has to be out of Kuwait. I wish now I had been a little more explicit in my first announcement on what I meant by mutually convenient dates. But I was not then, but now . . . and am not . . . not now prepared to have this man manipulate the purpose of the Secretary of State's visit. So we will . . . we have made an offer of many, many dates, but remember the United Nations resolution calls for total withdrawal by this date.

Q. And does your statement today indicate that you would not accept January 5th or 6th?

A. We've offered 15 days, and he ought to get moving and do something reasonable, if he really wants to move for peace.

Q. Mr. President, is there a date at which you would withdraw the offer to meet? The senators this morning say you're willing to forgo talks now.

A. Well, we're not going to doom them on terms that . . . that are . . . would appear to the world to be an effort to circumvent the United Nations resolution. I mean, he's got a massive force there, and force has to be out on the 15th of January under the United Nations resolutions. So we'll see . . . we'll see how it goes. I . . . I'm . . . I would say that we've given so many alternatives here that he ought to stay with . . . accept one of these. If he's serious.

Q. Is there a deadline for him to accept your offer?

A. No, we're not putting down deadlines on it. The Aziz meeting is on hold, I guess. I mean, I say I guess because we've made clear to them that its kind of a home-and-home arrangement here.

Q. You've said the deadline is real, so that means you think you have carte blanche to start a war after January 15th, or on January 15th?

A. I'm saying that the United Nations resolution is very clear as it regards January 15th, and I will continue now to work for a peaceful solution.

Q. Well, do you think you can go to war after that? Is that right?

A. What do you mean, can go to war?

Q. You can start a war.

A. I . . . I think that the United Nations resolutions should be fully implemented.

Q. Mr. President, when Congress comes back in January, will you ask Congress for specific authority to take offensive action?

A. I . . . we're talking about that, and I'm very pleased with the support we've had in Congress, and I'm very pleased with the level of support from the American people. You see, as these hostages have come home, I think the people have understood—the American people—much more clearly what's at stake. As they've seen the testimony about the brutality to the Kuwaiti people that was so compelling at the United Nations, I think people have said wait a minute, this policy deserves support. So I am pleased with the support I think that's being manifested in more support by the Congress. But I will be talking to the leaders, continuing to consult. And what I . . . I told the leaders in the Cabinet Room a few weeks ago: If you want to come here and strongly endorse what I am doing or endorse the United Nations resolution, I welcome that, because I think that would send a very strong, clear signal to the world.

Q. Well, sir, why are you afraid to go before Congress and consult with them and get their advice and get their approvals?

A. Hey, listen, Sarah, I was consulting with them as recently as this morning . . . five members of Congress. And we will continue to consult with them.

Q. Are you saying if Saddam Hussein won't meet by January 3rd, there simply will be no meeting?

A. I'm saying that he . . . we've given him 15 dates, and he ought to take one of them. I don't like to draw deadlines in the sand here. But I . . . there'd have to be some compelling reason for me to change it, because I don't want to move this up against the United Nations deadline. If you'll read the U.N. resolutions, you'll see that he should be totally out, totally out of Kuwait by January 15th. That's a massive undertaking. . . .

Q. Mr. President, if I may follow up?

A. Yeah?

Q. Are you saying that you may meet January 4th or 5th?

A. I'm not saying that. You're saying that. I've put it as clearly as I can. I hope there's no obfuscation.

Reference: New York Times, 15 December 1990, A6.

Statement by the North Atlantic Council Meeting in Ministerial Session at NATO Headquarters, 18 December 1990

1. Iraq's invasion and brutal occupation of Kuwait represent a flagrant violation of international law and the Charter of the United Nations and pose a fundamental challenge to international order. We condemn Iraq's persistent contempt for the Resolutions of the United Nations Security Council, which reflect the overwhelming solidarity and commitment of the international community. Iraq's behaviour threatens peace. It jeopardizes the unprecedented opportunity for the United Nations to realise the original vision of its role in promoting global peace and stability.

2. The responsibility now lies with the government of Iraq to ensure peace by complying fully with the mandatory United Nations decisions. Iraq has at last released the foreign citizens whom it had, illegally, detained as hostages. However, complete Iraqi withdrawal from Kuwait and the restoration of the sovereignty and legitimate government of Kuwait are unequivocal conditions for a peaceful solution. There can be no partial solutions.

3. We firmly support Resolution 678 and all other relevant Resolutions adopted by the Security Council and reiterate our hope that their implementation can be achieved by peaceful means. We are confident that a contact between the Presidency of the European Community and the Foreign Minister of Iraq, among other initiatives, can make a contribution to this purpose. We also encourage action by the UN Secretary General to this end. In particular, we support efforts for a dialogue, such as those made by President Bush, to provide Iraq, through direct high-level contacts, with the clearest possible understanding of the consequences of further postponing the fulfillment of its obligations. We agree that Iraq must not use these initiatives to delay meeting the January 15th date established by the United Nations.

The countries of the Gulf region, and in particular the Arab countries, also continue to bear a special responsibility in the efforts toward a solution.

4. Security Council Resolution 678 has authorised the use of all necessary means if Iraq does not comply before that date, and has expressly called on all governments to provide appropriate support in implementing the Resolutions adopted by the Security Council. Our countries will continue to respond positively to this United Nations request. Each of us, to the best of our ability, undertakes to provide further support for this continuing effort, in line with evolving requirements. Furthermore, each of us will continue to maintain and enforce the economic sanctions and to provide financial assistance to those countries most directly affected.

5. We note that the crisis in the Gulf poses a potential threat to one of our Allies having common borders with Iraq (Turkey), and we reaffirm our determination to fulfill the commitments stipulated in Article 5 of the Washington Treaty whereby an armed attack against one of our states shall be considered an attack against them all. We reiterate our firm commitment to the security of the entire Southern Region, the strategic importance of which is highlighted by this crisis.

Reference: NATO Review 38, 6 (December 1990): 5.

Statement by the Iraqi Government on United States and Iraq Talks, 4 January 1991

The following is the text of the Iraqi government's official announcement that it was accepting the Bush administration's plan to send representatives to meet in Geneva, Switzerland, on 9 January 1991.

Tariq Aziz told [the] Iraqi News Agency that the "American Administration linked its new offer to hold a meeting in Switzerland, as it did previously, with a series of arrogant statements which express the bad intentions of this Administration.

"Iraq has always stressed and would like to stress how its constant attitude, namely that it does not fear pressure and does not determine its attitude under threats and intimidation. Despite this bad way used by the American Administration, Iraq out of respect to world public opinion and to recognized norms of dealing between nations and not out of appreciation to the position taken by the American Administration and its bad attitude, has responded positively to the American proposal. And we have informed the American side of our approval of holding a meeting between myself and Minister Baker on January 9 in Switzerland.

"I was prepared to go to Washington and to receive Minister Baker in Baghdad if the American Administration acted in a courteous manner and respected the internationally recognized rules with regard to fixing dates for heads of states' meetings with other nations' envoys."

About what will take place at the meeting, Mr. Aziz said Iraq will stress in this meeting its constant principled attitude in rejecting threats. Iraq will also stress adherence to its rights and its readiness to strongly defend them.

"I will also seek to know whether the other side is ready to work for [the] realization of peace and security in the whole region on the basis of fairness and justice.

"In the forefront of the causes which need fairness and justice is the Palestinian question and the right of the Palestinian people in establishing its free state on the land of Palestine with Jerusalem as its capital."

Mr. Aziz said that the Iraqi authorities have informed the American side of Iraq's position as above stated.

About a statement made by European officials and the U.N. Secretary General about their desire to visit Iraq the Minister said, "Iraq welcomes anyone who wishes to visit Iraq to hold a serious dialogue to realize peace in the whole region."
Reference: New York Times, 5 January 1991, A5.

President Bush's Press Conference, 4 January 1991

The following are excerpts from a press conference held by President George Bush on the South Lawn of the White House as he was preparing to leave for Camp David.

Let me just make a brief statement and take a couple of questions, then I've got to be on my way. But, as you all know, Iraq has accepted my initiative for a meeting between Secretary Baker and Foreign Minister Aziz. The

meeting will take place on Wednesday, January 9th, in Geneva. And this is a useful step.

I hope that Iraq's acceptance of the meeting indicates a growing awareness of the seriousness of the situation and a willingness to heed the international community's will as expressed in 12 United Nations Security Council resolutions. There can be no compromise or negotiating on the objectives contained in those U.N. resolutions. And so it is now for Saddam Hussein to respond to the international community's plea for reason.

I took this initiative with the view of going the extra mile to achieve a peaceful solution to the current crisis in the gulf. Secretary Baker's mission to Geneva is to convey to Iraq the gravity of the situation and the determination of the international community to overcome Iraq's aggression against Kuwait. Iraq knows what is necessary: the complete and unconditional and immediate withdrawal of all Iraqi forces from all of Kuwait and the restoration of the legitimate Government of Kuwait.
Q. Mr. President, do you back up Baker's statement that there would be no retaliation against Iraq if it complies with the resolutions?
A. Well, I think its been made clear to Iraq, not only by Secretary Baker but by others, that if they totally comply, they will not be attacked. And, as I have said, when they totally withdraw, there still remains some problems to be solved, but they will not be under attack . . .
Q. Mr. President, what is in the letter you are sending to Saddam Hussein, and are you willing to have Secretary Baker go to Baghdad if that proves an option?
A. Well, the answer to your question is that the letter has not been finalized yet. I'm working on it. I have a copy I'm carrying with me now. I want to talk to the Secretary of State some more about it. And the second part of the question is no.
Q. [Inaudible] Secretary of State Baker to speak eye to eye with Saddam Hussein, when he was willing to meet you on the 12th, you're willing to talk on the 9th. Why not wait three days and have that direct meeting?
A. Well, because we, we have, we've exhausted that option. We put forward 15 different dates, and I believe that the message that both Secretary Baker and I want to convey can be done in this manner.
Q. You said you wanted him speaking directly and not through these intermediaries . . .
A. Well, that was rejected by the Iraqi president and so we're going to try it this way, and I hope that it'll have the same result.
Q. In diplomacy, as you so well know, it is often the art of give and take. The Iraqis are already saying that they will talk about getting out of Kuwait, but they also want to talk in Geneva about the Palestinian problem, about Israel's occupation of the West Bank. How do you—how are you instructing Secretary Baker to handle that portion of—

A. I don't need to instruct him because he and I are in total sync on this and so are the rest of the alliance. There will be no linkage on these two questions . . .

Q. If I may follow up, Mr. President, quite apart from linkage, whether it's called linkage or not, the Iraqis want to pursue these discussions. Is there room for some discussion on these other—

A. There will be no linkage on these other issues, or we can't tell anybody what he's—can bring up at a discussion, but there will be no linkage.

Q. Mr. President, if at the meeting on the 9th there seems to be progress being made, but it's not finished, would you delay resorting to the use of force while these talks continued?

A. That is a little hypothetical for me to respond, and I'm not going to take any hypothetical questions on this, because I don't want to show any deviation from the coalition's determination to see these United Nations resolutions implemented.

Q. Mr. President, is Secretary Baker prepared to discuss with Tariq Aziz further steps on the Arab-Israeli issue, the Palestinian question?

A. No, I don't think he's prepared to do that.

Q. Are you more optimistic now about the chances for peace, now that there is a meeting set up?

A. Well, I haven't gotten pessimistic about it. But time is going on here, and the coalition remains united in every way on these U.N. resolutions. But I think you'd have to view this as a positive step, and I was pleased that the proposal has been accepted.

Q. Mr. President, do you think that finally Saddam Hussein has gotten the message?

A. Well, I don't think he has gotten the message, and of course the purpose here is that he does get the message. So let's hope that it will work. I will say, just to be realistic about it, that there have been many meetings with Tariq Aziz, and heretofore the message has not been gotten. But Jim Baker is quite persuasive; he is a man of great conviction on this question. And I think that this represents a real opportunity for the Iraqis to understand how serious this coalition partner is about seeing those resolutions fully implemented.

Q. Mr. President, does your meeting tomorrow with Pérez de Cuéllar offer some new hope?

A. Well, I don't—I can't say that. I don't want to mislead the American people or the people around the world that are concerned, growing increasingly concerned about this situation.

But I go back with Pérez de Cuéllar a long time. We were ambassadors at the United Nations together in 1971 or 2. And I've known him and I know him very favorably, and I have great respect for what he has tried to do, including a trip to that area of the Middle East to make the Iraqis understand that the United Nations was serious.

And I talked to him in Paris, and I'm very anxious to see him and to compare notes with him. But I can't—I don't want to mislead you in answering the question. I don't have in mind a new initiative. But I do think that he stays in close touch with it. I heard what he had to say yesterday about things he is doing privately, keeping up with the key players on this gulf situation. And so I think it's more of getting together and comparing notes.

And he knows of my determination and our coalition position. So it won't—I don't need to reiterate that here. But I think it's more getting together. And if some new initiative he has in mind, I'm most anxious to hear what it might be.

Reference: "Remarks by Bush at News Conference," *New York Times,* 5 January 1991, A4.

Radio Address by President Bush, 5 January 1991

President George Bush delivered this talk to the American people during his weekly radio address from the White House.

As the new year begins, new challenges unfold—challenges to America and the future of the world. Simply put, 1990 saw Iraq invade and occupy Kuwait. 1991 will see Iraq withdraw, preferably by choice; by force, if need be. It is my most sincere hope [that] 1991 is a year of peace. I've seen the hideous face of war and counted the costs of conflict in friends lost. I remember this all too well, and have no greater concern than the well-being of our men and women stationed in the Persian Gulf. True, their morale is sky-high. True, if they are called upon to fight the aggressors, they will do their job courageously, professionally and, in the end, decisively. There will be no more Vietnams.

But we should go the extra mile before asking our servicemen and women to stand in harm's way. We should, and we have. The United Nations, with the support of the United States, has already tried to peacefully pressure Iraq out of Kuwait, implementing economic sanctions, and securing the condemnation of the world in the form of no less than 12 resolutions of the U.N. Security Council.

This week, we've taken one more step. I have offered to have Secretary of State James Baker meet with Iraqi Foreign Minister Tariq Aziz in Switzerland. Yesterday, we received word that Iraq has accepted our offer to meet in Geneva.

This will not be secret diplomacy at work. Secretary Baker will restate, in person, a message for Saddam Hussein: withdraw from Kuwait unconditionally and immediately, or face terrible consequences.

Eleven days from today, Saddam Hussein will either have met the United Nations deadline for a full and unconditional withdrawal, or he will have once again defied the civilized world. This is a deadline for Saddam Hussein to comply with the United Nations resolution, not a deadline for our own armed forces. Still, time is running out. It's running out because each day that passes brings real costs.

Saddam already poses a strategic threat to the capital cities of Egypt, Saudi Arabia, Turkey, Israel and Syria, as well as our own men and women in the gulf region. In fact, Saddam has used chemical weapons of mass destruction against innocent villagers, his own people. Each day that passes brings Saddam Hussein further on the path to developing biological and nuclear weapons and the missiles to deliver them. If Saddam corners the world energy market, he can then finance further aggression, terror and blackmail. Each day that passes increases Saddam's worldwide threat to democracy.

The struggling newborn democracies of Eastern Europe and Latin America already face a staggering challenge in making the transition to a free market. But the added weight of higher oil prices is a crushing burden they cannot afford. And our own economy is suffering, suffering the effects of higher oil prices and lower growth stemming from Saddam's aggression.

Each day that passes, Saddam's forces also fortify and dig in deeper into Kuwait. We risk paying a higher price in the most precious currency of all—human life—if we give Saddam more time to prepare for war. And each day that passes is another day of fear, suffering, and terror for the people of Kuwait, many who risked their lives to shelter and hide Americans from Iraqi soldiers. As the Emir of Kuwait said to our Vice President just last week, those who advocate waiting longer for sanctions to work do not have to live under such brutal occupation.

As I have discussed with members of Congress just two days ago, and in our many consultations, economic sanctions are taking a toll, but they are still not forcing Saddam out of Kuwait. Nor do we know when or even if they will be successful. As a result, America and her partners in this unprecedented coalition are sharing the burden of this important mission; and we are ready to use force to defend a new order emerging among the nations of the world, a world of sovereign nations living in peace.

We have seen too often in this century how quickly any threat to one becomes a threat to all. At this critical moment in history, at a time the cold war is fading into the past, we cannot fail. At stake is not simply some distant country called Kuwait. At stake is the kind of world we will inhabit.

Last Thanksgiving, I broke bread with some of our men and women at the front lines. They understand why we are in Saudi Arabia, and what we may have to do. I witnessed courage unfazed by the closeness of danger, and determination undiminished by the harsh desert sun. These men and women are America's finest. We owe each of them our gratitude and full support. That is why we must stand together, not as Republicans or Democrats, conservatives or liberals, but as Americans.

Reference: New York Times, 6 January 1991, A4.

President Bush's Message to the Coalition Nations on the Gulf Crisis, 8 January 1991

Recorded 6 January 1991 at Camp David, Maryland, this speech by President George Bush was broadcast on 8 January 1991 by the U.S. Information Agency's WORLDNET satellite network.

More than five months ago in the early morning hours of August 2nd, Iraqi forces rolled south and the rape of Kuwait began. That unprovoked invasion was more than an attack on Kuwait, more than the brutal occupation of a tiny nation that posed no threat to its large and powerful neighbor. It was an assault on the very notion of international order.

My purpose in speaking to you, the people of the countries united against this assault, is to share with you my view of the aims and objectives that must guide us in the challenging days ahead. From the center of the crisis in the Middle East, to people and countries on every continent, to the families with loved ones held hostage, to the many millions sure to suffer at the hands of one man with a stranglehold on the world's economic lifeline, Iraq's aggression has caused untold suffering, hardship and uncertainty.

In the more than five months since August 2nd, Iraqi troops have carried out a systematic campaign of terror on the people of Kuwait—unspeakable atrocities against men and women, and among the maimed and murdered, even children. In the more than five months since August 2nd, Iraq's action has imposed economic strains on nations large and small—among them some of the world's newest democracies at the very moment they are most vulnerable. And yet, Iraq's aggression did not go unchallenged.

In the five months since August 2nd, the world has witnessed the emergence of an unprecedented coalition against aggression. In the United Nations, Iraq's outlaw act has met a chorus of condemnation in 12 resolutions with the overwhelming support of the Security Council. At the moment, forces from 27 nations—rich and poor, Arab and Muslim, European, Asian, African and American—stand side by side in the gulf, determined that Saddam's aggression will not stand.

Letter from President Bush to Congressional Leaders, 8 January 1991

On 8 January 1991, President George Bush sent a letter to the congressional leaders, George J. Mitchell (D–Maine), Senate Majority Leader; Robert J. Dole (R–Kansas), Senate

Minority Leader; Thomas S. Foley (D–Washington), Speaker of the House of Representatives; and Robert H. Michel (R–Illinois), House Minority Leader, calling for the passage of a congressional resolution authorizing the United States to go to war in the Persian Gulf. The following is the text of that letter.

The current situation in the Persian Gulf, brought about by Iraq's unprovoked invasion and subsequent brutal occupation of Kuwait, threatens vital U.S. interests. The situation also threatens the peace. It would, however, greatly enhance the chances for peace if Congress were now to go on record supporting the position adopted by the U.N. Security Council on 12 separate occasions. Such an action would underline that the United States stands with the international community and on the side of law and decency; it also would dispel any belief that may exist in the minds of Iraq's leaders that the United States lacks the necessary unity to act decisively in response to Iraq's continued aggression against Kuwait.

Secretary of State Baker is meeting with Iraq's Foreign Minister on January 9. It would have been most constructive if he could have presented the Iraqi Government a Resolution passed by both Houses of Congress supporting the U.N. position and in particular Security Council Resolution 678. As you know, I have frequently stated my desire for such a Resolution. Nevertheless, there is still opportunity for Congress to act to strengthen the prospects for peace and safeguard this country's vital interests.

I therefore request that the House of Representatives and the Senate adopt a Resolution stating that Congress supports the use of all necessary means to implement Security Council Resolution 678. Such action would send the clearest possible message to Saddam Hussein that he must withdraw without condition or delay from Kuwait. Anything less would only encourage Iraqi intransigence; anything else would risk detracting from the international coalition arrayed against Iraq's aggression.

I am determined to do whatever is necessary to protect America's security. I ask Congress to join with me in this task. I can think of no better way for Congress to express it support for the President at this critical time. This truly is the last best chance for peace.
Reference: "Bush's Letter to Congressional Leaders," New York Times, 9 January 1991, A6.

Letter from President Bush to Saddam Hussein, 9 January 1991

On 9 January 1991, Secretary of State James Baker met with Iraqi Foreign Minister Tariq Aziz in Geneva, Switzerland, as a last-ditch attempt to stave off war in the Persian Gulf. Baker attempted to present Aziz with a letter that President George Bush wrote to Saddam Hussein. After reading the letter, Aziz refused to accept it. Three days later, the White House released the text of the letter.

Dear Mr. President:
We stand today at the brink of war between Iraq and the world. This is a war that began with your invasion of Kuwait; this is a war that can be ended only by Iraq's full and unconditional compliance with U.N. Security Council Resolution 678.

I am writing to you now, directly, because what is at stake demands that no opportunity be lost to avoid what would be a certain calamity for the people of Iraq. I am writing as well because it is said by some that you do not understand just how isolated Iraq is and what Iraq faces as a result. I am not in a position to judge whether this impression is correct; what I can do, though, is try in this letter to reinforce what Secretary of State Baker told your Foreign Minister and eliminate any uncertainty or ambiguity that might exist in your mind about where we stand and what we are prepared to do.

The international community is united in its call for Iraq to leave all of Kuwait without condition and without further delay. This is not simply the policy of the United States; it is the position of the world community, as expressed in no less than 12 Security Council resolutions.

We prefer a peaceful outcome. However, anything less than full compliance with U.N. Security Council Resolution 678 and its predecessors is unacceptable. There can be no reward for aggression. Nor will there be any negotiation. Principle cannot be compromised. However, by its full compliance, Iraq will gain the opportunity to rejoin the international community. More immediately, the Iraqi military establishment will escape destruction. But unless you withdraw from Kuwait completely and without condition, you will lose more than Kuwait. What is at issue here is not the future of Kuwait—it will be free, its government will be restored—but rather the future of Iraq. This choice is yours to make.

The United States will not be separated from its coalition partners. Twelve Security Council resolutions, 28 countries providing military units to enforce them, more than 100 governments complying with sanctions—all highlight the fact that it is not Iraq against the United States, but Iraq against the world. That most Arab and Muslim countries are arrayed against you as well should reinforce what I am saying. Iraq cannot and will not be able to hold on to Kuwait or exact a price for leaving.

You may be tempted to find solace in the diversity of opinion that is American democracy. You should resist any such temptation. Diversity ought not to be confused with division. Nor should you underestimate, as others have before you, America's will.

Iraq is already feeling the effects of the sanctions mandated by the United Nations. Should war come, it will be a far greater tragedy for you and your country. Let me state, too, that the United States will not tolerate the use of chemical or biological weapons, support of any kind for terrorist actions, or the destruction of Kuwait's oilfields and installations. The American people would demand the strongest possible response. You and your country will pay a terrible price if you order unconscionable actions of this sort.

I write this letter not to threaten, but to inform. I do so with no sense of satisfaction, for the people of the United States have no quarrel with the people of Iraq. Mr. President, U.N. Security Council Resolution 678 establishes the period before January 15 of this year as a "pause of good will" so that this crisis may end without further violence. Whether this pause is used as intended, or merely becomes a prelude to further violence, is in your hands, and yours alone. I hope you weigh your choice carefully and choose wisely, for much will depend upon it.

Reference: "Text of Letter from Bush to Hussein," *New York Times*, 13 January 1991.

Remarks by Secretary of State Baker Following Collapse of Peace Talks, 9 January 1991

Following the breakdown of negotiations between Secretary of State James Baker and Foreign Minister Tariq Aziz of Iraq, Baker appeared before reporters in Geneva, Switzerland. His remarks follow.

I have just given President Bush a full report of our meeting today. I told him that Minister Aziz and I had completed a serious and extended diplomatic conversation in an effort to find a political solution to the crisis in the gulf. I met with Minister Aziz today not to negotiate, as we had made clear we would not do, that is, negotiate backwards from United Nations Security Council resolutions, but I met with him today to communicate. And "communicate" means listening as well as talking. And we did that, both of us.

The message that I conveyed from President Bush and our coalition partners was that Iraq must either comply with the will of the international community and withdraw peacefully from Kuwait or be expelled by force.

Regrettably, in over six hours of talks, I heard nothing today that suggested to me any Iraqi flexibility whatsoever on complying with the United Nations Security Council resolutions.

There have been too many Iraqi miscalculations. The Iraqi Government miscalculated the international response to the invasion of Kuwait, expecting the world community to stand idly by while Iraqi forces systematically pillaged a peaceful neighbor. It miscalculated the

response, I think, to the barbaric policy of holding thousands of foreign hostages, thinking that somehow cynically doling them out a few at a time would somehow win political advantage, and it miscalculated that it could divide the international community and gain something thereby from its aggression.

So let us hope that Iraq does not miscalculate again. The Iraqi leadership must have no doubt that the 28 nations which have deployed forces to the gulf in support of the United Nations have both the power and the will to evict Iraq from Kuwait.

The choice is Iraq's. If it should choose to continue its brutal occupation of Kuwait, Iraq will be choosing a military confrontation which it cannot win, and which will have devastating consequences for Iraq.

I made these points with Minister Aziz not to threaten but to inform, and I did so with no sense of satisfaction. For we genuinely desire a peaceful outcome, and as both President Bush and I have said on many occasions, the people of the United States have no quarrel with the people of Iraq.

I simply wanted to leave as little room as possible for yet another tragic miscalculation by the Iraqi leadership. And I would suggest to you, ladies and gentlemen, that this is still a confrontation that Iraq can avoid.

The path of peace remains open, and that path is laid out very clearly in 12 United Nations Security Council resolutions adopted over a period of over five months. But now the choice lies with the Iraq leadership. The choice really is theirs to make. And let us all hope that that leadership will have the wisdom to choose the path of peace.

Questions and Answers

Q. What do you—what do your allies plan to do next to bring this message home?

A. After five months and 12 United Nations Security Council resolutions, it seems to me that it is almost evident that the time for talk is running out. It's time for Iraq to act, and to act quickly by getting out of Kuwait. But this is a coalition, and we are seeking to implement solemn resolutions of the United Nations, and so perhaps there may be a way that the Secretary General of the United Nations could use his good offices here in the remaining six or so days that we have left. I will say that—I've already mentioned that I didn't hear anything that to me demonstrated flexibility, nor did I hear any new proposals.

Q. Could you run through for us—you spoke for six hours—could you give us a sense of how the discussions evolved over those six hours? What did you begin with? What did he counter with? Why did you feel it necessary after two hours to call the President?

A. Well, we broke for lunch. And I think this is—I think this meeting is sufficiently important that I should call the President, and so I did. Just as I did as soon as we were finished.

But I began by saying that I was here to—not to negotiate but to communicate as I've just told you. That I was here for serious dialogue in an effort to find a political and peaceful solution, but that they should not expect that we would be prepared to walk backwards from U.N. Security Council resolutions, and that the terms of those resolutions had already been set.

And I told the minister I wanted to handle the meeting in whatever way he wanted, and I gave him the choice, and he chose for me to go first, just as he—I gave him the choice as well as to how to report to you. And he suggested that I come down here first.

So that's how we got where we are tonight. But let me say that I talked to him about—about how we saw the situation; about the history of the Security Council resolutions; about what I thought could happen in the event of observance of those resolutions; and what I feared what would happen in the event of Iraq's nonobservance of those resolutions.

He then presented the position of the Government of Iraq. And he will be down here in a few moments and he can—now we can't run through six hours of dialogue here. Nobody else will get to ask any questions.

Q. One quick follow-up. How detailed were you about the extent of force that would be used against Iraq if it does not comply with the U.N. resolutions by January 15th?

A. Well, I didn't give—I didn't get into things that would properly be in the realm of operational security matters. I hope I—I hope I effectively made the case with respect to what at least our opinion was of the 28-nation multinational force that is there in the gulf.

Q. Mr. Secretary, you have said in the past that you would seek approval for the use of force at the highest levels. Are you now at that stage in the process in which you will be seeking the use of force from other governments?

A. No, but the clock is ticking on, and I made that point to the minister today. As far as we are concerned, we have not taken—the President of the United States, who alone, in our executive branch, under our system, can make that decision, but has not taken that decision. And I'm not aware that any governments have.

Q. Mr. Secretary, in the remaining six days before the U.N. deadline, would you welcome an initiative by some other European allies or even Arab countries, such as Algeria, that perhaps include sending a European foreign minister to Baghdad to seek [a] peaceful resolution?

A. Well, this is an international coalition. Let me say it one more time. And therefore, as I've just indicated to you, it's an international coalition seeking to implement solemn resolutions of the world's peacekeeping and security body. And therefore there might, it seems to me, be some useful purpose served by perhaps the Secretary General's good offices. But I said last night,

and I have said for months, we welcome any and all diplomatic efforts to solve this crisis peacefully and politically. We want it solved peacefully and politically.

I'm disappointed, of course, that we did not receive any indications today whatsoever of any flexibility in the position of Iraq. So we welcome any and all diplomatic efforts. We do think if they are efforts by members of the international coalition that the message should be uniform, as it has been for five months, and it should not be [a] mixed message. But we want a peaceful and political solution.

Q. Mr. Secretary, can you tell us, you keep saying you saw no indication of flexibility. Did the Foreign Minister actually tell you that Iraq intends to keep Kuwait, and will not withdraw from Kuwait?

A. He did not make that statement, but he did not indicate that there was any chance that they would withdraw.

Q. Mr. Secretary, what did you tell the Foreign Minister about the willingness of the American people to go to war and the impact of political pressure on the President's decision-making?

A. I said don't miscalculate the resolve of the American people, who are very slow to anger, but who believe strongly in principle and who believe that we should not reward aggression and that big countries with powerful military machines should not be permitted to invade, occupy, and brutalize their peaceful neighbors.

Q. Mr. Secretary, you've told us what you didn't hear. You didn't hear any flexibility, and you told us that there was quite a bit of discussion of history. Could you tell us what you did hear? Did you hear justifications from the Foreign Minister? Did you hear a repeat of what they've been saying in public for some time?

A. I heard some things that I quite frankly found very hard to believe, but I will let him go into the detail here. But I heard, for instance, that their action in invading Kuwait was defensive in nature, and they were being threatened by Kuwait. And I will tell you the same thing I told the minister, which is I find it very hard to believe that any nation in the world will believe that.

Q. Mr. Secretary, even though you did spend six hours here today talking to Foreign Minister Aziz, in the past five and [a] half months you haven't had much contact with Iraq. What's to prevent the historians of this conflict from concluding that there was a failure of diplomacy here and we slid toward war without trying?

A. Well, there's been a lot of conversations with the leadership of Iraq, all to no avail. The Secretary General has already had one failed mission. There have been any number of Arab efforts to solve this crisis, all to no avail. There have been efforts by others, other Western governments. The Soviet Union has tried very hard—they've had meetings. We have now had a meeting. And so, you know, people can write whatever they decide they might want to write, but the truth of the matter is we have been very, I think—the international coalition—very responsible and measured in our approach to this. We have not, as some might suggest, gone off half-cocked. We have gone through the United Nations patiently working for consensus within the Security Council and it is only after five and a half months and the passage of 12 Security Council resolutions that we find ourselves at the point of [the] use of force. So I think that there's been more diplomacy exercised in this crisis than in almost any that I can think of. And the one thing that I would ask you all not to do is to equate diplomacy and appeasement. We made that mistake in the [19]30s. At least for our part, we don't intend to make it again.

Q. Mr. Secretary, did Minister Aziz make a specific proposal under which Iraq would get out of Kuwait, however unacceptable it was to you? Was there a specific proposal?

A. No. There was no specific proposal. He restated the positions that Iraq has stated publicly in the past. He defended their action in invading and occupying Kuwait. He explained how he feels that it was justified, and again, he'll be down here, and you can ask him yourselves.

Q. Mr. Secretary, you made it clear that you were not going to Baghdad. But did you and the Foreign Minister talk about future diplomatic contacts at your level between the United States and Iraq? Or did this one six-and-a-half hour meeting represent the conclusion of diplomatic initiatives by the United States?

A. Well, we will maintain our diplomatic contacts through our chargé in Baghdad until the 12th of January. I asked for, and received, the personal assurance of the minister that Joe Wilson and the four other Americans in our embassy there will be permitted to leave Baghdad on the 12th of January, and will not be restrained from so doing.

Q. Mr. Secretary, your mood, if I may say, seems pretty somber at this point. Can you describe your state of mind and your mood after what has occurred today?

A. Somber.

Q. Somber?

A. You got it.

Q. You're advising an evacuation?

A. I'm not saying that. I'm telling you that we have asked for and received assurances for our remaining five diplomatic personnel to leave on the 12th of January, which is a date that you well know is very close to the January 15th deadline, and happens to be the date that Iraq has been insisting on for three months for the meeting.

Q. Mr. Secretary, can you tell us now about the letter from President Bush; was it in fact in Arabic, what was the tone of it, did it contain graphic military scenarios intended to intimidate?

A. I regret to inform you . . . that the minister chose not to receive the letter from President Bush. He read it very slowly and very carefully. But he would not accept it, nor would the Iraqi Embassy in Washington accept an Arabic courtesy translation. You will have to ask the minister why he did not accept the letter.

My own opinion, for what it's worth, and it's only an opinion, was that he came here not authorized to accept a letter, that walked away from the United Nations resolutions, which is something that we cannot, and of course will not, do.

Q. Mr. Secretary, did you spell out your vision of what the gulf would look like if they withdrew peacefully? In other words, some of the restrictions that you have talked about that must be imposed upon Iraq, even if they did withdraw? Did you lay that plan out for him in some way?

A. Yes. I did in my original presentation this morning and I can't—I don't have time to go through all of that with you now, but that falls right in the category of the assurance that there would not be military force used against Iraq by the United States if they withdrew from Kuwait and permitted the restoration of the legitimate Government of Kuwait.

Q. Did you talk about the nuclear weapons, the chemical weapons, the size of the Iraqi military, things that are of concern to many in the western coalition beyond the occupation of Kuwait?

A. We had a full discussion of the questions about weapons of mass destruction. I pointed out the interest of the United States as we've expressed before in addressing that subject. And we talked about the presence, the multinational presence there, and the fact that President Bush has said that we do not desire nor want a permanent military ground presence in the Middle East—I mean, in the gulf, that we are not—we want to see our troops come home just as fast as the security situation will allow.

Q. Mr. Secretary, was there any single issue on which the difference between the United States and Iraq was narrowed during this six and a half hours?

A. Well, let me say that I think the discussion I've already indicated was a serious one. I think that the tone of it was good, as good as you could expect under the circumstances. We weren't pounding the table and shouting at each other; it was a very reasoned and I think responsible discussion by two diplomats who really would like to find a peaceful and political solution to this problem. But I've already said to you I did not detect flexibility in the position of Iraq, as they have stated it over the past several days.

Now, again I invite you to my opening statement: We still have six days. I just hope that they will think about this meeting, that they will focus on it, that when Foreign Minister Aziz gets back and reports to his president, that perhaps there could be some change in their position. But there cannot be a negotiation here because the terms of the United Nations Security Council resolutions were worked out in the debate in the United Nations, and the international coalition is bound to those resolutions.

Reference: "Remarks by Baker at News Conference in Geneva on Standoff in the Gulf," *New York Times,* 10 January 1991, A15, A16.

Press Conference of Tariq Aziz in Geneva, Switzerland, 9 January 1991

Following his meeting with Secretary of State Baker, Foreign Minister Tariq Aziz of Iraq met with reporters. Here are excerpts from his remarks.

When I arrived last night in Geneva, I said that I have come with open-mindedness, and that was my intention. And I also came in good faith. The most important fact about these talks I would like to draw your attention to is that they are taking place after five months of the occurrence of the latest events in the gulf.

If we had an earlier opportunity, several months ago, I told the Secretary that we might have been able to remove a lot of misunderstandings between us— there was a chance, or there is a chance, for that. Because he spoke at length about his government's assumptions of miscalculations by Iraq—and when I came to that point, I made it clear to him that we have not made miscalculations. We are very well aware of the situation. We have been very well aware of the situation from the very beginning.

And I told him that we have heard a lot of talk on his side and on the side of President Bush that the Iraqis have not got[ten] the message, they don't know what's going around them. . . . I told him if we had met several months ago, I would have told you that we do know everything. We know what the deployment of your forces in the region mean; we know what the resolutions you imposed on the Security Council mean; and we know all the facts about the situation—the political facts, the military facts, and the other facts, so talking about miscalculating is incorrect.

I hear Secretary Baker describing our meeting in form and I say also that from the professional point of view, it was a serious meeting. We both listened to each other very carefully. We both gave each other enough time to explain the views we wanted to explain—to convey the information we wanted to convey. From this aspect, about this aspect of the talks, I am satisfied.

But we had grave, or big differences about the issues we addressed. Mr. Baker reiterated the very well-known American position. He is interested in one question only; that's the situation in the Gulf, and the Security Council resolutions about that situation. I told him very clearly, and I repeated my idea and explained

it at length, that what is at stake in our region is peace, security and stability. What's at stake is the fate of the whole region, that region which has been suffering from wars, instabilities, hardships, for several decades.

If you are ready to bring about peace in the region— comprehensive, lasting, just peace to the whole region of the Middle East—we are ready to cooperate. I told him I have no problem with the international legality. I have no problem with the principles of justice and fairness. . . . We have been seeking for decades to have those principles respected and implemented in our region. But they have not been respected and implemented by the Israelis, and in that, they have got a continuous, strong American support. If the American Administration changes its position and works with us and with the other parties concerned in the region to bring about peace, comprehensive, lasting, just peace, we will be very glad and very enthusiastic to participate in that effort.

Concerning the new world order, or the international world order, I said I have no problem with that order. And we would love to be partners in that order. But that order has to be implemented justly, and in all cases, not using that order in a single manner, in a selective manner, in a selective manner, impose it on a certain case . . . and neglect the other issues and not show sincerity and seriousness about implementing it in other issues.

He said that he does not believe that what happened on the 2nd of August and later was for the cause of the Palestinian question, or to help the Palestinians. I explained to him the history of Iraq's interest in the Palestinian question. I explained to him that the Palestinian question is a matter of national security to Iraq. If the Palestinian question is not resolved, we do not feel secure in our country, because there have been wars in the past. Iraq participated in those wars, Israel attacked Iraq in 1981, and we were expecting [an] Israeli attack on Iraq this year—last year, in March and April [of] last year we were expecting such an attack. . . . Therefore it is a matter of Iraqi security as well as Arab security to see that the Palestinian question is solved according to . . . principles of justice and fairness.

And I told him that the United States actually implemented [an] embargo on Iraq before the 2nd of August. We had dealings with the United States in the field of foodstuffs; we used to buy more than a billion dollars of American products. And we were faithful and accurate in our dealing with the American relative institutions. Early in 1990, the American Administration suspended that deal, which was profitable to both sides. And we were denied food from the United States.

Then the United States Government decided to deny Iraq the purchase of a very large list of items.

That was done also by the British government and other western governments. So the boycott was there before the 2nd of August. The threat to the security of Iraq was there before the 2nd of August. The threat to the Palestinians was there before that date. The threat to the security of Jordan was there before that date.

If the matter is the implementation or the respect of . . . Security Council resolutions, we have a number of resolutions about the Palestinian question. They have been neglected for decades. The last two important resolutions, 242 and 338. The first was adopted in 1967, the other in 1973, and they are not yet implemented. And the United States and members of the coalition . . . have not sent troops to impose the implementation of those resolutions. They have not taken measures against Israel . . .

On the contrary, the United States government has covered the Israeli position, protected it politically at the Security Council and that's very well known to everybody. And the United States Government still supplies Israel with military and financial means to stick to its intransigence. So if the matter is respect of international law, Security Council resolutions, we would like you to show the same attention to all Security Council resolutions. And if you do that, a lot of differences between us will be removed.

When we discuss the question of the mass destruction of weapons, I told him in 1990 when this question was raised very, very strongly by the American administration, we made it public . . . that Iraq is ready to join an agreement to eliminate all mass destruction weapons in the whole region, including nuclear weapons, biological weapons and chemical weapons.

And I told the secretary that you only concentrate on what Iraq has and you don't show any concern about what Israel has. Israel does have nuclear weapons, and you cannot give me any assurances that Israel is not going to use them against us or against other Arabs. The only assurance—credible assurance—is that we reach an agreement on the elimination of all mass destruction weapons. And I told him, you have got a pledge from me to that, and my guess is that you cannot get such a pledge from the foreign minister of Israel or from his prime minister.

This raises, as well as the attitude towards the Security Council resolutions, the question of double standards. I told him we in Iraq and in the Arab world feel strongly against the double standards you used in addressing the questions in the region. When it comes to Israel, you are calm. . . . You can wait for months and years to try to persuade. If they are not persuaded . . . you don't do anything. You continue your support. But when it comes to Arabs, there you raise the stick. And we are fed up with this policy of double standards. We shall not accept to be treated as a nation of underdogs. We are a proud nation, we have our history, we have

our contribution to human civilization, and we would like to be treated in a dignified and just manner.

Concerning the threats—or no threats, which the Secretary referred to and has addressed to you—the tone of his language was diplomatic and polite. I reciprocated. But the substance was full of threats. And I told him, also in substance, that we would not yield to threats. We would like to have genuine constructive dialogue . . . in order to make peace in the region and between our two nations.

You hear that I declined to receive the letter from President Bush to my president. At the beginning of the meeting, Secretary Baker told me that he carries a letter from his President to my President, and he handed over a copy to me. I told him I want to read this letter first. And I read it . . . carefully and slowly, and I knew what it was about. I told him I am sorry, I cannot receive this letter.

And the reason is that the language in this letter is not compatible with the language that should be used in correspondence between heads of state. I have no objection that Mr. Bush would state his position very clearly. . . . But when a head of state writes to another head of state a letter, and if he really intends to make peace with that head of state or reach genuine understanding, he should use polite language. . . . Therefore, because the language of that letter was contrary to the traditions of correspondence between heads of state, I declined to receive it.

Questions and Answers

Q. Mr. Minister, would Iraq agree to leave Kuwait if promised an international conference on the question of Palestine?

A. I did not put it that way. I heard such a question during Mr. Baker's meeting with you. I told the secretary that if you are ready to respect and implement international legality, the principles of justice and fairness as far as all the issues in the region are concerned, you will find us very cooperative.

Q. Do you believe that war with the United States is inevitable?

A. Well, that is up to the American administration to decide. I told Mr. Baker that we are prepared for all expectations. We have been prepared from the very beginning . . . if the American administration decides to attack Iraq militarily, Iraq will defend itself in a very bold manner.

Q. Mr. Foreign Minister, in your opening statement, and in fact up to this very moment, you have not mentioned Iraq's annexation of Kuwait. I'm curious to know whether you actually ever discussed the question of withdrawal from Kuwait during the course of the six or so hours of talks with Secretary Baker.

A. Yes. Mr. Baker spoke a lot about the situation in the gulf, and I made our position very clear. I told him this situation is part and parcel of a general situation in the region. If you are ready to address it on the same principles, on the same criteria, I am ready to do the same.

Q. Mr. Foreign Minister, if the war starts in the Middle East, in the gulf, will you attack Israel?

A. Yes, absolutely. Yes.

Q. Foreign Minister, there have been quotes from Baghdad . . . questioning America's will and its resolve, particularly given its Vietnam experience. I wonder if you would give us your reading of America's will.

A. We have prepared ourselves for the worst from the very beginning. Therefore, we are not making miscalculations about that. But at the same time, I am telling you now that any support in the United States or elsewhere for the cause of peace is a noble phenomenon, and such a noble phenomenon has to be appreciated. We do appreciate the reasonable statements made by American individuals, by American politicians, about the situation in the region. . . .

Q. Mr. Minister, are there circumstances under which Iraq would withdraw from Kuwait, and if so, can you tell us what they would be?

A. I'm not going to answer hypothetical questions.

Q. Mr. Minister, before leaving Baghdad, you said you would have new proposals and ideas. What you've just said this evening you've said many, many times before. Why did you have no new proposals or ideas?

A. I raised a lot of ideas with Mr. Baker. I told him, why don't you work with us together and with the other parties to bring about a comprehensive peaceful settlement to the whole region? . . .

I raised with the secretary the question of the Arab solution. I told him why are you against the Arab solution? And he said that the majority of the Arab countries are against the so-called Arab solution. I told him, wait a minute. I will count one country after the other who has shown interest in an Arab solution, and when I counted the states . . . the number was 11. And this shows that there is a majority among the Arab world to try an Arab solution. But he strongly refused that path, and he even denied that there is an Arab solution—the idea of an Arab solution. I told him there is an Arab solution. Why not? This is an Arab problem . . . and what's wrong if a number of leaders in the Arab world meet and try to find solutions to this problem? And there is no contradiction between this and then taking that solution to the international organization and seek some sort of an endorsement to it. And there is a precedent in that—a very recent precedent. We have the situation in Lebanon . . . and it has been dealt with several times by the Security Council and by other international bodies. He says that this is the international community versus Iraq, this is the coalition versus Iraq. I told him, but the meeting is between you and me. The fact that the foreign minister of Iraq and the secretary of the United States are meeting here in Geneva discussing the situation shows that this is a confrontation

between Iraq and the United States. You have your allies on your side, and we do have allies on our side. You can count a bigger number. You have the capabilities, and we all know how that number of the coalition was increased. A lot of money—billions of dollars—were spent to create that coalition. We are not—we don't have such money to make a parallel coalition. But those who are supporting Iraq—they are supporting it genuinely. . . . And I told him, who are the staunchest supporters of Iraq now. The people of Palestine in the occupied territories. Those people were the most affected financially by the events in the gulf. And in spite of their financial and economic hardships, they support Iraq. Why? Because they find in this conflict, a golden chance for themselves that their country, their land—they themselves—might be liberated.

References: "Excerpts from Iraqi Foreign Minister's News Session after Geneva Talks," *New York Times,*10 January 1991, A15; "Aziz: 'I Made Clear That We Have Not Made Miscalculations,'" *Washington Post,* 10 January 1991, A26.

President's Bush Press Conference, 9 January 1991

Following the collapse of talks in Geneva between Secretary of State James Baker and Foreign Minister Tariq Aziz of Iraq, President George Bush held a press conference in the White House to discuss the discourse. Following are excerpts from the conference.

I have a brief opening statement, and then I will take a few questions. I have spoken with the Secretary of State, Jim Baker, who reported to me on his nearly seven hours of conversation with the Iraqi Foreign Minister, Tariq Aziz. Secretary Baker made it clear that he discerned no evidence whatsoever that Iraq was willing to comply with the international community's demand to withdraw from Kuwait and comply with the United Nations resolutions.

Secretary Baker also reported to me that the Iraqi Foreign Minister rejected my letter to Saddam Hussein, refused to carry this letter and give it to the President of Iraq. The Iraqi Ambassador here in Washington did the same thing. This is but one more example that the Iraqi Government is not interested in direct communications, designed to settle the Persian Gulf situation. The record shows that whether the diplomacy is initiated by the United States, the United Nations, the Arab League, or the European Community, the results are the same, unfortunately. The conclusion is clear: Saddam Hussein continues to reject a diplomatic solution.

I sent Secretary Jim Baker to Geneva, not to negotiate, but to communicate, and I wanted Iraqi leaders to know just how determined we are that the Iraqi forces leave Kuwait without condition or further delay. Secretary Baker made clear that by its full compliance with the 12 relevant United Nations Security Council resolutions, Iraq would gain the opportunity to rejoin the international community. And he also made clear—he also made clear how much Iraq stands to lose if it does not comply.

Let me emphasize that I have not given up on a peaceful outcome. It's not too late. I've just been on the phone subsequent to the Baker press conference with [Saudi] King Fahd, with [French] President Mitterrand, to whom I've talked twice today, [Canadian] Prime Minister Brian Mulroney, and others are contacting other coalition partners to keep the matter under lively discussion. It isn't too late. But now, as before, as it's been before, the choice of peace or war is really Saddam Hussein's to make. And now I'd be glad to take a few questions.

Questions and Answers

Q. You said in an interview last month that you believed in your gut that Saddam Hussein would withdraw from Kuwait by January 15th. After the failure of this meeting today, what does your gut tell you about that, and in your gut, do you believe that there is going to be war or peace?

A. I can't misrepresent this to the American people. I am discouraged. I watched much of the Aziz press conference and there was no discussion of withdrawal from Kuwait. The United Nations resolutions are about the aggression against Kuwait. They're about the invasion of Kuwait, about the liquidation of a lot of the people in Kuwait. It's about the restoration of the legitimate Government to Kuwait. And here we were listening to a 45-minute press conference after the Secretary stated—Secretary of State of the United States had a six-hour—six hours worth of meetings over there and there was not one single sentence that has to relate to their willingness to get out of Kuwait.

And so, Terry, I have to say I certainly am not encouraged by that, but I'm not going to give up, and I told this to our coalition partners, and I'll be talking to more of them when I finish here. We've got to keep trying. But this was—this was a total stiff-arm, this was a total rebuff.

Q. . . . Have you decided in your mind to go to war if he's not out of there by the 15th?

A. I have not made up my decision on what and when to do. I am more determined than ever that the United Nation's resolutions, including 678, be—is implemented fully.

Q. Aziz made a pledge that he would not make the first attack. Would you match that? And also, what's wrong with a Middle East conference if it could avoid a bloody war?

A. No, I wouldn't make it, and we oppose linkage. The coalition opposes linkage, and the argument with Saddam Hussein is about Kuwait. It is about the invasion of Kuwait, the liquidation of a member of the United Nations, a member of the Arab League. And it has long been determined by not just the Security Council but by the entire United Nations, that this is about Kuwait.

And that is the point that was missing from his explanations here today. And so there will be no linkage on these items, and that's been the firm position of all of the allies—those with forces there—and indeed, of the United Nations, the General Assembly. So when he talked about his allies there, I don't know who stood up at the General Assembly of the United Nations and stood against the resolution that so overwhelmingly passed condemning Iraq. So there will be no linkage, put it that way.

Q. Tariq Aziz, on the subject of the letter, suggested that it was rude in its use of language and somehow inappropriate to a diplomatic communication. I wonder, sir, if you are willing to release the letter now that it has been—run its course apparently, and if—whether you are or not, would you characterize it for us and tell us what it said.

A. Well, let me first describe why I wanted to send the letter. It has been alleged, fairly or unfairly, that those around Saddam Hussein refuse to bring him bad news, or refuse to tell it to him straight. And so I made the determination that I would write a letter that would explain as clearly and forcefully as I could exactly what the situation is that he faces. The letter was not rude. The letter was direct. And the letter did exactly what I think is necessary at this stage. But to refuse to even pass a letter along seems to me to be just one more manifestation of the stonewalling that is taking place. We gave him 15 dates for the secretary of state to meet with him, and he's off meeting with Mr. A, Mr. B, Mr. C, and has no time for that. So the letter was proper. I've been around the diplomatic track for a long time. The letter was proper. It was direct. And it was what I think would have been helpful to him to show him the resolve of the rest of the world, certainly of the coalition.

In terms of releasing it, Brit, I haven't given much thought to that. It was written as a letter to him. But let me think about it. I might be willing to do it, I might now. I just don't know. If I thought it would help get the message out to him and through an indirect way, maybe it makes some sense. Although we've been saying essentially the same thing over and over again that was in the letter.

Q. Was the refusal by the ambassador here to even accept the letter—was that prior to or simultaneous with the refusal of Tariq Aziz?

A. I think it was after . . . the letter had been rejected . . . at the table there in Geneva. It's just one more effort to try to get this direct communication to him.

Q. Mr. President, there are reports that you are considering a call-up of up to a million reservists to reinforce the forces that are serving in the Persian Gulf. What can you tell us about that?

A. I can tell you nobody's ever suggested that to me.

Q. Is there any reserve call-up being contemplated?

A. I'll tell you what I'll do. I'll ask the Secretary of Defense [Dick Cheney] to respond to that question when I get finished here.

Q. Can you tell us what your attitude now is about the use of force resolution that you asked for yesterday with the Congress?

A. Well, I had a good meeting with certain members of Congress. I have talked to all four leaders this afternoon—Senator [George] Mitchell, Senator [Robert] Dole, Speaker [Thomas] Foley. Congressman [Robert] Michel—I talked to him in person here—and I'm not sure where it stands . . . I am anxious to see and would certainly welcome a resolution that says, "We are going to implement the United Nations resolutions to a 'T'."

I don't think it's too late to send a consolidated signal to Saddam Hussein, and I think that would be a consolidated signal. I think it would be helpful still. . . .

So, I don't know exactly where it stands, but I know that there is a good feeling up there. I think people see that the American people are supportive of the policy of this country. I think they see that we have tried the diplomatic track. I hope they know that I am as committed to peace as anyone. But I hope they also know that I am firmly determined to see that this aggression not stand.

And I think they're backing me in that. So maybe that ingredient, which hasn't always been quite as clear as it is now, will help us as this . . . proper debate goes forward in the Congress.

Q. Constitutionally, sir, do you think you need such a resolution, and if you lose it, would you be bound by that?

A. I don't think I need it. I think [Defense] Secretary Cheney expressed it very well the other day. There are different opinions on either side of this question, but Saddam Hussein should be under no question on this. I feel that I have the authority to fully implement the United Nations resolutions.

Q. And on the question of being bound—the second part of that?

A. I still feel that I have the constitutional authority, many attorneys having so advised me.

Q. You talk about [that] you don't want this to be another Vietnam. . . . If the Congress of the United States refuses to give you a resolution, refuses to . . . even give you a Gulf of Tonkin–type resolution, how can you go to war?

A. I don't think they're going to refuse. . . . I would just repeat for the record that there have been a lot of uses of force in our history and very few declarations of war. But I have tried. I have done more consultation with the Congress than any other president. Some of these Democratic members have told me that. And I have tried to reach out to them in various ways, and I will continue to do it because I want to see a solid front here as we stand up to this aggressor.

I think he [Saddam] doesn't think that force will be used against him. I think he's misinterpreted the debate. I also think he's under a delusion about what would happen if a conflagration breaks out. I believe that firmly, and I've had many, many people whom I respect tell me that. So, I would hope that what we're talking about here would dissuade him from that.

Q. You said that the coalition is united against any linkage on the Palestinian question. You talked to François Mitterrand twice today but in public he says he is for this international peace conference, and he seems to have no objection at all if Saddam Hussein wants to use that as a fig leaf to pull out of Kuwait. You do have an objection. Mitterand also says that apparently the European Community foreign ministers want to meet with Aziz, apparently in Algiers. What if they go in there and say, "Well, we have no objection to an international peace conference on the Mideast?"

A. The foreign ministers of the EC have been very solid, and so has President François Mitterrand, that there will be no linkage. So you're asking me a hypothetical question that . . . I won't have to answer because he's not going to do that.

Q. He said today he disagrees with you.

A. The French government and the United States government over the years have had some differences in how the best way to bring peace to the Middle East is. We had a very active initiative underway by Jim Baker, but that doesn't have anything to do with the invasion of Kuwait. And François Mitterrand knows that it doesn't have to do with the invasion of Kuwait and the aggression against Kuwait, and I know he knows this and he's been very forthright about it.

But yes, he's very frank in saying countries have a different approach to how you solve another very important problem. . . . I am going to avoid linkage.

I listened to that Aziz meeting, and all he tried to do is obfuscate, to confuse, to make . . . everybody think this had to do with the West Bank, for example. And it doesn't. It has to do with the aggression against Kuwait, the invasion of Kuwait, the brutalizing of the people in Kuwait. And it has to do with a new world order, and that world order is only going to be enhanced if this newly activated peacekeeping function of the United Nations proves to be effective. That is the only way the new world order will be enhanced.

Q. You say that Saddam Hussein doesn't understand yet. Why not a meeting face-to-face?

A. Because he's had every opportunity, and he keeps stiff-arming. We finally said, "This is the last step." We tried 15 dates in Baghdad. We tried to set up these meetings. And now we tried this one, and there wasn't one single reason to make me think another meeting between the United States and Saddam Hussein would do—and the Iraqis would do any good at all. If I felt it would, fine; but it will not.

I talked to the secretary general of the United Nations today, and there is a chance that he might undertake such a mission. Certainly, we'd have no objection.

There's one other reason, and I cite that because this is not Iraq against the United States, it is Iraq against the rest of the world. It is the United Nations that passed 12 resolutions, not the United States. It is the General Assembly of the United Nations, 100-plus countries, standing solidly against the dictator. And therefore, it doesn't need to be a bilateral negotiation here. We tried that, and we were stiff-armed by an intransigent foreign secretary.

And so, the answer is if diplomacy can be effective now, let's keep it in the context in which these resolutions were passed. And I would hope that maybe it would have an effect, but . . . I'd have to level with the American people. Nothing I saw today—nothing—leads me to believe that this man is going to be reasonable. . . . I have less of a feeling that . . . he'll come around, but we ought to keep trying. We ought to keep trying right down to the wire.

Q. You repeated, "Keep trying," and you cited the secretary general of the United Nations; Secretary of State Baker cited him three times. What exactly could his mission be if there is no alternative to what Secretary Baker laid out?

A. I'm not sure. . . . What would a mission of Jim Baker have been? It might have been to convince the man that he is up against an immovable force. He's up against something that is not going to yield. He is up against a situation under which there will be no compromise, and there will be none. . . . I don't think he has felt that force will be used against him, and . . . I think he has felt that if it were he'd prevail. And he's wrong on both counts.

Q. Mr. President, there have been reports that Saddam believes that if it comes to war, even if he's driven out of Kuwait militarily, he can survive in power. Is he wrong?

A. I think he's wrong on all of his assumptions about what would happen if it came to war, God forbid.

Q. Would he be killed, Mr. President?

A. Huh?

Q. Would he be killed?

A. I'm not going to answer that. I don't know the answer to that question.

Q. You seem to have ruled out further diplomacy as a . . .

A. No. You missed what I said . . . about the secretary general, possibly. The EC has tried . . . , and, indeed, we see Aziz saying no, he wouldn't meet with the foreign ministers. You've seen President Chadli Benjedid of Algeria try. I told the congressman: I want to see us go the last step for peace. I want to use everything at my

power to encourage people to try. And, indeed, there have been.

The Arab League has tried. Over and over again, people have tried. And they run up against the same answer. I remember the speculation that came out here in our papers, in this country, about a visit by a French delegate that was going over there. The hopes were raised. Nothing happened. So I just had to argue with the premise, because there has been a lot of diplomacy, and there may be more.

Q. Sir, you seem to very skeptical that further diplomacy would work, and yet you've said here today that you haven't given up on a peaceful solution. I wonder where it is you find there's hope for a peaceful solution.

A. I'm not sure I have great hope for it. But I think when human life is at stake, you go the extra mile for peace. And that's what we have tried to do. And I will continue to think of reasons—I told President Mitterrand. I said, look, if you think of a new approach, or I do, please let's one or the other get on the phone and try. But we remain determined that these resolutions are going to be complied with. I am very concerned that sanctions—I know sanctions alone aren't going to get this job done. And so we are pushing here—and that's what the Baker meeting with Aziz was about. I'm not going to give up, though.

Q. A lot of people, in looking at this situation on the outside will say, there must be more than this. There must be some backchannel diplomacy. There must be something going on. We can't be rushing headlong into war this way. Can you tell that there is nothing—that it is what we appear to be getting, and if Saddam isn't going to move, then we're going to war?

A. I'm not going to use that phrase. I am going to say if Saddam doesn't move, we are going to fully implement resolution 678, and it will be fully complied with. But I wish I could tell you I'm more hopeful. There is no back channel. We've tried it directly. I've had to level, and properly so, with our coalition partners as to what I'm doing, and they've leveled with us, leveled with the United Nations Security Council members who are not involved in the coalition with force; for example, the Soviets. And a lot of avenues have been tried. But I can't tell you that there's any hidden agenda out there, secret negotiations. There is not. And it wouldn't be right for us to be off telling you one thing openly here and then going around behind a corner with some secret channel. So, I would like to say, if there's any feeling that that's happening, it isn't happening.

Q. The entire hope for peace then rests on Saddam backing off from—

A. And it has since August 2nd—exactly. Because this aggression is not going to stand.

Q. Mr. President, you said when you first proposed high-level talks between Iraq and the United States that it was because you were convinced the message had not gotten through, had not gotten across. Are you now convinced that the message has gotten across?

A. Well, I did listen carefully to Mr. Aziz, who I thought spoke quite well—I didn't agree with what he's trying to do, obviously to confuse the issue by refusing to discuss the issue at hand, which is the invasion of Kuwait, but I thought he did it well. And I thought he kind of sent a signal that they do understand what's up against them. But I still don't believe that they think the world coalition will use force against them. I may be wrong, but that's what I think in here. And I also still believe, as I said earlier, that he somehow has this feeling that he will prevail or that he will prolong. This will not be that.

Q. When you were listening to the foreign secretary Aziz, did you get any kind of particular feelings of anger or—

A. No, I didn't. I thought it was a very rational presentation, but wrong. . . . I must say I thought his style was good. . . . When I talked to Jim [Baker], he said, "Look, the man presented his case." Clearly, we didn't agree with it. I thought he was quite complimentary of the way the secretary of state did it.

So the atmospherics, I think, were all right. But he doesn't have it. He doesn't understand it. At least from what he said, he doesn't, because this is not about some other question of linkage. This is about the invasion and the aggression about Kuwait, the dismantling of Kuwait, the brutality about Kuwait.

And so I didn't get a sense of security from listening to that, but I will say that I thought that he presented his views in a reasoned, reasonable way. He had a tough agenda. He had some tough talking points in there. He works for a tough man.

Q. What, exactly, are you trying to convey here to Saddam Hussein on what he does have to lose? Is it the decimation of his society? Is it the liquidation of the military? Is it losing his own power? Can you be specific on this?

A. I can't be more specific, but I can be that . . . he will get out of Kuwait, and he will get out of Kuwait entirely, and he will get out of Kuwait without concession. That, I think, is the underlying part of the message.

Q. Mr. President, [on] the question of Israel, Tariq Aziz was emphatic that if Iraq is attacked, Israel will be attacked. What are your obligations to Israel? Are you prepared to fight a war throughout the Middle East?

A. That is too hypothetical a question for me to answer. We are prepared to do what we need to do to fully implement [U.N. resolution] 678, and I would think that he would think long and hard before he started yet another war. There is one war on—that's his war against Kuwait, that's his aggression against Kuwait. And I don't think he wants to start another one. So I'm not going to buy into that hypothesis. But the United States

would obviously feel that that was a most provocative act—most provocative.

Q. If I may, I don't believe it was a hypothetical question. The question was, what are your obligations to Israel?

A. We have friends all over the world. We have friends in this coalition. And I'm determined that the United States fulfill our obligations there. And clearly if a friend in that area were attacked, wantonly attacked, for no cause whatsoever, not only the United States but I think many people around the world would view that as a flagrant provocation. And I will leave it stand right there. Thank you all very much. Thank you.

Remarks of Secretary of Defense Dick Cheney

Q. Secretary Cheney, will you come and answer the question?

A. The question was on possible additional reserve call-up authority. Under the authority that we're currently using, I'm authorized by a delegation from the president to use up to—to call up to 200,000 reservists for up to 180 days. That authority for some of those reservists who have been called begins to expire in February, and so what we currently have in the works is a provision that would use a different provision of the statute that would allow us to keep reservists on active service for as long as two years, and to call under that provision up to one million additional reservists. We have no intention of calling one million reservists, but that's the provision that's available for me to be able to extend those people in critical skills whose services are now being utilized, and whom we would like to keep for this period of time so we don't have to release them immediately back to reserve status.

References: *New York Times,* 10 January 1991, A16; *Washington Post,* 10 January 1991, A27.

Bush News Conference after the Congressional Vote To Authorize War, 12 January 1991

I have a brief statement, and then I'll be glad to take a few questions.

First, let me just say that I am gratified by the vote in the Congress supporting the United Nations Security Council resolution. This action by the Congress unmistakably demonstrates the United States' commitment to the international demand for a complete and unconditional withdrawal from Kuwait.

This clear expression of the Congress represents the last best chance for peace. As a democracy, we've debated this issue openly and in good faith, and as President, I have held extensive consultations with the Congress.

We have now closed ranks behind a clear signal of our determination and our resolve to implement the United Nations resolutions. Those who may have mistaken our democratic process as a sign of weakness now see the strength of democracy. And this sends the clearest message to Iraq that it cannot scorn the January 15th deadline. Throughout our history, we have been resolute in our support of justice, freedom and human dignity.

The current situation in the Persian Gulf demands no less of us and of the international community. We did not plan for war, nor do we seek war. But if conflict is thrust upon us, we are ready and we are determined. We've worked long and hard as have others, including the Arab League, the United Nations, the European Community, to achieve a peaceful solution.

Unfortunately, Iraq has thus far turned a deaf ear to the voices of peace and reason. Let there be no mistake: peace is everyone's goal. Peace is in everyone's prayers. But it is for Iraq to decide."

Questions and Answers

Q. Mr. President, does this mean now that war is inevitable?

A. No.

Q. And have you made the decision in your own mind?

A. No, it does not mean that war is inevitable. And I have felt that a statement of this nature by both houses of the United States Congress was, at this late date, the best shot for peace. And so let us hope that that message will get through to Saddam Hussein.

Q. Have you made the decision in your own mind?

A. I have not because I still hope, hope, that there will be a peaceful solution.

Q. Mr. President, there's only three days left until the deadline, which isn't enough time for Saddam Hussein to pull out his troops. In fact, you, yourself, wouldn't let Jim Baker go to Baghdad on this date because there wouldn't be enough time. Do you see the possibility of anything happening in these last few days that could avert war or any chance . . . that he will pull his troops out?

A. Well, in terms of the chance, I'd have to say I don't know, and in terms of what could avert war, you might say an instant commencement of a large scale removal of troops with no condition, no concession, and just heading out would be . . . the best and only way to avert war, even though it would be at this date I would say almost impossible to fully comply with the United Nations resolutions.

Q. Mr. President, are you satisfied that countries in the international coalition like France, Syria and Egypt will take part in offensive operations in the event of hostilities in the Gulf?

A. Yes.

Q. The second part of that question: Sir, you've said that if hostilities come, it will not be another Vietnam. What kind of assumptions are you making about the duration of the conflict, and can you assure the American people that hostilities will not expand beyond the current period of operations?

A. Well, I am . . . I am not making any assumptions in terms of numbers of days. But I have said over and over again that the differences between what is happening in the gulf and what happened in Vietnam are enormous in terms of the coalition aligned against the Iraqis, in terms of the demographics, in terms of the United Nations action and, I am convinced, in terms of the force that is arrayed against Iraq. So I just don't think there is a parallel. . . . I have gone over all of this with our Secretary of Defense and with the Chairman of the Joint Chiefs and all three of us . . . are determined to keep casualties to an absolute minimum.

Q. The polls have shown [that] people support moving fairly quickly after the 15th. Would that be your intention?

A. Well, I have said and without trying to pin it down, or in any sense go beyond what I'm about to say, rather sooner than later. And I got into a discussion, and I know that's perhaps not of much help. But I think the worst thing you'd want to do is if a determination was made to use force to signal when you might be inclined to act. That would not be . . . that would . . . that would, in my view, put the lives of coalition forces needlessly at risk.

Q. The crackdown was still going on today in Lithuania. What is your answer to those who say that you are putting Lithuania and the Baltics under the rug because of the Persian Gulf?

A. Well, I don't think that's true. I've had an opportunity to express myself directly to President Gorbachev on that. We had a statement on it. The Soviets know our position clearly. So I don't . . . think that's a fair charge at all.

Reference: New York Times, 13 January 1991, A10.

Joint Congressional Resolution on the Use of Force in the Persian Gulf, 12 January 1991

To authorize the use of United States Armed Forces pursuant to United Nations Security Council Resolution 678:

WHEREAS the Government of the Iraq without provocation invaded and occupied the territory of Kuwait on August 2, 1990; and

WHEREAS both the House of Representatives (in House Joint Resolution 658 of the 101st Congress) and the Senate (in Senate Con. Resolution 147 of the 101st Congress) have condemned Iraq's invasion of Kuwait and declared their support for international action to reverse Iraq's aggression; and

WHEREAS Iraq's conventional, chemical, biological, and nuclear weapons and ballistic missile programs and its demonstrated willingness to use weapons of mass destruction pose a grave threat to world peace; and

WHEREAS the international community has demanded that Iraq withdraw unconditionally and immediately from Kuwait and that Kuwait's independence and legitimate government be restored; and

WHEREAS the U.N. Security Council repeatedly affirmed the inherent right of individual or collective self-defense in response to the armed attack by Iraq against Kuwait in accordance with Article 51 of the U.N. Charter; and

WHEREAS, in the absence of full compliance by Iraq with its resolutions, the U.N. Security Council in Resolution 678 has authorized member states of the United Nations to use all necessary means, after January 15, 1991, to uphold and implement all relevant Security Council resolutions and to restore international peace and security in the area; and

WHEREAS Iraq has persisted in its illegal occupation of and brutal aggression against Kuwait; Now, therefore, be it

Resolved by the Senate and House of Representatives of the United States in America in Congress assembled,
Section 1.
SHORT TITLE
This joint resolution may be cited as the "Authorization for Use of Military Force against Iraq Resolution."
Section 2.
AUTHORIZATION FOR USE OF U.S. ARMED FORCES
(a) Authorization.—The President is authorized, subject to subsection (b), to use United States Armed Forces pursuant to United Nations Security Council Resolution 678 (1990) in order to achieve implementation of Security Council Resolutions 660, 661, 662, 664, 665, 666, 667, 669, 670, 674, and 677.
(b) Requirement for Determination that Use of Military Force Is Necessary.—Before exercising the authority granted in subsection (a), the President shall make available to the Speaker of the House of Representatives and the President pro tempore of the Senate his determination that—

(1) the United States has used all appropriate diplomatic and other peaceful means to obtain compliance by Iraq with the United Nations Security Council resolutions cited in subsection (a); and (2) that those efforts have not been and would not be successful in obtaining such compliance.
(c) War Powers Resolution Requirements.—

(1) Specific Statutory Authorization.—Consistent with section 8(a) of the War Powers Resolution, the Congress declares that this section is intended to constitute specific statutory authorization within the meaning of section 5(b) of the War Powers Resolution.

(2) Applicability of Other Requirements.—Nothing in this resolution supersedes any requirement of the War Powers Resolution.
Section 3.
REPORTS TO CONGRESS
At least once every 60 days, the President shall submit to the Congress a summary on the status of efforts to

obtain compliance by Iraq with the resolutions adopted by the United Nations Security Council in response to Iraq's aggression.

Secretary of Defense Cheney's Remarks on the Attack on Iraq, 16 January 1991

On 16 January 1991, Secretary of Defense Dick Cheney delivered some remarks to reporters at the Pentagon regarding the opening air strikes on Iraq. Following that, Cheney and Joint Chiefs of Staff Chairman General Colin L. Powell answered some questions from the reporters assembled. Herewith are Cheney's remarks, as well as excerpts from the question and answer period.

Ladies and gentlemen, I know you all heard the speech a short time ago by the president. And while there is not a great deal we can add now we did want to be as forthcoming as we can with you.

At 7 o'clock tonight, as you all know by now, Eastern time, 3 o'clock Thursday morning in the gulf, the armed forces of the United States began an operation at the direction of the President to force Saddam Hussein to withdraw his troops from Kuwait and to end his occupation of that country.

At the direction of the President, I signed the execute order yesterday afternoon to undertake this operation subject to certain conditions. It was to begin only after we'd met the terms of the resolution passed last Saturday by the Congress. Those conditions have been complied with and proper notice has been given as required. And the operation was not to take place if there had been any last-minute diplomatic breakthroughs.

The operation under way tonight, taking place in the pre-dawn darkness of the Persian Gulf, involves allied Air Forces of four nations: the United States, the United Kingdom, Saudi Arabia, and Kuwait. As they undertake their missions, they do so after months of careful planning. At the direction of the President, great care has been taken to focus on military targets, to minimize U.S. casualties, and do to everything possible to avoid injury to civilians in Iraq and Kuwait.

The targets being struck tonight are located throughout Iraq and Kuwait. Our focus is on the destruction of Saddam Hussein's offensive military capabilities, the very capabilities that he used to seize control of Kuwait and that make him a continuing threat to the nations of the Middle East. These are the same capabilities that now threaten American and allied forces in the gulf. Our goal, the same one we have maintained throughout Operation Desert Shield, is to liberate Kuwait and enforce the resolutions of the U.N. Security Council.

This portion of the campaign directed against Saddam Hussein's offensive military force is an enormously complex undertaking. It involves all of the services of the United States military and hundreds of U.S. and allied aircraft. It is an ongoing operation and we must therefore limit the kind and the amount of information that we provide in these early stages.

This obviously is different from what happened in Panama in December of 1989, where most of the operation was over by the morning of the first day. We understand your need for information about what will happen next and we are well aware of our obligation to keep the American people informed. But you must also understand that we cannot talk about future operations without putting at risk the safety of those who will have to carry them out.

I believe I can speak for all of us at the Pentagon tonight when I say that we had hoped to settle this matter peacefully. This has clearly been an agonizing decision for the president and the Congress of the United States. And we've reached the point of committing our forces to battle very reluctantly only after the most careful consideration. But no one should doubt our ability and our resolve to carry out our missions and to achieve our objective.

I have great confidence in the professionalism and the dedication and the determination of the men and women of our armed forces. They are, without question, the finest young sailors, airmen and marines this nation has ever sent in harm's way. I want to assure all Americans that we will do our very best to carry out the president's orders as quickly and efficiently as possible and at the lowest cost possible. We'd be happy to respond to a few questions.

Questions and Answers

Q. General Powell, can you describe the Iraqi Air Force's resistance, if any, their losses so far and to what extent do you think that you've already achieved air superiority there?

Powell: The operation's only 3 1/2 hours old, so I'm not quite prepared to take on your second question. So far there has been no air resistance.

Q. Have there been any casualties so far?

Cheney: We will at the appropriate time be releasing information on casualties. We're not prepared to release any specifics now. I will simply say that at preliminary reports, we have received in terms of the success of the operation—and that includes the possibility of casualties—have been very, very encouraging. The operation appears to have gone well.

Q. Was there an Iraqi attempt—was there an Iraqi attempt to launch a missile, sir?

Powell: We've had reports of missile launches but none of them have been confirmed.

Q. What about the—what about the Scuds in Western Iraq at those air bases on the border? Have you got any reading on that? Those are fairly high priority targets.

Powell: Yes, they are a fairly high priority target.

Q. And how did you do?

Cheney: I'm not prepared [to report on] how we did or what we've done . . .

Q. A follow up, a follow up on this. At the end of this operation, this phase of the operation when you get a little better picture could you come back or have one of your staff come back and give us a briefing on it?

Powell: You'll be getting regular briefings and we'll be . . . as the secretary said, we're going to be as forthcoming as we possibly can while at the same time preserving operational security.

Q. Mr. Secretary, are you confident that your . . . that your targeting of command and control sites has left Saddam Hussein the ability to, No. 1, know what's happening to his forces? And No. 2, to communicate to you that he wants to quit if he decides so?

Cheney: I don't have any information at this point on the overall effectiveness of the operation. What I said was the preliminary reports are very positive but we are in the earliest stages of this and therefore, there is not a lot of detailed information we can give you on what the effect of the bombing campaign has been on specific strategic categories of targets.

Reference: "Cheney's Remarks on Attack on Iraq," *New York Times*, 17 January 1991, A17.

Statement by General Schwarzkopf on the Start of the Air War, 16 January 1991

On 16 January 1991 General H. Norman Schwarzkopf, commander-in-chief of the U.S. Central Command, released a communiqué announcing the beginning of the air war against Iraqi forces. Herewith is the text of that communiqué.

Soldiers, sailors, airman and marines of the United States Central Command:

This morning at 0300 we launched Operation Desert Storm, an offensive campaign that will enforce the United Nations resolutions that Iraq must cease its rape and pillage of its weaker neighbor and withdraw its forces from Kuwait. The President, the Congress, the American people and indeed the world stand united in their support for your actions.

You are a member of the most powerful force our country, in coalition with our allies, has ever assembled in a single theater to face such an aggressor. You have trained hard for this battle and you are ready. During my visits with you, I have seen in your eyes a fire of determination to get this job done quickly so that we may all return to the shores of our great nation. My confidence in you is total. Our cause is just! Now you must be the thunder and lightning of Desert Storm. May God be with you, your loved ones at home, and our country.

Reference: "The General: 'A Fire of Determination,'" *New York Times*, 17 January 1991, A17.

President Bush's Address to the American People on the Commencement of War in the Gulf, 16 January 1991

Just two hours ago, allied air forces began an attack on military targets in Iraq and Kuwait. These attacks continue as I speak. Ground forces are not engaged.

This conflict started August 2nd when the dictator of Iraq invaded a small and helpless neighbor, Kuwait—a member of the Arab League and a member of the United Nations—was crushed; its people brutalized. Five months ago, Saddam Hussein started this cruel war against Kuwait. Tonight, the battle has been joined.

This military action, taken in accordance with United Nations resolutions and with the consent of the United States Congress, follows months of constant and virtually endless diplomatic activity on the part of the United Nations, the United States, and many, many other countries. Arab leaders sought what became known as an Arab solution, only to conclude that Saddam Hussein was unwilling to leave Kuwait. Others traveled to Baghdad in a variety of efforts to restore peace and justice. Our Secretary of State, James Baker, held an historic meeting in Geneva, only to be totally rebuffed. This past weekend, in a last-ditch effort, the Secretary-General of the United Nations went to the Middle East with peace in his heart—his second such mission. And he came back from Baghdad with no progress at all in getting Saddam Hussein to withdraw from Kuwait.

Now the 28 countries with forces in the Gulf area have exhausted all reasonable efforts to reach a peaceful solution—have no choice but to drive Saddam from Kuwait by force. We will not fail.

As I report to you, air attacks are underway against military targets in Iraq. We are determined to knock out Saddam Hussein's nuclear bomb potential. We will also destroy his chemical weapons facilities. Much of Saddam's artillery and tanks will be destroyed. Our operations are designed to best protect the lives of all the coalition forces by targeting Saddam's vast military arsenal. Initial reports from General Schwarzkopf are that our operations are proceeding according to plan.

Our objectives are clear: Saddam Hussein's forces will leave Kuwait. The legitimate government of Kuwait will be restored to its rightful place, and Kuwait will once again be free. Iraq will eventually comply with all relevant United Nations resolutions, and then, when peace is restored, it is our hope that Iraq will live as a peaceful and cooperative member of the family of nations, thus enhancing the security and stability of the Gulf.

Some may ask: Why act now? Why not wait? The answer is clear: The world could wait no longer. Sanctions, though having some effect, showed no signs of accomplishing their objective. Sanctions were tried for well over five months, and we and our allies concluded that sanctions alone would not force Saddam from Kuwait.

While the world waited, Saddam Hussein systematically raped, pillaged, and plundered a tiny nation, no threat to his own. He subjected the people of Kuwait to unspeakable atrocities—and among those maimed and murdered, innocent children.

While the world waited, Saddam sought to add to the chemical weapons arsenal he now possesses, an infinitely more dangerous weapon of mass destruction—a nuclear weapon. And while the world waited, while the world talked peace and withdrawal, Saddam Hussein dug in and moved massive forces into Kuwait.

While the world waited, while Saddam stalled, more damage was done to the fragile economies of the Third World, emerging democracies of Eastern Europe, to the entire world, including to our own economy.

The United States, together with the United Nations, exhausted every means at our disposal to bring this crisis to a peaceful end. However, Saddam clearly felt that by stalling and threatening and defying the United Nations, he could weaken the forces arrayed against him.

While the world waited, Saddam Hussein met every overture of peace with open contempt. While the world prayed for peace, Saddam prepared for war.

I had hoped that when the United States Congress, in historic debate, took its resolute action, Saddam would realize he could not prevail and would move out of Kuwait in accord with the United Nations resolutions. He did not do that. Instead, he remained intransigent, certain that time was on his side.

Saddam was warned over and over again to comply with the will of the United Nations: Leave Kuwait, or be driven out. Saddam has arrogantly rejected all warnings. Instead, he tried to make this a dispute between Iraq and the United States of America.

Well, he failed. Tonight, 28 nations—countries from five continents, Europe and Asia, Africa, and the Arab League—have forces in the Gulf area standing shoulder to shoulder against Saddam Hussein. These countries had hoped the use of force could be avoided. Regrettably, we now believe that only force will make him leave.

Prior to ordering our forces into battle, I instructed our military commanders to take every necessary step to prevail as quickly as possible, and with the greatest degree of protection possible for American and allied service men and women. I've told the American people that this will not be another Vietnam, and I repeat this here tonight. Our troops will have the best possible support in the entire world, and they will not be asked to fight with one hand tied behind their back. I'm hopeful that this fighting will not go on for long and that casualties will be held to an absolute minimum.

This is an historic moment. We have in this past year made great progress in ending the long era of conflict and cold war. We have before us the opportunity to forge for ourselves and for future generations a new world order—a world where the rule of law, not the law of the jungle, governs the conduct of nations. When we are successful—and we will be—we have a real chance at this new world order, an order in which a credible United Nations can use its peacekeeping role to fulfill the promise and vision of the U.N.'s founders.

We have no argument with the people of Iraq. Indeed, for the innocents caught in this conflict, I pray for their safety. Our goal is not the conquest of Iraq. It is the liberation of Kuwait. It is my hope that somehow the Iraqi people can, even now, convince their dictator that he must lay down his arms, leave Kuwait, and let Iraq itself rejoin the family of peace-loving nations.

Thomas Paine wrote many years ago, "These are times that try men's souls." Those well-known words are so very true today. But even as planes of the multinational forces attack Iraq, I prefer to think of peace, not war. I am convinced not only that we will prevail, but that out of the horror of combat will come the recognition that no nation can stand against a world united. No nation will be permitted to brutally assault its neighbor.

No president can easily commit our sons and daughters to war. They are the Nation's finest. Ours is an all-volunteer force, magnificently trained, highly motivated. The troops know why they're there. And listen to what they say, for they've said it better than any President or Prime Minister ever could.

Listen to Hollywood Huddleston, Marine lance corporal. He says, "Let's free these people, so we can go home and be free again." And he's right. The terrible crimes and tortures committed by Saddam's henchmen against the innocent people of Kuwait are an affront to mankind and a challenge to the freedom of all.

Listen to one of our great officers out there, Marine Lieutenant Walter Boomer. He said: "There are things worth fighting for. A world in which brutality and lawlessness are allowed to go unchecked isn't the kind of world we're going to want to live in."

Listen to Master Sergeant J. P. Kendall of the 82nd Airborne: "We're here for more than just the price of a gallon of gas. What we're doing is going to chart the future of the world for the next 100 years. It's better to deal with this guy now than five years from now."

And finally, we should all sit up and listen to Jackie Jones, an Army lieutenant, when she says, "If we let him get away with this, who knows what's going to be next?"

I have called upon Hollywood and Walter and J. P. and Jackie and all their courageous comrades-in-arms to do what must be done. Tonight, America and the world are deeply grateful to them and to their families. And let me say to everyone listening or watching me tonight: When the troops we've sent in finish their work, I am determined to bring them home as soon as possible.

Tonight, as our forces fight, they and their families are in our prayers. May God bless each and every one of them, and the coalition forces at our side in the Gulf, and may He continue to bless our nation, the United States of America.

Reference: The Persian Gulf Crisis: Relevant Documents, Correspondence, Reports, Report prepared by the Subcommittee on Arms Control, International Security and Science of the Committee on Foreign Affairs, U.S. House of Representatives, June 1991, 129–131.

Executive Order 12743 of 18 January 1991

On 18 January 1991, President George Bush signed this directive ordering the Ready Reserve of the U.S. armed forces to active duty.

By the authority vested in me as President by the Constitution and the laws of the United States of America, including the National Emergencies Act (50 U.S.C. 1601 et seq.), and section 301 of title 3 of the United States Code; in furtherance of Executive Order 12722, dated August 2, 1990, which declared a national emergency to address the threat to the national security and foreign policy of the United States posed by the invasion of Kuwait by Iraq; and, in accordance with the requirements contained in section 301 of the National Emergencies Act, 50 U.S.C. 1631, I hereby order as follows:

Section 1. To provide additional authority to the Department of Defense and the Department of Transportation to respond to the continuing threat posed by Iraq's invasion of Kuwait, the authority under section 673 of title 10, United States Code, to order any unit, and any member not assigned to a unit organized to served as a unit, in the Ready Reserve to active duty (other than for training) for not more than 24 consecutive months, is invoked and made available, according to its terms, to the Secretary concerned, subject, in the case of the Secretaries of the Army, Navy, and Air Force, to the direction of the Secretary of Defense. The term "Secretary concerned" is defined in section 101(8) of title 10, United States Code, to mean the Secretary of the Army with respect to the Army; the Secretary of the Navy with respect to the Navy, the Marine Corps, and the Coast Guard when it is operating as a service in the Navy; the Secretary of the Air Force with respect to the Air Force; and, the Secretary of Transportation with respect to the Coast Guard when it is not operating as a service in the Navy.

Section 2. To allow for the orderly administration of

personnel within the armed forces, the authority vested in the President by section 527 of title 10, United States Code, to suspend the operations of section 523–526 of title 10, United States Code, regarding officer strength and officer distribution in grade, is invoked to the full extent provided by the terms thereof.

Section 3. To allow for the orderly administration of personnel within the armed forces, the authority vested in the President by section 644 of title 10, United States Code, to suspend the operation of any provision of law relating to the promotion, involuntary retirement, or separation of commissioned officers of the Army, Navy, Air Force, or Marine Corps, is invoked to the full extent provided by the terms thereof.

Section 4. The Secretary of Defense is hereby designated and empowered, without approval, ratification, or other action by the President, to exercise the authority vested in the President by sections 527 and 644 of title 10, United States Code, as invoked in sections 2 and 3 of this order, to suspend the operation of certain provisions of law.

Section 5. The authorities delegated by sections 1 and 4 of this order may be redelegated and further subdelegated to civilian subordinates who are appointed to their offices by the President, by and with the advice and consent of the Senate.

Section 6. This order is intended to improve the internal management of the executive branch, and is not intended to create any right or benefit, substantive or procedural, enforceable at law by a party against the United States, its agencies, its officers, or any person.

Briefing by General Schwarzkopf and Lieutenant General Horner on the War's First 36 Hours, 18 January 1991

On 18 January 1991, General H. Norman Schwarzkopf, Commander-in-Chief of the U.S. Central Command (CENT-COM), and Lieutenant General Charles Horner, Joint Coalition Force Air Component Commander (CENTAF, the Air Force element of CENTCOM) appeared in Riyadh, Saudi Arabia, to brief reporters on the first 36 hours of the air war. Herewith appear excerpts of that briefing.

Schwarzkopf: Let me just start by saying, as you all know, we are 36 hours into Operation Desert Storm. I would tell you that to date, the campaign is going just about exactly as we expected it to go.

As in the early days of any battle, the fog of war is present, but I would tell you that having been in the outset of several battles myself, and having been at the early hours of the Grenada campaign, I would tell you that we probably have a more accurate picture of what's going on in Operation Desert Storm than I have ever had before in the early hours of a battle. That pic-

ture's not perfect, but I think it's pretty good, and I want to just kind of bring you up to date on where we are at the present time.

As far as air operations are concerned, we are flying a total of about 2,000 air sorties of all types each day. More than 80 percent of all of those sorties have successfully engaged their targets. The sorties are being flown by United States Air Force, Navy, the Marines and some Army. We also have six other nations that are involved with us in this coalition—Saudi Arabia, Kuwait, the United Kingdom, the Canadians, the French, and the Italians have all participated in the air campaign to date. In addition to flying offensive operations, they are also flying defensive air operations over Saudi Arabia to protect the kingdom and also protect, naturally, our forces that are here.

To date [Friday, 18 January, 7 A.M. EST], we have lost seven aircraft: two United States Navy aircraft, one F-18 and one A-6, one Air Force F-15, one Kuwait A-4, two British Tornadoes, and the most recent one was an Italian Tornado. In regard to the disposition of the pilots, we are carrying all of the pilots as missing in action. However, we now have pretty good information that the Kuwaiti pilot is probably safe in the hands of the Kuwait resistance.

At sea, of course, in addition to flying against the targets that the Navy is taking on, the Navy is also in the business of protecting the fleet, both with their ships and with their aircraft aloft. We are tracking any potential adversaries that look like they're coming out to threaten the ships, and we're engaging those as required. This morning the Navy has engaged three enemy patrol boats and either disabled them or sunk them. In addition to that, we have increasing numbers of amphibious ships moving into the gulf area at this time.

On the ground, of course, the United States Army and the United States Marine Corps is continuing to defend Saudi Arabia. They are also repositioning our forces for further action. To date, there has been no direct hostile confrontation on the ground. However, yesterday there was a slight artillery duel—artillery on the part of the enemy, who was immediately reacted to by our air [forces] and the artillery was silenced during that duel. We had two Marines that were lightly wounded in action.

Of course the significant news today, I'm sure you all know about, but there were seven Scuds fired early this morning against Israel, and there was one Scud fired against Dhahran. The one Scud missile that was fired against Dhahran was destroyed by a United States Army Patriot missile. Fortunately, the seven missiles that were fired against Israel I would characterize as having yielded absolutely insignificant results. And as a result I think to date we can say that the enemy Scud campaign has been ineffective.

Now for the good news. As you know, finding the fixed-missile launchers is a relatively easy business, but finding the mobile launchers is like finding a needle in a haystack, as you can well imagine. This morning the United States Air Force found three mobile erector launchers with missiles on board inside Iraq. These launchers were obviously aimed at Saudi Arabia, given their positions. Those three mobile electric launchers have been destroyed.

In addition to that, at the same time, we found eight more mobile erector launchers in the same location. We are currently attacking those launchers, and we have confirmed—confirmed—the destruction of three more of those mobile erector launchers, and we are continuing to attack the others. And I assure you we will attack them relentlessly until we are either prevented from attacking them any further by weather, or we have destroyed them all.

In concluding my remarks, I want to make just two points. The first point is the one that you've heard from the Secretary of Defense and the chairman of the Joint Chiefs of Staff, but I think it bears repeating. And that's that we are only 36 hours into what is a campaign. The President of the United States said that this is not Panama, it will not be over in a day. And it certainly won't. So we are just continuing on this campaign, and the campaign will continue until we have accomplished our objectives.

The second point I would like to make is that we are doing absolutely everything we possibly can in this campaign to avoid injuring or destroying innocent people. We have said all along that this is not a war against the Iraqi people. And I think very shortly you're going to hear a little bit more about what we're doing to try and avoid hurting innocent people.

At this point, I'd like to introduce Lieutenant General Chuck Horner. Chuck Horner is the commander of the United States Central force—Central Command air forces. Since August we have been planning this campaign. And I think the one person who is . . . could be considered the architect of the entire air campaign as it's being conducted today is Chuck Horner. He is certainly the one person more than anyone else who is responsible for the magnificent airmen who are out there conducting this campaign today. He is a superb leader.

Horner: Thank you, General Schwarzkopf. The objectives of the air campaign were set out by General Schwarzkopf in August. And we've worked hard to bring together this very complex and very large campaign plan. We've been able to integrate all our forces, because we all fly off a common air-tasking order. And you've heard that we have forces from all the services in the United States plus many countries in the multinational force. We've been able to execute because we've trained very hard. And you'll find sorties where a Saudi aircraft will be dropping bombs and be es-

corted by an American fighter, provided support by other aircraft, such as from the countries mentioned.

There's no doubt that our air defense and our awareness of what's going on on the air battlefield are a result in large measure because of what the AWACs provides us and the defense that aircraft such as the F-14 and the F-15 provide our forces. In has been in some respects a technology war, although it is fought by men and women.

What I have now to show you are some film clips of some actual weapons delivery. . . . These first two will be F-111 deliveries using laser-guided bombs. This is a runway at an airfield halfway between Baghdad and Kuwait. The center of the runway is the end point. This is where the laser designator is pointed. This is taken at night with infrared sensors, and there the bomb goes off in the center of the runway, and the heat shows up as white. And now you'll see the pilot switch to higher magnification and as he flies away from the target. This is the smoke plume from the bomb, and there's the crater.

The next one is a Scud storage building in Kuwait. . . . Again, the pilot has released his bombs about two miles away. He's banking away from the target, leaving the target area, 'lasing' the target, and you'll see two bombs fly into the door of the storage bunker. And you'll be able to count each bomb . . . one, two. Those are 2,000-pound bombs.

This is the air defense headquarters in the vicinity of Baghdad. These are air shafts that provide [the] best access into this concrete structure. . . . The debris comes out the door from the bomb going into this lead-in air shaft . . .

This is another air-defense sector over the western part of Iraq. It's already been struck by a 117 [F-117]. This is a team effort The second aircraft comes through, and this part of the building here provides some structural weakness that will be exploited in this attack, and the bomb will hit in this area here.

And this is my counterpart's headquarters in Baghdad. This is the headquarters of the air force . . . the airplane overflies the building and drops the bomb down through the center of the building.

If we have any success in this air campaign, I can attribute it in large measure to the freedom with which we've been allowed to plan the campaign. We've had stringent guidance with regard to civilian damage, things of that nature. But the President, down through the Secretary of Defense, Chairman Powell and General Schwarzkopf, have been the key reason we've been able to plan a very efficient military campaign within the guidelines that they've set forth to us.

Questions and Answers

Q. Sir, does the Iraqi attack on Israel change at all the war aims of the United States in this campaign?

Schwarzkopf: No. Our objectives are exactly the same ones that were announced by the President of the

United States quite some time ago that were in fact the resolutions of the United Nations. And our objectives continue to remain exactly the same.

Q. Since the Scud attack on Tel Aviv yesterday, is there a change in the targeting of Saddam Hussein himself? Yesterday General Powell said he was not a specific target. Has that changed?

Schwarzkopf: We are not trying to kill any particular person. One of our aims all along has been to make sure that it's very difficult for the leadership to have any impact upon the decision-making process of the subordinate units, and there are several different ways we're going about doing that. We're not targeting any specific person to kill them.

Q. General, do you have any theories about the subdued nature of the response of the Iraqis so far?

Schwarzkopf: I think that General Powell has expressed it first of all in the fact that we probably achieved a degree of surprise, of tactical surprise, that we were trying to achieve. I think secondly once again Secretary Baker stated, after his Geneva press conference, I think that quite frankly that the Iraqis just had no concept whatsoever of what they were getting involved with when it comes to taking on the coalition forces.

Q. Have you detected any movement by the Iraqi armored forces?

Schwarzkopf: Nothing significant.

Q. I'm wondering; we hear varying degrees of percentages, that the planes hit 80 percent; some have said 50 percent. Of these—now the targets we're talking about, I'm wondering first of all, how many targets have we hit?

Horner: The bombing percentages you see are a function of the number of targets targeted versus the numbers that were hit. The difference in those numbers are people who did not get to the target because of weather or enemy defenses caused them to miss the target, things of that nature. It was kind of relevant to his question about the subdued nature of the Iraqi response. I'd like to take him along on one of the sorties; it might change his opinion of the "subdued nature."

Q. A question for General Horner, please. Can you give us some idea of what the state of Iraqi air force is like right now: how many planes destroyed, how many immobilized, because you've got runways that you've destroyed, how many fled to the north; some general order of magnitude on it?

Horner: It's obvious that I'd like to keep track of that. Unfortunately, a lot of their aircraft are in hardened shelters. We attack the shelter, and we really don't know the results on the aircraft.

Q. How far, roughly, are you into your campaign, the aerial bombardment campaign? And secondly, could you tell us how successful the Tornadoes, the British Tornadoes, have been, and whether the JP-233 has come up to expectations?

Schwarzkopf: Fine. We're exactly as far as we expected to be 36 hours into the campaign. You want to take the other question?

Horner: The Tornado obviously is very important to the campaign that's being performed by Saudi Arabia, Britain, and Italy. The reason it's so important, because it gives us the capability to penetrate the high, well-defended areas. And you're absolutely right, the 233 has done very well on the airfield attacks.

Q. General Horner, how many of the aircraft that we have lost have been lost to enemy fire, how many to missiles? And what is the status of the Iraqi antiaircraft missile defenses now? This is supposedly a high-priority target system. Can you give us something on that?

Horner: In terms of losses, we don't know. But we suspect one to SAMs, and the rest to triple A [antiaircraft artillery]. With regard to the air defenses, in some areas they are probably the most difficult air defenses assembled in the world. In other areas, they're not quite that difficult. And obviously, that's going to be a very strenuous campaign, achieving complete control of the air.

Q. Once you get on the ground, once you get forward, who is going to do the actual fighting on the allied side? Is there a special focus on the Arab units to do that?

Schwarzkopf: No, this is a coalition operation, and everybody that's involved in this coalition is planning to take part. It's just as it has been from the very beginning. Yes.

Q. How is the coordination of the various forces actually working? Could you give us a little insight into that?

Schwarzkopf: Well, I think I'd let General Horner answer that from the standpoint of the air campaign because this is, as you can well imagine—seven different nations and coordinating the air strikes and the type of aircraft that are being used is a rather difficult proposition. Whether it's effective or not I will leave to him.

Horner: It's effective.

Q. Well, my question, sir, is exactly how is it being done?

Horner: What you do . . .

Q. It seems like an enormous effort and . . .

Horner: It is an enormous effort. Of course now we have a lot of computers, and you can bring together the tens of thousands of minor details, radio frequencies, altitudes, tanker rendezvous, bomb configurations, who supports who, who's flying escort, who's—there are just thousands and thousands of details, and we work them together as one group, put them together in what we call a common air-tasking order, and it provides a sheet of music that everybody sings the same song off.

Q. We know something of what's happening in Baghdad, but we know very little of what's happening inside Kuwait. Can you give us any picture of what you're attacking and how it's going in Kuwait itself, around Kuwait City?

Schwarzkopf: As I said, I think the best answer to that is: it's going just about as we expected. We haven't run into anything that we didn't expect. As a matter of fact, the situation is probably a little bit better than what we expected inside Kuwait.

I'd just like to close with one last comment that I think is important to remember, and that's that the courage and the professionalism that's been exhibited by all of the people that have been involved in this campaign in the last 36 hours is nothing short of inspirational. I think we should all be very, very proud, every country should be very, very proud of the young men that have been up in those aircraft, the young women that have been up in the aircraft, and the way that they've done their jobs. And I have every confidence that as they gain more experience, they're just going to be better than the great job they've already done.

Reference: "The U.S. Commanders: Excerpts from Briefing by Two Generals on War's First 36 Hours," *New York Times*, 19 January 1991, A11.

President Bush's Press Conference on Israel and Operation Desert Storm, 18 January 1991

On 18 January 1991, President George Bush held a press conference and discussed issues relating to the opening strikes of the Persian Gulf War, as well as the Scud missile attacks on Israel. Herewith are excerpts of the conference.

We're now some 37 hours into Operation Desert Storm and the liberation of Kuwait, and so far so good. U.S. and coalition military forces have performed bravely, professionally and effectively.

It is important, however, to keep in mind two things: First, this effort will take some time. Saddam Hussein has devoted nearly all of Iraq's resources for a decade to building up this powerful military machine. And we can't expect to overcome it overnight, especially as we want to minimize any harm done to innocent civilians. And second, we must be realistic. There will be losses. There will be obstacles along the way. And war is never cheap or easy.

And I say this only because I am somewhat concerned about the initial euphoria in some of the reports and reactions to the first day's developments: No one should doubt or question the ultimate success, because we will prevail. But I don't want to see us get overly euphoric about all of this.

Our goals have not changed. What we seek is the same as what the international community seeks, namely, Iraq's complete and unconditional withdrawal from Kuwait and then full compliance with the Security Council resolutions. I also want to say how outraged I am by Iraq's latest act of aggression, in this case against Israel. Once again, we see that no neighbor of Iraq is safe, And I want to state here publicly how much I appreciated Israel's restraint from the outset, really from the very beginning of this crisis.

Prime Minister Shamir and his Government have shown great understanding for the interests of the United States and the interests of others involved in this coalition. Close consultations with Israel are continuing; so, too, are close consultations with our coalition partners.

Just a few minutes ago, I spoke to Prime Minister Brian Mulroney of Canada, and in that vein I also had a long and good conversation this morning with Soviet President Gorbachev, in which we thoroughly reviewed the situation in the gulf. And, of course, I took the opportunity to express again my concern, my deep concern, over the Baltics and the need to insure that there is a peaceful resolution to the situation there.

Let me close here by saying how much we appreciate what our fighting men and women are doing. This country is united. Yes, there is some protest, but this country is fundamentally united—and I want that message to go out to every kid over there serving this country. I saw in the paper a comment by one who worried from seeing demonstrations here and there in this country on television, that that expressed the will of the country. And so to those troops over there, let me just take this opportunity to say: your country is supporting you. The Congress overwhelmingly endorsed that.

Let there be no doubt in the minds of any of you. You have the full and unified support of the United States of America. So I salute them. They deserve our full support, and they are our finest.

Questions and Answers

Q. Mr. President, has the United States asked Israel not to retaliate against Iraq for its attack? What commitment has the United States received in these consultations that we've had with Israel, and how long do you think Israel can stay on the sidelines if these attacks continue?

Bush: These questions, questions of what we're talking to Israel about right now, I'm going to keep confidential. There's no question that Israel's Scud attack, the Scud attack on Israel, was purely an act of terror. It had absolutely no military significance at all, and it was an attack that is symptomatic of the kind of leader that the world is now confronting in Saddam Hussein—and again, I repeat, the man who will be defeated here. But Israel has shown great restraint, and I've said that. I think we can all understand that they have their own problems that come from this. But I don't want to go further into it, because we are right in the midst of consultations with Israel. I think they, like us, do not want to this war widened, and yet they are determined to protect their own population centers. And I can tell you that our defense people are in touch with our commanders to be sure that we are doing the utmost we can to suppress any of these missile sites that might wreak havoc, not just on Israel, but on other countries not involved in this fighting. So I'm going to leave it there. And I am confident that this matter can be resolved.

Q. Are you worried that it could change the course of the war?

Bush: I think that we ought to guard against anything that can change the course of the war, and so I think everybody realizes what Saddam Hussein was trying to do—to change the course of the war, to weaken the coalition, and he's going to fail. And I want to say: when the Soviet Union made such a strong statement, that was very reassuring, and we are in close touch with our coalition partners, and this coalition is not going to fall apart. I'm convinced of that.

Q. Mr. President, two days ago, you launched a war, and war is inherently a two-way street. Why should you be surprised or outraged when there is an act of retaliation?

Bush: Against a country that's innocent and is not involved in it, that's what I'm saying. Israel is not a participant, Israel is not a combatant, and this man has elected to . . . to launch a terrorist attack against the population centers in Israel with no military . . . no military design whatsoever. And that's why—it is an outrage, and the whole world knows it, and the whole world is . . . most of the countries of the world are speaking out against it. There can be no . . . no consideration of this in anything other than condemnation.

Q. Why is it that any move, or yet move for peace, is considered an end run at the White House these days?

Bush: Well, you obviously . . . what was the question? End run?

Q. Yes. That is considered an end run, that people who still want to find a peaceful solution seem to running into a brick wall.

Bush: Oh, excuse me. The world is united, I think, in seeing [that] these United Nations resolutions are fulfilled. Everybody would like to find a way to end the fighting, but it's not going to end until there's total agreement, total . . . total cooperation with and fulfillment of those U.N. resolutions. This man is not going to pull a victory off by . . . by trying to wage terrorist attacks against a country that is not a participant in all of this, and I'm talking about Israel. And so I think everyone would like to see it end, but it isn't going to end short of the total fulfillment of our objectives.

Q. Mr. President, do you have any message of reassurance to the people of Israel that the restraint shown by their Government doesn't place them in risk?

Bush: I think they know of our determination to safeguard them following this attack or prior to this attack. And we are going to be redoubling our efforts in the

darnedest search-and-destroy effort that's ever been undertaken in that area. And I hope that that is very reassuring to the citizens of Israel.

Q. Mr. President, are you trying to caution against overconfidence with your statement in . . . by concern that Saddam Hussein may have a lot more staying power than was originally thought, or is it based on an upcoming land warfare that is apt to be protracted?

Bush: No. I don't think there's any conclusion that he has a lot more staying power than anybody thought. But I—what I'm cautioning against is a mood of euphoria that existed around here yesterday because things went very, very well—from a military standpoint, exceptionally well. And this was received around the world with joy. But I just would caution again that it isn't going to be that easy all the time; we have not changed our assessment as to how difficult the task ahead is.

Q. Sir, will you be able to tell Prime Minister Shamir with any confidence that you have knocked out these missile sites?

Bush: Well, the problem, John, on that is we can tell him with confidence what we've done in terms of some of the missile sites, but not all, because you're dealing with mobile missiles that can be hidden. I'm getting a little off my turf here, because I vowed to permit the Defense Department to respond to these military questions. But I think that one is rather clear: that when you can hide a mobile missile the way they've done, it's awfully hard to certify that all of them have been taken care of.

Q. Mr. President, granted, you say, there are some rough days ahead, but there has also been a considerable amount of discussion as to the relatively unexpectedly low rate of response on the part of the Iraqis. You've had some briefings on this. What are your thoughts? What do you think explains this?

Bush: Well, I don't know, but my thoughts are that as each hour goes by, they are going to be relatively less able to respond, and I say that with no bravado; I just simply say that because that's what's happening over there. So there has been a . . . he may well have been holding his mobile missiles back, for example, wheeling them out there when he thinks they'll be undetected, and then firing a few of these missiles into the heart of downtown Haifa to try to make some political statement. There may be some more of that ahead, maybe aimed at other countries; who knows? But in terms of his ability to respond militarily, I can guarantee the world that as every hour goes by, he is going to be less able to respond, less able to stand up against the entire world . . . the world opinion as expressed in these United Nations resolutions.

Reference: "The President: Excerpts from the Remarks by Bush on Israel and the War against Iraq," *New York Times,* 19 January 1991, A12.

Letter from President George Bush to Speaker of the House Thomas S. Foley Notifying Congress on the Use of U.S. Forces in the Persian Gulf, 18 January 1991

Dear Mr. Speaker: On January 16, 1991, I made available to you consistent with section 2(b) of the Authorization for Use of Military Force Against Iraq Resolution (H.J. Res. 77, Public Law 102-1), my determination that appropriate diplomatic and other peaceful means had not and will not compel Iraq to withdraw unconditionally from Kuwait and meet the other requirements of the U.N. Security Council and the world community. With great reluctance, I concluded, as did the other coalition leaders, that only the use of armed force would achieve an Iraqi withdrawal together with the other U.N. goals of restoring Kuwait's legitimate government, protecting the lives of our citizens, and reestablishing security and stability in the Persian Gulf region. Consistent with the War Powers Resolution, I now inform you that pursuant to my authority as Commander in Chief, I directed U.S. Armed Forces to commence combat operations on January 16, 1991, against Iraqi forces and military targets in Iraq and Kuwait. The Armed Forces of Saudi Arabia, Kuwait, the United Kingdom, France, Italy, and Canada are participating as well.

Military actions are being conducted with great intensity. They have been carefully planned to accomplish our goals with the minimum loss of life among coalition military forces and the civilian inhabitants of the area. Initial reports indicate that our forces have performed magnificently. Nevertheless, it is impossible to know at this time either the duration of active combat operations or the scope or duration of the deployment of U.S. Armed Forces necessary fully to accomplish our goals.

The operations of the U.S. and other coalition forces are contemplated by the resolutions of the U.N. Security Council as well as H.J. Res. 77, adopted by Congress on January 12, 1991. They are designed to ensure that the mandates of the United Nations and the common goals of our coalition partners are achieved and the safety of our citizens and Forces is ensured.

As our united efforts in pursuit of peace, stability, and the security in the Gulf continue, I look forward to our continued consultation and cooperation.

Reference: The Persian Gulf Crisis: Relevant Documents, Correspondence, Reports, prepared by the Subcommittee on Arms Control, International Security and Science of the Committee on Foreign Affairs, U.S. House of Representatives, June 1991, 132.

Excerpts of Interviews with American Prisoners of War Held by Iraq, 20 January 1991

On 20 January 1991, Iraq broadcast interviews it conducted with seven men who were later identified as allied prisoners of war. The questioner of the prisoners is unidentified. Herewith are excerpts from the interviews, carried by CNN, of six of those prisoners.

First Prisoner

Q. Would you tell us your rank and name?

A. Lieutenant Colonel Clifford [inaudible; he is believed to be Marine Lieutenant Colonel Clifford M. Acree of Oceanside, California].

Q. What's your age?

A. Thirty-nine.

Q. What's your unit?

A. V.M.O. 2.

Q. You are the commander of that unit?

A. Yes, I am.

Q. Your mission?

A. Observation and reconnaissance.

Q. How your aircraft has been shot down?

A. I was flying a mission in southern Kuwait and was shot down by a surface-to-air missile.

Q. Do you have a message?

A. I would like to tell my wife and family that I'm alive and well.

Second Prisoner

Q. Would you tell us your rank and name?

A. My name is Lieutenant Jeffrey Norton Zaun, United States Navy.

Q. Your age?

A. I am twenty-eight.

Q. Your unit?

A. I am from Attack Squadron 35 on the USS *Saratoga*, the Red Sea.

Q. Your type of aircraft?

A. I'm flying the A-6E Intruder attack aircraft.

Q. Your mission?

A. My mission was to attack the H3 airfield in southern Iraq.

Q. Alone?

A. I flew as part of a formation of four aircraft in order to commit this attack.

Q. What do you think, Lieutenant, about this aggression against Iraq?

A. I think our leaders and our people have wrongly attacked the peaceful people of Iraq.

Q. Do you have a message?

A. Yes, I would like to tell my mother and my father and my sister that I am well treated and that they should pray for peace.

Third Prisoner

Q. Would you tell me about your rank, name and nationality?

A. O.K. My name is Maurice Cocciolone. And I'm captain from Italian Air Force.

Q. What is your age?

A. I am thirty years old.

Q. Tell us about your unit.

A. My unit is the 155 Squadron that is now in the base of Emirates—[the] United Arab Emirates.

Q. What was your mission?

A. To attack the forces of missiles in the southern region of Iraq.

Q. How have you been shot down?

A. We don't know exactly. It was right away fired from the ground. We don't know exactly what was it. These was firing from the ground from Iraq.

Q. What is your opinion about the war and the aggression against Iraq?

A. Well, the war is based on a bad reason . . . to solve a question, a political question. War . . . a bad thing in front of you. So I think the best solution of peace . . . would be to find a political peaceful means of bringing this situation to the end.

Q. You have a message to send.

A. O.K. I think the only message [I] would like to tell my political leaders that to solve question by war is always mad . . . And also, I have something to tell my parents, to my family. Don't be worried, I am pretty fine here. They are well taking care of me. Thank you.

Fourth Prisoner

Q. About your rank, name and nationality?

A. My name is Guy Hunter, Jr. I'm a warrant officer. I am an American.

Q. Your age?

A. Forty-six.

Q. Your unit?

A. D.M.O. 2 in the Marine Corps.

Q. Your type of aircraft?

A. OV-10 Bronco.

Q. What was your mission?

A. Against Iraqi troops in southern Iraq.

Q. How have you been shot down?

A. I am not certain. We were flying, and all of a sudden, a left bang off the left wing, uh, a large bang off the left wing, and the plane began to crash.

Q. What's your opinion of this aggression against Iraq?

A. I think this war is crazy and should never have happened. I condemn this aggression against peaceful Iraq.

Q. Do you have a message to send?

A. Yes, sir, I do. To my wife and children, I miss you very much. I'm in good hands and being treated well. To the children, please study hard in school.

Fifth Prisoner

Q. What is your rank, name and nationality?

A. My name is Flight Lieutenant Adrian John Nichols. I'm British.

Q. Your age?

A. Twenty-seven.

Q. Your unit?

A. Fifteenth Squadron.

Q. Type of aircraft?

A. Tornado.

Q. What was your mission?

A. To attack an Iraqi airfield.

Q. How were you shot down?

A. I was shot down by an Iraqi system. I do not know what it was.

Q. What do you think of this war against Iraq?

A. I think this war should be stopped. I do not agree on this war with Iraq.

Q. Do you have a message?

A. Mom and Dad, if you are listening, everything is okay here. Please pray for me. We shall be home soon.

Sixth Prisoner

Q. Tell me about your rank, name, and nationality.

A. My name is Flight Lieutenant Peters. I'm British.

Q. Your age?

A. Twenty-nine.

Reference: New York Times, 21 January 1991, A7.

Address by Saddam Hussein ("The Mother of All Battles" Speech), 20 January 1991

The following is an excerpted version of the so-called Mother of All Battles speech delivered by Saddam Hussein that was broadcast on Baghdad radio and subsequently translated by the Reuters news service.

O Glorious Iraqis, O holy warrior Iraqis, O Arabs, O believers wherever you are, we and our steadfastness are holding. Here is the great Iraqi people, your brothers and sons of your Arab nation and the great faithful part of the human family. We are all well. They are fighting with unparalleled heroism, unmatched except by the heroism of the believers who fight similar adversaries. And here is the infidel tyrant whose planes and missiles are falling out of the skies at the blows of the brave men. He is wondering how the Iraqis can confront his fading dreams with such determination and firmness.

After a while, he will begin to feel frustrated, and his defeat will be certain, God willing. . . . We in Iraq will be the faithful and obedient servants of God, struggling for his sake to raise the banner of truth and justice, the banner of 'God is Great.' Accursed will be the lowly.

At that time, the valiant Iraqi men and women will not allow the army of atheism, treachery, hypocrisy, and [word unknown] to realize their stupid hope that the war would only last a few days or weeks, as they imagined and declared. In the coming period, the response of Iraq will be on a larger scale, using all the means and potential that God has given us and which we have so far only used a part. Our ground forces have not entered the battle so far, and only a small part of our air force has been used.

The army's air force has not been used, nor has the navy. The weight and effect of our ready missile force has not yet been applied in full. The fact remains that the great divine reinforcement is our source of power and effectiveness. When the war is fought in a comprehensive manner, using all resources and weapons, the scale of death and the number of dead will, God willing, rise among the ranks of atheism, injustice, and tyranny.

When they begin to die and when the message of the Iraqi soldiers reaches the farthest corner of the world, the unjust will die and the 'God is Great' banner will flutter with great victory in the mother of all battles. Then the skies in the Arab homeland will appear in a new color and a sun of new hope will shine over them and over our nation and on the good men whose bright lights will not be overcome by the darkness in the hearts of the infidels, the Zionists, and the treacherous, shameful rulers, such as the traitor Fahd.

Then the door will be wide open for the liberation of beloved Palestine, Lebanon, and the Golan. Then Jerusalem and the Dome of the Rock will be released from bondage. The Kaaba and the Tomb of the Prophet Mohammed, God's peace and blessings be upon him, will be liberated from occupation and God will bestow upon the poor and needy the things that others owed them, others who withheld from them what they owed them as God had justly ordained, which is a great deal.

Then [words unknown], the good men, the holy warriors, and the faithful will know the truth of our promise to them that when the forces of infidelity attack the Iraqis, they will fight as they wished them to fight and perhaps in a better way, and that their promise is of faith and holy war. It remains for us to tell all Arabs, all the faithful strugglers, and all good supporters wherever they are: You have a duty to carry out holy war and struggle in order to target the assembly of evil, treason, and corruption everywhere.

You must target their interests everywhere. It is a duty that is incumbent upon you, and that must necessarily correspond to the struggles of your brothers in Iraq. You will be part of the struggle of armed forces in your holy war and struggle, and part of the multitude of faith and the faithful. If the opposing multitude captures you, you will be prisoners in their hands, even if they refuse to admit this in the communiqués and statements.

You will inevitably be released when the war ends, in accordance with international laws and agreements which will govern the release of prisoners of war. In this way you will have pleased God and honored, with your slogans and principles, the trust given to you.

God is great, God is great, God is great, and accursed be the lowly.

Reference: Micah L. Sifry and Christopher Serf, *The Gulf War Reader: History, Documents, Opinions* (New York: Times Books, 1991), 315–316.

Executive Order 12744 of 21 January 1991

President George Bush signed this executive order designating the Arabian Peninsula areas, airspace, and adjacent waters as a combat zone.

By the authority vested in me as President by the Constitution and the laws of the United States of America, including section 112 of the Internal Revenue Code of 1986 (26 U.S.C. 112), I hereby designate, for purposes of that section, the following locations, including the airspace above such locations, as an area in which Armed Forces of the United States are and have been engaged in combat:

—the Persian Gulf

—the Red Sea

—the Gulf of Oman

—that portion of the Arabian Sea that lies north of 10 degrees north latitude and west of 68 degrees east longitude

—the Gulf of Aden

—the total land areas of Iraq, Kuwait, Saudi Arabia, Oman, Bahrain, Qatar, and the United Arab Emirates.

For the purposes of this order, the date of the commencing of combatant activities in such zones is hereby designated as January 17, 1991.

Letter from Iraqi Foreign Minister Aziz to UN Secretary-General Pérez de Cuéllar, 24 January 1991

On 24 January 1991, Iraqi Foreign Minister Tariq Aziz sent a letter to United Nations Secretary-General Javier Pérez de Cuéllar detailing what Aziz claimed were "heinous premeditated crimes" against the Iraqi people.

Mr. Secretary General,

Since the imperialist United States, NATO and Zionist aggression against our country began at 0230 hours on 17 January 1991, the attacking forces have been committing heinous premeditated crimes against Iraqi citizens and against the economic, cultural, scientific and religious assets of our great people, which is one that has made a centuries-old contribution to human civilization.

On all occasions—in the course of our meeting at Amman on 31 August 1990 and during your visit to Baghdad on 11 and 12 January 1991—we have constantly indicated and have explained to you in a clear and detailed manner that the basic fact with regard to the events which preceded and followed 2 August 1990 is that the imperialist United States, NATO and the Zionist alliance and its treacherous adherents among the regimes of the region have had the objective, as they continue to do, of destroying resurgent Iraq, which is pursuing a free and independent policy and which proudly rejects imperialist and Zionist hegemony over the region and over its resources. Everything that has happened has taken place within the framework of a conspiracy hostile to the hopes of peoples for freedom, sovereignty, independence and relations of equality, which are the very principles and objectives for the achievement of which the United Nations is supposed to have been established.

The deliberate and brutal attacks launched on behalf of the United Nations by the forces of the criminal Zionistimperialist alliance on civilian economic, humanitarian, medical, cultural and religious targets and on citizens and their families in all parts of Iraq—documented examples of which are provided to you in the present letter—give cogent proof of the fact that the Governments participating in this alliance have the sole objective of taking vengeance on the proud people of Iraq and its militant leadership because of their opposition to the imperialist goals of those Governments.

It is indeed shameful for the United Nations that these premeditated crimes should be committed under the cover provided by resolutions adopted by the Security Council. The most recent of these is Security Council resolution 678 (1990), which the United States of America succeeded in having adopted by means of pressure, blackmail and bribery. The facts with respect to the receipt of bribes by State members of the Council and by leaders in those States are common knowledge.

Hundreds of millions of people in the world, in Asia, Africa and Latin America, who have suffered from the oppression and crimes of the former colonialists and the new imperialists, are today finding the so-called new international order of which the arrogant former colonialists and the new imperialists are speaking to be a dark age of intimidation and threats against those people aspiring to freedom and independence and fighting for relations of equity. The removal of the balancing role formerly played by the Soviet Union opens wide the way for the arrogant former colonialists and new imperialists once again to impose hegemony and intimidation, not only by the use of new and innovative methods, as is well known, but also by the old methods, namely aggression and open military occupation. What is new is that the colonialist technique as witnessed in past centuries has this time been used under the cover provided by iniquitous resolutions fabricated in the name of the United Nations which the Government of the imperialist colonialist alliance succeeded in having adopted by means of pressure, intimidation, blackmail and bribery.

The States that endorsed those resolutions for the motives indicated and you, personally, bear responsibility to history and to humankind for the heinous crimes being committed against the noble people of Iraq who are fighting for their freedom. Examples are given hereunder of the savage and premeditated acts of aggression committed by the aggressor forces between 17 and 21 January 1991.

[signed] Tariq Aziz,

Deputy Prime Minister and Minister for Foreign Affairs
Baghdad Governorate
17 January 1991
1. A pasteboard factory and plastic foam factory at Za'faraniyah bombed.
2. Homes in the Urdunn, Bunuk and Wahda quarters set on fire.
3. The Postal Department at Bab al-Mu'zzam set on fire and two citizens wounded.
4. A civilian vehicle set on fire near Al-Sha'b bridge.
5. The civil defense center for the Abu Ghurayb area bombed.
6. Abu Nawwas Street bombed.
18 January 1991
1. A clinic bombed; one killed and 10 wounded and four ambulances damaged.
2. The 7 Nisan residential area bombed; seven killed.
3. The residential Kasrah area bombed.
4. The vegetable-oil factory bombed.
5. Al-Sha'b sports stadium bombed.
19 January 1991
1. The Iwadiyah area bombed, resulting in the wounding of one citizen, the collapse of a restaurant and damage to neighboring shops.
2. The Ma'rifah residential district bombed; three wounded.
3. A building in the Kasrah area bombed; four civilians killed.
4. The Madinat Saddam residential area bombed; two homes damaged.
5. The Jazirat Baghdad tourist center bombed; two killed and seven wounded; one home destroyed.
6. A building under construction for the Council of Minister bombed.
7. The Al-Rashid Hotel area bombed; four homes damaged.
8. The Iraqi Museum bombed; six killed and 10 wounded; large scale damage to the museum building.
21 January 1991
1. Five killed and homes damaged in a residential neighborhood in Baghdad.
2. The Civil Defense Directorate in the Al-Sha'b area bombed; two of the staff killed and five wounded; five vehicles damaged.
22 January 1991
1. Homes in the 52 Street area bombed; two killed and three wounded.
2. Residential neighborhoods bombed in Nuayrah, Kiyyarah, the Qadisiyah quarter and the Dur al-Shuhada' quarter.
3. Madinat Saddam bombed and homes set on fire.
4. The Karradat Maryam area bombed; two killed and four wounded; four homes destroyed; a number of neighboring homes damagaed.
23 January 1991

Residential neighborhoods in the Waziriyah area and the Amin II area bombed.

Salah al-Din Governorate

17 January 1991

One killed and nine wounded in the Khudayrah area of the Balad district as a result of the explosion of time-delay bombs dropped from aircraft.

21 January 1991

1. Air attack on the Biji-Qaryat al-Bujwari district, wounding six.

2. Attack on the Dur district, in the heavily populated southern region, killing 22 and wounding 33 and causing large-scale damage to 112 homes and 30 vehicles and damage to the Al-Abbasi Mosque.

3. Missile falling in a field in the Faris district, killing one woman and wounding two other citizens, one a woman.

4. The Tikrit district bombed with cluster bombs dropped by two BRM-3A/As.

22 January 1991

Residential centers bombed in the town of Tikrit and the Samarra and Biji districts.

Ninawa Governorate

19 January 1991

The historic St. Thomas Church bombed and damaged.

Wasit Governorate

17 January 1991

Air attack on the provincial capital, killing nine and wounding nine others and damaging eight homes.

18 January 1991

Attack on the residential neighborhoods in the city of Kut, killing a woman and wounding 29 other citizens and damaging six homes and six civilians government offices.

Babil Governorate

18 January 1991

1. Residential areas bombed in the Latifayah sub-district; one woman wounded; a home damaged.

2. Attacks on the Musayyib district, damaging homes there.

19 January 1991

The provincial capital and the Musayyib, Mahmudiyah and Iskandiriyah area were subjected to air attacks in which the textile plant at Hillah was damaged and two of the workers were killed and 14 wounded and homes in Mahmudiyah were damaged.

21 January 1991

1. The health center in the provincial capital bombed from the air; 24 wounded; extensive damage to the building, the Civil Defense Directorate building and neighboring homes.

2. The Tall al-Dhahab area bombed; one wounded; homes damaged.

22 January 1991

Residential area bombed in the Mahmudiyah and Musayyib districts and the Iskandariyah sub-district; four civilians wounded.

Anbar Governorate

19 January 1991

1. A food storage warehouse containing vegetable-oil and rice for the civilian inhabitants bombed in the Abu Ghurayb area.

2. Residential centers bombed in the Bubali area of the provincial capital; four children and two women killed; 16 other citizens wounded, including six women and five children; two homes destroyed; and a fire started.

3. The Nukhaym sub-district bombed; 25 killed; nine wounded.

20 January 1991

1. Attack on the phosphate plant at Qa'im, killing three and wounding others.

2. A warehouse containing foodstuffs, meat and vegetable-oil bombed at Ramadi; two killed and seven wounded.

21 January 1991

1. The Hit district bombed; one killed and three wounded; homes damaged and destroyed; two civilian vehicles destroyed.

2. The Azrakiyah area in the Saqlawiyah sub-district bombed; a woman killed and four other citizens wounded.

3. A home hit by a missile fired by an aircraft, killing three and wounding nine, all of them women and children.

4. A home hit by a missile fired by an aircraft, destroying a house and a civilian vehicle.

5. An infant formula factory bombed in the Abu Ghurayb area.

6. A poultry farm bombed in the provincial capital.

Qadisiyah Governorate

17 January 1991

1. Residential centers in the provincial capital bombed; four killed and 23 wounded.

2. A residential building bombed; the governorate office building, the civil defense building, a number of shops and houses and four civilian vehicles and an ambulance set on fire.

19 January 1991

1. The State Vehicle Company complex bombed.

2. The food storage warehouse and flour factory bombed; damage caused; 10 killed and 22 wounded; two homes in the Mu'allimin quarter destroyed.

Muthanna Governorate

18 January 1991

1. Air attack on civilian area in the Qal'at Salih and Kahla' districts, killing four in the Ka'bi area and wounding five others.

2. The sugar factory bombed.

Najaf Governorate

18 January 1991

Agglomerations of nomadic Bedouin bombed in the Huwaymal area near Umm Tayyarah, 20 killed, including 12 children and 5 women.

21 January 1991

1. The Kufa cement factory bombed.

2. The water purification plant for the civilian inhabitants bombed; five killed including a woman, and 22 wounded.

3. Residential neighborhoods in the cities of Najaf and Kufa bombed; 14 killed, including four children and three women; 24 wounded, including three children and 16 women; a number of homes destroyed and damaged in the Amir quarter of Najaf, where 130 citizens were killed, and in the Al-Mutanabbi quarter of Kufa.

Dhi Qar Governorate

17 January 1991

Air attacks, killing two and wounding five in the Batha'Qaryat Al Budayr area and wounding two and damaging two homes and a vehicle in the provincial capital.

18 January 1991

Spherical bombs dropped on the Suq al-Shuyukh and Batha' areas, killing two and wounding two.

19 January 1991

One child killed in the Budur area during an air attack.

Karbala' Governorate

19 January 1991

1. Residential neighborhoods bombed in the provincial capital.

2. The Karbala' cement factory bombed, causing large-scale damage.

22 January 1991

Another residential neighborhood bombed in the provincial capital.

Basra Governorate

17-19 January 1991

1. The provincial capital bombed, including area of the city of Basra, Barjasiyah and Al-Asma'i and neighboring residential apartments, and Atabat Bin Ghazwan; 28 wounded; 40 shops and some homes and civilian vehicles damaged.

2. The Harithah and Assafiyah area bombed; six killed and 11 wounded, including a child aged three; six homes, an apartment and sour shops destroyed; six shops and 15 vehicles damaged.

3. The Faw district bombed; one wounded; 40 homes damaged.

4. The Qurnah district bombed; 17 killed and another 17 wounded; 12 homes destroyed; six civilian vehicles damaged.

Reference: "Letter to the U.N. Secretary-General from Mr. Tariq Aziz, Deputy Prime Minister and Minister for Foreign Affairs of Iraq, dated 24 January 1991," in Moore, Fred, comp., *Iraq Speaks: Documents on the Gulf Crisis* (Palo Alto, CA: privately printed, 1991), 82–84.

President Bush's Press Conference, 25 January 1991

On 25 January 1991, just nine days into the air war, President George Bush held a press conference, excerpts of which appear below.

Q. Mr. President, what can you do about the Iraqi dumping of oil in the gulf? Is there any way you can offset it, or . . .

Bush: Well, there's a lot of activity going on right now, trying to figure out what the best course of action is to clean this mess up, to stop this spill.

Saddam Hussein continues to amaze the world. First, he uses these Scud missiles that have no military value whatsoever. Then he uses the lives of prisoners of war, parading them and threatening to use them as shields. Obviously, they have been brutalized. And now he resorts to enormous environmental damage in terms of turning loose a lot of oil. No military advantage to him whatsoever in this. Absolutely not. It has nothing to do with that.

And so I don't know—I mean, he clearly is outraging the world, but back to your question. There were some meetings that were concluded about two hours ago. A course of action that I will not comment [on]—I think is close to agreement. I'm not going to comment on what it is, but I can assure you that every effort will be made to try to stop this continuing spill into the gulf and also to stop what has been done from moving [Iraqi troops] further south.

It's a little hard to do when the man has taken over this other country, Kuwait, and is using their assets in this way. But we will try hard, and you can rest assured that the scientists and the oil people, the military, are all involved—and the Saudis and the Kuwaitis, and the U.S. side are all involved in the closest consultation.

Q. Are you speaking of a retaliation?

Bush: No, I'm speaking on what we do about this spill right now. We'll get to that later.

Q. Mr. President, you said the other night that no one should cry for Saddam Hussein when he's brought to justice. Do you envision a war-crimes trial for Saddam? And also, can you say categorically that when this is all over Saddam will not be allowed to remain in power?

Bush: No, I'm staying with our objectives. And the violation of the Geneva Conventions are clear and we'll have to see how that works out, and have to see what a post-liberation Kuwait looks like there, in Iraq. But our objectives remain the same.

Q. As you pointed out, Saddam has done a number of things, none of them really a military offensive. Are you coming to the conclusion that he's not going to fight?

Bush: No, I haven't reached that conclusion at all. Because these Scud missiles, attacks, certainly invite instant retaliation, if you can find the mobile launchers, and we're keeping on in that quest, as I indicated the other day. I think what he's trying to do is rally support in some of the countries where he may have some. I think he's trying with the attacks on Israel to divide the coalition and to mount anti-Israel sentiment in parts of the world. What he doing when you dump oil reserves out, unless he's trying to show how tough he will be for Saudi Arabia or something like that, I can't figure out what he's doing when he brutally parades American prisoners. I can't figure that out either, or British prisoners, or an Italian airman. But it is not—it is not a performance that is winning him any points anywhere, in my view.

Q. Mr. President, the reports from Israel now indicate that the injuries to civilians, perhaps deaths, may have been caused by Patriot missiles themselves not striking their targets—or at least if they struck them, parts of them fell back on the civilian population, which raises anew the question of the sufficiency of the Patriot missile and the question about whether you are now contemplating additional measures to try to deal with the obviously persistent problem.

Bush: We are certainly dealing with that all the time, and we want to find ways to stop—we want to find ways to stop these brutal, senseless, non-military-value attacks on civilian populations.

Q. What is the sense of your level of confidence in the Israelis continuing to show restraint here? Obviously, it can't be any easier for them now.

Bush: No, although I felt I might be asked that question walking in here, and I'm still not certain that we know all the details, exactly what happened on this.

I will again express enormous confidence in the Patriots. They're doing very, very well. But whether this was debris falling down from an intercept or not, I simply don't want to comment because we don't yet know it for sure.

Q. Sir, one more try on Saddam Hussein. Given that your military commanders have said that they're hoping that this army quits rather than fights and results in a bloody ground offensive, why wouldn't it be entirely militarily appropriate to target Saddam Hussein?

Bush: Because we're not in the business of targeting Saddam Hussein. I've set out our goals, and I think that I will say this: as I said the other day in echoing my support for what Prime Minister Major of the United Kingdom said, no one will weep when he's gone. But having said that, we have spelled out our objectives and I will stay with them. But who knows what would happen if he left today. I would like to think that what I have said over and over again would resonate in Iraq, and that is that we have no arguments with the people of Iraq. We don't want to see a destabilized Iraq when this is all over. But we also don't want to see a continuation of the aggression. We will not tolerate continuation of this brutality. So we have a mix of problems, but the problems are not with the people in the streets of Baghdad.

Q. Mr. President, a couple of questions as to how the

gulf relates domestically. First of all, can you give the American people some sense of what this war is going to cost? Especially insofar as you and your Secretary of State are turning to allies and coalition partners and others to defray some of this cost, what are your projections, what sense can you give the American people? And, secondly, on the domestic front, how do you respond to Clayton Yeutter and others who are seeking to turn this issue politically against many Democrats who may have voted against the force resolution?

Bush: On the first part of it, I would leave that to the Pentagon. That is still being computed. That will be presented obviously to the United States Congress, that not only has a right to know, but has the prime obligations when it turns to funding these matters. I am very pleased with the cooperation and participation from foreign countries. I think Jim Baker today had or will have a statement regarding Kuwait[i] participation. You saw yesterday what the Prime Minister of Japan stepped up to the plate to do, and we salute that. There will be more such information forthcoming, hopefully next week. So the burden sharing, which is very, very important, is coming along pretty well, and Congress is very interested in this, and of course I'm very interested in it. So we'll be presenting that, along with the cost figures, to the Congress. But I can't give you the specific figures yet.

Q. Can I ask you for the second part of that question?

Bush: Oh, yes. My position on this is that this is not a partisan effort. I thought Lee Hamilton answered that question pretty well. I can't remember exactly what he said, but he said, look, I'm prepared to defend my vote one way or another, and I think everybody views it that way.

Q. Thank you, sir. Next Tuesday night when you go and give the State of the Union message in that great hall of the House where there's a joint session of the House and Senate, all of the members there, all the Cabinet, the Supreme Court, the diplomats and your wife and yourself—and that presents a great opportunity for terrorists, if they could get by. Why don't you give the State of the Union message quietly from the White House?

Bush: Well, many Presidents have given a State of the Union message by post office—you know, messenger, sent it up there. And I don't know that any have been done from the White House. But if I, you know, when I go to the Capitol, put it that way, I will have total confidence in the security apparatus of this country. It doesn't bother me one single bit. And I know this man has sponsored terrorism and we continue to be safeguarding in every way we can against it, but the Capitol of the United States will be secure and the people that are there will be safe. And so it doesn't—it just doesn't worry me, Sarah. Maybe it should. I'm not a fatalist exactly about this, because I think we are doing things to keep the Capitol, the people's Capitol, secure.

Q. But remember the man [inaudible] who shot up the Capitol?

Bush: Yes. Every once in a while you find some outbreak. None quite like that, though. That was probably the most violent. But it doesn't concern me. I'll be standing up there giving that speech with total confidence and the men and women of our security system, they're the best and so, see, that's why I hadn't considered changing. I am not going to be held a captive in the White House by Saddam Hussein of Iraq. And you can make a note of that one. We're going about our business and the world goes on.

Somebody asked me a while back about the Super Bowl. You think we ought to cancel the Super Bowl because of this situation? One, the war is a serious business and the nation is focused on it. But two, life goes on. And I'd say one thing—the kids over there in the Gulf—somebody told me to stop saying 'kids.' They look like kids to me, frankly. But I say it with great affection. I say it with affection. But the boys, the men and women in the Gulf, they want to see this game go on. They're going to get great instant replays over there. And so life goes on.

And this is a priority: getting this war concluded properly. But we are not going to screech everything to a halt in terms of our domestic agenda. We're not going to screech everything to a halt in terms of the recreational activities, and I cite the Super Bowl, and I am not going to screech my life to a halt out of some fear about Saddam Hussein.

Reference: "The White House: Excerpts from Bush's Remarks on Moves in Gulf," *New York Times,* 26 January 1991, A5.

Saddam Hussein's Interview on the War with Peter Arnett of CNN, 28 January 1991

Correspondent Peter Arnett of CNN held an informal interview with Saddam Hussein on 28 January 1991; only the excerpts of Hussein's comments were printed in the New York Times.

What we say is that light comes through the dark, penetrates the dark. As much as—whenever the American Administration expects that it is filling Baghdad or covering Baghdad with darkness, then the light that exists, that fills the breasts of the Iraqi people, the light, which is based on deep conviction in God, the one and only. What is important to us is that the darkness which the American Administration wants to see penetrate to the brains, to the minds, to the hearts, to the conscience of the people, is a darkness that has no place in the people—amongst the people of Iraq.

But as regards your questions. . . . Have they really won the first round? Or have they in fact—all they have reaped is the shame from the very moment they decided to launch their aggression.

You see, in fact, they were defeated, they were dealt a defeat the moment they signed the decision to launch the aggression, because they have signed a wrong, an unjust decision.

. . . Because victory and winning is not just in winning one particular or single battle or losing that one. But winning, in gaining the satisfaction, the pleasure of God, the one and only, and in winning the hearts of the people, first gaining the satisfaction of God the one and only, and secondly, winning the hearts of the people.

The pleasure of God, the blessings of God, and have they gained or won the hearts of the people? This is the criteria which we adopt, we at least adopt.

The most important thing is that our people now—our people now has never been—has never been as pure in its soul as it is now and throughout its history, and our armed forces have never been determined as they are now, throughout the history, and throughout the difficult circumstances in which—through the difficult situations with which they have dealt.

The important thing is that Iraq and Iran are two neighboring Muslim countries. And regardless or the circumstances of the past, these—these facts shall remain the most important in the relationship between the two countries.

And it is only natural that is—if it were only natural that if a certain [unintelligible] Iraqi aircraft found it under certain circumstances necessary that it should go down in a neighboring country's airport, an Islamic country, in this particular Islamic country or the other, then this could happen in the light of this spirit and in the light of this picture.

The facts that cannot be denied, the facts that have not been denied by Western media, are that there were Iraqi tankers loaded with crude oil, and they were attacked and sunk by the American forces. And—and the fact that the United States has not denied that they have attacked these tankers, and they knew these tankers were loaded with oil. And in addition to this fact, there is the other fact, which is that the United States armed forces have attacked oil installations which they themselves have not denied have done.

But when the Iraqis, if the Iraqis were to use oil for self-defense, including the use of oil in waters, then the Iraqis shall be justified for taking such an action. And it is certain that the future will show which part—what action for which the United States is responsible, and what action for which Iraq is responsible.

You, I do not—I do not want to insult anybody here. But this is the word one has to use. This is what we find in the dictionary, whoever—a liar is a man who doesn't tell the truth. The fact is that the Iraqi Army is there in Kuwait. And I'm sure that you as Americans can imagine that the offensive will be launched against the armed forces.

Where did it start on the night of the 16th—on the

night of the 17th? No attack was launched against armed forces in our 19th province. But he started his attack on Baghdad. And not against the military forces, but against our [unintelligible] installations and economic installations. . . . Didn't you—hasn't it become certain to you now that the battle that is started now is not really for Kuwait, it's not a battle over Kuwait, but for other reasons?

And we also said do not delude yourselves into believing that once the war started it would be—it would end in a matter of hours or days or weeks. It wouldn't be a war of weeks.

Do you remember what the Western leaders including President Bush were saying? They were saying that they would enter this war without a single American getting wounded. Has this been the case? We're only at the very outset of this war, only 10 days. Is it true that no Americans have been wounded? So what would happen if war were to expand or to begin taking its more comprehensive form?

I shall tell you that the problem here and now is not one of who has more weaponry or more weapons. In order to decide who will lose and who will win, it's based on who has the devil on his side and who has God on his side.

But if I were to take you around our antiaircraft men that you would see that each one will be proud for what he has done in the defense of Iraq and in defense of the values in which he believes.

In some situations the vultures were coming like rain. Our antiaircraft men were showered with bombs on occasion. But they never relinquished their guns. They never left their places, especially on the early days of fighting, first and second and third and fourth.

Through these pictures you could rest—you could rest assured about the answer as to how the result of the outcome of the confrontation on land is going to be. That is if the forces in question were to launch an offensive against our faithful men in the 19th province.

Do you remember what we said about keeping the foreign guests in this country, that it was being done to prevent war, and that if we were to keep them here, it may prevent war? What the hypocritical politicians, or the hypocrites of politics in the West said at the time—they said that keeping the foreign guests here would in fact itself lead to war, will cause the war to happen, but letting them go would prevent war from happening.

Now, this is past us, this is beyond us. We never repent any decision which we take and we have not repented the decision to let the foreigners go.

But if—but had we kept those 5,000 individuals from the West and Japan here, would Bush still have attacked Baghdad? When we decided to allow the foreigners, Western foreigners, to leave, we were not afraid of any action or any decision being taken against us.

What I said was that we shall use the weapons that shall equate the weapons that are used against us. We shall use the weapons that shall be equitable to the weapons used against us. But in any case, and under any circumstance, we shall never relinquish Iraq.

All of the force that is now being used against Baghdad, that is now attacking Baghdad, is Israel. What interest would you as an American have to come to attack Baghdad unless it is the Zionist influence that has played its role in the corridors of the U.S. Administration and led to this attack, this aggression being waged? . . .

This war that is being waged against us is a Zionist war. Only here, Zionism is fighting us through American blood, through your blood. And if Zionism is not using now some of its weapons, then the Zionists want to keep these weapons in order to be master of the situation, in order to be the dominant power in the area once the war has come to an end.

Zionism is fighting us. And had it not been for the Zionist influence, you would not have come here to occupy the land of our sanctity, the land of the tomb of Mohammed, and the land of the Muslims everywhere and to commit this aggression against Iraq and against Baghdad.

Reference: "Excerpts from Saddam Hussein's Comments on the Gulf War," *New York Times,* 31 January 1991, A13.

State of the Union Address, 29 January 1991

On 29 January 1991, President George Bush went before a joint session of Congress to deliver the annual State of the Union Address, delivered this time as the nation was at war. The relevant portions of his speech are included here.

Mr. President [Vice President Dan Quayle] and Mr. Speaker [Thomas S. Foley, D-Washington] and members of the United States Congress, I come to this house of the people to speak to you and all Americans, certain that we stand at a defining hour.

Halfway around the world we are engaged in a great struggle in the skies and on the seas and sands. We know why we're there. We are Americans, part of something larger than ourselves. For two centuries, we've done the hard work of freedom. And tonight we lead the world in facing down a threat to decency and humanity.What is at stake is more than one small country; it is a big idea: a new world order where diverse nations are drawn together in common cause to achieve the universal aspirations of mankind: peace and security, freedom and the rule of law. Such is a world worthy of our struggle, and worthy of our children's future.

The community of nations has resolutely gathered to condemn and repel lawless aggression. Saddam

Hussein's unprovoked invasion, his ruthless, systematic rape of a peaceful neighbor, violated everything the community of nations holds dear. The world has said this aggression would not stand, and it will not stand.

Together, together, we have resisted the trap of appeasement, cynicism and isolation that gives temptation to tyrants. The world has answered Saddam's invasion with 12 United Nations resolutions, starting with a demand for Iraq's immediate and unconditional withdrawal, and backed up by forces from 28 countries of 6 continents. With few exceptions, the world now stands as one.

The end of the cold war has been a victory for all humanity. A year and a half ago, in Germany, I said that our goal was a Europe whole and free. Tonight, Germany is united. Europe has become whole and free, and America's leadership was instrumental in making it possible.

Our relationship to the Soviet Union is important, not only to us but to the world. That relationship has helped to shape and other historic changes. But, like many other nations, we have been deeply concerned by the violence in the Baltics, and we have communicated that concern to the Soviet leadership. The principle that has guided us is simple: our objective is to help the Baltic peoples achieve their aspirations, not to punish the Soviet Union. In our recent discussions with the Soviet leadership we have been given representations which, if fulfilled, would result in the withdrawal of some Soviet forces, a reopening of dialogue with the republics, and a move away from violence. We will watch carefully as the situation develops. And we will maintain our contact with the Soviet leadership to encourage continued commitment to democratization and reform. If it is possible, I want to continue to build a lasting basis for U.S-Soviet cooperation, for a more peaceful future for all mankind.

The triumph of democratic ideas in Eastern Europe and Latin America, and the continuing struggle for freedom elsewhere all around the world all confirm the wisdom of our nation's founders. Tonight, we work to achieve another victory: a victory over tyranny and savage aggression.

We in this Union enter the last decade of the 20th century thankful for our blessings, steadfast in our purpose, aware of our difficulties, and responsive to our duties at home and around the world. For two centuries, America has served the world as an inspiring example of freedom and democracy. For generations, Americas has led the struggle to preserve and extend the blessings of liberty. And today, in a rapidly changing world, American leadership is indispensable. Americans know that leadership brings burdens and sacrifices. But we also know why the hopes of humanity turn to us. We are Americans; we have a unique re-

sponsibility to do the hard work of freedom. And when we do, freedom works.

The conviction and courage we see in the Persian Gulf today is simply the American character in action. The indomitable spirit that is contributing to this victory for world peace and justice is the same spirit that gives us the power and the potential to meet our toughest challenges at home.

We are resolute and resourceful. If we can selflessly confront evil for the sake of good in a land so far away, then surely we can make this land all that it should be.

If anyone tells you that America's best days are behind her, they're looking the wrong way. . . .

This nation was founded by leaders who understood that power belongs in the hands of the people. And they planned for the future. And so must we, here and all around the world.

As Americans, we know that there are times when we must step forward and accept our responsibility to lead the world away from the dark chaos of dictators toward the brighter promise of a better day. Almost 50 years ago, we began a long struggle against aggression and totalitarianism. Now we are facing another defining hour for America and the world.

There is no one more devoted, more committed to the hard work of freedom than every soldier and sailor, every marine, airman and coastguardsman—every man and woman now serving in the Persian Gulf. Oh, how they deserve—what a fitting tribute to them. You see, what a wonderful, fitting tribute to them. Each of them has volunteered, volunteered to provide for this nation's defense. And now they bravely struggle to earn for America, for the world and for future generations, a just and lasting peace. Our commitment to them must be the equal to their commitment to their country. They are truly America's finest.

And the war in the Gulf is not a war we wanted. We worked hard to avoid war. For more than five months we, along with the Arab League, the European Community, [and] the United Nations, tried every diplomatic avenue. U.N. Secretary General Peréz de Cuéllar; Presidents Gorbachev, Mitterrand, Özal, Mubarak and Benjedid; Kings Fahd and Hassan [of Morocco], Prime Ministers Major and Andreotti [of Italy], just to name a few, all worked for a solution. But time and again Saddam Hussein flatly rejected the path of diplomacy and peace.

The world well knows how this conflict began, and when: it began on August 2nd, when Saddam invaded and sacked a small, defenseless neighbor. And I am certain of how it will end. So that peace can prevail, we will prevail.

[Applause] Thank you. Tonight I am pleased to report that we are on course. Iraq's capacity to sustain war is being destroyed. Our investment, our training, our planning, all are paying off. Time will not be Saddam's salvation. Our purpose in the Persian Gulf remains constant: to drive Iraq out of Kuwait, to restore Kuwait's legitimate government and to insure the stability and security of this critical region. Let me make clear what I mean by the region's stability and security. We do not seek the destruction of Iraq, its culture or its people. Rather, we seek an Iraq that uses its great resources not to destroy, not to serve the ambitions of a tyrant, but to build a better life for itself and its neighbors. We seek a Persian Gulf where conflict is no longer the rule, where the strong are neither tempted nor able to intimidate the weak. Most Americans know instinctively why we are in the gulf. They know we had to stop Saddam now, not later. They know that this brutal dictator will do anything, will use any weapon, will commit any outrage, no matter how many innocents suffer. They know we must make sure that control of the world's oil resources does not fall into his hands only to finance further aggression. They know that we need to build a new, enduring peace, based not on arms races and confrontation but on shared principles and the rule of law.

And we all realize that our responsibility to be the catalyst for peace in the region does not end with the successful conclusion of this war.

Democracy brings the undeniable value of thoughtful dissent, and we've heard some dissenting voices here at home, some—a handful, reckless, most responsible. But the fact that all voices have the right to speak out is one of the reasons we've been united in purpose and principle for 200 years.

Our progress in this great struggle is the result of years of vigilance and a steadfast commitment to a strong defense. And now, with remarkable technological advances like the Patriot missiles, we can defend against ballistic missile attacks aimed at innocent civilians.

Looking forward, I have directed that the SDI [Strategic Defense Initiative] program be refocused on providing protection from limited ballistic missile strikes, whatever their source. Let us pursue an SDI program, that can deal with any future threat to the United States, to our forces overseas, and to our friends and allies.

The quality of American technology, thanks to the American worker, has enable us to successfully deal with difficult military conditions and help minimize precious loss of life. We have given our men and women the very best. And they deserve it.

We all have a special place in our hearts for the families of our men and women serving in the gulf. They are represented here tonight by Mrs. Norman Schwarzkopf. We are all grateful to General Schwarzkopf and to all those serving with him. And I might also recognize one who came with Mrs. Schwarzkopf, Alma Powell, the wife of the distin-

guished Chairman of the Joint Chiefs. And to the families let me say our forces in the gulf will not stay there one day longer than is necessary to complete their mission.

The courage and the success of the RAF pilots, of the Kuwaiti, Saudi, French, the Canadians, the Italians, the pilots of Qatar and Bahrain; all are proof that for the first time since World War II the international community is united. The leadership of the United Nations, once only a hoped-for ideal, is now confirming its founders' vision.

And I am heartened that we are not being asked to bear alone the financial burden of this struggle. Last year our friends and allies provided the bulk of the economic costs of Desert Shield, and now, having received commitments of over $40 billion for the first three months of 1991, I am confident they will do no less as we move through Desert Storm.

But the world has to wonder what the dictator of Iraq is thinking. If he thinks that by targeting innocent civilians in Israel and Saudi Arabia that he will gain advantage, he is dead wrong. And if he thinks that he will advance his cause through tragic and despicable environmental terrorism, he is dead wrong. And if he thinks that by abusing the coalition prisoners of war he will benefit, he is dead wrong. We will succeed in the Gulf. And when we do, the world community will have sent an enduring warning to any dictator or despot, present or future, who contemplates outlaw aggression. The world can therefore seize this opportunity to fulfill the long-held promise of a new world order where brutality will go unrewarded, and aggression will meet collective resistance.

Yes, the United States bears a major share of leadership in this effort. Among the nations of the world only the United States of America has both the moral standing and the means to back it up. We are the only nation on this earth that could assemble the forces of peace.

This is the burden of leadership, and the strength that has made America the beacon of freedom in a searching world. This nation has never found glory in war. Our people have never wanted to abandon the blessings of home and work for distant lands and deadly conflict. If we fight in anger, it is only because we have to fight at all. And all of us yearn for a world where we will never have to fight again.

Each of us will measure within ourselves the value of this great struggle. Any coast in lives—any cost—is beyond our power to measure. But the cost of closing our eyes to aggression is beyond mankind's power to imagine.

This we do know: Our cause is just. Our cause is moral. Our cause if right.

Let future generations understand the burden and blessings of freedom. Let them say, "We stood where duty required us to stand." Let them know that, together, we affirmed America and the world as a community of conscience.

The winds of change are with us now. The forces of freedom are together, united. And we move toward the next century, more confident than ever, that we have the will at home and abroad to do what must be done: the hard work of freedom.

May God bless the United States of America. Thank you very, very much. Thank you all. Thank you.

Reference: "Transcript of President's State of the Union Message to Nation," *New York Times,* 20 January 1991, A12.

President Gorbachev's Statement on the Persian Gulf Conflict, 9 February 1991

On 9 February 1991, Soviet President Mikhail Gorbachev delivered a statement in which he warned the United States and its coalition allies not to exceed the United Nations' mandate to force Iraqi troops out of Kuwait, while at the same time calling on both sides to resume diplomatic talks to bring a swift end to the conflict. Excerpts of his statement, which were provided by the official Soviet press agency TASS, appear below.

The developments in the gulf zone are taking an ever more alarming and dramatic turn. The war, the largest during the past several decades, is gaining in scope. The number of casualties, including among the civilian population, is growing. Combat operations have already inflicted enormous material damage. Whole countries—first Kuwait, now Iraq, then, perhaps, other countries—are facing the threat of catastrophic destruction . . .

The Soviet leadership reiterates its commitment, in principle, to the U.N. Security Council resolutions, which reflect the will of the majority of countries and the hopes of nations for [a] new world order that would rule out aggression and infringement on other countries' territory and natural resources.

However, the logic of the military operations and the character of the military actions are creating a threat if going beyond the mandate, defined by those resolutions.

Provocative attempts to expand the scope of the war, to draw Israel and other countries into it, thus giving the conflict another destructive dimension, the Arab-Israeli one, are also extremely dangerous.

Judging by some statements on a political level and those made on influential mass media organs, attempts are being made to condition people by both sides of the conflict to the idea of a possibility, and permissibility, of the use of mass destruction weapons. If this happened, the whole of the world politics, the world community in general, would be shaken to the foundations.

The only conclusion comes from historic responsibility, common sense and humaneness: to put to use all levers of a political settlement on the basis of the Security Council resolutions.

In this critical moment I appeal publicly to the Iraqi President, urging him to analyze again what is at stake for his country, to display realism which would make it possible to take the path of a reliable and just peaceful settlement. I shall immediately send my personal representative [Yevgeni Primakov] to Baghdad to meet President Hussein.

By taking these steps, we want, acting jointly with Arab and other Muslim countries, with European and Asian countries, with the United States in the first place, with all permanent members of the Security Council, not only to help overcome the state of war as soon as possible, but also to begin preparing a solid and equitable security system in that region . . .

The security system should include, of course, the settlement of the Arab-Israeli conflict and the Palestinian problem. The countries of the region should play a decisive role in this process. Iraq should hold a worthy place in the postwar settlement. Its people cannot bear responsibility for the past developments. They deserve sympathy, compassion and support . . .

I repeat that in order to make a breakthrough to peace in the Near and Middle East, it is necessary to put out the flame of war in the gulf as soon as possible . . . This is the most important thing now.

Reference: "Excerpts from Statement by Gorbachev on the Gulf," *New York Times,* 10 February 1991, A19.

Speech by Saddam Hussein to the Iraqi People, 10 February 1991

On 10 February 1991, Saddam Hussein went on Baghdad radio to deliver an address, excerpts of which appear below. Picked up in Nicosia, Cyprus, the speech was translated by the Associated Press.

Iraqis, your enemy believed it was capable of achieving its goals and reversing the course of history, and when he failed, he resorted to direct armed aggression. Here we are in the fourth week of this aggression with the Iraqis becoming more firm in their faith, and shining out more in front of the whole world.

The resistance of our heroes to the warplanes and rockets of aggression and shame is the strongest indication of the steadfastness, faith and light in the hearts of Iraqis and their great readiness not to give up the role willed to them by God, the will to which they responded faithfully and obediently.

All the good people will be victorious in Iraq, and victory will restore to the Iraqis all the requirements for a free and honorable living that they will merit as a reward for their patience and steadfastness.

Those who look for triumph should search for it not outside the great chapter of time that has elapsed, because it exists in each hour of the confrontation, in each day and week since the first hour of the siege . . . since the first day of the armed confrontation until the last day and hour, God willing.

Those who question when and how aggression was defeated should see it in the first moment that the President of the so-called greatest country was forced—as he said—to take the decision of war after the decision of the embargo instead of dialogue, and to ally against us those whom he did bring together when America's power looked so small to him, or thus God willed it.

With this he lost his prestige and made America lose its prestige as the biggest, or greatest, nation, as he calls it.

Bush lost his prestige when he lost conviction and lost the ability to convince through dialogue in order to avoid the course of using arms.

He lost prestige when he brought in the arms which the West had intended against the Warsaw Pact, against one of the countries of the third world, which is an Arab country.

Reference: "Iraqi Statement: Excerpts from Saddam Hussein's Speech," *New York Times*, 11 February 1991, A14.

Executive Order 12750 of 14 February 1991

This executive order was signed by President George Bush to designate the Arabian peninsula areas, airspace, and adjacent waters as the "Persian Gulf Desert Shield Area."

By the authority vested in me as President by the Constitution and the laws of the United States of America, including section 7508 of the Internal Revenue Code of 1986 (26 U.S.C. 7508), I hereby designate, for purposes of that section, the following locations, as the Persian Gulf Desert Shield area in which any individual who performed Desert Shield service (including the spouse of such individual) is entitled to the benefits of section 7508 of the Internal Revenue Code of 1986:
    —the Persian Gulf
    —the Red Sea
    —the Gulf of Oman
    —that portion of the Arabian Sea that lies north of 10 degrees north latitude and west of 68 degrees east longitude
    —the Gulf of Aden
    —the total land areas of Iraq, Kuwait, Saudi Arabia, Oman, Bahrain, Qatar, and the United Arab Emirates.

President Bush's Statement on the Start of the Ground War, 23 February 1991

On 23 February 1991, President Bush returned to the White House from the presidential retreat at Camp David to brief reporters and the nation on his thoughts as to the start of the ground war against Iraqi positions in Kuwait.

Yesterday, after conferring with my senior national security advisers and following extensive consultations with our coalition partners, Saddam Hussein was given one last chance, set forth in very explicit terms, to do what he should have done more than six months ago: withdraw from Kuwait without condition or further delay and comply fully with the resolutions passed by the United Nations Security Council.

Regrettably, the noon deadline passed without the agreement of the government of Iraq to meet the demands of United Nations Security Council Resolution 660, as set forth in the specific terms spelled out by the coalition to withdraw unconditionally from Kuwait.

To the contrary, what we have seen is a redoubling of Saddam Hussein's efforts to destroy completely Kuwait and its people.

I have therefore directed General Norman Schwarzkopf, in conjunction with coalition forces, to use all forces available, including ground forces, to eject the Iraqi Army from Kuwait.

Once again, this was a decision made only after extensive consultations within our coalition partnership. The liberation of Kuwait has now entered a final phase. I have complete confidence in the ability of the coalition forces swiftly and decisively to accomplish their mission.

Tonight as this coalition of countries seeks to do that which is right and just, I ask only that all of you stop what you were doing and say a prayer for all the coalition forces, and especially for our men and women in uniform, who this very moment are risking their lives for their country and for all of us.

May God bless and protect each and every one of them and may God bless the United States of America.

Thank you very much'

Reference: " 'One Last Chance,' Now 'the Final Phase,' " *New York Times*, 24 February 1991, A1.

Statement by President Bush and Official White House Statement on Iraqi Failure To Withdraw from Kuwait, 23 February 1991

On 23 February 1991, President George Bush spoke for a few moments to reporters on his reaction to the Iraqi refusal to withdraw all troops from Kuwait before the deadline imposed before the ground war would commence; later, White House Press Secretary Marlin Fitzwater read an official White House statement on the matter.

Bush Statement
We regret that Saddam Hussein took no action before the noon deadline to comply with the United Nations resolutions. We remain determined to fulfill the U.N. resolutions. Military action continues on schedule and according to plan.

White House Statement

CENTCOM reports that they have detected no military activity which would indicate any withdrawal of Saddam Hussein from Kuwait. Similarly, there has been no communication between Iraq and the United Nations that would suggest a willingness to withdraw under the conditions of the coalition plan. Iraq continues its scorched-earth policy in Kuwait, setting fire to oil facilities.

It's a continuing outrage that Saddam Hussein is still intent upon destroying Kuwait and its people, still intent upon inflicting the most brutal kind of rule on his own population, yet appears to have no intention of complying with the U.N. resolutions. Indeed, his only response at noon was to launch another Scud missile attack on Israel. The coalition forces have no alternative but to continue to prosecute the war.

As we indicated last night, the withdrawal proposal the Soviets discussed with Tariq Aziz in Moscow was unacceptable because it did not constitute an unequivocal commitment to an immediate and unconditional withdrawal. Thus, the Iraqi approval of the Soviet proposal is without effect.

President Bush today spoke with Prime Minister [Toshiki] Kaifu of Japan, President Özal of Turkey and President Gorbachev of the Soviet Union. The phone call from President Gorbachev occurred at 11:15 A.M. and lasted for approximately 28 minutes. President Gorbachev informed the president that he had talked to Prime Minister Major and President Mitterrand about his plan. Both of the allied leaders indicated full support for the coalition withdrawal plan. President Bush thanked President Gorbachev for his extensive efforts and reflected our general disappointment that Saddam Hussein has chosen not to respond positively.

Reference: *New York Times,* 24 February 1991, A19.

Statement of Tariq Aziz in Moscow, 23 February 1991

On 23 February 1991, Iraqi Foreign Minister Tariq Aziz, attempting to broker a peace deal with the Soviets, gave a statement to reporters in Moscow on his talks with Soviet leaders.

Last evening, the Soviet Government declared a proposal about the situation in the gulf region and in order to achieve a peaceful settlement to that situation in accordance with the U.N. resolutions. You are familiar with the points of that declaration, but anyhow, I am going to reiterate those points in English.

First, Iraq agrees to comply with Resolution 660 and therefore to withdraw immediately and unconditionally all its forces from Kuwait to the positions in which they were located on the first of August 1990.

Second, the withdrawal of the forces shall begin on the day following the cease-fire and the cessation of all military operations on land, sea and in the air.

Third, the withdrawal shall be completed within a period of 21 days, including the withdrawal from the city of Kuwait [Kuwait City] within the first four days of the said period.

Four, immediately upon the completion of the withdrawal of the troops from Kuwait, the grounds for which all the other resolutions of the Security Council were adopted will have been removed, and thereby those resolutions will cease to operate.

Five, all prisoners of war shall be released and repatriated within three days of the cease-fire and the cessation of all military operations.

The last point, the sixth, the cease-fire and withdrawal shall be confirmed, verified and supervised by observers and/or a peacekeeping force as determined by the Security Council.

These are the points of the plan, or the initiative that was declared by the Soviet Government last evening. I am here to tell you that the Iraqi Government fully endorses this plan and fully supports it.

Last night the Revolution[ary] Command Council issued a statement saying that Iraq supports the Soviet initiative and it appreciates the Soviets' efforts to reach a peaceful settlement to the situation. And we particularly appreciate the efforts of His Excellency, President Mikhail Gorbachev and his Government in this regard.

The second point I would like to address is the allegations made by the American Government yesterday that Iraq has created a new ecological situation in Kuwait, and you are aware of those allegations. My Government has strongly denied those allegations in the statement made last night. And the Iraqi Government asks the Security Council to establish immediately a committee to investigate the situation in Kuwait. If the American authorities would like to use this pretext to justify their aggressive position, such a pretext has no grounds.

Reference: *New York Times,* 24 February 1991, A19.

Executive Order 12752 of 25 February 1991

This administrative directive was issued by President George Bush to establish a program of health services for troops who served in Operation Desert Storm.

By the authority vested in me as President by the Constitution and the laws of the United States of America, including the National Emergencies Act (50 U.S.C. 1601 et seq.), section 5011A of title 38 of the United States Code, and pursuant to the national emergency declared with respect to Iraq in Executive Order No. 12722 of August 2, 1990, it is hereby ordered that, in the event that the Department of Veterans Affairs is requested by the Department of Defense to furnish care and services to members of the United States Armed Forces on active duty in Operation Desert Storm, the

Secretary of Veterans Affair may, pursuant to this order, enter into contracts with private facilities for the provision of hospital care and medical services for veterans to the fullest extent authorized by section 5011A(b)(1)(2) of title 38 of the United States Code.

White House Response to the Order for an Iraqi Withdrawal from Kuwait, 25 February 1991

Following Iraq's announcement that it was ordering all of its troops to withdraw "to the positions in which they were before the 1st of August 1990," the White House issued, through press secretary Marlin Fitzwater, a statement on the matter.

We continue to prosecute the war. We have heard no reason to change that. And because there is a war on, our first concern must be the safety and security of United States and coalition forces.

We don't know whether this most recent claim about [an] Iraqi withdrawal is genuine. We have no evidence to suggest the Iraqi army is withdrawing. In fact, Iraqi units are continuing to fight. Moreover, we remember when Saddam Hussein's tanks pretended to surrender at Khafji, only to turn and fire. We remember the Scud attacks today, and Saddam's many broken promises of the past. There are at least 22 dead Americans tonight who offer silent testimony to the intentions of Saddam Hussein.

The statement out of Baghdad today says that Saddam Hussein's forces will fight their way out of retreating. We will not attack unarmed soldiers in retreat, but we will consider retreating combat units as a movement of war.

The only way Saddam Hussein can persuade the coalition of the seriousness of his intentions would be for him to personally and publicly to agree to the terms of the proposal we issued on February 22. And because the announcement from Baghdad referred to the Soviet initiative, he must personally and publicly accept explicitly all relevant U.N. Security Council Resolutions, including especially U.N. Security Council Resolution 662, which calls for Iraqi rescission of its purported annexation of Kuwait, and the United States—I'm sorry, U.N. Security Council Resolution 674, which calls for Iraqi compensation to Kuwait and others.

That's the end of the statement. I might just add that the president met with his national security advisers for approximately an hour and fifteen minutes this evening to consider this matter, and the president has returned to his residence.
Reference: Washington Post, 26 February 1991, A6.

Iraqi Order To Withdraw from Kuwait, 26 February 1991

At 1:35 A.M. Baghdad time on 26 February (5:35 P.M. EST,

25 February), Baghdad Radio announced Saddam Hussein's order to Iraq's troops in Kuwait to fully and unconditionally withdraw from all of Kuwait. Herewith is the text of that order, monitored in Nicosia, Cyprus, and translated by the Associated Press.

An official spokesman announces the following:
In the name of God, the almighty, the compassionate;

Our armed forces have completed their duty of jihad, of rejecting compliance with the logic of evil, force and aggression. They have been engaged in an epic, valiant battle which will be recorded by history in letters of light.

The leadership has stressed its acceptance to withdraw in accordance with U.N. Security Council Resolution 660 when it agreed to the Soviet peace proposal. On this basis, and in compliance with this decision, orders were issued to the armed forces for an organized withdrawal to the positions in which they were before the 1st of August 1990.

This is regarded as a practical compliance with Resolution 660.

The spokesman emphasized that our forces, which have proved their fighting and steadfastness ability, will confront any attempt to attack them while implementing the withdrawal order.

They will fight with force and courage to make their withdrawal organized and honorable.

The Iraqi New Agency has learned that the Foreign Minister [Tariq Aziz] informed the Soviet ambassador of this decision, which constitutes a compliance with the U.N. Security Council's resolution 660. The Foreign Minister asked that a message be conveyed from leader President Saddam Hussein and the Revolutionary Command Council to President Gorbachev requesting him to exert efforts at the U.N. Security Council to achieve a cease-fire and put an end to the criminal behavior of the United States and its allies and collaborators.
Reference: Washington Post, 26 February 1991, A6.

Iraqi Letters of Capitulation to the United Nations, 27 February 1991

On 27 February 1991, Iraq's foreign minister, Tariq Aziz, circulated two letters, conceding Iraqi compliance with relevant UN resolutions, among other United Nations members.

I have the honor to notify you that the Iraqi Government reaffirms its agreement to comply fully with Security Council Resolution 660 (1990). The Iraqi armed forces have started to withdraw to the positions which they were in prior to August 1, 1990. It is hoped that the withdrawal will be fully completed in the next few hours, notwithstanding the continued attacks by American and other forces on the Iraqi armed forces during the withdrawal process.

I would like to inform you further that the Iraqi Government agrees to comply with Resolutions 662 (1990) and 674 (1990) if the Security Council adopts a resolution providing for an immediate cease-fire and the cessation of all military operations on land, at sea and in the air and if it is deemed that the bases on which Security Council Resolutions 661 (1990), 665 (1990) and 670 (1990) were adopted no longer exist and that those resolutions consequently are no longer in effect.

The Iraqi Government also affirms its full readiness to release all the prisoners of war immediately after the cease-fire and return them to their home countries within a very short period of time in accordance with the Third Geneva Convention of 1949, under the auspices of the International Committee of the Red Cross.

I should be grateful if you would kindly bring this letter immediately to the attention of the Security Council and have it circulated as a document of the Security Council.

I have the honor to inform you officially that the Government of Iraq agrees to comply fully with United Nations Security Council Resolution 660 and all other U.N. Security Council resolutions.

You are kindly requested to inform the Security Council members and to circulate this letter as an official document of the Security Council.

Reference: New York Times, 28 February 1991, A10.

General H. Norman Schwarzkopf, CENTCOM Briefing, Riyadh, Saudi Arabia, 27 February 1991

General Schwarzkopf: Good evening, ladies and gentlemen. Thank you for being here.

I promised some of you a few days ago that as soon as the opportunity presented itself, I would give you a complete rundown of what we were doing, and more important, why we were doing it—the strategy behind what we were doing. I've been asked by Secretary Cheney to do that this evening, so if you will bear with me, we're going to go through a briefing. I apologize to the folks who won't be able to see the charts, but we're going to go through a complete briefing of the operation.

This goes back to August 7th through January 17th. As you recall, we started our deployment on August 7th. Basically what we started out against was a couple of hundred thousand Iraqis that were in the Kuwait theater of operations. I don't have to remind you all that we brought over, initially, defensive forces in the form of the 101st, the 82nd, the 24th Mechanized Infantry division, the 3rd Armored Cavalry, and in essence, we had them arrayed to the south, behind the Saudi task force. Also Arab forces were arrayed in de-

fensive positions over here in this area. That, in essence, is the way we started.

In the middle of November, the decision was made to increase the force because by that time, huge numbers of Iraqi forces had flowed into the area, and generally in the disposition as they're shown right here. Therefore we increased the forces and built up more forces.

At this time we made a deliberate decision to align all of those forces within the boundary looking north toward Kuwait—this being King Khalid Military City over here. So we aligned those forces so it very much looked like they were all aligned directly on the Iraqi position.

We also at that time had a very active naval presence out in the Gulf, and we made sure that everybody understood about that naval presence. One of the reasons why we did that is it became apparent to us early on that the Iraqis were quite concerned about an amphibious operation to liberate Kuwait—this being Kuwait City. They put a very heavy barrier of infantry along here, and they proceeded to build an extensive barrier that went all the way across the border, down and around and up the side of Kuwait.

Basically, the problem we faced was this: When you looked at the troop numbers, they really outnumbered us about three-to-two, and when you consider the number of combat service support people we have—that's logisticians and that sort of thing in our armed forces—we were really outnumbered two-to-one. In addition to that, they had 4,700 tanks versus our 3,500 when the build-up was complete, and they had a great deal more artillery than we do.

I think any student of military strategy would tell you that in order to attack a position you should have a ratio of approximately three-to-one in favor of the attacker. In order to attack a position that is heavily dug in and barricaded such as the one we had here, you should have a ratio of five-to-one. So you can see basically what our problem was at that time. We were outnumbered three-to-two, at a minimum as far as troops were concerned, we were outnumbered as far as tanks were concerned, and we had to come up with some way to make up the difference.

I apologize for the busy nature of this chart, but I think it's important for you to understand exactly what our strategy was. What you see here is a color coding where green is a go sign, or a good sign, as far as our forces are concerned; yellow would be a caution sign; and red would be a stop sign. Green represents enemy units that have been attrited below 50 percent strength; the yellow are units that are between 50 and 75 percent strength; and of course the red units that are over 75 percent strength.

What we did, of course, was start an extensive air campaign. One of its purposes, I told you at the time, was to isolate the Kuwaiti theater of operations by taking out all the bridges and supply lines that ran between the north and the southern part of Iraq. That was to prevent reinforcements and supplies reaching the southern part of Iraq and Kuwait. We also conducted a very heavy bombing campaign, and many people questioned why. This reason is that it was necessary to reduce these forces down to strength that made them weaker, particularly along the front-line barrier that we had to go through.

We continued our heavy operations out in the sea because we wanted the Iraqis to continue to believe that we were going to conduct a massive amphibious operation in this area. I think many of you recall the number of amphibious rehearsals we had—including Imminent Thunder, which was written about quite extensively for many reasons. But we continued to have those operations because we wanted him to concentrate his forces—which he did.

I think this is probably one of the most important parts of the entire briefing. As you know, very early on we took out the Iraq Air Force. We know that he had limited reconnaissance means. Therefore, when we took out his air force, for all intents and purposes we took out his ability to see what we were doing down here in Saudi Arabia. Once we had taken out his eyes, we did what could best be described as the "Hail Mary Play" in football. I think you recall when the quarterback is desperate for a touchdown at the very end, what he does is send every receiver way out to one flank, and they all run down the field as fast as they possibly can into the end zone, and he lobs the ball. In essence, that's what we did.

When we know that he couldn't see us anymore, we did a massive movement of troops to the extreme west, because at that time we knew that the vast majority of his forces were still fixed in this area. Once the air campaign started, they would be incapable of moving out to counter this move even if they knew we made it. There were some additional troops out in this area, but they did not have the capability or the time to put in the barrier that had been described by Saddam Hussein as an absolutely impenetrable tank barrier. I believe those were his words.

So this was an extraordinary move. I must tell you, I can't recall any time in the annals of military history when this number of forces have moved over this distance to put themselves in a position to be able to attack. But what's more important, not only did we move the troops out there, but we literally moved thousands and thousands of tons of fuel, of ammunition, of spare parts , of water, and of food, because we wanted to have enough supplies on hand so if we launched this and got into a slug-fest battle, which we very easily could have, we'd have enough supplies to last for 60 days. It was a gigantic accomplishment, and I can't

give credit enough to the logisticians and the transporters who were able to pull this off, for the superb support we had from the Saudi government, the literally thousands and thousands of drivers of every national origin who helped us in this move out here. And of course, great credit goes to the commanders of these units who were also able to maneuver their forces out here into position.

As a result, by February 23rd, their front lines had been attritted down to a point where all of these units were at 50 percent or below. The second level, basically, that we had to face, and these were the real tough fighters we were worried about right here, were attritted to someplace between 50 and 75 percent. Although we still had the Republican Guard located here and here, and part of the Guard in this area we continued to hit the bridges all across this area to make absolutely sure that no more reinforcements came into the battle. This was the situation on February 23rd.

I shouldn't forget our forces. We put them deep into the enemy territory. They went out on strategic reconnaissance for us, and they let us know what was going on out there. They were our eyes, and it's very important that I not forget those folks.

This was the morning of the 24th. Our plans initially had been to start over here in this area and do exactly what the Iraqis thought we were going to do. That's taken them head-on in their most heavily defended area. Also, at the same time we launched amphibious feints and navel gunfire so that they continued to think we were going to be attacking along the coast, and therefore fixed their forces in this position. Our hope was that by fixing these forces, we would basically keep the forces here, and they wouldn't know what was going on out in this area. I believe we succeeded in that very well.

At four o'clock in the morning, the 1st and 2nd marine divisions launched attacks through the barrier system. They were accompanied by the U.S. Army Tiger Brigade of the 2nd Armored Division. At the same time, over here, two Saudi task forces also launched a penetration through this barrier. But while they were doing that, the 6th French Armored Division, accompanied by a brigade of the 82nd Airborne, also launched an overland attack to their objective up in this area, al-Faman Airfield. We were held up a little bit by the weather, but by eight o'clock the 101st Airborne air assault launched an air assault deep in enemy territory to establish a forward operating base in this location right here. Let me talk about each one of these moves.

First of all, the Saudis over here on the east coast did a terrific job. They went up against the very tough barrier systems; they breached the barrier very effectively; they moved out aggressively and continued their attacks up the coast.

I can't say enough about the two Marine divisions.

They did an absolutely superb job in breaching the so-called impenetrable barrier. It was a classic military breaching of a very tough minefield, barbed wire, fire trenches type barrier. They went through the first barrier like it was water. They went across into the second barrier line, even though they were under artillery fire at the time, and they continued to open up that breach. Then they brought both divisions streaming through that breach. A textbook operation, and I think it will be studied for many years to come as the way to do it.

I would also like to say that the French did a superb job of moving out rapidly to take their objective out here, and they were very successful, as was the 101st. Again, we still had the special forces located in this area.

What we found was that as soon as we breached these obstacles here and started bringing pressure, we started getting a large number of surrenders. I talked to some of you about that when I briefed you on the evening of the 24th. We also found that these forces were meeting with a great deal of success.

We were worried about the weather. It was going to get pretty bad the next day, and we were worried about launching this air assault. We also started to have a huge number of atrocities of the most unspeakable type committed in downtown Kuwait City, including reports that the desalinization plant had been destroyed. When we heard that, we were quite concerned. Based upon that, and the situation as it was developing, we made the decision that rather than wait until the following morning to launch the remainder of these forces that we would go ahead and launch them that afternoon.

This was the situation you saw the afternoon of the 24th. The Marines continued to make great progress through the breach and were moving rapidly north. The Saudi task force on the east coast was also moving rapidly north. We launched another Egyptian-Arab force in this location, and another Saudi force in this location—again, to penetrate the barrier. But as before, these assaults were to make the enemy continue to think that we were doing exactly what he wanted us to do. That meant a very tough mission for these folks.

At the same time, we continued to attack with the French. We launched an attack on the part of the entire 7th Corps where the 1st Infantry Division had gone through, breached an obstacle and mine-field barrier here, established quite a large breach through which we passed the 1st British Armored Division. At the same time we launched the 1st and 3rd Armored divisions. Because of the way our deception plan was working, we didn't even have to worry about a barrier. We just went right around the enemy and were behind him in no time at all. The 2nd Armored Cavalry Division and the 24th Mech Division was also launched out here in the far west. I ought to talk about the 101st because this is an important point.

Once the 101st had their forward-operating base established, they then launched into the Tigris-Euphrates Valley. There are a lot of people who are still saying that the object of the United States of America is to cause the downfall of the entire country of Iraq. Ladies and gentlemen, when we were here, we were 150 miles from Baghdad. What's more, there was nobody between us and Baghdad. If our intention had been to overrun and destroy Iraq, we could have done it unopposed, for all intents and purposes, from this position at that time. That was not our intention; we have never said it was our intention. It was truly to eject the Iraqis out of Kuwait and destroy the military power that had come in.

So this was the situation at the end of the afternoon of February 24th.

The next two days went exactly like we thought they would. The Saudis continued to make great progress on the eastern flank, keeping the pressure off the Marines flank. The special forces started operating small-boat operations in this area to help clear mines, but also to threaten the flanks here and to continue to make them think that we were going to conduct amphibious operations. The Saudi and Arab forces that took these two initial objectives turned to come in on the flank heading toward Kuwait City. The British passed through and continued to attack up this flank. Of course, the VII Corps came in and attacked in this direction shown here. The 24th Infantry Division made an unbelievable move all the way across into the Tigris-Euphrates Valley, and proceeded in blocking this avenue of egress, which was the only one left because we continued to make sure that the bridges stayed down. So there was no way out once the 24th was in this area, and the 101st continued to operate in here. The French, having succeeded in achieving all their objectives, then set up a flank guard position here to make sure no forces could get us from the flank.

By this time we had destroyed, or rendered completely ineffective, over 21 Iraqi divisions.

Of course, that brings us to today. We now have a solid wall across the north of the 18th Airborne Corps consisting of the units shown right here, attacking straight to the east. We have a solid wall here, again of the VII Corps also attacking straight to the east. The forces that they are fighting right now are the forces of the Republican Guard.

Today we had another significant day. The Arab forces coming from both the west and east closed in and moved into Kuwait City, where they are now in the process of securing it. The 1st Marine Division continues to hold Kuwait International Airport. The 2nd Marine Division continues to hold a position that blocks any egress out of the city of Kuwait, so no one can leave. To date we have destroyed to rendered inoperable—I don't like to say destroyed because that gives you visions of absolutely killing everyone, and that's not what we're doing. But we have rendered completely ineffective over 29 Iraqi divisions. The gates are closed.

We continue, of course, high-level air power. The air has done a terrific job from start to finish in supporting the ground forces, and we also have had great support from the Navy—both in the form of naval gunfire and in support of carrier air.

That's the situation at the present time.

Peace is not without a cost. These have been the U.S. casualties to date. I would just like to comment briefly about the casualty chart. The loss of one human life is intolerable to any of us who are in the military. But casualties of that order of magnitude, considering the job that's been done and the number of forces involved, is almost miraculous, even though it will never be miraculous to the families of those people.

This is what's happened to date with the Iraqis. They started with over 4,000 tanks. To date, we have over 3,000 confirmed destroyed—and I do mean destroyed or captured. As a matter of fact, that number is low because you can add 700 to that as a result of the battle that's going on right now with the Republican Guard. That number is very high, and we've almost completely destroyed the offensive capability of the Iraqi forces in the Kuwaiti theater of operations. The armored-vehicle count is also very high, and of course, you can see we're doing great damage to the artillery. The battle is still going on, and I suspect that these numbers will mount considerably.

I wish I could give you a better number than this, to be honest with you. This is just an estimate sent to us by the field today at noon time. The problem is, the prisoners out there are so heavy and obviously we're not going around and counting noses at this time to determine precisely what the number is. But we're confident that we have well over 50,000 prisoners of war at this time, and that number is mounting.

I would remind you that even as we speak, there is fighting going on out there. Even as we speak, there are incredible acts of bravery going on. This afternoon we had an F-16 pilot shot down. We had contact with him, he had a broken leg on the ground. Two helicopters from the 101st, they didn't have to do it, but they went in to try to pull that pilot out. One of them was shot down, and we're still in the process of working through that. But that's the kind of thing that's going on out on that battlefield right now. It is not a Nintendo game—it is a tough battlefield where people are risking their lives at all times. There are great heroes out there, and we ought to all be very, very proud of them.

That's the campaign to date. That's the strategy to date. I'd now be happy to take any questions anyone might have.

Q: I want to go back to the air war. The chart you

showed with the attrition rates of the various forces was almost the exact reverse of what most of us thought was happening. It showed the front-line troops attritted to 75 percent or more, and the Republican Guard, which gained a lot of public focus when we were covering the air war, attritted less than 75. Why is that?

A: Let me tell you how we did this. We started, of course, against the strategic targets. I briefed you on that before. At the same time we were hitting the Republican Guard. But the Republican Guard, you must remember, is mostly a mechanized armor force that is very well dug in and very spread out. So in the initial stages of the game, we were hitting the Republican Guard heavily, but we here hitting them with strategic-type bombers rather than pinpoint-precision bombers.

For lack of a better word, what happened is the air campaign shifted from the strategic phase into the theater. We knew all along that this was the important area. The nightmare scenario for all of us would have been to go through, get hung up in this breach right here, and then have the enemy artillery rain chemical weapons down. So one of the things that we felt we must have established was as much destruction as we could possibly get of the direct support artillery that would be firing on that breach. That's why in the latter days, we punished this area very heavily, because that was the first challenge. Once we got through this and were moving, then it's a different war. Then we're fighting their kind of war, and that's what we didn't want to have to do.

At the same time, we continued to attrit the Republican Guard, and that's why I would tell you that, again, the figures we're giving you are conservative. They always have been conservative. But we promised you at the outset we weren't going to give you anything inflated, but the best we had.

Q: Hussein seems to have about 500 to 600 tanks left out of more than 4,000. I wonder if an overview, despite these enormously illustrative pictures, you could say how long would it be before the Iraqi army could ever be a threat to the region again?

A: There's not enough left at all for Hussein to be an offensive regional threat. As you know, he has a very large army, but most of what is left north of the Tigris-Euphrates Valley is an infantry army. It's not an armored heavy army, which means it really isn't an offensive army. So it doesn't have enough left, unless someone choose to rearm them in the future.

Q: You said the Iraqis have got these divisions along the border which were seriously attritted. It figures to be about 200,000 troops that were there. You've go 50,000 prisoners. Where are the rest of them?

A: There were a large number of dead in these units—a very, very large number of dead. When we went into the units ourselves, we even found them in the trench lines. There were very heavy desertions. At one point we had reports of desertion rates of more than 30 percent of the units along the front. As you know, we had quite a large number of POWs that came across, so I think it's a combination of desertions, of people that were killed, of the people that we've captured, and of some other people who are just flat still running.

Q: It seems you've done so much that the job is effectively done. His forces are, if not destroyed, certainly no longer capable of posing a threat to the region. They seem to want to go home. What more has to be done?

A: To accomplish the mission that I was given, I have to make sure that the Republican Guard is rendered incapable of conducting the type of heinous acts that they've conducted so often in the past. What has to be done is for these forces to continue to attack across here and put the Republican Guard out of business. We're not in the business of killing them. We have psy-ops aircraft up. We're telling them over and over again, all you've got to do is get out of your tanks and you will not be killed. But they're continuing to fight, and as long as they do, we're going to continue to fight with them.

Q: That move on the extreme left which got within 150 miles of Baghdad, was it also a part of the plan that the Iraqis might have thought it was going to Baghdad, and would that have contributed to the deception?

A: I wouldn't have minded at all if they'd gotten nervous about it. I mean that very sincerely. I would have been delighted. Frankly, I don't think they ever knew it was there until the door had already been closed on them.

Q: I'm wondering how much resistance there still is in Kuwait, and I'm wondering what you say to people who would say the purpose of this war was to get the Iraqis out of Kuwait, and they're now out. What would you say to that public that is thinking that right now?

A: I would say there was a lot more purpose to this war than just get the Iraqis out of Kuwait. The purpose of this was to enforce the resolutions of the United Nations. There are some twelve different resolutions of the United Nations, not all of which have been accepted by Iraq to date, as I understand it. But I've got to tell you, as a military commander, my job is not to go ahead and at some point say that's great, they've just now pulled out of Kuwait—even though they're still shooting at us, they're moving backward, and therefore I've accomplished my mission. That's not the way you fight it, and that's not the way I would ever fight it.

Q: You talked about heavy press coverage of Imminent Thunder early on, and how it helped fool the Iraqis into thinking that it was a serious operation. I wondered if you could talk about other ways in which the press contributed to the campaign.

(Laughter)

A: First of all, I don't want to characterize Imminent Thunder as being only a deception, because it wasn't. We had every intention of conducting amphibious operations if they were necessary, and that was a very real rehearsal—as were the other rehearsals.

Q: What kind of fight is going on with the Republican Guard? And is there any more fighting going on in Kuwait, or is it essentially out of the action?

A: No. The fight against the Republican Guard right now is a classic tank battle. You've got fire and maneuver. They are continuing to fight and shoot at us as our forces move forward, and our forces are in the business of outflanking them, taking them to the rear, using our attack helicopters and advanced technology. One of the things that has prevailed, particularly in this battle, is our technology. We had great weather for the air war, but for the last three days, it's been raining, it's been dusty, there's black smoke and haze in the air. It's an infantryman's weather—God loves the infantryman, and that's just the kind of weather the infantryman likes to fight in. But our sights have worked fantastically well in their ability to acquire enemy targets through that kind of dust and haze. The enemy sights have not worked that well. As a matter of fact, we've had several anecdotal reports today of enemy who were saying to us that they couldn't see anything through their sights and all of a sudden their tank exploded when their tank was hit by ours.

Q: Can you tell us why the French, who went very fast in the desert in the first day, stopped (inaudible) and were invited to stop fighting after 36 hours?

A: That's not exactly a correct statement. The French mission on the first day was to protect our left flank. We wanted to make sure we confined this battlefield— both on the right and the left—and we didn't want anyone attacking the main attack on their left flank. So the French mission was not only to seize Al Salman, but to set up a screen across our left flank, which was vital to ensure that we weren't surprised. So they definitely did not stop fighting. They continued to perform their mission, and they performed it extraordinarily well.

Q: The Iraq Air Force disappeared very early in the air war. There was speculation they might return and provide cover during the ground war. Were you surprised they never showed themselves again?

A: We were not expecting it, but we never discounted it, and we were totally prepared in the event it happened.

Q: Have they been completely destroyed? Where are they?

A: There's not an airplane flown. A lot of them are dispersed throughout civilian communities in Iraq. We have proof of that.

Q: How many divisions of the Republican Guard now are you fighting, and any idea of how long that will take?

A: There were a total of five of them up here. One of them we probably destroyed yesterday. We probably destroyed two more today. I would say that leaves us a couple that we're fighting right now.

Q: I realize a great deal of strategy and planning took place, but did you think this would turn out to be such a cakewalk as it seems? And second, what are your impressions of Saddam Hussein as a military strategist? (Laughter)

A: First of all, if we had thought it would be such an easy fight, we definitely would not have stocked 60 days' worth of supplies on these log bases. As I've told you, it is very important that a military commander never assume away the capabilities of his enemy. When you're facing an enemy that is over 500,000 strong, has the reputation they've had of fighting for eight years, being combat-hardened veterans, has a number of tanks and the type of equipment they had, you don't assume away anything. So we certainly did not expect it to go this way.

As far as Saddam Hussein being a great military strategist, he is neither a strategist, nor is he schooled in the operational arts, nor is he a tactician, nor is he a general, nor is he a soldier. Other than that, he's a great military man. I want you to know that. (Laughter)

Q: I wonder if you could tell us anything more about Iraqi casualties on the battlefield. You said there were large numbers. Are we talking thousands, tens of thousands? Any more scale you can give us?

A: I wish I could answer that question. You can imagine, this has been a very fast-moving battle, as is desert warfare. As a result, even today when I was asking for estimates, every commander out there said we just can't give you an estimate. We've gone by too quickly.

Q: Very quickly, the special-operations folks—could you tell us what their role was?

A: We don't like to talk a lot about what special operations do, as you're well aware. But in this case, let me just cover some of the things they did. First of all, with every Arab unit that went into battle, we had special-forces troops with them. Their job was to travel right down at the battalion level as the communicators with friendly English-speaking units that were on their flanks. They could also call in air strikes as necessary, could coordinate helicopter strikes, and that sort of thing. That's one of the principal roles they played, and it was a very important role. Second, they did a great job in strategic reconnaissance for us. Third, special forces were 100 percent in charge of the combat search and rescue, and that's a tough mission. When a pilot gets shot down in the middle of nowhere, surrounded by the enemy, and you're the folks required to go in after them, that is a very tough mission. Finally, they also did some direct-action missions, period.

Q: General, there have been reports that when the Iraqis left Kuwait City, they took with them a number of the Kuwaiti people as hostages. What can you tell us about this?

A: We've heard that they took up to 40,000. I think you've probably heard what the Kuwaitis who were left in the city have stated. So I don't think there's any question that a very large number of young Kuwaiti males have been taken out of that city within the last week or two. But that pales to insignificance compared to the absolutely unspeakable atrocities that occurred in Kuwait in the last week. The people that did that are not a part of the same human race that the rest of us are. I've got to pray that that's the case.

Q: Could you give us some indication of what's happening to the forces left in Kuwait? What kind of forces are there, and are they engaged at the moment?

A: I'm not even sure they're here. I think they're probably gone. At most there are pockets of people who are just waiting to surrender as soon as somebody uncovers them. What we're really faced with is fighting the Republican Guard heavy mech and armor units that are there. Basically, what we want to do is capture their equipment.

Q: General, not to take anything away from the Army and the Marines on the breaching maneuvers, but many of the reports from your field commanders and soldiers are indicating that these fortifications were not as intense or as sophisticated as they were led to believe. Is this a result of the pounding that they took, or were they perhaps overrated in the first place?

A: Have you ever been in a mine field?

Q: No.

A: All there has to be is one mine, and that's intense. There were plenty of mines out there, plenty of barbed wire. There were fire trenches, most of which we set off ahead of time. But the Egyptian forces still had to go through some fire trenches. There were a lot of booby traps, a lot of barbed wire—not a fun place to be. I have to tell you, probably one of the toughest things that anyone ever has to do is to walk into something like that and go through it. And while you're going through it and clearing it, at the same time you're probably under fire by enemy artillery. That's all I can say.

Q: Was it less severe than you had expected? You were expecting even worse, in other words.

A: It was less severe than we expected, but one of the things I contribute to that is the fact that we went to extensive measures to make it less severe.

Q: Is the Republican Guard your only remaining military objective in Iraq? I gather there have been some heavy engagements. How would you rate this army you face—from the Republican Guard on down?

A: Rating an army is a tough thing to do. A great deal of the capability of an army is its dedication to its cause and its will to fight. You can have the best equipment in the world, the largest numbers in the world, but if you're not dedicated to your cause, then you're not going to have a very good army.

One of the things we learned immediately prior to the initiation of the campaign—it contributed, as a matter of fact, to the timing of the ground campaign—is that so many people were deserting. What's more, the Iraqis brought down execution squads whose job was to shoot people in the front lines. I have to tell you, a soldier doesn't fight very hard for a leader who is going to shoot him on a whim. That's not what military leadership is all about. So I attribute a great deal of the failure of the Iraqi Army to their own leadershap. They committed them to a cause that they did not believe in. They are all saying they didn't want to be there, they didn't want to fight their fellow Arabs, they were lied to when they went into Kuwait, and then after they got there, they had a leadership that was so uncaring that they didn't properly feed them, didn't properly give them water, and in the end, kept them there only at the point of a gun.

The Republican Guard is entirely different. They are the ones that went into Kuwait in the first place. They get paid more, get treated better. Oh, by the way, they also were well to the rear so they could be the first ones to bug out when the battlefield started folding, while these poor fellows up here who didn't want to be here in the first place bore the brunt of the attack. But it didn't happen.

Q: Can you tell us something about the British involvement, and perhaps comment on today's report of ten dead through friendly fire?

A: The British have been superb members of this coalition from the outset. I have a great deal of admiration and respect for all of them and particularly General Sir Peter [Delabiyea], who is not only a great general but has also become a close personal friend of mine.

They played a key role in the main attack. What they had to do was go through this breach in one of the tougher areas. Iraqis had reinforced here, and the Brits had to go through the breach and then fill up the block so that the main attack could continue on without forces over here, the mechanized forces over here, attacking that main attack in the flank. That was a principal role of the British. They did it magnificently, and then they immediately followed up in the main attack, and they're still up there fighting right now. So they did a great job.

Q: The 40,000 Kuwaiti hostages taken by the Iraqis, where are they right now? That's quite a few people. Are they in the line of fire? Do we know where they are?

A: No, no. We were told—and a lot of this is anecdotal—that they were taken back to Basra, and some of them were taken all the way to Baghdad. We were also told a hundred different reasons why they were taken. Number one, to be a bargaining chip if the time came

when bargaining chips were needed. Another one was for retribution, because of course, at that time Iraq was saying that these people were not Kuwaitis but citizens of Iraq, and therefore they could do anything they wanted to with them. I just pray that they'll all be returned safely before long.

Q: The other day on television, the Soviet Deputy Foreign Minister said that they were talking already about re-arming the Iraqis. There's some indication that the United States as well needs to have a certain amount of armament to retain a balance of power. Do you feel that your troops are in jeopardy finishing this off when already the politicians are talking about re-arming the Iraqis?

A: I certainly don't want to discuss [inaudible] because that's way out of my field. I would tell you that I'm one of the first people that said it's not in the best interest of peace in this part of the world to destroy Iraq, and I think the President of the United States has made it clear from the outset that our intention is not to destroy Iraq or the Iraqi people. I think everyone has every right to legitimately defend themselves. But the one message came through loud and clear, over and over, to the pilots that have flown in against their military installations: their war machine definitely was not defensive, and they demonstrated that more than adequately when they overran Kuwait and then called it a great military victory.

Q; Before starting the land phase, how much were you concerned by the Iraqi planes coming back from Iran? And do we know what happened to the Iraqi helicopters?

A: As I said before, we were very concerned about the return of the Iraqi planes from Iran, but we were prepared for it. We have been completely prepared for any type of air attack the Iraqis might throw against us, and we're still prepared for it. We're not going to let down our guard for one instant, so long as we know that capability is there, until we're sure this whole thing is over.

The helicopters are another interesting story, and we know where the helicopters were. They traditionally put their helicopters near some of their other outfits, and we tracked them carefully. What happened is despite the fact that the Iraqis claim that we indiscriminately bombed civilian targets, they took their helicopters and dispersed them all over the civilian residential areas just as fast as they possibly could. Quite a few of them were damaged on airfields—those that we could take on airfields—but the rest of them were dispersed.

Q: You mentioned the Saudi armed forces. Could you elaborate about their role on the first day?

A: The Saudi Army, as part of the eastern task force, had to attack up the coast to pin the enemy in this location. We had the Marine attack, and of course we were concerned about those Iraqi forces hitting the flanks. That's one of the things you just don't want to have happen to your advancing forces. The Saudi forces had a tough mission because they were being required to wage the kind of fight that the Iraqis wanted. It was a very, very tough mission. I should point out that the eastern task force wasn't only the Saudis but Kuwaitis, Egyptians, Syrians, the Emiris from United Arab Emirates, Bahrainis, Qataris, and Omanis, and I apologize if I've left anybody out, but it was a great coalition of people, all of whom did a fine job.

Q: Is there anything left of the Scuds or chemical capability?

A: I don't know, but we're sure going to find out if there's anything left. The Scuds that were being fired against Saudi Arabia came from right here. So obviously we're going to check on it when we finally get to that location.

Q: Could you tell us in terms of the air war, how effective was it in speeding up the ground campaign? Obviously, it's gone much faster than you ever expected. As a second part of that, how effective do you think the air/land battle campaign has been?

A: The air war, obviously, was very effective. You just can't predict about things like that. You can make your best estimates at the outset as to how quickly you will accomplish certain objectives, but a lot depends on how resilient the enemy is, how well dug in they are. In the earlier phases we made great progress in the air war. In the later stages, we didn't make much progress because frankly, the enemy had burrowed down into the ground. That, of course, made the air war tougher, but when you dig your tanks in and bury them, they're no longer tanks. They're now pillboxes. That then makes a difference in the ground campaign. When you don't run tanks for a long time, they have a lot of maintenance problems, seal problems and that type of thing. So the air campaign was very successful and contributed a great deal.

How effective was the air/ground campaign? I think it was pretty effective myself. I don't know what you all think.

Q: As you look down the road, can you tell us what you think would be a reasonable size for the Iraq Army, and can you tell us roughly what the size is now if the war were to stop this evening?

A: With regard to size right now, at one time Saddam Hussein was claiming that he had a 7,000,000-man army. If he did, they've still got a pretty big army out there. The effectiveness of that army is an entirely different question.

With regard to the size of the army he should have, that's not my job to decide that. An awful lot of people live in this part of the world, and I would hope that is a decision arrived at mutually by all the Arab world to contribute to peace and stability. That's the best answer I can give.

Q: Is there a military or political explanation as to why the Iraqis did not use chemical weapons?

A: We had a lot of questions about that, and I don't know the answer. I just thank God that they didn't.

Q: Is it possible they didn't use them because they didn't have time to react?

A: You want me to speculate, I'd be delighted to. Nobody can ever pin you down when you speculate. Number one, we destroyed their artillery. We went after their artillery big-time and they had major desertions. That's how they would have delivered their chemical weapons. Either that or by air, and we all know what happened to the air.

Other people speculate that their chemical weapons degraded, and because of the damage we did to their chemical-production facilities, they were unable to upgrade the chemicals within their weapons. That was one of the reasons, among others, that we went after their chemical-production facilities early on in the strategic campaign.

I'll never know the answer to that question, but as I say, thank God they didn't.

Q: Are you still bombing in northern Iraq? If you are, what's the purpose of it now?

A: Exactly the same thing we were trying to achieve before. The war is not over, and you have to remember, people are still dying out there. Those people that are dying are my troops, and I'm going to continue to protect those troops in every way I possibly can until the war is over.

Q: Are you going to try to bring to justice the people responsible for the atrocities in Kuwait City? And also, could you comment on the friendly-fire incident in which nine British were killed?

A: On the first question, we have as much information as possible on those people that were committing the atrocities, and we're using a screening process. Whenever we find those people that committed atrocities, we separate them out. We treat them no differently than any other prisoner of war, but the ultimate disposition of those people, of course, may be quite different than the way we treat any other prisoner of war.

With regard to the unfortunate incident yesterday, the only report we have is that two A-10 aircraft came in and attacked two British armored scout cars. That's what caused the casualties. There were nine KIA. We deeply regret that. There's no excuse for it. I'm not going to apologize for it. I will say that because of the number of extremely complicated maneuvers being accomplished out here, because of the extreme diversity of our forces, because of the radical differences in language of our forces, and the weather conditions and everything else, I feel that we were lucky that we did not have more of this type of incident. We went to extraordinary lengths to prevent that type of thing from happening. It's a terrible tragedy, and I'm sorry that it happened.

Q: (inaudible)

A: I don't know, I'm sorry. I don't believe so because the information I have is that a forward air controller was involved in directing that, and that would indicate that it was probably during the afternoon. But it was when there was very close combat going on out there.

Q: The United Nations General Assembly was talking about peace. As a military man, you look at your challenge, and you can get some satisfaction out of having achieved it. Is there some fear on your part that there will be a cease-fire that will keep you from fulfilling the assignment that you have? Do you fear that there will be some political pressure brought on the campaign?

A: I think I've made it very clear to everybody that I'd just as soon the war had never started, and I'd never lost a single life out there. That was not our choice. We've accomjplished our mission, and when the decision-makers agree that there should be a cease-fire, nobody will be happier than me.

Q: We were told today that an A-10 returning from a mission discovered and destroyed 16 Scuds. Is that a fact, and where were they located?

A: Most of those Scuds were located in western Iraq. We went into this war with intelligence estimates that I have since come to believe were grossly inaccurate. Either that, or our pilots are lying through their teeth, and I choose to think the former rather than the latter, particularly since many of the pilots have backed up what they've been saying by film and that sort of thing. In any case, last night the pilots had a very successful afternoon and night against the mobile erector launchers. Most of them in western Iraq were reportedly used against Israel.

Q: You've said many times in the past that you do not like body counts. You've also told us tonight that enemy casualties were very large. I'm wondering with the coalition forces already burying the dead on the battlefield, will there ever be any sort of accounting or head counts made?

A: I don't think there's ever been in the history of warfare, a successful count of the dead. That's because it's necessary to lay those people to rest, for a lot of reasons, and that happens. So I would say that no, there will never be an exact count. Probably in the days to come, you're going to hear many, many stories—either overinflated or underinflated, depending upon who you hear them from. The people who will know best, unfortunately, are the families that won't see their loved ones come home.

Q: If the gate is indeed closed, as you said several times, and the theories about where these Kuwaiti hostages are—perhaps Basra, perhaps Baghdad—where could they be? A quick second question: was the timing for the start of the ground campaign a purely military choice, or was it a military choice with political influence on the final choice of dates?

A: When I say the gate is closed, I don't want to give you the impression that absolutely nothing is escaping. Quite the contrary. That doesn't mean that civilian vehicles aren't escaping, that innocent civilians aren't escaping, or unarmed Iraqis—that's not what I'm talking about. I'm talking about the gate that is closed on their war machine.

As for the timing for the beginning of the ground campaign, we made a military analysis of when it should be conducted. I gave my recommendation to the Secretary of Defense and General Colin Powell, they passed that recommendation on to the President, and he acted upon that recommendation. Why, do you think we did it at the wrong time? [Laughter]

Q: I'm wondering if your recommendation and analysis were accepted without change.

A: I'm very thankful for the fact that the President of the United States has allowed the United States military and the coalition military to fight this war exactly as it should have been fought. The President in every case has taken our guidance and our recommendations to heart and has acted superbly as the commander-in-chief to the United States.

Thank you very much.

Reference: Pyle, Richard, *Schwarzkopf: The Man, the Mission, the Triumph* (New York: Signet, 1991).

Address by President Bush to the American People on the End of the War, 27 February 1991

Kuwait is liberated. Iraq's army is defeated. Our military objectives are met. Kuwait is once more in the hands of Kuwaitis in control of their own destiny. We share in their joy, a joy tempered only by our compassion for their ordeal.

Tonight, the Kuwaiti flag once again flies above the capital of a free and sovereign nation, and the American flag flies above our embassy.

Seven months ago, America and the world drew a line in the sand. We declared that the aggression against Kuwait would not stand, and tonight America and the world have kept their word. This is not a time of euphoria, certainly not a time to gloat, but it is a time of pride, pride in our troops, pride in the friends who stood with us in the crisis, pride in our nation and the people whose strength and resolve made victory quick, decisive and just.

And soon we will open wide our arms to welcome back home to America our magnificent fighting forces. No one country can claim this victory as its own. It was not only a victory for Kuwait, but a victory for all the coalition partners. This is a victory for the United Nations, for all mankind, for the rule of law, and for what is right.

After consulting with Secretary of Defense Cheney, the Chairman of the Joint Chiefs of Staff General Powell, and our coalition partners, I am pleased to announce that at midnight tonight, Eastern Standard Time, exactly 100 hours since ground operations commenced and six weeks since the start of Operation Desert Storm, all United States and coalition forces will suspend offensive combat operations.

It is up to Iraq whether this suspension on the part of the coalition becomes a permanent cease-fire. Coalition political and military terms for a formal cease-fire include the following requirements:

Iraq must release immediately all coalition prisoners of war, third country nationals, and the remains of all who have fallen.

Iraq must release all Kuwaiti detainees.

Iraq must also inform Kuwaiti authorities of the location and nature of all land and sea mines.

Iraq must comply fully with all relevant United Nations Security Council resolutions. This includes a rescinding of Iraq's August decision to annex Kuwait and acceptance in principle of Iraq's responsibility to pay compensation for the loss, damage and injury its aggression has caused.

The coalition calls upon the Iraqi government to designate military commanders to meet within 48 hours with their coalition counterparts at a place in the theater of operations to be specified to arrange for military aspects of the cease-fire.

Further, I have asked Secretary of State Baker to request that the United Nations Security Council meet to formulate the necessary arrangements for this war to be ended.

This suspension of offensive combat operations is contingent upon Iraq's not firing upon any coalition forces and not launching Scud missiles against any other country. If Iraq violates these terms, coalition forces will be free to resume military operations.

At every opportunity I have said to the people of Iraq that our quarrel was not with them but instead with the leadership and above all with Saddam Hussein. This remains the case. You, the people of Iraq, are not our enemy. We do not seek your destruction. We have treated your P.O.W.s with kindness.

Coalition forces fought this war only as a last resort and look forward to the day when Iraq is led by people prepared to live in peace with their neighbors.

We must now begin to look beyond victory in war. We must meet the challenge of securing the peace. In the future, as before, we will consult with our coalition partners.

We've already done a good deal of thinking and planning for the post-war period and Secretary Baker has already begun to consult with our coalition partners on the region's challenges. There can be and will be no solely American answer to all these challenges, but we can assist and support the countries of the region and be a catalyst for peace.

In this spirit, Secretary Baker will go to the region next week to begin a new round of consultations. This war is now behind us. Ahead of us is the difficult task of securing the potentially historic peace. Tonight, though, let us be proud of what we have accomplished. Let us give thanks to those who risked their lives. Let us never forget those who gave their lives.

May God bless our valiant military forces and their families and let us all remember them in our prayers.

Good night and may God bless the United States of America.

References: *New York Times,* 28 February 1991, A12; *Washington Post,* 28 February 1991, A27 & A34.

Cease-Fire Order to Iraqi Troops, 28 February 1991

On 28 February 1991, as its troops were in full flight from all points in Kuwait, the Iraqi military broadcast the following order over Baghdad Radio.

The aggressors imagined that through the Iraqi command decision to withdraw from Kuwait they were able to put our armed forces in a position that is contrary to the military and manly values for which the men of the mother of battles are known in this great showdown.

Many battles occurred in Basra district and other places in our great Iraq's territories after the withdrawal.

Due to faith in our capability that is able to teach the enemy forces lessons that will make them worried militarily and politically if the war continued, Bush announced his decision early this morning.

We are happy for the halt in fighting, which will save the blood of our sons and the safety of our people after God made them victorious by faith against their evil enemies and save the blood of the sons of humanity who suffered due to Bush and his traitorous agents.

Therefore, orders were issued to all our units at the battlefront not to open fire. God is great.

Reference: " 'Orders . . . Not To Open Fire,' " *Washington Post,* 1 March 1991, A28.

Iraqi Agreement To Obey United Nations Resolutions, 3 March 1991

On 3 March 1991, Foreign Minister Tariq Aziz of Iraq sent a letter, excerpted here, to the president of the United Nations Security Council and the United Nations Secretary General, declaring Iraq's intention to comply with United Nations resolutions passed by the Security Council since the Iraqi invasion of Kuwait, including Resolution 686, adopted on 2 March 1991 by a vote of 11–1 (Cuba voting no, with China, India, and Yemen abstaining).

Mr. President and Mr. Secretary General,
I have the honor to inform you that the Iraqi

government has taken note of the text of Security Council Resolution 686 (1991) and that it has agreed to fulfill its obligations under the said resolution. We hope that the council, in its turn, will interact in an objective and honorable manner, pursuant to the provisions of international law and the principles of equity and justice, with our faithful and—to the extent that we are able—speedy fulfillment of those obligations.

You and the members of the Security Council are well aware of the manner in which the American forces and their partners in the military operations against Iraq have implemented Security Council Resolution 678 (1990) [which authorized the use of force to drive Iraqi troops from Kuwait], and of the major losses which Iraq has suffered to its infrastructure, economic, civilian, cultural and religious property [and] basic public services . . .

Despite these facts, Resolution 686 (1991) has ignored the Iraqi people's suffering and the imposition on Iraq alone of a long series of obligations . . .

We record these facts for history and for the attention of those members of the Security Council and the international organization—and those elements of international public opinion—who have a conscience. Our agreement to fulfill our obligations under this resolution stems from our determination to refute the pretexts which some may employ in order to persist in their aggression against Iraq and to inflict further harm on its people.

Iraq hopes that the Security Council will ensure the adoption of a resolution proclaiming an official cease-fire and the cessation of all military operations on land, at sea and in the air, as well as the immediate withdrawal of the foreign military forces stationed without any justification in various regions of Iraq.

Iraq also hopes that the Security Council will proceed to declare, with all possible speed, the basis for its adoption of Security Council resolution 661 (1990) [imposing trade sanctions against Iraq], 665 (1990) and 670 (1990) [both of which established a naval blockade of Iraq] as having elapsed, with the result that the resolutions become null and void.

Tariq Aziz, Foreign Minister

Reference: "Iraq 'To Fulfill Its Obligations,'" *Washington Post*, 4 March 1991, A16.

Statements by General Schwarzkopf and Saudi General bin Sultan on the Iraqi Cease-Fire Agreement, 3 March 1991

On 3 March 1991, after the Iraqis agreed to cease-fire terms at Safwan, Iraq, General H. Norman Schwarzkopf and Saudi Lieutenant General Khalid bin Sultan met with reporters and issued a statement. Herewith are those remarks.

SCHWARZKOPF STATEMENT

Let me just say that we have just completed what I think were very frank, very candid and very constructive discussions with the Iraqi military. The purpose of this meeting, as stated previously by the president of the United States, was so that we could agree on certain conditions that were necessary to continue with a cessation of hostilities and the cessation of coalition offensive operations.

I am very happy to tell you that we agreed on all matters. Some of the subjects that were discussed were control measures to insure that units, armed units of the coalition do not come in contact with armed units of the Iraqi military that result in any more deaths.

We have received information on the location of minefields in Kuwait and minefields in international waters so that we can begin operations to make those areas safe.

We have also made it very clear that upon the signing of a cease-fire, but not before, all coalition forces will be drawn back from Iraqi territory that we currently occupy.

The most important point that we discussed was the immediate release of all prisoners of war. We have agreed that this release should be immediate. We have agreed that the details of this release must be worked out by the International Red Cross. But both sides have agreed that we will do everything we can to work with the Red Cross to as rapidly as possible determine locations and times. We have also asked that as a token of good faith on both sides that we have a symbolic release immediately. And I feel sure based upon our discussions that such a symbolic release should take place.

We have provided the Iraqis with the names of all of the missing in action, and we have asked for as much information as we could get concerning those missing in action. We have also asked them to provide us with the names of anyone who may have died while in their, in their custody. And we have also asked for the return of the remains.

I would just say that I think we have made a major step forward in the cause of peace. And I have every expectation that if we continue the open and frank and cooperative dialogue that we had today, and I would say very candidly that the Iraqis came to discuss and to cooperate with a positive attitude, that we are well on our way to a lasting peace.

KHALID BIN SULTAN STATEMENT

I think we should consider today as a memorable, historic day. And I hope that peace will last in the Middle East and the whole world. The attitude today, I concur with General Schwarzkopf that it was excellent. We have all the answers for all our questions. The delegation, the Iraqi delegations were willing to, not only to answer, but to satisfy us in every request we had.

I believe that also we have Saudi border outside the theater of operations also we discussed, and it is secured. And for Kuwait, I would like just to emphasize what General Schwarzkopf said, that we have a good, big number of detainees from Kuwait which I hope it will come very soon.

Reference: "Generals' Statements: Statements by U.S. and Saudi Commanders," *New York Times,* 4 March 1991, A8.

Address by President Bush to Joint Session of Congress, 6 March 1991

On the night of 6 March 1991, President George Bush delivered an address before a joint session of Congress in which he discussed the conclusion of the Persian Gulf War.

Speaker of the House Foley: Mr. President, it is customary at joint sessions for the chair to present the president to the members of Congress directly and without further comment. But I wish to depart from tradition tonight and express to you on behalf of the Congress and the country and through you to the members of our armed forces our warmest congratulations on the brilliant victory of the Desert Storm operation.

Members of Congress, I now have the high privilege and distinct honor of presenting to you the President of the United States.

President George Bush: Mr. President, Mr. Speaker, Members of Congress: Five short weeks ago, I came to this House to speak to you about the State of the Union. We met then in a time of war. Tonight, we meet in a world blessed by the promise of peace.

From the moment Operation Desert Storm commenced on January 16, until the time the guns fell silent at midnight one week ago, this nation has watched its sons and daughters with pride—watched over them with prayer. As Commander-in-Chief, I can report to you: Our Armed Forces fought with honor and valor. As President, I can report to the Nation: Aggression is defeated. The war is over.

This is a victory for every country in the coalition, and for the United Nations. A victory for unprecedented international cooperation and diplomacy, so well led by our Secretary of State James Baker. It is a victory for the rule of law and for what is right.

Desert Storm's success belongs to the team that so ably leads our Armed Forces: our Secretary of Defense and our Chairman of the Joint Chiefs, Dick Cheney and Colin Powell.

And of course, this military victory also belongs to the one the British call the "Man of the Match": the tower of calm at the eye of Desert Storm, General Norman Schwarzkopf.

And let us not forget Saudi General Khalid, or Britain's General de la Billière, or General Roquejoffre of France, and all the others whose leadership played such a vital role. And most importantly, all those who served in the field.

I thank the members of this Congress; support here for our troops in battle was overwhelming. And above all, I thank those whose unfailing love and support sustained our courageous men and women: I thank the American people.

Tonight, I come to this House to speak about the world—the world after war.

The recent challenge could not have been clearer. Saddam Hussein was the villain; Kuwait the victim. To the aid of this small country came nations from North America and Europe, from Asia and South America, from Africa and the Arab world—all united against aggression.

Our uncommon coalition must now work in common purpose to forge a future that should never again be held hostage to the darker side of human nature.

Tonight in Iraq, Saddam walks amidst ruin. His war machine is crushed. His ability to threaten mass destruction is itself destroyed. His people have been lied to—denied the truth. And when his defeated legions come home, all Iraqis will see and feel the havoc he has wrought. And this I promise you: For all that Saddam has done to his own people, to the Kuwaitis, and to the entire world, Saddam and those around him are accountable.

All of us grieve for the victims of war, for the people of Kuwait and the suffering that scars the soul of that proud nation. We grieve for all our fallen soldiers and their families, for all the innocents caught up in this conflict. And yes, we grieve for the people of Iraq, a people who have never been our enemy. My hope is that one day we will once again welcome them as friends into the community of nations.

Our commitment to peace in the Middle East does not end with the liberation of Kuwait. So tonight, let me outline four key challenges to be met:

First, we must work together to create shared security arrangements in the region. Our friends and allies in the Middle East recognize that they will bear the bulk of the responsibility for regional security. But we want them to know that just as we stood with them to repel aggression, so now America stands ready to work with them to secure the peace.

This does not mean stationing U.S. ground forces on the Arabian peninsula, but it does mean American participation in joint exercises involving both air and ground forces. And it means maintaining a capable U.S. naval presence in the region, just as we have for over 40 years. Let it be clear: our vital national interests depend on a stable and secure Gulf.

Second, we must act to control the proliferation of weapons of mass destruction and the missiles used to deliver them. It would be tragic if the nations of the Middle East and Persian Gulf were now, in the wake of war, to embark on a new arms race. Iraq requires special vigilance. Until Iraq convinces the world of its peaceful intentions—that its leaders will not use new revenues to rearm and rebuild its menacing war machine—Iraq must not have access to the instruments of war.

Third, we must work to create new opportunities for peace and stability in the Middle East. On the night I announced Operation Desert Storm, I expressed my hope that out of the horrors of war might come new momentum for peace. We have learned in the modern age—geography cannot guarantee security and security does not come from military power alone.

All of us know the depth of bitterness that has made the dispute between Israel and its neighbors so painful and intractable. Yet, in the conflict just concluded, Israel and many of the Arab states for the first time found themselves confronting the same aggressor. By now, it should be plain to all parties that peacemaking in the Middle East requires compromise. At the same time, peace brings real benefits to everyone. We must do all that we can to close the gap between Israel and the Arab states, and between Israelis and Palestinians. The tactics of terror lead nowhere—there can be no substitute for diplomacy.

A comprehensive peace must be grounded in United Nations Security Council resolutions 242 and 338 and the principle of territory for peace. The principle must be elaborated to provide for Israel's security and recognition, and at the same time for legitimate Palestinian political rights. Anything else would fail the twin tests of fairness and security. The time has come to put an end to the Arab-Israeli conflict.

The war with Iraq is over. The quest for solutions to the problems in Lebanon, in the Arab-Israeli dispute, and in the Gulf must go forward with new vigor and determination. I guarantee you: No one will work harder for a stable peace in the region than we will.

Fourth, we must foster economic development for the sake of peace and progress. The Persian Gulf and Middle East form a region rich in natural resources with a wealth of untapped human potential. Resources once squandered on military might must be redirected to more peaceful ends. We are already addressing the immediate economic consequences of Iraq's aggression. Now, the challenge is to reach higher—to foster economic freedom and prosperity for all people of the region.

By meeting these four challenges we can build a framework for peace. I have asked Secretary of State Baker to go to the Middle East to begin this process. He will go to listen, to probe, to offer suggestions, and to advance the search for peace and stability. I have also asked him to raise the plight of the hostages held in Lebanon. We have not forgotten them. We will not forget them.

To all the challenges that confront this region of the world, there is no single solution, no solely American answer. But we can make a difference. America will work tirelessly as a catalyst for positive change.

But we cannot lead a new world abroad if, at home, it's politics as usual on American defense and diplomacy. It's time to turn away from the temptation to protect unneeded weapons systems and obsolete bases. It's time to put an end to micro-management of foreign and security assistance programs, micro-management that humiliates our friends and allies and hamstrings our diplomacy. It's time to rise above the parochial and the pork barrel, to do what is necessary, what's right, and what will enable this nation to play the leadership role required of us.

The consequences of the conflict in the Gulf reach far beyond the confines of the Middle East. Twice before in this century, an entire world was convulsed by war. Twice this century, out of horrors of war hope emerged for enduring peace. Twice before, those hopes proved to be a distant dream, beyond the grasp of man.

Until now, the world we've known has been a world divided, a world of barbed wire and concrete block, conflict and Cold War.

Now, we can see a new world coming into view. A world in which there is the very real prospect of a new world order. In the words of Winston Churchill, a "world order" in which "the principles of justice and fair play . . . protect the weak against the strong.<193." A world where the United Nations, freed from Cold War stalemate, is poised to fulfill the historic vision of its founders. A world in which freedom and respect for human rights find a home among all nations.

The Gulf War put this new world to its first test. And my fellow Americans: We passed the test.

For the sake of our principles, for the sake of the Kuwaiti people, we stood our ground. Because the world would not look the other way, Ambassador Al-Sabah, tonight Kuwait is free.

Tonight, as our troops begin to come home, let us recognize that the hard work of freedom still calls us forward. We've learned the hard lessons of history. The victory over Iraq was not waged as "a war to end all wars." Even the new world order cannot guarantee an era of perpetual peace. But enduring peace must be our mission.

Our success in the Gulf will shape not only the new world order we seek but our mission here at home.

In the war just ended, there were clear-cut objectives, timetables and, above all, an overriding imperative to achieve results. We must bring that same sense of self-discipline, that same sense of urgency, to the way we meet challenges here at home.

In my State of the Union address and in my budget, I defined a comprehensive agenda to prepare for the next American century.

Our first priority is to get this economy rolling again. The fear and uncertainty caused by the crisis in the Gulf were understandable. But now that the war is over, oil prices are down, interest rates are down, and confidence is rightly coming back. Americans can move forward to lend, spend and invest in this, the strongest economy on Earth.

We must also enact the legislation that is key to building a better America. For example: In 1990, we enacted an historic Clear Air Act. Now we've proposed a National Energy Strategy. We passed a Child Care bill that put power in the hands of parents. Today, we're ready to do the same thing with our schools, and expand choice in education. We passed a Crime bill that made a useful start in fighting crime and drugs. This year we're sending to Congress our comprehensive crime package to finish the job. We passed the landmark Americans With Disabilities Act. Now we've sent forward our Civil Rights bill. We also passed the Aviation bill. This year we've sent up our new Highway bill. And these are just a few of our pending proposals for reform and renewal.

Tonight, I call on Congress to move forward aggressively on our domestic front. Let's begin with two initiatives we should be able to agree on quickly: transportation and crime. And then let's build on success with those and enact the rest of our agenda. If our forces could win a ground war in 100 hours, then surely the Congress can pass this legislation in 100 days. Let that be a promise we make tonight to the American people.

When I spoke in this House about the state of our Union, I asked all of you: If we can selflessly confront evil for the sake of good in a land so far away, then surely we can make this land all that it should be. In the time since then, the brave men and women of Desert Storm accomplished more than even they may realize. They set out to confront an enemy abroad, and in the process they transformed a nation at home.

Think of the way they went about their mission: with confidence and quiet pride. Think about their sense of duty, about all they taught us, about our values, about ourselves.

We hear so often about young people in turmoil; how our children fall short; how our schools fail us; how American products and American workers are second class. Well, don't you believe it. The America we saw in Desert Storm was first class talent.

And they did it using America's state-of-the-art technology. We saw the excellence embodied in the Patriot missile and the patriots who made it work.

And we saw soldiers who know about honor and bravery and duty and country and the world-shaking power of their simple words.

There is something noble and majestic about the pride, about the patriotism we feel tonight.

So, to everyone here, and everyone watching at home, think about the men and women of Desert Storm. Let us honor them with our gratitude. Let us comfort the families of the fallen and remember each precious life lost.

Let us learn from them as well. Let us honor those who have served us by serving others.

Let us honor them as individuals—men and women of every race, all creeds and colors—by setting the face of this Nation against discrimination, bigotry and hate.

I'm sure many of you saw on television the unforgettable scene of four terrified Iraqi soldiers surrendering. They emerged from their bunker, broken, tears streaming from their eyes, fearing the worst. And then there was the American soldier. Remember what he said? He said: "It's okay. You're all right now. You're all right now."

That scene says a lot about America, a lot about who we are. Americans are a caring people. We are a good people, a generous people. Let us always be caring and good and generous in all we do.

Soon, our troops will begin the march we've all been waiting for—their march home. I have directed Secretary [of Defense] Cheney to begin the immediate return of American combat units from the Gulf.

Less than two hours from now, the first planeload of American soldiers will lift off from Saudi Arabia headed for the U.S.A. It will carry men and women of the 24th Mechanized Infantry Division bound for Fort Stewart, Georgia. This is just the beginning of a steady flow of American troops coming home.

Let their return remind us that all those who have gone before are linked with us in the long line of freedom's march. Americans have always tried to serve, to sacrifice nobly for what we believe is right.

Tonight, I ask every community in this country to make this coming 4th of July a day of special celebration for our returning troops. They may have missed Thanksgiving and Christmas, but I can tell you this: For them and for their families, we can make this a holiday they'll never forget.

In a very real sense, this victory belongs to them—to the privates and the pilots, to the sergeants and the supply officers, to the men and women in the machines, and the men and women who make them work. It belongs to the regulars, to the reserves, to the Guard. This victory belongs to the finest fighting force this nation has ever known.

We went halfway around the world to do what is moral and just and right. We fought hard, and—with others—we won the war. We lifted the yoke of aggression and tyranny from a small country that many Americans had never even heard of, and we ask nothing in return.

We're coming home now, proud, confident, heads high. There is much that we must do at home and abroad. And we will do it. We are Americans.

May God bless this great nation—the United States of America.

Reference: The Persian Gulf Crisis: Relevant Documents, Correspondence, Reports (Washington, DC: Government Printing Office, 1991), 253–258.

Executive Order 12754 of 12 March 1991

This presidential dictate, issued by President George Bush, established the Southwest Asia Service Medal for service during Operation Desert Storm.

By the authority vested in me as President by the Constitution and the laws of the United States of America, including my authority as Commander in Chief of the Armed Forces of the United States, it is hereby ordered as follows:

Section 1. There is established, with suitable appurtenances, the Southwest Asia Service Medal. It may be awarded to members of the Armed Forces of the United States who participated in military operations in Southwest Asia or in the surrounding contiguous waters or in air space on or after August 2, 1990, and before a terminal date to be prescribed by the Secretary of Defense.

Section 2. The Southwest Asia Service Medal may be awarded posthumously to any person covered by, and under the circumstances described in, section 1 of this order.

Section 3. The Secretaries of the Military Departments, with the approval of the Secretary of Defense, and the Secretary of Transportation with respect to the Coast Guard when it is not operating as a service in the Navy, are directed to prescribe uniform regulations governing the award and wearing of the Southwest Asia Service Medal.

Saddam Hussein's Address to the Iraqi People on the Insurrection, 16 March 1991

On 16 March 1991, Saddam Hussein addressed the Iraqi people on the Shi'ite unrest in the south and the Kurdish upheaval in the north. The address, of which excerpts appear here, was carried live on CNN in the United States and was transcribed by the New York Times.

The painful events which took place in the country recently have prevented me from speaking to you at the time immediately after the height of the aggression and while the country from the extreme north to the extreme south and from the extreme east to the extreme west, while it was subjected to aggression by 30 states, and while our cities and villages were bleeding as a result of the brutal aggression which was targeted against the whole of Iraq and its sons and was targeted against the lives and properties of all Iraqis and what

they had built over decades with sweat, effort and creativity.

At this time, in particular, there were infiltrators from outside who were hordes of hateful traitors, people who had forged Iraqi IDs to sow devastation in a number of Iraqi cities and villages in the south, supported by rioters who were misled in the Basra, Amara, and Nasirya, Karbala, Najaf, and Hilla. These traitors launched attacks against some of the isolated units and military barracks retreating under fire of the aggression. They seized weapons and equipment and set the people's properties on fire. They plundered the premises of the state, schools, and hospitals, home of the citizens, and violated honor. They even burned civil records and records of the property register, records of marriage and inheritance in state departments.

Through dastardly, treacherous methods, they resorted to killing some officials in the state and the party, some officers and some citizens in those cities.

With God's aid, we have crushed the sedition in the cities of the south. And with the aid of those loyal, of good will, in all parts of Iraq, we are able to uproot the remnants of destruction and treason. . . . However, this honorable, patriotic approach must not discourage us from analyzing the negative phenomena, identifying their sources and their positions, and delving into the reasons behind them, and tracking the roots of bad education and orientation. O, glorious Iraqis everywhere on the beloved land of Iraq, all of us in Iraq feel that we are entering a new phase in our national life. It is a difficult phase, which will include a lot of bitterness, and will involve great sacrifices and serious losses.

Dear brothers, while we embark on construction, this new phase must be based on new bases in our national political life. As in the other aspects of our life, we had been preparing since 1979 to enter a new political phase. But the circumstances of foreign aggression against our country in 1980, which lasted for a very long period, prevented us from embarking on seeking and acting to establish the new political frameworks needed by the phase and the requirements of progress.

Once that aggression was over, we immediately began to reconstruct and began to restore the bases of peace while we were preoccupied with great national and pan-Arab concerns. And according with their priorities, we in the leadership discussed what we should do in this regard. In 1990, we had planned for a new phase in our political life, a phase which will witness the establishment of new institutions and new formulae for national action, based essentially on the principle of political pluralism, and in a clear framework of national unity and national responsibility, we declared a draft for a new constitution for the country, predicated on this basis and open for discussion.

It was intended that we were to start last fall to resume the discussion of the constitution in the state orders and to organize a referendum thereon, and to start building the institutions flowing from it. However, these events of August and thereafter prevented these actions.

Our decision as a leadership to build a democratic society based on the constitution and the rule of law and on institution and political pluralism now has been our determination before in the year 1990 is a decisive, irrevocable decision.

The first step that we will take on the path to build this new phase is the appointment of a new ministry that takes upon itself as a priority task the task of reconstruction and the provision of basic services to the citizens and to cooperate in its discharge of duties with the leadership and to resume the discussion of the draft constitution and to organize a referendum thereon, and the building of institutions flowing therefrom.

Reference: "Excerpts from the Address by Hussein on Iraq's Unrest," *New York Times,* 17 March 1991, A17.

United Nations Report on Humanitarian Assistance to Iraq, 22 March 1991

On 22 March 1991, the United Nations Security Council responded to a report from Under Secretary Martii Ahtisaari, in which he called for the elimination of all restrictions of food and other humanitarian assistance placed on Iraq by the Security Council, by voting to ease the sanctions, allowing for the shipment of such goods as fuel for generators, agricultural machinery, and equipment for the reconstruction of water purification and sewage treatment facilities destroyed in the Gulf War. Herewith are excerpts of Under Secretary Ahtisaari's report.

Nothing that we had seen or read had quite prepared us for the particular form of devastation which has now befallen the country. The recent conflict has wrought near-apocalyptic results upon the infrastructure of what had been, until January 1991, a rather highly urbanized and mechanized society. Now, most means of modern life support have been destroyed or rendered tenuous. Iraq has, for some time to come, been relegated to a pre-industrial age, but with all the disabilities of post-industrial dependency on an intensive use of energy and technology.

There is much less than the minimum fuel required to provide the energy needed for movement or transportation, irrigation or generators for power to pump water and sewage. For instance, emergency medical supplies can be moved to health centers only with extreme difficulty and, usually, major delay. Information regarding local needs is slow and sparse.

Most employees are simply unable to come to work. Both the authorities and the trade unions estimate that approximately 90 per cent of industrial workers have been reduced to inactivity and will deprived of income

as of the end of March. Government departments have at present only marginal attendance.

Food is currently made available to the population both through Government allocations and rations, and through the market. The Ministry of Trade's monthly allocation to the population of staple food items fell from 343,000 tons . . . to 182,000 tons when rationing was introduced [in September 1990], and was further reduced to 135,000 tons in January 1991 (39 percent of the pre-sanctions level).

While the mission was unable to gauge the precise quantities still held in Government warehouses, all evidence indicates that flour is now at a critically low level, and that supplies of sugar, rice, tea, vegetable oil, powdered milk and pulses [legumes] are currently at critically low levels or have been exhausted. Distribution of powdered milk, for instance, is now reserved exclusively for sick children on medical prescription.

Livestock farming has been seriously affected by sanctions because many feed products were imported. The sole laboratory producing veterinary vaccines was destroyed during the conflict, as inspected by the mission. The authorities are no longer able to support livestock farmers in the combat of disease, as all stocks of vaccines were stated to have been destroyed in the same sequence of bombardment on the center, which was an F.A.O. regional project.

The country has had a particular dependence upon foreign vegetable seeds, and the mission was able to inspect destroyed seed warehouses. The relevant agricultural authorities informed the mission that all stocks of potatoes and vegetable seeds had been exhausted. Next season's planting will be jeopardized if seeds are not provided by October 1991.

This year's grain harvest in June is seriously compromised for a number of reasons, including failure of irrigation/drainage (no power for pumps, lack of spare parts); lack of pesticides and fertilizers (previously imported), and lack of fuel and spare parts for the highly mechanized and fuel-dependent harvesting machines. Should this harvest fail, or be far below average, as is very likely barring a rapid change in the situation, widespread starvation conditions become a real possibility.

The mission recommends that, in these circumstances of present severe hardship and in view of the bleak prognosis, sanctions in respect of food supplies should be immediately removed, as should those relating to the import of agricultural equipment and supplies. The urgent supply of basic commodities to safeguard vulnerable groups is strongly recommended.

With the destruction of power plants, oil refineries, main oil facilities and water related chemical plants, all electrically operated installations have ceased to function. Diesel-operated generators were reduced to operating on a minimum basis, their functioning affected by lack of fuel, lack of maintenance, lack of spare parts and nonattendance of workers.

The supply of water in Baghdad dropped to less than 10 liters per day but has now recovered to approximately 3040 liters in about 70 percent of the area (less than 10 percent of the overall previous use).

As regards sanitation, the two main concerns relate to garbage disposal and sewage treatment. In both cases, rapidly rising temperatures will soon accentuate an existing crisis. Heaps of garbage are spread in urban areas and collection is poor to nonexistent. The collection is hampered by lack of fuel, lack of maintenance and spare parts and lack of labor, because workers are unable to come to work. Incinerators are in general not working, for these same reasons, and for lack of electric power. Insecticides, much needed as the weather becomes more torrid, are virtually out of stock because of sanctions and a lack of chemical supplies . . .

Iraqi rivers are heavily polluted with raw sewage, and water levels are unusually low. All sewage treatment and pumping plants have been brought to a virtual standstill by the lack of power supply and the lack of spare parts. Pools of sewage lie in the streets and villages. Health hazards will build in weeks to come.

As regards the displaced and the homeless, the authorities themselves have not yet been able fully to assess the impact of the recent hostilities. They have, however, calculated that approximately 9,000 homes were destroyed or damaged beyond repair during the hostilities, of which 2,500 were in Baghdad and 1,900 were in Basra. This has created a new homeless potential of 72,000 persons.

Official help is now hampered by the conditions described throughout this report and, especially, a virtual halt in the production of local building materials and the impossibility to import. The input of essential materials should be permitted.

It will be difficult, if not impossible, to remedy these immediate humanitarian needs without dealing with the underlying need for energy on an equally urgent basis. The need for energy means, initially, emergency oil imports and the rapid patching up of a limited refining and electricity production capability, with essential supplies from other countries. Otherwise, food that is imported cannot be preserved and distributed, water cannot be purified, sewage cannot be pumped away and cleansed, crops cannot be irrigated, medicines cannot be conveyed where they are required, needs cannot be effectively assessed. It is unmistakable that the Iraqi people may soon face a further imminent catastrophe, which could include epidemic and famine, if massive life-supporting needs are not rapidly met. The long summer, with its often 45 or even 50 degree temperatures (113 to 122 degrees Fahrenheit), is only weeks away. Time is short.

Reference: "Excerpts from U.N. Report on Need for Humanitarian Assistance in Iraq," *New York Times,* 23 March 1991, A5.

David Frost Interview with General Schwarzkopf, 27 March 1991

On 27 March 1991, General H. Norman Schwarzkopf was interviewed by David Frost on the program Talking with David Frost *in which the general questioned whether the United States had ended the ground war against Iraqi forces in Kuwait and Iraq too early, touching off a heated controversy that lasted for several days. Herewith are excerpts from that interview.*

Frost: How were you consulted about the cease-fire? I mean, how did it happen?
Schwarzkopf: . . . After the third day, as I say, we knew we had them [the Iraqis]. I mean we had closed the back door. The bridges across the Tigris and Euphrates were out. We had cut Highway 8 that ran up the Tigris and Euphrates valley on this side of the river. There was no way out for the, I mean, they could go through Basra. There were a few bridges going across Al Fao [the Al Fao peninsula], to the Al Fao. But there was nothing else and it was literally about to become the battle of Cannae, a battle of annihilation . . .

I reported that situation to General [Colin] Powell. And he and I discussed, have we accomplished our military objectives? And the answer was yes. . . . The enemy was being kicked out of Kuwait, was going to be gone from Kuwait. We had destroyed the Republican Guard as a militarily effective force.
Frost: Had you totally destroyed it? I mean in the sense Egypt and Syria wanted to carry on and destroy it a bit more, didn't they?
Schwarzkopf: Well, yeah. I mean, it is a question of how do you define the word destroy. The Republican Guard was a militarily ineffective force. And we had inflicted great damage upon them and they had been routed. Now, I obviously—you know we didn't destroy them to the very last tank. And again, this is a point that I think may be lost on a lot of people. That was a very courageous decision on the part of the President to also stop the offensive. You know, we didn't declare a cease-fire. What we did is, we suspended military operations. Frankly, my recommendations had been, you know, continue the march. I mean we had them in a rout and we could have continued to, you know, reap great destruction upon them. We could have completely closed the door and made it in fact a battle of annihilation. And the President, you know, made the decision that, you know, we should stop at a given time, at a given place that did leave some escape routes open for them to get back out and I think it was a very humane decision and a very courageous decision on his part also. Because it's, you

know, it's one of those ones that historians are going to second guess, you know, forever . . .

Frost: A very courageous decision, and a very real debate, really, that between, on the one hand, completely dispensing with the Republican Guard so it could never be used again, as you were recommending, another 24 hours, versus the humanitarian decision . . .

Schwarzkopf: I, I don't think you should put it in the context of [the] Republican Guard because they, remember, were the ones who were mostly to the rear and a lot of them had bugged out already. I mean, they had long since, ah, I think once they discovered that their flank, ah, up Route 8 was blocked and they weren't gonna, I think some of them had long since escaped. Matter of fact, they were north of the river and we probably, [in] another 24 hours, we could have inflicted terrible damage on them with air attacks and that sort of thing on the far side of the river. But nowhere near the devastation we were inflicting upon . . . the troops on this side of the river.

Reference: "Excerpts from the Schwarzkopf Interview," *New York Times*, 28 March 1991, A18.

Executive Order 12771 of 25 July 1991

This executive decree was issued by President George Bush to revoke all previous executive orders with respect to Kuwait.

By the authority vested in me as President by the Constitution and the laws of the United States of America, including the International Emergency Economic Powers Act (50 U.S.C. 1701 et seq.), the National Emergencies Act (50 U.S.C. 1601 et seq.), section 301 of title 3 of the United States Code, and the United Nations Participation Act (22 U.S.C. 287c),

I, George Bush, President of the United States of America, find that the expulsion from Kuwait of Iraq's occupation forces, the restoration of Kuwait to its citizens, and the reinstatement of the lawful Government of Kuwait eliminate the need for Executive Order No. 12723 of August 2, 1990, entitled "Blocking Kuwaiti Government Property," and Executive Order No. 12725 of August 9, 1990, entitled "Blocking Kuwaiti Government Property and Prohibiting Transactions with Kuwait." These orders were issued to protect the assets of the Government of Kuwait which were subject to United States jurisdiction, and to prevent the transfer of benefits by United States persons to Iraq based upon its invasion of Kuwait. Those orders also implemented the foreign policy and protected the national security of the United States, in conformity with applicable resolutions of the United Nations Security Council. Finding continuation of these orders unnecessary, I hereby order:

Section 1. Executive Order No. 12723 and Executive Order No. 12725 are hereby revoked. This revocation shall not affect the national emergency declared in Executive Order No. 12722 to deal with the unusual and extraordinary threat to the national security and foreign policy of the United States posed by the policies and action of the Government of Iraq.

Section 2. This revocation shall not affect:

(a) any action taken or proceeding pending and not finally concluded or determined on the effective date of this order;

(b) any action or proceeding based on any act committed prior to the effective date of this order; or

(c) any rights or duties that matured or penalties that were incurred prior to the effective date of this order.

Section 3. This order shall take effect immediately.

Iraqi Letter to the United Nations, 25 September 1991, and the Security Council's Official Reply

On 24 September 1991, Iraq detained 44 nuclear inspectors sent by the United Nations to Baghdad and prohibited them from taking copies of nuclear-related documentation that they had discovered, triggering an international crisis. The following letter was delivered to the Security Council president, Jean-Bernard Mérimée, by Iraq's ambassador to the United Nations, Abdul Amir al-Anbari, on 25 September 1991; the same day, Ambassador Mérimée delivered the Security Council's approved response.

Mr. President,

On instructions from my Government, I have the honor to inform you as follows:

1. With a view to solving the problem [of the detainment of the inspectors] satisfactorily and avoiding any difficulties, Iraq wishes Mr. Rolf Ekeus to go to Baghdad so that we may discuss with him ways of remedying the current situation and so that the modalities for the use of German helicopters may be considered.

2. Should Mr. Ekeus not go to Baghdad within 48 hours, the Iraqi authorities insist that the Iraqi side and the inspection team jointly draw up a record of all the documents and photographs taken by the team before the team is authorized to remove anything whatsoever from the site.

3. The Iraqi authorities do not and will not acknowledge any document or photograph that has not been entered in the record jointly drawn up by the two parties. Any allegation based on documents or photographs that have not been entered in the joint record will be indicative of a premeditated intention to prejudice Iraq's interests.

Iraq once again strongly protests at the inspection team's actions, particularly those of the leader of the team, Mr. David Kay. Moreover, we reiterate what we have already indicated to Mr. Rolf Ekeus, namely, that

the main source of the difficulties being encountered is the fact that inspection missions are entrusted to a large number of United States nationals. These United States nationals simply implement the policies of their Government, which persists in violating both the letter and the spirit of the resolutions of the Security Council and imposes its hostile policies on the Iraqi leadership.
Thank you,
Abdul Amir al-Anbari,
Iraqi Ambassador to the United Nations

Mr. Abdul Amir al-Anbari,
In reply to your letter dated 25 September 1991, I have the honor to inform you on behalf of the Security Council of the following:

1. The Council deplores Iraq's repeated violations of its obligations under resolutions 687 and 707 and reiterates its demand that the inspectors of the Special Commission and the International Atomic Energy Agency be released immediately with all the material they hold. The Council has no objection to the immediate establishment in this particular case of a joint inventory, in the presence of Iraqi officials, enabling the inspection team to fulfill the responsibility entrusted to it by the Security Council.

2. Mr. Ekeus has already contacted your mission on the modalities and scheduling of the next inspection missions, which will use helicopters of the Special Commission.

3. The Council reaffirms its strong support for the items of the Special Commission and the International Atomic Energy Agency, whose members are highly conscious of their responsibilities as international civil servants and are performing difficult tasks with the full authority of the Security Council in accordance with the Charter of the United Nations.
Thank you,
Jean-Bernard Mérimée,
President, United Nations Security Council
Reference: New York Times, 27 September 1991, A8.

Executive Order 12776 of 8 October 1991

President George Bush signed this directive to extend the National Defense Service Medal to members of the Reserve components of the armed forces who served during the Persian Gulf crisis.

By the authority vested in me as President by the Constitution and the laws of the United States of America, and as Commander in Chief of the Armed Forces of the United States, it is hereby ordered as follows:

Section 1. Under such regulations as the Secretaries of the Army, Navy, and Air Force, or the Secretary of Transportation with regard to the Coast Guard when it is not operating as a service in the Navy, may severally

prescribe, and subject to the provisions of this order, the National Defense Service Medal, as established by Executive Order 10448, as amended, may be awarded to members of the Reserve Components of the Armed Forces of the United States, as dilineated by section 261 of title 10 of the United States Code.

Section 2. The National Defense Service Medal, as authorized in the first section of this order, may be awarded to an individual who was a member in good standing of a Reserve Component of the Armed Forces of the United States during a period designated by the Secretary of Defense as the period of the Persian Gulf crisis for the purposes of this order.

Section 3. The National Defense Service Medal may be awarded posthumously to a member of the Reserve Component of the Armed Forces of the United States who satisfies the requirements for such award under this order and under regulations promulgated pursuant to section 1 of this order.

Executive Order 12790 of 3 March 1992

Signed on 3 March 1992 by President George Bush, this dictate amended the order that established the Southwest Asia Service Medal on 12 March 1991.

By the authority vested in me as President by the Constitution and the laws of the United States of America, and as Commander in Chief of the Armed Forces of the United States, it is hereby ordered that Executive Order No. 12754 of March 12, 1991, be amended as follows:

Section 1. Section 1 is amended by deleting the second sentence "Armed Forces" and by inserting in lieu thereof "Uniformed Services."

Sec. 2. Section 3 is amended to read: "The Secretaries of the Military Departments, with the approval of the Secretary of Defense; the Secretary of Transportation, with respect to the Coast Guard when it is not operating as a service in the Navy; the Secretary of Commerce, with respect to the National Oceanic and Atmospheric Administration; and the Secretary of Health and Human Services, with respect to the Public Health Service, are directed to prescribe uniform regulations governing the award and the wearing of the Southwest Asia Service Medal."

Speech and Report of Senator Shelby on the Persian Gulf War Syndrome, 17 March 1994

On 17 March 1994, Senator Richard Shelby of Alabama, then a Democrat and later a Republican, took to the Senate floor and spoke on his inquiry into the link between possible uses of chemical and biological weapons during the Persian Gulf War and so-called Persian Gulf War Syndrome, a number of unexplained illnesses that have struck Persian Gulf War veterans and their families. Herewith are Senator

Shelby's remarks as they appeared in the Congressional Record.

Mr. President, I am here today to issue a report following my investigation into the possible presence of chemical and biological weapons agents in the theater of operations during the Persian Gulf War. Additionally, I will discuss the possible connection between service in the Persian Gulf and the unexplained illness affecting thousands of veterans and their families.

When Iraqi forces, at the direction of Saddam Hussein, crossed into Kuwait on August 2, 1990, they set off a chain reaction of events that resulted in the assembling of the largest coalition of forces since the Second World War. Countries that had been on opposite sides of the cold war were now joined with the expressed goal of driving Saddam Hussein's troops out of Kuwait.

The United States led this effort with over 600,000 members of our armed services, including over 200,000 reservists.

At the time of the Iraqi invasion, there was a strong belief among the coalition forces that chemical and even biological agents would be used as weapons by Iraq.

Within a year after the highly successful Desert Storm operation, reports surfaced of a mystery illness affecting many veterans, primarily members of the National Guard and Reserve, who served in Saudi Arabia.

This group is experiencing symptoms commonplace to many known illnesses. However, in the case of the Gulf War veterans, we have not been able to diagnose the causes of the illnesses and the illnesses themselves have not responded to any known treatments.

I have seen firsthand the devastating, frustrating, and debilitating effects that this illness has had on many of these veterans. Citizens who were once healthy and able-bodied can no longer hold jobs or participate as active members of society.

Little progress has been made even though Congress mandated the establishment of a Desert Shield-Desert Storm registry, and treatment centers were created for the Gulf War syndrome. Veterans, increasingly frustrated by the inability of the Department of Veterans Affairs to treat their illness, began to seek treatment outside of the Department of Defense and Department of Veterans Affairs medical community.

My involvement in this issue has spanned two years.

Early on, I met with a group of veterans after a town meeting that I held and pledged that I would do everything in my power to get them proper treatment and to find the causes of their ailments.

The anxiety and fear experienced by our ill veterans was intensified throughout this period by constant reports in foreign and domestic media about the presence of chemical weapons agents during the Gulf War.

I cannot imagine a greater fear than that experienced by someone who suffers from a mysterious illness and believes it may have been caused by exposure to chemical weapons.

As chairman of the Subcommittee of Force Requirements and Personnel of the Senate Armed Forces Committee, I heard from afflicted veterans and saw firsthand the symptoms of these ailments.

Following this hearing, Dr. Charles Jackson of the Tuskegee Alabama Veterans Center diagnosed a patient as suffering from Gulf War Syndrome and chemical-biological warfare exposure. In response to this announcement and pressure from Congress, the Department of Veteran Affairs established a pilot program to test Persian Gulf veterans for possible exposure to chemical weapons agents.

As a result of these events, Senator Sam Nunn, chairman of the Committee on Armed Services, sent me, along with people on our staff and the people from the DOD, to Europe and then to the Middle East to investigate the possible presence of chemical and biological weapon agents during Operation Desert Storm, as well as the possible connection between service in the Persian Gulf and the unexplained illness affecting thousands of veterans.

Mr. President, I went to Europe to determine the validity of the two then-reported detections of chemical warfare agents by Czech soldiers. Instead, there were not only two, but five separate detections of chemical weapons agents in the Persian Gulf.

No one with whom I spoke could provide a solution to the mysterious illness; however, they could not rule out a possible link between the presence of chemical agents and the Gulf War Syndrome. Only the U.S. Department of Defense and the British government have denied that chemical agents could have caused the illness.

In light of my involvement, I have come to five major conclusions which I would like to share with you today.

First, I have no doubt that chemical agents, accurately verified by the Czech chemical detection units, were present in the theater of operations during the Persian Gulf War.

Both Czech and French forces detected and verified the presence of nerve and mustard gases at low levels during Desert Storm.

Second, we may never be able to determine the origin of these chemical agents. While I believe that we can rule out Iraqi Scud or Frog missiles, and Iraqi artillery, there still exist several possibilities. For example, the low-level chemical presence could have resulted from United States or coalition forces bombing Iraqi chemical weapons facilities or caches of Iraqi weapons on the Saudi border.

It is also feasible that a cloud of nerve agent, dissipating in intensity, could have travelled under the correct climate conditions. There is also the possibility of a training accident involving chemical agents among coalition forces. Finally, it is possible that the detections were the result of Saudi officials attempting to test the abilities of the Czechs whom they had engaged to assist in chemical detections.

Third, although a direct connection between the existence of low levels of chemical agents in the theater of operations and the Persian Gulf Syndrome cannot be established at this time, such a connection cannot and should not be discounted. Little information is available on exposure to low levels of chemical agents, but I believe that the work being done at Walter Reed Army Medical Center is on the right track in this area. We must give it our full support.

Fourth, the Department of Defense has proven reluctant to pursue or, in certain instances, to provide the information necessary to prove or disprove allegations about the presence of chemical agents in the theater of operations. After my contact with our allies, we found that various chemical detections were reported to central command headquarters and were included in operational logs. Only then, and after travelling half-way around the world, did Department of Defense officials admit that they had been aware of these same instances.

While I have not yet determined the reason for this apparent aversion to full disclosure by DOD, the staff working on this issue from our committee has been constantly challenged by the Department's evasiveness, inconsistency, and reluctance to work toward a common goal here.

Finally, Mr. President, and I believe alarmingly, the Persian Gulf medical records of members of the 24th Naval Reserve Battalion are inexplicably missing from their files.

Mr. President, despite the Czech and French detections and numerous reports, the Department of Defense is still reluctant to admit that there were chemical weapons agents present in the Persian Gulf. I cannot understand why they have taken this stand since we fully expected to be confronted with chemical weapons when we went there.

I can only conclude, Mr. President, that when dealing with the Department of Defense on this issue, you have to ask the right question to receive the right answer. I do not believe they understand that we are only seeking the truth in a way to help our veterans. Therefore, I am going to continue to ask question after question until we find the right answer from DOD.

Mr. President, I ask unanimous consent that, following my remarks, first, a copy of my letter to Sam Nunn, chairman of the Committee on Armed Services, be printed in the Record; second, a copy of my interim report provided in December [1993] to Senators Nunn

and Thurmond be printed in the Record; third, a copy of my report on my trip to the Middle East to continue the investigation into the Persian Gulf Syndrome; and, fourth, my conclusions and recommendations in detail on the Persian Gulf Syndrome be printed in the Record.

There being no objection, the material was ordered to be printed in the Record, as follows:

U.S. Senate
Committee on Armed Services
Washington, D.C., March 16, 1994

Hon. Sam Nunn,
Chairman, Committee on Armed Services, U.S. Senate,
Washington, D.C.,

Dear Mr. Chairman:

I am enclosing a full report of our investigation of the issues related to the possible presence of chemical and biological weapons agents in the theater of operations during Desert Storm and the possible connection between service in the Persian Gulf and the unexplained illness affecting thousands of veterans. This report includes:

Tab A: Interim report of European trip to investigate the Persian Gulf War Syndrome.

Tab B: Report of Middle East trip to continue the investigation into the Persian Gulf War Syndrome.

Tab C: Conclusions and Recommendations.

Tab D: Floor Statement regarding our investigation of the Persian Gulf Syndrome on behalf of the Committee on Armed Services.

Iraq entered the conflict with a demonstrated chemical weapons capability—having used chemical weapons indiscriminately during the Iran-Iraq War, not only against the Iranians, but also against the Iraqi Kurds. Iraq was also suspected of developing a biological weapons capability, most likely anthrax and botulism. As the coalition formed to fight Iraq's aggression, Saddam Hussein made inflammatory statements implying that he was willing to use these weapons to defeat the coalition by inflicting mass casualties.

With this knowledge and Saddam Hussein's threatening statements, the coalition forces strongly believed that Iraq would use chemical and biological weapons should there be a war. An array of defensive measures were adopted including an air campaign against all known chemical and biological weapons sites intended to disrupt Iraq's ability to use its chemical and biological weapons arsenal and signal to Iraqi military leaders that it would be in their best interest to disobey any orders from Saddam Hussein to use chemical and biological weapons. Additionally, U.S. officials repeatedly made statements that the use of chemical and biological weapons would be taken very seriously.

While the threat of the use of chemical or biological

weapons against the coalition forces was prevalent throughout the conflict, we received no indication from the Department of Defense that during or in the aftermath of the Persian Gulf conflict Iraqi forces used either chemical or biological warfare agents or that coalition forces discovered any stocks of chemical or biological warfare agents.

Within a year after the highly successful Desert Storm operation, reports surfaced of a mystery illness affecting many veterans of the war. Symptoms included: joint pain, fatigue, headaches, decreased short-term memory, rashes, painful burning muscles, sleep disorders and diarrhea. While individually these manifestations are common to many illnesses, these particular series of ailments did not respond to any known treatments.

The National Defense Authorization Act for Fiscal Year 1992 required the establishment of a registry of all U.S. armed forces in the theater of operations during Operation Desert Storm who may have been exposed to fumes from burning oil well fires. Despite the establishment of this registry and the registry established by the Veterans Affairs Committee of all participants in both Desert Shield and Desert Storm, little progress has been made on either the causes or the treatment of this mysterious disease. As a result, veterans have been seeking treatment outside of the Department of Defense and Department of Veterans Affairs medical community.

As the Chairman of the Subcommittee on Force Requirements and Personnel, I conducted a hearing on June 30, 1993, on military medical health care. I included a panel of Gulf War veterans consisting of Congressman Stephen Buyer of Indiana; Army Staff Sergeant Kerry Riegel; Petty Officer Sterling Sims, a member of the 24th Construction Battalion of the Naval Reserve; and Sergeant Willie Hicks, a member of the 644th Ordnance Company of the Alabama Army National Guard.

Just days before, a leading U.S. newspaper published a report that U.S. forces may have been exposed to chemical warfare agents during Desert Storm. In testimony, both Petty Officer Sterling Sims and Sergeant Willie Hicks spoke in great detail about their possible exposure to chemical attacks.

On July 2, 1993, the Czech News Agency reported that Czechoslovakian military units detected chemical warfare agents, both nerve gas and mustard agent, in the Saudi theater of operations during the opening days of the air war against Iraq. G-series nerve gas was found by a Czech chemical detection unit attached to Saudi troops in the area of Hafar al-Batin on January 19, 1991. Mustard agent was found in a 20 x 200-centimeter patch in the desert north of King Khalid Military City on January 24, 1991. A report of these detections was forwarded to the Department of Defense by the Czech government.

This announcement by the Czech News Agency led to a series of meetings with Department of Defense officials, including Undersecretary of Defense John Deutsch. While Department of Defense officials maintained that they had no evidence of any chemical weapons attacks by Iraq during the Gulf War, the Department of Defense could not confirm or deny the presence of chemical warfare agents at low levels in the theater of operations.

It was in response to these events that you authorized my travel to the Czech Republic, the United Kingdom and France during the period of November 28 through December 5, 1993, and to Saudi Arabia, Syria, Egypt, Israel and Morocco from January 3 to January 15, 1994. I was accompanied by Dr. Edwin Dorn, then Assistant Secretary of Defense for Personnel and Readiness, on the first leg of this investigation. Major General Ronald Blanck, commander of Walter Reed Army Medical Center, travelled with me on both legs of this journey.

In preparation for the trips, I, and members of my personal staff and the Committee on Armed Forces staff received a briefing from Department of Defense officials. Upon our return, I asked my personal staff and the SASC [Senate Armed Services Committee] staff to meet again with Department of Defense officials in an attempt to answer questions and inconsistencies which arose as a result of information learned from these trips.

The following report provides details of my contacts with high-level representatives of the coalition forces, several inescapable conclusions, and a floor statement addressing this issue.
Sincerely,
RICHARD SHELBY.
U.S. Senate,
Committee on Armed Services
Washington, D.C.

Memorandum to Senator Nunn and Senator Thurmond.
From: Senator Shelby.
CC: Senator [Dan] Coats. [of Indiana]
Subject: Report on trip to investigate "Persian Gulf Syndrome."
The following is a report on my trip to investigate issues related to the possible presence of chemical/biological weapons agents in the theater of operations during the Persian Gulf War, and any possible connection between service in the Persian Gulf War and the illness among U.S. veterans referred to as the Persian Gulf Syndrome. The trip included visits to Prague, Czech Republic; London, England; and Paris, France. Members of the Codel included two members of my personal staff, who serve as S. Res. to the SASC (Terry Lynch and Tom Young) and four members of the SASC

staff with responsibilities in the area of manpower, personnel and chemical/biological defense (Charles Abell, Monica Chavez, P. T. Henry, and Frank Norton).

Additionally, the Codel included representatives from DOD (Assistant Secretary of Defense [Personnel and Readiness] Ed Dorn; Major General Ron Blanck, Commander, Walter Reed Army Medical Center; and Colonel John Spiegel, military assistant to ASD Dorn).

Although the trip was productive, our investigation is incomplete. I believe a trip to the Middle East to meet with our coalition allies stationed in the areas in question is necessary to resolve key questions about the possible presence of chemical agents in the theater of operations and the possible causes of the Persian Gulf Syndrome.

The following is a summary of what the Codel learned during its trip.

RHEIN MAIN AIRPORT, WEST GERMANY

Enroute to Prague, the Codel had a layover in Frankfurt, West Germany, during which the Codel met with the Deputy Chief of Staff for Operations (DCSOPS) and representatives from the Headquarters of the U.S. Army Europe (USAREUR), and received a briefing on the military and civilian draw down in Europe. During the briefing, the USAREUR representatives provided their assessment of possible chemical weapons use/employment during the Persian Gulf War.

The USAREUR representatives offered the following information:

On January 19, 1991, a Czech chemical unit detected G-series nerve agents in two locations on January 19 in concentrations which were militarily insignificant. U.S. chemical reconnaissance troops were called in to verify the detection and were unable to detect any agent at either of the two locations.

On January 24, 1991, a Czech chemical unit detected mustard gas agent in a wet sand patch, measuring 2 meters by 60 centimeters, 2 kilometers north of King Khalid Military City (KKMC). (Note: Other sources would place this detection 10 kilometers north of KKMC.)

On January 17, 1991, the U.S. bombed a chemical weapons munitions storage site at An Nasiryah, located 200 kilometers from the Saudi-Iraq border. The U.S. does not believe this action was the cause of the January 19 detection of nerve agent by the Czech chemical unit.

The USAREUR representatives believe that the Saudis had an underground chemical training facility in the vicinity of the "wet spot," which could account for the small amount of chemical agents detected.

The USAREUR representatives also believe that the chemicals detected may have been part of an attempt on the part of the Saudis to test the capabilities of the Czech chemical units. The briefers did not offer any information on where the Saudis would have gotten the chemical weapons agents.

PRAGUE, CZECHOSLOVAKIA

While in Prague, the Codel met with members of the Czech chemical unit that served in the Persian Gulf: Colonel Kozak, Chief of the Chemical Troops; Lieutenant Colonel Smehlik, Senior Chemical officer in the Persian Gulf; Major Zilinsky and Captain Ferus, leaders of the Czech chemical units in the Persian Gulf during the operations.

The following is a summary of what was learned in the discussions with the members of the Czech chemical unit:

The Czechs initially had 169 members in their chemical detection unit that deployed to the Persian Gulf. That number subsequently increased to approximately 190. These forces included chemical, medical, and other support personnel. The Czech chemical unit was under contract to the Saudi government to provide chemical weapons/agent detection to the Saudi government during the Persian Gulf War.

On January 19, 1991, Czech chemical units that were working with the 4th and 20th Saudi brigades and were separated by approximately 20 kilometers, made three nearly simultaneous detections of a low concentration of G-series nerve agent in the air. The Czechs consider the three nearly simultaneous detections to be one event. The Czechs indicated that the detections took place in the late afternoon and that the event lasted approximately 40 minutes. The Czechs determined that, at ground level at the time of the event, the wind was blowing from the northwest. The Department of Defense had previously advised the Committee [on Armed Services] that the prevailing winds were blowing northeastward.

The Czechs took air samples from two of three locations, and verified the contents of the air samples in their mobile laboratory to contain G-series nerve agent. The Czechs were not able to distinguish between sarin or soman. LTC Smehlik indicated, however, that they had excluded V-series agents. These air samples were sent back to then Czechoslovakia [now the Czech Republic], and are no longer available, as they have been used up. An air sample from the third location was not taken for the purpose of verification because the Czech chemical unit was moving at the time of the alarm.

(NOTE: In the U.S., G-series nerve agents sarin and tabun are considered to be nonpersistent, evaporating at the same rate as water. VX, a persistent nerve agent, evaporates much more slowly, and spills of liquid VX can persist for a long time under average weather conditions.)

Captain Ferus, a leader of one of the Czech chemical units, informed us that on January 24, 1991, he was summoned by Saudi officials to an area 10 kilometers north of KKMC. His unit was accompanied to the area by Saudi soldiers, where he was asked to check the area for chemical agents. His unit detected mustard agent in the sand. No sample was taken because the presence of mustard agent was confirmed on the spot using a portable laboratory kit.

LTC Smehlik informed the Codel that he had recently learned that there had been another detection of mustard agent in the air near the Engineer School in KKMC 23 days prior to the detection on January 24. LTC Smehlik indicated that an air sample was taken, verified by the mobile laboratory, and forwarded to Czechoslovakia. This sequence of events was confirmed for the Codel by the Czech warrant officer who reported the actual detection.

The Czechs believe both detections of mustard agent to have been at levels that presented no danger to the health and safety of the troops in the area, and were, therefore, militarily insignificant.

Colonel Kozak informed the group that Czech units did not have any chemical agents in the Persian Gulf and they did not use live agents during their training with the Saudis.

The chemical detection equipment used by the Czechs consisted of Czech and Russian equipment of 1970s and 1980s vintage, yet, according to the Czechs, has a much lower threshold level for detection of chemical agents than does U.S. chemical detection equipment. The equipment used by the Czechs includes the GSP-11, a chemical agent detector/alarm which provides continuous monitoring capability; the portable CHP-71, a chemical analyzer used as a backup for the GSP-11; a portable laboratory which uses a litmus paper detection method, as well as other wet chemical analysis; and a mobile laboratory. We were told by the Czechs that the U.S. had arranged to examine the above-mentioned equipment and that the equipment would be shipped to Edgewood Arsenal for testing.

During the conduct of discussions with representatives of the Czech military, several events were mentioned which were anecdotal in nature and based on hearsay. There is no documentary evidence of these matters. Nonetheless, I believe they merit further consideration.

LTC Smehlik claimed that an air sample of the mustard agent detected in the air in KKMC prior to January 24, 1991, was given to a U.S. special forces member. In subsequent discussions with the Codel staff, Smehlik indicated that the individual in question could also have been an intelligence specialist.

LTC Smehlik also mentioned that he had heard the Egyptians had detected mustard agent in the air in the vicinity of KKMC. Representatives of the French military offered the same thoughts on Egyptian detections.

GREAT BRITAIN

The Codel met with Dr. Graham Pearson, Director General, Chemical and Biological Defence Establishment; Mr. Brian Pitts, Surgeon General's Office; Ms. Jill Ferguson; LTC John Esmonde-White; and Colonel Christopher Box.

There were approximately 42,000 British soldiers who served in the Persian Gulf War. The representatives of the British government the Codel met were not very helpful.

They do not believe that the Czech units detected the presence of any chemical weapons, nerve or mustard agents, in the Persian Gulf. They spent a considerable amount of effort attempting to find plausible means of discrediting the Czech reports.

The British government does not recognize any possibility of any connection between service in the Persian Gulf and any illness that cannot be explained by conventional medical diagnosis. The British have about 30 veterans from the Persian Gulf with medical problems. These medical conditions are not considered peculiar to their service in the Persian Gulf. British citizens have, however, set up a Persian Gulf Families Hot Line, located in Gloucester, England, that serves as a clearinghouse for those who believe they have illnesses related to their service in the Persian Gulf. I met with Mr. Raymond Donn, a solicitor from Manchester, England, who is in the process of filing a class action suit against the British government to obtain compensation for these veterans. Mr. Donn informed me that there could be as many as 500 sick British veterans.

The British government does not recognize Multiple Chemical Toxicity/Sensitivity as a valid concept. Additionally, the representatives with whom the Codel met believe the Persian Gulf Syndrome is the result of American veterans attempting to increase their medical and disability benefits. The Codel was advised that the United States did not have to invent a new environmental disease to explain the symptoms being experienced by American veterans.

PARIS, FRANCE

While in Paris, the Codel met with Lieutenant Colonel Gerrard Emile Ferrand, a French Army infantry officer who served in the Persian Gulf. The French had about 12,000 personnel in the Gulf.

Colonel Ferrand informed the Codel that the French had detected nerve and mustard agent at a Logistics Facility approximately 26 or 27 kilometers south of KKMC on the evening of January 24th or 25th. He indicated that the wind at ground level had been from the north—from Iraq. French chemical alarms were activated at two locations approximately 100 meters apart. Colonel Ferrand, who arrived at the location about 30 minutes after the initial alarm, indicated that litmus badges on the protective suits worn by French troops registered the presence of mustard agent. They contacted a Czech chemical unit and asked it to conduct tests to verify presence of the chemical agents. The Czech chemical unit arrived about 2 hours later, confirmed the presence of a mustard agent and a nerve agent—either soman or tabun—and decontaminated the area.

Colonel Ferrand also noted that, about 2 or 3 days later the French chemical alarms were again activated in the same area. At this time, the wind had shifted and was from the south. The French were unable to determine what chemical agent was present. They again asked the Czech chemical units for assistance, but none responded.

Colonel Ferrand reported both these events to the French command located at Riyadh. Colonel Ferrand believes these reports were forwarded to CENTCOM headquarters.

Members of the Codel also met with representatives of the French military medical community, including Major General Lauric, head of the French Military Medical Service. The French have no empirical evidence on which to base a connection between service in the Persian Gulf and any illness that cannot be explained by conventional diagnosis. The French veterans were all volunteers from the Rapid Reaction Corps and the French Foreign Legion. As such, these individuals had spent considerable time in Africa and other areas which would have exposed them to hostile environmental influences, and, perhaps, made them less susceptible to environmental factors in the Persian Gulf. The French are, however, monitoring the medical conditions of their veterans.

(NOTE: In discussions with the members of the Czech chemical unit, they did not mention any contact with the French concerning a detection of either or both nerve agent or mustard agent. The French had no knowledge of the Czech chemical agent detections.)

QUESTIONS THAT REMAIN TO BE ANSWERED
1. Did any of the coalition allies serving in the Persian Gulf have chemical weapons in the theater of operations or conduct chemical weapons training using live agents or simulants?
2. Did representatives of any of the coalition allies receive any air samples from the Czechs while in the Gulf? Specifically, did a U.S. Special Forces soldier or Intelligence Community member receive an air sample from the Czech chemical defense unit?
3. Did any member of the allied coalition receive reports, other than the report of the January 19 event, from any coalition partner of a detection of chemical agents including any reports of chemical agents at a level considered to be militarily insignificant and no threat to the safety or health of U.S. troops, or other coalition personnel?

4. What were the true weather (wind) conditions during the period in question. There is a discrepancy regarding the reported wind directions during the time various detections were made.

RECOMMENDATION
1. In order to complete the investigation of possible presence of chemical/biological agents in the Persian Gulf and the possible causes of the Persian Gulf Syndrome, it is necessary for me to visit with members of the allied coalition and meet with the appropriate representatives of their foreign and defense ministries. Coalition allies stationed in the area in question include Morocco, Syria, Egypt, and Saudi Arabia. Additionally, it would be useful to meet with appropriate defense and intelligence community representatives from Israel regarding any information they might have about the possible use of chemical weapons. I believe it would be in the Committee's interest for me to travel to the Middle East for this purpose during the first two weeks of January 1994.
2. Prior to my travelling to the Middle East, the Department of Defense should provide maps to the Committee showing locations of battalion-level and above units during the period from January 17, 1991, through February 1, 1991. Additionally, the Department of Defense should provide maps showing the dates, times, and locations of all bombings of chemical production or storage facilities and ammunition storage areas.
U.S. Senate,
Committee on Armed Services
Washington, D.C., February 28, 1994

Memorandum to Senator Nunn and Senator Thurmond.
From: Senator Shelby.
CC: Senator Coats.
Subject: Report on trip to Middle East to continue the investigation into the Persian Gulf Syndrome.
Upon the completion of my trip in December to Czechoslovakia, the United Kingdom and France to investigate issues related to the possible presence of chemical/biological weapons agents in the theater of operations during the Persian Gulf War, and any possible connection between service in the Persian Gulf War and the illness among U.S. veterans referred to as the Persian Gulf Syndrome, I informed you that I believed the investigation would not be complete without meeting other coalition allies stationed in the theater of operations. On January 315, I travelled to Riyadh, King Khalid Military City, and Jubail, Saudi Arabia; Damascus, Syria; Cairo, Egypt; Tel Aviv and Jerusalem, Israel; and Rabat, Morocco, to continue my investigation into this matter.

Members of the Codel included two members of my personal staff who serve as S. Res. to the SASC (Terry

Lynch and Tom Young), four members of the SASC staff with responsibilities in the area of manpower, personnel and chemical/biological defense (Charles Abell, Monica Chavez, P. T. Henry, and Frank Norton) and a representative from the Department of Defense (Major General Ron Blanck, Commander, Walter Reed Army Medical Center).

I believe the investigation of this issue has been productive and is complete, to the extent that the Congress can conclude the investigation. This report summarizes our meetings and discussions in the Middle East and North Africa with coalition allies on the possible presence of chemical agents in the theater of operations and the possible causes of the Persian Gulf Syndrome.

RIYADH AND JUBAIL, SAUDI ARABIA
On January 4–6, we visited Riyadh, King Khalid Military City (KKMC), and Jubail, Saudi Arabia, and met with several high-ranking members of the Saudi Arabian military, and civilian representatives of the firms located in the Jubail industrial region.

RIYADH
Major General Nazir Abd-Al Azziz al-Arfaj, Director of Military Intelligence and Security, advised the Codel that, on January 19 and 24, the dates when very low levels nerve agent and mustard agent were detected and verified by the Czech chemical units, the Czechs reported this to the Saudi Arabian military. In the absence of any evidence of a delivery vehicle (missile, bomb, etc.), the Saudis determined that these low levels did not pose a threat to the public health or to animals. He provided the following additional information:

To date, no Saudi military personnel or civilians have complained of illnesses that can be attributed to service in the theater of operations during the Persian Gulf War.

The Saudi Arabian government has no evidence of the use of biological agents during the Persian Gulf War, although the United Nations subsequently discovered evidence of research and development on biological agents.

On January 24, 1991, the French reported a possible chemical agent detection to the Saudis (the wet spot north of KKMC) who then contacted the Czech chemical defense unit. The Czechs detected and verified the presence of mustard agent on the ground. This incident was reported by the Saudis to CENTCOM Headquarters. U.S. personnel were sent to the area in question but were unable to detect a chemical agent.

Saudi intelligence had no information to offer regarding the possible source of the low-level chemicals.

When the wet spot was located (later determined by the Czech chemical defense unit to be mustard agent), the Saudi troops did not don chemical defense gear.

The Saudis do not believe the symptoms suffered by the U.S. soldiers are a result of exposure to chemical weapons. Major General Nazir Abd-Al Azziz al-Arfaj indicated that the Saudis did not have chemical agents or simulants and did not know if the other coalition forces had chemical agents in the theater. It is possible that the Egyptians and Syrians could have had chemical agents/weapons, but the Saudi military personnel do not have offensive chemical weapons in the area and did not conduct defensive chemical weapons training. He did, however, believe the reports of the Czech and French detections.

With regard to assistance from the Chinese, Major General Nazir Abd-Al Azziz al-Arfaj indicated that, while the Saudis have a relationship with the Chinese government because of the CSS-2 missiles, the Chinese military had no liaison in the theater of operations during the Persian Gulf War.

General Mohammed Saleh al Hammad, Chief of Staff, Minister of Defense Education, had very little to offer regarding the subject of the Codel's inquiry. He expressed confidence in the reliability of the Czech and French detections. When asked about from where the nerve agent and mustard agent could have come, he stated that he had no idea. He speculated, however, that they could have come from either friendly or aggressor forces. He also speculated that perhaps the U.S. military brought it.

KING KHALID MILITARY CITY (KKMC)
On January 6, the Codel flew to King Khalid Military City, where mustard agent had been detected in two locations. The Codel met with Major General Al Alhami, Northern Area Commander, who commanded KKMC during the Persian Gulf War.

General Al Alhami indicated that, during the war, he received no evidence of any detections of chemical agents nor of any medical problems that could be viewed as unusual. He indicated that, every time the Iraqis fired Scuds, all troops donned MOPP chemical protective gear (MOPP gear includes a full body suit and mask with hood). Additionally, he had no recollection of the French reporting their detection of mustard agent to the KKMC Headquarters.

He has no knowledge of the Saudis, U.S. or Syrians, or any coalition forces, having chemical agents/weapons with their forces during the Persian Gulf War.

JUBAIL INDUSTRIAL CENTER
Also on January 6, the Codel travelled to the Jubail Industrial Center to discuss the possibility of industrial chemical releases during the Persian Gulf War. The Codel met with Mr. Terry Velanzano of the Jubail Planning Group and a number of officials from the various civilian industrial concerns located at Jubail. Most of those with whom the Codel met were present at Jubail during the war.

The industrialists advised the Codel that there were no instances in which industrial chemicals were released either intentionally or unintentionally during the periods of time when coalition forces were located in the Jubail region. They specifically denied the intentional release of chemicals from pressurized systems in response to warnings of Scud attacks.

The industrialists also advised the Codel that there were no and are no instances of medical ailments among the Jubail work force and their families that could be construed as unusual or in any way linked to chemical agents during the war.

DAMASCUS, SYRIA

In Damascus, the Codel met with Major General Mohmend Zughaybi, Chief of Medical Service, Ministry of Defense; General Yaff, Director, Shrian Hospital; Mr. Assan, Assistant Director, and Mr. Amur, Director, Department of Americas, Ministry of Foreign Affairs; and Dr. Nejdi Jazzar, Assistant Secretary for American Affairs, Ministry of Foreign Affairs.

The Chief of Medical Services initially emphasized that he had no knowledge of Syrian chemical agents, weapons, their capabilities or of a Syrian chemical defense program. However, toward the end of the meeting, he responded affirmatively that Syrian troops conducted chemical defense training, but do not use chemical agents/weapons or simulants in that training. He later told the Codel that Syrian chemical defense equipment was of Eastern European origin. He indicated that the Syrians did not conduct any chemical defense exercises training in the theater of operation using chemical agents or chemical simulants.

General Zughaybi indicated that Syrian troops were stationed near Hafir al Batin. He remarked that U.S. troops panicked when the chemical alarms went off. He also indicated that, when the Syrian troops responded to the chemical alarms, they only put on masks, not protective suits.

He advised the Codel that, to his knowledge, the Syrians were not aware of any coalition allies having chemical weapons in the theater of operation, and that, although other Arab countries have chemical weapons, he did not think Syria has chemical weapons.

General Zughaybi was not aware of the Egyptians or Saudis being informed of chemical agent detections, or whether they complained that they were not informed.

The diseases suffered by the Syrian military personnel who participated in the Persian Gulf War are similar to symptoms of illness that occur in peacetime.

General Zughaybi asked General Blanck whether the diagnosis was PTS (post traumatic stress), or psychological. General Blanck replied that he believed it was organic. Additionally, General Zughaybi added that he did not know about the long-term effects of exposure to chemical agents—or rather, the occupance of symptoms long after exposure to low levels of chemical agents. He did add, however, that Syrian military personnel have a different psychological mindset to the desert. The underlying inference to be drawn is that, in his opinion, the Persian Gulf Syndrome may in fact be psychological in origin.

CAIRO, EGYPT

On January 9, the Codel travelled to Cairo, Egypt. While in Cairo, the Codel received a country team briefing from U.S. Embassy personnel. Senator Shelby met with President Mubarak.

On January 10, the Codel met with Lieutenant General Salah Halaby, Chief of Staff, Egyptian Armed Forces, and his staff. General Halaby advised the Codel that Egypt had its own chemical defense unit, which was very good, but he had no recollection that they had detected any chemical agents during the Persian Gulf War.

General Halaby indicated that Egypt's chemical defense equipment is from Eastern Europe and from the West, and that their detection equipment is more sophisticated than the Czech equipment. The Egyptians use an American chemical agent alarm (the M-1) and a Russian chemical agent detector (the bulb and probe). The Egyptians also use chemical-agent detection strips. He further indicated that the Egyptian chemical defense unit took air samples every day and night to check for changes.

He suggested that the chemicals detected were not chemical warfare agents, but industrial chemicals or substances used in the construction and structure of the A-10 aircraft. (An A-10 crashed near KKMC during the time frame when KKMC detections were made.) He did not believe the aircraft carried chemical weapons or chemical agents.

General Halaby and his staff commented that Egypt has no chemical weapons, only chemical defense equipment (protective gear). He said that, although Egyptian troops conduct chemical defense training, they do not use chemical simulants in their training other than tear gas. General Halaby was not aware of the Syrians having had chemical agents/weapons in the theater. He was certain that no Iraq aircraft or artillery (which could have been used to deliver chemical agents) had crossed the border.

He asked whether the illnesses suffered by the U.S. troops resulted from their exposure to depleted uranium.

The Egyptian troops were located approximately 6 miles north of the French troops in KKMC. At one point, General Halaby said they were not aware of the detection of chemical agent by the Czech chemical defense unit, but later in the interview, he acknowledged that they were aware of the detections but did not verify any chemical agents or equipment. General Halaby commented that he knew that chemical agents alarms could be tripped off by cigarette smoke. He suggested that the French and Czech detections could have been false alarms because the atmosphere was so full of petrochemical smoke.

PRESIDENT MUBARAK

President Mubarak acknowledged that Egypt had some chemical weapons. He speculated that perhaps the chemical agents about which the Codel was concerned came from Iran. He then discussed with Senator Shelby general foreign policy issues related to U.S. relations with Egypt, the peace process between Israel and Syria, as well as Egypt's relations prior to the Persian Gulf War.

JERUSALEM, ISRAEL

In Jerusalem, the Codel met with an intelligence officer of the Israeli Defense Force. He indicated that he was aware of chemical agents being used by Iraq during the Iran-Iraq War, and did not understand why they were not used in the Gulf War. He believed that it was very significant that no chemical weapons or delivery systems were found in the theater following the war. He surmised that there had been no preparation for their use or they were withdrawn prior to D-Day.

The Israeli officer indicated that he did not believe the Iraqis had a chemical weapons project underway but cautioned that they could restart one at any moment.

The Israeli officer also noted that the symptoms of the Persian Gulf illness did not fit any of the symptoms traditionally associated with exposure to chemical agents. He offered that, perhaps, the United States should focus some attention on biological agents. He was convinced that the Iraqis had a small biological weapons capability but indicated that no biological weapons or delivery systems had been found.

He indicated that the Israelis believed the Czech chemical units to be very proficient and that their equipment is very good. He noted, however, the prevalence of false alarms.

He suggested that we study the symptoms of those exposed to chemical agents during the Iran-Iraq War and that we discuss the Persian Gulf Syndrome with Iranian doctors.

Contrary to information provided to the Codel in other countries, the Israeli officer indicated that all the coalition forces, especially Egypt and Syria, use chemical agent simulants in their training.

RABAT, MOROCCO

On January 13, the Codel travelled to Rabat, Morocco. In preparation for our meetings with Moroccan government officials, the U.S. Embassy conducted a coun-

try team briefing and informed us that during the Persian Gulf War, Morocco and Saudi Arabia had a bilateral agreement which placed Moroccan military personnel under the authority of the Saudi military. Morocco sent a motorized infantry unit from the Western Sahara to the vicinity [of] a petrochemical facility north of Jubail about 50 kilometers from the Kuwait border.

In Rabat, the Codel met with Colonel Major Mohammed Beuboumaudi, Inspector, Military Health Services. He indicated that no Moroccan military personnel saw any chemical weapons or equipment. He mentioned that, on one occasion, his troops went to check the location in which an artillery shell exploded for chemical agent. There were no indications of any chemical agents present.

The Moroccan troops did not experience any illnesses symptomatic of exposure to chemical agents. Additionally, he pointed out that Moroccan troops were acclimated to service in the desert. The inference here being the possible psychological or environmental origin of the Persian Gulf Syndrome.

With regard to the origin of Moroccan military chemical defense equipment, he indicated that they used chemical detection badges and gas masks provided by the Saudi military. He noted that Morocco was a signatory of the Chemical Weapons Convention (CC).

In response to questions regarding the presence of chemical agents or weapons in the theater of operations, and knowledge as to whether coalition allies possessed chemical weapons or agents, Colonel Major Beuboumaudi provided negative responses. He indicated that he was not aware of Moroccan troops participating in chemical defense training with simulants during the Persian Gulf War.

The Codel also met with [the] deputy minister of foreign affairs, who reiterated the comments made by Colonel Major Beuboumaudi regarding the Morocco military personnel's not being aware of the presence of chemical weapons/agent in the theater of operations and not having any knowledge of other coalition allies in possession of chemical weapons/agents in the theater of operation.

CONCLUSIONS AND RECOMMENDATIONS ON THE PERSIAN GULF SYNDROME

After numerous congressional hearings, after many meetings with officials of the Department of Defense and Department of Veterans [Affairs] officials and after two trips abroad I have come to the following conclusions regarding the possible presence of chemical/biological weapons agents in the theater of operations during the Persian Gulf War, and [the] possible connection between service in the Persian Gulf War and the illness among U.S. veterans referred to as the Persian Gulf Syndrome.

1. Chemical agents were present in the theater of operations during the Persian Gulf War. These chemical agents were accurately verified by the Czech Chemical Units and reported to CENTCOM Headquarters.

On this vital issue I have no doubt. Czech and French forces detected both nerve gas and mustard agent at low levels during the early days of Desert Storm. In each instance, these chemical agents were verified by Czech equipment. The Codel had the opportunity to view this equipment and received a demonstration. Department of Defense officials have informed us that the Czech detection equipment, which is more sensitive than U.S. equipment, is more than adequate and that Czech personnel are well trained.

2. The origin of these chemical agents cannot be determined.

Although I have also concluded that we may never be able to determine the origin of these chemical agents there are several plausible scenarios. I believe that we can rule out Iraqi Scud or Frog missiles. We can also rule out Iraqi artillery—the distance from the Iraqi border is too far. The presence of low-level chemical weapons agents could have resulted from U.S. or coalition forces bombing either Iraqi chemical weapons facilities or caches of Iraqi weapons on the Saudi border. Hafar al-Batin is approximately 100 miles from the Saudi/Iraqi border. A cloud of nerve agent, dissipating in intensity, could possibly have travelled under the correct climate conditions to Hafar al-Batin. There is also the possibility of an accident involving chemical agents among coalition forces. Finally, it has been offered that these detections, especially those in Hafar al-Batin and the detection of the mustard agent on the ground north of KKMC, were the result of Saudi officials attempting to test the abilities of the Czechs who they had engaged to assist Saudi troops in chemical detections.

3. While a direct connection between the existence of low levels of chemical agents in the theater of operations and the Persian Gulf Syndrome cannot be established based on the information available at the time, such a connection cannot and should not be discounted.

This is the most difficult issue that confronted my investigation. There is very little information available on studies of exposure to low levels of chemical agents. I am confident that the work being accomplished under Major General Ronald Blanck, USA, Commander, Walter Reed Army Medical Center, is on the right track. I urge the Department of Defense and the Department of Veterans Affairs to finalize a case definition for the Gulf War Syndrome. The Department of Defense and the Department of Veterans Affairs should initiate a serious project which focuses on the long-term effects of exposure to low levels of chemical agents. Additionally, the Department of Defense and the Department of Veterans Affairs must cut through bureaucratic red tape and seek all possible medical treatments for the Gulf War Syndrome.

4. The Department of Defense has proven reluctant to pursue or, in certain instances, to provide the information necessary to prove or disprove allegations about the presence of chemical agents in the theater of operations during the Persian Gulf War. The reason for this apparent aversion to full disclosure has not been determined. Staff working on this issue were constantly challenged by the Department's evasiveness, inconsistency, and reluctance to work together toward a common goal.

Several examples will illustrate this point:

During a briefing I attended on November 19, 1993, Dr. John Deutsch, the Undersecretary of Defense for Acquisition, advised that, while the Department could neither confirm nor deny the Czech detections and verifications, the Department position was that categorically there were no chemical warfare agents present in the theater of operations.

Having been advised by the Department of Defense that it had no information to offer regarding the possible presence of chemical warfare agents in the theater of operations, I determined, with your concurrence, to travel to Europe and the Middle East to pursue this matter with our allies. Only after the Committee staff confronted the Department regarding specific events that I learned about during these travels, did the Department acknowledge that it had been aware of these same events.

Similarly, it was only after my contact with our allies revealed that they had, in fact, reported various chemical detections to the Central Command Headquarters, that the Department acknowledged evidence of this reporting in the operational logs.

On page 45 of the history of the 2nd Marine Division in Operation Desert Shield and Desert Storm, which was published by the Marine Corps' History and Museum Division, there is a detailed incident in which Marines of the 2nd Marine Division detected mustard agent. I am at a loss to explain how an official Marine Corps publication can document such an event and the Department of Defense could deny any evidence regarding chemical weapons in the theater of operations.

This passivity on the part of the Department when combined with rather obvious attempts to dissuade the Committee staff from the need for further investigation typifies the Department's attitude toward the Committee on this matter.

REPORT AND CONCLUSIONS ON THE PERSIAN GULF SYNDROME
(By Senator Richard C. Shelby)

When Iraqi forces, at the direction of Saddam Hussein, crossed into Kuwait on August 2, 1990, they set off a chain reaction of events that resulted in the assembling of the largest coalition of forces since the Second World War. Countries that had been on opposite sides of the cold war were now joined with the expressed goal of driving Saddam Hussein's troops out of Kuwait.

Soldiers, sailors, airmen and marines were sent to Saudi Arabia from all over the globe. The U.S. led this effort with over 600,000 members of our armed service, including over 200,000 reservists. Troops were sent from Great Britain, France, Italy, Egypt, Syria, Morocco, and many other nations. Czechoslovakia, at the behest of the Saudi Arabia government, provided chemical warfare detection units.

There was a strong belief among the coalition forces that chemical and even biological agents would be used as weapons by Iraq should the coalition forces invade Kuwait and Iraq. Iraq was known to possess G-series nerve and mustard agents and it was believed that they also possessed anthrax and possibly other biological agents. After all, Saddam Hussein had freely and indiscriminately used chemical weapons, delivered in artillery shells and dropped as bombs, during his war with Iran, not only against Iranians, but also against Kurds.

When Desert Storm began on January 17, 1991, there was obvious concern among coalition forces about Saddam Hussein's reaction to allied air strikes. U.S. bombing was stealthy and effective, knocking out Iraqi communications in the first hours of the war and Saddam Hussein's nuclear and chemical warfare factories were targeted and destroyed. Additionally, B-52s bombed Iraqi positions along the Kuwaiti and Iraqi borders with Saudi Arabia.

Saddam Hussein responded by launching Scud missiles toward Saudi Arabia and Israel. Because there was always the possibility of an Iraqi launch of a Scud armed with a chemical warhead, gas masks and chemical protection suits were donned at the first sign of attack. These Scud attacks were met with moderate success by U.S. Patriot missile batteries. With the exception of one missile which landed on a company of Pennsylvania reservists, the Scuds had more success as a weapon of terror than as a weapon of physical destruction.

On February 24, 1991, coalition forces began the ground phase of the campaign as they charged into Iraq and Kuwait. Within 100 hours Kuwait was in the hands of the coalition, and what was left of Saddam Hussein's forces were fleeing toward Baghdad. A great victory had been won. General Norman Schwarzkopf, Commander in Chief of [the] U.S. Central Command, and General Colin Powell, Chairman of the Joint Chiefs of Staff, were heroes and by the end of May 1991 the vast majority of U.S. troops were home.

However, by the summer of 1992, Gulf War veterans, primarily members of the National Guard and Reserves, were relating stories of a mystery illness affecting many who had served in Saudi Arabia. Symptoms included: joint pain, fatigue, headaches, decreased short-term memory, unexplained rashes, painful burning muscles, sleep disorders and diarrhea. While most of us have experienced similar symptoms at one time or another, these ailments were not responding to treatment.

In response to possible Gulf War–related illness, the Senate Armed Services Committee included a provision in the Department of Defense Authorization Act for Fiscal Year 1992 that established a registry for members of our armed forces who served in the Persian Gulf theater of operations and may have been exposed to fumes from burning oil wells. The smoke from oil well fires, deliberately set by Iraqi soldiers as they retreated from Kuwait, caused acute respiratory problems which could result in long-term health problems. However, none of these sick veterans were among those who had been exposed to smoke from oil well fires. To assist in the investigation of this issue, a Desert Shield/Desert Storm registry was established in the Department of Veteran Affairs Authorization Bill for Fiscal Year 1993.

By January 1993, the veterans were becoming increasingly frustrated by the inability of the Veterans Department to treat their illnesses. I met with a group of Alabama veterans after a town meeting that I held in Bessemer and pledged that I would do everything in my power to get them proper treatment and to find the cause of their ailments.

In February 1993, I met with Secretary of Veterans Affairs Jesse Brown and received his pledge to assist those veterans. Following this meeting, the Department of Defense and the Department of Veterans Affairs announced that centers would be established for the treatment of what had become known as the Gulf War Syndrome. However, when little progress was made, veterans were prompted to seek treatment outside of the Department of Defense and Department of Veterans Affairs medical community.

As chairman of the Subcommittee of Force Requirements and Personnel, I included a panel of Gulf War veterans consisting of Congressman Stephen Buyer of Indiana; Army Staff Sergeant Kerry Riegel; Petty Officer Sterling Sims, a member of the 24th Construction Battalion of the Naval Reserve; and Sergeant Willie Hicks, a member of the 644th Ordinance Company of the Alabama Army National Guard in my June 30, 1993, hearing on military medical health care.

Just days before the hearing, a leading U.S. newspaper published a report that U.S. forces may have been exposed to chemical warfare agents during Desert Storm, and testimony from both Petty Officer Sterling

Sims and Sergeant Willie Hicks confirmed the possibility of their exposure to chemical attacks while serving in the Persian Gulf War.

I believe the most dramatic event of the investigation occurred in the early morning hours of January 20, 1991, when an explosion went off in the sky above Jubail along the northeast coast of Saudi Arabia, alerting Seabees in the 24th Construction Battalion to don their chemical defensive gear. After the all-clear signal was given, a group of Seabees were hit with a burning mist that smelled of ammonia and caused their khaki, colored t-shirts to turn purple.

On July 2, 1993, possibly responding to reports in American newspapers, the Czech News Agency reported that Czechoslovakian military units had detected chemical warfare agents, both nerve gas and mustard agents, in Saudi Arabia during the opening days of the air war against Iraq. Nerve gas was detected by a Czechoslovakian unit attached to the Saudi troops in the area of Hafar al-Batin on January 19, 1991, and mustard agent was allegedly detected in a 20 x 200-centimeter patch in the desert north of King Khalid Military City on January 24, 1991. A report of these detections was supposedly forwarded to the U.S. Department of Defense by the Czech government.

This announcement led to a series of meetings with Department of Defense officials, which continued throughout the fall of 1993 and included a meeting with Undersecretary of Defense John Deutsch. Although a multitude of chemical alarms were sounded during Operation Desert Storm, the Department of Defense maintained that they had no evidence of any chemical weapons attacks by Iraq during the Gulf War and they could not confirm the detection of chemical warfare agents. While Department of Defense officials did not deny that the Czechs had detected chemical warfare agents at low levels, they could not or would not confirm the presence of chemical warfare agents in the theater of operations.

On October 27, 1993, Dr. Charles Jackson of the Tuskegee, Alabama, Veterans Medical Center diagnosed a patient as suffering from Gulf War Syndrome and Chemical-Biological Warfare Exposure. In response to both this announcement and pressure from Congress, Secretary Brown announced, on November 1, 1992, that the Department of Veterans Affairs was establishing a pilot program in Birmingham, Alabama, to test Persian Gulf veterans from Alabama and Georgia for exposure to chemical weapons agents, and on November 10, 1993, Secretary of Defense Les Aspin announced a blue-ribbon task force, headed by Dr. Josh Letterberg, to study the Gulf War Syndrome.

It was in response to these events that Senator Sam Nunn, Chairman of the Committee on Armed Services, sent me to both Europe and the Middle East to investigate all issues related to the possible presence of chemi-

cal and biological weapon agents in the theater of operations during Operation Desert Storm and the possible connection between service in the Persian Gulf and the unexplained illness affecting thousands of veterans. . . .
Reference: "Senator Shelby's Conclusions on the Persian Gulf Syndrome," *Congressional Record—Senate,* 17 March 1994, S3098-S3106.

Index of Chemical Agents Purchased or Formulated by Iraq, 25 May 1994

On 25 May 1994, after conducting lengthy hearings on possible chemical shipments to Iraq from the United States, the U.S. Senate Committee on Banking, Housing and Urban Affairs released an extensive report which detailed such shipments and their possible effect on what is called "Gulf War Syndrome." The following verbatim descriptions of chemicals that were shipped to Iraq were part of that report.

CHEMICAL AND NERVE AGENTS

Sarin (GB): A colorless and practically odorless liquid, Sarin dissolves well in water and organic solvents. The basic military use of Sarin is as a gas and a persistent aerosol. A highly toxic agent with a clearly defined myopic effect, symptoms of intoxication appear quickly without any period of latent effect. Sarin has cumulative effects—that is, a slow rate of detoxification independent of its method of entry into the body. According to Joachim Krause and Charles K. Mallory in *Chemical Weapons in Soviet Military Doctrine: Military and Historical Experience, 1915–1991,* the progressive signs of initial Sarin intoxication include myosis (contraction of the pupil), photophobia, difficulty [in] breathing, and chest pain.

Soman (GD): A neuro-paralytic toxic agent. Soman is a transparent, colorless, involatile liquid smelling of camphor. Soluble in water to a limited degree, Soman is absorbed into porous and painted surfaces. Soman is similar to Sarin in its injurious effects, but more toxic. When it acts on the skin in either droplet or vapor form, it causes a general poisoning of the organism.

Tabun (GA): A neuro-paralytic toxic agent. Tabun is a transparent, colorless liquid. The industrial product is a brown liquid with a weak sweetish smell; in small concentrations it smells of fruit, but in large concentrations it smells of fish. Tabun dissolves poorly in water but well in organic solvents; it is easily absorbed into rubber products and painted surfaces. Injury occurs upon skin contact with Tabun vapor and droplets. The symptoms of injury appear almost immediately. Marked myosis occurs.

VX: This colorless, odorless, liquid has a low volatility and is poorly soluble in water, but dissolves well in organic solvents. The danger of pulmonary VX intoxication is determined by meteorological conditions and the delivery method used. VX is thought to be very effective against respiratory organs when in the form of a thinly dispersed aerosol. The symptoms of VX intoxication are analogous to those of other nerve agents, but their development is markedly slower. As with other nerve agents, VX has a cumulative effect.

VESICANTS AND BLOOD AGENTS

Lewisite: A vesicant toxic agent, industrial lewisite is a dark-brown liquid with a strong smell. Lewisite is a contact poison with practically no period of latent effect. Lewisite vapors cause irritation to the eyes and upper respiratory tract. According to the Center for Disease Control, lewisite would cause stinging and burning. Its smell, generally characterized as the strong smell of geraniums, could be confused with the smell of ammonia (the reaction to which is regulated by pain fibers rather than smell). Iraqi stores of lewisite were not located after the war, according to the Department of Defense.

Cyanogen Chloride: The French first suggested the use of cyanogen chloride as a toxic agent. U.S. analysts have reported that it is capable of penetrating gas mask filters. Partially soluble in water, it dissolves well in organic solvents. It is absorbed easily into porous materials; its military state is a gas. Cyanogen chloride is a quick acting toxic agent. Upon contact with the eyes or respiratory organs, it injures immediately. Lethal exposures result in loss of consciousness, convulsions and paralysis.

Hydrogen Cyanide: A colorless liquid smelling of bitter almonds, hydrogen cyanide is a very strong, quick-acting poison. Hydrogen cyanide affects unprotected humans through the respiratory organs and during the ingestion of contaminated food and water. It inhibits the enzymes which regulate the intra-cell oxidant-restorative process. As a result, the cells of the nervous system, especially those affecting breathing, are injured, which in turn leads to quick death. An important feature of hydrogen cyanide is the absence of a period of latent effect. The military state of hydrogen cyanide is a gas. The toxic and physiologic properties of hydrogen cyanide permit it to be used effectively in munitions—predominantly in rocket-launched artillery. Death occurs after intoxication due to paralysis of the heart. Non-lethal doses do not cause intoxication.

BLISTER AGENTS

Mustard Gas: This is a colorless, oily liquid which dissolves poorly in water, but relatively well in organic solvents, lubricant products, and other toxic agents. The injurious effect of mustard gas is associated with its ability to inhibit many enzyme systems of the body. This, in turn, prevents the intra-cell exchange of chemicals and leads to necrosis of the tissue. Death is associated mainly with necrosis of the tissue of the central nervous system. Mustard gas has a period of latent effect (the first signs of injury appear after 2-12 hours), but does not act cumulatively. Its does not have any known antidotes. In military use it can come in gas, aerosol, and droplet form. It therefore acts through inhalation, cutaneously, perorally and directly through the blood stream. The toxic and physico-chemical properties of mustard gas allow it to be used in all type of munitions.

BIOLOGICAL MATERIALS

Bacillus Anthracis (Anthrax bacillus): Anthrax is a disease-producing bacteria identified by the Department of Defense in *The Conduct of the Persian Gulf War: Final Report to Congress* as being a major component in the Iraqi biological warfare program.

Anthrax is an often-fatal infectious disease due to [the] ingestion of spores. It begins abruptly with high fever, difficulty in breathing, and chest pain. The disease eventually results in septicemia (blood poisoning), and the mortality is high. Once septicemia is advanced, antibiotic therapy may prove useless, probably because exotoxins remain, despite the death of the bacteria.

Clostridium Botulinum (Botulism): A bacterial source of botulinum toxin, which causes vomiting, constipation, thirst, general weakness, headache, fever, dizziness, double vision, dilation of the pupils and paralysis of the muscles involving swallowing. It is often fatal.

Histoplasma Capsulatum: Causes a disease superficially resembling tuberculosis that may cause pneumonia, enlargement of the liver and spleen, anemia, an influenza-like illness and an acute inflammatory skin disease marked by tender red nodules, usually on the shins. Reactivated infection usually involves the lungs, the brain, spinal membranes, heart, peritoneum, and the adrenals.

Brucella Melitensis: A bacteria which can cause chronic fatigue, loss of appetite, profuse sweating when at rest, pain in [the] joints and muscles, insomnia, nausea, and damage to major organs.

Clostridium Perfringens: A highly toxic bacteria which causes gas gangrene. The bacteria produce toxins that move along muscle bundles in the body, killing cells and producing necrotic tissue that is then favorable for further growth of the bacteria itself. Eventually, these toxins and bacteria enter the bloodstream and cause a systemic illness.

References: *U.S. Chemical and Biological Warfare-Related Dual Use Exports to Iraq and Their Possible Impact on the Health Consequences of the Persian Gulf War,* a Report of Chairman Donald W. Riegle, Jr. and Ranking Member Alfonse M. D'Amato of the Committee on Banking, Housing and Urban Affairs with Respect to Export Administration, 103d Congress, 2d Session, 25 May 1994, 28–38.

Testimony of U.S. Ambassador to the United Nations Albright to the Senate Foreign Relations Committee, 21 March 1995

On 21 March 1995, United States Ambassador to the United Nations Madeleine K. Albright appeared before the

Senate Committee on Foreign Relations to testify on a number of subjects dealing with the proposed Peace Powers Act (S.5) and the National Security Revitalization Act (H.R.7). In her comments, excerpted from the full testimony but with her observations on Iraq appearing in full here, she discussed the possible lifting of sanctions on Iraq.

Over the past month, I have visited or spoken with the leaders of most Security Council members to lock in support for our policy of maintaining sanctions against Iraq. My goal was to counter growing pressure to ease sanctions, coming particularly from countries with an economic interest in resuming business with Iraq. The results were heartening. The strong American resolve that I was able to convey on behalf of the President, coupled with the compelling information we were able to share concerning Iraqi activities, caused skeptics to become fence-sitters, and fence-sitters to hop down on our side of the pickets. On March 13, the Council decided to extend sanctions unchanged for another two months.

This is not, however, the end of the story. We continue to be accused in some quarters of indifference to the hardships suffered by the Iraqi people, and of having moving the goalposts in terms of what is required to ease or lift sanctions later this spring.

This is not a time for America to be taking the United Nations for granted. Our position on Iraqi sanctions is rooted in concern for the security of friends in a region of strategic importance. It is based on our continued well-founded suspicion of the intentions of the Iraqi regime. It reflects our support for strengthening international standards of human rights and law. And it is based on the facts.

Iraq's compliance with U.N. Security Council resolutions since 1991 has been and remains meager, sporadic, selective, and incomplete. When Iraq has complied, it has done so only as a result of concerted pressure from the international community.

Weapons of Mass Destruction
Chairman [Rolf] Ekeus of the U.N. Special Commission (UNSCOM) has expressed repeatedly his concern that Iraq has not come clean about all of its past weapons programs, noting that Iraqi disclosures about its weapons of mass destruction programs often are like the tales of 1,001 Arabian nights; they change every time U.N. inspectors confront Iraqi officials with new information.

Iraq refused to provide any cooperation to UNSCOM until November 1993. Even after this time, it declined to provide any comprehensive information about biological weapons, claiming it had no offensive BW program, but only a nascent, defensively oriented research program.

On February 27, Ekeus told the Security Council

that Iraq had imported 22 tons of biological medium, a growth culture needed in small quantities for civilian use, but useful in massive quantities only for BW. Iraq has not provided a convincing explanation of why it imported this material, what it was used for and why they have not been able to turn it over to UNSCOM. Until these matters are cleared up, we must proceed on the assumption that the material was either turned into weapons or used for a program to do so.

The fact is that the U.S. intelligence community believes that Iraq may be hiding equipment and materials belonging to each of its weapons of mass destruction programs. And we believe that if the oil embargo is lifted unconditionally, Baghdad could well order the departure of U.N. inspectors. Under those circumstances, Iraq would be able to begin producing Scud missiles within one year; it would be able to rebuild its biological weapons program in less than one year and its chemical warfare program in two to three years. In five to seven years, it could build a nuclear device.

Lest there be doubt about its intentions, Iraq continues to devote money and manpower to rebuilding its infrastructure for its weapons of mass destruction and conventional weapons programs. The Al Kindi missile research and development facility, for example, supported many Iraqi weapons programs before the war. The facility was damaged heavily during Operation Desert Storm but has largely been rebuilt and even expanded since then. The facility has been under U.N. supervision, but could easily be converted to support prohibited weapons programs.

The Habbiniyah II facility produced CW agent precursor chemicals before Desert Storm. The Iraqis have rebuilt the main production building and the chlorine plant and have added a phenol production line as well as a ferric chloride line. These production lines contain dual-use equipment that could easily be converted to CW agent or precursor chemical production.

Return of Captured Military Equipment
Iraq's claim that it retains only a few pieces of damaged Kuwaiti combat equipment is false.

• For example, Iraq claims that it has only four of the more than 200 BMP-2 armored personnel carriers that it stole from Kuwait.

• The truth is that Iraq still has more than 200 of these captured Kuwaiti vehicles, and many other Kuwaiti weapons, which it used to threaten Kuwait last October.

Terrorism
Iraq has continued to use terror as an instrument of state. Last April, Iraqi intelligence officers murdered Talib al-Suhayl, an Iraqi oppositionist in Beirut.

Repression of the Iraqi People

Finally, Iraq has refused to comply with the U.N. Security Council resolution 688 and has continued to repress its own people.

• The United Nations Special Rapporteur for human rights in Iraq reports that there is no evidence of significant improvement of Iraq's human rights record, which is among the world's worst, and that in some areas Iraq's record has worsened.

• In the north, Saddam's economic blockade of the three Kurdish provinces is now in its third year, and Baghdad's shut-off of electrical power to Dahuk province is in its second year.

• In the south, the repression of the marsh Arabs continues. At least 700 hamlets have been destroyed by government forces since 1991. The drying of the marshes threatens to extinguish a centuries-old culture and typifies the brutality of Saddam Hussein's regime.

Impact of Sanctions

The sanctions regime has had a dramatic impact on Iraq's economy. The dinar, which traded 40 to the dollar in January 1993 and 150 to the dollar in January 1994, now trades at about 1200 to the dollar.

Iraqi Construction—the Palaces

Nevertheless, Saddam has refused to implement U.N. Security Council resolutions 706 and 712, which allow limited oil exports under U.N. supervision, and he has devoted considerable resources to rebuilding the Iraqi military and his own palaces.

• Iraq has constructed 50 new palaces or luxury residences since the end of Desert Storm at a cost of over $1.5 billion. There are now 78 such palaces or residences in Iraq for use by Saddam, his family, or close supporters.

For example, the Mosul palace complex includes two areas; one with five palaces and two offices or apartment buildings; the other with three completed palaces and a fourth under construction on a newly excavated, man-made lake. The estimated postwar cost of expanding this complex is between $170–$230 million.

One of the largest and most elaborate palaces in Iraq is in the Lake Tharthar complex; its estimated size is about 300,000 square feet—about five times the size of the White House and one and one-half [times] the size of Versailles. Other buildings on the compound—including residences and service and security facilities—add at least another 150,000 square feet to the complex. The estimated cost of this complex is $180–$240 million.

An additional $230–$310 million has been spent expanding the Baghdad Republican Palace.

America's Position

In summary, our position on Iraq sanctions has been consistent, principled and grounded in a realistic and hard-won understanding of the nature of the Iraqi regime. We are determined to ensure that Iraq's government is not allowed to resume building weapons of mass destruction; and we will continue to condemn its use of terror against others and against its own people. Iraqi complaints about the unfairness of all this remind me of the story about the schoolboy who came home with his face damaged and his clothes torn. When his mother asked him how the fight started he said, "It started when the other guy hit me back."

It is not our intention that the people of Iraq should suffer for the sins of their government; but make no mistake, the responsibility for those hardships rests not with the U.N. or with the United States, but with the dictatorial, luxury-loving elite in Iraq.

Reference: Testimony of U.S. Ambassador to the United Nations Madeleine K. Albright to the Senate Foreign Relations Committee, Hearing on the Peace Powers Act and The National Security Revitalization Act, United States Senate Committee on Foreign Relations, Tuesday, 21 March 1995, 14–17.

Chronology of the Persian Gulf War

636 The Zoroastrians of Persia and Arab tribes recently converted to Islam fight at Qadissiyat. This epic battle, won by the Arabs, is later hailed by *Saddam Hussein*.

1534 The Ottoman Turks overrun Baghdad, subjugating much of what is now *Iraq* and remaining in authority in the area until 1918.

1752 The al-Sabahs are established as the rulers of *Kuwait* under Sheik Sabah bin Jabir al-Sabah.

1869 The opening of the Suez Canal makes Mesopotamia and the once-closed Arab world accessible to trade.

1871 Sheik Abdullah ibn Sabah al-Sabah of Kuwait is relegated to the status of a provincial governor of *Basra*.

1899 Sheik Mubarak ibn Sabah al-Sabah, the ruler of Kuwait, enters into an agreement with the British under which Kuwait becomes a protectorate.

1913–1914 Kuwait is declared an independent state under British protection.

1914 Britain joins with Sharif Hussein of Mecca, king of the Hashemites (and a descendant of the prophet Muhammad) to establish British influence in the Transjordan area.

1916 *9 May.* Under the *Sykes-Picot-Sazanov Agreement,* the Allied Powers fighting in World War I secretly agree to divide the Middle East into "spheres of influence" following the end of the war.

1918 *3 October.* Ottoman Empire authority over the Arabs ends as a Bedouin army led by *Faisal I,* leader of the Arab insurrection against Turkish domination, enters Damascus.

1919 Saudi Arabian religious fundamentalists overrun Kuwait but are driven out by British troops, who seal the Saudi-Kuwait border for the next 20 years.

1920 *April.* Under the *San Remo Agreement,* the League of Nations mandates Iraq, Transjordan, and Palestine to *Great Britain* and *Syria* and Lebanon to France. *King Faisal* of Damascus objects to French rule over Syria.

2 June. Iraqi tribes begin a revolution against British rule that lasts until October.

24 July. The French army enters Damascus and topples Faisal, commencing the French mandate of Syria.

August. The remains of the Ottoman Empire, ruled by the Turks in Constantinople (now Istanbul) accept the *Treaty of Sèvres,* in which the Turks are ordered to relinquish all authority over the *Kurds* as a people. The treaty is never ratified by Turkey and is replaced by the *Treaty of Lausanne* in 1923.

1921 *27 August.* The British establish Faisal, the former Syrian king, as their puppet leader in Iraq and install him as the first king of Iraq.

1922 *10 October.* The Anglo-Iraqi Treaty is signed by Percy Zachariah Cox, Britain's representative in the *Persian Gulf,* and King Faisal of Iraq, allowing Great Britain to become a major factor in Iraqi affairs.

1923 *April.* The *Treaty of Uqair* establishes the boundaries of Kuwait, Iraq, and Saudi Arabia.

24 July. Representatives of the British Empire, France, Italy, Japan, Greece, Romania, and the confederation of ethnic states in the Balkans that eventually evolve into Yugoslavia sign the Treaty of Lausanne, which consolidates the ideas of the 1920 *Treaty of Sèvres* and gives Turkey a fair share of its border with Iraq.

1925 *Oil* is discovered in Iraq.

1932 *3 October.* Under British sponsorship, Iraq becomes a member of the League of Nations, the first Arab country to do so.

1933 King Faisal of Iraq dies; his son Ghazi succeeds him.

1936 *October.* A military coup d'état in Iraq is led by Bakr Sidqi, who forces Prime Minister Yassin al-Hashemi to resign.

1937 King Ghazi of Iraq advocates the absorption of Kuwait and criticizes the Kuwaiti ruler as an outdated feudal monarch.

28 April. According to his biography, Saddam Hussein is born in a small village near the northern Iraqi town of Tikrit.

August. Bakr Sidqi is assassinated by dissident Iraqi army officers.

1939 King Ghazi of Iraq dies in a car accident; his father's cousin, Abdul Illah, is designated as regent for Ghazi's son, Faisal.

1941 *8 June–12 July.* British occupation of Syria. With the aid of French troops in the area, the British attempt to circumvent a possible German invasion of the area by occupying parts of Syria, but later withdraw.

1945 Establishment of the *League of Arab States;* the initial members are Egypt, Iraq, *Jordan,* Lebanon, *Saudi Arabia,* Syria, and *Yemen.*

1947 *Michel Aflaq* forms the *Ba'ath* party in Syria. Its influence later spreads to Iraq.

1948 *17 September.* Swedish diplomat Count Folke Bernadotte of Wisborg, representing the *United Nations* in settling the Palestine question, and his aide Col. Andre Serot of France are assassinated by three

Jewish terrorists in Jerusalem, setting the stage for the formation of *Israel.*

1951 The U.S. Army Corps of Engineers begins construction of the Saudi airfield at *Dhahran,* the first such American action in Saudi Arabia.

1951–1954 Sometime during this period, the Iraqi branch of the Ba'ath party is founded.

1952 Iraq announces its claim to Kuwait, but is warned by the British government against any invasion.

1953 King Ghazi's son Faisal is installed as King *Faisal II* of Iraq.

1955 *24 February.* The Pact of Mutual Cooperation, also known as the *Baghdad Pact,* is signed between Turkey and Iraq.

4 April. The Baghdad Pact is signed between Great Britain and Iraq, clearing the stage for full British involvement in Iraqi internal and military affairs.

1958 First cousins *Hussein ibn Talal,* king of Jordan, and Faisal II, king of Iraq, briefly unite their nations in the Arab Federal State. Prime Minister Nuri as-Said of Iraq asks Kuwait to join the union, but the offer is rejected.

14 July. A group of communists and followers of Egypt's Gamel Abdel Nasser led by Iraqi military officer *Abdul-Karim Qassem* overthrow the pro-British Iraqi government of Premier Nuri as-Said. As-Said and King Faisal II are executed in the uprising. It is reported that two Americans in Iraq—Eugene Burns, a writer, and George Colley, a construction engineer—are dragged into the streets and killed by rampaging mobs.

1959 *16 March.* An economic delegation from Iraq signs an Agreement of Technical and Economic Cooperation with the *Soviet Union,* indicating a complete break with the West. The Soviets lend the Iraqis 550 million rubles for internal improvements such as bridges and agricultural development.

24 March. Iraqi leader Qassem announces that Iraq will withdraw from the Baghdad Pact on 24 February 1960.

1961 *19 June.* Great Britain terminates the 1899 agreement with Kuwait and declares the emirate to be an independent nation.

26 June. Iraqi leader Qassem declares that Kuwait is part of Iraq, the first such signal that Iraq intends to lay claim militarily to that nation. Great Britain and the Arab League respond by sending troops to defend Kuwait's sovereignty.

1963 *8 February.* Ba'athist coup in Iraq. Ten thousand people are killed in the first week; nine months of bloodshed follow before the Ba'athists lose their grip on power in November. Iraqi leader Qassem is executed by the coup plotters.

14 May. Kuwait is admitted to the United Nations as its 111th member.

4 October. The new Iraqi government announces that Qassem's claim on Kuwait was in error and that it recognizes Kuwait's independence as a separate nation.

1 November. Abd al-Salaam Arif stages a bloodless coup in overthrowing the Ba'athists.

1964 *26 May.* Iraq signs an agreement with Egypt to establish a joint presidential committee and military command.

October. Saddam Hussein is involved in a failed coup attempt. He is captured, found guilty, and ultimately spends two years in prison.

1967 Iraq severs diplomatic relations with the United States over its support of Israel during the Six Day War.

4 June. Iraq signs a defense pact with Egypt and Jordan.

1968 *17 July.* A bloodless coup returns the Ba'athists to power. It is led by *Ahmad Hassan al-Bakr,* who is named president; Saddam Hussein is named assistant general secretary of the Ba'ath party.

1969 *30 July.* Iraq signs a defense pact with Syria.

1972 *9 April.* Iraq signs a 15-year treaty of friendship with the Soviet Union.

December. Iraqi construction crews begin to build a road two miles inside Kuwait at *Samita.*

1973 *March.* Iraq presents Kuwait with a treaty that gives Iraq comprehensive rights to drill oil inside Kuwait, including oil export facilities. Kuwait refuses to sign it.

20 March. Kuwaiti soldiers attempt to stop construction work by Iraqi soldiers at Samita. The Iraqis fire on the Kuwaitis, starting a small skirmish in which two Kuwaitis and one Iraqi are killed. An Iraqi patrol later shells a Kuwaiti border post at Umm Qasr.

5 April. Mediation by Foreign Minister Abdel Halim Khaddam of Syria and Secretary-general Mahmoud Riad of the Arab League leads to an Iraqi pullout from Samita.

1974 Saddam Hussein, deputy chairman of Iraq's *Revolutionary Command Council,* describes Iraq's relations with the United States in a frank speech: "There is no contradiction between our decision to sever diplomatic relations with America and to deal commercially with some American companies....The presence of these American companies will never open the door to a change in our political program."

1975 *6 March.* Signing between *Iran* and Iraq of the *Algiers Agreement:* Iraq gives up its territorial desires in the area in exchange for a small piece of the *Shatt al-Arab Waterway* and Iranian aid in destroying the Kurds in Iraq. The treaty is signed by the shah of Iran and Saddam Hussein, vice-chairman of Iraq's Revolutionary Command Council.

18 November. France and Iraq sign the Franco-Iraqi Nuclear Cooperation Treaty. Under the terms of the pact, France agrees to build the Tammuz nuclear breeder at

Tuwaitha (the plant is soon named after its actual site, *Osirak*) and train 600 Iraqi nuclear technicians.

1976 Sybetra, a Belgian company, begins work on a phosphate mine in the western Iraqi desert near the village of Shab al-Hiri. Sybetra also signs a contract to build a fertilizer plant at Al Qaim, with the proviso that the plant would be fortified with heavy concrete walls.

1977 The United States and Bahrain sign an agreement allowing for the leasing of docking and shore facilities by American forces stationed in the Middle East. France sells Iraq 36 *Mirage F-1s* for $1.8 billion.

July. A joint Iraqi-Kuwaiti committee is established to resolve the border problems arising from the 1973 Samita incident.

1978 Iraq signs a deal with the Soviet Union; for $3 billion, the USSR sells to Iraq 138 *MiG-23* and MiG-27 fighter/bombers, *Scud missile* launchers, troop and equipment transports, and MI8 transport helicopters.

October. The Ayatollah Ruhollah Khomeini is expelled from his exile in Iraq.

26 October. Iraq signs a treaty with Syria for mutual defense and joint military action. The treaty is abandoned in 1979.

1979 The Carter administration puts Iraq on its list of terrorist nations.

February. The Islamic Revolution breaks out in Iran. In the commotion, Iraq sees a growing opportunity to capture the contentious Shatt al-Arab Waterway.

7 April. The completed nuclear reactor due to be shipped from France to Iraq in two days is destroyed by an explosion. Israel's Mossad intelligence agency is suspected, but no evidence is ever found.

28 July. The *New York Times* reports a rift in the leadership of the Iraqi Revolutionary Command Council, and that "tens and perhaps more than a hundred arrests" have occurred following opposition to Saddam Hussein's leadership.

14 December. According to the *New York Times*, "Iran announces, but then denies, that it is has been invaded by Iraq."

1980 *23 January.* In a speech before a joint session of Congress, President Jimmy Carter outlines his policy on American interests in the Persian Gulf. "Let our position be absolutely clear. Any attempt by any outside forces to gain control of the Persian Gulf region will be regarded as an assault on the vital interest of the United States of America. Any such assault will be repelled by any means necessary, including military force," he declares.

February. Saddam Hussein discloses his National Covenant, in which he vows the "renunciation of the use of force by any Arab country against another and the resolution of all inter-Arab disputes by peaceful means."

March. The Carter administration accuses Italy of supplying Iraq with nuclear equipment. Italy responds that it did so with the agreement of the U.S. government.

8 April. Iran's Ayatollah Khomeini denounces Saddam Hussein and calls on the Iraqi army and Iraqi dissidents to overthrow his regime. In response, Saddam allows training of Iranian exiles in Iraq to fight the Iranian government.

9 April. Iraqi Shi'ite dissidents Mohammed Baqir al-Sadr and his sister, Bint al-Huda, are executed by the Iraqi government in what is considered a prelude to the Iraqi invasion of Iran.

14 June. Unknown assassins murder Yahia El-Meshad, head of Iraq's nuclear power program, in his hotel room in Paris. Again, French authorities suspect the Israeli Mossad, but no evidence is ever found, nor is anyone arrested for the crime.

10 July. A dozen American F-4E jets arrive in Egypt to train with the Egyptian air force, the first time American troops practice with an Arab army.

4 September. Iraq alleges that Iranian military units have attacked the Iraqi border town of Khanaqin.

7 September. Iraq abrogates the 1975 Algiers Agreement with Iran.

22 September. Iraqi troops invade Iran, touching off one of the bloodiest wars of the twentieth century. In honor of the Arab victory over the Persians in the 636 A.D. battle of Qadissiyat, Saddam Hussein calls his 1980 offensive "Qadissiyat Saddam."

23 September. The United States and the Soviet Union declare their individual neutrality in the *Iran-Iraq War.* However, over the next several years, both countries send arms and materiel to both Iran and Iraq.

28 September. The United Nations Security Council votes unanimously on a resolution that calls for both Iran and Iraq to "refrain immediately from the further use of force."

29 September. Iran refuses to consider a cease-fire offer from the Iraqis. "There is no question of a cease-fire for us," declares Ali Akbar Hashemi Rafsanjani, speaker of the Iranian Majlis (Parliament).

30 September. Iranian jets fly over Iraq's Osirak nuclear site and fire several missiles at the reactor. Iran later denies that the attack ever happened, and the failed assault is blamed on Israel. An Iraqi newspaper states: "The Iranian people should not fear the Iraqi nuclear reactor, which is not intended to be used against Iran, but against the Zionist enemy."

4 October. Jordan becomes the first Arab country to announce its support for Iraq in the Iran-Iraq War.

November. The United States and Egypt conduct joint military exercises under the code name *Operation Bright Star,* the first time American troops train in an Arabian desert atmosphere. They are joined by troops from *Oman,* Somalia, and the Sudan.

25 December. The U.S. General Accounting Office reports that it accidentally approved a license for a shipment of General Electric frigate turbines to Iraq.

1981 *7 June.* Israeli planes attack and destroy the Iraqi nuclear power plant at Osirak. Although condemned internationally at the time, this action has wide-ranging implications for the crisis that eventually consumes the Persian Gulf.

16 July. Minister of Information Muhammad Abdu Yamani of Saudi Arabia announces that his country, in a gesture of friendship to a neighbor Arab state, will offer to pay the entire cost of rebuilding Iraq's destroyed Osirak nuclear power facility.

8 August. Crown Prince Fahd of Saudi Arabia proposes a seven-point peace plan for the Middle East; he says that the Camp David accords between Israel and Egypt "are futile as a framework for a just and comprehensive peace." Israel decries the plan as "unacceptable."

September. Iranian troops attack and bomb the Kuwaiti oil installations at Umm al-Aish, near the Iraqi border. In protest, Kuwait temporarily withdraws its ambassador to Iran.

1 October. President Ronald Reagan warns that "there's no way the United States could stand by and see that [Persian Gulf oil] taken over by anyone that would shut off that oil."

6 October. President Anwar el-Sadat of Egypt is assassinated by Muslim extremists in Cairo. His vice president, *Hosni Mubarak,* is named as his successor.

13 October. In a national referendum, Hosni Mubarak is elected president of Egypt.

28 October. Defense Minister Ariel Sharon of Israel charges the United States with supplying sensitive military equipment to Iraq that might be turned against Israel.

29 October. President Reagan reassures Israel that the United States is "fully committed" to making sure Israel retains "its military and technological edge" over its Arab neighbors after the Senate votes 52–48 to allow Saudi Arabia to purchase $8.5 billion in AWACS jets. The U.S. Senate also votes 52–48 to sell $8.5 billion worth of sophisticated aircraft and other military equipment, including five AWACS jets, to Saudi Arabia.

8 November. In a televised address to the Egyptian people, President Hosni Mubarak declares that Egypt is "an African state" and would "never be within the orbit of this or that country, or this bloc or that bloc."

17 November. Iran's Ayatollah Khomeini denounces the Saudi peace plan generated on 8 August as "contrary to Islam."

27 December. Iraq settles its boundary dispute with Saudi Arabia.

1982 Iraqi troops are pushed back to Iraq's prewar border with Iran.

26 February. In a change of policy, the U.S. State Department drops Iraq from its list of terrorist nations, paving the way for American exports of food and technological materials to Iraq. Kuwait attempts to mediate the Iran-Iraq War, but is unsuccessful.

March. Iran unleashes Operation Undeniable Victory against Iraq, a turning point in the Iran-Iraq War. Iran is able to drive Iraqi troops deeply back into Iraq and split the Iraqi army at a cost of untold thousands of lives.

April. The Reagan administration announces the sale to Iraq of up to a dozen Lockheed LL-100 transports and five Boeing jets.

June. Iran's offensive, launched in March, causes Iraq to ask the United Nations to negotiate a settlement, and to declare its willingness to withdraw all Iraqi troops from Iranian soil.

6 June. Israel launches Operation Galilee to drive Syrian and Palestinian fighters from Lebanon.

July. Iran launches Operation Ramadan near Basra: The Iranian army utilizes Pasderan (Revolutionary Guard) forces and Basij volunteers, including some nine-year old boys, to invade Iraqi minefields and other fortifications. The numbers of dead are considered staggering, although no firm numbers are ever revealed.

September. Some American lawmakers object to the removal of Iraq from the State Department list of terrorist states because of the return of terrorist Abu Nidal to *Baghdad.*

3 September. Israel's Operation Galilee ends in failure as it negotiates a withdrawal of PLO fighters from Beirut to safety.

October. Six Construct International, also known as Sixco, a Belgian construction concern, finishes work on the Al Qaim chemical complex on Iraq's western border with Syria and begins to build the secret complex known only as Project 505, where within six underground bases Iraq will house its planes and pilots in the event of a nuclear attack. The Iraqi government announces that it possesses a chemical weapon capable of killing 100,000 people in a single attack.

21 November. Foreign Minister *Tariq Aziz* of Iraq accuses the United States of supplying military equipment to Iran that is being used in the Iran-Iraq War.

15 December. The U.S. Department of Agriculture announces $210 million in Commodity Credit Corporation (CCC) loans to Iraq for the purchase of food in the United States.

1983 The Iranians unleash three additional "human waves" at Iraq, all with little or no success but with massive casualties. The Iran-Iraq War settles into a World War I type of stalemate and attrition.

Summer. Undersecretary for Foreign Affairs Ismat Kittani of Iraq visits the United States to improve U.S.-Iraqi relations.

July. KBS, a Dutch company, ships 500 tons of thiodigycol from Phillips Petroleum in Belgium to Baghdad. When mixed with hydrochloric acid, thiodigycol turns into mustard gas.

December. Special Middle East envoy Donald Rumsfeld visits Baghdad to improve U.S.-Iraqi relations. For the first time Iraq uses yperite, a form of mustard gas, against waves of attacking Iranian troops.

1984 Sometime during this year, the Reagan administration tilts toward Iraq in its war with Iran, secretly deciding to share "limited intelligence" with Baghdad. This cooperation would continue until just before Iraq's invasion of Kuwait in 1990.

February. Assistant Secretary of State Richard Murphy visits Baghdad in one of the final acts before Baghdad and Washington restore relations. Iraqi troops spray canisters of poison gas on Iranian troops in the Howeiza marshes near the Majnoon Islands. Medics arriving on the scene find the affected Iranians vomiting, their skin turning red, and then dying in horrible pain.

March. The world press begins to report that Iranian soldiers have been attacked by chemical weapons. Secretary-general *Javier Pérez de Cuéllar* of the United Nations sends a team of investigators to Iraq to discover the truth. The team finds Iranians who have been victims of a chemical attack, as well as an Iraqi chemical bomb assembled in Spain by a company called Explosivas Alevesas, but shipped from the Torrejon Air Base, an American site, in Spain.

April. Iraq's State Enterprise for Pesticide Production (SEPP) asks Melchemie, a Dutch enterprise, for phosphorus oxyxchloride, which can be used to produce the toxic agent tabun; the Dutch company tries, but is unsuccessful in finding someone to sell the chemical to Iraq.

19 June. The U.S. Export-Import Fund loans $84 million to Iraq to construct an oil pipeline.

20 June. After Rep. Howard Berman (D–CA) attempts to have Iraq reclassified as a terrorist state, Secretary of State George Shultz writes him, "The legislation you proposed would be seen and resented in Baghdad as a foreign attempt to dictate Iraqi policy, severely disrupting our diplomatic dialogue."

October. Bell Helicopter Textron signs a deal to sell Iraq 45 commercial helicopters.

13 November. The United States and Iraq resume diplomatic relations.

November. In order to placate the West, Saddam Hussein deports several member of the Abu Nidal terrorist group from Iraq. He later invites them to return. Carlos Cardoen, a Chilean arms dealer, delivers cluster bomb fuses to Iraq with zirconium contents made by Teledyne Industries Inc. and the International Signals Corporation, both American companies.

1985 *13 March.* Iraq begins a massive chemical attack on Iranian troops, killing about 5,000 soldiers.

26 March. Secretary of State George Shultz discusses the use of chemical weapons with Foreign Minister Aziz of Iraq. The U.S. government officially condemns the use of such weapons; however, at the same time, it increases U.S. Export-Import loans from $35 million in 1985. By 1990 the amount will increase to $267 million.

25 May. A suicide bomber from the Muslim fundamentalist group Islamic Holy War rams his dynamite-laden car into the motorcade of Emir Sheik Jaber al-Ahmed al-Sabah, killing himself, two bodyguards, and a bystander, but only slightly wounding the emir.

July. Assistant Secretary of Defense Richard Perle signals the first official U.S. government concern about Iraq; he writes to Secretary of Defense Caspar Weinberger that "there is a body of evidence indicating that Iraq continues to actively pursue an interest in nuclear weapons.… In the past Iraq has been somewhat less than honest in regard to the intended end-use of high technology equipment."

15 August. Iraq uses French-made AS-30L laser-guided "smart" bombs to attack Iran's Kharg Island oil terminal, the first time such weapons have been used in wartime. The lasers in the weapons are manufactured by Martin Marietta.

1986 *9 February.* In one of the bloodiest battles of the Iran-Iraq War, Iraqi troops capture the Fao Peninsula.

27 October. The British Broadcasting Corporation television program "Panorama" presents "The Secrets of Samarra," an inside investigative look at Iraq's main chemical-producing plant on the Tigris River northwest of Baghdad.

3 November. A Lebanese news magazine, *Al Shiraa,* discloses that the United States has been shipping weapons to Iran, uncovering what is later known as the Iran-Contra Affair.

18 November. Saddam Hussein writes to President Reagan, registering his objection to the sale of American military hardware to Iran. Assistant Secretary of State Murphy writes to Secretary of State Shultz: "Saddam Hussein's letter…is a measure of the intense anger and sense of betrayal felt by the Iraqis.… Although the equipment transferred to Iran from U.S. stock was apparently limited in type and amount, it is difficult to refute the Iraqis' underlying accusation— that the U.S. has armed Iran to kill Iraqis."

1987 *3 March.* Iraq renegotiates its $500 million debt to Western banks.

7 March. To discourage the destruction of oil tankers by Iranian mines, the United States announces that it will escort Kuwaiti oil tankers through the Persian Gulf after reflagging them with the American flag.

2 April. The Reagan administration refuses to approve the sale of *C-130 Hercules Transports* to Iraq, but does consent to supply Baghdad with satellite photos of Iranian troop movements.

17 May. An Iraqi *Exocet missile* slams into the frigate USS *Stark,* killing 37 American sailors. Iraq apologizes for the incident.

15 August. Saddam Hussein boasts of the successful test firing of the Iraqi Scud missile variant called the al-Hussein.

2 November. In an embarrassing incident, the frigate USS *Carr* fires on what it suspects is an Iranian gunboat in the Persian Gulf; in actuality, it is an unarmed fishing vessel. An Indian crew member is killed.

1988 *February.* In a raid of a company called Paimpex in Rome, Italian police find 28 tons of cluster bombs ready for shipment to Iraq. Originally built by Chilean arms dealer Carlos Cardoen, they are later found to have been paid for with loans from the Banca Nazionale de Lavoro, an Italian bank.

29 February. Iraq launches the first of nine missiles in what will be called "The War of the Cities," striking Tehran and causing an untold number of civilian casualties.

17–18 March. Iraq attacks Kurds sympathetic with Iran. The key target is the border village of Halabja, where some 70,000 civilians are attacked with cyanide gas. Some 5,000 men, women and children are killed, and 7,000 more are maimed for life.

17 April. Iraq launches a massive assault to recapture the strategic Fao Peninsula from Iran by using vital satellite reconnaissance photos from the United States. Iran accuses the United States of providing Iraqi troops with helicopter protection.

25 April. The Iraqi military tests the al-Abbas, an Iraqi-built variant of the Soviet Scud missile.

3 July. In the Persian Gulf, the USS *Vincennes* shoots down an Iranian jetliner, killing all 290 men, women, and children aboard. Although the United States claims that it fired fearing a repeat of the 1987 *Stark* incident, it is learned four years later that the ship was in territorial Iranian waters, was in pursuit of Iranian gunboats, and mistakenly thought that the jetliner was an Iranian F-14.

14 July. Vice President *George Bush,* in the midst of his presidential campaign, makes a historic appearance before the UN Security Council to defend the United States in the *Vincennes* incident.

20 August. The Iran-Iraq War ends in a stalemate brokered by the United Nations. Although Saddam Hussein claims victory, his nation has suffered 420,000 casualties (120,000 dead and 300,000 wounded militarily, an untold number of dead and wounded civilians, plus 70,000 prisoners of war still held by Iran), and is saddled with a debt of $80 billion and reconstruction costs estimated at more than $320 billion. Because Iraqi access to the Persian Gulf is limited to the ruined Shatt al-Arab Waterway, Iraqi representatives meet with officials from Kuwait to demand from that country the long-term lease of Bubiyan and Warba islands; the talks go nowhere. Iraq comes under increasing criticism for its use of chemical weapons during the war; however, American exports in food and technology continue, reaching more than $1 billion in CCC loan guarantees for fiscal years 1988 and 1989.

December. Iraq again demands long-term leases to Bubiyan and Warba islands. Kuwait refuses.

1989 *14 January.* The *Times* of London reports that the British Department of Trade and Industry allowed British companies, through a legal license, to ship to Iraq thousands of pounds of the basic ingredient to manufacture the nerve gas sarin since 1983.

17 January. Officials in the Reagan administration confirm the ABC news report that Iraq was building *chemical and biological warfare* plants that could produce anthrax, typhoid, and cholera.

18 January. Quoting Israeli intelligence authorities, Radio Luxembourg reports that West German scientists, along with counterparts from Cuba and East Germany, have been in Iraq for several years helping the Iraqis construct the Zaafaraniya germ warfare plant at Salman Pak, 8 miles south of Baghdad.

23 January. In an interview, Chancellery Minister Wolfgang Schaeuble of West Germany denies that his nation has been involved in aiding Iraq's buildup of chemical and biological weaponry.

25 January. Sen. John McCain (R–AZ) claims that the United States has shipped to Iraq bacteria viruses 10 times more lethal than anthrax. "We know that Iraq has already misused international agreements to obtain [the] tularemia virus from the U.S.... We have every reason to assume that Iraq may soon weaponize two of the three most lethal biotoxins—anthrax and tularemia," McCain charges.

29 January. The *Washington Post* reports that the U.S. State Department is investigating Sen. McCain's claim that Iraq has obtained the tularemia virus.

30 January. U.S. Customs announces the arrests of Nicholas J. Defino, an officer of the Nu Kraft Mercantile Corporation of New York, and Frans Van Anraat, a Dutch agent for Nu Kraft, on charges of purchasing 500 tons of the chemical agent thiodiglycol from Alcolac International, illegally shipping them to Jordan, and then rerouting the shipment to Iraq. Executives of Alcolac plead guilty to one count of violating U.S. export laws by also shipping thiodiglycol to Iran.

February. For the third and last time, Iraq demands leases to Bubiyan and Warba islands. Kuwait again refuses. At this time, U.S. intelligence sources detect the construction of fixed ballistic missile launchers in the Western part of Iraq.

9 February. In testimony before the Senate Committee on Governmental Affairs, CIA Director William Webster alleges that Iraq has generated "several thousands of tons of chemical agents."

28 March. The U.S. Department of State announces that it has approved an Iraqi offer of $27.3 million as compensation for the 37 men killed in the May 1987 attack on the frigate USS *Stark*.

3 June. Iranian leader Ayatollah Khomeini dies in Tehran, setting off a quick but frenzied attempt to grab power.

4 June. An Assembly of Experts, composed of Iranian Shi'ite authorities, selects President Hojatolislam Seyed Ali Khamenei as Iran's supreme religious leader.

23 June. Michel Aflaq, founder of Syria's Ba'ath party and a leading authority in Iraq, dies in a Paris hospital.

28 July. Iranian Majlis speaker Hojatolislam Ali Akbar Hashemi Rafsanjani is elected president of Iran. He is sworn in on 3 August.

4 August. FBI agents raid the American offices of the Banca Nazionale de Lavoro (BNL), an Italian bank. The agents find evidence in the Atlanta branch that the bank has been sending billions of dollars in illegal loans to Iraq.

17 August. A clandestine missile plant near the Iraqi town of Hilla explodes, killing perhaps a thousand Iraqis.

September. The Kuwaiti Emir, Sheik Jaber al-Ahmad al-Sabah, travels to Baghdad where Saddam Hussein bestows on him the Rafadin Medal, Iraq's highest award.

2 October. President Bush secretly signs National Security Directive 26, a proclamation of American policy in the Persian Gulf region following the end of the Iran-Iraq War. It thus become official policy that "the United States government should propose economic and political incentives for Iraq to moderate its behavior and to increase our influence with Iraq."

3 October. The U.S. Department of Agriculture suggests that the government issue $1 billion in loan credits to Iraq. Because of the burgeoning BNL scandal, the Treasury Department refuses to issue the loan credits. Instead, USDA offers $400 million in credits.

6 October. Iraqi Foreign Minister Aziz meets with Secretary of State *James Baker* to push the U.S. government into issuing an additional $500 million in commodity credits to Iraq.

8 October. The Iraqis threaten to default on the payment of prior loans from the United States if the nation is not extended more credit.

13 October. Secretary James Baker becomes aware of an internal State Department memo which alleges that Iraq is using farm credits to purchase equipment for its nuclear weapons program. The memo's authors states that "If smoke indicates fire, we may be facing a four-alarm blaze in the near future." Nonetheless, Baker decides to push for the issuance of more farm credits to Iraq.

31 October. Baker impels Secretary of Agriculture Clayton Yeutter to issue further loan credits to Iraq.

5 December. Iraq tests a rocket with three stages.

1990 *January*. Investigators going over BNL's files discover more than $3 billion in loans in Iraq.

5 January. The official Iraqi news agency INA reports that Saddam Hussein's automobile is in a serious accident, although Saddam is unharmed; however, Iraqi dissidents claim that four assassins sprayed the car with machine gun fire in an unsuccessful assassination attempt.

19 February. In a speech before the Arab Cooperation Council, Saddam Hussein declares that American troops should be removed from the entire Persian Gulf region.

11 March. Accusing him of spying for the West and Israel, Iraq sentences Iranian-born British journalist *Farzad Bazoft* to death.

15 March. Ignoring pleas of leniency from around the world, Iraq executes Farzad Bazoft.

16 March. Iraq is condemned around the world for its execution of Farzad Bazoft. British Prime Minister *Margaret Thatcher* calls the murder "an act of barbarism"; however, the British government's $400 million line of credit for commodities is not canceled.

17 March. An estimated 100,000 Iraqi demonstrators march through the streets of Baghdad and surround the British Embassy to condemn the United Kingdom's protest against the hanging of Farzad Barzoft.

28 March. Six suspects are arrested in London trying to smuggle American-made nuclear triggers to Iraq.

30 March. *Dr. Gerald Bull*, who had been helping the Iraqis acquire a "supergun" to fire missiles about 1,000 miles, is mysteriously assassinated in Brussels, Belgium.

April. The U.S. Department of Agriculture, citing gross irregularities in its records, ends its CCC loan program with Iraq. The program, from fiscal 1983 until fiscal 1990, had lent Iraq some $4.5 billion in food credits.

2 April. In a fiery speech, Saddam Hussein proclaims that if Israel attacks Iraq, he will "burn half" of the Jewish state with chemical weapons.

12 April. British inspectors seize parts of Dr. Gerald Bull's supergun that are on their way to Iraq. Sens. Robert Dole (R-Kansas), Howard Metzenbaum (D-Ohio), Alan Simpson (R-Wyoming), and Frank Murkowski (R-Alaska) meet with Saddam Hussein in Baghdad to reassure him on American intentions as to his nation. Metzenbaum lauds Saddam that " I am now aware that you are a strong and intelligent man and that you want peace," while Simpson tells the Iraqi leader that " I believe that your problems lie with the Western media and not with the U.S. government."

16 April. Speaking on Radio Baghdad, Saddam Hussein denounces Western criticism of the construction of Iraqi strategic weapons and the country's poor human rights record as a pretext for another Israeli assault on his nation. He proclaims that any such attack would be met with chemical weapons.

18 April. Saddam Hussein, in a speech, declares, "He who launches an aggression against Iraq or the Arab nation will now find someone to repel him. If we can strike him with a stone, we will. With a missile, we will…and with all the missiles, bombs, and other means at our disposal."

25 April. The *U.S. Central Command (USCENTCOM)* commences a program called Iraq Regional Warning Problem to expand the accumulation of intelligence in Iraq.

8 May. Saddam Hussein declares that he has obtained an American-made trigger used to set off nuclear weapons.

21 May. USCENTCOM appraises the developing trouble spot that is the border between Iraq and Kuwait and estimates that "Iraq is not expected to use military force to attack Kuwait or Saudi Arabia to seize disputed territory or resolve a dispute over oil policy."

3 June. The Ayatollah Ruhollah Khomeini dies in Iran.

28 June. The *Wall Street Journal* publishes a lengthy interview that reporter Karen Elliott House conducted in Baghdad with Saddam Hussein. The Iraqi leader tells House that the influx of Soviet Jews into Israel is leading the region to "inevitable" conflict. His response to the charge that he is considered by his friends and enemies alike as the Butcher of Baghdad: "Weakness doesn't assure achieving the objectives required by a leader." Saddam's lack of mentioning Kuwait as one of his nation's difficulties is glaring.

July. The American military conducts a secret wargame called Internal Look which indicates that while Saudi Arabia could be defended from a mythical Iraqi invasion, the cost in American casualties would be high.

1 July. Saddam Hussein declares that his nation has binary chemical weapons and calls them "a deterrent sufficient to confront the Israeli nuclear weapon."

12 July. Officials meet at the White House to consider a request from the *United Arab Emirates* that two *KC-135 refueling tankers* be deployed to buttress the UAE air force.

14 July. Syria's President Hafez al-Assad visits Egypt for the first time since 1977, when Egypt signed a peace accord with Israel.

17 July. Saddam Hussein accuses several Persian Gulf states of "stabbing Iraq in the back" with a "poisoned dagger" by exceeding oil production quotas, thus reducing world oil prices and Iraq's ability to recover financially from the Iran-Iraq War. He estimates that such "backstabbing" has cost Iraq $89 billion between 1981 and 1990, and an additional $14 billion if it was allowed to continue.

18 July. In a letter from Iraqi Foreign Minister Tariq Aziz to the Arab League, Iraq accuses Kuwait of stealing Iraqi oil, building military installations, and refusing to cancel loans it had made to Iraq during the Iran-Iraq War. Iraq also identifies Kuwait and the United Arab Emirates as the two Arab nations that had been exceeding their OPEC-imposed quotas for oil production. Iraq threatens to take action if these events are not halted. In the United States, USCENTCOM issues a Worldwide Warning Indicator Monitoring System (WWIMS) status change to reflect growing concern over Iraq's intentions in its dispute with Kuwait.

19 July. Saddam Hussein is declared President-for-life by the Iraqi Parliament, which is dominated by Hussein's Ba'ath Party. Observers see this as an indication that Hussein's earlier promise to conduct free elections was a lie. Kuwait sends a letter to the Arab League that states that Iraq has frequently violated Kuwaiti territory and has refused repeatedly to settle long-standing border disputes. USCENTCOM receives its first intelligence reports of Iraqi troop movements near the Kuwait border.

21 July. The Kuwaiti government sends a message to UN Secretary-general Javier Pérez de Cuéllar on recent developments. Iraq again accuses Kuwait of implementing an "imperialist" plan to destroy Iraq. USCENTCOM detects 3,000 military vehicles moving from Baghdad on the roads to Kuwait.

22 July. Iraqi Foreign Minister Aziz arrives in Cairo to meet with Egyptian President Mubarak. Saddam Hussein apparently welcomes Mubarak's role as mediator in the growing crisis.

23–28 July. USCENTCOM plans for a possible Iraqi invasion of Kuwait using some 300,000 troops and 640 combat aircraft.

23 July. The *Defense Intelligence Agency (DIA),* after appraising Iraq's military strengths and weaknesses, officially discounts the possibility of an Iraqi invasion of Kuwait. The Pentagon orders two KC-135 refueling aircraft to Al Dahfra Airport in the United Arab Emirates in response to an official UAE request for the planes. The maneuver is dubbed *Operation Ivory Justice.*

24 July. Western military attachés crossing from Kuwait to Iraq on their way to Baghdad see 2,000 to 3,000 Iraqi army vehicles moving toward the Kuwaiti border, while military satellites detect the movement of 30,000 elite army troops to the border as well. Most of these troops are located in the southern city of Basra, but others, about 8,000, are discovered to be near Bubiyan and Warba Islands and have bridge assembly equipment. President George Bush puts U.S. warships in the Persian Gulf on alert. The Kuwait government activates a full military alert and dispatches the nation's small military force to the Iraqi border. Egyptian President Hosni Mubarak visits Iraq and Kuwait. After meeting with the Kuwaiti Emir, Mubarak flies to Jiddah to meet with King Fahd of Saudi Arabia to discuss the conflict. Mubarak seems to calm the crisis at first when he gets both sides to agree to meet in Saudi Arabia to iron out any problems. Later, after Mubarak has left Iraq, the official Iraqi news agency repeats earlier accusations of Kuwait's "aggression."

25 July. Saddam Hussein asks to meet with U.S. Ambassador *April Glaspie.* Conflicting sources later report that Glaspie assured the Iraqi president that the United States would not become involved militarily in an Iraqi-Kuwaiti border dispute. Glaspie later denies any such assurance. The White House announces that the United States is sending two aerial refueling planes to the area, and will deploy additional combat ships to join those ships already in the Persian Gulf region. Bush Administration officials announce their willingness to use military force to defend the flow of oil through the Strait of Hormuz. The government of Kuwait fully mobilizes its 20,000-man armed forces.

26 July. The 87th session of the *Organization of Petroleum Exporting Countries (OPEC)* meets after two days of preliminary talks. Ministers declare the benchmark price for oil will be $21 per barrel and announce a production ceiling of 22.491 million barrels per day, hoping to respond to one of Iraq's complaints.

27 July. The U.S. House of Representatives and Senate vote to impose economic sanctions on Iraq because of Iraq's human rights violations and the increasingly hostile policies of Saddam Hussein's government. The Bush Administration opposes the sanctions. The Senate votes to cut $700 million in Department of Agriculture loan guarantees that Iraq has used in the past to purchase American wheat, rice, lumber, and cattle. The House votes to allow the Secretary of Agriculture to waive sanctions if he determines them to be more harmful to American farmers than to Iraq. OPEC confirms its decision to set a target oil price at $21 per barrel and set a production ceiling at 22.5 million barrels per day. Saudi Arabian oil minister Hisham Nazir calls the agreement historic due to the high level of commitment by all 13 member countries. American analysts claim the arrangement is reached as a result of Iraq's threat of force against those who might disagree or violate the accord.

28 July. Iraq reacts to American sanctions by declaring that those members of the Congress who voted in favor of them were directed by "a fear of Zionism," while commending members who voted against sanctions, saying that they represent the real interests of the American people.

30 July. Iraq secretly triples, up to 100,000, the number of troops along the Kuwaiti border. Egyptian President Mubarak later discloses angrily that during his mission of peace to Baghdad Saddam Hussein had promised that he would not invade Kuwait. American analysts continue to state privately and in official reports to government leaders that Iraq's military actions are a form of intimidation rather than a prelude to invasion.

31 July. Communications between Iraqi and Kuwaiti delegations that begin in Saudi Arabia are mediated by Saudi King Fahd. It is reported that Iraq takes a hard line, calling for compensation from Kuwait for seizing what it claims is Iraqi territory and stealing $2.4 billion worth of oil from disputed oil fields along their common border, while also demanding that Kuwait cancel Iraq's estimated $10 billion war debt. USCENTCOM reports to the White House and the Pentagon that an Iraqi invasion of Kuwait is imminent. The Defense Intelligence Agency, in a reversal, agrees with the USCENTCOM assessment. Some pizza parlors around the White House get calls for deliveries to the presidential mansion of a large number of pizzas, tipping off many that a major crisis is at hand.

1 August. Talks to end the dispute between Iraq and Kuwait end with "no agreement" between the two countries, according to Iraq's Deputy Prime Minister Sa'dun Hammadi. Further meetings are not scheduled, although there are suggestions that the talks be held in Baghdad. In discussions with American Secretary of Defense *Dick Cheney, General H. Norman Schwarzkopf,* the commander-in-chief of the U.S. Central Command (US-CINCCENT), predicts that any invasion of Kuwait would probably end with the taking of the disputed Rumaila (or Rumailya) oil field and Bubiyan Island; a blueprint of potential American air strikes against Iraqi military targets in the event of Americans being drawn into such a conflict is presented.

2 August. Iraqi troops sweep into Kuwait, encountering little or no resistance, and occupy the entire nation in a matter of hours. The emir of Kuwait and his family flee before his nation is enveloped. A new provisional government—reportedly consisting of Kuwaiti revolutionaries opposed to the ruling al-Sabah family—is installed as the puppet government of Kuwait. Iraq claims that this newly installed *Provisional Free Government of Kuwait* has requested military assistance from Iraq, and that it will eventually hold elections in Kuwait. In one of its first acts, the new Kuwaiti "government" confiscates all the assets of the al-Sabah family. Iraq issues a summons for Arab unity and declares the Kuwaiti situation an "internal matter." In the United States, President George Bush issues Executive Order 12722, which freezes all Iraqi assets in the United States, bans all trade and transactions with Iraq, and forbids air or sea travel to Iraqi ports, and Executive Order 12723, which freezes all Kuwaiti assets in the United States. The president also orders the aircraft carrier *Independence* to the Arabian Sea. The U.S. House of Representatives immediately passes an economic sanctions bill, effectively to formulate the president's order into statutory law. The Senate passes a resolution that supports the president's executive order. The UN Security Council adopts Resolution 660, which calls for the unconditional withdrawal of Iraqi troops from Kuwait. The vote is 14-0, with Yemen abstaining. Following the U.S. lead, France and Great Britain freeze all Kuwaiti and Iraqi assets in their respective countries. The Soviet Union halts the supply of arms to Iraq. In response to these moves, Iraq immediately halts its debt repayment to the United States. The Islamic Conference Organization condemns Iraq's invasion of Kuwait. Baghdad Radio, in a statement apparently issued by Saddam Hussein, warns that "our [Iraqi] armed forces will close in an iron rank against those who try to challenge us and will make Iraq and Kuwait a graveyard for those who launch any aggression."

3 August. The United States and the Soviet Union mutually solicit the international community to end all arms shipments to Iraq. The United States also proposes UN action that would bring about a complete economic boycott of Iraq. Panama and Nicaragua denounce the Iraqi military action. American allies Italy, Germany, Belgium, and Japan announce that they will freeze all Kuwaiti assets. Turkey denounces the Iraqi invasion as an unjust act. Iraq deploys armored brigades along the Saudi border and sends reinforcement troops into Kuwait. Saudi Arabia hastily schedules a summit meeting in Jiddah between Arab leaders and Saddam Hussein. The exiled Kuwaiti emir refuses to attend while Kuwait remains occupied. Across the Arab world, there is a lack of consensus among Iraq's neighbors on a single course of action. Algeria, Morocco, and Syria individually denounce the Iraqi invasion. Egypt alone demands the immediate withdrawal of Iraqi troops. The Arab League Council votes in favor of a Saudi-proposed resolution that condemns Iraq's action in Kuwait and calls for the immediate withdrawal of Iraqi troops. Iraq ignores the resolution. Yemen, Jordan, Iraq, the Palestine delegation, Sudan, and Mauritania abstain. Libyan delegates walk out before the vote. Iraq announces its intent to withdraw troops from Kuwait on 5 August. However, it announces that the provisional government, which the United States has denounced as a puppet regime, will remain in control. Oil prices rise to $24.49 per barrel. According to press reports, 120 Iraqi military officers are executed by an Iraqi firing squad for opposing the invasion of Kuwait. Britain sends two warships to the Middle East, with France sending a single warship.

4 August. A proposed Arab summit, to be held in Jiddah, Saudi Arabia, collapses after PLO Chairman *Yasir Arafat* appears in Egypt with what he calls a "peace plan" by Libyan President Muammar el-Qaddafi. Baghdad television announces that the new Kuwaiti "government" is led by Col. Ala Hussein Ali, who holds the positions of prime minister, commander-in-chief of the armed forces, minister of defense, and interior minister. Eight other men are also named. Analysts note that all nine men are Iraqi military officers or mayors of Iraqi cities, and that Col. Ali is a son-in-law of Saddam Hussein, which Iraq angrily denies. The new provisional government announces that it was forming a "popular Arab army" to be open to all Arabs who wished to defend Iraq and Kuwait. Baghdad announces the release of 11 American oil workers who had disappeared during the invasion. The British Defense Ministry demands the release of 35 British servicemen acting as advisers to the Kuwaiti government who had been grabbed and apparently taken to Baghdad. In Rome, the 12-member *European Economic Community* imposes a boycott on oil imports from Iraq and Kuwait and ends all sales of European arms and other military equipment to Iraq. Jordan's King Hussein comes to Saddam Hussein's defense, saying that the Iraqi leader is a "patriot" for the majority of those in the Arab world. Yemen's President Ali Abdul Saleh expresses approval of Iraq's invasion on Baghdad television. Syria, Iraq's mortal enemy, de-

nounces the action and calls for the immediate withdrawal of Iraqi troops. Saudi Arabia mobilizes its air and ground forces to stem any possible Iraqi invasion after reports come in that Iraqi troops have taken portions of the neutral zone between Saudi Arabia and Iraq. Iraq denies the charges. French Foreign Minister Roland Dumas announces that France would consider joining in a *naval blockade* of Iraq.

5 August. President Bush declares that Iraq's invasion of Kuwait "will not stand." He demands a complete Iraqi withdrawal from Kuwait and says that the United States will not recognize the puppet regime installed there. Defense Secretary Dick Cheney travels to Saudi Arabia to confer with the Saudis on confronting the Iraqi threat. China announces that it has halted arms shipments to Iraq. Japan agrees to halt all oil imports from Iraq and Kuwait.

6 August. The UN Security Council passes the sweeping Resolution 661 on a vote of 13-0-2, which prohibits all UN members from importing any Iraqi or Kuwaiti products, and prevents transfers of funds to either country. All five permanent members of the Security Council vote in favor of the broad economic sanctions, while Cuba and Yemen abstain. Witnesses report heavy Saudi Arabian air activity at the airport near the capital of Riyadh. Reports from a secret airbase in the Saudi Arabian desert mention that 200 to 300 Saudi tanks are seen heading toward the Iraqi frontier. In Kuwait, 366 American, Britons, Germans, and other Westerners are rounded up at hotels, workplaces, and even on an airplane at Kuwait's airport and put on buses for destinations unknown. Egypt mobilizes its armed forces to deal with a possible Iraqi invasion of Saudi Arabia. In Baghdad, U.S. diplomat Joseph Wilson is summoned to a meeting with Saddam Hussein and warned against "any act that might endanger the region's peace and security." Hussein further orders the populace of Baghdad to begin to practice mass evacuation techniques, advising his nation over radio to be alert at any time for an American attack. Iraq shuts down one of the two parallel pipelines that cross into southern Turkey due to the lack of storage space for pumped oil, a direct result of the United Nation's economic boycott, which within 48 hours has cut Iraq's daily export of oil by 40 percent. The United States increases its naval force in the Middle East for a possible blockade to enforce trade sanctions. France and Great Britain agree to increase their naval presence as well. Secretary of State Cheney meets in Riyadh with Saudi King Fahd, who requests American military troops to be stationed in Saudi Arabia to defend his nation from the threat of a potential Iraqi attack. In Moscow, American Secretary of State James Baker and Soviet Foreign Minister Eduard Shevardnadze issue a joint statement denouncing the Iraqi invasion of Kuwait as "crude," "tragic," and "a violation of international law." Both men, in unison, warn Baghdad of "very serious consequences" if it did not comply with the UN mandate and withdraw from Kuwait as soon as possible. World oil prices rise to $26.05 per barrel.

7 August. The United States, in responding militarily to Iraq's invasion of Kuwait, begins to fully implement what is to become *Operation Desert Shield*, with the main mission to enforce the sanctions against Iraq and stave off an Iraqi invasion of Saudi Arabia. President Bush announces that American forces are being sent to Saudi Arabia to provide land, air, and naval protection to the Arab state. The aircraft carrier USS *Dwight Eisenhower* is sent through the Suez Canal, while the USS *Independence* arrives at the Gulf of Oman, and the USS *Saratoga*, carrying 2,100 Marines, and the battleship USS *Wisconsin* depart from the eastern United States to the Persian Gulf region. 48 F-15C Eagle fighters from the 1st Tactical Fighter Wing's 27th and 71st squadrons under the command of Col. John M. "Boomer" McBroom head to Saudi Arabia with only a few hours' notice. The 82nd Airborne Division, headquartered at Fort Bragg, North Carolina, the 24th Mechanized Infantry Division at Fort Stewart, Georgia, and the 101st Airborne Division at Fort Campbell, Kentucky, as well as Marine units, are placed on standby status. Egyptian President Mubarak rejects a request from Defense Secretary Dick Cheney for the use of military facilities in Egypt. Turkey bans imports of Iraqi oil and closes down a second oil pipeline from Kirkuk to Yumurtahk. Iraq threatens to attack Saudi Arabia if it shuts down the pipeline that runs through its territory. Switzerland bans all trade and financial transactions with either Iraq or Kuwait, the first time since World War II that Switzerland participates in an international trade embargo. Sweden likewise announces economic sanctions against Iraq and Kuwait. China announces its disapproval of any military intervention in the Middle East, but recognizes Saudi Arabia's sovereign right to request aid. Israel praises American intervention in the situation. Iraq pronounces Kuwait a "republic" and declares the end of the emirate. Jordan announces its nonrecognition of the new Kuwaiti republic. The *Gulf Cooperation Council (GCC)* calls on Iraq to withdraw its forces in accordance with the resolutions of the Arab League, the statement of the Islamic Conference Organization, and the resolutions of the United Nations. It announces that the GCC will not recognize any government formed as a result of the aggression. Iraq reportedly deploys surface-to-surface missiles in southern Iraq, within striking distance of Riyadh, the Saudi capital, and several oil fields. Frenchmade Iraqi Mirage F1 planes and *MiG-29 Fulcrums* are reported seen at airfields in southern Iraq.

8 August. Iraq announces its annexation of Kuwait, and Saddam Hussein issues a boast that Iraq is not afraid of American firepower. "All the fleets and squadrons of aircraft…will not shake a single palm frond in Iraq," he brags. Kuwait's government-in-exile asks the United Nations to hold a special session of the Security Council to declare the Iraqi annexation invalid. In Washington, President Bush declares that "a line has been drawn in the sand" that Iraq must not cross. He outlines four priorities: (1) the immediate, unconditional, and complete withdrawal of Iraqi forces from Kuwait; (2) the restoration of Kuwait's legitimate government; (3) the commitment of the American government to the security and stability of the Persian Gulf; (4) protection of Americans abroad. The operation, first called "Peninsula Shield," is renamed "Desert Shield." Bush waives implementation of the Metzenbaum Amendment, which limits the number of American F-15 aircraft sent to Saudi Arabia to 60. The Pentagon announces that American forces sent so far to Saudi Arabia will reach 50,000 within the month. Assistant Secretary of State for Near Eastern Affairs John H. Kelly is sent to Syria to elicit Damascus's help in isolating Iraq. The Pentagon orders the 82nd Airborne, elements of the 101st Airborne, and the 24th Mechanized Infantry Division to Saudi Arabia. Five AWACS jets arrive in Saudi Arabia and 4,000 Marines arrive as well, with some being deployed near the oil terminal at Khafji. Britain agrees to send air and naval forces to join the multinational effort to defend Saudi Arabia. West Germany, Italy, and Spain agree to give American transport planes use of their airspace and bases in the movement of troops to Saudi Arabia. Greece and Egypt authorize American planes to use their airspace but not their bases for the transport of personnel and equipment to the Persian Gulf. Japan and the European Community express support for President Bush's decision to send troops. The Soviet Union remains silent on the entire issue of the buildup, in essence giving its tacit support. According to French press sources, American and British citizens in Saudi Arabia are advised by their embassies to leave the country. A 10-year old American girl, Penelope Nabokov, one of the Americans held against their will, is released from a Baghdad hotel and takes shelter in the American Embassy in Baghdad. Other Americans, as well as Westerners from various countries, remain under detention in various locations in Iraq. Iraq's Revolutionary Command Council (RCC) announces the unification of Iraq and Kuwait. Col. Ala Hussein Ali is appointed Deputy Prime Minister of Iraq following the merger of the two nations. Iraq reiterates that it will respect its nonaggression treaty with Saudi Arabia. Tunisia announces its continued support for Iraq, and some Mauritanians join the new military force that Iraq has formed in Kuwait. Egypt calls for an emergency Arab summit to be held in Cairo. Oil prices fall to an average $26 a barrel. Turkish Prime Minister *Turgut Özal* announces the closing of the Iraqi oil pipeline to Turkey.

9 August. Day one of Operation Desert Shield. Meeting for a two-day summit in Cairo, 13 of the 21 Arab League members, agree to send military forces to aid Saudi Arabia and other Gulf states to protect against a potential Iraqi invasion of the entire Gulf region, while 12 of the members vote to condemn Iraq's invasion of Kuwait and demand a return of Kuwait's ruler. The Arab summit breaks up when the head of Kuwait's "interim government," Col. Ala Hussein Ali, arrives and takes the Kuwaiti seat. President Bush sends a letter "consistent with the War Powers Resolution" notifying Congress of the deployment of troops to the Persian Gulf, but says that he does not believe involvement in hostilities was imminent. The United States calls for other nations to send ground forces to aid in the defense of Saudi Arabia. U.S. Secretary of State James Baker meets with President Turgut Özal of Turkey to persuade him to allow American planes to be used in operations against Iraq, if the need should arise. Özal, sensitive to his country's geographical proximity to Iraq, defers a decision. Iraq seals off its borders to all foreigners except diplomats, effectively trapping an estimated 550 Americans in Iraq and another 3,000 Americans in Kuwait. The UN Security Council votes 15 to 0 to declare Iraq's annexation of Kuwait null and void. Jordanian Foreign Minister Marwan Qassem declares that Jordan will recognize the UN boycott of Iraq, and closes the port of Aqaba to goods destined for Iraq. It is reported that two Soviet warships have traveled through the Suez Canal on their way to the Persian Gulf; however, the Soviets state that they will not participate in military intervention in the Gulf, adding that they oppose force and unilateral actions. Unconfirmed reports state that the Iraq Petroleum Company (IPC) oil pipeline that travels from Iraq through Syria to the Mediterranean Coast might be reopened; Syria had closed the IPC pipeline during the Iran-Iraq War. The Islamic Liberation Front announces its support for Iraq, becoming the first armed Palestinian organization to side with Saddam Hussein. The PLO remains uncommitted.

10 August. The American Tactical Information Broadcast System (TIBS) becomes operational. F-16C and D Falcons, part of the 363rd Tactical Reconnaissance Wing from Shaw Air Force Base in South Carolina, as well as C-130E Hercules cargo craft from the 317th Tactical Airlift Wing at Pope Air Force Base in North Carolina, begin arriving in Saudi Arabia as some of the first units to make up Operation Desert Shield. The Commander-in-Chief of the U.S. Central Command, General H. Norman Schwarzkopf, issues an Operation Order (OPORD) for Desert Shield which sketches a plan for a "three-phase concept of operations-deterrence, interdiction of advancing forces, and restoration of the border." Forces from the Royal Saudi Arabian Air Force, the U.S. Air Force, and the U.S. Navy conduct Exercise Arabian Gulf to coordinate air procedures in the Persian Gulf theater of operations. Meeting in emergency session in Cairo, the Arab League considers the deteriorating situation in the Gulf. Iraqi Foreign Minister Tariq Aziz, sitting as a representative of his nation, tells the delegates that the summit is a waste of time unless American troops are forced to leave the area. After Iraqi delegate Taha Yassin Ramadan tells the delegates that Iraq cannot leave Kuwait because "Kuwait is part of Iraq," and Saddam Hussein calls for a "*jihad*" (holy war) against the emirates and monarchies of the Persian Gulf, the league votes 12-3 to condemn the invasion of Kuwait, demand an immediate withdrawal from Kuwait, call for the restoration of the emir to his throne, and endorse Saudi Arabia's request for more American troops. Only 12 members of the 21-member league vote

for the resolution, while Iraq, Libya, and the PLO vote against it, with Yemen and Algeria abstaining. Tunisia's representative is not present, and Sudan, Jordan, and Mauritania take no position. A PLO-inspired resolution calling for all issues to be discussed relevant to the Middle East before any action is taken is not brought to a vote. The Iraqi government demands that all foreign governments close their embassies in Kuwait. The United States, Japan, and the European Community refuse, while the Soviet Union issues no formal statement. Assistant Secretary of State John H. Kelly meets with Syrian President al-Assad in Damascus to secure Syrian support for American policy in the Gulf.

11 August. British, Moroccan, and Egyptian troops arrive in Saudi Arabia. Several American diplomats, along with former hostage Penelope Nabokov, cross from Iraq into Jordan. Hosni Mubarak claims that there is "no hope" of peacefully ending the crisis with an Iraqi withdrawal from Kuwait. Crowds in Jordan, Mauritania, and Yemen denounce American troops in the Gulf and condemn Mubarak and Saudi King Fahd as American puppets. British citizen Dennis Croskery is shot and killed by Iraqi troops while trying to escape from Kuwait.

12 August. Saddam Hussein offers to withdraw from Kuwait in exchange for an Israeli pullout from the West Bank, Golan Heights, and Gaza Strip, and a Syrian withdrawal from Lebanon. This diplomatic move to link the Kuwaiti crisis with Israeli and Syrian land issues fails. A second Operation Arabian Gulf, utilized to coordinate combat air patrols over the Gulf region, is conducted. President Bush orders the Navy to halt all Iraqi imports and exports, but does not use the word "blockade." The United States says that it is acting on a request by the exiled government of Kuwait to enforce the United Nations sanctions under Article 51 of the UN Charter. Secretly, the United States initiates *Operation Stigma*, a total and complete arms embargo against Iraq. The U.S. Department of Defense establishes the *National Media Pool,* consisting of 17 members of the American press, to travel to Saudi Arabia. The first U.S. casualty in Operation Desert Shield, Air Force Staff Sgt. John Campisi, is killed in Saudi Arabia when he is struck by a military vehicle.

13 August. The United States demands of Jordan that its close its port of Aqaba to all ships carrying cargo destined for Iraq. At the same time, Jordanian King Hussein meets in Baghdad with Saddam Hussein. Four *MH-53 Sea Dragon* helicopters arrive in Riyadh as part of a special operations force. The Pentagon announces that American troops are landing "practically every ten minutes" in Saudi Arabia. Britain and Australia join the US naval blockade of all Iraqi ports of entry, while other nations in the UN Security Council—including France, the Soviet Union, Canada, and Malaysia—refuse to participate unless the United Nations votes in favor of joint action under Article 42. Pakistan agrees to send ground troops to Saudi Arabia. The Netherlands and Belgium consent to send naval forces to join the multinational armada. Saudi Arabia prevents the first Iraqi tanker from loading oil at the Red Sea port of Yanbu by refusing tug boat assistance. Thousands of Palestinians demonstrate in the West Bank and Gaza Strip against American intervention in Arab affairs. Japanese Prime Minister Toshiki Kaifu cancels his Middle East trip, during which he was scheduled to meet with leaders of the Gulf states. Japanese Foreign Minister Taro Nakayama is sent to the Gulf in his place. The National Media Pool sets up operations in Dhahran, Saudi Arabia, by establishing the *Joint Information Bureau (JIB)* in the Dhahran International Hotel.

14 August. The five permanent members discuss how a coordinated blockade can be established under the direction of the United Nations. Syrian troops begin arriving in Saudi Arabia, as well as over 1,000 Moroccan troops. The U.S. Army Forces Central Command Forward (ARCENT FWD) and the U.S. Air Force Central Command Directorate of Electronic Combat (USCENTAF/EF) are established in Saudi Arabia. Italy decides to send two frigates and a supply ship to the Eastern Mediterranean. More than 10,000 Tunisians demonstrate in Tunis in support of Iraq and denounce American military intervention in the Gulf.

15 August. Saddam Hussein suggests a peace initiative to Iran that includes the withdrawal of Iraqi troops from the Shatt al-Arab Waterway, the recognition of disputed prewar borders, and the release of all prisoners of war. Iran accepts the terms, freeing up Iraqi troops to move from the Iranian front into Kuwait. One thousand Syrian troops arrive in the Kuwaiti Theatre of Operations. Iraq calls thousands of Western hostages "restrictees" and announces that they might be used as bargaining chips during the crisis. The Soviet Foreign Ministry announces that Iraq had changed its mind regarding the evacuation of Soviet citizens and would allow only women and children to depart, leaving some five thousand Soviet men in detention in Iraq. Brazilian and Indian men and women are allowed to leave; Brazil declares that it will maintain diplomatic relations with Iraq for the time being. Jordan's King Hussein arrives in the United States for high-level talks with President George Bush. Turkish ships enforcing the embargo turn away two ships headed for Iraq with food. Rumors fly that an Iraqi freighter laden with East German military equipment is headed for Iraq.

16 August. President George Bush authorizes the use of American forces in carrying out the embargo against Iraq. The Joint Chiefs of Staff immediately begins carrying out the order. The British stop the departure of a ship from Britain carrying unidentified cargo bound for the Jordanian port of Aqaba. Iraqi commanders in Kuwait order all American and British citizens, estimated to be about 6,500, to assemble at two hotel sites in Kuwait City, and warns of dire consequences if they refuse.

17 August. Thirty-five American diplomats, sent to visit Americans held at the Al-Rashid hotel in Baghdad, are turned away by Iraqi authorities. President George Bush warns that any movement of the hostages consti-

tutes "a contravention of international law." The Iraqi Ambassador to the United States calls the delay in releasing the American hostages part of the Iraqi "bureaucracy." "We are in an emergency situation that you, the United States, created," explains Ambassador Mohammed al-Mashat on ABC's "Good Morning America." Two American U2 aircraft arrive in the Kuwaiti Theatre of Operations. American ships enforcing the embargo stop two Iraqi ships, but allow them to continue after determining that they are not carrying embargoed goods. *Qatar* announces that American troops will be stationed in their country at Doha. For the first time in history, the *Civil Reserve Air Fleet (CRAF)* is activated; 38 private American airliners are put into service transporting American troops to the Gulf. Gen. H. Norman Schwarzkopf, USCINCCENT (U.S. Commander in Chief, U.S. Central Command) is briefed on possible Iraqi targets that would be destroyed in a potential air campaign over Iraq. He names the plan for such an attack *Operation Desert Storm.* Although Iraq releases 1,000 Iranian POWs, Iran announces that it will sell oil to Japan to make up for the loss of Iraqi crude. American Secretary of Defense Dick Cheney flies to Saudi Arabia to supply the Saudi government with the newest variants of the F-15 aircraft. Radio Baghdad taunts American troops in the desert. "Didn't you hear that the sand dunes in the desert move, and they have swallowed up many people and they will swallow you?"

18 August. After the guided missile frigate USS *Reid* fires on the Iraqi tanker *Khanaqin* in the Persian Gulf (another tanker is later fired on in the Gulf of Oman), the Iraqi government calls the embargo "an act of war," and declares that food will be withheld from foreign hostages. Iraq also declares that the 10,000 Western hostages it holds as "guests" will be moved to military, oil, and other potential attack sites as "shields." As part of their peace agreement, Iraq begins to withdraw troops from the disputed areas along the Iran-Iraq border. The COMUSAFCENT (Commander, U.S. Air Force Central Command), Lt. Gen. Charles Horner, reports that the United States does not have enough forces in Saudi Arabia to stop a full-scale Iraqi invasion of the Arabian peninsula. He suggests that halting such an advance would require "a heavy reliance" on air power.

19 August. Saddam Hussein offers to release all Western hostages if American troops leave Saudi Arabia. White House press secretary Marlin Fitzwater says of the offer, "It seems we're getting a daily seminar of Iraqi ridicule these days. This one doesn't have much relationship at all to our objectives." Saddam Hussein does announce on Iraqi television that as a goodwill gesture he is releasing 600 hostages from Austria, Finland, Portugal, Sweden, and Switzerland. Iraqi troops in Kuwait demand that all Americans in Kuwait surrender at designated sights. Some Americans hold out in their apartments. The U.S. Navy intercepts the Cypriot freighter *Dongala* outside the port of Aqaba carrying material bound for Iraq.

20 August. C-21A *Learjets* and C-130 Hercules aircraft start STAR (scheduled tactical airlift) flights to rush emergency supplies to the Kuwaiti Theater of Operations. Libyan President Col. Muammar el-Qaddafi condemns the use of Westerners as shields and offers Libyan troops to the United Nations for use in the crisis.

21 August. Saddam Hussein declares that the seizure of Westerners in Iraq and Kuwait was done to prevent American aggression, and warns of a "great tragedy" if the United States attacks Iraq. The first *F-117A Stealth Fighters* arrive in the Kuwaiti Theater of Operations. A variety of U.S. Air Force and Coast Guard transport, tanker, and electronic warfare aircraft are dispatched to Riyadh Air Force Base, Saudi Arabia.

22 August. President George Bush signs Executive Order 12727, which calls the selected reserve of the U.S. armed forces to active duty. Writes the president, "I hereby determine that it is necessary to augment the active armed forces of the United States for the effective conduct of operational missions in and around the Arabian Peninsula." He also issues Executive Order 12728, which delegates the president's authority to suspend any provision of law relating to the promotion, retirement, or separation of members of the armed forces. Brig. Gen. Buster Glosson is named COMUSAF-CENT FWD (Commander, U.S. Air Force Central Command Forward, in charge of the Air Force units in the forward area). Oil prices rise to $31.22 a barrel. The second American casualty of Operation Desert Shield, Navy Electrician's Mate 3rd Class Daniel M. Jones, is killed when he is electrocuted in an accident aboard the USS *Antietam*.

23 August. Saddam Hussein appears on Iraqi television for 40 minutes with a group of British hostages, sparking outrage in the Western world. He is seen chatting with the people he calls "guests" and says to the group, "If I were not so busy, I would have liked to have lunch with you." American Secretary of Defense Dick Cheney announces troop call-up ceilings of 25,000 for the Army, 6,300 for the Navy, 3,000 for the Marines, and 14,500 for the Air Force. The United States evacuates Marine guards and some diplomats and their families from the American embassy in Kuwait while claiming that any order to fully abandon the embassy would be defied. The European Community votes to defy the order as well, leaving India and Lebanon as the only nations to comply and formally close their Kuwaiti posts. Iraq calls the failure of Western nations to close the Kuwaiti embassies "an act of aggression." Jordan claims that it will comply with the UN embargo of Iraq if it receives $2 billion in compensation from the United Nations.

25 August. The UN Security Council votes 13-0 to approve military action in the embargo against Iraq. Saddam Hussein dismisses the vote as part of an American plot. "Whoever collides with Iraq will find columns of dead bodies that have a beginning but will not have an end," he warns. In Kuwait, water and electric supplies are cut to all embassies in an effort to close

the missions. In Kuwait City, 20 Japanese and 4 Britons are flushed out of their hiding spaces. *Bahrain* secretly allows the United States to base C-130 Hercules aircraft at the clandestine Bateen Air Force Base, which is normally used as a supply dump. Kurt Waldheim, president of Austria, becomes the first Western head of state to visit Baghdad since the start of the Gulf crisis.

26 August. Kurt Waldheim departs from Iraq with 95 Austrian hostages given to him as a goodwill gesture. Fifty-two of the 55 dependents of U.S. Embassy personnel from Kuwait are allowed to leave by road to Turkey. UN Secretary General Javier Pérez de Cuéllar announces that he will meet with Iraqi Foreign Minister Tariq Aziz in Jordan to attempt to end the crisis. The Soviet Union declares that its ships in the Persian Gulf region will not use force to stop Iraqi ships attempting to break the embargo. In towns on the Syrian-Iraqi border, Syrian troops open fire and kill a number of Syrians protesting Syria's decision to oppose Iraq in the Gulf crisis. Israel announces that it will block the shipment of Palestinian-made goods to Jordan for transport to Iraq. Over 300 American and foreign reporters have converged on Saudi Arabia; because of this, the U.S. Department of Defense's National Media Pool is discontinued. A new system of pool reporters assigned to different combat units is instituted with the help of the Joint Information Bureau (JIB).

27 August. Iraq orders all of its ships not to resist if Americans board them for inspection. The U.S. Department of State orders 36 members of the Iraqi Embassy in Washington to leave the United States by Thursday, 30 August.

28 August. Iraq declares that Kuwait is its nineteenth province. Saddam Hussein renames Kuwait City "Kadhima" and names the province after himself.

29 August. In Baghdad, CBS's Dan Rather interviews Saddam Hussein, who dismisses the potential threat of an American air war. "There is no powerful and quick strike that any nation could deliver, whatever their overall power. The United States depends on the Air Force. The Air Force has never decided a war in the history of wars," the Iraqi leader declares.

An Air Force *C-5A Galaxy Transport*, conveying material to the Coalition forces in the Gulf, crashes on takeoff from Ramstein Air Force Base in West Germany, killing 13 of the 17 Americans aboard, the first air fatalities of Operation Desert Shield.

30 August. During a press conference, President Bush demands "the immediate and unconditional withdrawal of Iraqi forces from Kuwait," among other objectives. In an address on Radio Baghdad, Saddam Hussein proclaims, "If war breaks out between the United States and Iraq…I think that the United States will no longer be superpower number one. And the harm that will inflicted on the invaders will be even more severe that what they experienced in Vietnam, and Iraq will come out on top." Soviet Deputy Foreign Minister Aleksandr Belonogov, who has been working with the Coalition to coordinate the Soviet response to the Gulf crisis, criticizes the presence of American troops in the Gulf area.

31 August. Iraq announces that 237 selected women and children being held as hostages, including 14 Americans, will be released only in exchange for Iraqis in Britain and France who Iraq claims are being held against their will. Britain and France respond that these unnamed Iraqis are stranded only because their airline tickets on the boycotted Iraqi Airways are no good and they have no way to get home. The USS *Biddle* intercepts and boards the Iraqi merchant ship *Al Karamah*, and, after finding it empty, allows it to proceed. U.S. government officials tell the *Washington Post* that President George Bush has decided to forgive Egypt's $7.1 billion military debt in recognition of their assistance in the Gulf crisis. The *New York Times* reports that an additional $1 billion is being sent to Israel to reinforce that nation's defense against a possible Iraqi attack.

1 September. The United States and the Soviet Union announce that Presidents George Bush and *Mikhail Gorbachev* will meet in a summit in Helsinki, Finland, on 8 and 9 September. American civil rights leader the Rev. Jesse Jackson arrives in Baghdad and meets with Saddam Hussein; later, Jackson leaves Iraq with 330 Western hostages, including 102 Americans, given to Jackson as "a humanitarian measure."

2 September. About 750 Western hostages, including 230 Americans, are permitted to leave Iraq.

3 September. Iraq tightens the restrictions for the release of hostages by forcing them to leave only on Iraqi Airways flights or by land to Jordan.

4 September. The American guided missile destroyer USS *Goldsborough*, patrolling the Gulf of Oman, stops and boards the Iraqi cargo ship *Zanoobia*. After being diverted to the Port of Muscat in *Oman*, the *Zanoobia* is found to be carrying tea to the Iraqi port of Basra.

6 September. The African nation of Senegal agrees to send troops to the Persian Gulf as part of the international Coalition.

7 September. The exiled emir of Kuwait promises the United States $2.5 billion, and an additional $2.5 billion for Egypt, Jordan, and Turkey.

Presidents Bush and Gorbachev meet in Helsinki, Finland. Main topic of discussion: the Persian Gulf crisis and how the world will react to Saddam Hussein's refusal to comply with UN resolutions demanding a withdrawal from Kuwait. In their joint statement released at the end of the summit, the two men write, "Our preference is to resolve the crisis peacefully, and we will be united against Iraq's aggression as long as the crisis exists. However, we are determined to see this aggression end, and if the current steps fail to end it, we are prepared to consider additional ones consistent with the U.N. Charter." American Secretary of State James A. Baker III completes three days of meetings with Egyptian President Hosni Mubarak and Saudi King Fahd, in which the three men agree that there will be no negotiations with Iraq regarding regional issues until Iraqi troops withdraw from Kuwait.

9 September. Iraqi Foreign Minister Aziz flies to Iran to meet with Iran Foreign Minister Ali Akbar Velayati to coordinate Iraqi efforts to circumvent the economic embargo.

10 September. Iran and Iraq restore full diplomatic relations. Saddam Hussein offers free Iraqi oil to any nation that sends ships to take it away. However, because of the embargo, no ship will be able to leave with the oil, and the offer is refused.

11 September. President Bush tells a joint session of Congress that "We will not let this aggression stand." The president outlines four objectives in Operation Desert Shield: (1) the complete, unconditional withdrawal of Iraqi troops from Kuwait; (2) the restoration of Kuwait's legitimate government; (3) the assurance of stability in the Persian Gulf; and (4) the protection of American citizens abroad, particularly in Kuwait and Iraq.

12 September. Joint Chiefs of Staff Chairman *Colin Powell* visits the Kuwaiti Theater of Operations (KTO).

14 September. Great Britain announces that it is sending the British 7th Armoured Brigade to the Gulf. Iraqi troops forcibly enter the French Embassy in Kuwait City and detain four French citizens; Iraqi troops also enter the embassies of Belgium, Canada, and the Netherlands. The Iraqi government announces a cut of 50 percent in food rations for its citizenry because of the economic embargo.

15 September. French President *François Mitterrand* denounces the Iraqi invasion of his nation's embassy in Kuwait. In response, he pledges 4,000 French troops to the international Coalition in the Gulf. Gen. Michael Dugan, Air Force Chief of Staff, in an interview with the *Washington Post*, explains that a massive air war against Iraqi assets in both Kuwait and Iraq was the battle plan that was shaping up. Further, he declares that if such a war were to break out, the Coalition would target Saddam Hussein and his family.

16 September. Iraqi television broadcasts, unedited, a speech by President George Bush, in which the president explains to the Iraqi people why American troops are in the Persian Gulf. Iraq opens the border between Kuwait and Saudi Arabia, prompting thousands of frightened Kuwaitis to flee. Italy expels the Iraqi military attaché, while France expels 29 Iraqi diplomats. The Coalition's 1,000th ship intercept occurs when the destroyer USS *O'Brien* stops the Bahamian-flagged *Daimon*.

17 September. American Secretary of Defense Cheney relieves General Dugan of his command, calling his disclosure of the American plan of battle, as well as the possible targeting of Saddam Hussein and his family, "poor judgment." Great Britain expels eight Iraqi diplomats.

18 September. Saudi Arabia and the Soviet Union restore full diplomatic relations for the first time in 50 years. The Saudis subsequently invite the Soviets to send troops to the Gulf as part of the international Coalition. Turkey announces the extension of the Defense and Economic Cooperation Agreement it had signed with the United States to allow American planes to attack Iraq from Turkish bases.

22 September. The Iraqi government releases what it alleges is a transcript of a dialogue held 25 July 1990 between Saddam Hussein and U.S. Ambassador to Iraq April Glaspie, in which Glaspie tells Saddam that the United States has "no opinion of the Arab-Arab conflicts, like your border disagreement with Kuwait." Glaspie denies the substance of the conversation.

23 September. Saddam Hussein threatens to attack Saudi Arabian oil fields and Israel if Iraq is "strangled" by the economic embargo.

24 September. In a speech opening the session of the UN General Assembly, French President Mitterrand suggests that if Iraq withdraws from Kuwait, all of its concerns will be open for discussion.

25 September. Soviet Foreign Minister Eduard Shevardnadze tells the UN General Assembly that "war may break out in the gulf region any day, any moment" and warns the members that "we should remind those who regard aggression as an acceptable form of behavior that the United Nations has the power to suppress acts of aggression."

27 September. Iran and Great Britain restore full diplomatic relations, cut off in 1988 when Iran threatened the life of *Satanic Verses* author Salman Rushdie.

30 September. An Air Force *F-15E Eagle* crashes during training exercises in the Saudi desert, killing Maj. Peter S. Cook, the pilot, and Capt. James B. Poulet, the navigator and weapons system officer.

1 October. President George Bush speaks to the UN General Assembly. He condemns Iraq's invasion of Kuwait but, like French President Mitterrand a few days earlier, claims that all of Iraq's interests in the region would be addressed if it pulled out of Kuwait. In his speech, he declares, "…As I said last month, the annexation of Kuwait will not be permitted to stand. And this is not simply the view of the United States. It is the view of every Kuwaiti, the Arab League, the United Nations. Iraq's leaders should listen. It is Iraq against the world." Israel announces that it is distributing gas masks to all of its 4.6 million citizens. In Saudi Arabia, *Operation Camel Sand*, a deceptive attempt to convince the Iraqis that American forces would attempt to liberate Kuwait from the sea, begins.

8 October. An *RF-4C Phantom* reconnaissance craft belonging to the Alabama Air National Guard crashes in southern Saudi Arabia on a training mission, killing Maj. Barry K. Henderson, the pilot, and Maj. Stephen G. Schramm, the navigator. Later that evening, two Marine Corps *UH-1N Huey Iroquois* helicopters crash into the North Arabian Sea while conducting a

night exercise, killing all eight men aboard. American deaths during Operation Desert Shield reach 29.

10 October. An *F-111F Aardvark* bomber crashes in Saudi Arabia on a training mission, killing Capt. Frederick A. Reid, the pilot, and Capt. Thomas R. Caldwell, the weapons system officer.

17 October. The Japanese Diet begins parliamentary debate on the use of Japanese troops in the Persian Gulf as part of the Coalition but only in a noncombat role.

18 October. A ministerial meeting of the Arab League in Tunis, Tunisia, is split over the Persian Gulf crisis. Convened to condemn Israel for the Temple Mount killings of 19 Arabs on 8 October, the conference votes down a PLO-sponsored resolution to likewise condemn the United States, 11–10. Voting against the resolution were Bahrain, Djibouti, Egypt, Kuwait, Lebanon, Oman, Qatar, Saudi Arabia, Somalia, Syria, and the United Arab Emirates. Farouk Kaddoumi, known as the PLO's "foreign minister," calls those countries "America's Arabs."

20 October. More than 5,000 people march through the streets of New York City protesting the American buildup in the Persian Gulf.

25 October. CIA Director William Webster says in an interview that "I find no real confidence that that area [the Persian Gulf] will ever be secure again as long as he [Saddam Hussein] is there unless there is some countervailing force present in the area, whether it's regional security or some other means, or unless he has been disassociated with his instruments of mass destruction in one form or another."

27 October. In an interview, Soviet President Mikhail Gorbachev implies that the Iraqi government may be "reconsidering" its position on whether to withdraw from Kuwait. Soviet diplomats at the United Nations ask that body to delay any consideration of a resolution condemning Iraq's failure to withdraw from Kuwait in response to Soviet envoy Yevgeni Primakov's trip to Baghdad to iron out a possible withdrawal initiative after an invitation by Saddam Hussein. Skepticism abounds when, during a press conference, Iraqi Information and Culture Minister Latif Nassif Jassim tells reporters that "Kuwait is province No. 19" and that "the Americans must leave the region." The Center for Defense Information in Washington, D.C., a private think tank, releases a report showing that the United States could suffer from 2,000 to 12,000 military deaths if war breaks out in the Persian Gulf.

30 October. President Bush is questioned by lawmakers when he meets with 15 congressional leaders from both parties in an informal session at the White House. In Baghdad, the Iraqi news service INA announces that Saddam Hussein has put his military commanders on "extreme alert" against a possible U.S. attack in the next several days. The Iraqis also announce the release of all 256 French hostages because they feel French President Mitterrand's 24 September speech before the United Nations was conciliatory. Aboard the amphibious assault ship USS *Iwo Jima*, a boiler pipe accident kills ten sailors. In another accident, a Marine is killed and three more are injured when their Humvee vehicle overturns on a sand dune. American deaths in Operation Desert Shield rise to 42. According to the *Wall Street Journal*, foreign workers and freed hostages report that the living conditions of hostages still in Iraq are deteriorating.

31 October. Saddam Hussein invites the families of those held hostage in Iraq to visit with them.

1 November. Iraq announces that in response to a call from the Arab-American Reconciliation Society, it is releasing four American hostages. In denying that the captives are being treated badly, Minister of Information and Culture Latif Nassif Jassim says, "All the Americans at sites have complete freedom. They can watch TV, read books and read newspapers. They also enjoy the friendship of Iraq forces." Amnesty International calls upon King Fahd to investigate reports that hundreds of Yemeni workers forced to leave Saudi Arabia are being tortured. Large numbers of Syrian troops move into combat-ready positions in Saudi Arabia.

3 November. American Secretary of State James Baker heads off on an eight-day trip to American allies to consult them on the buildup in the Persian Gulf. His first stop is Bahrain. Saddam Hussein announces that an undefined number of European hostages in Iraq now have "the right to choose leaving Iraq or staying, according to their desire." National Assembly of Iraq Speaker Saadi Mahdi Saleh lays out an offer to release the remaining hostages "if two of the following states give guarantees not to resort to the military option: China, France, Germany, Japan, and the Soviet Union…," and if the five permanent members of the UN Security Council agree "to keep away from a military settlement of the Gulf crisis and [attempt] a peaceful solution." Former Japanese Prime Minister Yasuhiro Nakasone arrives in Baghdad to meet with Saddam Hussein to get the remaining Japanese hostages released.

4 November. Secretary of State James Baker meets with Saudi King Fahd in Riyadh, where they agree on a framework for the command and control of American and Saudi forces in Saudi Arabia.

5 November. Former West German Chancellor Willy Brandt arrives in Baghdad to accompany German hostages home. Congress enacts the Iraq Sanctions Act of 1990 as part of the Foreign Operations Appropriation Act.

6 November. The Pentagon announces that 824 Marine reservists from units in 14 states have been called up for duty, the first time they have been used in the Persian Gulf crisis. From London, the Associated Press announces that *Jane's Defence Weekly*, a British military magazine, has obtained Soviet spy photos that show Iraqi forces mining uranium in the Gara Mountains, 40 miles south of the Turkish border.

8 November. The Bush Administration announces that an additional three Army divisions, three aircraft carriers and accompanying task forces, and a second battleship will be deployed to the Persian Gulf to supplement the power of U.S. forces in the area. In Moscow, Secretary of State Baker meets with Soviet Foreign Minister Eduard Shevardnadze, who says, "a situation may emerge which effectively would require" the use of military force to expel Iraqi troops from Kuwait, and he adds that "I would advise against looking for some differences in the positions between the Soviet Union and the United States." In Japan, the ruling Liberal Democratic Party rejects a plan to send Japanese forces to the Persian Gulf in a noncombat role.

10 November. Secretary of State Baker ends his consultation junket to Coalition allies and reports that many want economic sanctions to have more time before a military option is instituted.

12 November. The *Detroit News* reports that many Democrats and Republicans in Congress have become alarmed by President Bush's moves toward war and are seeking ways to challenge him. At their annual meeting in Washington, the National Conference of Catholic Bishops vote 249–15 for a resolution calling for a peaceful solution to the Gulf crisis. "We fear that [to] resort to war…could cost many lives and raise serious moral questions," says Archbishop Roger Mahoney of Los Angeles, author of the resolution. In Baghdad, former New Zealand Prime Minister David Lange announces that all 16 New Zealanders in Iraq will be released to him. Responding to Saddam Hussein's 31 October invitation, 12 relatives of hostages tell the *Washington Post* that they will head to Iraq to visit their families.

15 November. President Bush leaves for a nine-day trip to Europe and to visit American troops in the Persian Gulf for Thanksgiving. *Operation Imminent Thunder*, a tactical exercise like its earlier counterpart Operation Camel Sand, begins. The largest exercise yet involving American military forces, it is staged just 25 miles from the Kuwaiti border. Iraq calls the drill "a provocative act." *USA Today* reports that Secretary of State Baker is trying to convince the five permanent members of the UN Security Council to vote for a resolution authorizing force against Iraq before Yemen takes the chair as head of the council on 1 December.

17 November. President Bush speaks to a crowd of more than 100,000 in Wenceslas Square in Prague, Czechoslovakia, where he tells them, "As you undertake political and economic reform, know one thing: America will not fail you in this decisive moment. America will stand with you." The crowd roars back, "Long Live Bush" and "U.S.A." Writing for the Iraqi armed forces newspaper *Al-Qadisiyah* in the article entitled "The American Decision and the Crisis of War or No War," Staff Maj. Gen. Mundhir Abdul-Rahman Ibrahim writes that Iraqi defensive moves have "rendered the chances of [Coalition] success…less likely." He chides that the "fresh [American] reinforcements rushed to the area will fail to be of any significant effect," and that Iraq enjoys "the element of surprise...the edge in land forces in terms of numbers, equipment...full experience...[and] the ability to transfer the field of battle beyond the immediate theater of operations."

18 November. President Bush meets with West German Chancellor Helmut Kohl to discuss the Coalition.

19 November. At the Conference on Security and Cooperation in Europe (CSCE) gathering in Paris, President Bush starts the first of two days of summitry with Soviet President Gorbachev in which the two men will sign a NATO and Warsaw Pact conventional arms limitation treaty. The *Wall Street Journal* reports that the Soviet Union has failed to agree to back a U.S.-sponsored resolution calling for the use of force in the Gulf, although the issue of whether the Soviets totally disagree with such a declaration, or are divided on certain details, is unclear. Iraq announces that because of the American build-up in Saudi Arabia, it is sending 250,000 more troops to Kuwait and will be calling up an additional 100,000 to defend the Iraqi nation.

20 November. The *Washington Post* and the *Miami Herald* report that talks at the CSCE meeting have brought the United States and the Soviet Union "closer" to agreement on a UN resolution requiring force to expel the Iraqis from Kuwait. In Washington, D.C., 45 Democrats (44 from the House and 1 from the Senate), led by Rep. Ron Dellums (D-California), sue in federal court to enjoin President Bush from going to war in the Gulf unless he gets congressional approval. The Iraqi Assembly votes to release all German hostages; it calls the move "a message of encouragement to the people of Europe to take more independent actions and stand against the arrogant position of the Americans who are calling for war."

21 November. President Bush arrives in Saudi Arabia to spend time with the troops for Thanksgiving. He meets with Saudi King Fahd to inspect and review Coalition plans for war.

22 November. Thanksgiving. President Bush dines with American troops in Saudi Arabia. He tells them, "We won't pull punches. We are not here on some exercise. This is a real world situation. And we are not walking away until the invader is out of Kuwait." In Baghdad, Iraqi Minister of Information and Culture Latif Nassif Jassim delivers a Thanksgiving message to the American people: "We wish peace everywhere and for everybody. But if anybody imagines that he can undermine Iraq and he can attack Iraq, I say, go and drink the water of the sea." In Yemen, President Ali Abdullah Saleh, meeting with Secretary of State James Baker, criticizes the deployment of American and other Coalition troops on Saudi soil. He declares that these foreign troops have "complicated the problem rather than solved it," and calls for an Arab solution to the crisis.

23 November. In Cairo, President Bush meets with Egyptian President Hosni Mubarak to discuss the Gulf situation.

24 November. In a hastily scheduled meeting, President Bush flies to Geneva, Switzerland, where he meets with Syrian President Hafez al-Assad. Al-Assad assures Bush, the *Miami Herald* reports, "of Syria's support for U.S. policy in the Persian Gulf crisis and agreed to continue a 'dialogue' with American officials over Syria's alleged involvement in terrorist activities."

27 November. The Senate Armed Services Committee and the House Banking Committee open hearings on U.S. engagement in the Persian Gulf. While several administration officials, including Secretary of Defense Cheney and Joints Chiefs Chairman Powell, do not appear, former CIA Director James Schlesinger testifies, opining that the because of the sanctions against it, the Iraqi economy "is rapidly becoming a basket case." Sen. Edward Kennedy (D-Massachusetts) tells the Senate committee, "The case for using force has not been made. The sanctions are not only working well, but they should be given more time to work effectively." In moving testimony before the UN Security Council, several Kuwaiti refugees verify that Iraqi troops have raped and pillaged their nation.

28 November. In a press conference in Omaha, Nebraska, Sen. Bob Kerrey (D-Nebraska) calls for a reduction in U.S. troop strength in the Persian Gulf. "Do we really want to die to re-establish the Emir in Kuwait?" he questions. In a statement that he issues to the Senate Armed Services Committee hearing, Kerrey writes, "The administration policy...is pushing us into a war we could avoid, reopening social divisions we have only recently healed and undermining public support for a sound and sustained foreign and military policy."

29 November. The UN Security Council votes 12–2 to authorize the use of military force to expel Iraqi forces from Kuwait. Yemen and Cuba vote against the measure, while China abstains. In Washington, D.C., former Navy Secretary James Webb, Jr., tells the Senate Armed Services Committee that the Bush administration should reinstitute the draft. "If the President wishes to attack a million-man army, he cannot count on a two-day bombing campaign and be home by February," Webb tells the senators. "If a bombing campaign does not work, there is no way to predict the direction or the duration of a war in this region."

30 November. In a press conference, President Bush offers talks with the Iraqi government, pledging to send Secretary of State Baker to Baghdad to meet with Foreign Minister Aziz. He declares that "I will do my level best to bring those kids home without one single shot fired in anger." He adds, "We're in the Gulf because the world must not and cannot reward aggression. And we're there because our vital interests are at stake. And we're in the Gulf because of the brutality of Saddam Hussein." In a startling and unexpected move, Iraqi authorities in Kuwait visit the besieged American Embassy in Kuwait City and deliver a basket of fruit, vegetables, and cigarettes.

1 December. Iraq accepts President Bush's offer to resolve the Persian Gulf crisis as an opportunity to have "a serious and deep dialogue." However, the statement, released by the Revolutionary Command Council, reiterates that "Palestine and the other occupied Arab territories remain before our eyes and at the forefront of the issues that we will discuss in any dialogue." A PLO spokesman in Tunis, Yasir Abed Rabbo, says that "the U.S. President's decision is a step in the right direction." In an interview with CNN, Vice President *Dan Quayle* restates American policy: "Palestine is not an issue on the table. The issue on the table is Saddam Hussein's invasion of Kuwait…You're not going to link Palestine up to Saddam's invasion of Kuwait."

3 December. Baghdad Radio reports that "1,416 children under the age of five have died recently" due to the medicine shortage created by the international sanctions placed on Iraq. The release can not be independently verified, but it is reported that medicine is not covered by the embargo. Soviet television, quoting Aeroflot's Baghdad representative, Aleksandr Kirichenko, relates that 1,000 Soviet citizens in Iraq—nearly a third of the Soviets in that country—would be allowed to leave. *USA Today* publishes a poll showing that President Bush's approval rating has risen to 57 percent.

4 December. One hundred seventy-seven members of the House Democratic Caucus vote for a resolution calling on the Bush Administration not to go to war without congressional approval. Thirty-seven Democrats vote against the measure. In Canberra, Australian Prime Minister Bob Hawke, defending the deployment of Australian ships to aid the Coalition in the Persian Gulf, tells Parliament, "I know there will be some who will ask why we should contribute when others do not. The essential answer is this—that what others do or don't do does not obviate our responsibility to judge for ourselves what is right, and what is in our interests, and to act accordingly…There are even those who have purported to base their assessment of the Gulf situation on the presumption of moral equivalence between the U.S. and Iraqi positions…Let there be no ambiguity here—no 'mindless muddying' of the waters. If it comes to conflict, the international community will not be the aggressor. The United States and the other allies will not be the aggressor. The aggressor is the nation that took, occupied and annexed Kuwait in August." In Ankara, Turkish President Turgut Özal is reported to have urged his nation's military to dispatch a small number of troops to Saudi Arabia to help the Coalition effort while making Incirlik Air Force Base available to the United States.

6 December. Saddam Hussein calls for the release of all Western hostages held in Iraq and Kuwait. In an announcement covered by Iraqi government radio, he alludes to "positive changes" in the United States; he argues that "the reasons for which the foreigners were prevented from travel have been diminished" and that they "have been replaced by something more powerful: a change in the American public opinion." He offers no evidence of this. According to the Associated Press, Iraq's ambassador to the United Nations, Abdul

Amir al-Anbari, remarks that he would like to see all of the hostages home by Christmas. A senior Egyptian military official tells the *Washington Post* that "Saddam wants to transfer [the upcoming talks] to negotiations. He's playing with American public opinion."

7 December. The U.S. Department of State announces that after all foreign "shields" are released from custody in Iraq and Kuwait all U.S. Embassy staff in Kuwait will be evacuated and the embassy closed. White House spokesman Marlin Fitzwater says of the action, "The personnel there have performed courageously and at great personal sacrifice. They really deserve to go out when all the other citizens go out."

8 December. Twenty-three Americans classified as "hostages" fly out of Baghdad on a private jet chartered by former Texas Governor John Connally. In Baghdad, the Iraqi government announces that it has rejected the dates of 20 December, 21 December, 22 December, and 3 January for a meeting between Secretary of State Baker and Foreign Minister Aziz, instead proposing 12 January. National Security Advisor *Brent Scowcroft* calls the move "another ploy that he [Saddam Hussein] is trying to use to drag things out and to avoid seriously facing up to what the world community is demanding that he do."

10 December. One hundred fifty two American "hostages" arrive at Andrews Air Force Base in Maryland, leaving the number left in captivity about 600, of which 400, the U.S. government estimates, will remain with family in Iraq and Kuwait. Iraqi Minister of Information Latif Nassif Jassim declares that any thoughts of an Iraqi withdrawal from Kuwait before the 15 January deadline are "nothing but dreams and wishful thinking…We will not compromise one iota…Not an inch [of Kuwait] can be relinquished." Declaring the day to be Human Rights Day, President George Bush speaks of Iraq's attack on Kuwait: "What has happened to Kuwait is more than an invasion. It is a systematic assault on the soul of a nation." The U.S. government estimates that the buildup so far in the Gulf has cost $27 billion.

12 December. Iraqi state radio reports that Saddam Hussein has fired 70-year-old Minister of Defense Gen. Abdel-Jaber Khalil Shanshal and replaced him with Maj. Gen. Saadi Toma Abbas, who is reported to be in his mid-50s. Abbas, a hero of the Iran-Iraq War, is the current inspector general of the armed forces and a former deputy chief of staff.

13 December. A *New York Times/CBS Poll* finds that 45 percent of the American public want to start the war on the 15 January deadline, while 48 percent indicate a willingness to let the deadline slip and let the sanctions take their course. The last flight to leave Iraq, sponsored by the United States, arrives in Frankfurt, West Germany, carrying Ambassador *W. Nathaniel Howell* and 31 other Americans from Kuwait and Iraq, as well as 96 others, including Britons, Canadians, Italians, and Japanese. Algerian President Chadli Benjedid, in Tehran, is told by Saudi officials not to come to Riyadh unless Saddam Hussein, whom Benjedid had just visited, is prepared to withdraw unconditionally from Kuwait. In an interview carried by the Iraqi press agency INA, Saddam Hussein says that his country desires a peaceful end to the Persian Gulf crisis but will go to war if the alternative is foreign domination of both Iraq's land and its oil. "We want peace, endeavor to achieve it, and work to reach a point where no one of us brandishes his sword against the other. But if the enemies want to push affairs to a military duel, then by God's help we would win and would walk over their corpses and tread on their heads."

14 December. President George Bush announces that Iraq must agree to talks to mediate the Gulf crisis no later than 3 January and puts on hold any possibility of further talks. The *New York Times* says that the moves "indicate that what is at issue between the two sides is not so much conflicting schedules but conflicting strategies." Assistant Secretary of Defense for Public Affairs Pete Williams issues a draft memo outlining his proposal for American media coverage if a war breaks out. It includes how many reporters could operate in the war zone, what pools they would belong to, and what security restrictions they would have to obey. Williams's memo is roundly criticized by American media executives.

15 December. Iraq announces that because of the dispute over dates for a summit between Secretary of State Baker and Foreign Minister Aziz, any such talks are postponed indefinitely. From Baghdad, Algerian President Chadli Benjedid admits that further talks to induce an Iraqi withdrawal from Kuwait will prove fruitless. He comments that the only hope "in this new unstable world is through the restoration of Arab unity," which can be accomplished "only on the basis of mutual respect and legitimacy which protects our people from injustice." Some Middle East experts decipher Benjedid's comments to mean that he had promised Iraq diplomatic efforts to solve its problems with Kuwait if it withdrew. In Tehran, Sudanese President Omar Hassan al-Bashir calls for "the necessity of a complete withdrawal of Iraqi forces from Kuwait and of the foreign forces from the region."

17 December. In an article in the Syrian government newspaper *al-Jumhuriya*, Abu Abbas, mastermind of the 1985 *Achille Lauro* hijacking, warns that if the United States and its allies attack Iraq, "Palestine [sic] groups" will "attack American and Western targets." He declares that "among those targets are U.S. installations and interests spread all over the globe."

19 December. Publicly, President Bush is told by high-ranking American military officers that American troops in the Persian Gulf may not be ready for combat by 15 January. Lt. Gen. Calvin Waller, deputy commander of U.S. troops, says that it could be mid-February before all 430,000 troops presently in the Gulf are adequately prepared for battle. In a shocking move during a speech before the Soviet Parliament, Soviet Foreign Minister Eduard Shevardnadze resigns, warning his country

of "revolutionary forces" that want to take over and destroy Mikhail Gorbachev's reforms.

22 December. In one of the worst accidents of Operation Desert Shield, a ferry carrying more than 100 sailors from Haifa in Israel to the USS *Saratoga* capsizes, killing 19 men and raising the death toll from the deployment to 73.

27 December. In an interview, Saddam Hussein declares that "if aggression were to take place, we should assume that Israel has taken part in it. Therefore, without asking any questions we will strike at Israel. If the first strike is dealt to Baghdad or the front, the second strike will target Tel Aviv."

28 December. A 17-ship flotilla, led by the aircraft carriers USS *America* and USS *Theodore Roosevelt*, leave from the Norfolk Naval Base in Virginia, headed for the Persian Gulf. U.S. forces in the Gulf are put on alert when Iraq tests a ballistic missile inside its borders, which does not threaten the deployment in Saudi Arabia. The German magazine *Der Spiegel* reports that more than 100 German companies have been implicated in building up Iraq's conventional weapons capability. The Soviet Union assures the Bush Administration that Soviet policy toward the situation in Iraq will not change even though Foreign Minister Shevardnadze has resigned.

29 December. Appearing on NBC's *Meet the Press*, Sen. Bob Dole of Kansas says, "The American people are not yet committed to war, and they want to make certain that President Bush has done everything, pursued every avenue for peace, before the firing starts." Echoing those sentiments on CBS' *Face the Nation*, Reps. Les Aspin of Wisconsin and Lee Hamilton of Indiana caution that a meeting with the Iraqi government "is really a precondition" to going to war. Vice President Dan Quayle meets in Riyadh with Saudi King Fahd and Saudi Deputy Prime Minister Crown Prince Abdullah, requesting that the Saudis and Kuwaitis bear a greater burden of the financial cost of the military buildup in the Gulf.

1991 *1 January.* Iraqi television shows a videotape of Saddam Hussein visiting with his troops in Kuwait for the New Year; the Iraqi leader tells his officers that "it is not easy for us to see one of you wounded. But God willing everything will be O.K., Palestine and Jerusalem will be liberated and you will see it with your eyes."

2 January. President Hosni Mubarak of Egypt warns Iraq that a "sea of blood" will flow if it does not withdraw from Kuwait.

3 January. The *New York Times* quotes several senior diplomats who say that the Iraqi government will move its bureaucracy out of Baghdad before 15 January. King Hussein of Jordan travels to London for talks with British leaders on the Gulf crisis. The *Washington Post* reports that NATO has approved a request from Turkey for the deployment of 42 fighter aircraft and more than 470 personnel from the rapid reaction force from NATO's Allied Commander in Europe Mobile Force to protect that nation from a possible Iraqi attack.

4 January. Iraq's Tariq Aziz releases a statement in which he agrees to meet with Secretary of State Baker in Geneva on 9 January, but he chastises the "arrogant statements which express the bad intentions of this Administration." Aziz further demands that any potential Iraqi withdrawal from Kuwait be linked with the establishment of a Palestinian state "with Jerusalem as its capital." Foreign Ministers of the European Community meet in Luxembourg to discuss the Gulf crisis.

5 January. The Iraqi government dismisses the 15 January deadline for a pullout from Kuwait. Information Minister Latif Nassif Jassim says of the decision, "Dates set by Bush only exist in his mind and imagination, and we don't recognize them." In Baghdad, Saddam Hussein meets with French parliament member Michel Vauzelle for 4 1/2 hours. Some diplomats acknowledge that secret negotiations, involving an Iraqi withdrawal from Kuwait in exchange for a conference regarding its pre-invasion grievances, are under way. Iraqi television announces that Saddam Hussein will speak the next day on the anniversary of Iraq's Army Day.

6 January. In a speech to Iraqi troops in Kuwait to celebrate Army Day, Saddam Hussein declares that "in this struggle that you are leading, you are fighting against social and economic oppression, against discrimination…against the oppression practised by foreign powers…against double standards, corruption and hegemony." Israeli jets attack a PLO base in southern Lebanon, killing one guerrilla and wounding six. In a press conference in Riyadh, Saudi King Fahd tells a reporter that he feels Saddam Hussein will bow to pressure and withdraw from Kuwait by 15 January.

7 January. The Pentagon announces that six Iraqi pilots commanding an equal number of Iraqi helicopters defected to Saudi Arabia, marking a significant "psychological war gain," reports the *New York Times.* The United Nations requests that all of its nonessential staff leave Israel. After complaints from various news organizations, the Pentagon revises its rules for reporters in Saudi Arabia. Further protests result.

8 January. Secretary of State Baker and Foreign Minister Aziz arrive in Geneva, Switzerland, in preparation for the next day's meeting. In Washington, D.C., President Bush sends a letter requesting a vote on a war resolution to the Congressional leadership, telling them, "It would…greatly enhance the chances for peace if Congress were now to go on record supporting the position adopted by the U.N. Security Council." This is the first time such a letter has been sent to Congress since the passage of the Tonkin Gulf resolution in 1964. Rep. Les Aspin, Chairman of the House Committee on Armed Services, releases a report entitled, "The Military Option: The Conduct and Consequences of War in the Persian Gulf," a white paper that discusses a scenario on which the U.S. and its Coalition allies can win a war against Iraq. "When Congress votes this week on authorizing the use of military force to push the Iraqis out of Kuwait, this is the military campaign they will be voting on," relates Aspin. In Riyadh, Saudi

officials report that King Fahd believes that Iraq will not withdraw from Kuwait peacefully and must be forced out. Ezzet Ibrahim, vice chairman of Iraq's Supreme Revolutionary Council, becomes the highest ranking Iraqi official to visit Iran to normalize relations between the two enemies. The Pentagon retracts its earlier report that six Iraqi helicopters had defected to Coalition forces.

9 January. After meeting for 6 1/2 hours, Baker and Aziz fail to agree on an Iraqi withdrawal from Kuwait, pushing the world closer to war. After attempting to deliver a letter to Aziz for Saddam Hussein, Baker is rebuffed. After the conference breaks up, Baker says to reporters, "Regrettably…I heard nothing that suggested to me any Iraqi flexibility whatsoever." He adds, "The choice [to withdraw] is Iraq's. If it should choose…to continue its brutal occupation of Kuwait, Iraq will be choosing a military confrontation which it cannot win and which will have devastating consequences for Iraq." Aziz, joined in the Iraqi entourage by Saddam Hussein's brother, Barzan Tikriti, reports on the outcome of the meeting, " I told Mr. Baker that we are prepared for all expectations. We have been prepared from the very beginning. If they decide to attack Iraq, we will not be surprised. We have our experience in war. And I told him that if the American administration decides to attack Iraq militarily, Iraq will defend itself in a very bold manner…We are a courageous nation and we deeply feel that we have been treated unjustly…We have prepared ourselves for the worst from the beginning." In response to a reporter's question on whether Iraq would attack Israel if war erupted, Aziz replies, "Yes, absolutely. Yes." The *Miami Herald* reports President Bush to say, "I can't misrepresent this to the American people. I am discouraged." Baker, in a cautionary move, orders Joseph Wilson, the senior American diplomat in Baghdad, to close the U.S. Embassy there and evacuate the rest of the staff. French President François Mitterrand, in a press conference, declares that France would attempt to settle the Persian Gulf crisis until the morning of 16 January.

10 January. The U.S. Congress begins its historic debate on whether to authorize American forces to go to war. Sen. George Mitchell (D-Maine) sets the tone when he says, "Prematurely abandoning the sanctions and immediately going to war involves risk. The risk of human life. How many young Americans will die? That's the risk—the terrible risk." Arab diplomats report that Saddam Hussein plans to wait "a day or two" after the 15 January deadline to propose a withdrawal from Kuwait while calling for an international conference to address the Palestinian issue. UN Secretary-general Javier Pérez de Cuéllar leaves New York for a meeting with Saddam Hussein in what is considered a last-ditch attempt to peacefully solve the Persian Gulf crisis. In mock exercises performed by American troops in California on Iraq ground targets constructed with the use of satellite photos, some U.S. forces suffered more than 50 percent losses. Central Intelligence

Agency Director William Webster reports that the CIA has made this assessment of the situation: "even if sanctions continue to be enforced for an additional six to 12 months, economic hardship alone is unlikely to compel Saddam to retreat from Kuwait." Secretary of State James Baker prepares to head for Europe to brief American allies on Bush Administration plans for war in the Gulf.

11 January. On the third and last day of a conference of more than 1,000 Islamic scholars in Baghdad, Saddam Hussein talks of solving the Palestinian problem "according to international law or not." The *New York Times* reports that senior UN diplomats have asked Secretary-general Javier Peréz de Cuéllar to appeal to Saddam Hussein to leave Kuwait in exchange for a vague promise regarding an international conference on other problems in the Middle East to be held at a later date.

12 January. Congress votes to authorize the United States to go to war against Iraq. The vote is 52–47 in the Senate and 250–183 in the House. In the Senate, 42 Republicans are joined by 10 Democrats to vote for the resolution. Only 2 Republicans, Mark Hatfield of Oregon and Charles Grassley of Iowa, vote against the declaration. In a press conference, President Bush hails the vote as "the last best chance for peace." UN Secretary-general Peréz de Cuéllar arrives in Baghdad from Amman, Jordan. In Damascus, Syrian President Hafez al-Assad appeals to Saddam Hussein to withdraw from Kuwait before war starts. In Baghdad, the last American officials in the Iraqi capital haul down the American flag from the U.S. Embassy and depart silently for Europe. The Iraqi government announces that the Iraqi National Assembly will be convened in emergency session the following day to consider ways to react to the threat of war.

15 January. The U.S. Department of Defense issues a memo outlining 12 areas of security issues that cannot be covered by reporters. Between 2 August and 15 January, 103 American combatants have been killed in the gulf conflict.

16 January. The UN deadline for an Iraqi pullout from Kuwait passes. President Bush issues an order giving the go-ahead for U.S. forces to attack Iraqi positions by air. An hour before the first attack, the president notifies the congressional leadership of his order. In the first attack, four *MH-53J Pave Low* helicopters escort eight *AH-64 Apache* helicopters in a raid of Iraqi radar installations inside Iraq in what is dubbed Task Force Normandy. F-117A Stealth fighters attack military and economic positions around Baghdad. The attack is seen and reported on by American correspondents holed up in Baghdad's al-Rashid Hotel. Among the reports are live broadcasts by ABC's Gary Shepard, who is on the air live with Peter Jennings on the *World News Tonight,* and CNN's Bernard Shaw, Peter Arnett, and John Holliman, who vividly describe from their hotel room the waves of attacks on Baghdad by F-117 Stealth fighters. The first American casualty of the war, Lt. Cmdr. Michael Scott Speicher, is shot

down over the Persian Gulf when his *F/A-18C Hornet* is hit by a surface-to-air missile.

17 January. U.S. bombers attack and destroy the Iraqi nuclear research center at Tuwaitha. A plane carrying 126 members of the press cleared by the U.S. Department of Defense arrives in Saudi Arabia.

18 January. Two Scud missiles crash into Tel Aviv and Haifa, threatening to bring Israel into the war. The first Coalition prisoners of war, Lt. Col. Clifford M. Acree and Chief Warrant Officer Guy L. Hunter, Jr., are taken captive when their *OV-10 Bronco* observation craft is shot down by a missile over southern Kuwait. Another flight, a Navy *A-6E Intruder* carrying Lt. William T. Costen and Lt. Charles Turner, is shot down over Kuwait, with no word of their fate. Two other Coalition craft are lost, including an *F-4G Phantom II Wild Weasel* (which ran out of fuel), and an Italian *Tornado* with both crew members taken prisoner. Attacks by Coalition planes exceed 1,000 sorties per day.

19 January. The U.S. sends to Israel two *Patriot* batteries for defense against Scud missile attacks. Col. David W. Eberly, USAF, and Maj. Thomas E. Griffith, Jr., USAF, are shot down. They are among a number of Coalition crews captured. Several Iraqi aircraft are downed by Coalition aircraft. Eberly and Griffith later reveal that after their plane crashed they evaded capture by Iraqi forces for two days. Iraq orders all foreign journalists out of the country, except for CNN's Peter Arnett and his crew, as well as several Jordanian reporters. In Amman, Jordan, King Hussein calls for a cease-fire in the conflict, saying that he is trying to prevent a "tragic disaster." The *Tomahawk Land Attack Missile* (TLAM) is used for the first time in the Persian Gulf war by planes (by U.S. Navy A-6s and A-7s) and by submarines (fired by the USS *Louisville* and the USS *Pittsburgh*) against Iraqi targets. The USS *Nicholas* captures 22 Iraqi *enemy prisoners of war (EPWs)* from oil platforms in the Persian Gulf.

20 January. The world is stunned when Iraq releases videotape of six bruised and beaten Allied POWs, identified as American Lt. Col. Clifford M. Acree, American Chief Warrant Officer Guy L. Hunter, Jr., American Lt. Jefferson N. Zaun, Flight Lt. John Peters (RAF, Great Britain), Flight Lt. Adrian Nichols (RAF, Great Britain), and Capt. Maurice Cocciolone (Italian Air Force). Iraq announces that these captured airmen would be scattered "among scientific and economic targets, as well as among other selected targets." In a speech delivered by Saddam Hussein on Baghdad Radio, the Iraqi leader tells his people that "you must target their [the Coalition's] interests everywhere" and explains that only a fraction of Iraq's weapons have been used so far.

21 January. President Bush attacks the Iraqi use of POW footage as a violation of the Geneva Convention. Assistant Secretary of Defense for Public Affairs Pete Williams announces that the news media cannot film the coffins of American casualties arriving at Dover Air Force Base in Delaware. The Military Traffic Management Command (MTMC) facility in Istanbul, Turkey, is the subject of a bombing, the first known case of terrorist activity against the Coalition forces. Thirty-seven Patriots are fired at 10 different Scuds fired at Riyadh and Dhahran. The 22 EPWs captured by the USS *Nicholas* on 19 January are deposited with the EPW camps.

22 January. Iraq releases a another videotape of what it claims are two captured American pilots. American officials identify them as Maj. Jeffrey Scott Tice and Maj. Harry Michael Roberts, listed as missing on 20 January. Their capture brings the number of POWs held by Baghdad to nine, including five Americans. The Pentagon also acknowledges that 18 Coalition airplanes have been brought down, including 9 American planes; 24 Coalition pilots, including 13 Americans, are listed as missing in action. Iraq claims it has 20 Coalition pilots as prisoners and announces that it will scatter the prisoners among economic and military targets as shields. British Prime Minister *John Major* denounces Saddam Hussein as "immoral" and "a man without pity" for his treatment of Coalition prisoners of war. Iraq is reported to have blown up the Kuwaiti oil installations in the Walfra oilfields. An Iraqi Scud missile avoids being destroyed by a Patriot missile and slams into a suburb of Tel Aviv, killing three and wounding 96. The American ships USS *Philadelphia* and *Spruance* attack the Bayji oil refinery with Tomahawk Land Attack Missiles.

23 January. The U.S. Senate votes 99–0 (Senate Concurrent Resolution 5), and the House votes 418–0 (House Concurrent Resolution 48) to condemn Iraq for its treatment of war prisoners. White House Press Secretary Marlin Fitzwater denounces CNN for Peter Arnett's report on the bombing of the Iraqi "baby milk factory." Iraq launches its fourth Scud attack on Saudi Arabia, but the assault is deterred by a Patriot missile. Joint Chief of Staff Chairman Gen. Colin Powell announces that the allies have achieved air superiority over Kuwait and Iraq, and will continue to destroy Iraq's military capability from the air while concentrating on severing supply lines from Iraq to Kuwait.

24 January. CBS announces that reporter Bob Simon and his crew are missing. It is later discovered that the men had traveled against military restrictions to the Saudi-Iraqi border, where they were captured. The allies retake Qaruh Island, the first Kuwaiti ground to be recaptured. A Saudi pilot shoots down two Iraqi planes. Six Scuds are launched at Saudi Arabia and Israel. The *Washington Post* reports that Israel has announced that it will not intervene in the war. The *New York Times* reports that Iraq is cutting off gasoline supplies to its people to conserve its dwindling reserves.

25 January. The United States accuses the Iraqis of environmental terrorism when an oil slick appears from several tankers destroyed by the Iraqis at the Kuwaiti port of Nina Al Ahmadi. In a skirmish, American ships confront an Iraqi vessel laying mines near Sea Island Terminal, setting the terminal on fire. Iranian President Hashemi Rafsanjani tells a prayer meeting at Tehran University that Iran will remain neutral in the

Persian Gulf war. According to the *New York Times*, the Soviet independent news agency Interfax is reporting that several Soviet Defense Ministry sources are saying that Saddam Hussein has in the past few days had several of his top commanders shot because of heavy losses suffered by Iraq in the first week of the war. The U.S. European Command reports that 28 Patriots were fired at the 7 Scuds fired at Israel, destroying all of the missiles.

26 January. Saudi officials caution that oil released from Kuwait's Sea Terminal Island oil terminus is heading for Saudi beaches. An unknown number of American F-111s from the Saudi Air Force Base at Taif attack the Al Ahmadi oil refinery to stop the flow of oil into the Persian Gulf. Five Scud missiles are fired at Tel Aviv and Haifa in Israel, and Riyadh in Saudi Arabia, and all are intercepted by Patriot missiles or land in noncivilian areas. Three Iraqi planes are shot down, bringing the total to 45. Several planes from the Bahraini Air Force fly their first offensive mission of the war, striking an antiship missile site inside Kuwait. The *New York Times* reports that U.S. military authorities have concluded that Iraqi forces cannot be defeated by air power alone.

27 January. Utilizing GBU-15 smart bombs, several American Air Force F-111 fighters bomb the manifolds on Kuwaiti oil stations to stop the flow of oil into the Persian Gulf. Saudi experts estimate that more than a million barrels (45 million gallons) of oil a day is flowing into the Persian Gulf due to Iraqi sabotage. American military officials warn that an ecological disaster is in the making. The London *Sunday Times* reports that American intelligence has detected "increased activity" at the Iraqi main chemical-producing plant at Samarra. U.S. Command believes that 58 Iraqi aircraft have fled to Iran, including several French-built Mirage F-1s with the capability of carrying Exocet antiship missiles. Ending an eight-day assault, the 2nd Battalion of the 7th Air Defense Artillery of the U.S. Air Force reports that it has found and destroyed 10 Scud missiles.

28 January. About 80 Iraqi jets have moved to safety in Iran. The Saudis estimate the Persian Gulf oil spill to contain more than 11 million barrels (450 million gallons) of oil. In a letter to Javier Pérez de Cuéllar, Iraq claims that Coalition bombing has so far killed 324 civilians and wounded an additional 416, but offers no evidence. The United States and Soviet Union jointly announce that a meeting scheduled for 11–13 February between President Bush and Soviet President Gorbachev has been postponed. Four Patriots are fired at a Scud hurled at Riyadh, while a second Scud is allowed to fall untouched in an unpopulated section of Israel.

29 January. In his State of the Union message, President Bush tells the American people that "together, we have resisted the trap of appeasement, cynicism and isolation that gives temptation to tyrants." U.S. officials estimate the number of Iraqi jets flying to safety in Iran has increased to 90, up about 10 from the previous day. In a letter to the United Nations, Iran insists that, due to its neutral status in the conflict, all Iraqi planes would be impounded until after the war. Allied planes fly over 2,600 missions this day. It is reported that in one engagement, a convoy of Iraqi military vehicles was attacked and destroyed by Coalition fighters on 28 January. Baghdad Radio reports that an unnamed Coalition pilot, taken to the Ministry of Industry, was killed in a raid on that building. Iraqi armored forces launch attacks at al-Khafji and al-Wafrah; a quick Coalition response prevents any forward advance. In Oman, 6,000 American Marines participate in Exercise Sea Soldier IV.

30 January. Iraqi tank forces attack Coalition forces at al-Khafji, killing 12 U.S. Marines and wounding two others in the first ground skirmish of the war. Secretary of Defense Cheney secretly dispatches the Delta Force to the Persian Gulf to aid in the hunt for Scud launchers.

31 January. Saudi forces announce the recapture of the city of al-Khafji. Iraqi forces in southern Kuwait come under brutal assault by American *B-52* bombers. American POW Col. David Eberly is moved to an Iraqi prison dubbed "The Biltmore." The Pentagon announces that an Air Force *AC-130A/H Spectre gunship* is lost.

1 February. The Pentagon confirms that an AC-130A/H Spectre gunship has been shot down over Kuwait, with 14 men aboard.

2 February. General Schwarzkopf decides against an amphibious landing to liberate Kuwait and turns instead to a plan for a ground attack of Iraqi positions. The *New York Times* reports that France has consented to allow American B-52s to travel through French airspace from Britain en route to the Middle East. Two Scuds, fired at Israel, are allowed to crash into an unpopulated area near Tel Aviv. A third Scud, fired at Riyadh, is intercepted by two Patriot missiles, although the wreckage crashes into a residential area, causing minor casualties.

3 February. USCENTAF reports that three Scuds and two mobile erector-launchers have been destroyed by F-15 fighters. Marine Cpl. Albert G. Haddad is killed in a helicopter crash; he is the only Arab-American to die during Operations Desert Shield and Desert Storm.

4 February. A letter signed by 21 House members is sent to CNN President Tom Johnson denouncing Peter Arnett's reports from Baghdad.

6 February. USCINCCENT reports that an estimated 118 Iraqi aircraft have fled to Iran. More Scuds and their launch towers are destroyed by F-15E "Scud Busting" aircraft.

9 February. Three Patriot surface-to-air missiles are fired at a Scud heading toward Tel Aviv.

10 February. Secretary of State Dick Cheney returns to the United States after a tour of Saudi Arabia and announces that the air war must continue before the ground war proceeds.

11 February. Three Patriots are fired at a Scud heading toward Tel Aviv, destroying it in the air. Soviet envoy Yevgeni Primakov arrives in Baghdad to negotiate an Iraqi withdrawal from Kuwait.

13 February. In what was to become the most controversial incident of the war, two laser-guided bombs dropped from F-117A Stealth fighters slam into the hardened Iraqi bunker called al-Firdos, killing several hundred Iraqi civilians. U.S. authorities claim that the bunker is an intelligence center shielded with civilians.

15 February. Saddam Hussein, in a broadcast on Baghdad Radio, reports on "Iraq's readiness to deal with Security Council Resolution No. 660 of 1990 with the aim of reaching an honorable and acceptable political solution, including [the] withdrawal" from Kuwait. The United States rejects the overture. A Scud fired at an unknown destination in Saudi Arabia falls harmlessly into the Persian Gulf or near al-Jubayl.

16 February. F-15E fighters report three Scuds and four launchers have been destroyed. Three additional Scuds are fired at Israel: one is destroyed by two Patriots, one is lost, and a third hits an unpopulated area of Israel.

18 February. A Soviet peace proposal is offered that aims to end the war in exchange for a promise of Iraqi security and a conference on Middle East issues.

19 February. A Scud fired at Israel is destroyed by a Patriot.

20 February. The Senate Governmental Affairs Committee begins to hold hearings of the Pentagon's rules on media access during the war.

21 February. Patriots are employed to destroy two Scuds fired at King Khalid Military City in Saudi Arabia and one discharged at Bahrain.

22 February. President Bush issues an ultimatum to Iraq: withdraw from Kuwait by noon 23 February or American troops would commence the ground war. The Soviet peace proposal, only four days old but rejected by all sides, is revised to exclude any promise of a Middle East peace conference. USCENTAF and USNARCENT aircraft destroy four Scuds and eight mobile launchers.

23 February. Two Scuds, one fired at Kfia, Saudi Arabia, and a second at Tel Aviv, are not engaged.

24 February. The ground war (G-Day) begins. Resistance is light as Coalition troops storm across the Saudi-Kuwaiti border into areas once occupied by the Iraqis. Iraqi troops confronted by Coalition forces buckle, resulting in thousands of Iraqi prisoners of war in the first day of fighting. Individual Scuds are fired at Riyadh (two) and King Khalid Military City, but both are destroyed by Patriots. Secretary of Defense Cheney suspends media access and briefings until reports begin to come in on the success of the ground war.

25 February. Less than 24 hours after the start of the ground war, Saddam Hussein announces that Iraqi troops will withdraw immediately in compliance with UN Security Council Resolution 660. A Scud missile, either hit by a Patriot and not fully destroyed, or totally missed, slams into a military barracks, killing 28 American servicemen and women in the worst single incident of casualties for the Coalition during the war.

26 February. Iraqi troops are in full flight from Kuwait; CBS reporter Bob McKeown becomes the first Western journalist to enter Kuwait City. The VII Corps of the U.S. Army clashes with the Republican Guard in the battle of 73 Easting.

27 February. President Bush announces that the war will end at midnight, and declares that the goal of Kuwaiti liberation has been accomplished. Two F-111F fighter jets attack the North Taji command bunker with 4,700 pound laser-guided GBU-28 bombs, apparently destroying the target. Nine British soldiers are killed when an American *A-10* fires on infantry fighting vehicles (IFVs) belonging to the Royal Regiment of Fusiliers in one of the worst *friendly fire* incidents of the war. General Schwarzkopf conducts what becomes known as the *"Mother of All Briefings."*

28 February. The Persian Gulf War ends at 12 midnight EST. In the BNL loan case, Attorney General Richard Thornburgh announces several indictments.

1 March. The first reports of a revolt by Shi'ite Muslims in the city of Basra are circulated. The United States reopens its embassy in Kuwait under the leadership of Ambassador Edward W. Gnehm, Jr. President Bush tells reporters that "By God, we've licked the Vietnam syndrome once and for all!"

2 March. The UN Security Council approves, by a vote of 11 to 1 (Cuba) with three abstentions (China, India, and Yemen), Resolution 686, which lays out a formal agreement for the end of hostilities in the Gulf while calling on Iraq to implement all previous twelve resolutions. CBS reporter Bob Simon and his crew are released by the Iraqi government.

3 March. General Schwarzkopf, accompanied by Lt. Gen. Sir Peter de la Billière, British commander in the Gulf, Lt. Gen. Michel Roquejoffre, French commander in the Gulf, and Prince Gen. Khalid bin Sultan, head of Saudi forces, meet with Lt. Gen. Sultan Hashim Ahmad, chief of Iraqi military operations, and Lt. Gen. Saleh Abbud Mahmud, commander of the Iraqi 3rd Corps in Kuwait, at the captured Iraqi airfield of Safwan, three miles north of the Kuwait-Iraq border, to discuss a permanent cease-fire. The Iraq government announces that it intends "to fulfill its obligations" under Resolution 686 passed by the UN Security Council. Kuwaiti soldiers search through the Palestinian district in Kuwait City for suspected collaborators.

4 March. Iraq discloses that it has 36 prisoners of war: 21 Americans, 12 Britons, 2 Italians, and 1 Kuwaiti. The first 10 prisoners are released to the custody of the International Committee of the Red Cross. Sheik

Saad al-Abdallah al-Sabah, the Kuwaiti Crown Prince and premier, returns to Kuwait. Near Basra, *New York Times* reporter Chris Hedges is taken captive by Iraqi soldiers battling Shi'ite rebels.

5 March. The remaining 26 allied POWs are released. Baghdad Radio announces that the annexation of Kuwait has been declared null and void and that all property seized by Iraqi forces in Kuwait after 2 August 1990 would be returned. The U.S. government announces that U.S. casualties during the ground war total 115 killed and 300 wounded.

6 March. President Bush delivers an address to a joint session of Congress and tells the American people that "aggression is defeated. The war is over." American troops begin to return home. Ali Hassan Majid, a cousin of Saddam Hussein's who is believed responsible for the chemical weapons attack on the city of Halabja in 1988 and the civilian administrator of Kuwait from August to November 1990, is named Iraqi Interior Minister. British Defense Secretary Tom King reports that the Coalition has not yet decided on the final disposition of Iraqi prisoners of war who refuse to return home.

7 March. The Kurdish insurgency begins. Fifteen Iraqi cities are threatened by the counteraction. Iraq releases 1,700 Kuwaiti prisoners.

8 March. During Friday prayers at Tehran University, Iranian President Hashemi Rafsanjani warns Saddam Hussein "not to color the streets with [the] blood" of rebel Shi'ite civilians. He urges Hussein "to submit to the will of the people" and remove himself from the Iraqi leadership. "Now that the Iraqi people are ready to take over a ruined country from you and rebuild it, you should welcome this offer," Rafsanjani says. In Baghdad, the Iraqi leadership expels all Western journalists from the capital and at the same time deploys troops around the streets of Baghdad, signifying that Saddam Hussein intends to crush the rebellion and does not want it broadcast. The Iraqi government releases *New York Times* correspondent Chris Hedges.

9 March. President Bush warns Saddam Hussein not to use chemical weapons against the Shi'ite rebellion.

10 March. The 21 Americans held as prisoners of war by Iraq return to the United States.

12 March. The Red Cross informs the U.S. government that Iraq has offered to return the remains of 14 Coalition servicemen. Among them is Navy Lt. William T. Costen, killed when his A-6 Intruder was shot down 18 January. Others include five Britons. The Pentagon announces that it has found and identified the body of Capt. David Spellacy, who was killed when his OV-10 Bronco observation plane was shot down over Kuwait by Iraqi ground fire on 25 February. The removal of the names of Costen and Spellacy leave 21 Americans still listed as missing in action, a number which includes 14 who apparently perished when their AC-130A/H Spectre gunship was shot down over Kuwait 31 January. Iraqi opposition leaders report that

Iraqi troops loyal to Saddam Hussein have attacked Shi'ite rebels in the Shi'ite Muslim holy cities of Karbala and Najaf. Gen. Norman Schwarzkopf takes a tour of the liberated Kuwait City.

14 March. Upon orders from President Bush, elements of the 101st Airborne and the 1st Cavalry advance 30 miles deeper into Iraq to take up new positions in what is viewed as an attempt to increase pressure on the government of Saddam Hussein. More than a dozen of the 21 former American prisoners of war hold press conferences, in which they tell of being treated "with compassion" by their Iraqi captors, excluding occasional beatings during interrogations. Maj. Jeffrey S. Tice, shot down on 20 January, reports that he suffered electric shock torture to make him talk. Emir Sheik Jaber al-Ahmed al-Sabah, the leader of Kuwait, quietly returns to his shattered country. Caryle Murphy of the *Washington Post* is awarded the George Polk Award for her reports from inside Kuwait after the Iraqi invasion.

15 March. Kurdish guerrillas announce that they control most of northern Iraq. A Turkish newspaper, *Gunes,* reports that Iraqi troops are crossing into Turkey waving white flags of surrender and that at Habur, a major border crossing between Turkey and Iraq, the Iraqi flag has been replaced by the red, yellow, and green Kurdish flag.

16 March. In order to bolster his beleaguered government, Saddam Hussein promises the Iraqi people that he will reform the Iraqi political system to allow for the freedom of speech, freedom of the press, and a new, more liberal constitution. In his address, carried live on Baghdad television and radio, Saddam says, "Iraqis will find in this new era more liberty to express their wills and their interests through political parties, societies, and the press." In Bermuda, where he is meeting with British Prime Minister John Major, President Bush dismisses the pledge, saying that "his [Saddam Hussein's] credibility is zilch, zero, zed." At "Checkpoint Charlie," inside what is called Coalition-occupied Iraq, American troops stop and arrest a group of Iraqi soldiers trying to smuggle 500 pounds of explosives into Kuwait hidden in bags of rice. The *Oakland Tribune* shows Princess Alia, daughter of Jordan's King Hussein, taking part in a march in Amman to raise money for Iraqi relief. In eastern Saudi Arabia, a cannon is sounded, starting the month-long Muslim observance of Ramadan.

20 March. In the first aerial dogfight since the end of the war, a U.S. F-15C shoots down an Iraqi SU-22 after the jet violates the prohibition against flights of fixed-wing aircraft. In Washington, D.C., former U.S. Ambassador to Iraq April Glaspie testifies before the Senate Foreign Relations Committee that during her 25 July 1990 meeting with Saddam Hussein, she told the Iraqi leader directly that the United States would defend Kuwait sovereignty as well as American interests in the area against Iraqi aggression; she denies that the

discussion matched a purported transcript released by Iraq on 22 September 1990.

21 March. U.S. human rights organizations condemn Kuwaiti troops and police for arresting, beating, and in some cases executing Palestinians in Kuwait who are suspected of collaborating with the Iraqis during the occupation.

22 March. The U.S. Senate appropriates $42.6 billion to cover the cost of the war. It also clears the way for $5.4 billion as a "dire emergency" to be used for war veterans, as well as aid to Israel and Turkey. Massoud Barzani, the head of the Kurdish rebellion, calls on other opposition leaders to meet with him and help form a provisional Iraqi government. He also states that 95 percent of the northern area of Iraq is controlled by the rebels. Tehran Radio reports that rioting has spread to Baghdad and that Saddam Hussein has declared a state of national emergency, but the report cannot be independently verified. Fighting intensifies near *Mosul* and Khanaquin in northern Iraq, while Shi'ites rebel against Republican Guard troops in the holy city of Najaf.

23 March. As the rebellion against his authority spreads, Saddam Hussein reshuffles his cabinet, resigning the prime ministership to name Deputy Prime Minister Sa'dun Hammadi, a Shi'ite Muslim, as the new prime minister. Foreign Minister Tariq Aziz is named deputy prime minister. Hammadi's promotion is seen as an overture to the rebelling Shi'ites in southern Iraq. Interior Minister Ali Hassan Majid is retained in his post.

25 March. Newsweek reports that in southern Iraq, Republican Guard troops are viciously attacking Shi'ite rebels, strafing civilians with tanks, burning alive wounded rebels, and hanging those who surrendered. The newspaper *al-Qadissiya* calls the insurrection "the gravest conspiracy in [Iraq's] contemporary history." Detectives hired by the Kuwaiti government to track down assets stolen by Iraq during the occupation announce that they have found that Saddam Hussein has secreted $2.4 billion in 40 banks around the world in accounts not frozen by Western governments after the Kuwaiti invasion. The detectives also announce that Saddam had "skimmed" an additional $10 billion from Iraq's oil revenues from 1979 to 1989. Further, they found that Iraqi front companies owned $1 billion in shares of European concerns, including a more than 8 percent ownership of France's Hachette, the world's sixth largest publisher.

26 March. The *New York Times* reports that U.S. officials concede that the Shi'ite revolt in southern Iraq may be close to collapsing under the weight of Republican Guard attacks and that the Kurds in the north will not hold out much longer. Iraq tells the United Nations that it is ready to return to Kuwait some 1.2 million ounces of gold bullion, worth about $457 million, which it stole during the occupation. Iraq also offers to return commemorative coins and Kuwaiti money worth $1.8 billion.

27 March. In an interview with David Frost, Gen. H. Norman Schwarzkopf declares that he wanted to crush the Iraqis the same way that Hannibal annihilated the Romans army at the battle of Cannae in 216 B.C., but that President Bush stopped him. Secretary of Defense Dick Cheney disagrees, issuing a statement in which he declares that Schwarzkopf "raised no objections" at the time his opinion was requested on the subject of ending the war before the Republican Guard could be fully destroyed.

28 March. Iraqi forces make major advances on the Kurdish rebellion.

29 March. The *Associated Press* reports Kurdish claims that rebels have recaptured the vital oil center of Kirkuk, although the Iraqi government dismisses the claim.

30–31 March. The Kurdish rebellion collapses. As Kurdish refugees flee before Iraq battalions, the first reports come in of massive refugee shifts to the mountains of northern Iraq and southern Turkey.

1 April. The Turkish government frantically appeals to the world to help the Kurdish refugees. The U.S. Army announces plans to withdraw 20,000 U.S. troops from the Kuwaiti Theater of Operations.

2 April. The Pentagon concedes that Iraqi government troops have retaken the towns of Erbil, Dahuk, and Zakhu, all in northern Iraq, leaving the Kurds in control only of the provincial capital of Sulaimaniya, near the Iranian border. The Iraqi army also demolishes the town of Tuz Khurmatu in retaliation for civilians there supporting the insurgency. The major powers on the UN Security Council ignore calls from Turkey and France to take up the issue of the Iraqi refugees, instead concentrating on putting together the details for a resolution effectively ending the Persian Gulf War.

3 April. Major Kurdish rebel activity ceases. The UN Security Council passes Resolution 687, which offers to end the war against Iraq and lift some of the sanctions if the Iraqis accept strict military and financial conditions.

4 April. President Bush is criticized for allowing the Kurdish insurgency to collapse without American aid. He replies, "We're not going to get sucked into this by sending precious American troops into battle."

5 April. The Iraqi government completely crushes all Kurdish resistance; 300,000 Kurdish refugees move toward southern Turkey, while a similar number shift into western Iran. The United States begins *Operation Provide Comfort,* which aims to provide humanitarian aid (food, water, basic medical assistance, and shelter) to the Kurdish refugees who have fled the Iraqi army.

6 April. Iraq accepts UN Resolution 687, adopted on 3 April.

10 April. The U.S. government warns Saddam Hussein not to disrupt or thwart any of the relief measures involved in Operation Provide Comfort. Meanwhile, Maj. Sadi Sadeq al-Maruyyati, an Iraqi army

doctor inside the Kurdish refugee camp of Uzumlu, Turkey, located about 35 miles west of the town of Cukurca, tells the Associated Press, "In two or three days, thousands of children will die of gastroenteritis [diarrhea] and pneumonia." The UN Security Council members settle on imposing a cease-fire at 10 a.m. on 11 April. Congress enacts the *Operation Desert Shield/Desert Storm Supplemental Appropriations Act of 1991,* which procures supplemental appropriations for Operations Desert Shield and Desert Storm, as well as establishing a Persian Gulf Regional Defense Fund with an additional $15 billion in appropriations to pay for military operations in the Persian Gulf area.

12 April. Iraqi Foreign Minister Ahmad Hussein Khuddayer al-Sammaraei calls on Iran to return all 148 Iraqi aircraft that it is holding, which Iraq says includes 33 planes that are attached to Iraqi Airlines; Iran retorts that it has only 22 Iraqi fighter aircraft and that any others Iraq claimed it had must have been shot down by allied pilots. Although Iran says that it will return the 22 planes if requested to through the United Nations, some intelligence sources report that Iran has begun to repaint the captured planes with the markings of the Iranian Air Force.

13 April. Iran announces that more than one million Shi'ite and Kurdish refugees have passed into Iran, with more expected every day. UNIKOM, the UN Iraq-Kuwait Observation Mission, arrives in Kuwait City with 1,440 members.

17 April. A "safe zone" for Kurdish refugees is established; relief camps for the estimated 850,000 refugees are initiated by the United States.

21 April. Gen. H. Norman Schwarzkopf arrives back to CENTCOM headquarters in Tampa, Florida, to a cheering crowd of several thousand. The Reuters news service reports that a Gallup poll of Americans finds that 55 percent don't think that the United States won the war, while 51 percent would support further military action to drive Saddam Hussein from power.

29 April. The *Washington Post* reports that Kurdish *peshmerga* (Arabic: "Those who confront death") guerrillas are blocking Kurdish refugees from returning to their villages in Iraq so that they can resume their war against the Iraqi government.

8 May. New York Newsday, citing confidential sources, reports that on 2 March, two days after the Allied cease-fire, the 24th Mechanized Infantry Division, known as the "Victory Division," was attacked by elements of the elite Hammurabi Division of the Iraqi Republican Guard; during the 24-hour battle, the Americans destroyed 247 Iraqi tanks and 500 military transports and more than 3,000 Iraqi soldiers were taken prisoner. "We really waxed them," one commander was quoted as saying of the clash, which was originally reported as a small attack.

9 May. UN Secretary-general Javier Pérez de Cuéllar, visiting the White House, tells President Bush that the Iraqi government had rejected an American proposal to station UN peacekeeping troops in the Kurdish areas of northern Iraq, warning that American troops may have to stay in the area for an extended period of time. Secretary of Defense Cheney, after meeting with Persian Gulf leaders, tells reporters in Ireland on his way home that the Gulf states involved in Operation Desert Storm have agreed to store American military hardware in the area, allowing for a continued American presence in the region. The Kuwaiti government announces that trials of suspected collaborators will begin on 12 May.

13 May. The U.S. military hands over control of the Kurdish refugee encampments to the United Nations.

15 May. Atomic specialists from the United Nations begin the process of inspecting and cataloging Iraq's nuclear sites and chemical weapons storehouses.

18 May. Kurdish leader Massoud Barzani announces that he has reached an agreement with the Iraqi government in which a Kurdish autonomous region will be carved out of northern Iraq, although the control over crucial oil properties in the area are still under debate. As part of the agreement, Iraqi troops are seen abandoning army posts near the Kurdish village of Dohuk.

19 May. After a short delay, Kuwait begins the trials of suspected collaborators.

22 May. The U.S. Senate passes an appropriation bill which clears $572 million, mostly for refugee assistance.

4 June. The *Los Angeles Times,* quoting American officials, reports that a top Iraqi scientist defected in May and told Pentagon experts that much of Saddam Hussein's nuclear program survived the Persian Gulf War.

8 June. A huge victory parade is held in Washington, D.C., for returning American troops.

9 June. A Kuwaiti martial law court sentences Manki Shimmiri, a technician in the Kuwaiti Air Force, to death for collaborating with the Iraqis during the occupation. U.S. Ambassador to Kuwait Edward W. Gnehm, Jr., warns the Kuwaitis that human rights must be respected and that the world was monitoring the trials.

13 June. The last troops involved in the ground war part of Operation Desert Storm return to the United States.

18 June. Iraq frees Douglas Brand, a 31-year old British engineer sentenced to life for spying, after Saddam Hussein receives a personal appeal from former British Prime Minister Edward Heath.

23 June. The Commerce Department starts an investigation into whether department officials altered documents on sales of "military-useful technology" to Iraq so that such documents would not seem incriminating when investigated by Congress. The bodies of two BBC newsmen lost in northern Iraq are identified. Nick Della Casa and Charles Maxwell were in northern Iraq near the Turkish border in March filming Kurdish refugees fleeing from Iraqi troops when they disappeared. Both were shot to death, and their bodies were found 23 May. A third member of the crew, Rosanna Della Casa, who is Maxwell's sister, remains missing.

24 June. Iraqi Minister of Industry Amer Asadi reports that the Coalition bombing destroyed major sections of Iraq's electricity grid and that the country is undergoing a major crisis in restoring power to the Iraqi people.

25 June. The *New York Times* reports that an international alliance of *minesweepers* from the Coalition nations has cleared most of the 1,200 mines off Kuwait's coast.

26 June. The Bush Administration presents photos to the UN Security Council showing Iraq using evasive techniques to move and hide sensitive uranium enriching equipment from UN inspectors. Kuwait's prime minister, Crown Prince Saad al-Abdullah al-Salem, a member of Kuwait's ruling family, orders that all collaborators sentenced to death will be spared.

27 June. Secretary of State James Baker accuses Iraq of "extraordinarily serious" violations by moving equipment before examination by UN inspectors. Iraq's ambassador to the United Nations, Abdul Amir al-Anbari, reports that the equipment being moved "could be anything, like office furniture."

28 June. Iraqi troops fire over the heads of UN inspectors as they prepare to inspect nuclear equipment at Fallujah, east of Baghdad. President Bush tells reporters that "we can't allow this." The UN Security Council issues a unanimous statement demanding that Iraq allow the inspectors unlimited and safe access to the equipment. It expresses "grave concern" at Iraq's "flagrant violations" of the cease-fire order as well as all relevant UN Security Council resolutions.

29 June. Kuwait ends martial law. President Bush, in an interview, accuses Saddam Hussein of "cheating and lying and hiding" on the issue of inspections. He declares that he has the authority to order further strikes against Iraq if it does not comply with UN resolutions, although such an option has not been discussed as yet. Kurdish opposition leaders reject an autonomy agreement with the Iraqi government. More than 1,200 Kuwaitis waiting in a camp just inside Kuwait flee into Iraq, fearing that they will be labeled as collaborators.

28 July. Kuwait exports its first oil since the invasion.

18 September. The UN Security Council permits Iraq to sell $1.6 billion in oil to purchase food supplies and other essentials. Iraq refuses to comply, noting that the request earmarks a portion of the money to compensate Kuwaiti victims of the invasion.

23 September. Iraqi troops detain 40 UN atomic inspectors after they discover in a Baghdad building critical documents dealing with the Iraqi nuclear power program. A UN official discloses that the team secretly copied many of the documents and spirited them out of the country without the Iraqis' knowledge. The Bush Administration asks Saudi Arabia to allow the United States to station additional military aircraft and Patriot missile batteries in the desert kingdom.

24 September. Iraq unconditionally agrees to allow UN inspectors to fly inside Iraq using UN helicopters. In congressional testimony, Charles E. Allen, interim head of the CIA, reveals that as early as January 1990, he and other top CIA officials were warning the Bush Administration that Iraq might invade Kuwait, but that such warnings were ignored.

4 October. Four Israeli F-15 fighters make an unauthorized reconnaissance flight over Iraq. The Iraqis complain to UN Secretary-general Pérez de Cuéllar, and the United States decries the Israeli move.

7 October. Kurdish guerrillas execute 60 Iraqi soldiers captured during Iraq's sweep of northern Iraq against Kurdish separatists. Massoud Barzani, leader of one of the Kurdish groups, condemns the killings.

6 November. The last of the Kuwaiti oil fires is extinguished. The total cost of the operation to date: $1.5 billion.

23 November. Iraq releases British businessman Ian Richter, imprisoned since 1985 for bribery. Although the British government denies that it made a deal for Richter's release, the British government does allow Iraq access to $125 million (70 million pounds) of its assets frozen in August 1990 by Prime Minister Thatcher to purchase food and medicine.

5 December. Congress passes Public Law 102-190, the *National Defense Authorization Act,* which mandates that the Department of Defense establish a registry of soldiers complaining of symptoms from being exposed to burning oil.

1992 *9 January.* The Associated Press, citing a General Accounting Office draft memo, reports that while *M-1A1 Abrams tanks* and *M-2 Bradley IFVs* were "highly effective" during the Persian Gulf War, continuation of the conflict past its actual cease-fire would have left these vehicles facing "disastrous supply shortages." A report by Greenpeace, prepared by former Army intelligence officer William Arkin, claims that 70,000 Iraqi civilians were killed by Coalition bombing during the Persian Gulf War.

12 January. U.S. *News & World Report* reports that "several weeks before the Persian Gulf War started, U.S. intelligence agents inserted a computer virus into a network of Iraqi computers tied to that country's air defense system" by smuggling it in a printer that was subsequently shipped to Iraq.

26 January. Seymour Hersh of the *New York Times* writes that in interviews conducted over the past two months with former State Department, White House, and intelligence officials, he has learned that the Reagan Administration was providing highly classified intelligence to Iraq in 1982—two years earlier than previously thought.

5 February. The UN Security Council votes to maintain sanctions against Iraq, citing continuing failure to submit to the monitoring of the destruction of weapons of mass destruction.

26 February. Iraq announces its refusal to allow a team of inspectors from the United Nations to begin the dismantling of Scud missile plants and other Scud missile mechanics.

28 February. The UN Security Council condemns Iraq and rejects arguments from Iraqi envoy Tariq Aziz that Iraq has carried out its obligations under the cease-fire declaration. The Security Council sets 26 March as the deadline for Iraq to establish a program of destroying Scud missile and nuclear facilities in Iraq.

19 March. Iraq discloses that it had hidden 89 Scuds and other such missiles after the close of the Gulf war and had concealed these from UN inspectors.

20 March. Iraq agrees to fully comply with the UN resolutions demanding it reveal its missiles and nuclear weapons sites.

5 April. Iranian warplanes attack anti-Iranian rebels backed by Iraq at bases near the Iran-Iraq border in the first skirmish between the two nations since the end of the Iran-Iraq War.

16 April. The UN Kuwaiti-Iraq Border Commission defines the border between the two nations and awards Kuwait much of the disputed Rumailya oil field and a part of the Iraqi seaport of Umm Qasr.

19 May. Kurds in northeastern Iraq hold their first free elections to elect candidates to an autonomous Kurdish legislature.

22 May. The Kurdish elections end in a draw. The Democratic Party of Kurdistan and the Patriotic Union of Kurdistan agree to share power.

4 June. The Iraqi Kurdistan National Assembly meets for the first time as an autonomous body. Jawhar Namiq Salem, an economist, is elected speaker.

26 June. The Turkish Parliament approves a plan to allow American and Coalition military forces to stay in the country for six more months to protect the Kurds in northern Iraq.

2 July. Rumors fly that disaffected members of the Republican Guard unsuccessfully attempted to assassinate Saddam Hussein, with hundreds, perhaps thousands, of officers purged and murdered.

3 July. The Iraqi government denies any attempted coup had taken place the previous day.

9 July. Twenty Democrats on the House Judiciary Committee request Attorney General William P. Barr to appoint an independent counsel to investigate the prewar relationship between the United States and Iraq.

3–4 August. About 2,000 U.S. Marines and other troops land in Kuwait to begin two weeks of joint American-Kuwaiti military exercises.

10 August. Attorney General Barr rejects the request for an independent counsel, calling the accusations of American participation in the buildup of the Iraqi military "vague and conclusory."

21 August. Operation Provide Relief begins.

26 August. President George Bush warns Iraq that Iraqi aircraft flying over southern Iraq to attack Shi'ites will be shot down by allied aircraft.

27 August. Operation Southern Watch begins.

4 September. David Kay, the head of the UN Iraqi weapons inspection team, announces that all nuclear material and other weapons have been cleared from Iraq.

10 September. Iran seizes and annexes three islands in the Persian Gulf that it has jointly ruled with the United Arab Emirates since 1971. The UAE and other Persian Gulf states protest the annexation.

23–27 September. More than 30 Iraqi Kurdish groups meet in northeastern Iraq and agree on a plan to topple Saddam Hussein from power.

14 October. In a letter to Attorney General William Barr, Sen. David Boren (D-Oklahoma), chairman of the Senate Intelligence Committee, requests the appointment of a special prosecutor to examine whether the United States was involved in the use of Banca Nazionale del Lavoro (BNL) loans to Iraq.

16 October. Attorney General Barr names former federal Judge Frederick B. Lacey to investigate claims that the United States was involved in using BNL funds for loans to Iraq.

4 November. Congress passes Public Law 102-585, The Veterans Health Care Act of 1992, which establishes the *Veterans Persian Gulf Health Registry* in the Department of Veterans Affairs.

9 December. Special prosecutor Frederick Lacey releases a 190-page reporting clearing the United States in the BNL banking controversy.

13 December. Operation Restore Hope begins.

27 December. An American F-16 shoots down a single Iraqi warplane after it strays into the protected southern region of Iraq.

1993 *8 January.* The United Nations condemns Iraq's proclamation that it would no longer allow UN inspectors to fly around Iraq in UN helicopters.

9 January. American officials believe, through the use of reconnaissance, that Iraq has complied with the 6 January demand that it remove surface-to-air missiles south of the 36th parallel.

10 January. Kuwait discloses that 250 Iraqi troops crossed into the Iraq-Kuwait demilitarized zone to retrieve Iraqi arms and other equipment at Umm Qasr, a former Iraqi military base. The zone is set to become official Kuwaiti territory on 15 January. Kuwaitis fill their gas tanks so that they might be able to flee south if another Iraqi invasion occurs. The *New York Times* reports that Abdul-Jabbar Mohsen, chief press secretary

to Saddam Hussein, wrote in the Iraqi newspaper *al-Jumhouriya* that the people of Iraq "have no choice but to resist and fight for survival."

11 January. The Bush Administration announces that Iraq has moved the controversial SAM missile batteries from the disputed Shi'ite zone in the south to the protected zone north of the 32nd parallel in northern Iraq. In the second incident in two days, 250 more Iraqis, this time civilians, cross into the Iraq-Kuwait demilitarized zone to recover what Iraq says are its armaments at Umm Qasr. The UN Security Council condemns the incursions, warning of "serious consequences" if they do not stop.

12 January. The *New York Times* reports that President Bush, in the final days of his administration, has planned a retaliatory strike on Iraq for the defiance of UN resolutions and the demand to withdraw SAM missile batteries, and the two incursions of Iraqi troops into Kuwait.

13 January. About 80 warplanes (aided by 30 support aircraft) from the United States, France, and Great Britain attack various targets inside Iraq, mostly below or at the key line at the 36th parallel. They include radar stations at al-Amara, Najaf, Samawa, and at the Tallil Air Base near Nasiriya, as well as missile sites near Tallil and Basra. Among the planes which took part in the attack were F/A-18 Hornets, F-111F Aardvarks, F-117A Stealth fighters, French Mirage 2000s, British Tornadoes, and A-6 Intruders. In a fiery speech after the attack, Saddam Hussein beseeches his followers to "fight on against the aggressors so that the Iraqi airspace from the north to the south, from the east to the west, is turned into fiery lava." In an editorial published in the Iraqi government paper *al-Jumhouriya*, Abdul-Jabbar Mohsen, press secretary for Saddam Hussein, writes that "Kuwait is part of Iraq. This is an historic fact, and international treaties and world conspiracies cannot change the facts of history forever." He adds that "Kuwait shall return to Iraq in defiance of the Security Council and America." For the fourth time, Iraqis travel to the disputed zone of Umm Qasr to retrieve materiel. In a press conference, President Bush reports that "the coalition did the right thing [in attacking Iraq]." British Prime Minister John Major says that "we didn't take this action lightly." In Paris, a statement from the French Ministry of Defense simply declares, "It's a simple operation, a raid that's aimed at putting a halt to the intolerable provocations of Iraq so that Saddam Hussein will understand." To back up the Coalition action, President Bush orders that 1,250 American troops would be sent to Kuwait, bolstering about 300 Special Forces troops already in Kuwait training Kuwaiti soldiers. Kuwait places its armed forces on alert for a possible Iraqi invasion or other military action. Sheik Ali al-Sabah, Kuwait's defense minister, says that his nation's forces were "coordinating with the allied forces to handle any possible attack."

14 January. The Pentagon announces that while only one of the four missile sites targeted during the previous day's attack on Iraq was destroyed, two air-defense command facilities were damaged, and in addition Iraq was forced to dismantle the other three missile batteries. Iraq's state television network pronounces that 19 soldiers and 2 civilians were killed in the raid. The Iranian news agency IRNA runs a statement from President Hashemi Rafsanjani in which he calls the attack "a shameful act." However, the Iranian leader also chides the Iraqi government for bringing the situation down on its people. "The Iraqi Government's biggest mistake was that it turned its back on the [Iraqi] people and disregarded them," Rafsanjani's statement read. "When a government is representative of its people, no enemy would dare have bad intentions against them." In an interview published in the *New York Times*, President-elect Bill Clinton proclaims that he is not "obsessed" with Saddam Hussein and that "he indicated that he was ready for a fresh start with Saddam."

15 January. Iraq announces its refusal to guarantee the security of UN inspectors who come to Iraq. Calling the new action "disturbing," the Bush Administration puts American forces on alert for another attack on Iraq to make it comply. President-elect Bill Clinton claims that the *New York Times* "misrepresented his words" in yesterday's interview and that he had "no intention" of opening a new era of friendship with Iraq.

16 January. Iraq pushes the Coalition to the brink of further military action by agreeing to guarantee the safety of UN inspectors, in exchange for the UN aircraft staying out of the *no-fly zone* south of the 36th parallel. The United Nations rejects the plan. "What is unacceptable is the imposition of conditions," a Bush Administration official says.

17 January. Upon the orders of President Bush, American ships in the Persian Gulf and the Red Sea fire approximately 40 Tomahawk Land Attack Missiles (TLAMs) at the Zaafaraniya military complex, a key component in the Iraqi nuclear weapons program located about 8 miles south of Baghdad. The *New York Times*, in its 18 January edition, says of the compound, "The multi-billion dollar Zaafaraniya complex, which Pentagon officials said contains about two dozen buildings, covers an area of 2,200 by 900 feet. The complex, just north of the Tigris River and near the highway from Baghdad to Salman Pak, was not a target during the Gulf War." In a blistering speech to the Iraqi people, Saddam Hussein tells them to prepare for a "final and decisive chapter that will be the end of all chapters." Prior to that attack, an American F-4G Phantom II Wild Weasel assaulted and destroyed an Iraqi SA-6 SAM missile battery with a HARM air-to-surface antiradiation missile after the battery locked on to planes patrolling the southern no-fly zone. An hour and 40 minutes later, an Iraqi *MiG-23 Flogger* was shot down by an AMRAAM missile fired by an American F-16 after the Iraqi plane flew ten miles into the no-fly zone. During another incursion into the former Iraq-Kuwait demilitarized zone by Iraqi troops, Kuwaiti border

guards lying in wait open fire, killing one Iraqi soldier. American administration officials, speaking on condition of anonymity, tell the *New York Times* that President Bush was prepared to attack Iraq again on 15 January, but was cautioned against the move by British Prime Minister Major. Such an attack would have involved striking targets north of the 32nd parallel.

18 January. Coalition warplanes strike at Iraq for a third time in a week. Ten F-15Es, four F-16s, and four British Tornadoes depart from a base in Saudi Arabia to hit the missile batteries at Tallil, Najaf, and Samawa that escaped complete destruction in the first attack on 13 January. Further, four American ships in the Persian Gulf and the Red Sea fire 45 cruise missiles at the Zaafaraniya military complex near Baghdad, apparently destroying it completely. One cruise missile is apparently hit by Iraqi ground fire, crashing into the Rashid Hotel in Baghdad and causing the deaths of three Iraqi workers at the building. At the time of the attack by the planes, an American F-15 becomes entangled in a dogfight with an Iraqi MiG-23 Flogger; the F-15 fires two missiles at the plane, but its destruction is not confirmed. Soviet Foreign Minister Andrei Kozyrev calls the deaths of civilians "especially regrettable" and asks for an emergency meeting of the UN Security Council.

19 January. Making overtures to the new president of the United States, Bill Clinton, Iraq announces that all UN arms inspectors would be allowed to fly into Baghdad and around the country in UN helicopters and airplanes; in addition, a cease-fire is ordered against patrolling American aircraft. Three incidents around Iraq break the silence: An American F-4G Phantom II Wild Weasel, picking up indications that an Iraqi radar-seeking site 14 miles east of Mosul is homing in on American planes, fires a HARM antiradiation missile at the battery. An hour later, an American F-16 comes under attack from an Iraqi antiaircraft battery near the Saddam Hydroelectric Dam, 25 miles north of Mosul. Two hours later, two American F-16s are attacked by an Iraqi antiaircraft battery 12 miles north of Mosul. In all three incidents, the American planes do not receive damage and return to base. For the first time, King Fahd tells his cabinet that he is uneasy about continued Coalition attacks against Iraq. Qatar, a Coalition ally, denounces the repeated attacks. A Qatari newspaper, *Al-Arab*, which apparently reflects the government's opinion, editorializes that it hoped the new Clinton Administration would demonstrate "a greater ability to co-exist with others, without demonstrations of arrogant power and the policies of settling accounts that was [*sic*] practiced by the previous Administration." Turkish Prime Minister Suleyman Demirel flies to Damascus to enlist Syrian support to end the Kurdish separatist movement. Iraq puts on display the destroyed Zaafaraniya complex to visiting reporters. While the Pentagon alleges the plants there were employed in the making of electromagnetic isotope separators used to produce enriched uranium for nuclear weapons, the plant general director, Yihya Nassif, reports that the factory was "vital for the reconstruction of Iraq after the gulf war" and that it was "involved in the manufacture of everything from toothpaste to cylinder beads."

21 January. Acting under the final orders of the Bush Administration, an American F-4G Phantom II Wild Weasel and an F-16, escorting a French Mirage 2000 reconnaissance plane 10 miles south of Mosul, attack an Iraqi SAM missile battery with a HARM missile and cluster bombs. The Iraqi Foreign Ministry claims that the missile and bombs missed the target and hit a residential area, destroying a fertilizer factory. The 52-member UN nuclear weapons inspection team arrives in Baghdad.

22 January. For the second time in two days, an American F-4G Phantom II Wild Weasel attacks an Iraqi antiaircraft battery, this time one 15 miles east of Mosul.

23 January. Three Navy aircraft—an A-6 Intruder bomber and two F/A-18 Hornets—flying over Nasiriya in southern Iraq are attacked by an Iraqi antiaircraft battery; the A-6 drops a laser-guided bomb on the target, allowing all three craft to return to the aircraft carrier USS *Kitty Hawk* safely.

4 March. Two Pakistani soldiers belonging to UNIKOM, the UN Iraq-Kuwait Observation Mission, are arrested by the Iraqis at the Iraq-Kuwait border.

April. UN weapons inspectors in Iraq confirm that Iraq has been producing forms of mustard gas and such toxic agents as sarin and tabun at a vast chemical weapons complex at Muthanna, 65 miles northwest of Baghdad.

14–17 April. Former President George Bush tours Kuwait. Iraqi agents smuggled into Kuwait and armed with explosives attempt but fail to assassinate the former president.

2 May. The Kuwaiti government announces that to symbolically renounce all possible ties to Iraq, it will construct a 120-mile ditch along its border with Iraq. The ditch, calculated to be about 9 feet deep and 16 feet wide, would also have a hill on the Kuwaiti side about 12 feet tall.

7 May. A Department of Veterans Affairs Blue Ribbon panel meets to discuss the mysterious diseases plaguing Gulf War veterans.

9 June. The House Committee on Veterans Affairs Subcommittee on Oversight and Investigation on Health Care of Persian Gulf Veterans meets.

23 June. American intelligence detects a movement of Iraqi arms and men toward the border with Iran in what some are calling an attempt to head off an Iranian invasion of eastern Iraq.

26 June. Armed with evidence that the Iraqi government supported a potential assassination attempt on President George Bush during his visit in April, the United States initiates a missile attack on Baghdad. Ships in the Red Sea launch 23 Tomahawk cruise missiles at the headquarters of the Iraqi intelligence service in downtown Baghdad.

24 August. Husham el-Shawi, the Iraqi ambassador to Canada, and Hamid el-Jabouri, who retired the previous week as Iraq's ambassador to Tunisia, announce in London that they are defecting to the West. They join the Iraqi ambassadors to the Netherlands and Spain, as well as Mohammed el-Mashat, former Iraqi ambassador to Austria, Great Britain, and the United States, who have defected since the start of the Persian Gulf War.

9 September. Israel and the Palestine Liberation Organization recognize each other's legitimacy. Prime Minister Yitzhak Rabin and PLO Chairman Yasir Arafat exchange letters calling for the end of their nearly 30-year war.

1 October. Funding is approved for a scientific study of Gulf War–related illnesses to be performed by the National Academy of Sciences and the Institute of Medicine (NAS/IOM).

16 October. The Blue Ribbon panel meeting to discuss the illnesses of Gulf War veterans is formally chartered as the Persian Gulf Expert Scientific Committee.

17 November. The official Iraqi government newspaper *al-Jumhouriya* asserts that Iraq's "dignity and honor" are being violated by Kuwait and that Iraq would fight such dishonor with "a wall of bodies and a sea of blood." In an article by editor Salah Muktiar, the paper calls the Kuwaitis "worms and snakes" and claims that Iraq is preparing to respond to "the provocative behavior of Kuwait [*sic*] rulers, which includes flagrant violations of Iraq."

10 December. Undersecretary of Defense John Deutsch forms the Defense Science Board Task Force in Chemical Weapons (DSCTFCW) under the leadership of Nobel laureate Joshua Lederberg.

20–22 December. The Gulf Cooperation Council meets in Riyadh for its fourteenth session; it calls "for Iraq to respect the sovereignty and independence of Kuwait and for [the] acceptance of international borders as stated by United Nations Security Council Resolution 833."

21 December. The Defense Science Board Task Force in Chemical Weapons is expanded to include health effects on Gulf War veterans.

1994 *13 February.* The Voice of the Iraqi People, a covert radio station inside Iraq, reports that Saddam Hussein is still trying to hide chemical and biological weapons materials from UN inspectors.

25 February. The *San Francisco Chronicle* reports that three years after the liberation of their country, "Kuwaitis [are] dissatisfied with their lot."

14 April. Two F-16 fighters shoot down two friendly Blackhawk helicopters, killing 15 American and 11 British, French, and Turkish troops in an accident near Irbil in northern Iraq in what is called the *Dinarte Incident.*

25 May. In a testy hearing before the Senate Banking Committee, Undersecretary of Defense Edwin Dorn is ridiculed by committee members for asserting that *Gulf War Syndrome* was not caused by Iraqi gas attacks. In a joint statement issued by Secretary of Defense William Perry and Joint Chiefs of Staff chairman John Shalikashvili, the two men call Persian Gulf veterans' health concerns "top priorities" for the Pentagon.

29 May. Saddam Hussein announces that he is firing his foreign minister, Ahmed Hussein Khudayir al-Samarral, and is taking over the office himself. Khudayir is allowed to keep his alternate post of finance minister. The move is interpreted to mean more repression for the Iraqi people amongst the outcries against the deteriorating Iraqi economy, worsened by nearly four years of UN sanctions.

4 June. A Kuwaiti court sentences five Iraqis and one Kuwaiti to death for conspiring to assassinate former President George Bush.

14 June. In a broadcast monitored in Cyprus, Iraqi Trade Minister Mohammed Mehdi Saleh warns that under decree No. 59, issued on 4 June, Iraqi farmers face amputation of their hands if they fail to sell all of their cereal harvests to the government.

23 June. The Defense Science Task Board on Persian Gulf War Health Effects, an offshoot of the Defense Science Board Task Force in Chemical Weapons, reports that it can find no credible evidence that Gulf War–related activities are the cause of so-called Gulf War Syndrome. "We could find no persuasive evidence of the use of chemicals in that theater," reports panel chairman Joshua Lederberg.

13 July. The Pentagon announces that human error, particularly by AWACs technicians, caused the Dinarte incident in April in which 26 U.S. and allied troops were killed.

25 July. Israeli Prime Minister Yitzhak Rabin and Jordan's King Hussein end their nations' nearly half-century-old conflict by signing an accord pledging to work together for peace.

4 August. The General Accounting Office, in a report to the Senate Veterans Committee, explains that the Pentagon offered troops little if any protection from the potential of Iraqi gas attacks during the Persian Gulf War, although the report stresses that there is no evidence that any gas attacks actually happened.

14 August. A Bangladeshi warrant officer, a member of the UN Iraq-Kuwait Observer Mission (UNIKOM) to monitor the Iraq-Kuwait border, is shot and killed on the Safwan-to-Baghdad highway on the Iraqi side of the border in the first incident of its kind in which a member of UNIKOM is killed. The assailants escape.

26 August. The Pentagon offers the families of the 11 non-American servicemen killed in the Dinarte incident $100,000 each.

29 August. A military panel recommends courts martial for AWACs technicians involved in the Dinarte incident.

October. The Italian journal *Panorama* announces that "Spring, 1995, is the earliest Iraq can expect the UN Security Council to lift international sanctions that prevent the country from exporting oil." Russia's *Izvestia* reports that it has learned of a deal proposed by Iraqi Deputy Prime Minister Tariq Aziz in July for Iraq to repay Moscow its $7 billion debt if the Yeltsin government pushes for an end to sanctions.

4 October. Saddam Hussein denounces the UN sanctions against his country, declaring that "the Iraqi people will render helpless those harboring ill intentions."

7 October. Military satellites and other intelligence sources pick up signs that some 10,000 Iraqi troops from the Hammurabi Division of the Republican Guards have been moving toward the Kuwaiti border for the past week. To counter the potential threat, President Bill Clinton orders the aircraft carrier USS *George Washington* to move from the Adriatic Sea to the Persian Gulf and dispatches 2,000 Marines on board the USS *Tripoli* to the area, beginning what is to be known as *Operation Vigilant Warrior.*

8 October. The United States accelerates the sending of up to 4,000 Marines to the Persian Gulf. Iraq threatens to pull out of the United Nations. The government newspaper *al-Jumhouriya* reports that "we [Iraq] are not seeking war or military confrontation at all, but we need to put an end to the suffering of our people by lifting the sanctions through any means."

9 October. The United States picks up its movement of troops and planes to the Persian Gulf: American Secretary of Defense William J. Perry orders squadrons of F-15s, F-16s, A-10s, and AWACs radar planes to defend Kuwait from an Iraqi invasion. Already dispatched to the Gulf by the United States are 12,000 troops, the cruiser USS *Leyte Gulf,* carrying 122 cruise missiles, the destroyer USS *Hewitt,* carrying 73 cruise missiles, and an amphibious assault group. The British pledge six Tornado fighters, while the French send nine Mirage 2000 fighters. American Secretary of State Warren Christopher warns the Iraqi regime that it "would pay a horrendous price" if it invaded Kuwait again. Baghdad Radio accuses the West of trying to destroy the Iraqi people, and that the embargo had subjected them to "an injustice of unprecedented proportions."

10 October. The *International Herald Tribune* reports on the formation of units of thousands of "Saddam Commandos," who vow to fight to the death to remove UN sanctions against their country.

11 October. The *New York Times* reports that even though the Iraqi army seem to be moving away from the Kuwaiti border, the United States continues to inundate the area with American troops and materiel. Rolf Ekeus, head of the UN Special Commission on Iraq, reports to the Security Council on Iraq's attempts to comply with UN resolutions; Ekeus calls the report "fundamentally positive."

12 October. Tension among the former Coalition allies bubbles forth: French Defense Minister François Léotard suggests that the American buildup in the Persian Gulf is "not unconnected to [American] domestic politics"; Russian Foreign Minister Andrei Kozyrev announces that he will go to Baghdad to try and settle the latest crisis. The United States floats an idea to require Republican Guard troops to be permanently banned from the southern Iraqi zone. The Kuwaiti government, anxious over possible Iraqi war movements, presses for a full accounting of the 609 Kuwaiti citizens believed held in Iraqi prisons since the end of the Persian Gulf War.

13 October. The official Iraqi press agency, INA, releases an Iraqi-Russian statement in which Iraq declares that it is ready to accept and recognize Kuwait's sovereignty and the borders that were established following the Gulf War cease-fire. "Iraq has stated it is ready to settle the issue of recognizing the sovereignty and borders of Kuwait in accordance with UN Security Council Resolution 888," the statement asserts. The commander of United forces in the Gulf, Gen. J. H. Binford Peay III, announces that the deployment of American forces to Kuwait, estimated at about 25,000, would "slow at the margins" because of the Iraqi withdrawal that seemed to be taking place. Secretary of Defense William J. Perry proclaims that the United States will store a division's worth of armored equipment and other materiel in Kuwait and Saudi Arabia even if Iraq completes its withdrawal. The *International Herald Tribune* reports that Klaus-Dieter von Horn, a Middle Eastern affairs official at the German Economics Ministry, said in an interview that his country was waiting eagerly to begin the rebuilding of Iraq's infrastructure, but that because of the current crisis, "the likelihood of sanctions being lifted anytime soon has shrunk."

15 October. The UN Security Council votes unanimously (15–0) to condemn the Iraqi troop movements that threaten Kuwait. The threat of a second Iraqi invasion of Kuwait diminishes. Russian Foreign Minister Andrei V. Kozyrev visits Kuwait to discuss his negotiations with Saddam Hussein to recognize Kuwait's borders.

16 October. A proposal by the British to force the Iraqis to notify the allies two weeks before any future troop movements jeopardizes French support of the resolution and is dropped. In an interview with the official Iraqi news agency, INA, Iraqi Minister of Culture and Information Hamed Hamadi announces that the "military force whose presence in the south was the subject of the big storm raised by the Americans has moved to rear positions after completing its training operation according to orders that have been issued." The Iraqi press reacts to the crisis: the Ba'ath party organ *al-Thawra* editorializes that "the storm was stirred for reasons relating to his [President Clinton's] shaky popularity in American public opinion"; the government newspaper *al-Jumhouriya* denounces King Hussein of Jordan for condemning the Iraqi troop movements.

17 October. *U.S. News & World Report* reports that challenges in the Iraqi military to his leadership led Saddam Hussein to provoke "an international confrontation."

20 October. The Pentagon announces that because Iraq's threat to Kuwait has abated, 1,000 American troops put on high alert to be sent to the Persian Gulf are being removed from the alert. The USS *Eisenhower* leaves for the Persian Gulf with 500 women aboard as part of the crew.

21 October. Counselor to the Attorney General John M. Hogan, in an action backing up the findings of Judge Frederick Lacey in December 1992, releases his report clearing the United States in the BNL controversy. The report is initially classified.

26 October. The *Washington Times* reports that "President Saddam Hussein's eldest son, Uday, has criticized Iraq's foreign-policy makers, saying they had gained nothing from the United Nations in return for scrapping Iraq's weapons of mass destruction. Uday, who publishes Iraq's most popular newspaper, *Babel*, suggested…that Iraqi foreign policy has remained in a whirlpool…'We go to New York and come back with nothing,' Uday said…of Mr. [Tariq] Aziz's repeated trips to New York to lobby for easing UN sanctions."

28 October. President Bill Clinton visits with American troops in Kuwait and is awarded the Mubarak Medal, Kuwait's highest civilian honor, by Emir Jabir al-Ahmadal-Jabir al-Sabah.

5 November. The Associated Press reports that more than 100 American, British, and Kuwaiti soldiers practice maneuvers in the Kuwaiti desert.

9 November. Sources suggest that after a two-hour meeting with Soviet Foreign Minister Kozyrev, and a month of intensive negotiations by the Russians, Saddam Hussein indicates that he is ready to abide by the UN mandate and formally recognize Kuwait as a separate nation, with established borders to also be recognized. From Nicosia, Cyprus, comes word that several Iranian fighter planes have bombed bases in northern Iraq belonging to an Iranian Kurdish dissident group. The group says that the bases, at Koi Sanjaq and Taqtaq, were hit by an "intensive" attack.

10 November. Iraq agrees to recognize Kuwait. The Iraqi National Assembly votes to acknowledge "the sovereignty of the state of Kuwait, its territorial integrity and independence," and would respect the "inviolability" of the Kuwaiti-Iraq border as established by the United Nations. The official Iraqi news agency, INA, condemns Iran's attack on Kurds in northern Iraq and claims that civilian targets were struck. Iran's Islamic Republic News Agency (IRNA) calls the bases headquarters of "counterrevolutionaries."

12 November. Baghdad Radio reports the explosion of two bombs near the Baghdad Hotel, killing the bomber and wounding three students, an hour after another bomb exploded in the Ur district of Baghdad, wounding three other students.

13 November. The Clinton Administration reports that American Ambassador to the United Nations Madeleine Albright plans to tell the UN Security Council that intelligence has found Iraqi leaders, including Saddam Hussein, have built luxurious palaces while the Iraqi people have suffered from economic sanctions.

24 November. The Kurdistan Democratic Party and the Patriotic Union of Kurdistan, the two main Kurdish guerrilla factions, sign a peace agreement ending fighting in a Kurdish-held enclave in northern Iraq that has killed some 4,000 people in the past few months.

4 December. In an article in the Swedish journal *Svenska Dagbladet*, Saddam Hussein's half-brother, Barzan Ibrahim al-Tikriti, head of Iraq's UN headquarters in Geneva, admits that the 1990 invasion of Kuwait was a mistake. "I wish it would not have happened, since the consequences have been terrible for the Iraqi people," he says.

6 December. The Kuwaiti Parliament, in a blow to Muslim fundamentalists, votes down a bill to segregate male and female students in the classrooms, libraries, and restaurants at Kuwait University.

12 December. Newsweek reports that the U.S. Navy is attempting to stop the smuggling of oil from Iraq to Iran.

25 December. The London *Observer* reports that "U.N. weapons inspectors in Iraq believe that Saddam Hussein is failing to disclose a significant biological-weapons program."

1995 *10 January.* U.S. Ambassador to the United Nations Albright displays for the Security Council photos of Iraqi troops armed with captured Kuwaiti arms moving toward the Kuwaiti border in the crisis that developed in October 1994.

16 January. The Hogan Report on the BNL loan controversy, submitted in October 1994, is declassified and released to the public.

17 January. The *Washington Post* reports that Polish intelligence officers in Baghdad helped six American CIA agents escape from inside occupied Kuwait through Iraq to asylum in Turkey in October 1990. The action was one of three where the Polish government worked behind the scenes to help Westerners, including Britons, escape from the Iraqi occupation.

18 January. Iran's official news agency, IRNA, reports that plots to kill Saddam Hussein and his son Odai have been uncovered. Travelers from Iraq say that 20 Iraqi air force and army officers, including Gen. Mohammed Mathlum al-Deleimi of the air force, were part of the plot and were executed on 7 January.

26 January. Teledyne Industries Inc. pleads guilty, and agrees to pay a fine of $13 million, to charges that from 1982 until 1989 it transported 120 tons of zirconium to Carlos Cardoen, a Chilean arms dealer, who in turn repackaged the zirconium as cluster bombs that were then sold to Iraq.

16 February. The *New York Times* reports that "Iraq has set up a secret system over the past year to export crude oil and refined products to bypass the United Nations sanctions barring such sales."

19 February. The London *Sunday Times* reports that Gen. Wafiq al-Samarra'i, the highest-ranking Iraqi military officer to defect to the West, is telling Western intelligence that after the Persian Gulf War Saddam Hussein secreted at least 80 Scud missiles, as well as modified al-Hussein Scuds, and 200 anthrax bombs that he buried in the Salah Ad Din region of northern Iraq, near Saddam's hometown of Tikrit.

27 February. The White House says that President Clinton will have the United States veto any UN Security Council resolution that lifts sanctions against Iraq. The United States claims that Russia and France are pushing for a lifting of sanctions so that they can negotiate billions of dollars in trade with Iraq if that country is allowed to sell its oil for profit. Rolf Ekeus, head of the UN Special Commission on Iraq, reports that Iraq could be hiding 20–30 metric tons of material to make biological and chemical weapons. Sources relate that a burgeoning spy scandal, uncovered earlier in the week, in which France demanded the expulsion of five Americans from the country, may be tied to an American investigation into whether France has renewed trading with Iraq in violation of the UN sanctions. A report prepared by former Dutch foreign minister Max van der Stoel for the UN Commission on Human Rights on the condition of human rights in Iraq calls the situation "heinous." "It is simply shocking that near the end of the 20th century, any state should so publicly and unashamedly incorporate heinous practices into its law," van der Stoel says. A car bomb explodes in the main market of the northern Iraqi city of Zakhu, killing 54 people and wounding 80 more. The attack is blamed on Kurdish rebels.

5 March. The *New York Times* reports that after a week-long trip with stopovers in seven nations, Madeleine Albright, U.S. ambassador to the United Nations, has convinced a majority of members of the UN Security Council that because Iraq is rebuilding its military capability, missile capacity, and chemical weapons potential, any move to end UN sanctions would be premature.

6 March. Responding to criticism from the National Academy of Sciences that he is doing nothing to help Gulf War veterans, President Bill Clinton announces that he will convene a panel of eminent scientists, doctors, veterans, and "other citizens" to study the problem more closely, although the names of the panel members are not released at this time.

11 March. Oil executives from several nations meet in Baghdad as the Iraqi government displays its potential for selling oil after international sanctions are lifted.

12 March. In Saudi Arabia, Secretary of State William Christopher meets with Saudi officials to ensure

Saudi support for continued international sanctions against Iraq.

13 March. The UN Security Council decides not to lift sanctions against Iraq. On this day, two McDonnell-Douglas civilian employees working in Kuwait to service F/A-18 Hornets drive their white jeep toward the UNIKOM forces at the Iraq-Kuwait border. They accidentally cross into Iraqi territory at Umm Qasr, where they are arrested and taken away. This story is not revealed for five days.

17 March. The story surfaces concerning the two McDonnell-Douglas workers taken prisoner by Iraq. Nizar Hamdoon, the Iraqi ambassador to the United Nations, states: "The two men crossed into Iraq illegally and are now in the custody of our government." He added that the Iraqi government was investigating the circumstances of the capture, and was in contact with the International Committee of the Red Cross (ICRC). The *New York Times* reports that Deputy Prime Minister Tariq Aziz has won the support of the Vatican to overturn crippling UN sanctions.

18 March. In the first official comment regarding the two Americans captured at the Iraq-Kuwait border, Vice President Taha Yassin Ramadan of Iraq reports while his government acknowledges holding the men, "nothing much will happen to them."

19 March. Concern grows over the fate of the two as-yet-unidentified aerospace workers held by Iraq. The United States asks the ICRC for help in obtaining their release. Michel Bordaux of the ICRC tells Britain's ITN News, "The delegation in Baghdad has presented a request to the Iraqi authorities so that delegates of our delegation can visit those two gentlemen, and we are waiting for an answer." The United States also requests the aid of the Polish government, whose embassy in Baghdad houses the interests section of the United States (the interest section is where the United States conducts business in the absence of a formal embassy), established since the severing of ties between Baghdad and Washington. Several sources speculate that Saddam Hussein may be holding the two men as leverage to get UN sanctions on Iraq lifted. A Kuwaiti newspaper reports that the two men were arrested when they panicked and tried to flee from an Iraqi checkpoint after realizing they had driven across the border. Defense Secretary William Perry, meeting with the Saudi defense minister, displays satellite photos showing that Iraq is rebuilding its military to prewar levels. Perry is reassured by the Saudis that they will allow the United States to station arms and other materiel on Saudi soil, in a reversal of their previous stand. Saddam Hussein inaugurates a bridge over the Tigris River, the last to be rebuilt of the 133 bridges destroyed by the Coalition during the Gulf War.

20 March. Backed by F-16 fighter jets and other American-made military equipment, 35,000 Turkish troops march across the Turkey-Iraq border at Zakhu in the Allied no-fly zone to attack and destroy Kurdish separatist bases. After a briefing by Prime Minister Tansu Ciller of Turkey, President Clinton does not criticize the invasion. Secretary of Defense Perry, in Kuwait, calls on Iraq to release the two Americans, identified as David Daliberti, 41, of Jacksonville, Florida, and William Barloon, 39, of Minneapolis, Minnesota. He admits that while the Iraqis have the authority to hold the men, they are taking advantage of "an innocent mistake." Perry visits the al-Jebar Air Base in Kuwait to examine Kuwaiti defensive measures.

21 March. U.S. Ambassador to the United Nations Madeleine Albright tells the Senate Foreign Relations Committee, "If the oil embargo is lifted unconditionally, Baghdad could well order the departure of UN inspectors. Under those circumstances, Iraq would be able to begin producing Scud missiles within one year; it would be able to rebuild its biological weapons program in less than a year, and its chemical warfare program in two to three years. In five to seven years, it could build a nuclear device." She displays photographs of several Iraqi chemical and biological weapons installations, destroyed or damaged during the Gulf War by the Coalition, that appear to have been rebuilt completely.

22 March. American officials, speaking on the basis of anonymity, tell CNN correspondent Wolf Blitzer that analysts inside the U.S. government believe that two coups have been attempted against Saddam Hussein this year and that political unrest, added to the unstable Iraqi economic situation, is making Hussein more vulnerable to revolution every day. They speculate that if Iraq does not foresee a lifting of UN sanctions, the Iraqi leader might use a military option instead of diplomacy. Secretary of State Perry, visiting Abu Dhabi on the last leg of his six-day Persian Gulf tour, tells reporters that Iran is arming small islands that it holds in the strategic Strait of Hormuz, the mouth of the Persian Gulf near Oman, with 155mm gas-laden shells, particularly on Abu Musa, near the United Arab Emirates. In the past Iran has been accused of deploying on these small islands antiship and antiaircraft missiles, including Chinese-made Silkworms. "We really do not know why Iran would choose to deploy chemical weapons there, but we consider it a very negative factor, and a very threatening action on their part.... It is a deployment far beyond any reasonable defensive requirement that Iran has, and it can only be regarded, I believe, as a potential threat to shipping in the area," Perry tells reporters. The 18-ship U.S. contingent in the area monitors the deployment carefully. Iranian ambassador to the United Nations Kamal Kharrazi tells ABC News, "It is basically nonsense, in terms of military knowledge and sense, to deploy chemical weapons on the islands; what's the use of it?" Turkish soldiers in northern Iraq search for rebels of the Kurdistan Workers Party, or PKK, a Marxist dissident group. Secretary of State Warren Christopher, meeting with Foreign Minister Alain Juppé of France, is told that the invasion "breaks basic principles of international law."

23 March. For the first time Iraq allows two Polish diplomats to visit with detainees David Daliberti and William Barloon, and they are reported to be in satisfactory condition. Iraqi trade minister Mohammed Mehdi Saleh confirms that the two Americans are safe and are being treated well. As to when they would be released, Saleh replied that "the Iraqi people have been hostages for five years" to a UN trade embargo. For the fourth day, Turkish troops pound PKK rebel positions with artillery and air strikes. Turkey's European allies are beginning to criticize the operation because of purported human rights violations.

25 March. American detainees Daliberti and Barloon are put on trial, found guilty of illegally entering Iraq, and sentenced to eight years in prison. American reaction when the news of the trial comes out is explosive.

May. Saddam Hussein removes his half-brother, Watban Ibrahim Hassan, as interior minister for unknown reasons.

15 June. Iraqi dissidents report that tribal leaders, joined by soldiers who oppose Saddam Hussein's regime, formed the so-called July 14 Tank Battalion and attacked a radio transmitter at Abu Ghraib near Baghdad on 14 June, but were repulsed by pro-Saddam forces.

16 June. Quoting a dispatch from the official Iraqi news agency INA, the official Ba'ath party newspaper *al–Thawra* calls the stories of a clash near Baghdad between pro- and anti-Saddam forces "lies." "Their [the Western press] last lie is an indication of stupidity and rancor on Iraq," the paper declares.

17 June. The *Washington Times* reports that a classified UN joint report prepared in May 1995 by UNICEF, the World Health Organization, and the World Food Council declares that up to 4 million Iraqi children are dependent on food distribution handouts and that up to one million of these are in danger of starvation.

19 June. In a report prepared by UN weapons inspector Rolf Ekeus, the UN Special Commission declares that it has found evidence that Iraq is withholding information on its biological weapons program.

20 June. A military court acquits Capt. James Wang of criminal charges in the shootdown of two American helicopters over northern Iraq in April 1994. Youssef Ibrahim of the *New York Times* reports that 150 officers and soldiers of a mutinous Iraqi army unit that was involved in a clash with government forces on 14 June have been executed and that further purges are possible.

5 July. UN weapons inspector Rolf Ekeus dramatically reports that on Saturday, 1 July, Iraqi officials admitted that they had at one time produced "large quantities" of deadly agents used to manufacture botulism and anthrax spores. The Iraqis further admitted that the BW research began at a plant at Muthanna in 1985.

16 July. Iraq releases American prisoners David Daliberti and William Barloon after 124 days in captivity. The two Americans are pardoned after Saddam Hussein meets with Congressman Bill Richardson (D–New Mexico). Saddam tells Richardson that he wished that other heads of state would observe humanitarian considerations, a surreptitious appeal for Western governments to lift the embargo on Iraq. After the men are moved to the Polish Embassy in Baghdad, Barloon thanks Richardson for "coming and getting us." Daliberti says that it is "a wonderful day." Secretary of State Warren Christopher, appearing on NBC's *Meet the Press,* dampens speculation that the U.S. government traded for the men. "No letter was delivered, no concessions were made; he wasn't authorized to negotiate; he simply went there on a private humanitarian mission," he says. On CNN, historian Phebe Marr speculates that Saddam acted because 17 July is the anniversary of the Ba'ath takeover, and he would "appear magnanimous rather than weak, rather than giving into the Americans" on the issue of the two captives. Saddam calls on the United States to end sanctions, and promises that there will be no more information provided to the United Nations on its weapons programs until they are lifted.

17 July. Former captives Barloon and Daliberti take a 14-hour drive to freedom in Amman, Jordan. Richardson tells ABC News that while there was not a quid pro quo for the release of the two men, he did talk with Saddam about the United States easing sanctions on Iraq. "It could be that the Iraqis are positioning themselves for a push to lift the sanctions, and to do that they've created a more favorable atmosphere, at least internationally, with this humanitarian release, but they're going to have take some concrete steps before I believe the Security Council moves," Richardson says in a telephone interview from the Jordanian capital.

22 July. The *Economist* magazine reports that Saddam Hussein has removed his defense minister, Ali Hassan Majid, from power. Hassan Majid had been, according to the magazine, "[Saddam's] best and most brutal henchman. He saw to the mass gassing of Kurdish villagers in 1988–89 (earning him the name 'Chemical Ali'); he was governor of occupied Kuwait in 1990 ([where he became known as] 'the butcher of Kuwait'); and he put down the [Shi'ite and Kurdish] uprisings in 1991." The reasons for his removal remain a mystery.

23 July. David Daliberti, accompanied by his wife, arrives back home in Jacksonville, Florida.

30 July. Saddam Hussein, in a bizarre and unexpected move, pardons all political prisoners held in Iraqi jails, leading to further speculation that he is trying to get support to end crippling sanctions adopted against his country.

2 August. Kuwait recalls the Iraqi invasion on its fifth anniversary.

References

Atkinson, Rick, *Crusade: The Untold Story of the Persian Gulf War* (Boston: Houghton Mifflin, 1993); Baker, David, *Flight and Flying: A Chronology* (New York: Facts on File, 1994); Bennis, Phyllis, and Michel Moushabeck, eds., *Beyond the Storm: A Gulf Crisis Reader* (New York: Olive Branch Press, 1991); Bloom, Saul, et al., eds., *Hidden Casualties: Environmental, Health and Political Consequences of the Persian Gulf War* (Berkeley, CA: North Atlantic Books, 1994); *Congressional Quarterly Almanac*, 102d Congress, 1st Session, 1991 (Washington, DC: Congressional Quarterly, 1992), 440–441; *Congressional Quarterly Almanac*, 102d Congress, 2d Session, 1992 (Washington, DC: Congressional Quarterly, 1993), 545–555; Fialka, John J., *Hotel Warriors: Covering the Gulf War* (Washington, DC: Woodrow Wilson Center Press, 1992); *Gulf War Air Power Survey* (Washington, DC: Government Printing Office, 1993); *Operation Desert Shield/Desert Storm*, Hearings before the Committee on Armed Services, U.S. Senate, 102d Congress, 1st Session, 1991; Sciolino, Elaine, *The Outlaw State: Saddam Hussein's Quest for Power and the Gulf Crisis* (New York: John Wiley & Sons, 1991); Stasio, Renee L., *Iraq's Invasion of Kuwait: A Review of Events*, Congressional Research Service Issue Brief, September 1990; *U.S. Chemical and Biological Warfare–Related Dual Use Exports to Iraq and Their Possible Impact on the Health Consequences of the Persian Gulf War*, Report of Chairman Donald W. Riegle, Jr., and Ranking Member Alfonse M. D'Amato of the Committee on Banking, Housing and Urban Affairs with Respect to Export Administration, U.S. Senate Report, 103d Congress, 2d Session, 25 May 1994, 20–23.

Bibliography

Abrams, Irwin, *The Nobel Peace Prize and the Laureates: An Illustrated Biographical History, 1901–1987* (Boston: G. K. Hall, 1988).

Abu-Hakima, Ahmad Mustafa, *The Modern History of Kuwait* (London: Luzac, 1983).

Abu Jaber, Kamel, *The Arab Ba'th Socialist Party: History, Ideology, and Organization* (Syracuse, NY: Syracuse University Press, 1966).

Adams, James, *Bull's Eye: The Assassination and Life of Supergun Inventor Gerald Bull* (New York: Times Books, 1992).

Adams, Michael, ed., *The Middle East* (New York: Facts on File, 1988).

Adler, Bill, *The Generals: The New American Heroes—The Commanders behind Desert Storm: General H. Norman Schwarzkopf and General Colin Powell* (New York: Avon Books, 1991).

Adler, Tina, "Desert Storm's Medical Quandary: Do Iraqi Chemical and Biological Agents Explain Gulf War Syndrome?" *Science News* 145:25 (18 June 1994), 394–395.

Al-Khalil, Samir, *Republic of Fear: The Inside Story of Saddam's Iraq* (Berkeley: University of California Press, 1989; New York: Pantheon Books, 1990, reprint).

Albright, David, and Mark Hibbs, "Hyping the Iraq Bomb," *Bulletin of the Atomic Scientists* 47:2 (March 1991).

———, "Iraq and the Bomb: Were They Even Close?" *Bulletin of the Atomic Scientists* 47:2 (March 1991).

Allen, Thomas B., "Turkey Struggles for a Balance," *National Geographic* 185:5 (May 1994), 2–36.

Allen, Thomas B., F. Clifton Berry, and Norman Polmar, *CNN: War in the Gulf: From the Invasion of Kuwait to the Day of Victory and Beyond* (Atlanta, GA: Turner Publishing, 1991).

Allman, T., "Arafat in the Storm" *Vanity Fair* 57:5 (May 1994), 116–123, 179–187.

Almond, Denise L., ed., *Desert Score: Gulf War Weapons* (Washington, DC: Carroll Publishing Company, 1991).

Amnesty International, *Iraq: Evidence of Torture* (London: Amnesty International Publications, 1981).

Apostolo, Georgio, *The Illustrated Encyclopedia of Helicopters* (New York: Bonanza, 1984).

Arms, Thomas S., *Encyclopedia of the Cold War* (New York: Facts on File, 1994).

Arnett, Peter, *Live from the Battlefield: From Vietnam to Baghdad—35 Years in the World's War Zones* (New York: Simon & Schuster, 1994).

Ascherio, Albert, et al., "Effect of the Gulf War on Infant and Child Mortality in Iraq," *New England Journal of Medicine* 327:13 (24 September 1992), 931–936.

Ashley, Steven; and C. P. Gilmore, "Finally: Stealth!" *Popular Science* 233:1 (July 1988), 45–51, 94–95.

Atkinson, Rick, *Crusade: The Untold Story of the Persian Gulf War* (Boston: Houghton Mifflin, 1993).

Azzi, Robert, "Saudi Arabia: The Kingdom and Its Power," *National Geographic* 158:3 (September 1980).

Bakan, S., et al., "Climate Response to Smoke from Burning Oil Wells in Kuwait," *Nature* 361:6325 (30 May 1991), 367–371.

Banks, Arthur S., ed., *Political Handbook of the World: 1993* (Binghamton, NY: CSA Publications, 1993).

Batatu, Hanna, *The Old Social Classes and the Revolutionary Movements of Iraq: A Study of Iraq's Old Landed and Commercial Classes and of Its Communists, Ba'thists and Free Officers* (Princeton, NJ: Princeton University Press, 1978).

Behrens, Carl, Robert Bamberger, and Marc Humphries, *Oil and Iraq's Invasion of Kuwait*, Report of the Congressional Research Service, 7 September 1990.

Bennis, Phyllis, and Michel Moushabeck, eds., *Beyond the Storm: A Gulf Crisis Reader* (New York: Olive Branch Press, 1991).

Bey, Midhat Ali Hadyar, *The Life of Midhat Pasha: A Record of His Services, Political Reforms, Banishment, and Judicial Murder* (London: John Murray, 1903).

Birtles, Philip, and Paul Beaver, *Missile Systems* (Shepperton, Surrey, UK: Ian Allen, 1985).

Blake, Bernard, ed., *Jane's Weapon Systems, 1988–89* (Coulsdon, Surrey, UK: Jane's Information Group, 1988).

Boyne, Walter J., *The Weapons of Desert Storm* (Lincolnwood, IL: Publications International, 1991).

Brooks, Richard, Skip Hiser, and T. K. Hohl, "If It Was There, P-3s Found It," *U.S. Naval Institute Proceedings* 118:8 (August 1991), 41–43.

Broughton, Jacksel M., "Wasted Air Power: Doing It Right in the Persian Gulf Highlighted What Went Wrong in the Air War over North Vietnam," *Vietnam* 7:2 (August 1994), 18–24.

Brown, R. A., comp., *United States Naval Forces in Desert Shield and Desert Storm* (Washington, DC: Naval Historical Center, Contemporary History Branch, 1993).

Browning, K. A., et al., "Environmental Effects from Burning Oil Wells in Kuwait," *Nature* 351:6325 (30 May 1991), 363–367.

Bulkeley, Rip, and Graham Spinardi, *Space Weapons: Deterrence or Delusion?* (Totowa, NJ: Barnes & Noble Books, 1986).

Bullock, John, *The Persian Gulf Unveiled* (New York: Congdon & Weed, 1984).

Busch, Noel F., "Ibn Saud: *Life* Visits Arabia," *Life* 14:22 (31 May 1943), 69–88.

Bush, George, with Victor Gold, *Looking Forward* (New York: Doubleday, 1987).

Butson, Thomas G., *Gorbachev: A Biography* (New York: Stein & Day, 1985).

Byron, Lord, *The Poetical Works of Byron* (Boston: Houghton Mifflin, 1975).

"Calculating the Costs of the Gulf War," *Congressional Quarterly's Research Reports* 1991:10 (15 March 1991).

Canby, Thomas Y., "After the Storm," *National Geographic* 180:2 (August 1991), 2–35.

Caprara, Giovanni, *Space Satellites: Every Civil and Military Satellite of the World since 1957* (New York: Portland House, 1986).

CARDRI (Committee against Repression and for Democratic Rights in Iraq), *Saddam's Iraq: Revolution or Reaction?* (London: Zed Books, 1990).

Carter, E. W. III, "Blockade," *U.S. Naval Institute Proceedings* 116:11 (November 1990), 42–47.

Carus, Seth, *The Genie Unleashed: Iraq's Chemical and Biological Weapons Programs* (Washington, DC: Washington Institute for Near East Policy, 1989).

Chadwick, Frank, *The Desert Shield Fact Book* (Bloomington, IL: Game Designers' Workshop, 1991).

Chubin, Shahram, *Iran's National Security Policy: Capabilities, Intentions & Impact* (Washington, DC: Carnegie Endowment for International Peace, 1994).

Cigar, Norman, "The Soviet Navy in the Persian Gulf: Naval Diplomacy in a Combat Zone," *Naval War College Review* XLII:2 (Spring 1989), 56–88.

Clancy, Tom, *Armored Cav: A Guided Tour of an Armored Cavalry Regiment* (New York: Berkley Books, 1994).

Cleveland, William L., *A History of the Modern Middle East* (Boulder, CO: Westview, 1994).

Cochran, Darrell, "100 Hours to Victory," *Soldiers* 46:5 (May 1991), 9–13.

Cohen, Roger, and Claudio Gatti, *In the Eye of the Storm: The Life of General H. Norman Schwarzkopf* (New York: Farrar, Straus & Giroux, 1991).

Collins, Joseph J., "Desert Storm and the Lessons of Learning," *Parameters: U.S. Army War College Quarterly* XXII:3 (Autumn 1992), 83–95.

Collins, Louise Mooney, and Lorna Mpho Mabunda, *The Annual Obituary 1993* (Detroit: St. James Press, 1994).

Commire, Anne, ed., *Historic World Leaders* (Detroit: Gale, 1991).

Committee To Review the Health Consequences of Service during the Persian Gulf War Medical Follow-up Agency, the Institute of Medicine, *Health Consequences of Service during the Persian Gulf War: Initial Findings and Recommendations for Immediate Action* (Washington, DC: National Academy Press, 1995).

Corelli, Rae, "The Threat of Gas Attacks: It Changed the Way People Live," *Maclean's* 107:7 (18 February 1991), 34–35.

Cottrell, Alvin J., gen. ed., *The Persian Gulf States: A General Survey* (Baltimore, MD: Johns Hopkins University Press, 1980).

Covey, Dana C., "Offering a Helping Hand in Iraq," *U.S. Naval Institute Proceedings* 118:5 (May 1992), 106–109.

Creveld, Martin Van, "The Persian Gulf Crisis of 1990–91 and the Future of the Morally Constrained War," *Parameters: U.S. Army War College Quarterly* XXII:2 (Summer 1992), 21–40.

Crystal, Jill, *Kuwait: The Transformation of an Oil State* (Boulder, CO: Westview Press, 1992).

Cullen, Tony, and Christopher F. Foss, eds., *Jane's Land-Based Air Defence, 1989–90* (Coulsdon, Surrey, UK: Jane's Information Group, 1989).

Cushman, John H., "Joint, Jointer, Jointest," *U.S. Naval Institute Proceedings* 118:5 (May 1992), 78–85.

Dane, Abe, "America's Secret Commandos," *Popular Mechanics* 169:9 (September 1992), 25–32, 116.

——, "The Army's Newest Killer Chopper," *Popular Mechanics* 168:7 (July 1991), 26–29.

——, "Report from Charlie Battery," *Popular Mechanics* 168:4 (April 1991), 23–28, 126.

Dann, Uriel, *Iraq under Qassem: A Political History, 1958–1963* (New York: Frederick A. Praeger, 1969).

Darwish, Adel, and Gregory Alexander, *Unholy Babylon: The Secret History of Saddam's War* (New York: St. Martin's Press, 1991).

Daume, Daphne, ed., *1982 Britannica Book of the Year* (Chicago: Encyclopaedia Britannica, 1982).

David, H. W. C., and J. R. H. Weaver, eds., *The Dictionary of National Biography Volume 1912–1921* (London: Oxford University Press, 1980).

DeAtkine, Norvell B., "The Middle East Scholars and the Gulf War," *Parameters: U.S. Army War College Quarterly* XXIII:2 (Summer 1993), 53–63.

Degenhardt, Henry W., ed., *Revolutionary and Dissident Movements: An International Guide* (New York: Longman, 1988).

De la Billière, Sir Peter, *Storm Command: A Personal Account of the Gulf War* (New York: HarperCollins Publishers, 1992).

Delery, Tom, "Away, the Boarding Party!" *U.S. Naval Institute Proceedings* 117:5 (May 1991), 65–71.

Devlin, John F., *The Ba'th Party: A History from Its Origins to 1966* (Stanford, CA: Hoover Institution Press, 1976).

Di Rita, Larry, "Exocets, Air Traffic, & the Air Tasking Order," *U.S. Naval Institute Proceedings* 118:8 (August 1992), 59–63.

Dickson, Harold R. P., *Kuwait and Her Neighbours* (London: Allen & Unwin, 1956).

Dickson, Paul, *War Slang: American Fighting Words and Phrases from the Civil War to the Gulf War* (New York: Pocket Books, 1994).

Diller, Daniel C., ed., *Russia and the Independent States* (Washington, DC: Congressional Quarterly, 1993).

Dockery, Kevin, *SEALs in Action* (New York: Avon Books, 1991).

Doder, Dusko, and Louise Branson, *Gorbachev: Heretic in the Kremlin* (New York: Viking, 1990).

Dougherty, Vice Adm. William A., "Storm from Space," *U.S. Naval Institute Proceedings* 118:8 (August 1992), 48–52.

Dowd, Maureen, and Thomas L. Friedman, "The Fabulous Bush & Baker Boys," *New York Times Magazine*, 6 May 1990.

DuBois, Thomas R., "The Weinberger Doctrine and the Liberation of Kuwait," *Parameters: U.S. Army War College Quarterly* XXI:4 (Winter 1991–1992), 24–38.

Dunn, Vice Adm. Robert F., "Early Gulf War Lessons," *U.S. Naval Institute Proceedings* 117:3 (March 1991), 25.

Dunnigan, James F., and Austin Bay, *From Shield to Storm: High-Tech Weapons, Military Strategy, and Coalition Warfare in the Persian Gulf* (New York: William Morrow, 1992).

Dupuy, Trevor N., *Future Wars: The World's Most Dangerous Flashpoints* (New York: Warner Books, 1993).

Dupuy, Trevor N., et al., *How To Defeat Saddam Hussein: Scenarios and Strategies for the Gulf War* (New York: Warner Books, 1991).

The European Parliament (Luxembourg: Secretariat of the European Parliament, Directorate-General for Information and Public Relations, 1980).

Evans, Frank, "*Princeton* Leaves the War," *U.S. Naval Institute Proceedings* 117:7 (July 1991), 70–72.

Farah, Caesar E., *Islam: Beliefs and Observances* (Hauppauge, NY: Barrons Educational Series, 1987).

Farouk-Sluglett, Marion, and Peter Sluglett, *Iraq since 1958: From Revolution to Dictatorship* (London: I. B. Tauris, 1990).

Fernea, Robert A., and Wm. Roger Louis, *The Iraqi Revolution of 1958: The Old Social Classes Revisited* (London: I. B. Tauris, 1991).

Fialka, John J., *Hotel Warriors: Covering the Gulf War* (Washington, DC: Woodrow Wilson Center Press, 1992).

Field, John Osgood, "From Food Security to Food Insecurity: The Case of Iraq, 1990–91," *GeoJournal* 30:2 (June 1993), 185–194.

Field, John Osgood, and Robert M. Russell, "Nutrition Mission to Iraq: Final Report to UNICEF by Tufts University, August 14, 1991."

———, "Nutrition Mission to Iraq for UNICEF," *Nutrition Reviews* 50:2 (February 1992), 41–46.

Finnie, David H., *Shifting Lines in the Sand: Kuwait's Elusive Frontier with Iraq* (Cambridge, Mass.: Harvard University Press, 1992).

Fischer, John, "The Editor's Easy Chair: The Shah and His Exasperating Subjects—A Report from Iran, Part II," *Harper's* 230:1379 (April 1965).

Fischer, Mary A., "Dying for Their Country" *GQ* 64:5 (May 1994), 146–153, 203–207.

Flint, Julie, "The Lion and the Wolf," *New Statesman & New Society*, 22 January 1993, 16–17.

Foss, Christopher F., *Jane's Main Battle Tanks* (London: Jane's Publishing Group, 1986).

Foss, Christopher F., ed., *Jane's Armour and Artillery, 1992–93* (Coulsdon, Surrey, UK: Jane's Information Group, 1992).

Francillon, Rene J., *Grumman Aircraft since 1929* (Annapolis, MD: Naval Institute Press, 1989).

———, *McDonnell Douglas Aircraft since 1920* (London: Putnam & Company, 1979).

Frederick, T. J., and P. N. Nagy, "So Where Were All the RO/ROs?" *U.S. Naval Institute Proceedings* 118:5 (May 1992), 124–127.

Freedman, Lawrence, and Efraim Karsh, *The Gulf Conflict: Diplomacy and War in the New World Order, 1990–1991* (Princeton, NJ: Princeton University Press, 1993).

Friedman, Alan, *Spider's Web: The Secret History of How the White House Secretly Armed Iraq* (New York: Bantam Books, 1991).

Friedman, Norman, *Desert Victory: The War for Kuwait* (Annapolis, MD: Naval Institute Press, 1991).

Froggett, Steve, "Tomahawk in the Desert," *U.S. Naval Institute Proceedings* 118:1 (January 1992), 71–75.

Fromkin, David, *A Peace To End All Peace: The Fall of the Ottoman Empire and the Creation of the Modern Middle East* (New York: Avon Books, 1989).

Gardner, Dana, "How Patriot Launched the Smart War Era," *Design News* 44:8 (22 April 1991), 66–70.

Gascoigne, Bamber, *Encyclopedia of Britain* (New York: Macmillan Publishing Company, 1993).

Geyer, Alan, and Barbara G. Green, *Lines in the Sand: Justice and the Gulf War* (Louisville, KY: Westminster/John Knox Press, 1992).

Gibson, Andrew E., "After the Storm," *Naval War College Review* XLV:3 (Summer 1992), 21–27.

Gorbachev, Mikhail, *Perestroika: New Thinking for Our Country and the World* (New York: Harper & Row, 1988).

Gowers, Andrew, and Tony Walker, *Behind the Myth: Yasser Arafat and the Palestinian Revolution* (New York: Olive Branch Press, 1991).

Graves, William, "Iran: Desert Miracle," *National Geographic* 147:1 (January 1975).

Graz, Liesl, *The Turbulent Gulf* (London: I. B. Tauris, 1990).

Green, Fitzhugh, *George Bush: An Intimate Portrait* (New York: Hippocrene Books, 1989).

Gunston, Bill, *An Illustrated Guide to Modern Bombers* (New York: Prentice-Hall, 1988).

———, *An Illustrated Guide to Modern Fighters and Attack Aircraft* (New York: Prentice-Hall, 1987).

———, *An Illustrated Guide to USAF: The Modern US Air Force* (New York: Prentice-Hall, 1991).

Gunston, Bill, cons. ed., *The Encyclopedia of World Air Power* (New York: Crescent, 1980).

Hallion, Richard P., *Storm over Iraq: Air Power and the Persian Gulf War* (Washington, DC: Smithsonian Institution Press, 1992).

Harris, Kenneth, *Thatcher* (Boston: Little, Brown and Company, 1988).

Harrison, P. W., "The Situation in Arabia," *Atlantic Monthly*, December 1920, 849–855.

Hart, Alan, *Arafat: Terrorist or Peacemaker?* (London: Sidgwick & Jackson, 1984).

Hawley, T. M., *Against the Fires of Hell: The Environmental Disaster of the Gulf War* (New York: Harcourt Brace Jovanovich, 1992).

Hedges, Stephen J., Peter Cary, Eleni Dimmler, and Kyrill Belianinov, "The Other Problem in the Persian Gulf," *U.S. News & World Report*, 14 November 1994, 87–88.

Hein, Steven L., "Coasties in the Persian Gulf," *U.S. Naval Institute Proceedings* 116:11 (November 1990), 118–119.

Helmreich, Paul C., *From Paris to Sèvres: The Partition of the Ottoman Empire at the Peace Conference of 1919–1920* (Columbus: Ohio State University Press, 1974).

Henderson, Simon, *Instant Empire: Saddam Hussein's Ambition for Iraq* (San Francisco: Mercury House, 1991).

Heppenheimer, T. A., "Stealth: First Glimpses of the Invisible Aircraft Now under Construction," *Popular Science* 229:3 (September 1986), 74–79, 115–116.

Hewins, Ralph, *A Golden Dream: The Miracle of Kuwait* (London: W. H. Allen, 1963).

Hickman, William F., "Confrontation in the Gulf: Unintended Consequences," *Naval War College Review* 44:1 (Winter 1991), 49–61.

Hiro, Dilip, "Anti-Western Feeling in the Arab World Can Only Escalate," *New Statesman & New Society*, 22 January 1993, 17.

———, *The Longest War: The Iran-Iraq Conflict* (New York: Routledge, Chapman & Hall, 1991).

Hitchens, Christopher, "Struggle of the Kurds," *National Geographic* 182:2 (August 1992), 32–61.

Hobbs, David, *An Illustrated Guide to Space Warfare* (London: Salamander Books, 1986).

Hogg, Ian V., ed., *Jane's Infantry Weapons, 1993–94* (Coulsdon, Surrey, UK: Jane's Information Group, 1993).

Holden, David, and Richard Johns, *The House of Saud: The Rise and Rule of the Most Powerful Dynasty in the Arab World* (New York: Holt, Rinehart & Winston, 1981).

Horne, Charles F. III, "Mine Warfare Is with Us and Will Be with Us," *U.S. Naval Institute Proceedings* 117:7 (July 1991), 63.

Institute of Medicine, *Health Consequences of Service during the Persian Gulf War: Initial Findings and Recommendations for Immediate Action* (Washington, DC: National Academy Press, 1995).

"Iraq and Beyond: PostCold War Military Choices," *Congressional Quarterly's Editorial Research Reports* 1:42 (16 November 1990).

"Israel's 40-Year Quandary," *Congressional Quarterly's Editorial Research Reports* 1:14 (15 April 1988).

"The JDW Interview: Major General Khalifa Ibn Ahmed al-Khalifa, Bahraini Minister of Defence," *Jane's Defence Weekly* 14:14 (4 April 1992), 592.

Javits, Jacob K., with Don Kellerman, *Who Makes War: The President versus Congress* (New York: William Morrow, 1973).

Jones, Joseph, *Stealth Technology: The Art of Black Magic*, edited by Matt Thurber (Blue Ridge Summit, PA: Tab Books, 1989).

Jordan, John, *An Illustrated Guide to Modern Destroyers* (New York: Prentice-Hall, 1986).

———, *An Illustrated Guide to Modern Naval Aviation and Aircraft Carriers* (New York: Prentice-Hall, 1983).

Junor, Penny, *Margaret Thatcher: Wife, Mother, Politician* (London: Sidgwick & Jackson, 1983).

Kaiser, Robert G., *Why Gorbachev Happened: His Triumphs, His Failure, and His Fall* (New York: Simon & Schuster, 1992).

Kaplan, Roger, "Vichy François," *American Spectator* 28:2 (February 1995), 42–45.

Karsh, Efraim, and Inari Rautsi, *Saddam Hussein: A Political Biography* (New York: Free Press, 1991).

Keegan, John, *World Armies* (Detroit, MI: Gale Research Company, 1983).

Kelly, Michael, "In Gaza, Peace Meets Pathology" *New York Times Sunday Magazine,* 27 November 1994, 56–63, 72–79, 96–97.

Kindsvatter, Peter S., "VII Corps in the Gulf War: Deployment and Preparation for *Desert Storm,*" *Military Review* LXXII:1 (January 1992), 2–16.

———, "VII Corps in the Gulf War: Ground Offensive," *Military Review* LXXII:2 (February 1992), 16–37.

Kinross, Lord John Patrick Douglas Balfour, *The Ottoman Centuries: The Rise and Fall of the Turkish Empire* (New York: William Morrow, 1977).

Klare, Michael T., "Fueling the Fire: How We Armed the Middle East," *Bulletin of the Atomic Scientists* 47:1 (January/February 1991), 19–26.

Krosney, Herbert, *Deadly Business: Legal Deals and Outlaw Weapons—The Arming of Iran and Iraq, 1975 to the Present* (New York: Four Walls Eight Windows, 1993).

Kutyna, Donald J., "SPACECOM: We Lead Today, but What about Tomorrow?" *Defense '91,* July/August 1991, 20–29.

Lacey, Robert, *The Kingdom: Arabia and the House of Sa'ud* (New York: Avon Books, 1981).

Lambert, Mark, ed., *Jane's All the World's Aircraft, 1991–92* (Coulsdon, Surrey, UK: Jane's Information Group, 1991).

———, *Jane's All the World's Aircraft, 1993–94* (Coulsdon, Surrey, UK: Jane's Information Group, 1993).

Landersman, S ., "Professional Notes: Will Hussein Use Gas?" *U.S. Naval Institute Proceedings* 117:2 (February 1991), 84–87.

Lantos, Tom, "Will Saddam Strike Again?" *Reader's Digest* 144:865 (May 1994), 99–103.

Lauterpacht, E., et al., eds., *The Kuwait Crisis: Basic Documents* (Cambridge, UK: Grotius Publications, 1991).

Lewytzkyj, Borys, ed., *Who's Who in the Soviet Union* (Munich, Germany: K. G. Saur, 1984).

Licatovich, Bill, "Iraqi Propaganda Ploys," *Soldiers* 46:1 (January 1991).

Livingstone, Neil C., and David Halevy, *Inside the PLO: Covert Units, Secret Funds, and the War against Israel and the United States* (New York: William Morrow, 1990).

Lloyd, T. O., *The British Empire, 1558–1983* (New York: Oxford University Press, 1984).

Long, Franklin, Donald Hafner, and Jeffrey Boutwell, *Weapons in Space* (New York: W. W. Norton, 1986).

Lunt, James, *Hussein of Jordan: Searching for a Just and Lasting Peace* (New York: William Morrow, 1990).

MacArthur, John R., *Second Front: Censorship and Propaganda in the Gulf War* (New York: Hill & Wang, 1992).

McDowell, David, *The Kurds: A Nation Denied* (London: Minority Rights Publications, 1992).

Mackey, Sandra, *The Saudis: Inside the Desert Kingdom* (Boston: Houghton Mifflin, 1987).

McKinnon, Dan, *Bullseye: Iraq* (New York: Berkley Books, 1987).

Marr, Phebe, *The Modern History of Iraq* (Boulder, CO: Westview Press, 1985).

Martin, J. M., "(Mines:) We Still Haven't Learned," *U.S. Naval Institute Proceedings* 117:7 (July 1991), 64–68.

Matarr, Philip, "The PLO and the Gulf Crisis," *Middle East Journal* 48:1 (Winter 1994), 31–46.

Maynes, Charles William, "Dateline Washington: A Necessary War?" *Foreign Policy* 82:(Spring 1991).

Mazarr, Michael J., Don M. Snider, and James A. Blackwell, Jr., *Desert Storm: The Gulf War and What We Learned* (Boulder, CO: Westview Press, 1993).

Medvedev, Zhores A., *Gorbachev* (New York: W. W. Norton, 1986).

Metz, Helen Chapman, ed., *Iraq: A Country Study* (Washington, DC: U.S. Government Printing Office, 1990).

The Middle East and North Africa 1989 (London: Europa, 1988).

Miller, David, *An Illustrated Guide to Modern Sub Hunters* (London: Salamander Books, 1984).

Miller, Judith, "Syria's Game: Put On a Western Face," *New York Times Magazine,* 26 January 1992, 12–20, 49.

Miller, Judith, and Laurie Mylroie, *Saddam Hussein and the Crisis in the Gulf* (New York: Times Books, 1990).

Mollins, Carl, "Countdown to Battle," *Maclean's* 107:7 (18 February 1991), 26–28.

Montgomery, Glenn, "When the Liberation of Kuwait Began," *U.S. Naval Institute Proceedings* 117:4 (April 1991), 51–52.

Morelock, J. ., *The Army Times Books of Great Land Battles from the Civil War to the Gulf War* (New York: Berkley Books, 1994).

Moritz, Charles, ed., *Current Biography Yearbook,* various years (New York: H. W. Wilson).

Morrow, Bruce, et al., "Mikhail Gorbachev: Man of the Decade," *Time,* 4 January 1990, 42–45.

Mostyn, Trevor, exec. ed., *The Cambridge Encyclopedia of the Middle East and North Africa* (Cambridge, UK: Cambridge University Press, 1988).

Munro, David, ed., *Chambers World Gazetteer: An A–Z of Geographical Information* (Edinburgh: W&R Chambers, 1988).

Napier, Kenneth, "With the British in the Gulf," *U.S. Naval Institute Proceedings* 117:6 (June 1991), 65–66.

Netton, Ian Richard, ed., *Arabia and the Gulf: From Traditional Society to Modern States* (Totowa, NJ: Barnes & Noble Books, 1986).

Northcutt, Wayne, *Mitterrand: A Political Biography* (New York: Holmes & Meier, 1992).

Ogden, Chris, *Maggie: An Intimate Portrait of a Woman of Power* (New York: Simon & Schuster, 1990).

Osmańczyk, Edmund Jan, *The Encyclopedia of the United Nations and International Agreements* (Philadelphia: Taylor & Francis, 1985).

Padilla, R. A., "F/A-18Ds Go to War," *U.S. Naval Institute Proceedings* 118:8 (August 1991), 40.

Pagonis, William G., *Moving Mountains: Lessons in Leadership and Logistics from the Gulf War* (Boston: Harvard Business School Press, 1992).

Palmer, Michael A., *Guardians of the Gulf: A History of America's Expanding Role in the Persian Gulf, 1833–1992* (New York: Free Press, 1992).

Palmer, R. R., and Joel Colton, *A History of the Modern World* (New York: Knopf, 1984).

Pardew, James W., Jr., "The Iraqi Army's Defeat in Kuwait," *Parameters: U.S. Army War College Quarterly* XXI:4 (Winter 1991–1992), 17–23.

Paxton, John, *Companion to Russian History* (New York: Facts on File, 1983).

Peebles, Curtis, *Battle for Space* (New York: Beaufort Books, 1983).

Pelletiere, Stephen C., and Douglas V. Johnson II, *Lessons Learned: The Iran-Iraq War* (Carlisle Barracks, PA: U.S. Army War College Strategic Studies Institute, 1991).

Pelletiere, Stephen C., Douglas V. Johnson II, and Leif R. Rosenberger, *Iraqi Power and U.S. Security in the Middle East* (Carlisle Barracks, PA:, U.S. Army War College Strategic Studies Institute, 1990).

Perry, William J., "Desert Storm and Deterrence," *Foreign Affairs* 70:4 (Fall 1991), 66–82.

Phillips, Andrew, "Doctors in the Desert: Canada's Medics Report for Duty," *Maclean's* 107:7 (18 February 1991), 32.

———, "Facing the Enemy: A Report from the Kuwaiti Front," *Maclean's* 107:7 (18 February 1991), 30–31.

Pipes, Daniel, and Patrick Clawson, "Ambitious Iran, Troubled Neighbors," *Foreign Affairs: America and the World 1992/93* 72:1 (January 1993), 124–141.

Polmar, Norman, *The Naval Institute Guide to the Ships and Aircraft of the U.S. Fleet* (Annapolis, MD: Naval Institute Press, 1993).

———, *Ships and Aircraft of the U.S. Fleet* (Annapolis, MD: Naval Institute Press, 1987).

Polmar, Norman, ed., *World Combat Aircraft Directory* (Garden City, NY: Doubleday, 1976).

Prados, Alfred B., and Clyde R. Mark, *Iraq-Kuwait Crisis: U.S. Policy and Options,* Report of the Congressional Research Service, 30 August 1990.

Prater, Phil, "Night Moves in the Gulf," *Soldiers* 46:5 (May 1991), 14–16.

Pyle, Richard, *Schwarzkopf: The Man, the Mission, the Triumph* (New York: Signet, 1991).

Quinn, Hal, "Preparing for Horror: Suffield's Secrets Protect Troops," *Maclean's* 107:7 (18 February 1991), 36.

Raviv, Dan, and Yossi Melman, *Every Spy a Prince: The Complete History of Israel's Intelligence Community* (Boston: Houghton Mifflin, 1990).

Reader's Digest Natural Wonders of the World (Pleasantville, NY: Reader's Digest Association, 1980).

Russell, Malcolm B., *The First Modern Arab State: Syria under Faysal, 1918–1920* (Minneapolis: Bibliotheca Islamica, 1985).

Rahman, Fazlur, *Islam* (Chicago: University of Chicago Press, 1979).

Rajaee, Farhang, ed., *The Iran-Iraq War: The Politics of Aggression* (Gainesville: University Press of Florida, 1993).

Rankin, A. G., and R. G. Smith, "Australian Divers Clear Mines," *U.S. Naval Institute Proceedings* 117:7 (July 1991), 74.

Rees, Elfan Ap, *World Military Helicopters* (London: Jane's Publication Company, 1986).

Reich, Bernard, ed., *Political Leaders of the Contemporary Middle East and North Africa: A Biographical Dictionary* (Westport, CT: Greenwood Press, 1990).

Renshon, Stanley A., ed., *The Political Psychology of the Gulf War: Leaders, Publics, and the Process of Conflict* (Pittsburgh: University of Pittsburgh Press, 1993).

Rodriguez, George, and Robert Ruby, "Taking Down the Oil Platforms," *U.S. Naval Institute Proceedings* 117:4 (April 1991), 53.

Rush, Alan, *Al-Sabah: History and Genealogy of Kuwait's Ruling Family, 1752–1987* (London: Ithaca Press, 1987).

Said, Edward, "Second Thoughts on Arafat's Deal," *Harper's* 288:1724 (January 1994), 16–18.

Scales, Robert H., Jr., *Certain Victory: The United States Army in the Gulf War* (Washington, DC: Office of the Chief of Staff, United States Army, 1993).

Schloesser, Jeffrey, "The Limits of Power: America's 20 Years in the Gulf," *Military Review* LXXII:1 (January 1992), 17–29.

Schmidt-Hauer, Christian, *Gorbachev: The Path to Power* (Topsfield, MA: Salem House Publishers, 1986).

Sciolino, Elaine, *The Outlaw State: Saddam Hussein's Quest for Power and the Gulf Crisis* (New York: John Wiley & Sons, 1991).

Sea Power: The Official Publication of the Navy League of the United States 37:1 (January 1994).

Seale, Patrick, *Asad: The Struggle for the Middle East* (Berkeley: University of California Press, 1988).

Shane, Peter M., and Harold H. Bruff, *The Law of Presidential Power: Cases and Materials* (Durham, NC: Carolina Academic Press, 1988).

Sharpe, Richard, ed., *Jane's Fighting Ships 1990–91* (Coulsdon, Surrey, UK: Jane's Information Group, 1990).

———, *Jane's Fighting Ships 1993–94* (Coulsdon, Surrey, UK: Jane's Information Group, 1993).

Sheehy, Gail, *The Man Who Changed the World: The Lives of Mikhail S. Gorbachev* (New York: HarperCollins Publishers, 1990).

Shimoni, Yaacov, *Biographical Dictionary of the Middle East* (New York: Facts on File, 1991).

———, *Political Dictionary of the Arab World* (New York: Macmillan Publishing Company, 1987).

Shlapak, David A., and Paul K. Davis, "Possible Postwar Force Requirements for the Persian Gulf: How Little Is Enough?" Report N-3314-CENTCOM/JS, Rand Corporation (Santa Monica, CA), 1991.

Shrader, Charles R., "Friendly Fire: The Inevitable Price," *Parameters: U.S. Army War College Quarterly* 22:3 (Autumn 1992), 29–44.

Shutler, General Philip, "Future Shield/Future Storm," *Naval War College Review* XLV:1 (Winter 1992), 100–102.

Sifry, Micah L., and Christopher Serf, eds., *The Gulf War Reader: History, Documents, Opinions* (New York: Times Books, 1991).

Simon, Bob, *Forty Days* (New York: G. P. Putnam's Sons, 1992).

Small, Richard, "Environmental Impact of Fires in Kuwait," *Nature* 350:6313 (7 March 1991), 11.

Smallwood, William L., *Warthog: Flying the A-10 in the Gulf War* (McLean, VA: Brassey's, 1993).

Smith, David O., "The Postwar Gulf: Return to Twin Pillars?" *Parameters: U.S. Army War College Quarterly* XXI:2 (Summer 1991), 51–60.

Smith, Hedrick, ed., *The Media and the Gulf War* (Washington, DC: Seven Locks Press, 1992).

Smith, Perry M., *How CNN Fought the War: A View from the Inside* (New York: Carroll Publishing Group, 1991).

Smyth, Gareth, "Divided in Unity," *New Statesman & New Society*, 22 January 1993, 18.

Spick, Mike, *An Illustrated Guide to Modern Fighter Aircraft* (New York: Prentice-Hall, 1987).

"State of the United Nations: Decline or Regeneration in the Next Fifty Years," Report of the 29th United Nations of the Next Decade Conference, 19–24 June 1994. Courtesy of the Stanley Foundation, Muscatine, IA.

Stiner, Carl W., "The Strategic Employment of Special Operation Forces," *Military Review* LXXI:6 (June 1991), 2–13.

Stitt, Iain P. A., cons. ed., *The Arthur Anderson European Community Sourcebook* (Chicago: Triumph Books, 1991).

Stockdale, Vice Adm. James, "POWs: Silence Is Not Golden," *U.S. Naval Institute Proceedings* 117:3 (March 1991), 29–30.

Summers, Harry G., Jr., *On Strategy II: A Critical Analysis of the Gulf War* (New York: Dell Publishing, 1992).

———, "Leadership in Adversity: From Vietnam to Victory in the Gulf," *Military Review* LXXI:5 (May 1991), 2–9.

Swan, Tony, "Earth Mover: The Civilian Hummer—For Those Who Would Go Where No 4x4 Has Gone Before," *Popular Mechanics* 169:6 (June 1992), 27–30.

Sweetman, Bill, and James Goodall, *Lockheed F-117A: Operation and Development of the Stealth Fighter* (Osceola, WI: Motorbooks International, 1990).

Szafranski, Richard, "Desert Storm Lessons from the Rear," *Parameters: U.S. Army War College Quarterly* XXI:4 (Winter 1991–1992), 39–49.

Tarr, David R., and Bryan R. Daves, eds., *The Middle East* (Washington, DC: Congressional Quarterly, 1986).

Taylor, John W. R., ed., *Jane's All the World's Aircraft*, various years (London: Jane's Yearbooks).

Taylor, John W. R., and Kenneth Munson, "Gallery of Middle East Airpower," *Air Force* 77:10 (October 1994).

Taylor, John W. R., and Gordon Swanborough, *Military Aircraft of the World* (New York: Charles Scribner's Sons, 1979).

Telhami, Shibley, "Israeli Foreign Policy after the Gulf War," *Middle East Policy* 1:2 (1992), 85–95, 192–193.

Terry, James P., "The Environment and the Laws of War: The Impact of Desert Storm," *Naval War College Review* XLV:1 (Winter 1992), 61–67.

Timmerman, Kenneth R., *The Death Lobby: How the West Armed Iraq* (Boston: Houghton Mifflin Company, 1991).

Twinam, Joseph Wright, "The Gulf Cooperation Council since the Gulf War: The State of the States," *Middle East Policy* 1:4 (1992), 96–115.

U.S. News & World Report, *Triumph without Victory: The History of the Persian Gulf War* (New York: Times Books, 1993).

Villiers, Alan, *Sons of Sinbad* (New York: Charles Scribner's Sons, 1969).

Vronskaya, Jeanne, with Vladimir Chuguev, *A Biographical Dictionary of the Soviet Union, 1917–1988* (London: K. G. Saur, 1989).

Wallach, Janet, and John Wallach, *Arafat: In the Eyes of the Beholder* (New York: Lyle Stuart, 1990).

Walmer, Max, *An Illustrated Guide to Strategic Weapons* (New York: Prentice-Hall, 1988), 43.

Werrell, Kenneth P., "Air War Victorious: The Gulf War vs. Vietnam," *Parameters: U.S. Army War College Quarterly* XXII:2 (Summer 1992), 41–54.

Wiener, Robert, *Live from Baghdad: Gathering News at Ground Zero* (New York: Doubleday, 1992).

Williams, Marjorie, "Jim Baker Is Smooth, Shrewd, Tough and Coolly Ambitious. That Is Why Washington Loves Him," *Washington Post Magazine*, 29 January 1989, 16–22, 36–38.

Woodward, Bob, and David S. Broder, *The Man Who Would Be President: Dan Quayle* (New York: Simon & Schuster, 1992).

The Worldmark Encyclopedia of the Nations: United Nations (New York: Worldmark, 1988).

Yearbook of the United Nations 1992 (Dordrecht, The Netherlands: Martinus Nijhoff Publishers, 1993).

Yenne, Bill, *McDonnell Douglas: A Tale of Two Giants* (New York: Crescent Books, 1985).

Young, Hugo, *The Iron Lady: A Biography of Margaret Thatcher* (New York: Farrar, Straus & Giroux, 1989).

Zacks, Yuval Joseph, "Operation *Desert Storm*: A Just War?" *Military Review* LXXII:1 (January 1992), 30–35.

Zahlan, Rosemarie Said, *The Creation of Qatar* (London: Croom Helm, 1979).

———, *The Making of the Modern Gulf States* (London: Unwin Hyman, 1989).

Government Documents

Access to Oil: The United States' Relationships with Saudi Arabia and Iran (Washington, DC: U.S. Government Printing Office, 1977).

Developments Concerning National Emergency with Respect to Kuwait, Communication from the President of the United States Transmitting a Report on Developments since His Last Report on August 9, 1990, Concerning the National Emergency with Respect to Kuwait, Pursuant to 50 U.S.C. 162(a) (Washington, DC: U.S. Government Printing Office, 1991).

The Gulf Crisis: Finding a Peaceful Solution: A Special Report (Washington, DC: United States Institute of Peace, 1990).

The Iraqi Army: Organization and Tactics (Fort Irwin, CA: National Training Center, 1991).

Jordan: Suspension of U.S. Military Assistance during the Gulf Crisis (Gaithersburg, MD: General Accounting Office, 1992).

Military Assistance to Saudi Arabia, Communication from the President of the United States Transmitting a Report on the Deployment and Mission of the United States Armed Forces in Response to the request received from the Government of Saudi Arabia (Washington, DC: Government Printing Office, 1990).

Mroczkowski, Dennis P. *U.S. Marines in the Persian Gulf, 1990–1991* (Washington, DC: History and Museums Division, Headquarters, U.S. Marine Corps, 1993).

The Persian Gulf Crisis: Relevant Documents, Correspondence, Reports (Washington, DC: U.S. Government Printing Office, 1991).

Quilter, Charles J. II. *U.S. Marines in the Persian Gulf, 1990–1991: With the Marine Expeditionary Force in Desert Shield and Desert Storm* (Washington, DC: History and Museums Division, Headquarters, U.S. Marine Corps, 1993).

Report on Kuwait, Communication from the President of the United States Transmitting a Report that the Operations Conducted by Coalition Forces to Liberate Kuwait Have Been Successful, Pursuant to Public Law 102-1 (Washington, DC: U.S. Government Printing Office, 1991).

United States Arms Sales to the Persian Gulf: Report of a Study Commission to Iran, Kuwait, and Saudi Arabia, May 22–31, 1975: Pursuant to H. Res. 315 (Washington, DC: U.S. Government Printing Office, 1976).

United States Central Intelligence Agency, *The World Factbook 1994* (Washington, DC: Government Printing Office, 1994).

United States Congress. House. *Asian Response to the Crisis in the Persian Gulf*, Hearing before the Subcommittee on Asian and Pacific Affairs of the House Committee on Foreign Affairs, 101st Congress, 2d Session, September 19, 1990 (Washington, DC: U.S. Government Printing Office, 1991).

———. *Briefing on Operation Desert Shield: Costs and Contributions*, Hearing before the House Committee on the Budget, 102d Congress, 1st Session, January 4, 1991 (Washington, DC: U.S. Government Printing Office, 1991).

———. *Consideration of Draft Legislation on the Situation in the Persian Gulf*, Markup before the House Committee on Foreign Relations, 102d Congress, 1st Session, on H. Con. Res. 1, January 9, 1991 (Washington, DC: U.S. Government Printing Office, 1991).

———. *Cost of Operation Desert Shield and Desert Storm and Allied Contributions*, Testimony before the House Committee on the Budget by Frank C. Conahan, assistant comptroller general, National Security and International Affairs Division, General Accounting Office, 15 May 1991.

———. *Crisis in the Persian Gulf*, Hearings and Markup before the Committee on Foreign Affairs, House of Representatives, 101st Congress, 2d Session, September 4 and 27, and October 18, 1990 (Washington, DC: U.S. Government Printing Office, 1990).

———. *Crisis in the Persian Gulf: Sanctions, Diplomacy, and War*, Hearings before the Committee on Armed Services, House of Representatives, 101st Congress, 2d Session, Hearing Held December 4, 5, 6, 12, 13, 14, 17, 19, and 20, 1990 (Washington, DC: U.S. Government Printing Office, 1991).

———. *Defense for a New Era: Lessons of the Persian Gulf War*, Report of the House Armed Services Committee, 1992.

———. *Effectiveness of the U.S. Civil Reserve Air Fleet Program*, Hearing before the Subcommittee on Investigations and Oversight of the Committee on Public Works and Transportation, House of Representatives, 101st Congress, 2d Session, October 10, 1990 (Washington, DC: U.S. Government Printing Office, 1991).

———. *Energy Impact of the Persian Gulf Crisis*, Hearing before the House Committee on Energy and Commerce, 102d Congress, 1st Session, January 9, 1991 (Washington, DC: U.S. Government Printing Office, 1991).

———. *Energy Policy Implications (Economic and Budgetary) of the Middle East Oil Crisis,* Hearing before the Task Force on Community Development and Natural Resources of the House Committee on the Budget, 101st Congress, 2d Session, October 24, 1990 (Washington, DC: U.S. Government Printing Office, 1991).

———. *Human Rights Abuses in Kuwait and Iraq,* Hearing before the House Committee on Foreign Affairs, 102d Congress, 1st Session, January 8, 1991 (Washington, DC: U.S. Government Printing Office, 1991).

———. *Intelligence Successes and Failures in Operations Desert Shield/Storm,* Report of the Oversight and Investigations Subcommittee of the House Committee on Armed Services, 103d Congress, 1st Session, 1993. (Washington, DC: U.S. Government Printing Office, 1993)

———. *The Military Option: The Conduct and Consequences of War in the Persian Gulf,* a white paper of the House Committee on Armed Services, Representative Les Aspin, chairman, 8 January 1991.

———. *U.N. Role in the Persian Gulf and Iraqi Compliance with U.N. Resolutions,* Hearing before the Subcommittee on Europe and the Middle East and on Human Rights and International Organizations of the House Committee on Foreign Affairs, 102d Congress, 1st Session, April 23, July 18, and October 21, 1991 (Washington, DC: U.S. Government Printing Office, 1992).

———. *Use of Chemical Weapons in Desert Storm,* Hearing before the Oversight and Investigations Subcommittee of the House Committee on Armed Services, 103d Congress, 1st Session, 1994 (Washington, DC: U.S. Government Printing Office, 1994)

United States Congress. Senate. *Civil War in Iraq: A Staff Report to the Committee on Foreign Relations, United States Senate* (Washington, DC: U.S. Government Printing Office, 1991).

———. *Crisis in the Persian Gulf Region: U.S. Policy Options and Implications,* Hearings before the Senate Committee on Armed Services, 103d Congress, 2d Session, September 11, 13; November 27, 28, 29, 30; and December 3, 1990 (Washington, DC: U.S. Government Printing Office, 1991).

———. *The Future of Saudi Arabian Oil Production,* Staff Report to the Subcommittee on International Economic Policy of the Senate Committee on Foreign Relations, (Washington, DC: U.S. Government Printing Office, 1979).

———. *Is Military Research Hazardous to Veterans' Health? Lessons Spanning Half a Century,* Staff Report of the Senate Committee on Veterans' Affairs, Senate Report 103-97, 103d Congress, 2d Session, 1994 (Washington, DC: U.S. Government Printing Office, 1994).

———. *Joint Chiefs of Staff Briefing on Current Military Operations,* Hearing before the Senate Committee on Armed Services, 103d Congress, 2d Session, 1994 (Washington, DC: U.S. Government Printing Office, 1994).

———. *Oil Prices and Supplies in the Wake of the Persian Gulf Crisis,* Hearings before the Senate Committee on Governmental Affairs, 103d Congress, 2d Session, 1991 (Washington, DC: U.S. Government Printing Office, 1991).

———. *Operation Desert Shield/Desert Storm,* Hearings before the Senate Committee on Armed Services, 103d Congress, 1st Session, 1991 (Washington, DC: U.S. Government Printing Office, 1991).

———. *U.S. Chemical and Biological Warfare–Related Dual Use Exports to Iraq and Their Possible Impact on the Health Consequences of the Persian Gulf War,* Report of Chairman Donald W. Riegle, Jr., and Ranking Member Alfonse M. D'Amato of the Committee on Banking, Housing and Urban Affairs with Respect to Export Administration, 103d Congress, 2d Session, 25 May 1994 (Washington, DC: U.S. Government Printing Office, 1994).

United States Department of Defense. "Conduct of the Persian Gulf War: Final Report to Congress (Pursuant to Title V of the Persian Gulf Conflict Supplemental Authorization and Personnel Benefits Act of 1991)," Report by the Department of Defense, April 1992.

———. *Gulf War Air Power Survey. Volume I: Planning Report and Command and Control Report; Volume II: Operations Report and Effects and Effectiveness Report; Volume III: Logistics Report and Support Report; Volume IV: Weapons, Tactics, and Training Report and Space Report; Volume V: Statistical Compendium and Chronology* (Washington, DC: Government Printing Office, 1993).

———. "Persian Gulf Veterans' Problems," Report of the Persian Gulf Veterans Coordinating Board, 13 December 1994.

United States Department of Defense, *Soviet Military Power 1986* (Washington, DC: Government Printing Office, 1986), 77

United States Department of Defense. Brinkerhoff, John R., "United States Army Reserve in Operation Desert Storm—The Case of the Unit that Was Not Called: The 377th Theater Army Area Command," Monograph of the Department of the Army, Army Reserve—Program Analysis and Evaluation Division (DAAR-PAE), 1991.

———, "United States Army Reserve in Operation Desert Storm—Civil Affairs in the War with Iraq," Monograph of the Department of the Army, Army Reserve—Program Analysis and Evaluation Division (DAAR-PAE), 1991.

———, "United States Army Reserve in Operation Desert Storm—Countering the Terrorist Threat: The 3rd Battalion, 87th Infantry," Monograph of the Department of the Army, Army Reserve—Program Analysis and Evaluation Division (DAAR-PAE), 1993.

———, "United States Army Reserve in Operation Desert Storm—Enemy Prisoner of War Operations: The 800th Military Police Brigade," Monograph of the Department of the Army, Army Reserve—Program Analysis and Evaluation Division (DAAR-PAE), 1992.

———, "United States Army Reserve in Operation Desert Storm—Engineer Support at Echelons above Corps: The 416th Engineer Command," Monograph of the Department of the Army, Army Reserve—Program Analysis and Evaluation Division (DAAR-PAE), 1992.

———, "United States Army Reserve in Operation Desert Storm—Port Operations," Monograph of the Department of the Army, Army Reserve—Program Analysis and Evaluation Division (DAAR-PAE), 1991.

———, "United States Army Reserve in Operation Desert Storm—The Signal Support Dilemma: The 335th Signal Command," Monograph of the Department of the Army, Army Reserve—Program Analysis and Evaluation Division (DAAR-PAE), 1992.

———, "United States Army Reserve in Operation Desert Storm—Strategic Intelligence Support: Military Intelligence Detachments for the Defense Intelligence Agency," Monograph of the Department of the Army, Army Reserve—Program Analysis and Evaluation Division (DAAR-PAE), 1991.

United States Department of Defense. Brinkerhoff, John R., and Theodore S. Silva, "United States Army Reserve in Operation Desert Storm—Ground Transportation Operations," Monograph of the Department of the Army, Army Reserve—Program Analysis and Evaluation Division (DAAR-PAE), 1994.

United States Department of Defense. Scales, Robert H., "Certain Victory" (Washington, DC: Office of the Chief of Staff, U.S. Army, 1993).

United States Department of Defense. Seitz, John, and Theodore S. Silva, "United States Army Reserve in Operation Desert Storm—Installation Operations," Monograph of the Department of the Army, Army Reserve—Program Analysis and Evaluation Division (DAAR-PAE), 1994.

United States Department of Defense. Silva, Theodore S., "United States Army Reserve in Operation Desert Storm—Augmenting the Training Base: The Army Reserve in Support of TRADOC," Monograph of the Department of the Army, Army Reserve—Program Analysis and Evaluation Division (DAAR-PAE), 1994.

United States Department of Defense and Department of Veterans Affairs Interagency Persian Gulf Veterans Coordinating Board, "Report on Persian Gulf Veterans Problems," December 1994, 8 pages.

United States Department of Justice, "Banca Nazionale del Lavoro (B.N.L.) Task Force: Final Report to the Attorney General, Janet Reno" (reported 21 October 1994; declassified 15 January 1995).

United States Department of State. Bureau of Public Affairs. "Background Notes: Iraq," August 1982.

United States Department of Veterans Affairs, "VA Fact Sheet: VA Programs for Persian Gulf Veterans," November 1994, 8 pages.

United States Government Accounting Office. "Desert Shield/Storm Air Mobility Command's Achievements and Lessons for the Future: Report to the Chairman, Committee on Armed Services, U.S. Senate" (Gaithersburg, MD: United States General Accounting Office, 1993).

———. "Operation Desert Storm: Questions Remain on Possible Exposure to Reproductive Toxicants," Report to the Chairman, Committee on Veterans' Affairs, U.S. Senate, Report GAO/PEMD-94-30 (August 1994).

———. "Operation Desert Storm: Questions Remain on Possible Exposure to Reproductive Toxicants," Report to the Chairman, Committee on Veterans' Affairs, U.S. Senate, August 1994, 14–19.

Illustration Credits

All illustrations were provided by AP/Wide World Photos, except the following:

2 Courtesy Grumman Corporation.

3 Cmdr. John Leenhouts, U.S. Navy. DN-SC-91-03749.

4 G. Cinelli Phan, U.S. Navy. DN-ST-10592.

10 U.S. Air Force. DF-ST-91-05061.

12 U.S. Air Force. DF-ST-91-06340.

13 Lt. Comdr. Ken Neubauer, U.S. Navy. DN-SC-92-03278.

14 Comdr. John Leenhouts, U.S. Navy. DN-SC-91-05319.

17 U.S. Air Force. DF-ST-91-05070.

18 CWO2 Tony A. Alleyne, U.S. Navy. DN-SC-92-06308.

21 Staff Sgt. Dean Wagner, U.S. Air Force. DF-ST-92-09233.

25 CWO Ed Bailey, U.S. Navy.

39 U.S. Air Force. DF-ST-92-07819.

48 PH3 Brad Dillon, U.S. Navy. DN-SN-91-09307.

57 Airman 1st Class Fisher, U.S. Air Force. DF-ST-91-03415.

58 Sgt. Prentes Tramble, U.S. Air Force. DF-ST-92-07611.

66 JO2 Pete Hatzakos, U.S. Navy. DN-SC-91-07402.

76 Department of Defense. DN-SC-93-05051.

86 U.S. Army.

88 Courtesy Grumman Corporation.

89 Courtesy Grumman Corporation.

92 Lt. Steve Gozzo, Department of Defense. DN-SC-93-03891.

97 Master Sgt. Sutherland, U.S. Air Force. DF-ST-83-05382.

98 Courtesy Grumman Corporation.

99 Tech. Sgt. H. H. Deffner, U.S. Air Force. DF-ST-92-07383.

100 Courtesy Grumman Corporation.

101 Sgt. Kimberly Yearyean, U.S. Air Force. DF-ST-92-08446.

111 U.S. Marine Corps. DM-ST-91-11761.

113 Staff Sgt. Glenn B. Lindsey, U.S. Air Force. DF-ST-82-10231.

154 Courtesy Grumman Melbourne Systems.

160 Comdr. John Leenhouts, U.S. Navy. DN-SC-91-04959.

173 Sgt. Brian Cumper, U.S. Army. DA-ST-07355.

174 U.S. Army.

175 CWO2 Ed Bailey, USNR. DN-SC-91-10908.

192 JO1 Joe Gawlowicz, U.S. Navy. DN-SC-91-08119.

193 Staff Sgt. F. Lee Corkran, U.S. Air Force. DF-ST-92-07749.

222 U.S. Army.

229 Courtesy *Soldiers*.

241 OS2 John Bouvia, U.S. Navy. DN-SC-92-08705.

260 SSG Martello, U.S. Army.

274 JO1 Joe Gawlowicz, U.S. Navy. DN-ST-92-00821.

275 JO2 Pete Hatzakos, U.S. Navy. DN-SC-91-09815.

278 U.S. Navy. DN-SN-91-08885.

280 Department of Defense. DD-ST-91-07798.

281 U.S. Army.

284 PH2 Rudy D. Pahoyo, U.S. Navy. DN-SN-93-01471.

285 U.S. Army.

296 OS2 John Bouvia, U.S. Navy. DN-SC-92-02874.

Index

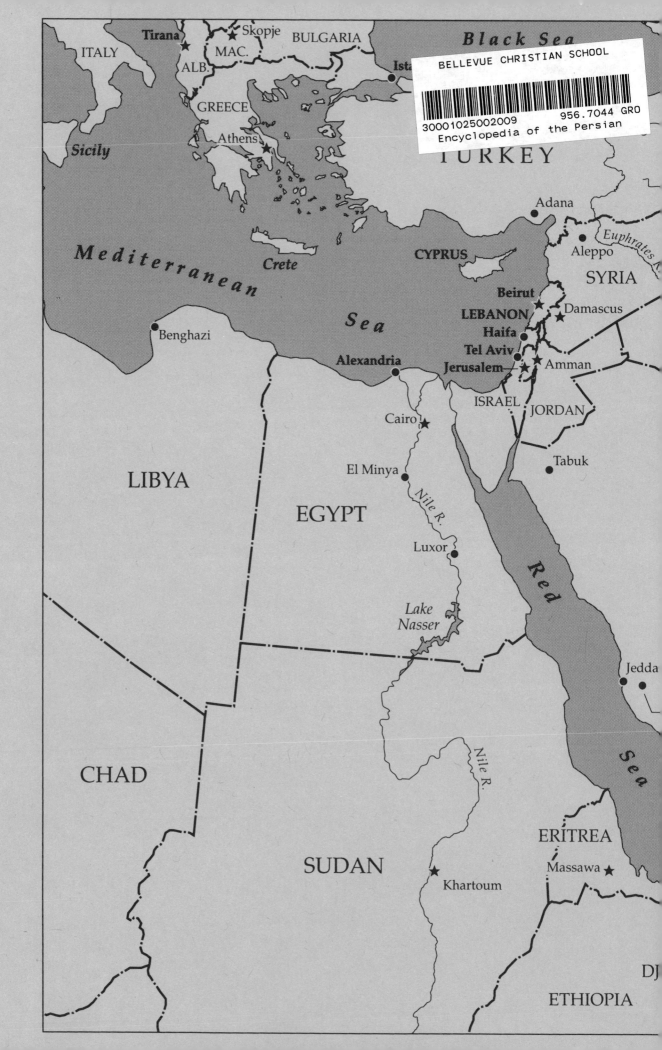